D1252469

Current Biography Yearbook 2018

H. W. Wilson

A Division of EBSCO Information Services, Inc.

Ipswich, Massachusetts

GREY HOUSE PUBLISHING

SEVENTY-NINTH ANNUAL CUMULATION—2018

International Standard Serial No. 0084-9499

International Standard Book No. 978-1-68217-641-2

Library of Congress Catalog Card No. 40-27432

Current Biography Yearbook, 2018, published by Grey House Publishing, Inc., Amenia, NY, under exclusive license from EBSCO Information Services, Inc.

CONTENTS

LIST OF BIOGRAPHICAL SKETCHES

List of Biographical Sketches

LIST OF OBITUARIES

List of Obituaries

List of Obituaries

Current Biography Yearbook 2018

Virgil Abloh

Date of birth: September 30, 1980
Occupation: Fashion designer

In March 2018, the internationally recognized French fashion house Louis Vuitton made headlines when it named American designer Virgil Abloh artistic director of its menswear line. The move was in some ways an unlikely one, as Abloh was both a relatively new designer and particularly active within the realm of streetwear, a segment of fashion that differed significantly from earlier incarnations of the Louis Vuitton brand in terms of its aesthetic, relative practicality, and appeal to young people and people of color. However, some in the fashion industry were less surprised by Abloh's selection, which signaled a desire among Louis Vuitton's leadership to tap into new trends and schools of thought and thereby ensure the longevity of the 164-year-old brand. "The first thing I am going to do is define new codes," Abloh told Vanessa Friedman and Elizabeth Paton for the *New York Times* (26 Mar. 2018) of his plans for the menswear line. "My muse has always been what people actually wear, and I am really excited to make a luxury version of that."

Active within the fashion community since the early aughts, Abloh had no formal training in clothing design and instead entered the field after completing degrees in civil engineering and architecture. Through his longtime creative partnership with hip-hop artist and fashion devotee Kanye West, Abloh made a name for himself in streetwear and went on to open his first store, the streetwear boutique RSVP Gallery, in 2009. After designing a short-lived fashion line known as Pyrex Vision, Abloh established a new label, Off-White, in 2013 and worked extensively to explore and promote his design aesthetic through its men's, women's, and furniture collections. "I don't come from where I'm supposed to come from," he told Diane Solway for *W* magazine (20 Apr. 2017). "So I have to prove that this is design, that this is art, that this is valid." Indeed, the popularity of Off-White and Abloh's hiring at Louis Vuitton have aptly demonstrated his success in that endeavor, and an exhibition dedicated to his work was scheduled to open at

GSAPPstudent, via Wikimedia Commons

the Museum of Contemporary Art in Chicago in June 2019.

EARLY LIFE AND EDUCATION

Abloh was born on September 30, 1980, near Chicago, Illinois, to parents who had immigrated to the United States from Ghana. His mother worked as a seamstress, and Abloh would later credit her with laying the foundation for his later work in fashion. His father managed a paint company. Abloh grew up with his parents and sister in Rockford, a town in north-central Illinois, where he attended Boylan Catholic High School.

As a teenager, Abloh was interested in athletic pursuits, including soccer and skateboarding. He also enjoyed music and developed an interest in deejaying, which he practiced on the weekends during his high school years. Despite such interests, however, Abloh did not initially consider pursuing a career in the arts, and he would later come to consider his teenage self's skepticism a source of inspiration. "I'm always trying to prove to my 17-year-old self that I can do creative things I thought weren't possible," he told Solway. After graduating from Boylan Catholic in

1998, Abloh enrolled in the University of Wisconsin–Madison, where he earned his bachelor's degree in civil engineering in 2003. He went on to enroll in a graduate program in architecture at the Illinois Institute of Technology, completing his master's degree in 2006.

EARLY CAREER

While living in Chicago after completing his bachelor's degree, Abloh began to explore the field of design independently, creating his own graphic T-shirts and launching his own website. A crucial point in Abloh's career trajectory came in 2002, when he began what would become a long-term affiliation with the hip-hop artist Kanye West. A Chicago native, West had been working as a music producer since the 1990s and by 2002 was beginning to establish himself as a rapper in his own right. After capturing West's attention with his design work, Abloh formed a productive creative partnership with the artist, for whom he would create album art, set designs, and merchandise. Abloh was named creative director of West's agency, Donda, in 2010 and was nominated for a 2011 Grammy Award for art direction on West and fellow rapper Jay-Z's album *Watch the Throne*.

Abloh and West particularly connected over their shared interest in fashion and made headlines with their appearances at major fashion-industry events such as Paris Fashion Week. "We were a generation that was interested in fashion and weren't supposed to be there," he told Solway. "We saw this as our chance to participate and make current culture. In a lot of ways, it felt like we were bringing more excitement than the industry was." Not content to be solely consumers of fashion, Abloh and West both completed a six-month internship at the Italian fashion company Fendi in 2009.

The year 2009 also saw the opening of RSVP Gallery, a store in Chicago's Wicker Park neighborhood owned by Abloh, Marc Moran, and Don C. Specializing in streetwear, RSVP Gallery was quickly established as a venue for high-profile fashion-related events and as the launching point for products designed or inspired by hip-hop artists and other cultural influencers. The store also introduced some of Abloh's early fashion designs, including his Pyrex Vision collection of screen-printed shirts in 2012. For Abloh, the continued success of RSVP Gallery and his own design projects represent part of a shift in the fashion industry, which was transitioning from an industry of which trends set and controlled by established companies, publications, and celebrities to one in which young consumers and online influencers could alter the fashion landscape overnight. The industry's gatekeepers "lost their footing," he told Zach Baron for *GQ* magazine (1 Aug. 2016). "It's raining. Kids can push them over. I know kids who are half my age who

can kill a brand on a whim, make it uncool if they want to."

OFF-WHITE

Following the success of Pyrex Vision, Abloh founded his next streetwear label, Off-White, in Milan, Italy, in 2013. As the label's designer, he sought to continue to popularize high-end streetwear as well as to emphasize the legitimacy of that segment of the fashion industry, which had long been dismissed by the industry's gatekeepers. "In a large part streetwear is seen as cheap," Abloh opined to Christopher Morency for the *Business of Fashion* (29 Sept. 2016). "What my goal has been is to add an intellectual layer to it and make it credible." Having demonstrated an affinity for repurposing and reinterpreting existing clothing and imagery with Pyrex Vision, Abloh continued in that vein with Off-White and also went on to collaborate with established brands such as Nike, Levi's, and Jimmy Choo. Abloh cites a wide range of influences—from Renaissance painter Caravaggio to luxury brand Balenciaga to skateboarder brand Supreme to the Women's March on Washington—and freely mixes the images and ideas inspired by them.

After launching with menswear, Off-White introduced its first women's collection in 2014 and made its Paris Fashion Week debut that year. For Abloh, selling both men's and women's lines better enabled Off-White to reach its core audience, which included "girls wearing Céline and their boyfriend's [Nike] Air Force Ones," as he explained to Matthew Schneier for the *New York Times* (5 Nov. 2014). "My premise is to create a brand that's immersed in this young fashion customer," he told Schneier. "Me, as a designer, that's what I draw from, that's the culture that I'm a part of: the music, the restaurants, the Chateau [Marmont] to the Mercer. That sort of premise, that's where I'm at." Abloh launched a furniture collection under the Off-White brand, Grey Area, in 2016.

As Abloh established Off-White as an influential force in the streetwear sphere, the label earned extensive acclaim from both streetwear aficionados and the fashion-industry establishment: Abloh was named a finalist for the prestigious LVMH Young Designers Prize in 2015, and Off-White won the British Fashion Award in the urban luxe category in 2017.

LOUIS VUITTON

Although Abloh enjoyed running his own label, he long aspired one day to helm one of the fashion industry's large companies. "We've all got our little pontoon boats or whatever. Some might be bigger than others. The fashion house is the ocean cruise," he told Baron. He added, "It's got 7,000 people on it. You're steering it. That's my goal. I want to do that." A turning point in

Abloh's career came in March 2018, when he was selected to replace designer Kim Jones as artistic director for menswear for Louis Vuitton, a long-established fashion house and part of the LVMH group, which also owns Christian Dior, Fendi, Givenchy, and Bulgari, among other luxury fashion, jewelry, and cosmetics brands. "This opportunity to think through what the next chapter of design and luxury will mean at a brand that represents the pinnacle of luxury was always a goal in my wildest dreams," Abloh told Friedman and Paton following the company's announcement that he had taken the position. "And to show a younger generation that there is no one way anyone in this kind of position has to look is a fantastically modern spirit in which to start."

Accepting the Louis Vuitton position not only represents a major next step for Abloh but also marks the first time an African American has attained such a post in the European luxury fashion industry. The move has also enabled Abloh to rethink the brand's approach to menswear and draw from his extensive experience interacting with young fashion-forward streetwear buyers. Among other goals, he hoped to drum up interest in the Louis Vuitton brand among younger consumers, make clothing that reflects the realities of twenty-first-century life, and improve the brand's communications strategy and engagement with global issues. Abloh's first menswear collection for Louis Vuitton, the Spring 2019 collection, debuted in Paris in June 2018. That year, he was named among *Time* magazine's hundred most influential people of the year.

PERSONAL LIFE

Abloh met his future wife, Shannon, while they were in high school. The couple married in 2009 and have two children. Abloh was based in Chicago for much of his career but planned to move to Paris after joining Louis Vuitton.

Abloh has also retained a passion for deejaying, which he has described as similar in some ways to his design work. "You have three minutes to read the room, play a song, and impress the crowd. Then you have to figure out how to style this group of songs together so it's one point of view," he told Solway. "I'm literally just litmus-testing the culture." Abloh performs globally, both under his own name and under the stage name Flat White.

SUGGESTED READING

Baron, Zach. "The Life of (Virgil) Abloh." *GQ*, 1 Aug. 2016, www.gq.com/story/virgil-abloh-profile. Accessed 13 July 2018.

Friedman, Vanessa, and Elizabeth Paton. "Louis Vuitton Names Virgil Abloh as Its New Men's Wear Designer." *New York Times*, 26 Mar. 2018, www.nytimes.com/2018/03/26/ business/louis-vuitton-virgil-abloh.html. Accessed 13 July 2018.

Morency, Christopher. "The Unlikely Success of Virgil Abloh." *Business of Fashion*, 29 Sept. 2016, www.businessoffashion.com/articles/intelligence/the-unlikely-success-of-virgil-abloh-off-white. Accessed 13 July 2018.

Schneier, Matthew. "Virgil Abloh, Kanye West's Creative Director, Puts Street Wear in the Spotlight with His Off-White Line." *New York Times*, 5 Nov. 2014, www.nytimes.com/2014/11/06/fashion/virgil-abloh-kanye-wests-creative-director-street-wear-Off-White-Label.html. Accessed 13 July 2018.

Singer, Olivia. "Virgil Abloh: The *Vogue* Interview." *Vogue*, 26 Mar. 2018, www.vogue.co.uk/article/virgil-abloh-vogue-interview-april-issue. Accessed 13 July 2018.

Solway, Diane. "Virgil Abloh and His Army of Disruptors: How He Became the King of Social Media Superinfluencers." *W*, 20 Apr. 2017, www.wmagazine.com/story/virgil-abloh-off-white-kanye-west-raf-simons. Accessed 13 July 2018.

Yotka, Steff. "A Brief History of Virgil Abloh's Meteoric Rise." *Vogue*, 28 Mar. 2018, www.vogue.com/article/virgil-abloh-biography-career-timeline. Accessed 10 July 2018.

—*Joy Crelin*

Joshua Abrams

Date of birth: 1973
Occupation: Composer, musician

Jazz musician and composer Joshua Abrams is best known for performing with his collective, the Natural Information Society, beginning in the early 2010s, though he got his start in the Chicago jazz world nearly two decades earlier. The band is organized around Abrams's guimbri, a three-stringed Moroccan bass lute. The guimbri is an instrument central to Gnawa music, which developed for spiritual healing among enslaved black Africans in North Africa. Abrams's music with the Natural Information Society combines Gnawa elements with minimalist American jazz to create a repetitious yet meditative groove. "I like music with an undulating repetition, so that it sounds like it's repeating but there's constant change," he told Stuart Broomer for *Musicworks Magazine* (Fall 2015). He describes the group's work not in terms of making music, but "collectively building sonic environments," he told Will Schube in an interview for the blog *Bandcamp Daily* (16 May 2017). "We're weaving the music together as an ensemble, and once everyone's up to speed on a composition there's room for everyone to improvise and make choices

Hreinn Gudlaugsson, via Wikimedia Commons

within it." The band's 2017 album, *Simultonality*, is also arguably its most successful, exhibiting the cohesion formed among the band after years of play.

MUSICAL EDUCATION

Abrams was born in Boston, Massachusetts, in 1973. He grew up in Philadelphia, Pennsylvania, where he made his auspicious musical start as an original member of the hip-hop group the Roots. Founded by Ahmir Khalib "QuestLove" Thompson and Tariq "Black Thought" Trotter as high schoolers, the Square Roots (as they were then called) busked on street corners in the late 1980s. Abrams, nicknamed the Original 808 for the bass-toned drum machine, played bass for the group and appeared on their 1993 debut, *Organix*. Around the same time, he performed in a chamber group conducted by the experimental composer Earle Brown. In the biography for his website, Abrams describes both experiences as "formative."

Abrams enrolled at Northwestern University in Evanston, Illinois, outside of Chicago, in 1991. Within a few years, Abrams became a fixture of the Chicago music scene. "For me, jazz is a social music and you gain some of the most important experience while you're actually working," he told Broomer of his musical education. "In Chicago at that time, there were still working bands, and I got to play often with members of different generations, which is different from learning jazz in college and then playing mostly with peers." He cited the tenor saxophonist Lin Halliday and the guitarist Bobby Broom as particularly influential.

EARLY CAREER IN CHICAGO

By the mid-1990s, Abrams was serving as the house bassist for the Velvet Lounge, a renowned jazz nightclub in Chicago's South Loop owned by tenor saxophonist Fred Anderson. Abrams also played in bands and recorded with such artists as composer and cornetist Rob Mazurek, the experimental rock band Joan of Arc, jazz pioneer Roscoe Mitchell, and the Montreal-based chamber-rock collective Godspeed You! Black Emperor.

In the late 1990s, Abrams joined the minimalist band Town and Country, with Ben Vida on guitar and trumpet, Liz Payne on contrabass, and Jim Dorling on harmonium. Abrams played not only bass for Town and Country, but also piano, drums, and a variety of melodic percussion instruments. The band released a handful of albums, including *It All Has to Do with It* (2000) and the better-received *Up Above* (2006), throughout the early aughts.

Around 1998, Abrams formed a jazz/rock trio called Sticks and Stones along with drummer Chad Taylor and alto saxophonist Matana Roberts. The three met playing at the Velvet Lounge and went on to release *Sticks and Stones* in 2002 and *Shed Grace* in 2004.

In 2002, Abrams released a solo album called *Busride Interview*, for which he sampled and mixed instrumental music, electronic sound, and field recordings. The following year, he released *Cipher* under the name Josh Abrams through Delmark Records. He recorded it with an improvisational acoustic quartet including guitarist Jeff Parker, trumpeter Axel Dörner, and clarinetist-saxophonist Guillermo Gregorio. Aaron Steinberg, who reviewed the album for *Jazz Times* (1 Mar. 2004), wrote that Abrams allows each band member to shine, remarking, "With a light hand, Abrams steers the group through everyone's comfort zones."

In the years following, Abrams tried his hand at hip-hop production and released two albums under the stage name Reminder—*Continuum* and *West Side Cabin*—in 2005 and 2007, respectively. Around this time, from 2004 to 2008, Abrams also played a weekly club date with Parker and with John Herndon of the post-rock group the Tortoises.

ADOPTING THE GUIMBRI

Abrams began playing the guimbri on a trip to Morocco in 1998. "I had the chance to hear Gnawa music live in Marrakesch's Jemaa El Fna. In Essaouira, I met Maâlem Najib Soudani, who gave me a basic understanding of the instrument, as well as my first guimbri," he recalled to Broomer. Abrams wondered if it was right for him as a white man and outsider to continue to play the culturally significant instrument back in Chicago, but legendary jazz drummer Hamid Drake, who had recorded with renowned

Moroccan musician Mahmoud Ghania, encouraged him to pursue it. Enjoying making music with Drake, Abrams agreed.

In 2007, Abrams made his first guimbri recording—featuring the musicians of Town and Country and others under the name DRMWPN (pronounced "Dream Weapon"): a live LP recording called *Bright Blue Galilee*. His second recording playing the guimbri was a free jazz piece that year called "Sakti/Shiva," on the LP *From the River to the Ocean*, as a member of a Drake and Anderson ensemble.

NATURAL INFORMATION SOCIETY

Abrams's best known and most successful project, the Natural Information Society, got an important boost through a fortuitous connection. In 2008 and 2009, Abrams, vibraphonist Jason Adasiewicz, guitarist Emmett Kelly, and drummers Frank Rosaly and Noritaka Tanaka recorded solo, trio, and quartet psychedelic pieces drawing on Abrams's past influences and featuring his Gnawa-inspired guimbri playing. The result would be the album *Natural Information*.

After playing a show with the folk musician Bonnie "Prince" Billy, Abrams struck up a conversation with Eremite Records founder Michael Ehlers. Ehlers mentioned that he was moving cross-country. Abrams, thinking that the company was on hiatus, gave Ehlers a demo of the album to listen to on the drive. "In retrospect, I think he feared it was a pitch; he told me he had stopped the label so I didn't have any expectations when I passed it to him," Abrams recalled to Schube. "Ironically, on that ride, he got really into the recording and asked if he could release it on vinyl. That became the first record, and it all went from there." *Natural Information* was released under Abrams's name through Eremite Records in 2010.

The Natural Information Society is based on Abrams's three principles of "focus, continuity, and repetition," Schube noted. These goals invoke both the ceremonial tradition of the guimbri and the minimalism of certain forms of experimental jazz. Ben Ratliff, who reviewed *Natural Information* for the *New York Times* (19 Sept. 2010), described it as "one of the rough gems of the post-everything musical era." Ratliff observed, "Every piece . . . is quiet and commanding, bound by its own mysterious glue."

Abrams and the Natural Information Society released their second album, *Representing*, in 2012. Abrams made the album in his apartment, bringing in different small ensembles to record. That year, the Natural Information Society officially coalesced around a core duo of Abrams and Rosaly.

LATER ALBUMS

In 2015 the Natural Information Society—by then a revolving group of musicians that include Abrams, Rosaly, Kelly, drummer Mikel Avery, autoharpist Ben Boye, and percussionist Lisa Alvarado on gong and harmonium—began to tour. They released a two-disc album called *Magnetoception* the same year. The album featured longer grooves like the long, understated, drone-heavy "By Way of Odessa." "Although the music is hypnotic," Bill Meyer wrote in his review for *Dusted* magazine (8 June 2015), "trance doesn't lead to easy bliss. The guitars add grit as well as languor, commanding sharpened attention rather than drift. The Gnawa use their music to banish demons and ease suffering; Abrams uses his to draw us into a state that is altered but quite alert."

Automaginary, a collaboration between Natural Information Society and the ambient rock duo Bitchin Bajas, was also released in 2015. Aaron Leitko, who reviewed that record for *Pitchfork* magazine, rated it 7.9 out of 10.

When Abrams and the Natural Information Society's album *Simultonality* was released in 2017, *Rolling Stone* magazine named one of the 20 Best Avant Albums of the year. Marc Masters echoed Abrams's views on the joy of repetition when he wrote in *Pitchfork* (6 Apr. 2017) that *Simultonality* creates "a sound that moves forward while simultaneously seeming to freeze time." Masters wrote, "Abrams' simple figures can continually hold attention across long stretches because his tone is so rich and multi-layered. Throughout *Simultonality*, his playing forms the foundation of each song, offering his bandmates a core around which they can circle, fly, digress, and connect."

In 2018, Abrams received a Foundation for Contemporary Arts grant in recognition of his innovation in music and sound.

COMPOSING FOR THE BIG SCREEN

Abrams is also a film score composer, working primarily with the documentary filmmaker Steve James. James contacted Abrams after listening to *Natural Information*. Abrams agreed to compose the score for James's *The Interrupters* (2011), a documentary about a group of Chicago antiviolence activists—six weeks before the film premiered at the Sundance Film Festival. Abrams worked with James again in 2014, composing the score for *Life Itself*, a biopic about the film critic Roger Ebert, then recently deceased.

Eremite Records released the two scores together as an album in 2015. Reviewing that album for *Pitchfork* (4 Nov. 2015), Leitko wrote: "Watching the films, Abrams' music is never intrusive. It enhances a scene, but never forces a mood. And while it's probably not the first place you'd turn to experience his work, it provides an example of his stylistic reach and musical ability." Abrams also composed the scores for Bill Siegel's documentary *The Trials of Muhammad Ali* (2013) and James's Academy Award–nominated short *Abacus: Small Enough to Jail* (2016).

PERSONAL LIFE

Abrams lives in Chicago with his spouse, Lisa Alvarado, a fellow musician in the Natural Information Society and visual artist. In 2017, Alvarado presented her first New York solo exhibit, *Sound Talisman*, featuring the painted textiles used as backdrops for the Natural Information Society's performances. She also designs the group's cover art.

SUGGESTED READING

Abrams, Joshua. "Joshua Abrams Is a Focused Force in Jazz and Film Scoring." Interview by Will Schube. *Bandcamp Daily*, 16 May 2017, daily.bandcamp.com/2017/05/16/joshua-abrams-interview. Accessed 15 July 2018.

Broomer, Stuart. "Joshua Abrams' Natural Information Society." *Musicworks Magazine*, vol. 123, Fall 2015, www.musicworks.ca/featured-article/joshua-abrams%E2%80%99-national-information-society. Accessed 15 July 2018.

Leitko, Aaron. Review of *Music for Life Itself & The Interrupters*, composed by Joshua Abrams. *Pitchfork*, 4 Nov. 2015, pitchfork.com/reviews/albums/21177-music-for-life-itself-the-interrupters. Accessed 15 July 2018.

Masters, Marc. Review of *Simultonality*, by the Joshua Abrams and the Natural Information Society. *Pitchfork*, 6 Apr. 2017, pitchfork.com/reviews/albums/22964-simultonality. Accessed 15 July 2018.

Meyer, Bill. Review of *Magnetoception*, by Joshua Abrams and the Natural Information Society. *Dusted*, 8 June 2015, dustedmagazine.tumblr.com/post/121024570127/joshua-abramsmagnetoception-eremite. Accessed 15 July 2018.

Ratliff, Ben. "Surfboards, Harmonies and Sheet Metal." Review of *Natural Information*, by Joshua Abrams, et al. *New York Times*, 19 Sept. 2010, www.nytimes.com/2010/09/19/arts/music/19playlist.html. Accessed 15 July 2018.

Steinberg, Aaron. Review of *Cipher*, by Joshua Abrams. *Jazz Times*, 1 Mar. 2004, jazztimes.com/reviews/countercurrents/josh-abrams-cipher. Accessed 15 July 2018.

SELECTED WORKS

Natural Information, 2010; *Representing*, 2012; *Magnetoception*, 2015; *Simultonality*, 2017

—*Molly Hagan*

Joseph Acaba

Date of Birth: May 17, 1967
Occupation: Astronaut

Although many of the United States' astronauts are drawn directly from the military and the scientific community, Joseph Acaba came from a less common source: a middle-school classroom. A former math and science teacher, he was one of three educators accepted in 2004 into a new National Aeronautics and Space Administration (NASA) program focused on training teachers to travel into space as mission specialists. Although NASA's program might seem unusual to some, Acaba found his teaching background to be an asset to his work. "I think the teaching profession really gets you pretty well qualified to become an astronaut," he told Clara Moskowitz for *Space.com* (28 Sept. 2012). "It may not seem that way, but schoolteachers every day, they're in a stressful environment, every day is different, and you need to cope with a wide range of people and different experiences."

Acaba's academic background in geology and years of service in the US Marine Corps Reserve and the Peace Corps also helped prepare him for his first trip to the International Space Station (ISS), taken via the space shuttle *Discovery* in 2009. Following the success of his first mission, Acaba returned to the ISS for an extended expedition in 2012, living aboard the station for several months. He again traveled to the ISS aboard a Russian *Soyuz* spacecraft in September 2017 for an expedition scheduled to last until February 2018. Although far from Earth, Acaba found

By NASA [Public domain], via Wikimedia Commons

an exciting temporary home in space. "Looking out the window, you have a view you can't get anywhere else on Earth, so I don't think we ever get tired of that," he told William Harwood for *CBS News* (12 Sept. 2017). "But we also have the usual, we watch movies, you have a telephone, you can call your family and friends, just living up there every day is pretty fun."

EARLY LIFE AND EDUCATION

Joseph Michael Acaba was born on May 17, 1967, in Inglewood, California. The third of four children born to Ralph and Elsie Acaba, Puerto Ricans who had moved to the mainland, he grew up primarily in the Southern California city of Anaheim. A young child during key moments in the US space program, he developed an interest in space travel early in life thanks, in part, to family members who owned reel-to-reel recordings of events such as the 1969 first moon landing. "My grandfather and my father were really interested in the Apollo missions and so they'd show us those tapes," he recalled in a NASA preflight interview (5 Jan. 2009). "Even though I wasn't watching them live, I did feel like I was at that time and that really got me thinking about space." Acaba was also an avid reader of science fiction, which further sparked his interest. "That opened up just tons of possibilities and it kind of got me thinking about maybe someday becoming an astronaut," he said in the interview.

Acaba attended Esperanza High School in Anaheim, where he particularly enjoyed taking hands-on courses such as metal shop. He graduated from the school in 1985. Acaba initially planned to enroll in a technical school, but his father persuaded him to consider a university instead. He ultimately chose to attend the University of California in Santa Barbara to study geology. While an undergraduate, Acaba enrolled in the US Marine Corps Reserves alongside a group of his friends. He spent six years in the reserves, during which he completed his undergraduate and graduate degrees. Acaba earned his bachelor's degree from the University of California in 1990 and a master's degree in geology from the University of Arizona (UA) in 1992. He would later pursue graduate studies in education through Texas Tech University's distance learning program, earning a master's degree in that area in 2015.

EARLY CAREER

After graduating from UA, Acaba initially found a job in hydrogeology, a field that focuses on water found below the ground. He worked primarily in California, where he dealt with issues such as pollutant runoff. In 1994, he left his job to join the Peace Corps. As a volunteer with the service organization, Acaba spent two years in the Dominican Republic, where he taught local students about the environment. He developed a love of teaching during that time and began to consider pursuing work in the educational field following his return to the United States. However, he did not immediately find teaching work after leaving the Peace Corps, instead serving for a time as island manager for the Caribbean Marine Research Center (CMRC) in the Bahamas. Acaba later moved to Florida, where he found an environmental job dealing with shoreline vegetation.

Acaba began to exercise his love of teaching in the classroom in the late 1990s, first taking a job at Florida's Melbourne High School, in Brevard County. After a year, he moved to Dunnellon Middle School, where he taught science and mathematics to seventh- and eighth-grade students. During his time at the school, Acaba cofounded a science center that focused on hands-on learning. He remained at Dunnellon Middle School for four years.

BECOMING AN ASTRONAUT

In 2003, the National Aeronautics and Space Administration (NASA) announced it was launching a new initiative to train a select group of teachers as astronauts, with the goal of promoting space exploration among students and forging connections between schools and NASA's programs. Unlike the Teacher in Space program of the 1980s, which was canceled following teacher Christa McAuliffe's death in the 1986 *Challenger* disaster, the Educator Astronaut Project would train the teachers extensively as astronauts so they would be able to carry out key mission duties in addition to participating in educational programs. Acaba, then working at Dunnellon Middle School, was intrigued by the prospect of becoming an astronaut. "When I saw the announcement, I felt that everything I had done to this point was in preparation for this job," he said, as quoted in a NASA press release (3 June 2004). He was ultimately chosen for the program, becoming one of three educators selected to join the eleven-member 2004 astronaut candidate class.

Following his selection, Acaba traveled to Houston, Texas, to undergo training at the Lyndon B. Johnson Space Center in Houston. The training programs at the space center included scientific, flight, and survival training, among other efforts. Acaba completed his training in 2006 and spent the next years working for NASA while waiting for his opportunity to travel into space as a mission specialist. The opportunity came in 2009, when Acaba was assigned to the crew of the space shuttle *Discovery* for a two-week mission known as STS-119. "It was very cool to find out," he said of the announcement in his 2009 NASA preflight interview. "It was kind of that same feeling that I got when I received the phone call asking me if I wanted to come and become an astronaut—just something that's almost unbelievable, the realization of a dream and just a very happy moment."

Discovery launched from Florida's John F. Kennedy Space Center on March 15, 2009, carrying Acaba and his six crewmates as well as solar arrays and other equipment bound for the International Space Station (ISS). Upon leaving Earth's atmosphere, Acaba became the first person of Puerto Rican heritage to go into space, a milestone he celebrated by bringing a Puerto Rican flag with him. The shuttle reached the ISS on March 17, and Acaba and his colleagues began to carry out a variety of duties aboard and around the station, including spacewalks. Acaba completed two spacewalks over the course of the mission. The crew left the ISS on March 25 and landed in Florida on March 28.

FURTHER MISSIONS

Following his first flight into space, Acaba remained deeply involved with US and international spaceflight efforts, working in the ISS's Earth-based operations department as well as at the Russian cosmonaut-training center Star City. He made his second trip to the ISS in May of 2012, traveling from the Baikonur Cosmodrome in Kazakhstan aboard a Russian *Soyuz* spacecraft. Acaba served as flight engineer for the mission, known as Expedition 31/32. Unlike during his previous trip, which lasted only a matter of weeks, Acaba and his colleagues spent several months aboard the ISS, conducting a variety of scientific experiments. "The duration's a big thing," he explained in a NASA preflight interview (20 Mar. 2012). "When you do a shuttle flight, you know, it's two weeks, you're jam-packed and, you're just there and you're working hard and I don't think you get the opportunity to really enjoy living in space, which is going to be great now."

In addition to the scientific efforts taking place during the mission, Acaba's time at the ISS was particularly significant because it encompassed the first test mission of the *Dragon* spacecraft, created by the company SpaceX. That craft reached the ISS not long after Acaba's arrival. It delivered a variety of supplies to the space station, representing a new means of keeping the ISS fully stocked with equipment and living essentials. Acaba returned to Earth in September 2012.

Acaba again returned to the ISS in September of 2017 as a crewmember for Expedition 53/54. During the mission, which was planned to conclude in February 2018, Acaba and his colleagues were tasked with carrying out experiments related to areas such as cosmic rays, fiber optics, and bone cell growth. Acaba was particularly excited about the fact there were now four astronauts staffing the laboratory operated by the US Operating Segment (USOS). "Having four USOS crew members on board, it gives you a lot more opportunities, not only to maintain the space station but then do the science we're up there for," he explained to Harwood. "I think the number I heard is somewhere around eight hundred more hours of utilization. That's a big chunk of science we're going to be able to do." In addition to carrying out experiments and other tasks within the ISS, Acaba remained committed to education during his time on the ISS, posting intriguing information about space-station life on the social networking site Twitter and recording educational videos.

PERSONAL LIFE

Acaba has three children. He is a lifelong fan of the Anaheim-based Los Angeles Angels baseball team. Acaba also enjoys outdoor activities such as scuba diving, hiking, kayaking, biking, and camping.

A resident of the Houston area since his time in astronaut training, Acaba was one of many residents of that region whose homes were flooded when Hurricane Harvey approached Texas in August 2017. Acaba was out of the country at the time, preparing for his third trip to the ISS, and friends and neighbors gathered to mitigate the flood damage to his house. "It was a huge relief to know that there were people at home, taking care of me," he told Marcia Dunn for the *Orlando Sentinel* (20 Sept. 2017). Then, when Puerto Rico was devastated by Hurricane Maria the next month, Acaba offered words of encouragement from aboard the ISS.

SUGGESTED READING

Acaba, Joseph. "Preflight Interview: Joe Acaba." *NASA*, 20 Mar. 2012, www.nasa.gov/mission_pages/station/expeditions/expedition31/acaba_interview.html. Accessed 12 Jan. 2018.

Acaba, Joseph. "Preflight Interview: Joseph Acaba, Mission Specialist." *NASA*, 5 Jan. 2009, www.nasa.gov/mission_pages/shuttle/shuttlemissions/sts119/interview_acaba.html. Accessed 12 Jan. 2018.

Dunn, Marcia. "Puerto Rican Astronaut Gets Double Dose of Hurricanes." *Orlando Sentinel*, 20 Sept. 2017, www.orlandosentinel.com/news/space/go-for-launch/os-puerto-rico-hurricane-astronaut-20170920-story.html. Accessed 12 Jan. 2017.

"Florida Teacher Selected as Astronaut Candidate." *NASA*, 3 June 2004, www.nasa.gov/home/hqnews/2004/jun/HQ_04178_minority_feature_acaba.html. Accessed 12 Jan. 2017.

Harwood, William. "Soyuz Launches with Space Station Crew Looking Forward to Expanded Research." *CBS News*, 12 Sept. 2017, www.cbsnews.com/news/

space-station-crew-looks-forward-to-expand-ed-research/. Accessed 12 Jan. 2018.

Marcial Ocasio, Jennifer A. "Puerto Rican Astronaut Joseph Acabá Embarks on Third Trip into Space." *Orlando Sentinel*, 13 Sept. 2017, www.orlandosentinel.com/news/space/go-for-launch/os-puerto-rican-astronaut-joseph-acaba-20170912-story.html. Accessed 12 Jan. 2018.

Moskowitz, Clara. "'Avengers' in Space: NASA Astronaut Recounts Movie Nights and Life in Orbit." *Space.com*, 28 Sept. 2012, www.space.com/17804-astronaut-joe-acaba-life-space.html. Accessed 12 Jan. 2018.

—Joy Crelin

Elliot Ackerman

Date of birth: April 12, 1980
Occupation: Author

A long line of famed American novelists have written about their experiences in combat—Ernest Hemingway, Joseph Heller, Kurt Vonnegut, and Tim O'Brien, to name just a few—but few have written so eloquently from the perspectives of the citizens of the countries in which they were fighting. Enter Elliot Ackerman, a US Marine veteran and recipient of the Silver Star, with tours of duty in the wars of Iraq and Afghanistan, who has penned two critically acclaimed novels about life in the modern Middle East. His debut effort, *Green on Blue* (2015), looks at the experiences of a young Afghan soldier who has spent his entire life immersed in a state of continual war; his second novel, *Dark at the Crossing* (2017), details the trials of an Iraqi American who fought in the Iraq War and then seeks to join the rebels in the Syrian Civil War. Although each novel is a fictionalized account of modern-day events, both are infused with Ackerman's great care in describing the lives of the kinds of people he knew and fought alongside during his military career. For the author, capturing these lives and experiences in words is one of the most important things he could do with his life. "There are these moments in the military where you're present at these enormous intersections of history and humanity," he said to Megan O'Grady in an interview published in *Vogue* (17 Feb. 2015). "I came out of the end of that and I just wanted to write. If you do it well, you know it will last. It can't get blown away like everything else." Ackerman's work has appeared in the *New York Times*, the *New Yorker*, the *Atlantic*, and the *New Republic*, among other publications. His short fiction has been included in *The Best American Short Stories*.

EARLY LIFE AND EDUCATION

Elliot Ackerman was born on April 12, 1980, and lived in Los Angeles, California, until the age of nine. At that time his father, Peter Ackerman, a financier and longtime chair of the board of advisors at the Fletcher School of Law and Diplomacy at Tufts University, had taken a position at his firm's branch in London. With his mother, the author Joanne Leedom-Ackerman, and his older brother, Nate, Elliot Ackerman disembarked in England, where he came to love skateboarding.

Ackerman recalled in a piece he wrote for the *New York Times Magazine* (5 Dec. 2014): "Southbank, at an eastern bend in the Thames, is the center of British skateboarding. Sheltered from London's incessant rain by an undercroft, the space has stairs, ledges and a large, smoothly paved expanse that sweeps into a three-sided bank. Graffiti artists worked there unmolested, homeless people slept in the corners, the sidewalk smelled faintly of urine and the continuous crashing of skateboards left your head ringing. I loved it."

At age fifteen, Ackerman returned with his family to the United States, settling in Washington, DC. In 1998 he entered Tufts University, where he enrolled in a program at the Fletcher School that allowed him to earn a bachelor's degree from Tufts and a master's degree from Fletcher in five years total. He studied international affairs, which appealed to him greatly, and participated in the Reserve Officers' Training Corps (ROTC) program, joining the US Marines as an infantry officer upon graduation in 2003—the year a US–led coalition invaded Iraq.

A CAREER OF SERVICE

"My father understood my decision to go somewhere and prove myself. The military is, for all its quirks, a place where no one cares where you're from," he said to Megan O'Grady for *Vogue*. "For my mother, it was more difficult. That being said, she tapped incredible reserves of strength, becoming someone I could always talk to about the challenges of combat. She knows my most difficult war stories, ones where I lost friends, ones where I still question some of the decisions I made. But I don't think her emotional trajectory is unique. Whether your mother is a novelist like mine or a third-generation military wife, the idea of a son or daughter being in mortal danger is terrifying."

Ackerman felt he needed to serve in the military because he wanted to do something meaningful with his life at a unique moment in US history. He wrote in a piece for *Vogue* (17 Feb. 2015): "I chose to serve because I didn't want to spend my early 20s scouring spreadsheets at a bank or making photocopies at a law firm. For better or worse, I wanted a job with actual responsibility, where my performance really mattered, and it did in the Marines; it mattered in terms of lives."

Ackerman would go on to serve five tours of duty during his time in the Marines. He served two tours in Iraq in 2004 and 2005, including in the second battle of Fallujah. For his actions as a platoon commander in that battle, he earned a Purple Heart, for shrapnel wounds, and the Silver Star—the country's third-highest military award—for valor.

In 2005 he was also sent stateside, to aid in the recovery efforts following Hurricane Katrina, which had devastated the Gulf Coast region. A year later he was serving in the Mediterranean, where he evacuated US citizens from Beirut during the Israeli war in Lebanon. He was then deployed to Afghanistan for two years, where he worked as a combat advisor for Afghan troops. He left the Marine Corps as a captain in 2008, then moved to the Central Intelligence Agency (CIA) from 2009 to 2011, working on counterterrorism in the Middle East.

In 2011 Ackerman helped his father establish a nonprofit organization called Americans Elect, which encouraged third-party candidates to run for the presidency in 2012. In 2012, Ackerman was one of just fifteen people selected to join the prestigious White House Fellow program. During the yearlong fellowship, he worked on veterans' employment issues. In 2013 he moved to Turkey to work for a humanitarian aid consulting firm monitoring the conflict in Syria, and to gather material for his fiction.

ACCLAIMED NOVELIST

Unlike the novels of many military veterans, Ackerman's debut, *Green on Blue* (2015), does not focus on the experiences of an American soldier in a combat zone, but rather on the life of a modern Afghan soldier living in a nation long torn by war. The novel is narrated by the young Aziz, who describes the complex set of circumstances that led to his becoming a soldier seeking to avenge his brother's wounding in a bazaar bombing. Aziz was raised in the period after the Soviet-Afghan War ended in 1989; he lived a peasant's life alongside his parents and his older brother, Ali. When the Taliban destroy their village and take their parents and other villagers away, the boys are forced to beg in the streets. Eventually they get work making deliveries, and Aziz gets an education at a madrassa, but all of that comes to an end following Ali's wounding after US forces arrive in late 2001. Aziz declares vengeance for his brother's mutilation, leading him to join the Special Lashkar, a military unit working alongside the Americans. His new position leads him to confront the man who ordered the attack that injured his brother—and to navigate the perilous shifting alliances in the war against the Taliban.

Green on Blue earned considerable acclaim upon its publication. In a review for the *Christian Science Monitor* (27 Mar. 2015), Katherine A. Powers declared that Ackerman's debut demonstrated "what it means to live in a country in a state of perpetual war among ever-mutating alliances, in which everyone is forced to choose sides. But here, no side is what it seems, except as a target for destruction—and, as it happens, the potential means of a livelihood. . . . Elliot Ackerman, who served five tours of military duty in Iraq and Afghanistan, knows the territory and has not, it would seem, come away with feelings of national accomplishment." A critic writing for *Kirkus Reviews* (7 Dec. 2014) declared: "Ackerman writes in a deliberately flat style that emphasizes personalities rather than military action—and he does justice to the political and moral difficulties of contemporary Afghanistan."

Ackerman's sophomore effort, *Dark at the Crossing* (2017), explores the world of the Syrian Civil War and the tumult facing its participants. In it we meet Haris Abadi, an Iraqi who worked as an interpreter with US special operations forces during the Iraq War and has since become an American citizen. As the war in Syria begins in earnest, he finds himself drawn back to the Middle East, in hopes of aiding the militants looking to overthrow the regime of Syrian president Bashar al-Assad. Abadi tries to enter Syria through Gaziantep, Turkey, but is turned away at the border. Here he meets a Syrian exile named Amir. Haris, however, begins to form a deep connection with Amir's wife, Daphne. The trio agree to attempt to enter Syria together, even if it means working with the Islamic State (referred to in the novel as Daesh, the acronym of the group's Arabic name).

Major media outlets again praised Ackerman's work as a novelist. Brian Turner remarked in the *Washington Post* (24 Jan. 2017) that "while Ackerman's experiences surely filter the narrative of Haris Abadi's story, the author's hand fades as we're transported beyond the horizon of our own lives. It's impossible not to consider the millions of people involved in years of conflict in Syria. *Dark at the Crossing* is not only a fictional meditation on remorse, betrayal, love and loss, but also a journey that returns us to the beautiful and broken world we live in." Similarly, Lawrence Osborne proclaimed in the *New York Times* (1 Feb. 2017): "'Dark at the Crossing' is unusual in that few of its characters are Western—a bold move in a culture obsessed with 'appropriation.' Whether this makes them convincing to an Arab ear is hard to say, but Ackerman's decision is clearly motivated by empathy and a desire not to tell his story through characters thinking and speaking his own language."

Dark at the Crossing was a finalist for the 2017 National Book Award.

PERSONAL LIFE

Ackerman and his wife, Xanthe Scharff Ackerman—a journalist and executive director of the Fuller Project for International Reporting—have two children and until recently lived in Istanbul, Turkey, where he conducted research and reported on the Syrian Civil War.

SUGGESTED READING

Ackerman, Elliot. "Safe on the Southbank." *The New York Times*, 5 Dec. 2014, www.nytimes.com/2014/12/07/magazine/safe-on-the-southbank.html. Accessed 24 Jan. 2018.

Ackerman, Elliot. "Veteran and Novelist Elliot Ackerman on the Moment He Was Ready to Leave War." *Vogue*, 17 Feb. 2015, www.vogue.com/article/elliot-ackerman-iraq-afghanistan-veteran-essay. Accessed 24 Jan. 2018.

Ackerman, Elliot. Review of *Green on Blue*, by Elliot Ackerman. *Kirkus Reviews*, 17 Feb. 2015, www.kirkusreviews.com/book-reviews/elliot-ackerman/green-on-blue/. Accessed 24 Jan. 2018.

O'Grady, Megan. "Five-Tour Veteran Elliot Ackerman Charts New Territory in a Charged New Novel, *Green on Blue*." Review of *Green on Blue*, by Elliot Ackerman. *Vogue*, 17 Feb. 2015, www.vogue.com/article/veteran-elliot-ackerman-green-on-blue-book. Accessed 24 Jan. 2018.

Osborne, Lawrence. "A Story of Chaos at the Border of Turkey and Syria." Review of *Dark at the Crossing*, by Elliot Ackerman. *The New York Times*, 1 Feb. 2017, www.nytimes.com/2017/02/01/books/review/dark-at-the-crossing-elliot-ackerman.html. Accessed 24 Jan. 2018.

Powers, Katherine A. "'Green on Blue' Tells a Powerful, Tragic Story of War in Afghanistan, as Seen by a Young Afghan." Review of *Green on Blue*, by Elliot Ackerman. *The Christian Science Monitor*, 27 Mar. 2015, www.csmonitor.com/Books/Book-Reviews/2015/0327/Green-on-Blue-tells-a-powerful-tragic-story-of-war-in-Afghanistan-as-seen-by-a-young-Afghan. Accessed 24 Jan. 2018.

Turner, Brian. "What Drives an American to Fight in Syria?" Review of *Dark at the Crossing*, by Elliot Ackerman. *The Washington Post*, 24 Jan. 2017, www.washingtonpost.com/entertainment/books/what-drives-an-american-to-fight-in-syria/2017/01/23/e55737d0-e1aa-11e6-a547-5fb9411d332c_story.html. Accessed 24 Jan. 2018.

SELECTED WORKS

Green on Blue, 2015; *Dark at the Crossing*, 2017; *Waiting for Eden*, 2018

—Christopher Mari

José Altuve

Date of birth: May 6, 1990
Occupation: Baseball player

Houston Astros second baseman José Altuve could be considered the living embodiment of persistence. A lifelong baseball lover who first learned to play from his father while growing up in Venezuela, Altuve tried out for the Astros as a teenager but was turned away, purportedly because of his below-average height. Upon returning to the tryouts, however, Altuve impressed the team's representatives with his strong batting skills, winning himself a place in the organization. Several years in the minor leagues followed, and he was promoted to the majors in July 2011. The Astros finished the season with the worst record in Major League Baseball (MLB) and remained in last place for the next two seasons. Altuve and his teammates, however, persevered, and their ongoing efforts not only led to impressive statistics—Altuve had the highest batting average in the American League (AL) in 2014, 2016, and 2017—but also enabled the Astros to secure the franchise's first World Series victory in 2017. Although Altuve was pleased with the team's success, he remained focused on setting new goals. "I'm happy and all that," he told Tom Verducci for *Sports Illustrated* (5 Dec. 2017), "but I feel like, 'OK, we have to move

By Keith Allison, via Wikimedia Commons

forward, and next year is another year.' I mean, we are World Series champions forever. Everybody knows that. But I want to win multiple World Series."

EARLY LIFE AND EDUCATION

José Carlos Altuve was born on May 6, 1990, in Puerto Cabello, Venezuela, to Carlos Altuve and Lastenia Linares. Altuve's father worked at a chemical company as an assistant to an engineer; his mother was a homemaker. He grew up in the city of Maracay. Altuve learned to play baseball as a child, initially playing the game with his father. He went on to play extensively during his early years in Maracay, a city that had once been home to successful major-league players such as Miguel Cabrera. Major-league teams actively recruited players from Venezuela, and the Houston Astros operated a training school and summer and winter-league teams in the country.

He attended a tryout for the Astros at the age of sixteen but was reportedly asked to leave, a decision Altuve—who as an adult stands at about five feet six inches—attributed to his small stature. Although he initially considered giving up, his father encouraged him to persevere and show the Astros' representatives that he was a talented batter. Altuve returned to the tryouts the next day, uninvited, where he was given the opportunity to show off his skills. "I remember this guy, a big prospect, was on the mound—a big lefty throwing gas," he recalled to Verducci. "I was like, He's going to throw you a first-pitch fastball. If you don't hit it, you're done." Altuve hit that pitch and the next, aptly demonstrating his capabilities. Following his tryout, Altuve signed with the Astros as an amateur free agent in 2007, receiving a signing bonus of only $15,000.

MINOR LEAGUES

After signing with the Astros organization, Altuve began his professional baseball career in 2007, as a member of the Venezuelan Summer League Astros, the team's international rookie-level affiliate. He appeared in sixty-four games and achieved a batting average of .343. Altuve spent the 2008 season and the beginning of 2009 with the Greeneville Astros, the rookie-level affiliate in the Appalachian League, before moving to the Tri-City ValleyCats, a class-A short-season team, in August 2009. He played with two teams during the 2010 season, spending April through July with the class-A Lexington Legends and August and September with the class-A-advanced Lancaster JetHawks. Altuve also participated in the Venezuelan Winter League during the late fall and early winter of 2010.

Altuve viewed his time in the minor leagues as a valuable learning experience that particularly prepared him to face some of the trickiest challenges facing major-league batters. "I kept listening in the minor leagues, and even earlier than that," he told Verducci, "people would say, 'If you don't hit the fastball, you're not going to get to the big leagues.' Every game you're going to get a fastball. I haven't seen a guy that throws twenty breaking balls out of twenty pitches. One or two of those are going to be a fastball. And you have to be ready to hit it." Indeed, Altuve demonstrated that he was ready to hit whatever came at him during his final season in the minor leagues, achieving batting averages of .408 over fifty-two games with the JetHawks and .361 over thirty-five games with the double-A Corpus Christi Hooks in the spring and summer of 2011.

HOUSTON ASTROS

In 2011, Altuve was called up to the major leagues, making his debut with the Astros on July 20. Over the course of his first season, Altuve played in fifty-seven games with the Astros and managed 26 runs and 61 hits in 221 at bats. Despite his relatively quick adjustment to major-league play, the Astros as a whole struggled during the season and ended with a win-loss record of 56–106, the worst in the major leagues. The following two seasons were dismal for the Astros as well, and the team again ranked last in the major leagues in both 2012 and 2013. During that period, Altuve worked to improve his play, and in 2012, he was selected as a reserve player for his first All-Star Game. Following the 2012 season, the Astros moved from the National League (NL) to the American League (AL), becoming a member of the AL West division, all within MLB.

Despite the challenges the Astros faced during Altuve's early years with the team, he remained optimistic about the franchise's outlook. "In 2011, we lost 100 games, 2012 and 2013 [too]. But I cannot lie—I believe in the process. I believe in what Jeff Luhnow and Jim Crane used to [tell] me, like, 'Hey, we're gonna win one day. We're gonna become a really good team,'" he said, as quoted by Michelle R. Martinelli in *For the Win* (2 Nov. 2017). "I was like, OK, now I want to get better every single day to be part of that team when they become good." To that end, Altuve dedicated the period between the 2013 and 2014 season to improving his batting skills as well as his overall physical fitness and nutrition.

ON THE RISE

The 2014 season marked a turning point both for the Astros as a whole and for Altuve in particular. Although the team was still unable to achieve a positive win-loss record, the Astros ranked higher than several other MLB teams by the end of the season with a record of 70–92. Altuve played a substantial role in the team's relative success, achieving a batting average of .341, the highest among all AL players during that season. Altuve also led the league in stolen bases (56) and hits (225), setting a new Astros record for hits in a single season. In recognition of his achievements during the season, Altuve received his first Silver Slugger Award in November of that year.

The following season represented another leap forward for the Astros, as the team ended the season with an 86–76 record, finishing second in the AL West. Altuve amassed the most hits (200) and at bats (638) in the league over the course of the regular season. He also achieved the highest fielding percentage among all AL second basemen with .993, earning the 2015 Gold Glove Award for his fielding work. Following the conclusion of the regular season, the Astros secured the team's first Wild Card berth in a decade. Altuve and his teammates played a successful Wild Card Game against the New York Yankees and earned a spot in the American League Division Series (ALDS). Although the Astros ultimately lost the ALDS to the Kansas City Royals, the team's postseason campaign demonstrated that Altuve's optimism was well founded.

Although the Astros failed to return to the playoffs in 2016, the season was a professionally rewarding one for Altuve. He led the AL in hits (216) and batting average (.338). Altuve received several awards for his performance, including the 2016 Lou Gehrig Memorial Award, and was particularly honored to be selected as Sporting News' 2016 Major League Player of the Year, a title voted on by professional baseball players. "I really appreciate that from my teammates and players on other teams. These are the kind of things that make you keep getting better," he told Brian McTaggart for *MLB* (27 Oct. 2016). "You wake up every morning and realize you won this award by the players, and you want to keep getting better. Not only for the team, but for the fans and for everybody that's been [helping] you."

WORLD SERIES WIN, MVP

During the 2017 season, the Astros achieved a win-loss record of 101–61, finishing first in the AL West. Altuve once again ended the season with the highest batting average (.346) and most hits (204) in the AL. The Astros secured a spot in the postseason and entered the ALDS, facing off against the Boston Red Sox. Altuve hit three home runs in the first game of the ALDS, which the Astros ultimately won, 3–1. Moving onward into the American League Championship Series (ALCS), the Astros defeated the Yankees by a single game, winning the team's first AL pennant and second pennant ever. The Astros then competed against the Los Angeles Dodgers in the World Series, playing a full, seven-game series. Altuve scored four runs over the course of the series and most notably caught the final out of game seven, securing the Astros' victory.

The first World Series win in franchise history, the Astros' 2017 victory was in many ways the culmination of years of effort and persistence on the part of Altuve and his teammates. "This year, I felt something in spring training in the locker room," he said following the World Series, as quoted by Martinelli. "I saw a good chemistry between everybody—players, coaches everybody. And we only talked about winning, winning, winning. That's all we wanted to do, and now we're here." In recognition of his work during the regular season and postseason, Altuve was the recipient of several awards, including the AL Hank Aaron Award and the Babe Ruth Award. He was most notably named Most Valuable Player (MVP) in the American League. "I wasn't expecting this," he told Richard Justice for *MLB* (16 Nov. 2017) after receiving the honor. "I think my teammates made this for me. They made me an MVP."

In March 2018, Altuve signed a five-year, $151 million contract extension with the Astros that would keep him with the team through 2024. His 2018 season started off strong with a 4–1 game against the Texas Rangers on March 29 of that year. He continued to play regularly throughout the season but injured his knee that July and was placed on the ten-day disabled list for the first time in his MLB career.

PERSONAL LIFE

Altuve met his wife, Nina, while they were both in high school. They live in the Houston area with their daughter, Melanie.

SUGGESTED READING

"Jose Altuve Reportedly Agrees to 5-Year, $151 Million Extension with Astros." *ESPN*, 16 Mar. 2018, www.espn.com/mlb/story/_/id/22797342/houston-astros-extend-jose-altuve-5-year-deal. Accessed 10 Aug. 2018.

Justice, Richard. "MVP: Stanton by a Nose, Altuve Towers over AL." *MLB*, 16 Nov. 2017, www.mlb.com/news/giancarlo-stanton-jose-altuve-win-mvp-awards/c-262040670. Accessed 10 Aug. 2018.

Martinelli, Michelle R. "Jose Altuve on Astros' Road to World Series Champs: 'I Believe in the Process.'" *For the Win*, 2 Nov. 2017, ftw.usatoday.com/2017/11/jose-altuve-houston-astros-world-series-dodgers-trust-the-process-video. Accessed 10 Aug. 2018.

McTaggart, Brian. "Altuve Wins Sporting News' MLB Player of the Year." *MLB*, 27 Oct. 2016, www.mlb.com/news/jose-altuve-wins-sporting-news-player-of-year/c-207313826. Accessed 10 Aug. 2018.

Putterman, Alex. "Jose Altuve, Baseball's Unlikeliest Superstar." *The Atlantic*, 6 Oct. 2017, www.theatlantic.com/entertainment/archive/2017/10/jose-altuve-baseballs-unlikeliest-superstar/542139/. Accessed 10 Aug. 2018.

Span, Emma. "Little Big League: How Jose Altuve Became an Unlikely Batting Champ." *Sports Illustrated*, 17 Dec. 2014, www.si.com/mlb/2014/12/17/jose-altuve-houston-astros-batting-champ. Accessed 10 Aug. 2018.

Verducci, Tom. "SI's 2017 Sportsperson of the Year: José Altuve Defied Odds to Bring Houston Hope . . . and a Title." *Sports Illustrated*, 5 Dec. 2017, www.si.com/sportsperson/2017/12/05/jose-altuve-2017-sportsperson-of-the-year-houston-astros. Accessed 10 Aug. 2018.

—*Joy Crelin*

Craig Anderson

Date of Birth: May 21, 1981
Occupation: Hockey player

Unlike many players in the National Hockey League (NHL), Craig Anderson has taken a somewhat roundabout route to major-league success. A talented goalkeeper who excelled in junior-level hockey in his teens, he was drafted by the NHL's Calgary Flames in 1999 but ultimately did not sign a contract with the team, returning instead to the junior-level Guelph Storm. A second chance came in 2001, when he was drafted by the Chicago Blackhawks. Anderson struggled to find his footing during his time with the Blackhawks and continued to experience

By Michael Miller (Own work), via Wikimedia Commons

difficulties after moving to the Florida Panthers and the Colorado Avalanche. An early 2011 trade to the Ottawa Senators, however, proved to be a turning point for Anderson. In the years since joining the team, he has achieved impressive statistics, recording the league's highest save percentage in the 2012–13 season, and been awarded the prestigious Bill Masterson Memorial Trophy—a far cry from his loss-plagued early seasons in the NHL. "I think the game is so mental and has such a learning curve," Anderson explained to Adrian Dater for the *Denver Post* (1 July 2009). "For me, it wasn't a long time, but it did take a few years."

EARLY LIFE AND EDUCATION

Craig Peter Anderson was born on May 21, 1981, in Park Ridge, Illinois, to Holly and Richard Anderson. His mother was a teacher who later became a real estate agent, while his father worked in accounting and later operated a wire manufacturing company. Anderson grew up in the Chicago suburbs of Northbrook and Barrington, where he began playing sports at a young age. As a child, he sometimes played hockey with his brother, Jon, who would later go on to play professional baseball for several minor-league affiliates of the Boston Red Sox. Anderson also played the saxophone and was an avid fan of car racing, an interest he inherited from his father.

Demonstrating a talent for hockey, Anderson focused on that sport during his teen years, playing youth hockey with teams such as the Chicago Jets and the Chicago Freeze. As he entered his late teens, he was faced with making the difficult choice between attending college and playing hockey on that level or beginning his professional career in major junior hockey, a category that was open generally to players in their late teens and offered player stipends. While the decision was an important one, Anderson felt that success was possible either way. "The bottom line is if you're good enough to make it, you're going to make it, whether you go to college or if you go to junior," he told Terry Frei for the *Denver Post* (9 Oct. 2009). "For me, I felt I needed to get away and get a little bit of a stronger challenge." In 1998 Anderson opted to pursue his career in professional hockey immediately, entering the Ontario Hockey League (OHL) Priority Selection, the draft for one of Canada's major junior–level hockey leagues.

EARLY CAREER

In the tenth round of the OHL Priority Selection, Anderson was drafted by the Guelph Storm. Aware that playing for a major junior team and thus forfeiting his ability to play at the college level was a potentially risky move, he negotiated with the Storm to ensure that if he did not sign a professional contract, the team would pay for four years of college expenses. "If you didn't make it, if you got injured, there still was that safety net. For me, it worked out really well," he told Frei (9 Oct. 2009). Anderson later completed two years of college while in between contracts. After joining the Guelph Storm, he played in more than one hundred games for the team over three seasons.

In 1999, Anderson entered the NHL Draft. He was selected by the Calgary Flames in the draft's third round. While waiting to come to an agreement with the Flames, he continued to play for the Storm, distinguishing himself as a talented goaltender. He was named OHL Goaltender of the Year following the 2000–2001 season and appeared on that year's OHL All-Star Team. Anderson was unable to agree to a contract with the Flames, however, and they did not sign him. He then reentered the NHL Draft in 2001 and was selected by the Chicago Blackhawks in the third round.

JOINING THE NHL

Upon joining the Blackhawks organization, Anderson was first assigned to the Norfolk Admirals, a developmental affiliate within the American Hockey League (AHL). During the 2001–2002 season, he played in twenty-eight games with the team during his debut season, achieving a record of nine wins, thirteen losses, and four ties and a save percentage of .886. Following the regular season, Anderson joined his new teammates in the AHL playoffs with the goal of claiming the Calder Cup, the AHL equivalent of the NHL's Stanley Cup. However, the Admirals were eliminated in first round of the playoffs. Anderson returned to the Admirals for

much of the 2002–2003 season and again accompanied the team to the playoffs, in which the Admirals advanced to the second round before being defeated by the Houston Aeros. He also played six games for the Blackhawks during the season, making his NHL debut in November of 2002. Although initially pleased to be playing in Chicago, Anderson soon discovered that being close to home also meant being close to distractions. "To play near home in front of friends and family was neat in a way," he told Frei for the *Denver Post* (14 Nov. 2009), "but I found that being real young, you haven't learned the pro game and you haven't learned how to block out the outside factors."

Anderson split his time between the Admirals and the Blackhawks during the 2003–2004 season, playing thirty-seven games with the Admirals and twenty-one with the Blackhawks. His NHL record that season was poor: the Blackhawks won only six of the games in which Anderson appeared. The 2004–2005 NHL season was canceled due to a ten-month labor dispute, so Anderson spent the entire season with the Admirals. Following the season, the team entered the AHL playoffs once more, but was eliminated in first round by the Philadelphia Phantoms, who went on to win the 2005 Calder Cup. In his final season with the Blackhawks, Anderson played in twenty-nine games, all of them with the NHL team. He struggled to succeed as a goaltender, winning only six games and posting a disappointing save percentage of .886. Anderson has noted that his experience with the Blackhawks made it difficult for him to establish himself as a goaltender worth signing. "It's tough for a goalie to get any credibility when you're on a bad team and losing all the time," he said, as quoted by Jonas Siegel for the *Canadian Press* in *CBC Sports* (1 May 2017).

FROM FLORIDA TO COLORADO

In 2006 Anderson was traded to NHL's Florida Panthers. He initially joined the Rochester Americans in the AHL, playing thirty-four games with the team during the 2006–2007 season and accompanying the team into the first round of the AHL playoffs. He performed well during his five games with the Panthers during the season, achieving a save percentage of .931, and became determined to earn a permanent spot on the Panthers. "I was going to prove to everyone, not just Florida, that I was the best American League goalie and I deserved a shot somewhere," he recalled to Frei (14 Nov. 2009). Anderson joined the Panthers for the following two seasons, playing in seventeen games in the 2007–2008 season and in thirty-one in 2008–2009.

Following the end of the 2008–2009 season, Anderson became a free agent, or a player permitted to sign with any team that makes an offer.

He promptly joined the Colorado Avalanche, signing a two-year, $3.6 million contract with the team. "It's a dream come true," he told Dater, of the move to Colorado. "It was the place I wanted to be, a city I've always loved. I think it's a great opportunity for me." During his first season with the Avalanche, Anderson played in seventy-one games and achieved a record of thirty-eight wins and twenty-five losses. The team qualified for the playoffs in 2010 but lost to the San Jose Sharks in the Western Conference quarterfinals. Anderson's 2010–2011 season with the Avalanche proved far less successful than his first: losses outnumbered wins, and Anderson managed a save percentage of only .897, his lowest in several seasons.

OTTAWA SENATORS

In February 2011, the Colorado Avalanche traded Anderson to the Ottawa Senators. For Anderson, the change in team gave him another opportunity to make a first impression as a goalkeeper. "Any time you can get that new first impression it gives you an opportunity to open up people's eyes and say, 'Hey, this is who I am,'" he told Siegel. His attempt to make a new impression paid off: during his first season with the Senators, Anderson won eleven out of eighteen games, with only five losses, and achieved a new career high save percentage of .939. The following season, he won thirty-three of the sixty-three games played and later accompanied the team to the quarterfinals of the playoffs. The 2012–2013 season was shortened due to another NHL lockout, the second in a decade. Anderson nevertheless performed well during the abbreviated season, achieving a new career milestone with a .941 save percentage, the highest in the NHL that season. In the playoffs, the Senators defeated the Montreal Canadiens in the quarterfinal but lost to the Pittsburgh Penguins in the conference semifinal.

Anderson's strong performance with the Senators during his first several seasons with the team, including the 2013–2014 season, made him a valuable member of the team, and Senators' management was motivated to keep him with the organization. In August 2014, he signed a $12.6 million contract extension, committing himself to the team through 2017–2018 season. Following the contract extension, Anderson continued to make a valuable contribution to the team, including playing in the playoffs yet again in 2015.

During the 2016–2017 season, Anderson took a two-month leave of absence from the Senators while his wife was undergoing treatment for cancer. Returning to the team with her encouragement, he finished off the season strong and proceeded into the playoffs, in which the Senators defeated the Boston Bruins and New York Rangers in the first two rounds before being beaten 4–3 by Pittsburgh in the conference finals. In recognition of Anderson's dedication to the sport of hockey, the Professional Hockey Writers' Association awarded him the Bill Masterton Memorial Trophy in June 2017. Several months later, Anderson again extended his contract with the Senators, signing a two-year, $9.5 million agreement. "Ottawa has been a home for me since I got here. Welcomed me with open arms," he said, as quoted by Don Brennan for the *Ottawa Citizen* (11 Sept. 2017), after signing the contract extension. "I've set some pretty good roots here, as far as just getting used to the town, getting used to the fans and really enjoying my time here." Anderson started the 2017–2018 season off with three wins out of five games, including a 3–1 victory over the Detroit Red Wings.

PERSONAL LIFE

Anderson and his wife, Nicholle, were married in 2010. They have two sons, Levi and Jake, and own a home in Coral Springs, Florida. In the fall of 2016, Nicholle Anderson was diagnosed with a rare throat cancer and subsequently began treatment, during which time Anderson took a leave of absence from the Senators. She was declared cancer free in May 2017.

SUGGESTED READING

Brennan, Don. "Anderson Remains Focused through Hurricanes, Contract Status." *Ottawa Citizen*, 11 Sept. 2017, ottawacitizen.com/sports/hockey/nhl/senatorsextra/anderson-remains-focused-through-hurricanes-contract-status. Accessed 12 Nov. 2017.

"Craig Anderson of Senators Wins Masterton Trophy." *NHL.com*, 21 June 2017, www.nhl.com/news/craig-anderson-wins-masterton-trophy/c-290049476. Accessed 12 Nov. 2017.

Dater, Adrian. "Avs' New Goalie Up for No. 1 Task." *The Denver Post*, 1 July 2009, www.denverpost.com/2009/07/01/avs-new-goalie-up-for-no-1-task. Accessed 12 Nov. 2017.

Frei, Terry. "Avalanche's Craig Anderson at Home in Net, Windy City." *The Denver Post*, 9 Oct. 2009, www.denverpost.com/2009/10/09/avalanches-craig-anderson-at-home-in-net-windy-city/. Accessed 12 Nov. 2017.

Frei, Terry. "Avs Looking Up to Anderson." *The Denver Post*, 14 Nov. 2009, www.denverpost.com/2009/11/14/avs-looking-up-to-anderson/. Accessed 12 Nov. 2017.

Garrioch, Bruce. "On Mother's Day, Senators Take Time to Relax and Reflect." *Ottawa Citizen*, 14 May 2017, ottawacitizen.com/sports/hockey/nhl/senatorsextra/on-mothers-day-senators-take-time-to-relax-and-reflect. Accessed 12 Nov. 2017.

Siegel, Jonas. "Senators' Craig Anderson Took Long Road in Building Credibility." *CBC Sports*, 1 May 2017, www.cbc.ca/sports/hockey/nhl/craig-anderson-road-to-success-1.4093510. Accessed 12 Nov. 2017.

—*Joy Crelin*

Caitriona Balfe

Date of birth: October 4, 1979
Occupation: Actor

Irish-born Caitriona Balfe, who spent several years modeling for top brands before breaking into acting, is best known for her portrayal of Claire Beauchamp Randall, the time-traveling protagonist of the hit television show *Outlander*, which premiered on the Starz network in 2014 and quickly gained millions of fervent fans. Based on the beloved Diana Gabaldon novels and adapted by screenwriter Ronald D. Moore of *Battlestar Galactica* fame, *Outlander* has largely satisfied the expectations of readers insistent on adherence to the original novels and has charmed initially skeptical critics. "The series, which involves time travel and 18th-century Scottish politics, is so hard to classify," Richard Lawson wrote for *Vanity Fair* (5 Aug. 2014). "It's a little of everything, but not entirely anything. *Outlander*'s mix of genres and tones is strange, but it's nonetheless a disarmingly enjoyable series."

Balfe—who has earned multiple awards and nominations, including a British Academy of Film and Television Arts (BAFTA) Scotland Award, for her portrayal of Claire—acknowledges that the series contains genre elements that some find easy to disparage. In an interview with Lisa Rosen for the *Los Angeles Times* (28 May 2015), she joked about how often her character's bodice has been torn. "It's the go-to thing in 1743," she quipped. Still, she believes *Outlander* and its characters also resonate on a more meaningful level. "You see this woman who can really do anything," she explained to Rosen about Claire. "One thing that I struggled with a little bit, but also loved about her so much, is just her lack of self-pity. She has this mettle where, no matter what kind of trauma befalls her, she gets right back up and meets the next day with the same kind of gumption and ferocity." Although Balfe has praised Gabaldon for creating such a popular and relatable character, many reviewers have commended the actor herself for elevating the role. In a critique for the industry publication *Backstage* (1 Apr. 2015), Tim Grierson wrote, "'Outlander' is an ostensibly lush period-piece-within-a-period-piece drama

By Christine Ring, via Wikimedia Commons

that's consistently richer and thornier than its romance-novel trappings suggest. And much of the credit goes to Balfe."

EARLY YEARS

The middle child of seven, Caitriona Balfe was born on October 4, 1979, in Dublin, Ireland. She was raised in the small village of Tydavnet, in County Monaghan. Her father, now retired, was a member of the Republic of Ireland's national police force, and during the Troubles, as the decades-long conflict between Catholics and Protestants in Northern Ireland was known, he often feared for his safety. "I remember a woman coming to our door one time to tell us that 'our kind,' meaning cops and their families, were not wanted in Monaghan," the actor recalled to Patricia Danaher for the *Irish Daily Mail Weekend* (30 Sept. 2017). "My father would work crazy long shifts because at that point there was 24-hour border patrol and he was head sergeant in the area."

Despite the strife, the family ultimately became a fixture in the community; Balfe's father became involved in local amateur theatrics, and she credits her early love of acting to his example. Eager to win a share of attention in her large, discordant family, Balfe became something of a ham. At around the age of seven, she got involved in a local youth theater, portraying Mr. Bumble in a stage production of *Oliver!* There was no movie theater in her small village, and she vividly remembers being allowed to take the bus for the first time to one in a neighboring town. "*Robin Hood* was the first film I ever saw in the cinema—Kevin Costner in all his glory on the big screen!" she told Danaher. Still, in retrospect, she appreciates growing up in Tydavnet. "At the end of the day, I'm a country girl who grew up climbing trees and mucking out," she expressed to Danaher. "We grew up on the poetry of Patrick Kavanagh and the landscape of Monaghan is very much imprinted in me."

MODELING CAREER

Though she had always hoped, little could Balfe have known at the time that she would become quite the world traveler. She briefly attended the Dublin Institute of Technology, where she studied acting; however, one day, when she was collecting money for charity outside of the Swan Centre, a large shopping mall in the suburb of Rathmines, she was approached by a modeling agent. A few part-time modeling stints in Dublin followed. Then, lured by the prospect of traveling, she convinced her parents to allow her to drop out of school to try modeling for a year when a scout invited her to work in France. "I was 19 and going to live abroad for the first time—and not just anywhere, but in Paris," she wrote in a personal essay for the *New York Times* (3 Oct. 2017). "The city of love and culture, of Yves Saint Laurent, Gertrude Stein and the Louvre. It was about as far away from my tiny village in Ireland as I could imagine."

The initial reality of being in Paris, however, did not match Balfe's dreams. "My first month was much harder than I expected," she wrote in her *New York Times* piece. "The constant stream of rejection from castings started to wear me down. I got lost constantly. No one understood my halting, embarrassing attempts at speaking French." Eventually, though, she began to adapt to the city and to win assignments, eventually modeling and walking the runway for a wide variety of fashion houses, including Kenzo, Moschino, Givenchy, Marc Jacobs, Dolce & Gabbana, Alberta Ferretti, Louis Vuitton, and Chanel.

Balfe also appeared on the covers of such glossy magazines as *Vogue* and *Elle*, and the planned one-year hiatus from acting school had turned into a break of almost a decade—one that saw her visiting world capitals and living in countries such as Italy and Japan before she ultimately settled in New York City. Her father was supportive, albeit sometimes discomfited by the garments she was modeling. In 2002, she had appeared in the annual televised Victoria's Secret fashion show.

During this period, fashion journalists often referred to Balfe as Ireland's first official supermodel. However, with the acting bug still niggling at the back of her mind, she never felt fully satisfied by her modeling career: "It was never something that I wanted to do. It was never a dream of mine and I found it very stifling and limiting," she explained to Patrick Freyne for the *Irish Times* (11 Aug. 2012). Finally, in 2009, after years of modeling, she moved from New York to Los Angeles to pursue her original dream.

ACTING CAREER BEGINS

Balfe spent her first several months in Los Angeles determinedly trying to break into the acting world on her own, taking classes at the Sanford Meisner Center and other studios. Despite her fear that she would be too old to catch the eye of casting agents or directors, she found her first role relatively quickly: a nonspeaking part in the 2011 science-fiction blockbuster *Super 8*, written and directed by veteran J. J. Abrams, who ensured that the studio pulled strings to get her the appropriate work visa. Her next screen credits included a few episodes of the television miniseries *The Beauty Inside* (2012), the web series *H+* (2012–13), the heist film *Now You See Me* (2013), and the prison thriller *Escape Plan* (2013), starring Sylvester Stallone and Arnold Schwarzenegger.

Balfe was still relatively unknown by the time Moore, his casting director and producers, and Gabaldon had been searching for some time for the best actor to fill one of the only major roles left vacant in the upcoming television adaptation *Outlander*, that of Claire; however, they would later express in interviews that Balfe had immediately caught their attention. After viewing her audition tape, she was asked to read lines with Sam Heughan, the actor chosen to play the young Scottish warrior Jamie. Their chemistry, which many critics have since noted, was palpable. "The casting of Claire Randall was a long and difficult one because the role is so crucial to the success of our show. . . . Caitriona wasn't on anyone's radar, she wasn't on any list, but when we saw her audition tape, we immediately knew she was someone special," Moore explained, as quoted by Nellie Andreeva in *Deadline Hollywood* (11 Sept. 2013).

OUTLANDER

By September 2013, Balfe's casting in the series that would introduce her to legions of fans and change the course of her career had been announced. The first season, which premiered on August 9, 2014, follows the adventures of Claire, a nurse in post–World War II Great Britain. On a vacation to the Scottish Highlands with her historian husband (Tobias Menzies), Claire unwittingly touches an enchanted stone and is transported back to 1743, where she meets Fraser. The action builds up to a battle between the Highlanders and the British as seen through the eyes of a woman from the 1940s.

Though the successful series largely became her focus, in 2015 Balfe appeared in the film *The Price of Desire* and in 2016 she had a role in the thriller *Money Monster*, helmed by George Clooney and Julia Roberts. Meanwhile, recognition of her performance as Claire in *Outlander* over subsequent seasons had earned her two People's Choice Awards, two Saturn Awards, a BAFTA Scotland Award, and three Golden Globe Award nominations by 2018. Season 4 of the show is set to premiere in the fall of 2018, and Starz announced earlier that year that *Outlander* has already been renewed for a fifth. Each season of the program is adapted from one book in Gabaldon's series; with the author having penned eight Outlander books by early 2018, fans have been hopeful that Starz will adapt them all. Balfe remains thrilled at the prospect of continuing the show: "How do we keep the writing fresh, how do we keep the story fresh, how do we let these characters evolve and explore other facets of their life," she asked rhetorically in an interview with Emily Longeretta for *Us Weekly* (23 Mar. 2018). "That's what excited me as an actor, is being able to just explore new things."

PERSONAL LIFE

At the 2018 Golden Globes ceremony, Balfe confirmed that she was engaged to be married to record producer Tony McGill, whom she had met through a mutual friend. The announcement took many observers by surprise, as the couple had only rarely been spotted together before then.

Balfe is a patron of the organization World Child Cancer. In April 2018, she ran the London Marathon on behalf of the group.

SUGGESTED READING

Balfe, Caitriona. "Caitriona Balfe: The First Time I Left Home (and Fell in Love)." *The New York Times*, 3 Oct. 2017, www.nytimes.com/2017/10/03/arts/television/caitriona-balfe-outlander.html. Accessed 1 May 2018.

Balfe, Caitriona. "Caitriona Balfe Serves Up an Insider's View of *Outlander*." Interview by Lisa Rosen. *Los Angeles Times*, 28 May 2015, www.latimes.com/entertainment/envelope/emmys/la-en-st-caitriona-balfe-20150528-story.html. Accessed 1 May 2018.

Danaher, Patricia. "It's a Long Way from the Stoney Grey Soil of Monaghan." *Irish Daily Mail Weekend*, 30 Sept. 2017, pp. 2–3.

Grierson, Tim. "The Gorgeous Determination of Caitriona Balfe." *Backstage*, 1 Apr. 2015, www.backstage.com/interview/gorgeous-determination-caitriona-balfe. Accessed 1 May 2018.

Lawson, Richard. "*Outlander* Refuses to Define Itself, and That's a Good Thing." Review of *Outlander*, developed by Ronald D. Moore. *Vanity Fair*, 5 Aug. 2014, www.vanityfair.com/hollywood/2014/08/outlander-review. Accessed 1 May 2018.

Longeretta, Emily. "*Outlander*'s Caitriona Balfe and Sam Heughan on Keeping It Steamy through 'Domestic' Relationship in Season 4." *Us Weekly*, 23 Mar. 2018, www.usmagazine.com/entertainment/news/how-outlanders-claire-jamie-keep-the-romance-alive-in-season-4. Accessed 1 May 2018.

SELECTED WORKS

Super 8, 2011; *The Beauty Inside*, 2012; *Escape Plan*, 2013; *Outlander*, 2014– ; *Money Monster*, 2016

—Mari Rich

Jesse Ball

Date of birth: June 7,1978
Occupation: Author

Critically acclaimed American novelist, poet, and short-story writer Jesse Ball has drawn comparisons to surrealist and experimental authors like Franz Kafka and Italo Calvino. According to Jill Owens for *Powell's Books Blog* (5 Mar. 2018), Ball's work "stretches the boundaries of what fiction can do—his spare, poetic prose encompasses philosophy as much as plot and his novels contain an enduring and appealing strangeness, often presented through mysteries or puzzles." Ball began his career as a poet before publishing his debut novel, *Samedi the Deafness*, in 2007

By Papermoth via Wikimedia Commons

and has since produced a prolific and equally acclaimed output of work, including more than a half-dozen novels, several short-story and poetry collections, and various collaborative works.

Ball's novels are marked by their integration of narrative and poetic conventions and concentrate on such themes as truth, memory, language, love, and empathy. In an interview with *Chicago Magazine* (27 June 2016), Ball told Joe Meno, "Books should have a purpose. Books should be practical in some sense. Because [in life] you are going to be racked with grief and afflicted by mortal things, horrific things that you can't even predict."

EARLY LIFE AND EDUCATION

Born the second of two sons in 1978 in New York, Jesse William Ball grew up in Port Jefferson, Long Island. His father, Robert, worked as a social service administrator, and his mother, Catherine, was a librarian. Both were avid readers and helped inspire his early interest in books. When Ball was a boy, his father gave him a copy of John Gardner's 1971 novel *Grendel*, which retells the Old English epic *Beowulf* from the perspective of the monster. Tackling the power of literature and myth and the timeless battle of good versus evil, the book left a lasting impression on him.

For Ball, books provided solace during times of difficulty. His brother, Abram, had Down syndrome and experienced a wide range of medical problems. Consequently, Ball spent much of his childhood in hospitals, where he often read to the "humming of machines," namely the sound of Abram's ventilator, as he noted to Meno. "He couldn't really communicate very much," he added, "but he could smile, demonstrate emotion." Abram underwent dozens of surgeries and lived on a ventilator for years before dying in 1998 at the age of twenty-four; their father had died a few years before.

Ball has said that he shared a close bond with Abram, whose rich vision of life would form the core of his writing, which initially began as a clandestine endeavor. At age twelve he started composing poems for himself. Uninterested in sharing his work, Ball continued to write in secret throughout adolescence. It was not until he attended Vassar College in Poughkeepsie, New York, that he began distributing self-bound manuscripts of his works. This was "a turning point for me," he told Tom Lynch in a profile for *Newcity* (24 Feb. 2009). "I was as much of a writer then as I was ever going to be."

After graduating from Vassar in 2000, Ball enrolled at Columbia University, where he pursued an MFA. While there he met the renowned poet Richard Howard. The onetime poet laureate of New York State helped Ball publish and wrote the foreword to his first book of poetry, *March Book*, in 2004.

POET TO NOVELIST

March Book, which is divided into five sections of loosely linked poems, marked the beginning of what Ball described to Owens as his "lyrical phase." Many of Ball's early works are characterized by an "intensity of lyrical expression," as he explained, and were also partly inspired by his fascination at the time with "strange things, coincidences, and the natural revelatory content of coincidence."

Following *March Book*'s publication, Ball traveled widely, living at various times in France, Spain, Scotland, and Iceland, where he met his first wife, Thordis Bjornsdottir, a poet and author. Ball collaborated with Bjornsdottir on a collection of short stories and drawings called *Vera & Linus* (2006). Containing disturbingly surreal scenes that evoke the short stories of Franz Kafka, the collection follows a pair of eponymous lovers, Vera and Linus, whose childlike inclination for play is nothing more than scenery in a sinister fairy-tale world shaped by violence and cruelty.

Echoes of Kafka also show up in Ball's debut novel, *Samedi the Deafness*, which was published in 2007 to widespread critical acclaim. Written while Ball resided at Hawthornden Castle in Scotland, this paranoid meditation on the nature of lying and truth-telling revolves around a mnemonist named James Sim, who becomes embroiled in a game of murder and betrayal after being abducted and taken to a "verisylum," a sanitarium for chronic liars. Mixing classical narrative techniques with conventions from poetry, such as line breaks in some sections, it showcases the experimental style for which Ball would become known.

In 2008 Ball won the Plimpton Prize for his story "The Early Deaths of Lubeck, Brennan, Harp, and Carr," which appeared in *The Paris Review*'s Winter 2007 issue. The following year saw the publication of his novel *The Way through Doors* (2009), whose paragraphs are line-numbered like a poem. It tells the story of a municipal inspector, Selah Morse, who witnesses a young woman run over by a taxicab and rushes her to the hospital. Masquerading as her boyfriend, Morse beguiles the amnesia-plagued woman with stories to help her regain her memory after she is erringly released into his care.

DYSTOPIA AND CRIME

Ball's novel *The Curfew* (2011) upends the tropes of dystopian fiction with a minimalist take on the genre. The novel centers on the relationship between William Drysdale and his mute eight-year-old daughter, Molly, who live in a totalitarian state with a "huge death cell" at its center. Drysdale, a former concert violinist, writes epitaphs for the gravestones of the deceased, among whom may be his beloved wife. After receiving a clue about her fate, Drysdale sets out to find her, leaving Molly in the care of a puppeteer neighbor, Mr. Gibbons, and his wife. In his absence, Molly and Mr. Gibbons put on a bleak puppet play that channels the past, present, and future.

Featuring many of Ball's stylistic signatures, including clipped sentences, short paragraphs, and sparsely detailed scenes, *The Curfew* received mostly positive reviews from critics for its compelling look at the underlying horrors of oppression. In a review for the *New York Times* (26 Aug. 2011), author William Giraldi called the novel "a spare masterwork of dystopian fiction, a fevered prose poem of society strangled by nefarious rule." Critic Veronica Scott Esposito for the *Los Angeles Review of Books* (26 Sept. 2011), however, found fault with Ball's minimalism and gimmicky authorial choices (for example, the use of enjambment), which came at the sacrifice of plot and character development.

Notwithstanding, Ball's profile on the national literary scene rose further with his next novel, *Silence Once Begun* (2014). A deliberate departure from his early lyrical works, the novel chronicles the life of Oda Sotatsu, a solitary twenty-nine-year-old Japanese thread salesman who confesses to a series of scandalous crimes that he did not commit. Narrated by an obsessed journalist, appropriately named Jesse Ball, it is largely presented as a series of question-and-answer interviews with witnesses, offering a range of conflicting perspectives on Oda, who, after being arrested and jailed, keeps a steadfast silence even in the face of execution.

Redefining the conventional crime thriller, *Silence* drew comparisons to Japanese director Akira Kurosawa's iconic film *Rashomon* (1950) in its expert handling of the subjectivity of truth. James Wood, writing for the *New Yorker* (10 Feb. 2014), commented that one of the novel's achievements "is the way that Ball enriches his metafictional restlessness with the humane curiosity that sometimes struggled for air in the more gamelike grid" of his previous novels. The novel was finalist for the 2014 *Los Angeles Times* Book Prize and the 2015 New York Public Library Young Lions Fiction Award.

GAINING NATIONAL PROMINENCE

Ball's daring and unconventional approach to the narrative form was again evident in his fifth published novel, *A Cure for Suicide* (2015), which mostly consists of dialogue. Returning to the theme of memory, the novel focuses on a man identified as "the claimant," who is brought to a strange village to recover after almost dying of an illness. There, he encounters an unnamed female "examiner," who teaches him the basic functions of living. The examiner's true intentions are called into question, however, after he meets an enchanting young woman at a party named Hilda.

Combining "the simplicity of a fable and the drama of a psychological thriller," as novelist Sarah Gerard wrote in a review for the *New York Times* (24 July 2015), *Cure* was widely praised for its stripped-down exploration of some of life's deepest questions. It was long-listed for the 2015 National Book Award.

In 2016 Ball received a Guggenheim Fellowship for fiction and produced his sixth novel, *How to Set a Fire and Why*. Written as a diary, the novel centers on a disturbed teenager, Lucia, who must navigate the trials of adolescence after her father dies and her mother descends into mental illness. She does so, rebelliously, after falling in with a secret group of arsonists at her high school. Some critics likened Ball's precocious, wickedly funny Lucia to a female version of Holden Caufield, the protagonist of J. D. Salinger's seminal 1945 novel, *Catcher in the Rye*.

Ball followed this up with a darkly humorous short-story collection, titled *The Deaths of Henry King* (2017). It was written in collaboration with the author Brian Evenson and features illustrations by Lilli Carré. Later in 2017, Ball was named one of America's best young novelists by the prestigious British literary magazine *Granta*.

HONORING HIS BROTHER

Ball's 2018 novel *Census* further represents his shift toward more character-driven and emotionally affecting stories. Inspired by his brother, the novel portrays the relationship between a widowed father and his son, who has Down syndrome. After the father, a former surgeon, is diagnosed with a terminal heart condition, he takes a job as a census taker for a shadowy government entity and embarks on a road trip with his son. Along the way, the two encounter a wide cast of unique characters, who must agree to have their lowest rib tattooed.

Census features a heartfelt introduction from Ball, who expresses his intention to write a true-to-life story about what it is like to love a person with Down syndrome. Settling on a "hollow" conceit, the novel, which is narrated by the father, depicts the son only from the vantage point of other characters. Neither the father and son are named, and save for the novel's introduction, the words "Down syndrome" never appear. The places they travel through, meanwhile, are only identified by their letters, ranging from A to Z. Ball told Owens, "Many of the books that I write are parables of a sort . . . my fiction is largely nonfictional, because it's at the crossing of roads where life occurs."

Featuring episodic chapters written in spare, aphoristic prose, *Census* was universally well-received by critics. In a review for the *Guardian* (14 Apr. 2018), author James Lasdun described it as a "high-concept fable" and observed, "It isn't a polemic about special needs, but a detailed and moving portrayal of a kind of radical innocence, one that brings both the cruelty and the kindness in the world around it into sharp focus." Meanwhile, Parul Sehgal, writing for the *New York Times* (6 Mar. 2018), opined that it was Ball's "most personal and best to date," adding that it contained "signature surreal flourishes" that were reminiscent of works by the Italian writer Italo Calvino.

OTHER WORK

In addition to writing, Ball joined the faculty at the School of the Art Institute of Chicago in 2007. While there, he has developed and taught innovative classes on such topics as lying, lucid dreaming, and walking. Despite his initial reservations about teaching, Ball told Meno that he has striven to cultivate students' interests to help them become better writers.

Much has been written about Ball's lightning-fast manner of working. He typically writes his novels with little planning in only one to three weeks, hanging up manuscript pages around him as they are completed. Largely eschewing revision, he has claimed that most of his works have been published in their original first-draft form.

PERSONAL LIFE

Ball resides in Chicago and has been married twice.

SUGGESTED READING

Ball, Jesse. "Powell's Interview: Jesse Ball, Author of Census." Interview by Jill Owens. *Powell's Books*, 5 Mar. 2018, www.powells.com/post/interviews/powells-interview-jesse-ball-author-of-census. Accessed 26 Aug. 2018.

Lasdun, James. "*Census* by Jesse Ball Review—A Moving Portrayal of Radical Innocence." *The Guardian*, 14 Apr. 2018, www.theguardian.com/books/2018/apr/14/census-jesse-ball-review-downs-syndrome-novel-human-empathy. Accessed 26 Aug. 2018.

Lynch, Tom. "Where Dreams Lie: Inside the Strange Compelling Worlds of Jesse Ball." *Newcity*, 24 Feb. 2009, newcity.com/2009/02/24/where-dreams-lie-inside-the-strange-compelling-worlds-of-jesse-ball. Accessed 26 Aug. 2018.

Meno, Joe. "Inside the Bizarre, Brilliant World of Jesse Ball." *Chicago Magazine*, 27 June 2016, www.chicagomag.com/Chicago-Magazine/July-2016/Jesse-Ball. Accessed 26 Aug. 2018.

Sehgal, Parul. "A Widower and His Son Find Cruelty on the Road in Census." Review of *Census*, by Jesse Ball. *The New York Times*, 6 Mar. 2018, www.nytimes.com/2018/03/06/books/review-census-jesse-ball.html. Accessed 26 Aug. 2018.

Wood, James. "But He Confessed." Review of *Silence Once Begun*, by Jesse Ball. *The New Yorker*, 10 Feb. 2014, www.newyorker.com/magazine/2014/02/10/but-he-confessed. Accessed 26 Aug. 2018.

SELECTED WORKS

Samedi the Deafness, 2007; *The Curfew*, 2011; *Silence Once Begun*, 2014; *A Cure for Suicide*, 2015; *How to Set a Fire and Why*, 2016; *Census*, 2018

—Chris Cullen

Barry Barish

Date of birth: January 27, 1936
Occupation: Physicist

In September 2015, the Laser Interferometer Gravitational-Wave Observatory (LIGO) locations in Hanford, Washington, and Livingston, Louisiana, detected something unusual in the cosmos: gravitational waves, phenomena caused by major events in space such as the collision of black holes. The discovery was a significant one within the physics community, as the existence of gravitational waves had been predicted nearly one hundred years before but had long remained unconfirmed. Among the primary scientists credited for the discovery was Barry Barish, a researcher who had served as the project's director for nearly a decade and who in 2017 shared the Nobel Prize in Physics with fellow scientists Kip Thorne and Rainer Weiss.

Barish, whom fellow Nobel laureate Thorne called "the most brilliant leader of large science projects that physics has ever seen" in a California Institute of Technology (Caltech) news release (3 Oct. 2017), has had a long career in physics, contributing to particle physics research at institutions such as Fermilab and Italy's Gran Sasso National Laboratory and leading efforts to design innovative new particle accelerators. A longtime member of the Caltech faculty, Barish taught at the institution for nearly four decades before his retirement in 2005. Although he has frequently argued that the 2017 Nobel Prize should truly recognize the hundreds of scientists who contributed to LIGO rather than only three, Barish acknowledges that his newfound recognition gives him a platform to discuss issues of concern to him, such as climate change. "I think that there's a need in our society for scientists to take a stand on certain kinds of issues," he

told Calla Cofield for *Space.com* (4 Oct. 2017). "I am appreciative that [after winning the prize] I have a little more power in my research, but I think there's another part of it that I hope I can live up to."

EARLY LIFE AND EDUCATION

Barry Clark Barish was born on January 27, 1936, in Omaha, Nebraska. He spent his early years in Omaha with his parents, Harold and Lee Barish. The family moved to California in the mid-1940s, settling in the Los Feliz neighborhood of Los Angeles. Barish attended public schools in the Los Angeles area, including Monroe Elementary School, King Junior High School, and John Marshall High School. As a child and teenager, Barish developed an interest in science and mathematics but also dreamed of becoming a writer, an ambition that lessened after an unpleasant experience reading the nineteenth-century Herman Melville novel *Moby-Dick* in high school.

Barish's parents had not attended college themselves but valued education highly, and they encouraged their son to become the first in his family to pursue a college education. Barish initially hoped to attend the California Institute of Technology (Caltech) but ultimately enrolled in the University of California, Berkeley, where he first focused on engineering. He was not particularly interested in the field but thought that it was a more practical field of study than physics. "I had thought that unless you were [physics pioneer Albert] Einstein or something, you didn't do things like physics. It was engineering that you did," he recalled to Shirley K. Cohen for the

Caltech Oral History Project (1998). Within his first semester, Barish determined that he was not well suited for engineering, and he switched his focus to physics after that point. As a senior, he had the opportunity to participate in a research project at the Lawrence Radiation Laboratory, beginning what would become a long career in physics research. He earned his bachelor's degree from Berkeley in 1957.

After completing his undergraduate studies, Barish remained at Berkeley to complete his PhD. Although he had the opportunity to join established research groups at the university, he instead opted to pursue his thesis research largely on his own. "I decided I would just go off and do something that I thought I knew hadn't been done, and wanted to do myself, on the 184-inch cyclotron at Berkeley," he told Cohen. Barish's research fell within the field of high-energy particle physics, which deals primarily with subatomic particles and their interactions. He completed his thesis research by 1962, earning his doctorate in physics that year.

ACADEMIC CAREER

After completing his doctorate, Barish remained at Berkeley as a research assistant into 1963. As a member of physicist Burton Moyer's research group, he assisted in carrying out research using the Bevatron particle accelerator at the Lawrence Radiation Laboratory, later renamed the Lawrence Berkeley National Laboratory. While serving as a research assistant, Barish met Alvin Tollestrup, a particle physicist and associate professor at Caltech. Tollestrup recruited Barish to join that institution, and Barish began a research fellowship at Caltech in 1963.

Although Barish's research work took him to a variety of institutions both within and outside of the United States, he devoted his academic career to Caltech, where he was hired as an assistant professor in 1966. He was promoted to associate professor in 1969 and to full professor in 1972. In 1991, he was named the Ronald and Maxine Linde Professor of Physics, a title he held until his retirement. Since 2005, he has held the title of Ronald and Maxine Linde Professor of Physics, Emeritus.

Barish enjoyed teaching both undergraduates and graduate students, although he has noted that his research responsibilities often prevented him from taking on as many graduate students as he would have liked. Although some have questioned his decision to spend his entire career at one institution, he is adamant that his choice was the correct one. "Caltech's been a very good place for me. I've thrived here. I don't have fantasies that I would have done better somewhere else in terms of being able to realize myself," he explained to Cohen. "I was lucky to be able to do physics. And the one job that I had worked out well for me."

RESEARCH

Much of Barish's early research continued to focus on high-energy particle physics, and he conducted research at major institutions such as New York's Brookhaven National Laboratory and Illinois's Fermi National Accelerator Laboratory, better known as Fermilab. In California, he carried out research at the Stanford Linear Accelerator Center, and he also worked for a time at the Gran Sasso National Laboratory in Italy. In addition to his primary scientific interest, Barish devoted a portion of his career to searching for the hypothetical elementary particles known as magnetic monopoles.

As Barish's career progressed, he came to recognize that he was particularly suited for managing large-scale research projects—a tricky process, with differing perspectives, research goals, and personalities involved. "Scientists, especially physicists, we're presumptuous and think we can do everything better than everybody else," he confessed to Cofield. "One thing that I realized early is, I had some talent managing and organizing things." Barish realized that although he naturally seemed to have a talent for organizing projects, there was already a large body of work concerning management techniques. "Why should I reinvent the wheel? People [already] know how to do this," he recalled to Cofield. "So I actually spent a lot of time reading about how professional managers work."

Over the decades, Barish became known as a talented manager as well as an influential researcher, and he took on leadership roles in a variety of projects. At Caltech, he served as principal investigator for the Caltech High Energy Physics Group from 1984 to 1996. He was also involved in the design process for multiple proposed particle accelerators, including the Superconducting Super Collider, which was planned to be constructed in Texas. The project was canceled by the US Congress in 1993, after a portion of the planned facility had already been constructed. Barish later served as director of the design effort for the International Linear Collider, a particle accelerator proposed to be built in Japan.

LIGO

In 1994, Barish took on what would become one of the defining roles of his career when he joined the LIGO project as principal investigator. The project, a collaboration between Caltech and the Massachusetts Institute of Technology (MIT), was launched in the 1980s with the goal of establishing observatories that would be used for the detection of cosmic gravitational waves. Such waves, the result of cosmic events such as

the collision of black holes, were first predicted by Albert Einstein in 1916, but Einstein believed that it would be impossible to detect them from Earth. The scientists affiliated with LIGO sought to detect and prove the existence of gravitational waves that, in turn, could be used to learn more about the cosmos.

Prior to Barish's involvement, the struggling LIGO project had not yet established its observatories and was in danger of being shut down. Barish took a month to decide whether he wanted to join the project, ultimately concluding that it had potential. "I decided to take LIGO on, but not because I had convinced myself that it could succeed or that it was in good shape underneath," he explained to Cohen. "It was more the opposite—that I couldn't convince myself that I couldn't make it work; I couldn't convince myself that it was rotten." After three years as principal investigator, Barish became the director of LIGO and also founded the LIGO Scientific Collaboration, an international team of researchers. Over the course of his tenure, he oversaw the creation of observatories in Washington and Louisiana, which began searching for gravitational waves in the 2000s. Barish stepped down as director of LIGO in 2006 but remained a researcher with the project and in 2013 joined the LIGO Scientific Collaboration Executive Committee.

On September 14, 2015, LIGO made its first detection of gravitational waves, which researchers later announced were the result of a collision between two black holes that took place 1.3 billion years before the waves were detected by LIGO's instruments. Researchers announced their findings to the public in February 2016, stunning the scientific community with proof that the waves Einstein had predicted not only existed, but could be detected. The team went on to detect additional waves in December 2015 and January 2017. In August 2017, both LIGO and the European Gravitational Observatory's Virgo instrument detected gravitational waves caused by the collision of neutron stars. Light from the collision was also detected by researchers.

NOBEL PRIZE

On October 3, 2017, the Royal Swedish Academy of Sciences announced that Barish was one of three scientists who would receive the Nobel Prize "for decisive contributions to the LIGO detector and the observation of gravitational waves," as reported on the award's official website. In addition to being the most prestigious prize in the field of physics, the Nobel Prize also grants a monetary award, which in 2017 amounted to 9 million Swedish krona, or more than 1.1 million US dollars. Barish and fellow Caltech researcher Kip Thorne, who holds the title of Richard P. Feynman Professor of Theoretical

Physics, Emeritus, each received one-quarter of the award, while the remaining half was awarded to Rainer Weiss, an emeritus professor of physics at MIT.

Although honored to receive the prize, Barish was not entirely convinced that the recognition should have gone to him specifically. "It's a combination of being thrilled and humbled at the same time, mixed emotions," he told Dennis Overbye for the *New York Times* (3 Oct. 2017) following the announcement. "This is a team sport, it gets kind of subjective when you have to pick out individuals." Barish has argued that the credit for LIGO's success lies with more than one thousand individual scientists who have made substantial contributions to the complex and long-running project.

PERSONAL LIFE

Barish met his wife, psychoanalyst and professor Samoan Barish, while they were both graduate students at Berkeley. They have two children and live in Santa Monica, California. Barish is an avid reader and cyclist.

SUGGESTED READING

Barish, Barry. Interview with Shirley K. Cohen. *Oral History Project, California Institute of Technology Archives*, 1998, oralhistories.library.caltech.edu/178/1/Barish_OHO.pdf. Accessed 14 Dec. 2017.

"Barry C. Barish—Facts." *Nobelprize.org*, 2017, www.nobelprize.org/nobel_prizes/physics/laureates/2017/barish-facts.html. Accessed 14 Dec. 2017.

"Caltech Scientists Awarded 2017 Nobel Prize in Physics." *Caltech*, 3 Oct. 2017, www.caltech.edu/news/barish-and-thorne-awarded-nobel-prize-physics-52463. Accessed 14 Dec. 2017.

Cho, Adrian. "Will Nobel Prize Overlook Master Builder of Gravitational Wave Detectors?" *Science*, 27 Sept. 2016, www.sciencemag.org/news/2016/09/will-nobel-prize-overlook-master-builder-gravitational-wave-detectors. Accessed 14 Dec. 2017.

Cofield, Calla. "Gravitational-Wave Scientists: Q&A with Nobel Winners Kip Thorne and Barry Barish." *Space.com*, 4 Oct. 2017, www.space.com/38360-q-a-with-ligo-nobel-prize-winners.html. Accessed 14 Dec. 2017.

Hoban, Virgie. "Big Science in Action: Nobel Laureate Barry Barish Helped Open a New Window on the Universe." *California*, 2017, alumni.berkeley.edu/california-magazine/winter-2017-power/big-science-action-nobel-laureate-barry-barish-helped-open-new. Accessed 14 Dec. 2017.

Overbye, Dennis. "2017 Nobel Prize in Physics Awarded to LIGO Black Hole Researchers." *New York Times*, 3 Oct. 2017, www.nytimes.com/2017/10/03/science/nobel-prize-physics.html. Accessed 14 Dec. 2017.

—*Joy Crelin*

Janine Sherman Barrois

Occupation: Television writer, producer, and showrunner

Janine Sherman Barrois, who has spent around two decades in the television industry working behind the scenes as a writer and producer on a variety of shows, has been increasingly mentioned as part of the small, but powerful, coterie that includes Shonda Rhimes and Ava DuVernay. Beginning in 2017, she has gained greater attention for her role as an executive producer and the showrunner of the edgy, popular TNT television series *Claws*, which follows the adventures of five women working at a Florida nail salon who become involved in laundering money for a bogus pain-treatment clinic. Remarking on her success for *MADE* (20 May 2017), A. J. Linton wrote, "From writing scripts for the Wayans to producing iconic shows like *Criminal Minds* and *ER*, Janine has carved a lane for herself while simultaneously creating a path for aspiring showrunners of color."

Barrois often stresses to interviewers the importance of diversity both in front of and behind the cameras and, in putting together the cast and crew for *Claws*, she made a concerted effort to be as inclusive as possible. A point of pride

Photo by Amanda Edwards/Getty Images

for her, the show has particularly won praise for its depiction of a group of strong and diverse female characters. "In *Claws* the women are front and center. They want power and are not looking to men to help them get it," she explained to Laura Broman for *Romper* (9 June 2017). "These women are essentially unsung heroes in terms of race, gender, and class."

"Like anyone, I've faced challenges when going for top tier opportunities. . . . But what I can say is that the landscape has evolved and horizons have broadened," she stated to Linton.

EARLY YEARS AND EDUCATION

Janine Sherman Barrois grew up in eastern Massachusetts and has one older brother. As a teenager, she moved with her family to Reston, Virginia, and while in high school, she worked on the student newspaper. She quickly discovered, however, that she preferred narrative storytelling to journalism.

Upon entering Howard University, a historically African American school in Washington, DC, she majored in communications, thinking that she might one day pen scripts about crime, politics, and other weighty topics. (She had always been a fan of police dramas like *Hill Street Blues*, which she watched with her father and brother.) By coincidence, her Howard roommate was the daughter of director Gilbert Moses, who had cofounded the pioneering African American drama company known as the Free Southern Theater. He advised Barrois to switch her major to English as this would allow her to read more widely and subsequently become a better storyteller. She did so, while minoring in film studies; she found the advice invaluable and now recommends that any aspiring young writer read as much as possible from a range of genres.

Upon graduating from Howard, Barrois moved to Los Angeles. In relating this decision, made with her roommate, to Linton, she said, "At a certain point during our undergraduate career, we both decided that we needed to take a leap of faith and move to Hollywood to pursue a career in screenwriting." A few lean years followed, during which time she ate a lot of inexpensive ramen noodles, as she has recalled, and took on a series of odd jobs; she was fired from one of these—a gig assisting comedian, producer, and writer Judd Apatow—because of her inability to proofread accurately.

Barrois applied multiple times to the Warner Bros. Television Writers' Workshop, an esteemed program that allows aspiring television writers to hone their craft. Highly selective, the workshop accepts only eight participants each year out of a pool of more than 2,500. Although she was turned down initially, once she partnered with another writer to apply, they were accepted as a team and secured an agent.

FINDING HER FOOTING IN TELEVISION

Warner Bros. was deeply invested in mentoring its workshop participants and finding them positions on shows once they had completed the program. Barrois landed a job writing for *Lush Life*, a new Fox series created by Yvette Lee Bowser about two mismatched roommates. It aired in 1996 for only four episodes.

Following the disappointment of *Lush Life's* cancellation, Barrois cowrote a pilot with Damon Wayans, who had gained fame in the early 1990s as the cocreator and star of the hit sketch-comedy series *In Living Color*. Although the series, *413 Hope St.*, about a crisis center serving inner-city youth, was canceled by Fox after ten episodes that finished airing in early 1998, Barrois had been tapped to work on *The Jamie Foxx Show*, which starred Foxx as an aspiring actor from Texas who settles in Los Angeles to pursue an entertainment career, supporting himself in the meantime by working in his aunt and uncle's hotel. She wrote several episodes between 1997 and 1999 before going on to pen and dabble in producing episodes of Eddie Murphy's animated project *The PJs*, a family-friendly show about the superintendent in a public housing project, from 1999 to 2000.

Although Barrois appreciated the chance to work with such popular comedians as Wayans, Foxx, and Murphy, she had long wanted to work on more gritty, dramatic projects. After she and her writing partner wrote a film script that was never picked up but attracted the attention of high-profile producer John Wells, she was invited to write for his NBC show *Third Watch*—a series revolving around the exploits of a group of New York City police officers, firefighters, and paramedics—beginning in 2000, and she jumped at the chance. Though this meant the amicable breakup of her writing partnership as her partner left after working on one season to return to comedy, Barrois embraced the genre. In 2001, she began producing the show as well, and she was ultimately promoted to co-executive producer, thanks, in part, to the mentorship of Wells. Of her experience working for the veteran, she stated to Linton, "I learned the true value of perseverance, because this business is not easy to survive in at all."

EARNING RECOGNITION THROUGH *ER* AND *CRIMINAL MINDS*

Barrois next worked with Wells on the highly regarded medical drama *ER*, a show that she had always admired. She wrote and produced numerous episodes between 2005 and 2009, despite having been initially daunted at the fact that many of the crew had been working together on the long-running series for years. In 2006, she was a finalist for the Humanitas Prize in the sixty-minute category for her writing for the episode "Darfur." Finding herself in greater demand following her time on *ER*, though she was itching to get a show of her own developed, she inked a deal with CBS to get further exposure as a writer and executive producer on another hit show, *Criminal Minds*, whose protagonists are the elite profilers of the FBI's Behavioral Analysis Unit. In 2014, she was a recipient of a National Association for the Advancement of Colored People (NAACP) Image Award for best dramatic writing for her work on the episode "Strange Fruit."

She remained with the show, which allowed her to delve into the world of serial killers and other dangerous criminals, until 2015, when she was again approached by Warner Bros. Television, whose executives had kept an eye on her work. It was a difficult decision to leave a show as interesting and successful as *Criminal Minds*. "The hardest thing about taking a risk is that it's so much easier when you hate your day job," she recalled to Lisa Bonner for *Ebony* (28 July 2015). Warner Bros., however, made her an offer that included possibilities of development and perks such as her own bungalow on the studio lot, and she made the leap. She explained to Bonner, "I was literally in the parking lot shaking. Actually I never in my wildest dreams thought I'd get this offer. I went in my office and cried, I couldn't believe it."

She was even more thrilled when she first read a draft of the script for *Claws*, written by Eliot Laurence, and she did not hesitate to accept the offer to serve as the showrunner and an executive producer for the series. "It was just so bold and refreshing. . . . I loved the Florida noir aspect and the humor and the drama it possessed. That, and the idea that it was centered on these five cool fierce women," she explained to Kellee Terrell for the website *HelloBeautiful* (15 July 2018).

RUNNING THE SHOW

Once arrangements had been made with the TNT network and before carefully selecting the cast, Barrois traveled to Florida, where the story is set, to scout locations to serve as inspiration for the show, which takes place in and around a fictional salon owned by head manicurist Desna (Niecy Nash) and operated with the help of her ex-alcoholic best friend Jennifer (Jenn Lyon); Ann, a baseball bat–wielding lesbian (Judy Reyes); Polly, a preppy ex-con (Carrie Preston); and Virginia, a young, sexy ex-stripper (Karrueche Tran). Despite the exaggerated nature of some of the show's plotlines, settings, and costumes, Barrois did not want to simply make frothy, mindless television. "[We want] to show young women that you can get whatever you want in this world; that you can have a crew that supports you and roots you on, that wants you to win and that's going to sit in the front row

watching the movie of your life cheering you on," she explained to Aramide Tinubu for *Ebony* (23 June 2017).

In the summer of 2017, *Claws* premiered to high ratings that it sustained throughout its first season, and although some reviewers had difficulty getting past the show's over-the-top nature, most appreciated what Kevin Fallon cited in his review for the *Daily Beast* (7 June 2017) as its "'*Steel Magnolias* meets *Breaking Bad*'" ethos. "There is style and there is fun, and there may be an instinct to dismiss the show for those reasons. Just as for certain audiences (yours truly included), there is an instinct to embrace the show for a slew of other reasons, including the cast, the feminism, the nails, and the baseline camp of it all," he wrote. After being renewed for a second season that aired in the summer of 2018, it was announced that the show was also being renewed for a third season.

Additionally, Barrois made her directorial debut in 2018, with the short film *French Fries*. Part of the Shatterbox series of shorts by female directors, the picture tells the story of a young African American couple as they struggle to repair their failing marriage. "Directing fulfills that desire to not only write the story but tell the story, visually," she told Regina R. Robertson for *Essence* (11 June 2018).

PERSONAL LIFE

Barrois is married to the animation artist Lyndon Barrois.

SUGGESTED READING

Barrois, Janine Sherman. "*Claws* Showrunner, Janine Sherman Barrois, Adds a New Title to Her Resume." Interview by Regina R. Robertson. *Essence*, 11 June 2018, www.essence.com/entertainment/claws-showrunner-janine-sherman-barrois-interview. Accessed 1 Aug. 2018.

Barrois, Janine Sherman. "*Claws* Showrunner Janine Sherman Barrois on Creating 'Florida Noir.'" Interview by Sonia Saraiya. *Variety*, 15 June 2017, variety.com/2017/tv/news/claws-showrunner-janine-sherman-barrois-1202467941/. Accessed 1 Aug. 2018.

Barrois, Janine Sherman. "A Conversation with Hollywood Power Player: Janine Sherman Barrois." Interview by A. J. Linton. *MADE*, 30 May 2017, www.made-magazine.com/conversation-hollywood-power-player-janine-sherman-barrois/. Accessed 1 Aug. 2018.

Barrois, Janine Sherman. "Janine Sherman Barrois Sharpens Her Pen for TV." Interview by Lisa Bonner. *Ebony*, 28 July 2015, www.ebony.com/entertainment-culture/behind-black-hollywood-janine-sherman-barrois-sharpens-her-pen-for-tv. Accessed 1 Aug. 2018.

Broman, Laura. "Janine Sherman Barrois Flips Female Stereotypes in TNT's *Claws*." *Romper*,

9 June 2017, www.romper.com/p/janine-sherman-barrois-flips-female-stereotypes-in-tnts-claws-63258. Accessed 1 Aug. 2018.

Fallon, Kevin. Review of *Claws*, created by Eliot Laurence. "*Claws*: The New *Breaking Bad* Takes Place at a Nail Salon." *The Daily Beast*, 7 June 2017, www.thedailybeast.com/claws-the-new-breaking-bad-takes-place-at-a-nail-salon. Accessed 1 Aug. 2018.

SELECTED WORKS

The Jamie Foxx Show, 1997–99; *The PJs*, 1999–2000; *Third Watch*, 2000–05; *ER*, 2005–09; *Criminal Minds*, 2010–15; *Claws*, 2017–

—*Mari Rich*

Pushpa Basnet

Date of birth: 1983
Occupation: Social worker, activist

Photo by Michael Loccisano/Getty Images for Turner

Nepal, a small landlocked country between China and India, is home to eight of the world's highest mountains, including Mount Everest. One of the poorest countries in the world as measured by gross domestic product (GDP) per capita, it is also home to more than seventy prisons housing some 19,000 inmates, despite a capacity of just over 10,000. Nepal's overcrowded prisons are not repositories just for convicted criminals; a large percentage of inmates are those still awaiting trial. More disturbingly, parents sent to prison with no provisions for the care of their children must in some cases bring their children with them. The Nepali government estimates there are around eighty children in the country imprisoned along with parents who have no family members or friends available to serve as guardians.

Social worker Pushpa Basnet has made it her life's purpose to save as many of these young people as possible. She is the founder of the Butterfly Home, a residential facility, learning center, and surrogate family for Nepali children with incarcerated parents. "It's not fair for children to live in the prison because they haven't done anything wrong," Basnet told CNN reporter Kathleen Toner in 2012. "My mission is to make sure no child grows up behind prison walls."

Basnet was chosen as CNN's 2012 Hero of the Year, a designation honoring everyday people who make great humanitarian contributions to the world. At the star-studded ceremony marking the event, actor Susan Sarandon presented Basnet with the award, saying: "Most people see an injustice, get upset, do a short-term something and move on. Because to do more would mean interrupting their lives. Pushpa dared to forge a new path, against all odds, to give incarcerated children an education and a future. To give them love and build their self-esteem. To give them hope. She does all this without any claim to their future. I believe she has taken the definition of mother to a new level."

In 2016 Basnet—who is called "Mamu" (meaning "Mommy") by the well over one hundred children she has helped since launching her organization in 2005—became CNN's first-ever superhero, a special honor given to commemorate the Hero campaign's tenth anniversary.

EARLY YEARS AND EDUCATION

Pushpa Basnet was born in 1983 in Kathmandu, the capital of Nepal. She has one older brother and one younger sister. She has described herself to journalists as a relatively headstrong child. "I did what I wanted to do," she recalled to Sharika Nair for the Indian website *YourStory* (28 Mar. 2017). "I hated studies and loved arts and crafts. I liked to cook. But most of all, I loved cycling and would constantly be roaming around."

Her father was a businessman who traveled regularly for work, and the family often accompanied him. Basnet has described him as an undemonstrative and sometimes stern man; however, she has also praised him for treating his daughters and son equally and for allowing all three of them similar freedoms, despite Nepalese society's patriarchal culture.

Basnet, an admittedly indifferent student for much of her early academic career, attended a boarding school in Kathmandu. She flunked the math portion of an exam required for graduation, and her parents were fearful of what might become of her. Her father was leaving for a business trip when he got word of her failure, Basnet recalled to Nair. "He was crying while leaving and he was worried about my future."

Basnet had to wait a year to retake the exam, which she then passed. During that year, she decided to volunteer at an orphanage in Kathmandu and became interested in social work. Upon finishing secondary school, she entered St. Xavier's College, a highly regarded Jesuit school in Kathmandu. According to the school's mission statement, students are expected "to use their God-given talents not only for personal fulfillment, but also for service unto others."

Basnet took that ethos to heart, and despite her parents' fears she would be unable to earn a good living in the field, she chose to major in social work. "I had a very fortunate life, with a good education," Basnet explained to Toner. "I should give it to somebody else."

One day, as part of her coursework, Basnet and her classmates visited a women's prison in Kalimati, a section of Kathmandu known predominately for its massive wholesale fruit and vegetable market. She was dismayed by the dirty, crowded conditions at the prison and horrified to discover children living alongside their imprisoned parents. When the visit was over and she turned to go, a nine-month-old girl grabbed her shawl and smiled charmingly at her. "I felt she was calling me," Basnet recalled to Toner.

When she told her parents about her experience, they assured her she would forget all about the child in a few days. However, Basnet found herself unable to stop thinking about the plight of the imprisoned children. They could remain there only until the age of eight, she learned, and if a home could not be found by then, they faced life on the streets or in an orphanage. On the bright side, "At least the children are safe inside the prison," she explained to Nair. "With unreliable relatives, they could be abused or trafficked." Still, Basnet wanted to help. In 2005, when she was just twenty-one years old, she did so.

ACTIVISM

That year, Basnet launched a day-care service, the Early Childhood Development Center. Many of the prisoners were reluctant to hand their children over to the care of a woman in her early twenties, and prison officials were similarly suspicious. "When I started, nobody believed in me," Basnet admitted to Toner. "People thought I was crazy. They laughed at me."

Finally, five frightened but excited children were placed in her care on a trial basis. Basnet would arrive at the prison each weekday morning, take her new charges to a small building she had rented, and return them to the prison in the afternoon. She scraped to finance the project with the help of sympathetic friends, selling pieces of her own jewelry to raise money, and furnishing the space with castoff furniture from her parents.

Basnet's program was the first of its kind in Kathmandu, and as word of it spread, increasing numbers of children from diverse backgrounds—Muslim, Buddhist, and Hindu—were entrusted to her care. She dreamed of doing even more, however, particularly after some of her original children aged out of the system and were taken from their parents to be placed in orphanages. Unhappy with the conditions in the orphanages she toured, Basnet opened a residential facility for the older children in 2007, living there herself to care for dozens of young residents at a time. "We do cooking, washing, shopping," she told Toner. "It's amazing, I never get tired. The (children) give me the energy. . . . The smiles of my children keep me motivated."

When she was chosen from a field of 45,000 nominees as the CNN Hero of the Year in 2012, she used the $300,000 she received to expand her operation, beginning construction of a building she named the Butterfly Home. "My children are like butterflies—right now they are caterpillars," she told Edward Barsamian for *Vogue* (13 Mar. 2014), explaining the choice of name.

In 2014 the Butterfly Home became the subject of a short documentary film, *Waiting for Mamu*, directed by Thomas Morgan. Morgan had been inspired to make the film after meeting Basnet during a program that brought leaders of nongovernmental organizations (NGOs) from around the world to study and network in the United States. The film, which enjoyed the backing of Sarandon and filmmaker Morgan Spurlock, garnered the audience award at that year's Traverse City Film Festival and met with a positive reception at other festivals as well.

SETBACKS AND REBUILDING

Tragedy struck Nepal on April 25, 2015, when a devastating earthquake rocked the central part of the country, killing 9,000 people and damaging more than 600,000 structures in Kathmandu and surrounding towns. Among the buildings severely damaged was the Butterfly Home, still under construction and previously due to open in October. Undaunted, Basnet and the children set up tarps in a nearby field, where they lived while additional funds were raised and repairs made.

Today, younger residents attend an on-site learning center, while older ones walk to a nearby public school. All have access to a well-equipped library and comfortable sleeping quarters, and all learn English, math, and computer skills. Extracurricular activities include arts and crafts, camping, and martial arts, which Basnet believes helps them deal with issues of grief and anger.

Basnet is adamant the children maintain contact with their parents, with the goal of re-uniting families as soon as possible. If a parent is incarcerated in a local prison, she arranges regular visits, and for those far away, she encourages the children to write regularly. She has also launched an initiative to teach parents to make various handicrafts, which she then sells to make money to run the Butterfly Home. "Often, they think that they're useless because they're in prison," Basnet told Toner. "I want to make them feel that they are contributing back to us." Once they are released, parents can also use their newly learned skills to support their families.

In addition to running the Butterfly Home, Basnet provides fresh milk, clothes, and medical supplies to children whose parents choose to keep them in prison, and she continues to finance school tuition for Butterfly Home alumni after they have rejoined their families.

PERSONAL LIFE

Basnet has stated her intention to remain unmarried, in order to devote herself fully to her mission. Her younger sister, Purnima, is also a trained social worker and serves as an integral part of the Butterfly Home.

SUGGESTED READING

Barsamian, Edward. "Nepalese Social Worker Pushpa Basnet Honored Last Night at Neuehouse." *Vogue*, 13 Mar. 2014, www.vogue.com/article/pushpa-basnet-nepalese-social-worker-waiting-for-mamu. Accessed 6 Jan. 2018.

Campbell, Charlie. "Child Support." *Time*, 9 Jan. 2014, time.com/4216/child-support/. Accessed 6 Jan. 2018.

Dhakal, Sanjaya. "Pushpa Basnet: Nepal's 'Mamu' Wins CNN Hero Award." *BBC News*, 4 Dec. 2012, www.bbc.com/news/world-asia-20579801. Accessed 6 Jan. 2018.

Nair, Sharika. "From Failing Her Math Board Exam to Becoming a CNN Superhero, Pushpa Basnet's Journey." *YourStory*, 25 Mar. 2017, yourstory.com/2017/03/pushpa-basnet/. Accessed 6 Jan. 2018.

Restauri, Denise. "A Girl from Nepal Takes Kids out of Prison and Becomes Their Mother. A Personal Story." *Forbes*, 20 Jan. 2014, www.forbes.com/sites/deniserestauri/2014/01/20/a-girl-from-nepal-takes-kids-out-of-prison-and-becomes-their-mother-a-personal-story/#76cbe92d2f2a. Accessed 6 Jan. 2018.

Toner, Kathleen. "Pulling Children out of Nepal's Prisons." *CNN*, 22 Nov. 2016, www.cnn.com/2012/03/15/world/cnnheroes-basnet-nepal-prisons/index.html. Accessed 6 Jan. 2018.

Welinder, Shelby. "One Woman's Perseverance in Nepal: The Story of Pushpa Basnet." *Conscious*, consciousmagazine.co/one-womans-perseverance-in-nepal-the-story-of-pushpa-basnet/. Accessed 6 Jan. 2018.

—*Mari Rich*

Natalie Batalha

Date of birth: ca. 1966
Occupation: Astrophysicist

Astrophysicist Natalie Batalha was named one of the hundred most influential people in the world by *Time* magazine in 2017, but as her work has demonstrated, her influence has truly reached far beyond Earth itself. As a mission scientist and later a project scientist for the National Aeronautics and Space Administration (NASA), Batalha contributed to the launch of the Kepler space observatory in 2009 and played a crucial role in interpreting the data the spacecraft amassed—data that enabled the Kepler team to confirm the existence of thousands of planets orbiting faraway stars. "We have found lava worlds with one hemisphere that's an ocean—an ocean not of water but of molten rock. We have found disintegrating planets literally breaking up before our eyes," Batalha told Pat Brennan for the *NASA Kepler* blog (6 Apr. 2017) of the team's extrasolar findings. "We have found circumbinary planets, planets that are orbiting not one, but two stars. We find planets as old as the galaxy itself." Although finding planets that might seem straight out of science fiction was exciting for the researchers, even more significant were the planets most like Earth: small, rocky planets orbiting within the so-called habitable zone that allows for the presence of liquid water and, potentially, life.

A graduate of the doctoral program in astrophysics at the University of California, Santa Cruz, Batalha originally specialized in studying stellar activity. She joined the Kepler project in 1999 and quickly became a key member of the team, which was headed by principal investigator William Borucki and based out of NASA's Ames Research Center. Following the launch of the spacecraft, Batalha not only spearheaded data analyses but also communicated many of the team's findings to the public, including the confirmation of rocky planet Kepler 10-b in 2011. Through her work, she hopes to advance the scientific understanding of the galaxy and to highlight the characteristics that make Earth itself particularly rare. "Searching for potentially habitable worlds makes one appreciate just how precious living worlds are," she said in a NASA

Wikimedia Commons

Peggy Townsend for the University of California, Santa Cruz's *Newscenter* (13 June 2017). "I thought, though mysterious, the universe is not just chaos. It's not a collection of meaningless, random events. If we can uncover the secrets of the universe through numbers, then what limits are there to what we can learn?"

BECOMING A SCIENTIST

Fueled by her burgeoning fascination with physics, Batalha explored the field further over the course of her time at Berkeley. A key point for her came during the summer she spent as an intern at the Wyoming Infrared Observatory. "Up to this point, I didn't understand what it meant to do research," she explained in an interview for NASA's website (6 Mar. 2009). "The professor I worked for gave me a challenging problem to solve, and the process of figuring out a solution to the problem was fun. . . . It made me re-think what I perceived to be my strengths and weaknesses." Following her return to Berkeley, Batalha found work in the laboratory of astronomer Gibor Basri. She earned her bachelor's degree in physics from Berkeley in 1989.

Over the next eight years, Batalha pursued graduate studies in astrophysics, splitting her time between the United States and Brazil, where her astrophysicist husband was working at the time. She earned her master's degree in astrophysics from the Observatório Nacional in Rio de Janeiro in 1992 and went on to work toward her doctorate at the University of California, Santa Cruz, where she was advised by astronomy and astrophysics professor Steven Vogt. Her research focused primarily on sunspots occurring in stars younger than the Sun. She completed her PhD in 1997 and a postdoctoral fellowship in Rio.

Although Batalha's chief focus was stellar activity, she became intrigued by the search for exoplanets that was taking place during her years as a doctoral student. The existence of exoplanets—planets located outside of the solar system to which Earth belongs—had long been suspected but was not confirmed until the early 1990s, and in 1995, a team of European researchers confirmed the existence of a planet orbiting a star like the Sun. Batalha, who attended the conference in Florence, Italy, where that discovery was presented, became further intrigued by the search when she learned about the use of transit photometry. That method detects planets orbiting stars by observing changes in a star's brightness when a planet passes between that star and Earth. Batalha later contacted William Borucki, a researcher who was using transit photometry to search for exoplanets, to discuss possible interference from sunspots, and Borucki ultimately

news release (20 Apr. 2017). "I hope that the discoveries from the Kepler spacecraft inspire people to learn more about other planets, and, in turn, make us love this one all the more."

EARLY LIFE AND EDUCATION

Batalha was born Natalie Marie Stout around 1966. She grew up in northern California, where she lived with her parents, Doug and Linda, and her brother, Trevor. As a teenager, Batalha admired astronaut Sally Ride, the first woman from the United States to travel into space. Although she excelled in math, she was not yet drawn to a career in science; instead, she considered becoming a gymnast and, later, becoming a philosopher. Batalha attended schools within California's Richmond Unified School District and cheered in high school. She has cited the space shuttle program, Catholic catechism, and Carl Sagan as early influences that affected her future course.

After graduating from high school, Batalha became the first in her family to attend college when she matriculated at the University of California, Berkeley. She initially planned to major in business with the encouragement of her parents, who believed that major would be key to future career success. Not long after beginning her studies, however, Batalha realized that her dream was to work for NASA and, to that end, enrolled in an introductory physics class. Although she found the class itself difficult, Batalha was drawn to the possibilities the field of physics presented. "When I saw the universe could be represented through numbers and equations, it blew me away," she recalled to invited her to join the research effort known as the Kepler mission.

KEPLER

Batalha joined Borucki's team as a National Research Council postdoctoral fellow, in 1999. Since the 1980s, Borucki had been working on a proposed project in which a space observatory would be launched into orbit around the Sun, where it would collect data on the brightness of stars within a specific area of the Milky Way that could then be analyzed as part of the search for exoplanets. Upon joining the small team dedicated to that effort, based at NASA's Ames Research Center in northern California, Batalha put her expertise in stellar activity to use to improve the effectiveness of the proposed project. Although NASA had rejected the proposal on multiple occasions, in December 2001 the project was selected as a mission to be carried out within NASA's Discovery program.

In addition to her work at the Ames Research Center, Batalha found a position as an associate professor at San José State University. She enjoyed teaching and remained at the university for ten years, dividing her time between the university and Ames. Batalha decreased her teaching schedule as the Kepler project progressed, eventually joining the Astrophysics Branch of the Ames Research Center's Space Sciences Division. In addition to preparing for the eventual launch of the Kepler spacecraft, she worked on a related project in which the team analyzed data collected by the Vulcan photometer, a detector that measured the brightness of stars from its position at Lick Observatory on California's Mount Hamilton. Batalha held several titles over her years with the research team, including mission scientist and deputy science team director, and she was named project scientist for the Kepler mission in August of 2016.

LAUNCH AND FINDINGS

After decades of planning, the Kepler spacecraft launched into space aboard a Delta II rocket on the night of March 6, 2009. Named for the German astronomer Johannes Kepler (1571–1630), the spacecraft consisted of a photometer used to measure the brightness of stars as well as mechanisms that controlled the positioning of the device. While orbiting the Sun, Kepler was tasked with observing about 170,000 stars located in a particular section of the Milky Way. The data it collected was transmitted back to Earth, where Batalha and her colleagues analyzed it to locate planets. They were particularly interested in rocky planets—planets that, like Earth, are composed of solid materials such as rock and metal—as gas giants and related types of planets were easier to discover.

The team's years of effort proved successful: in January 2011, the team announced that they had confirmed the existence of Kepler-10b, the first known rocky planet discovered outside of Earth's solar system, thanks to analysis led by Batalha. Over the following years, she and her colleagues confirmed thousands of additional planets, thirty of which appeared to be less than twice the size of Earth and orbiting within what is known as the habitable zone, the range of distances from their star that allows for surface water to exist as a liquid rather than as ice or gas. In addition to confirming simply that such planets exist, the findings enabled researchers to draw further conclusions. Data collected through Kepler about thousands of planets have enabled Batalha and her colleagues to estimate how many habitable-zone planets may exist in the galaxy: "We have learned that every star has at least one planet, and that there are tens of billions of potentially habitable, Earth-size planets," Batalha explained to Brennan. The original Kepler mission ended in May 2013, but Batalha and her colleagues continued to analyze the data it accumulated as the spacecraft made further observations through what became known as the K2 mission.

RECOGNITION AND FUTURE GOALS

Due to the success of the Kepler project, Batalha has received a great deal of recognition for her work, both within the scientific community. In 2011, she received the NASA Exceptional Public Service Medal for both leadership on Kepler and her efforts to communicate the team's findings to the public. The Harvard-Smithsonian Center for Astrophysics awarded her the 2017 Lecar Prize in recognition of her contributions to the study of exoplanets. That year also saw Batalha's inclusion in *Time* magazine's list of the world's hundred most influential people in 2017, alongside fellow exoplanet researchers Guillem Anglada-Escudé and Michaël Gillon.

Despite having contributed to numerous discoveries through the Kepler mission, Batalha remains intent upon learning more about the galaxy. She has served as a member of the advisory committee for the James Webb Space Telescope, a space observatory scheduled for launch in 2019, as well as the Astrophysics Advisory Committee to the NASA Science Mission Directorate. In April 2015, she became one of three leaders of NASA's newly established Nexus for Exoplanet System Science interdisciplinary project, which seeks to identify exoplanets that may support life. For Batalha, Kepler's findings have played a key role in that search. "Knowing there are many potentially habitable worlds catalyzes the search for life in a very tangible way," she told Brennan.

PERSONAL LIFE

Batalha and her husband, fellow astrophysicist Celso Correa Batalha, met while they were both working in Basri's laboratory at Berkeley and married in 1989. They have four children, the oldest of whom followed in her parents' footsteps by earning a PhD in astrophysics and astrobiology in June 2017. Batalha lives in Danville, California.

SUGGESTED READING

Batalha, Natalie. "A Star among Planet-Hunters, Natalie Batalha." Interview by Pat Brennan. *NASA Kepler*, NASA, 6 Apr. 2017, blogs. nasa.gov/kepler/2017/04/06/a-star-among-planet-hunters-natalie-batalha. Accessed 9 Feb. 2018.

"Bay Area Native Takes Road Less Traveled to NASA's Kepler Mission." 6 Mar. 2009, *NASA*, 7 Aug. 2017, www.nasa.gov/centers/ames/research/2009/batalha.html. Accessed 9 Feb. 2018.

Ferris, Timothy. "Meet Natalie Batalha, the Explorer Who's Searching for Planets across the Universe." *Smithsonian Magazine*, Dec. 2017, www.smithsonianmag.com/science-nature/natalie-batalha-explorer-searching-planets-across-universe-180967220. Accessed 9 Feb. 2018.

"Kepler Scientist on *Time* Magazine's Most Influential List." *NASA*, 20 Apr. 2017, www.nasa.gov/feature/ames/kepler/kepler-scientist-on-time-magazine-most-influential-list. Accessed 9 Feb. 2018.

Kwok, Roberta. "The Stars Her Destination." *California Magazine*, Nov.–Dec. 2008, alumni.berkeley.edu/california-magazine/november-december-2008-stars-berkeley/stars-her-destination. Accessed 9 Feb. 2018.

Townsend, Peggy. "Looking for Life." *University of California Santa Cruz Newscenter*, Regents of the University of California, 13 June 2017, news.ucsc.edu/2017/06/batalha-natalie-time-100.html. Accessed 9 Feb. 2018.

—*Joy Crelin*

Gage Skidmore [CC BY-SA 3.0], via Wikimedia Commons

Lake Bell

Date of birth: March 24, 1979
Occupation: Actor, director

Lake Caroline Bell has won acclaim as an actor, writer, director, and producer of television shows and films. She told Mark Peikert for *Backstage* (8 Aug. 2013), "[Directing] suits me. It's multifaceted, multidimensional, and requires so much focus and energy, but it is intense creativity. It's like exercising every muscle of creativity at all times." She also serves on the board of Women in Film, an organization that advocates for changes in culture and policy in the treatment of women in the screen industries. The group is dedicated to achieving parity for women in pay, representation on screen, and opportunity. Noted for her work in comedy, Bell is aware of the need for kindness, even in that genre. As she told Meredith Goldstein for the *Boston Globe* (10 Aug. 2013), "I don't like the trend in comedy to be mean spirited or to laugh heartily at someone else's expense. It personally doesn't turn me on. I'm really jazzed to make films that make people feel good."

EARLY LIFE AND EDUCATION

Bell's parents, who divorced when she was a child, provided her with plenty of material for her career, she claims. Her father, Harvey Siegel, is a real estate developer and her mother, Robin Bell, is an interior designer. Bell, who has an older brother, caught the acting bug by age four, as she told Peter Martin for *Esquire* (May 2014), "I was tirelessly motivated, because I felt very clear about what I wanted to do. I didn't fully understand what it meant to be an actor, but I knew it was someone who gets to play different characters, gets to pretend to be in different worlds, and gets to make people laugh or feel."

At thirteen, Bell worked for a family as an au pair in France; the job also provided Bell with her first plane trip. When she was fourteen, Bell left her home in Vero Beach, Florida, where her mother had moved when Bell was twelve, to attend the Chapin School in New York City. She also participated in an exchange student program in France.

Bell believes her writing career began during her high school days, in letters to her mother. She told Martin, "My mother is a beautiful writer. Writing letters back and forth with her was an athletic endeavor, and it became something I really looked forward to." From writing letters to keeping a journal was an easy step for Bell. She also began directing a few plays while in high school.

Bell attended Skidmore College in upstate New York for a year to appease her parents. She then studied acting in London at Rose Bruford College of Theatre and Performance, from which she graduated in 2002.

EARLY CAREER

Bell moved to Los Angeles after graduation. Her intention was, as she told Mary Pols for *Time* (19 Aug. 2013), "to go straight to the big time, funding my acting career with this supplemental career as a voice-over artist. Then I realized, obviously, you can't just roll into that. It is just as hard as becoming a . . . movie star. I ended up being a hostess at a place where they serve boiled eggs at the bar."

Although she had roles on the television shows *ER* (2002), *Surface* (2005–6), *Miss Match* (2003), *The Practice* (2004), *Surface* (2005–6), and *Boston Legal* (2004–6), Bell began getting serious attention for her role in HBO's *How to Make It in America* (2010–11).

In 2009 Bell was cast in the film *It's Complicated* as the young, second wife of Alec Baldwin's character, competing with Meryl Streep as the first wife. She describes the character as "kind of cold," and admits difficulty in being cast in scenes with Streep, her hero. As she told Willa Paskin for *New York* (7 Feb. 2011), "On my first day, [director] Nancy Meyers had to pull me aside and say, 'You need to get it together.' I just couldn't find the power . . ."

WORST ENEMY

Bell wrote and directed *Worst Enemy*, a 2011 short film about a woman who is trapped in a girdle, as an experiment. Her agent had advised her to do a short project before attempting a full-length feature. The film, which Bell financed, went to Sundance Film Festival.

She is sensitive to the amount of effort required for a film, as she told Michelle Lanz and Cameron Kell for *The Frame* (31 Aug. 2015). "To get a great project off the ground, it takes years. It just does. And I have a great respect for the process, which includes the writing process, the development process, the casting, the producing—all of it."

IN A WORLD . . .

In 2013 Bell starred in and directed a movie she had written about the world of voice-overs, *In a World . . . .* She wrote the script in secret; when she showed it to her agent, he suggested she direct it. Bell and her husband also painted the fake Picassos and Keith Haring art used in the film.

The movie was screened first at Sundance Film Festival, where it won the Waldo Salt Screenwriting Award: U.S. Dramatic. It was released to theaters in the summer. In its first weekend, showing in only three theaters, it grossed a more-than-respectable $71,000.

Addressing the sexism in voice-over work, Bell wrote of the conflict between a woman breaking into work as a voice-over artist and her successful father, played by the famed actor and voice artist Fred Melamed. She played the daughter, Carol, whose own struggling career in voice-over work for movie trailers suddenly takes off, creating friction between the characters. As A. O. Scott wrote for the *New York Times* (8 Aug. 2013), the movie is not only a coming-of-age story, but also "a show-business satire, a family drama, a feminist parable, and a sweet romantic comedy. Not that any of these labels can do justice to the originality of Ms. Bell's creative voice."

Voice-over work had been Bell's first ambition when she left London for Hollywood, not realizing the competitive nature and biases of the industry. Yet she is honest about wanting voice-over work herself, telling Amanda Dobbins for *New York Magazine* (19 Aug. 2013), "This [movie] is a 93-minute audition to the voice-over world, hoping they will hear me."

"They" did hear. Bell was cast as the voice of Chloe, the fluffy gray cat, in the 2016 animated film *The Secret Life of Pets*. Bell is obsessed with dialects and accents; her favorite accent is cockney for the muscular effort it requires.

MORE FILMS

Bell starred in the 2014 Disney film *Million Dollar Arm*, which was based on a true story. Jon Hamm played the role of J. B. Bernstein, a sports agent looking for the next great talent. He creates a reality TV competition show in India and finds two amazingly talented adolescent boys who know how to bowl in cricket but know nothing of baseball. Bernstein brings them to the United States to learn about baseball and play in the major leagues. During the adventure, Bernstein also meets Brenda, played by Bell, who becomes his wife.

Bell was a lead actor appearing with Simon Pegg in the British romantic comedy *Man Up*. Tess Morris wrote the script for the film, which opened in 2015. Morris was at a low point in both her professional and personal life when a man walked up to her and asked if her name was Clare. Although Morris admitted she was not, she thought the idea of an accidental blind date was a great seed for a comedy.

Bell took the role of Nancy, the female lead, who takes another woman's blind date to find her perfect match. She drew praise for her British accent, in addition to the liveliness she brought to the movie. As Andrew Lapin wrote for *National Public Radio* (13 Nov. 2015), "With a lot of help from Bell and Pegg, the movie cheerfully suggests it's possible to stage a lighthearted romance without dropping off your brain beforehand."

I DO . . . UNTIL I DON'T

Bell wrote, directed, and starred in the 2017 film *I Do . . . Until I Don't*, which follows three married couples being pursued by a woman with a negative view of marriage. She is making a documentary to defend her presupposition that marriage should be a seven-year renewable commitment.

Bell began the film's script after finishing the final draft of *In a World . . . .* During the writing, she met her future husband, and the experience added depth to what she had first considered to be an unromantic romantic comedy. She set the film in Vero Beach, which she knew well, in part, because she loved the colors.

The film is, in Bell's opinion, an antidote to the negativity of contemporary life. As she told Kevin Lincoln for *Vulture* (28 Aug. 2017), "It's very hopeful and very kind-spirited, and it was always intended that way, but it's just resonant in a different way in this time. Because the message is about being kind, and having a respectfulness to an institution and a concept of being loyal to someone . . . .."

Bell also directed six episodes of *Childrens Hospital*, the Emmy Award–winning television comedy on the cable network Adult Swim, which ran from 2008 until 2016.

PERSONAL LIFE

In June 2013, Bell married tattoo and fine artist Scott Campbell, whom she met on the set of *How to Make It in America*. Rob Corddry, Bell's costar, officiated at the ceremony. Six years later, she finally permitted Campbell to place tattoos on her body—two geometric designs, one on each shoulder. The couple has two children, a daughter and a son. After the birth of her daughter, Nova, Bell told Lanz and Kell, "Before my daughter, I definitely was a workaholic. And I still am, and that's a part of the texture of who I am, but I had no idea that I would consider my daughter in every breath that I take."

Bell's movie idol is Lauren Bacall. As she told Rebecca DiLiberto for *Instyle* (Mar. 2006), "She had that sexy, smoky elegance. That's the epitome of cool." Bell also regularly watches the romantic comedy *Moonstruck* because of Cher's performance. Bell became a vegan after doing a detox diet to get in shape for her film stunts; she eats meat only when traveling to other countries.

SUGGESTED READING

Bell, Lake. "Lake Bell on the Challenges of Navigating Motherhood, a Film Career and Being a Workaholic." Interview by Michelle Lanz and Cameron Kell. *The Frame*, 31 Aug. 2015, www.scpr.org/programs/the-frame/2015/08/31/44310/lake-bell-on-the-challenges-of-navigating-motherho/. Accessed 15 Jan. 2018.

Carbone, Nick, et al. "Pop Chart." *Time*, 19 Aug. 2013, p. 50. *Academic Search Ultimate*, www.search.ebscohost.com/login.aspx?direct=true&db=asn&AN=89629789. Accessed 7 Feb. 2018.

DiLiberto, Rebecca. "Lake Bell of Surface." *Instyle*, vol. 13, no. 3, Mar. 2006, p. 394. *Biography Reference Bank*, www.search.ebscohost.com/login.aspx?direct=true&db=f6h&AN=20561265. Accessed 7 Feb. 2018.

Lapin, Andrew. "A Smarter Romantic Comedy in *Man Up*." Review of *Man Up*, directed by Ben Palmer. *National Public Radio*, 13 Nov. 2015, www.npr.org/2015/11/13/455750161/a-smarter-romantic-comedy-in-man-up. Accessed 30 Jan. 2018.

Martin, Peter. "The Many Talents of Lake Bell." *Esquire*, 8 Mar. 2014, www.esquire.com/entertainment/a32857/lake-bell-photos-interview-0514/. Accessed 3 Jan. 2018.

Paskin, Willa. "Saved by the Bell." *New York*, vol. 44, no. 4, 7 Feb. 2011, p. 70. *Biography Reference Bank*, www.search.ebscohost.com/login.aspx?direct=true&db=f6h&AN=57771046. Accessed 7 Feb. 2018.

Peikert, Mark. "Lake Bell Is Not Your Sexy Baby." *Backstage*, vol. 54, no. 32, 8 Aug. 2013, pp. 20–23. *Business Source Premier*, www.search.ebscohost.com/login.aspx?direct=true&db=bth&AN=89672339. Accessed 7 Feb. 2018.

SELECTED WORKS

It's Complicated, 2009; *In a World . . .* , 2013; *Million Dollar Arm*, 2014; *Man Up*, 2015; *I Do . . . Until I Don't*, 2017

—Judy Johnson

Robin Benway

Date of birth: 1978
Occupation: Author

Since the publication of her first novel, *Audrey, Wait!* (2008), Robin Benway has been a best-selling author of young-adult (YA) fiction. She is also the winner of the 2017 National Book Award for Young People's Literature for *Far from the Tree*, her compelling novel about a trio of siblings adopted into different families. Benway's novels are notable in that they have all been written from the first-person perspective, which is how she claims her characters come to her—speaking to her directly. Her fans and critics have commended her for the realistic way she portrays the lives of teenagers. She believes she is aided in her writing by the fact that her teenage experiences remain fresh in her mind. In an interview with Agatha French for the *Los Angeles Times* (9 Nov. 2017), Benway said, "It's such an emotional time . . . you feel things so strongly, whether it's romance or sadness or uncertainty. . . . I think that's what YA really captures, whether it's a dystopian novel or it's a romantic comedy, there's always going be heightened emotion because it's not so much the setting or the plot. It's about the feeling."

EARLY LIFE, EDUCATION, AND CAREER

Robin Benway was born in 1978 and grew up with her brother in Orange County, California. Although she did not know any writers growing up, the idea of writing appealed to her for a long time. She attended New York University (NYU) in New York City, where she was the 1997 recipient of the Seth Barkas Prize for Creative Writing. She then transferred to the University of California, Los Angeles (UCLA), from which she graduated with a Bachelor of Science degree in sociology.

Following her graduation, Benway embarked on a career as a publicist in book publishing. From March 1999 to May 2001 she was a publicity assistant at Ballantine Publishing in Santa Monica, California. She then became the West Coast publicist for Alfred A. Knopf, a position she held until December 2001. From February 2003 to October 2003 she was the director of publicity for Book Soup, Inc., based out of West Hollywood and Costa Mesa, California. She followed that job with a position as the West Coast sales representative for the Pearson Technology Group, based in Los Angeles. She held that position from March 2004 to October 2005.

Benway enjoyed the work, particularly as it allowed her to have contact with so many talented and well-known authors. For a time, she toyed with the idea of becoming a writer herself, then decided to take a year off to see if she could make it as an author—even though she did not know how to write a book and did not have any fully fleshed-out ideas. In an interview with Sue Corbett for *Publishers Weekly* (4 June 2015), Benway recalled: "I had a great job but it wasn't right for me. So I decided to apply to MFA programs and I wrote a story from the perspective of a ten-year-old girl as part of the application process. I didn't get into any of the programs but I had already quit my job and I realized I wasn't going to ever have a better chance to try to do what I wanted to do, which was write. And writing that story [with the ten-year-old character] made me realize I like writing in a younger voice."

AUDREY, WAIT!

Benway then learned of a UCLA Extension class in young-adult literature being taught by Rachel Cohn. It began on the day her unemployment was to start. Seeing this as a good omen, she enrolled in the class. As part of the course, she was required to write the first chapter of a young-adult novel. The first chapter of what would become *Audrey, Wait!* came to her fairly quickly. When the novel was about half complete, Benway sent it to a literary agent, with Cohn's aid and encouragement. The agent was impressed with Benway's work and offered to represent her. *Audrey, Wait!* was then bought by editor Kristen Pettit at Razorbill on March 2, 2007.

Audrey, Wait! had been inspired by Benway's love of music. After sixteen-year-old Audrey breaks up with her musician boyfriend, Evan, she is shocked to discover that the song he writes about her becomes an enormous hit, heard everywhere. The song's popularity brings with it some unexpected fame for Audrey herself, who attempts to lead a normal life while at the same time being chased by paparazzi. A critic for *Kirkus Review* (15 Mar. 2008) noted: "This profusion of teen wit . . . both quells the mayhem of Audrey's life and holds the story together. Readers won't find much substance here but they will find entertainment, well pitched to the target audience of mid-teen girls. A pleasant little romp."

OTHER NOVELS

Benway followed her debut novel with *The Extraordinary Secrets of April, May & June*, which was first published in 2010. The three titular characters are sisters who are contending with some major changes in their lives: a new school, their parents' divorce, and newfound magical powers. The powers give April the ability to see the future; May the ability to disappear; and June to read other people's thoughts. Throughout the book, each sister takes a turn narrating their story, describing how their new abilities have impacted their lives in unexpected ways.

In *Publishers Weekly* (5 July 2010), a reviewer said: "Benway . . . proves that her own extraordinary ability is her sense of humor; if secondary characters feel contrived to move the plot along, Benway otherwise executes her premise with panache, such as the way the sisters' powers pair with their personalities."

Benway's next two novels, *Also Known As* (2013) and *Going Rogue* (2014), focus on the adventures of teenager Maggie Silver, a professional safecracker and the daughter of international spies. In the first novel, Maggie is uncomfortable with her parents' lifestyle, traveling the world to stop crimes, because it never allows her to have enough time to make friends or have a boyfriend. But then Maggie gets her first solo assignment at a private school in New York City, where she must acquire the information she needs while at the same time trying not to reveal who she really is. *Going Rogue* finds Maggie still in New York, where she has settled down to a new life with a steady boyfriend and friends, but then the worst happens: her parents are accused of theft, and Maggie herself must come to their aid. Both novels were cheered by critics and fans for their humor, realistic and relatable characters, and mystery.

Benway's next novel, *Emmy & Oliver*, was published in 2015 and took on the difficult topic of child kidnapping. Emmy and Oliver are the very best of friends up until the second grade, when Oliver is kidnapped by his father. When he is finally returned to his mother a decade later, Emmy still lives next door and finds herself trying to come to terms with what happened to Oliver and how it has impacted all their lives. Benway explained to Corbett why she was motivated to write a novel with such a difficult subject as *Emmy & Oliver*: "I don't have kids but a lot of my friends now have two- and three- and four-year-olds and I have been watching that incredible bond develop between them. At the same time, because I write for teenagers, I'm also always thinking about what happens when that bond is severed, when those kids grow up and start moving away from their parents. From that I started thinking about what would happen if the bond is instantly severed, like, in Oliver's case, because a parent takes a child and goes into hiding."

WINNER OF THE NATIONAL BOOK AWARD

Benway's latest novel, *Far from the Tree*, garnered serious attention upon its publication in 2017. The book itself took a while to germinate. Benway had been working on a new book idea with little luck. She told her editor that she was not going to meet her deadlines. Then, just a week later, she was in a parking lot and heard a song by Florence + The Machine and had a revelation. The book, she suddenly realized, was about adoption. In short order she and her editor had worked out the idea: the book would be about an adopted teenage girl named Grace giving her own child up for adoption. Grace learns from her adoptive parents that she has two biological siblings: Maya, a year younger, and Joaquin, who is older. When they meet, they begin to develop a new understanding of what makes up a family—and what makes up their own personal and ethnic identities. (Of the three, only Joaquin identifies as Latino.)

Benway was praised for the deft way in which she handled her characterizations as well as for the considerable research she undertook to explore the issues of race and class when it came to adoption in the United States. The book received numerous stellar reviews upon its publication. In the *Los Angeles Times*, for example, French praised the novel, writing "Well-plotted and told from multiple perspectives, *Far from the Tree* pairs pitch-perfect teenage voices with an empathy for their real pain and complex struggles."

Benway found out that she had been long-listed for the National Book Award for Young People's Literature on the day she was helping her mother move into a new condominium. On November 15, 2017, she learned that she had won the coveted prize, for which she received a bronze medal and statue, along with $10,000. During her acceptance speech, Benway talked about members of her family who had inspired her throughout her life. Benway recalled, as quoted by Colin Dwyer for *NPR* (15 Nov. 2017), how her grandmother taught her that "creativity is not inspiration, it's not that bolt of lightning. . . . It's about getting up and making the coffee and getting to work to find the room that that lightning lit up for them for that one moment."

OTHER ACCOLADES

Benway's novels have been published in multiple languages and in twenty countries and have made the *New York Times* Best Sellers list on numerous occasions. In addition to winning the National Book Award, she has received the following awards for *Audrey Wait!*: the 2008 Blue Ribbon Award from the Bulletin for the Center for Children's Books; the 2009 American Library Association (ALA) Best Fiction for Young Adults; and the 2014 Popular Paperbacks for Young Adults Top Ten list selected by the Young Adult Library Services Association.

PERSONAL LIFE

Benway enjoys music and has shared playlists that have inspired her writing on her website. She lives in Los Angeles, California, with her dog, Hudson, whom she credits with helping her relax about upcoming publishing deadlines.

SUGGESTED READING

"About Robin." *Robin Benway*, www.robinben-way.com/about/. Accessed 1 Mar. 2018.

Benway, Robin. "Q & A with Robin Benway." Interview by Sue Corbett. *Publishers Weekly*, 4 June 2015, www.publishersweekly.com/pw/by-topic/childrens/childrens-authors/article/67017-q-a-with-robin-benway.html. Accessed 1 Mar. 2018.

Dwyer, Colin. "Jesmyn Ward, Frank Bidart, Masha Gessen and Robin Benway Win National Book Awards." *NPR*, 15 Nov. 2017, www.npr.org/sections/thetwo-way/2017/11/15/564479979/jesmyn-ward-frank-bidart-masha-gessen-and-robin-ben-way-win-national-book-awards. Accessed 2 Apr. 2018.

French, Agatha. "In Her Sixth Book for Teens—*Far from the Tree*, a National Book Award Finalist—Robin Benway Strikes at the Heart." *Los Angeles Times*, 9 Nov. 2017, www.latimes.com/books/la-ca-jc-robin-benway-20171109-story.html. Accessed 1 Mar. 2018.

Gómez, Sarah Hannah. "Robin Benway Opens Up about Her National Book Award–Winning YA Novel." *School Library Journal*, 10 Jan. 2018, www.slj.com/2018/01/teens-ya/robin-benway-opens-national-book-award-winning-ya-novel/#. Accessed 5 Mar. 2018.

Review of *Audrey, Wait!*, by Robin Benway. *Kirkus Review*, 15 Mar. 2008, www.kirkus-reviews.com/book-reviews/robin-benway/audrey-wait/. Accessed 5 Mar. 2018.

"The Extraordinary Secrets of April, May & June." Review of *The Extraordinary Secrets of April, May & June*, by Robin Benway. *Publishers Weekly*, 5 July 2010, www.publishersweek-ly.com/978-1-59514-286-3. Accessed 1 Mar. 2018.

SELECTED WORKS

Audrey, Wait!, 2008; *The Extraordinary Secrets of April, May & June*, 2010; *Also Known As*, 2013; *Going Rogue*, 2014; *Emmy & Oliver*, 2015; *Far from the Tree*, 2017

—Christopher Mari

Mookie Betts

Date of birth: October 7, 1992
Occupation: Baseball player

Hard-playing outfielder Mookie Betts almost immediately became a key component of the Boston Red Sox after first joining the team, originally as a second baseman, in the 2014 season. After switching to the outfield, first as a center fielder and then in right, Betts demonstrated the overall offensive and defensive skills to be a cornerstone of the organization for years to come. In just his first three-and-a-half big-league seasons, he became a two-time All-Star and most valuable player (MVP) runner-up, with two Gold Glove Awards and a Silver Slugger Award to his name. By the end of the 2017 regular season, he had already racked up a .292 batting average, 78 home runs, and 310 runs batted in (RBIs).

Even as a young player, Betts maintains a self-possession and ease that many older veterans have never mastered, suggesting to many baseball observers that he could be one of the faces of the sport, drawing the attention of a new generation to Major League Baseball (MLB). "He's got every attribute that would fit that 'face of baseball,' from his great talent, the excitement he creates on the field, how he does everything incredibly well," teammate David Price said to Nick Cafardo for the *Boston Globe* (19 Feb. 2017). "His personality is one that everybody loves and can feel comfortable with. He's a winner. He does everything he can, whether it be in the outfield, the plate, the base paths to win a game."

EARLY LIFE AND EDUCATION

Mookie Betts was born Markus Lynn Betts on October 7, 1992, in Nashville, Tennessee. His parents, Willie Betts and Diana Benedict, recalled that even as a toddler he always wanted to play with a ball—and run everywhere once he learned how. He lived in Murfreesboro until age ten. After his parents separated, he moved with his mother to Brentwood, on the border

Wikimedia Commons

of Nashville. His father lived nearby and often drove him to baseball games throughout his youth.

By the time he entered Overton High School as a freshman, Betts' local reputation as a highly driven talent was well established. He was seen as a team player who worked well with others, but his innate skills made him stand out. Part of his success was his ability to study something, then imitate and often improve upon it. "His dad is good at that," his mother recalled to Jen McCaffrey for *MassLive* (15 July 2015). "They can both pick up stuff. He can probably fix anything. They just watch stuff and be able to fix a hole or repair something. It goes beyond sports." Among Betts' skills: solving a Rubik's Cube in about two minutes.

Still, baseball emerged as Betts' primary showcase. As a high school junior, he batted .549 with 6 homers, 37 RBIs, and 24 stolen bases. As a senior, he batted .509 with 39 RBIs and 29 stolen bases. With numbers like those, the scouts from several big league teams began coming around to see if he really had what it took to play in the majors. Danny Watkins, an area scout for the Boston Red Sox, saw Betts play at age seventeen and eighteen. He liked what he saw but wanted to make sure both Betts and his family knew what it meant to go pro, and that the young player would be able to handle it. "You're talking about potentially changing or altering this kid's direction in life," Watkins explained to McCaffrey. "Since the time he was young, the thinking is high school, college, then a profession. So you're talking about giving them the chance to alter that and so you really want to focus in more on their family life, their home life, how stable has it been, how mature is this guy going to be when he gets out on his own."

After some soul searching, Betts and his family decided to take the shot at skipping college to go pro. However, they also wanted to make sure he would be comfortable financially if things did not work out, and he needed to go back to school. In the 2011 MLB Draft, Betts was taken by the Red Sox in the fifth round, number 172 overall. The team gave him a $750,000 bonus, well over normal for such a relatively low draft spot, signaling their high hopes for the unproven prospect.

MINOR LEAGUE SENSATION

Betts's first full season in the minor leagues, 2012, was a bit of an adjustment period. With the Lowell Spinners, playing shortstop as well as his more natural second base position, he found his offensive numbers slumping considerably from the astronomical highs he had maintained in high school. But he kept at it and made the adjustments necessary to allow his promotion to the Single-A Greenville Drive at the start of the

2013 season. From there he climbed the ranks of the Red Sox farm system quickly, moving to the Salem Red Sox in July 2013 and earning several awards as a breakout player.

Betts started the 2014 season at the double-A level with the Portland Sea Dogs. After just fifty-four games, he found himself promoted to Triple A with the Pawtucket Red Sox, where he continued to excel. He also began training as an outfielder in anticipation of eventually joining Boston's major-league club, where second base was occupied by franchise stalwart Dustin Pedroia. When asked what accounted for his rapid success in the minors, Betts remained humble. "I think just hard work, taking a lot of swings, preparing myself," Betts said to Ben Watkins for *Rolling Stone* (13 Jan. 2016). "I got put in a situation where there were the right coaches around me. I credit them and all of the hard work I put in for my success."

In late June 2014 Kevin Boles, Pawtucket's manager, called Betts back to the field after a game. He had gone home but returned quickly, worried that he had gotten into trouble. Shortly after he arrived Boles gave him the good news: Betts had been called up and would make his major-league debut with the Red Sox against their hated rivals, the New York Yankees, at Yankee Stadium on June 29. "I thought I was going to be a lot more excited than I was but I was like 'Alright,' and started packing my stuff," Betts recalled of his promotion to McCaffrey. "It seemed like everyone else was a lot more excited than I was. I don't know if it was because I was nervous or something. That night I didn't get a whole lot of sleep."

EMERGING ALL-STAR

During the 2014 season, Betts would go back down to the minors a couple more times, but he stuck with the Red Sox permanently after his final call up on August 18. During that first season in the big leagues, he played in a total of fifty-two games, racking up five homers and a batting average of .291. He filled in at second base occasionally, but primarily played center field and some games in right field.

For most of the 2015 season, his first full season in the majors, Betts was Boston's starting center fielder. He also batted mainly in the leadoff spot and quickly impressed fans with his offensive abilities. By the end of the season he had a batting average of .291, with 18 homers and 77 RBIs. Equally impressive were his forty-two doubles and eight triples, along with 21 stolen bases. Yet even as a superstar in the making, Betts was characteristically humble about his accomplishments, noting the importance of sustained success. "You get lucky and do it once," he told Watkins. "My plan is to be consistent. I don't necessarily want to have better numbers than I did last year. I just want to be consistent. That's all. If I can do that same thing or somewhere close to it every year, I'll have a pretty decent career and be able to play for a long time."

During the 2016 season Betts would not only be consistent, he would improve on those numbers and be named to the All-Star Game for the first time in his career. He switched from center to right field to make room for fellow young sensation Jackie Bradley Jr. (the pair, along with shortstop Xander Bogaerts and later fellow outfielder Andrew Benintendi, would become known as Boston's "Killer B's"). Betts became the first major leaguer to reach two hundred hits in 2016, and finished the regular season with an MLB-leading 359 total bases. His other statistics were equally terrific: a .318 batting average, 31 homers, 113 RBIs, 42 doubles, and 5 triples along with excellent defense. His offensive performance helped the Red Sox win the American League East Division with a 93–69 record, but the team lost in a three-game sweep to the Cleveland Indians in the first round of the playoffs. During the off-season, Betts was named the runner up for the league's MVP award in recognition of his all-around excellence. He also won a Gold Glove Award for defense and a Silver Slugger Award for offense as a right fielder.

RED SOX CORNERSTONE

Coming off his superb 2016 campaign, Betts was established as a staple of the Red Sox lineup and one of the brightest young talents in all of baseball. With the retirement of many stars of the previous generation, including Red Sox slugger David Ortiz, the team and the league looked for fresh faces to attract a new wave of fans. Many in the sports media speculated that Betts—young, gifted, humble, approachable—was ideally positioned to serve as a sort of ambassador for baseball to young people. Many considered him an inspiration to young African Americans, among whom baseball had lost popularity to other sports. "I have learned to accept that I'm a role model for some people," Betts told Alex Speier for the *Boston Globe* (22 Mar. 2017). "I embrace it. I try to be the best I can be, smile, have fun playing the game, and make little aspects of the game enjoyable. That way, younger kids can go out, love playing the game, do things to have fun."

Betts continued to excel offensively and defensively in 2017, though his numbers dipped from the previous year. Carrying over from September 12, 2016, he maintained an impressive streak of 129 consecutive plate appearances without striking out through April 19, 2017. He was again nominated for the All-Star Game. He completed the 2017 season with a .264 batting average—considerably lower than normal for him—but still with a solid 24 homers, 102 RBIs,

46 doubles, and a pair of triples. He finished sixth in MVP voting and won his second Golden Glove. The Red Sox again won their division, but again were eliminated in the first round of the playoffs, losing to the eventual World Series champion Houston Astros in four games.

Following the 2017 season, Betts was eligible to pursue a raise through arbitration for the first time. In that system, if the player and the team cannot agree on a salary, an independent third party chooses between both camps' recommended figures, based on the player's past performance and potential. Betts and the Red Sox agreed to go to arbitration rather than negotiate at all, with the team offering $7.5 million for 2018 and Betts's management asking for $10.5 million. Both represented considerable increases from his $950,000 salary in 2017, reflecting his star status. In January 2018 the judges ruled in favor of Betts, making him the second-highest paid player of those in their first arbitration-eligible year, after Kris Bryant of the Chicago Cubs, who had negotiated for $10.85 million earlier that month.

PERSONAL LIFE

In addition to being an exceptional ballplayer, Betts earned attention for his skill in bowling—a pastime that his mother encouraged since he was very young. He has bowled multiple perfect games and competed in the Professional Bowlers Association (PBA) World Series of Bowling. "I have no idea what it is about bowling," Betts told Watkins. "It's just a love I have for it. I can't even explain why. Bowling is just fun for me."

SUGGESTED READING

Cafardo, Nick. "Is Mookie Betts the Few 'Face of Baseball?'" *The Boston Globe*, 19 Feb. 2017, www.bostonglobe.com/sports/redsox/2017/02/19/mookie-betts-new-face-baseball/VzUbXtqdB3mrBG0nBPIINN/story.html. Accessed 2 Mar. 2018.

Kepner, Tyler. "Red Sox Hew Rough Diamonds into Bats That Are a Cut Above." *The New York Times*, 3 June 2016, www.nytimes.com/2016/06/04/sports/baseball/boston-red-sox-mookie-betts-xander-bogaerts-jackie-bradley-jr.html. Accessed 2 Mar. 2018.

Lauber, Scott. "Mookie Betts Awarded $10.5 Million in Arbitration." *ESPN*, 31 Jan. 2018, www.espn.com/mlb/story/_/id/22276032/red-sox-outfielder-mookie-betts-awarded-105-million-arbitration. Accessed 2 Mar. 2018.

McCaffrey, Jen. "The Story of Mookie Betts' Rise from Nashville to Boston Red Sox Franchise Cornerstone." *Mass Live*, 15 July 2015, www.masslive.com/redsox/index.ssf/2015/07/boston_red_sox_mookie_betts.html. Accessed 2 Mar. 2018.

"Mookie Betts, Stats, Fantasy & News." *MLB*, m.mlb.com/player/605141/mookie-betts. Accessed 2 Mar. 2018.

Speier, Alex. "Mookie Betts Is Just Happy to Be One of the New Faces of Baseball." *Boston Globe*, 22 Mar. 2017, www.bostonglobe.com/sports/redsox/2017/03/22/mookie-betts-happy-one-new-faces-baseball/Wloi7QIUC84a-SOIm9aEYPJ/story.html. Accessed 2 Mar. 2018.

Watkins, Ben. "Bowling with Mookie Betts: Red Sox Star Is on a Roll." *Rolling Stone*, 13 Jan. 2016, www.rollingstone.com/sports/features/bowling-with-mookie-betts-red-sox-star-is-on-a-roll-20160113. Accessed 2 Mar. 2018.

—*Christopher Mari*

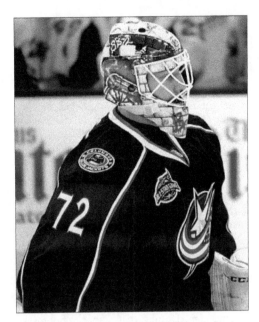

Sergei Bobrovsky

Date of birth: September 20, 1988
Occupation: Hockey player

For National Hockey League (NHL) goaltender Sergei Bobrovsky, the most important part of any hockey game is "the atmosphere in the hockey arena," he told Timur Ganeev for *Russia Beyond* (24 Dec. 2014). "There is a full house at every match," he explained to Ganeev. "In the NHL you're always playing in a full stadium, and that really makes me happy." Indeed, a significant portion of the fans filling the stadiums in which Bobrovsky plays are likely there to see Bobrovsky himself. Since debuting with Ohio's Columbus Blue Jackets in 2013, Bobrovsky—known to fans and teammates as Bob—has established himself as a valuable contributor to the team's success on the rink, earning widespread recognition for his skills as a goalie.

Born and raised in what is now Russia, Bobrovsky began his professional career playing with Metallurg Novokuznetsk in the Kontinental Hockey League and, despite his eligibility, was not selected by an NHL team during the 2006 draft. He joined the NHL in 2010, signing with the Philadelphia Flyers as a free agent. After two seasons with that team, Bobrovsky was traded to Columbus, where he achieved league-best statistics, won two Vezina Trophies, and was selected for multiple All-Star teams. For Bobrovsky, however, his past struggles and achievements are both distractions from what truly matters. "It doesn't matter what happened yesterday," he said, as quoted by Brian Compton for *NHL.com* (12 Apr. 2017). "Tomorrow is most important."

EARLY LIFE

Bobrovsky was born on September 20, 1988, in Novokuznetsk, a Siberian city then part of the Soviet Union and later part of Russia. His father, Andrey, was a coal miner, and his mother, Larisa, worked in metal fabrication. Bobrovsky credits his parents with helping him develop the toughness and strong work ethic crucial to his success in professional hockey.

A fan of hockey from early childhood, Bobrovsky was inspired by the NHL highlights that he saw on television and especially admired the impressive saves achieved by professional goaltenders. He began playing hockey at the age of six but did not initially take on the role of goaltender, as his parents were averse to the idea. However, he eventually began playing in that position to meet the needs of his team. "Our goalie fell ill, and we were scheduled to play the next day. We didn't have a second goalie, and the coach asked whether I wanted to go in goal. I agreed," he recalled to Ganeev. "I liked it, and I've stayed in goal ever since."

Goaltenders require a great deal of equipment to perform their roles, and while Bobrovsky's parents bought some of it, they were unable to afford all the protective pads and other items their son needed. To ensure that the talented young athlete could play, his early coach Alexei Kitsyn took on the task of making Bobrovsky's pads and glove. "He made it. By himself. By his hands," Bobrovsky told Aaron Portzline for the *Columbus Dispatch* (18 Jan. 2015). "It sounds crazy. If you know how some kids today get the best gear, how much money they spend . . . and that's how it started for me."

EARLY CAREER

Bobrovsky played in a variety of junior-level competitions and in 2007 made his professional hockey debut as a member of Metallurg Novokuznetsk, a team then within the Russian Superleague. In 2008 Metallurg Novokuznetsk joined the recently formed Kontinental Hockey League (KHL), which encompasses ice hockey teams from countries throughout Europe and Asia. Bobrovsky spent several seasons as a goaltender for Metallurg Novokuznetsk in addition to participating in international competition. He represented Russia in the 2008 International Ice Hockey Federation World Junior Championship (also called the IIHF World Under 20 Championship), where Russia placed third.

Although Bobrovsky was a successful player in the KHL, he aspired to play hockey in the United States. "My only dream was to play in the NHL," he told Ganeev. He had been eligible to be drafted by an NHL team during the 2006 NHL Draft, but had not been selected by any team. Despite that setback, Bobrovsky remained on the radar of NHL talent scouts, and his strong performance with Metallurg Novokuznetsk meant that he was a strong prospect for teams seeking new goalies. One such team was the Philadelphia Flyers, whose European scout Ken Khudyakov brought Bobrovsky to the team's attention. Bobrovsky signed a three-year contract with the Flyers as a free agent in May 2010.

PHILADELPHIA FLYERS

During his first training camp and preseason in the NHL, Bobrovsky impressed Flyers leadership with his strong performance. He maintained a record of three wins, zero losses, and one tie during the preseason and achieved an impressive average save percentage of .939. Although the team's leaders initially planned to send Bobrovsky to a developmental team and later considered adding him to the main Philadelphia Flyers team as a backup goaltender, they ultimately tasked him with serving as a starting goaltender after an established goalie was injured during training camp.

Having learned that he would be starting goalie only hours before the game, Bobrovsky made his NHL regular season debut on October 7, 2010, in the season opener against the Pittsburgh Penguins. The Flyers won that game, with Bobrovsky blocking 29 of the 31 shots taken against him. Over the remainder of the season, he played in 54 games for the Flyers, starting 52 of them, and achieved a save percentage of .915. He was named rookie of the month for November 2010. At the end of the regular season, Bobrovsky accompanied the Flyers to his first playoffs, during which he appeared in 6 games. The team was successful in the first round of the tournament, defeating the Buffalo Sabres in the Eastern Conference quarterfinals, but went on to lose the conference semifinals to the Boston Bruins.

A backup goaltender during his second season with the Flyers, Bobrovsky played in only 29 of the 2011–12 season's 82 games, starting 25 of them and tallying a save percentage of .899. During the playoffs, the Flyers beat the Penguins in the conference quarterfinals but lost to the New Jersey Devils in the semifinals. Dissatisfied with being a backup goaltender, Bobrovsky made Flyers leadership aware that he would likely leave the team after his contract was up, and he was subsequently traded to the Columbus Blue Jackets in June 2012. Although his departure from his first NHL team was due in part to his desire for further opportunities, he remained conscious of the important role the Philadelphia Flyers had played in his career. "I always, always appreciate the Flyers' organization and what they've done for me," Bobrovsky told Randy Miller for *NJ.com* (8 Dec. 2014). "It was a huge experience for me and I appreciate that."

MOVE TO COLUMBUS

The 2012–13 NHL season did not begin in October, as originally scheduled, due to the 2012–13 NHL lockout, a labor dispute over revenue sharing, salary caps, and related issues. During the lockout, Bobrovsky signed with the KHL team SKA St. Petersburg and played for that franchise until the NHL schedule resumed. He made his debut with the Columbus Blue Jackets on January 19, 2013, in a successful game against the Nashville Predators. Bobrovsky played in 38 games during the shortened season, achieving a career-high save percentage of .932. The Blue Jackets did not qualify for the playoffs that year, but Bobrovsky himself received significant recognition for his work on the ice, including a spot on the NHL All-Star Team for the 2012–13 season. He also won that season's Vezina Trophy, awarded by the NHL to the goaltender voted best in the league. Having established himself as a valuable contributor to the Blue Jackets, he signed a two-year, $11.25 million contract with the team in the summer of 2013.

Over the next seasons, Bobrovsky offered up a generally strong performance. He played 58 games in the 2013–14 season, including 32 wins, and achieved a save percentage of .923. In the winter of 2014, he took time off from NHL play to compete in the Winter Olympics in Sochi, Russia, with the Russian men's hockey team. The team's loss to Finland in the quarterfinals was disappointing for the players and for the host country, but Bobrovsky was determined to overcome that disappointment. "It's already behind us," he told the *Canadian Press* (26 Feb. 2014). "Right after the games, I felt empty and

I felt bad. But that's already past." Two months after the Olympics, Bobrovsky went to his first NHL playoffs with the Blue Jackets, the team's first since switching from the Western Conference to the Eastern Conference in 2013. The team was ultimately defeated by the Penguins, 4 games to 2.

COLUMBUS BLUE JACKETS

During the 2014–15 season, Bobrovsky played in 51 games, winning 30 of them, and had a save percentage of .918. In January 2015, he signed a four-year, $29.7 million contract that would keep him with the Blue Jackets through the 2018–19 season. "I'm really happy to stay with the team and this organization," he said, as quoted by Pierre LeBrun for *ESPN* (10 Jan. 2015). "They were great to me and it's great to be a Blue Jacket for four more years."

The following season was challenging for Bobrovsky, who experienced multiple groin injuries and spent several weeks off the ice. He ultimately played in only 37 games that season and achieved a disappointing win-loss ratio of 15–19 and the lowest save percentage in several seasons. However, he rebounded in the 2016–17 season, playing in 63 games. He won 41 of the games in which he played, contributing to a 16-game win streak that was the second-longest ever achieved in the NHL. At .931, Bobrovsky's save percentage was the highest in the league that season, and he also led the league in lowest goals against average in NHL with 2.06. Although the Blue Jackets were again defeated by the Penguins in the playoffs, the season was a particularly successful one for Bobrovsky, who played in the 2017 All-Star Game and won his second Vezina Trophy. His achievements were particularly striking in comparison to his struggles the previous season, which for Bobrovsky had proved to be a valuable learning experience. "There were lessons from last season," he said, as quoted by Compton. "The rest of it you try to throw in the garbage, reset your mind, relax, and get ready for what's next."

Bobrovsky started the 2017–18 season off strong on October 6, 2017, with a shutout game against the New York Islanders. He played in 38 games through January 12, 2018, winning 21 of them and achieving a total of 4 shutouts. On January 2, 2018, he became the fourth Russian-born goalkeeper to win 200 games in the NHL. "It's definitely a good milestone, I would say," he told Brian Hedger for the official website of the *Columbus Blue Jackets* (3 Jan. 2018). However, he did not view that milestone as an excuse to slack off on the ice. "I'm still in the process and progress, and I don't really have time to feel satisfied by that," he told Hedger.

PERSONAL LIFE

Bobrovsky married his wife, Olga Dorokova, in 2011. He lives in Columbus during the NHL season and often visits Russia during the off-season. An avid traveler, he particularly enjoys visiting museums.

SUGGESTED READING

Bobrovsky, Sergei. "Sergei Bobrovsky: 'I Had One Dream: To Play in the NHL.'" Interview by Timur Ganeev. *Russia Beyond*, 24 Dec. 2014, www.rbth.com/sport/2014/12/24/sergei_bobrovsky_i_had_one_dream_to_play_in_the_nhl_40883.html. Accessed 12 Jan. 2018.

Canadian Press. "Sergei Bobrovsky Over Olympic Disappointment, Looking to Lead Jackets' Late Push to Playoffs." *The Hockey News*, 26 Feb. 2014, www.thehockeynews.com/news/article/sergei-bobrovsky-over-olympic-disappointment-looking-to-lead-jackets-late-push-to-playoffs. Accessed 12 Jan. 2017.

Compton, Brian. "Sergei Bobrovsky Top Pick in Vezina Trophy Race." *NHL.com*, 12 Apr. 2017, www.nhl.com/news/columbus-blue-jackets-sergei-bobrovsky-is-top-pick-for-vezina-trophy/c-288672188. Accessed 12 Jan. 2018.

Hedger, Brian. "Mr. 200: Bobrovsky's Milestone Another Reminder of His Skill, Importance." *Columbus Blue Jackets*, 3 Jan. 2018, www.nhl.com/bluejackets/news/columbus-blue-jackets-bobrovsky-200/c-294629490. Accessed 12 Jan. 2018.

LeBrun, Pierre. "Sergei Bobrovsky Gets $29.7M." *ESPN*, 10 Jan. 2015, www.espn.com/nhl/story/_/id/12143599/sergei-bobrovsky-signs-four-year-contract-extension-columbus-blue-jackets. Accessed 12 Jan. 2018.

Miller, Randy. "Columbus Blue Jackets Goalie Sergei Bobrovsky Wanted to Leave Flyers, but Had No Rift with Ilya Bryzgalov." *NJ.com*, 8 Dec. 2014, www.nj.com/flyers/index.ssf/2014/12/columbus_blue_jackets_goalie_sergei_bobrovsky_wanted_to_leave_flyers_but_had_no_rift_with_ilya_bryzg.html. Accessed 12 Jan. 2018.

Portzline, Aaron. "Blue Jackets: Team's Three All-Stars Inspired by Parents, Coaches." *The Columbus Dispatch*, 18 Jan. 2015, www.dispatch.com/bluejacketsxtra/content/stories/2015/01/18/blue-jackets-all-stars.html. Accessed 12 Jan. 2018.

—*Joy Crelin*

Devin Booker

Date of birth: October 30, 1996
Occupation: Basketball player

Basketball player Devin Booker "always wanted to be one of those players that can turn around the franchise," as he told Marc J. Spears for the *Undefeated* (5 Apr. 2018). After reaching the National Basketball Association (NBA) with the Phoenix Suns, he worked to do just that. A talented shooting guard and sometimes point guard who previously played for the University of Kentucky Wildcats, Booker dedicated himself to improving the standing of the struggling team, which had not won an NBA championship at any point in its first five decades of existence. Although he faced challenges, including injuries and the team's streak of losing seasons, his emergence as a high-scoring star brought optimism. "I knew from day one that there wasn't going to be success right off the bat," he told Spears. "There was going to be some ups and downs, but also hopefully it's all up from here."

The son of retired professional basketball player Melvin Booker, the younger Booker grew up both playing and studying basketball and impressed onlookers with his achievements on the court in high school. In a single season at the University of Kentucky he drew the attention of numerous professional teams, including the Suns, who selected him as the thirteenth overall pick in the 2015 NBA Draft. He was named to the NBA All-Rookie First Team before truly breaking out as a star in his second and third years, including with an eye-opening seventy-point game in March 2017. Driven by a competitive nature, Booker became known for performing well against the best players in the game. "When I go against [the superstars], there's a fire in my eye, 'cause those are the top guys in the League, and that's the position I'm trying to get in," he told Adam Figman for *Slam* (15 Nov. 2017). "Every time I get a chance to play against those guys, I'm not backing down."

EARLY LIFE AND EDUCATION

Devin Armani Booker was born on October 30, 1996, in Grand Rapids, Michigan, to Melvin Booker and Veronica Gutierrez. His father was a professional basketball player who played for several NBA teams during the mid-1990s and went on to play internationally. Booker spent his childhood in Grandville, a suburb of Grand Rapids, where he lived with his mother and half siblings Davon and Mya. Summers were often spent visiting his father, and Booker at times had the opportunity to travel abroad while his father was playing overseas.

While basketball was one of Booker's main focuses from an early age, academics were also

By Keith Allison, via Wikimedia Commons

a high priority in his household. "Coming home with all straight A's, most of my life, that was the expectation from my parents," he told Spears. "It wasn't even anything we talked about; that was instilled in me at a young age." He would later credit his parents' approach to his education with teaching him the discipline that would be key to his success as a basketball player.

Booker spent his freshman year of high school at Grandville High School, where he quickly progressed through the school's freshman, junior varsity, and varsity basketball teams. He then moved to the city of Moss Point, Mississippi, to live with his father, who had retired from international basketball. He began to attend and play basketball at Moss Point High School, where his father hoped he would learn to play the sport in a new way thanks to the tougher urban environment. "He needed to be challenged," Booker's father told Figman. "It's nothing against suburban basketball, but it's a little different in the hood. It's just something that made him better. It's just another challenge that he took upon. And he took over the area. Took over the state, actually."

A significant asset to his team, Booker drew widespread attention for his work on the court and as a senior was named to the 2014 McDonald's All-American Boys Game roster. He also attended several high-profile basketball training camps, including ones endorsed by NBA superstars such as Lebron James and Kevin Durant, further honing his skills. Booker graduated from Moss Point High School in 2014.

UNIVERSITY OF KENTUCKY

Heavily scouted by college athletic programs throughout his high school career, Booker ultimately decided to attend the University of Kentucky and play for the dominant Wildcats men's basketball team. He made valuable contributions during his first and only season with the team, achieving a total of 381 points, fifty-three free throws, seventy-six rebounds, and forty-two assists over the course of thirty-eight games played. The team went undefeated during the regular season and ended the season ranked number one in the Southeastern Conference (SEC). Booker was named to the All-SEC Freshman Team and the All-SEC Second Team, and also earned the SEC Sixth Man of the Year award.

In the spring of 2015, the Kentucky Wildcats entered the National Collegiate Athletic Association (NCAA) Division I basketball tournament. They remained unbeaten through the initial rounds, and defeated Notre Dame University in the Elite Eight stage of the tournament to proceed to the Final Four, where they faced the University of Wisconsin–Madison Badgers in the national semifinals. The Wildcats ultimately were eliminated by the Badgers in their first losing game of the season.

Although Booker initially planned to play several years of college basketball before attempting to begin a professional career, his strong performance during his freshman season at the University of Kentucky made him the focus of significant attention from NBA teams. He ultimately opted to enter the 2015 NBA Draft along with several of his college teammates, leaving the University of Kentucky after only a year. On June 25, 2015, Booker was selected by the Phoenix Suns as the thirteenth overall draft pick.

JOINING THE SUNS

Following the NBA Draft, Booker signed a four-season contract with the Suns. He made his debut with the team in the season opener on October 28, 2015, against the Dallas Mavericks. Although the Suns lost that game by sixteen points, Booker contributed significantly while coming off the bench, scoring fourteen points during his twenty-one minutes in play.

Over the remainder of the 2015–16 season, Booker continued his strong play, appearing in almost every game. He even took on a starting role after teammate Eric Bledsoe had to undergo knee surgery two months into the season, and his scoring increased with the greater playing time. Midway through the season he also participated in All-Star Weekend events, playing in the Rising Stars Challenge and setting a record as the youngest player to compete in the three-point contest, where he came in third. Across the course of his rookie year, Booker posted per-game averages of 27.7 minutes played, 13.8 points, 2.8 free throws, 2.5 rebounds, and 2.6 assists per game.

For Booker, joining the Suns presented an opportunity to play a critical role in a struggling team's comeback. Although the team had existed since 1968, the franchise had never won an NBA championship. In addition, although the team had flourished at various points in its existence, it had declined significantly since its last division title in 2007. In light of such challenges, Booker devoted himself both to helping the team and to establishing himself as a key player. "I'm just trying to get a chance to play. Just trying to be out on the court," he told Spears of his early seasons with the team. "I was trying to solidify that I wasn't just a backup plan." Widely recognized for his strong performance during his debut season, Booker was named to the 2016 All-Rookie First Team and ended up in fourth place in voting for the Rookie of the Year Award.

DISAPPOINTMENT AND DETERMINATION

Booker continued to improve in his second year in the NBA. During the 2016–17 season, he played in seventy-eight games with the Suns, starting all of them, and averaged thirty-five minutes per game. He had an average of 22.1 points, 4.7 free throws, 3.2 rebounds, and 3.4 assists per game and made the tenth-most two-point field goal attempts of any player in the NBA. In addition to his solid overall statistics, Booker at times astonished onlookers with particularly impressive feats on the court. On March 24, 2017, he scored seventy points in a single game while facing off against the Boston Celtics, becoming just the sixth player to ever reach that mark. "That was a special game," he recalled to Figman. "Some games I surprise myself."

Despite such efforts from Booker, however, the Suns continued to struggle as a team—they even lost Booker's seventy-point game. They finished the season with the worst record in the Western Conference and the second-worst record in the NBA. Though Booker began to be recognized as a potential All-Star, with superstars James and Durant among those praising him, his position on a losing team kept his profile relatively low.

The subsequent season was similarly challenging for both the Suns and for Booker. His efforts to improve the team's standing were hampered by multiple injuries, including an adductor strain that forced him to take several weeks off. He went on to injure his hand later in the season and was forced to sit out the Suns' last dozen games. When he was able to play, Booker made a strong showing, averaging 34.5 minutes, 24.9 points, 5.4 free throws, 4.5 rebounds, and 4.7 assists over fifty-four games. Nevertheless, the Suns finished the season with a 21–61 record, last in both the Western Conference and the NBA. Booker was deeply disappointed by the team's season, having hoped that the Suns would be able to "make that jump" into a higher level of play, as he told Spears. "We fell super short," he added. "Being a competitor, being a winner most of my whole life, it's really hard."

Following the 2017–18 season, Booker was adamant that he would do everything possible to reverse the Suns' fortunes. "I'm done with not making the playoffs," he told the Associated Press, as reported by *NBC Sports* (12 Apr. 2018). "This is probably my last year ever not making the playoffs. If that's putting pressure on myself, I'm going to take this summer and work that hard so that it doesn't happen again." In addition to setting that goal, Booker faced questions about his future with the franchise, as his rookie contract would expire after the next season. Much speculation surrounded his contract negotiation, his eligibility for a maximum deal, and his desire to play with stronger teammates. Suns executives noted they would give their star a say in the franchise's offseason moves, and Booker, in turn, reiterated his desire to make things work in Phoenix. "When that time comes I'll have to make a decision," he told Scott Bordow for *AZcentral* (30 Mar. 2018) of a potential contract extension. "I've always said this is the place I want to be."

PERSONAL LIFE

Booker bought a home in Phoenix, contributing to media speculation that he meant to stay with the Suns long-term. Having intended to major in computer science in college, he later discussed his interest in finishing his bachelor's degree. Outspoken about a variety of issues, he often particularly expressed his opposition to the practice of prohibiting college athletes from being paid for their work. Booker, whose half-sister has the genetic disorder microdeletion syndrome, formed a bond with a fan with Down syndrome, inviting her to team events and other outreach activities.

SUGGESTED READING

Bordow, Scott. "Phoenix Suns Star Devin Booker Says Coaching Search Secondary to Acquiring Better Talent." *AZcentral*, 30 Mar. 2018, www.azcentral.com/story/sports/nba/suns/2018/03/30/phoenix-suns-devin-booker-coaching-search-jay-triano-ryan-mcdonough/474037002/. Accessed 9 June 2018.

Figman, Adam. "Savage Mode." *Slam*, 15 Nov. 2017, www.slamonline.com/nba/devin-booker-interview-cover-story/. Accessed 9 June 2018.

Pekale, Zach. "ESPN: Might Not Be Right Time for Suns to Pay Devin Booker." *Arizona Sports*, 30 Mar. 2018, arizonasports.com/story/1480240/espn-might-not-right-time-suns-pay-devin-booker/. Accessed 9 June 2018.

Spears, Marc J. "Devin Booker Aims to Rise with Suns." *The Undefeated*, 5 Apr. 2018, theundefeated.com/features/devin-booker-aims-to-rise-with-phoenix-suns/. Accessed 9 June 2018.

Stephenson, Creg. "Moss Point's Devin Booker Has the Name and the Game." *GulfLive.com*, 20 Jan. 2012, blog.gulflive.com/mississippi-press-sports/2012/01/moss_points_devin_booker_has_t.html. Accessed 9 June 2018.

"Suns' Devin Booker: 'This Is Probably My Last Year Ever Not Making the Playoffs.'" *NBC Sports*, 12 Apr. 2018, nba.nbcsports.com/2018/04/12/suns-devin-booker-this-is-probably-my-last-year-ever-not-making-the-playoffs/. Accessed 9 June 2018.

Zimmerman, Kevin. "Suns Draft Pick Devin Booker Groomed to Play Professionally." *Fox Sports*, 26 June 2015, www.foxsports.com/arizona/story/suns-nba-draft-devin-booker-groomed-professional-melvin-booker-062615. Accessed 9 June 2018.

—*Joy Crelin*

Boyko Borisov

Date of birth: June 13, 1959
Occupation: Prime Minister of Bulgaria

A black-belt holder in karate and a former bodyguard turned politician, Boyko Borisov is the prime minister of Bulgaria. He began serving a second term in 2014. He had previously stepped down before the completion of his first term following street demonstrations in 2013.

EARLY LIFE AND EDUCATION

Boyko Borisov was born on June 13, 1959, in Bankya, Bulgaria. The older of two children born to Veneta Borisova, a nursery school teacher, and Metodi Borisov, an officer at the Ministry of Internal Affairs, Borisov grew up in the small village of Bankya. As a teen, he studied karate and participated in tournaments, eventually reaching the high-ranking level of seventh dan. He later coached the Bulgarian national karate team and served as a referee at international tournaments.

Borisov studied fire techniques and safety at the Higher Special School of the Ministry of Interior, a specialized higher education institution devoted specifically to training state officials for various offices and roles. After graduating in 1982 with a degree in firefighting equipment and fire safety and achieving the rank of lieutenant, Borisov worked for the Ministry of Interior's fire department in the Bulgarian capital city of Sofia. He started as a platoon commander and rose to the position of company commander.

After leaving the fire department in 1985, Borisov joined the faculty as a lecturer at the Higher Institute for Police Officers Training and Scientific Research. He also took courses and earned a PhD in the psychological and physical training of operatives. In 1990 Borisov left his teaching position, and the following year he founded a security and personal protection firm, IPON-1. The firm prospered and gained several high-profile clients, including Todor Zhivkov (1911–1998), the former communist dictator of Bulgaria, and Simeon Saxe-Coburg-Gotha, who was king of Bulgaria from 1943–1946 and became the country's prime minister in 2001.

POLITICAL CAREER

Borisov entered politics in 2001 when he was appointed secretary general of the Ministry of Interior by a presidential decree. He simultaneously received the rank of colonel. The position was an influential and powerful one, with Borisov responsible for fighting crime and corruption. The position also was a very public one, and Borisov received extensive media coverage, gaining a reputation for being tough on crime while becoming a media celebrity at the same time.

In 2005 Borisov ran on Prime Minister Saxe-Coburg-Gotha's ticket for a seat in parliament. After winning the election, he was sworn in, but he filed his resignation in September and stepped down two weeks later.

Borisov then ran as an independent candidate for mayor of Sofia to replace the previous mayor who had resigned mid-term. Having gained prominence—and immense publicity—as the country's top crime fighter and media darling, he was hugely popular and won by a landslide.

A year after winning the election, Borisov founded a new political party, the center-right Citizens for European Development of Bulgaria (GERB). In 2007 Borisov ran for re-election as mayor of Sofia and once again easily won despite a poor record of addressing many of the city's problems, such as municipal corruption and poor garbage collection.

Two years later Borisov announced his intent to run for prime minister. During his campaign he promised to solve Bulgaria's economic crisis, combat corruption, and restore the country's place within the European Union (EU). Bulgaria had joined the EU in 2007, but after failing to take sufficient measures to reduce crime and corruption, the EU withheld hundreds of millions of euros aid. Already the poorest country in the EU, the blocked aid plunged Bulgaria into a deep economic crisis.

GERB won the July 2009 election, and Borisov became the prime minister. Despite his campaign promises Borisov failed to make significant changes, and in February 2013 social unrest erupted with citizens protesting in the streets and demanding that the country's poverty rates, austerity measures, and substandard living standards be addressed by the government. Borisov stepped down as prime minister that month.

In October 2014 Bulgaria held a snap election, and Borisov was once again elected prime minister. He took office on November 7, 2014 and formed a coalition government with the Reformist Bloc. During his second term as prime minister, he stressed his intent to solve the country's economic woes and mend relations with the EU. He achieved some progress by implementing an infrastructure project, but as of mid-2015 he had failed to make education, pension, or health care reforms.

IMPACT

Despite his popularity Borisov has failed to deliver on his campaign promises. Bulgaria continues to be plagued with corruption and financial problems. The EU considers Bulgaria one of its most corrupt members. In response to repeated EU warnings, Borisov announced in mid-2015 a restructuring of agencies to fight corruption. Whether he will be able to make significant policy changes to oust corruption in Bulgaria is unknown.

PERSONAL LIFE

Borisov has one child, a daughter, Veneta, from a marriage that ended in divorce. He lives with his domestic partner, Tsvetelina Borislavova, the chief executive officer of a private investment company.

SUGGESTED READING

"Boyko Borisov (MR)." *NATO.* NATO Parliamentary Assembly, 30 May 2011. Web. 12 Oct. 2015.

"Boyko Borisov." *Government of Bulgaria.* Council of Ministers of the Republic of Bulgaria, 2015. Web. 12 Oct. 2015.

Brunwasser, Matthew, and Dan Bilefsky. "After Bulgarian Protests, Prime Minister Resigns." *New York Times.* New York Times, 20 Feb. 2013. Web. 12 Oct. 2015.

"Bulgarians Prefer the Mellower Borisov 2.0—Poll." *Sofia Globe.* Sofia Globe, 21 Apr. 2015. Web. 12 Oct. 2015.

Day, Matthew. "Seven Things You Didn't Know about Boiko Borisov." *Telegraph.* Telegraph Media Group, 7 Oct. 2014. Web. 12 Oct. 2015.

"Who Is Who: Bulgaria's New Prime Minister Boyko Borisov." *Sofia News Agency.* Novinite JSC, 21 July 2009. Web. 12 Oct. 2015.

Williams, Matthias, and Catherine Evans. "Bulgaria's Prime Minister Boiko Borisov." *Reuters.*

Thomson Reuters, 7 Nov. 2014. Web. 12 Oct. 2015.

—*Barb Lightner*

By Keith Allison, via Wikimedia Commons

Alex Bregman

Date of birth: March 30, 1994
Occupation: Baseball player

With his relatively slight build, Alex Bregman of the Houston Astros never fit the prototype of a Major League Baseball (MLB) third baseman. Throughout every level of his playing career, however, he excelled no matter where he played thanks to a work ethic often described as legendary. Known as "a true baseball rat" who "loves the game, loves practice, loves being around his teammates," as Astros manager A. J. Hinch described him to Hillel Kuttler for the *Jewish Telegraph Agency* (27 Mar. 2018), Bregman used his dedication to develop all-around offensive and defensive skills and quickly emerged as one of the brightest young talents in the game.

Bregman enjoyed a decorated three-year career as a shortstop at Louisiana State University (LSU) before being selected by the Astros second overall in the 2015 MLB Draft. During a rapid rise through the Astros' farm system he was gradually transitioned to third base, and in July 2016, he made his major-league debut. Building on his solid rookie campaign, he firmly entrenched himself as the Astros' everyday third baseman in 2017. That postseason, Bregman emerged as a star with a talent for clutch play, recording several pivotal hits and defensive gems that helped propel the Astros to their first-ever World Series title. To many observers, the championship was just the beginning of Bregman's potential. "You're talking about a 23-year-old kid who plays like a 30-year-old veteran," teammate José Altuve—himself a frequent All-Star and Most Valuable Player (MVP) candidate—told Jorge L. Ortiz for *USA Today* (31 Oct. 2017). "He hits homers, he steals bases. I remember when I was 23 and I wasn't as good as him, so I feel like he's going to be a superstar."

EARLY LIFE

Of Russian Jewish heritage, Alexander David Bregman was born on March 30, 1994, in Albuquerque, New Mexico, and grew up with baseball in his blood. His grandfather, Stanley Bregman, was a prominent attorney who served as general counsel for the MLB's Washington Senators. Bregman's father, Sam, and his uncle, Ben, played baseball for the University of New Mexico.

Along with his younger siblings, Jessica and A. J., Bregman was raised in the affluent Northeast Heights section of Albuquerque. He started playing T-ball at the age of four, and in his first game, wowed attendees by turning an unassisted triple play. Throughout his youth he honed his baseball skills by repeatedly throwing a baseball against the brick wall behind his family's house. Bregman's parents, who are both lawyers, aided his development by playing catch with him and throwing him batting practice on a regular basis. As Sam Bregman explained to Ross Dellenger for the Baton Rouge, Louisiana, *Advocate* (15 June 2015) about his son, "He's like every other kid, except he's obsessed with the game of baseball."

Bregman rooted for the Arizona Diamondbacks and dreamed of one day following in the footsteps of his idol, the New York Yankees' superstar shortstop Derek Jeter. Those dreams gradually began to crystallize when, at age eight, he joined the Albuquerque Baseball Academy, an elite training program for cultivating baseball talent. The academy soon became Bregman's second home.

BASEBALL OBSESSION

Bregman quickly separated himself from his peers with an unrelenting work ethic that reached legendary status among his family, friends, and teammates. By age thirteen, he was waking up each day at five o'clock in the morning to go to the batting cages before school. His father recalled to Kuttler that "he'd hit in the batting cages until he got calluses."

When Bregman was in junior high school, he took part in a baseball camp held at the University of New Mexico, where the school's head baseball coach, Ray Birmingham, discussed the need for dedication to achieve greatness. Taking Birmingham's lecture to heart, Bregman immersed himself even more in his baseball training; he often spent so much time practicing that facility workers would have to send him home. In an interview with the Brooklyn-based Jewish weekly *The Vues* (31 Oct. 2017), Bregman said, "My personal belief is that everyone is created equally. In my opinion, talent doesn't exist. I think it comes down to being obsessed with what you want to be. If you are obsessed with what you want to be, you will find a way to make it happen."

Bregman's unwavering mindset translated to remarkable success on the field. As a freshman at Albuquerque Academy, he earned a spot on the varsity team as a shortstop and helped lead the Chargers to the Class 4A state title. His all-around versatility, along with his exceptional knowledge of strategy and opposing players' tendencies, eventually prompted coaches to move him to catcher, which was his primary position in high school. He caught the attention of scouts around the country during his junior year, when he posted an astonishing .678 batting average and hit a state record nineteen home runs.

COLLEGE STANDOUT

Bregman entered his senior season at Albuquerque Academy as a highly touted prospect. He hoped to be selected in the first round of the 2012 MLB Draft, but those hopes were dashed after he fractured the middle finger on his right throwing hand during the first week of the season. The freak injury, which occurred while he was fielding grounders before a game, limited him to just six games that season and adversely affected his draft stock. He was ultimately selected by the Boston Red Sox in the twenty-ninth round of the draft.

Because he was passed over in the first round, Bregman opted to go with his backup plan of attending Louisiana State University (LSU), in Baton Rouge, Louisiana. He chose the school because of its storied baseball program, regarded as among the best in the country. Playing under coach Paul Mainieri, Bregman earned the Tigers' starting shortstop spot as a freshman, winning a three-way battle over two other top players. "Bregman was going to be our shortstop, just because I just thought he had the superior leadership skills, and he was the most vocal and just brought all the intangibles that I wanted," Mainieri told Evan Drellich for the *Houston Chronicle* (13 June 2015). "He had this aura about him, of fearlessness and attacking attitude."

Bregman rewarded Mainieri's faith in him by establishing himself as one of the best college shortstops in the country. As a freshman he batted .369 and finished second in the nation with 104 base hits. He helped lead LSU to the College World Series (CWS) for the first time since 2009, earned All-American honors, and was recognized as the Southeastern Conference (SEC) Freshman of the Year, among other honors. The Tigers earned another CWS berth during Bregman's junior season, in which he led the SEC with thirty-eight stolen bases and finished second in the league with twenty-two doubles.

During his three seasons at LSU, Bregman dazzled coaches and teammates not just with his skills, but also with his extreme practice habits, perpetually optimistic attitude, and tireless approach to the game. "Smartest college player I've ever seen," Bregman's assistant coach at LSU, Will Davis, told Dellenger. "He's so in tune with the game, it's ridiculous. Most people that have the intelligence level of a coach aren't good. He has the intelligence level, baseball IQ of a coach, and he's really good."

HOUSTON ASTROS

Recognizing his many attributes, the Houston Astros selected Bregman with the second overall pick in the 2015 MLB Draft. The team awarded him a contract that included a $5.9 million signing bonus. Bregman became the highest-drafted player from New Mexico and the highest-drafted position player in LSU history. Upon being drafted, he acknowledged that attending LSU proved to be the difference in making him a surefire top pick.

As many expected, Bregman rapidly ascended through the Astros' farm system, rising from Class A to Class AAA ball in less than a year. During that time the Astros gradually transitioned him to third base, largely due to the team already having two highly touted players at shortstop and second base in Carlos Correa and José Altuve, respectively. Bregman opened the 2016 season with the Astros' class AA squad, the Corpus Christi Hooks, before being promoted to the AAA Fresno Grizzlies of the Pacific Coast League. After hitting .333 with six home runs and fifteen runs batted in (RBIs) in eighteen games with the Grizzlies, he was added to the Astros' big-league roster in late July.

Bregman made his MLB debut at third base in a game against the Yankees. Despite going hitless in his first seventeen major-league at-bats, he began to show flashes of his potential after second-year Astros manager A. J. Hinch moved him up to the number-two spot in the lineup. He finished his rookie season with a .264 batting average, eight home runs, thirteen doubles, and thirty-four RBIs in forty-nine games, forty of which he started at third base.

That performance helped position the up-and-coming Astros for a playoff berth, but the team faltered down the stretch, finishing third in the AL West Division with an 84–78 record. Bregman was nonetheless recognized as a promising player to watch. He was named *USA Today* Minor League Player of the Year, becoming the first player in franchise history to receive the honor.

STAR IN THE MAKING

In March 2017, Bregman played for Team USA at that year's World Baseball Classic (WBC). The team won its first WBC title after defeating Puerto Rico 8–0 in the final. The youngest member of the team, Bregman received just four at-bats during the competition while serving in a backup role. Still, he impressed US national team manager Jim Leyland with his grit and determination. "He's one hell of a player," Leyland told Ortiz of Bregman. "He's very aggressive on both offense and defense. He comes every day to beat you. I really like him a lot."

Bregman carried over that laser-like focus into the 2017 season, which saw him solidify his place on an Astros' infield that was arguably the most formidable in the game. He appeared in a team-leading 155 games during the regular season, in which he batted .284 with nineteen homers, seventy-one RBIs, thirty-nine doubles, five triples, and seventeen stolen bases, and posted an .827 on-base plus slugging (OPS) percentage. His doubles total was ninth-best in the AL and his OPS ranked third among AL third basemen. Meanwhile, he led all third basemen with a .970 fielding percentage, making just ten errors in 337 total chances and further illustrating his seamless transition to the position.

Bregman's production helped add another dimension to an already potent Astros' offense that led the majors in a number of offensive categories. The Astros won the AL West with a 101–61 record, marking their second-highest win total in franchise history. Rallying in the aftermath of Hurricane Harvey, which devastated the Houston metropolitan area, the Astros surged into the 2017 postseason, where Bregman achieved a breakthrough performance. In eighteen postseason starts at third, he recorded four homers and ten RBIs, as well as several clutch hits and game-saving defensive plays, one of which came during the Astros' series-clinching game 7 victory over the Yankees in the AL Championships Series (ALCS). As Astros pitcher Justin Verlander, the 2017 ALCS MVP, put it to Ortiz, Bregman "thrives in big moments. When the pressure is on he's a guy you want in your corner."

WORLD SERIES CHAMPION AND BEYOND

Bregman's memorable postseason performance continued as the Astros reached the 2017 World Series against the Los Angeles Dodgers. He hit two home runs in the series, as well as a walk-off single in the bottom of the tenth inning of game 5 to give Houston a three-to-two game advantage. He was just the second-ever player to have an RBI in his first five World Series appearances. The Astros ultimately won in seven games to secure their first World Series title in franchise history.

Entering the 2018 season, Bregman expressed his desire to help the Astros repeat as World Series champions. "There are a lot of things I want to accomplish in this game," he explained to Kuttler. "Winning is right there at the top." Though back-to-back MLB titles are uncommon, many analysts felt young stars like Bregman gave Houston a strong chance. Hinch summed up for Kuttler the widespread enthusiasm over Bregman's potential: "While he's established himself as a major league player . . . he's not even close to what he's going to be."

PERSONAL LIFE

Bregman earned a reputation as a friendly and helpful teammate, comfortable interacting with anyone. He began learning Spanish from a young age in school, and after joining the Astros organization he made a concerted effort to improve his command of the language to better communicate with his many Latino teammates. He has also been involved in charitable activities, and launched the foundation AB for AUDS, dedicated to helping children with autism and Down syndrome.

SUGGESTED READING

Dellenger, Ross. "June 2015: Alex Bregman's Dedication to Baseball Has LSU Aiming for Its 7th College World Series Title." *The Advocate*, 15 June 2015, www.theadvocate.com/baton_rouge/sports/lsu/article_05993e4c-0f7b-54c7-8c64-09c149a8f5b5.html. Accessed 12 June 2018.

Drellich, Evan. "All-or-Nothing Approach Defines Draftee Bregman." *Houston Chronicle*, 13 June 2015, www.houstonchronicle.com/sports/astros/article/All-or-nothing-approach-defines-Bregman-6326005.php. Accessed 12 June 2018.

"Getting to Know Houston Astros Alex Bregman." *The Vues*, 31 Oct. 2017, thevuesonline.com/articles/getting-to-know-houston-astros-alex-bregman/. Accessed 12 June 2018.

Kuttler, Hillel. "Alex Bregman Is Baseball's Next Jewish Star." *Jewish Telegraphic Agency*, 27 Mar. 2018, www.jta.org/2018/03/27/arts-entertainment/alex-bregman-is-baseballs-next-jewish-star. Accessed 12 June 2018.

Ortiz, Jorge L. "Houston's Other Star: Alex Bregman Emerging as Postseason Hero." *USA Today*, 31 Oct. 2017, www.usatoday.com/story/

sports/mlb/2017/10/31/alex-bregman-emerging-postseason-hero/815089001/.   Accessed 12 June 2018.

—*Chris Cullen*

By Keith Allison [CC BY-SA 2.0], via Wikimedia Commons

Zach Britton

Date of birth: December 22, 1987
Occupation: Baseball player

Zach Britton, an All-Star left-handed pitcher for the Baltimore Orioles, is one of Major League Baseball's (MLB) best closers. Britton spent five years in the minor leagues and another three years bouncing between leagues before gaining control of his 96-mph power sinker and becoming the Orioles' full-time closer in 2014. In 2016, Britton led the American League (AL) in saves, converting all 47 save opportunities. He finished the season with a .54 earned run average (ERA). In 2017, he set an AL record after converting his 55th consecutive save. His perfect streak ended a month later, leaving his official tally at sixty. As a high school player in Texas, Britton never expected to make it to the majors, and certainly not as a closer. The Orioles, who drafted Britton in 2006, are equally surprised by the path Britton's career has taken. "If anyone's ever told you they thought this was going to happen, I'd think they'd be crazy," Dave Wallace, the Orioles pitching coach, told Eduardo A. Encina for the *Baltimore Sun* (5 Apr. 2016). "None of us knew really. It was an opportunity, a guy with great stuff and makeup. He's found a role, or a role has found him, however way you want to put it. . . . Once in a while something like this comes along and it's tremendous."

EARLY LIFE

Britton was born in Panorama City, California, on December 22, 1987. He has two older brothers, Clay and Buck. Britton began his pitching career in Hart Little League. As a teenager, he joined the junior varsity team at Canyon High School in Santa Clarita as a pitcher and outfielder. His freshman year, Britton was named the team's most valuable player, but his parents, Greg and Martha, recall his dangerously competitive spirit. When Britton was fifteen, he ran full speed into a stadium light post chasing after a foul ball during a batting contest at practice. The accident put him in the hospital with a fractured skull, a fractured right collarbone, a separated shoulder, and bleeding in his brain. Doctors told Britton's parents that it might be necessary to drill into Britton's skull to stop the swelling, but that such a surgery might affect Britton's motor skills or even leave him paralyzed. Luckily,

the swelling went down on its own and surgery became unnecessary. After Britton's brush with fate, the young player went against his doctors' orders, calling his baseball coach and telling him that he was medically cleared to play—a lie. Britton's parents were furious. "He's scared us a few times with his intensity," Greg Britton told Kevin Van Valkenburg for the *Baltimore Sun* (26 Apr. 2011). Still, Britton was able to return to the pitcher's mound later that year.

When Britton was sixteen, his family moved to Texas. He began playing for the Weatherford High School Kangaroos, one of the best teams in the state. He quickly made a name for himself with his fastball, but was also an all-state outfielder. The doggedness that nearly killed him became an asset, if a stressful one. "He would give up a home run to a guy and we would still win the game, but Zach would be talking about that home run," Jason Lee, one of Britton's coaches at Weatherford told Brittany Ghiroli for *MLB.com* (15 Apr. 2011). "He would be happy we won, but he'd be like, 'When I see that guy next, he's not going to beat me.' He was fixated on constantly improving." Texas A&M University recruited Britton as an outfielder during his senior year, and he made plans to bunk his freshman year with future Dodgers pitcher Clayton Kershaw. Only a week before the MLB Draft did Britton consider that he might have any shot at going pro. Rumors circulated that the Washington Nationals were considering taking him in the first few rounds. Britton was surprised; his death-defying injuries several years earlier would normally be enough to give any major-league team pause. The Baltimore Orioles decided to take a chance on Britton, selecting him in the third round of the 2006 draft, eighty-fifth, as a pitcher.

MINOR LEAGUE CAREER

Britton's professional career got off to a rocky start. He first played for the Bluefield Blue Jays, a Rookie-level team in the Appalachian League; then team manager Gary Allenson recalled Britton as unfocused, more concerned with watching his family film his game on their home movie camera than with playing the game itself. Britton was a volatile player, unable to control his emotions when things went wrong—and early on, things went wrong a lot. Britton went 0–4 with a 5.29 ERA in 11 starts with Bluefield in 2006. He was frequently booed off the field. The young player was also, Britton admitted later, depressed, living on his own for the first time. However, things began looking up after a fortuitous accident in 2007, when Britton was playing for the short-season Single-A Aberdeen IronBirds in the New York–Penn League.

As the story goes, then pitching coach Calvin Maduro tried to teach Britton a cut fastball (a pitch that breaks toward the pitcher's glove side as it reaches home plate) to add to his repertoire. Britton could not seem to master it. His attempts to throw a cutter did not "cut" in one direction, they sank. Thus, Britton stumbled into his own version of a pitch called a power sinker, one of the most difficult in the game to master. "At the time, I was just looking for a something that, as a pitcher, gave me confidence," he recalled to Van Valkenburg. "Something I could throw in situations where, in the past, if I had guys on base, I would give up those runs. That pitch was able to get me out of those situations." Britton did not, at first, know why the pitch worked so well for him or even exactly how he did it, but experimentation with pressure points helped make it his own. The velocity of his throws steadily increased. The same season, Britton added two more pitches, a slider and a change-up, to his repertoire. He ended the 2007 season with the IronBirds with a 3.68 ERA in 15 games.

Britton moved on to a full-season team in 2008, the Single-A Delmarva Shorebirds in the South Atlantic League. For the second time after the IronBirds, Britton, still a teenager, was the youngest player on the team. He enjoyed his best minor league season yet, pitching a career-high 147.1 innings and lowering his ERA to 3.12. He was striking out more batters, but he was walking a lot of them, too, a fact that troubled major league scouts. In 2009, continuing to move up the ladder in the Orioles franchise, Britton joined the Class A-Advanced Frederick Keys in the Carolina League. There, he notched a 2.70 ERA. Britton was promoted twice in 2010, first to the Double-A Bowie Baysox in the Eastern

League, and then, mid-season, to the Triple-A Norfolk Tides in the International League. He played games for both teams again in 2011, and in April, received an unexpected call-up to the majors.

BALTIMORE ORIOLES

Britton made his debut with the Orioles on April 3, 2011, in a game against the Tampa Bay Rays at Tropicana Field. He was thinking that day of a close family friend named Sandi Stephens who had died in a car accident in 2007. Shortly after her death, Britton, an amateur artist, drew a picture of Sandi riding a horse. He had the picture silk-screened onto a t-shirt, and wears it underneath his jersey every time he pitches. "I know this may sound cheesy, but I feel like I've done really well since I've worn that shirt," he told Ghiroli. (He has multiple identical shirts, and once paid a clubhouse attendant $100 to ship him another after misplacing one at an away game with Norfolk.) Before the game on April 3, he texted his mother to tell her that he was dedicating his debut to Sandi. It was not a perfect game—Britton was unable to gain enough control over his sinker to land a strikeout, though he did grind out three strikeouts with his slider. Britton won five of his first six starts with the team, but in July, he was unexpectedly sent back to Double-A Bowie. Some observers speculated that the demotion was strategic, but Britton was disappointed to be relegated to the uncertain and precarious position of being a player caught between two leagues. "It's more frustrating for me, because it's not where I want to be and there's no [set plan]," Britton told Jeff Zrebiec for the *Baltimore Sun* (9 July 2011). "I feel like I'm kind of in-between like la-la-land. Almost like, you are throwing here and what's happening after that? So it's frustrating to say the least."

Britton's 2012 season was plagued by a shoulder injury. He began the season in the minor leagues and made his season debut with the Orioles in mid-July. He played only a handful of games and posted a disappointing 5.07 ERA. He made a better start in the minor leagues in 2013, and was called up again in April. He began the 2014 season with the Orioles and crucially, worked with pitching coach Dave Wallace and bullpen coach Dom Chiti to gain control of his pitches by throwing to a small strike zone constructed with strings. Visualization transformed the way he thought about his game, he told Tyler Kepner for the *New York Times* (25 Aug. 2016). "That drill really helped me understand what my pitch is actually doing," he said. Britton was named the Orioles' full-time closer in May 2014, and threw his sinker with a new and deadly consistency. He helped the Orioles sweep the Detroit Tigers in the American League Division Series (ALDS) and posted a cool 1.65 ERA. Britton made his first All-Star Game appearance in July 2015, and finished the season with a 1.92 ERA.

Britton enjoyed a record-breaking 2016, when he allowed only four earned runs the entire season. There was a four-month stretch, between April 30 and August 24, during which he allowed no earned runs at all, making him one of the most efficient closers in the league. Of 47 save opportunities that year—including one in the 2016 All-Star Game—Britton converted every one, leading the AL in saves. He ended the season with a .54 ERA, won the Mariano Rivera Award, given to the best reliever in the AL, and placed fourth in the Cy Young Award voting. Britton began the 2017 season with a shoulder injury, but, in July, made AL history, converting his 55th consecutive save in a win against the Houston Astros. His streak ended in August; his record stands at 60 consecutive saves. (The major-league record is eighty-four.) He finished the season with a 2.89 ERA.

PERSONAL LIFE

Britton married Courtney Leggett, a California lawyer, in 2011. They have two young children, Zander and Zilah. His brother Buck was drafted by the Orioles in 2008 and has been a minor-league infielder since then.

SUGGESTED READING

Encina, Eduardo A. "Orioles Closer Zach Britton Rises Only after He Embraced the Sinker." *The Baltimore Sun*, 5 Apr. 2016, www.baltimoresun.com/sports/orioles/bs-sp-orioles-britton-0406-20160405-story.html. Accessed 13 Nov. 2017.

Ghiroli, Brittany. "Britton Beats the Odds, Boosts the O's." *MLB.com*, 15 Apr. 2011, m.orioles.mlb.com/news/article/17805926//. Accessed 12 Nov. 2017.

Kepner, Tyler. "With a Pinpoint Sinker, Zach Britton Raises His Cy Young Award Chances." *The New York Times*, 25 Aug. 2016, www.nytimes.com/2016/08/26/sports/baseball/zach-britton-baltimore-orioles-cy-young-award-chances.html. Accessed 13 Nov. 2017.

Van Valkenburg, Kevin. "Great Find and Terrible Loss Have Buoyed Orioles' Britton." *The Baltimore Sun*, 26 Apr. 2011, www.baltimoresun.com/sports/orioles/bal-great-find-and-terrible-loss-have-buoyed-orioles-britton-20120131-story.html. Accessed 12 Nov. 2017.

Zrebiec, Jeff. "Orioles Demote Zach Britton to Double-A Bowie." *The Baltimore Sun*, 9 July 2011, www.baltimoresun.com/sports/orioles/bs-sp-orioles-britton-0710-20110709-story.html. Accessed 13 Nov. 2017.

—*Molly Hagan*

Malcolm Brogdon

Date of birth: December 11, 1992
Occupation: Basketball player

Although many aspiring athletes might be in a rush to enter the realm of professional competition, basketball player Malcolm Brogdon has demonstrated that sometimes, taking one's time can be worth the wait. Drafted by the Milwaukee Bucks in 2016 at the age of twenty-three, he entered the National Basketball Association (NBA) after having played a full four seasons for the University of Virginia, where he also earned a bachelor's and stayed an extra year for a master's degree. In an age when most NBA stars are drafted before finishing school, Brogdon would credit his complete college experience with helping him to develop his skills and confidence both on the court and off. Upon joining the Bucks for the 2016–17 season, he soon established himself as a valuable contributor to the team, winning the trust of his teammates and coaches. "I think the biggest compliment they can give me is having the confidence in me at the end of games for me to have the ball and to make decisions and to create for them and to create my own shot and finish games," he told James Herbert for *CBS Sports* (13 Apr. 2017). "That's the biggest compliment I can get from anybody." With the support of his teammates, Brogdon offered up a strong performance during his debut professional season, for which he was named the NBA's 2016–17 Rookie of the Year.

A talented player from an early age, Brogdon initially attracted widespread notice

By Thomson200 [CC0], via Wikimedia Commons

while playing high school basketball near Atlanta, Georgia, where he grew up in a family that emphasized the importance of public service and doing good both in local communities and abroad. In keeping with that upbringing, Brogdon sought to use his newfound fame for good after joining the NBA, supporting a variety of charitable causes and speaking out about social and political issues that concern him. "I'm a huge believer in karma," he told Tom Pipines for Milwaukee's *Fox 6 Now* (14 Dec. 2016). "What you do, what you put into the world, it's going to come back around if you do good. Whenever I can touch and I can impact a younger life, I try to do it because that's how I would have wanted to be treated."

EARLY LIFE AND EDUCATION

Malcolm Moses Brogdon was born on December 11, 1992, in Atlanta, Georgia. His mother, Jann Adams, was an assistant professor in the department of psychology at Morehouse College at the time of his birth and would later serve in other positions at that institution, including department chair and associate dean of mathematics and science. His father, Mitchell Brogdon, was a lawyer and trial mediator. Brogdon's parents divorced when he was eleven years old, and Brogdon and his two older brothers subsequently lived with their mother in Atlanta.

Throughout Brogdon's early years, his parents strongly emphasized the importance not only of education but also of public service. That focus ran in his extended family: his maternal grandfather, John Hurst Adams, had been a leader in the civil rights movement as well as a bishop in the African Methodist Episcopal Church. To ensure that her children gained a better understanding of the lives of other people, Brogdon's mother moved her family from a middle-class neighborhood to a low-income neighborhood in Atlanta and instilled in the children an understanding that one's worth was not tied to one's income or career. "My mom has taught me and my brothers . . . to not identify yourself as your profession," Brogdon explained to C. Isaiah Smalls for the *Undefeated* (6 Oct. 2017). "It's more so what type of person you are, what type of character you have and how you treat your fellow man." Brogdon was particularly influenced by service-oriented trips he took to the African countries of Ghana and Malawi, which sparked his desire to combat poverty on a global scale.

Brogdon demonstrated athletic prowess from an early age, playing sports such as soccer and basketball. He soon began to focus primarily on the latter and sought to emulate established basketball players both on the court and off. "For me the big thing was what are they working on—not just what are they doing when the lights are on, but what are they doing when no one's watching, how are they training, how did they get this good?" he told Herbert of his learning process. "What you realize is a lot of guys were just working extremely hard. They were willing to push themselves to the limits that other guys weren't and be uncomfortable when they were training and working out. And that's what I started to do." His intensive off-the-court work paid off during his years playing basketball for the Greater Atlanta Christian School, which won multiple Class AA state championships during his tenure on the team. Brogdon graduated from the school in 2011.

UNIVERSITY OF VIRGINIA

After graduating from high school, Brogdon enrolled in the University of Virginia to study history, turning down offers from several other schools, including Harvard University. Although many aspiring professional basketball players enter the NBA draft during their college years, Brogdon chose to remain in school to complete not only his undergraduate studies but also a graduate degree. Although his choice left some observers in the media skeptical about his chances of playing professionally, Brogdon considers his time studying and playing college-level basketball to have been key to his later success. "It helps you mature and form an identity and know who you are coming into the highest level of basketball," he explained to Jeff Zillgitt for *USA Today* (5 Jan. 2017). "I didn't let it deter me at all or hurt my confidence."

Throughout his five years at the University of Virginia, Brogdon was a key member of the school's men's basketball team, the Cavaliers, which plays within Division I of the National Collegiate Athletic Association (NCAA). He played in 28 games during his first season with the team, amassing a total of 188 points, 78 rebounds, and 38 assists before breaking his foot near the end of the season. The injury forced him to undergo foot surgery in March of 2012, and he subsequently sat out what would have been his sophomore season to recover. Brogdon came back strong in the 2013–14 season, becoming a starting player in 37 games and leading the team in average points scored per game. He continued to improve even further during his final two seasons with the Cavaliers, earning recognition from organizations such as the National Association of Basketball Coaches (NABC), the Associated Press (AP), and the University of Virginia Alumni Association. He was twice named an All-American, and became the first player to earn both the Atlantic Coast Conference's (ACC) Player of the Year and Defensive Player of the Year awards in the same season in 2016.

In addition to amassing impressive statistics during the regular college basketball season, Brogdon accompanied the Cavaliers to the NCAA Tournament on several occasions. In the 2016 tournament, the team advanced to the Elite Eight round of play before being eliminated by Syracuse University. In recognition of his contributions to the team, the Cavaliers retired Brogdon's jersey number, fifteen, in February of 2017. Brogdon earned his master's degree in public policy from the University of Virginia's Batten School of Leadership and Public Policy in 2016.

MILWAUKEE BUCKS

In June 2016, Brogdon was chosen in that year's NBA Draft. However, he was not taken as quickly as his decorated college career might have suggested. Despite positive attention from several teams prior to the draft, team after team passed on him due to concerns over his earlier foot injury, his relatively old age compared to most draftees, and other factors. Finally selected by the Milwaukee Bucks as the sixth pick in the second round and the thirty-sixth overall pick, he signed a three-year contract with the team shortly thereafter.

Brogdon made his debut with the Bucks on October 26, 2016, in a game against the Charlotte Hornets, coming off the bench. Although Milwaukee lost that game by 11 points, Brogdon nevertheless had the opportunity to show off his skills, contributing a solid 8 points, 6 rebounds, and 5 assists. Before long he had established himself as a valuable bench contributor and fill-in starter. He ultimately played in 75 of the team's 82 games during the 2016–17 season, starting 28 of them, and achieved a per-game average of 10.2 points, 2.8 rebounds, and 4.2 assists as well as a free throw percentage of .865. Although he proved he was capable of triple-doubles and other flashy statistical achievements on occasion, his greatest asset was his deep basketball knowledge. "I play the game thinking the game first," he told Herbert. Propelled by the contributions of Brogdon and other young players including Giannis Antetokounmpo and Khris Middleton, the Bucks made it to the first round of the 2017 NBA Playoffs but lost to the Toronto Raptors, 2–4.

Brogdon's strong effort during his debut season with the team did not go unnoticed, with analysts and fellow players alike praising both his work ethic and his in-game contributions. He was selected to play in the Rising Stars game at the All-Star Weekend in the middle of the season. Then, in June 2017, he was named the NBA's Rookie of the Year after being selected to the All-Rookie First Team. The news was surprising to some, as Brogdon was the first player not drafted in the first round to claim that title in more than fifty years. He was also the first Bucks player to be named Rookie of the Year since

future Hall of Fame player Kareem Abdul-Jabbar won in 1970 and one of the oldest ever to win the award. For Bucks leadership, however, the recognition was the culmination of Brogdon's impressive work and dedication. "Malcolm worked tirelessly to improve his game and became a valuable contributor," head coach Jason Kidd said in an announcement posted on the Bucks' NBA website (26 June 2017). "In fact, he was so reliable it was easy to forget that he was a rookie." Brogdon, who noted in the announcement that he was "humbled and honored," credited his achievements to the influence of his teammates and coaches as well as his mother.

The 2017 basketball season started off strong for the Bucks, with a win against the Boston Celtics in which Brogdon scored 19 points. To meet the needs of his team, he transitioned from the position of point guard to that of shooting guard early in the season. In January, he set a new career high in scoring, with 32 points in a game against the Phoenix Suns. By the beginning of February 2018, just before the All-Star break, he was recording averages of 13.5 points, 3.4 rebounds, and 3.3 assists and a free throw percentage of .882—all except assists registering above his rookie levels. Milwaukee remained in the playoff hunt despite inconsistent play and the firing of Kidd midseason.

PERSONAL LIFE

Long involved in public-service efforts, Brogdon remained deeply interested in working for a variety of worthy causes, both during his professional basketball career and afterward. He particularly expressed his interest in founding a nonprofit or nongovernmental organization dedicated to fighting global poverty as well as food and water insecurity, which he witnessed firsthand during his childhood trips to countries in Africa. After gaining fame in the NBA, Brogdon also sought to use his greater public profile to speak out against issues such as racism and white supremacy. "I think it's our duty, I don't think it's something we really have a choice to do," he told *Sports Illustrated*, as quoted by Jeremy Woo (16 Aug. 2017). "If you have a platform, you should speak out. It's the morally right thing to do."

SUGGESTED READING

Gardner, David. "Malcolm Brogdon Knows His Impact Can Extend Well beyond the Hardwood." *Sports Illustrated*, 30 Oct. 2015, www.si.com/college-basketball/2015/10/30/malcolm-brogdon-virginia-cavaliers-acc-preview. Accessed 12 Jan. 2018.

Herbert, James. "For Your Consideration: Malcolm Brogdon, the Improbable Rookie of the Year Choice." *CBS Sports*, 13 Apr. 2017, www.cbssports.com/nba/news/for-your-consideration-malcolm-brogdon-the-improbable-rookie-of-the-year-choice/. Accessed 12 Jan. 2017.

"Malcom Brogdon Wins NBA Rookie of the Year." *NBA: Milwaukee Bucks*, NBA Media Ventures, 26 June 2017, www.nba.com/bucks/malcolm-brogdon-wins-nba-rookie-year. Accessed 12 Jan. 2018.

Pipines, Tom. "'He's Been a Leader:' Bucks Rookie Malcolm Brogdon Born to Make a Difference Both on and off the Court." *Fox 6 Now*, 14 Dec. 2016, fox6now.com/2016/12/14/hes-been-a-leader-bucks-rookie-malcolm-brogdon-born-to-make-a-difference-both-on-and-off-the-court/. Accessed 12 Jan. 2018.

Smalls, C. Isaiah, II. "NBA Rookie of the Year Malcom Brogdon Is Woke." *Undefeated*, 6 Oct. 2017, theundefeated.com/features/nba-rookie-of-the-year-malcolm-brogdon-is-woke/. Accessed 12 Jan. 2018.

Woo, Jeremy. "Ex-UVA Star Malcolm Brogdon Speaks Passionately on Charlottesville." *Sports Illustrated*, 16 Aug. 2017, www.si.com/nba/2017/08/16/malcolm-brogdon-charlottesville-stick-sports-si-now. Accessed 12 Jan. 2018.

Zillgitt, Jeff. "Malcolm Brogdon, the Bucks' Second-Round Pick, Was Steal of the NBA Draft." *USA Today*, 5 Jan. 2017, www.usatoday.com/story/sports/nba/columnist/jeff-zillgitt/2017/01/05/milwaukee-bucks-malcolm-brogdon-nba-draft-virginia-acc/96214318/. Accessed 12 Jan. 2018.

—*Joy Crelin*

By thedemonhog, via Wikimedia Commons

Aline Brosh McKenna

Date of birth: August 2, 1967
Occupation: Screenwriter, producer

"Thin people who want to be in love and their concerns about their love life—that's not a very dynamic want," screenwriter Aline Brosh McKenna told Susan Dominus for the *New York Times* (25 Aug. 2011). Indeed, although romantic relationships are paramount in some of Brosh McKenna's earliest projects, her best-known film and television work has focused largely on the relationships between her protagonists and their careers and obligations. "There's a spectrum of urgency, and wanting to find someone is a not-very-directed goal," she told Dominus. "Whereas, 'I need to get through this year and then get promoted,' or 'If we don't get the ratings up the show will close down'—there's an urgency."

Perhaps best known as screenwriter of the 2006 film *The Devil Wears Prada* and showrunner for the critically acclaimed television series *Crazy Ex-Girlfriend* (which first aired in 2015 and was renewed for a fourth season in early 2018), Brosh McKenna began her screenwriting career as the writer of numerous rejected pilots before moving into film with features such as 1999's *Three to Tango*. Following *The Devil Wears Prada*, she wrote the original screenplays for films such as *27 Dresses* and *Morning Glory* and also contributed to adapted works such as 2011's *We Bought a Zoo* and the 2014 film version of the musical *Annie*. For Brosh McKenna, the key to her success has, in part, been the intriguing yet relatable challenges that face her protagonists, some of which have been drawn from the lives of those around her. "I write about things I'm interested in and hope other people will be interested, too," she told *Working Mother* (13 Oct. 2010). "I have many fabulous friends struggling with really interesting things."

EARLY LIFE AND EDUCATION
Brosh McKenna was born Aline Brosh in France on August 2, 1967. She was one of two children born to an Israeli engineer father and a French mother who worked for a time as a midwife; in interviews, she has explained that this multicultural upbringing had a lasting impact on her identity and work. Her family moved to the United States when she was less than a year old, settling in Fort Lee, New Jersey. The family moved throughout New Jersey during her childhood, and she spent many of her early years in Montvale, where her parents purchased a farm property. "Everyone else in the neighborhood had regular houses with regular lawns, but we had this rambling property with a stream

running through it and a pond we skated on in the winter," she recalled to Naomi Pfefferman for the *Jewish Journal* (31 Dec. 2011). "What we started to learn from the responsibility of taking care of animals was profound. You become very matter of fact about rats and all the denizens of the barn, and you do have a different connection to life and death."

As a teenager, Brosh McKenna attended Saddle River Day School, a preparatory school in northern New Jersey. After graduating from high school, she enrolled at Harvard University to study literature. Active in Harvard's theatrical and literary extracurricular organizations, she directed plays and wrote for the *Harvard Crimson* student newspaper. She also worked on what would be her first major project during her years at Harvard, writing the humorous book *A Coed's Companion: Everything a Smart Woman Needs to Know about College* with roommate Stacie Lipp. She earned her bachelor's degree from Harvard in 1989, and *A Coed's Companion* was published the following year.

EARLY CAREER

Following her graduation from Harvard, Brosh McKenna moved to New York City, where she worked to establish herself as a freelance magazine writer. Although she succeeded in finding some work, her attempt to progress in New York's notoriously competitive magazine-publishing industry was largely unsuccessful. "Of all the things I've tried to do in my adult life that I've failed at, that was the worst," she told Pfefferman. Interested in potentially writing for film or television, she enrolled in a six-week screenwriting class at New York University (NYU), during which she wrote a screenplay that won her representation by an agent. Having discovered a talent for screenwriting, she moved to Los Angeles to pursue a career in that field.

During Brosh McKenna's early years in Los Angeles, she succeeded in selling her first film screenplay as well as her first television pilot. However, despite such apparent success, she struggled to progress beyond that point, as studios purchased but ultimately discarded her pilots. "Every season your beloved pilot becomes garbage, never to be seen again, and I never got used to that," she told Alison Herman for the *Ringer* (9 Nov. 2017). Although she did earn a television writing credit in 1995, after rewriting one of her rejected pilots to be an episode of the sitcom *All-American Girl,* she ultimately moved away from television and concentrated her efforts on film. She made her feature-film debut in 1999 with *Three to Tango,* a romantic comedy cowritten with Rodney Patrick Vaccaro and starring Matthew Perry, Neve Campbell, and Dylan McDermott. She followed that film with the 2004 romantic comedy *Laws of Attraction,*

cowritten with Robert Harling and starring Julianne Moore and Pierce Brosnan.

THE DEVIL WEARS PRADA

Brosh McKenna became particularly well known as a screenwriter in 2006, following the release of *The Devil Wears Prada.* The film, an adaptation of a 2003 novel by Lauren Weisberger that was widely considered to have been loosely based on the author's time as an assistant to *Vogue* editor Anna Wintour, stars Anne Hathaway as Andrea ("Andy") Sachs, the young assistant and Meryl Streep as intimidating fashion editor Miranda Priestly. The fifth screenwriter hired to adapt the novel, Brosh McKenna took a different approach than her predecessors, balancing the narrative's serious and comedic elements while focusing particularly on protagonist Andy's relationship with her job. *The Devil Wears Prada* won praise from many critics following its release, earning Streep an Academy Award nomination for her performance as Priestly. Brosh McKenna herself was nominated for best adapted screenplay from the Writers Guild of America in recognition of her work.

With *The Devil Wears Prada,* Brosh McKenna established herself as a screenwriter who focuses on realistic challenges that women face in their everyday lives, a reputation she continued to build through her next two films, *27 Dresses* (2008) and *Morning Glory* (2010). "In *Prada,* she's thrust into a world and expected to be a type of person that she didn't even know existed," she told Jenna Milly for *Script* (18 Nov. 2010) in a conversation about her films' protagonists. "In *27 Dresses,* she's been brought up to show how she can serve other people. In *Morning Glory,* she's been underestimated. I try to look for things myself or my friends have really experienced. What are some of the challenges these women would be facing? That's where I start."

Although her films often feature romantic elements, Brosh McKenna has rejected the label of romantic comedy and has stressed that the primary relationship in many of her films is that between a woman and her career. "The women have goals that are not strictly speaking romantic," she explained to Dominus. Her 2011 film *I Don't Know How She Does It,* an adaptation of a 2002 novel by Allison Pearson, further explored that area, focusing on a woman's efforts to balance her family life with her career goals.

WIDE-RANGING PROJECTS

In addition to *I Don't Know How She Does It,* the year 2011 saw the premiere of another film written by Brosh McKenna, *We Bought a Zoo.* Cowritten with director Cameron Crowe and based on a 2008 memoir by Benjamin Mee, the film focuses on a family's efforts to revitalize the zoo on their newly purchased property. She was also hired to rewrite the screenplay for the 2014 film *Annie*, a contemporary adaptation of the 1977 musical of the same name. She went on to share the screenwriter credit with the film's director, Will Gluck.

Alongside such efforts, Brosh McKenna spent several years developing a live-action adaptation of the Disney animated classic *Cinderella* (1950), in which she hoped to present a more independent and action-oriented incarnation of the character. However, her project ultimately fell through, and the live-action *Cinderella* adaptation released in 2015 was created without her involvement. Although she was disappointed by the fate of the project, she noted in interviews that such disappointments are simply part of making films in the twenty-first century. "What I realized is, corporations have exigencies that have nothing to do with writing," she told Herman. "They kind of needed to make a Cinderella that was recognizably a Cinderella, which I completely understand." In 2013, Disney had announced that Brosh McKenna had also been hired to draft a screenplay for a live-action film based on *101 Dalmatians* villain Cruella de Vil.

CRAZY EX-GIRLFRIEND

Although Brosh McKenna had switched her focus from television to film by the late 1990s, she returned to the medium in 2015 with the premiere of the musical comedy series *Crazy Ex-Girlfriend* on the CW network. Cocreated with lead actor and comedian Rachel Bloom, *Crazy Ex-Girlfriend* follows a woman named Rebecca Bunch who abruptly moves from New York to California to win back an ex-boyfriend from her teen years. Having become so invested in and passionate about the project from its creation, Brosh McKenna decided to serve as showrunner for the show and also made her directorial debut with a 2016 episode of the series. "Because I had gotten to a certain level as a screenwriter, I think I came into it with a degree of confidence from people," she told Herman of the show's origins. "Which might've been somewhat unearned, because I hadn't run a pilot in fifteen years. And then once we did the pilot, I hadn't ever run a series."

Blending comedy, musical numbers, and candid discussions of topics such as sexuality and mental health, *Crazy Ex-Girlfriend* is unique among television comedies, a characteristic that Brosh McKenna has linked, in part, to the degree of creative control that she and Bloom had over the series from the beginning. "There's not one thing in there that anybody made us do, and I kind of think you can tell," she told Herman. *Crazy Ex-Girlfriend* was received well by critics during its first season, and Bloom won the 2016 Golden Globe Award for best actress in a television comedy or musical for her portrayal of Rebecca. The show continued to earn critical acclaim over the subsequent seasons and was renewed for a fourth and reportedly final season in April 2018.

In addition to running *Crazy Ex-Girlfriend*, Brosh McKenna has partnered with several of the show's writers and producers to develop film and television projects through her production company. She signed a two-year development deal with CBS Television Studios in March 2017. She also published her first graphic novel, a contemporary adaptation of the nineteenth-century Charlotte Brontë novel *Jane Eyre*, in the fall of that year.

PERSONAL LIFE

Brosh McKenna met her husband, Will McKenna, while living in New York. They have two sons, Charlie and Leo. They live in the Los Angeles area.

SUGGESTED READING

Bendheim, Kim. "Aline Brosh McKenna '89." *Harvardwood*, 1 Nov. 2006, www.harvardwood.org/mp200611. Accessed 17 Apr. 2018.

Brosh McKenna, Aline. "Up Early with *Morning Glory* Writer Aline Brosh McKenna." Interview by Jenna Milly. *Script*, 18 Nov. 2010, www.scriptmag.com/features/up-early-with-morning-glory-writer-aline-brosh-mckenna. Accessed 17 Apr. 2018.

Dominus, Susan. "If Cinderella Had a Blackberry. . . ." *The New York Times*, 25 Aug. 2011, www.nytimes.com/2011/08/28/magazine/if-cinderella-had-a-blackberry.html. Accessed 17 Apr. 2018.

Herman, Alison. "How Aline Brosh McKenna Reinvented the Romantic Comedy—for TV." *The Ringer*, 9 Nov. 2017, www.theringer.com/tv/2017/11/9/16625682/aline-brosh-mckenna-profile. Accessed 17 Apr. 2018.

"Making Movies with Aline Brosh McKenna." *Working Mother*, 13 Oct. 2010, www.workingmother.com/2010/10/home/making-movies-aline-brosh-mckenna. Accessed 17 Apr. 2018.

Pfefferman, Naomi. "The Cinderella Stories of Aline Brosh McKenna." *Jewish Journal*, 31 Dec. 2011, jewishjournal.com/mobile_20111212/99652/. Accessed 17 Apr. 2018.

SELECTED WORKS

Three to Tango (with Rodney Patrick Vaccaro), 1999; *Laws of Attraction* (with Robert Harling), 2004; *The Devil Wears Prada*, 2006; *27 Dresses*, 2008; *Morning Glory*, 2010; *I Don't Know How She Does It*, 2011; *We Bought a Zoo* (with Cameron Crowe), 2011; *Annie* (with Will Gluck), 2014; *Crazy Ex-Girlfriend* (with Rachel Bloom), 2015–

—*Joy Crelin*

Rachel Brosnahan

Date of birth: December 15, 1990
Occupation: Actor

Actor Rachel Brosnahan is proof that a performer's talent can turn a small role into something much greater. An actor since her late teens, Brosnahan first gained widespread attention in her early twenties for her performance as Rachel Posner in the political drama series *House of Cards*. The character of Posner was initially intended to appear in just two episodes and have only five lines. However, Brosnahan's compelling performance prompted the show's writers to rework their plans for the character, ultimately making her a core part of the show for the next season and creating a powerful sendoff for the character. Brosnahan ended up earning an Emmy nomination for the performance. For Brosnahan herself, her time on *House of Cards* was both a major turning point in her career and a life-changing experience. "To be a part of something with [director] David Fincher and [actor] Robin Wright, it was mind-blowing," she told Jackson McHenry for *Vulture* (29 Nov. 2017). "[Showrunner] Beau Willimon took such a chance on me."

Beginning in 2017, Brosnahan again captured the attention of viewers and critics with her starring role in *The Marvelous Mrs. Maisel*, a television series from acclaimed creator Amy Sherman-Palladino. Set in the late 1950s, the show follows Brosnahan's character, Midge Maisel, as she begins a career in stand-up comedy following the abrupt dissolution of her marriage. The role was a challenging and rewarding one for Brosnahan, who was particularly intrigued by her character's strong will. "I've never played a character so confident," she explained to Elisabeth Donnelly for *Vanity Fair* (17 Mar. 2017). "Midge's confidence is boundless, and that was a big challenge for me—the way that she speaks, the inflection, her patterns. She's able to hold on because of this single-mindedness. When she sets onto something, she will not stop until she gets it." The series premiered on Amazon's streaming service to widespread critical acclaim, and Brosnahan won the Golden Globe Award for best actress in a comedy for her work.

EARLY LIFE AND EDUCATION

Rachel Elizabeth Brosnahan was born on December 15, 1990, in Milwaukee, Wisconsin. Her family moved to Illinois when she was four years old, and she grew up in the city of Highland Park, a northern suburb of Chicago. Brosnahan's mother, Carol, was a homemaker, while her father, Earl, worked in publishing. She had two younger siblings, Lydia and Alec;

By Mingle Media TV, via Wikimedia Commons

her aunt is the clothing and accessories designer Kate Spade.

As a child and teenager, Brosnahan enjoyed a variety of sports, including snowboarding and wrestling. She started acting at an early age, beginning with roles in school plays, and later attended the Broadway Bootcamp acting camp. Although her parents were somewhat skeptical of her hope to pursue acting as a career, they encouraged her to work toward her goals. "My dad said, you know, if you want to do it, then prove it," she recalled to Rachel Syme for the *New York Times Magazine* (28 Nov. 2017). "And I started saving money for acting classes."

After graduating from Highland Park High School in 2008, Brosnahan enrolled in New York University (NYU) to study acting at the university's Tisch School of the Arts. Through the university's partnership with the Lee Strasberg Theatre and Film Institute, she studied the acting techniques pioneered by Strasberg, which are commonly known as Method Acting. She graduated from NYU in 2012.

EARLY CAREER

Brosnahan launched her acting career in her late teens, beginning with a small part in the horror film *The Unborn* in 2009, booked while she was still in high school. Also in 2009 she appeared in the comedy *The Truth About Average Guys* and performed in the play *Up* with Chicago's Steppenwolf Theatre Company. Over the following years, Brosnahan found work in a variety of television series, appearing in episodes of shows such as *Gossip Girl*, *The Good Wife*, and *CSI: Miami*.

For Brosnahan, her early career gave her the opportunity both to build her résumé and to explore her options as a performer. "Early on, you don't have the luxury of a lot of choices," she told McHenry. "Sometimes you're forced to do things that will advance your career and not necessarily things that fulfill you artistically, but I've been fortunate to do a lot of both." In addition to her television work, Brosnahan appeared in several independent films such as the 2011 drama *Coming Up Roses*, in which she starred alongside veteran performer Bernadette Peters. Her first appearance in a bigger-budget production was the 2013 supernatural romance *Beautiful Creatures*, which helped raise Brosnahan's profile despite receiving mixed reviews. She also continued to perform on stage, appearing in the Broadway revival of the play *The Big Knife* in 2013.

HOUSE OF CARDS

During Brosnahan's senior year at NYU, she was cast in what initially was to be a small role in the political drama series *House of Cards* on the online streaming service Netflix. Her performance so impressed the series' writers and showrunner Beau Willimon, however, that they expanded her role. Brosnahan's character, Rachel Posner, went on to become a key part of the show's first season by playing a crucial role in protagonist Frank Underwood's plot to manipulate and later bring about the downfall of a fellow politician. Brosnahan reprised the role of Posner in the show's second season, which focused significantly on the character's complex relationship with Underwood's second-in-command, played by actor Michael Kelly. Many critics noted that the chemistry between Brosnahan and Kelly proved to be a highlight of the show.

As a drama focusing on the machinations of ambitious characters who will stop at nothing to achieve their goals, *House of Cards* features numerous dramatic character sendoffs. Brosnahan's final episode as Posner is no exception, and the actor did not even learn of her character's demise until the last minute. "It's devastating on the one hand, because this has been the most incredible experience I've ever had," she recalled to Mehera Bonner for *Marie Claire* (11 Mar. 2015) of the moment she learned of her character's fate. "But I do think Rachel's death makes the most sense for the story, and I'm not sure it could have ended any other way. Everyone on this show is kind of a ticking time bomb." In recognition of her performance in that final episode, Brosnahan was nominated for the 2015 Emmy Award for guest actress in a drama.

FILM AND TELEVISION PROJECTS

Following her debut on *House of Cards*, Brosnahan found steady work, appearing in a wide range of television projects. She completed an arc on the series *The Blacklist* in 2014 and that year also costarred in the series *Black Box*, which was canceled after a season. She likewise appeared in the 2014 miniseries *Olive Kitteridge*, which won the Emmy Award for outstanding limited series. Beginning in 2014, Brosnahan costarred as Abby Isaacs in *Manhattan*, a series set in the 1940s focusing on the lives of those involved with the Manhattan Project, which resulted in the United States' production of atomic weapons. "I was such a nerd when it came to researching for that show," she recalled to McHenry. "I read every book about the wives of Los Alamos." In addition to deepening her knowledge of the Manhattan Project, Brosnahan's work on Manhattan instilled in her a love of period pieces. *Manhattan* ended in 2015, after its second season. Brosnahan later made her first appearance in an Amazon original television series in 2016 with her role in director Woody Allen's *Crisis in Six Scenes*.

In addition to television, Brosnahan remained active in films, appearing in works such as *Louder than Bombs* (2015) and *Burn Country* (2016) and *The Finest Hours* (2016). In the 2016 film *Patriots Day*, which chronicles the 2013 Boston Marathon bombings, Brosnahan was tasked with portraying Jessica Kensky, a woman who lost a leg in the bombings. To prepare for the role, Brosnahan spent time with Kensky and her husband and learned about their experiences firsthand. "They were so forthcoming with this intense, immense, unspeakable tragedy that they are still experiencing the effects of," she told Donnelly. "I'm in awe of Jessica every day." Brosnahan also returned to the stage during that period, starring as Desdemona in a New York Theatre Workshop production of William Shakespeare's *Othello* from late 2016 to early 2017.

THE MARVELOUS MRS. MAISEL

A major turning point in Brosnahan's career came in 2017, when her new television series, *The Marvelous Mrs. Maisel*, premiered on Amazon's streaming service. Created by Amy Sherman-Palladino, best known for creating the series *Gilmore Girls*, the series takes place in the New York City of the late 1950s. Brosnahan's character, Midge Maisel, is a privileged homemaker whose life is upended by the discovery that her husband has been having an affair. After an impromptu drunken performance at a comedy club reveals her potential as a performer, Midge embarks on a career in stand-up comedy. Although Brosnahan had little experience with comedy prior to that point, she immediately found herself drawn to the role of Midge. "I realized I had never read a woman who is so unapologetically confident. Genuinely so. I've certainly never played one," she told McHenry. "That felt important to me, to represent that kind of woman who is more in line with the kinds of women that I know and love. It feels radical in a way that it shouldn't anymore."

To prepare for the role, Brosnahan researched the comedy of the 1950s extensively and particularly focused on the work of female comedians of the 1950s and 1960s such as Jean Carroll and Joan Rivers. She likewise noted in interviews that some elements of her portrayal of Midge were based on her own grandmother. However, despite her character's immersion into the world of comedy, Brosnahan has repeatedly denied having any interest in performing stand-up as herself. "I get to f—— it up and try again. There's an audience that is paid to laugh at my jokes. I'm playing a character while I'm doing stand-up," she told McHenry. "Real stand-ups, man, they're playing themselves. I'd be far too terrified."

Following its premiere in March 2017, the pilot of *The Marvelous Mrs. Maisel* earned critical acclaim as well as significant attention from Amazon Prime subscribers and was subsequently ordered to series. The full series premiered in November of that year. Well received by both viewers and critics, *The Marvelous Mrs. Maisel* won the Golden Globe Award for best comedy following its first season, and Brosnahan took home the Golden Globe for best actress in a comedy series. The series' second season began filming in early 2018.

PERSONAL LIFE

Brosnahan lives in the Harlem neighborhood of New York. She is in a relationship with fellow actor Jason Ralph, who worked with Brosnahan on *Manhattan* and on the 2014 independent film *I'm Obsessed with You (But You've Got to Leave Me Alone)*.

SUGGESTED READING

Brosnahan, Rachel. "'Marvelous Mrs. Maisel' Star Rachel Brosnahan: 'I Would Be So Traumatized If I Did My Own Standup.'" Interview with Debra Birnbaum. *Variety*, 11 Dec. 2017, variety.com/2017/tv/news/rachel-brosnahan-marvelous-mrs-maisel-amy-sherman-palladino-1202636508/. Accessed 11 May 2018.

Brosnahan, Rachel. "Rachel Brosnahan Auditioned for *The Marvelous Mrs. Maisel* While Terribly Sick." Interview with Jackson McHenry. *Vulture*, 29 Nov. 2017, www.vulture.com/2017/11/rachel-brosnahan-marvelous-mrs-maisel-interview.html. Accessed 11 May 2018.

Brosnahan, Rachel. "Why 'House of Cards' Star Rachel Brosnahan Is Team Claire." Interview with Mehera Bonner. *Marie Claire*, 11 Mar. 2015, www.marieclaire.com/celebrity/news/a13676/why-house-of-cards-star-rachel-brosnahan-is-team-claire/. Accessed 11 May 2018.

Crowder, Courtney. "Rachel Brosnahan, from Highland Park to 'House of Cards.'" *Chicago Tribune*, 19 Feb. 2014, articles.chicagotribune.com/2014-02-19/entertainment/ct-rachel-brosnahan-house-of-cards-interview-20140219_1_francis-underwood-corey-stoll-beau-willimon. Accessed 11 May 2018.

Donnelly, Elisabeth. "Take Rachel Brosnahan, Please." *Vanity Fair*, 17 Mar. 2017, www.vanityfair.com/hollywood/2017/03/rachel-brosnahan-marvelous-mrs-maisel-amy-sherman-palladino-amazon. Accessed 11 May 2018.

Rodriguez, Briana. "Rachel Brosnahan: A New Chapter." *Backstage*, 13 Dec. 2017. www.backstage.com/interview/rachel-brosnahan-new-chapter/. Accessed 11 May 2018.

Syme, Rachel. "Rachel Brosnahan's Comic Timing." *The New York Times Magazine*, 28 Nov. 2017. www.nytimes.com/2017/11/28/magazine/rachel-brosnahans-comic-timing.html. Accessed 11 May 2018.

SELECTED WORKS

Beautiful Creatures, 2013; *House of Cards*, 2013–15; *The Blacklist*, 2014; *Black Box*, 2014; *Manhattan*, 2014–15; *Patriots Day*, 2016; *The Marvelous Mrs. Maisel*, 2017–

—*Joy Crelin*

Brothers Osborne

Occupation: Music group

JOHN OSBORNE
Date of birth: April 27, 1982
Occupation: Lead guitarist, backing vocalist

T. J. OSBORNE
Date of birth: November 18, 1984
Occupation: Lead vocalist, rhythm guitarist

When the country duo, the Brothers Osborne, (siblings John and T. J. Osborne) released their debut album in 2016, many hailed them as a refreshing change from the other acts popular in the genre at that time. "As the industry experiences backlash to the wildly popular 'bro-country' style, audiences are ready for something different. Enter the Brothers Osborne," Emily Yahr wrote for the *Washington Post* (20 Jan. 2016), referring to a subgenre of country music typically sung by white, male recording artists. "Is everyone really driving a pickup truck down to the river to drink beer with a pretty girl wearing tight jeans?"

Photo by Jason Kempin/Getty Images

By contrast, as Jewly Hight wrote for the *New York Times* (12 Apr. 2018), the Brothers Osborne "decided to commit to a musical identity they could inhabit convincingly." Explaining that much modern country music relies on drum machines and synthesizers, Hight continued, "The one they chose—a groove-driven, occasionally jammy singing-and-shredding duo—has made for a rather exotic presence in contemporary country over the last half-decade." T. J., the duo's vocalist, told Hight, "We really wanted to drive that into people's minds really early in our career that John isn't holding a guitar so that we can call ourselves a duo. He literally is every bit of another singer in the group, with his hands."

The brothers' debut album, *Pawn Shop*, landed on the Billboard Top Country Albums chart at number three; spawned the hit singles "Stay a Little Longer," "Rum," "21 Summer," and "It Ain't My Fault"; and earned them Country Music Association (CMA) awards as best vocal duo in both 2016 and 2017, as well as CMA honors for the music video for "It Ain't My Fault," which the Association deemed 2017 video of the year. The duo was also recognized as best of the year by the Academy of Country Music (ACM) at their awards ceremony in early 2018.

Some industry observers were surprised that "It Ain't My Fault" was not the subject of a backlash from country music fans, who often skew to the right politically, since the video depicts an armed robber in a Donald Trump mask who is captured by police when he runs into a high brick wall. (Other robbers dressed as former Presidents Clinton, Bush, and Obama are able to make their escapes.) "We come from a very blue-collar, red part of the country, and we were like the lonely liberals in that town," John Osborne told Chris Willman for *Variety* (29 Apr. 2018). "But the thing is, we were best friends with all of these people. We still are." He continued, "Our intentions are always pure. It's never to divide anyone. It's never to poke the hornet's nest. It's just to remind people that you can stay awake, or wake up, and it's okay to speak, as long as it has a positive outcome." Even if their political views were to negatively affect their career, however, T. J. told Hight that he would not be bothered by it. "I love playing music, and I want to do it for the rest of my life, but I don't play music so I can be rich and famous," he said. "I play it because I like playing music—and I can be a plumber and play music, too."

EARLY LIFE AND EDUCATION

John Thomas Osborne (known as John) was born on April 27, 1982, and Thomas John Osborne (known as T. J.) was born on November 18, 1984. Their father (also named John Thomas) has joked to interviewers that his wife, Tricia, went into labor with T. J. while the couple were watching a football game between the Philadelphia Eagles and the Washington Redskins, and they were too distracted to think of an entirely new name. T. J. and John are two of five siblings; they have one brother and two sisters. The elder John Thomas and Tricia raised their family in the tiny Maryland fishing town of Deale, on the Chesapeake Bay. Yahr explained that the culture there is "an unusual hybrid of Northeastern attitude and Southern charm." "We used to get asked a lot why we got into country music being from Maryland," John Osborne told Yahr. "It's really country around here—but instead of farms, we have water. It's the same kind of mentality, the same blue-collar, hard-working town."

The elder John Thomas worked as a plumber, and his sons helped from the time they became able to fetch tools and wiggle into whatever tight space required it. Money was often scarce. "There were times when T.J. and I would come home from school and all of our electricity would be off because our folks had a hard time paying the electric bill," John recalled to Taylor Weatherby for *Billboard* (1 May 2018). "And instead of crying about it, our dad would turn it into a really fun game of hide-and-go-seek in the dark." T. J. added, "We had no idea that we were poor. We just thought that was just life."

The duo's parents were avid music fans, and Tricia often wrote songs late into the night after her children had gone to sleep. She made periodic trips to Nashville to try to sell the tunes, to no avail. Undeterred, the couple hosted massive music jams on the weekends for friends and neighbors and built a reel-to-reel recording studio in their backyard shed. Instruments, including multiple guitars and mandolins, were strewn through the house.

When his boys reached their teens, John Sr. recruited them to form a trio, which he called Deuce and a Quarter. Besides jamming at home, the three often played covers of Merle Haggard and Lynyrd Skynyrd songs at local venues, including the Deale firehouse. In addition to Deuce and a Quarter, John and T. J. played in a band called Jax 'n' Jive, which won the Battle of the Bands competition at Anne Arundel County's Southern High School in 1999.

By then, John had developed into a talented guitarist, studying the technique of such artists as the Allman Brothers, Jimi Hendrix, and Eric Clapton for hours in the cramped bedroom he shared with his brother. He took formal lessons on the double bass and was once named "Teen of the Week" by a local newspaper for his contributions to the school orchestra. Although he was recruited by Catholic University and George Washington University, John chose to attend Belmont University in Nashville, wanting to be near the country-music hub. Neighbors in Deale held a benefit to raise money for his travel expenses, and he arrived in 2002. In 2004, the year he graduated, T. J. came to Nashville as well.

MUSIC CAREER

Initially, John played with a band called King-Billy, whereas T. J. tried forging a solo career. On occasion, they played together, and, as T. J. recalled to Weatherby, "People kept always mentioning, 'The energy between the two of you is really cool to watch.' We'd never even noticed it because we'd been doing it our whole lives." Tricia had for years encouraged them to perform professionally together—pushing them, somewhat to their amusement, to compete on *American Idol*.

In 2011 they finally began working together officially, signing a publishing deal for their original songs. The following year they signed a recording contract with EMI Records. The Brothers Osborne were not an instantaneous hit, and industry insiders, hearing their name, sometimes became confused because a bluegrass duo called the Osborne Brothers had recorded in the 1960s and '70s.

In early 2014 they released the upbeat single "Let's Go There," which peaked in the mid-thirties on the country charts, and then followed that up with "Rum," which did slightly better. Although they appeared on several "ones to watch" lists compiled by music journalists, the record company declined to back a full-length album by the duo. "We were watching artists that were getting signed a year or two years after us just fly by us on the charts," T. J. admitted to Hight. In late 2014, the label did release a five-track extended play (EP), and the third track, "Stay a

Little Longer," did well enough to capture the attention of label executives. The track was cowritten with hit-maker Shane McAnally, who was known for his work with such chart-toppers as Kelly Clarkson, Kenny Chesney, and Luke Bryan. It also garnered a 2015 Grammy nomination for Best Country Duo/Group Performance, the first of several nominations in that category for the brothers.

In 2016, with the help of high-powered producer Jay Joyce, the duo released their full-length debut, *Pawn Shop*. In addition to garnering the Brothers Osborne their CMA and ACM awards for best vocal duo, the album was named one of the top ten country albums of the year by the editors of *Rolling Stone* (7 Dec. 2016), who wrote: "Leave it to a pair of hard-drinking, blue-collar siblings from Maryland to show Nashville that not all bros are boors. With the Jay Joyce–produced *Pawn Shop*, buttery-smooth singer T.J. Osborne and guitar shaman John Osborne deliver a debut album that's full of greasy licks, back-porch arrangements and surprisingly vulnerable vocals."

The Brothers Osborne's sophomore effort, *Port Saint Joe*, came in 2018. It received equally laudatory attention, with Ann Powers opining for the NPR (National Public Radio) show *First Listen* (12 Apr. 2018), "Unlike much radio-friendly country, *Port Saint Joe* feels loose, unfettered by samples and studio tricks. . . . It's more groove-based, conjuring thoughts of what Pearl Jam might have sounded like had that band come out of Nashville instead of Seattle."

The brothers were proud of how they had matured musically in the intervening years. "We've progressed a lot," John asserted to Weatherby. "All those little things that we did, from hanging out on the bus together, to playing a show out in the middle of a cornfield, to jamming during sound check—all of those little things add up to a really, really big impact on what you do creatively."

PERSONAL LIFE

In mid-2015 John Osborne married fellow singer-songwriter Lucie Silvas, holding a small spur-of-the-moment ceremony in their living room and exchanging candy rings instead of real ones. They informed their fans of the nuptials a week later, via social media.

The brothers have remained very close to their family, crediting their parents with fostering their love of music. "One of the best parts about our success is that our family gets to enjoy it with us," John told Weatherby. "They deserve credit, too." They often take their parents to awards shows.

SUGGESTED READING

Duvall, Erin. "Brothers Osborne Have the Same Name, Just Flipped, Because There Was a Football Game On." *One Country*, 28 Sept. 2016, www.onecountry.com/country-artists/brothers-osborne/brothers-osborne-dad-explains-names/. Accessed 7 May 2018.

Hight, Jewly. "Brothers Osborne Want to Bring Guitar Heroes Back to Nashville." *The New York Times*, 12 Apr. 2018, www.nytimes.com/2018/04/12/arts/music/brothers-osborne-port-saint-joe.html. Accessed 7 May 2018.

Jackson, Alex. "Deale's Brothers Osborne Show Off Their Hometown in Video for Hit Country Song." *Capital Gazette*, 28 Apr. 2012, www.capitalgazette.com/news/ph-ac-cn-brothers-osborne-0808-20140808-story.html. Accessed 7 May 2018.

Osborne, John, and T. J. Osborne. "Country's Brothers Osborne on Looser New Album, Politics, Pot and Unexpected Popularity." Interview by Chris Willman. *Variety*, 29 Apr. 2018, variety.com/2018/music/news/brothers-osborne-interview-1202791387/. Accessed 7 May 2018.

Powers, Ann. "There's More than Just Weed, Willy and Whiskey to Brothers Osborne." Review of *Port Saint Joe*, by the Brothers Osborne. *First Listen*, NPR, 12 Apr. 2018, www.npr.org/2018/04/12/601109262/first-listen-brothers-osborne-port-saint-joe. Accessed 7 May 2018.

Weatherby, Taylor. "How Brothers Osborne's Humble Upbringing Led to Recording in a Beach House and Making Their Success a Family Affair." *Billboard*, 1 May 2018, www.billboard.com/articles/columns/country/8359707/brothers-osborne-interview-port-saint-joe-album-family. Accessed 7 May 2018.

Yahr, Emily. "Meet the Brothers Osborne, the Embodiment of Country Music's Evolution." *The Washington Post*, 20 Jan. 2016, www.washingtonpost.com/lifestyle/style/meet-the-brothers-osborne-the-embodiment-of-country-musics-evolution/2016/01/20/b8d0ffda-b950-11e5-99f3-184bc379b12d_story.html. Accessed 7 May 2018.

—*Mari Rich*

Kane Brown

Date of birth: October 21, 1993
Occupation: Singer

In 2017, Kane Brown became the first country artist in history to top all five of *Billboard*'s main

Photo by John Shearer/Contour by Getty Images

country charts at the same time. By the time he was twenty-four years old, he had amassed a following of millions of loyal fans, not only through the traditional channels of success in country music, but by initially posting videos of himself singing country classics on social media sites like Facebook and YouTube. Brown has stated that part of his impact was due to people's preconceived notions that the tattooed multiracial young man would be a rapper. Instead, Brown began belting out country classics in a rich baritone voice. After releasing the extended play record (EP) *Closer* (2015), Brown was signed by the major country label RCA/Sony Music Nashville in 2016 and released another EP, *Chapter 1* (2016), as well as the full-length album *Kane Brown* (2016). All three releases reached the top ten of the country charts. Despite the naysayers who doubted he could last in the mostly white country music scene, many industry insiders perceived him as part of the future of country music. "I just want people to know that I'm a good person, and I'm not a thug like everybody thinks I am," he said to Cindy Watts for the *Tennessean* (1 Dec. 2016). "I feel like I have my loved ones, but I have a lot of haters, too."

EARLY LIFE AND EDUCATION

Kane Allen Brown was born in Chattanooga, Tennessee, on October 21, 1993. His father was African American and Cherokee; his mother was white. He was raised primarily by his mother and grandparents in often impoverished conditions. On occasion, when between places to live, he and his mother lived out of their car. Despite their difficulties, his mother raised him with a core morality, which he has claimed helped to keep him away from drugs and guns during his formative years. "I always look at it like, 'Stuff happens for a reason,'" he said prior to the debut of his full-length album, as quoted by Watts. "I feel like God put me in places in life to learn, and it was getting me ready for now. Now I get to tell it, and show people what's wrong and what's right."

While growing up primarily in rural Georgia, Brown contended with a physically abusive stepfather, whom his mother later divorced, and classmates who often mocked his ethnic background. He received some stability and support from his great-grandfather, who owned a small general store until a big-box store effectively put him out of business. "He owned this store called the Cold Spot and every day after school I would go and sit in there and just hang out with him and he would teach me everything," Brown said in an interview with Jon Freeman for *Rolling Stone* (2 Dec. 2016). "Teach me life, pretty much—how to run the store, what goes where, how to clean up, how to sweep. Every day I'd go in there and get minnows and worms and I'd take my pop, which is my granddad, and we'd go fishin' every day."

He was also supported by a friend in his school choir, singer Lauren Alaina, who was later a runner-up on the television show *American Idol* and developed a successful country music career in her own right. "She's always had this amazing voice and then she went on *American Idol* and she really convinced me to sing," he explained to Jon Freeman for *Rolling Stone*. "I was always a shy kid in choir and I would always hum and she was like, 'Sing for me' and she was like, 'You have a beautiful voice.'"

AN INTERNET SENSATION

In eleventh grade, Brown won a talent contest with his version of the country song "Gettin' You Home (The Black Dress Song)" by Chris Young. Before performing, he was taunted with racial slurs by classmates; by the end of the song, his rich country baritone had won them over and he performed an encore. During his senior year of high school in 2013, he began posting videos of himself online performing hits by country greats like Chris Young, Brantley Gilbert, and George Strait. The videos brought him an ever-growing online following of mostly female fans who were amazed that Brown—whom many initially believed to be a rapper due to his appearance—could perform so many country classics.

The positive online feedback encouraged and inspired him. While working a series of jobs for companies like FedEx and Target, he auditioned for *The X Factor* and *American Idol*. Although he didn't make the cut for *American Idol* and left *The X Factor* after producers attempted

to put him in a boy band, his online presence continued to grow. He continued posting videos of himself singing country songs, and, before long, he had tens of thousands of followers and his videos had gotten millions of views on YouTube and Facebook.

As his online popularity grew, Brown decided to record his own EP, with the aid of GoFundMe and Kickstarter campaigns. Titled *Closer*, the EP was released in June 2015. It debuted at number twenty-two on the Billboard Top Country Albums chart on June 22 and then peaked at number seven. His success began to draw the attention of record companies in Nashville.

SIGNING WITH RCA/SONY MUSIC NASHVILLE

Even after the success of *Closer*, it took some time for Brown to get signed to a record deal. The creation of new country stars has historically been a long, step-by-step process. With an online fan base and already popular EP, Brown had found success outside of the country music production system, but producers were wary of signing him.

In the fall of 2015, Brown sat down for the first time with a professional Nashville songwriter, Josh Hoge. Although Hoge stated he initially did not want to work with Brown, he later saw both Brown's talent and potential. Hoge took an idea Brown had about a break-up and helped him to pen "Used to Love You Sober." Weeks later the song had amassed a million views on Facebook. When it was released on iTunes, it sold 38,000 copies in two days and soon hit the top of the country singles chart.

In early 2016, Brown signed with RCA/Sony Music Nashville. Randy Goodman, the chief executive of Sony Music Nashville, said of Brown to Emily Yahr for the *Washington Post* (8 Dec. 2016): "He didn't have the financial means to even get a guitar until later on when he started working. And because he's a biracial young man coming into what is typically a white world in country music, I think he comes to it with a bit of personal trepidation." Goodman had Brown record a second EP, *Chapter 1*, which was released in March 2016. Like its predecessor, it shot up the country charts, peaking at number three on the Billboard Top Country Albums chart on April 9, 2016. *Chapter 1* includes the singles "Used to Love You Sober" and "Last Minute Late Night." "Used to Love You Sober" became Brown's first song to reach the Billboard Hot Country Songs chart, peaking at number fifteen.

KANE BROWN

During the summer of 2016, Brown opened for country band Florida Georgia Line on their summer tour, where he garnered praise from country fans. He then returned to the studio to record his first full-length album, for which he cowrote seven of the record's eleven tracks. "It's totally different from anything I've released so far," Brown told Gary Graff for *Billboard* (2 Dec. 2016). "It's pretty much autobiography. A lot of the songs you learn more about me growing up and see what a hard time I've been through, from bullying to being broke to child abuse, and learning from it and being a bigger man today, a better man. It's pretty much my childhood on that record. I'm glad I'm letting it go, all that stuff from the past, by singing about it."

Produced primarily by Dann Huff, the self-titled *Kane Brown* was released in December 2016; its tracks strike a balance between contemporary country, with songs like "Learning," and classic country, with cuts like "Cold Spot" and "Granddaddy's Chair." Other songs include the singles "Thunder in the Rain" and "What Ifs," duetting with his friend Alaina on the latter. "What Ifs" became a certified platinum single and reached number one on the Billboard Hot Country Songs chart. The album itself debuted on the Billboard 200 at number ten; a deluxe version of the album, which contained four new songs, including the number-one hit single "Heaven," was released in October 2017 and hit number five on the Billboard 200 and number one on the Top Country Albums chart.

In October 2017, Brown became the first country artist ever to lead all five of *Billboard*'s main country charts: Top Country Albums, Hot Country Songs, Country Airplay, Country Digital Song Sales, and Country Streaming Songs. He was especially proud of "What Ifs" hitting the top of the charts. "I've had a good-size fan base for a while," Brown said to Jim Asker for *Billboard* (17 Oct. 2017). "Now that I'm with RCA, they were able to get radio onboard and it's just really awesome to see their support and 'What Ifs' going to No. 1." The same year, he was nominated for the Academy of Country Music (ACM) Award for New Male Vocalist of the Year, a nomination he received again in 2018.

In 2018, Brown won his first CMT Award for Collaborative Video for "What Ifs." The single "Lose It," was released on June 7, 2018, followed by the single "Weekend" on August 8. Around the same time, it was announced that Brown's second album would be released on November 9, 2018.

PERSONAL LIFE

Brown lives in the Nashville area with his fiancé, singer Katelyn Jae.

SUGGESTED READING

Asker, Jim. "Kane Brown Becomes First Artist to Simultaneously Lead Five Country Charts." *Billboard*, 17 Oct. 2017, www.billboard.com/articles/columns/chart-beat/8005648/ kane-brown-what-if-country-charts-record. Accessed 31 July 2018.

"Bio." *Kane Brown*, 2018, meetkanebrown.com/bio/. Accessed 14 Aug. 2018.

Freeman, Jon. "Kane Brown on Personal New Album, Why He Won't Sing First Hit: Ram Report." *Rolling Stone*, 2 Dec. 2016, www.rollingstone.com/music/music-country/kane-brown-on-personal-new-album-why-he-wont-sing-first-hit-ram-report-104768/. Accessed 31 July 2018.

Graff, Gary. "Kane Brown on His Self-Titled Debut: 'It's Pretty Much My Childhood on That Record.'" *Billboard*, 2 Dec. 2016, www.billboard.com/articles/columns/country/7581640/kane-brown-album-childhood-debut. Accessed 31 July 2018.

Hermanson, Wendy. "Kane Brown Announces New Album, Reveals Release Date." *Taste of Country*, 7 June 2018, tasteofcountry.com/kane-brown-2018-album-release-date/. Accessed 2 Aug. 2018.

Watts, Cindy. "Raising Kane Brown: Biracial Singer Forges Own Path in Country Music." *Tennessean*, 1 Dec. 2016, www.tennessean.com/story/entertainment/music/2016/12/01/raising-kane-brown-biracial-singer-forges-own-path-country-music/93490558/. Accessed 31 July 2018.

Yahr, Emily. "Kane Brown Could Be the Future of Country Music. So Why Is the Industry Skeptical?" *The Washington Post*, 8 Dec. 2016, www.washingtonpost.com/lifestyle/style/kane-brown-could-be-the-future-of-country-music-so-why-is-the-industry-skeptical/2016/12/07/8e1eb296-bc51-11e6-91ee-1adddfe36cbe_story.html?utm_term=.fd0db881b2e7. Accessed 31 July 2018.

SELECTED WORKS

Closer, 2015; *Chapter 1*, 2016; *Kane Brown*, 2016

—*Christopher Mari*

Millie Bobby Brown

Date of birth: February 19, 2004
Occupation: Actor

In the summer of 2016, subscribers of the streaming service Netflix turned the TV series *Stranger Things* into a pop culture phenomenon. A pastiche of horror, science fiction, the novels of Stephen King, and the cinema of the 1980s, *Stranger Things* was a near-instant success, averaging around 14 million viewers in its first season, according to data compiled by Symphony

By Gage Skidmore [CC BY-SA 2.0], via Wikimedia Commons

Technology Group. And although fans of the series lauded the four young boys who played the leads, arguably the show's breakout character was Eleven, a young girl who has incredible powers and who has spent her entire life in a lab being used as a psychic weapon by the government. As played by actor Millie Bobby Brown, Eleven is at first frightened and vulnerable. Over the course of the show's eight episodes, she becomes stronger and more confident, even drawing the attraction of Mike Wheeler, the de facto leader of the gang of boys at the center of the action. "Eleven . . . resonates because she is different," Brown told Joe Utichi for *Deadline* (11 Aug. 2017). "She's an outcast, she's a freak, and that is why people relate to her. People love her for being a freak and for being different, and Mike loves her for being a unique character. That's, I think, why people related to her so much."

The role of Eleven is, to date, the biggest of Brown's acting career, which began in 2013 with a role on the TV series *Once Upon a Time in Wonderland* and continued with a series of smaller parts in both commercials and prime-time television series. The success of the show has brought her to an entirely different level of fame, with lucrative film and TV offers coming in regularly. However, having come from humble beginnings, with a family that moved around a great deal, Brown has remained grounded. "You know, I'm just a thirteen-year-old like any other thirteen-year-old, so I just plan on living my life and take it step-by-step," she told Sarah Cristobal for *InStyle* (5 Oct. 2017). "Hopefully in five years' time I will be in college. No, let's say eight years . . . unless I get a really good movie."

EARLY LIFE AND EDUCATION

Millie Bobby Brown was born on February 19, 2004, in Marbella, Malaga, Spain, the third of four children of Kelly and Robert Brown. When Millie was four, her father's real estate business was forced to close. Her parents then moved the family back to their native England, settling in the coastal town of Bournemouth, Dorset. At that young age, Brown was already feeling the urge to be a performer. "I wanted to be a singer when I was three," she told Lynn Hirschberg for *W* magazine (29 June 2017). "I just started like humming, and I was really bad, and then I just started to like train myself." This craving for the spotlight fully took root when Brown was a student at Pokesdown Primary School, where she performed in the annual Nativity play and a talent show as well. "Even at five years old she was happy to stand up on a stage singing in front of 450 people," Gemma Hill, a teacher at the school, told Tom Leonard for the *Daily Mail* (22 Feb. 2017). "She always had that natural confidence. She was brilliant; she looked like a little star."

After four years in England, Brown and her family moved to Orlando, Florida, where her parents started a teeth-whitening business. As an outlet for her creative energies, Brown began taking acting classes in a weekend workshop. "It was acting, dancing, singing four hours every Saturday," she told Clemmie Moodie for the *Daily Mail* (7 Dec. 2016). "There was a showcase and an agent said she wanted to represent me."

Encouraged by the agent's endorsement, the Brown family decided to give their daughter's acting career a shot, selling everything they had to relocate the family to Los Angeles.

EARLY CAREER

At first, Brown enjoyed some success in Hollywood, landing a commercial for Publix cupcakes and earning the role of a young Alice on the ABC series *Once Upon a Time in Wonderland*, a spinoff of the popular series *Once Upon a Time*. Although the role was intended as a one-off, Zack Estrin, the showrunner for *Once Upon a Time in Wonderland*, was so impressed with Brown's work that he wrote an episode with the sole intention of bringing the character back. "She walked on the set like she was born on it," Estrin told Gregory E. Miller for the *New York Post* (15 Sept. 2017). "She was the most confident child I had ever seen. I remember turning to her parents going, 'You guys better get ready.' It was obvious even then . . . I had to let them know they had a unicorn."

After *Once Upon a Time in Wonderland* was canceled, Brown won the role of Madison, a young girl whose body becomes the vessel for a reincarnated serial killer on the BBC America series *Intruders*. Unfortunately, the show was also canceled after only one season. Following the demise of *Intruders*, Brown landed small roles on such TV series as *NCIS*, *Grey's Anatomy*, and *Modern Family*. However, larger roles continued to elude her. When she was passed over for the lead in Steven Spielberg's 2016 adaptation of Roald Dahl's *The BFG*, she feared that her acting career might be over after only a few years. "I was devastated," she told Caroline Graham for the *Daily Mail* (6 Aug. 2016). "I wasn't getting work. I thought I was done."

To make matters worse, the time in Los Angeles was stretching the family's finances, to the point that they were relying on Brown's manager to lend them money just to get by. Eventually, they were forced to return to England, further shattering Brown's hopes of making it as an actor. She continued to audition, but was told by one casting agent that she was "too mature and grown up." That same day, she auditioned for *Stranger Things*.

STRANGER THINGS

The first audition for the role that would change her life was an emotional one for Brown, as she had just been rejected for another role. Her *Stranger Things* audition required her to cry, and, after the events of the day, Brown had no difficulty in summoning tears. Her audition so impressed the producers that she was invited back for a second one, and then had a meeting via Skype with the show's creators, Ross and Matt Duffer. Brown was flown to Los Angeles for her final audition, and it was there that she learned from the Duffer brothers what she would have to do if she got the part. According to a story Brown relayed in various interviews, she was standing in the room with the show's creators when Ross Duffer went over to her and placed his hand on Brown's head, making a buzzing sound like an electric clipper. When Brown asked what the gesture was supposed to mean, Duffer informed the young actor that, should she get the role, she would be required to shave her head.

Brown's parents balked at the suggestion, but Brown herself saw no problem with it, seeing it as a trait that was reflective of her own personality. "I wasn't worried about my hair at all," she told Vanessa Lawrence for *W* (3 Oct. 2016). "I don't care what I look like; it's how people think of me. And I do care how people think of me. I want people to say, 'Oh, she's nice,' rather than, 'Oh, she's so pretty.'"

Once Brown landed the role of Eleven, she embarked on a crash course of 1980s cinema, binge-watching such films as *The Goonies* (1985), *E.T.* (1983), *Poltergeist* (1982), and *Stand by Me* (1986). She also immersed herself in other paraphernalia of the decade. On the set one day, she recalled seeing a device that she could not identify, which her father informed her was a record player. Brown became so enamored with the record player that her parents bought her one for Christmas that year.

On set, Brown found it harder to bond with her child costars, primarily because they were all boys and had formed a sort of club. However, she did find a kindred spirit in Winona Ryder, the actor who plays the mother of Will Byers, whose disappearance is the framework for the entire series. Brown had been a fan of Ryder's prior to working with her on *Stranger Things*, and recalled how the two would often spend time together between takes. Having been a child actor herself, Ryder often would impart advice to Brown on how to navigate the pitfalls of show business.

Stranger Things debuted on Netflix on July 15, 2016, with all eight episodes of the series released on the same day. It was an almost immediate success, with critics praising the show's nostalgic tone as well as its unique story. Much of the acclaim went to the show's cast, particularly its five young stars. Reviewers were especially laudatory when it came to Brown. Writing in the *New Yorker* (22 Aug. 2016), Emily Nussbaum called her performance "career-launching," and observed, "Her head shaved, her face grave, she's silent for much of the series, but she bends the story toward her, through fearless emotional transparency."

In addition to becoming a highly blogged-about show, *Stranger Things* also worked its way into the cultural zeitgeist in other ways. As the show grew in popularity, supermarkets saw a rise in the sales of Eggo waffles, which were the favorite food of Brown's character, Eleven. The Eggo craze grew to such an extent that the Kellogg Company supplied a vintage Eggo commercial to be used in the teaser trailer for the second season of *Stranger Things*, which aired during the 2017 Super Bowl.

Brown's character particularly resonated with fans, so much so that, "Eleven" Halloween costume (inspired by the bad dress and wig her friends cobble together to disguise her) was, according to the fashion site Lyst, the most popular costume choice of 2016.

FUTURE ROLES

The success of *Stranger Things* propelled Brown into a new level of stardom. For her work as Eleven, she was nominated for an Emmy Award for Outstanding Supporting Actress in a Drama Series. She lost the award to Ann Dowd, who won for *The Handmaid's Tale*, but, had she won, she would have been the youngest Emmy winner in history.

In 2019, Brown will appear in a starring role in *Godzilla: King of the Monsters*, a sequel to 2014's *Godzilla*. She also appeared in the second season of *Stranger Things*, which debuted on Netflix on October 27, 2017. The season featured a more prominent role for her character, having Eleven leave the small town of Hawkins, Indiana, where the series is set, in search of her missing mother. "It's more of a coming-of-age story for her," Brown told Patrick Gomez for *People* (27 Oct. 2017). "She's trying to be a normal teenager. . . . That's something I'm also going through right now."

As was the case with the inaugural season, critics again praised Brown for bringing new depth to her character. "When it comes to range and growth," wrote Dominic Patten for *Deadline* (25 Oct. 2017), "Millie Bobby Brown proves that her resonating performance as Eleven in Season 1 was a sign of a star, not a one-hit wonder."

PERSONAL LIFE

Although Brown's career is currently on an upward trajectory, she has tried to remain anchored and not allow herself to fall prey to the trappings of stardom. Her family still insists on her doing chores around the house and are very careful with how she dresses and how much makeup she is allowed to wear. Additionally, Brown herself says she, unlike many kids her age, doesn't spend time on her phone or on social media. "At the end of the day, I just do my job, I love my art," she told Colleen Nika for *Dazed* (22 Nov. 2016). "I genuinely want to change the world. I'm very generous and I really want people to see that I am—that's really it."

SUGGESTED READING

Brown, Millie Bobby. Interview. By Maddie Ziegler. *Interview*, 24, Oct. 2016, www.interviewmagazine.com/culture/millie-bobby-brown. Accessed 20 Oct. 2016.

Lawrence, Vanessa. "Like Eleven, Millie Bobby Brown Can Be Very Badass." *W*, 3 Oct. 2016, www.wmagazine.com/story/like-eleven-millie-bobby-brown-can-be-very-badass. Accessed 13 Oct. 2017.

Leonard, Tom, "From Bournemouth to Beverly Hills." *Daily Mail*, 22 Feb. 2017, www.dailymail.co.uk/femail/article-4250624/Millie-Bobby-Brown-Stranger-Things-BANKRUPT-moving-LA.html. Accessed 13 Oct. 2017.

Miller, Gregory E. "At 13, 'Stranger Things' Star Millie Bobby Brown Is an Icon in the Making." *New York Post*, 15 Sept. 2017, nypost.com/2017/09/15/at-13-stranger-things-star-millie-bobby-brown-is-an-icon-in-the-making/. Accessed 10 Nov. 2017.

Nika, Colleen. "Millie Bobby Brown: True Heroine." *Dazed*, 22 Nov. 2016, www.dazeddigital.com/artsandculture/article/33765/1/millie-bobby-brown-stranger-things. Accessed 14 Oct. 2017.

Niven, Lisa. "When Vogue Met Millie Bobby Brown." *Vogue*, 22 Sept. 2016, www.vogue.co.uk/article/when-vogue-met-millie-bobby-brown. Accessed 13 Oct. 2017.

Patten, Dominic. "'Stranger Things 2' Review: Return of the Duffer Bros' Upside Down Is Top Notch." Review of *Stranger Things*, directed by the Duffer Brothers. *Deadline*, 25 Oct. 2017, deadline.com/2017/10/stranger-things-2-review-duffer-brothers-millie-bobby-brown-david-harbour-winona-ryder-netflix-video-1202194576/. Accessed 25 Oct. 2017.

SELECTED WORKS

Once Upon a Time in Wonderland, 2013; *Intruders*, 2014; *NCIS*, 2014; *Modern Family*, 2015; *Grey's Anatomy*, 2015; *Stranger Things*, 2016– ; *Godzilla: King of the Monsters*, 2019

—*Jeremy Brown*

Sterling K. Brown

Date of birth: April 5, 1976
Occupation: Actor

Like many actors, Sterling K. Brown toiled in small, little-noticed roles for many years. That changed, seemingly overnight, when he played young lawyer Christopher Darden in the 2016 FX miniseries *American Crime Story: The People v. O. J. Simpson*, based on the true story of the famed football player on trial for murder. Brown won a Primetime Emmy Award for outstanding supporting actor in a limited series or movie for his sensitive portrayal, and the following year, he again appeared on stage to accept an Emmy Award—this one in the category of outstanding lead actor in a drama series, for his work in the NBC hit *This Is Us*. That victory marked the first time in almost two decades that a black leading actor had garnered the coveted prize, and critics almost universally agreed that his nuanced performance as family man Randall Pearson on *This Is Us* was exceedingly deserving of the honor.

As explained in the pilot of the show, Randall had been adopted as an infant by a white family, grieving over the loss of one of their triplets during childbirth. They fully embrace him as their own, referring to the trio of children as "the Big Three," and over the course of the show the audience becomes privy to the joys and burdens of raising a large, multiracial family. "I'm not trying to pat Hollywood on the back too much, but the power of a story well told moves the needle," Brown told Debra Birnbaum for *Variety* (20 Sept. 2017). "It changes the way in which we interact and see society. I think Randall Pearson coming into people's houses may offer the opportunity

By Blairali [CC BY-SA 4.0], via Wikimedia Commons

to say, 'That guy is more like me than I would have thought.' The next time they come across another African American male they may not cross the street. They may not pretend like they don't see him. They may actually look him in the eye and say hello."

EARLY LIFE

Sterling Kelby Brown was born on April 5, 1976, in St. Louis, Missouri, to Sterling Brown Jr. and Aralean Banks Brown. He has two brothers, Armand and Robert, and two sisters, Angela and Ariel, and the children grew up in the suburb of Olivette. Brown, who was known by his middle name as a child, enjoyed a particularly close relationship to his father and often tells interviewers of fond memories the two shared: being excited to find a one-hundred-dollar bill lovingly hidden under his plate of French toast during a birthday breakfast as a surprise, for example, or watching the popular television shows of the era, such as *Hill Street Blues* and *Barney Miller*, together. "My dad was a reactive kind of guy, similar to me; we let our emotions flow relatively easily," he recalled to Birnbaum. "So the fact that I had him as an example, I never was caught up with this idea that I have to be a strong, silent type. If you feel something, just feel it."

Brown's father died of complications from a heart attack when he was just forty-five years old. Brown was ten at the time. The actor told Natalie Stone for *People* magazine (21 Sept. 2016), "He gave me ten of the best years that a kid could ever have. And I never doubt that he loved me unequivocally, unconditionally." At sixteen, he began using the name Sterling, instead

of Kelby, in his father's honor. During his first Emmy acceptance speech, he addressed his father directly, saying, "I love you. Sterling Brown Jr. I changed what people called me at age sixteen so I could hear your name every day of my life."

Brown attended Mary Institute and St. Louis Country Day School, where he participated in athletics and appeared in student productions. "I discovered that I love being on stage in high school. My first play was *Godspell*—I was a member of the ensemble," he recalled to Matt Grobar for *Deadline Hollywood* (23 Aug. 2017). "One night in particular, people were standing up and applauding. . . . It was the first time I'd experienced a high outside of athletics. I was a basketball player, football player. But this high was so pure—you get bit, and you just keep chasing that."

EDUCATION

Despite his love of the spotlight, when Brown—who worked at a country club and a lumberyard to earn money as a teen—entered Stanford University, he opted to major in economics. "In the application essay I wrote to get into Stanford, I talked about how I was going to own one outlet of every popular fast-food chain, so that I'd be constantly be in competition with myself," he laughed to Chuck Barney during an interview for the *Mercury News* (9 Mar. 2017). "I didn't think it would be prudent to pursue [acting] as a career possibility."

During his freshman year at Stanford, however, Brown was approached by drama professor Harry Elam Jr., who visited the Ujamaa dorm, one of the university's themed residences, looking for black students to appear in a production of the August Wilson play *Joe Turner's Come and Gone*. He tapped Brown for the role of Herald Loomis and was impressed by his performance. "He told me, 'I know you don't plan on majoring in [theater], but you might just want to hang around the drama department and have some fun with it, because you've got some talent,'" Brown recalled to Barney.

Brown was intrigued by the prospect but uncertain about whether to actually switch majors, given the idiosyncrasies of Stanford's aspiring thespians. "I remember doing my first acting class, and they start beating their chests and shaking their arms, and I'm like, 'Ehhhh, I don't know if this is for me,'" he admitted to Laura Shin for the *Stanford Alumni Magazine* (Sept./ Oct. 2011). He ultimately became convinced, however, that his passion resided with theater. "I realized that every time I did a play, my grades got better," he told Barney. "That's because it fed my soul. It took a couple of years for me to figure out that my hobby really was my calling."

Brown graduated from Stanford with an acting degree in 1998, and in 2001 he earned an MFA degree from New York University's Tisch School of the Arts. Classmates recall that he exercised his voice by reciting tongue twisters and often tried on different accents or physical mannerisms while walking the city streets or riding the subway. (That ability for mimicry was on full display when he appeared in a 2009 Public Theater production of Tarell Alvin McCraney's The Brother/Sister Plays that found him imitating two gossipy church ladies, chiding a young boy for his misbehavior and speaking in tongues.)

PROFESSIONAL ACTING CAREER

Brown began to find small professional roles after graduating from NYU, appearing in productions of The Resistible Rise of Arturo Ui and Twelfth Night in 2002 and landing a bit part in the 2002 romantic comedy Brown Sugar starring Taye Diggs and Sanaa Lathan. His first acting job paid him three hundred dollars a week. The single room he rented in Harlem cost eighty-five dollars a week, and he has recalled to journalists that he spent hours riding a city bus that summer just to enjoy the air conditioning.

Most often auditions ended in frustration. "It's like a boxer," Brown told Gail Pennington for the St. Louis Post-Dispatch (2 Feb. 2016). "You keep jabbing and jabbing until hopefully you have an opportunity for a hook or straight right." That opportunity seemed to come in 2007, when he began appearing in the role of psychiatrist Roland Burton, the husband of a lieutenant colonel suffering from posttraumatic stress disorder in the long-running Lifetime Network series Army Wives, which aired until 2013. He found it gratifying to be approached on the street by military personnel or their spouses, who sometimes explained to him how much the show, and his work in it, meant to them. The response made him appreciate his chosen profession even more. "This isn't like for other people where they have to go to work," he told Shin. "I get to go to work."

Brown took occasional other roles during his time on Army Wives. He had guest roles in such television series as Eli Stone, Medium, and The Good Wife, and played a recurring character, Detective Cal Beecher, in the CBS show Person of Interest in 2012 and 2013. He could be seen on the big screen in the 2011 comedy film Our Idiot Brother, starring Paul Rudd, and the little-seen 2013 thriller The Suspect alongside Mekhi Phifer.

Brown continued to book guest roles on other series once Army Wives was off the air; he made appearances in episodes of NCIS, The Mentalist, Masters of Sex, Castle, and Criminal Minds, among others. Although those jobs kept him in the public eye—as did his small role in the 2016 Tina Fey film Whiskey Tango Foxtrot—it was his portrayal of Christopher Darden in American Crime Story: The People v. O. J. Simpson that took his career to a new level.

BREAKOUT ROLES

He had just performed multiple roles in a challenging production of Hamlet alongside his wife and Andre Holland and had appeared as the lead in the Suzan-Lori Parks play Father Comes Home from the Wars when he was asked to audition for The People v. O. J. Simpson. "I took on the mountain and made it to the top," he said of his roles in Hamlet and Father Comes Home to Anne Thompson for IndieWire (15 Aug. 2016). "I went in with a different feeling. Sometimes I felt like I was fighting to get into the room. Now I had a sense of belonging; I was not a neophyte; I recognized that I have things of worth that I can bring to the table." Thanks, in part, to that new confidence and attitude, Brown landed the Emmy Award–winning part, and soon after that he was cast in the show that has brought him even greater acclaim and fame: This Is Us.

Although some critics have dismissed the series as saccharine or overblown, This Is Us has been a massive hit with the public, and even those reviewers who are cynical have applauded the humanity and relatable nature of its characters. "Watching This Is Us is like getting beaten up with a pillow soaked in tears," James Poniewozik opined in a review of the show for the New York Times (19 Sept. 2016) while praising Brown's display of "tightly wound, complicated passion."

Now, with a second Emmy to his credit, Brown has been appearing in larger parts in major projects. In 2017 he played Joseph Spell, a man who has been accused of rape, in the Thurgood Marshall biopic Marshall, and he has a strong supporting role in the eagerly anticipated Marvel superhero film Black Panther, due for release in 2018.

PERSONAL LIFE

In 2007 Brown married actor Ryan Michelle Bathe, whom he had met while they were both freshmen at Stanford University. Bathe has appeared on This Is Us and Army Wives alongside her husband, among other television credits. They have two sons, Andrew and Amaré.

SUGGESTED READING

Barney, Chuck. "This Is Us: Former Bay Area Resident Sterling K. Brown Feels 'Blessed beyond Words.'" The Mercury News, 9 Mar. 2017, www.mercurynews.com/2017/03/09/this-is-us-sterling-k-brown-feels-blessed-beyond-words. Accessed 2 Nov. 2017.

Birnbaum, Debra. "Sterling K. Brown Opens Up about His Historic Emmy Win in Morning-After Interview." Variety, 20 Sept. 2017, variety.com/2017/tv/news/sterling-k-brown-emmys-1202563894. Accessed 2 Nov. 2017.

Brown, Sterling K. "*This Is Us* Star Sterling K. Brown on His Own Father-Son Story and Acting as a Calling." Interview by Matt Grobar. *Deadline Hollywood*, 23 Aug. 2017, deadline.com/2017/08/this-is-us-sterling-k-brown-emmys-interview-randall-pearson-1202149446. Accessed 2 Nov. 2017.

Pennington, Gail. "St. Louisan Relives Simpson Trial in *People v. O. J.*" *St. Louis Post-Dispatch*, 2 Feb. 2016, www.stltoday.com/entertainment/television/gail-pennington/st-louisan-relives-simpson-trial-in-people-v-o-j/article_422f0f08-3c68-514c-99c9-f9f37f45e437.html. Accessed 2 Nov. 2017.

Shin, Laura. "Now Playing." *Stanford Alumni Magazine*, Sept./Oct. 2011, alumni.stanford.edu/get/page/magazine/article/?article_id=44011. Accessed 2 Nov. 2017.

Stone, Natalie. "Sterling K. Brown Explains the Heartwarming Reason He Changed His Name as a Teenager." *People*, 21 Sept. 2016, people.com/tv/sterling-k-brown-reveals-why-he-changed-his-name-as-a-teenager. Accessed 2 Nov. 2017.

Thompson, Anne. "How *The People v. O. J. Simpson* Changed Everything for Breakout Star Sterling K. Brown." *IndieWire*, 15 Aug. 2016, www.indiewire.com/2016/08/the-people-v-oj-simpson-sterling-k-brown-interview-emmys-this-is-us-marhsall-1201717054. Accessed 2 Nov. 2017.

SELECTED WORKS

Army Wives, 2007–13; *Whiskey Tango Foxtrot*, 2016; *American Crime Story: The People v. O. J. Simpson*, 2016; *This Is Us*, 2016– ; *Marshall*, 2017

—Mari Rich

Kris Bryant

Date of birth: January 4, 1992
Occupation: Baseball player

EARLY LIFE AND EDUCATION

Kristopher Lee Bryant was born on January 4, 1992, in Las Vegas, Nevada, to Mike and Susie Bryant. His father is a former minor league baseball player with the Boston Red Sox who later became a baseball hitting coach in Las Vegas. Bryant's father began coaching his hitting technique when Bryant was five years old.

Playing baseball at Bonanza High School in Las Vegas, Bryant drew media attention and the praise of his coaches. In his high school career, he hit a batting average of .418 with twenty-five home runs and eighty-five runs batted in (RBI).

Bryant was a successful student in high school as well, and earned the ranking of salutatorian upon graduation, an honor he forfeited to another student. He told reporters in 2010 that, while playing professional baseball was his life-long dream, he was proud of doing well in school and was anticipating attending college.

His success as a high school player earned Bryant a full scholarship to the University of San Diego. He played National Collegiate Athletic Association (NCAA) baseball for the San Diego Toreros. He batted .365 his freshman year and .366 his sophomore year. His junior year (and final year with the Toreros) he hit the record-breaking thirty-one home runs. While in college, Bryant was Baseball America's 2013 College Player of the Year.

MAJOR LEAGUE PLAYER

Having completed three years of college during which he was a standout player for the Toreros, Bryant entered Major League Baseball (MLB) as an exciting prospect and was projected to be a first-round draft selection. The Chicago Cubs drafted Bryant with the second overall pick in the first round of the 2013 MLB First-Year Player Draft. At six feet five inches, Bryant was quickly identified as a strong hitter with a fluid swing, which experts speculated would become more powerful with training.

Bryant ascended quickly through the Chicago Cubs' organization, beginning in the AA Minor League, advancing to AAA and on to the team's MLB starting roster in 2015. At the end of the 2014 season, Bryant was named USA Today's Minor League Player of the Year.

Prior to making the Cubs' starting roster, Bryant was demoted to the minor leagues after spring training for the 2015 season despite his success in the minor leagues and during the training season. Journalists and sports analysts speculated that the demotion was related not to his performance, but to his contract. By moving Bryant into the minor leagues, the 2015 season did not count toward Bryant's contract, and the Cubs earned an extra year of Bryant's performance against his five-year agreement. His demotion only lasted eleven days. He was called up to the major league team toward the end of April 2015 to take the place of third baseman Mike Olt, who was put on the disabled list.

In his first full season with the Cubs, Bryant was an acclaimed player, hitting with a .275 batting average and scoring twenty-six home runs. His performance earned him the title of National League Rookie of the Year.

Reporters and members of MLB have remarked on Bryant's positive, humble personality. Bryant described himself as a perfectionist in a

2014 interview and acknowledged the difficulty of seeking perfection in a sport in which the best players only earn hits on three out of ten attempts.

ESPN called Bryant's rookie season a "virtuoso performance," and noted that aside from his twenty-six home runs, Bryant was also very strong in batting average on balls in play (BABIP), an advanced baseball metric that subtracts home runs from a player's batting average. Bryant's BABIP of .375 was the fifth best in all of professional baseball in 2015.

Despite his success as a rookie, Bryant felt that there was room for improvement in his batting performance. He had the league's highest rate of swings and misses on pitches, at 34.9 percent. He has emphasized his strikeout rate as an area in which he intends to make improvements. In the 2016 preseason, Bryant began work on changing his swing to flatten his home runs into line drives, rather than high, deep shots, which are more susceptible to strong winds.

Bryant has advocated for MLB to change its requirements for incoming player draft eligibility, arguing that players should be required to attend college for at least one year before entering the MLB Draft. In 2015 he told the *Huffington Post* he believes baseball prospects should be aware that baseball careers don't always work out, and it's important to have "something to fall back on."

On April 4, 2016, Bryant played his first opening day game with the Cubs. The Cubs defeated the Anaheim Angels in California 9–0.

IMPACT

As National League Rookie of the Year in 2015, Bryant became widely known as an emerging star in MLB. His hitting power and early training from his father have been noted as factors in his quick rise to becoming one of the league's top home run hitting prospects.

Bryant has said that he hopes to help the Chicago Cubs win a World Series title, which the team has not achieved since 1908.

PERSONAL LIFE

Bryant was pleased to be drafted by the Chicago Cubs, noting that his mother was born in Chicago. When he's not playing baseball, Bryant enjoys playing golf, spending time with his family, and watching movies.

SUGGESTED READING

Bauman, Mike. "Cubs Prospect Kris Bryant Mature beyond His Years." *MLB.Com.* MLB Advanced Media, 13 July 2014. https://www.mlb.com/cubs/news/cubs-third-baseman-kris-bryant-showing-hes-a-complete-baseball-player/c-124094212. 25 June 2018.

Brewer, Ray. "All Eyes on Bonanza Slugger Kris Bryant, a Likely First-Round Draft Pick." *Las Vegas Sun.* Greenspun Media Group, 6 Mar. 2010. https://lasvegassun.com/news/2010/mar/06/all-eyes-bonanza-slugger-kris-bryant-likely-first-/. 25 June 2018.

Bryant, Kris. "Kris Bryant Talks Taylor Swift, Sandlot and Cubs World Series." Interview by Andy Gray. *Sports Illustrated.* Time, 22 July 2015. https://www.si.com/extra-mustard/2015/07/22/cubs-kris-bryant-taylor-swift-sandlot-world-series. 25 June 2018.

Gebreyes, Rahel. "Chicago Cubs' Kris Bryant Thinks College Should Be Mandatory for MLB Players." *Huffington Post.* https://www.huffingtonpost.com/entry/kris-bryant-mlb-baseball-college_us_566a07dee4b080eddf57b64d, 11 Dec. 2015. Web. 25 June 2018.

Gonzalez, Mark. "Kris Bryant Learning All the Angles, Including an Adjustment on His Swing." *Chicago Tribune.* Tribune Publishing, 24 Mar. 2016. http://www.chicagotribune.com/sports/baseball/cubs/ct-kris-bryant-swing-cubs-spring-spt-0325-20160324-story.html. 25 June 2018.

"Kris Bryant." *ESPN.* ESPN Internet Ventures, 4 Apr. 2016. http://www.espn.com/mlb/player/_/id/33172/kris-bryant. 25 June 2018.

Rothkranz, Lindzy. "Kris Bryant: 5 Fast Facts You Need to Know." *Heavy.* Heavy, 17 Apr. 2015. https://heavy.com/sports/2015/04/kris-bryant-stats-bio-contract-college-school-draft/. 25 June 2018.

—*Richard Means*

BTS

Occupation: Music group

Jin
Date of birth: December 4, 1992
Occupation: Singer

Suga
Date of birth: March 9, 1993
Occupation: Rapper

J-Hope
Date of birth: February 18, 1994
Occupation: Rapper and dancer

RM
Date of birth: September 12, 1994
Occupation: Rapper

J
Date of birth: October 13, 1995
Occupation: Singer

V
Date of birth: December 30, 1995
Occupation: Singer

Jungkook
Date of birth: September 1, 1997
Occupation: Singer

BTS is the most popular Korean pop band in the world. (Their name is an acronym for Bangtan Boys, or Bangtan Sonyeondan, "Bulletproof Boy Scouts," in Korean.) Members include leader RM (formerly Rap Monster), Jin, Suga, J-Hope, Jimin, V, and Jungkook. In 2017, they became the first K-pop group to ever win a Billboard Music Award, for Top Social Artist, an honor given to artists with high fan engagement on social media. They won the same award again the following year. Comedian Ellen DeGeneres, who hosted the group on her daytime talk show in 2017, compared their arrival in the United States to that of the Beatles in 1964. Some considered the comparison hyperbole, but there is no denying that BTS inspires in their fans emotions reminiscent of Beatlemania. Since their first single "No More Dream" in 2013, BTS has enjoyed a feverishly loyal fanbase called ARMY, short for Adorable Representative M.C for Youth. American music fans might be familiar with the fervid Beyhive, Beyoncé's core fanbase. The two groups

share a depth of devotion to their idols. In June 2018, ARMY and the Beyhive joined forces to stream "Apes——," the new Beyoncé and Jay-Z song, and "Fake Love," the new BTS single, in an effort to make both artists chart higher. When BTS performed at the 2017 American Music Awards, they set a Guinness World Record for Twitter engagement. *Time* magazine listed them among their 25 Most Influential People on the Internet in 2017.

The members of BTS—three rappers and four singers; all, in the tradition of boy bands, formidable dancers—write most of their own songs, and fans, Chris Martins wrote for *Rolling Stone* (19 Dec. 2017), "appreciate . . . [the] empathy, honesty, and independence" conveyed in their lyrics. Martins described their sound as a crowd-pleasing combination of rap, electronic dance music (EDM), R & B, and pop. K-pop is a bit like the American teen pop of the late 1990s and early 2000s: brash and shiny. BTS fits this mold, but they also defy it. They are presented, Sheldon Pearce wrote for *Pitchfork* (24 May 2018), "as the art-house alternative to K-pop's manic energy: a modish, dilettantish, act whose music is a vehicle for large artistic choices and statements." Pearce referenced the video for the group's song "Blood Sweat & Tears," which features a museum filled with real works of art and Nietzsche quotes etched in stone.

THE BAND MEMBERS

RM, originally known as Rap Monster, was born Kim Namjoon on September 12, 1994. He grew up in Ilsandong-gu, northwest of Seoul. RM, who became fluent in English from watching

AJEONG_JM, via Wikimedia Commons

subtitled DVDs of the American sitcom *Friends*, has an IQ of 148. He scored in the top 1.3 percent in the country on his university entrance exams—despite spending most of his high school career scribbling rap lyrics in his notebooks. RM began rapping at thirteen, and before BTS, was a member of a hip-hop crew called Daenamhyup, in which he went by the name Runch Randa. He enjoys a thriving solo career outside of BTS. He has collaborated with such major Korean acts as the hip-hop group MFBTY (My Fans [Are] Better Than Yours) and producer Primary. He has also collaborated with American artists such as DC–based rapper Wale and the rock band Fall Out Boy. RM released a solo mixtape called *RM* in 2015; *SPIN* magazine named it one of their fifty best hip-hop albums of the year.

Suga was born Min Yoon-gi on March 9, 1993, and grew up in Daegu, South Korea's third largest city. He grew up poor, and, like RM, began rapping at an early age. As a teenager, he was a member of an underground rap crew called D-Town, or Daegu-Town, under the name Gloss. He is the most politically outspoken member of BTS. "If we don't talk about these issues, who will? Our parents? Adults? So isn't it up to us? That's the kind of conversation we have [in the band]: who knows best and who should talk about the difficulties our generation faces? It's us," he told Crystal Tai for the *South China Morning Post* (26 May 2018). In 2016, Suga released a self-titled mixtape under the alias Agust D. On it, Suga wonders if his BTS success sells out his unground roots; he also raps about his struggles with depression and obsessive-compulsive disorder. This is a particularly strong example of Suga's frankness, as mental illness and mental health care are highly stigmatized in Korea.

J-Hope was born Jung Ho-seok on February 18, 1994. He grew up in the southwestern city of Gwangju. Often referred to as the group's "dancing king," J-Hope became known as an up-and-coming dancer after winning a national dance competition in 2008. Martins described him as a "bubbly ham." J-Hope released a solo mixtape called *Hope World* in 2018. Elements of the tape are inspired by the Jules Verne classic *Twenty-Thousand Leagues under the Sea*.

Jin, the oldest member of the group, was born Kim Seok-jin on December 4, 1992. He grew up in Gwacheon, south of Seoul. He was discovered by a talent agent as a university student and asked to audition for BTS. He graduated with a degree in acting from Konkuk University in 2017. Jin has a solo ballad called "Awake" on the BTS album *Wings*.

V was born Kim Tae-hyung to a family of farmers on December 30, 1995. He was born in Daegu as well, and also spent some of his childhood in Geochang. He is also an actor, appearing in the Korean television period drama *Hwarang*, which aired from 2016 to 2017.

Jimin was born Park Jimin on October 13, 1995. He grew up in Busan, on South Korea's northeast coast. He trained as a modern dancer before joining BTS.

Jungkook was born Jeon Jungkook in Busan on September 1, 1997. The band's youngest member, he joined BTS when he was just fifteen. He graduated from high school in 2017.

THE MAKING OF BTS

RM was the first official member of BTS. He was recruited by a small management company called Big Hit Entertainment in 2010. For two years, the group consisted of the three rappers: RM, Suga, and J-Hope, who joined up in that order. RM was worried the group would never get off the ground. "New members weren't being recruited, so I felt anxious and restless," he told the Korean *Sports Seoul*, as quoted by Colette Bennett for the *Daily Dot* (12 May 2016). "People around us kept asking, 'When in the world are you debuting?'" Jungkook, who had received offers from seven other talent agencies, joined BTS and Big Hit Entertainment in 2013. Members Jin, V, and Jimin followed soon after. They released 2 *Cool 4 Skool*, the first of a mini-album trilogy, in 2013. They rounded out the trilogy with *O!RUL8,2?* later in 2013 and *Skool Luv Affair* in 2014.

The video for their debut single, "No More Dream," featured the boys wearing gold chains and bandanas, mimicking the visual style of black American hip-hop culture. K-pop and Korean hip-hop have an uneasy relationship with black culture in general. Stars have a disturbing penchant for wearing blackface, and RM himself once demonstrated his ability to "talk black" on air. In 2014, BTS traveled to Los Angeles to film a reality television show called *BTS American Hustle Life*. Led by rappers Coolio and Warren G, the group participated in a rigorous hip-hop boot camp to understand the genesis of rap music.

LOVE YOURSELF: TEAR AND OTHER ALBUMS

Around the same time, the group began to write more of their own material. They released their first full-length album, *Dark & Wild*, in 2014. Their second album, *Wings* (2016), drew inspiration from Hermann Hesse's 1919 coming-of-age novel *Demian*, which explores truth and illusion. "Maybe it's risky to bring some inspiration from novels from so long ago, but I think it paid off more," RM told Martins. He compared the BTS artistic universe to the ever-expanding world of the *Star Wars* films. The group's body of work, Suga told Martins, "draws from our personal lives and interests, we can expand it as much as we want and it's not alien for us." In 2017, BTS released *Love Yourself: Her*. Their lead single, "DNA," peaked at number sixty-seven on the US Billboard Hot 100 chart, making it the highest-charting single for a K-pop group ever, and the second Korean-language song to appear on that chart at all. (Korean solo artist PSY earned a number two hit with the ubiquitous "Gangnam Style" in 2012.) *Billboard* magazine (13 Dec. 2017) named "DNA" number forty-nine on their list of the best songs of 2017. Caitlin Kelley described the song as "a rich concoction of soft rock and brain-burrowing EDM-pop." The same year, *Billboard* also ranked the song forty-ninth on its list of the 100 Greatest Boy Band Songs of All Time. The album's second single, the boastful "Mic Drop," was inspired by former US president Barack Obama's mic drop at the White House Correspondent's Dinner in 2016.

Calling BTS one of the "brightest lights" in the K-pop genre, Jon Caramanica, for the *New York Times* (20 Sept. 2017), praised the band's ease with slower songs demonstrated on *Love Yourself: Her*. BTS "is capable of the flamboyance and sometimes manic energy that can dominate and typify much of K-pop, [but] it's just as comfortable with a more tranquil approach," he wrote. Both Pearce and Caramanica noted how well the seven members play off each other's unique talents. On the song "Best of Me," written with Andrew Taggart of the Chainsmokers, Jimin and Jungkook "sing back to back, two shades of tender in a tug of war," also noted Caramanica. While the last song, "Outro: Her," features the three rappers, each showcasing "a different approach: Rap Monster with bluster, Suga with slick talk and J-Hope with tricky double-time rhymes," Caramanica wrote, concluding of the song and BTS as a collective: "But there's no sense of muscling for turf—just the easy swagger of artists who know they're in control."

BTS's album *Love Yourself: Tear*, mostly about the grief of lost love, was released in 2018. When the first single, "Fake Love," premiered on YouTube, it was the biggest twenty-four-hour debut of the year and the third biggest twenty-four-hour debut of all time, with 35.9 million views in a single day. The album itself, Pearce wrote, "aims for cohesion and produces fun, prismatic songs in the process." *Love Yourself: Tear* debuted at number one on the US Billboard 200 album chart, the first Korean album ever to top the chart and the first non-English album to do so in more than twelve years.

SUGGESTED READING

Bennett, Colette. "How BTS Is Changing K-pop for the Better." *Daily Dot*, 12 May 2016, www.dailydot.com/upstream/bts-kpop-korean-boy-band/. Accessed 2 July 2018.

Caramanica, Jon. "BTS Takes a Different Approach to K-pop: Ease." Review of *Love Yourself: Her*, by BTS. *New York Times*, 20 Sept. 2017, www.nytimes.com/2017/09/20/arts/music/bts-love-yourself-her-review.html. Accessed 5 July 2018.

Kelley, Caitlin. "Billboard's 100 Best Songs of 2017: Critic's Picks." *Billboard*, 13 Dec. 2017, www.billboard.com/articles/news/list/8063600/100-best-songs-of-2017-critics-picks. Accessed 2 July 2018.

Pearce, Sheldon. Review of *Love Yourself: Tear*, by BTS. *Pitchfork*, 24 May 2018, pitchfork.com/reviews/albums/bts-love-yourself-tear/. Accessed 3 July 2018.

Martins, Chris. "Inside BTS-Mania: A Day in the Life of the K-Pop Superstars." *Rolling Stone*, 19 Dec. 2017, www.rollingstone.com/music/music-features/inside-bts-mania-a-day-in-the-life-of-the-k-pop-superstars-129689/. Accessed 1 July 2018.

Tai, Crystal. "Suga from K-pop Giants BTS—His Life, His Loves and His Solo Works." *South China Morning Post*, 26 May 2018, www.scmp.com/culture/music/article/2147605/suga-k-pop-giants-bts-his-life-his-loves-and-his-solo-works. Accessed 2 July 2018.

SELECTED WORKS

Dark & Wild, 2014; *Wings*, 2016; *Love Yourself: Her*, 2017; *Love Yourself: Tear*, 2018

—*Molly Hagan*

Tarana Burke

Date of birth: September 12, 1973
Occupation: Activist

Tarana Burke is a civil rights activist and social justice organizer best known for coining the phrase "me too" in 2006 as a way for survivors to safely share their experiences of sexual assault. In 2017, after the publication of two explosive articles detailing the years-long abuses of movie producer Harvey Weinstein, actor Alyssa Milano made a Twitter post encouraging people to reply with "me too" if they have also experienced sexual harassment or assault; this soon evolved into the Twitter hashtag #MeToo. Milano, who hoped to raise awareness about the ubiquity of sexual harassment and sexual assault, was unaware that Burke had been using the phrase in her work for ten years. Determined not to let her work be erased, Burke staged a successful online campaign to connect her work with young women of color to a national awakening spurred by the Weinstein allegations. In doing so, she transformed a hashtag into a movement.

The #MeToo movement has felled a number of famous men, but perhaps more importantly, it has transformed the way people of all genders view their own experiences and their relationships to structures of power. At the end of the year, Burke and a group of women dubbed the Silence Breakers were named *Time* magazine's Person of the Year. "It made my heart swell to see women using this idea—one that we call 'empowerment through empathy'... to not only show the world how widespread and pervasive sexual violence is, but also to let other survivors know they are not alone," Burke wrote in two successive Twitter posts on October 15, 2017, as quoted by Abby Ohlheiser for the *Washington Post* (19 Oct. 2017).

Burke, who has been a grassroots community organizer since she was a teenager, founded a nonprofit organization for sexual assault survivors called Just Be Inc. in 2003; the organization was renamed Me Too in 2006. She is also the senior director of Girls for Gender Equity, a Brooklyn-based organization that is "committed to the physical, psychological, social, and economic development of girls and women," according to its website. In addition, Burke worked as a consultant on the 2014 film *Selma* and is the creator and author of *She Slays*, a fashion blog dedicated to "forty and over, stylish women who are still vibrant and fun while being savvy and practical."

EARLY LIFE AND EDUCATION

Burke was born on September 12, 1973 and grew up in the West Bronx in New York City. Her family has long been involved in working for social justice. Speaking to J'na Jefferson for *Vibe* magazine (3 Apr. 2018), Burke described her grandfather as a "Garveyite" (a follower of the radical Pan-Africanist Marcus Garvey) and her mother as a "womanist"; a term coined by writer Alice Walker. Womanism centers on the experiences of black women in a larger struggle for gender equality.

Thanks to these familial influences, Burke was an avid reader of social justice literature by the time she was in seventh grade, devouring classics such as Alex Haley's *Roots: The Saga of an American Family* (1976) and Ivan Van Sertima's *They Came before Columbus: The African Presence in Ancient America* (1976). Her favorite authors included Toni Morrison, Maya Angelou, and Zora Neale Hurston. Burke's reading inspired her to join an international youth organization called the 21st Century Youth Leadership Movement to learn about grassroots community organizing when she was fourteen years old. A few years later, in 1989, she helped counter Donald Trump's media campaign against the Central Park Five, a group of young black and Hispanic men who were accused of raping a white woman in Central Park. Despite overwhelming evidence of their innocence—and their later exoneration due to DNA evidence and the confession of the actual perpetrator—Trump purchased a full-page advertisement in New York newspapers doubling down on their guilt and calling for their execution. Burke helped organize a rally in response to the ads.

Burke attended Alabama State University and then Auburn University in Montgomery. After graduating in 1996 with a degree in political science, she took a job with the 21st Century Youth Leadership Movement in Selma, Alabama. There, she met a thirteen-year-old whom she publicly identifies only as Heaven. "People would call her trouble," Burke said to Ohlheiser. "And she was trouble, because she was a survivor." One day, Heaven sought out Burke and told her about the sexual violence she had experienced. But Burke, as she admitted to Ohlheiser, "was not ready" for Heaven's pain. "When she disclosed, I rejected her," Burke recalled. She never saw Heaven again.

For years after the encounter, Burke was wracked with guilt. She asked herself, "Why couldn't you just say 'me too'?" Burke is a survivor herself—she was raped by a friend when she was six, molested for years by a neighbor as a teenager, and raped by an acquaintance as an adult. Her experience with Heaven left her thinking about the transformative possibilities of empathy.

JUST BE INC.

Burke began researching what resources were available to young sexual assault survivors. When she went to a local rape crisis center, she told Nikki Ogunnaike for *Elle* (19 Oct. 2017), the woman in charge told her that they only took clients based on referrals from the police station. "So I was like let me get this straight. If I go to you and I need some help, I need to go to the police first? She said 'yes'. . . . I was blown by that," Burke recalled. "I couldn't imagine anybody in my circle, any young person I worked with, any older person voluntarily going through that process."

Burke thought about her own work as an organizer and decided to apply those skills to creating resources for survivors. "As an organizer, we don't wait for people to come to us and say help us organize something, we go out into the community and we bring the skills to a group of people to organize themselves," she said to Ogunnaike. "And I felt like I needed to bring this to the marginalized among us because they're not going to seek out these services." In 2003 Burke founded the nonprofit organization Just Be Inc. to help women, particularly young women of color like Heaven, heal from sexual assault and find self-worth in a world that seeks to degrade and devalue them.

Burke and her team gave young women a language with which to share their experiences, but it was the power of community that was the most effective aspect of the organization's work. "You could have pain you're experiencing without having the words to describe it, because no one taught it to you," she said to Jefferson. "So we started off giving them language, then, we gave them possibility. I could stand up and say, 'I'm Ms. Tarana, this happened to me, too.' And that always got them. That was the hook." In 2006, Burke created a MySpace page for young women to share their own "me too" stories. The same year, she officially changed the name of the organization from Just Be Inc. to Me Too.

In 2008 Burke moved to Philadelphia, where she worked for several nonprofit groups, including the Art Sanctuary, which seeks to "use the power of Black Art to transform individuals, create and build community and foster cultural understanding," according to its website. She also met and worked with educator and filmmaker Aishah Shahidah Simmons.

CREATION OF #METOO

In early October 2017, the *New York Times*, followed a few days later by the *New Yorker*, broke a major story accusing movie producer Harvey Weinstein of numerous instances of sexual harassment and sexual assault over decades of his career. The outing of Weinstein's crimes, and the chilling measures he purportedly took in order to commit them, led to a furious outpouring on social media platforms, particularly Twitter. People were angered not just by the abuse, but also by the ways in which Weinstein, and the larger Hollywood machine, sought to ostracize women who tried to speak out against it. Survivors outside of Hollywood—many but not all of them women—took to Twitter to air their righteous rage.

In an effort to harness this energy, actor Alyssa Milano posted on Twitter (15 Oct. 2017): "If you've been sexually harassed or assaulted write 'me too' as a reply to this tweet." Hours later, more than forty thousand users had replied, many using the hashtag #MeToo. Milano hoped the words would suggest the ubiquity of sexual violence and sexual intimidation, a cause related to but not quite the same as Burke's intention to foster interpersonal expressions of empathy.

RESPONSE TO #METOO

"Initially I panicked," Burke recalled to Sandra E. Garcia for the *New York Times* (20 Oct. 2017), of her reaction upon first seeing the hashtag. "I felt a sense of dread, because something that was part of my life's work was going to be co-opted and taken from me and used for a purpose I hadn't originally intended." On her own Twitter account, she posted a video of herself talking about her work with Me Too from 2014. "It's a natural response that people are expressing experiences like that, so I can't say people stole this from me, but what I *can* say is that there is work behind this," she said to Ogunnaike. "This is not a moment, there is a movement and there's a body of work, and I really want people to understand that it's bigger than a hashtag."

Other Twitter users, many of them black women, rushed to elevate Burke's work. Days later, Milano began publicly crediting Burke as the true founder of the movement. It was a familiar story with a surprisingly happy ending; veteran black women organizers often find themselves and their work eclipsed by white activists new to a cause.

Burke embraced the movement, though she is careful to voice her critiques of it as well. It is important for Burke that #MeToo move beyond mass disclosure and toward healing, which for Burke would involve more conversations about consent and accountability on the part of perpetrators. "The onus is always on women," she said to Ogunnaike. "The onus is always on us to tell our stories, to elevate the conversation, for us to keep the conversation going and talk about our pain and to constantly put our trauma out front in order for people to believe us. That's why I say this is about survivors talking to each other because we need to focus on each other."

The #MeToo movement made Burke a national figure almost overnight. She and other activists and survivors who spoke out, including actor Ashley Judd and software engineer Susan Fowler, were named *Time* magazine's Person of the Year in 2017. (They were collectively called the Silence Breakers.) Burke also appeared at the Golden Globe Awards and the Academy Awards in 2018.

PERSONAL LIFE

Burke has an adult daughter named Kaia Burke. Kaia, like her mother, is an activist and a survivor.

SUGGESTED READING

Burke, Tarana. "Tarana Burke Started the #MeToo Movement 10 Years Ago." Interview by Nikki Ogunnaike. *Elle*, 19 Oct. 2017, www.elle.com/culture/a13046829/tarana-burke-me-too-movement-10-years-ago. Accessed 6 July 2018.

Garcia, Sandra E. "The Woman Who Created #MeToo Long Before Hashtags." *New York Times*, 20 Oct. 2017, www.nytimes.com/2017/10/20/us/me-too-movement-tarana-burke.html. Accessed 6 July 2018.

Jefferson, J'na. "A Long Road Ahead: #MeToo Founder Tarana Burke on Sexual Assault, Stigmas and Society." *Vibe*, 3 Apr. 2018, www.vibe.com/featured/tarana-burke-me-too-feature. Accessed 6 July 2018.

Ohlheiser, Abby. "The Woman behind 'Me Too' Knew the Power of the Phrase When She Created It—10 Years Ago." *Washington Post*, 19 Oct. 2017, www.washingtonpost.com/news/the-intersect/wp/2017/10/19/the-woman-behind-me-too-knew-the-power-of-the-phrase-when-she-created-it-10-years-ago. Accessed 6 July 2018.

Wellington, Elizabeth. "Tarana Burke: Me Too Movement Can't End with a Hashtag." *Philly.com*, 23 Oct. 2017, www.philly.com/philly/columnists/elizabeth_wellington/philly-me-too-movement-founder-tarana-burke-20171023.html. Accessed 6 July 2018.

—*Molly Hagan*

Jimmy Butler

Date of birth: September 14, 1989
Occupation: Basketball player

By Catherine Salaün, via Wikimedia Commons

Professional basketball player Jimmy Butler is thankful for the challenges he has faced throughout his life. "I love what happened to me," he told Chad Ford for *ESPN* (18 June 2011). "It made me who I am." While many athletes have overcome personal hardships to achieve success in their respective sports, Butler's own challenge was a particularly harsh one: at the age of thirteen, he was rendered homeless after his mother expelled him from their home, forcing Butler to take shelter with various friends over the next several years. After a friend's family took him in permanently, Butler was able to focus his attention further on the sport of basketball, beginning a journey that would take him first to Tyler Junior College and later to the National Basketball Association (NBA).

A successful basketball player in high school, Butler played one season for Tyler before transferring to Marquette University, where he demonstrated his talents as a member of the university's Golden Eagles. He was drafted by the Chicago Bulls in 2011 and spent six seasons with the team, setting new personal bests and competing in multiple playoff tournaments before being traded to the Minnesota Timberwolves. Upon his debut with the Timberwolves in October 2017, Butler brought his skills on the court to the team as well as his sense of ambition. "I'm not going to say, 'Hey, if we make the playoffs, then oh, what a great season. Let's just make the playoffs and then get swept,'" he told Jace Frederick for the *Pioneer Press* (18 Oct. 2017) of his aspirations. "I want to win a championship."

EARLY LIFE AND EDUCATION

Jimmy Butler III was born on September 14, 1989, in Houston, Texas. He was one of four children born to Londa and Jimmy Butler. Butler's father left the family when Butler was a small child, and when Butler was thirteen years old, his mother forced him to leave their home, reportedly saying that she did not like the look of him and that he, therefore, had to go. Over the following several years, Butler moved between his friends' homes, finding numerous places to stay but no permanent home. He eventually befriended fellow teenager Jordan Leslie, whose family—particularly his mother, Michelle Lambert—took Butler in and accepted him as one of their own.

Although Butler's challenging teen years proved a topic of interest among many sports fans and journalists, Butler has noted that he does not want to be defined by such experiences. "That hasn't gotten me to where I am today," he told Bryan Smith for *Chicago* magazine (19 Oct. 2015). "I'm a great basketball player because of my work. I'm a good basketball player because of the people I have around me. And if I continue to be stuck in the past, then I won't get any better. I won't change, I'll get stuck as that kid."

Butler attended Tomball High School in Tomball, Texas, where he played for the Cougars basketball team. He served as captain of the team during his senior year, during which he also averaged 19.9 points per game. Butler graduated from Tomball in 2007.

COLLEGE BASKETBALL

Although Butler hoped to play basketball for a four-year college or university after high school, he was unable to secure a scholarship to do so and instead enrolled in Tyler Junior College, a two-year school in Tyler, Texas. As a member of the college's basketball team, Butler impressed both fans and college scouts, averaging 18.1 points per game during his first season. His performance on the court attracted attention from college basketball programs, and after being scouted by Marquette University, Butler decided to move to Wisconsin to enroll in and play basketball for Marquette.

Butler majored in communication studies and became a key member of the Golden Eagles basketball team during his three years at Marquette. During his first year on the team, he averaged only 5.6 points per game, far below his average at Tyler Junior College. In the 2009–10 season, however, he increased his per-game average to 14.7, and his final season at Marquette saw him achieve a per-game average of 15.7 points during thirty-seven games. He also achieved averages of 34.6 minutes played per game, 6.1 rebounds, and 2.3 assists over the course of his final season.

While Butler's talent for his sport was evident, he consistently attributed his college success to the influence of his teammates, whom he credited with teaching him to be a true team player. "I was tutored by the best," he explained to Ford. "Those guys taught me so much about how to play and how to be a man. I knew that to be successful, I had to be more than a scorer. I had to become a leader. . . . I wanna be that glue guy, I want to be a guy my team and my coach can count on."

CHICAGO BULLS

In the summer of 2011, Butler entered the NBA Draft, through which he hoped to be selected to play professionally for an NBA team. For Butler, the moment was the culmination of years of hard work and a repudiation of anyone who had ever doubted him. He recalled being told in high school that he was too short and too slow for the game. "My whole life, people have doubted me. . . . They didn't know my story. Because if they did, they'd know that anything is possible," he told Ford. "Who would've thought that a small-town kid would become a halfway decent player in college and now has a chance to be drafted in the NBA? That's my chip. That's what motivates me. I know I can overcome anything if I just take everything one day [at a] time." On June 23, 2011, Butler was selected by the Chicago Bulls in the first round of the draft. He signed a contract with the team in December of that year.

Butler made his NBA debut on January 1, 2012, in a home game against the Memphis Grizzlies. The Bulls won the game 104–64, and Butler, a reserve player during the game, contributed 2 points and 2 rebounds. Over the course of his debut season, Butler played in a total of forty-two games and averaged 8.5 minutes played, 1.3 rebounds, 0.3 assists, and 2.6 points per game. Following the conclusion of the season, Butler competed in his first play-offs, appearing in three of the Bulls' games against the Philadelphia 76ers before the team's first-round elimination. Over the course of the next two seasons, Butler adjusted further to professional play and improved his statistics, managing averages of 8.6 points per game in the 2012–13 season and 13.1 points per game in 2013–14. The Bulls competed in the play-offs after both seasons, making it to the conference semifinals in 2013.

PROFESSIONAL BASKETBALL

Throughout his seasons with the Bulls, Butler found a new home in the city of Chicago and took inspiration from the team's dedicated fan base. "The city just embraced me," he told K. C. Johnson for the *Chicago Tribune* (23 June 2017). "The fan base, I feel like I grew so much as a person and player in my six years there. They did so much for me and gave me an opportunity to be as great as I could make myself. They made me want to win." During the 2014–15 season, Butler led the NBA in minutes per game, ranked fifth in free throws, and made a substantial contribution to the Bulls with an average of 20.0 points per game. The recipient of that season's award for most-improved player, Butler was also selected for the 2015 NBA All-Star Game, his first of four consecutive selections between 2015 and 2018. During the play-offs, the Bulls again progressed to the conference semifinals before their defeat by the Cleveland Cavaliers. In July 2015, Butler signed a $95 million contract extension with the Bulls that had the potential to keep him with the team for an additional five years.

Although the 2015–16 season was less successful for the Bulls, which finished ninth in the Eastern Conference and failed to earn a spot in the play-offs, Butler put forth a strong performance, averaging 20.9 points, 5.3 rebounds, and 4.8 assists over the course of the season. He exceeded all three of those statistics in the 2016–17 season, achieving new personal records of 23.9 points, 6.2 rebounds, and 5.5 assists per game. He also ranked third in the NBA for free throw attempts. After the end of the season, the Bulls competed in the first round of the play-offs but were defeated by the Boston Celtics, four games to two.

In addition to playing with the Bulls, Butler represented the United States in international competitions, most notably the Olympic Games. In 2016, he accompanied the US men's basketball team to the Summer Olympics in Rio de Janeiro, Brazil, where he competed in all the team's games. Butler helped the team defeat Serbia in the final game of the tournament, claiming a gold medal for the United States.

MINNESOTA TIMBERWOLVES

In June 2017, after six seasons with the Bulls, Butler was traded to the Minnesota Timberwolves. He made his season debut with the team on October 18, 2017, in a game against the San Antonio Spurs. Although the Timberwolves lost that first game by eight points, Butler's performance that season was strong and featured averages of 22.2 points, 5.3 rebounds, and 4.9 assists. Although the team achieved a strong enough record to earn a spot in the play-offs in the spring of 2018, Butler expressed doubts about the team's championship chances. "I don't think we play hard enough right now," he told David Aldridge for the *NBA* website (26 Feb. 2018). "I don't think we guard the way we're supposed to in order to win." However, Butler remained optimistic that improvements were possible. "It starts with everybody as an individual," he told Aldridge. "If you can say you're giving your all . . . we're going to be in a good position to win."

In February 2018, Butler injured his knee in a game against the Houston Rockets. He underwent meniscus surgery shortly afterward and ultimately missed seventeen games while recovering from his injury. Butler returned to the court on April 6 for a successful game against the Los Angeles Lakers, one of the final games of the season. Less than two weeks after his return, Butler embarked on his first attempt at playoff success with the Timberwolves, facing off against the Rockets in the first round of the 2018 championship.

PERSONAL LIFE

Butler lived in the River North neighborhood of Chicago before moving to Minnesota. In addition to basketball, he enjoys playing games such as dominoes. Although passionate about his sport, Butler has explained in interviews that he does not plan to devote his entire life to basketball. "If I'm just known for being a basketball player, then my career wasn't the right thing," he told Frederick. "I give so much of my life to this game, to take my mind away from it, I have to do something else I love."

SUGGESTED READING

"Bulls Sign Rookie Guard Jimmy Butler." *NBA*, 9 Dec. 2011, www.nba.com/bulls/bulls-sign-rookie-guard-jimmy-butler.html. Accessed 13 Apr. 2018.

Butler, Jimmy. "For Jimmy Butler, It's All about Winning with the Timberwolves." Interview by Jerry Zgoda. *StarTribune*, 22 Jan. 2018, www.startribune.com/ for-jimmy-butler-it-s-all-about-winning-with-the-timberwolves/470414053. Accessed 13 Apr. 2018.

Butler, Jimmy. "Morning Tip Q&A: Jimmy Butler." Interview by David Aldridge. *NBA*, 26 Feb. 2018, www.nba.com/article/2018/02/26/morning-tip-qa-jimmy-butler-minnesota-timberwolves. Accessed 13 Apr. 2018.

Ford, Chad. "Jimmy Butler Finds a New Home, Hope." *ESPN*, 18 June 2011, www.espn.com/nba/draft2011/columns/story?columnist=ford_chad&page=Butler-110618. Accessed 13 Apr. 2018.

Frederick, Jace. "Meet Jimmy Butler, the Basketball-Obsessed Alpha the Timberwolves Needed." *Pioneer Press*, 18 Oct. 2017, www.twincities.com/2017/10/17/meet-jimmy-butler-the-basketball-obsessed-alpha-the-timberwolves-needed. Accessed 13 Apr. 2018.

Johnson, K. C. "Jimmy Butler on Trade to Timberwolves: 'Nothing Ever Shocks Me.'" *Chicago Tribune*, 23 June 2017, www.chicagotribune.com/sports/basketball/bulls/ct-jimmy-butler-timberwolves-trade-20170623-story.html. Accessed 13 Apr. 2018.

Smith, Bryan. "It's Good to Be Jimmy Butler." *Chicago*, 19 Oct. 2015, www.chicagomag.com/Chicago-Magazine/November-2015/Jimmy-Butler. Accessed 13 Apr. 2018.

—*Joy Crelin*

Daniel Caesar

Date of birth: April 5, 1995
Occupation: Singer-songwriter

Daniel Caesar is an independent Canadian singer-songwriter with famous fans that include R & B singer Mary J. Blige, producer Rick Rubin, and former president Barack Obama, who included two of Caesar's songs—"Blessed" and "First World Problems" with Chance the Rapper—on his list of favorite songs of 2017. Caesar's debut album *Freudian* (2017) garnered two Grammy nominations—one for Best R & B Performance for "Get You" featuring Kali Uchis (which peaked at number eleven on the *Billboard* charts) and another for Best R & B Album. The Oshawa-born singer comes from a musical family; his father, Norwill Simmonds (Caesar's given name is Ashton Simmonds), is a gospel singer. Although Caesar can be compared to such artists as Frank Ocean or the Weeknd, his music stands apart for its clear gospel influence. But Caesar's influences run deeper than that. A fallout with his family and the Seventh-Day Adventist Church in which he was raised led him to leave home after high

Photo by Scott Legato/Getty Images

of whom were raised in the tight-knit community of the church. Caesar wrote his first song when he was in the eighth grade. Called "Shy That Way," it was inspired by Caesar's crush on a classmate named Bethany. It sounded similar to songs by then-popular singer-songwriters such as John Mayer and Jason Mraz, though Caesar's access to popular music was limited. "We had some Stevie Wonder and Luther Vandross, but there's a lot of hip-hop and other black music that I just never grew up on," he explained to Anupa Mistry for the *Fader* (5 Apr. 2016). "My parents didn't listen to anything other than black gospel."

PRAISE BREAK

Caesar attended high school at Kingsway College, a private Christian school in Oshawa, working alongside some of his classmates in a lumberyard each day before class. But he was beginning to chafe against his small town and his family's religion. His dissatisfaction came to a head in tenth grade, when he started smoking pot and listening to Pink Floyd. He failed choir class and got expelled after he got caught selling a small amount of weed. He completed high school by homeschooling. During his graduation week, Caesar and his parents had a falling out. "It was an amalgamation of things," he told Mistry. "They weren't going to let me go to the parties during grad week—they didn't want me to do anything bad before school ended—and my dad had told me to clean up my room and I didn't. So I came home one day and all my s—— was in garbage bags," he recalled. Caesar spent the summer with a friend in the suburbs of Toronto. Then he got a job as a dishwasher at an expensive restaurant downtown and began couchsurfing. Some nights he slept on park benches. Though Caesar's living situation was precarious, he found time to write music. He joined a group of like-minded musicians, including rapper Sean Leon, called the IXXI Collective.

Working with Grammy-nominated producers Jordan Evans and Matthew Burnett, Caesar recorded his first EP, *Praise Break*, during a two-month period in 2014. It was released the same year, alongside a three-track EP called *Birds of Paradise*. *Praise Break* was originally titled *Pseudo* (after one of the seven tracks), and explored a perceived inauthenticity that Caesar encountered when he moved to Toronto. But ultimately Caesar decided the phrase "praise break" fit his outlook better. "It's like a double entendre," he told Pastuk of the title. "My entire life I was brought up religious and now I'm taking a break from it." A "praise break" is also a term that refers to the moment when a religious congregation is overcome by joy and interrupts a service to offer ecstatic praise. *Rolling Stone* offered its own kind of praise for the seven-song EP, naming

school and rough it in Toronto, where he stayed committed to his artistic vision.

He released his first EP, *Praise Break*, in 2014. When an interviewer suggested that Caesar had left home as a form of rebellion against his parents, the singer offered a thoughtful response. "I had to leave because I wanted to make music, and they didn't want me to do that," he told Slava Pastuk for *Noisey* (2 Oct. 2014). "I'm not making music because it will piss my parents off, I'm making music because I want to. . . . I say it's not rebellion [because] I'm doing what makes me happy and they just don't like that." (Caesar and his parents have since reconciled.) Caesar exhibits a willingness to be vulnerable in his music as well as interviews. "It's like I'm presenting myself, saying, 'Do your worst to me.' But that's the highest reward, because I think the things that I feel are all things that everybody feels, but don't want to say," he told Ryan B. Patrick of the Canadian music magazine *Exclaim!* (7 Dec. 2017).

EARLY LIFE AND EDUCATION

Caesar was born Ashton Simmonds on April 5, 1995, in Scarborough in east Toronto, though he was raised in Oshawa, a small, predominantly white Toronto suburb. His father Norwill Simmonds is a gospel singer who released his first album when he was a high school student in Jamaica. Caesar recorded a duet with his father called "Give Me Jesus" when he was sixteen; it appears on *Can You Feel His Love?*, a 2012 album by Simmonds. Caesar's mother Hollace, like his father, is a committed Seventh Day Adventist. Caesar is the second of four brothers, all it one of their 20 best R & B albums of 2014. Charles Aaron, writing for that publication (15 Dec. 2014), cited the "delicate care" taken with the album's "vivid ambience," adding that "Caesar's languidly powerful vocals (recorded mostly in the living room of co-producer Jordan Evans)" were evidence "that we're witnessing the dawn of an abiding talent." The album samples the late folk singer Jeff Buckley and makes a reference to the classic film *Casablanca*, which Caesar had first seen the year before. The iconic Humphrey Bogart line, "We'll always have Paris," inspired him to write a song of the same name on the spot. Mistry, who wrote about Caesar's work for *Pitchfork* (6 Nov. 2015), described the album as "stunning," and "a slow, contemplative push back at obedient worship and theological rigor."

FREUDIAN

Caesar released his second EP, *Pilgrim's Paradise*, in 2015. The record, produced by Jordan Evans and Matthew Burnett, dealt with similar themes of love and loss of faith. On the song "Death and Taxes," Caesar sings, "Surely my sins have found me out / God rest my soul, but show me out / Spit on my grave but kiss my mouth." Zach Frydenlund, who reviewed the EP for *Complex* (11 Nov. 2015), described Caesar's sound as a cross between John Mayer and R & B singer John Legend. Caesar told Frydenlund that the songs on the EP were "a self-pilgrimage." "I'm finding my way through my songs," he said. "I'm not sure I know exactly what matters in life yet, but I know what doesn't."

Caesar and his team of collaborators released his debut album *Freudian* in August 2017. The album's lead single, "Get You" featuring pop singer Kali Uchis, was a breakout hit. It peaked at number five on the Billboard Hot R & B Songs chart. "It was kind of like, this is our moment. We knew that if we put out a subpar project, we could lose all the momentum," he told Patrick of *Freudian*. Luckily, critics and fans did not find the album subpar. Most of its songs are inspired by a tumultuous romantic relationship from Caesar's early Toronto days. He samples two well-known gospel songs—Kirk Franklin's "Hold Me Now" and Kyle David Matthews's "We Fall Down"—on songs about romantic love. Briana Younger, who reviewed *Freudian* for *Pitchfork* (26 Aug. 2017), wrote that their inclusion is "emblematic of the synergistic relationship between gospel and R & B," which Caesar embraces on the album. "Caesar's balance between sacred elements and secular sentiment . . . is what sets him apart," she wrote. "There's something visceral about the sound of an organ or a polyphonic choir, or admitting to a lover that they 'saved [your] soul like Jesus.' Put those things next to bluesy guitars and expressions of carnal desire, and the result feels as contradictory as love itself—divine and discordant at the same time. This is right where *Freudian* lands," she wrote. Younger also praised Caesar's featured guests, including Uchis, Syd of the band the Internet, and R & B singer H.E.R. Stacy-Ann Ellis of *Vibe* magazine (29 Aug. 2017) described the latter collaboration—"The Best Part" with H.E.R.—as "the album's most affecting song and most loving ballad."

Freudian received a boost thanks to support from the streaming service Apple Music. Apple Music also made a short documentary about Caesar's life as part of their Up Next series. The singer's stock continued to rise after he premiered a track called "First World Problems" with Chance the Rapper on *The Late Show with Stephen Colbert* in September. In November, *Freudian* received two Grammy nominations. Caesar was overwhelmed by his rapid rise, but as he told Patrick at the end of the year, fame "hasn't gotten that crazy yet." He added, "Whatever happens, happens. I can't be living in fear. I did that for so long."

PERSONAL LIFE

Caesar lives in the Rosedale neighborhood of Toronto.

SUGGESTED READING

Aaron, Charles. "20 Best R & B Albums of 2014: Daniel Caesar, 'Praise Break' EP." Review of *Praise Break*, by Daniel Caesar. *Rolling Stone*, 15 Dec. 2014, www.rollingstone.com/music/music-lists/20-best-rb-albums-of-2014-168202/daniel-caesar-praise-break-ep-227407/. Accessed 14 Aug. 2018.

Ellis, Stacy-Ann. "On 'Freudian,' Daniel Caesar Baits Us Back into Savoring the Tender Bits of Love." Review of *Freudian*, by Daniel Caesar. *Vibe*, 29 Aug. 2017, www.vibe.com/2017/08/daniel-caesar-freudian-album-review/. Accessed 14 Aug. 2018.

Frydenlund, Zach. "Premiere: Drift Away with Daniel Caesar's 'Pilgrim's Paradise' EP." Review of *Pilgrim's Paradise*, by Daniel Caesar. *Complex*, 11 Nov. 2015, www.complex.com/music/2015/11/daniel-caesar-new-ep-premiere-stream-pilgrims-paradise. Accessed 14 Aug. 2018.

Mistry, Anupa. "Daniel Caesar's Stripped-Down Soul Music Sounds Like Home." *Fader*, 5 Apr. 2016, www.thefader.com/2016/04/05/daniel-caesar-interview. Accessed 14 Aug. 2018.

Pastuk, Slava. "Daniel Caesar's Reign of Freedom." *Noisey*, 2 Oct. 2014, noisey.vice.com/en_ca/article/rm8y86/daniel-caesar-interview. Accessed 14 Aug. 2018.

Patrick, Ryan B. "Daniel Caesar on Leaving the Church, the Rise of Toronto and His Amazing 2017." *Exclaim!* 7 Dec. 2017, exclaim.ca/music/article/

daniel_caesar_on_leaving_the_church_the_ rise_of_toronto_and_his_amazing_2017. Accessed 14 Aug. 2018.

Younger, Briana. "Daniel Caesar, *Freudian*." Review of *Freudian*, by Daniel Caesar. *Pitchfork*, 26 Aug. 2017, pitchfork.com/reviews/albums/daniel-caesar-freudian/. Accessed 14 Aug. 2018.

SELECTED WORKS

Praise Break, 2014; *Pilgrim's Paradise*, 2015; *Freudian*, 2017

—*Molly Hagan*

John Carreyrou

Date of birth: ca. 1973
Occupation: Journalist

"Among the many hot streaks in investigative journalism, it would be hard to top John Carreyrou's ongoing run," Brad Hamilton wrote for the *Hatch Institute* website (21 May 2018). Hamilton, who referred to Carreyrou as "the *Wall Street Journal*'s deep-dive ace," traced the beginning of that run to 2003, when the reporter was part of a team that earned the paper a Pulitzer Prize for its work on a series about corporate scandals. Carreyrou followed that achievement with a host of others, all for work with the *Wall Street Journal* (*WSJ*): in 2003 he also won a German Marshall Fund Peter R. Weitz Journalism Prize for excellence in reporting on European affairs, and the following year he was part of a team that won the same prize again. In 2015 he was part of the team that won a second Pulitzer—this one for a project that exposed Medicare fraud.

In 2016 Carreyrou received the sixty-seventh annual George Polk Award in Journalism for Financial Reporting, in recognition of his breaking coverage of Theranos Inc., a Silicon Valley startup that falsely claimed to have developed technology that would allow hundreds of different lab tests and health screenings to be conducted with just a few drops of blood. His hard-hitting series of articles, published in the *WSJ* in late 2015, detailed the secretive inner workings of the company and the motives of its founder, Elizabeth Holmes, who had siphoned hundreds of millions of dollars from several high-profile investors, including Betsy DeVos and Carlos Slim; attracted fawning coverage in such respected outlets as the *New Yorker*; lured establishment figures like Henry Kissinger and George Shultz to sit on the Theranos board; and persuaded major drugstore chain Walgreens to set up blood-drawing clinics using the still untested technology in its stores.

Before faulty and misleading results sent several panicked people to their local emergency rooms, Holmes, as Roger Lowenstein wrote for the *New York Times* (21 May 2018), "was feted as a biomedical version of Steve Jobs or Bill Gates, a wunderkind college dropout who would make blood testing as convenient as the iPhone."

In 2018 Carreyrou expanded upon his coverage in a book, *Bad Blood: Secrets and Lies in a Silicon Valley Startup*, which quickly landed on the New York Times Best Seller list. Just weeks after the book's publication, Holmes was indicted on charges of criminal fraud. In a review for the *Financial Times* (9 July 2018), David Crow remarked on that indictment—which followed years of Holmes casting aspersions on the *WSJ* and threatening legal action: "*Bad Blood* is already out of date. Subsequent editions of this riveting story . . . will have to include a victory lap from investigative journalist John Carreyrou."

EARLY LIFE AND EDUCATION

Carreyrou's father is the respected French journalist Gérard Carreyrou, whose storied career has included stints at the radio station Europe 1, the television network TF1, and the newspaper *France-Soir*. His mother is the former Jane Evans, a native of Long Island, New York, who had studied French at Stanford University and attended the Sorbonne in Paris before embarking on a career as a language teacher.

The couple had married in 1971, and John Carreyrou was born a couple of years later in New York but was raised in France. He returned to the United States for college, graduating from Duke University in 1994 with a bachelor's degree in political science and government.

JOURNALISM CAREER

Carreyrou sought to follow in his father's footsteps as a journalist, and after graduating, he took a job at Dow Jones Newswires. In 1999 he joined the staff of the *Wall Street Journal* (*WSJ*), operating out of the paper's bureau in Brussels, Belgium. His star steadily rose at the venerable media outlet. In 2001 he was assigned to the Paris bureau, where he covered a range of topics, from business to global terrorism, and within two years, he had been appointed deputy bureau chief for southern Europe.

In October 2002, the paper published the article "Damage Control: How Messier Kept Cash Crisis at Vivendi Hidden for Months," an exposé Carreyrou had helped author on the financial woes of Paris-based media conglomerate Vivendi SA and the machinations of its beleaguered CEO, Jean-Marie Messier. That coverage, part of a series on corporate scandals, contributed to the *WSJ*'s 2003 Pulitzer win for explanatory reporting. Carreyrou also received high-level plaudits for his contributions to a five-part 2003 series titled "The Disintegration of the Trans-Atlantic Relationship over the Iraq War." (Carreyrou's portion was an examination of the Normandy region's complex emotional responses to American military might—from gratitude for US actions in World War II to opposition to the ongoing war in Iraq.)

Later in the 2000s Carreyrou moved back to the United States to join the paper's staff in New York, and there he began covering the medical and pharmaceutical industries. Those topics were, as he explained to Kara Swisher for Vox Media's *Recode Decode* podcast (3 June 2018), "what appealed to me the most coming back from Europe as a foreign correspondent." He continued, "I knew I'd have to specialize. When you're abroad, you get to cover everything. When you're back in the states, you obviously have a narrower slice of real estate that you're given, and so I wanted that slice to be interesting and really engaging to me."

He ultimately became chief of the paper's New York–based health and science bureau, and in 2015 he shared another Pulitzer Prize, this one for his part in the investigative series "Medicare Unmasked," which revealed fraud and abuses in the system that cost taxpayers billions of dollars.

THERANOS

In late 2014 Carreyrou read "Blood, Simpler: One Woman's Drive to Upend Medical Testing," a *New Yorker* profile of young tech entrepreneur Elizabeth Holmes, who was purportedly developing a device that would allow medical personnel to run an unheard-of range of lab tests using just a small sample of blood from a finger prick. She compared the practice of drawing multiple tubes of blood to torture and claimed that her company, Theranos, would not only disrupt the entire industry but change countless people's lives.

Although the article had been penned by well-regarded journalist Ken Auletta and the *New Yorker* was renowned for its stringent fact-checking, something about it felt off to Carreyrou. "It was clear that Theranos hadn't done any peer review [studies] and was jealously guarding its secret recipe, which I thought was weird," he recalled to Brad Hamilton for *Medium*. "Because in medicine, any real innovation goes through scientific journals." Carreyrou admits, however, that he might not have followed through on that nagging feeling had it not been validated a few months later by a pathologist he had met while working on the Medicare story. After finding out that the man shared his misgivings, Carreyrou aired his thoughts in a blog post. Comments flooded in, including one from a reader who could put the reporter in touch with Richard

Fuisz, a doctor and inventor whom Holmes had sued for purportedly stealing patent information. Fuisz, in turn, connected Carreyrou with one of Holmes's former lab directors, and the investigation snowballed from there.

Using information gleaned from the former employee as well as from sites like LinkedIn, Carreyrou amassed a group of sources who, while fearful of retaliation, felt an obligation to expose the malfeasance at the company. They painted a clear picture of a CEO whose obsessive desire to emulate tech titans like Steve Jobs (whose customary black turtlenecks she even habitually mimicked) had led her to mislead investors and business partners about the ability of her company's technology to produce accurate blood test results. Among the most high-profile sources was former Theranos employee Tyler Shultz, the grandson of George Shultz, a former secretary of state who had joined Holmes's board.

Theranos fired back with threats of legal action. Additionally, Holmes asked Rupert Murdoch, who owns the *WSJ* and had invested in Theranos, to prevent the publication of the article, and she arranged for several of Carreyrou's sources to be put under surveillance. "There were stressful moments," the journalist admitted to Alexis Buisson for the online publication *Frenchly* (23 June 2018). "The *Wall Street Journal* is in the habit of giving those who are the subject of an article lots of time to respond. In this case, they took advantage of that to threaten me and my sources."

BAD BLOOD

Despite that intimidation, Carreyrou pressed on, and in late 2015 the *WSJ* began publishing his reportage. When the first piece appeared in October, Holmes gathered Theranos employees and reaffirmed that they were changing the world, and that Carreyrou and the *WSJ* had gotten the story utterly wrong. The meeting ended with employees starting an obscene rhyming chant invoking Carreyrou's name. "I thought it was ridiculous, but I didn't think too much about it at the time because I was working on other articles on the case," he told Buisson. "This chant is emblematic of how Theranos works. They had committed fraud, but that didn't prevent them from being arrogant and denigrating everyone."

In 2016, thanks to mounting public pressure, Theranos began correcting tens of thousands of blood tests that had been conducted on trusting consumers, and by 2017 the company had closed its last lab. In March 2018 the Securities and Exchange Commission sued Holmes and former Theranos president Ramesh "Sunny" Balwani (with whom she had been romantically involved), for fraud. To settle the civil case, Holmes agreed to give up control of the company and pay a $500,000 fine. Three months later, as *Bad Blood*, Carreyrou's book-length treatment of the Theranos matter, was hitting best-seller lists, Holmes and Balwani were indicted on criminal charges of defrauding investors and deceiving patients and doctors.

Bad Blood is set to be made into a film; the screenplay is being penned by Vanessa Taylor, who cowrote the big-screen hit *The Shape of Water*, and it will be directed by Adam McKay. Jennifer Lawrence is slated to star as Holmes.

Carreyrou has given a great deal of thought to why so many savvy and intelligent people were duped by Holmes and riveted by her vision. "She capitalized on this yearning there was, in Silicon Valley and beyond, to see a woman break through in this man's world," he explained to Scott Simon on National Public Radio's *Weekend Edition Saturday* (23 June 2018). "If you look back over the past thirty years, all these tech founders that have gone on to be billionaires and icons were all men. Elizabeth Holmes was going to be that first [woman] tech founder who became a billionaire."

PERSONAL LIFE

Carreyrou is married to *Bloomberg News* editor Molly Schuetz. The couple live in the Brooklyn neighborhood of Park Slope with their three children. Carreyrou, an avid soccer fan, roots for the French national team.

SUGGESTED READING

Buisson, Alexis. "Meet John Carreyrou, the Reporter Who Exposed Theranos and Shook Silicon Valley." *Frenchly*, 23 June 2018, frenchly.us/franco-american-journalist-john-carreyrou-shakes-silicon-valley. Accessed 2 Aug. 2018.

Carreyrou, John. Interview by Brad Hamilton. *The Hatch Institute*, 21 May 2018, thehatchinstitute.org/all-stories/john-carreyrou. Accessed 2 Aug. 2018.

Carreyrou, John. Interview by Kara Swisher. *Recode Decode*, Vox Media, 3 June 2018, www.recode.net/2018/6/3/17422498/wsj-investigative-journalist-john-carreyrou-theranos-blood-health-care-recode-decode. Accessed 2 Aug. 2018.

Carreyrou, John. "Reporter John Carreyrou on the 'Bad Blood' of Theranos." Interview by Scott Simon. *Weekend Edition Saturday*, NPR, 23 June 2018, www.npr.org/2018/06/23/622795416/reporter-john-carreyrou-on-the-bad-blood-of-theranos. Accessed 2 Aug. 2018.

Crow, David. Review of *Bad Blood: Secrets and Lies in a Silicon Valley Startup*, by John Carreyrou. *Financial Times*, 9 July 2018, www.ft.com/content/20855a62-803d-11e8-8e67-1e1a0846c475. Accessed 2 Aug. 2018.

Knibbs, Kate. "How John Carreyrou Exposed the Theranos Scam." *The Ringer*, 22 May 2018, www.theringer.com/2018/5/22/17378494/bad-blood-theranos-john-carreyrou-interview. Accessed 2 Aug. 2018.

Lowenstein, Roger. "How One Company Scammed Silicon Valley. And How It Got Caught." Review of *Bad Blood: Secrets and Lies in a Silicon Valley Startup*, by John Carreyrou. *The New York Times*, 21 May 2018, www.nytimes.com/2018/05/21/books/review/bad-blood-john-carreyrou.html. Accessed 2 Aug. 2018.

—*Mari Rich*

Horacio Cartes

Date of birth: July 5, 1956
Occupation: President of Paraguay

Horacio Cartes is the president of Paraguay and a multimillionaire businessman. His victory in the April 21, 2013, presidential elections marked the Colorado Party's return to power.

EARLY LIFE AND EDUCATION

Horacio Manuel Cartes Jara, known as Horacio Cartes, was born in Asunción, Paraguay, on July 5, 1956. The son of Ramón Telmo Cartes Lind, a former airplane pilot, and Elva Jara Lafuente, he is one of four children. His father, who owned and operated the Paraguayan franchise of Cessna, an aircraft manufacturer, encouraged him as a child to pursue aeronautical engineering. After studying at some of the most prestigious, private secondary schools in Asunción, Cartes attended the Spartan School of Aeronautics (now the Spartan College of Aeronautics and Technology) in Tulsa, Oklahoma.

When he returned to Paraguay at the age of nineteen, Cartes turned his attention to entrepreneurship, a pursuit that would eventually make him one of the wealthiest citizens of Paraguay. Among his first ventures was a currency exchange business that would later become the powerful Banco Amambay. Eventually, his business empire, known as the Grupo Cartes conglomerate, consisted of more than two-dozen companies, including agricultural enterprises, beverage companies, and tobacco manufacturers.

Throughout his professional career, Cartes has been the target of several criminal investigations, including currency fraud, drug trafficking, and money laundering. He has never been formally charged.

POLITICAL CAREER

Cartes's career in politics began in 2009 when he joined the center-right Colorado Party. The Colorado Party was in the midst of a political crisis having just been ousted from executive power for the first time in sixty-one years in Paraguay, thirty-five of which were spent supporting Alfredo Stroessner's military dictatorship. In 2008 the Colorado Party had lost the presidency to the more leftist, ideological government of Fernando Lugo, a former bishop.

Prior to joining the Colorado Party, Cartes had no interest in politics and was not even registered to vote. He has said in interviews that his decision to run for president was based on a desire to curb the leftward direction of Paraguayan politics, which he felt had started to emulate Hugo Chavez's government in Venezuela. The Colorado Party accepted Cartes as their 2013 presidential candidate, waiving the mandate that all candidates must be party members for at least ten years to run.

With the motto of "New Directions," Cartes's presidential campaign was based largely on economic promises. His solutions to rebuild Paraguay's economy included raising private capital to improve the country's infrastructure, modernizing the country's public enterprises, and creating jobs for ordinary citizens. Additionally, he promised voters that the Colorado Party had changed and that his own personal fortune would make him immune to bribery and corruption as president.

Cartes's primary opponent during the presidential election, which was held on April 21, 2013, was Efraín Alegre of the Liberal Party. After winning nearly 46 percent of the vote, Cartes was sworn into office on August 15, 2013; Alegre came in second with 37 percent. The event marked the second time in the nation's 202 years of independence that a new leader peacefully assumed power from an opposition party. At his inauguration, Cartes stated that he was not in politics to become wealthier or to further his career, but to serve the Paraguayan people and improve conditions for future generations. In his first year of presidency, he was able to successfully restore Paraguay's relations with its regional neighbors Bolivia and Venezuela.

In March 2014, thousands of Paraguayan citizens took to the streets to protest Cartes's privatization plan. The plan consisted of new "public-private" laws that allowed for private, foreign companies to invest in Paraguay's public infrastructure, assets, and services in exchange for owning concessions and charging fees. In interviews, Cartes has said that he based his privatization plan off of similar economic policies in Chile and Brazil. Protestors responded to the plan by going on strike and demanding that instead of privatization, Cartes ensure a better welfare system, a 25 percent raise in minimum salaries, the end of violence against peasants, and agrarian reform. Cartes attempted to mollify protestors by raising the minimum wage by 10 percent. However, protests against his government have continued.

As Paraguayan presidents are constitutionally restricted to a single five-year term, Cartes is set to resign after the 2018 general election.

IMPACT

Although controversial, Cartes's staunchly pro-business approach to government has been effective in creating economic growth. By touting Paraguay as "Latin America's best hidden treasure" to foreign investors and restoring the country's membership in the free trade regional bloc of Mercosur, he has facilitated significant economic growth.

PERSONAL LIFE

Horacio Cartes is married to María Montaña de Cartes. They have a son and two daughters.

SUGGESTED READING

Cartes, Horacio. "An Interview with Horacio Cartes: The New Face of the Colorados." *Economist*. Economist Newspaper, 17 Dec. 2013. Web. 17 Dec. 2015.

Gilbert, Jonathan, and Jonathan Watts. "Horacio Cartes Wins Paraguay Election." *Guardian*. Guardian News and Media, 21 Apr. 2015. Web. 17 Dec. 2015.

"Horacio Cartes Wins Paraguay Presidential Election." *BBC*. BBC, 22 Apr. 2013. Web. 17 Dec. 2015.

Romero, Simon. "Conservative Tobacco Magnate Wins Presidential Race in Paraguay." *New York Times*. New York Times, 21 Apr. 2013. Web. 17 Dec. 2015.

Stocker, Ed. "Horacio Cartes: Millionaire. Criminal. Business Titan. Homophobe. The Next President of Paraguay?" *Independent*. Independent.co.uk, 19 Apr. 2013. Web. 17 Dec. 2015.

—*Emily E. Turner*

Yvonne Chaka Chaka

Date of birth: March 18, 1965
Occupation: Singer; activist

Although not well known by mainstream audiences in the United States, Yvonne Chaka Chaka is an icon in her native South Africa. As a recording artist, she was an influential figure in the country's dance-music scene during the 1980s and 1990s, helping to make what is

By World Economic Forum, via Wikimedia Commons

widely described as "bubblegum disco" the predominant sound of the era. The upbeat music also became associated with the battle to abolish apartheid, a cause to which Chaka Chaka developed strong ties. She has also been lionized for her activism in other areas, leading campaigns against malaria, hunger, childhood marriage, and other such societal ills. Dubbed "the Princess of Africa" for both her stardom and her social efforts, she has received such honors as the World Economic Forum's 2012 Crystal Award and the 2017 BET (Black Entertainment Network) International Global Good Power Award.

Chaka Chaka views music as a force for good in the world and a powerful vehicle for change. "I worked hard, and I think how I did it was always remembering you need to keep your feet firmly on the ground and respect your art," she told Guguleth Mhlungu for the South African site *News24* (22 Mar. 2015). "Your art is important. You can also let your art work for you. I never thought I would be in the same room as [former Secretary-General of the United Nations] Ban Ki-moon, or singing for Queen Elizabeth, or having dinner with Oprah, or being invited to the White House, but my work as a musician made that all possible."

EARLY LIFE AND EDUCATION

The future singer was born Yvonne Machaka in 1965 in the Dobsonville area of Soweto, a township near the South African capital of Johannesburg (and later incorporated into the city). Under the segregated apartheid regime, Soweto was exclusively black. Her father, Puti, died when she was young. Although he had

been a talented musician whom Chaka Chaka would credit with inspiring her, he was unable to achieve his own dreams of fame before his untimely death. Her mother, Sophie, was left to bring up Chaka Chaka and her sisters, Doreen and Refiloe, alone, earning what she could as a house cleaner. Chaka Chaka has recalled that some nights, supper consisted of only gravy and *pap* (a type of porridge). On good days, Sophie brought home leftover food given to her by her employers, and the siblings often foraged in the local fields for *morogo*, a leafy green also known as African spinach.

Adding to the family's troubles, Chaka Chaka suffered from seizures as a child, forcing her mother to take her to various clinics. One day, in desperation, her mother took her instead to a Pentecostal church to try the power of prayer, and soon after, the condition went away. Though Chaka Chaka admits the possibility that she would have outgrown the seizures regardless, she continues to maintain a deep spirituality.

As a child, Chaka Chaka banged on empty cans to make music and sang into a broken broom handle, pretending it was a microphone. She later joined her church's choir, where she stood out for her talent and love of performing. She soon began to draw attention, and in 1981 she appeared on the televised talent show *Sugar Shack*, becoming reportedly the first young black person to be featured on South African television. However, that distinction meant little to her, she would later say, as her family did not own a television set.

Chaka Chaka's original professional goal was to become an accountant, while her mother hoped she would be a lawyer. Her musical career ultimately turned her away from those pursuits, but she later advanced her education. From 1990 to 1993, Chaka Chaka attended the University of South Africa (UNISA), where she earned certificates in adult education and local government management and administration. She would also earn a certificate of speech and drama from Trinity College, London, in 1997.

MUSICAL BREAKTHROUGH

With significant attention on her vocal talents following her television appearance, Chaka Chaka launched what would turn out to be a meteoric musical career while still in her teens. She burst onto the scene in 1984, at the age of nineteen, with an infectious disco-tinged single, "I'm in Love with a DJ." Other successful singles followed, building on and becoming influential parts of the developing "bubblegum" sound. Her debut album, *Thank You Mr. DJ*, came out shortly after, and quickly achieved double-gold status. A string of other hit albums followed, including *Sangoma* (1987) and *I'm Burning Up* (1987), making her a major star throughout much of

Africa and earning international attention as well. A savvy businessperson and aware that musical success could be fleeting, Chaka Chaka launched her own company, Chaka Chaka Promotions, and her own music label, Chaka Chaka Music.

Chaka Chaka's early songs were influenced by mbaqanga (a musical style rooted in Zulu culture with jazz influence), but featured English lyrics and modern synthesizer beats. The singles were played on heavy rotation on South African radio, many of them reaching near-legendary status, including, for example, "Umqombothi." A paean to the titular African beer brewed with maize and sorghum malt, it was released in 1988 and later featured on the soundtrack to the 2004 Don Cheadle movie *Hotel Rwanda*. The song features a bouncy tune and simple, lighthearted lyrics, such as, "I work hard every day to make my beer/ Wake up early every morning to please my people with African beer."

As those lines might attest, Chaka Chaka feels a deep connection to her homeland and has made a point of demonstrating her African pride in her music. When offered a chance to move to Paris to record and perform, she declined. Her works, while still catchy and upbeat, eventually became more politically aware and indicative of national pride, such as *I Cry for Freedom* (1988) and *The Power of Afrika* (1996). Chaka Chaka also met the jailed anti-apartheid activist Nelson Mandela, who wrote her a note from prison thanking her for the music that helped him and his fellow political prisoners get by. Frightened of the South African secret police, Chaka Chaka chewed up and swallowed the note on her way home. However, she would draw much inspiration from Mandela, and worked closely with him following his release from prison in 1990.

ACTIVISM

Chaka Chaka took a brief hiatus from recording music in the mid-1990s, and during this time she increased her social activism. Her many initiatives eventually earned her as much attention as her music into the twenty-first century. After apartheid was finally dismantled and Mandela became president of South Africa in 1994, she developed a relationship with the beloved leader that she likened to a father-daughter connection, which inspired her to further pursue humanitarian causes. When Mandela later launched his 46664 initiative, a series of concerts aimed at raising awareness of HIV/AIDS, she served as an ambassador for the project and performed alongside such international artists as Beyoncé Knowles, Peter Gabriel, Bono, Jimmy Cliff, and others. The title of her 2012 album *Amazing Man* refers to Mandela, who died the year after its release.

After one of Chaka Chaka's backup singers died of malaria in 2004, she was horrified to learn that the mosquito-borne disease was killing more than a million people each year in sub-Saharan Africa, many of them children. She agreed to serve as a UNICEF Goodwill Ambassador focused on eradicating the deadly but preventable illness and participated in Roll-Back Malaria, a collaboration between the World Bank, United Nations, World Health Organization, and other organizations. By 2007 Chaka Chaka had launched her own charitable organization, the Princess of Africa Foundation, taking its name from a nickname given to her by devoted fans. The group is active in areas of healthcare, sanitation, and education, and distributes medication, vaccines, mosquito netting, and other needed supplies. Chaka Chaka's humanitarian work was chronicled in the 2010 documentary *The Motherland Tour: A Journey of African Women*, which showcases frontline healthcare providers working under the auspices of her foundation.

Although she has won numerous awards for her music—including best female artist of the year honors at the South African Music Awards (equivalent in prestige to a Grammy)—Chaka Chaka has said that she is proudest of the many laurels she has received for her social activism. These include the Rotary Paul Harris Fellowship Award and the 2012 World Economic Forum Crystal Award, the latter of which she was the first African woman to receive. "I know what it is like to sleep without food. I know what is like not to have," she wrote on her foundation's website. "My mum taught me that when you die you are never going to take anything with you. So when I have, I share with others."

AN AFRICAN ICON

In the 2010s Chaka Chaka remained best known for her early genre-defining hits and her dedicated humanitarian work. However, she also continued to routinely perform to sold-out crowds and was known for being warm and approachable to her fans. "I don't see the reason why I should have bodyguards stop the same people who buy my music when they want to greet me," she explained to Mthokozisi Dube for the South African publication the *New Age* (7 Feb. 2017). "They sacrifice and take their time to come to my shows. Surely, they deserve some respect."

Chaka Chaka's warm personality as the Princess of Africa has helped ensure her continued status as a widely known and respected figure. Often mentioned as one of the most credible and trusted stars in South Africa, she has also been celebrated for her business acumen. She has owned a series of companies, including an IT firm and a luxury auto dealership; represented various advertising campaigns; and also remained in the public eye through occasional television and film appearances. In 2001 the editors of the South African *Star* named her among the nation's top one hundred heroes. She was also presented with the position of honorary colonel in the South African air force due to her expertise in communication and outreach.

Yet despite all her accomplishments, Chaka Chaka has not rested on her laurels or even slowed down. She continues to intertwine her music and her activism in pursuit of her goal of improving society. "I have learnt that after 21 years of freedom and democracy, there are still injustices," she explained to Mhlungu. "When I started singing music, I reflected the injustices of the time. Now we have a new set of challenges. . . . So, I still have a lot to do through—and with—my music."

PERSONAL LIFE
In 1989 Chaka Chaka married Mandlalele "Tiny" Mhinga, a doctor she met through one of her sisters. As a prince of the Shangaan tribe, Mhinga was entitled to take multiple wives. However, Chaka Chaka told journalists that she forbade such a practice, and she has spoken out against other traditional marital customs, such as child brides. She has described how she and Mhinga worked through jealousy issues to enjoy an exceptionally strong, complementary relationship. She likes to cook while he takes care of the ironing, for example, and they enjoy golfing together.

The couple has four sons: Ningi, Mfumu, Nandla, and Themba. "I always remind my boys that everything they have is a blessing and not their right," Chaka Chaka told Shirley Genga for *Standard Digital* (4 July 2010). "They must understand that in life, they need to work hard if they want to live a good life."

SUGGESTED READING
"African Pop Legend Yvonne Chaka Chaka: I Won't Allow My Husband a Second Wife." *The Telegraph*, 11 Dec. 2012, www.telegraph.co.uk/women/9738593/African-pop-legend-Yvonne-Chaka-Chaka-I-wont-allow-my-husband-a-second-wife.html. Accessed 4 Dec. 2017.

Chaka Chaka, Yvonne. "Chaka Chaka: I Have Achieved My Destiny." Interview by Shirley Genga. *Standard Digital*, 4 July 2010, www.standardmedia.co.ke/lifestyle/article/2000013065/chaka-chaka-i-have-achieved-my-destiny. Accessed 4 Dec. 2017.

Chaka Chaka, Yvonne. "A Year of Milestones for the Princess of Africa." Interview by Gugulethu Mhlungu, *News24*, 22 Mar. 2015, www.news24.com/Arc4. Accessed 4 Dec. 2017.

Dube, Mthokozisi. "Big Interview: Yvonne's African Love Affair." *The New Age*, 7 Feb. 2017, www.thenewage.co.za/big-interview-yvonnes-african-love-affair/. Accessed 4 Dec. 2017.

Makgalemele, Thembisile. "A Great Career, Marriage and Family: How Did She Do It?" *Drum*, 16 Apr. 2015. *PressReader*, www.pressreader.com/south-africa/drum/20150416/282664685905988. Accessed 4 Dec. 2017.

"Yvonne Chaka Chaka" *Who's Who Southern Africa*, whoswho.co.za/yvonne-chaka-chaka-4645. Accessed 4 Dec. 2017.

SELECTED WORKS
Thank You Mr. DJ, 1987; *Sangoma*, 1987; *I'm Burning Up*, 1987; *I Cry for Freedom*, 1988; *The Power of Afrika*, 1996; *Back on My Feet*, 1997; *Yvonne and Friends*, 2001; *Kwenzenjani?*, 2002; *Celebrate Life*, 2006; *Amazing Man*, 2012

—Mari Rich

Timothée Chalamet

Date of birth: December 27, 1995
Occupation: Actor

Prior to early 2017, Timothée Chalamet was a largely unknown actor who was recognized primarily for his season-long arc on the Showtime television series *Homeland* (2001–) in 2012 and an award-winning stage performance in the Off-Broadway play *Prodigal Son*. However, his life and career changed forever in January of that year, when the film *Call Me by Your Name* (2017) premiered at the Sundance Film Festival. Directed by Luca Guadagnino and based on a novel by André Aciman, the film starred Chalamet as Elio, a young man living in Italy who falls in love with visiting American graduate student Oliver, played by Armie Hammer. Chalamet's performance in the film captured the attention of critics and film viewers, and he went on to be nominated for numerous awards, including the Academy Award for best actor, in recognition of his strong and emotionally affecting performance.

Raised in New York City and exposed to theater and the other performing arts from a young age, Chalamet attended the renowned Fiorello H. LaGuardia High School of Music & Art and Performing Arts and began acting in television and film as a teenager, appearing in shows such as the comedic drama *Royal Pains* (2009–16) and *Homeland* and films such as *Men, Women & Children* (2014) and *Interstellar* (2014). Amid his breakthrough with *Call Me by Your Name*, he also appeared in the Academy Award–nominated film *Lady Bird* (2017) and the Western *Hostiles* (2017). Despite his abrupt increase in fame due

Photo by Axelle/Bauer-Griffin/FilmMagic/Getty Images

to such projects, Chalamet remains focused primarily on the craft of acting itself. "It's the one thing I'm good at," he told Vanessa Lawrence for *W* (8 Feb. 2016). "It's the one thing that fulfills me."

EARLY LIFE AND EDUCATION

Timothée Hal Chalamet was born on December 27, 1995, in New York. His mother, Nicole Flender, was a former dancer and Broadway performer who later became a real estate broker and a member of the Actors' Equity Association National Council, while his father, Mark Chalamet, worked as an editor. Chalamet and his older sister, Pauline, grew up in the Hell's Kitchen neighborhood of Manhattan and spent their summers in France, their father's native country. As the child of a former performer, a grandchild of screenwriter Harold Flender, and a theatergoing resident of New York City, Chalamet was exposed to the performing arts at an early age. He frequently attended plays with his family during his early life and played piano as a child, a skill he would later relearn for his role in the film *Call Me by Your Name*. Also an avid soccer player, Chalamet coached a children's team while in France and aspired to play professionally until determining that he was not physically suited to such a career.

As a teenager, Chalamet attended Fiorello H. LaGuardia High School of Music & Art and Performing Arts, a prestigious institution known for producing numerous successful actors, artists, and musicians. Chalamet later noted in interviews that he nearly failed to gain admission to LaGuardia due to his poor behavior in

middle school and was admitted only after receiving a recommendation from a teacher. During his years at LaGuardia, he participated in the school's theater program and began acting steadily. Chalamet later credited his time at the school with developing his acting abilities. "To be in that environment at that age?" he told Paul Flynn for *GQ UK* (17 Sept. 2017). "You know, college are the formative years for a lot of people but to have that experience from thirteen through seventeen, for better or for worse, to have someone in your ear going 'feel, feel, feel, stop inhibiting, feel, feel, feel,' it's helped me a lot as an actor." Chalamet graduated from LaGuardia in 2013.

Although already working as an actor, Chalamet enrolled in Columbia University after graduating from high school with the encouragement of his parents, who reminded him of the importance of having a backup plan. However, he dropped out of university after a year. "I just kind of floundered," he told *Interstellar* costar Matthew McConaughey for *Interview* (2 June 2017). "Columbia takes a wholehearted academic commitment that I think I have in me, but it was just not where my mind was at the time."

EARLY CAREER

Long exposed to the world of the performing arts, Chalamet began acting in commercials as a child and began appearing in short films by his early teens. He made his television debut in a 2009 episode of the long-running television series *Law & Order* (1990–2010). In 2012, he appeared in multiple episodes of the series *Royal Pains* and in eight episodes of the Showtime drama *Homeland*. Having previously worked on two television films, Chalamet made his feature-film debut in *Men, Women & Children* in 2014. Over the subsequent years, Chalamet took on roles in several films, including both major productions and independent works. In 2014, he appeared in the Christopher Nolan–helmed science fiction film *Interstellar*, playing the teenage incarnation of a character played as an adult by actor Casey Affleck. He costarred in the 2015 independent film *One and Two* and that year was also a member of the ensemble Christmas film *Love the Coopers*, while in 2016, he costarred in *Miss Stevens*, an independent comedy about high school students and their teacher at a drama competition.

In addition to his film work, Chalamet at times performed on stage and garnered attention for his lead role in the play *Prodigal Son*, which opened Off-Broadway in February 2016. Written and directed by award-winning playwright John Patrick Shanley, the play featured Chalamet in the lead role of Jim, a troubled teenager inspired, in part, by Shanley himself. Chalamet identified with the character, whose behavior he has linked to his own poor behavior during his early life. "I naturally have a me-against-the-world mentality and I've been fighting it since I was thirteen," he told Lawrence. "It's felt like it's only gotten me in lonely, angry places. And here is an opportunity to exorcise these demons in the healthiest context available, through the guidance of someone who had the same mentality [and] has made it to the other side a really joyous, noble guy." Chalamet received widespread critical acclaim for his performance and in May of 2016 won the Lucille Lortel Award for Outstanding Lead Actor in a Play.

CALL ME BY YOUR NAME
A key moment in Chalamet's career came in 2013, when he first met with director Luca Guadagnino. Guadagnino was planning to direct the film *Call Me by Your Name*, based on the novel by André Aciman, and at that time was seeking out both funding for the film and the right actor to play the character of Elio, one of two young men who fall in love over the course of the summer in Italy during the 1980s. Upon meeting Chalamet, Guadagnino was impressed by the actor's personality and dedication to his craft. "I saw an incredibly articulate, bright, smart, artistically ambitious young man, someone who not only had a sense of self that was completely unnarcissistic but had ambition to make sure his art as an actor was shining on-screen," the director told Julie Miller for *Vanity Fair* (5 Dec. 2017). Chalamet was unofficially cast in the project, which did not begin filming until 2016.

Prior to the start of filming, Chalamet traveled to the filming location in Italy to study Italian, piano, and guitar, skills he needed to master for the film. Over the course of the shoot, he became close friends with costar Armie Hammer, who plays American graduate student Oliver, and was particularly excited to work alongside actor Michael Stuhlbarg, who plays Elio's father and whom Chalamet had seen in plays in New York earlier in life. Following the film's completion, *Call Me by Your Name* premiered at the Sundance Film Festival in January 2017. The film screened at many additional US and international festivals before its limited release in US theaters in November 2017.

Call Me by Your Name received critical acclaim following its premiere, and critics focused particularly on Chalamet's performance as Elio. He earned numerous award nominations for his work, including an Academy Award nomination for best actor in a leading role that made him the youngest actor to be nominated in that category since 1944. Although thrilled by the nominations, Chalamet noted that he was less interested in awards and recognition than he was in the process of making the film. "What this movie's been already is so above and beyond I think any

of our wildest dreams," he told Anna Menta for *Newsweek* (24 Nov. 2017). "The experience of getting to shoot it was the main appeal. And the reception it's been getting is above and beyond our wildest dreams." Guadagnino later revealed in interviews that he hoped to direct a sequel to the film, and Chalamet expressed his interest in reprising the role of Elio.

OTHER PROJECTS
The year 2017 also saw the release of the coming-of-age film *Lady Bird*, which, like *Call Me by Your Name*, proved to be an Academy Award contender. Chalamet played a supporting role in the film, which starred Saoirse Ronan in the title role. He likewise had a supporting role in the Western *Hostiles*, which premiered at the Telluride Film Festival in the fall of 2017 and arrived in US theaters in early 2018.

In addition to his already-released projects, Chalamet received a great deal of attention for his upcoming films, not all of it positive. As the Me Too and Time's Up movements against sexual abuse and harassment in Hollywood and society gained traction in 2017 and 2018, he faced questions about his decision to appear in the Woody Allen film *A Rainy Day in New York*, which was scheduled for release in 2018. After learning more about the allegations against Allen, who was accused of molesting his adopted daughter when she was a child, Chalamet announced that he would donate his salary from the film to charities dealing with sexual assault and related issues. "I am learning that a good role isn't the only criteria for accepting a job," he wrote in a statement, as quoted by Steph Harmon for the *Guardian* (16 Jan. 2018). "That has become much clearer to me in the past few months, having witnessed the birth of a powerful movement intent on ending injustice, inequality and above all, silence."

Also in 2018, Chalamet was scheduled to appear in the films *Hot Summer Nights*, which had premiered at the South by Southwest Film Festival the previous year, and *Beautiful Boy*, in which he plays a young man who is addicted to methamphetamine. "I've never given myself more to any project in my life. I lost twenty pounds to do it," he told Menta. "We really gave it everything, we laid it all on the line. It's a really powerful and moving memoir." In early 2018, it was also announced that Chalamet would star in the Netflix film *The King* as Henry V of England.

PERSONAL LIFE
Chalamet lives in New York.

SUGGESTED READING
Chalamet, Timothée. Interview by Matthew McConaughey. *Interview*, 2 June 2017, www.

interviewmagazine.com/film/timothee-chal-amet. Accessed 9 Mar. 2018.

Chalamet, Timothée. "Timothée Chalamet on 'Call Me by Your Name,' Vulnerability, and That Peach Scene." Interview by Anna Menta. *Newsweek*, 24 Nov. 2017, www.newsweek.com/timothee-chalamet-interview-call-me-your-name-720407. Accessed 9 Mar. 2018.

Flynn, Paul. "Timothée Chalamet and Armie Hammer on Friendship, the Oscars and That Peach Scene." *GQ UK*, 17 Sept. 2017, www.gq-magazine.co.uk/article/armie-hammer-timothee-chalamet-interview. Accessed 9. Mar. 2018.

Harmon, Steph. "Timothée Chalamet: 'I Don't Want to Profit from my Work on Woody Allen's Film.'" *The Guardian*, 16 Jan. 2018, www.theguardian.com/film/2018/jan/16/timothee-chalamet-i-dont-want-to-profit-from-my-work-on-woody-allens-film. Accessed 9 Mar. 2018.

Lawrence, Vanessa. "Actor Timothée Chalamet Is Young and Wise." *W*, 8 Feb. 2016, www.wmagazine.com/story/actor-timothee-chalamet-prodigal-son. Accessed 9 Mar. 2018.

Miller, Julie. "Inside Timothée Chalamet's Overnight Breakout." *Vanity Fair*, 5 Dec. 2017, www.vanityfair.com/hollywood/2017/12/timothee-chalamet-call-me-by-your-name-breakout-star. Accessed 9 Mar. 2018.

"Timothée Chalamet Interview: Working with Greta Gerwig on *Lady Bird* and His Oscar Nomination for *Call Me by Your Name*." *The Times*, 4 Feb. 2018, www.thetimes.co.uk/article/timothee-chalamet-interview-greta-gerwig-lady-bird-oscar-nomination-call-me-by-your-name-qz3vk63p5. Accessed 9 Mar. 2018.

SELECTED WORKS

Homeland, 2012; *Men, Women & Children*, 2014; *Interstellar*, 2014; *One and Two*, 2015; *Love the Coopers*, 2015; *Miss Stevens*, 2016; *Call Me by Your Name*, 2017; *Lady Bird*, 2017; *Hostiles*, 2017

—Joy Crelin

Kam Chancellor

Date of birth: April 3, 1988
Occupation: Football player

Over the course of his eight seasons in the National Football League (NFL), the Seattle Seahawks' strong safety Kam Chancellor was one of the most dominant and respected defensive players in the game. An unheralded 2010 fifth-round draft pick out of Virginia Tech University, Chancellor earned the Seahawks' starting strong

By Mike Morris via Wikimedia Commons

safety spot in just his second season in 2011 and quickly emerged not only as a game-changing playmaker, but also as a galvanizing team leader. He established himself as the tone-setting enforcer of an imposing Seahawks' secondary that became known as the "Legion of Boom," one that played an integral role in the Seahawks making consecutive Super Bowl appearances following the 2013 and 2014 seasons. Often saving his best play for big games, Chancellor had a standout performance in Super Bowl XLVIII to help the Seahawks win their first-ever NFL title. He earned four career Pro Bowl selections (2011, 2013–15) and was also a two-time second-team All-Pro selection (2013–14).

Nicknamed "Bam Bam," Chancellor, who wore a helmet with a menacing tinted visor, earned a fearsome reputation around the NFL for his bone-rattling hits, each one of which were "a half-second of chaos," as Robert Mays wrote for *Grantland* (29 Jan. 2015). His presence in the middle of the field was such that opposing receivers would often change their routes simply to avoid getting into violent collisions with him. Chancellor's ultraphysical and unrelenting style of play took an equal toll on his own body, however, and resulted in his enduring multiple injuries during his career. A severe neck injury suffered during the 2017 season ultimately prompted Chancellor to announce his retirement from football in July 2018.

EARLY LIFE AND EDUCATION

Kameron Darnel Chancellor was born on April 3, 1988, in Norfolk, Virginia. Along with his three brothers and two sisters, he grew up in Norfolk's Park Place neighborhood, a crime-plagued area located on the west side of the city. Chancellor was raised by his mother, Karen Lambert, who worked multiple jobs at a time to help the family make ends meet. He has said that his biological father was never in the picture and that he met him only once.

Growing up without a father figure, Chancellor was forced to step into that role for his two younger brothers at an early age. He and his siblings found a common outlet in sports, which kept them off the streets and out of trouble. Gravitating toward football and basketball, Chancellor began playing in recreational leagues as a boy and quickly displayed natural athleticism.

Chancellor did his part to contribute to the family finances, taking a job at a local barbershop when he was just ten years old. Charged with menial tasks like sweeping the floors and taking out the trash, he would use his earnings to buy food for his brothers and sisters. Chancellor explained to Gregg Bell for the *Olympian* (7 Sept. 2016) that having to get a job early and help his family made him stronger as a person, teaching him how to be "the guy that likes to lead by example."

ROAD TO THE NFL

Chancellor's reputation as a lead-by-example type in the athletic realm began to take shape in junior high. By then, he had already become one of Norfolk's best football and basketball players. He went on to star in both sports at Maury High School. As a quarterback for the school's football team, Chancellor awed coaches and teammates with his dual-threat abilities as a passer and runner. Meanwhile, he excelled on the basketball court with his ability to dunk and grab rebounds from opponents with ease.

During his senior football season, Chancellor passed for more than 2,000 yards and rushed for 500 yards, en route to leading Maury to a 10–2 record and an appearance in the Group AAA Division 5 playoffs. It was during those playoffs when he first displayed glimpses of his potential as a safety, which he occasionally split time at in high school in addition to his quarterback responsibilities. In his senior year he accepted a scholarship offer to play quarterback at Virginia Tech University, in Blacksburg.

Chancellor's time playing quarterback quickly came to an end, however, once he arrived at Virginia Tech in the fall of 2006. Intrigued by his size, coaches auditioned Chancellor at the cornerback position and were impressed enough to convert him into a full-time defender soon thereafter. After playing cornerback and the rover position—a safety-linebacker hybrid—during his freshman and sophomore seasons, respectively, Chancellor was moved to safety full-time as a junior. In four seasons with the Hokies, he started

forty-one of fifty-four career games, recording 208 tackles and six interceptions.

Entering the 2010 NFL Draft, Chancellor was projected by scouts and analysts to be an early-round selection. Some teams, however, expressed concerns about his flexibility due to his six-foot-three-inch height, which is considered tall for an NFL safety. Consequently, he dropped to the fifth round of the draft. He was selected 133rd overall by the Seattle Seahawks, who used their first-round pick that year to select the Texas Longhorns' free safety Earl Thomas. At Chancellor's first NFL training camp, he put to rest any doubts about his ability.

ALL-PRO ENFORCER

As a rookie during the 2010 season, Chancellor played mostly on special teams while getting acclimated to the NFL game under the tutelage of veteran strong safety Lawyer Milloy. He appeared as an extra defensive back in various team defensive packages. Finishing second on the Seahawks with 11 special-teams tackles, Chancellor "definitely was a young guy on a mission," as Milloy put it to Mays, referring to his pupil's unwavering eagerness to learn. The Seahawks won the National Football Conference (NFC) West Division with a 7–9 record and advanced to the second round of the playoffs, becoming the first team with a sub-.500 regular-season record to accomplish both feats.

When Milloy retired that offseason, Chancellor assumed his starting strong safety role. He was also charged by the Seahawks' head coach Pete Carroll with taking Milloy's place as vocal leader of the Seahawks' defense. He soon proved his leadership abilities, starting fifteen games in 2011 and earning his first career Pro Bowl selection after finishing second on the team in tackles (97) and interceptions (four).

During the 2012 season, Chancellor firmly established himself as one of the top safeties in the game. Capable of effectively and forcefully playing both the run and the pass, he became the enforcer of a formidable Seahawks secondary that included Thomas and cornerbacks Richard Sherman and Brandon Browner. Together, the quartet came to be known around the league as the "Legion of Boom," a nickname inspired by their propensity to "lay the boom" on opponents, as Chancellor first mentioned in a radio interview prior to that season.

Chancellor himself earned the nickname "Bam Bam" for his tendency to obliterate opponents with ultraviolent hits. One of the first of these to gain him leaguewide fame occurred during a 2012 week-sixteen contest against the San Francisco 49ers, in which he upended the 49ers' tight end Vernon Davis as he tried to make a sideline catch. He amassed 101 combined tackles that season for a dominant Seahawks defense that led the NFL in fewest points allowed. The Seahawks finished with an 11–5 record and returned to the playoffs after a one-year absence.

SUPER BOWL CHAMPIONS

The Seahawks would again lead the league in scoring defense in 2013, 2014, and 2015. Those years saw the team emerge as a perennial title contender, thanks largely in part to Chancellor and his defensive backfield mates. In 2013, they played a pivotal role in the Seahawks advancing to the Super Bowl, as the team also led the league in total defense, passing defense, total takeaways, and turnover margin. Chancellor started all sixteen games for the second consecutive season and recorded 99 tackles and three interceptions. He earned his second career Pro Bowl nod and received the first of two straight second-team All-Pro selections.

In Super Bowl XLVIII, Chancellor helped set the tone early after delivering a crushing hit to the Denver Broncos' wide receiver Demaryius Thomas in the game's opening minutes. The Seahawks would thoroughly dominate the Broncos for the remainder of the game, defeating them 43–8 to earn the franchise's first NFL title. Chancellor finished with 10 combined tackles, an interception, and two passes defensed, but was forced to spend the ensuing three days in a hospital to recover from trauma and internal bleeding. Recognizing his willingness to sacrifice his body on every play, the Seahawks awarded him a five-year, $34 million contract extension that offseason, during which he underwent hip surgery.

In 2014, Chancellor was voted a defensive team captain and helped the Seahawks return to the Super Bowl. After fully recovering from hip surgery and from a nagging groin injury that sidelined him for two games, he returned to form during the second half of that season. He had one of the most memorable games of his career during a matchup against the Carolina Panthers in the NFC divisional playoff round. He recorded 11 combined tackles, a ninety-yard interception return for a touchdown, and two perfectly timed leaps over the Panthers' offensive line to block a field goal attempt. After the game, Richard Sherman said that Chancellor "damages people's souls," as quoted by Tony Drovetto for *Seahawks.com* (10 Jan. 2015). "He plays in a dark place. We feed off of him all game long. He's an intimidator, aggressive ball player, and he plays by the rules."

In Super Bowl XLIX, Chancellor recorded 10 tackles despite suffering a medial-collateral ligament injury in his knee just two days before the game. The Seahawks, though, failed to win a second consecutive NFL title after losing to the New England Patriots, 28–24, on a dramatic last-minute touchdown.

EARLY RETIREMENT

During the 2015 offseason, Chancellor, who also had bone spurs in his feet and balky ankles, opted not to have surgery on his knee. However, he resolved to negotiate a better contract with the Seahawks to ensure financial security for his long-term future, which was already in jeopardy due to his injuries. The team initially resisted his demands, forcing him to hold out for the first fifty-three days of the 2015 season.

After the Seahawks opened that season 0–2, Chancellor returned to the team. The Seahawks won eight of their last ten games to finish with a 10–6 record but were eliminated from playoff contention after losing to the Panthers, 24–31, in the NFC divisional round. Though receiving a fourth career Pro Bowl nod for his regular-season performance, Chancellor acknowledged that his holdout was a mistake, having an adverse effect on the team's chemistry. "I learned that this is a business. This is the NFL. But more importantly, it's about a brotherhood," he told Bell.

Chancellor was again named a defensive team captain prior to the 2016 season, in which he was limited to twelve games due to injuries. In August 2017, he earned his long-awaited contract extension from the Seahawks, agreeing to terms on a three-year deal that included $25 million in guaranteed money. Chancellor appeared in just nine games that season, which was abruptly cut short after he sustained a serious neck injury while making an awkward tackle in the waning moments of Seattle's week-ten 22–16 victory over the Arizona Cardinals.

In July 2018, Chancellor announced his commitment to retiring from football after a series of neck scans showed inadequate progress, creating a heightened risk of paralysis if he continued playing. Later that month he was placed on the Seahawks' reserve/physically-unable-to-perform list for the 2018 season after being deemed medically ineligible to play by team doctors. Because he remains on the team's payroll, he is eligible to receive $12 million in guaranteed money for the last two years of his 2017 contract.

PERSONAL LIFE

Off the field, Chancellor has been known for his many charitable endeavors, which include founding the Kam Cares Foundation, which helps benefit underprivileged children in Seattle and in the Norfolk/Hampton Roads area where he grew up. In July 2017, Chancellor married his longtime girlfriend, Tiffany Luce, in a ceremony held at the Terranea Resort outside of Los Angeles, California. He is a dedicated Christian.

SUGGESTED READING

Bell, Gregg. "What Kam Chancellor Learned Holding Out Last Year." *The Olympian,* 7

Sept. 2016, www.theolympian.com/sports/nfl/seattle-seahawks/article100088142.html. Accessed 28 Aug. 2018.

Drovetto, Tony. "Richard Sherman on Kam Chancellor: 'He Damages People's Souls.'" *Seahawks.com*, 10 Jan. 2015, www.seahawks.com/news/richard-sherman-on-kam-chancellor-he-damages-people-s-souls-115406. Accessed 28 Aug. 2018.

Mays, Robert. "Beware the Visor." *Grantland*, ESPN Internet Ventures, 29 Jan. 2015, grantland.com/features/kam-chancellor-seattle-seahawks-super-bowl/. Accessed 28 Aug. 2018.

Phillips, Michael. "For Chancellor, Success Means Helping Family." *Richmond Times-Dispatch*, 31 Jan. 2014, www.richmond.com/sports/professional/football/superbowl/for-chancellor-success-means-helping-family/article_e42509ab-3e7b-531b-b093-a50830b-6db4f.html. Accessed 28 Aug. 2018.

Robertson, Jimmie. "Humble Beginnings." *Inside Hokie Sports*, 11 Aug. 2009, inside.hokiesports.com/issues/2.1/20090811aae.php. Accessed 28 Aug. 2018.

Saslow, Eli. "Leading the Boom." *ESPN*, 30 Nov. 2016, www.espn.com/espn/feature/story/_/id/18158453/how-kam-chancellor-became-soul-seattle-seahawks. Accessed 28 Aug. 2018.

—*Chris Cullen*

Photo by Stefanie Keenan/Getty Images for *W* Magazine

Hong Chau

Date of birth: 1979
Occupation: Actor

Hong Chau first came to the attention of audiences in the second season of the critically acclaimed HBO television series *Treme* (2010–13), which followed its characters as they tried to rebuild their lives in post–Hurricane Katrina New Orleans. She remained with the series until it ended, then landed her first feature-film role—a small part in Paul Thomas Anderson's noir-inflected comedy-drama *Inherent Vice* (2014). Subsequent job offers were few and far between; in the year following the film's release, she could not land a single film audition. That all changed when she was cast as political dissident Ngoc Lan Tran in Alexander Payne's genre-bending science-fiction satire *Downsizing* (2017).

Tran, Chau has said, is a character that any actor would be lucky to play. "She gets to be funny. She gets to be a pain. . . . She gets to be heroic," she said to Rebecca Ford for the *Hollywood Reporter* (5 Sept. 2017). "You don't get that all in one character often." Even more important, according to Chau, is that a character such as

Tran—a disabled Vietnamese woman—is placed in the spotlight at all. "We have seen glimpses of this character but only in the background," she said to Lisa Rosen for the *Los Angeles Times* (21 Dec. 2017), "so to give a character like this the screen time and the attention and the complexity is what I have been waiting for, as not just an actor, but as a person who loves film."

EARLY LIFE

Hong Chau's parents and older brother fled Vietnam in 1979, during the tumultuous period following the end of the Vietnam War. Chau's mother was six months pregnant with her when they made their treacherous escape as part of the massive group generally referred to as the "boat people." (Historians estimate that some two million Vietnamese fled the brutal Communist regime between 1975 and 1995, with eight hundred thousand risking a voyage across the South China Sea to other countries on crowded, unsafe vessels that were regularly attacked by pirates.) Chau's mother gave birth to her while the family was living in a refugee camp in Thailand. Her father had been shot by government guards as they raced to the water, and he was so bloodied that the malefactors who attacked their boat did not deign to search his pockets, leaving the family in better shape than many in the refugee camp as they retained a small amount of money.

During Chau's infancy, a Vietnamese Catholic church located in New Orleans, Louisiana, sponsored the family and arranged for them to move to the United States. The trip marked the first time they had been on an airplane. The Chaus initially lived with a Vietnamese family who had arrived in New Orleans a few years previously before striking out on their own. Chau's parents, who spoke no English, took on menial service jobs to make a life for themselves and their children. They later ran a neighborhood bodega. On occasion, they received public assistance, including reduced-price school lunches for their children.

Chau grew up speaking Vietnamese and remains fluent in the language. Speaking to Jodi Guglielmi for *People* magazine (5 Jan. 2018), she revealed that she did not start learning English until she entered school, and that she has still never spoken English to her parents. "I'm so grateful that they continued to speak Vietnamese with me and didn't really abandon our culture," she said.

EDUCATION

Growing up, Chau attended a succession of New Orleans public schools, including Eleanor McMain Secondary School and Benjamin Franklin High School, before graduating from the Louisiana School for Math, Science, and the Arts, a public and selective magnet boarding school located in Natchitoches, four hours from the city. While in school, she did not participate in drama classes or student productions, choosing instead to compete in events such as the Science Olympiad.

Nor did she ever consider an acting career. "Growing up the way I did, being an actor in Hollywood was definitely never a plausible career choice at all," Chau recalled to Guglielmi. Deeply introverted, she began to take public speaking and improvisation classes as a way to combat her shyness. "It was never about becoming an actor," she said. "I started going on auditions just as a dare to myself—that was like my version of *Fear Factor*."

After high school, Chau attended Boston University with the assistance of a federal Pell Grant. She initially studied creative writing, but when her parents worried about the impracticality of that major, she switched to film studies, reasoning that the subject would allow her to be involved in storytelling of another sort. "I chose film because it's a trade," she said to Taryn Nobil for *Variety* (8 Dec. 2017). "I was wrong about it being practical." With a new goal of becoming a documentary filmmaker, Chau took on several student internships, including one cleaning lenses and filters at a camera company and one working for renowned documentary filmmaker David Sutherland.

EARLY CAREER

Upon graduating, Chau accepted an entry-level job at PBS but wondered if she was truly on the right path. While in college, she had acted in several of her friends' student film projects, prompting one professor to tell her she was "pretty good" and "should stick with it," as she recalled to Dave Walker for the New Orleans *Times-Picayune* (18 Nov. 2012). With this encouragement, she moved to New York, where she worked a series of odd jobs while taking acting lessons. She eventually signed with an agent and began winning small roles. "A lot of it was student films and bad Off-Off-Broadway," she said to Walker. "You meet lots of great people that way, doing really awful things together."

Chau's first major role came in 2006, when she costarred in *Finding My America*, a quasi-reality miniseries produced by the now-defunct ImaginAsian TV. In it, she and actor Jackie Chung played two friends on a road trip from New York to San Francisco. "If you log the hours and divide it by the money," she said to Walker, "it paid 25 cents an hour."

Work in commercials followed, as did a number of one-off television roles that "might not have necessarily had an ethnicity attached to them, but they'd be for the barista, the waitress or the cop," as she said to Patrick Ryan for *USA Today* (21 Dec. 2017). Among those roles, she played a masseuse in a 2008 episode of *The Sarah Silverman Program* (2007–10), a cook in a 2010 episode of the hit sitcom *How I Met Your Mother* (2005–14), and a lab technician in a 2010 episode of the crime procedural *NCIS* (2003–). She also landed a recurring role as Specialist Wing in the short-lived science-fiction web series *Trenches* (2010).

TREME AND OTHER WORK

In 2011 Chau began appearing in the HBO television drama *Treme*, fortuitously set in her hometown of New Orleans. In it, she played Linh, the daughter of a Vietnamese fisherman who becomes enmeshed in a relationship with a drug-addicted street musician. "I was excited there would be a Vietnamese character on the show, regardless of whether I would play the character or not. You never see that, especially a fishing family," she said to Walker.

Following the end of the series in 2013, Chau made her big-screen debut—once again playing a masseuse—in *Inherent Vice*, adapted from the 2009 Thomas Pynchon novel of the same name. Although most reviews focused on leads Joaquin Phoenix and Josh Brolin, reviewer Germain Lussier, writing for the blog */Film* (19 Nov. 2014), praised "newcomer Hong Chau in the film's most bat-s—— but memorable role."

Auditions were still few and far between, however. "I did a regional car commercial and an internet potato chip commercial," she recalled to Bruce Fretts for the *New York Times* (25 Dec. 2017). "I was seriously thinking I needed to quit and get a serious job where I can feed myself and it doesn't kill my soul."

She was heartened, however, to win a recurring role on the little-seen NBC series *A to Z* (2014–15), and in 2015 she returned to the world of Off-Broadway to appear in the premiere run of *John*, by Pulitzer Prize winner Annie Baker. Chau credits the experience with strengthening her acting chops in advance of her breakthrough role. "[*John*] was three-and-a-half hours long, with two intermissions, and it had only four characters, so there was a lot to do," she said to Fretts. "It was my first time having a meaty role. Because of that play, I was not nervous before *Downsizing*. I was ready. It came at the right time in my life."

Chau also raised her profile significantly with a supporting role in the first season (initially billed as a miniseries) of David E. Kelley's HBO series *Big Little Lies* (2017–), which starred Nicole Kidman and Reese Witherspoon. But it was her role as Ngoc Lan Tran that would catch the attention of critics and earn her numerous award nominations.

DOWNSIZING

When Chau first heard that director Alexander Payne was working on a new film, a science-fiction social satire, she knew she wanted to be a part of it; Payne, as she told Mike Scott for the *Times-Picayune* (13 Dec. 2017), "was at the top of" her "secret little dream list" of directors to work with. "I thought, 'Oh, maybe there's a lab tech with a line or two,' because I had been trained to think so small in regards to how I look and what I can play—or what people will allow me to play," she said to Ford. To her surprise, while reading the script, she discovered that the female lead was a Vietnamese political activist named Ngoc Lan Tran, who is shrunk down to a fraction of her size by the Vietnamese government as punishment and escapes to the United States in a shipping box, sustaining injuries during the voyage that result in the amputation of her leg.

Near the end of 2015, Chau wrangled an audition for the part. "It was *right* before Thanksgiving, and [casting director John Jackson] told me, 'What you did was lovely, but you won't hear anything for another two months,'" she recalled to Kate Erbland for *IndieWire* (21 Dec. 2017). Two days later, Payne met with her in person; about a week after that, he called her to personally offer her the role.

To play Tran, a native Vietnamese speaker who began learning English as an adult, Chau modeled her accent and speaking patterns on those of her parents and others she knew while growing up in the heavily Vietnamese area of New Orleans East. She also worked with a Toronto-based amputee consultant and spent time in a rehabilitation center to portray a person more accurately and respectfully wearing

an ill-fitting prosthetic. "That was the huge responsibility that I felt, it wasn't so much about, 'oh, this is an Asian character, so I need to do it this way or that way,' or that it was specifically a disabled character. It was *all* those things, and yet the focus of the story wasn't about any one of those things, it just took somebody as they were and let them be the character," she said to Erbland.

Starring alongside Chau is Matt Damon, playing a hapless occupational therapist who has voluntarily undergone the groundbreaking shrinking process. Although scientists initially invented "downsizing" as a means to combat climate change—and are horrified that it is being used by governments to quell dissidence—Damon's character does so for economic reasons: a dollar goes much further in the bucolic miniaturized communities that have been built to accommodate the doll-sized people.

Chau earned numerous plaudits for her emotive acting, including a 2018 Virtuosos Award from the Santa Barbara International Film Festival and nominations for the 2017 Golden Globe, Critics' Choice Movie, and Screen Actors Guild (SAG) Awards for best supporting female actor. Amid these honors, however, she also received criticism for her character's strong Vietnamese accent and broken English, which many saw as playing to Asian stereotypes.

Chau has remained steadfast in defending her portrayal of Tran, often calling out the assumptions underlying the criticism. "I've had so many interviews with people about the accent, the accent, the accent," she said to Boris Kachka for *Vulture* (12 Dec. 2017). "It's a necessary conversation but not a very fun conversation. Because when I look at my parents, I don't see a stereotype. . . . Those seem like very innocent questions [about the character's background and accent], but the overall effect of having to answer that is a bit dehumanizing to me, because I have to sit there and explain to another human being why somebody who looks like me and sounds like my parents deserves to exist onscreen."

PERSONAL LIFE

Chau lives in Los Angeles with her dog, Kobe. She remains close to her parents, who evacuated to Dallas, Texas, after the family's home was destroyed by Hurricane Katrina in 2005, and who have since opened a bodega. "They're always in my life," she said of her parents to James Mottram for the *Independent* (21 Jan. 2018). "I am who I am because of them and whatever strength or ability to not shrink comes from them. . . . They have had such a hard life and yet they laugh the hardest."

SUGGESTED READING

Chau, Hong. "*Downsizing*'s Hong Chau Is Sick of Talking about That Accent." Interview by Boris Kachka. *Vulture*, New York Media, 12 Dec. 2017, www.vulture.com/2017/12/downsizing-q-and-a-with-hong-chau.html. Accessed 5 June 2018.

Erbland, Kate. "*Downsizing* Breakout Hong Chau on Her Controversial Accent and Playing a Disabled Character Respectfully." *IndieWire*, Penske Business Media, 21 Dec. 2017, www.indiewire.com/2017/12/downsizing-hong-chau-controversial-accent-disabled-character-1201909841/. Accessed 5 June 2018.

Ford, Rebecca. "Hollywood's Next Big Thing: *Downsizing* Breakout Hong Chau on Asian Typecasting and Working with Matt Damon." *The Hollywood Reporter*, 5 Sept. 2017, www.hollywoodreporter.com/news/hollywoods-next-big-thing-downsizing-breakout-hong-chau-asian-typecasting-working-matt-damon-1034594. Accessed 5 June 2018.

Fretts, Bruce. "*Downsizing* Actress Breaks Through, for Better and Worse." *The New York Times*, 25 Dec. 2017, www.nytimes.com/2017/12/25/movies/hong-chau-downsizing-stereotyping.html. Accessed 5 June 2018.

Guglielmi, Jodi. "Five Things to Know about *Downsizing* Star and Golden Globe Nominee Hong Chau." *People*, 5 Jan. 2018, people.com/movies/five-things-to-know-about-downsizing-star-and-golden-globe-nominee-hong-chau/. Accessed 5 June 2018.

Walker, Dave. "Actress Hong Chau Brings New Orleans Background to Role as *Treme*'s Linh." *The Times-Picayune*, 18 Nov. 2012, www.nola.com/treme-hbo/index.ssf/2012/11/actress_hong_chau_brings_new_o.html. Accessed 5 June 2018.

SELECTED WORKS

Treme, 2011–13; *Inherent Vice*, 2014; *A to Z*, 2014–15; *Big Little Lies*, 2017; *Downsizing*, 2017; *Duck Butter*, 2018

—Mari Rich

Luke Combs

Date of birth: March 2, 1990
Occupation: Singer, songwriter

Though self-made singer and songwriter Luke Combs is still relatively new to the industrial country music scene, he has made an undeniable impression in a short amount of time. In addition to featuring three successive number-one singles, his debut full-length album, *This One's*

clintonbrannen, via Wikimedia Commons

for You, reached the top spot on the Billboard Top Country Albums chart and stayed there for a total of six weeks following its release in June 2017. Critics, several of whom considered the record one of the genre's best of the year, have noted that Combs's unique, fresh look and style have helped him to stand out in a saturated market. "There's a perception these days (not entirely unfounded) that country music rewards its male performers for following a particular formula. The combination of gleaming, rhythmic Top 40 hooks, flirtatious frat-party swagger and small-town backdrops has served as a pattern in the industry, largely because it works," Jewly Hight wrote in a review of *This One's for You* for National Public Radio (25 May 2017). "For Luke Combs, though, demonstrating current pop fluency *and* a connection with the sturdy contributions of previous generations of country performers aren't mutually exclusive propositions."

Having struggled independently for years to find his way and have his music shared with the world, Combs himself has expressed some astonishment at his newfound fame. Referencing the 2017 Country Music Association (CMA) Awards, where he received a nomination for that year's best new artist and served as a presenter, he told Nancy Kruh for *People* (10 Dec. 2017), "A year ago I was watching TV, eating pizza at a buddy of mine's house, and we were talking about how I was hopefully going to be there next year." He intends, he has said, to always keep his humble beginnings in mind. Additionally, he is savvy enough to know that his image, including his scruffy beard, likely holds a key to his popularity and relatability. "I think my cool factor is not having one," he quipped to Chris Parton for *Rolling Stone* (30 Jan. 2017).

EARLY LIFE AND EDUCATION

Luke Combs was born on March 2, 1990, and largely raised in Asheville, North Carolina. His parents have said that he began singing at a very young age, evincing a fondness for country star Vince Gill, whose name he mispronounced as "Vince Skittles." He sang in his middle school chorus, and he continued to perform once he entered Asheville's A. C. Reynolds High School, where he also played on the football team.

After graduating from Reynolds in 2008, Combs entered Appalachian State University in Boone, North Carolina, studying first business (despite his dislike of math) and then switching to criminal justice. He played on the school's rugby team and, as he has admitted, shunned most of his homework in favor of video games. He also rediscovered his love for country music in earnest, particularly when he was encouraged to listen to the new Eric Church album.

Restless during one summer break as his friends stayed in their respective college towns, he decided to learn to play the guitar that his parents had bought him several years prior, gradually teaching himself the chords. "I've always been a small goals kind of guy," he recalled to Parton. "When I picked up guitar it wasn't like, 'Ok, I'm going to be Kenny Chesney.' It was like, 'I want to play a chord,' and then it was like, 'I want to play another one, then play a song, then sing while playing the song.'"

STRIKING OUT ON HIS OWN

Juggling school and work, Combs began landing gigs playing and singing a combination of cover songs and original compositions at local venues in his home state. Living in an apartment over a bar called Town Tavern, he worked as a bouncer there (in addition to being employed at an Izod store) to earn extra money. One night, after assuring the manager that the noise would not bother the upstairs tenant, since he was, in fact, the tenant in question, he auditioned by singing the Garth Brooks hit "Friends in Low Places." That unassuming bar became one of his first regular gigs, and other local venues continued to follow. Because of his reputation as "the ball cap-wearing, fun-time guy whom everyone knew," as Cindy Watts wrote for the *Tennessean* (29 June 2017), his friends eagerly attended those early shows, and his fan base grew exponentially. Talking to Watts about the dingy unit above the Town Tavern, he joked, "208 Faculty Street, Apartment 3, where the dreams came true."

Despite that humorous self-deprecation, his ambition had been sparked by his local successes, and after visiting Nashville during spring break in 2013, he began posting clips of himself covering popular country songs on social media. He gradually reached about thirty thousand followers, self-released an EP—titled *The Way She Rides*—that sold thousands of copies in early 2014, and began attracting hundreds of fans to his live performances. "I didn't even know what a tour manager was, but I was the tour manager, booking agent, all that stuff," he recalled to Parton. "I wasn't overwhelmed because I enjoyed doing it." In the summer, he independently released a second EP, *Can I Get an Outlaw*.

In the fall of 2014, just a few credits shy of earning his college degree, reinforced by the financial success of his EPs and facing the end of his apartment lease, he dropped out of school and moved to Nashville to pursue a music career in earnest. "I got to this point where I was like, I can't expand what I'm doing musically, as far as a career, from this small mountain town in North Carolina; I've hit the glass ceiling if I stay in this town," he explained to Gayle Thompson for the website *The Boot* (2 June 2017).

BREAKING THROUGH WITH "HURRICANE"

In late 2014, a few months after he had moved to Nashville, known colloquially as Music City for its status as the seat of American country music, Combs was introduced to songwriters Taylor Phillips, who also hailed from North Carolina, and Thomas Archer. The three collaborated on the tune "Hurricane," which is narrated by a man who is simply trying to relax at a bar when his ex-lover suddenly walks in. The song was inspired by one of their friend's breakup. Combs intended the track to be part of a new, self-released six-song EP that would be produced by country music veteran Scott Moffatt. (Reportedly, the two sealed their deal in the parking lot of a Nashville Waffle House.)

The singer was shocked when Moffatt informed him that the tracks would need to be "mastered," the process of fine-tuning audio elements and fixing minor flaws. Previously, he had never mastered his self-released music, and he was dismayed to learn that the going rate for professional mastering was $200 a song, which he did not have. He ultimately decided to get "Hurricane" ready for release as a single, in hopes that it would earn him enough to master the other tracks; he and his cowriters were not prepared for the runaway, breakout success that the song would become.

"Hurricane" appeared on iTunes in June 2015 and sold some fifteen thousand copies during the first week alone, landing at number forty-six on the Billboard Hot Country Songs chart. The revenue from those sales easily allowed Combs to finish and release the rest of the EP (titled *This One's for You*) later that year. He then toured in support of the EP, and his social media presence continued to grow. By the fall of 2016, "Hurricane" had been streamed more than twenty million times, and Combs had been cited by several industry publications as an artist to watch. "I guess I [don't] focus too much on why they like it," he told Emily Yahr for the *Washington Post* (1 June 2017). "I'm just glad they do."

A LABEL AND A DEBUT ALBUM

In October 2016, Combs was signed to major label Columbia Nashville in partnership with River House Artists. The label immediately re-released "Hurricane" as a single, which reached the top of the Billboard Country Airplay Chart in May 2017. In June, his full-length debut album, also titled *This One's for You*, came out, claiming the number-one spot on the Billboard Top Country Albums chart, going gold within just months, and becoming the top-selling debut from a country artist in 2017. The editors of *Rolling Stone* (5 July 2017) included it on their list of "25 Best Country and Americana Albums of 2017 So Far," writing, "New artists' debut albums are rarely so cohesive, engaging and altogether satisfying. But Combs hits all those marks on *This One's for You*."

Further living out his dream, Combs, who had begun opening for fellow country artist Brantley Gilbert on an arena tour early in the year, joined him for a summer leg before beginning his first major headlining tour that fall. "When I come do a show, I want people in the crowd to go, 'Man, he seems like a genuine, nice guy that I could sit down and have a beer with,'" he told Steve Wildsmith for the Blount County *Daily Times* (25 Jan. 2017) of his performance philosophy. Subsequent hit singles from *This One's for You* have included "When It Rains It Pours" and "One Number Away," which, like "Hurricane," reached number one on the Billboard Country Airplay chart. In May 2018, Combs, Jason Aldean, and Lauren Alaina joined forces for a tour, which kicked off in Kansas City. That summer, approximately one year after the original release of the full-length version of *This One's for You*, he also reissued the album as *This One's for You Too* with five new songs added.

PERSONAL LIFE

As of mid-2018, Combs was dating Nicole Hocking. Following the success of his debut album, he had given some of his new fortune to his parents, helping his father to be able to retire, and he was reportedly looking to buy a house in the Nashville area.

On October 1, 2017, Combs played at the Route 91 Harvest Festival in Las Vegas, Nevada. After he finished his set, he wandered over to the main stage with his manager to watch headliner Aldean play. He was standing on the side of the stage when a gunman began shooting from a high floor of the Mandalay Bay Resort & Casino across from the festival, killing dozens of people and wounding hundreds more. Because of his proximity, Combs was interviewed widely in the wake of the massacre, and he described thinking at first that the gunfire was stage pyrotechnics. Refusing to be cowed by the harrowing event, he paid tribute to the victims with a performance on *Jimmy Kimmel Live!* hours after the incident and continues to tour widely.

SUGGESTED READING

Hight, Jewly. Review of *This One's for You*, by Luke Combs. *NPR*, 25 May 2017, www.npr.org/2017/05/25/529538447/first-listen-luke-combs-this-ones-for-you. Accessed 10 June 2018.

Kruh, Nancy. "Inside Luke Combs' Fast Rise from Couch Potato to CMA Awards Nominee." *People*, 10 Dec. 2017, people.com/country/luke-combs-fast-rise-couch-potato-to-cma-awards-nominee/. Accessed 10 June 2018.

Parton, Chris. "Inside 'Hurricane' Singer Luke Combs' Unlikely Success." *Rolling Stone*, 30 Jan. 2017, www.rollingstone.com/music/music-country/inside-hurricane-singer-luke-combs-unlikely-success-129126/. Accessed 10 June 2018.

Roland, Tom. "Newcomer Luke Combs Blows into Mainstream with 'Hurricane.'" *Billboard*, 25 Oct. 2016, www.billboard.com/articles/columns/country/7550035/newcomer-luke-combs-blows-into-mainstream-with-hurricane. Accessed 10 June 2018.

Watts, Cindy. "Luke Combs Forges Own Path, Finds Hurricane of Fame." *Tennessean*, 29 June 2017, www.tennessean.com/story/entertainment/music/cma-music-festival/2017/06/29/luke-combs-forges-own-path-finds-hurricane-fame/387163001/. Accessed 10 June 2018.

Wildsmith, Steve. "Rising Star: Luke Combs Stays True to His Humble North Carolina Roots." *The Daily Times*, 25 Jan. 2017, www.thedailytimes.com/entertainment/rising-star-luke-combs-stays-true-to-his-humble-north/article_48c83998-25fa-57ca-b3d7-820a565fd020.html. Accessed 10 June 2018.

—*Mari Rich*

Beth Comstock

Date of birth: August 30, 1960
Occupation: Business executive

Beth Comstock has ranked on *Forbes* and *Fortune* magazines' lists of the world's most powerful

By Joi Ito [CC BY 2.0], via Wikimedia Commons

women multiple times. The first female vice chair in the history of the multibillion global conglomerate General Electric (GE), Comstock ascended to that post in August 2015 and took charge of GE Business Innovations, with her responsibilities encompassing corporate marketing and communications, sales, and other vital areas of the company, such as GE Lighting, with three billion dollars in annual sales. Business journalists have noted that stakeholders have been counting on Comstock to not only run GE's legacy lighting business but to bring GE more fully into the modern era.

"It's all part of her realization that there's a new chapter for marketing, and new tools for marketing, which are fundamentally about connecting disparate data and operations and people, and they have invaded practically everything," Steven Butler wrote for the online news site *OZY* (25 Jan. 2016). "In Comstock's case, it creates a spread that has seemingly no limits in a company whose products range from gas turbines and light bulbs to locomotives." Comstock herself remarked to Daniel Long in an interview for *W & M* (19 Aug. 2016), a magazine published by her alma mater, the College of William and Mary: "We're sort of at the intersection of industrial and digital. . . . It's about being an engine of progress for the world."

In October 2017, Comstock announced her intention to retire from GE at the end of the year—a move she says will allow her to pursue new career paths. Whatever she chooses to do next, industry insiders agree that she has made an indelible mark on GE. "When you achieve a first within a company that started with Edison's

light bulb, suffice it to say, you've done something," Long wrote.

EARLY YEARS AND EDUCATION

Elizabeth J. Comstock grew up in Winchester, Virginia, a close-knit town nestled in the Shenandoah Valley. Her father, Gene, was a dentist, and her mother, Shelby, was a teacher. While her father was somewhat quiet and introspective, her mother was jokingly known as the unofficial "mayor" of Winchester because of her winning nature, friendliness, and involvement in the community. Comstock has quipped that if her mother sat next to a stranger on an airplane, she would know their entire life story by the end of the flight. "My parents had a strong influence on my leadership style as my father is more reserved and creative, while my mom is very outgoing," Comstock told Dan Schawbel for *Forbes* (20 Oct. 2016). "While I more naturally sided with my father's tendencies, I recognized the advantages that come with my mom's inquisitive and talkative style and have tried to combine both into my own leadership."

Comstock has described her childhood as relatively idyllic, with plenty of neighborhood friends, Girl Scouts, and cheerleading. "I was involved in pretty much anything you could get involved in," she recalled to Butler. She attended the College of William and Mary, in Williamsburg, Virginia, where she majored in biology, thinking she might become a doctor or science journalist. "I never expected biology to play out in my marketing and business career," she told Long, "but biology's taught me a lot about ecosystems and the way the world collaborates. For any system to work well, each thing has to have its role, and one depends on the other. It's good to be reminded of that in business."

Upon graduating in 1982, Comstock decided to try her hand at television news rather than following a path directly related to science or medicine. She found work at a television service in Richmond, Virginia, working in various capacities behind the scenes and occasionally appearing on camera to report on the state government. With an eye to advancing to a full-time, on-air gig, she began inundating the news director of a high-profile station with phone calls and audition tapes, and she has told interviewers that his brutal rejection turned out to be a favor that helped her develop backbone and tenacity.

EARLY BUSINESS CAREER

Comstock next embarked on a series of jobs in communications and public relations at a variety of large media companies. In 1990 she joined Turner Broadcasting, where she oversaw CNN, TNT, and TBS. From 1996 to 1998 she served as a senior vice president of corporate communications at NBC News, a post that she had some trepidation about accepting. Mainstream network news was not considered a growth industry then, and her mentors advised her it could prove to be a bad career move to take the position, which had remained open for more than six months. Still, she decided to make the leap, reasoning that she would be able to shake things up and make her own mark in the position.

NBC was then owned by GE, a company with a long and storied history. It had been incorporated back in 1892 with the merger of inventor Thomas Alva Edison's Edison General Electric Company and two competitors. (Edison had founded his original firm, the Edison Electric Light Company, in 1878, in order to market the incandescent lamp and other products. After 1892, he remained on as a consultant.)

Comstock did, in fact, make a mark at NBC, helping to launch MSNBC, a cable and satellite television network providing news coverage and political commentary. In 1998 Comstock became the vice president of corporate communications at GE. "I got to work with two legendary businessmen: [former GE chairman] Jack Welch and [Microsoft founder] Bill Gates," she said during a Wharton Leadership Lecture at the University of Pennsylvania, as quoted on the school's website (8 May 2013). "I was a small town girl with no graduate degree, but GE turned into my finishing school, my business school, all because I took a challenge."

CHIEF EXECUTIVE

In 2003 Comstock ascended to chief marketing officer at GE, the first person to be given that title at the company in more than twenty years. In that post, she oversaw marketing and sales development and was responsible for cross-business programs within the massive conglomerate. Under her leadership, she shepherded the eighteen-month development of a new slogan, moving the company from its venerable, twenty-four-year old slogan "We Bring Good Things to Life" to "Imagination at Work." As she explained in her Wharton lecture, "We really felt this brought back the spirit of Thomas Edison. You have to have passion and curiosity to succeed in what we believe we are—a company that brings products into a quickly moving world."

In 2006 Comstock became the president of Integrated Media at NBC Universal, in which capacity she oversaw the company's digital efforts, including the preliminary stages of the streaming service Hulu and the acquisition of the now-defunct iVillage.com, a media company aimed at women. In 2008 Comstock became the chief marketing and commercial officer at GE, charged with a wide-ranging portfolio of duties, including growth and innovation initiatives in such areas as health and sustainability. She has told journalists of the company's efforts to make the world greener and healthier with pride, pointing to its work with technologies like high-tech batteries, cell phone grids, and simpler ultrasound machines that can be more easily used in developing countries. Those initiatives resonated deeply with her and spoke to her longtime interest in science and technology. "My career trajectory makes no sense. Absolutely no sense," she marveled to Lena Dunham in an interview for *Lenny* magazine (19 July 2016). "I got out of school thinking I was going to be a doctor. Then I really wanted to be a science reporter, so I got into media. But I was horrible on camera. Really horrible, really bad. I learned that I was much better behind the scenes. So I got into marketing. One thing leads to another, and I worked my way through NBC. Then I end up at GE, which was the last place on earth I expected to be. But it makes a lot of sense. I love science. My science background is a thread that goes through my career."

VICE CHAIR AT GE

Comstock reached the pinnacle of her career at GE in August 2015, when she was named vice chair. In this position, she took charge of finding and leading new growth opportunities. "She's morphed into the person who's digitizing GE businesses," business analyst Nicholas Heymann explained to Butler. "She laid the groundwork for the rebirth of GE." Although some of her efforts fell flat—her belief in a failed startup named Quirky, in which GE invested $30 million, was derided by business analysts, for example—Comstock found it invigorating to be on the frontlines. "I think this idea of what it means to be a digital industrial company is very exciting," Comstock told Long. "In bringing the Internet to industry, we have the ability to connect every piece of machinery—a jet engine, a wind turbine. . . . Over time you can start to predict when things are going to happen and make companies more efficient."

Comstock also oversaw the introduction of lean-startup principles to several industrial teams at GE, an initiative that was so successful it spread to multiple GE units and ultimately to the company's top executives. "Such experiments were unorthodox at GE," Geoff Colvin wrote in an article for *Fortune* (14 Sept. 2016). "But Comstock—direct, fast-paced, articulate—has a way of making the ambitious and unorthodox sound logical and matter-of-fact, even obvious."

In October 2017 Comstock, who is also a member of Nike's Board of Directors and a trustee of the Cooper Hewitt Smithsonian Design Museum, announced that she would be leaving GE within a few months. "I love the company, its people and purpose. I am proud to have been a part of shaping its future," she wrote in a post to

Facebook (6 Oct. 2017). "Now it's time for me to do one of the things I love to do—explore what's next. This time for me. Among those things, I am finishing a book, appropriately enough, about change." Insiders speculate that the move, part of a wider executive shakeup at GE, came because of falling stock valuation and subsequent streamlining and cost-cutting measures.

PERSONAL LIFE

Comstock's first marriage ended in divorce when she was in her mid-twenties. She later married businessman Chris Travers. She has two adult daughters.

SUGGESTED READING

Butler, Steven. "The Woman Who's Lighting Up the Digital World for GE." *OZY*, 25 Jan. 2016, www.ozy.com/rising-stars/the-woman-whos-lighting-up-the-digital-world-for-ge/66602. Accessed 2 Nov. 2017.

Colvin, Geoff. "How Beth Comstock Is Lighting Up GE." *Fortune*, 14 Sept. 2016, fortune.com/beth-comstock-general-electric-most-powerful-women. Accessed 2 Nov. 2017.

Comstock, Beth. "Beth Comstock: Being an Introverted Leader in an Extroverted Business World." Interview by Dan Schawbel. *Forbes*, 20 Oct. 2016, www.forbes.com/sites/danschawbel/2016/10/20/beth-comstock-being-an-introverted-leader-in-an-extroverted-business-world/2/#2f94a5561c6f. Accessed 2 Nov. 2017.

Comstock, Beth. "Beth Comstock of General Electric: Granting Permission to Innovate." Interview by Adam Bryant. *The New York Times*, 17 June 2016, www.nytimes.com/2016/06/19/business/granting-permission-to-try-something-new.html. Accessed 2 Nov. 2017.

Dunham, Lena. "The GE Executive Pulling Women Up the Ladder with Her." *Lenny*, 19 July 2016, www.lennyletter.com/work/interviews/a390/ge-executive-pulling-women-up-the-ladder-with-her. Accessed 2 Nov. 2017.

Long, Daniel. "Bright Lights, Big Apple." *W&M Alumni Magazine*, 19 Aug. 2016, www.wm.edu/news/stories/2016/bright-lights,-big-apple.php. Accessed 24 Oct. 2017.

Sellers, Patricia. "GE Names a New Vice Chair, and She Is . . ." *Fortune*, 1 Sept. 2015, fortune.com/2015/09/01/ge-comstock-vice-chair. Accessed 2 Nov. 2017.

—*Mari Rich*

Jack Conte

Date of birth: July 12, 1984
Occupation: Entrepreneur; musician

Jack Conte is an American entrepreneur and musician best known for making up one half of the indie-pop musical duo Pomplamoose. A graduate of Stanford University, Conte was among the first wave of artists in the mid-2000s to launch a musical career through social media networks. With fellow Stanford alumnus Nataly Dawn, who would become his wife, he formed Pomplamoose in 2008. Releasing one-of-a-kind "video songs" on the video-sharing site YouTube, the group quickly became an Internet sensation and generated millions of followers. They went on to release several digital download albums, most notably *Tribute to Famous People* (2010), which features their signature covers of hit pop songs.

Although Pomplamoose enjoyed success as an independent musical entity, the challenges of maintaining that success prompted Conte to cofound Patreon, a crowdfunding platform, in 2013. The start-up soon developed a reputation as one of the most innovative companies of its kind, enabling artists to earn regular incomes while simultaneously maintaining their creative control. In an interview with Vanessa Hua for *Stanford Magazine* (Mar./Apr. 2015), Conte explained, "As an independent creator, I did everything as a business owner. Doing a start-up, it's like being a musician, but a little easier because people help you."

By https://www.flickr.com/photos/ninja-bear/ via Wikimedia Commons

EARLY LIFE AND EDUCATION

Jack Conte was born on July 12, 1984, in San Francisco, California. He grew up just north of the city in the Marin County town of Corte Madera. Along with his sister, Conte was raised in a musical family. His father, a doctor, was a jazz piano player, and his mother, a nurse, was a jazz singer. Both of his parents performed together and instilled in him an early love of music. At age six he started playing the piano, learning the blues scale from his father.

Conte's parents nurtured his many creative endeavors, which included making films and videos. When Conte was seventeen, he began work on a Claymation video, titled "Black Hat White," which took a total of four summers to complete. The experience introduced him to the intricacies of video production, for which Pomplamoose would later become known. He went on to study music composition at Stanford University, located approximately an hour south of his home in California's Silicon Valley.

At Stanford, Conte started teaching himself the guitar and drums. "After that it snowballed into all the other random instruments," he noted to Jim Aikin for *Keyboard* (31 Jan. 2011), "which I really don't play—I just hack my way through." Playing in various bands, Conte became an early proponent of the video-sharing site YouTube, launched in 2005, which he began using intensively, along with other social media networks, to help broaden his musical exposure. He also produced music for himself and others. Among these collaborators was Nataly Knutsen, who he first met during a gig at CoHo, Stanford's campus coffeehouse.

Connecting over their complementary musical tastes, Conte and Knutsen, who eventually adopted the stage name Nataly Dawn, soon began dating. The couple pursued separate musical projects before they started making YouTube videos together in 2007. By that time Conte had graduated from Stanford and gotten a contract job making corporate videos for Google. He turned down an opportunity to study film at the University of Southern California (USC) after becoming intrigued by YouTube's do-it-yourself (DIY) potential. "It got to be a great community," Conte said of the video site to Ian S. Port for the *Dallas Observer* (24 Feb. 2011). "I thought it was going to be a sort of MySpace-y business thing, and it turned out that it was something really special."

MAKINGS OF AN INTERNET SENSATION

Recognizing their own special partnership and encouraged by the response to their YouTube videos, Conte and Dawn formed Pomplamoose in 2008. As Pomplamoose (the name of an English play based on the French word for grapefruit) the two created a repertoire of songs, both originals and covers, that were marked by their quirky jazz-pop melodies and multi-instrument layering. Port wrote that the duo's original songs "drift among musical styles, threading a deep appreciation for vintage pop and jazz through organ-driven rock, funky R&B and delicate folk."

Pomplamoose is widely credited with popularizing a medium that the band dubbed the "video song," presenting an unvarnished look at the music-making process. Unlike conventional music videos, video songs, according to specific rules created by Conte and Dawn, do not feature lip-syncing or hidden sounds; the videos are shot as the music tracks are being recorded. "We start recording right away," Conte told Aikin. "We don't, like, orchestrate the song first and then go back and film and re-record everything." Both Conte and Dawn sing and play a wide variety of instruments on the tracks. Conte drew on his music background to fill many roles, leading Port to describe him as "a musical Swiss Army knife, the kind of person who can write an arrangement for string ensemble, lay down a densely syncopated drum track and perform complex passages on the piano with aplomb."

Pomplamoose quickly won a strong following on YouTube, where many of their video songs went viral. In 2009 the duo released their self-titled debut album, *Pomplamoose*. Though the album was a digital-only release, accompanying YouTube videos to its songs generated millions of views, helping Conte and Dawn sell approximately 100,000 songs in MP3 format the year of its release. Concurrently, Conte's profile rose through his own independent music projects. He put out two EPs, *Nightmares and Daydreams* and *Sleep in Color*, and three digital download volumes of his video songs between 2007 and 2008. One of those songs, "Yeah Yeah Yeah," featured an accompanying video using stop-motion animation that proved popular.

CARVING AN INDEPENDENT PATH

Later in 2009 Pomplamoose experienced a significant uptick in popularity after Conte and Dawn decided to record covers of well-known pop songs. Among these were a whimsical riff on superstar Beyoncé's number-one hit "Single Ladies (Put a Ring on It)," which soon earned millions of views. The song appears on Pomplamoose's second album, *Tribute to Famous People* (2010), an album of covers that also includes inventive spins on Lady Gaga's "Telephone," Michael Jackson's "Beat It," and Edith Piaf's "La Vie en Rose," the latter of which features Conte playing an ominous-sounding accordion and xylophone.

Made available for purchase through Apple's iTunes store and other digital download sites such as E-Junkie, the cover album sold around 30,000 tracks within a month. It continued to sell well over the following months, enabling both Conte and Dawn to earn enough income to pursue their music careers full-time. Pomplamoose's strong digital sales, coupled with their massive YouTube presence, resulted in them receiving offers from major record companies. However, Conte and Dawn declined them, instead choosing to maintain financial independence and full creative control over their music. They did, however, record a series of holiday songs for a 2010 advertising campaign by automaker Hyundai. That deal gave them greater financial means to pursue their music and exposed them to an even wider audience, though some fans disapproved of the commercial focus.

Pomplamoose released two more digital-only albums, *The Album You Bought at Our Show (Thanks for That)* and *Hey It's Pomplamoose* in 2011 and 2012, respectively. Although the duo remained resolute and committed to keeping their DIY self-sufficiency, download sales of their songs gradually tapered off, forcing them to draw on other revenue sources. Unlike most musicians, however, they largely eschewed live performances, giving only a handful during the first years of their existence. The challenges of running an independent online music business took a toll on Conte and Dawn, and their output of new material declined. They eventually put Pomplamoose on hiatus so both could pursue more creatively fulfilling solo projects.

Conte reached a turning point in his career in 2013, while he was self-financing an extravagant music video. Taking three months to complete and costing more than ten thousand dollars, the video, an electronic, dancing, music (EDM)-inspired number titled "Pedals," features dancing robots and a replica of Han Solo's Millennium Falcon cockpit from *Star Wars*, which Conte built by hand. Though the video was enthusiastically received by fans, it generated only a pittance from YouTube advertising revenue. "It was this rock-bottom moment for me as a creator," Conte told Kathleen Chaykowski for *Forbes* (28 Feb. 2018).

CROWDFUNDING FOR THE LONG-TERM

The "Pedals" experience prompted Conte to form the crowdfunding startup company Patreon, which would help artists like himself get paid for their creative efforts. He cofounded the company, which went live in May 2013, with his Stanford roommate Sam Yam, who had previously helped establish the mobile advertising platform AdWhirl. Unlike crowdfunding sites like Kickstarter and Indiegogo, which feature one-time fundraising campaigns, "Patreon is a website that helps artists make money," as Conte put it to Ryan Tate for *Wired* (22 Oct. 2013). "It's crowdfunding on an ongoing basis for a creator." The company is built around a pledging system

in which fans, or "patrons," pay monthly subscriptions to support their favorite artists. The company welcomes a wide swath of creators, including musicians, writers, podcasters, animators, photographers, and game designers, who can sign up for free.

Conte's gamble that fans would be willing to pay for such a service paid off, and within months after launching, Patreon had already lined up millions in investments from venture capitalists. Despite starting with only three artists, the website was soon used by more than a million fans and an estimated 50,000 creators, with notable names including ukulele performer Cynthia Lin, a cappella group Pentatonix, Chilean illustrator Fran Meneses, and the veteran journalist Tom Merritt. In return for pledging a monthly or per-piece amount of their choosing, fans can be offered exclusive perks, which include everything from live music lessons to unique works.

Pomplamoose also returned to activity in 2013 and made full use of Conte's other venture. The band allowed their Patreon subscribers to download original songs and gave them access to music and video production tutorials, among other things. Subscriber pledges helped Conte and Dawn cover both cost-of-living and business expenses. The importance of Patreon particularly hit home for the duo in the fall of 2014, when they lost money on a twenty-three-city tour despite amassing nearly $100,000 in ticket sales. Conte documented the experience in a blog post that drew considerable backlash, with commenters criticizing his finances and his honesty. He viewed the controversy as further proof of the importance of a tool like Patreon. The bulk of Pomplamoose's revenue soon came from the website, bolstered by additional sales from iTunes and the music licensing platform Loudr. Still, running a media company along with an indie band continued to be challenging. "It's like pushing a boulder up the hill, seven days a week," he told Hua. "But it's been wonderful learning how to do it."

By 2018, Patreon had grown into a San Francisco–headquartered company with one hundred employees and was being valued at an estimated $400 million. Conte announced plans to expand Patreon overseas, where as many as forty percent of its subscribers resided. He also expected the company to eventually foray into small-business services like ticketing and merchandizing. As he told Chaykowski, "Artists don't have to starve anymore."

PERSONAL LIFE

In May 2016, following a short engagement, Conte and Dawn married. The couple split their time between San Francisco and California's

Sonoma County, where they built a home recording studio.

SUGGESTED READING

Aikin, Jim. "Pomplamoose on Reinventing Music Video." *Keyboard*, 31 Jan. 2011, www.keyboardmag.com/artists/pomplamoose-on-reinventing-music-video. Accessed 20 Sept. 2018.

Chaykowski, Kathleen. "Digital Medici: How This Musician-Turned-Entrepreneur Plans to Save Creators from Advertising." *Forbes*, 28 Feb. 2018, www.forbes.com/sites/kathleenchaykowski/2018/02/13/digital-medici-how-this-musician-turned-entrepreneur-plans-to-save-creators-from-advertising. Accessed 20 Sept. 2018.

Hua, Vanessa. "Funds from Fans." *Stanford Alumni*, Mar./Apr. 2015, alumni.stanford.edu/get/page/magazine/article/?article_id=77268. Accessed 20 Sept. 2018.

Port, Ian S. "Pomplamoose's DIY Revolution." *Dallas Observer*, 24 Feb. 2011, www.dallasobserver.com/music/pomplamooses-diy-revolution-6420868. Accessed 20 Sept. 2018.

Tate, Ryan. "The Next Big Thing You Missed: 'Eternal Kickstarter' Reinvents Indie Art." *Wired*, 22 Oct. 2013, www.wired.com/2013/10/big-idea-patreon/. Accessed 20 Sept. 2018.

SELECTED WORKS

Pomplamoose, 2009; *Tribute to Famous People*, 2010; *The Album You Bought at Our Show (Thanks for That)*, 2011; *Hey It's Pomplamoose*, 2012

—*Chris Cullen*

Auli'i Cravalho

Date of birth: November 22, 2000
Occupation: Actor

Auli'i Cravalho is an actor best known for voicing the title character in the Disney film *Moana* (2016). The Hawaiian-born Cravalho won the role when she was just fourteen years old; the film, which became the second-highest-grossing five-day Thanksgiving opener of all time, premiered a day after her sixteenth birthday. Drawn from Polynesian history and mythology, *Moana* is set about two thousand years ago, on a fictional island in the central Pacific Ocean. In it, Moana, the teenage daughter of the island chief, embarks on an adventure to save her people. Cravalho stars alongside Dwayne "The Rock" Johnson, who plays a demigod named Maui.

Photo by Paul Archuleta/FilmMagic

Moana was popular with audiences and praised by critics. It was nominated for two Academy Awards, for best animated feature and best original song, the latter for the song "How Far I'll Go," written by Pulitzer Prize–winning *Hamilton* creator Lin-Manuel Miranda and performed by Cravalho.

Cravalho, who began her senior year of high school in fall 2017, originally planned to study biology or law, but since the release of *Moana* her acting career has flourished. In 2017 she was cast in the new NBC musical drama series *Rise*. The show, slated to premiere in March 2018, is based on the 2013 nonfiction book *Drama High*, by Michael Sokolove, about a working-class town's celebrated high school theater program and the drama teacher who leads it. Cravalho plays one of the students in the program.

EARLY LIFE

Cravalho, known by her family as Chloe, was born in Kohala, on the island of Hawaii, on November 22, 2000. She is of native Hawaiian, Portuguese, Puerto Rican, Irish, and Chinese descent. An only child, she grew up climbing avocado trees and directing plays in her backyard. She and her mother, Puanani, moved to Mililani, on the island of Oahu, when she was nine.

Cravalho's extended family is filled with singers and musicians. Her grandmother wrote Hawaiian music, her uncles performed as a band called the Freitas Brothers in the 1980s, and one of her cousins also auditioned for the role of Moana. In an interview with Julie Kosin for *Harper's Bazaar* (30 Nov. 2016), Cravalho joked that she was belting tunes "straight out of the womb." She added, "I think I've always been singing. I actually credit my singing voice to my mom because she wouldn't give me a pacifier when I was a baby, so I screamed and screamed and screamed and I developed wonderful lungs." She has also been dancing hula, a traditional Polynesian dance, since she was five.

Cravalho attends Kamehameha Schools Kapālama, a private all-Hawaiian school in Honolulu. "We learn everything about being Hawaiian," she said to Diane Daniel for the *New York Times* (17 Nov. 2016). "We have a really deep respect for the water and the land. We say 'mauka to makai,' mountains to ocean. I believe if you take care of the ocean, the ocean will take care of you in return." Cravalho, like the character Moana, feels a deep personal connection to the water, having grown up swimming, surfing, playing water polo, and paddling with a team in an outrigger canoe. "I'm . . . a klutz on land," she confessed to Daniel, "so water is my thing."

MOANA AUDITION

Cravalho was a freshman in high school when she first heard about a casting call for a new Disney movie called *Moana*. "I admit that when I first heard about the film I was a little bit wary," she said to Don Wallace for *Honolulu* magazine (1 Nov. 2016)—partly because she feared she was not talented enough for the role and partly because she worried that Disney might not treat Polynesian culture with respect. In addition, she told Kosin, "the main auditions were happening during my freshman year of high school. Freshman year of high school is confusing as it is, and I decided I was going to focus on school." However, Cravalho did audition with a group of friends for a chance to perform at a charity event for the nonprofit organization Kids for Cause. They did not get the gig, but the person evaluating the auditions, Rachel Sutton, turned out to also be the casting director for *Moana*. Sutton contacted Cravalho and asked if she would consider auditioning for the film. Cravalho set aside her fears and said yes.

Disney brought her and her mother to Los Angeles, where Cravalho was the last actor to read for the role of Moana, on the last day of auditions. During her last callback via Skype, the production team asked her to deliver a particular line as if she had just learned that she had gotten the part. After a few more directives, they officially awarded her the role. The video of the audition, in which Cravalho tearfully calls her mother from her school's music room to share the news, went viral.

The film's writer-director duo, John Musker and Ron Clements, were impressed by Cravalho's "fearlessness." "She has a playful, mischievous wit," Musker said to Mike Gordon for the *Honolulu Star-Advertiser* (8 Oct. 2015).

"She can project vulnerability, she doesn't seem intimidated at all by the challenges ahead, and her Polynesian background has helped shape her connection to family, hard work, and music. These are all qualities she shares with Moana."

MAKING MOANA

The character Moana is unique among Disney princesses in that her story arc does not contain a love story. "That's because the journey that Moana goes on—of self-discovery—doesn't need a love interest," Cravalho explained to Kosin. "Finding yourself is something you do all on your own, and it's *for* you—not for anyone else. While others may help you along the way, never forget that the journey is for you."

In the movie, Moana is next in line to become chief of her village, but she is drawn to the mystery and promise of the ocean. No one in Moana's village ventures far into the Pacific, but times are growing desperate: crops are failing, fish are dying, and no one seems to know why. It is up to the adventurous Moana to journey across the dangerous ocean to find Maui and make him return a precious gem so that the world will be in harmony again. Moana's journey is a hero's quest; along the way, she must discover her true self, which also means discovering the true nature of her culture and her navigator ancestors.

The movie also explores issues of sustainability. "You've got to give back," Musker said to Kelly McEvers for NPR's *All Things Considered* (23 Nov. 2016). He added, "We heard a phrase when we were in the South Pacific: you don't own the land, the land owns you. And I think, you know, we sort of took that to heart."

Cravalho grew up hearing the myths described in the film, but she was less familiar with the process of making a movie. "The most challenging part was figuring out how to be comfortable in a recording booth," she said to Kosin. "I wasn't sure how to act with cameras on me—they usually put cameras [in the booth] so the animators can watch and add more lifelike facial expressions to the character. I wasn't used to that whole 'lights, camera, action' thing." Later, publicity for the film took Cravalho all over the world. She was particularly excited for trips to cold-weather cities, because it allowed her to wear elegant coats and scarves that are too warm for Hawaii.

FILM RELEASE AND AFTERMATH

Moana, which premiered a day after Cravalho's sixteenth birthday, enjoyed one of the best Thanksgiving openings of all time. Critics praised the film and Cravalho's performance as the plucky Moana. In her review for the *Verge* (26 Nov. 2016), Tasha Robinson wrote that *Moana* felt like the apotheosis of the best Disney plots and heroines and praised Moana as "a fully rounded character with an idealized yet believable body, flaws that she acknowledges and fights, and a resourcefulness that makes her admirable even when she's failing."

Moana was nominated for two Academy Awards, including the award for best original song for "How Far I'll Go," which Cravalho sings in the film. She performed the song at the Academy Awards ceremony in February 2017, alongside dancers waving flowing flags that represented ocean waves. The performance won her accolades, despite one of the flags hitting her in the face while she was singing.

Soon after her Academy Awards performance, Cravalho landed a starring role in the new NBC musical drama Rise. The show is based on the true story of a Pennsylvania drama teacher named Lou Volpe, as recounted in the book Drama High: The Incredible True Story of a Brilliant Teacher, a Struggling Town, and the Magic of Theater (2013), by journalist Michael Sokolove, one of Volpe's former students. Set in a struggling working-class town, the show will tackle serious issues such as alcoholism, poverty, and homelessness. Cravalho plays a character named Lillette Suarez. Other stars include Josh Radnor, best known for his role in the sitcom How I Met Your Mother (2005–14), and film veteran Rosie Perez. The show is slated to premiere in March 2018.

In November 2017, it was announced that Cravalho would reprise her role as Moana in the Hawaiian-language dub of the film.

PERSONAL LIFE

Cravalho works hard to balance her acting career with her schoolwork and her social life. She generally avoids social media and has said that she is happy without a driver's license, at least for the time being. "My mom and I had a very intense conversation" about driving, she said to Mike Miller for People (23 Nov. 2016). "I was like, 'You know I appreciate all the gifts that you've given me. You don't need to give me a car. . . . You can take me where I need to go. We will jam in the car together and when I want to come home, you got to come home with me, okay?'"

She is still considering pursuing science as a career, if perhaps later than she had originally planned. "Someday," she said to Wallace, "when I'm not running around, when I'm not getting on planes 24/7, I would like to develop a sunscreen that wouldn't harm the reef."

SUGGESTED READING

Cravalho, Auli'i. "Auli'i Cravalho on Voicing Moana and Feeling Like Beyoncé." Interview by Julie Kosin. Harper's Bazaar, 30 Nov. 2016, www.harpersbazaar.com/culture/film-tv/news/a19148/aulii-cravalho-moana-interview/. Accessed 18 Dec. 2017.

Cravalho, Auli'i. "What to See in Hawaii? Ask Auli'i Cravalho of Disney's Moana." Interview by Diane Daniel. The New York Times, 17 Nov. 2016, www.nytimes.com/2016/11/20/travel/hawaii-aulii-cravalho-of-moana-disney.html. Accessed 18 Dec. 2017.

Cravalho, Auli'i, and John Musker. "Moana Actress Grew Up with the Polynesian Myth That Inspired the Movie." Interview by Kelly McEvers. NPR, 23 Nov. 2016, www.npr.org/2016/11/23/503066811/moana-actress-grew-up-with-the-polynesian-myth-that-inspired-the-movie. Accessed 18 Dec. 2017.

Gordon, Mike. "Mililani Teen Lands Lead in Disney's Moana." Honolulu Star-Advertiser, 8 Oct. 2015. Newspaper Source Plus, search.ebscohost.com/login.aspx?direct=true&db=n5h&AN=2W63608965909&site=ehost-live. Accessed 18 Dec. 2017.

Miller, Mike. "All about Auli'i Cravalho, the Amazing 16-Year-Old Voice of Disney's Moana." People, 23 Nov. 2016, people.com/movies/all-about-aulii-cravalho-the-amazing-16-year-old-voice-behind-moana/. Accessed 19 Dec. 2017.

Robinson, Joanna. "How Pacific Islanders Helped Disney's Moana Find Its Way." Vanity Fair, 16 Nov. 2016, www.vanityfair.com/hollywood/2016/11/moana-oceanic-trust-disney-controversy-pacific-islanders-polynesia. Accessed 18 Dec. 2017.

Wallace, Don. "Moana Star Auli'i Cravalho Is Not Your Average Disney Princess." Honolulu, 1 Nov. 2016, www.honolulumagazine.com/Honolulu-Magazine/November-2016/Moanas-Aulii-Cravalho-is-Not-Your-Average-Disney-Princess/. Accessed 19 Dec. 2017.

—Molly Hagan

Anthony Davis

Date of birth: March 11, 1993
Occupation: Basketball player

For New Orleans Pelicans forward Anthony Davis, the basketball court is more than simply the venue where his sport is played. "I like to use the court as my safe haven; it kind of eases everything I'm going through and releases everything in my mind," he told Khalil Garriott for the website of the energy drink company Red Bull (20 Oct. 2016). "I just think about the ball and the rim and the floor, what's on the floor, who's on the floor—that's it. Anything that goes on in the outside world is forgotten." Indeed, Davis's approach to his sport has been undoubtedly successful. A

By Ian McCormick via Wikimedia Commons

lifelong basketball player who played a single season for the University of Kentucky, he was selected as the number-one National Basketball Association (NBA) Draft pick in the summer of 2012 and shortly thereafter won an Olympic gold medal as a member of the US men's basketball team. Upon joining the New Orleans Hornets (soon renamed the Pelicans), Davis immediately established himself as a strong addition to the team and put forth impressive efforts on the court during both regular NBA seasons and the playoffs. While he hopes one day to win the championship for the first time in the franchise's history, he plans to "take it year by year and just see," as he told Rachel Nichols for *ESPN* (20 Feb. 2018).

EARLY LIFE AND EDUCATION

Anthony Marshon Davis Jr. was born in Chicago, Illinois, on March 11, 1993, to Erainer and Anthony Davis Sr. He grew up in Chicago's Englewood neighborhood, where he lived with his parents, his twin, Antoinette, and his older sister, Iesha. The family eventually moved to the suburb of Orland Park. As a child and teenager, Davis spent time playing basketball with his cousins, one of whom, Keith Chamberlain, went on to play professional basketball abroad.

Davis attended Perspectives Charter School, for sixth through twelfth grades, which his parents determined offered smaller class sizes and a higher-quality education than the local public schools. Despite such benefits, the school's athletic programs and facilities were limited; notably, the school had no basketball court, and the basketball team traveled around Chicago to play

at different venues. As a member of the Perspectives basketball team, however, Davis did not allow such challenges to prevent him from playing the game. "We had reversible uniforms before senior year. And we'd wear all different types of shoes; not really looking like a team. But we didn't let that stop us from playing basketball," he told Jimmy Smith for *NOLA.com* (7 Oct. 2012). "We really all just stuck with it and persevered through the whole situation."

Despite the skill and talent he demonstrated on the court, Davis largely escaped the notice of scouts through much of his high school career. That began to change in his last two years of high school, when he grew seven inches in a short period of time, reaching a height of six feet ten. "It made the game a lot easier for me," he told Elena Bergeron for *ESPN* (30 Dec. 2011). "I didn't have to try to shoot floaters over these giant guys." After his junior basketball season, he joined the Amateur Athletic Union team Meanstreets. A local fan of high school basketball posted video footage of Davis's play online, and colleges began to take notice. Davis ultimately chose to commit to playing for the University of Kentucky following his graduation in 2011. He was named a McDonald's All American in 2011.

NCAA AND OLYMPIC CHAMPION

Following his graduation from high school, Davis enrolled in the University of Kentucky and joined the Kentucky Wildcats men's basketball team. A strong competitor within Division I of the National Collegiate Athletic Association (NCAA), the team represented an exciting new world for Davis, who, despite his skills, was unaccustomed to winning games. "Never won in my life, like, ever. Except AAU, but even then we weren't that good," he recalled to Lang Whitaker for *GQ* (27 June 2012). "And then when I was at Kentucky, we'd go on fifteen-game winning streaks, and I'd be like, 'What?' I didn't know how to respond."

Over the course of his freshman season with the Wildcats, Davis played in forty games and averaged 14.2 points, 10.4 total rebounds, and 1.3 assists per game. In recognition of his performance on the court, he was named to the NCAA AP All-America first team and named the Southeastern Conference Player of the Year, among other honors. During the 2012 NCAA tournament, the Wildcats dominated the championship, in which they beat the Kansas Jayhawks by eight points. Davis led the team in rebounds and assists during the final game, held in New Orleans in April 2012, but set an NCAA championship record with six points, sixteen rebounds, five assists, six blocks, and three steals, all in a single game. He was named most outstanding player of the championship, an achievement earned by only three other freshmen.

In the summer following his sole season in Kentucky, Davis joined the US men's basketball team as a replacement for injured player Blake Griffin. During July and August 2012, he traveled to London, England, to play basketball in that year's Olympic Games. Performing well throughout the tournament, the team won the gold medal after beating Spain in the final stage of the competition. The experience was a formative one for Davis, who later told interviewers that he would rather win another Olympic gold medal than be named the NBA's most valuable player (MVP). Davis went on to represent the United States in additional international events, including the 2014 International Basketball Federation (FIBA) World Cup, in which his team placed first.

NEW ORLEANS

After playing for Kentucky for one season, Davis entered the 2012 NBA Draft in the hope of being selected to play for a professional basketball team. In the weeks leading up to the draft, he became the center of attention within the sports media as commentators attempted to predict his fate in the draft. The experience was a strange one for Davis. "I'm just trying to take it all in," he told Michael Lee for the *Washington Post* (10 June 2012). "I used to just look at all types of magazines and say, 'I wish it was me on this cover.' I had no thought of ever being here right now." On June 28, 2012, the New Orleans Hornets selected Davis as the first overall pick in the draft.

Davis made his debut with the Hornets on October 31, 2012, in a game against the San Antonio Spurs. During his debut season, he played in sixty-four games with the team and averaged 13.5 points, 8.2 rebounds, and one assist per game. For his first several seasons, Davis played in the position of power forward, although he started playing center in late 2015. Following the 2012–13 season, the Hornets organization changed the team's name to the New Orleans Pelicans, and Davis and his teammates competed under that name from that point on.

Over the next several seasons, Davis established himself as a key member of the Pelicans and a strong player as compared to his fellow NBA athletes. During the 2013–14 season, he was selected for the All-Star Game, his first of many. The following season, Davis led the NBA in blocks, two-point field goals, and player efficiency, establishing a pattern of dominance in those areas that continued throughout the next seasons. The year 2015 proved to be particularly significant for Davis, as the Pelicans qualified for the playoffs for the first time in his tenure with the team. Despite their efforts, however, the Pelicans fell to the Golden State Warriors in the first round of the competition; the Warriors went on to be a frequent obstacle between the Pelicans and success in the playoffs. "It's really tough because they play so well as a team," Davis explained to Angel Diaz for *Complex* (30 July 2018). "They move the basketball, have the best shooters in the game, the best scorer in the game; you really have to play a perfect game. When they make their runs, you have to be poised enough to combat them." Despite such setbacks, Davis repeatedly distinguished himself as an essential part of the Pelicans, and in July 2015, he signed a five-year contract extension with the team worth $145 million.

CHALLENGES AND ASPIRATIONS

The 2015–16 season was challenging for Davis, who was a consistently strong performer on the court but ultimately played in only sixty-one games during the season, as knee and shoulder injuries forced him to end his season early in March 2016. Nevertheless, Davis took his recovery period as an opportunity to improve his overall physical fitness. Following his return to play at the start of the 2016–17 season, he played in seventy-five games and achieved per-game averages of 28 points scored and 11.8 rebounds, his highest to that date. He was named most valuable player of the 2017 NBA All-Star Game.

During the 2017–18 NBA season, the Pelicans faced a variety of challenges, including the absence of injured center DeMarcus Cousins. Despite such setbacks, the team performed well and ended the season ranked second in the Southwest Division, earning a spot in the playoffs. During the playoffs, the team defeated the Portland Trail Blazers four games to none in the first round. Davis made a particularly strong contribution during the competition, leading the team in points and rebounds in multiple games. The Pelicans then moved on to the conference semifinals, where they fell to the Golden State Warriors, the eventual winners of the NBA finals.

Although appreciative of the opportunity to play in the NBA playoffs, Davis has noted in interviews that he is dissatisfied with merely competing in—and not winning—the tournament. "I've done that before, and nobody talks about it. Nobody talks about it at all," he told Nichols. "I feel like we can do more. We have to. You know, they all say basketball is a game of runs. This might be our run. You know, you don't know, and you just got to play it out and see where it goes from there." Going into the 2018–19 season, the Pelicans were the focus of widespread speculation due to rumors that Davis could be traded to another franchise, although some sports commentators argued that New Orleans would be unlikely to agree to such a trade.

PERSONAL LIFE

Since joining the Pelicans, Davis has developed a deep appreciation of the city of New Orleans. "The food is amazing," he told Diaz. "The atmosphere and the people too. There's no place like it." Although he has noted that he intends to continue playing basketball for the foreseeable future, Davis has also expressed interest in one day returning to college and completing his degree, with the goal of continuing his career in basketball off the court. "When this is all over, I still want to go back to high school and coach, probably for my old high school team," he told Smith.

SUGGESTED READING

"Anthony Davis: Pelicans Would Have Contended for Title If DeMarcus Cousins Not Hurt." *ESPN*, ESPN Internet Ventures, 20 Feb. 2018, www.espn.com/nba/story/_/id/22517944/anthony-davis-says-new-orleans-pelicans-made-nba-finals-demarcus-cousins. Accessed 14 Sept. 2018.

Bergeron, Elena. "Anthony Davis Is NEXT." *ESPN*, ESPN Internet Ventures, 30 Dec. 2011, www.espn.com/espn/next2012/story/_/id/7390571/cbb-kentucky-anthony-davis-next-espn-magazine. Accessed 14 Sept. 2018.

Davis, Anthony. "Anthony Davis Tells Us DeMarcus Cousins 'Went from a Teammate to an Enemy.'" Interview by Angel Diaz. *Complex*, 30 July 2018, www.complex.com/sports/2018/07/anthony-davis-demarcus-cousins. Accessed 14 Sept. 2018.

Davis, Anthony. "The Man, the Myth, the UnibrowTM: A GQ+A with Anthony Davis." Interview by Lang Whitaker. *GQ*, 27 June 2012, www.gq.com/story/anthony-davis-nba-draft-number-one-pick-interview. Accessed 14 Sept. 2018.

Lee, Michael. "NBA Draft: Anthony Davis Learned How to Play Big When He Had to Play Small." *The Washington Post*, 10 June 2012, www.washingtonpost.com/sports/nba-draft-anthony-davis-learned-how-to-play-big-when-he-had-to-play-small/2012/06/10/gJQAAyyJTV_story.html. Accessed 14 Sept. 2018.

Smith, Jimmy. "Anthony Davis' Perseverance Paid Off in His Journey from Chicago to New Orleans Hornets." *NOLA.com: The Times-Picayune*, 6 Oct. 2012, www.nola.com/hornets/index.ssf/2012/10/anthony_davis_rise_to_top_pick.html. Accessed 14 Sept. 2018.

—*Joy Crelin*

Felicia Day

Date of birth: June 28, 1979
Occupation: Actor

In her 2015 memoir, *You're Never Weird on the Internet (Almost)*, Felicia Day describes herself as "situationally famous," which might be true if she were only known for her supporting roles in such television series as *Buffy the Vampire Slayer*, *Dollhouse*, *Eureka*, and *Supernatural*. But to the many fans who are familiar with her work on Internet-based projects, she is a giant, best known for her work in front of and behind the camera in web series such as *Dr. Horrible's Sing-Along Blog* (2008), *The Guild* (2007–13), and *Dragon Age: Redemption* (2011), in which Day portrays the elf Tallis. In 2012 Day launched her own YouTube channel, Geek & Sundry, which is dedicated to such "geeky" pursuits as comic books, video games, romance novels, tabletop games, and sketch comedy. A megahit in niche markets, the channel has proved such a powerhouse that it was acquired by Legendary Entertainment in 2014. Although enormously popular on the convention circuit and among her legion of fans, Day remains unknown in the more mainstream entertainment industry. She recalled to Monica Hesse for the *Washington Post* (3 Apr. 2012): "Whenever I go to a meeting at a studio lot, it's always the IT guy or the assistant or the accountant who knows me. And then the executives look at me, like, 'I don't know why I'm meeting with you.'"

By Felicia Day [CC BY 2.0], via Wikimedia Commons

EARLY LIFE AND EDUCATION

Felicia Day was born Kathryn Felicia Day in Huntsville, Alabama, on June 28, 1979. She was homeschooled throughout much of her childhood, which greatly influenced her creative development. In an interview with John Gaudiosi for *Crave* (26 Aug. 2015), she said of her homeschooling: "It had a huge impact on life. I was not raised around other children and my two conduits to other people were doing community theater as a kid and using the Internet to talk to people in the very early days on CompuServe and Prodigy. That connection around the things that I loved primarily, not just the things around me, encouraged me to really find my place amongst the subjects that I loved more than just random people."

And video games became a central focus of her life. She and her brother played text adventures and role-playing games (RPGs) together on the family's table-sized "laptop." "That really was our escape," she told Gaudiosi. "When we finally got dial-up Internet we connected with people around the video games we loved, especially Ultima."

Having performed as a musician and an actor from an early age, she enrolled at the University of Texas at Austin at age sixteen. There she double-majored in violin and mathematics. Although she loved both subjects, math was always her backup plan. Her passion was for performance—which led her to pursue an acting career in Hollywood.

EARLY CAREER

Like many young actors, Day found herself getting small guest-starring roles on television series and in films. She also found that Hollywood tended to micromanage her looks. Several casting directors suggested she get a nose job or fix her teeth to improve her chances of getting bigger parts, but Day wanted most of all to be herself. Her first major reoccurring role came in 2003 on *Buffy the Vampire Slayer* as Vi, one of the show's "slayerettes." Her time spent on that series would begin her longtime association with writer-director Joss Whedon. For Whedon she appeared as Penny in *Dr. Horrible's Sing-Along Blog* (2008), a musical-comedy web miniseries he wrote and directed, and as the character Mag on his series *Dollhouse* (2009–10). She is also known for her work as Holly Marten on the series *Eureka* (2011–12) and for her reoccurring role as Charlie Bradbury on *Supernatural* (2012–15).

BUILDING AN ONLINE EMPIRE

While Day was able to pay her bills as a working actor, she was also tinkering with a TV pilot she had been writing about a group of gamers, based on her own experiences playing *World of Warcraft*. Unfortunately, the idea found little interest in Hollywood. Then a friend suggested she produce the show herself online. Day liked the idea; she and a producing partner pooled their money and filmed three episodes in their own homes.

The Guild premiered on YouTube in July 2007 and ran for six seasons, ending in 2013. The series—about a gamers' guild called the Knights of Good—was unapologetically geeky and appealed to a niche audience who ate up every episode. Before long, the series was receiving sponsorship deals with companies such as Microsoft and Sprint, and Day herself was becoming an enormous draw at conventions such as San Diego Comic-Con. In the series, Day played Cyd, an introvert who details the hours she and her fellow gamers spend playing a fantasy massively multiplayer online role-playing game (MMORPG) called *The Game*.

In addition to being a financial success, *The Guild* won multiple honors during its six-season run, including a YouTube Video Award, a South by Southwest Greenlight Award, a Yahoo! Video Award, and numerous Streamy and International Academy of Web Television (IAWTV) awards. Seemingly all in a moment, Day was a sensation. "Suddenly, these offers were flooding in from everywhere. Television. Huge opportunities. I wasn't ready for that. I hadn't defined what I loved enough to be able to handle that," she recalled to Hesse. "I had to ask myself, 'Where do I want my life to go?' . . . With mainstream acting, I already knew how that path would end."

In March 2012, Day announced that she would be starting her own YouTube channel, Geek & Sundry, as part of YouTube's $100 million original-content channel initiative. The company hoped to use the initiative to develop artistic credibility in its web video format.

Day brought the production of *The Guild* over to her new channel. She also produced three new series for the channel: *The Flog*, which she hosted; *Sword & Laser*, which was hosted by Veronica Belmont and Tom Merritt; and *Tabletop*, which was hosted by actor Wil Wheaton, best known for his starring role as Wesley Crusher on *Star Trek: The Next Generation*. The latter show was developed because of Wheaton's passion for tabletop games—a love that Day now shares. She told Eris Walsh for the Mary Sue (22 Sept. 2015): "[Wil Wheaton] really introduced me to this whole world, and the fact that his enthusiasm made me enthusiastic, which made me enthusiastic to share it with everybody, was really kind of a big driving force within the last couple years of my life."

For two years Geek & Sundry was funded by YouTube. Its popularity surged during that time: roughly 1.4 million subscribers to its YouTube network and Hulu channel and more than 12 million fans on social media. In 2014 Legendary Entertainment acquired Geek & Sundry for an undisclosed sum, but allowed Day to maintain creative control over the channel as she continued to produce additional series, such as *Critical Role*, *Titansgrave*, *Super Fun Awesome Party Game Time*, *Game Engine*, and *ESCAPE!* The channel has also spawned numerous merchandising opportunities, including a Dark Horse Comics series based on *The Guild*.

PENNING A MEMOIR

In 2015, Day took the publishing world by storm when she released her memoir *You're Never Weird on the Internet (Almost)*, which became a *New York Times* Best Seller. In it, she detailed her homeschooled origins in Alabama and how she began to embrace her "uncool" side through the development of the Internet, which matured with her throughout her youth. The book also discusses how she forged her own path in the entertainment industry because she grew tired of being typecast as a "crazy cat-lady secretary." She also confronts her struggles with gaming addiction, depression, and anxiety in a forthright but humorous manner. In an interview with Jevon Phillips for the *Los Angeles Times* (10 Aug. 2015), Day explained why she took on the daunting task of writing a memoir in her thirties: "What I wanted to do was open the door to this new world, which is digital media, since my life is exactly the same years as the emergence of the Internet. . . . It's like the industrial revolution, a technological revolution, and hopefully it opens doors for people rather than closes them. That's why I wanted to have that message of openness and creativity and expressing yourself—the Pollyanna view of technology."

In addition to being a best seller, *You're Never Weird on the Internet (Almost)* met with a considerable amount of critical acclaim. Reviewing the book, Kelly Lawler remarked in *USA Today* (11 Aug. 2015): "Written in her engaging and often hilarious voice, it's just downright fun to read." Lawler notes that Day's use of the kind of slang and casual writing styles often seen on social media "might seem gimmicky, but Day makes it feel so natural that you forget that not every book includes annotated pictures of the author as a child or passages about video games that SEE INTO YOUR SOUL."

CONTINUED ACTING CAREER

Although Day has become a successful businesswoman and web video producer, she continues to act. In 2017 she joined the cast of the revival of *Mystery Science Theater 3000*, a show from the 1990s in which a janitor trapped aboard a space station is forced to watch awful B-movies as a part of a pair of mad scientists' plot to take over the world. In the revival, which premiered on Netflix, Day plays Kinga, the granddaughter and daughter of the mad scientists from the original series. "She is very insecure, doesn't have a lot of self-confidence, and is overcompensating in a lot of ways," Day said of her character, as quoted by Aaron Sagers for *SyFyWire* (1 June 2017). "Her grandiose plans are only happening because she's surrounded by yes-people."

Day's other major acting role is on *The Magicians*, a fantasy show on SyFy that is based on the acclaimed trilogy of novels by Lev Grossman. Day joined the cast in the show's third season as Poppy, a character who is an expert in dragons. "I am thrilled to join *The Magicians* this season," Felicia Day told Alicia Lutes for the *Nerdist* (7 Nov. 2017). "The show is one of my favorites, the cast is incredible to work with, and showrunner, Sera Gamble, is one of my Hollywood heroes. I can't wait for fans to meet Poppy!" The third season of *The Magicians* premiered in January 2018.

SUGGESTED READING

"About." *Official Website of Felicia Day*, Feliciaday.com/. Accessed 11 Dec. 2017.

Day, Felicia. "Interview | Felicia Day: The Actress on Her Online Entertainment Empire." Interview by John Gaudiosi. *Crave*, 26 Aug. 2015, www.craveonline.com/design/894721-interview-felicia-day-actress-online-entertainment-empire. Accessed 11 Dec. 2017.

Day, Felicia. "Felicia Day Lets the World Know That 'You're Never Weird on the Internet (Almost).'" Interview by Jevon Phillips. *Los Angeles Times*, 10 Aug. 2015, beta.latimes.com/books/jacketcopy/la-et-jc-felicia-day-youre-never-weird-on-the-internet-almost-20150727-story.html. Accessed 11 Dec. 2017.

Day, Felicia. "An Interview with the Queen of Geek: Felicia Day." Interview by Eris Walsh. *The Mary Sue*, 22 Sept. 2015, www.themarysue.com/felicia-day-interview/. Accessed 11 Dec. 2017.

Hesse, Monica. "Felicia Day: A Rising Star for the Internet Geek." *The Washington Post*, 3 Apr. 2012, www.washingtonpost.com/lifestyle/style/felicia-day-a-rising-star-for-the-internet-geek/2012/04/03/gIQAHpnEtS_story.html. Accessed 11 Dec. 2017.

Lawler, Kelly. "Day's Story Is Anything but 'Weird.'" Review of *You're Never Weird on the Internet (Almost)*, by Felicia Day. *USA Today*, 20 Aug. 2015, www.usatoday.com/story/life/books/2015/08/11/review-felicia-day-youre-never-weird-internet-almost-memoir/31104167/. Accessed 11 Dec. 2017.

Sagers, Aaron. "Mad About Felicia Day: MST3K's Supervillain Speaks." *SyFyWire*, 1 June 2017, www.syfy.com/syfywire/mst3k-felicia-day-interview. Accessed 11 Dec. 2017.

SELECTED WORKS

Buffy the Vampire Slayer, 2003; *The Guild*, 2007–13; *Dr. Horrible's Sing-Along Blog*, 2008; *Eureka*, 2011; *Supernatural*, 2012–15; *Mystery Science Theater 3000*, 2017–

—Christopher Mari

Angus Deaton

Date of birth: October 19, 1945
Occupation: Economist

Angus Deaton is a professor of economics and international affairs at Princeton University. He was awarded the 2015 Nobel Memorial Prize in Economic Sciences for his expansive research in economic studies, including how individual consumption affects economic policy and the use of household surveys in assessing aggregate data.

EARLY LIFE AND EDUCATION

Angus Stewart Deaton was born on October 19, 1945, in Edinburgh, Scotland. He studied at Fettes College in Edinburgh as a Foundation Scholar from 1959 to 1964 and took an active part in the college community as a school prefect, president of the Paramecium Society discussion group, and a member of the rugby team.

Deaton earned his bachelor's (1967), master's (1971), and doctoral (1974) degrees at Cambridge, and from 1967 to 1968 he worked in the Economic Intelligence Department of the Bank of England. His thesis, "Models of Consumer Demand and Their Application in the United Kingdom," was completed in 1975. In 1976, he began working as a professor of econometrics at the University of Bristol and published his influential paper "An Almost Ideal Demand System" in the *American Economic Review* in 1980. The paper analyzed consumer demand for specific products and how consumers are affected by public and private policies that alter market supply and demand.

Deaton served as a visiting professor at Princeton University in New Jersey from 1979 to 1983. In 1983, the university appointed him the Dwight D. Eisenhower Professor of International Affairs and Economics. The following year he became the editor of the Economic Society's publication, *Econometrica*. He also served as the associate editor of the *Pakistan Development Review* from 1990 to 1997 and the *World Bank Research Observer* from 1991 to 2007.

LIFE'S WORK

Angus Deaton is a British-American economist renowned for his contribution to development economics, particularly the theory of consumption, savings, and the economics of well-being. One of his first major contributions to the field was his study of the evolution of consumer demand in the United Kingdom during the first seventy years of the twentieth century. Titled "The Analysis of Consumer Demand in the United Kingdom," the paper won Deaton the Econometric Society's first Frisch Medal, which was awarded in 1978. He and his colleagues continued to expand on the analysis of consumer demand, and their work led to the consumer demand model known as An Almost Ideal Demand System (AIDS), which has since become the standard model for economists studying consumer behavior. Deaton first presented the model in a 1980 issue of the *American Economic Review*, and it became groundbreaking in the field of economics and has since been applied to various branches, including the determination of consumption rates. His approach to consumption has helped expand economists' views on the analysis of individual households, rather than focusing primarily on larger economic issues such as gross domestic product (GDP).

Deaton published another innovative study, "Why Is Consumption So Smooth?" (1989), which was first published in the *Review of Economic Studies* and introduced the concept known as the Deaton Paradox. This paradox states that consumer consumption is not altered by drastic shocks to consumer income. This was an important factor for economists to expand their understanding of the actions of consumers, and it also challenged the existing permanent income hypothesis, which proposed that consumers spend according to their lifetime income.

Deaton produced several household survey studies in the 1990s, including his book *The Analysis of Household Surveys* (1997), which looks at how surveys can be used to analyze economic policy issues, especially in developing countries. Deaton's book helped lay the groundwork for economists to use relevant statistics compiled from household surveys to improve policies. The book marked a shift in economic focus for Deaton toward the subjective well-being of the consumer.

In the early 2000s, Deaton began to study how to measure and reduce global poverty and income inequality, chiefly in India and Africa, with the belief that those who are born in wealthy countries have a "moral obligation to reduce poverty and ill health" in other parts of the world. In these studies, Deaton stressed the importance of household surveys to accurately measure the prevalence of poverty. Studying the opposite side of the economic spectrum, he published a paper in August 2010 suggesting that an individual's happiness increases with income.

Throughout his research and work as an educator, Deaton has served on numerous councils and associations. He became a member of the Chief Economist's Advisory Council in 2001, and in 2007, he became a senior research scientist for the Gallup Organization, a management consulting company. Two years later he was elected president of the American Economic Association. He was awarded the 2015 Nobel Memorial Prize in Economic Science for his study of consumption as it relates to poverty and welfare.

IMPACT

Through his research, Deaton has furthered several fields of economic studies, including microeconomics, econometrics, and development economics. He has shifted the focus of economic studies from large aggregates to individual households and placed particular emphasis on consumer well-being rather than on measuring consumer income.

PERSONAL LIFE

Deaton was married to American Mary Ann Burnside until her death from breast cancer in 1975. They had two children who both attended Princeton University. Deaton is married to Anne Case, a fellow economics professor at Princeton.

SUGGESTED READING

Appelbaum, Binyamin. "Nobel in Economics Given to Angus Deaton for Studies of Consumption." *The New York Times*, 12 Oct. 2015, www.nytimes.com/2015/10/13/business/angus-deaton-nobel-economics.html. Accessed 23 Aug. 2018.

Bird, Mike. "This Is Why Angus Deaton Just Won the Nobel Prize in Economics." *Business Insider*, 12 Oct. 2015, www.businessinsider.com/who-is-angus-deaton-2015-nobel-prize-in-economics-winner-2015-10. Accessed 23 Aug. 2018.

Cassidy, John. "Angus Deaton: A Skeptical Optimist Wins the Economics Nobel." *New Yorker*. Condé Nast, 12 Oct. 2015, www.newyorker.com/news/john-cassidy/angus-deaton-a-skeptical-optimist-wins-the-economics-nobel. Accessed 23 Aug. 2018.

Judd, J. Wesley. "A Conversation with Nobel Prize Winner Angus Deaton." *Pacific Standard*, psmag.com/economics/interview-with-angus-deaton. Accessed 23 Aug. 2018.

Timiraos, Nick. "Nobel Prize in Economics: Who Is Angus Deaton?" *Wall Street Journal*, 12 Oct. 2015, blogs.wsj.com/economics/2015/10/12/nobel-prize-in-economics-who-is-angus-deaton. Accessed 23 Aug. 2018.

SELECTED WORKS

The Analysis of Household Surveys: A Microeconomic Approach to Development Policy, 1997; "An Almost Ideal System," 1980; "Why Is Consumption So Smooth?," 1989; "Household Surveys, Consumption, and the Measurement of Poverty," 2003; *The Great Escape: Health, Wealth, and the Origins of Inequality*, 2013

—*Patrick G. Cooper*

Guy Delisle

Date of birth: January 19, 1966
Occupation: Graphic novelist

Some graphic novelists might seek to make broad statements about a country's history, culture, or politics when creating a travelogue, but Guy Delisle takes a more personal approach. A published cartoonist since the mid-1990s, the Canadian-born artist and writer became well known early in the twenty-first century with the publication of his first two graphic novels, *Shenzhen* and *Pyongyang*, which document his experiences visiting and working in the titular Chinese and North Korean cities. His later graphic novels *Burma Chronicles* and *Jerusalem* take a similar approach, documenting Delisle's everyday life as he navigates new cities and cares for his young children during his longtime partner's assignments to those regions for Doctors Without Borders (Médecins Sans Frontières; MSF). "My books are always at pavement level," he explained to Rachel Cooke for the *Guardian* (31 May 2012). "That's what I do."

Originally an animator by trade, Delisle is known for creating intriguing, amusing, and

By Selbymay, via Wikimedia Commons

expressive works that convey a great deal of information through their characteristic simplicity. "The challenge is not to explain too much," he told Cooke. He added, "If I need to draw a little arrow, or a map, then I do. If you did those things in a documentary, it would look like a PowerPoint presentation. But in a comic, it's fine." In addition to his travelogues, Delisle has authored several humorous collections of comics about parenting as well as a series focusing on a fictional detective. His graphic novel *Hostage*, his first nonfiction work to focus on another individual's experiences, was published in English in 2017.

EARLY LIFE AND EDUCATION
One of four children, Delisle was born in 1966, in the Canadian city of Charlesbourg, Quebec (now a borough of Quebec City). His mother, Lucienne, was a teacher, while his father, André, worked as a technical draftsman. Delisle began reading comics as a child and was particularly interested in the comics known as *bandes dessinées*, French-language works created primarily by French and Belgian writers and artists. Among the comics he enjoyed during that period were *Les Aventures de Tintin* (*The Adventures of Tintin*), created by Belgian cartoonist Hergé, and *Astérix*, originally helmed by René Goscinny and Albert Uderzo. As Delisle grew older, he enjoyed the work of comics artists such as Moebius, who was particularly known for experimenting with visual styles.

Delisle also became interested in the field of animation early in life and aspired to become an animator. After graduating from high school, he eventually attended Ontario's Sheridan College to pursue animation studies. Following his time at Sheridan College, Delisle took a position with the Montreal-based animation company Ciné-Groupe from 1986 to 1988. He then left Canada to travel and pursue animation opportunities abroad, particularly in Europe.

EARLY CAREER
After leaving Canada, Delisle lived for a time in Germany, working in Munich and Berlin, and later moved to France, where he worked for studios such as Folimage. He also spent a year teaching animation on the island of La Réunion, a French overseas department east of Madagascar. Over the course of his years in animation, Delisle found that the European animation industry was in the midst of a transition in which domestic studios were closing and animation work was instead being outsourced, primarily to countries in Asia. Speaking of that transitional period, he told Noel Murray for the *AV Club* (30 Apr. 2012): "It wasn't animation anymore, it was just supervising. There's not a lot of animation in France like there used to be, because there were

studios all over the place . . . and now they're all gone. They don't exist anymore; everything is outsourced in animation." Due to the rise of outsourcing, Delisle was tasked with traveling to China and North Korea to oversee projects being animated there, an experience that would form the basis of his first two graphic novels.

Long intrigued by comics, Delisle began creating his own in the early 1990s during his years in animation, building upon his knowledge of animation techniques to create short visual stories. "I was thinking, maybe we could use the movement in some stories to try to describe just a moment in one page or so," he recalled to Kenan Kocak in an interview for *European Comic Art* (Sept. 2014). "It would be nice to shrink time or compress time on just one page or have the time, for example, a year, passing from one image to another one, very quickly or very slowly. So I played with that in my short stories." By the mid-1990s Delisle began publishing short comics in *Lapin*, an independent French comics magazine.

SHENZHEN AND PYONGYANG
Delisle is perhaps best known for his many graphic novels documenting his travels to and life in various countries. The first, *Shenzhen*, was published in French in 2000 and in English as *Shenzhen: A Travelogue from China* in 2006. Originally a short graphic story published in a comics magazine, Delisle soon decided to expand the work into a full graphic novel chronicling three months spent in the titular Chinese city in the late 1990s, during which time he worked with a Chinese animation studio on behalf of a Belgian production company. *Shenzhen* particularly features Delisle's observations of Chinese business life.

Delisle later spent two months on a similar assignment in North Korea, which he documented in his 2003 graphic novel *Pyongyang*. Published in English as *Pyongyang: A Journey through North Korea* in 2007, the work earned critical acclaim and in 2006 was nominated for the prestigious Eisner Award for best reality-based work. Although both *Shenzhen* and *Pyongyang* reflect Delisle's firsthand experiences in those cities, he was careful to note that his graphic novels do not attempt to present a portrait of a city or country as a whole. "It's not a documentary for sure," he told Hillary Brown for *Paste* magazine (2 May 2017). "People just walk around with me, and I show them the few things that I have noticed and that I think are interesting or weird or funny to show, and I put all that together in the book, after I have taken notes."

BURMA CHRONICLES AND JERUSALEM
After quitting the animation industry, Delisle continued to travel alongside his partner,

Nadège Souprayenmestry, a Frenchwoman from La Réunion who worked as an administrator for MSF and was assigned to countries such as Burma, also known as Myanmar. Delisle's *Burma Chronicles* (2008; *Chroniques birmanes*, 2007) documents their year living in the city of Yangon (formerly Rangoon), during which Delisle cared for their young son and explored the city while Nadège worked. In 2008, the family moved to Israel and spent a year living in East Jerusalem, a disputed area of the city considered by some to belong to Israel and by others to Palestine. Delisle initially documented his time there in a visual blog but ultimately adapted his experiences into a fourth travel-oriented graphic novel, *Jerusalem: Chronicles from the Holy City* (2012; *Chroniques de Jérusalem*, 2011). *Jerusalem* was well received following its publication and won the Fauve d'Or, the prize for the best comics album, at the 2012 Angoulême International Comics Festival.

Because of the political and military tensions in some of the countries Delisle has written about, his graphic novels have often drawn comparisons to more journalistic graphic works by cartoonists such as reporter Joe Sacco. Delisle, however, does not consider himself to be a journalist or his comics to be journalistic works. He prefers to think of his work as ethnography. "I go in a country where I don't know anything about it, and I just spend a year trying to understand what's going on," he explained to Brown. "That's what I like about autobiography. The reader knows where the information comes from because I describe myself. They know that I'm not a specialist of the Middle East. I'm not an adventurer. I'm just an ordinary guy."

OTHER GENRES
In addition to his well-known travelogues, Delisle created numerous additional graphic works representing a variety of tones and genres. His books *Aline et les autres* (1999) and *Albert et les autres* (2001) were published in English as *Aline and the Others* (2006) and *Albert and the Others* (2007) and feature bizarre and sometimes macabre cartoon portraits of women and men. Delisle is likewise the author and illustrator of the three installments in the *Inspecteur Moroni* series (2001–4), about a fictional police detective.

Delisle, inspired by his son, wrote two child-focused works, *Louis au ski* (*Louis Skiing*) (2005) and *Louis à la plage* (*Louis at the Beach*) (2008). He later went on to create the three-volume *Le guide du mauvais père* (2013–15), which was published in English as *A User's Guide to Neglectful Parenting* (2013), *Even More Bad Parenting Advice* (2014), and *The Owner's Manual to Terrible Parenting* (2015). The latter series features fictionalized versions of Delisle, his partner, and their two children, and he described the works to Kocak as "some kind of autobiography."

HOSTAGE
Perhaps Delisle's most ambitious project to date, his 2016 graphic novel, *S'Enfuir: Récit d'un otage*, took more than a dozen years to come to fruition. Published in English as *Hostage* in 2017, the graphic novel tells the story of Christophe André, an MSF administrator who was abducted and held hostage for nearly four months in 1997. After learning about the incident, Delisle met with André through a mutual friend and took extensive notes on his story with the goal of presenting it in graphic-novel form. The two corresponded over fifteen years, until the project was done. *Hostage* represented a new step for Delisle, who had previously presented only his own experiences in his long-form works. "I think I must have been afraid to work on this book because it was something else who had to talk about their story. It was a different process," he recalled to Alex Wong for the *Comics Journal* (2 June 2017).

Making effective use of Delisle's characteristically simple style of illustration, *Hostage* calls attention to the mindset and emotions of its central figure, transporting its readers into the room where André was held captive. "I knew I had to do an immersive type of book," Delisle told Wong. "I wanted the reader to really suffocate with him, to stay with him and just show how you survive in that situation where you have no control of your life." Critics widely praised Delisle's approach to presenting André's story, and *Hostage* was named one of the year's best books or best graphic novels by publications such as the *Globe and Mail*, the *Washington Post*, and the *Boston Globe*.

PERSONAL LIFE
Delisle settled in Montpellier, France, in 1991. Since returning from Jerusalem, he, Nadège, and their children, Louis and Alice, have made it their permanent home. Although he is best known for his travelogues, he has noted in interviews that settling in one place was in some ways a relief. "The kids were a bit bigger and we knew we wouldn't do that for our lives. So, it was the time for us to stop and it was a good time, because everybody is happy with that situation," he told Kocak. "Maybe when I get old, I'll have some very interesting experience, and I might do one [another travelogue]. But now, it's very nice for me to do different books because . . . it's nice to change and have different styles."

SUGGESTED READING
Cooke, Rachel. "Guy Delisle: 'The Challenge Is Not to Explain Too Much.'" *The Guardian*, 31 May 2012, www.theguardian.com/

books/2012/may/31/guy-delisle-jerusalem-review-interview. Accessed 9 Mar. 2018.

Delisle, Guy. "'I Wanted the Reader to Really Suffocate with Him': A Guy Delisle Interview." Interview by Alex Wong. *The Comics Journal*, 2 June 2017, www.tcj.com/a-guy-delisle-interview. Accessed 9 Mar. 2018.

Delisle, Guy. "Interview: Cartoonist Guy Delisle on Crafting His Masterwork of Captivity and Freedom, 'Hostage.'" Interview by Hillary Brown. *Paste*, 2 May 2017, www.pastemagazine.com/articles/2017/05/cartoonist-guy-delisle-on-learning-to-empathize-wi.html. Accessed 9 Mar. 2018.

Delisle, Guy. Interview by Kenan Kocak. *European Comic Art*, vol. 7, no. 2, Sept. 2014, pp. 90–114. *Berghahn*, berghahnbooks.com/blog/interview-with-guy-delisle. Accessed 9 Mar. 2018.

Delisle, Guy. Interview by Noel Murray. *AV Club*, 30 Apr. 2012, www.avclub.com/guy-delisle-1798231305. Accessed 9 Mar. 2018.

Köhler, Nicholas. "Guy Delisle: Stranger in Strange Lands." *Maclean's*, 26 Apr. 2012, www.macleans.ca/culture/books/a-stranger-in-strange-lands. Accessed 9 Mar. 2018.

SELECTED WORKS

Shenzhen (*Shenzhen: A Travelogue from China*), 2000; *Pyongyang* (*Pyongyang: A Journey through North Korea*), 2003; *Chroniques birmanes* (*Burma Chronicles*), 2007; *Chroniques de Jérusalem* (*Jerusalem: Chronicles from the Holy City*), 2011; *Le guide du mauvais père* (*A User's Guide to Neglectful Parenting, Even More Bad Parenting Advice, The Owner's Manual to Terrible Parenting*), 2013–15; *S'Enfuir: Récit d'un otage* (*Hostage*), 2016

—*Joy Crelin*

Rafael Devers

Date of birth: October 24, 1996
Occupation: Baseball player

Rafael Devers is a third baseman and power hitter for the Boston Red Sox who made his major-league debut in the middle of the 2017 season. Born and raised in the Dominican Republic, he was first discovered by a Red Sox scout at age fourteen and signed with the team two years later as a top international prospect. After spending several years working his way up through the minor leagues, Devers was called up, earlier than the team intended, for his skills as a third baseman. Devers had been a prominent minor-league talent, and Red Sox management tried to play down his major-league debut. This hedging

By Keith Allison, via Wikimedia Commons

seemed silly several weeks later when Devers stunned onlookers with a game-tying home run against the New York Yankees, forcing the game into extra innings. By the postseason, baseball pundits were hailing his potential, anointing him the Red Sox's next great heavy hitter.

"From the first day when I got signed, [reaching the major leagues has] always been my goal," Devers said to Christopher Smith for the website *MassLive.com* (23 Apr. 2018), with some assistance from a translator. "I knew the talent that I had and I have. And I knew that I had the talent to make it there. I just knew I had to work every single day to make that a reality. And I never put pressure on myself no matter how many people were talking about me. I just took every day and worked as hard as I could each day." In 2018, his first full major-league season, Devers continued to impress. At an away game in April, he hit the first grand slam (home run with bases loaded) of his career, becoming the youngest Red Sox player to land such a hit since 1965.

EARLY LIFE

Rafael Devers Calcaño was born in Sánchez, a coastal town in the Samaná province of the Dominican Republic, on October 24, 1996, to parents Lucrecia García and Rafael Devers. He grew up in Sánchez and then in Santo Domingo, the country's capital city, where he often tagged along to his father's amateur baseball games. "I can't even remember the first time I went to a stadium, but I have been playing baseball as long as I can remember," Devers said to Marly Rivera in a Spanish-language interview for *ESPN* (5 Aug. 2017) that was later translated into

English. He added, "I started to play baseball because my dad played baseball, and he always brought me along to watch the games, and when practice was over, the parents would let us play there."

Devers's parents divorced when he was seven, and he mostly lived with his father, a shop owner, though he remained close with his mother. Like many Dominicans, Devers grew up playing vitilla, a version of stickball played with a broomstick for a bat and a water jug cap as a ball. The game is so popular in the Dominican Republic that a handful of Dominican major-league players credit it for their skill, because the cap is so small and moves so unpredictably. It was Devers's fellow vitilla players who first gave him the nickname Carita, or "Baby Face," because of his young-looking visage; the name stuck.

GETTING SCOUTED

Devers began playing for several little-league teams in Santo Domingo when he was fourteen, and he caught the attention of major-league scouts right away. Manny Nanita, a Dominican-based scout for the Boston Red Sox, first noticed Devers at a team practice on a field near a horse track in Santo Domingo. "What I first noticed was that Devers looked different than the rest of the players during batting practice," Nanita recalled to Jen McCaffrey for *MassLive.com* (28 Aug. 2017). "He was squaring the ball up most of the time and driving it where it was pitched, but what really caught my attention was seeing him face pitchers, he was so focused and confident in his ability to hit that it looked like a battle between him and the pitcher." After the practice was over, Nanita introduced himself to Devers and his father and then immediately contacted Eddie Romero, then the Red Sox's director of international scouting (later an assistant general manager for the team). Nanita continued to watch Devers play for the next year and a half.

When Romero finally saw Devers play, he was impressed. "A lot of times you hear hyped guys and all this, but when we went to see [Devers] it was legit," he said to McCaffrey. Romero noticed that Devers was playing against boys that were often three or four years older and holding his own. He told Nanita to sign him. By that time, other teams, including the Arizona Diamondbacks and the Toronto Blue Jays, were also interested, but Devers was loyal to Nanita, the first scout who had ever reached out to him. Among scouts, Devers was considered the most advanced left-handed hitter on the international market. Devers signed with the Boston Red Sox for $1.5 million in August 2013, when he was just sixteen.

MINOR LEAGUES

Devers began his professional baseball career at the Red Sox Dominican Academy in El Toro, about thirty-five minutes from Santo Domingo. Romero described the academy to McCaffrey as "pro baseball 101." Participants lift weights and practice every day, play three or four games a week, and are required to learn English. José Zapata, who manages the Dominican Summer League (DSL) at the academy, became Devers's first manager. "First thing I saw about him was his talent," Zapata wrote of Devers in an email to McCaffrey. "Especially his swing when he was taking batting practice in that first week of work. It was pretty easy coaching him. . . . He showed great effort to work every day." Devers worked hard with Zapata to improve his defensive skills, with impressive results: over twenty-eight games, he led the DSL Red Sox in batting average (.337), slugging percentage (.538), and on-base percentage (.445).

After half a year with the academy, Devers made his American debut with the Gulf Coast League (GCL) Red Sox, a rookie-league team in Fort Myers, Florida, in July 2014. At the time, he was already ranked number 11 among Red Sox prospects. During his time with the GCL, Devers led his team in runs batted in (RBIs; thirty-six) and was among the top ten in the league for batting average (.312) and slugging percentage (.484). The league named him to the 2014 postseason All-Star Team.

In 2015 Devers was promoted to the South Atlantic League (SAL), a Class A minor league, and moved to South Carolina to play for the Greenville Drive. At eighteen, he was one of the youngest players in the minor leagues. Nelson Paulino, Devers's hitting coach with the Drive, echoed Zapata's assessment of Devers as a player, telling Scott Keepfer for the *Greenville News* (10 July 2015), "He tries to get better, day by day."

In July 2015, the same month that he recorded his first career home run, Devers was invited to play in the All-Star Futures Game in Cincinnati, Ohio. The game is for the best prospects in minor league baseball; Devers, the second-youngest player in that year's game, was awed by his invitation. "Last year I watched the Futures Game on TV," he said to Keepfer, through a translator. "This year's I'm going to be playing in the game, and that makes me proud." Devers finished the season with a .288 batting average, a .443 slugging percentage, and seventy RBIs.

In 2016, Devers was promoted yet again, this time to the Carolina League's Salem Red Sox, a Class-A Advanced team in Salem, Virginia. For the first time in Devers's brief career, he really struggled. Romero, speaking to McCaffrey, speculated that Devers's slump came from the cold weather and "historically . . . tough league." Or perhaps Devers's work ethic had gotten the best of him; as Romero said, "Every hitting coordinator that went in there said he's just trying to do too much."

By late May, Devers had gone four hitless games. He decided to focus on his defense, and Salem manager Joe Oliver supported him. "I had a lot of faith that he was going to start to swing the bat," Oliver said to Aaron McFarling for the *Roanoke Times* (6 Sept. 2016). "I really did. I had seen him for a little bit in spring training and instructional league and had a pretty good idea what he was like when he was really good. You just don't forget how to hit like that." Indeed, he did not. Devers batted .326 in the last eighty-eight games, finishing the season with a batting average of .282, seventy-one RBIs, and eleven home runs. He was named to the Carolina League's postseason All-Star Team.

BOSTON RED SOX

In 2017, Devers was invited to spring training with the Red Sox. He began the season with the Double-A Eastern League Portland Sea Dogs in Maine, with whom he played seventy-seven games with a .300 batting average, a .575 slugging percentage, and eighteen home runs. He earned another invitation to the All-Star Futures Game, and many speculated that after the All-Star break, Devers would be promoted directly to the major leagues. Red Sox management had other ideas. Devers played nine games with the Triple-A International League Pawtucket Red Sox in Rhode Island.

Devers finally made his major-league debut in a game against the Seattle Mariners in Seattle on July 25, 2017. The team had planned on keeping Devers in the minors for a bit longer, but a series of unfortunate events left the Boston Red Sox in need of a third baseman, and Devers was called up early. The team minimized his debut. "It's important to note, while there's going to be a lot of focus on his arrival here, he is a young player," former coach John Farrell said to Scott Lauber for *ESPN* (24 July 2017). "There are going to be some ups and downs that we'll live with and experience, but the time has come for Devers to meet his mark. The ability to drive the ball is there. I think we have to temper our expectations when he comes here."

After a hitless debut, Devers hit three home runs in his first nine games. In August, he dazzled baseball fans with a game-tying home run in a tense game against the New York Yankees. The explosive play in the ninth inning, which sent the game into extra innings, was a record breaker; the pitch came in at nearly 103 miles an hour, the fastest pitch for a home run since 2008. It was also the first home run that Yankees pitcher Aroldis Chapman had allowed since the

World Series the previous season. "I'm here for a reason," Devers said after the game, speaking to Peter Abraham for the *Boston Globe* (17 Aug. 2017) with the assistance of a translator. "I've never been afraid on the baseball field. I want the chance to show what I can do."

In fifty-eight games, Devers closed the 2017 season with a .284 batting average, a .482 slugging percentage, ten home runs, and thirty RBIs. In game three of the American League Division Series against the Houston Astros, Devers became the youngest Red Sox player to hit a postseason home run. His two-run go-ahead shot gave the Red Sox their first lead of the series to win the game.

Devers started off the 2018 season similarly strong. On April 18, at an away game against the Los Angeles Angels, he hit his first career grand slam, batting in four runs in a single play—a career high—and landing his third home run in less than a month. That night, he became the youngest Red Sox player to hit a grand slam since twenty-year-old Tony Conigliaro in 1965.

PERSONAL LIFE

Devers has a young daughter, Rachell, who lives with her mother in the Dominican Republic, and whose image he has tattooed on his left arm. "She motivates me a lot," he said of his daughter to Peter Abraham for the *Boston Globe* (17 Aug. 2017). "I want to do the best I can for her. She's my reason for being in the world."

SUGGESTED READING

Abraham, Peter. "Just 20, Rafael Devers Is Showing Advanced Talent and Poise." *The Boston Globe*, 17 Aug. 2017, www.bostonglobe.com/sports/redsox/2017/08/17/just-rafael-devers-showing-advanced-talent-and-poise/o2NTbqwtlWioJtgVhMqk2L/story.html. Accessed 16 May 2018.

Devers, Rafael. "Rafael Devers, Boston Red Sox Slugger: 'Nothing Better Could've Happened in My Life Than My Daughter.'" Interview by Christopher Smith. *MassLive.com*, Advance Publications, 23 Apr. 2018, www.masslive.com/redsox/index.ssf/2018/04/rafael_devers_boston_red_sox_s_1.html. Accessed 16 May 2018.

Devers, Rafael. "Rafael Devers on Playing against His Heroes, for His Favorite Team and Being Nicknamed 'Baby Face.'" Interview by Marly Rivera. *ESPN*, 5 Aug. 2017, www.espn.com/mlb/story/_/id/20256476/rookie-rafael-devers-settles-third-base-boston-red-sox. Accessed 17 May 2018.

Keepfer, Scott. "The Future Is Now: Drive's Rafael Devers Has Look of Fast-Rising Star." *The Greenville News*, 10 July 2015, www.greenvilleonline.com/story/sports/baseball/greenville-drive/2015/07/10/

future-now-drives-rafael-devers-look-fast-ris-ing-star/29966877/. Accessed 15 May 2018.

Lauber, Scott. "Red Sox Promote Top 3B Prospect Rafael Devers." *ESPN*, 24 July 2017, www.espn.com/mlb/story/_/id/20140832/boston-red-sox-calling-top-prospect-rafael-devers. Accessed 15 May 2018.

McCaffrey, Jen. "Scouting Rafael Devers: How the Boston Red Sox Found a 14-Year-Old Future Phenom in the Dominican Republic." *MassLive.com*, Advance Publications, 28 Aug. 2017, www.masslive.com/redsox/index.ssf/2017/08/rafael_devers_boston_red_sox.html. Accessed 15 May 2018.

McFarling, Aaron. "Devers' Play Delivers Constant Comfort to Salem Red Sox Roster." *The Roanoke Times*, 6 Sept. 2016, www.roanoke.com/sports/baseball/devers-play-delivers-constant-comfort-to-salem-red-sox-roster/article_23bb52eb-2909-585f-a87c-b6e-94f5acd09.html. Accessed 15 May 2018.

—*Molly Hagan*

Jessica Diggins

Date of birth: August 26, 1991
Occupation: Cross-country skier

In February 2018, Jessica "Jessie" Diggins made history when she crossed the finish line for the Olympic cross-country skiing ladies' team sprint competition, claiming a first-place finish and a gold medal alongside teammate Kikkan Randall. The pair were the first American women ever to win Olympic medals for the sport of cross-country, or Nordic, skiing, and their gold medal was only the second medal won by any American for that sport. Although Diggins competed in several additional ski events at the Olympics and came close to medaling in several of them, she was particularly thrilled to have won the gold for her team sprint with Randall, with whom she had previously achieved success at the International Ski Federation's World Cup and World Championship events. "Just having it happen at a team event means so much more to me than any individual medal ever would," she told Tom Dougherty for *NBCOlympics.com* (21 Feb. 2018).

A skier since she was barely old enough to walk, Diggins competed extensively on the high school level and later turned down a college scholarship to pursue a career as a professional athlete. In addition to skiing with club teams such as the Central Cross Country Ski Association and Stratton Mountain School elite teams, she joined the US national ski team in 2011 and went on to represent the United States in a variety of international competitions, including the 2014 Winter Olympics in Sochi, Russia. Despite her professional focus, however, Diggins has noted that she performs best when she focuses on her enjoyment of the sport rather than on the goal of winning. "When I'm having fun, that's when I'm dangerous on the race course," she told Rachel Blount for the Minneapolis *Star Tribune* (22 Feb. 2018). "And if one too many people says, 'OK! I believe it! You're going to go win it,' then it becomes less fun. Because winning is not the full end game for me."

EARLY LIFE AND EDUCATION

Jessica "Jessie" Diggins was born on August 26, 1991, in St. Paul, Minnesota, to Clay and Deborah Diggins. She grew up in Afton, Minnesota, with her parents and her sister, Mackenzie. Her parents were avid cross-country skiers, and they introduced Diggins to that sport at a very young age. "From when I was a baby, they would put me in their backpack and go on their ski dates every weekend," she recalled to the hosts of the NPR program *Wait Wait . . . Don't Tell Me!* (3 Mar. 2018). "And so I grew up, you know, pulling on my dad's hair telling him to mush like he was a sled dog or something." When Diggins was still a small child, the family joined the Minnesota Youth Ski League, and she began learning to ski herself before even beginning school. The love of skiing also extended to Diggins's maternal grandparents, and the family often gathered to ski together during the winters.

Although Diggins was "mostly in it for the hot chocolate" during her early life, as she told Hanna Howard for *Teen Vogue* (14 Feb. 2018), she later developed an interest in cross-country

By Cephas, via Wikimedia Commons

ski racing, particularly after joining her high school's ski team. Diggins likewise participated in athletic activities such as swimming and track and played the violin for a time before focusing primarily on skiing. She graduated from Stillwater Area High School in 2010.

EARLY CAREER

By her preteen years, Diggins demonstrated not only an affinity for skiing but also the qualities that would make her a strong competitor in the sport. "It became evident she had a combination of talent and drive," her mother told Dan Emerson for *St. Croix Valley Magazine* (Jan. 2017). She began competing against high school students while in seventh grade and won her first high school race at the Snowflake Nordic Ski Center in Duluth, Minnesota. As a skier for Stillwater Area High School, Diggins earned her school multiple state titles. Following her graduation in 2010, Diggins joined the Central Cross Country Ski Association's elite CXC Team, with which she competed for two seasons. She later joined the Stratton Mountain School T2 elite team, which would remain her club team into 2018. In 2011, she was selected to join the US national women's cross-country ski team.

Although Diggins was offered a scholarship to Northern Michigan University after high school, she opted to defer admission for a year to ski full time and determine whether she wanted to pursue a full-time career in the sport. She achieved significant success as a skier during that period, which led her to put plans to attend college aside for the time being. "I got on the US Ski Team, and I was like, 'You know what? School's always going to be there, but I have this shot,'" she told Howard of her decision. Diggins later took some online classes through Westminster College and was particularly intrigued by subjects such as sociology and psychology, but skiing remained her primary focus.

As a skier, Diggins particularly enjoys participating in distance races. "It's just you and the course, and no games or tactics with other skiers . . . just skiing your heart out," she told Emerson. She also performed particularly well in sprints and would go on to distinguish herself as a particularly strong competitor in team sprint events.

NATIONAL COMPETITOR

Joining the US national team, Diggins found herself among a group of experienced skiers whose leadership skills and ski talents made them excellent mentors for a young athlete. "Everyone on the team is a leader in a different way," she explained to Howard. She continued, "Some people are really good at being the emotional team leader or the inspirational team leader, or someone's an incredible listener and they can

get anyone to feel better. And so I love looking at all my teammates, and being the youngest on the World Cup circuit, I see them as these awesome older sisters." Diggins found success when competing along with Randall, who in 2009 had become the first American woman to medal at the International Ski Federation (FIS) Nordic World Ski Championships.

Throughout her years as a professional skier, Diggins has regularly competed in FIS Cross-Country World Cup events. She earned her first team first-place finish alongside Randall in 2012, winning a team sprint event in Quebec City, Quebec, Canada. Her first major individual victory came in early 2016, when she claimed first place in an FIS Stage World Cup five-kilometer freestyle event in Toblach, Italy. In January 2018, she earned her first non-stage World Cup first-place finish in Seefeld, Austria, in a ten-kilometer freestyle mass start competition.

Diggins competed in her first FIS Nordic World Ski Championships in February 2011, achieving her best performance in the four-by-five-kilometer relay, in which she placed ninth. She returned to the biennial championships in 2013 and made history when she and Randall claimed the gold medal in the team sprint, becoming the first Americans to do so. Subsequent world championships saw Diggins claim second place in the individual ten-kilometer and sprint freestyle events as well as third in the 2017 team sprint. The 2017 sprint freestyle event was particularly significant for the US team, as Diggins and Randall took second and third place, respectively, thus having two American women medal for the second consecutive championship. "It seemed like we made it," Diggins told Rachel Axon for *USA Today* (24 Feb. 2017). "It's been a lot of hard work to get here, and it was just this really cool team pride moment."

OLYMPIC GOLD

In addition to her success in FIS-sponsored international competitions, Diggins entered a variety of US events as well as international competitions run by different athletics bodies. She made her first Olympic appearance with the US national team in 2014, competing at the Winter Games in Sochi, Russia. During that competition, she placed thirty-eighth in the thirty-kilometer mass start event, thirteenth in the sprint freestyle event, and eighth in the four-by-five-kilometer relay and the fifteen-kilometer skiathlon.

In February 2018, Diggins traveled to Pyeongchang, South Korea, to compete in her second Winter Olympics. She put forth a greatly improved performance from her previous Olympic outing, placing seventh in the thirty-kilometer mass start event, sixth in the classic sprint, and fifth in the four-by-five-kilometer relay, ten-kilometer freestyle, and skiathlon. On February 21, Diggins participated in the ladies' team sprint free competition, in which pairs of skiers alternated to sprint through six laps. Paired with Randall, Diggins helped claim first place in the second heat of the semifinals, and the duo went on to face off against several serious competitors, including former Olympic gold medalist Marit Bjørgen of Norway, in the finals.

Over the course of the event, Diggins pushed herself hard to claim the greatest Olympic finish yet for her team. "In that last corner, I don't know what I was thinking, except, 'Go! Go! Go!'" she told Blount. "You're going to have to dig really deep. I was in a lot of pain, for sure. But when your team is counting on you, you've got to give it everything you have." Diggins and Randall ended the event with a total time of 15:56.47, 0.19 seconds ahead of Swedish skiers Charlotte Kalla and Stina Nilsson. For Diggins, the realization that she and Randall had claimed first place was stunning. "I was like, 'Did we just win the Olympics?'" she told Blount. "And she was like, 'Yeah.'"

A significant milestone in Diggins's skiing career, the pair's gold-medal finish was a major achievement for the US national team as well. They were the first American women to win an Olympic cross-country ski medal and likewise claimed what was only the United States' second Olympic medal in that sport, following the silver medal won by skier Bill Koch in 1976. In recognition of her achievements, Diggins was selected to serve as the United States' flag bearer during the closing ceremonies.

PERSONAL LIFE

Diggins spends her summers training in Stratton, Vermont, and her winters competing in FIS World Cup competitions, primarily in Europe. In addition to skiing, she enjoys such activities as swimming, cliff-jumping, and dance. "I really love trying to learn hip-hop, and I'm not very good at it, let's just get that out of the way, but you don't have to be great at something to totally love it," she told Howard. Diggins has expressed an interest in becoming a children's dance teacher following her retirement from skiing.

SUGGESTED READING

Axon, Rachel. "U.S. Women Make History at Cross Country Skiing World Championships." *USA Today*, 24 Feb. 2017, www.usatoday.com/story/sports/olympics/2017/02/24/jessie-diggins-kikkan-randall-silver-bronze-cross-country-skiing-world-championships/98364702. Accessed 12 May 2018.

Blount, Rachel. "Jessie Diggins Propels U.S. to First Gold in Cross-Country Skiing History." *Star Tribune*, 22 Feb. 2018, startribune.com/diggins-propels-u-s-to-first-gold-in-cross-country-skiing-history/474683283. Accessed 12 May 2018.

Diggins, Jessica. "An Interview with Jessie Diggins, Winter Olympics 2018 Cross-Country Skier." Interview by Hanna Howard. *Teen Vogue*, 14 Feb. 2018, www.teenvogue.com/story/jessie-diggins-cross-country-skiing-team-usa-olympics-q-and-a/amp. Accessed 12 May 2018.

Diggins, Jessica. "Not My Job: Cross-Country Skier Jessie Diggins Gets Quizzed on Skee-Ball." Interview by Peter Sagal et al. *Wait Wait . . . Don't Tell Me*, NPR, 3 Mar. 2018, www.npr.org/2018/03/03/590247178/not-my-job-cross-country-skier-jessie-diggins-gets-quizzed-on-skee-ball. Accessed 12 May 2018.

Dougherty, Tom. "U.S. Ends 42-Year Olympic Cross-Country Medal Drought with Historic Gold." *NBCOlympics.com*, 21 Feb. 2018, www.nbcolympics.com/news/us-ends-42-year-olympic-cross-country-medal-drought-historic-gold. Accessed 12 May 2018.

Emerson, Dan. "Afton's Jessie Diggins Is a Star on the U.S. Nordic Ski Team." *St. Croix Valley Magazine*, Jan. 2017, stcroixvalleymag.com/afton%E2%80%99s-jessie-diggins-star-us-nordic-ski-team. Accessed 12 May 2018.

"Olympian with Northland Roots: Jessie Diggins Grew Up in Skiing Family." *Duluth News Tribune*, 16 Feb. 2018, www.duluthnewstribune.com/lifestyle/family/4404326-olympian-northland-roots-jessie-diggins-grew-skiing-family. Accessed 12 May 2018.

—Joy Crelin

Skylar Diggins-Smith

Date of birth: August 2, 1990
Occupation: Basketball player

Skylar Diggins-Smith is a Women's National Basketball Association (WNBA) All-Star point guard for the Dallas Wings, formerly known as the Tulsa Shock. Diggins-Smith was drafted third overall by the Shock in 2013, behind WNBA legends Brittney Griner of the Phoenix Mercury and Elena Delle Donne of the Washington Mystics. Before that, she was a college superstar. At Notre Dame, she led her team to three National Collegiate Athletic Association (NCAA) Final Four games and two championship games. She is the only player, male or female, in Notre Dame history to earn over 2,000 points, 500 rebounds, and 500 assists. She is also the school's all-time leading scorer, with 2,357 career points. Coach Muffet McGraw's characterization of

BDZ Sports [CC BY-SA 4.0], via Wikimedia Commons

her at the time is apt. McGraw told Ann Hardie for *Notre Dame Magazine* (Winter 2012–13) that Diggins-Smith "is the face of women's college basketball."

Despite an injury in 2015, Diggins-Smith has become extraordinarily popular during her four years as a professional baller. She has appeared at Fashion Week, at the Grammy Awards, in the pages of *Vogue* and has posed for *Sports Illustrated*'s swimsuit issue. In 2016, she published a young adult book based on her life called *The Middle School Rules of Skylar Diggins*. The book is part of a series about the childhoods of famous athletes by author Sean Jensen. It was illustrated by her husband, Daniel Smith. Diggins-Smith is the only female athlete signed to rapper Jay-Z's Roc Nation Sports (she calls herself the "Princess of Roc Nation"). The agency has brokered deals for her with Nike (where she has a line of headbands) and BodyArmor sports drink, but also Neiman Marcus, Nordstrom, and Sprint. Building her brand has taken real effort, Mina Kimes for *ESPN* (13 May 2016) pointed out: unlike a male basketball star, Diggins-Smith's fame "isn't a side effect of her labor, transmitted passively to millions via their TV sets at night." Her personal brand is truly "a project" and "a job that she approaches with the same intensity she displays on the court."

In her work as a businesswoman, Diggins-Smith hopes to bring more attention to the WNBA. She is also being pragmatic; female players do not enjoy the same salaries or benefits that male players do. In her retirement, still several years down the road, Diggins-Smith hopes to transform herself into a mogul. This ambition,

too, is in line with her brand. Diggins-Smith often uses the phrase "beauty and the beast" on social media. "A lot of times they don't talk about women athletes . . . having both," she told Kimes. "But you can have both. You can be a feminine woman and a beast on the court. You don't have to choose."

EARLY LIFE

Diggins-Smith was born in South Bend, Indiana, on August 2, 1990. Shortly after her birth, Diggins-Smith's parents separated. She lived with her mother, Renee Scott, in a town near South Bend called Mishawaka. When she was three years old, her father, Tige Diggins, gave her a basketball hoop. The young Diggins-Smith was ecstatic. Her father coached her in the sport, as did Maurice Scott, Diggins-Smith's stepfather. Scott was the director of the nearby Martin Luther King Jr. Recreation Center. Diggins-Smith played her first games at the center, with Scott as her coach. She soon began playing seriously with a travel league, her work ethic inspired by her mother. "She'd tell us [Diggins-Smith and her stepsiblings], 'Don't say I can't. Say I'll try,'" Diggins-Smith recalled to Mike Lopresti for *USA Today* (5 Mar. 2013). Determination and an aversion to losing were ingrained in Diggins-Smith from an early age. After a poor performance at the Amateur Athletic Union (AAU) National Championships when she was eleven years old, her stepfather, who was also her coach at the time, caught her up late one night reviewing hours of game tape. The next year, when Diggins-Smith was twelve, she led her team, the Lady Soldiers, to a national championship.

By the time Diggins-Smith was in eighth grade, Notre Dame University had already expressed interest in offering her a scholarship. She played for the Washington High School Panthers in South Bend. After losing the state championship her freshman year in 2006, Diggins-Smith led the team to a championship in 2007, scoring a state finals record 17 rebounds and 27 points. She was named Gatorade State Girls' Basketball Player of the Year in 2008 after averaging 29.5 points, 7.6 rebounds, 4.5 assists and 3.9 steals a game. In the summer, she led the USA Women's Under-18 National Team to a gold medal at the International Basketball Federation (FIBA) Under-18 Championship in Buenos Aires, Argentina. In 2008, her junior year, she was ranked number one as a point guard and number three overall in her class. In 2009, she was named the Gatorade National High School Athlete of the Year. She was also named Most Valuable Player (MVP) at both the McDonald's High School All-America Game and the Women's Basketball Coaches Association (WBCA) High School All-America Game. (The last time a player accomplished that feat was in 2004.)

Diggins-Smith briefly considered committing to Stanford University, before accepting a scholarship at her hometown Notre Dame prior to graduating in 2009.

STARDOM AT NOTRE DAME

Surprisingly, Diggins-Smith, who graduated with a degree in management-entrepreneurship, spent much of her freshman year at Notre Dame on the bench. "I went in there with so much hype from the South Bend community, and now this," she recalled to Hardie. But by the end of the next year, Diggins-Smith was a starter, and, thanks to social media, a national phenomenon, receiving encouraging tweets from fans like rapper Lil' Wayne and singer Chris Brown. That year, she hit 1,000 career points mid-season (only the second player in school history to do so in their sophomore year), and led the Irish to the 2011 NCAA championship, where they lost to Texas A&M. Diggins-Smith was selected to the 2011 State Farm Coaches' All-America team. She and Griner were the only two sophomores chosen for the elite ten-player squad. Diggins-Smith and the Irish returned to the NCAA championship in 2012, only to lose to Baylor. That year, she was the first Notre Dame player ever selected as the recipient of the Nancy Lieberman Award, presented to the NCAA's top point guard. She was also named Big East Player of the Year. (She won both prestigious awards again the following year.) The Irish returned to the Final Four in 2013, but ultimately lost to the UConn Huskies. Diggins-Smith was particularly devastated by the loss. In four years, she had failed to lead the Irish to a championship title. Huskies coach Geno Auriemma, she recalled to Nick Combs for the blog *Slap the Sign* (2013), pulled her aside to set the record straight: "He told me not to let this game define my legacy and said I have done more for the sport than some people who have won four national championships."

WNBA CAREER

Diggins-Smith was selected third in the 2013 WNBA draft by the Tulsa Shock. She struggled to adjust to her new career during her rookie season, but received the WNBA Most Improved Player (MIP) Award after her second season in 2014. That year, she started all 34 games, and led the team in scoring (20.1 points), assists, steals and minutes. She led the entire league in minutes, placed second overall in scoring and fourth overall in assists. In 2015, Diggins-Smith was averaging about 17 points a game when an anterior cruciate ligament (ACL) tear in June put an abrupt end to her season. (WNBA seasons run from May to September.) To add insult to injury, the tear came after Diggins-Smith scored a season-high 31 points in a winning game against the Seattle Storm. Before her injury Diggins-Smith had considered playing in China. Most WNBA players, whose salaries are capped at $110,000, play overseas in the off-season to make extra money. Diggins-Smith, who spends her off-seasons pursuing her various business endeavors and training, was hoping that time in China would polish her game in time for the 2016 Olympics, but the ACL tear saw her cut from the Olympic team. Her road to recovery was long and difficult. She returned to South Bend, while the Shock announced that it was moving the franchise to Dallas. Diggins-Smith began her career with the new Dallas Wings in 2016 in a limited role thanks to her ongoing recovery, but signed a contract extension to play with the team through 2019. In 2017, Diggins-Smith was back on her A-game. In a June game against the San Antonio Stars, Diggins-Smith scored a franchise-record seven three-pointers. Later that season, she was voted to the 2017 All-Star Team.

The same year—2017—Diggins-Smith teamed up with Crystal McCrary, who produced and directed the 2013 documentary *Little Ballers*, to produce a three-part documentary series called *Little Ballers Indiana* for Nickelodeon. The miniseries follows an AAU team of eleven- and twelve-year-old girls. The team, called the Sky Digg Ballers, is sponsored by Diggins-Smith and coached by her stepfather. The series is about basketball, De Elizabeth wrote for *Teen Vogue* (27 Feb. 2017), "But make no mistake: the message of *Little Ballers* will hit home for everyone, regardless of whether or not they ever played sports. It is refreshing to witness a story of girls discovering solidarity through a sport, and how that sportsmanship translates into the bigger themes of life."

PERSONAL LIFE

Diggins-Smith met Daniel Smith, a graphic artist and former football player who is also a South Bend native, at the University of Notre Dame. They were married at the Museum of Contemporary Art Chicago in spring 2017.

SUGGESTED READING

Combs, Nick. "Skylar Diggins: The South Bend Kid, the Notre Dame Legend." *Slap the Sign*, 8 Apr. 2013, slapthesign.com/2013/04/08/skylar-diggins-the-south-bend-kid-the-notre-dame-legend/. Accessed 15 Jan. 2018.

Elizabeth, De. "Nickelodeon to Premiere Three-Part Docu-Series, 'Little Ballers Indiana.'" *Teen Vogue*, 27 Feb. 2017, www.teenvogue.com/story/nickelodeon-premiere-three-part-docu-series-little-ballers-indiana. Web. 15 Jan. 2018.

Hardie, Ann. "Being Skylar Diggins." *Notre Dame Magazine*, Winter 2012–13, magazine.nd.edu/news/being-skylar-diggins/. Accessed 15 Jan. 2018.

Kimes, Mina. "How Skylar Diggins Is Building a Brand That Transcends the WNBA." *ESPN*, 13 May 2016, www.espn.com/wnba/story/_/id/15472015/dallas-wings-star-skylar-diggins-wants-change-marketing-game-wnba-players. Accessed 15 Jan. 2018.

Lopresti, Mike. "Skylar Diggins' Notre Dame Legacy Goes beyond Twitter, Final Four." *USA Today*, 5 Mar. 2013, www.usatoday.com/story/sports/ncaaw/bigeast/2013/03/05/skylar-diggins-notre-dame-fighting-irish/1965359/. Accessed 15 Jan. 2018.

—*Molly Hagan*

Julie Dillon

Date of birth: January 30, 1982
Occupation: Artist

Julie Dillon is a three-time Hugo Award–winning illustrator. The science fiction and fantasy artist's work has appeared on the covers of games, novels, music albums, and magazines. She began her freelance career in 2006, and won her first Chesley Award in 2011. (The Chesley Awards, from the Association of Science Fiction and Fantasy Artists, recognize achievement in science fiction and fantasy illustration.) Dillon was first nominated for the prestigious Best Professional Artist Award at the Hugo Awards in 2013, making her the first female artist nominated in the category since Rowena Morrill in 1986. She went on to win the award in 2014, 2015, and 2017. The Hugo Awards, the science fiction/fantasy (SFF) genre's longest-running award, were roiled by controversy during this time. The same year that Dillon was first nominated, a right-wing contingent of mostly male fans called the Sad Puppies exploited the Hugo Awards' nomination system to favor candidates of their own choosing. The Sad Puppies formed in reaction to the Hugo Awards' tentative embrace of work featuring and created by women and people of color. The SFF genre has long been dominated by white male creators and stories featuring white men. The Puppies viewed the shift away from this tradition as an assault on the genre's core values. (There is a long and rich history of women and people of color creating SFF stories and art, but the Puppies saw the Hugos' recognition of this work as politically motivated.) The Puppies' campaign came to a vitriolic climax (and spectacular demise) in 2015, the same year Dillon won Best Professional Artist for a second time and African American author N. K. Jemisin won Best Novel.

Dillon is an important player in this larger story because her work is part of a new guard. Her illustrations feature women, often women of color, as heroes of their various and beguiling worlds. "Everyone has an important viewpoint to offer the world," Dillon told Galen Dara for *Fantasy Magazine* (1 Oct. 2014), when asked about what advice she would give aspiring female artists. "And if your chosen field doesn't tend to have many voices like yours, your unique viewpoint is all the more valuable (even if everyone doesn't see it that way right away)."

EARLY LIFE AND EDUCATION

Dillon was born on January 30, 1982. As a teenager, the young SFF fan drew fan art and copied images from her Magic: The Gathering cards using pencil, charcoal, and watercolor. (Magic is a popular trading card game that was first produced in the early 1990s.) Inspired by the explosive popularity of anime in the late 1990s, Dillon set aside her pencils and brushes and made the leap into digital art. "I saved up and got a tablet and a copy of [Adobe] Photoshop and got to work," she told illustrator Kiri Leonard in an interview for Leonard's personal blog (8 May 2014). "I don't know that working digitally was necessarily a choice of one medium over another, so much as it was just the teenage me trying to be like all the other cool kids and then just getting used to working that way." In the early 2000s, Dillon found the digital concept art community online. Concept artists make illustrations that tell a story through their depiction of characters and settings, and could serve as the basis for a movie or video game. She found this community of artists through forum posts on a now defunct website called Sijun. Art, particularly digital art using Photoshop, became Dillon's passion, but she was unconvinced that she could make it her career. Thus, she chose to attend Sacramento State University as a computer science student. In class, she doodled in the margins of her notebooks. Feeling ill at ease in the major, Dillon switched her degree to technical theater. After a few years, this life course, too, felt wrong.

Dillon earned her BFA degree in fine art from Sacramento State University in 2005, but her training, she told the British digital art magazine *Imagine FX* (29 Jan. 2016), left much to be desired. The program was, she said, "at best unhelpful. At worst, it was discouraging and damaging." Her professors were curiously "anti-illustration" and "anti-traditional skill building," she recalled. Even with a degree, she lacked training in anatomy, color theory, and composition. After graduation, she focused on making a living, taking local art classes when she could, and continuing to create work for herself in her spare time. Eventually, she decided she would have to take herself seriously as an artist to succeed. She enrolled in classes a few hours away at serious art schools, the Academy of Art University in San Francisco and Watts Atelier of the Arts in Encinitas. Her professional career began in 2006.

ARTISTIC VISION

For the first six months of her career as a freelance illustrator, Dillon hunted for jobs, sent out her portfolio, and contacted art directors. No one expressed any interest in working with her. She almost quit, but then *Dragon* magazine, a now defunct publication about the role-playing game Dungeons and Dragons, contacted her. The magazine hired her to design characters for an article. The assignment was the true beginning of Dillon's professional career. Her work for *Dragon* led to work with other clients, including Tor Books and the game-publishing company Wizards of the Coast. Still, Dillon told *Imagine FX*, it took her several years to make a living from illustration alone.

Dillon works on multiple projects at a time. She schedules her days efficiently, brainstorming concepts and drawing sketches in the morning and completing detail work in the evening. She works entirely in digital media. Dillon explained her process of realizing her client's vision to *Imagine FX*: "I start with a general concept or feeling I want to convey. Sometimes the composition jumps right in my head, exactly the way I want it. But often I have to brainstorm a little bit to figure out the best way to approach the concept, to best express the idea I want to express." Sometimes, when Dillon presents a sketch to a client, they decide to move in a different direction. Such was the case with a painting called *Ariadne*, which grew from a rejected idea about the mythological princess Ariadne. In the story, Ariadne gives Theseus a ball of thread to help him find his way through the labyrinth to slay the beastly Minotaur. Dillon imagined Ariadne (and her red ball of thread) making the way through the maze herself, with the Minotaur looming, larger-than-life, beyond the horizon line.

The painting, which was composed using a fish-eye grid, is a good representation of Dillon's unique sensibility. Magical elements are often represented using abstraction. In *Alice*, Alice of *Alice in Wonderland* slices her way through an avalanche of life-sized playing cards with a knife. Dillon is perhaps best known, however, for her use of vibrant color. Her palette tends toward complimentary purples and golds. "I like those brighter color schemes because they are so lively and energetic and eye catching," she told Loraine Sammy for *Apex Magazine* (4 Mar. 2014). An illustration called *Fortune's Favored* features a dark-skinned woman leaping from a tower and swinging above city rooftops on a rope of flags. It is notable for its swirling composition and bright pinks, purples, oranges, and golds. The grisly *Space Sirens* depicts shadowy space monsters draining the life from human astronauts. In contrast to its subject matter, the painting is backlit by brilliant greens, pinks, blues, and oranges.

Dillon draws inspiration from such artists as Alphonse Mucha and John William Waterhouse. Mucha was a Czech Art Nouveau and Symbolist painter who died in 1939. His work, in the Neoclassical style, often depicted mythic or haloed women emerging from an ornate frame, but his masterpiece, a series of large-scale paintings called *The Slav Epic*, also bears a remarkable similarity to Dillon's work in both color (purples and golds) and composition. In some of Dillon's compositions, such as *Cosmic Traveler*, the painting appears to ripple outward from a focal point, playing on the magic of circles and halos. This choice mimics the overt geometric shapes in Mucha's work.

The influence of Waterhouse, a Romantic painter who died in 1917, is equally recognizable in Dillon's work. Waterhouse painted figures, mostly women, from Greek mythology and medieval legend. Unlike Mucha, he preferred to set his characters in realistic scenes. His Celtic figures, with their long, draping skirts and cascading hair, are playfully interpreted in some of Dillon's paintings, such as *Slumbering Naiad*. Her evocative *Surface* is reminiscent of Waterhouse's painting of William Shakespeare's Ophelia, a character from *Hamlet* who drowned herself in a river.

In 2014, buoyed by her first Hugo Award for Best Professional Artist, Dillon started a Kickstarter fundraising page to finance her first book, a collection of paintings called *Imagined Realms: Book 1*. The fundraiser quickly exceeded its goal. Dillon self-funded a second book, *Imagined Realms Book 2: Earth and Sky*, in 2015. Dillon won her third Hugo Award for Best Professional Artist in 2017. She also illustrated the cover for a collection called *Catalysts, Explorers and Secret Keepers: Women of Science Fiction* (2017).

PERSONAL LIFE

Dillon, who enjoys hiking, gardening and volunteering at a local equine rescue organization, lives in Northern California.

SUGGESTED READING

Bell, Julie, et al. "Artist Spotlight: Women in Fantasy Illustration Roundtable." Interview by Galen Dara. *Fantasy Magazine*, 1 Oct. 2014, www.fantasy-magazine.com/new/artist-spotlight/artist-spotlight-women-in-fantasy-illustration-roundtable/. Accessed 14 Jan. 2018.

Dillon, Julie. "Interview with Julie Dillon." *Apex Magazine*, 4 Mar. 2014, www.apex-magazine.com/interview-with-julie-dillon/. Accessed 14 Jan. 2018.

Dillon, Julie. "Women in Fantasy Illustration: Julie Dillon." Interview by Kiri Leonard. *Kiri*, 8 May 2014, kirileonard.com/women-fantasy-illustration-julie-dillon/. Accessed 13 Jan. 2018.

"Julie Dillon." *Imagine FX*, 29 Jan. 2016, www.pressreader.com/australia/imagine-fx/20160129/281500750264595. Accessed 13 Jan. 2018.

—*Molly Hagan*

Grigor Dimitrov

Date of birth: May 16, 1991
Occupation: Tennis player

In November 2017, tennis player Grigor Dimitrov surprised fans and sports commentators when he defeated all opponents to win the Nitto ATP Finals, a prestigious tournament within the Association of Tennis Professionals (ATP) World Tour. His win occurred during his first appearance at the Finals, making him the first player to win during a debut appearance there in nearly two decades. Dimitrov's success at the Finals likewise marked his fourth World Tour title of 2017, an impressive achievement following two years of disappointment on the court.

A tennis player since early childhood, Dimitrov first gained widespread attention in 2008, when he won the junior boys' singles championship at Wimbledon. He launched his professional tennis career in entry-level men's tournaments, became a frequent competitor in the ATP World Tour by 2011, and began amassing tour titles in 2013, a trend he hopes to continue. However, although Dimitrov has demonstrated both the desire and the talent to win multiple ATP World Tour titles, he seeks to balance that drive with a sense of flexibility and a genuine love of the game. "I'm just going a little bit with the flow," he told Reem Abulleil for *Sport360* (15 Nov. 2017). "I'm just focusing on what I'm doing right now, I'm not thinking of the ranking or the points."

EARLY LIFE AND EDUCATION

Grigor Dimitrov was born on May 16, 1991, in Haskovo, Bulgaria. He grew up in that city, in a neighborhood that he described to Joe Shute for the *Telegraph* (5 June 2015) as tough. "It wasn't easy to walk out on the street," he told Shute. "There were always things happening around. It was a mixture of crime and an unsafe environment."

Dimitrov's parents, Dimitar and Maria, were both heavily involved in sports: his father coached tennis, and his mother, a former

By Joshua Sadli [CC BY-SA 2.0], via Wikimedia Commons

volleyball player, was a sports instructor. Dimitrov began playing tennis himself at the age of three, under the tutelage of his father, who remained his coach during the player's early career. "Throughout the summer we would be out there on the court at the hottest times of the day but I loved it," he recalled to David Cox for the *Financial Times* (15 Aug. 2014). "I was enjoying it so much and I think that's what made us work so well together. We were pulling each other up and striving for greatness."

Although Dimitrov learned a great deal about tennis through his father's instruction, the family ultimately determined that he should undertake further training outside of Bulgaria. He left the country as a teenager to train abroad, including at the Sánchez-Casal Academy in Barcelona, Spain, for the 2007–8 season. During that time, Dimitrov rebelled against the rules but nevertheless managed to hone his skills with the goal of making the transition into professional play.

EARLY CAREER

Dimitrov began playing tennis professionally at the age of sixteen, launching his career on the Futures circuit of tournaments. Organized by the International Tennis Federation (ITF), the Futures tournaments are geared toward players in the preliminary stages of their professional careers. Dimitrov played in ITF events in 2007 in Bulgaria and Spain. He made his debut appearance on the ATP World Tour, the highest-level professional circuit, in April 2008, playing in the first qualifying round of the Barcelona Open. Over the course of that year, he went on to appear in ITF events, as well as mid-level ATP Challenger Tour and a select few ATP World Tour competitions. He won his first ITF event in February of that year, defeating Carlos Gonzalez de Cueto in the final of the Spain F5 competition, and claimed additional victories at Spain F20 Futures, Spain F34 Futures, and Spain F35 Futures during the months that followed.

Perhaps the most exciting moment in Dimitrov's career to that point came in the summer of 2008, when he played in the junior boys' singles championships at Wimbledon. Hosted in London, England, since 1877, the adult Wimbledon championships are among four events known as tennis's Grand Slam tournaments, which also include the Australian Open, the French Open, and the US Open. Although not conveying the same level of prestige as its adult counterpart, the junior Wimbledon competition was a meaningful one for Dimitrov, who defeated Finnish player Henri Kontinen to claim the title. In addition to representing a major milestone in his career, the win reinforced his commitment to professional tennis. "The first thought when I was lifting the trophy was that I want [to] make it to the top," he told Pritha Sarkar for *Reuters* (27 June 2015). "I want to win the real thing." Dimitrov went on to win the junior US Open boys' singles title later that year. His seemingly effortless performance earned him the moniker Baby Fed, a reference to longtime tennis champion Roger Federer.

Over the next several years, Dimitrov competed in a variety of events, primarily on the ITF circuit and the ATP Challenger Tour. He entered two Grand Slam tournaments in 2009, the US Open and Wimbledon, but was eliminated in the second qualifying round and the first round, respectively. Dimitrov won his first ATP Challenger Tour event in Geneva, Switzerland, in August of 2010 and achieved two additional back-to-back Challenger Tour victories in Bangkok, Thailand, in September.

WORLD TOUR AND OLYMPIC COMPETITION

By 2011, Dimitrov had become a fixture on the ATP World Tour and consistently competed in Grand Slam tournaments, although he had yet to proceed past the second round of any of those events. In addition to his professional play, he represented Bulgaria at the 2012 Olympic Games in London, competing in the men's singles tennis competition. At the Olympics, he defeated Lukasz Kubot of Poland in the round of sixty-four but lost to Gilles Simon of France in the round of thirty-two.

In October 2013, Dimitrov claimed his first ATP World Tour title at the Stockholm Open in Sweden. Over the year following his first ATP World Tour win, Dimitrov made a particularly strong showing on the court, claiming three additional World Tour titles. His string of victories began in March 2014, when he won in Acapulco, Mexico, and he went on to win the BRD Năstase Țiriac Trophy in Bucharest, Romania, the following month. In June, Dimitrov won London's Queen's Club Championships. He also achieved his best Grand Slam finishes yet that year, reaching the quarterfinals of the Australian Open in January and setting a new personal record in July after making it to the semifinals at Wimbledon.

Yet Dimitrov struggled in 2015. During that year, he played more than twenty matches but won no ATP World Tour titles and was unable to progress past the semifinals in any singles tournaments in which he competed. Although he made it to the finals of several events the following year, including the Istanbul Open and the China Open, he again claimed no tour titles. He also had a somewhat disappointing performance in the Olympic Games in Rio de Janeiro, Brazil, where he was eliminated from the men's singles tournament in the round of sixty-four.

Despite such challenges, Dimitrov viewed tournaments from which he was eliminated early as valuable teaching tools. "The matches are good to watch so you can see how the players are in certain situations—how they play, for example, in the moments of a big match," he explained to Christopher Bollen, *Interview*, (18 July 2016). "Those are the moments when you rely on yourself. You can't rely on your coach or anyone else to scout that."

TURNING POINT

A turning point in Dimitrov's career came in 2017, during which he put forward an impressive performance that overcame the disappointments of the previous two years. He began the year by winning the Brisbane International early in January, defeating Japanese tennis star Kei Nishikori to claim his first World Tour title since 2014. He went on to compete in his second semifinal match at the Australian Open and in February won Bulgaria's Sofia Open. In August of 2017, Dimitrov won his third title of the year at the ATP World Tour Masters 1000 Cincinnati.

Dimitrov has attributed his improved performance to an intentional effort to set concrete goals with his team, which since August 2016 has included successful coach Daniel "Dani" Vellverdú. "It was basically about simplifying everything as much as possible, from my fitness, to the on-court work to the off-court work," he explained to James Buddell for the *ATP World Tour* website (8 Nov. 2017). "Setting regular targets—short-, medium- and long-term—has helped to develop my confidence and consistency."

In November of 2017, Dimitrov made his first appearance in the Nitto ATP Finals, an event considered within the tennis community to be the highest-level professional tournament outside of the Grand Slam competitions. "The [Nitto ATP] Finals is a very special place for anybody," he told Buddell. "I've definitely always wanted to go there and be a part of that elite group." During the competition, which took place in London, he defeated Dominic Thiem of Austria, David Goffin of Belgium, and Pablo Carreño Busta of Spain in round-robin matches before overcoming US player Jack Sock in the semifinals. In the finals, Dimitrov again faced off against and ultimately beat Goffin to claim the title, his fourth that year.

Dimitrov started 2018 off strong, making it to the semifinals of the Brisbane International and to the quarterfinals of the Australian Open, both in January. Fueled by his success in 2017, he hoped to achieve even more over the course of the year. "I want to try to improve at tournaments I didn't do well at in 2017. I want to do better at the Grand Slams," he said in an interview for the *ATP World Tour* website (11 Feb. 2018). "That's the priority for any top player."

PERSONAL LIFE

Dimitrov maintains a residence in Monte Carlo, Monaco, but spends much of his time living out of hotels while traveling to compete. "I've never really settled in one place," he told Bollen. "I think with each year, I'm starting to feel it more and more, you know, to come back home and be like, [*sighs*] 'Okay, this is home. You can drop your stuff.'"

Although increasingly successful on the tennis court, Dimitrov has noted in interviews that he one day intends to step away from the sport to pursue other interests. "For some people it is their life but I don't see tennis being that forever," he explained to Shute. "Right now this is my priority and what I want to do. I'm winning and my goals are far ahead but after that I'm done with tennis. I like designing, creating and working on new things." Dimitrov has designed his own racket for Wilson as well as athletic apparel in partnership with Nike and enjoys painting.

Dimitrov reportedly dated American tennis star Serena Williams in 2012, and then her rival, Maria Sharapova, from 2012 to 2015. In late 2015, he became involved with singer Nicole Scherzinger.

SUGGESTED READING

Abulleil, Reem. "Grigor Dimitrov Interview: Every Loss Hurts More, Every Win I Appreciate More." *Sport360*, 15 Nov. 2017, sport360.com/article/tennis/255267/atp-finals-grigor-dimitrov-interview-on-conquering-his-demons-practicing-with-rafael-nadal-and-more. Accessed 9 Feb. 2018.
Buddell, James. "Grigor Dimitrov: Leaving No Stone Unturned." *ATP World Tour*, 8 Nov. 2017, www.atpworldtour.com/en/news/dimitrov-nitto-atp-finals-2017-programme. Accessed 9 Feb. 2018.
Cox, David. "Interview: Grigor Dimitrov." *Financial Times*, 15 Aug. 2014, www.ft.com/content/aa338f54-2277-11e4-9d4a-00144feabdc0. Accessed 9 Feb. 2018.
Dimitrov, Grigor. "Getting Personal with Grigor Dimitrov." Interview by Stanley Kay. *Sports Illustrated*, 29 Aug. 2017, www.si.com/tennis/2017/08/29/grigor-dimitrov-rafael-nadal-us-open-racket-the-notebook. Accessed 9 Feb. 2018.
Dimitrov, Grigor. Interview. By Christopher Bollen. *Interview*, 18 July 2016, www.interviewmagazine.com/culture/grigor-dimitrov. Accessed 9 Feb. 2018.
Sarkar, Pritha. "Acrobatic Dimitrov Hopes to Turn Wimbledon Upside Down." Reuters, 27 June 2015, www.reuters.com/article/us-tennis-wimbledon-dimitrov/acrobatic-dimitrov-hopes-to-turn-wimbledon-upside-down-idUSKBN0P70LA20150627. Accessed 9 Feb. 2018.
Shute, Joe. "Grigor Dimitrov: '500 Roses Are the Most I've Ever Sent Maria Sharapova at Once.'" *The Telegraph* [UK], 5 June 2015, www.telegraph.co.uk/sport/tennis/11643242/Grigor-Dimitrov-500-roses-are-the-most-Ive-ever-sent-Maria-Sharapova.html. Accessed 9 Feb. 2018.

—Joy Crelin

Jennifer Doudna

Date of birth: February 19, 1964
Occupation: Scientist

Jennifer Doudna is an American biochemist who codeveloped the CRISPR-Cas9 gene-editing technology.

EARLY LIFE AND EDUCATION

Jennifer Doudna was born on February 19, 1964, in Washington, DC. When she was seven, she and her family moved to Hilo, Hawaii. Her father took a job at the University of Hawaii at Hilo as a professor of literature. Her mother was a community college professor of history.

Doudna developed an interest in science as a child, and she cites many activities as inspirations for her future career. When she was in sixth grade, she read *The Double Helix* (1968) by James D. Watson and was enthralled by Watson's account of the discovery of the double helix configuration of DNA. She deepened her interest in science by working one summer in the lab of a family friend studying worms and mushrooms.

Doudna attended Pomona College in Claremont, California, and received a bachelor's degree in chemistry in 1985. There she studied under several professors who instilled in her an interest in research. She then studied at Harvard University under Jack W. Szostak, a 2009 Nobel laureate. She received her doctorate in biochemistry in 1989.

A CAREER IN SCIENCE

While a doctoral student at Harvard, Doudna earned distinction for coauthoring an article with Szostak that reported their findings on the catalysis of a ribozyme on various RNA substrates. The study was significant in that it provided support for the catalytic property of RNA. Doudna continued her research in self-replicating RNA as a postdoctoral research fellow in Szostak's lab until 1991. She then joined the lab of Thomas R. Cech, a 1989 Nobel laureate for chemistry, at the University of Colorado Boulder as a Lucille P. Markey Scholar in biomedical science.

From 1994 to 2002, Doudna worked at Yale University in the Department of Molecular Biophysics and Biochemistry, first as an assistant professor, and from 2000 on as the Henry Ford II Professor of Molecular Biophysics and Biochemistry. While her early research focused on the structure of RNA, her later research focused more on viral RNAs, hoping an understanding of their function could lead to new medical treatments of viruses such as hepatitis.

Doudna began working as an investigator for the Howard Hughes Medical Institute in 1997 and was a visiting professor at Harvard University from 2000 to 2001. During the late 1990s and early 2000s, she achieved several distinctions. In 1996, she and Cech published the structure of the P4-P6 domain, the first image of a large structure of RNA other than tRNA. She was awarded the Searle Scholar Award in 1996, the National Academy of Sciences Award for Initiatives in Research in 1999, the Alan T. Waterman Award in 2000, and the American Chemical Society Eli Lilly Award in Biology in 2001. She joined the National Academy of Sciences (NAS) in 2002.

Also in 2002, Doudna became a professor of cell biology and molecular biology at the University of California, Berkeley. She also joined the faculty of the Biophysics Group at the university and became a faculty scientist at the Physical Biosciences Division of the Lawrence Berkeley National Laboratory.

In 2005, Doudna began studying microbes that had an unusual sequence of DNA called clustered regularly interspaced short palindromic repeats (CRISPR). The sequences repeated and between the duplicate sequences were stretches of DNA that had been invaded by viruses. Doudna studied the virus-infected stretches to identify how viruses are able to change DNA.

While at a conference in Puerto Rico in 2011, Doudna met French microbiologist Emmanuelle Charpentier, who was also doing research on CRISPR sequences. They decided to collaborate and, together with postdoctoral researchers, they discovered a way to edit genes by splicing a genome and deleting or adding pieces of DNA. They published a description of their gene-editing technique, called CRISPR-Cas9, in *Science* in August 2012. In January 2013, they reported a demonstration of their technique using human cells.

In December 2012, George Church of Harvard University and Feng Zhang of Broad Institute simultaneously published independent papers reporting their demonstrations of the technique. Because they published their demonstrations before Doudna, Charpentier, and their team, they were recognized as the inventors of this technique by the US Patent Office and awarded several patents. Doudna and Charpentier contested the patents and a patent fight resulted, with the University of California and the Broad Institute taking their case for intellectual property rights to federal court.

Doudna and Charpentier have received numerous awards for their development of the CRISPR-Cas9 technique, including the 2014 Breakthrough Prize, the 2015 Gruber Genetics Prize, and the 2016 Canada Gairdner Award.

IMPACT

The development of CRISPR-Cas9, nicknamed DNA scissors, has proven to be a breakthrough technique in genome studies. It has led to the creation of new companies using the technique and the proliferation of novel studies in genomic engineering and disease therapies. Doudna formed two companies: Caribou Biosciences, devoted to research techniques, and Intellia Therapeutics, aimed at medical therapies and in vivo therapeutic development. Researchers around the world are using CRISPR-Cas9 to better understand genetic diseases, while others are using it for nonhuman applications, such as disease resistance in plants. In 2015, concerns over the use of CRISPR-Cas9 to genetically alter human embryos led Doudna and other biologists to call for a moratorium on using the technique for this purpose.

PERSONAL LIFE

Doudna is married to Jamie Cate, a scientist and professor at the University of California, Berkeley. They have a son, Andrew, and live in California.

SUGGESTED READING

"Jennifer A. Doudna." *University of California, Berkeley.* Regents of the University of California, 17 Sept. 2015. Web. 2 May 2016.

"Jennifer A. Doudna, Ph.D.: Investigator/1997–Present." *Howard Hughes Medical Institute.* HHMI, n.d. Web. 2 May 2016.

"Jennifer Doudna." *Gruber Foundation.* Gruber Foundation, 2015. Web. 2 May 2016.

Marino, Melissa. "Biography of Jennifer A. Doudna." *Proceedings of the National Academy of Sciences of the United States of America.* National Academy of Sciences, 7 Dec. 2004. Web. 2 May 2016.

Pollack, Andrew. "Jennifer Doudna, a Pioneer Who Helped Simplify Genome Editing." *New York Times.* New York Times, 11 May 2015. Web. 2 May 2016.

Sanders, Robert. "Jennifer Doudna, Cosmology Teams Named 2015 Breakthrough Winners." *Berkeley News.* UC Regents, 10 Nov. 2014. Web. 2 May 2016.

Wolfe, Alexandra. "Jennifer Doudna: The Promise and Peril of Gene Editing." *Wall Street Journal.* Dow Jones. 11 Mar. 2016. Web. 2 May 2016.

—*Barb Lightner*

Marcus du Sautoy

Date of birth: August 26, 1965
Occupation: Mathematician

"Mathematics is not only about utility," mathematician Marcus du Sautoy wrote in an essay for *Prospect* magazine (19 May 2016). "It's also about wonder and beauty." Indeed, du Sautoy has devoted much of his professional life to sharing the wonder and beauty of his field with the public through books, television programs, and public lectures and performances. A longtime researcher into subjects such as symmetry, du Sautoy became a professor of mathematics at the University of Oxford in 2005 and was named Simonyi Professor for the Public Understanding of Science in 2008. As Simonyi Professor, he has worked extensively to communicate the history, mechanisms, and applications of mathematics to audiences that may be disinterested in—or even hostile toward—the field. He has earned widespread recognition for his work, including entry into the prestigious Order of the British Empire and Royal Society. For du Sautoy, teaching the public the fascinating secrets of mathematics and science has rendered his own field not only more visible but also more appealing within society. "There's a geek chic about it now," he told Andrew Pettie for the *Telegraph* (26 July 2011).

Photo by David Levenson/Getty Images

"Science is cool. In fact, I'm no longer embarrassed to tell people that I'm a mathematician."

EARLY LIFE AND EDUCATION

Marcus Peter Francis du Sautoy was born in London, England, on August 26, 1965. He and his younger sister grew up in the town of Henley-on-Thames, where they lived with their parents, Bernard and Jennifer. Du Sautoy's father worked with computers, while his mother had previously worked for the British government's Foreign Office but left her position to care for the children. In addition to being influenced by his parents, who nurtured his analytical and creative sides, du Sautoy grew up admiring his grandfather Peter du Sautoy, who had served as an editor and later chairman for the publishing company Faber and Faber.

As a child and teenager, du Sautoy enjoyed music and began to play the trumpet. He was likewise interested in languages, in part, because of a misconception regarding his mother's former profession. "My mother worked for the Foreign Office and I was convinced—wrongly as it turns out—that she was a secret agent," he recalled to Robin McKie for the *Guardian* (1 Nov. 2008). "So I began learning different languages so I could be a spy as well. But I found it frustrating: all those irregular verbs and nouns. There was no pattern." He would later contrast the seemingly patternless nature of most languages with the "logical and consistent" nature of mathematics, which he described to McKie as "the perfect language."

du Sautoy initially struggled with mathematics in school, unable to connect in a meaningful way with the forms of arithmetic taught in the classroom. However, a turning point came when a teacher told him about some of the broader applications of mathematics and recommended an array of reading material that sparked du Sautoy's interest in the field. He was further inspired by a 1978 lecture delivered by mathematician Christopher Zeeman for the Royal Institution Christmas Lecture series, to which du Sautoy himself would contribute a series of lectures in 2006. After winning a scholarship to Wadham College, part of the University of Oxford, in 1983, du Sautoy pursued undergraduate and graduate studies in mathematics, earning his doctorate in the subject in 1989.

ACADEMIC AND RESEARCH CAREER

After completing his doctorate, du Sautoy traveled to Israel for a time, working at the Hebrew University in Jerusalem. Following his return to the United Kingdom, he held fellowships at a variety of institutions, including Queen Mary University of London. He joined All Souls College, Oxford, as a postdoctoral research fellow in 1990 and would later serve there as a Fifty-Pound Fellow and a Quondam Fellow. Du Sautoy also held posts as a Royal Society University Research Fellow at both Oxford and the University of Cambridge and became a fellow of Wadham College, Oxford, in 2002. He went on to serve as a Professorial Fellow of New College, Oxford.

As a researcher, du Sautoy's mathematical interests include prime numbers, which he described to McKie as "the atoms of arithmetic," and the concept of symmetry. "I'm trying to understand what symmetrical objects exist in mathematics and in nature—not just in three dimensions but in higher dimensions as well," he told Eleanor Hayes for *Science in School* (22 May 2012). In communicating such subjects to the general public, du Sautoy stresses the multitude of forms in which symmetry appears in nature and in society, including crystal structures, viruses, visual art, and music. To explore symmetry in his own research, he makes use of mathematical expressions such as zeta functions. Du Sautoy has published a variety of scholarly works on symmetry and related topics, including *Analytic Pro-p Groups* (1999) and *Zeta Functions of Groups and Rings* (2008).

A professor of mathematics at the University of Oxford since 2005, du Sautoy took on a second prestigious post in 2008, when he was appointed the Simonyi Professor for the Public Understanding of Science. Du Sautoy was the second scholar to hold that position, which had been funded by, and named for, computer scientist Charles Simonyi, and first filled by biologist Richard Dawkins. As Simonyi Professor, du Sautoy worked in both the University of Oxford's Mathematical Institute and the Department of Continuing Education and was tasked with communicating scientific concepts to general audiences. Du Sautoy also holds honorary doctorates from institutions such as Queen Mary University of London and the University of Liverpool and has served as a visiting professor at institutions in France, Israel, Australia, and elsewhere.

MATH AMBASSADOR

Du Sautoy has long sought to communicate scientific and mathematical concepts—and the relevance of the fields of science and mathematics themselves—to audiences and has devoted himself primarily to that effort since taking on the position of Simonyi Professor. "I think science is a foreign land for many people, so I think of my role as an ambassador's job," he explained to Pettie. Du Sautoy is particularly concerned about what he described to Pettie as an ongoing "breakdown in dialogue between scientists and the rest of society," which has resulted in some members of the public becoming distrustful of scientific knowledge and even arguing that subjects such as mathematics are irrelevant and should no longer be taught in schools. "We need scientists and mathematicians explaining why they are excited about their subjects but also why they are important for solving social problems, informing political debate and for the economy," he told Pettie.

To that end, du Sautoy has become well known in the United Kingdom for his publications, media appearances, and events such as public lectures, many of which focus on the history, real-world applications, and enduring relevance of mathematics. In addition to his scholarly books and papers, du Sautoy is the author of several popular science books, including *The Music of the Primes: Why an Unsolved Problem in Mathematics Matters* (2003), about an unproven mathematical conjecture known as the Riemann hypothesis, and *Finding Moonshine: A Mathematician's Journey through Symmetry* (2008), which deals with du Sautoy's life as a mathematician in addition to the history of the study of symmetry. His 2010 work *The Number Mysteries: A Mathematical Odyssey through Everyday Life* discusses several of mathematics' famous unsolved problems, while *What We Cannot Know: Explorations at the Edge of Knowledge* (2016) deals with areas of knowledge that du Sautoy identifies as potentially beyond human understanding. He has also contributed writing to a variety of edited works, including essays on the topic of symmetry in art.

MATHEMATICS ON TELEVISION

In addition to authoring a variety of mathematical works for general audiences, du Sautoy has become particularly known as a television presenter, having hosted or cohosted game shows such as *Mind Games* (2004–6) and *Dara Ó Briain: School of Hard Sums* (2012–14) as well as a variety of televised documentary series. His 2005 documentary *The Music of the Primes* was based on his book of the same title, while the lecture series *The Num8er My5teries*, delivered as part of the Royal Institution Christmas Lecture series in 2006 and broadcast online and on television, covered similar topics to his later book *The Number Mysteries: A Mathematic Odyssey Through Everyday Life*. He has appeared in many installments of the BBC2 documentary series *Horizon* (2009–13) and has also starred in works that blend his passions for mathematics and music, including 2012's *Maestro at the Opera*, which chronicles his attempt to learn opera conducting.

du Sautoy gained significant attention for his four-part documentary series *The Story of Maths* (2008) and the three-part series *The Code* (2011), the latter of which seeks to promote an understanding of the mathematical concepts, such as fractals and ratios, underlying much of the world. "My big thesis is that although the world looks messy and chaotic, if you translate it into the world of numbers and shapes, patterns emerge and you start to understand why things are the way they are," he explained to Pettie. His 2015 documentary *The Secret Rules of Modern Living: Algorithms* further emphasized the role mathematics play in everyday life, exploring the many functions of mathematical algorithms.

Alongside his television work, du Sautoy has made extensive radio appearances and has written articles for publications such as the London *Times*, *Wired*, the *Guardian*, and *New Scientist*. He has delivered a variety of public lectures, including a 2009 TED Talk on symmetry, and has performed original stage productions at events such as England's Glastonbury Festival. In recognition of his work as a researcher and as an ambassador for mathematics, du Sautoy was named an officer of the Order of the British Empire in 2010. He was also the recipient of the 2001 Berwick Prize and received the 2009 Faraday Prize from the Royal Society. He was elected to the prestigious Royal Society in 2016.

PERSONAL LIFE

Du Sautoy met his wife, Shani Ram du Sautoy, while living in Israel. They married in 1994. The couple lives in North London and have three children, Tomer, Magaly, and Ina. Their second son, Jonathan, was stillborn.

In addition to his passion for mathematics, du Sautoy is a lover of music, which he has often linked to his field of study. "I've always been convinced that mathematics and music share much in common," he told McKie. "As I sit at my desk, there is often music playing as I try to battle away with the latest mathematical conundrum that I'm wrestling with." He is also an avid fan of the soccer team Arsenal and has played soccer with the club team Recreativo Hackney, the members of which have prime numbers on their jerseys.

SUGGESTED READING

Adar, Shaul. "Fearful Symmetry." *Haaretz*, 22 Oct. 2010, www.haaretz.com/1.5129341. Accessed 9 Feb. 2018.

du Sautoy, Marcus. "A Beautiful Mind." Interview by Pritha Kejriwal. *Kindle*, 2 Dec. 2012, kindlemag.in/a-beautiful-mind/. Accessed 9 Feb. 2018.

du Sautoy, Marcus. "If I Ruled the World: Marcus du Sautoy." *Prospect*, 19 May 2016, www.prospectmagazine.co.uk/magazine/if-i-ruled-the-world-mathematics-euclid. Accessed 9 Feb. 2018.

du Sautoy, Marcus. "My Family Values." Interview by Juliet Rix. *The Guardian*, 11 Sept. 2009, www.theguardian.com/lifeandstyle/2009/sep/12/my-family-values-marcus-du-sautoy. Accessed 9 Feb. 2018.

Hayes, Eleanor. "Career Interview: Marcus du Sautoy." *Science in School*, 22 May 2012, www.scienceinschool.org/2012/issue23/dusautoy. Accessed 8 Feb. 2018.

McKie, Robin. "A Mathematician Who's in his Prime." *The Guardian*, 1 Nov. 2008, www.theguardian.com/education/2008/nov/02/maths-sautoy-dawkins-oxford-science. Accessed 9 Feb. 2018.

Pettie, Andrew. "Marcus du Sautoy Interview: 'There's a Geek Chic about Maths Now.'" *The Telegraph*, 26 July 2011, www.telegraph.co.uk/culture/tvandradio/8664235/Marcus-du-Sautoy-interview-Theres-a-geek-chic-about-maths-now.html. Accessed 9 Feb. 2018.

SELECTED WORKS

The Music of the Primes: Why an Unsolved Problem in Mathematics Matters, 2003; *Finding Moonshine: A Mathematician's Journey through Symmetry*, 2008; *The Number Mysteries: A Mathematical Odyssey through Everyday Life*, 2010; *What We Cannot Know: Explorations at the Edge of Knowledge*, 2016

—Joy Crelin

Jacques Dubochet

Date of Birth: June 8, 1942
Occupation: Biophysicist

In October 2017, Swiss biophysicist Jacques Dubochet was one of three scientists to receive the most prestigious award in their field: the Nobel Prize in Chemistry. A professor emeritus at

By Félix Imhof ©UNIL, 4 October 2017 [CC BY-SA 4.0], via Wikimedia Commons

Switzerland's Université de Lausanne (UNIL) at the time of the award, Dubochet earned recognition for nearly four decades of work in cryo–electron microscopy (cryo-EM), in which biological samples are frozen at extremely low temperatures before being examined with electron microscopes. Dubochet, a former researcher at the European Molecular Biology Laboratory (EMBL), is particularly known for his work with vitrified water—water that has been frozen so quickly that it forms a glassy substance rather than ice crystals—which, since the 1980s, has been foundational to cryo-EM. Although he shared the Nobel Prize with only two additional scientists, Dubochet has noted frequently in interviews that his discoveries have all resulted from collaborations with numerous other researchers.

EARLY LIFE AND EDUCATION
Dubochet was born on June 8, 1942, in Aigle, Switzerland, one of four children born to Jean-Emmanuel Dubochet and Liliane Dubochet-Baenziger. His father's work as an engineer prompted the family to move around Switzerland during Dubochet's early years, but Dubochet grew up primarily in the western canton of Vaud. As a young child, Dubochet's interest in science arose in part out of his fear of the dark. His learning that the sun will return each morning fueled a desire to learn more about the world, and he went on to conduct a variety of amateur experiments as a child. Although Dubochet would later become known for his collaborative approach to science, his younger self was "quite

asocial," he told Celia Luterbacher and Domhnall O'Sullivan for *Swissinfo* (4 Oct. 2017). "I had a lot of difficulty with the world," he added. "Every ten years, I found, it got a little better."

Upon beginning secondary school, Dubochet initially enrolled in a program focusing on literature. However, he quickly determined that that focus was too difficult for him and transferred to a science program. While in secondary school, Dubochet was diagnosed with dyslexia, becoming the first student in the canton to be diagnosed with the learning disorder. He initially treated his diagnosis as a "pillow for laziness," as he explained to Luterbacher and O'Sullivan, but continued to explore his interest in science and went on to enroll in the Ecole polytechnique de l'Université de Lausanne (now École polytechnique fédérale de Lausanne), from which he graduated with a degree in physics in 1967.

After leaving polytechnic school, Dubochet earned a certificate in molecular biology from the Université de Genève in 1969. From 1971 to 1974, Dubochet pursued doctoral studies first in Geneva and then at the University of Basel's Biozentrum, its department of molecular biology and biomedical research. He carried out his thesis research under the supervision of Eduard Kellenberger, an accomplished molecular biologist who cofounded the Biozentrum and the European Molecular Biology Organization. Dubochet earned his PhD around 1973 but continued his research at the Biozentrum until 1978.

EUROPEAN MOLECULAR BIOLOGY LABORATORY
In 1978, Dubochet joined the European Molecular Biology Laboratory (EMBL) as the leader of the laboratory's Structural and Computational Biology Unit. Founded in 1974 and headquartered in Heidelberg, Germany, the laboratory was then under the direction of Nobel Prize–winning biochemist John Kendrew, who recruited Dubochet for a project concerning cryo–electron microscopy (cryo-EM). A means of producing images of molecules such as proteins that have been frozen at very low temperatures, cryo-EM is an alternative to older means of imaging molecules. These means, including X-ray crystallography and traditional electron microscopy, were generally effective but not well suited for studying all samples. X-ray crystallography, for example, is most effective when used to study molecules that can be crystallized, which proteins in cell membranes cannot do, while traditional electron microscopy could damage the samples being studied. "Electrons are great: even a single molecule may leave a trace in their beam and electron microscopists have learned to make use of them with breathtaking effect," Dubochet explained to Rosemary Wilson and Adam Gristwood for *EMBL etc.*, the institution's news

site (24 Aug. 2015). "But they are also rather destructive: the column of an electron microscope must be under a vacuum, while risks of structural damage lurk around every corner." Of concern was the presence of water in some samples, as liquid water evaporates at a lower temperature when placed in a vacuum and, without water, the samples tend to dry out and collapse.

Over nine years at EMBL, Dubochet and his colleagues worked to address the problem of water in cryo-EM. Their research proved fruitful, revealing new ways of studying molecules. In 2015, he was awarded the EMBL's inaugural Lennart Philipson Award for his translational research.

WATER AND CRYO-EM

For Dubochet and his colleagues at the EMBL, the issue of water in cryo-EM presented a particularly tricky problem. Freezing samples suspended in water prevented the water from evaporating while under a vacuum, but the resulting ice crystals blurred images of the samples. A turning point came when Dubochet's colleague Alasdair McDowall experimented with liquid ethane to cool the samples, rather than the conventional liquid nitrogen. "I saw a well-formed drop that did not look like our familiar water droplets," Dubochet recalled in a 2011 retrospective article published in the *Journal of Microscopy*. The researchers assumed that the drop was some remaining ethane and allowed the sample to grow warmer. "Suddenly, we saw it change into small speckles that electron diffraction unmistakably identified as cubic ice that we were familiar with from previous experiments on vapor deposition on a cold substrate," Dubochet wrote. "Obviously, the droplet we took first for ethane was vitreous water."

Dubochet and his colleagues realized that the liquid ethane had frozen the sample so quickly that ice crystals did not have time to form. Instead, the water froze clear and glassy, a process known as "vitrification." As vitrified water did not form ice crystals that would distort the image, the sample could then be studied with an electron microscope. This important discovery proved controversial, however, and Dubochet and McDowall's initial attempt to publish on the subject was rejected, as journal publishers doubted that vitrification of water was possible. Ultimately their first paper on the subject, "Vitrification of Pure Water for Electron Microscopy," was published in the December 1981 issue of the *Journal of Microscopy*.

Throughout the following years, Dubochet and his colleagues explored new processes for preparing and studying cryo-EM samples, including thin-film vitrification, in which a thin film of water is placed over a supporting grid. Dubochet was particularly intrigued by cryo-electron microscopy of vitreous sections, or CEMOVIS. Many specimens of interest to researchers are too large to be frozen in a thin layer, so in CEMOVIS, researchers first vitrify the sample and then cut it into sections of suitable size to study. Although the work of Dubochet's team has been key to the development of CEMOVIS techniques, he has been quick to point out that such advances have not been miraculous leaps forward. "The progress came from a large [number] of incremental improvements affecting all the various steps of the specimen preparation protocol," he wrote for the *Journal of Microscopy*.

LAUSANNE

Dubochet remained at EMBL until 1987, when he left to teach at UNIL in Switzerland. There he also directed the institution's Centre of Electron Microscopy and the Laboratory of Ultrastructural Analysis. He served as president of the biology department between 1998 and 2002, when he visited Australia, Germany, and France on sabbatical. Dubochet published widely during his time at the university, authoring or coauthoring more than ninety articles over two decades.

Dubochet also taught courses both in his academic field and in philosophy and ethics, which he considered key to the education of future scientists. "I have devoted a lot of effort to the curriculum—biology and society—and Lausanne at that time was unique in developing this curriculum for all our students," he told Adam Smith for the *NobelPrize.org* website (4 Oct. 2017). He retired in 2007 and was named emeritus professor. In October 2017 he returned to the university to speak on the importance of good citizenship among scientists, a topic he described to Smith as "very close to [his] heart."

NOBEL PRIZE

On October 4, 2017, the Royal Swedish Academy of Sciences announced that Dubochet would share that year's Nobel Prize in Chemistry with Scottish biophysicist Richard Henderson of the Medical Research Council's Laboratory of Molecular Biology and German biophysicist Joachim Frank at Columbia University. They split the award money of 9 million Swedish kronor, or approximately $1.1 million. The three researchers were recognized for their varied contributions to cryo-EM: Henderson, initially a specialist in X-ray crystallography, determined how to use an electron microscope to view a protein at atomic resolution (that is, such that individual atoms are discernable), and Frank used an electron microscope and a computer to compose three-dimensional images of macromolecules such as ribosomes. Dubochet was specifically recognized for his water-vitrification method, which defied prior scientific assumptions about the capabilities of water.

Besides being significant in and of themselves, the advances made by Dubochet, Henderson, and Frank enabled widespread cryo-EM developments that, in turn, allowed researchers to better understand the workings of cells and to study specific specimens such as the Zika virus. "Soon there are no more secrets," Sara Snogerup Linse, the chair of the chemistry prize committee, said during the October 4 prize announcement. "Now we can see the intricate details of the biomolecules in every corner of our cells, in every drop of our body fluids. We can understand how they are built and how they act and how they work together." Dave Agard, a University of California biochemist, told Ben Guarino for the *Washington Post* that new medicines and vaccines may be developed because cryo-EM allows researchers to see the exact shape and composition of a complex biomolecule, and Stockholm University biochemist Peter Brzezinski foresees the possibility of its capturing molecular interactions in the future.

Dubochet is certainly aware of the significance of his work and grateful for the recognition he has received, yet he remains adamant that his accomplishments have truly resulted from decades of collaboration. "A scientific prize is an ambiguous thing," he told Luterbacher and O'Sullivan. "It puts forward an individual, whereas it should be putting forward a collective effort. I am not all alone!"

PERSONAL LIFE

Dubochet and his wife, an art historian and watercolorist named Christine, have a son, Gilles, and a daughter, Lucy. Dubochet lives in Morges, Switzerland, where he serves as a leftist city councilor. He enjoys socializing, the mountains, and nature.

SUGGESTED READING

Chang, Kenneth. "Nobel Prize in Chemistry Awarded for 3D Views of Life's Biological Machinery." *The New York Times*, 4 Oct. 2017, www.nytimes.com/2017/10/04/science/nobel-prize-chemistry.html. Accessed 12 Nov. 2017.

Dubochet, Jacques. "Cryo-EM—The First Thirty Years." *Journal of Microscopy* 245.3 (2011): 221–4. doi:10.1111/j.1365-2818.2011.03569.x. Accessed 12 Nov. 2017.

Dubochet, Jacques. Interview by Adam Smith. *NobelPrize.org*, 4 Oct. 2017, www.nobelprize.org/nobel_prizes/chemistry/laureates/2017/dubochet-interview.html. Accessed 12 Nov. 2017.

Guarino, Ben. "Three Biophysicists Win 2017 Nobel Prize in Chemistry for Imaging Molecules of Life." *The Washington Post*, 4 Oct. 2017, www.washingtonpost.com/news/speaking-of-science/wp/2017/10/04/2017-nobel-prize-in-chemistry-won-by-jacques-dubochet-joachim-frank-and-richard-henderson. Accessed 12 Nov. 2017.

Luterbacher, Celia, and Domhnall O'Sullivan. "Swiss Nobel Prize Winner Reacts with 'Great Gratitude.'" *Swissinfo*, 4 Oct. 2017, www.swissinfo.ch/eng/jacques-dubochet_swiss-nobel-winner-reacts-with--great-gratitude-/43571386. Accessed 12 Nov. 2017.

Stokstad, Erik, and Robert F. Service. "A Cold, Clear View of Life Wins Chemistry Nobel." *Science*, 4 Oct. 2017, www.sciencemag.org/news/2017/10/cold-clear-view-life-wins-chemistry-nobel. Accessed 12 Nov. 2017.

Wilson, Rosemary, and Adam Gristwood. "Celebrating Excellence." *EMBL etc.*, European Molecular Biology Laboratory, 24 Aug. 2015, news.embl.de/alumni/1508-kendrew-philipson. Accessed 12 Nov. 2017.

—*Joy Crelin*

Andrzej Duda

Date of birth: May 16, 1972
Occupation: President of Poland

Andrzej Duda became the sixth president of Poland in 2015 and has made sweeping reforms since taking office.

EARLY LIFE AND EDUCATION

Andrzej Duda was born on May 16, 1972, in Krakow, Poland. His parents, Jan Tadeusz Duda and Janina Milewska Duda, were both university professors. He attended Jan III Sobieski High School in Krakow, graduating in 1991. He then studied law at Jagiellonian University, receiving a master's degree in 1997. He taught legal studies at Jagiellonian University, where he completed a doctorate of law in 2005. Duda opened his own law practice in 2005.

POLITICAL CAREER

Duda joined the liberal Freedom Union party in the early 2000s. A few years later, he joined the conservative Law and Justice party. Following the party's victory in the 2005 parliamentary elections, he became an adviser to the party's parliamentary caucus.

Rising rapidly through the ranks, Duda served as the deputy justice minister from 2006 to 2007 and then became the undersecretary of state, or legal adviser to President Lech Kaczyński, in 2008. After Kaczyński died in a plane crash in April 2010 and Bronisław Komorowski of the center-right Civic Platform party became president, Duda resigned. Later that year, he was elected to the city council of Krakow.

In 2011 Duda was elected to the lower house of parliament, and he became the deputy chair of the constitutional accountability committee. He assumed a greater role in the Law and Justice party, becoming its spokesperson in November 2013. In May 2014 he was elected to the European Parliament, where he served on the committee on legal affairs.

Relatively unknown among the public and generally considered a behind-the-scenes politician, Duda's status changed in 2014 after Jarosław Kaczyński tapped Duda to run for the presidency in the 2015 elections. As a cofounder of the Law and Justice party and twin brother of the deceased president, Kaczyński's recommendation carried significant weight. Duda accepted the challenge and vowed to continue the former president's legacy and to carry out his political plans.

Duda's campaign targeted the public's discontent with the current government, and he ran on the values of the Law and Justice party's three pillars of a strong society: family, jobs, and security. He promised to help struggling citizens by lowering the recently increased retirement age, increasing the personal tax allowance, and subsidizing food for rural children. Duda appealed to people's patriotism and desire for Poland's interests to be a priority over Europe's interests. He proposed raising taxes on foreign-owned banks and supermarkets and improving relations with Eastern European countries such as Lithuania.

Despite polls predicting an easy victory for incumbent president Komorowski, Duda received nearly 35 percent of all the votes in the first round and won the runoff election in May 2015, receiving 51.5 percent of the votes to Komorowski's 48.5 percent. Duda's startling win caused concern among some political analysts and members of the European Union (EU), who feared his skepticism of the EU would upset Poland's relationship with the rest of Europe.

Sworn in on August 6, 2015, Duda renounced his party membership, saying he was a leader of all people in Poland. In his inaugural speech, he announced his intent to position Poland to play a greater role in the international community and to build a more powerful army. He also stated his desire for the North Atlantic Treaty Organization (NATO) to have a greater presence in Poland.

Although the president's role is primarily ceremonial in Poland, Duda is responsible for the country's foreign policy, heads its armed forces, appoints the head of the central bank, and can propose legislation and veto bills.

Within months of becoming president, Duda created a constitutional crisis in December 2015 when he swore in four new judges to the Constitutional Court of Poland, overriding judges who had been approved by the previous parliament, including two judges whose terms had not yet expired. This action came shortly after the Law and Justice party won the majority of votes in the October 2015 elections, giving it control of both houses of the parliament. With the Law and Justice party controlling the parliament and presidency, the only government body it did not have control of was the Constitutional Court—until Duda appointed judges loyal to the ruling government. The government defended Duda's action, saying it was necessary to allow the government to make the reforms it had promised voters. Opponents decried the action as it eliminated the constitutional checks and balances that prevent one party from assuming absolute power. In late December 2015 Duda also signed a controversial amendment changing the terms under which the Constitutional Court approved rulings. In January 2016 he created controversy again when he signed legislation giving the government full control of the state media.

IMPACT

Duda's election as president in May 2015 signaled a shift to the right in Polish politics that was realized when the Law and Justice party won the majority of parliament seats in the October 2015 national elections. While Duda has taken action to carry out some of his campaign promises—such as introducing a draft of a bill to lower the retirement age—numerous observers have expressed concern that the pace and nature of the reforms and new legislation are undermining Poland's constitution and threatening its democracy.

PERSONAL LIFE

Duda married Agata Kornhauser-Duda, a German teacher, in 1994. They have a daughter, Kinga.

SUGGESTED READING

"About Me." *President.Pl.* Govt. of Poland, n.d. Web. 12 Apr. 2016.

Foy, Henry. "Andrzej Duda, Accidental President." *Financial Times.* Financial Times, 29 May 2015. Web. 12 Apr. 2016.

Lyman, Rick. "Bronislaw Komorowski, Poland's President, Concedes Defeat to Right-Wing Challenger Andrzej Duda." *New York Times.* New York Times, 24 May 2015. Web. 12 Apr. 2016.

Scislowska, Monika. "Poland's President Signs Media Law despite EU Concerns." *AP.* Associated Press, 7 Jan. 2016. Web. 12 Apr. 2016.

Sobczky, Martin M. "Andrzej Duda Sworn In as Poland's New President." *Wall Street Journal.* Dow Jones, 5 Aug. 2015. Web. 12 Apr. 2016.

Szary, Wiktor. "Poland's New President Andrzej Duda Heralds Shift to the Right." *Reuters.* Thomson Reuters, 24 May 2015. Web. 12 Apr. 2016.

Szary, Wiktor, and Jakub Iglewski. "Poland's President Signs Disputed Amendment to Top Court Powers." *Reuters.* Thomson Reuters, 28 Dec. 2105. Web. 12 Apr. 2016.

—*Barb Lightner*

Erica Armstrong Dunbar

Date of Birth: circa 1970
Occupation: Author, professor

In 1796, a young enslaved woman named Ona Judge escaped slavery and fled northward, ultimately settling in New Hampshire. More than two hundred years later, historian Erica Armstrong Dunbar told Judge's story in the 2017 book *Never Caught: The Washingtons' Relentless Pursuit of Their Runaway Slave*, revealing not only why Judge made the courageous decision to claim her freedom but also the lengths to which her former owners—George and Martha Washington, then president and First Lady of the United States—would go to try to get her back. An expert in African American history and the author of the 2008 work *A Fragile Freedom: African American Women and Emancipation in the Antebellum City*, Dunbar sought not only to share Judge's extraordinary story with the world but also to highlight the risky lives of many African Americans during the late eighteenth and early nineteenth centuries. "What Ona's story tells us is not just the fragility of a fugitive's life, but of all black people's lives at that moment," she told Lucas Iberico Lozada for *Paste* (3 Mar. 2017). "Because you have to ask the question: How free is free if slavery exists right next door? What does your freedom mean if, at any moment, you can be captured against your will?"

Named the Charles and Mary Beard Professor of History at Rutgers University in 2017, Dunbar previously spent more than fifteen years at the University of Delaware, where she held the position of Blue and Gold Professor of Black American Studies and History prior to her departure. She has likewise served as director of the Library Company of Philadelphia's Program in African American History since 2011. As a historian, she seeks to increase the visibility of African American history, an understanding of which, she argues, is key to the United States' continued development. "There is absolutely no way we will ever come to a moment of reconciliation and real progress unless we recognize and accept the past for what it was," she explained to

Photo by Dimitrios Kambouris/Getty Images

Vanessa del Fabbro for *Richmond Magazine* (21 Apr. 2017). "If we want to understand our present and help shape the future in a progressive way we must engage the past, and that means the ugliness of slavery. Until we do, I am not sure we will get to the place that many of us wish us to be."

EARLY LIFE AND EDUCATION

Dunbar was born Erica Armstrong in the early 1970s to Frances and Jacob Armstrong. She and her twin sister, Nicole, grew up in Philadelphia, Pennsylvania. As a child, she was an avid reader and particularly enjoyed reading historical works based on true stories. She attended the Germantown Friends School, a private Quaker day school in Philadelphia's Germantown neighborhood, graduating in 1990.

After high school, Dunbar enrolled in the University of Pennsylvania (Penn) to study history, with the goal of eventually becoming an attorney. However, her aspirations began to shift during the summer before her freshman year, when she participated in a program then known as the Afro-American Studies Summer Institute. The program introduced her both to the academic field of history and to African American history, and proved highly influential. "What surprised me so much was that there was so much content I had never heard of," she told Robert DiGiacomo for the *Pennsylvania Gazette* (24 Apr. 2017). "By focusing on African-American history, it allowed me to have a better understanding of American history." Her newfound passion for history was shaped further through her association with Penn professor Evelyn Brooks Higginbotham, an accomplished scholar of African American history. Higginbotham encouraged Dunbar to become a historian and continued to mentor her even after leaving Penn for Harvard University.

In addition to the summer institute and the mentorship of Higginbotham, Dunbar has credited her development as an academic to the Mellon Mays Undergraduate Fellowship Program. "I can honestly say had I not been a Mellon Mays Undergraduate Fellow, there's no way I would have been an academic," she said in an interview for the website of the Andrew W. Mellon Foundation (Aug. 2017). "It was probably the single most important intervention in my life as a young adult and gave me permission to do what I love the most—reading, writing, thinking about history and, in particular, African American women's history." Thanks to such support, she focused on history and African American studies while at Penn, earning her bachelor's degree from the university in 1994. She went on to pursue graduate studies at Columbia University, where she held a Ford Foundation fellowship before completing her doctorate in 2000.

ACADEMIC CAREER AND PUBLICATION OF *A FRAGILE FREEDOM*

After completing her doctoral studies, Dunbar took a position at the University of Delaware, joining the institution in August 2000. As an assistant professor, she taught courses focusing primarily on African American history. In her third year at the university, she took a period of leave to work on her first book. She was also a participant in the Woodrow Wilson Career Enhancement Fellowship Program.

Over the course of her more than fifteen years at the University of Delaware, Dunbar established herself as a well-regarded professor as well as a leader in the field of history. She was promoted to associate professor of history and black American studies and granted tenure in 2007, and the following year, she was named a distinguished lecturer by the Organization of American Historians. Her first book, *A Fragile Freedom: African American Women and Emancipation in the Antebellum City*, was also published in 2008 by Yale University Press. Based in part on her doctoral thesis, the book focuses on the experiences of free African American women in northern cities, particularly Philadelphia, where they faced a variety of challenges related to race, gender, and class in an era of widespread social and economic change. In addition to bringing her research into the public eye, the publication of *A Fragile Freedom* further established Dunbar as an expert in African American women's history as well as the history of African Americans in Philadelphia.

Alongside her work as a professor and writer, Dunbar began serving as director of the Program in African American History at the Library Company of Philadelphia in 2011. The first person to hold that position, she became responsible for promoting the study of early African American history. In an interview for the Andrew W. Mellon Foundation website, she detailed the importance of her affiliation with the research library: "My position as director has allowed me to be around thinkers and people who are shaping the field of African American history. But it's also created an opportunity for me to give back." Among other efforts, the Program in African American History hosts conferences and other events, cosponsors the Race in the Atlantic World, 1700–1900 series with the University of Georgia Press, and offers a variety of fellowships in conjunction with the Andrew W. Mellon Foundation.

Having received recognition for her work as a professor such as the 2012 Ujima Award from the Department of Black American Studies, Dunbar went on to share her expertise in several documentary projects, including a PBS American Experience program on abolitionists, the documentary series *Philadelphia: The Great Experiment*, and the television genealogy series *Who Do You Think You Are?* She was named Blue and Gold Professor of Black American Studies and History at University of Delaware in March 2016 and in May of that year was officially promoted to full professor. In late 2016, she won the Lorraine A. Williams Leadership Award from the Association of Black Women Historians.

NEVER CAUGHT

Dunbar received her greatest recognition to date beginning in early 2017, with the publication of her book *Never Caught: The Washingtons' Relentless Pursuit of Their Runaway Slave, Ona Judge*. The book focuses on Ona Judge, also known as Oney Judge and Ona Judge Staines, an enslaved woman who was one of more than 150 slaves held by US president George Washington and his wife, Martha Washington. The child of an enslaved seamstress and a white indentured servant, Judge was one of Martha Washington's primary domestic slaves and, due to her role in the household, was one of a contingent of slaves brought from the Washingtons' Virginia home to the presidential residence in Philadelphia. Slavery was being legally phased out in Philadelphia at the time, but the Washingtons managed to exploit a legal loophole to avoid emancipating slaves such as Judge. In 1796, when Judge was in her early twenties, she learned that Martha Washington planned to give her to a family member as a wedding gift. Determined to avoid that fate, which would mean returning to Virginia, Judge fled Philadelphia and headed north, eventually settling in New Hampshire. Despite the Washingtons' efforts to recapture her, some of which violated federal fugitive slave laws, Judge avoided capture and remained in New Hampshire until her death in the mid-nineteenth century.

Dunbar first became aware of Judge's story while researching her doctoral thesis. As she searched through an electronic newspaper archive, she discovered a runaway slave advertisement offering a ten-dollar reward for Judge's return and became particularly intrigued when she realized that the Washingtons were the woman's former owners. "I said to myself: 'Here I am, a scholar in this field. Why don't I know about her?'" she recalled to Jennifer Schuessler for the *New York Times* (6 Feb. 2017). Although Dunbar did not incorporate Judge into her thesis or *A Fragile Freedom*, she later returned to the topic and spent several years researching what would become *Never Caught*.

In developing the book, Dunbar drew from historical records such as the runaway slave advertisement and George Washington's personal notes as well as interviews with Judge herself that were published in abolitionist newspapers in the mid-nineteenth century. The latter sources enabled Dunbar to reveal Judge's own perspective on events, insight she emphasized as rare under the circumstances. Overall, she sought to accessibly highlight lesser-known enslaved individuals who escaped slavery, as opposed to well-known figures, and to call attention to the Washingtons' slaveholding activities. "We have the famous fugitives, like Harriet Tubman and Frederick Douglass," she explained to Schuessler. "But decades before them, Ona Judge did this. I want people to know her story." Received well by critics, historians, and general audiences, *Never Caught* became a finalist for the National Book Award following its publication and in late 2017 was optioned for film. Meanwhile, following the end of the academic year, Dunbar had left the University of Delaware to take the position of Charles and Mary Beard Professor of History at New Jersey's Rutgers University.

PERSONAL LIFE
Dunbar met her husband, physician Jeffrey Kim Dunbar, in 1998. Their son, Christian, was born in 2004. She lives in Pennsylvania.

SUGGESTED READING
DiGiacomo, Robert. "Discovered—but Not Captured." *The Pennsylvania Gazette*, 24 Apr. 2017, thepenngazette.com/discovered-but-not-captured/. Accessed 12 Jan. 2018.

Dunbar, Erica Armstrong. "Freeing History: Erica Armstrong Dunbar." *The Andrew W. Mellon Foundation*, Aug. 2017, mellon.org/resources/shared-experiences-blog/freeing-history/. Accessed 12 Jan. 2018.

Dunbar, Erica Armstrong. "Q&A: Erica Armstrong Dunbar." Interview by Vanessa del Fabbro. *Richmondmag*, 21 Apr. 2017, richmondmagazine.com/arts-entertainment/q-a-erica-armstrong-dunbar/. Accessed 12 Jan. 2018.

Lozada, Lucas Iberico. "Erica Armstrong Dunbar Talks *Never Caught*, the True Story of George Washington's Runaway Slave." *Paste*, 3 Mar. 2017, www.pastemagazine.com/articles/2017/03/never-caught-erica-armstrong-dunbar.html. Accessed 12 Jan. 2018.

Schuessler, Jennifer. "In Search of the Slave Who Defied George Washington." *The New York Times*, 6 Feb. 2017, www.nytimes.com/2017/02/06/arts/george-washington-mount-vernon-slavery.html. Accessed 12 Jan. 2018.

—Joy Crelin

Jacqueline Durran

Date of birth: ca. 1966
Occupation: Costume designer

For costume designer Jacqueline Durran, the year 2017 was the culmination of two significant, yet very different, challenges. That year saw the release of two films featuring her costumes, the live-action Disney film *Beauty and the Beast* and the Winston Churchill biopic *Darkest Hour*—the former a brightly colored spectacle tasked with living up to its animated predecessor and the latter a period piece with an overall emphasis on realism and historical accuracy. Such divergent aesthetics and their associated restrictions might have stumped a lesser designer, but not Durran. "I like things that are puzzles, and I tend to think of costume design as a puzzle," she told Sarah Haight for *W* (1 Apr. 2008). "You're taking fabrics and a time period and a color scheme, and putting them together in a way that, presto, makes sense visually." As costume designer for both films, she created critically acclaimed costumes that not only met the specific needs of the films but also earned her two Academy Award nominations for Best Costume Design.

A film costuming professional since the late 1990s, Durran began her career first as an employee of a costume supplier and later as a wardrobe mistress and assistant costume designer for a variety of films. Rising to the position of costume designer, she established a productive working relationship with director Joe Wright, earning her first Academy Award nomination for her work on his 2005 adaptation of *Pride and Prejudice*. Over the following decade, she earned additional nominations for works such

Photo by Amanda Edwards/WireImage, via Getty Images

as Wright's *Atonement* (2007) and Mike Leigh's *Mr. Turner* (2014) and in 2013 won her first Academy Award for her work on Wright's *Anna Karenina* (2012). Although she is perhaps best known for working on period pieces featuring dramatic dresses, furs, jewels, and otherwise opulent attire, Durran has noted that the needs of each film outweigh any overarching sense of style. "I approach my movies from the point of view of the characters, to help tell their story," she told Haight.

EDUCATION AND EARLY CAREER

Although Durran would go on to establish herself as one of the most successful costume designers in Hollywood, she did not initially plan to pursue studies in that field. Upon completing secondary school, she enrolled in the University of Sussex to study philosophy, earning her bachelor's degree in that subject in 1988. Six years later, she enrolled in the Royal College of Art as a graduate student, studying the history of costume design. She earned her master's degree from the college in 1996.

Durran's career in costuming began when she found a job at the costume supplier Angels, which had been in business since the late nineteenth century. "I started to learn what the job entailed," she recalled to Trilby Beresford for *Amy Poehler's Smart Girls* (2 Mar. 2018). "I met costume designers and I worked with the costume designers and I started to see the difference between the costume designs' pattern work. And I learned about stitching and little things." She made her film costuming debut in

the late 1990s, when she served as wardrobe mistress for the 1999 film *Eyes Wide Shut*. Over the next several years, she gained further experience in costuming, serving as assistant costume designer for major films such as the James Bond film *The World Is Not Enough* (1999) and *Star Wars: Episode II—Attack of the Clones* (2002). She likewise formed some professional connections that would shape her career going forward, including a recurring association with filmmaker Sally Potter, serving as first assistant costume designer for *The Man Who Cried* (2000) and later as costume designer for the film *Yes* (2004).

In addition to Potter, Durran established a longstanding working relationship with filmmaker Mike Leigh during her early career, serving as second assistant costume designer for Leigh's period piece *Topsy-Turvy* (1999). She would later work with him on the films *All or Nothing* (2002) and *Vera Drake* (2004), for which she earned her first award for Best Costume Design from the British Academy of Film and Television Arts (BAFTA). Uncommonly, Leigh provides her no script. Rather, she explained to Tim Robey for the *Telegraph* (3 Feb. 2006), "How it works is that, after the actors have been rehearsing for a certain amount of time, they come to the costume department, and we ask them who the character is. We ask them where they would go to buy their clothes, how much money they would spend, etc." With such information in hand, the costume department then determines what those characters wear.

CRITICALLY ACCLAIMED COSTUMES

Already established as a talented costuming professional by the early 2000s, Durran gained notice midway through the decade for her work on the 2005 film *Pride and Prejudice*, for which she was nominated for the Academy Award for Best Costume Design for the first time. An adaptation of the 1813 Jane Austen novel of the same name, *Pride and Prejudice* was the feature-film directorial debut of Wright, with whom Durran would later collaborate on films such as *Atonement* (2007). She earned her second Academy Award nomination for that film, an adaptation of a 2001 novel by Ian McEwan. She went on to serve as costume designer for Wright's film *The Soloist* (2009) as well as the spy film *Tinker Tailor Soldier Spy* (2011), directed by Tomas Alfredson. At the same time, she had continued to work on Leigh's films, designing costumes for *Happy-Go-Lucky* (2008) and *Another Year* (2010).

In 2012, Durran's eye-catching costuming work again graced the screen in the film *Anna Karenina*, an adaptation of the Leo Tolstoy novel (1875–77), directed by Wright. Prior to the making of the film, Durran and Wright worked together to define the aesthetic that would form the basis of her overall approach to the film's costumes. "Joe always comes with a vision before we've even started," she told Julie Miller for *Vanity Fair* (25 Jan. 2013). "In our first meeting, he talked about how he wanted to pare down the costumes to the kind of essence to them." Focusing on iconic silhouettes, she mixed fashion influences from both the nineteenth and twentieth centuries to create costumes that reflected the opulence and drama characteristic of the film overall. In recognition of her work, she received the 2013 Academy Award for Best Costume Design. Received nearly a decade after her first nomination in that category, the award excited Durran but ultimately had little effect on her mindset or approach. "Winning an Oscar does give you a feeling of success that I'm not sure anything else can give you," she told Valli Herman for the *Los Angeles Times* (22 Mar. 2018). "You can't help but feel it's an achievement. On a day-to-day basis, I don't think much changes. I still work with the same directors and I try and do the same work."

Durran also won her second BAFTA Award and the Costume Designers Guild Award for Excellence in Period Film in recognition of her work on *Anna Karenina*; she had already been nominated for awards by both institutions (as well as others) for previous projects. Following the success of *Anna Karenina*, she was again nominated for an Oscar for *Mr. Turner* (2014), another collaboration with Leigh. She went on to design the costumes for a 2015 film adaptation of William Shakespeare's *Macbeth* (1623), directed by Justin Kurzel, and the Peter Pan adaptation *Pan* (2015), directed by Wright. Although she had not previously ventured into television costuming, she made her first entry into that medium with "Nosedive," an episode of the anthology series *Black Mirror* (2016) that was directed by Wright.

A PRODUCTIVE YEAR

The year 2017 saw the release of two films with costumes by Durran: *Beauty and the Beast*, the live-action adaptation of the 1992 animated Disney classic of the same name, and *Darkest Hour*, a period piece on British prime minister Winston Churchill's actions during World War II. Although not the first year in which multiple films featuring her work came out, it was the most successful to date, as she was nominated for the Academy Award for both. In addition to both earning her critical acclaim, the films each presented unique challenges due to their settings and restrictions. Designing the costumes for *Beauty and the Beast*, for example, was particularly daunting because of the iconic nature of many of the costumes from the 1992 film, particularly protagonist Belle's yellow ball gown. "Those costumes exist in people's imaginations

and all I wanted to do was to honor what they expect those costumes to be in a live action movie," she told Kara Warner for *People* (18 Mar. 2017). Practical considerations such as star Emma Watson's desire not to wear a corset likewise affected the design process, leading Durran to create costumes that allowed for greater movement than their animated counterparts.

Beauty and the Beast likewise presented challenges due to the film's use of computer-generated imagery (CGI) for some characters, including the Beast. As Durran and her team did not initially know that the Beast was going to be CGI, they created physical costumes that later had to be duplicated in CGI form. "The actual costume had to be photographed, the pattern and fabric, in the way we wanted it to be worn and then sent to the visual effects departments," she explained to Herman. "They re-created the costume on camera in CG from our existing item. They put the details into the computer program and then they can predict the movement of the costume based on the fabric and the action and work with it from that point."

For *Darkest Hour*, Durran's sixth film with Wright, the costuming team was tasked with presenting costumes that were as close to life as possible. "We decided early on that this film wasn't going to be stylized," she said in an interview for the *Focus Features* website (22 Dec. 2017). "So for me the work was getting the details of what people wore right and interpreting those back as closely as I could into the actors' costumes." To that end, she and her team purchased period-appropriate clothing made by some manufacturers known for outfitting Churchill during his lifetime. Although she ultimately lost the 2018 Oscar to fellow designer Mark Bridges, who won for his work on *Phantom Thread*, her impressive work on two vastly different films further emphasized her skill in tailoring her design approach to each specific project.

SUGGESTED READING

Durran, Jacqueline. "Following the Thread of History: A Q&A with Jacqueline Durran." *Focus Features*, 22 Dec. 2017, focusfeatures. com/article/craft_darkest-hour_jacqueline-durran. Accessed 12 May 2018.

Durran, Jacqueline. "How I Undressed Mr. Darcy." Interview by Tim Robey. *The Telegraph*, 3 Feb. 2006, www.telegraph.co.uk/culture/film/3649828/How-I-undressed-Mr-Darcy. html. Accessed 12 May 2018.

Durran, Jacqueline. "Meet Oscar Nominated Costume Designer Jacqueline Durran." Interview by Trilby Beresford. *Amy Poehler's Smart Girls*, 2 Mar. 2018, amysmartgirls.com/meet-oscar-nominated-costume-designer-jacqueline-durran-4ad3bef4cef6. Accessed 12 May 2018.

Haight, Sarah. "Dressing the Part." *W*, 1 Apr. 2008, www.wmagazine.com/story/hollywood-costumes. Accessed 12 May 2018.

Herman, Valli. "Want a Master Class in Movie Costumes? Revisit the Recent Work of Costume Designer Jacqueline Durran." *Los Angeles Times*, 22 Mar. 2018, www.latimes.com/fashion/la-ig-jacqueline-durran-20180322-htmlstory.html. Accessed 12 May 2018.

Miller, Julie. "Sketch to Still: How *Anna Karenina*'s Ill-Fated Heroine Came to Wear Unlucky Capes, Couture-Inspired Gowns, and $2 Million in Chanel Jewels." *Vanity Fair*, 25 Jan. 2013, www.vanityfair.com/hollywood/2013/01/anna-karenina-costume-designer-oscar-nominations-keira-knightley. Accessed 12 May 2018.

Warner, Kara. "Dressing Up a Classic: All about the *Beauty and the Beast* Costumes." *People*, 18 Mar. 2017, people.com/movies/beauty-beast-costumes-making-of-details. Accessed 12 May 2018.

—*Joy Crelin*

By Gage Skidmore, via Wikimedia Commons

Joel Edgerton

Date of birth: June 23, 1974
Occupation: Actor, screenwriter, director

Joel Edgerton has a name and face people *almost* know. Since the mid-1990s, he has found work in supporting roles in major films and television series, both here in the United States and in his native Australia, but it has not been until very recently—starting largely with the mixed martial arts film *Warrior* (2011) and running through performances such as his Golden Globe–nominated turn in *Loving* (2016)—that he has become something of a more high-profile actor in Hollywood. His success—as well as his continuing anonymity—has to do with the fact that he tends to blend into a role, submerging himself into it rather than exploding out of it. Despite this, he believes he is not very unlike other actors, who want to earn recognition for their work. "My theory about actors," he remarked in an interview with Matt Mueller for *Independent* (24 Oct. 2014), "is that we're all desperately insecure and we lacked love in our childhoods and so now we've got a job where we're seeking the attention of a lot of people."

Taking advantage of his increasing influence in Hollywood, Edgerton has also begun branching out into other creative outlets within the film industry in the form of writing and directing. After penning the screenplay for *Felony* (2013), which he also starred in, he went on to simultaneously occupy the positions of writer, star, and director for the thriller *The Gift* (2015). His debut directorial effort was largely well received by critics, and, expressing pride in that effort, he has acknowledged his versatile success: "I'm not on top of the mountain," he said to Angus Fontaine for *GQ Australia* (14 Oct. 2015). "But I've climbed high enough to get a good view of the action."

EARLY LIFE AND CAREER

The son of Marianne and Michael Edgerton, Joel Edgerton was born in Blacktown, New South Wales, Australia, on June 23, 1974. "I'm from a relatively small town and a rural place, and I think you see that in my hands and my face," he said to Zach Baron for *GQ* (6 Dec. 2016).

Growing up in the town of Dural, northwest of Sydney, he and his older brother, Nash, fell in love with filmmaking and acting at an early age, making their own films together. His parents believed in raising their children with traditional values. "I grew up being taught, 'do unto others as they would do unto you,'" he told Mueller. After attending the Hills Grammar School, and graduating in 1991, he became increasingly interested in pursuing a career as an actor, studying at the Nepean Drama School at the University of Western Sydney. Upon graduation, he found work in the Australian theater (including several well-received Shakespeare productions), television, and film industries beginning in the mid-1990s. With no real contacts of their own to help get them in the door, he and his brother, who had given up an education in electrical engineering to pursue a career as a stuntman, formed the collective Blue-Tongue Films and produced more serious short films to display their talents. He is perhaps best known for what would really be his breakout role of that period as William McGill in the Australian TV series *The Secret Life of Us* (2001–2), for which he won an award from the Australian Film Institute.

His first major supporting role in an American film production was playing Owen Lars, who would go on to raise Luke Skywalker in the original Star Wars films, in the second of the franchise's prequels, *Star Wars: Episode II—Attack of the Clones* (2002). In addition to reprising his role as Lars in *Star Wars: Episode III—Revenge of the Sith* (2005), he took on roles in several Australian and American films, including *Kinky Boots* (2005); *Smokin' Aces* (2006); *The Square* (2008), which he also helped write and was directed by his brother; *Separation City* (2009); and *Animal Kingdom* (2010). He explained to Fontaine that at that point, he could still never quite get himself to stay in Los Angeles on a permanent basis: "Instead I'd come to LA and dip my toe in, have a little paddle and then go home to work in the local theatre and TV scene. Looking back, that may have slowed my progress but it kept me sane. . . . That allowed me, psychologically, to distance myself from any expectation I had to succeed."

MOVING INTO THE MAINSTREAM

The 2011 film *Warrior*, in which Edgerton starred alongside Tom Hardy, brought him closer to the forefront of American cinemas when he played the fictional mixed martial arts fighter Brendan Conlon. His performance earned considerable praise from filmgoers and critics and helped to elevate his status in Hollywood. "I was always looking at the level up, the quality of scripts that was a little out of my reach. Movies like *Warrior* and *Animal Kingdom*, they lift you up so you can reach the better scripts," he told Charlie Teasdale for *Esquire* (15 Dec. 2017). He began appearing in significant supporting roles in big-budget films such as *Zero Dark Thirty* (2012), director Kathryn Bigelow's take on the ten-year manhunt for Osama bin Laden, and Baz Luhrmann's adaptation of F. Scott Fitzgerald's masterpiece novel *The Great Gatsby* (2013), in which he played Tom Buchanan, the husband of Daisy Buchanan (played by Carey Mulligan). He also appeared as Ramses in Ridley Scott's widely derided adaptation of the biblical story of Moses in *Exodus: Gods and Kings* (2014).

Despite the film's drubbing, Edgerton continued to be seen as an actor to watch, particularly after his turn as a detective in Sydney who accidently puts a newspaper boy in a coma in *Felony* (2013), a film he both wrote and produced. He was also lauded for his role in *Black Mass* (2015), as real-life Federal Bureau of Investigation agent John Connolly leading the manhunt of Boston gangster James "Whitey" Bulger (played by Johnny Depp). Remarking on his performance in the *New York Times* (18 Dec. 2015), Cara Buckley noted, "His swaggering, cock-of-the-walk depiction of the FBI agent John Connolly was one of the high points of *Black Mass*."

Perhaps Edgerton's most notable film of 2015 was *The Gift*, in which he costarred with Jason Bateman and Rebecca Hall. His directorial debut, he also wrote and coproduced the movie, a psychological thriller in which two men, Simon and Gordo, played respectively by Bateman and Edgerton, revisit the adversarial bully-and-abused relationship they had in high school when they reconnect decades later and place Simon's wife, Robyn (played by Hall), at the center of their renewed rivalry. Critics praised Edgerton's efforts on both sides of the screen, a dual role which, he told Tim Robey for the *Telegraph* (22 Nov. 2015), took some getting used to: "I worked hard at the script, did my homework, and then I allowed all the plagiarism from all the great directors I'd worked with to sort of soak in. I realised a week into shooting, because I was terrified, that I knew what I was doing. . . . I knew my camera instincts were right."

LOVING

In *Loving* (2016), Edgerton received some of the best notices of his career as an actor for his understated performance as Richard Loving, a real-life white bricklayer who fell in love with an African American woman named Mildred Jeter (played by Ruth Negga) in the 1950s. They married in Washington, DC, in 1958 and returned home to Virginia, where they were later arrested for violating the state's laws against interracial marriage. The couple, who were reserved and simply wanted to be left alone to live their lives, ultimately became the plaintiffs for the unanimous landmark 1967 US Supreme Court case *Loving v. Virginia*, which invalidated such state laws as unconstitutional.

Loving was written and directed by Jeff Nichols, with whom Edgerton had worked previously on the science-fiction film *Midnight Special*, which had come out earlier in 2016. Both lead actors received considerable acclaim for their restrained but effective performances: Edgerton earned a Golden Globe nomination for best actor in a drama while Negga earned best actress nominations for the Academy Awards and the Golden Globes. "These beautiful real people, who it's impossible not to fall in love with, were so quiet and shy and disinterested in being revolutionaries," Edgerton said during a press tour, as quoted by Stephanie Merry for the *Washington Post* (10 Nov. 2016). "Jeff, in a mission to tell that true story truthfully, had to remain authentic to that, and it meant that there was a screenplay that was only really dotted with dialogue."

LATEST PROJECTS

Edgerton also received praise for his performance in the postapocalyptic thriller *It Comes at Night* (2017), in which he starred as Paul, a father who is looking to keep his wife and son (played by Carmen Ejogo and Kelvin Harrison Jr.) safe in an isolated home. When a new family arrives at their doorstep, Paul reluctantly agrees to let them share the house with them, once he appears to be certain that they are free from whatever disease exists outside that has devastated the rest of humanity. The film, written and directed by Trey Edward Shults, received acclaim for its intense psychological horror, as well as for the performances of its main actors.

Another notable film of 2017 was *Bright*, a mash-up of a science-fiction and buddy-cop film, in which Edgerton costarred alongside Will Smith. The film is set in an alternate reality of modern Los Angeles, where humans like Smith's character Daryl Ward live alongside mythical creatures like orcs, centaurs, and elves. Ward is asked to partner with an orc, played by Edgerton, and before long, the duo need to recover a weapon of unspeakable power at large in the city. A Netflix original, the film was noted for the way it confronted the issue of race very directly, something that both Edgerton and Smith agreed appealed to them when they decided to come on board.

Edgerton looks to be busy in 2018 as well. His action-comedy film *Gringo*, directed by his brother Nash and costarring Charlize Theron and David Oyelowo, is due for release, as is *Red Sparrow*, a spy thriller costarring Jennifer Lawrence. Continuing to look for worthy projects to work on behind the camera as well, by the end of 2017 he was working on writing, directing, and starring in *Boy Erased*, the story of a Baptist preacher's son forced to undergo conversion therapy. The film is expected to hit theaters in 2018. Regarding being part of the project, he explained his view to Teasdale: "It's incredibly rewarding and satisfying to know that we're doing something important in terms of subject matter. . . . I really feel like every day we have the ability to change things; to change people's attitudes and change some people's lives by shining a light on something that's quite insidious."

PERSONAL LIFE

Notoriously private and a bit of a workaholic, Edgerton ended an engagement to fashion designer Alexis Blake in 2013 reportedly to focus on his career.

SUGGESTED READING

Baron, Zach. "The Understated Brilliance of Joel Edgerton." *GQ*, 6 Dec. 2016, www.gq.com/story/joel-edgerton-moty-profile. Accessed 11 Jan. 2018.

Fontaine, Angus. "Joel Edgerton on Overcoming Fear and Directing a Movie." *GQ Australia*, 14 Oct. 2015, www.gq.com.au/entertainment/film+tv/joel+edgerton+on+overcoming+fear+and+directing+a+movie,39635. Accessed 11 Jan. 2018.

Merry, Stephanie. "'Tell the Judge I Love My Wife': The Brilliant Simplicity of *Loving*." *The Washington Post*, 10 Nov. 2016, www.washingtonpost.com/lifestyle/style/tell-the-judge-i-love-my-wife-the-brilliant-simplicity-of-loving/2016/11/08/b08bc28e-a530-11e6-8fc0-7be8f848c492_story.html. Accessed 11 Jan. 2018.

Mueller, Matt. "*Felony* star Joel Edgerton Interview: Actors Are All 'Desperately Insecure.'" *Independent*, 24 Oct. 2014, www.independent.co.uk/arts-entertainment/films/features/hollywood-star-joel-edgerton-interview-actors-are-all-desperately-insecure-9816107.html. Accessed 11 Jan. 2018.

Robey, Tim. "Joel Edgerton: 'I Wasn't Pretty Enough for *Neighbours*.'" *The Telegraph*, 22 Nov. 2015, www.telegraph.co.uk/film/black-mass/joel-edgerton-interview/. Accessed 11 Jan. 2018.

Teasdale, Charlie. "Joel Edgerton Shows You How to Dress for Winter." *Esquire*, 15 Dec. 2017, www.esquire.com/uk/style/a14433635/netflix-bright-joel-edgerton/. Accessed 11 Jan. 2018.

SELECTED WORKS

Star Wars: Episode II—Attack of the Clones, 2002; *Warrior*, 2011; *Zero Dark Thirty*, 2012; *The Great Gatsby*, 2013; *The Gift*, 2015; *Black Mass*, 2015; *Midnight Special*, 2016; *Loving*, 2016; *It Comes at Night*, 2017; *Bright*, 2017

—Christopher Mari

Nima Elbagir

Date of birth: July 1978
Occupation: Journalist

Standing at six feet one inch tall, fluent in Arabic, and boasting a posh English accent, the Sudanese broadcast journalist Nima Elbagir "is really like no press-corps veteran you have ever met," as Andrew Billen declared for *Television Magazine* (June 2016). Known as a dogged, no-nonsense reporter, Elbagir has made a living documenting events in some of the world's

Photo by Mike Coppola/Getty Images for Peabody Awards

most inhospitable places. She is a London-based senior international correspondent for CNN, which she joined in 2011.

Mainly concentrating her reporting on Africa, Elbagir has broken a number of major stories for CNN, most notably an investigation into the Libyan slave trade that garnered widespread international attention in 2017. She has received numerous awards for her work and has drawn comparisons to her veteran CNN colleague Christiane Amanpour, a renowned British Iranian journalist and television host.

EARLY LIFE AND EDUCATION

Nima Elbagir was born in July 1978 in Khartoum, the capital city of Sudan. She has a brother and two sisters and was raised by devoutly religious Sunni Muslim parents, both of whom were journalists. In the 1980s, her father, Dr. Ahmed Abdullah Elbagir, founded the independent Sudanese newspaper *Al-Khartoum*; her mother, Ibtisam Affan, served as its publisher, becoming the first woman publisher in Sudan. Elbagir, though, had "a very all over the place upbringing," as she told Maggie Brown for the *Guardian* (27 Feb. 2016).

At the time of her birth, Elbagir's father was in prison for being a member of an opposition political party. He was released when Elbagir was three, and the family then fled to England. They returned to Sudan five years later, and Elbagir's parents set up their newspaper. In 1989, Omar al-Bashir took power in Sudan in a military coup, and *Al-Khartoum* was, along with other newspapers, seized and shut down. At the time, Elbagir's father was out of the country and opted not to return. The rest of the family was prevented from leaving, however, and it was not until Elbagir was fourteen that the family was reunited in Exeter, England.

Elbagir attended private day schools in and around Exeter, an experience that "left her with a middle-class English accent and a gift for self-effacement," as Billen noted. Despite admittedly being an apathetic and, at times, disruptive student, she did well enough on her A-level exams—the equivalent of a high school diploma in the United States—to win acceptance to the London School of Economics. There, she earned a degree in philosophy.

Upon graduating in 2001, Elbagir returned to Sudan to enter the family trade. By then, her parents had moved back to Khartoum and resumed publishing *Al-Khartoum* under strict censors. Initially encouraged to become a doctor, Elbagir has attributed her decision to become a journalist to "a genetic streak of stubbornness," as she put it to Brown. She received her first training at *Al-Khartoum*.

EARLY CAREER

In 2002, Elbagir got her professional start working as a correspondent for *Reuters* in Sudan; for the next three years, she served as a trainee journalist with the news agency. She made a name for herself after becoming one of the first to report about the genocidal conflict in Darfur, which began in February 2003 and has since resulted in the deaths of an estimated 300,000 people. Elbagir's experience in the western Sudanese region, which is one of the biggest recipients of economic aid in the world, taught her that "people will do something" if they are informed about such atrocities, as she recalled to Brown. "As a journalist," she added, "you have to believe your job is to illuminate, try and shine the light. . . . And then you have to trust."

Elbagir moved into broadcast journalism in 2005, when she joined *More4 News*, the digital offshoot of the UK's *Channel 4 News*. As an on-air reporter for *More4 News*, which folded in 2009, she landed a series of exclusive interviews, including one with former South African president Jacob Zuma ahead of his 2006 rape trial. Concurrently, Elbagir reported for *Channel 4 News*. In 2007, she traveled to Somalia's capital, Mogadishu, to chronicle the suffering of civilians there from lawlessness. That piece earned her two Foreign Press Association awards, for television news story of the year and journalist of the year, in 2008.

Gaining a reputation for insightful, well-informed reports, Elbagir began appearing on Channel 4's acclaimed documentary series *Unreported World*. Between 2008 and 2009, she presented episodes on the Janjaweed militia group in Darfur, mystical cults in Venezuela, and violent rebel groups in the Congo. She started freelancing for CNN in 2010, partly out of a desire to report on more foreign affairs. Over the next year, she covered several stories for the network, including ones on violence against women in Nigeria and the South Sudanese independence referendum.

FEARLESS ON THE FRONTLINES

Elbagir was appointed an international correspondent for CNN, based out of the network's bureau in Johannesburg, South Africa, in 2011, and moved to its bureau in Nairobi, Kenya, in 2013. Two years later, the network promoted her to senior international correspondent, a post she continues to hold.

Based in CNN's London bureau, Elbagir has specialized in breaking major news from Africa but has also covered top stories in other parts of the world. Often traveling to conflict zones that put her at great personal risk, she has won the respect of peers and colleagues alike for her intrepid reporting. In 2011, for example, she flew to Egypt to cover the massive political demonstrations in Cairo's Tahrir Square, even after it was revealed that a French television journalist and many other women had been sexually assaulted there. During the summer of 2012, she journeyed to civil war–torn Syria for a CNN undercover series called "Damascus Undercover," which offered a harrowing glimpse into life in the country. The report received an Overseas Press Club (OPC) Award for spot news reporting in 2013.

Elbagir demonstrated her fearlessness again in 2014, when she covered the Ebola virus epidemic in the West African country of Liberia. Risking exposure to the highly contagious and often deadly virus, she entered Liberia's quarantine zones to document the devastation wrought by the outbreak, which was the worst in history. Required to wear a biohazard suit, Elbagir was struck by the overwhelming smell of bleach upon arriving at the zones, which health workers kept in easily accessible buckets for quick decontamination purposes. She has said that she was driven to cover the outbreak after becoming disheartened by the tepid international response to the Horn of Africa famine, which she covered at its height in 2011.

The response to Elbagir's coverage of the schoolgirl kidnappings in Chibok, Nigeria, however, was different. Elbagir was the first international journalist to report from the northern Nigerian village from which 276 schoolgirls were abducted by the terrorist organization Boko Haram in April 2014. The report sparked an international effort, led by world leaders, to free the schoolgirls, as well as a social media campaign that helped rally support from numerous celebrities. In an article for the London *Evening Standard* (29 Feb. 2016), Elbagir, who won a 2014 Peabody Award for her reporting, told Sophia Sleigh that the kidnappings marked a "turning point" for news coverage of Africa.

EXPOSING MODERN SLAVERY

Elbagir has said that being a Sudanese, Arabic-speaking female journalist has helped her gain unprecedented access to people, places, and situations that are hard to reach for most Western journalists. As she noted to Brown, her race and unique background allows her "to disappear in so many communities. . . . I have been able to play those grey areas. Sometimes I feel the sheer novelty value of me disarms people."

These cultural advantages aided Elbagir in her months-long investigation in 2015 into people smuggling from Egypt to Italy. At that time, most African migrants, too traumatized after being subjected to inhumane treatment at the hands of their smugglers, were unwilling to go on record about their experiences, even after reaching safety. By 2016, however, migrants had started opening up to reporters, which strengthened Elbagir's ability to investigate reports about the existence of a slave trade in Libya.

After spending months building sources and evidence, Elbagir, her producer, Raja Razek, and photojournalist Alex Platt traveled to the Libyan capital of Tripoli in the fall of 2017. Using hidden cameras and pretending to be Sudanese women looking for their lost loved ones, Elbagir and Razek attended and filmed an auction where a dozen men were sold into slavery. Most of the men were immigrants from countries in sub-Saharan Africa who had failed to come up with the funds necessary to pay off their smugglers.

Shortly after witnessing the auction, Elbagir and her collaborators gained access to a Libyan immigration center. There, they encountered throngs of illegal immigrants who offered more shocking first-hand accounts of being sold as slaves. Elbagir's subsequent reports drew widespread global attention and led to follow-up investigations by the Libyan government and the United Nations. In 2018, Elbagir and Razek won a George Polk Award for foreign television reporting for the story. "When you are talking about slavery you are sticking your finger into so many open wounds," she explained to Al Tompkins for Poynter.org (21 Nov. 2017). "We were not just reporting a story, we were entrusted with proof that there are real human beings being sold."

In the spring of 2018, Elbagir followed up her Libyan slave-trade story with an exposé about the use of child labor in cobalt mining in the Democratic Republic of the Congo. The report prompted the German automotive group Daimler, which, like other car manufacturers, uses cobalt in the production of their clean-energy vehicles, to launch an audit into their supply-chain network.

COURAGE AND CHANGE

Working in a political climate that has repeatedly questioned the accuracy and credibility of news reports, Elbagir, whose employer CNN has received numerous charges of "fake news" by US President Donald Trump, has remained steadfast in her belief in the power of journalism. In an interview with Pete Vernon for the *Columbia Journalism Review* (11 May 2018), she explained, "When people want to establish that we are not to be believed and we are not to be trusted, it's because they know we are capable of changing the climate and the culture, and opening people's eyes in really powerful ways."

Elbagir's determination and courage have been recognized by the Royal Television Society, which named her its 2016 Specialist Journalist of the Year, and by the International Women's Media Foundation, which presented her with a 2018 Courage in Journalism Award.

PERSONAL LIFE

Elbagir lives with her husband, a British diplomat, in the Battersea district of southwest London.

SUGGESTED READING

Billen, Andrew. "Nima Elbagir: Winning Access to the Frontline." *Television Magazine*, Royal Television Society, June 2016, rts.org.uk/article/nima-elbagir-winning-access-frontline. Accessed 29 June 2018.

Brown, Maggie. "CNN Reporter's Award Draws Amanpour Comparison." *The Guardian*, 27 Feb. 2016, www.theguardian.com/media/2016/feb/27/cnn-reporters-award-draws-amanpour-comparison. Accessed 29 June 2018.

Elbagir, Nima. "CNN's Nima Elbagir on Slavery, Child Labor, and Reporting in the Age of Trump." Interview by Pete Vernon. *Columbia Journalism Review*, 11 May 2018, www.cjr.org/q_and_a/nima-elbagir-cnn.php. Accessed 29 June 2018.

Sleigh, Sophia. "Boko Haram Altered How We Cover Africa News, Says Top Reporter Nima Elbagir." *Evening Standard*, 29 Feb. 2016, www.standard.co.uk/news/world/boko-haram-altered-how-we-cover-africa-news-says-muslim-reporter-nima-elbagir-a3191451.html. Accessed 29 June 2018.

Tompkins, Al. "How CNN Documented Human Slave Auctions." *Poynter*, 21 Nov. 2017, www.poynter.org/news/how-cnn-documented-human-slave-auctions. Accessed 29 June 2018.

—*Chris Cullen*

Phil Elverum

Date of birth: May 26, 1976
Occupation: Musician

"If this music thing doesn't pan out for Phil [Elverum], his soft, measured speaking voice all but guarantees him a back-up career as a reference librarian or NPR commentator," Brian Howe quipped in a feature article for the influential music magazine *Pitchfork* (13 May 2008). Elverum, as Howe implies, is known for his understated sound, but he is far from a monochromatic performer. Identified strongly with his native Pacific Northwest, Elverum has recorded under multiple names, including the Microphones (1996–2002) and Mount Eerie (2003–present). "Regardless of the moniker, Elverum's collections include interlocking themes and references to earlier material, and are marked by a distinctive naturalistic, self-recorded lo-fi analog sound that mixes his whispered, gentle voice—which can also yell and bellow—with ambitiously varied instrumentation," Brandon Stosuy wrote for the *Believer* (July/Aug. 2009). "His work can be delicately spare or layered and noisy, often in the same song." In a profile for the *New Yorker* (6 Sept. 2017), Peter C. Baker noted that recording on his own label, P.W. Elverum & Sun, allowed the artist to follow "his personal musical compass wherever it leads him—from lo-fi contemporary folk to noise rock, electronica, and Norwegian doom metal."

Listeners also often comment on the beauty and poetic content of Elverum's lyrics. Stosuy,

By Frédéric Minne, via Wikimedia Commons

for example, described them as being focused on "memory, first-person storytelling, myth, naturalism, the everyday as sacred, and sense of place (in and out of Washington State)," while Baker opined that they were, at times, "reminiscent of the writings of [acclaimed Norwegian novelist] Karl Ove Knausgård: first-person, digressive narratives that pinball between the quotidian and the cosmic."

Elverum has received increased critical attention for his album, *A Crow Looked at Me* (2017), which serves as a meditation of sorts on the death of his wife, Geneviève Castrée, who had succumbed to pancreatic cancer in 2015, just months after giving birth to the couple's daughter. "This wasn't music I wanted to listen to casually," Baker wrote, reflecting, as many critics did, on the project's meaningfulness and importance.

EARLY YEARS

The artist was born Phil Elvrum. (He added the extra "e" to his last name later in life, after discovering during a trip to Norway that there was a town there spelled Elverum.) On his official website, he writes, "I don't think it's necessary for anyone to know my biographical details in order to relate to my music but I know that it's a common curiosity. . . . I personally don't care that much about people and wish that everyone else was a little more focused on the song, not the singer."

Almost everything written about him mentions Anacortes, the Washington town of just 16,000 inhabitants where he was born and where his family has lived for several generations: "I had the good fortune of growing up in a town where my great-great grandparents were some of the first Euro inhabitants," he explained to Stosuy. The earliest family members to settle in the town owned multiple canneries, making them among its wealthiest inhabitants. (Anacortes had been a major hub for fishing and canning but is known now mainly as being a point of departure for the ferry to the San Juan Islands.)

Elverum has told interviewers, perhaps apocryphally, that an eccentric great-grandmother and grandfather had raised a baby gorilla, who dressed in human clothing and played with the neighborhood children until it got too large and aggressive and was sent to a zoo in Seattle. Members of subsequent generations became teachers. "Not university professors, not super-scholars, but middle-school teachers. We read books," he told Stosuy, explaining that his parents gave him the middle name of Walter, in honor of the poet Walt Whitman.

Elverum, who worked at a local record store, recorded cassettes of his music as a teen, giving them basic titles like "Drums.Beats" and "4 Track Stuff." Although some of the young people in Anacortes chafed at the insularity and quiet of growing up in such a small town, Elverum did not share that attitude. "Hearing my classmates talk about, 'Oh, it's so boring. Nothing ever happens,' I just couldn't identify with that, because my friends and I were so busy with our cool projects like putting on shows, playing in bands, making tapes, recording, constantly doing crazy stuff, creating our own excitement," he recalled to Grayson Haver Currin for *Noisey* (24 May 2017). "It made me realize that . . . I could do that anywhere."

Elverum began touring as a musician right after graduating from high school, traveling with D Plus, a band he had formed. "Coming back from that [tour], it totally changed my understanding of life," he recalled to Howe. "It opened my world, to realize a person could live that way. Going back into a classroom felt so weird and wrong." Thus, while Elverum moved to Olympia, Washington, at age nineteen to attend college, he lasted just a short time before dropping out to pursue a music career on a full-time basis. He became an active participant in Olympia's thriving arts scene, and he could often be found in the studio at K Records, helping out and experimenting with his own music—although from time to time, when money was tight, he returned to Anacortes to work in the record store.

THE MICROPHONES

In 1999, according to most sources, K Records released Elverum's first full-length album, *Don't Wake Me Up*. Working with a small group of other vocalists and engineering the recording himself, he chose the name the Microphones. "What might first have appeared scattered or sloppy in execution eventually revealed an artist developing a tone that embraced the juxtaposition of harmony and dissonance, the extension and/or subversion of how instruments typically interact with voice and each other and the use of non-musical sounds to give songs a deeper context in time and space," Eric Hill wrote for the arts magazine *Exclaim!* (21 Mar. 2017) of that debut effort. (Other sources, with a more exhaustive view of the Northwest music scene of the era, state that at some point before *Don't Wake Me Up*, the Microphones had released a series of lo-fi cassettes on the local Knw-Yr-Own label, as well as a full-length album titled *Tests* (1998), on the Elsinor label.)

In quick succession, K Records released the EP *Moon, Moon* (1999), *It Was Hot We Stayed in the Water* (2000), and the somewhat confusingly named *The Glow, Pt. 2.* (2001). (An eleven-minute track on the previous album had been titled "The Glow.")

"While *It Was Hot We Stayed in the Water* expanded the Microphones' lo-fi, psych pop horizons, their sixty-six-minute epic *The Glow, Pt. 2* marks an even bigger departure," Heather Phares opined in an undated review for the online guide AllMusic. "The album revels in its kaleidoscopic sounds, spanning pastoral folky ballads, playful symphonic pop, and gusts of white noise. . . . Expansive yet accessible, indulgent yet unpretentious, *The Glow, Pt. 2* redefines the Microphones' fascinatingly contradictory music."

A different label, St. Ives, released the Microphones' next two projects, *Blood* (2001) and *Little Bird Flies into a Big Black Cloud* (2002), both of which came out in highly limited release, solely on vinyl; each copy of *Little Bird* featured a cover hand-painted by Elverum.

The Microphones returned to K Records for 2003's *Mount Eerie*, which earned rapturous reviews from many critics. Writing for *Pitchfork* (20 Jan. 2003), for example, Eric Carr asserted, "This is a massive artistic statement from The Microphones, and though it may be cryptic—even overwhelming at times—it remains warm and open, thanks to the stunning intimacy that has consistently been the group's hallmark. As the truth and meaning of the universe become manifest, *Mount Eerie* comforts, illustrating that comprehension isn't as important as acceptance."

The title of the album referred to the dramatically towering mountain (Mount Erie) on Fidalgo Island, where Anacortes is located, and Elverum subsequently decided to begin recording under an adaptation of that name.

MOUNT EERIE

Discussing the name change with Stosuy, Elverum said, "I love this place. It is home, in a deep way. The mountain (Mount Erie) is right in the middle of the island. . . . I grew up under it, staring at it every morning waiting for the school bus. It's a special place for me, and the mysterious beauty in the rock face is potent. It has a similar vibe to much of what I am trying to do in music."

In 2004 Elverum released his first recordings under the new name, a multipart project that included a limited-edition CD titled *Seven New Songs of Mount Eerie*, a twelve-inch vinyl record called *Mount Eerie Dances with Wolves*, and a live triple album recorded during a tour in Copenhagen. The following year he released what many fans consider the first official Mount Eerie release, *No Flashlight*, notable for including what amounted to an atlas of maps, photographs, and liner notes meant to help listeners delve deeper into the music. Subsequent releases also included elaborate or artistic packaging, which became something of a trademark, especially after the artist launched his own label, P.W. Elverum & Sun.

Mount Eerie, Pts. 6–7, came out in 2007, and the ten-inch vinyl picture disc included in the package was almost secondary to the hardcover book of Elverum's photographs it also contained. He followed that with *Lost Wisdom* (2008), a collaboration with singer Julie Doiron and guitarist Fred Squire; the double album *Wind's Poem* (2009), inspired by Nordic black metal; *White Stag* (2009); *Clear Moon* (2012); *Ocean Roar* (2012); *Pre-Human Ideas* (2013); and *Sauna* (2015).

Although Elverum earned consistently good reviews from the music cognoscenti, he has received the most mainstream attention to date for his 2017 album, *A Crow Looked at Me*, written in the wake of his wife's death from pancreatic cancer. He recorded the lo-fi effort in the room where she had slept towards the end of her life, using an acoustic guitar, one microphone, and a laptop, working mainly at night while their infant daughter was asleep.

"The resulting album, *A Crow Looked at Me*, sounds like an Elverum work," Jayson Greene wrote for *Pitchfork* (13 Mar. 2017). "The music is low and murmuring. His voice is hushed and conversational. The theme of impermanence can still be felt. But the difference between this album and everything else he's done is the difference between charting a voyage around the earth and undertaking it."

PERSONAL LIFE

Elverum—who in 2005 created a series of roughly sketched comics he dubbed *Fancy People Adventures*, which is still available online—continues to live in Anacortes with his daughter. His own parents live in the house he grew up in, not far away. He has told interviewers that he might move some day from Anacortes to one of the neighboring islands where he owns land, but he has said he intends to continue making music and various other forms of art.

Of his thirteen-year marriage to his late wife, Geneviève, he reminisced to Greene, "It always felt like we were two comets in the galaxy that happened to crash into each other in a meaningful way."

SUGGESTED READING

Baker, Peter C. "In a Room, Listening to Phil Elverum Sing about His Wife's Death." *The New Yorker*, 6 Sept. 2017, www.newyorker.com/culture/culture-desk/in-a-room-listening-to-phil-elverum-sing-about-his-wifes-death. Accessed 6 Feb. 2018.

Currin, Grayson Haver. "A Conversation with Mount Eerie's Phil Elverum on His Devastating New Album." *Noisey*, 24 May 2017, www.noisey.vice.com/en_us/article/wn9z54/a-conversation-with-mount-eeries-phil-elverum-on-his-devastating-new-album. Accessed 6 Feb. 2018.

Gotrich, Lars. "Mount Eerie Shares Heartbreaking 'Real Death.'" "All Songs Considered." *National Public Radio*, 25 Jan. 2017, www.npr.org/sections/allsongs/2017/01/25/511604857/mount-eerie-shares-heartbreaking-real-death. Accessed 6 Feb. 2018.

Greene, Jayson. "Death Is Real: Mount Eerie's Phil Elverum Copes with Unspeakable Tragedy." *Pitchfork*, 13 Mar. 2017, www.pitchfork.com/features/profile/10034-death-is-real-mount-eeries-phil-elverum-copes-with-unspeakable-tragedy/. Accessed 6 Feb. 2018.

Hill, Eric. "An Essential Guide to Mount Eerie, the Microphones and the World of Phil Elverum." *Exclaim!*, 21 Mar. 2017, www.exclaim.ca/music/article/an_essential_guide_to_mount_eerie_the_microphones_and_the_world_of_phil_elverum. Accessed 6 Feb. 2018.

Howe, Brian. "Microphones." *Pitchfork*, 13 May 2008, www.pitchfork.com/features/interview/6849-microphones. Accessed 6 Feb. 2018.

Stosuy, Brandon. "Phil Elverum [Phil Elverum [Mount Eerie, the Microphones, et al.]" *The Believer*, July/Aug. 2009, www.believermag.com/issues/200907/?read=interview_elverum. Accessed 6 Feb. 2018.

SELECTED WORKS

Don't Wake Me Up, 1999; *The Glow, Pt. 2*, 2001; *No Flashlight*, 2005; *Mount Eerie, Pts. 6–7*, 2007; *A Crow Looked at Me*, 2017

—*Mari Rich*

Joel Embiid

Date of birth: March 16, 1994
Occupation: Basketball player

Joel Embiid, nicknamed the Process, is a center for the Philadelphia 76ers (known by fans as the Sixers). Embiid was born and raised in Cameroon, and dreamed of becoming a soccer player. A fortuitous viewing of Kobe Bryant's most valuable player (MVP) performance in the 2010 National Bastketball Association (NBA) finals led him to consider another sport. He picked up a basketball in 2011. "Everything in my life happens really fast," he mused to Lee Jenkins for *Sports Illustrated* (26 Oct. 2016). Less than three years later, Embiid was selected third overall by the Philadelphia 76ers in the 2014 NBA draft. (He is the highest-drafted African-born player since Hasheem Thabeet, a Tanzanian player drafted by the Memphis Grizzlies in 2009.) It seemed like a Cinderella story. Embiid was poised to become an NBA superstar, but his

By Brent Burford [CC BY 2.0], via Wikimedia Commons

early NBA career was marred by injury and grief. A foot injury prevented Embiid from playing for two years, and the sudden death of his younger brother in an accident left Embiid wondering if moving so far from home to pursue a career in basketball was the right decision after all. Eventually, he decided to stay in Philadelphia, working through his injuries in tribute to his brother. Embiid's breakout 2016 season offered fans a glimpse of his greatness before another injury sidelined him, and in 2017, Embiid signed a five-year, $148 million contract extension with the Sixers.

While injuries kept him off the court, Embiid connected with fans through social media. He is a prolific user of Twitter, happy to profess his love for a mocktail called the Shirley Temple, and an Internet prankster who once live-tweeted preparations for an imaginary date with the singer Rihanna. He was introduced to social media's potential for comedy after the draft, when a tape delay made it appear as though Embiid was less than enthused to be joining the Sixers. His bored reaction became a meme. So, too, has Embiid's catchphrase, "Trust the Process." Fans have been known to shout it to Embiid in encouragement as he walks (or as in one viral video, runs) down the street. Embiid's career is just getting started; Clay Skipper, who interviewed Embiid for *GQ Magazine* (19 Oct. 2017), speculated that Embiid's impressive range of talents stand to make him "the future of the NBA."

EARLY LIFE AND INTRODUCTION TO BASKETBALL

Embiid was born in Yaoundé, the capital of Cameroon in West Africa, on March 16, 1994. His father, Thomas Embiid, is a colonel in the Cameroon military and a former handball champion. Embiid grew up with a younger sister, Muriel, and a younger brother, Arthur.

Embiid grew up in an upper-middle-class home. His mother, Christine, drove a Mercedes, and forbade him from playing sports—he liked volleyball and soccer best—until he had memorized the notes he had taken at school. His comfortable, unremarkable upbringing did not jive with his American teammates' ideas about what life looked like in Cameroon, or Africa, in general. Playing to their ignorance, and showcasing the sense of humor for which he is known, Embiid later convinced his college teammates that he killed a lion when he was six years old to prove that he was a man. Distressingly, they believed him. "Americans, they don't really have any idea of what's going on in the world," he told Adrian Wojnarowski for the *Woj Pod* podcast (11 Nov. 2016). "When they think about Africans, they think about . . . us running around with lions and tigers and all those other animals, so when I got to Kansas I kind of used that to my advantage . . . ."

Embiid was a good student at school in Yaoundé, and a superior midfielder on his soccer team. "It was a good environment, a good situation," Thomas Embiid told Jason King for the *Bleacher Report* (17 Nov. 2013). In 2010, Embiid watched Lakers shooting guard Kobe Bryant dominate the NBA finals against the Boston Celtics, and discovered a new interest in the sport. In July 2011, before Embiid's junior year of high school, a basketball camp was held in the area, but Embiid was too embarrassed by his lack of skill to sign up. As the story goes, his volleyball coach signed him up anyway. This series of events is remarkable considering the lack of enthusiasm for basketball in Cameroon. "There is only one sport in Cameroon," a Cameroonian basketball player named Melvin Eyabi told Jordan Ritter Conn for the now defunct sports website *Grantland* (27 June 2014). He was referring to the country's fervid enthusiasm for soccer. The camp was led by Luc Richard Mbah a Moute, a Cameroonian-born power forward for the Houston Rockets. Mbah a Moute was blown away by Embiid. The 6 feet 9 inches tall teen lacked training and finesse, but Mbah a Moute saw serious potential, and named Embiid one of the camp's top five players when the camp was over. This accolade came with an invitation to another camp, part of an NBA global outreach program called Basketball without Borders, in Johannesburg, South Africa.

HIGH SCHOOL AND COLLEGE CAREER

Embiid had intended to go to France and enroll at the National Institute of Sports and Physical Education (Institut national du sport et de l'éducation physique, INSEP) to play volleyball, but his success at the camp, and prodding from Mbah a Moute, convinced his father to give his blessing for Embiid to pursue a career in basketball. Embiid made the wrenching decision to move to the United States to attend Montverde Academy, a prep school in Florida and Mbah a Moute's own alma mater. "Just imagine walking away from your whole family like that," Embiid told King. "It's not easy." Though Embiid did not know it at the time, it was the last time he would ever see his brother.

In the United States, Embiid faced a steep learning curve. He spoke hardly any English—Cameroon is a predominantly French-speaking country—and worse, he had yet to get the hang of basketball. His high school teammates (aside from two players who were also from Cameroon) did not make Embiid's transition any easier. They teased him for his limited understanding of the game, but Embiid's coach, Kevin Boyle, gave them a stern warning. "Laugh all you want, but in five years, you're going to be asking him for a loan, because he's going to be worth about $50 million," he later recalled to King. "I told them, 'You have no idea how good that kid is going to be.'"

Embiid began his junior year playing for the school's junior varsity team; by his senior year, he was ranked among the top ten college prospects in America. By this time, he had transferred, again with the help of Mbah a Moute, to the Rock School in Gainesville, Florida. He studied tapes of NBA legend Hakeem Olajuwon, learning to mimic his moves with lethal precision. Bill Self, the coach at the University of Kansas, first saw Embiid play in the fall of his senior year in 2012. Embiid quickly became Self's top recruitment priority. Kansas is one of the best programs in the country, but Embiid was strongly considering the University of Florida and the University of Texas, Austin. After seeking the guidance of his coaches and Mbah a Moute, Embiid ultimately committed to Kansas. During Embiid's freshman year, Self compared Embiid to a "sponge," soaking up information and plays with ease. Self told King, "He has a natural feel, natural instincts. Of all the guys on our team, he's the most instinctive basketball guy we have." During his single year with the team, Embiid was named Big 12 Defensive Player of the Year, and averaged 11.2 points, 8.1 rebounds, and 2.6 blocks per game. In March, he suffered a stress fracture in his spine. Embiid missed both the Big 12 tournament and the National Collegiate Athletic Association (NCAA) tournament, where Kansas fell to Stanford in the third round.

TRUST THE PROCESS

Despite his back injury and a stress fracture in his right foot, Embiid was still considered a top prospect in the 2014 NBA draft. Embiid later revealed that he nearly elected to stay at Kansas for a second year. A mentor convinced him to leave. In June 2014, Embiid was selected third overall by the Philadelphia 76ers. (His Kansas teammate, Andrew Wiggins, went first to the Cleveland Cavaliers.) Embiid was elated, but his foot injury proved more problematic than he could have imagined. Embiid lost both his rookie and sophomore seasons to recovery. During this time, in October 2014, Embiid's brother, Arthur, died at the age of thirteen in an accident caused when an out-of-control truck crashed into his schoolyard. Between recovery and grief, it was a low and lonely period for Embiid.

In 2016, Embiid's third year in the league, he made his NBA debut in a preseason game against the Boston Celtics in October. He played for 13 minutes, scoring 6 points and 4 rebounds, and blocking 2 shots. "I was pretty nervous," Embiid said after the game, as reported by Jeff Goodman for *ESPN* (5 Oct. 2016). "I had trouble breathing, but once I got that first bucket, everything slowed down. I started seeing the game easier."

Embiid was named Eastern Conference Rookie of the Month in November and December 2016, and January 2017, making him the runaway favorite for Rookie of the Year. But on January 20, in a game against the Portland Trail Blazers, the unlucky Embiid sustained another injury, this time a slight meniscus tear in his knee. In March, the Sixers announced that Embiid's season was over. He had played just 31 games, but it was enough time for him to showcase the breadth of his talent. A mended Embiid made a spectacular preseason debut in October 2017, scoring 22 points and 7 rebounds in just 14 minutes of play against the Brooklyn Nets. In November, Embiid posted a career-high 46 points—the most by any Sixers player in over a decade—in a game against the Los Angeles Lakers. He also made 7 assists and blocked 7 shots; the last player to achieve that combination of stats in one game was Julius Erving in 1982. With the 2018 season just heating up, there is no telling what else the Process might accomplish.

SUGGESTED READING

Conn, Jordan Ritter. "Started from Yaoundé, Now He's Here." *Grantland*, 27 June 2014, grantland.com/features/joel-embiid-nba-draft-philadelphia-76ers-kansas-jayhawks/. Accessed 16 Jan. 2018.

Embiid, Joel. "Joel Embiid Is the Future of Basketball." Interview by Clay Skipper. *GQ Magazine*, 19 Oct. 2017, www.gq.com/story/ joel-embiid-the-process-interview. Accessed 16 Jan. 2018.

Goodman, Jeff. "Joel Embiid Scores 6 Points, Grabs 4 Boards in NBA Debut." *ESPN*, 5 Oct. 2016, www.espn.com/nba/story/_/ id/17716939/joel-embiid-makes-nba-debut. Accessed 16 Jan. 2018.

Jenkins, Lee. "Joel Embiid: 'I'm The Process.'" *Sports Illustrated*, 26 Oct. 2016, www.si.com/ nba/2016/10/26/joel-embiid-philadelphia-76ers-the-process. Accessed 16 Jan. 2018.

King, Jason. "Meet Kansas' Joel Embiid, a Cameroon Native Blossoming into a Top NBA Prospect." *Bleacher Report*, 17 Dec. 2013, bleacherreport.com/articles/1891203-meet-kansas-joel-embiid-a-cameroon-native-blossoming-into-a-top-nba-prospect. Accessed 16 Jan. 2018.

Wojnarowski, Adrian. "Joel Embiid and Brett Brown Join Woj." *Woj Pod*, 11 Nov. 2016, www.acast.com/theverticalpodcastwithwoj/ joel-embiid-and-brett-brown-join-woj. Accessed 16 Jan. 2018.

—*Molly Hagan*

Mathias Énard

Date of birth: January 11, 1972
Occupation: Author

"Mathias Énard is a French novelist who has gained recognition in Europe for the scale of his ambitions and the hurtling, anarchic energy of his prose," Robert F. Worth wrote for the *New York Times* (20 Feb. 2015). "He has a large appetite for disaster, and his books are packed with wars, massacres, terrorism—with human depravity of every kind. His sentences spin on and on, acquiring a giddy momentum as they lurch through gutters and brothels and kill zones."

Énard's books frequently draw upon themes of Orientalism, a field whose preeminent scholar was widely considered to be Palestinian American academic and literary critic Edward Said. Énard's most recent novel, 2015's *Boussole* (translated into English in 2017 as *Compass*), frequently cites Said's work, but Énard has admitted that it can be hard to pin down an exact definition of the term Orientalism, even though it is used to describe many of his own volumes. "If it's difficult to define the 'Orient,' then it's also complicated to know what 'Orientalism' means," he told Thea Lenarduzzi in an interview for *Five Books*. "It has many sides—the first is maybe the scientific, linked to the history of our knowledge of the Middle East: linguistics, archaeology, history, social sciences, etc. But there [are] also the arts: painting, travel literature, poetry and

By ActuaLitté [CC BY-SA 2.0], via Wikimedia Commons

even music have invented, as well as discovered, this distorted reality we call the 'Orient'—part dream, part object of desire, part violent representations and fantasies."

Despite winning the Prix Goncourt, one of France's highest literary honors, *Compass* frustrated some critics—largely because of the complexities of its themes. "Énard . . . occasionally overstuffs *Compass* with the kind of Orientalist arcana that might be better suited to a scholarly essay," Tobias Grey wrote for the *Financial Times* (10 Mar. 2017). "However, when he concentrates on storytelling, as he does in the novel's second half, there are passages of pure delight with rare insight into the human condition."

EARLY LIFE AND EDUCATION

Énard was born on January 11, 1972, in Niort, France. As a young man, he studied the history of Islamic art at the École du Louvre and Arabic and Persian at the Institut national des langues et civilisations orientales (Inalco), a school in Paris that had been designated in 1985 as a *grand établissement*, one of France's most prestigious institutions of research and higher education.

The Lebanese Civil War was nearing its end in 1990, but the city—once known for its cosmopolitan art and literary scenes as well as for its air of diversity and tolerance—was still in disarray. Thanks to a series of grants and academic exchanges, Énard subsequently traveled widely throughout the Middle East, visiting Egypt, Iran, and Syria, among other locales. Énard was fascinated by the beauty, volume,

cultural refinement, and diversity of Arabic and Persian literature.

In 2000, Énard settled in Barcelona, where he found work as a translator and began teaching Arabic as a faculty member at the Universitat Autònoma de Barcelona (UAB), a massive public institution of higher education generally considered to be one of the best in Spain.

LITERARY CAREER

In 2003 Énard published his first novel, *La perfection du tir* (*The Perfect Shot*), whose protagonist is a sniper serving in a civil war in an unnamed country. Although the book got little attention in the United States, it garnered the Prix des cinq continents de la francophonie in 2004, a literary prize administered by the Organisation internationale de la francophonie, which represents countries and regions in which French is the mother tongue or the majority of citizens are French-speaking. Énard followed his auspicious debut with the 2004 publication of *Remonter l'Orénoque* (Up the Orinoco), the tale of a love triangle set against the backdrop of the Amazon, and 2007's *Bréviaire des artificiers* (The artificer's breviary), a tongue-in-cheek fable about an apprentice terrorist.

ZONE

Énard's next book, *Zone* (2008), won him an American audience when it was translated into English by Charlotte Mandell and published in 2010 under the same title. The five-hundred-page book consisted of a single sentence: the interior monologue of French spy Francis Servain Mirković, as he journeys by train to the Vatican to hand over a dossier of war crimes committed in central Europe and the Mediterranean. In the process, he recalls his childhood, his time as a mercenary in a Croatian militia, his reading of the *Iliad*, the atrocities detailed in the dossier, and numerous other events that pop into his head. "Though the reader is marooned in Mirkovic's consciousness for more than 500 pages, the boundaries of his skull do not feel claustrophobic, because the mind at work in the novel is remarkably elastic," Stephen Burn wrote in a review for the *New York Times* (7 Jan. 2011). "The 150,000-word sentence that makes up Énard's erudite and ambitious novel is certainly an attempt to create a Flaubertian encyclopedia of our times at the end of a violent century. But this millennial archive also measures guilt—it passes sentence, as it were, on both the regrets and memories of Énard's narrator and the larger guilt and shame that he describes as 'the weight of Western civilization.'" *Zone* received multiple literary honors, including the Prix du Livre Inter and the Prix Décembre.

STREET OF THIEVES

Énard next garnered attention in the United States in 2014, when his novel *Rue des voleurs* (2012) was translated into English by Mandell and released in 2014 as *Street of Thieves*. The novel takes place during the Arab uprisings of 2011 and is narrated by a young Moroccan man named Lakhdar. "*Street of Thieves* is . . . modest in scope," Robert F. Worth wrote for the *New York Times* (20 Feb. 2015). "Énard is at his best when he takes his eyes off Literature and uses his narrative gifts to convey Lakhdar's adolescent yearnings: anguished love for his Spanish girlfriend and nostalgic loyalty to a childhood friend from Tangier who is slowly being radicalized by an Islamist sheikh. This second plotline, seen through Lakhdar's thoroughly lapsed but sympathetic perspective, is artfully told, and represents the kind of fiction one hopes will emerge, from Énard or others, after the tumult once known as the Arab Spring has receded a little further into the past." Among the literary laurels garnered by the novel were the Prix du Roman-News, Prix littéraire de la Porte Dorée, and le Choix Goncourt de l'Orient. Although the last-named prize carries the Goncourt name, it is administered not by the Société littéraire des Goncourt but by the Middle East Regional Directorate of the Agence universitaire de la francophonie.

PRIX GONCOURT

Énard would soon be honored by the Académie Goncourt, however. The influential French literary organization was founded by the author and publisher Edmond de Goncourt in 1903 to encourage the celebration of French writing and honor the memory of his late brother Jules. Each November, its members gather over a traditional lunch of lamb stew and olives at the Drouant restaurant, in Paris, to decide upon "the best and most imaginative prose work of the year," which is then awarded the Prix Goncourt, often called France's highest literary honor. In 2015, Énard's novel *Boussole* (2015) was chosen for the prize.

The book's protagonist, Franz Ritter, is a terminally ill Austrian musicologist in love with a woman named Sarah, a scholar of Orientalism. Calling the book "as much an essay, a compendium, a rant and a polemic as it is a work of fiction," Justin Taylor wrote for the *Los Angeles Times* (24 Mar. 2017), "Ritter spends a long dark night of the soul in his apartment in his home city—Vienna . . . in an insomniac reverie that pays homage to both *One Thousand and One Nights* and *In Search of Lost Time*. . . . If Scheherazade and Proust are the novel's East and West, its North and South are W.G. Sebald (erudite melancholia) and Thomas Bernhard (a blitzkrieg of spleen)." Referring to the English-language translation of the book, *Compass*, which was released in the United States in 2017, Taylor concluded, "*Compass* is as challenging, brilliant, and—God help me—important a novel as is likely to be published this year." *Compass* was shortlisted for the Man Booker Prize, and its Italian translation, *Bussola*, garnered the Premio Gregor von Rezzori (Gregor von Rezzori Award) at the Festival degli Scrittori (Festival of Writers) in Florence.

OTHER HONORS

Énard is a member of the editorial board of *Inculte* (*Uncultivated*), a French journal of literature and philosophy. In addition to his other honors, his 2010 work *Parle-leur de batailles, de rois et d'éléphants* (Tell them about battles, kings and elephants) was awarded the Lycéens Goncourt, which is judged by a panel of high school students. In 2017 he received the Leipzig Book Award for European Understanding, which is administered by the city of Leipzig, Germany, and includes prize money of 15,000 euros.

PERSONAL LIFE

Énard continues to live and teach in Barcelona, although in 2013 he accepted a writing residency in Berlin, Germany. He co-owns a Lebanese restaurant, Karakala, not far from his home.

SUGGESTED READING

Burn, Stephen. "River of Consciousness." Review of *Zone*, by Mathias Énard. *The New York Times*, 7 Jan. 2011, www.nytimes.com/2011/01/09/books/review/Burn-t.html. Accessed 7 Dec. 2017.

Cohen, Joshua. "A Prize-Winning French Novel about the Western Obsession with the East." Review of *Compass*, by Mathias Énard. *The New York Times*, 30 June 2017, www.nytimes.com/2017/06/30/books/review/compass-mathias-enard.html. Accessed 7 Dec. 2017.

Énard, Mathias. "The Separation Between Orient and Occident Is Entirely Artificial': An Interview with Mathias Énard." By Simon Leser. *Culture Trip*, 3 Aug. 2017, www.theculturetrip.com/europe/france/articles/the-separation-between-orient-and-occident-is-entirely-artificial-an-interview-with-mathias-enard/7. Accessed 7 Dec. 2017.

Lenarduzzi, Thea. "Mathias Énard on the 'Orient' and Orientalism." *Five Books*, 2018, https://fivebooks.com/best-books/orientalism-mathias-enard-man-booker. Accessed 7 Dec. 2017.

Taylor, Justin. "Winner of the Prix Goncourt, *Compass* by Mathias Énard Is Brilliant and Frustrating." Review of *Compass*, by Mathias Énard. *Los Angeles Times*, 24 Mar. 2017, www.latimes.com/books/jacketcopy/la-ca-jc-enard-compass-20170324-story.html. Accessed 7 Dec. 2017.

Willsher, Kim. "France's Top Literary Prize Awarded to Mathias Énard." *The Guardian*, 3 Nov. 2015, www.theguardian.com/books/2015/nov/03/frances-top-literary-prize-awarded-to-mathias-enard. Accessed 7 Dec. 2017.

Worth, Robert F. Review of *Street of Thieves*, by Mathias Énard. *The New York Times*, 20 Feb. 2015, www.nytimes.com/2015/02/22/books/review/street-of-thieves-by-mathias-enard.html. Accessed 7 Dec. 2017.

SELECTED WORKS

La perfection du tir (The Perfect Shot), 2003; *Remonter l'Orénoque (Up the Orinoco)*, 2004; *Bréviaire des artificiers (The artificer's breviary)*, 2007; *Zone*, 2008; *Rue des voleurs (Street of Thieves)*, 2012; *Boussole (Compass)*, 2015

—*Mari Rich*

Photo by Jared Siskin/Patrick McMullan via Getty Images

Awol Erizku

Date of birth: 1988
Occupation: Artist

Awol Erizku is a conceptual artist best known for his portraits of singer Beyoncé when pregnant with twins Rumi and Sir in 2017. The announcement photographs—one of which was, for a time, the most popular Instagram post ever with over eleven million "likes"—may have introduced Erizku and his work to a larger audience, but the multimedia artist and deejay was well known in art circles long before then. As an undergraduate student at the Cooper Union, Erizku won acclaim for a photograph called *Girl with a Bamboo Earring* (2009), which reimagines the subject of seventeenth-century Dutch painter Johannes Vermeer's *Girl with the Pearl Earring* as a young black woman. Alongside a series of photographs in a similar vein, Erizku's earliest work sought to "distill notions of black beauty and 'update' key canonical and contemporary works in Western art," Antwaun Sargent wrote in an interview for the *Fader* (14 Dec. 2016). Thanks to that series, he gained representation with a blue-chip New York gallery at age twenty-four.

Erizku began to broaden his artistic practice as a graduate student at Yale University, creating works that moved beyond the canvas and the camera lens. One of his shows, called *Make America Great Again*, was presented at the Ben Brown Fine Arts gallery in London in April 2017. It featured an American flag and red MAGA hats emblazoned with the image of a black panther, a reference to the radical black liberation party, the Black Panthers. Erizku is notable for his use of social media websites like Tumblr and Instagram. He operates an Instagram page according to standard gallery hours, alternating between public and private settings. Erizku also integrates music into his work, creating a mixtape for each solo show. Another 2017 show, *Purple Reign* at Stems, a gallery in Brussels, Belgium, featured work inspired by the Future mixtape of the same name.

EARLY LIFE AND EDUCATION

Erizku was born in Addis Ababa, Ethiopia, in 1988, but after coming to the States as an infant, he grew up in the Andrew Jackson Houses, a New York City housing project in the South Bronx. Erizku was interested in art at an early age, but a fortuitous incident in junior high set him on his future path. "Me and my friends were setting toilet paper on fire," he recalled to Kilo Kish for the website *Creators* (25 Nov. 2015). While awaiting punishment from the principal, he was instructed "to stay in that classroom," and it turned out to be a high school portfolio preparation class. They were preparing for LaGuardia and Art and Design—two competitive New York City arts high schools. Erizku joined the class, prepared a portfolio of drawings and paintings, and applied to the High School of Art and Design in Manhattan. He got in and was classmate with rapper A$AP Ferg.

Still, Erizku told Jori Finkel for the *New York Times* (10 Apr. 2017), that he never truly considered pursuing art professionally until an epiphany in an art history class. Art, he realized, was crowded with white faces. "We were looking at the painting 'The Girl with the Pearl Earring' and at that moment I felt I wanted to be an artist so I could bring more people who looked like me, my mother and my sisters, into history," he said. He realized this dream, quite literally, in a photograph he made while he was a painting student at the prestigious Cooper Union in New York. Erizku posed one of his sisters to look like the girl in the Vermeer painting. He called the arresting piece *Girl with a Bamboo Earring* (2009). The photograph, which was presented at a group show at the FLAG Art Foundation, effectively launched Erizku's career. Erizku completed the series by transforming other famous images. He reimagined, for example, Leonardo da Vinci's *Lady with an Ermine* as *Lady with a Pitbull* (2009). Other images feature young women sporting designer labels like their aristocratic predecessors flaunted silk and fur. "What saves the works from falling into a formulaic gimmick," Priscilla Frank wrote for the *Huffington Post* (22 June 2012), "is their cinematic intensity."

THE ONLY WAY IS UP

Erizku studied with multimedia artist Lorna Simpson and photographer Christine Osinski and worked as an assistant to photographer David LaChapelle. He earned his bachelor's degree in 2010, and two years later, enrolled in the graduate photography program at Yale. Erizku enjoyed his first solo show, featuring *Girl with a Bamboo Earring* and other photographs. Titled *Black and Gold*, it was presented at the Hasted Kraeutler Gallery in New York City in June and July of 2012.

Erizku earned his MFA degree in 2014, the same year he presented *The Only Way Is Up*, also at the Hasted Kraeutler. The show featured pieces like *Oh What a Feeling, aw, F——— It, I want a Trillion* (2014), an installation of seven stacked basketball hoops with 24-carat gold-plated nets. The title of the piece comes from the Jay-Z song "Picasso Baby," and the piece itself references a similar work called *Untitled (Stack)* by the late minimalist artist Donald Judd. But Erizku remains interested in changing the way artists talk about and contextualize their art. When he posted a photo of the work on his Tumblr account, he told Sargent for *Complex* (7 Aug. 2014), he was pleased by comments such as "It's like when you see a hot chick at a bar, and then you see her girlfriends," and "She got you going through all those hoops!" He concluded, "So you get all these various interpretations of the piece. And that is more satisfying to me than someone saying it's like a Donald Judd."

NEW FLOWER AND BAD II THE BONE

In 2015, Erizku debuted a short film called *Serendipity*, a collaboration with deejay MeLo-X, at the Museum of Modern Art (MoMa) PopRally event. The film features Erizku demolishing a bust of Michelangelo's *David* with a sledgehammer and installing one of Egyptian queen Nefertiti in its place. The performance was "my way of saying 'black lives matter' in a way only I knew how," he told Finkel. The same year, Erizku presented a solo exhibition, *New Flower: Images of the Reclining Venus*, at the FLAG Art Foundation in New York. The show featured photographs Erizku had taken on a trip to Addis Ababa in 2013. He hired several Ethiopian sex workers to pose for photographs reimagining two famous white nudes: Édouard Manet's *Olympia* and Jean-Auguste-Dominique Ingres's *La Grande Odalisque*. Each woman chose which painting she wished to emulate and whether to pose completely naked. Erizku produced the show's mixtape with deejay SOSUPERSAM. A critic for *Tadias*, a New York–based Ethiopian magazine, praised the show, writing, "Erizku stirs in us the possibility to reconceptualize the space for black beauty in the new global art history being made."

In 2016, Erizku presented the show *Bad II the Bone* at his own roving gallery space called the Duchamp Detox Clinic, named for the famous French conceptual artist Marcel Duchamp. The show featured a piece called *Ask the Dust*, an old red Porsche bursting with silk flowers, but was mostly comprised of pieces repurposing street signs and basketball hoops. Erizku told Sargent for *Vice* (14 Jan. 2016), that, in the manner of Duchamp, who famously displayed a urinal as a "readymade" piece of art, he was "taking the elements of the streets and bringing them back into abstraction."

MAKE AMERICA GREAT AGAIN

From November 2016 through early January 2017, Erizku presented *I Was Going to Call It Your Name, but You Didn't Let Me* at the Nina Johnson gallery in Miami, Florida. The show's central image was a hand holding a rose, an image synonymous with nail salons. In such instances, the hand is usually white; Erizku, in his paintings and neon sculptures, makes it various shades of brown. "What drew me to the ubiquitous nail salon sign at first was the fact that I never had seen a version with a black hand, and second, that it's weird that this motif doesn't communicate whether the hand is receiving the rose or giving it," he told Andrew Nunes for *Creators* (9 Dec. 2016). "The moment the hand is black, considering the racial tension and political climate of our country, it took on a whole new life and meaning, which was very exciting to me as the basis for a new body of work."

In April 2017, not long after Beyoncé's pregnancy announcement was published on the star's Instagram account, Erizku presented two solo shows. The first took its title from the campaign slogan of Donald Trump—*Make American Great Again*. He told Isobel Thompson for *Vanity Fair* (21 Apr. 2017) that he was "reclaiming" the phrase. Erizku, who often creates saleable merchandise for his shows, bought two hundred of the recognizable red baseball hats emblazoned with the phrase, stitching over the slogan with an image of a black panther, a nod to the radical black liberation party. "I'm putting it out there," he told Finkel, "because I'm black and I'm Muslim and this is everything Trump has tried to stand against."

That same week, Erizku presented *Purple Reign*. Each piece in the latter exhibit, including photographs and installations, was inspired by a song from rapper Future's 2016 mixtape of the same name.

PERSONAL LIFE

Erizku relocated to Southern California with his girlfriend, floral designer Sarah Lineberger, in 2014. The two have collaborated on numerous projects, including a series, begun in 2013, called *Dream and Nostalgia III* that features basketball hoops apparently overgrown with silk flowers. In 2016, the couple jointly created the piece *Ask the Dust*, which made an appearance in a photo from Beyoncé's pregnancy announcement series. Lineberger went on to design the floral arrangement for Beyoncé's birth announcement as well.

Erizku and Lineberger live in Los Angeles.

SUGGESTED READING

Erizku, Awol. "How Artist Awol Erizku Found Inspiration in His Favorite Songs." Interview by Antwaun Sargent. *The Fader*, 14 Dec. 2016, www.thefader.com/2016/12/14/awol-erizku-interview. Accessed 7 Aug. 2018.

Finkel, Jori. "Beyoncé's Pregnancy Photographer Is Opening an 'Anti-Trump' Show." *The New York Times*, 10 Apr. 2017, www.nytimes.com/2017/04/10/arts/design/beyonces-pregnancy-photographer-is-opening-an-anti-trump-art-show.html. Accessed 6 Aug. 2018.

Frank, Priscilla. "Awol Erizku's Remixed Classics Hit Hasted Kraeutler Gallery." *Huff-Post*, 22 June 2012, www.huffingtonpost.com/2012/06/22/awol-erizkus-remixed-clas_n_1606818.html. Accessed 7 Aug. 2018.

Kish, Kilo. "Awol Erizku Talks Creative Voice and Duchamp Detox Clinic." *Creators*, Vice Media, 25 Nov. 2015, creators.vice.com/en_us/article/4xqbaw/awol-erizku-talks-creative-voice-and-duchamp-detox-clinic. Accessed 9 Aug. 2018.

Sargent, Antwaun. "Artist Awol Erizku on Creating a New Way to Look at Race in Art." *Complex*, 7 Aug. 2014, www.complex.com/style/2014/08/awol-erizku-the-only-way-is-up. Accessed 9 Aug. 2018.

"Shaken & Stirred by Beauty: Review of Awol Erizku's New Flower (Addis Ababa) Exhibit." Review of *New Flower: Images of the Reclining Venus*, by Awol Erizku. *Tadias*, 21 Sept. 2015, www.tadias.com/09/21/2015/shaken-stirred-by-beauty-review-of-awol-erizkus-new-flower-addis-ababa-exhibit. Accessed 9 Aug. 2018.

Thompson, Isobel. "Awol Erizku, Beyoncé's Instagram Portrait Artist, Will Hate This Headline about His Trump-Inspired London Show." *Vanity Fair*, 21 Apr. 2017, www.vanityfair.com/style/2017/04/awol-erizku-trump-inspired-london-show-beyonce. Accessed 10 Aug. 2018.

SELECTED WORKS

Girl with a Bamboo Earring, 2009; *Lady with a Pitbull*, 2009; *Oh What a Feeling, aw, F—— It, I want a Trillion*, 2014; *Serendipity*, 2015; *Ask the Dust*, 2016

—*Molly Hagan*

Damien Escobar

Date of birth: June 13, 1988
Occupation: Musician

"Who's to say that if Bach were alive right now he wouldn't be playing hip-hop and blending everything?" Mary Zakheim wrote for the travel and culture blog *Miles Away* (Feb. 2017). "Damien Escobar . . . is in the 'Bach Would've Played Hip-Hop' camp. And so would anyone [be] who has listened to Escobar's enchanting fusion of classical violin over hip-hop beats."

Escobar got his start busking on New York City subways during his early teens with his brother, Tourie, who was also a classically trained violinist. The two later adopted the name Nuttin' But Stringz, became finalists on the televised competition *America's Got Talent*, and went on to perform in front of such luminaries as President Barack Obama, the royal family of Dubai, and Oprah Winfrey. That success was hard won, however. "It was a struggle," Escobar recalled to Allison Stewart for the *Chicago Tribune* (26 May 2016). "It was three years of people saying, 'No, this can't work. It's a gimmick, two black kids from Queens playing hip-hop on the violin.' We set out to prove everyone wrong, and we did."

Few critics now accuse Escobar, who started a solo career in 2014, of being a mere novelty. Echoing sentiments often expressed in reviews of his albums and live performances, Kandia Johnson wrote for *Black Enterprise* (22 June 2015), "His musical gift transcends race, gender, age and culture."

Photo by Marcus Ingram, via Getty Images

CHILDHOOD AND MUSICAL EDUCATION

Damien Escobar was born in 1988, two years after Tourie. Their mother, an elementary school teacher, raised them in the New York City borough of Queens, in a predominantly black section known as Jamaica. (The area has also been home to such popular black artists as 50 Cent and Nicki Minaj.) Tourie was enrolled in his public school's violin program, and as soon as Escobar turned eight years old—the minimum age for participation—he signed up as well. The two sometimes met with incomprehension or derision from peers, who wondered why they were not playing basketball or learning to program a drum machine. "I had to hide my instrument just to get to school every single day," Escobar recalled to Farai Chideya for the National Public Radio program *News and Notes* (1 Dec. 2006). "I was ashamed of it."

Despite that, he spent countless hours practicing, and when he was ten, his music teacher suggested he try out for a spot at the Juilliard School of Music. Some sources assert that he was, to that date, the youngest student ever accepted to the iconic institution, which he attended until he was thirteen. He next enrolled at the Bloomingdale School of Music, in Manhattan, where Tourie was also a student. He has admitted that he sometimes rebelled against the strictures of classical training, frustrating his teachers. "[One] said, 'You can't play that way. Bach wouldn't like that,'" Escobar recalled to Frank Chlumsky for *Interview Magazine* (26 Dec. 2016). "I'm like, 'Bach's been dead for like 400 years, for one. Two, in the 1600s Bach was

an innovator. He'd be doing the same s—— that I'm doing now. I am Bach.'"

Escobar and Tourie had begun to perform together when they were about ten and twelve, respectively. "I grew up in a household with a single mom who couldn't afford to give us the things that we wanted," he told Zakheim. "But she taught us how to go out and get it for ourselves." They did so by playing on New York City subways, choosing routes that ran through wealthier neighborhoods such as the Upper West Side and performing on the moving train cars, rather than on the platforms as many buskers did, to gain a captive audience.

Although they could sometimes go home with hundreds of dollars after playing just a few hours, Escobar felt drained by the intensity of studying at Juilliard and Bloomingdale, and when he was about fourteen, he abandoned his instrument altogether. One of the bleakest periods of his life ensued. He joined a neighborhood gang and, soon after, was arrested on a weapons charge. Kicked out of his high school, he was sent instead to a school for violent offenders. At just fifteen years old, he was facing seven years in prison, but a sympathetic judge sensed that he had contributions to make to society and decided to give him a second chance.

Relieved and grateful, Escobar reentered his old high school, and in 2003, he and Tourie decided to try to forge careers as professional musicians.

NUTTIN' BUT STRINGZ

The duo began calling themselves Nuttin' But Stringz and found a manager, James Washington, who was willing to promote their hard-to-classify blend of classical, hip-hop, R & B, pop, and jazz. They played at small venues and school assemblies around the city, and in December 2004 they placed third in a talent competition at the famed Apollo Theater in Harlem. That triumph in front of the Apollo's notoriously hard-to-please crowd gained them entrée to the city's larger, more well-known venues, such as Joe's Pub and the Hit Factory, and invitations poured in from the producers of *The Late Late Show with Craig Ferguson*, the *Tonight Show with Jay Leno*, and the *Ellen DeGeneres Show*. In mid-2006 they appeared briefly in the dance film *Step Up*, starring a young Channing Tatum, and later that year they released their well-received debut album, *Struggle from the Subway to the Charts*, which spawned two singles: an emotive cover of the Luther Vandross hit "Dance with My Father," and "Thunder," which was featured in that year's television coverage of the NCAA (National Collegiate Athletic Association) basketball tournament on CBS.

In 2007, with their star on the rise, the pair performed at the White House during Black

Music Month. (That annual celebration, which takes place each June, was launched by President Jimmy Carter in 1979, and in 2009, during the Obama administration, its official name was changed to African-American Music Appreciation Month.)

In 2008 Nuttin' But Stringz competed on NBC's popular show *America's Got Talent*, gaining increased national exposure and finishing in the top three. The celebrity judges were uniformly lavish in their praise, with one, Simon Fuller, asserting: "For emotions, for intensity, professionalism, for commanding the stage and electricity, you guys are my favorite act in the competition, you roasted it." Their website began receiving more than 10 million hits per week.

At what was perhaps the pinnacle of their popularity, they were invited to perform on January 18, 2009, at a Kennedy Center celebration of Martin Luther King Jr.'s birthday, and the following day they were featured at an inaugural ball hosted by the voter registration–focused nonprofit Declare Yourself, alongside Jamie Foxx, Maroon 5, and John Legend. Thanks to those successes, Escobar became relatively wealthy, buying a waterfront condominium in the trendy Williamsburg section of Brooklyn.

In 2012, the brothers stopped performing as Nuttin' But Stringz. "I think both of us wanted to walk away at that point," Escobar told Stewart. "You spend 10 years in a group with someone, you change over those 10 years. We started as kids, up until the point we were men. . . . We had two different stories we wanted to tell, and we couldn't get on the same page on a joint story we wanted to tell together."

A SECOND ROUGH PERIOD

Unsure of his ability to perform without Tourie, Escobar became unproductive and deeply depressed. He has told interviewers that his bank account quickly dwindled from six figures to zero, and his condo went into foreclosure. He spent several months homeless, sleeping and killing time on the subways where he had once busked. He later moved back in with his mother in Queens and visited a federal office to try to get public assistance. "So I'm in the welfare office and my brother and I, we had a McDonald's commercial on the air earlier in the year and I get in the office and guess what I saw on the damn TV," Escobar recalled to Zakheim.

Viewing that ironic incident as a wake-up call, Escobar began trying to piece his life back together, returning to school to get his real estate license and getting his first conventional job. One day, when he was late getting to the real estate office, his supervisor chided him. "She was saying to me, 'Damien, I don't care who you used to be.' And that really stuck with me," Escobar

continued to Zakheim. "I remember getting on the E train back to Jamaica and I remember thinking to myself, 'Do I really want to be a used-to-be guy?'"

When he arrived back at his mother's house, he picked up his violin and began playing again.

SOLO MUSIC CAREER

Escobar slowly built a fan base as a solo artist, going viral on YouTube with cover tunes of such artists as John Legend and Adele, and touring small venues and colleges. After President Obama was reelected, Escobar found the courage to perform in January 2013 at Russell Simmons's Hip-Hop Inaugural Ball. The following year he released his solo debut, *Sensual Melodies*, which he had recorded in his mother's basement. The album was downloaded more than 200,000 times and landed on the iTunes Top 100 chart. That year was also notable for his publication of a children's book, *The Sound of Strings*, which he based on his own life, and his appearance as part of Oprah Winfrey's "The Life You Want" motivational tour. He also went viral with a video in which, clad in a dark hoodie, he performed a haunting version of the old civil-rights anthem "We Shall Overcome," in honor of Mike Brown, Trayvon Martin, and other young black men who had been killed by police officers or vigilantes.

Escobar released the album *Boundless* in 2017. "*Boundless*, for me, it's kind of a double entendre," Escobar told Zakheim of his reasons for choosing that title. "There are no musical boundaries, there are no musical limits for me on this record. On the other side of it is, there's no boundaries to me—as a man, as a human being—it's kind of like a coming-of-age project, where I feel absolutely free."

PHILANTHROPY

Escobar's extensive philanthropic efforts include partnerships with such groups as the VH1 Save the Music Foundation, UNICEF, and Kennedy's Cause, a charity that benefits children with lymphatic malformation and that he got involved with because its young founder, Kennedy Hubbard, who suffers from the condition, is also a violinist. As a member of Nuttin' But Stringz, Escobar cofounded a nonprofit called Violins against Violence, which later morphed into a program called M.A.D.E. (Music and Arts with Damien Escobar), which aimed to introduce arts programs into urban communities. Distressed by the fact that money donated to schools was often not used for arts programming as intended, he began manufacturing his own line of student violins and donating those instead, as well as issuing grants to fund music-teacher salaries.

Escobar sits on the Board of Directors for the YMCA in his old neighborhood, and each year he mounts a benefit concert for the organization that raises tens of thousands of dollars. "Everybody who knows me knows that giving back to youth is my highest priority," he asserted to Kandia Johnson. Of his musical priorities, he explained to Johnson that his goal is to change mainstream attitudes about his instrument. "I'm not concerned about being the number one violinist in the world. I've been told that for many years," he said. "I'm not going to stop until you say Stevie Wonder and Damien in the same sentence or Damien Escobar and Drake in the same sentence."

PERSONAL LIFE

Escobar has two children: a daughter, who plays the violin, and a son, who is studying the piano. A doting father, he sometimes posts Facebook videos or Instagram photos featuring them.

SUGGESTED READING

Barker, Cyril Josh. "Damien Escobar's Sweet Sounds of Success." *New York Amsterdam News*, 30 Aug. 2013, amsterdamnews.com/news/2013/aug/30/damien-escobars-sweet-sounds-success/. Accessed 14 May 2018.

Escobar, Damien. "The Contemporary Violinist." Interview by Frank Chlumsky. *Interview Magazine*, 26 Dec. 2016, www.interviewmagazine.com/music/damien-escobar-faces-of-2017. Accessed 14 May 2018.

Escobar, Damien, and Tourie Escobar. "Nuttin' But Stringz: Hip-Hop Violin." Interview by Farai Chideya. *News and Notes*, NPR, 1 Dec. 2006, www.npr.org/templates/story/story.php?storyId=6565133. Accessed 14 May 2018.

Johnson, Kandia. "*BE* Modern Man: Meet Emmy Award-Winning Violinist Damien Escobar." *Black Enterprise*, 22 June 2015, www.blackenterprise.com/be-modern-man-meet-emmy-award-winning-violonist-damien-escobar/. Accessed 14 May 2018.

Stewart, Allison. "Damien Escobar Continues His Musical Journey after Nuttin' But Stringz Fades." *Chicago Tribune*, 26 May 2016, www.chicagotribune.com/entertainment/music/ct-damien-escobar-ott-0527-20160524-story.html. Accessed 14 May 2018.

Zakheim, Mary. "A Man, His Violin, and Some Sick Beats." *Miles Away*, Feb. 2017, www.cheapoair.com/miles-away/damien-escobar-interview/. Accessed 14 May 2018.

SELECTED WORKS

Struggle from the Subway to the Charts, 2006; *Sensual Melodies*, 2014; *Boundless*, 2017

—*Mari Rich*

Jackie Evancho

Date of birth: April 9, 2000
Occupation: Singer

Jackie Evancho first captivated television audiences as a ten-year-old opera-singing contestant on the fifth season of NBC's *America's Got Talent*. Her powerful voice catapulted her to a second-place finish and immediately drew comparisons to Scottish singing sensation Susan Boyle, runner-up from the third season of *Britain's Got Talent*. Since her near-win, Evancho has experienced a meteoric rise as a classical crossover artist, releasing seven studio albums, all of which have reached number one on the Billboard Classical Albums chart.

In her short yet storied career, Evancho has also achieved several milestones. Not only is she the youngest top-ten *Billboard* artist to date, but she also has the distinction of being the youngest solo platinum singer in the United States. Evancho made history again in April 2017, with a twelve-day engagement at New York City's Cafe Carlyle, in support of her album *Two Hearts* (2017). At seventeen, she became the youngest person ever to perform at the venue.

EARLY LIFE AND CAREER

Jacqueline Marie "Jackie" Evancho was born to Lisa and Michael Evancho on April 9, 2000, in Pittsburgh, Pennsylvania. She grew up alongside her three siblings, Juliet, Zachary, and Rachel, in the Pittsburgh suburb of Richland. Evancho first displayed an interest in performing at age

By Cynthia Moser [Public domain], via Wikimedia Commons

seven—a week before her eighth birthday. "It was after I saw the [2004] movie *Phantom of the Opera* with my family and fell in love with the music that I began singing those songs around the house," she shared with Christiana Keyes for *Naples Illustrated* (11 Jan. 2016). "My mom asked if I would want to do a local talent competition and I did. From that point forward it was about trying to get seen."

In April 2008, Evancho not only launched her own YouTube channel but also entered her very first competition: the Kean Idol Talent Search. Despite a lack of formal training, she reached the finals, ultimately finishing second to a twenty-year-old opera singer. She won second place again in the same competition the following year. Additionally, Evancho honed her vocal skills during a stint (2008–09) with the Children's Festival Chorus of Pittsburgh (now Pittsburgh Youth Chorus), as well as appearances in several 2009 showcases, including the popular Boston, Massachusetts–based cable series *Debra Crosby's TalentQuest Show*; WonderWorld TV's Golden Ribby Awards, also held in Massachusetts; and the USA World Showcase Talent Competition at the MGM Grand Las Vegas Hotel and Casino.

Evancho's efforts began to pay off. In October 2009, classical and New Age conductor-composer Tim Janis tapped her to perform the "Ave Maria" solo in his PBS special *Celebrate America*, which showcases talented high-school choirs. That same month, Evancho, an Eden Hall Upper Elementary School fourth-grader, performed alongside Grammy Award–winning producer David Foster at New Jersey's Prudential Center during his Hitman Tour, after reaching the finals of Foster's Hitman Talent Search contest. Evancho followed that up with the November 2009 independent release of her full-length debut album, *Prelude to a Dream*, a collection of mostly classical crossover cover songs from a range of artists including Josh Groban, Andrea Bocelli, and Martina McBride. The album debuted at number two on the Billboard Classical Album chart.

AMERICA'S GOT TALENT

By early 2010 Evancho had become a local fixture, singing the national anthem at the January inauguration for Pennsylvania Supreme Court Justice Joan Orie Melvin and the April opening day ceremony for the Pittsburgh Pirates at PNC Park. Evancho's life changed in late summer, when she successfully submitted a YouTube audition video for NBC's reality competition series *America's Got Talent* (*AGT*), after twice being rejected by the show's producers. As the top vote-getter among 20,000 YouTube submissions, Evancho automatically advanced to the *AGT* quarterfinals on August 10, 2010, competing against eleven other YouTube acts handpicked by the judges. Although her live rendition of Giacomo Puccini's aria "O Mio Babbino Caro" ("Oh My Dear Daddy") impressed the judging panel, it also sparked lip-syncing accusations. To address the rumors, Howie Mandel urged the ten-year-old to sing a cappella on the next day's live results show, during which she advanced to the second round of semifinals on August 31.

With her performance of "Time to Say Goodbye," the English version of Bocelli's "Con te partirò," Evancho earned a spot in *AGT's* Top 10, which aired the first week of September. After reaching the Final Four with her angelic, choir-backed rendition of Andrew Lloyd Webber's arrangement of "Pie Jesu" ("Holy Jesus"), Evancho performed two final numbers: "Ave Maria," accompanied by a choir, harpist, and string orchestra; and "Time to Say Goodbye," a guest duet with Sarah Brightman. Despite being the favorite to win, Evancho finished second to singer-songwriter Michael Grimm on the September 15 finale.

MAJOR-LABEL DEBUT

Evancho made her talk show debut on NBC's *The Tonight Show with Jay Leno* a week after the *AGT* season five finale and appeared on *The Oprah Winfrey Show* the following month. In October, Evancho signed a recording contract with Simon Cowell's Sony-owned Syco Music and also embarked on *AGT's* first-ever nationwide tour with her fellow Top 10 finalists. After the tour's conclusion in early November, she released her major-label recording debut, *O Holy Night* (2010), which took just three days to record and reached number two on the Billboard Top Holiday Albums chart a month later. Evancho promoted her Christmas-themed EP with performances at Pittsburgh's annual My Macy's Holiday Parade, Disney Parks Christmas Day Parade, as well as the Christmas tree lighting ceremonies at New York City's Rockefeller Center and Washington, DC. By early December 2010, *O Holy Night* had topped the Billboard Classical Albums chart and achieved platinum certification, making Evancho the youngest US solo artist ever to go platinum.

Evancho kicked off 2011 by performing the National Anthem at the National Hockey League's (NHL) Winter Classic. She gave her first professional concert in February, performing with the Houston Chamber Choir at St. Paul's Methodist Church before headlining Boca Raton, Florida's Festival of the Arts BOCA in March. Next came high-profile appearances at a Muhammad Ali charity event in late March, the May 25 farewell episode of Winfrey's talk show, and the season five live finale of *Britain's Got Talent*, where she performed "Nessun Dorma"

("Nobody Shall Sleep") from her upcoming album, *Dream with Me* (2011).

DREAM WITH ME

Dream with Me, produced by Foster, featured fourteen tracks including duets with fellow powerhouse divas Barbra Streisand and Susan Boyle. To promote her second full-length disc, Evancho made the talk-show rounds, appearing on NBC's *The Today Show*, ABC's *The View*, and CBS's *The Talk*. She also taped an accompanying PBS *Great Performances* special at the Sarasota, Florida–based Ringling Museum of Art that repeatedly aired throughout June. The following month, *Dream with Me* debuted at number two on the Billboard 200 and was certified gold; at the end of the month, Evancho launched her first solo US tour, a nearly year-long event comprised of eighteen orchestra-backed shows held at indoor and outdoor venues, including Pittsburgh's Benedum Center, New York City's Avery Fisher Hall, and Las Vegas's Mandalay Bay.

COLLABORATIONS AND CHART TOPPERS

In the fall Evancho returned to the *AGT* stage as a guest performer during the show's season six finale. She partnered with Tony Bennett on the classic "When You Wish Upon a Star," a track on the UK deluxe version of his *Duets II* disc (2011). Another collaboration was Evancho's first film role, costarring opposite Robert Redford in the thriller *The Company You Keep* (2012), which she filmed from late September until late November 2011. In the political drama, she plays a teenager whose recently widowed father (Redford) turns out to be a former 1960s radical.

After filming *The Company You Keep*, Evancho released *Heavenly Christmas* (2011), her third studio album and second collection of traditional holiday songs, which reached the top five of the Billboard Holiday Album Sales chart. The next month she briefly interrupted her Dream with Me Tour and made three concert appearances to support the album. Evancho closed out 2011 with the top two spots (*O Holy Night* and *Dream with Me*, respectively) on the year-end Billboard Classical Albums chart.

In January 2012, Evancho resumed the Dream with Me Tour, performing at Japan's Bunkamura Orchard Hall and subsequently returning to the United States; the tour concluded five months later, at New Jersey's Performing Arts Center (NJPAC). Los Angeles's Orpheum Theatre was the setting for her second PBS special, *Jackie Evancho: Music of the Movies*, which she taped in mid-June and which aired throughout August. Her renditions of classic Hollywood theme songs also became the basis of her next album, *Songs from the Silver Screen* (2012), and a two-year, twenty-two-city tour that kicked off in late August. *Songs from the Silver Screen* finally hit shelves in early October 2012 and weeks later topped the Billboard Classical Albums chart. The twelve-year-old Evancho finished the year with three albums on the top ten of the year-end Classical Albums chart (*Heavenly Christmas*, *Dream with Me*, and *Songs from the Silver Screen*, respectively).

Shortly after completing the first leg of her Songs from the Silver Screen Tour in late June 2013, Evancho sang the national anthem and performed "God Bless America" at the *A Capitol Fourth 2013 Independence Day Concert* in Washington, DC. She embarked on the second leg of her Songs from the Silver Screen Tour in early October 2013 and spent the rest of the year promoting the album, which ranked in the top five of the Billboard Classical Albums chart for 2013.

SWITCHING LABELS AND MUSICAL DIRECTION

Evancho made headlines in May 2014, when she left Syco and signed with Sony Music Masterworks. Along with her new label, Evancho adopted a more mature sound, reflected in the lead single for her next album: a haunting rendition of "The Rains of Castamere," an iconic theme song from HBO's fantasy drama *Game of Thrones*, which she unveiled in early June. After attending the Songwriters Hall of Fame Induction as a performer and presenter, Evancho released the follow-up track—*The Phantom of the Opera's* "Think of Me"—in mid-July. *Awakening*, Evancho's first album under Sony Masterworks' Portrait Records and fifth full-length disc, became available in late September; two weeks later it topped the Billboard Classical Albums chart. Evancho promoted the tracks from *Awakening*—a mix of classical pieces and covers of more contemporary tunes, such as U2's "With or Without You"—during her third PBS concert special, which aired in November. That same month she launched the Awakening Tour, spending nearly a year-and-a-half on the road. *Awakening* ended 2014 ranked at number eleven on the Billboard Classical Albums chart and cracked the top five at the close of 2015.

Evancho started increasingly experimenting with a pop sound. She followed up an August 2015 cover of Ed Sheeran's "All of the Stars" and a December 2015 cover of Taylor Swift's "Safe and Sound" with a remake of Sam Smith's "Writing's on the Wall," which she debuted in January 2016. Within four months Evancho had wrapped up her tour and released an original song: the piano ballad "Apocalypse." "I'm singing what I like. And the best thing about it is, I'm finding different sides of my voice with every new song I sing," she told Katie Atkinson for *Billboard* (19 Apr. 2018). "Everything sounds different, and it's really fun to find out new things about myself."

FACING BACKLASH

In July 2016 Evancho made her second appearance at PBS's *A Capitol Fourth* celebration in Washington DC. That fall she released her sixth studio album and second full-length holiday CD: *Someday at Christmas*, which featured a cover of the Stevie Wonder title tune, as well as collaborations with Placido Domingo and Il Volo. By December, Evancho, who was in the second month of a five-month tour, Live in Concert, had scored another number-one record, when *Someday at Christmas* reached the top of the Billboard Classical Albums chart.

Evancho's decision to sing the National Anthem at the January 2017 presidential inauguration earned her criticism from fans, however. They accused Evancho of hypocrisy and of being disloyal to her transgender older sister, Juliet, by performing for an administration whose vice-president elect has a history of anti-LGBTQ discrimination. At the time, Juliet was part of a lawsuit against her school district over its policy of not allowing transgender students to use the bathroom that matches their gender identity. After the Trump administration repealed federal protection for transgender students, Evancho unsuccessfully requested a meeting with Trump (via a February 27 tweet) to discuss the issue.

Despite concerns that the intense public scrutiny and fan criticism over Evancho's inauguration performance would jeopardize her career, she released her seventh studio album in March 2017. *Two Hearts* (2017), a two-disc CD of classical crossover tracks and five original pop tunes, features four songs that Evancho cowrote. A month later, as she kicked off a twelve-day engagement at New York City's Café Carlyle, *Two Hearts* became her seventh consecutive record to top Billboard Classical Albums chart. In May 2017, she embarked on a tour in support of the album that was scheduled to end in February 2019. She appeared in *Growing Up Evancho*, a one-hour TLC special about her and her family, in August 2017.

PERSONAL LIFE

Evancho, a 2018 high school graduate and aspiring actor, splits her time between her parents' home outside of Pittsburgh and a New York City apartment she shares with Juliet, an aspiring model.

SUGGESTED READING

Atkinson, Katie. "Jackie Evancho Trades Classical for Pop on Brand-New Song 'Apocalypse': Exclusive Premiere," www.billboard.com/articles/columns/pop/7334249/jackie-evancho-pop-debut-song-apocalypse-premiere. Accessed 10 August 2018.

Evancho, Jackie. "Jackie Evancho on Speaking Out through Music." Interview by Michel Martin and Victoria Whitley-Berry. *NPR Music*, 2 Apr. 2017, www.npr.org/2017/04/02/522237106/jackie-evancho-on-speaking-out-through-music. Accessed 14 Aug. 2018.

Evancho, Jackie. "Stealing the Show: Q&A with Jackie Evancho." Interview by Christiana Keyes. *Naples Illustrated*, www.naplesillustrated.com/2016/01/11/stealing-the-show-qa-with-jackie-evancho/. Accessed 10 August 2018.

O'Malley Greenburg, Zack. "Jackie Evancho: 14 Questions with the 30 under 30 Opera Prodigy." *Forbes*, 17 Nov. 2017, www.forbes.com/sites/zackomalleygreenburg/2017/11/17/jackie-evancho-14-questions-with-the-30-under-30-opera-prodigy. Accessed 14 Aug. 2018.

Sciullo, Maria. "Jackie Evancho: Little Girl with Big Voice." *Pittsburgh Post-Gazette*, 30 Aug. 2010, old.post-gazette.com/pg/10242/1083610-455.stm. Accessed 15 Aug. 2018.

SELECTED WORKS

Prelude to a Dream, 2009; *O Holy Night*, 2010; *Dream with Me*, 2011; *Heavenly Christmas*, 2011; *Songs from the Silver Screen*, 2012; *Awakening*, 2014; *Someday at Christmas*, 2016; *Two Hearts*, 2017

—*Bertha Muteba*

Eve Ewing

Date of birth: 1986
Occupation: Poet; sociologist

As a teenager, Eve Louise Ewing began her career as a sociologist by observing and analyzing her hometown, Chicago. As she told Susan Stamberg for NPR's Morning Edition (13 Feb. 2001), the city had long been segregated by ethnicity as well as race, "It's like a hundred years ago when people came, you know, from Ireland and Germany and Eastern Europe, they chose to live amongst each other . . . because, you know, they needed people who spoke the same languages, they wanted certain foods, they wanted to practice certain religions." Her interest in Chicago has led to her appointment as an assistant professor in the School of Social Service Administration at the University of Chicago. Ewing is also a writer. The American Library Association (ALA) honored her in 2018 with the Alex Award, given annually to ten books written for adults that also appeal to twelve- to eighteen-year-olds. Her winning work, *Electric Arches* (2017), is a compilation of both prose and poetry, along with artwork. Aware of her multiple interests and how

Photo by Daniel Barlow

difficult it can be to find names for all she does, she told Christopher Borrelli for the *Chicago Tribune* (22 Sept. 2017), "I'm intrigued with black intellectual history—people who did multifaceted work. W. E. B. Du Bois did fiction, journalism, early infographics. Zora Neale Hurston was a novelist and anthropologist. There's a pressure to compartmentalize, and like Whitman said, we contain multitudes."

CHILDHOOD AND EDUCATION

Ewing was born to a black mother, Sylvia, and a white father. Her maternal grandmother left Mississippi as part of the great African American migration to northern cities, in part fueled by the racist violence in the South. Her mother was at one time a radio reporter and producer in Chicago. She fostered Ewing's imagination when her daughter had nightmares, inviting her to create different, less frightening endings to the dreams. Her father was a caricature artist who set up at Navy Pier to draw portraits of tourists and a cartoonist. Their neighborhood was not the safest; there were broken sidewalks and street gangs. Her mother allowed her to ride her bicycle only one block and back, so to watch her.

She attended Northside College Preparatory, new at the time and the city's highest rated public school. Doing so required ninety minutes of commute time, which Ewing spent with her journal and a sketchbook. She was also involved in Young Chicago Authors.

Ewing was sensitive to criticism, as her mother told Borrelli, "You raise a child to have one foot on the ground and one in the sky, and

you worry if people get them. Eve was a golden child and teacher's favorite, but once she had a teacher who didn't love her. I worried she couldn't take criticism."

After graduation from high school, Ewing went on to the University of Chicago, earning a degree with honors in English language and literature in 2008. Her area of concentration was African American literature of the twentieth century. She also holds a master's degree in elementary education from Dominican University, from which she graduated in 2009, as well as a master's in educational policy and management from Harvard Graduate School of Education, earning the latter in 2013.

EARLY CAREER

Ewing returned to Chicago's public schools, where she worked as a teacher of English and science from 2008 to 2011. She took part in the teachers' strike of September 2012. That strike, created in the wake of budget cuts that dramatically affected black neighborhoods, instilled in her a desire to understand the sociology behind such decisions.

Having left her teaching position at Pershing West Middle School, in 2016 she earned a doctoral degree from Harvard Graduate School of Education. Her research focused on the intersections of culture, communication, and communities. She worked with adolescents on social change, particularly relating to environmental racism. In addition, she worked with young people on writing, particularly at slam poetry and spoken word events.

While at Harvard, Ewing's goal was to return to Chicago, despite the prevailing attitude that no one returns home following Harvard. As she told Kiese Laymon for *Guernica* (17 Oct. 2017), "I sat in Harvard for five years reading books about the corners and neighborhoods of my own hometown, where I had spent the preceding two-and-a-half decades. And then I just came back as soon as I could."

ELECTRIC ARCHES

In 2017 Ewing published *Electric Arches*, a collection of poetry, prose, and art that reflected her growing up in Chicago's Logan Square and Hermosa communities. She was influenced by Claudia Rankine's work, particularly *Citizen: An American Lyric* (2014), which Ewing read as she was working on her own collection. She asked some of her former students from Chicago public schools to choose the cover for the book; they selected a work by Brianna McCarthy, a Trinidadian artist, depicting a black girl with stars on her face.

Marwen Gallery in Chicago hosted a book launch party for *Electric Arches* in September 2017 and the 106 tickets for the event sold out in twelve hours. When Ewing reads from her book, people are moved, as she told Aimee Levitt for *Chicago Reader* (14 Sept. 2017), "I've been reading it out loud a lot. People cry a lot. I see them inside the poem while I'm talking, coming with me to another place and time." The book went into its second printing two weeks after its release.

As Borrelli reported, Ewing's writing partner, Hanif Willis-Abdurraqib, said, "A lot of her work deals with imagining a futuristic, fantastic Chicago, and it finds comfort in world-building, but still honors the real people who live there. . . . She's a perpetual optimist, an Afrofuturist who speaks to a Chicago that could be."

NO BLUE MEMORIES

With Nate Marshall, Ewing coauthored a biographical play about the life of Chicago poet Gwendolyn Brooks, who in 1950 became the first African American to win a Pulitzer Prize. Brooks also was granted more than seventy honorary degrees and was named Poet Laureate of Illinois. Ewing regards Brooks as a mentor not only in poetry, but also in community service. She used that experience to go a step further, creating a shadow puppet program with multimedia for Manual Cinema, which the Poetry Foundation commissioned to celebrate Brooks's centenary.

As Drew Dir, a cofounder of Manual Cinema and puppet designer for the show, told Borrelli, "The exciting thing about Eve is that she's this pastiche in a way, and that's sort of what we do, too. So she and Nate . . . never came in with this specific image to dictate to us. They instead had clear ideas of what Brooks's life and poetry meant to them—they're just instinctively collaborative."

Ewing and Marshall studied Brooks's archive, housed at the University of Illinois. Brooks lived on Chicago's South Side, in Bronzeville, where Ewing later taught. Ewing wanted to create a fuller portrait of the poet; much of her work and life post-1967 has not been fully explored. As she told Darcel Rockett for *Chicago Tribune* (13 Nov. 2017), "We don't have a Gwendolyn Brooks major motion picture. We don't have a 'Hamilton' for Gwendolyn Brooks. So I think for us, this is opening a conversation. We're trying to make an argument about the arc of her life and also trying to showcase some aspects of her life that maybe people are not aware of."

RESEARCH AND WRITING

Ewing focused her doctoral research on the effects of school closings in Chicago on the neighborhoods in which the schools had been located. The school at which she had taught in Bronzeville was one of the fifty Chicago schools that closed during Ewing's first year in the doctoral program.

As she told Jill Anderson for the *Harvard Graduate School of Education* website (2 June 2016), "I felt a moral imperative to make this the focus of my work. It was a devastating event for a lot of communities." She continued, explaining her motivation for pursuing her doctorate, "There was someone making decisions I didn't like and I thought, maybe, if I could get to the table, then I'd tell them that their ideas were bad. In retrospect, [what was happening had] a simple explanation, but part of my job now is to look at the frame, wall, and gallery. . . . Never lose sight of the picture or the frame."

Ewing was troubled by the methods by which decisions about school closings were made. School administrators and teachers were not asked for their input. Closing schools named for prominent African Americans had a negative impact on the neighborhoods.

After completing and defending her dissertation, Ewing returned to Chicago on a two-year Provost Career Enhancement Postdoctoral Scholar fellowship at the University of Chicago. Her primary work during this time was revising her doctoral dissertation, which won the Dissertation of the Year Award, to become a more mainstream publication. The university is publishing her work, *Ghosts in the Schoolyard: Racism and School Closings on Chicago's South Side*, in fall 2018.

In addition to that work, Ewing's research focused on three areas. One is the problem of lead contamination in more than one hundred Chicago schools. Ewing is looking for correlations with race and community in the contaminated areas. She is also working on a project for a racially diverse sample of middle schoolers on norms of consent in sexual relationships. Finally, Ewing is examining an Alternative School Attendance Project (ASAP), seeking to understand the factors that lead students who have had to leave traditional schools to attempt alternative schools to earn a high school diploma.

In 2017 Ewing also became a senior civic media fellow at the University of Southern California's Annenberg Innovation Lab.

LOVE FOR CHICAGO

Even as a fourteen-year-old, Ewing was passionate about Chicago. As she told Stamberg, "I love the diversity, I love the food, I love the art and I love the people. . . . There is a lot of history and there's a lot of variance and it's sort of revolutionary architecturally and I like the way there are old things mixed with new things."

Ewing has created opportunities for other people in the arts to flourish, including the Emerging Poets Incubator and the Chicago Poetry Block Party. She is also a member of the group Seven Scribes. In 2017 they collected short stories from each of the members, all of whom are emerging writers of color. The anthology is entitled *Beyond Ourselves*.

PERSONAL LIFE

Ewing identifies as African American. Her Twitter account, Wikipedia Brown, has more than 130,000 followers. With Hanif Willis-Abdurraqib, Ewing is half of Echo Hotel, a writing collective. She admits to a love of carne asada tacos and fried chicken. On her left arm is a tattoo that says, *Poetry is not a luxury*, which is a quotation from African American poet Audre Lorde. She told Borrelli that she dreams of being a recluse, saying, "After my 10th book I think I'm never leaving the house. I'm going full Salinger. I'll just come out occasionally to throw rocks. I can't wait to be a total weirdo." Ewing wrote an editorial for the *New York Times* entitled "Why Authoritarians Attack the Arts" decrying the Trump administration's proposal to defund National Endowment for the Arts (6 Apr. 2017), saying, "We need the arts because they make us full human beings. But we also need the arts as a protective factor against authoritarianism. In saving the arts, we save ourselves from a society where creative production is permissible only insofar as it serves the instruments of power."

SUGGESTED READING

Borrelli, Christopher. "Chicago Renaissance Woman Eve Ewing Is a Poet, Sociologist, Closet *Star Wars* Fan and Local Twitter Celebrity." *Chicago Tribune*, 22 Sept. 2017, www.chicagotribune.com/entertainment/ct-ent-eve-ewing-20170901-story.html. Accessed 14 Mar. 2018.

Ewing, Eve L. "Why Authoritarians Attack the Arts." *The New York Times*, 6 Apr. 2017, www.nytimes.com/2017/04/06/opinion/why-authoritarians-attack-the-arts.html. Accessed 20 Mar. 2018.

Laymon, Kiese. "Eve Ewing: Other Means to Liberation." *Guernica*, 17 Oct. 2017, www.guernicamag.com/eve-ewing-means-liberation/. Accessed 19 Mar. 2018.

Levitt, Aimee. "Chicago Is Eve Ewing's Home, and Her Art." *Chicago Reader*, 14 Sept. 2017, www.chicagoreader.com/chicago/eve-ewing-wikipedia-brown-twitter-electric-arches/Content?oid=30542198. Accessed 15 Mar. 2018.

Rockett, Darcel. "'No Blue Memories' Gives Glimpse of Gwendolyn Brooks' Literary Life, Legacy." *Chicago Tribune*, 13 Nov. 2017, www.chicagotribune.com/entertainment/theater/ct-ent-no-blue-memories-20171114-story.html. Accessed 21 Mar. 2018.

Stamberg, Susan. "Teenager on Chicago's Strengths & Appeal." *Morning Edition (NPR)*, 13 Feb. 2001, *Newspaper Source*, search.ebscohost.com/login.aspx?direct=true&db=nfh&AN=6XN200102131115. Accessed 22 Feb. 2018.

SELECTED WORKS

Electric Arches, 2017; *Beyond Ourselves*, 2017 (coeditor); *No Blue Memories: The Life of Gwendolyn Brooks*, 2017; *Ghosts in the Schoolyard: Racism and School Closings on Chicago's South Side*, 2018

—Judy Johnson

Ronan Farrow

Date of birth: December 19, 1987
Occupation: Journalist

In April 2018 journalist Ronan Farrow won a Pulitzer Prize for Public Service in recognition of his reporting on the credible allegations that Hollywood mogul Harvey Weinstein sexually assaulted numerous women in the film industry. Just months after that coverage, Farrow helped break the story of New York attorney general Eric Schneiderman, who was accused by multiple women of nonconsensual physical violence during sexual encounters. Although he also reports on other important matters—such as financial improprieties among President Donald Trump's appointees—Farrow has become perhaps most associated with reporting on sexual assault and the grassroots #MeToo movement, which encourages women to speak out about abuse they have suffered.

Some observers have posited that Farrow has a special affinity for those stories because of his own family history. His father, famed director Woody Allen, was accused in 1992 of molesting Farrow's adopted sister Dylan, then seven years old. That year Allen was also discovered to have taken nude photos of another of Farrow's adopted sisters, Soon-Yi Previn, and in 1997 he married her, despite having been a father figure to her for years and despite an almost four-decade difference in their ages. "You see early in life with that kind of a family background the way in which the most powerful men in America wield power for good and for ill," he told Marisa Guthrie for the *Hollywood Reporter* (10 Jan. 2018). "And probably, yes, the family background made me someone who understood the abuse of power from an early age."

In mid-2018 the editors of *Time* magazine named Farrow one of the 100 most influential people of the year, along with fellow journalists Jodi Kantor and Megan Twohey, who helped break the Weinstein story and shared in the Pulitzer. The citation stated, "Their hard work and impeccable journalism have changed

US Embassy Kyiv, Ukraine

attitudes, behavior, conversations, norms, laws and policies, yielding enormous personal and public good."

"If people are coming to me with stories that need telling and that can maybe make the world a better place in some small way if they are told, then I'm going to do everything in my power to expose those hard truths," Farrow asserted to Terry Gross for National Public Radio's *Fresh Air* (23 May 2018).

EARLY LIFE AND EDUCATION

Satchel Ronan O'Sullivan Farrow was born on December 19, 1987, in New York City. (Named in honor of baseball legend Satchel Paige, he began using his middle name as a young adult.) His mother is the actor Mia Farrow, who is best known for her starring role in the 1968 film *Rosemary's Baby*. Although she once told an interviewer that Ronan's father may have been singer Frank Sinatra, an ex-husband to whom she remained close, it is generally accepted that Allen is his father.

Mia Farrow and Allen met in 1979 and subsequently made more than a dozen movies together over the course of a twelve-year romantic relationship. They never married and maintained separate apartments on opposite sides of Central Park. Ronan was the couple's only biological child, but the family also included Mia Farrow's biological children from previous relationships and a number of adoptees, many of them from impoverished or war-torn countries. "For volume and variety, it's hard to match the Farrow household—it was a United Nations General

Assembly in the dining room," Jesse Lichtenstein wrote for the *New York Times* (3 Jan. 2014). After splitting with Allen, Mia Farrow adopted five more children, giving Ronan Farrow a total of thirteen siblings, some with severe disabilities or illnesses. (Three of them—Thaddeus, Lark, and Tam—are now deceased.)

Because of Allen's notoriety, the family was featured frequently in the tabloid press, and sometimes just entering Farrow's school building required powering through a crowd of paparazzi. After Mia Farrow and Allen had split and the investigation into Dylan's alleged molestation had ended with no criminal charges filed, she moved with the children to Frog Hollow, a home in rural Connecticut.

Preternaturally bright, Ronan Farrow—who loved natural history and delighted in keeping aquariums filled with bullfrogs and incubators of baby chicks in his room—skipped several grades. At around age nine he took the SAT, as the test was a requirement for gaining admission to Johns Hopkins' Center for Talented Youth program, which allows young people to take college-level courses over the summer. He scored well, allowing him to enroll in the program and leading people around him to suggest that he was already prepared to begin a college education. When he was eleven years old, he entered Bard College at Simon's Rock, an institution dedicated to allowing young people to begin their college studies early. (Even in that milieu, he stood out; the average age of entry is about sixteen.)

Farrow then transferred to the main campus of Bard College, where he earned an undergraduate degree in philosophy at the age of fifteen, becoming the school's youngest graduate ever. In 2009 he earned a law degree from Yale University and later passed the New York Bar.

PUBLIC SERVICE

From an early age Farrow traveled to developing countries with his mother, who was deeply engaged in humanitarian work, and he was moved to begin his own advocacy efforts. From 2001 to 2009, he served as a UNICEF Spokesperson for Youth, frequently speaking out on behalf of the children affected by the crisis then ongoing in Sudan's Darfur region, and while in law school he interned in the office of the chief counsel at the United States House Committee on Foreign Affairs.

It was while traveling in Sudan as a teen, as a volunteer for UNICEF, that Farrow contracted an infection in the bones of his leg. Between the ages of sixteen and twenty, he had multiple surgeries and was forced to use crutches or a wheelchair to get around. It had little effect on his drive and work ethic, however. He has self-deprecatingly recalled to interviewers the time he testified before US Congress while wearing comically baggy pants over the metal braces that had been drilled into his bone during one surgery. "I drew strength from my siblings, who had more permanent disabilities than I, and from every person I have met since grappling with this sort of a situation," he told Gross.

In 2009, the year he earned his JD, Farrow became a special adviser for humanitarian and NGO affairs in the office of diplomat Richard Holbrooke, then the special envoy for Afghanistan and Pakistan under President Barack Obama. Farrow, who considered Holbrooke an invaluable mentor, held that post for two years, serving as a point of contact between the White House and nongovernmental groups on the ground in the region.

In 2011 Secretary of State Hillary Clinton tapped Farrow to direct the State Department's Office of Global Youth Issues, and in that capacity, he was charged with empowering young people around the globe to drive economic and civic change.

JOURNALISM

After leaving government service in 2012, Farrow won a Rhodes Scholarship to attend Magdalen College, part of the University of Oxford, where he studied politics and international relations. Concurrently, he was dipping a toe into the world of journalism, penning essays and opinion pieces for such publications as *Foreign Policy*, the *Atlantic*, and the *Wall Street Journal*.

In early 2014 Farrow began hosting an MSNBC television news show called *Ronan Farrow Daily*, on which he discussed such weighty topics as terrorism and income inequality. "When we do a story, I want to make sure you walk away with the freshman-college knowledge, the cocktail-party take on it," he told Lichtenstein, "something that when you go to recount it to your friends, you know the basics and also you know what the future is, and if you happen to care about the issue, what you can do with that." The show had difficulty finding an audience, however, and it was canceled in early 2015.

Farrow remained at NBC as a news correspondent, and his investigative segments on topics such as worker safety and special-interest politics were shown on NBC's *Today* show and branded as "Undercovered with Ronan Farrow." In 2016 Farrow pitched the idea of a multipart series on sexual harassment in Hollywood. Actor Rose McGowan had tweeted about her own experiences, and although she did not mention Weinstein's name, insiders knew immediately to whom she was referring. Farrow persuaded McGowan, with whom he had become acquainted several years before, to sit for an interview, and he soon obtained interviews with several other accusers—as well as an explosive New York

Police Department tape of Weinstein admitting to assaulting model Ambra Battilana Gutierrez.

By some accounts, the network began having second thoughts about letting him pursue the story further, so powerful was Weinstein in the industry and so fierce his reputation. (NBC executives have denied that narrative.) Farrow found a more willing outlet in the *New Yorker*, which published his exposé on October 10, 2017, a few days after Jodi Kantor and Megan Twohey had published their similarly themed piece in the *New York Times*. "I'll forever be grateful to this incredible team at the *New Yorker*," he told Gross. "Every single person at every echelon of management there is a true journalist, and they stick up for dangerous and difficult stories. . . . [They] restored my faith in our profession, honestly."

Farrow, who has also penned columns in support of his sister Dylan, has gained a reputation for thoroughness and rigor, believing that he serves his sources best by investigating their claims in an almost legalistic manner. He is also known, however, for his empathy and sensitivity. "I absolutely feel an ongoing obligation to every source that was brave enough to help expose injustice," he told Andrew Anthony for the *Guardian* (14 May 2018). "I think if you ask any of the sources who have worked with me on these very difficult stories . . . they'll tell you I am there for them to take the late-night calls and there to work with them if there is fallout, and my heart breaks for them when there's a high cost of telling these stories."

Farrow has also written a book, *War on Peace: The End of Diplomacy and the Decline of American Influence*, which was published in early 2018. Anthony described it as "a compelling mixture of political analysis and personal anecdote written in a reflective, almost nostalgic tone that betrays none of the doubt and uncertainty or zeal and tunnel vision that are the common characteristics of youth."

PERSONAL LIFE

In addition to the Pulitzer Prize, Farrow's honors include the Cronkite Award for Excellence in Exploration and Journalism and Refugees International's McCall-Pierpaoli Humanitarian Award. He was also honored in 2018 by the Point Foundation, which recognizes advocacy for LGBTQ issues. Farrow, who has described himself as "part of the LGBT community," was recognized by the foundation both for his reporting on Weinstein and for his series of reports on the issues faced by transgender Americans.

Known for his formidable work ethic, he sometimes spends eighteen hours a day in the *New Yorker's* newsroom and has said that his social life is secondary to him. He is active on social media, however, and is known for his humorous and pithy posts; he has nearly 600,000 followers on Twitter.

SUGGESTED READING

Anthony, Andrew. "Ronan Farrow: Woody Allen, Harvey Weinstein and Me." *The Guardian*, 14 May 2018, www.theguardian.com/media/2018/may/13/ronan-farrow-interview-woody-allen-harvey-weinstein-me-too. Accessed 17 June 2018.

Farrow, Ronan. "Ronan Farrow: 'I Was Raised with An Extraordinary Sense of Public Service.'" Interview by Terry Gross. *Fresh Air*, NPR, 23 May 2018, www.npr.org/2018/05/23/613495834/ronan-farrow-i-was-raised-with-an-extraordinary-sense-of-public-service. Accessed 13 June 2018.

Glancy, Josh. "Ronan Farrow, the Reporter Son of Mia Farrow and Woody Allen, on How He Helped to Bring Down Harvey Weinstein." *Times* [London], 22 Apr. 2018, www.thetimes.co.uk/article/interview-ronan-farrow-the-reporter-son-of-mia-farrow-and-woody-allen-on-how-he-brought-down-harvey-weinstein-7m9gc7s3p. Accessed 13 June 2018.

Guthrie, Marisa. "Ronan Farrow, the Hollywood Prince Who Torched the Castle." *Hollywood Reporter*, 10 Jan. 2018, www.hollywoodreporter.com/features/ronan-farrow-hollywood-prince-who-torched-castle-1073405. Accessed 13 June 2018.

Lichtenstein, Jesse. "Ronan Farrow: Reluctant TV Star." *New York Times*, 3 Jan. 2014, www.nytimes.com/2014/01/05/magazine/ronan-farrow-reluctant-tv-star.html. Accessed 17 June 2018.

Schulman, Michael. "Ronan Farrow: The Youngest Old Guy in the Room." *New York Times*, 25 Oct. 2013, www.nytimes.com/2013/10/27/style/Ronan-Farrow-the-son-of-Mia-Farrow-steps-out-of-the-family-shadow.html. Accessed 13 June 2018.

Stampler, Laura. "10 Things You Need to Know About Ronan Farrow That Will Make You Feel Horribly Unaccomplished." *Time*, 18 Oct. 2013, newsfeed.time.com/2013/10/18/10-things-you-need-to-know-about-ronan-farrow-that-will-make-you-feel-horribly-unaccomplished/. Accessed 17 June 2018.

—*Mari Rich*

Emil Ferris

Date of birth: 1962
Occupation: Writer, cartoonist

Emil Ferris is a graphic novelist with an extraordinary personal story. The daughter of artists,

By Jody C., via Wikimedia Commons

Ferris spent her early adulthood working as a freelance illustrator and toy designer. In 2001, she was bitten by a mosquito at her fortieth birthday party. She contracted the West Nile virus, which led to meningitis and encephalitis that left her unable to walk, draw, and for a time, speak. Ferris taught herself to draw again, and after several years of painful recovery, decided to go to art school. A few years later, she earned her master's degree in creative writing, beginning a process that would eventually lead to the publication of her first graphic novel, *My Favorite Thing Is Monsters* (2016). In another brush with cruel fate, the book, once published, was nearly lost at sea when the ship that was carrying the first printing of her book was seized en route from South Korea to the United States. The book finally did make it into the hands of American readers, although several months late.

Framed as the 1968 notebook diary of a young girl named Karen, *My Favorite Thing Is Monsters* combines elements of Ferris's childhood—the Chicago neighborhood where she was raised, her Holocaust survivor neighbors, and her love of classic horror movie monsters—with the story of a murder. Divided into two parts—the conclusion was set to be published in 2018—the completed novel will total nearly 800 pages of ballpoint pen illustrations on lined notebook paper. Douglas Wolk of the *New York Times* (31 May 2017) praised Ferris's precise draftsmanship, calling *Monsters* "a startling demonstration of Ferris's range, power and ambition." Another *Times* book critic, Parul Sehgal, named it one of her favorite books of

2017, describing it as an "eerie masterpiece" (7 Dec. 2017). But perhaps the highest praise of all came from a fellow artist. Dana Jennings of the *New York Times* (17 Feb. 2017) reported that the legendary cartoonist Art Spiegelman, author of the Pulitzer Prize–winning graphic novel *Maus* (1973), called Ferris "one of the most important comics artists of our time."

EARLY LIFE

Ferris was born on the South Side of Chicago, Illinois, in 1962. She spent her earliest years in Albuquerque and Santa Fe, New Mexico, but her family returned to Chicago, settling in the Uptown neighborhood on the North Side, when Ferris was about five years old. Her parents met as students at the School of the Art Institute of Chicago. Her mother, Eleanor Spiess-Ferris, was a surrealist painter. Her father, Mike Ferris, was a toy designer who made the first Mickey Mouse telephone. Her brother Michael would become a sculptor. Unsurprisingly, art was an important part of Ferris's childhood. The family went to the Art Institute, one of the largest art museums in the country, the way "most families go to church," she recalled to Sam Thielman for the *Guardian* (20 Feb. 2017). "We sort of memorized paintings the way other kids memorized Bible verses." Her father also taught her an important technique she playfully calls "stealth drawing," she told Thielman. Father and daughter would board Chicago's public transit, the elevated train system called the El, and surreptitiously draw the faces of other passengers. Ferris continues to practice this technique, using the fruits of her labor in her work.

Ferris's young life was intellectually stimulating but largely sedentary. She was born with such severe scoliosis that she could not walk until she was almost three years old. A corrective surgery when she was ten put her in a body cast for nearly a year. Her disability, she has said, made her feel a bit like the monsters in her favorite horror films. In fact, like the young protagonist of her novel *My Favorite Thing Is Monsters*, Ferris desperately wanted to be a monster. As a child, she struggled with her conflicting sexual desires—Ferris is bisexual—and the disturbing correlation between female beauty and violence. "I saw that the beautiful women around me were often constrained not only by their beauty but by the way that being an object of male desire frequently caused violence in their lives," she told Thielman. "Being a monster seemed like the absolute best solution."

Ferris's fondness for dark stories was likewise born of a struggle to comprehend real-life horror. People were sometimes murdered in her neighborhood, and close friends, including Ferris herself, were victims of sexual violence. She once saw the body of a young boy who had fallen out of a window. Neighbors, many of whom were Holocaust survivors, were living reminders of the world's capacity for violence. The neighbors shared their stories with a young Ferris, who found the horrors they contained almost impossible to believe. Despite the depths from which it sprang, Ferris's love of monsters, and her gifts as a storyteller, won her friends as a student at Gale Elementary School in Rogers Park. She could not run and play with the other kids, but she could draw them to her by telling scary stories on the playground. This act of transformation—turning one kind of horror into another, more entertaining kind—is a hallmark of Ferris's work.

EARLY CAREER AND WEST NILE VIRUS

Ferris dropped out of high school when she was sixteen. She was briefly homeless before earning her GED certificate. She found work as a waitress and cleaned houses. At the time, Ferris hoped to be an actress. She studied with several theaters in Chicago, but later turned her attention to art, working as a freelance illustrator and artist. Like her father, she found success as a toy designer. She sculpted a line of Happy Meal prizes featuring characters from the Disney movie *Mulan* (1998) for fast-food company McDonald's. She also made a line of toys called Tea Bunnies for the Tokyo-based toy company Tomy.

Ferris, who was by this time raising a young daughter on her own, was making a decent living when an unlikely accident set her life on a different path. Ferris was bitten by a mosquito at her fortieth birthday party and contracted the West Nile virus—though she did not realize it at first. She fell ill with a fever that lasted for days. After arriving at the hospital, Ferris suffered from hallucinations only to wake up and realize that brain infections, meningitis and encephalitis, had left her almost completely paralyzed. She could not walk, move her right side—including her drawing hand—or speak.

Unable to work, Ferris and her daughter moved in with Ferris's mother. Ferris's recovery was slow, difficult, and painful, but it awakened a ferocious creative desire. She desperately wanted to regain "the ability to draw and walk and live and create," as she told Terry Gross for the National Public Radio (NPR) program *Fresh Air* (30 Mar. 2017). "It became clear to me that it was much more important to be generous and to do the best that I could and give something to the world." She added: "It is possible to leave this place without getting anything. And I didn't want that to be my trajectory."

With the help of her daughter, Ferris painstakingly re-taught herself to draw by duct-taping a pen to her hand. A few years later, she went back to school to study painting and animation at the School of the Art Institute of Chicago.

She earned her bachelor of fine arts degree in 2008. A few years after that, Ferris returned to the school to study creative writing. She earned her master of fine arts degree in 2011. Her thesis was the first few pages of what would become her first graphic novel, *My Favorite Thing Is Monsters*.

MY FAVORITE THING IS MONSTERS (2016)

Ferris brought together numerous influences for her graphic novel debut. As a child, Ferris's grandmother had sent her editions of Collier's illustrated novels of Charles Dickens. "I just wanted that experience: to write stories where the drawings were that articulated and atmospheric," she recalled to Thielman. Other artists who have inspired Ferris's work are stylistically diverse but illuminate Ferris's own unique style and the themes she uses that style to explore. Foremost among them is the German expressionist painter Otto Dix, an artist best known for his firsthand depictions of the horrors of World War I. Another inspiration was the artist George Grosz. Grosz was a German painter and caricature artist who also served in World War I. He spent his career making art that criticized the violence and greed of the era.

Ferris's work is also inspired by the work of other graphic novelists. "When I read [Spiegelman's] *Maus*," she told Jennings, "I realized you could tell a story of tremendous import using the graphic novel." *Maus* tells the story of Spiegelman's father, a Holocaust survivor, using cartoon mice. Ferris also has cited the work of Alison Bechdel, best known for her graphic memoir *Fun Home* (2006), which explores abuse and sexuality. Ferris's novel is a mystery story, but also a coming-of-age tale that touches on sexuality and the trauma of the Holocaust.

In it, a ten-year-old girl named Karen likes to imagine herself as a werewolf. A social misfit in a rough neighborhood, she finds solace in her drawing and watching horror films. She likes to visit her glamorous neighbor Anka, a Holocaust survivor. When Anka is found shot to death—a suicide, the police say—Karen takes it upon herself to solve the case. She uncovers more than she bargained for, including wrenching episodes from Anka's traumatic past. Ferris weaves together Karen's love of monsters with her discovery of true monstrousness. John Powers, who reviewed the book for *Fresh Air* (22 Feb. 2017), wrote that, despite the book's painful subjects, its power lies in its heart. "Ferris clearly knows all of Karen's emotions from deep within," Powers wrote. "Every page feels like it's been secreted from the very core of her being."

PERSONAL LIFE

Ferris, who suffers from chronic pain, walks with the aid of a cane, and sometimes uses a wheelchair. She lives in Evanston, Illinois, outside of Chicago.

SUGGESTED READING

Gross, Terry. "In 'Monsters,' Graphic Novelist Emil Ferris Embraces the Darkness Within." *Fresh Air*, National Public Radio, 30 Mar. 2017, www.npr.org/2017/03/30/522034367/in-monsters-graphic-novelist-emil-ferris-embraces-the-darkness-within. Accessed 6 Mar. 2018.

Jennings, Dana. "First, Emil Ferris Was Paralyzed. Then Her Book Got Lost at Sea." *The New York Times*, 17 Feb. 2017, www.nytimes.com/2017/02/17/arts/design/first-emil-ferris-was-paralyzed-then-her-book-got-lost-at-sea.html. Accessed 6 Mar. 2018.

Powers, John. "'My Favorite Thing is Monsters' Is a Dazzling, Graphic Novel Tour-de-Force." *Fresh Air*, National Public Radio, 22 Feb. 2017, www.npr.org/2017/02/22/516643494/my-favorite-thing-is-monsters-is-a-dazzling-graphic-novel-tour-de-force. Accessed 6 Mar. 2018.

Sehgal, Parul. "Times Critics' Top Books of 2017." *The New York Times*, 7 Dec. 2017, www.nytimes.com/2017/12/07/books/critics-favorite-books-2017.html. Accessed 6 Mar. 2018.

Thielman, Sam. "Emil Ferris: 'I Didn't Want to Be a Woman—Being a Monster Was the Best Solution.'" *The Guardian*, 20 Feb. 2017, www.theguardian.com/books/2017/feb/20/emil-ferris-my-favorite-thing-is-monsters-graphic-novel. Accessed 6 Mar. 2018.

Wolk, Douglas. "New Graphic Novels Detail Personal Journeys and Twists of Fate." *The New York Times*, 31 May 2017, www.nytimes.com/2017/05/31/books/review/summer-reading-new-graphic-novels.html. Accessed 6 Mar. 2018.

—Molly Hagan

Florida Georgia Line

Occupation: Band

TYLER HUBBARD

Date of birth: January 31, 1987
Occupation: Singer-songwriter, guitarist

BRIAN KELLEY

Date of birth: August 26, 1985
Occupation: Singer-songwriter, guitarist

Country music audiences were first captivated by Florida Georgia Line (FGL) in late 2012, when their

By Morgan Williams [CC BY 2.0], via Wikimedia Commons

debut single, "Cruise," topped the Billboard Country Airplay chart, making them the first duo or group since the Zac Brown Band achieved this feat in 2008. Their ode to the open road gained mainstream recognition the following year, reaching fourth on the Hot 100 with their "Cruise" remix version featuring the rapper Nelly. Because of the song's crossover success—and its focus on back roads, trucks, tailgates, drinking, and women—the duo quickly became the poster children for the so-called bro-country sound, influenced by hip hop and rock, that is reflected throughout their double-platinum debut album and their platinum-selling follow-up.

However, the duo embraced a more mature sound for their 2016 platinum disc, *Dig Your Roots,* which boasted a duet with idol Tim McGraw ("May We All"), as well as cross-genre collaborations with Ziggy Marley ("Life Is a Honeymoon") and nineties pop group Backstreet Boys ("God, Your Mama, and Me"). The pair has also lent their vocals to tracks by other pop artists, including Bebe Rexha's "Meant to Be," Hailee Steinfeld and Alesso's "Let Me Go," and the Chainsmokers' "Last Day Alive."

EARLY YEARS

Tyler Hubbard was born to Amy and Roy Wayne Hubbard on January 31, 1987. He grew up in Monroe, Georgia, with his siblings Cameron and Amelia. Sports quickly became Hubbard's first love. At age three he was introduced to dirt bikes by his father, the owner of a tree-cutting business.

Hubbard's passion for music surfaced during his teens. "I listened to a lot of worship music, but also a lot of country and any type of rhythmic music," he shared with Guy Little for *Acoustic Magazine* (6 Apr. 2015). While attending Loganville Christian Academy (LCA), Hubbard, who grew up listening to country legend Tim McGraw, rocker Lynyrd Skynyrd, and rapper Lil Wayne, penned lyrics and created beats for Ingenious Circuit, the hip-hop group he formed with some classmates. He also honed his singing abilities as the youth worship leader for the First Baptist Church of Loganville.

Like Hubbard, Brian Kelley, who was born on August 26, 1985, to Ed and Mary Margaret Kelley, hails from the South: Ormond Beach, Florida. Kelley also grew up playing sports, pitching for the Sandcrabs baseball team at Seabreeze High School in Daytona Beach.

Kelley's love of music began during his junior year. The sixteen-year-old convinced his father to buy him a hundred-dollar guitar from the Daytona Flea & Farmers Market. Another early influence was Kelley's older sister and frequent chaperone, Katherine, a country music enthusiast who often listened to Garth Brooks, Tim McGraw, and Kenny Chesney on her car radio. Kelley learned to play and write songs.

CROSSING PATHS

After graduating from LCA in 2005, Hubbard studied music business at Belmont University in Nashville, Tennessee, where he also led on-campus worship services. However, tragedy struck in February 2007, when Hubbard, who was visiting from school, witnessed his father's helicopter clip a tree and crash in the family's backyard during a failed landing. "I have that image ingrained in my brain forever of what we saw that day and how fragile the human body is and how fragile life is," he recalled to Alison Bonaguro for *CMT* (29 May 2014). Not long after his father's death, Hubbard experienced another life-changing event: his first encounter with future bandmate Brian Kelley, a transfer student from Florida State University (FSU).

Despite landing an athletic scholarship at FSU, Kelley saw little action. Instead he spent his downtime honing his songwriting and performing guitar at a local Baptist church in downtown Tallahassee. Following his sophomore season, Kelley switched to Daytona State College, where he earned his associate's degree in 2007 before transferring to Belmont. "I had a class with Tyler's good buddy, who introduced us. We hit it off musically," Kelley shared with Korina Lopez for *USA Today* (14 Oct. 2012). In an October 2012 interview for ESPN, Hubbard recalled hearing Kelley play worship music at church and liking his sound.

PURSUING THEIR PASSION

In 2009, following their graduation from Belmont, the duo set up residence together in Nashville and started working on songs, giving themselves two years to break into the country music scene. To support themselves, the pair painted houses, washed and detailed cars, and cut grass, while performing gigs at local venues. They also settled on a moniker for their band: Florida Georgia Line. "We had to stop showing up as Brian and Tyler, we needed a name, so we put our heads together and said, 'I want to represent where I'm from and you want to represent where you're from,'" Kelley told Ashleigh Schmitz for *Parade* (5 May 2014). "Two states got thrown out and the 'Line' and it kind of stuck."

In mid-December 2010, Florida Georgia Line (FGL), by then a popular fixture on the Southeast club circuit, had independently released and digitally distributed *Anything Like Me*, a debut EP boasting six songs the duo cowrote. Rock producer and songwriter Joey Moi, co-owner of independent music firm Big Loud Mountain, subsequently discovered them during a county fair. Under Moi's guidance, FGL began work on their next EP, drawing from various genres, including rock and hip-hop. They also signed with Big Loud Mountain in December 2011.

RECORD DEAL

The following April, "Cruise," the record's lead single, debuted on iTunes. *It'z Just What We Do*, FGL's second digital EP, hit the shelves in May, prior to their appearance at CMA (Country Music Association) Festival's BMI (Broadcast Music Inc.) Tailgate Party and at Willie Nelson's 2012 Country Throwdown Tour. The duo caught a break when John Marks, SiriusXM's senior director of country music programming, played "Cruise" in regular rotation on the Highway, a popular satellite radio channel featuring current hits and tracks from new country artists. The airplay helped "Cruise" sell nearly 200,000 copies in two months, attracting interest from several major record labels.

After signing with Big Machine Label Group in July 2012, FGL's career took off. "Cruise" was officially released to country radio in early August, prior to FGL's Grand Ole Opry debut on August 12. The duo spent the rest of the year opening for Jake Owen on the eleventh annual CMT on Tour. During that period, they not only unveiled their first full-length studio album, *Here's to the Good Times* (2012), but also scored their first number-one hit in December, when "Cruise" topped the Billboard Country Airplay and Hot Country Songs charts, supplanting country-pop superstar and labelmate Taylor Swift in the latter category. *Good Times* eventually climbed to the top five of the Billboard 200

by June 2013. For their next single, released in December 2012, the duo collaborated with Luke Bryan on another bro-country track: "This Is How We Roll," which topped the Hot Country Songs chart in late March.

COLLABORATION WITH NELLY

FGL kicked off 2013 as the opener for Bryan's Dirt Road Diaries Tour and then Swift's Red Tour. They also released "Get Your Shine On," which eventually reached number twenty-seven on the Billboard Hot 100 and made the top five of the Country Airplay chart. FGL's first chart-topper, "Cruise," subsequently found a wider audience after Monte Lipman, then chair and CEO of Universal Republic Records, approached hip-hop artist Nelly to remix it. "I listened to it, and I was like, 'First thing we gotta do is speed the beat up a little bit,'" the rapper told Adelle Platon for *Billboard* (1 June 2017). "They got somebody else to do the track and sped the beat up, and then I just went in and tried different variations of it until we came up with one that was really, really dope."

The new version of "Cruise" debuted on iTunes and pop radio on early April, the same month the duo claimed new artist and new vocal duo of the year 2012 honors at the 2013 Academy of Country Music (ACM) Awards. Even as FGL scored big again with "Get Your Shine On," response remained overwhelmingly positive for the "Cruise" remix, which reached fourth on the Hot 100 in July. While the accompanying video claimed CMT Music Awards for Breakthrough Video and Duo Video, "Cruise" was named single of the year by both the American Music Awards (AMAs) and the Country Music Association (CMA) Awards. It was also nominated for the 2013 Billboard Music Awards' top country song. The song ended the year in the top ten of the Hot 100, and FGL topped the Top Country Artists chart for 2013.

FGL achieved several other milestones in 2013, including a number-one album on the Top Country Albums chart, another chart-topping single ("Round Here") on Country Airplay, and their first-ever headlining tour, which ran from early October to mid-December. FGL was also named the vocal duo of the year by the CMAs and the ACMs.

BRO-COUNTRY

In January 2014 the duo made history when "Cruise" surpassed Lady Antebellum's "Need You Now" as the all-time best-selling country digital song. The summer anthem also gained notoriety in country music's male-dominated landscape, for popularizing hot trucks, dirt roads, tailgate parties, alcohol, and beautiful, scantily clad women—a trend first referred to as "bro-country" by music critic Jody Rosen for an August

2013 *Vulture* article that also referenced Jason Aldean, Jake Owen, and Luke Bryan. However, FGL was hesitant to categorize their music. "We definitely embrace it, [but] we don't really put ourselves in that box, or any sort of box," Hubbard told Brandon Friederich for *Maxim* (6 Jan. 2017). "We just do our own thing, and we don't really want to throw a label on our music."

From early May until late October, FGL, who were working on their second studio album, appeared with Aldean at all but two stops of his fifty-city Burn It Down Tour. When "Dirt" debuted in July 2014, the nostalgic, sentimental ballad (and lead single) was a clear departure from the up-tempo bro-country tunes featured on their previous record. However, the group had not completely abandoned bro-country, as reflected by the digital release of their follow-up, the reggae-tinged party anthem "Sun Daze," in October 2014. Audiences responded favorably to both songs, giving the duo consecutive number ones on Country Airplay. Response was equally positive for FGL's second studio album, *Anything Goes*, which topped the *Billboard* 200 within two weeks of its debut in mid-October. This was followed by the release of their singles "Sippin' on Fire" and the title track "Anything Goes" in October 2014; by mid-June 2015, "Sipping' on Fire" also topped the Country Airplay chart.

In addition to winning Top Country Song for "Cruise" at the 2014 Billboard Music Awards, FGL claimed their second vocal duo of the year honors at the CMAs and the ACMs, and Favorite Band, Duo or Group–Country at the AMAs. They also won CMT Music Awards for Duo of the Year for "Round Here" and Collaborative Video of the Year for "This Is How We Roll."

In 2015 FGL embarked on their worldwide Anything Goes Tour. On October 31, "Anything Goes" simultaneously reached the top ten on the Country Airplay and Hot Country Songs charts. FGL ended the year with several industry accolades under their belt: the Billboard Music Award for Top Country Artist, their third consecutive CMA Award for Vocal Duo of the Year, AMAs for Favorite Duo or Group–Country and Favorite Album–Country, and the CMT Music Award for Duo Video of the Year. In April 2016, they received the Recording Industry Association of America's diamond certification for "Cruise," sales, which had hit ten million units. By May 2016, the single "H.O.L.Y." had claimed the top of the Hot Country Songs chart, as "Confession," from their previous disc, became the duo's eighth number-one on Country Airplay.

MATURE SOUND

For their third studio album, *Dig Your Roots*, released in August 2016, the duo adopted a more mature sound. "It's an evolution," Hubbard

confided to Gary Graff for *Billboard* (25 Feb. 2016). He continued, "It's a little bit more real, a little bit more personal and there's a little bit more of a nostalgic feel." By May 2016, the album's single "H.O.L.Y.," released in advance of the rest of the album, had claimed the top of the Hot Country Songs chart. At around the same time, "Confession," from their previous disc, became the duo's eighth number-one on Country Airplay. *Dig Your Roots* produced two more chart-toppers: the Tim McGraw duet "May We All," and "God, Your Mama, and Me," another high-profile collaboration with the nineties pop group the Backstreet Boys. That year, they claimed ACM's vocal event of the year award and AMA's favorite duo prize. Not only did they finish the year ranked third among the Billboard Top Country Artists chart, but "H.O.L.Y." also topped the Country Digital Song Sales chart and won them their third CMT Music Award for Duo Video of the Year. FGL was back on the road in June 2017, kicking off their first stadium concert tour, the Smooth Tour, featuring Nelly and the Backstreet Boys.

OTHER VENTURES

In addition to making award-winning music, the duo has embarked on several related business ventures. In 2015 Kelley and Hubbard cofounded the music publishing firm Tree Vibez Music, with the mission of helping aspiring artists and songwriters of any genre. They were also inspired to create Old Camp Peach Pecan Whiskey, blending iconic flavors of their home states in a classic southern beverage. Distribution began in October 2016. Their entrepreneurism continued with a Nashville restaurant and bar, FGL House, opened the following May. In December 2017 the duo announced plans to create a retail and event space to house Tree Vibez Music, their Tribe Kelley Trading Post retail store, and a hub for creative professionals.

PERSONAL LIFE

Kelley, who married Brittney Marie Cole in December 2013, lives outside Nashville on thirty-two acres. Hubbard married Hayley Stommel in 2015 and also calls the Nashville area home.

SUGGESTED READING

Bonaguro, Alison. "Inside Fame Reveals Florida Georgia Line's Family Tragedy." *CMT*, www.cmt.com/news/1727825/inside-fame-reveals-florida-georgia-lines-family-tragedy. Accessed. 14 Dec. 2017.

Friederich, Brandon. "Florida Georgia Line on Their New Whiskey, Dream Musical Collaborations and Embracing 'Bro-Country.'" *Maxim*, 6 Jan. 2017, www.maxim.com/entertainment/florida-georgia-line-old-camp-whiskey-1-2017. Accessed 14 Dec. 2017.

Little, Guy. "Florida Georgia Line." *Acoustic Magazine*, 6 Apr. 2015, www.acousticmagazine.com/interviews/florida-georgia-line. Accessed 14 Dec. 2017.

Lopez, Korina. "On the Verge with Country Duo Florida Georgia Line." *USA Today*, 14 Oct. 2012, www.usatoday.com/story/life/music/2012/10/14/florida-georgia-line-country-duo-on-the-verge/1618911. Accessed 14 Dec. 2017.

Platon, Adelle. "Nelly Talks Smooth Tour with Florida Georgia Line and Making Records Country Fans Can Appreciate." *Billboard*, 1 June 2017, www.billboard.com/articles/columns/hip-hop/7817347/nelly-country-florida-georgia-line-smooth-tour. Accessed 14 Dec. 2017.

Schmitz, Ashleigh. "Brian Kelley Reveals How Florida Georgia Line Came Up with Their Band Name." *Parade*, 5 May 2014, parade.com/287930/ashleighschmitz/florida-georgia-lines-brian-kelley-we-want-to-be-bigger-than-the-music. Accessed 14 Dec. 2017.

SELECTED WORKS

Here's to the Good Times, 2012; *Anything Goes*, 2014; *Dig Your Roots*, 2016

—Bertha Muteba

By Tony Rich via Wikimedia Commons

Sabina-Francesca Foişor

Date of birth: August 30, 1989
Occupation: Chess player

In April 2017, chess player Sabina-Francesca Foişor competed in the US Women's Chess Championship, her ninth since her first appearance in the tournament in 2009. A strong player holding the World Chess Federation (FIDE) rank of Woman Grandmaster, she had experienced limited success in the US Women's Chess Championship to that point, finishing in no better than fourth place. The 2017 competition, however, proved to be a key turning point for Foişor: after progressing through the first ten rounds of the tournament, she claimed the championship after her final match enabled her to earn a total score higher than that of 2016 champion and former college chess teammate Nazí Paikidze. In addition to earning Foişor $25,000 in prize money, her victory solidified Foişor's status as a major competitor on the national and international stages.

For Foişor, success at the US Women's Championship and elsewhere was the result of a lifetime of training in the game of chess. The daughter of accomplished Romanian chess players Cristina and Ovidiu Foişor, she began

competing by the time she was five years old and had a successful career as a child and teenager, competing both in Romania and elsewhere in Europe. After earning a chess scholarship to the University of Maryland, Baltimore County (UMBC), the home of one of the United States' most prestigious chess programs, she moved to the United States and went on to establish herself not only as a valuable member of the UMBC chess team but also as a frequent competitor in events such as the Chess Olympiad and the Women's World Team Championship. Although Foişor has faced a variety of challenges in her chess career, most notably the death of her mother in early 2017, she has persevered and remained committed to the game to which she has devoted much of her life. "I believe to play chess well one must have an open mind and do things that really benefit them—regardless of their difficulties," she wrote in a blog post for the website of the *St. Louis Chess Club* (16 May 2018).

EARLY LIFE AND CAREER

Foişor, whose last name is sometimes written as Foisor, was born in Timişoara, Romania, on August 30, 1989. Her parents, Cristina and Ovidiu, were both chess players who held the rank of International Master and had experienced success both within Romania and on the international level: her father had won the Romanian chess championship in 1982, while her mother had won the national women's championship five times and competed in fourteen Chess Olympiads. As the child of two accomplished players, Foişor began playing chess herself at the age of four. "They decided it would be a good idea to teach me how to play chess," she recalled to Ryanne Milani for the *Baltimore Sun* (28 Apr. 2012). "It's a nice way to be together." Her younger sister, Mihaela-Veronica, also learned to play and would go on to hold the rank of Woman International Master.

Having demonstrated a talent for chess, Foişor began competing in tournaments by the time she was five years old and likewise began intensive training in the game. "When I was a kid, I used to work with my parents about five to seven hours a day," she told Milani. "I had to give up hanging out with my friends. I didn't do those things very often." Foişor's dedication and training took her to chess tournaments in Romania as well as other European nations with larger chess programs. "We were appreciated more abroad for some reason," she told Ben Johnson for the *Perpetual Chess Podcast* (2 May 2017). Foişor won a European championship for girls under the age of eight in 1997 and went on to compete in under-ten and under-twenty competitions within Romania. She placed third at the European championship for girls under fourteen in 2003 as well as at the under-eighteen girls' competition in 2007. In recognition of her strong chess rating, Foişor was granted the title of Woman International Master by the World Chess Federation (FIDE) in 2005. She was promoted to Woman Grandmaster, a title that is the highest title exclusively for women but is ranked lower than the gender-neutral titles of International Master and Grandmaster, in 2007.

COLLEGE CAREER

In 2008, Foişor moved to the United States to attend the University of Maryland, Baltimore County (UMBC), which had offered her a full chess scholarship. Since the 1990s, UMBC had actively recruited strong college-age chess players from around the world to compete for the institution, which developed a reputation as a major contender in events such as the Pan-American Intercollegiate Team Chess Championships. As a recipient of the university's Coca-Cola Chess Fellowship and later the Pepsi Chess Fellowship, Foişor had the opportunity to study at the university as well as to compete alongside other highly rated young chess players. Over the course of her time with the UMBC chess team, Foişor—whose nickname on the team was Sunshine—helped the team win the President's Cup in 2009 and accompanied her teammates to numerous intercollegiate competitions.

Despite UMBC's heavy focus on chess, Foişor has noted that she personally devoted herself more to her studies than to chess during her time at the university. "My parents were not so happy about it because my chess career basically stagnated a lot and actually . . . my rating went down over a hundred rating points," she told Johnson. "Chesswise it wasn't so great, but I thought it was really important to have an education as well." As an undergraduate, Foişor majored in modern language and linguistics with a focus on French. She also pursued minors in psychology and Russian language. After earning her bachelor's degree in 2012, Foişor remained at UMBC to pursue a master's degree in intercultural communications. She completed her graduate studies in 2014. After leaving UMBC, Foişor moved to Lubbock, Texas, and worked for a time at Texas Tech University.

NATIONAL AND INTERNATIONAL COMPETITION

While still an undergraduate student, Foişor made the decision to transfer from the Romanian chess federation to its US counterpart so that she could represent the United States in international competitions. After transferring in late 2008, she became a fixture on the US women's chess team and competed in several Chess Olympiads, team-based tournaments overseen by FIDE. The US women's team placed fifth in the 2010 Chess Olympiad, Foişor's first with the team. In addition to those events, Foişor began competing in the Women's World Team Championships in 2013 and regularly played in the US Women's Chess Championship, having made her first appearance in that tournament in 2009.

Although Foişor sought to continue her chess career while pursuing work outside of chess, striking a balance between those two worlds was not always possible. In 2016, she requested a leave of absence from her day job to compete in that year's US Women's Chess Championship. After her supervisor reportedly denied her request and told her that she had no chance of winning, Foişor quit. Although she later found another job, she went on to focus primarily on her chess career, which included teaching as well as playing. "I really enjoy teaching chess, and sometimes more than training myself," she told Johnson. "It's great to have been given the opportunity of learning to play chess and then getting so high. It's really important to share your knowledge with others." Foişor's work as a teacher has included online lessons as well as an in-person residency at the St. Louis Chess Club, and she also maintained a YouTube channel to which she posted videos analyzing chess games and techniques.

US WOMEN'S CHAMPION

Foişor and the international chess community suffered a loss in early 2017, when Foişor's mother, Cristina, died of cancer. Both Foişor and her mother had been scheduled to compete in the 2017 Women's World Chess Championships, held in Iran in February and March of that year, and had been excited to compete in the same tournament. Following her mother's death, Foişor decided to compete in the tournament as planned. Although she was eliminated early in the competition, Foişor remained focused on honoring her mother's memory and legacy, particularly as the US Women's Chess Championship approached. "I really wanted to try to stay strong and . . . work as much as I can so that I can somehow keep her memory alive," she explained to Johnson. "Being able to win the US Women's Championship was definitely a dream that both of us have had."

In April of 2017, Foişor traveled to St. Louis, Missouri, to compete against eleven other talented players in the US Women's Chess Championship. By the final round, the sole competitor standing between Foişor and the championship was presumed frontrunner Nazí Paikidze, the 2016 champion and a USBC graduate who had been a member of the chess team while Foişor was in graduate school. Paikidze lost to opponent Jennifer Yu in her final match, while Foişor defeated opponent Virkud Apurva in the eleventh round of the competition to claim first place and a prize of $25,000. Following her victory, Foişor was named to *Forbes*'s 2018 Thirty under Thirty in Games list and went on to be featured on the cover of *American Chess Magazine*.

Foişor's success at the 2017 championship reinforced her desire to focus primarily on her chess career. Although she was less successful at the 2018 US Women's Chess Championship, at which she placed fifth, she took that disappointment as a valuable lesson about her approach. "I took a little bit of time to think about what went wrong," she wrote in her blog post for the St. Louis Chess Club. "I started my chess preparation for this prestigious event in February; I ate healthy meals; I exercised and trained every single day; yet, toward the end of my games, I couldn't keep my calm and missed a lot of opportunities and tactical ideas." After comparing her preparation process in 2018 to her far more successful routine in 2017, Foişor attributed her diminished performance to a lax daily routine and insufficient focus on sleep, diet, and exercise, which she believes are essential to success in her field. As 2018 progressed, Foişor sought to take a more holistic approach to her mental and physical performance in the hope of experiencing further triumphs in competition.

PERSONAL LIFE

Foişor is engaged to Grandmaster Elshan Moradiabadi, whom she met in 2014. He has also served as her coach. Foişor and Moradiabadi live in Durham, North Carolina. In addition to playing and teaching chess, Foişor has a longstanding interest in language and linguistics and is fluent in four languages.

SUGGESTED READING

Foişor, Sabina-Francesca. "Follow Your Routine—In Life and Chess." *Saint Louis Chess Club*, 16 May 2018, saintlouischessclub.org/blog/follow-your-routine---life-and-chess. Accessed 10 Aug. 2018.

Foişor, Sabina-Francesca. Interview by Ben Johnson. *Perpetual Chess Podcast*, 2 May 2017, podtail.com/en/podcast/perpetual-chess-podcast/ep-22-woman-grandmaster-sabina-foisor/. Accessed 10 Aug. 2018.

McGourty, Colin. "US Championship 11: Foisor Triumphs, So Gambles." *Chess24*, 10 Apr. 2017, chess24.com/en/read/news/us-championship-11-foisor-triumphs-so-gambles. Accessed 10 Aug. 2018.

Milani, Ryanne. "Foisor Ready to Make Her Move." *The Baltimore Sun*, 28 Apr. 2012, www.baltimoresun.com/sports/outdoors/bs-sp-outdoors-chess-sabina-foisor-0429-20120428-story.html. Accessed 10 Aug. 2018.

Rosenwald, Michael S. "At College Chess's Final Four, Once-Dominant UMBC Is Now the Underdog." *The Washington Post*, 5 Apr. 2013, www.washingtonpost.com/local/at-college-chesss-final-four-once-dominant-umbc-is-now-the-underdog/2013/04/05/f0c5857e-9d46-11e2-a941-a19bce7af755_story.html. Accessed 10 Aug. 2018.

Shabazz, Daaim. "Championship Shows Changing Face of US Chess." *Chess Drum*, 17 Apr. 2017, www.thechessdrum.net/blog/2017/04/17/championship-shows-changing-face-of-u-s-chess/. Accessed 10 Aug. 2018.

Yermolinsky, Alex. "Sabina Foisor Is 2017 US Women's Champion!" *ChessBase*, 10 Apr 2017, en.chessbase.com/post/sabina-foisor-is-2017-us-women-s-champion. Accessed 10 Aug. 2018.

—*Joy Crelin*

Nick Foles

Date of birth: January 20, 1989
Occupation: Football player

The Philadelphia Eagles quarterback Nick Foles has experienced a career "of ultra-high highs and deep, deep lows," as Dan Graziano wrote for *ESPN* (22 Jan. 2018). An unheralded third-round pick by the Eagles in the 2012 National Football League (NFL) Draft, the six-feet-six Foles began his career in Philadelphia as a backup before enjoying a record-breaking 2013 season, in which he earned his first Pro Bowl selection. He struggled with inconsistency,

By Matthew Straubmuller, via Wikimedia Commons

however, during the 2014 season, which ended prematurely due to a broken collarbone. Forgettable one-season stints with the St. Louis (now Los Angeles) Rams and Kansas City Chiefs followed before Foles returned to the Eagles prior to the 2017 season. By then, according to Dan Wetzel for *Yahoo! Sports* (5 Feb. 2018), he was considered "nothing but a backup, a journeyman, another name in the NFL's parade of mediocre QBs."

Foles changed this league-wide perception of him in December 2017, when he was thrust into the Eagles' starting quarterback role after franchise star Carson Wentz suffered a season-ending knee injury. He galvanized top-seeded Philadelphia during the 2018 NFL postseason and ultimately helped lead the team to Super Bowl LII. There, the Eagles upset the New England Patriots, 41–33, to win their first-ever Super Bowl title. Foles won the Super Bowl Most Valuable Player (MVP) Award as one of only a few backup quarterbacks to win a championship, forever immortalizing himself among Eagles fans.

EARLY LIFE

The oldest of three children, Foles was born on January 20, 1989, in Austin, Texas, to Larry Foles, a highly successful restaurateur, and Melissa Foles. Though growing up privileged, Foles learned early on the value of hard work from his father, who worked upwards of eighty hours per week during his childhood. Foles applied that grounded mindset to athletics, in which he showed interest from an early age. "I guess sports was in his genes," his father told Rod Walker for the Baton Rouge, Louisiana, *Advocate* (3 Feb. 2018). "He would pick up a ball and have it in his hands all day long."

When Foles was a toddler, his father would drop Nerf balls on his head to develop his hand-eye coordination. Foles had natural athleticism and excelled at every sport he tried. As a youth he played football, basketball, and baseball, and was also involved in karate. By the time he reached middle school, however, he narrowed his focus to football and basketball. More physically imposing than his peers—he was over six feet tall by eighth grade—he was sometimes prohibited from playing on his age-level Pop Warner football teams because of his size. On the teams he did play, he distinguished himself as an even-keeled player who possessed maturity beyond his years.

HIGH SCHOOL CAREER

Foles attended Westlake High School in Austin, where he was a two-sport star in football and basketball. He was a three-year starter for the basketball team, twice earning team MVP honors and receiving all-district recognition as a junior during the 2005–6 season. Football, however, remained his top priority, and as a sophomore, he earned a rare spot on Westlake's elite varsity football team. Though Foles primarily played quarterback, coaches also had him divide time at the tight end position due to his size and athleticism. Foles nonetheless considered himself a quarterback, and thanks to his exceptional arm strength and pocket presence, he became the team's starter as a junior.

Adding toughness to his list of attributes, Foles played most of his senior season with a torn labrum in his throwing shoulder. Still, he led Westlake to a runner-up finish in the Class 5A state title game. In his two seasons as Westlake's signal-caller, Foles established school career records for passing yards (5,568) and passing touchdowns (56), surpassing marks initially held by Drew Brees, the perennial All-Pro quarterback for the NFL's New Orleans Saints. Yet despite those achievements, he was mostly overlooked by colleges with major football programs. Many dismissed him as slow-footed or attributed his success to his high school team's strong system rather than his own skills. He ultimately signed with Michigan State University. "Nick was always the underdog," his father explained to Walker. "Nobody ever took him serious, and I think that was because of his laid-back attitude."

COLLEGE SUCCESS AND NFL DRAFT

Things did not get any easier for Foles at Michigan State, which already had two future NFL starting quarterbacks on its depth chart in Brian Hoyer and Kirk Cousins. Foles saw playing time in the first game of the 2007 season but did not see the field again for the remainder of his freshman campaign. As a result, prior to his sophomore season, he transferred to the University of Arizona, where he felt he would have a better chance of starting. "I really think that you have moments in your life where you can go one way or you can go another," Foles explained to Reuben Frank for *NBC Sports Philadelphia* (23 July 2014).

Foles seized his moment at Arizona, but first had to win a spot on the team as a walk-on player. He was granted redshirt status, but in the fall of 2009, he lost a battle with Matt Scott to become the team's starting quarterback. Scott struggled in the first three games of that season, though, after which Foles became the starter, a position he would retain for the remainder of his college career. Despite being largely surrounded by mediocre talent, Foles put up stellar numbers in his three seasons as the Wildcats' quarterback, becoming the school's all-time leader in passing yards (10,011) and touchdowns (67). He led Arizona to consecutive bowl game appearances in 2009 and 2010, and as a senior in 2011 he threw for a school single-season record 4,434 yards and 28 touchdowns.

Still, Foles did not enter the 2012 NFL Draft as a highly coveted quarterback prospect. That year's draft class included several highly regarded quarterbacks, including top overall pick Andrew Luck as well as dual-threat prospects Robert Griffin III, Ryan Tannehill, and Russell Wilson. Foles fell to the third round, taken eighty-eighth overall by the Philadelphia Eagles on the potential of his arm strength and toughness.

EARLY NFL CAREER

Foles entered his rookie 2012 season as a backup to the Eagles' incumbent quarterback Michael Vick. He made his NFL debut in a week-ten matchup against the Dallas Cowboys, replacing Vick in the second quarter after Vick suffered a concussion. Foles started the Eagles' next six games and finished his rookie season with 1,699 passing yards, a team rookie record (he missed the season finale with a broken right hand). The Eagles lost all but one of his six starts, however, and finished with a dismal 4–12 record. The team's longtime head coach, Andy Reid, was fired at the end of the season and replaced by Chip Kelly, who had spent the previous four seasons at the helm of the University of Oregon.

Foles competed for the Eagles' starting quarterback job during the 2013 training camp. However, he was outperformed by Vick, who was named the starter to begin the season. Yet Foles found his way back onto the field due to another Vick injury and enjoyed a breakout 2013 season. In ten starts, he posted an 8–2 record, breaking several NFL records in the process. During

a week-nine game against the Oakland Raiders, Foles tied a league record with seven touchdown passes in a game and posted a rare perfect passer rating (158.3). He finished the season with twenty-seven touchdowns and only two interceptions, which was then the best touchdown-to-interception ratio in league history. He also led the NFL in passer rating (119.2), touchdown percentage (8.5) and yards per attempt (9.1).

Foles's performance helped guide the Eagles back to the play-offs, where they narrowly lost to the Saints in the first round. Foles was selected to his first Pro Bowl in 2014 and won the game's MVP honors after throwing for eighty-nine yards and a touchdown. The quarterback's sudden success, meanwhile, led to much talk of his future. Kelly even humorously addressed the speculation that Foles presented the future of the franchise by quipping that he would be the Eagles' quarterback "for the next thousand years."

DISCARDED JOURNEYMAN

Quips aside, Foles became the Eagles' clear-cut starter for the 2014 season after Vick left the team in free agency. Foles played in just eight games, however, before being sidelined the rest of the season with a broken collarbone. Though the Eagles went 6–2 in his starts, Foles failed to duplicate his success from the previous year and put up inconsistent numbers, throwing thirteen touchdowns and ten interceptions.

Foles's first tenure with the Eagles ended abruptly in March 2015, when he was unceremoniously traded to the St. Louis Rams in exchange for quarterback Sam Bradford. Shocked by the move, Foles struggled in his one season with the Rams. He threw ten interceptions and just seven touchdowns in eleven games during the 2015 campaign, in which he was benched twice due to poor play. That off-season the Rams, who finished with a 7–9 record, selected quarterback Jared Goff with the first overall pick in the draft. In response, Foles requested and was granted his release from the team.

Disillusioned and frustrated, Foles considered retiring from the game. "I knew I could still play . . . I just did not like football," he explained in an interview with his childhood friend Laura Bassett for *HuffPost* (2 May 2018). "I'd had enough. I'd lost the joy." Foles had a change of heart, however, after receiving words of encouragement from Reid. His former coach offered him a roster spot with the Kansas City Chiefs, where Reid had landed after being jettisoned by the Eagles. Foles signed a one-year contract with the Chiefs to serve as the backup quarterback, ultimately seeing action in just three games in 2016.

EAGLES REUNION

Despite his backup role, Foles would later claim that his time with the Chiefs helped restore his love for football. Upon becoming a free agent in 2017 he returned to the Eagles, signing a two-year, $11 million deal as a backup and veteran mentor for franchise quarterback Carson Wentz, the second overall pick in the 2016 draft. Foles was lured back to the team by second-year head coach Doug Pederson, himself a former NFL journeyman signal-caller, who had been the Eagles' quarterbacks coach in 2012.

Under the steady guidance of Pederson and the MVP-caliber play of Wentz, the Eagles opened the 2017 season in dominant fashion, winning ten of their first twelve games. Their season was thrown into jeopardy, however, when Wentz tore the anterior cruciate ligament (ACL) in his left knee in week fourteen, ending his campaign. Foles took over as starting quarterback, and the Eagles managed to win two of their final three games and secure the top playoff seed in the National Football Conference (NFC) with a 13–3 record. His uneven play in those games, however, fostered skepticism about the team's lofty postseason aspirations.

Undaunted, Foles helped the Eagles overcome the Atlanta Falcons and Minnesota Vikings, respectively, in the divisional play-off round and NFC Championship Game. The victories advanced the team to Super Bowl LII. "In sports, everything's a process, and you can't give up," Foles told Graziano. "Everyone, when it's a bad outing, wants to be really critical. But no one in the locker room doubted me."

UNLIKELY SUPER BOWL HERO

The Eagles entered Super Bowl LII as heavy underdogs to the defending champion New England Patriots, led by superstar quarterback Tom Brady. Yet Foles remained confident and composed. "This game was a microcosm of [Foles's] career," Wetzel wrote. "Little expected, except by him. Overlooked when compared to the other guy. Nothing to lean on but himself, his faith and those around him."

The Eagles nonetheless pulled off an unlikely 41–33 upset to win their first-ever Super Bowl and first league title since 1960. Leading the way was Foles, who threw for 373 yards and three touchdowns. He also added a one-yard touchdown reception on a trick play that would earn a place in Super Bowl legend as the "Philly Special," making him the first player in Super Bowl history to both throw and catch a touchdown pass. Foles was named MVP of the game, in which the Eagles and Patriots combined for an astonishing 1,151 total yards, the most in any game in NFL history.

Once again, Foles's success brought speculation about his future. During the 2018 off-season, he agreed to terms on a reworked contract with the Eagles that gave him a raise and provided an option to remain with the team in 2019. Yet with Wentz set to be ready to start the season, Foles was slotted back into the backup position. Discussing his role with the Eagles, he admitted to Bassett that it was "humbling" to lose his starting job even after leading the team to a Super Bowl title. "But it's good for me," he added. "I'm learning a lot about myself and growing in ways I never could imagine."

PERSONAL LIFE

Foles met his wife, Tori Moore Foles, a standout collegiate volleyball player, while the two were attending the University of Arizona. The couple married in 2014 and had a daughter, Lily, in 2017. Known for his deep Christian faith, Foles at one time expressed a desire to become a youth pastor after his football career.

SUGGESTED READING

Foles, Nick. "How Nick Foles Got Back Up." Interview by Laura Bassett. *Huff-Post*, 14 May 2018, www.huffington-post.com/entry/nick-foles-nfl-friends_us_5ae8e4cee4b00f70f0ecef79. Accessed 2 May 2018.

Frank, Reuben. "Arizona Transfer Put Nick Foles on Path to Eagles." *NBC Sports Philadelphia*, 23 July 2014, www.nbcsports.com/philadelphia/philadelphia-eagles/arizona-transfer-put-nick-foles-path-eagles. Accessed 14 May 2018.

Graziano, Dan. "From Backup to Eagles' Lead Dog: Nick Foles Is Win Away from Super Bowl Glory." *ESPN*, 22 Jan. 2018, www.espn.com/blog/nflnation/post/_/id/267300/backup-to-philadelphia-eagles-lead-dog-nick-foles-is-win-away-from-super-bowl-glory. Accessed 14 May 2018.

Walker, Rod. "Former Baton Rouge Restaurant Owner Larry Foles One Proud Dad on Super Bowl Sunday." *The Advocate*, 3 Feb. 2018, www.theadvocate.com/baton_rouge/sports/article_1e2158c4-08c0-11e8-8141-57cadb-2168ba.html. Accessed 14 May 2018.

Wetzel, Dan. "The Rise of Nick Foles: How a Journeyman QB Became a Super Bowl Hero." *Yahoo! Sports*, 5 Feb. 2018, sports.yahoo.com/rise-nick-foles-journeyman-qb-became-super-bowl-hero-065920628.html. Accessed 14 May 2018.

—*Chris Cullen*

Susan Fowler

Date of birth: ca. 1991
Occupation: Software engineer

In the late fall of 2015, University of Pennsylvania (Penn) graduate Susan Fowler started a new job as a software engineer at the ride-sharing company Uber. She was thrilled to join the company, which presented itself as devoted to innovation and offered numerous intriguing challenges to its many software engineers. However, she soon found that the popular technology company was home to a systemic sexual harassment and discrimination problem and that employees who reported incidents to human resources—among them Fowler herself—faced stonewalling at best and blatant retaliation at worst. Although she quickly found a new job and left Uber after just over a year, she felt a responsibility to share her experiences with the wider world. "When someone has crossed the line you need to take action and make sure it doesn't happen again," she told Kathleen Chaykowski for *Forbes* (10 Apr. 2018).

In February 2017, Fowler published a lengthy blog post outlining her experiences with harassment at Uber and the numerous ways in which management and the company's human resources department failed to address and ultimately exacerbated the unethical, and at times illegal, treatment she and her fellow female engineers faced. The blog post drew significant attention to the culture at Uber, prompting multiple investigations that in turn resulted in nearly two dozen employees being fired and its chief executive officer resigning. After the shake-up at Uber, Fowler remained committed to addressing issues such as harassment in the workplace and shedding light on the questionable labor practices at many technology companies. "Sunlight is the best medicine, as we all know," she told Chaykowski. "I'm sure the company I used to belong to can tell you that."

EARLY LIFE AND EDUCATION

Susan Fowler was born around 1991. The second of seven children, she grew up in Yarnell, Arizona. Her father was a Pentecostal preacher who also worked as a payphone salesman and later as a high school teacher, while her mother homeschooled the children before returning to the workforce when Fowler was about thirteen years old. In a post to her early blog *Fledgling Physicist* (12 Dec. 2013), Fowler described her household as "a poor home where paying your own way and being self-sufficient were more important than getting a normal education." Indeed, the young Fowler demonstrated a level of self-sufficiency far beyond what is typically expected of a young teenager. While her younger siblings began attending public school after their mother went back to work, she began to work full time (often as a babysitter or ranch hand) and embarked on an attempt to homeschool herself, primarily by reading books on topics such as philosophy, history, and foreign languages. "I tried to read the classics, would go to the library a lot, tried to teach myself things," she recalled to Maureen Dowd for the *New York Times* (21 Oct. 2017). "But didn't really have any direction. I really had this dream that someday I could be educated." Having decided to pursue a college education, she applied to a variety of institutions, including Arizona State University (ASU). Despite her lack of formal education, her self-designed curriculum and strong standardized test scores earned her admission to ASU on a scholarship.

Enrolling in ASU in 2009, Fowler initially studied philosophy, a subject that had long fascinated her. She soon developed an interest in astronomy and physics but could not enroll in many of the courses she wanted to take, as she lacked the prerequisite high school–level math and science knowledge. She transferred to Penn in 2011 and resumed her fight to study physics, once again taking much of her education into her own hands. "I spent every minute of my days trying to learn everything I had never been able to learn from 6th–12th grade physics and math," she wrote for *Fledgling Physicist*. "I had the most difficult time possible taking intro physics and the beginning calculus courses. I kept going. I knew that if I was ever going to learn this stuff, I had to learn it now." In addition to launching her *Fledgling Physicist* blog during that period, she succeeded in gaining admission to Penn's physics program. She graduated in 2014.

UBER

After graduation, Fowler moved to California to pursue work in computer science. She spent several months each at the companies Plaid and PubNub, where she worked as an engineer. Then, she joined Uber, best known for its eponymous ride-sharing service, in November 2015. Upon beginning work there, she spent several weeks in training before being allowed to choose the team she wanted to join. She chose a site reliability engineering (SRE) team, as its projects were within her area of interest and expertise.

Fowler's experience at Uber took a disconcerting turn on her first day with the SRE team, when she received a series of inappropriate messages from her manager. "He was in an open relationship, he said, and his girlfriend was having an easy time finding new partners but he wasn't," she recalled in a post to her newer blog, *Susan Fowler* (19 Feb. 2017), titled "Reflecting on One Very, Very Strange Year at Uber." "It was clear that he was trying to get me to have sex with him, and it was so clearly out of line that I immediately took screenshots of these chat messages and reported him to [human resources]." She expected that the human resources department at a company as large as Uber would be equipped to handle an incident of blatant sexual harassment. However, the human resources professionals refused to punish the manager and told Fowler that she could either switch teams or remain on the SRE team and risk receiving a negative performance review from the manager in question, which they said would not be considered retaliation. Fowler also alerted higher-level managers of the issue, but they disregarded her concerns. She ultimately left the team and joined a new SRE team with a different manager.

Over her subsequent months at Uber, Fowler became aware of other instances of harassment and discrimination and realized that there was a systemic problem that contributed to a dramatic decrease in the number of female engineers at the company. Meanwhile, she continued to face discriminatory treatment herself: among other incidents, management blocked her request to transfer to another team, citing performance issues that were not supported by her perfect performance score. She continued to be denied and even had a positive performance review negatively changed despite her efforts and accomplishments, which included writing the book *Production-Ready Microservices*, published by O'Reilly Media in 2016. After she reported additional incidents to human resources, her manager told her that if she reported anything else she would be fired, a threat that violated the law. Within a week, she received an offer for a new job outside of Uber, with the online payments start-up Stripe. She left Uber in December 2016, just over a year after she was first hired.

WHISTLE-BLOWER

Although Fowler had started a new job as founding editor in chief of the Stripe publication *Increment* in January 2017, she remained troubled by what she and her fellow female employees had experienced at Uber. She ultimately chose to discuss her experiences publicly in the hope of calling attention to the toxic culture present at Uber and other technology companies. "I knew I had to be super-careful about how I said it if I wanted anybody to take it seriously. A lot of women have been whistle-blowers in the past, and a lot of them have just gotten torn down and treated terribly," she told Dowd. Despite such worries, she remained determined to speak out. "If what people know you for is bringing light to an issue about bad behavior, about bad stuff going on and laws not being followed and people being treated inappropriately, why wouldn't I want that? That's a badge of honor," she explained to Dowd. "And I wasn't just

standing up for myself. I felt like I was standing up for everyone else that I was seeing at Uber who was mistreated."

In February 2017, Fowler published the nearly three-thousand-word blog post titled "Reflecting on One Very, Very Strange Year at Uber," in which she documented the discrimination and harassment she experienced at Uber. News of the blog post spread, and her story soon became the topic of discussion throughout the technology world and beyond. Considering her experiences, Uber launched two investigations into the culture at the company, and at least twenty Uber employees were eventually fired. The company's chief executive officer, Travis Kalanick, was likewise forced to step down from his position, as he had become closely linked with the discriminatory culture at Uber and was at times accused of perpetuating it. Coinciding with widespread discussions about sexual harassment throughout media and society, including the #MeToo movement, the events surrounding Uber had a significance that extended far beyond a single company.

IMPACT

After publishing her blog post, Fowler became the center of significant attention, and some publications and organizations praised her for her work in publicizing her experiences. Identified as one of the Silence Breakers who spoke out about sexual harassment and assault, she was recognized as one of *Time* magazine's people of the year for 2017. She was likewise named person of the year by the *Financial Times* and included on *Politico Magazine*'s list "50 Ideas Blowing Up American Politics (and the People behind Them)." She has sought to use her new-found platform to speak out against other abuses taking place within large technology companies, most notably forced arbitration, a policy that prevents workers from taking their current or former employers to court. "They [companies] know exactly how much it will take to get you to sign away your right to get you not to talk about your experience," she told Chaykowski about the issue. "It's corrupt, it's cruel and it ends up covering all of these problems up for years until again someone says, 'I don't care. Bring it on.'"

After leaving Uber, Fowler also served as an adviser for AllVoices, a tool enabling employees to report harassment or other issues anonymously. A longtime blogger, she further established herself as a writer, signing a contract to write a memoir in late 2017 and selling the film rights to her story to the production company Good Universe. Her career evolved further in July 2018, when she was hired as the new California-based technology opinion editor for the *New York Times*. In that role, she would be "responsible for commissioning—and sometimes writing—pieces on all the ways technology is shaping our culture, economy, relationships, politics, and play" and "bring[ing] her unique brand of courage, clarity of mind, and moral purpose" to the publication, according to a *New York Times* press release quoted by Avery Hartmans in *Business Insider* (23 July 2018). Fowler was set to begin her new role in September of that year.

PERSONAL LIFE

Fowler began dating her future husband, Chad Rigetti, in early 2016. Rigetti heads the California-based quantum-computing company Rigetti Computing. They live in Berkeley, California, with their daughter, Seymour. For Fowler, who was sometimes referred to as Susan Fowler Rigetti following her marriage, the birth of her child only increased her resolve to continue addressing issues of sexual harassment and discrimination in the workplace. "Now I'm just like, 'Got to make this world better so she doesn't have to deal with these things,'" she told Dowd.

SUGGESTED READING

Chaykowski, Kathleen. "Uber Whistleblower Susan Fowler on What Every Company Should Do to Stop Harassment." *Forbes*, 10 Apr. 2018, www.forbes.com/sites/kathleenchaykowski/2018/04/10/uber-whistleblower-susan-fowler-on-what-every-company-should-do-to-stop-harassment/#2bdec9a7384a. Accessed 10 Aug. 2018.

Dowd, Maureen. "She's 26, and Brought Down Uber's C.E.O. What's Next?" *The New York Times*, 21 Oct. 2017, www.nytimes.com/2017/10/21/style/susan-fowler-uber.html. Accessed 10 Aug. 2018.

Fowler, Susan. "If Susan Can Learn Physics, So Can You." *Fledgling Physicist*, 12 Dec. 2013, fledglingphysicist.com/2013/12/12/if-susan-can-learn-physics-so-can-you. Accessed 10 Aug. 2018.

Fowler, Susan. "Reflecting on One Very, Very Strange Year at Uber." *Susan Fowler*, 19 Feb. 2017, www.susanjfowler.com/blog/2017/2/19/reflecting-on-one-very-strange-year-at-uber. Accessed 10 Aug. 2018.

Hartmans, Avery. "The Engineer Who Blew the Whistle on Uber's Culture of Sexual Harassment Was Just Hired by the *New York Times*." *Business Insider*, 23 July 2018, www.businessinsider.com/uber-whistleblower-susan-fowler-rigetti-hired-new-york-times-tech-opinion-editor-2018-7. Accessed 10 Aug. 2018.

Levin, Sam. "Susan Fowler's Plan after Uber? Tear Down the System That Protects Harassers." *The Guardian*, 11 Apr. 2018, www.theguardian.com/technology/2018/apr/11/susan-fowler-uber-interview-forced-arbitration-law. Accessed 10 Aug. 2018.

—*Joy Crelin*

Sylvia Fowles

Date of birth: October 6, 1985
Occupation: Basketball player

"I hate being the focal point of a team sport," basketball player Sylvia Fowles told Seth Berkman for the *New York Times* (12 Sept. 2017). Indeed, as a child she was resistant to the idea of playing basketball at all, joining a team in eighth grade only after being encouraged by her mother and a prospective coach. Her talent for the sport was impossible to ignore, and an impressive high school career as well as four successful seasons with Louisiana State University's Lady Tigers made Fowles a focal point whether she liked it or not. Drafted into the Women's National Basketball Association (WNBA) in 2008, the six-feet-six center quickly established herself as a key member of the Chicago Sky and went on to excel as part of the Minnesota Lynx, to which she was traded in 2015.

Despite her success with the Sky and the Lynx, Fowles generally views herself as comparable to any other player. "I don't see myself doing too much different, except being consistent and being dominant," she told Berkman. Her fans, teammates, and coaches, however, have disagreed with Fowles's self-assessment, identifying her as one of the most significant players in the league. In recognition of her strong performance on the court, Fowles was named the WNBA's Most Valuable Player (MVP) in 2017.

By SusanLesch, via Wikimedia Commons

EARLY LIFE AND EDUCATION

Sylvia Shaqueria Fowles was born in Miami, Florida, on October 6, 1985. She grew up in Miami-Dade County, where she lived with her mother, Arrittio, and four older siblings. As a child, Fowles was exposed to basketball primarily through her older brothers, who played casual games with neighborhood friends. She quickly learned that the game could be harsh, particularly when her brother Morris was playing. "He'd see when I was about to cry and he'd tell me, 'I'll send you home if you cry,'" she recalled to Brian Kotloff for the *WNBA.com* (14 Oct. 2016). "I used to have to straighten out my act real quick and just suck it up and go out there to finish the game." Despite her early experiences with basketball, Fowles avoided playing the sport competitively as a child, instead trying out sports such as track and volleyball.

When Fowles was in middle school, a local basketball coach sought to convince her to join his basketball team and won the support of her mother, who encouraged Fowles to consider playing. She began playing basketball in eighth grade, playing on youth teams such as the Miami Suns, an Amateur Athletic Union (AAU) team. Fowles joined her school team while attending Miami Edison High School and continued playing after transferring to the Gulliver Preparatory School, earning state titles for both teams. She graduated from Gulliver Prep in 2004.

COLLEGE CAREER

As a successful high school player, Fowles was recruited to join various college-level basketball programs. While visiting Louisiana State University (LSU), she met LSU Lady Tigers guard Seimone Augustus, who was two years ahead of Fowles in school. Augustus, who hosted Fowles during her visit, was surprised by Fowles's calm demeanor—and her hobby of knitting. "She just sat there with her knit kit and knitted this sweater for the coaches," Augustus told Kotloff. "But then once she got to LSU and we actually got on the floor and played together, I'm like, 'Yo, totally different person.'" The two players became close friends, and their friendship would endure throughout years of playing for competing professional teams.

Having decided to attend and play basketball for LSU, Fowles enrolled in the university as a general studies major. With the LSU Lady Tigers, one of the many National Collegiate Athletic Association (NCAA) teams playing within the competitive Division I, Fowles had a highly successful college career, playing in the Final Four of the NCAA championship each year. During her time at LSU, Fowles set records for a variety of different statistics, including total number of points, rebounds, and blocked shots. She was recognized with various honors over the course of her college career, including being named to the 2008 All-America Team and selected as the Southeastern Conference's player of the week on multiple occasions. Considering her many contributions to LSU's basketball program, the university retired Fowles's jersey, number 34, in the fall of 2017.

CHICAGO SKY

In the spring of 2008, Fowles was selected as the second overall pick in the WNBA draft. Chosen by the Chicago Sky, she joined the team that year, playing in seventeen games over the course of the 2008 season. During the next several seasons, Fowles played in most of the Sky's regular-season games and tallied impressive statistics. She led the league in field goals and two-point field goals in 2011, in blocks in 2010 and 2011, and in total rebounds in 2013. Fowles signed a three-year contract with the Sky in 2012.

The year 2013 saw Fowles hit a new career milestone, advancing to her first WNBA playoffs during the postseason. Although the team was eliminated by the Indiana Fever in the conference semifinals, the experience was a significant one for Fowles, who would go on to make numerous appearances in the playoffs. The Sky performed better during the following postseason, defeating the Atlanta Dream and the Fever in the conference semifinals and finals, respectively. The team then moved on to the WNBA Finals, the Sky's first, but ultimately lost to the Phoenix Mercury.

MINNESOTA LYNX

Fowles spent seven productive seasons with the Sky, but by 2015, she found herself wanting to explore new opportunities. "I thought about how Chicago has come a long way . . . and how blessed I've been to be in Chicago for seven seasons, but that still didn't override me wanting to do new things," she told Patricia Babcock McGraw for the *Daily Herald* (8 May 2015). "I want to do something different." She requested to be traded to another team and announced that she planned to sit out the 2015 season if she was not traded.

In July 2015, the Chicago Sky's management announced that Fowles had been traded to the Minnesota Lynx. Fowles was thrilled to have been traded to the Lynx, for which Augustus had played since being drafted in 2006, and described the day of the trade as "the happiest day of [her] life," as quoted by Kotloff. Joining the team for the 2015 season, Fowles played in eighteen games during the regular season and achieved top-ten rebound percentages and field goal percentages despite her limited number of games. In her first postseason with the Lynx, Fowles played in ten games as the team moved past the Los Angeles Sparks and the Mercury to enter the WNBA Finals. The team beat the Fever 3–2, earning Fowles her first championship—and the WNBA Finals MVP award.

MOST VALUABLE PLAYER

Fowles was a major contributor to the Lynx during the 2016 and 2017 seasons, leading the league in two-point field goals, offensive rebounds, and blocks in 2017. The Lynx again advanced to the WNBA Finals in 2016 but were defeated by the Sparks, 3–2. After the Lynx lost the 2016 championship, the team's coach, Cheryl Reeve, encouraged Fowles—primarily a defensive player—to place more emphasis on offense. Fowles had sought to avoid "stepping on anybody's toes" upon joining the team, as she told Pat Borzi for *ESPN* (22 June 2017). However, Reeve's advice changed her outlook significantly. "She wanted me to step up and wanted me to be me and not worry about anything else," Fowles told Borzi.

During the 2017 season, Fowles took Reeve's encouragement to heart and recorded a strong performance that included an average of 18.9 points, 10.4 rebounds, and 2.0 blocks per game. Following the season, the Lynx returned to the playoffs and advanced to the WNBA Finals for the third consecutive year, this time achieving a 3–2 victory against the Sparks. Fowles played a key role in the 2017 playoffs, playing a total of 283 minutes and scoring 65 field goals, 105 rebounds, and 16 blocks. Based on her performance during the regular season and the playoffs, Fowles was named the WNBA's most valuable player for 2017. Having previously signed a two-year deal with the Lynx in 2016, Fowles signed an additional multiyear contract extension with the team that year. "It was a no-brainer," she said, as quoted by John Altavilla for the *Hartford Courant* (16 Sept. 2017. "I wanted to be here. And this is where I plan on being until I'm done."

INTERNATIONAL SUCCESS

In addition to playing on high school, college, and WNBA teams, Fowles represented the United States internationally while in college, competing as a member of the US Senior National Team. After beginning her professional career, she played for international teams during the WNBA's off season, a common practice among professional American players. Fowles has played with the Turkish team Samsun Canik Belediye and went on to play several off-seasons with China's Beijing Great Wall.

Fowles has also competed as a member of the US national women's basketball team in three consecutive Olympic Games. The team earned a gold medal during Fowles's Olympic debut at the 2008 games in Beijing and repeated that accomplishment in London, England, in 2012 and Rio de Janeiro, Brazil, in 2016. Although the US women's team was a favorite to win, Fowles calls attention to the hard work she and her teammates—and the members of the competing teams—put in. "It always looked as if we dominated from the outside but it is always a struggle," she said in an interview for the International Basketball Federation (*FIBA.com*) website (22 Aug. 2008). "Nothing is easy. Every team we have played has always given us a run."

PERSONAL LIFE

Although committed to additional seasons with the Lynx, Fowles has also put thought into her future career following her eventual retirement from basketball. She is working on an online degree in mortuary sciences from the American Academy McAllister Institute in New York, having had an interest in that field since childhood. In addition to basketball, she enjoys knitting, sewing, and drawing. She is active in a variety of charities, including the Sylvia Fowles Family Fund and Citizens United for Research in Epilepsy. Fowles owns a home in Cutler Bay, Florida.

SUGGESTED READING

Altavilla, John. "Sylvia Fowles: A Worthy WNBA MVP." *Hartford Courant*, 16 Sept. 2017, www.courant.com/sports/basketball/hc-wnba-playoffs-sylvia-fowles-0917-20170916-story.html. Accessed 12 Nov. 2017.

Berkman, Seth. "Sylvia Fowles, WNBA Star and Aspiring Funeral Director." *The New York Times*, 12 Sept. 2017, www.nytimes.com/2017/09/12/sports/basketball/wnba-sylvia-fowles-lynx.html. Accessed 12 Nov. 2017.

Borzi, Pat. "Minnesota's Sylvia Fowles Is the Frontrunner for WNBA MVP." *ESPN*, 22 June 2017, www.espn.com/wnba/story/_/id/19692223/minnesota-lynx-sylvia-fowles-frontrunner-wnba-mvp. Accessed 12 Nov. 2017.

Fowles, Sylvia. "USA—Fowles: 'It Looked as If We Dominated from Outside but It Is Always a Struggle." Interview. *FIBA*, 22 Aug. 2008, www.fiba.basketball/pages/eng/fe/08/olym/wom/news/inte/p/newsid/28329/FE_news_inteArti.html. Accessed 12 Nov. 2017.

Kotloff, Brian. "Meet Sylvia Fowles, Minnesota's Gentle Giant." *WNBA*, 14 Oct. 2016, www.wnba.com/news/sylvia-fowles-minnesota-lynx-wnba-finals-101416/. Accessed 12 Nov. 2017.

McGraw, Patricia Babcock. "Fowles Shocks Sky with Demand to Be Traded." *Daily Herald*, 8 May 2015, www.dailyherald.com/article/20150508/sports/150508775/. Accessed 12 Nov. 2017.

"Sylvia Fowles Donating Part of MVP Bonus to Cycles for Change." *ESPN*, 22 Sept. 2017,

www.espn.com/wnba/story/_/id/20781552/
sylvia-fowles-minnesota-lynx-donating-some-
wnba-mvp-bonus-cycles-change. Accessed 12
Nov. 2017.

—Joy Crelin

Shelly-Ann Fraser-Pryce

Date of birth: December 27, 1986
Occupation: Runner

When sprinter Shelly-Ann Fraser-Pryce qualified to compete for Jamaica at the 2008 Summer
Olympic Games in Beijing, China, many in the
world of track and field were surprised by her
apparent rise from obscurity. A longtime athlete who had competed extensively since high
school, Fraser-Pryce was ranked seventieth in
the world in her sport but was not yet considered
a potential Olympic contender. By the time of
the Olympics, however, she defied all naysayers
to claim a gold medal in the women's 100-meter
event at the games.

Over the subsequent years, Fraser-Pryce
made a name for herself as one of Jamaica's best
sprinters, winning gold medals at the IAAF (International Association of Athletics Federations)
World Championships in 2009, 2013, and 2015.
Upon her return to the Olympics in 2012, she
claimed an additional gold medal as well as two
silvers, and her performance in the relay and
100-meter events garnered her an additional silver and bronze in 2016. Although Fraser-Pryce
took a break from competing in 2017 while expecting her first child, she has made it very clear
that her previous accomplishments are just the
beginning. "I'm extremely hungry and wanting to
get back out there," she told Hubert Lawrence
for the *Gleaner* (10 Feb. 2018), "and I still think
there's a lot more to give."

EARLY LIFE AND EDUCATION

Fraser-Pryce was born Shelly-Ann Fraser in
Kingston, Jamaica, on December 27, 1986. She
grew up in Waterhouse, a low-income area of
Kingston with a reputation as a hotbed of violent crime. Fraser-Pryce spent much of her early
life living with her two brothers and her mother,
Maxine, who worked as a street vendor. Fraser-
Pryce has credited her mother's influence as well
as her involvement in athletics with helping her
overcome the challenges of her childhood. "I
didn't become just another Waterhouse statistic
but someone who could uplift the community,
who showed something good could come from
anywhere in Jamaica. Even the ghetto," she explained to Ian Chadband for the *Telegraph* (29
Oct. 2009).

By Arian Zwegers, via Wikimedia Commons

As a child, Fraser-Pryce demonstrated a talent for track and field, and she began competing by the age of ten. She competed extensively
in high school and under-eighteen events while
attending the Wolmer's High School for Girls
in Kingston, establishing herself as a talented
sprinter. After graduating from high school, she
enrolled in the University of Technology, Jamaica, to study child and adolescent development. She completed her degree in 2012 and
was named the university's official ambassador.
Fraser-Pryce later announced plans to pursue a
master's degree at the University of the West Indies and in 2016 was awarded an honorary doctorate from the university.

EARLY CAREER

After high school, Fraser-Pryce began working
with coach Stephen Francis, who has remained
her coach ever since. She trained primarily at
the MVP Track and Field Club in Kingston, a
facility known for producing many successful
Jamaican athletes. By 2007, she was competing
regularly in a variety of running events in international competition, including the 100-meter,
200-meter, and 4×100 relay events. In 2008,
she competed in numerous countries in addition
to Jamaica, including the United States, Brazil,
Italy, and Germany.

Although ranked seventieth in the world
among female sprinters prior to the 2008 national Olympic trials, Fraser-Pryce was not initially
regarded as a potential member of the Jamaican Olympic team, which observers expected
would include 2007 world champion Veronica

Campbell-Brown. However, Fraser-Pryce beat Campbell-Brown in the 100-meter event in the Olympic trials, placing among the top three sprinters in the event and earning the right to compete in that event at the Olympics. "A lot of people didn't want me to run, they said I was too young. But I didn't let it faze me that much," she told Anna Kessel for the UK *Observer* (8 May 2010). "I just knew I had to run because the rules guaranteed me a place on the team. I actually got a lot more determination because of it."

OLYMPIC DEBUT

In the summer of 2008, Fraser-Pryce traveled to Beijing, China, where she competed in both the women's 100-meter sprint event and the 4×100-meter relay at the Summer Olympic Games. Although the Jamaican team failed in the relay, Fraser-Pryce achieved an impressive performance from the start of the 100-meter competition, achieving a time of 11.35 seconds in the first round of the competition. She managed times of 11.06 and 11.00 in the quarterfinals and semifinals, respectively, and in the final round, Fraser-Pryce beat fellow Jamaican sprinters Sherone Simpson and Kerron Stewart to win the gold medal with a time of 10.78 seconds (Simpson and Stewart tied for silver). Fraser-Pryce was the first Jamaican woman to win the gold medal in the 100-meter sprint event, a milestone that was especially meaningful due to her relative inexperience in international competition and the public's initial reaction to her inclusion on the team.

Upon her return to Jamaica, Fraser-Pryce found herself suddenly a celebrity, having overcome adversity to claim one of the six gold medals won by Jamaican athletes during the 2008 games. She was particularly stunned to see that someone had painted her portrait on a wall in her childhood neighborhood of Waterhouse. "I was so shocked," she recalled to Kessel. "The only time they draw people on the wall where we live is when they're dead."

WORLD CHAMPION

Following her success at the Beijing Olympics, Fraser-Pryce continued to compete in Jamaica and abroad, achieving impressive results at competitions in Switzerland, Monaco, Italy, and Germany. At the 2008 IAAF World Athletics Final, held in September in Stuttgart, Germany, Fraser-Pryce placed first in the women's 100-meter event, with a time of 10.94 seconds. A year later, she represented Jamaica at the IAAF World Championships in Berlin, Germany, competing in the 100-meter and relay events. She contributed to the Jamaican team's gold-medal finish in the relay and also claimed an individual gold in the 100-meter event, achieving a time of 10.73 seconds in the final round.

Although she and her fellow female sprinters performed strongly at the World Championships and other competitions, Fraser-Pryce found that they did not receive nearly as much media attention as Jamaica's male athletes, including the highly successful sprinter Usain Bolt. "A lot of females don't get the recognition men do in track and field and that's weird," she told Kessel. "We work just as hard as them, we might not be breaking world records because they're so out of reach but we're still doing great things." Fraser-Pryce continued to work hard over the subsequent years, claiming gold medals in the 100-meter, 200-meter, and relay events at the IAAF World Championships in Moscow, Russia, in 2013. Two years later, she claimed her third gold medal in the 100-meter event at the World Championships in Beijing, completing the sprint in 10.76 seconds, 0.05 seconds ahead of silver medalist Dafne Schippers. She also helped win the Jamaican women's team's gold medal in the 4×100 relay for the third time. Asked about her experiences at the World Championships, Fraser-Pryce attributed her success to her intense training. "It's about hard work. It's about training through pain. It's about sacrifices," she explained to Sean Ingle for the *Guardian* (24 Aug. 2015).

RETURN TO THE OLYMPICS

Fraser-Pryce returned to the Summer Olympics in 2012, qualifying to participate in the 100-meter as well as the 200-meter and relay events at that year's games in London, England. She claimed a silver medal in the 200-meter race, finishing 0.21 second behind American sprinter Allyson Felix, and the Jamaican relay team itself took second place behind the United States. However, Fraser-Pryce once again dominated the 100-meter, overcoming American runner Carmelita Jeter and Jamaican teammate Campbell-Brown to claim the gold with a time of 10.75 in the final round.

Although Fraser-Pryce suffered a toe injury in 2016 that affected her performance, she nevertheless traveled to her third Olympic Games in the summer of that year, competing in the 100-meter and relay events in Rio de Janeiro, Brazil. Although the competition proved less successful for the athlete than her previous Olympic outings due in part to her injury, she nevertheless won a bronze medal in the 100-meter event and was pleased to see Jamaican teammate Elaine Thompson claim the gold in that race. Fraser-Pryce and her fellow members of the relay team likewise claimed a silver medal, placing second behind the United States. "Rio finally taught me who I was," Fraser-Pryce told Liam Flint for *Cross the Line* of her experience. "In life not everything is about us, it's about the people that we inspire."

MOVING FORWARD

In March of 2017, Fraser-Pryce announced that she would not be competing in the 2017 running season due to her pregnancy. "My focus heading into training for my 2017 season was on getting healthy and putting myself in the best possible fitness to successfully defend my [world 100-meter] title in London2017," she wrote on Facebook, as quoted by Nick Zaccardi for *NBC Sports* (8 Mar. 2017). "Moving forward on this journey, I look forward to seeing you all in 2018 when I return to competition." She resumed training in October 2017 and planned to return to competition in 2018.

In addition to running, Fraser-Pryce operates the Pocket Rocket Foundation, which provides high school scholarships to deserving student athletes. She also opened a café, Shelly's Café, on the University of Technology campus as well as launching a hair salon and the hair-care line Lady Shelly. "I am passionate about all of these things and am just one of those people who, if I say I am going to do something, I will give it one hundred and ten percent," she told Flint.

PERSONAL LIFE

Fraser-Pryce met her husband, Jason Pryce, while accompanying his sprinter friend Asafa Powell to a training session at the University of Technology. The couple married in 2011, and their son Zyon was born in August 2017.

In addition to her efforts on the track, Fraser-Pryce seeks to inspire her fellow Jamaicans to follow their dreams and avoid the pitfalls that could prevent their success. "It's Jamaican women and children who are my inspiration," she told Chadband. "I try to be an example for them, that they can still succeed. I can try to talk to them; finish high school, don't get pregnant at a young age, don't be hanging out on the streets. Just do your schoolwork, focus on a sport if you're good at it, do what I did."

SUGGESTED READING

Chadband, Ian. "Shelly-Ann Fraser's Rise from Poverty to One of the World's Best Sprinters Is Remarkable." *Telegraph*, 29 Oct. 2009, www.telegraph.co.uk/sport/olympics/6462382/Shelly-Ann-Frasers-rise-from-poverty-to-one-of-the-worlds-best-sprinters-is-remarkable.html. Accessed 9 Mar. 2018.

Fraser-Pryce, Shelly-Ann. "Jamaican Sprinter, Shelly-Ann Fraser-Pryce: 'I Had Never Dreamed That I Would Be an Olympian.'" Interview with Liam Flint. *Cross the Line*, www.xtheline.co.uk/shelly-ann-fraser-pryce/. Accessed 9 Mar. 2018.

Ingle, Sean. "Shelly-Ann Fraser-Pryce Powers to Third World Championships 100m Gold." *The Guardian*, 24 Aug. 2015, www.theguardian.com/sport/2015/aug/24/shelly-ann-fraser-pryce-wins-world-100m-gold. Accessed 9 Mar. 2018.

Kessel, Anna. "Olympic Champion Shelly-Ann Fraser Makes Fast Work of Fame Game." *Observer*, 8 May 2010, www.theguardian.com/sport/2010/may/09/shelly-anne-fraser-olympic-champion. Accessed 9 Mar. 2018.

Lawrence, Hubert. "Still Extremely Hungry—Fraser-Pryce." *Gleaner*, 10 Feb. 2018, jamaica-gleaner.com/article/sports/20180210/still-extremely-hungry-fraser-pryce. Accessed 9 Mar. 2018.

Williams, Ollie. "Rio 2016: Can Shelly-Ann Fraser-Pryce Beat Usain Bolt to Olympic History?" *CNN*, 18 July 2016, www.cnn.com/2016/07/18/sport/rio-2016-usain-bolt-fraser-pryce/index.html. Accessed 9 Mar. 2018.

Zaccardi, Nick. "Shelly-Ann Fraser-Pryce Announces Pregnancy." *NBC Sports*, 8 Mar. 2017, olympics.nbcsports.com/2017/03/08/shelly-ann-fraser-pryce-pregnant/. Accessed 9 Mar. 2018.

—Joy Crelin

Emily Fridlund

Date of birth: 1979
Occupation: Author

Emily Fridlund never expected to be nominated for the Man Booker Prize, one of the most prestigious literary awards given to works of English-language literature. Nevertheless, her debut novel, *History of Wolves* (2017), made its way first onto the Man Booker longlist and then onto the shortlist, alongside such literary heavyweights as Paul Auster and George Saunders. The novel's success elevated Fridlund's profile considerably; prior to the book's publication she had been quietly publishing her short fiction in literary journals for more than a decade. Since the publication of *History of Wolves*, however, her work has become more in demand. A collection of her short fiction was published under the title of *Catapult* in late 2017. That book also met with critical acclaim.

The thing that remains most remarkable about Fridlund—she is known for tight language and often dark takes on modern life in America—is that she hardly ever thinks about publication as she writes. She does not even outline. Language for her is a rhythm, and from that rhythm, she follows one sentence to the next until her story is complete. "So much of the writing process is sitting quietly in a chair, or wandering around outside," Fridlund said in an interview with Laurie Hertzel for the

Sydney Morning Herald (28 Sept. 2017). "It's such a quiet process, so internal and private. The vast majority of the time I didn't think about publication."

EARLY LIFE AND EDUCATION

The second of three children, Emily Fridlund was born in 1979 and grew up in Edina, Minnesota, a comfortable suburban town. She and her siblings lived next door to the house her grandfather built. An outdoorsy family, the Fridlunds spent many of their vacations on the North Shore of Lake Superior, where they often went camping. These vacations helped to form much of the backdrop to Fridlund's first novel.

Fridlund had loved the idea of being a writer ever since she was a little girl. In an interview for *SmokeLong Quarterly* (15 Sept. 2007), Fridlund recalled, "I suppose I'm one of those people who has been writing (generally badly) since I was arranging the furniture in my dollhouse, and perhaps because of this, calling myself a writer still feels awkward, even a little shameful—like admitting I play with dolls or toys, or worse, asking to be respected for taking my dolls so seriously."

She did her undergraduate work at two colleges, first at St. Olaf College in Minnesota, then at Principia College in Illinois, where she earned her bachelor's degree. She then studied fiction writing at the master of fine arts (MFA) program at Washington University in St. Louis. The experience proved transformative, particularly through her studies with the writers Marshall Klimasewiski and Kellie Wells. Fridlund told *SmokeLong Quarterly* that Klimasewiski and Wells "are both remarkable writers, stalking their separate fascinations in precise and often startling prose." Washington University's visiting writers program also gave Fridlund the opportunity to work for a shorter time with writers such as Peter Ho Davies and Joy Williams. She completed her MFA in 2004.

During this period of her life, she began publishing her own fiction in a number of literary journals, including the *Boston Review*, the *New Orleans Review*, *Quick Fiction*, *The Portland Review*, and *Beloit Poetry Journal*. She also taught, and spent a year teaching writing in Dalian, China. When she came back to the United States, she spent some time living in New Jersey, then moved to California, where she enrolled in a doctoral program at the University of Southern California. In 2014 she earned her PhD in literature and creative writing. She also continued to publish in literary journals, including *ZYZZYVA*, the *Southwest Review*, *FiveChapters*, and *Sou'wester*, among others.

HISTORY OF WOLVES

Fridlund's debut novel, *History of Wolves* (2017), began its life as a short story that she wrote in California one winter, thinking of how much she missed the snow in Minnesota, and particularly the North Woods. An invented town came to mind, in which lived a teenaged girl named Linda. "History of Wolves" won the 2013 McGinnis-Ritchie Award for Fiction. When the story was completed, Fridlund thought she was done with it, but after a time she found herself being drawn back to Linda's life in rural Minnesota and began to expand upon the original idea.

In the novel, readers are introduced to a first-person narrator named Linda. Linda tells her story both as a teenager who is raised in a now-defunct commune outside a small town in Minnesota and as a thirty-seven-year-old woman who has not gotten over either the tragic incidents that occurred so many years ago. When the story begins, Linda is not entirely sure if the people who are raising her are her parents or just the people who remained behind when the commune collapsed. Her peers think she's weird and call her "Commie" and "Freak." Linda, friendless and unsure of herself, takes to her new history teacher, Mr. Grierson, in part because of his efforts to seem cool to his students, but also because of the rumors that he is in a sexual relationship with one of her classmates, Lily. Curious, Linda manages to get Mr. Grierson to offer a ride to her and awkwardly attempts to seduce him. Later, Mr. Grierson is arrested for possession of child pornography. Then when a new family moves in across the lake from where Linda lives, she watches them through a telescope. Eventually she gets to know them: Patra, the mother; Paul, the four-year-old son; and Leo, the father, who is something of a mysterious presence. Linda becomes close to Patra and Paul and begins to babysit Paul. From them she learns that Patra is younger than her husband and is editing his manuscripts on astrophysics, and that Paul often talks about God, almost as if he is in a trance. Linda soon learns that much of Paul's talk has its origins in his father's belief in Christian Science.

The novel earned considerable acclaim upon its release and was shortlisted for the prestigious Man Booker Prize, one of the most respected literary awards for English-language writers, which carries a stipend of £50,000 (about US$65,000 in 2018). In a review for *NPR* (3 Jan. 2017), Michael Schaub called the novel "electrifying" and wrote: "The book doesn't follow the now-familiar narrative arc that other novels in the genre do. There's no moment of revelation at the end; if anything, the protagonist ends up more confused than she was at the beginning. Fridlund refuses to obey the conventions that her sometimes hidebound colleagues do, and her novel is so much the better for it."

Other reviewers, however, were less than enthusiastic. In a review for the *Irish Times* (14 Oct. 2017), Sarah Gilmartin wrote that "the novel's intensity [is] diluted by its two story strains. . . . But while the two plots might lessen the power of their individual stories, they work well in juxtaposition to highlight the novel's themes, namely the arbitrary nature of justice and the difference between action and thought." Jennifer Senior, for the *New York Times* (4 Jan. 2017), was more critical, writing that "'History of Wolves' contains the kernels of many possible novels, with lots of larger ideas to plumb . . . [but] all the ideas in the world can't make a great novel. It's what you do with them that matters."

CATAPULT

After the success of her debut novel, Fridlund published a slim collection of her short fiction, titled *Catapult*, in late 2017. The collection won the Mary McCarthy Prize in Short Fiction. The eleven stories were selected from the number of short stories that she had published over the years and provided readers with an insight into characters who are often dislocated from the worlds in which they live. Fridlund's language is often precise and quick, using a few details to flesh out personalities or circumstances. Among the characters who make up this collection are a childless woman, a teenage girl looking to lose her virginity, a woman who does not much care for her best friend, a man who has been deserted by his wife, and families upended by difficulties.

The collection was widely praised in literary circles. In her review for the *Atlantic* (Jan./Feb. 2018), Ann Hulbert called *Catapult* a "new dynamic collection of short stories [that revel] in discomfort and disorientation." A critic for *Kirkus Reviews* (6 Aug. 2017) called it "a collection of jarring and polished short fiction," adding that Fridlund's stories "evoke Flannery O'Connor's masterly way with grotesquery but deviate in Fridlund's contempt for faith."

PERSONAL LIFE

Fridlund, who is married and has a son named Eliot, is a visiting scholar at Cornell University in Ithaca, New York. She completed *History of Wolves* with the aid of a feminist grant from the Barbara Deming Memorial Fund, and her work has been nominated for two Pushcart Prizes, the 2013 Tartts First Fiction Award, the 2014 Noemi Book Award for Fiction, and the 2018 Sue Kaufman Prize for First Fiction from the American Academy of Arts and Letters, among other prizes.

SUGGESTED READING

Fridlund, Emily. Review of *Catapult*, by Emily Fridlund. *Kirkus Reviews*, 6 Aug. 2017, www.kirkusreviews.com/book-reviews/emily-fridlund/catapult-fridlund/ Accessed 26 June 2018.

Fridlund, Emily. "Powell's Interview: Emily Fridlund, Author of 'History of Wolves.'" By Jill Owens. *Powells.com*, 6 Jan. 2017, www.powells.com/post/interviews/powells-interview-emily-fridlund-author-of-history-of-wolves. Accessed 25 June 2018.

Fridlund, Emily. "Smoking with Emily Fridlund." Interview. *SmokeLong Quarterly*, 15 Sept. 2007, www.smokelong.com/smoking-with-emily-fridlund/. Accessed 25 June 2018.

Gilmartin, Sarah. Review of *History of Wolves*, by Emily Fridlund. *The Irish Times*, 14 Oct. 2017, www.irishtimes.com/culture/books/history-of-wolves-by-emily-fridlund-1.3240992. Accessed 25 June 2018.

Hertzel, Laurie. "Debut Novelist Emily Fridlund 'Didn't Expect' to Beat Stars to Man Booker Shortlist." *Sydney Morning Herald*, 28 Sept. 2017, www.smh.com.au/entertainment/books/debut-novelist-emily-fridlund-didnt-expect-to-beat-stars-to-man-booker-shortlist-20170928-gyq7hu.html. Accessed 25 June 2018.

Hulbert, Ann. "The Propulsive Power of *Catapult*." Review of *Catapult*, by Emily Fridlund. *The Atlantic*, Jan./Feb. 2018. https://www.theatlantic.com/magazine/archive/2018/01/emily-fridlund-catapult-review/546584/. Accessed 25 June 2018.

Schaub, Michael. "Beautiful, Icy 'History of Wolves' Transcends Genre." Review of *History of Wolves*, by Emily Fridlund. *NPR*, 3 Jan. 2017, www.npr.org/2017/01/03/507162378/beautiful-icy-history-of-wolves-transcends-genre. Accessed 25 June 2018.

Senior, Jennifer. "Review: A Teenager Bears Witness to Backwoods Intrigue in 'History of Wolves.'" Review of *A History of Wolves*, by Emily Fridlund. *New York Times*, 4 Jan. 2017, www.nytimes.com/2017/01/04/books/review-history-of-wolves-emily-fridlund.html. Accessed 25 June 2018.

—*Christopher Mari*

Fu Yuanhui

Date of birth: January 7, 1996
Occupation: Swimmer

For Chinese backstroke swimmer Fu Yuanhui, the sport of swimming is far more than an enjoyable activity. "I used to quite like it, but now

Photo by VCG/VCG via Getty Images

that it has become my career I can't say if I like it or not," she said in 2016, as reported by Jiayang Fan for the *New Yorker* (19 Aug. 2016). "It's become part of my life." Indeed, the sport has been a key part of Fu's life since she was five years old, when her parents encouraged her to begin swimming to improve her health. Over the next decade, the young athlete honed the skills that would win her a silver medal at the World Junior Swimming Championships in 2011 and the following year qualify her to compete in her first Summer Olympic Games. Later victories at events such as the World Championships and National Games of China further solidified Fu's status as a swimmer to watch and one of many successful swimmers to have come out of the prestigious Chen Jinglun Sports School.

Fu became particularly well-known in both China and abroad in 2016, when she claimed a bronze medal in the women's 100-meter backstroke event at the Olympic Games in Rio de Janeiro, Brazil. She subsequently drew international attention when she attributed her lackluster performance in a relay event to having her period, receiving widespread praise for her candid discussion of an issue that affects many young athletes but is not widely discussed. Following the Olympics, Fu embraced some aspects of her newfound celebrity, such as interacting with her many fans during online livestreams, while largely rejecting the other trappings of fame. "Though my popularity has grown, what people care most about is my personal life, rather than my swimming times. It made me feel like an entertainment star and laid great pressure on me,"

she told journalists, as reported by the website *Women of China* (11 Oct. 2016). "I am only an athlete. I'd like people to remember my name because of my capabilities, not in this way."

EARLY LIFE AND CAREER

Fu was born on January 7, 1996, in China. Her father, Fu Chungsheng, worked for a transportation company, while her mother worked for a hotel. Fu grew up in Hangzhou, a city in eastern China. As a young child, she struggled with asthma, and her parents encouraged her to begin swimming at the age of five in the hope that the exercise would improve her health. She quickly demonstrated a talent for the sport and soon began swimming as part of a local team. As her skills improved, Fu began an intensive training program at the Chen Jinglun Sports School in Hangzhou, a prestigious school known for training award-winning Chinese swimmers such as Olympic medalists Sun Yang and Luo Xuejuan. In addition to training as a swimmer, Fu studied exercise rehabilitation at Tianjin Medical University for a time.

As a teenager, Fu competed extensively in international swimming competitions, showcasing her talents in bouts against swimmers from around the world. She was particularly skilled in the backstroke and primarily competed in 50- and 100-meter backstroke events. In 2011, she entered the girls' 100-meter backstroke competition at the International Swimming Federation (FINA) World Junior Swimming Championships, ultimately winning a silver medal after finishing less than a second behind Ukrainian swimmer Daryna Zevina.

OLYMPIC DEBUT

Fu made her Olympic debut in 2012, after qualifying to compete in the women's 100-meter backstroke competition at the Olympic Games in London, England. During the early stages of the competition, Fu was not a leading competitor but performed well enough to secure a spot in the final round. She ultimately placed eighth in the event, with a time of 1:00.5. Over the subsequent years, Fu continued to progress on the international level and put forth strong performances at events such as the 2014 Asian Games in Incheon, South Korea, where she claimed gold medals for both the 50- and 100-meter backstroke.

Despite her increasing success as an athlete, Fu approached her swimming as a vocation and a means of serving her country rather than as a source of fame. "I'm a professional athlete, which is my job and duty," she said in an online livestream, as reported by Mo Xiaojun for *Women of China* (9 Jan. 2017). "In contrast to sportsmen and women in other countries, we are cultivated by our country and should repay its kindness. While fulfilling our duty, we also feel a sense of honor." Fu continued to represent China internationally at events such as the 2015 FINA World Championships, held in Kazan, Russia, in August of that year. During the FINA competition, Fu won the gold medal for the 50-meter backstroke, again demonstrating her dominance in that form of swimming. She also competed in the 4×100 medley relay and helped her team claim first place in that event.

RIO OLYMPICS

By 2016, Fu had long been established as an athlete to watch in the international swimming community; she gained a still greater international platform when she competed at the Olympics in Rio de Janeiro, Brazil. Much as in 2012, Fu faced the challenge of having to compete in the 100-meter backstroke rather than her preferred 50-meter race, as the latter was not an Olympic event. She trained extensively prior to the competition but doubted her chances for success. "I still had not dared to expect any breakthrough or good scores," she said, as reported by *Women of China* (11 Oct. 2016). Upon the start of the competition in August 2016, however, Fu ranked fourth in her heat and went on to perform well in the semifinals, claiming a spot in the final competition. She completed the final 100-meter backstroke event in 58.76 seconds, tying Canadian swimmer Kylie Masse for third place and claiming her first Olympic medal. Fu's surprised reaction to her performance garnered international attention and prompted some commentators to contrast her response to those of fellow swimmers such as Sun, who was reportedly deeply disappointed after winning a silver medal rather than a gold in one of his events.

Fu received further attention later in the Olympics after competing with her teammates in the women's 4×100 medley relay. In the final stage of the event, the team ultimately placed fourth, falling behind the Danish team by 0.17 seconds. Disappointed by her performance, Fu was candid about the factors that she believed prevented her from meeting her full potential. "It's because my period came yesterday, so I felt particularly tired—but this isn't an excuse, I still didn't swim well enough," she told journalists, as reported by Tom Phillips for the *Guardian* (15 Aug. 2016). Following that interview, Fu became the center of immediate international attention with many fans and journalists praising her for her willingness to discuss menstruation, which had long been a taboo topic in sports both in China and elsewhere in the world.

Following the 2016 Games, Fu became a widely known public figure in China and abroad and made a variety of public and media appearances. She became particularly known for her online livestreams, which were among the most popular such broadcasts in China. Fu also appeared in an episode of the reality show *Absolute Wild*, in which Chinese celebrities accompany British survival expert Bear Grylls into the wilderness.

CONTINUING COMPETITION

In addition to meeting her obligations as an Olympic medalist and public figure, Fu continued to compete in national and international swimming events following her 2016 success. At the 2017 FINA World Championships, held in July of that year in Budapest, Hungary, she participated in the 50-meter backstroke event and came within a fraction of a second of winning her second consecutive gold medal in the event. To Fu's disappointment, however, she ultimately finished 0.01 seconds behind Brazilian swimmer Etiene Medeiros to claim second place. "The Budapest setback was such a heavy blow to me," she later told *XinhuaNet* (3 Sept. 2017). "I felt like I dropped to the rock bottom both mentally and physically after that." Despite her disappointment in Budapest, Fu continued to push herself further and in September claimed the gold medal in the women's 100-meter backstroke at the National Games of China. "When I was so lost, I did not give up on myself. Instead I continue to work hard," Fu told *XinhuaNet* of her preparation for the competition. "My experience tells me that every drop of your sweat and every effort you make will eventually come back at some point in the form of a reward."

While competing in 2018, Fu faced an additional challenge in the form of a shoulder injury that had bothered her off and on since 2013 but became particularly troubling in the spring of 2018. While competing in the Chinese National Championships and Asian Games selection meet in April of that year, she was unable to qualify for the final stage of the 200-meter backstroke competition because of that injury and told journalists that she would seriously consider retiring from the sport if her shoulder did not recover. However, Fu returned to the pool for the 50-meter backstroke and placed first in the event with a time of 27.16, only one-tenth of a second slower than the standing world record. "I thought I would not stand on the podium this time since I was not in my best shape," she said after the competition, as reported by Loretta Race for *Swim Swam* (17 Apr. 2018). "But the result and full-house local fans boosted my confidence." Fu's gold-medal performance qualified her to compete in the 50-meter backstroke in the 2018 Asian Games, held in Indonesia in August and September of that year.

PERSONAL LIFE

When not competing, Fu enjoys reading and cooking and is particularly devoted to animal welfare. "When I attend training or competitions in other places, I often buy cat and dog food so I can feed stray animals when I see them," she said in a livestream, as reported by Mo on *Women of China*. "When I [see] animals in need of urgent help on the Internet, I want go to find them by plane. I can't bear to see the scene of people hurting animals. It makes me especially unwell." Fu has expressed interest in opening an animal shelter following her eventual retirement from swimming and has also raised the possibility of continuing her education.

SUGGESTED READING

"Adorable Swimmer Fu Yuanhui Wins Our Hearts Yet Again." *XinhuaNet*, 3 Sept. 2017, www.xinhuanet.com/english/2017-09/03/c136579615.htm. Accessed 13 July 2018.

"Chinese Swimmer Fu Yuanhui Wins Public's Heart for Rare Candor." *NBC Olympics*, 12 Aug. 2016, www.nbcolympics.com/news/chinese-swimmer-fu-yuanhui-wins-publics-heart-rare-candor. Accessed 13 July 2018.

Fan, Jiayang. "Fu Yuanhui Teaches China to Relax at the Olympics." *The New Yorker*, 19 Aug. 2016, www.newyorker.com/news/daily-comment/fu-yuanhui-teaches-china-to-relax-at-the-olympics. Accessed 13 July 2018.

"Fu Yuanhui: I Want to Be an Athlete, Not a Celebrity." *Women of China*, 11 Oct. 2016, www.womenofchina.cn/womenofchina/html1/people/sportswomen/1610/709-1.htm. Accessed 13 July 2018.

Mo Xiaojun. "Swimming Sensation Fu Yuanhui Live Streams Birthday Celebration for Fans." *Women of China*, 9 Jan. 2017, womenofchina.cn/womenofchina/xhtml1/people/sportswomen/1701/1385-1.htm. Accessed 13 July 2018.

Phillips, Tom. "'It's Because I Had My Period': Swimmer Fu Yuanhui Praised for Breaking Taboo." *The Guardian*, 15 Aug. 2016, www.theguardian.com/sport/2016/aug/16/chinese-swimmer-fu-yuanhui-praised-for-breaking-periods-taboo. Accessed 13 July 2018.

Race, Loretta. "Olympic Bronze Medalist Fu Yuanhui Battles Back from Shoulder Injury." *Swim Swam*, 17 Apr. 2018, swimswam.com/olympic-bronze-medalist-fu-yuanhui-battles-back-from-shoulder-injury. Accessed 13 July 2018.

—*Joy Crelin*

Rivka Galchen

Date of birth: April 19, 1976
Occupation: Writer

Canadian-born Rivka Galchen is a writer who has served as an assistant professor at Columbia University School of Arts and on the graduate faculty at New York University's School of Arts & Sciences. Yet her work often draws on her background in science, particularly her medical degree, as much as on the literary establishment. She uses this unique voice to explore deep themes and questions, especially in her critically praised fiction. "So much of medicine—most of it, really—doesn't crossword-puzzle out into a clean-edged diagnosis. Medicine explains things up to a point, and then hits a wall," Galchen told Alice Whitwham for the *Paris Review* (11 June 2014). "Fiction often does its best work in those same wide spaces where data starts to lose its conclusive usefulness."

Galchen's writing career began after she left medicine behind to study literature, and her debut novel, *Atmospheric Disturbances*, was published in 2008. Rave reviews and awards quickly followed. In 2010, that book won a William Saroyan International Prize for Writing, given to emerging authors by the Stanford University Libraries and the William Saroyan Foundation, and the *New Yorker* named Galchen one of twenty writers under forty to watch. Although she later branched out into nonfiction writing, she remained committed to the possibilities of fiction. As she told April Ayers Lawson for *Vice* (11 July 2014), "What is it that fiction can do well? . . . I think that has something to do with these spaces that are not better illuminated in other ways, these murky places that don't yield much to other forms of investigation."

EARLY LIFE AND EDUCATION

Galchen's parents emigrated to Canada from Israel in 1969, so that her father, Tzvi, could complete a postdoctoral program at the University of Toronto. Her parents were academics; her father in meteorology and her mother in computer programming. Galchen was born in Toronto, and had one older brother, Oren. Although her parents had expected to return to Israel, they moved instead from Toronto to Norman, Oklahoma, when Galchen was four years old. Theirs was essentially the only Jewish family in town, which gave her the feeling of being in exile; at home, her parents spoke Hebrew. The family traveled to Israel for visits most years, so she developed a close connection to that country.

Galchen's parents held her to high academic standards, and she did well in school. She went on to college at Princeton University, but initially rebelled against her parents' wishes for her to pursue science. Instead she earned her undergraduate degree in English, with famed author Joyce Carol Oates as her thesis advisor. However, she then bowed to family pressure and enrolled in the Mount Sinai School of Medicine, with a focus on psychiatry. "My mom begged me, basically, to study medicine, thinking I'd be unemployed otherwise," she told Sheldon Kirshner for *Canadian Jewish News* (4 Dec. 2008). "I wanted to make her happy. I was a yalda tova, a good girl."

Medical practice did not come naturally for Galchen; she often apologized to patients before giving them exams. After her second year she spent a year in Peru working on issues of public health, which she did enjoy. She also came to appreciate the unusually intimate atmosphere of hospitals for both staff and patients. But in general, she was unsatisfied and longed to return to creative writing, though her risk-averse nature led her to finish her degree. As she told Carolyn Kellogg for *Los Angeles Times* (1 May 2014), "I think I managed to stay unhappy for all of my medical education. That unhappiness was motivating. I felt like I was so young and so bitter!"

BEGINNING AS A WRITER

After five years at Mount Sinai, Galchen graduated with her medical degree in 2003 and immediately applied and was accepted to the creative writing program at Columbia University. With the reassurance that she was still in an academic setting, she gave herself a deadline to succeed or else return to medicine. She soon found herself much more at ease as she reentered the literary world. "I loved Columbia," she told Kirshner. "I made very close friends. I read a lot more deeply. Before Columbia, I felt desperately behind in my knowledge of literature. No one had ever told me about Ulysses." During her studies, she also taught a class in essay writing to undergraduates.

Galchen was named a Robert Bingham Fellow as she worked to complete her master of fine arts degree at Columbia. The fellowship gave her time to work on her first novel, which she began in 2004 and often wrote while sitting in the Hungarian Pastry Shop near her apartment in Manhattan. Soon after graduating in 2006, she also received a Rona Jaffe Foundation Writers' Award. The prize further enabled her to focus on finishing her book and getting it published.

While her first novel became her primary project, Galchen also wrote short fiction. She explained her take on the short story form to Whitwham: "Short stories feel found to me—I like that about them. Of course, they're actually not found, they're written, just as novels are written, but they seem to have a more dense and unchangeable core than novels do, or at least it seems like one reaches the immutable core faster."

ATMOSPHERIC DISTURBANCES

Once Galchen had started writing her first novel, "it very much wrote itself," as she told Kirshner. "It didn't develop in the direction of my plans." She eventually hired an agent, who helped convince her to leave behind the working title, *Open Letter to the Royal Academy of Meteorology*, and her next choice, *Fleas Mutely Festivaling*. She submitted the work for publication and within days it was accepted. The novel was released in 2008 as *Atmospheric Disturbances*.

The novel is a sort of mystery: the protagonist, a psychiatrist, believes his wife has been replaced by an almost exact duplicate and sets off on an international search to find his real wife. This basic structure supports a complex, intellectual narrative that many reviewers felt successfully continued the postmodern techniques of writers such as William Pynchon and Jorge Luis Borges. Notably, Galchen slyly inserts her father into the novel as a supporting character, and the plot often connects to his field of meteorology.

The critical response to *Atmospheric Disturbances* was overwhelmingly positive and launched Galchen to literary fame. Fellow author Vincent Scarpa wrote for Tin House (6 July 2016) that "the sentences sing, never losing their music even when they're a paragraph long, and feel perfected without ever feeling tweaked or overworked." The novel was nominated for many awards, including Canada's 2008 Rogers Writers' Trust Fiction Prize and the New York Public Library's 2009 Young Lions Fiction Award. In 2010 it won the William Saroyan International Prize for Writing, and it was instrumental in Galchen being named to the *New Yorker*'s list of young writers to watch that same year.

AMERICAN INNOVATIONS

Galchen's first collection of short stories, published in 2014, was inspired in part by her realization that all her favorite authors were male, and all their writing featured male narrators. Annoyed that she had not been exposed to more women writers, she embarked on a mission to subvert that paradigm. All of the short stories in the collection *American Innovations* have female narrators; all but one were inspired by short stories written by men, ranging from David Foster Wallace to Haruki Murakami. The opening sentence of "The Lost Order," for example, directly mirrors the opening of one of Murakami's stories, and "Wild Berry Blue" is similar in plot to James Joyce's "Araby."

Despite these inspirations and similarities, Galchen herself did not recognize the unifying theme in her short works until she had written most of the stories. She later referred to her writing style as a kind of sleepwalking. Four of the stories in the collection were previously published in the *New Yorker*. As Deborah Treisman, the fiction editor of that magazine, told Kellogg, "Rivka's stories can be challenging, because she doesn't pander to the reader: So much of it is about voice, and there's often a learning curve as you become attuned to the voice of a particular story. There's a real technical cleverness to what she does; she's also very funny, an acute observer of social ridiculousness, which makes the small flares of emotion all the more devastating."

American Innovations again brought Galchen much acclaim. For Women's History Month, critics at the *New York Times* chose the collection as one of fifteen works by women writers of the twenty-first century held up as significant contributions to fiction. "The DNA in these stories may be old, but Galchen has uncovered a new register and a new space for the domestic and the fantastic to meet," Parul Sehgal wrote for that newspaper (5 Mar. 2018). "There might be no better model for looking to the past in order to move forward."

LITTLE LABORS

Galchen's next book was *Little Labors* (2016), an extended essay about her first months with her baby daughter. She largely based the work on *The Pillow Book*, an eleventh-century text made up of a unique mix of observations and narrative by Sei Shōnagon, one of the ladies in waiting to the empress of Japan. Galchen had intended to do a critical study of *The Pillow Book* and another classic of Japanese literature, *The Tale of the Genji* by Murasaki Shikibu. The deadline for that piece happened to fall near the birth of her daughter, however, and the writing ended up taking her in a completely different direction.

In *Little Labors*, Galchen presents the point of view of a new mother, knowing that perspective will inevitably end with the passage of time. The short sections include everything from her deeply personal experiences with her own child to broad musings on cultural perceptions of babies. She does not name her daughter in the book, choosing instead to call her "the puma" until the baby begins to walk, when she becomes "the chicken"—hinting at the considerable humor throughout the book.

Like her previous works, *Little Labors* was praised by critics. As Scarpa wrote, "It is a work of stunning intersections between curiosity and scrutiny, between wandering and wondering, and to follow Galchen's mind as it moves through everything she's gathered to look at is a gift. Reading it, one feels the enlargement of one's heart and mind, which is the work of literature."

PERSONAL LIFE

Galchen is married to computer scientist Aaron Harnly. The couple had a daughter in 2013 and

gave her the middle name Spark in honor of writer Muriel Spark. Other women writers Galchen admires include Jane Bowles, Lydia Davis, Janet Frame, Helen DeWitt, and Marilynne Robinson. She told Andy Battaglia for the *Wall Street Journal* (30 June 2014) about her embrace of spontaneity in her everyday life: "I'm never planning an outfit in advance. I don't like to have a grocery list when I go to the supermarket. When I try to cook to a recipe, it doesn't go very well." This trait has carried over into her general outlook as well. "I like running up against the boundary of understanding, she told Battaglia. "There's honesty in getting really close to something but admitting that it's actually fading away. You realize it's pixilated. When you get close, the resolution only goes so far."

SUGGESTED READING

Battaglia, Andy. "Rivka Galchen, Author of 'American Innovations,' on Writing and Uncertainty." *The Wall Street Journal*, 30 June 2014, www.wsj.com/articles/rivka-galchen-author-of-american-innovations-on-writing-and-uncertainty-1404146536. Accessed 5 Sept. 2018.

Galchen, Rivka. "Dismissing the Captain: An Interview with Rivka Galchen." Interview by Vincent Scarpa. *Tin House*, 6 July 2016, tinhouse.com/dismissing-the-captain-an-interview-with-rivka-galchen/. Accessed 5 Sept. 2018.

Galchen, Rivka. "Field Geology: An Interview with Rivka Galchen." Interview by Alice Whitwham. *The Paris Review*, 11 June 2014, www.theparisreview.org/blog/2014/06/11/field-geology-an-interview-with-rivka-galchen/. Accessed 5 Sept. 2018.

Galchen, Rivka. "The Joy of Being Elusive and Unstable: An Interview with Author Rivka Galchen." Interview by April Ayers Lawson. *Vice*, 11 July 2014, www.vice.com/en_us/article/kwpnqz/the-joy-of-being-elusive-and-unstable-an-interview-with-author-rivka-galchen-711. Accessed 5 Sept. 2018.

Kellogg, Carolyn. "Rivka Galchen Talks about Putting a Female Twist on Iconic Stories." *Los Angeles Times*, 1 May 2014, www.latimes.com/books/jacketcopy/la-ca-jc-rivka-galchen-20140504-story.html. Accessed 5 Sept. 2018.

Kirshner, Sheldon. "Rivka Galchen's Journey to Literary Fame." *The Canadian Jewish News*, 4 Dec. 2008, www.cjnews.com/culture/books-and-authors/rivka-galchens-journey-literary-fame. Accessed 5 Sept. 2018.

Smith, Claiborne. "Rivka Galchen." *Kirkus*, 6 May 2014, www.kirkusreviews.com/features/rivka-galchen/. Accessed 5 Sept. 2018.

SELECTED WORKS
Atmospheric Disturbances, 2008; *American Innovations: Stories*, 2014; *Little Labors*, 2016.

—Judy Johnson

Alejandro García Padilla
Date of birth: August 3, 1971
Occupation: Governor of Puerto Rico

As the eleventh governor of the Commonwealth of Puerto Rico, Alejandro García Padilla has tackled several key issues, including calls to change the island's status as a territory and severe economic problems. In 2015 García Padilla announced that the commonwealth was unable to pay its debts and that he would not seek re-election in 2016.

EARLY LIFE AND EDUCATION
Alejandro García Padilla was born on August 3, 1971, in Coamo, Puerto Rico. His father was a World War II veteran who worked as a general manager of a manufacturing company. His mother was a homemaker. His parents had six children.

García Padilla earned a bachelor's degree in political science and economics from the University of Puerto Rico in 1994. Three years later, he earned a juris doctor degree from the Interamerican University of Puerto Rico. He began his career as a public servant by working as a law clerk for Puerto Rico's Court of Appeals. He also worked as a legislative aide, an attorney specializing in contracts and real estate in a private legal firm, a university professor at the Interamerican University School of Law, and a radio talk show panelist.

POLITICAL CAREER
García Padilla was appointed the secretary of the Department of Consumer Affairs in 2005. In 2007 he resigned and announced he was running for senator. He was elected to the Senate of Puerto Rico in 2008 and took office in January 2009. During his term in the Senate, he served on several committees, including those of governmental affairs, judicial affairs, and public safety. He also worked to promote bipartisan support for bills on university scholarships, pension benefits, and economic development.

In 2011 García Padilla was elected president of the Popular Democratic Party (PDP) and announced his plan to run for governor. He ran against incumbent governor Luis Fortuño, of the New Progressive Party. The gubernatorial campaign issues focused on Puerto Rico's status as a commonwealth territory, crime, and economic

issues. In 2012 Puerto Rico had high unemployment, high crime, high public debt, and growing discontent about its bleak economic conditions. Although Fortuño had implemented many economic austerity measures, Puerto Rico's unemployment rate remained above 13 percent, its government pension systems had a total unfounded liability of more than $37 billion, and its bonds had been downgraded to ratings slightly above junk. García Padilla campaigned against Fortuño's austerity measures. He promised to reduce public-sector job cuts, to create jobs, and to increase spending on education. He also helped to unite the PDP in its opposition to statehood.

The 2012 race for governor was a close one; García Padilla won the election by a narrow margin. In his inaugural speech in January 2013, García Padilla outlined the issues facing the commonwealth and promised to take action. He immediately created a fiscal stimulus plan, but within months, analysts criticized the plan as focused on short-term gains rather than long-term solutions. For example, García Padilla's plan included several public-works projects to improve the island's transportation infrastructure. Although these projects would create fifty thousand jobs, the jobs were not permanent.

In his 2014 State of the Commonwealth address, García Padilla cited his achievements since taking office as preparing a balanced budget and reducing government operating costs. He outlined his plan for economic recovery: to attract new industrial sectors to Puerto Rico, revitalize the tourist industry, increase government revenue through cutting operating costs, and strengthen the agricultural sector. In interviews later that year, García Padilla noted his accomplishments in job creations and judicial pension reform. He planned to promote economic growth through tax incentives and education scholarships and reduce the commonwealth's debt by increasing revenue through partial privatization of government utilities and additional pension reforms.

Three months later, García Padilla acknowledged that his fiscal measures were inadequate. In June 2015 he gave a speech to the public in which he stated that it was impossible for Puerto Rico to achieve economic recovery while also making payments on its public debts. He announced that the commonwealth was unable to pay its $72 billion debt and requested that it be allowed to restructure its debts under US bankruptcy laws. Although Puerto Rico is a territory of the United States, it is ineligible to file for bankruptcy under federal bankruptcy code. Following his speech, García Padilla assembled a group to prepare a five-year plan for restructuring Puerto Rico's debt.

On September 8, 2015, García Padilla gave a speech broadcast over television and online media in which he presented his fiscal reform plan. It outlined a series of economic reforms, including making public services more efficient, contracting some public services to for-profit companies, and increasing college tuitions. Most of these reforms required that creditors make sacrifices and forfeit billions of dollars in debt payments. Many of the reforms also were dependent on Congress passing legislation, such as changing federal bankruptcy codes to allow Puerto Rico to file for bankruptcy. In February 2016, García Padilla stated that Puerto Rico faced an impending humanitarian crisis if it was unable to reduce its debt. In March 2016, US Senate Democrats proposed two bills to restructure Puerto Rico's debt, but neither were likely to pass both houses of Congress.

IMPACT

García Padilla's refusal to pay Puerto Rico's debts and his request for debt restructuring are unprecedented for a US territory or state. Financial analysts predicted that the effects of the Puerto Rico debt crisis were likely to reverberate beyond the economic stability of Puerto Rico and have far-reaching effects on the US municipal bond market, constitutional issues, and the United States–Puerto Rico relationship. Because of the all-consuming nature of solving the debt crisis, García Padilla has stated that he will not run for reelection in 2016.

PERSONAL LIFE

García Padilla married Wilma Pastrana Jiménez in 2001. They have three children: Ana Patricia, Juan Pablo, and Diego Alejandro.

SUGGESTED READING

Corkery, Michael, and Mary Williams Walsh. "Puerto Rico's Governor Says Island's Debts Are 'Not Payable.'" *New York Times*. New York Times, 28 June 2015. Accessed on 10 Sept. 2015.

García Padilla, Alejandro. Interview. "Two Pearls." *Business Year.* Business Year, 2014. Accessed on 10 Sept. 2015.

Kuriloff, Aaron. "Puerto Rico Plan Calls for Spending Cuts, Tax Overhaul." *Wall Street Journal*. Dow Jones, 9 Sept. 2015. Accessed on 10 Sept. 2015.

"Update 1—New Governor Takes Office in Debt-Swamped Puerto Rico." *Reuters*. Thomson Reuters, 2 Jan. 2013. Accessed on 10 Sept. 2015.

Walsh, Mary Williams. "Democrats' Bills to Empower Puerto Rico Face Uphill Battle." *New York Times*. New York Times, 13 Mar. 2016. Accessed on 14 Mar. 2016.

Walsh, Mary Williams. "Puerto Rico Lays Out 5-Year Plan for Restructuring Its Debts." *New York Times*. New York Times, 9 Sept. 2015. Accessed on 10 Sept. 2015.

—*Barb Lightner*

Ross Gay

Date of birth: August 1, 1974
Occupation: Poet

Ross Gay is an award-winning American poet. He is also an artist, an editor, and a professor and has received several national fellowships.

EARLY LIFE AND EDUCATION

Ross Gay was born in Youngstown, Ohio, on August 1, 1974, the older of two sons in a working-class family. Gay grew up in an apartment complex located five miles outside of Philadelphia. His mother was a catalog copy editor and his father worked as a manager at a series of fast-casual restaurants. Gay has explained to interviewers that he attributes his unique perspective as a poet to the biculturalism of his childhood where he was influenced by both his father's personal history as an African American man from a steel town and his mother's experiences as a woman from a white farming community in Minnesota.

Throughout his youth, Gay was interested in a number of different activities including skateboarding, video games, and sports. Except for comic books, Gay was not interested in reading or writing until college. A natural athlete, Gay played football for Lafayette College while receiving his bachelor's degree in English and art. After graduating in 1996, he attended Sarah Lawrence College to pursue a masters of fine arts (MFA) degree in poetry. It was at Sarah Lawrence that he met the professors who would help him develop his voice as a writer, including Tom Lux and Gerald Stern. After completing his MFA, Gay went on to earn a doctorate in English from Temple University in 2006. His dissertation was entitled, "An American Drama: Black/White Interracial Desire Narratives, 1894–2003."

CAREER

Gay's career in academia began in the early 2000s while he pursued his doctorate from Temple. Gay returned to Lafayette College in the fall of 2001 as a humanities fellow and taught courses on writing, black authors, and the relationship between visual art and text. From 2005 to 2007, Gay worked as a faculty member at the low-residency MFA poetry program at New England College, taught poetry workshops and African

American literature at New Jersey's Montclair State University, and taught poetry at the University of Pittsburgh where he was a visiting assistant professor.

His first book, *Against Which* (2006), was a loose collection of poems that were united by the themes of violence, love, and loss. Reception of the book was positive, with critics praising the vibrancy of Gay's prose. *Against Which* explored a broad spectrum of topics, including the pain of slavery and childhood schoolyard fights. The literary world was introduced to Gay's stylistic tendency to transform mundane imagery into powerful commentary on the human existence. Additionally, one of the collection's most extolled poems, "How to Fall in Love with Your Father," was selected for publication by the Public Poetry Project of the Pennsylvania Center for the Book.

Gay's second book, *Bringing the Shovel Down* (2011), was written over the course of four years. Unlike *Against Which*, Gay wrote *Bringing the Shovel Down* with a deliberate framework in mind. It also differed greatly in its voice; where the speaker in *Against Which* speaks in highly metric spondees, Gay alternates between different voices and perspectives for each of the poems in *Bringing the Shovel Down*. The poems comprise mediations on ideas of violence, conscience, and the power of the state, and the volume was well-received by the literary community. The title poem, which is published in two versions in order to convey conflicted human ideals, has been a common point of praise among critics.

In 2007, Gay began working as an associate professor of English and associate director of creative writing at Indiana University Bloomington. It was at Bloomington that he discovered a passion for gardening, and his third collection of poetry, *Catalog of Unabashed Gratitude* (2015), reflects this by examining the natural world in a manner that has been compared to Walt Whitman. Determined to write a collection of poems that express his reverence for life, *Catalog of Unabashed Gratitude* explores the elements of Gay's life which he is most grateful. Rich in imagery and themes of gardening, the book has received the highest acclaim with many critics praising its sexual humor and sensory detail. The book became a finalist for the 2015 National Book Award and won the 2015 poetry prize from the National Book Critics Circle. On March 3, 2015, Gay won the Kingsley Tufts Poetry award, one of the most prestigious awards in poetry, along with its $100,000 prize.

IMPACT

Gay's unique poetic style, perspective, and prose have shaped the landscape of contemporary poetry in the United States. By using his writing to explore the experience of African American men living in a racist society, Gay has become an important voice in the twenty-first century civil rights movement. In 2015, he was nominated for a NAACP image award.

PERSONAL LIFE

Gay lives in Bloomington, Indiana, where he spends his time gardening, coaching basketball, and editing the chapbook presses *Q Avenue* and *Ledge Mule*. He is also the editor of the online sports magazine *Some Call It Ballin'*. He serves on the board of the Bloomington Community Orchard.

SUGGESTED READING

Cornish, Audie. *Rev. of Unabashed Gratitude,* by Ross Gay. *National Public Radio.* Natl. Public Radio, 17 Nov. 2016. Web. 11 Mar. 2016.

Gay, Ross. Interview by Joanna Penn Cooper. "A Conversation with Ross Gay." *Cortland Review.* Cortland Review, 15 Nov. 2008. Web. 11 Mar. 2016.

Gay, Ross. Interview by Kaveh Akbar. "'It's All So Goddamn Compelling': Ross Gay." *Dive Dapper.* Dive Dapper, 2 Nov. 2015. Web. 11 Mar. 2016.

Gay, Ross. "Some Thoughts on Mercy." *Sun Magazine.* Sun, July 2013. Web. 11 Mar. 2016.

Licad, Abigail. "Poet Ross Gay Is on a Roll: He Talks Gardens and Gratitude." *Los Angeles Times.* Los Angeles Times, 10 Feb. 2016. Web. 11 Mar. 2016.

SELECTED WORKS

Against Which, 2006; *Bringing the Shovel Down,* 2011; *Catalog of Unabashed Gratitude*, 2015

—*Emily Turner*

Roxane Gay

Date of birth: October 28, 1974
Occupation: Writer

Explaining the ardor of writer Roxane Gay's devoted fan base, Molly McArdle wrote for *Brooklyn Magazine* (22 Feb. 2017), "Gay sells hundreds of thousands of books, fills up dozens of auditoriums, attracts attention off and online not just because she's that good—though she is—but because her goodness cuts to the quick of human experience. Her work returns again and again to issues of power, the body, desire, trauma, survival, truth." In a profile for the *Guardian* (2 Aug. 2014), Kira Cochrane expressed similar sentiments, writing, "Gay has the voice of the friend you call first for advice, calm and sane as

By Slowking4, via Wikimedia Commons

Outside of her tightknit and loving family, Gay often felt shy and awkward. She spent much of her time reading and particularly loved *Nancy Drew* mysteries and the *Little House on the Prairie* series. She also harbored a seemingly improbable fondness for the Sweet Valley High series, books that followed the adventures of a pair of pert, blond twins from California. Gay explained in a 2011 essay "I Once Was Miss America" that to her and other girls of her age, the series reflected familiar hopes, fears, and aspirations, despite featuring almost uniformly financially secure, slim Caucasian characters. An imaginative child, she had by then been weaving tales of her own for several years: Gay has told interviewers that starting at about age four, she sketched out entire villages on napkins and created stories about the characters who lived in them.

At age twelve, Gay was brutally gang-raped by a group of boys in the woods near her home. In the aftermath, she became convinced that she had somehow invited the attack or deserved it, and that a girl as pathetic as she perceived herself to expect no better treatment from the world. The incident triggered a destructive cycle of binge eating. She writes in *Hunger*: "I was swallowing my secrets and making my body expand and explode. I found ways to hide in plain sight, to keep feeding a hunger that could never be satisfied—the hunger to stop hurting. I made myself bigger. I made myself safer." She continued to put on pounds over the next several years, despite her parents' entreaties and their willingness to send her to weight-loss programs.

EDUCATION

As a teen, Gay attended the prestigious Phillips Exeter Academy, a boarding school in Exeter, New Hampshire. Miserable, lonely, and believing that no one there could help her, she focused much of her energy on attaining stellar grades. Thanks to her academic achievement, she graduated in 1992 and was admitted to Yale University. There, she initially majored in premedical and biology studies, but soon switched to architecture and then to English. Concurrently, she fell in with the theater crowd and spent much of her free time building sets and running the sound and light boards during productions.

Gay dropped out of Yale at the beginning of her junior year to pursue a relationship with a forty-four-year-old whom she had met in an online chat room. Without telling her family or friends, she moved with him to Arizona and found work as a phone-sex operator. When she lost her home there, Gay headed to Minneapolis to embark on a short-lived romance with another person she had met online. After just a few weeks, she dejectedly called her family for help.

well as funny, someone who has seen a lot and takes no prisoners."

Gay, who teaches writing at Purdue University, is perhaps best known for her provocatively titled book *Bad Feminist: Essays* (2014), and *Hunger* (2017), a memoir that provides an unflinching look at what it means to move through the world as a woman of color and size. (Gay, who is of Haitian descent, stands six-feet-three and once weighed 577 pounds.) "Living in my body has expanded my empathy for other people and the truths of their bodies," she writes in *Hunger*. "Certainly, it has shown me the importance of inclusivity and acceptance." Despite the inherent kindness evident in much of her writing—and in her fans' frequently expressed warmth toward her—Gay is far from a Pollyanna. "If you bite, she will likely bite back," Marisa Meltzer warned in *Elle* (14 June 2017), "with not just fury but with a stroke of lightning-fast, spot-on rhetorical jujitsu."

EARLY LIFE

Roxane Gay was born in Omaha, Nebraska, on October 28, 1974. Her parents had immigrated to the United States from Haiti when both were nineteen years old. Her father, Michael Sr., was a civil engineer who helped construct tunnels, and her mother, Nicole, was a homemaker. The family moved often for her father's job, and lived at various times in Colorado, Illinois, Virginia, and New Jersey. Gay has two younger brothers, Joel and Michael Jr., and the siblings enjoyed a close relationship. Gay has described her parents as strict.

They had spent the year frantically looking for her, and her father flew her home to Omaha.

Gay went on to complete her bachelor's degree and then a master's degree in English at the University of Nebraska–Lincoln. In 2010 she earned a doctorate in rhetoric and technical communication from Michigan Technological University.

FORAY INTO WRITING

While earning her degrees Gay published several pieces of erotica under various pen names. As a graduate student in 2006 she also cofounded a literary magazine of experimental prose and poetry called *PANK*, and in 2010 she founded Tiny Hardcore Press, a small independent company that releases pocket-sized novellas and chapbooks that would be ignored by large, mainstream publishers. Her own essays soon began appearing regularly in such well-regarded publications as the *Rumpus* (where she became its founding essays editor), *Virginia Quarterly Review*, and *McSweeney's*. By some standards, she reached a pinnacle as a contributing writer in 2015, when she was invited to submit regular opinion pieces to the venerable *New York Times*.

Gay's first full-length book, *Ayiti*, a collection of stories about Haiti and its people, appeared in 2011. She followed that in 2014 with two other books: a novel titled *An Untamed State*, about the kidnapping of a wealthy Haitian American woman, and the essay collection *Bad Feminist*. While it received wildly varying reviews, most divided along ideological lines, *Bad Feminist* introduced Gay to a large, mainstream audience. In a review for *Slate* (5 Aug. 2014), Katy Waldman opined, "Much of what makes this book work—and the loose essays hang together—is Gay's wry and delightful voice," and agreed with Gay's assertion that one of feminism's "biggest failures involves not taking women of color, queer women, and transgender women seriously."

DIFFICULT WOMEN AND HUNGER

In January 2017 Gay published *Difficult Women*, a well-received book of short stories whose protagonists are troubled, unconventional, or obstinate—or some combination thereof. "The book is dedicated: 'For difficult women, who should be celebrated for their nature' but it is not quite a celebration but more of a history and a testament," Anna James wrote for the *Los Angeles Times* (12 Jan. 2017). "It feels like the book we have been waiting for Gay to write."

That June Gay published the memoir *Hunger: A Memoir of (My) Body*, which Adrienne Green deemed "a gripping book, with vivid details that linger long after its pages stop" in her review for the *Atlantic* (13 June 2017). *Hunger*, she noted, was not written to motivate, but Gay's

rejection of the social stigma around overweight and her vulnerability do inspire. Green concluded the book is "arresting and candid. At its best, it affords women, in particular, something so many other accounts deny them—the right to take up space they are entitled to, and to define what that means."

Despite the respect and critical acclaim the memoir garnered her, Gay suffered repeated indignities while promoting it. Mia Freedman, host of the Australian podcast *Mamamia*, introduced an interview they had recorded together by confiding to listeners that she feared Gay would not fit in the studio elevator, for example. Just ahead of her interview with the National Public Radio show *This American Life*, host Ira Glass exhorted his audience to "grab a Twinkie" during a station break.

HAVING A VOICE IN POP CULTURE

Gay considers social media a vital form of community and has more than 430,000 Twitter followers, who avidly read her thoughts on serious social, political, and literary topics, as well as on her favorite television shows and celebrities. In 2017 Gay received additional praise from the literary community when she announced that she was breaking with Simon & Schuster, after the company signed Alt-right provocateur Milo Yiannopoulos to a book deal. Even when the publisher withdrew the contract in the wake of statements Yiannopoulos made that appeared to condone pedophilia, Gay refused to let them off the hook, writing scathingly on Tumblr that Simon & Schuster had simply made a business decision that the poor publicity was costing them more than the book would ultimately earn. *Not That Bad: Dispatches from Rape Culture*, a book of essays Gay edited, was due to be published in 2018 by HarperCollins.

In addition to writing fiction and nonfiction, Gay became the first black woman ever to author a comic-book series for the iconic company Marvel. Co-created with the essayist Ta-Nehisi Coates and several other writers, the series *Black Panther: World of Wakanda* follows Ayo and Aneka, two members of the superhero Black Panther's elite female security force.

ACADEMIC CAREER

Gay began her teaching career in 2010, as an assistant professor of English at Eastern Illinois University. In 2014 she accepted a tenure-track position at Purdue University's College of Liberal Arts in Indiana, where she is now an associate professor of creative writing. "When I walk into the classroom, the students stare at me like I'm in charge," she humorously writes in *Bad Feminist*. "They wait for me to say something. I stare back and wait for them to do something. It's a silent power struggle. Finally, I tell them to do things and they do those things. I realize I am, in fact, in charge."

PERSONAL LIFE

Gay identifies as bisexual and prefers to shield her personal life and her romantic partner. Gay divides her time between Lafayette, Indiana, and Los Angeles.

SUGGESTED READING

Cochrane, Kira. "Roxane Gay: Meet the Bad Feminist." *The Guardian*, 2 Aug. 2014, www.theguardian.com/world/2014/aug/02/roxane-gay-bad-feminist-sisterhood-fake-orgasm. Accessed 13 Jan. 2018.

Gay, Roxane. "In *Hunger*, Roxane Gay Says What No One Else Will About Being Fat in America." Interview by Janelle Okwodu. *Vogue*, 18 June 2017, www.vogue.com/article/roxane-gay-interview-hunger-memoir. Accessed 13 Jan. 2018.

Gay, Roxane. "Talking with *An Untamed State* Author Roxane Gay." Interview by Jim Higgins. *Milwaukee Journal Sentinel*, 23 May 2014, archive.jsonline.com/entertainment/books/talking-with-an-untamed-state-author-roxane-gay-b99275236z1-260459921.html. Accessed 13 Jan. 2018.

Green, Adrienne. "The Boldness of Roxane Gay's *Hunger*." Review of *Hunger: A Memoir of (My) Body*, by Roxane Gay. *The Atlantic*, 13 June 2017, www.theatlantic.com/entertainment/archive/2017/06/the-boldness-of-roxane-gays-hunger/530067. Accessed 13 Jan. 2018.

McArdle, Molly. "The Rise of Roxane Gay." *Brooklyn Magazine*, 22 Feb. 2017, www.bkmag.com/2017/02/22/rise-roxane-gay. Accessed 13 Jan. 2018.

Meltzer, Marisa. "Roxane Gay's New Memoir about Her Weight May Be Her Most Feminist—and Revealing—Act Yet." *Elle*, 14 June 2017, www.elle.com/culture/a45920/roxane-gay-profile-hunger-memoir. Accessed 13 Jan. 2018.

Waldman, Katy. "It's Good to Be a 'Bad' Feminist." Review of *Bad Feminist*, by Roxane Gay. *Slate*, 5 Aug. 2014, www.slate.com/articles/double_x/doublex/2014/08/bad_feminist_by_roxane_gay_reviewed.html. Accessed 13 Jan. 2018.

SELECTED WORKS

Ayiti, 2011; *An Untamed State*, 2014; *Bad Feminist*, 2014; *Hunger: A Memoir of (My) Body*, 2017; *Difficult Women*, 2017

—*Mari Rich*

Red Gerard

Date of birth: June 29, 2000
Occupation: Snowboarder

As American snowboarder Red Gerard prepared to take his third and final run down the slopestyle course at the 2018 Winter Olympics, he did not fully expect to complete his run, let alone win a gold medal in his event. However, his years of training paid off, and an excellent third-run score earned Gerard the number-one place on the podium. "I can't believe I got to land my run," he told Ben Bloom for the UK *Telegraph* (11 Feb. 2018) after the fact. "Just to land a run would have been plenty for me and to get on the podium, but to get first is crazy." In addition to representing a major professional milestone for Gerard, who was then seventeen, his victory was particularly significant for the United States, as Gerard became the first US athlete to claim a gold medal at that year's games.

Growing up in a heavily snowboarding-oriented family, Gerard began snowboarding as a toddler and was competing before he had even entered his teens. After impressing onlookers at regional and junior-level events, he began competing on the International Ski Federation's Snowboard World Cup circuit in 2015 and won his first World Cup event two years later. A practitioner of both the slopestyle and big air forms of snowboarding, he has experienced success with the former, including at the Winter Olympics. Regardless of his success in competition, however, Gerard remained devoted to the spirit of his sport and valued fun and camaraderie far more highly than accolades—including his gold medal. "Honestly, I've just given [the medal] to my brother or my agent or something, and let them hold it because I'll probably just lose it," he told Sam Blum for *Thrillist* (7 Mar. 2018).

EARLY LIFE

Redmond "Red" Gerard was born in Westlake, Ohio, on June 29, 2000. His father, Conrad, worked in finance. His mother, Jen, ended up serving as his manager for much of his early career and later managed the business side of his sister Tieghan's food blog business, Half Baked Harvest. The second-youngest of seven children, Gerard spent his early childhood in Rocky River, a suburb of Cleveland, Ohio. His family made a trial move to Colorado in early 2008 and for a time split their lives between Ohio and Colorado towns such as Breckenridge and Frisco. The Gerards eventually settled in Silverthorne, a small town in Summit County.

Outdoor sports, including biking and dirt biking, were popular in the Gerard family. Most notably, however, several of Gerard's siblings, particularly older brothers Brendan and Trevor, were deeply immersed in snowboarding. Gerard began snowboarding himself at the age of two, but particularly began to hone his skills on the slopes after the move to Colorado, where he practiced at local resorts such as Copper Mountain. "I remember I used to bomb the hill and just slide out right to my butt," he told Blum of his early days snowboarding in Colorado. Forced to learn quickly to keep up with his older siblings, Gerard soon demonstrated his talent on the slopes, impressing his family. By the time he was a preteen, he focused primarily on practicing and competing in snowboarding. He soon withdrew from local schools and enrolled in online classes that better fit his schedule.

As Gerard progressed as a snowboarder, some of his most important training happened right at his family's home in Silverthorne. His brother Brendan first realized the hill in their backyard was ideally suited for a terrain park, and the family built features such as rails to practice tricks on. A dirt bike was converted into a rope tow, and the park—which eventually became known as Red's Backyard—proved highly popular with local kids. Despite the ease of access, the park was decidedly not for amateurs. "There's been some injuries, a lot of concussions," Gerard told Nick Zaccardi for *NBC Sports* (16 Oct. 2017). "I have ate some serious crap back there, for sure. It's a dangerous little park."

EARLY CAREER

As a child, Gerard initially drew the attention of the snowboarding community through videos of his exploits that his brothers recorded and posted on websites such as YouTube. By the time he was eleven, he was considered among the best young talents in the sport. "It's pretty fricken awesome," he told *Yobeat.com* (15 Feb. 2012) at the time. "I think it's pretty cool because all the websites are putting my videos up . . . Hardly anyone ever says anything bad, which is cool because people on websites can be mean."

Gerard began to compete in snowboarding events put on by the USA Snowboard and Freeski Association. In 2012 he participated in a team challenge at the extreme sports–oriented Winter X Games, winning a gold medal. Gerard's success as a young snowboarder also brought him to the attention of numerous potential sponsors, and by the age of eleven, he had secured a sponsorship with Burton Snowboards. He went on to be sponsored by brands such as Red Bull, Celtek, and Mountain Dew. While he noted in interviews as a preteen that he hoped to make "a lot of money" as a snowboarder, he explained to *Yobeat.com* that his true focus lay elsewhere. "I snowboard to have fun and ride with my brothers and to learn new tricks," he said.

Throughout his early career, Gerard focused primarily on the slopestyle form of snowboarding,

in which athletes navigate a course full of obstacles and jumps and are scored for their tricks. He was successful in that event, placing fourth in slopestyle at the International Ski Federation (FIS) Junior World Championships in 2015. Gerard competed in a variety of FIS events, primarily in the United States, during his early career and went on to join the US slopestyle snowboarding team.

INTERNATIONAL COMPETITION

Gerard began competing professionally on the FIS Snowboard World Cup circuit in 2015, first appearing at the World Cup competition at Cardrona Alpine Resort in New Zealand that August. He placed eleventh in the men's slopestyle event. He went on to appear in several World Cup events in 2016, including in Italy and South Korea. Although primarily known for competing in slopestyle events, he at times competed in big air events, which focused on large jumps that enabled snowboarders to perform complex aerial tricks. Gerard also appeared in a variety of other events, including the Burton US Open, where he placed fifth in slopestyle in 2016, and the Dew Tour.

The year 2017 was a particularly productive one for Gerard, who began the year with his first World Cup event podium appearance after placing third in slopestyle at Austria's Kreischberg resort in January. The following month, he won the slopestyle competition at Mammoth Mountain in California, another World Cup event as well as an Olympic qualifier. He then placed second in big air at a World Cup event in Milan, Italy, and ended the 2016–17 FIS Snowboard World Cup season ranked first in the slopestyle World Cup standings and fourth in freestyle overall.

Outside of the World Cup circuit, Gerard placed fourteenth in men's slopestyle at the Winter X Games in Aspen, Colorado, and ninth at the Norway X Games that year. He returned to the Winter X Games in Aspen in January 2018, placing fourth in the men's slopestyle competition. That month also saw him place first in slopestyle at the Snowmass World Cup event in Colorado. Not only was it Gerard's second World Cup win, but his victory guaranteed him a place on the US men's Olympic snowboarding team for the 2018 Winter Olympic Games, held in Pyeongchang, South Korea.

2018 OLYMPIC GAMES

Many athletes actively strive to compete in the Olympic Games, but Gerard displayed a notably relaxed attitude toward the competition. "I didn't really, to be honest, grow up watching the Olympics. It was always Dew Tour, X-Games, US Open and all that that I was watching," he told Karma Allen for *ABC News* (14 Feb. 2018). "So I didn't have as much pressure coming into it and it was just another event." Following his arrival in Pyeongchang, Gerard planned to compete in the slopestyle event, which had debuted at the Winter Olympics in 2014, and the big air event, which was making its Olympic debut that year.

On February 10, 2018, Gerard competed in a qualification heat that also included Kyle Mack, a fellow US competitor and Olympic roommate, earning himself a spot in the final round of the men's slopestyle competition. The next day, Gerard—wearing a jacket borrowed from Mack after oversleeping and misplacing his own that morning—faced off against ten other athletes in the final round.

Each snowboarder received three opportunities to earn the greatest number of points possible on the slopestyle course. Gerard crashed on both of his first two runs and sat in last place going into the final attempt. Despite the pressure, his third and final run down the course scored a total of 87.16 points, enough to send him into first place. He ultimately claimed the gold medal in the men's slopestyle event when the last few competitors failed to beat his score. He became the first American athlete to win a gold medal in the 2018 games, as well as the youngest-ever gold medalist in snowboarding and the first Winter Olympics gold medalist born in the 2000s. He went on to place fifth in the men's big air event, the final stage of which was held on February 24.

GOLD MEDALIST

Despite already being a well-known figure within the snowboarding community, Gerard's gold-medal performance in the Olympic slopestyle event made him an instant celebrity. Much media coverage centered on his candid reaction to his victory, his family's partying in Pyeongchang, and his generally laid-back personality. He appeared on national television programs and was featured in various internet memes. The sudden spotlight was somewhat challenging for Gerard, who typically preferred to focus on his sport. "It's definitely something new to me," he told Blum. "I just kind of got thrown into it and I'm just sort of in the process now."

However, Gerard was unambiguously excited about the recognition he received from the fast food chain Chipotle, which he had frequently cited in interviews as one of his favorite places to eat. In light of his 87.16 score on his final Olympic slopestyle run, the company offered Gerard eighty-seven free burritos. "Chipotle is a hero, I have free food there for a year and I can bring as many people as I want," he told *Pyramid Magazine* (2018) following that announcement.

Often asked in interviews about his plans following the Olympics, Gerard stressed that he hoped to work on filming snowboarding videos but also to remain active in competition. "I enjoy doing contests and I'm looking forward to doing them again," he explained to *Pyramid Magazine*. "I'll definitely do some filming but I like contests and the places they bring me to so I'll continue to ride them." In September 2018, he returned to the FIS World Cup circuit, competing in the big air event at Cardrona.

PERSONAL LIFE

In addition to snowboarding, Gerard skateboards and plays golf. He has noted in interviews that if he could not be a professional snowboarder, he would consider becoming a golfer. "I could just see myself out on the tees drinking an iced tea," he told Blum.

SUGGESTED READING

Allen, Karma. "Olympic Gold Medalist Red Gerard Recalls 'Hectic' Morning before Big Win." *ABC News*, 14 Feb. 2018, abcnews.go.com/Entertainment/olympic-gold-medalist-red-gerard-recalls-hectic-morning/story?id=53070408. Accessed 14 Sept. 2018.

Bloom, Ben. "Teen Prodigy Red Gerard Becomes First Winter Olympic Medallist Born in 2000s with Slopestyle Gold." *The Telegraph*, 11 Feb. 2018, www.telegraph.co.uk/winter-olympics/2018/02/11/teen-prodigy-red-gerard-becomes-firstwinter-olympic-medallist. Accessed 14 Sept. 2018.

Boyd, Taylor. "Red Gerard Is the New Face of Snowboarding, and That's a Good Thing." *Transworld Snowboarding*, 20 Feb. 2018, snowboarding.transworld.net/photos/red-gerard-is-the-new-face-of-snowboarding. Accessed 14 Sept. 2018.

Gerard, Red. "A Pre Teen Hump Day with Red Gerard." *Yobeat.com*, 15 Feb. 2012. yobeat.com/2012/02/15/a-pre-teen-hump-day-with-red-gerard. Accessed 14 Sept. 2018.

Gerard, Red. "Real Talk: Red Gerard Interview." *Pyramid Magazine*, 2018, www.pyramidmagazine.com/real-talk-interviews/real-talk-red-gerard-interview. Accessed 14 Sept. 2018.

Gerard, Red. "Teen Gold Medalist Red Gerard: I Might Not Have Said F*ck on TV after All." Interview by Sam Blum. *Thrillist*, 7 Mar. 2018, www.thrillist.com/amphtml/news/nation/red-gerard-interview-gold-medal-olympic-snowboarder. Accessed 14 Sept. 2018.

Zaccardi, Nick. "Red Gerard Is the New Face of US Slopestyle." *NBC Sports*, 16 Oct. 2017, olympics.nbcsports.com/2017/10/16/red-gerard-slopestyle-snowboarding. Accessed 14 Sept. 2018.

—Joy Crelin

Rachel Kaadzi Ghansah

Date of birth: ca. 1982
Occupation: Essayist

Rachel Kaadzi Ghansah won the 2018 Pulitzer Prize for Feature Writing for an essay called "A Most American Terrorist: The Making of Dylann Roof," about the white supremacist who fatally shot eight churchgoers and their pastor in cold blood at the historic Emanuel African Methodist Episcopal Church, or Mother Emanuel, in Charleston, South Carolina, in 2015. The essay, first published in *GQ Magazine* in 2017, also won a National Magazine Award. A collection of Ghansah's essays called *The Explainers and the Explorers* is forthcoming.

Ghansah's work often explores black art and the lives of African American artists such as Pulitzer Prize–winning rapper Kendrick Lamar, rapper Missy Elliott, and comedian Dave Chappelle. "I like writing about people who look like me and the people I know who don't have good pieces written about them, because we deserve it," Ghansah explained in a video blog for *PBS NewsHour* in February 2016. Ghansah cut her literary teeth working for the rap/hip-hop group the Roots in the early 2000s. One of Ghansah's former professors at Columbia University, the award-winning novelist Zadie Smith, penned an ode to her for the UK edition of *Elle* (6 Dec. 2016). "Her non-fiction reads like a rich fiction," Smith wrote. "It's uncommon to read a voice that mixes anger and joy so beautifully and with so much skill. She doesn't write rants, she writes eloquent, appreciative tirades. . . . The energy in her writing comes from a place of aesthetic delight."

By Andrew Lih, via Wikimedia Commons

EARLY LIFE

Ghansah was born in 1982 to a Ghanaian father and an African American mother, a professor from Louisiana. Ghansah spent her early childhood in Indiana and moved with her mother, her grandmother, and her sister to Philadelphia, Pennsylvania, when she was about eight or nine years old. She writes about her upbringing among female relatives and her maternal history in the 2012 essay "My Mother's House."

Ghansah recalls growing up under the guidance of her mother's intellectual and diverse group of friends. "I come from these interesting women coming together to create a pretty radical world for their children," she told Chloe Wayne Sultan for the website *Creative New York* (27 Apr. 2018). Surprisingly, given her upbringing in an academic house, it took Ghansah a painfully long time to learn how to read. Once she could, she recalled for *PBS NewsHour*, "I just started to read ravenously." Her early literary heroes included poet Sonia Sanchez (whom her mother knew and convinced to come guest-teach Ghansah's middle-school class), science-fiction writer Madeleine L'Engle, and historical fiction novelist Toni Morrison.

Ghansah graduated from a private high school in Philadelphia that she "hated," as she wrote in her essay "Don't Let the Green Grass Fool You," published in *Politico* (14 Dec. 2011). She longed to escape, she wrote. To that end, she dropped out of college and began working for Richard Nichols, the manager for the Philadelphia-based hip-hop group the Roots, in 2000.

WORK WITH THE ROOTS AND EDUCATION

Ghansah doggedly pursued the job with Nichols, procuring his phone number from a National Public Radio (NPR) producer she knew and calling him a handful of times before he agreed to meet with her. In that first meeting, Ghansah told Nichols that she was a published writer—a lie at the time, she wrote in the essay, but one that would become self-fulfilling. Ghansah was more interested in being a part of a cultural moment driven by hip-hop. Nichols became an important mentor to Ghansah, and she learned things from members of the Roots as well. Tariq "Black Thought" Trotter, she recalled to Sultan, encouraged her to expand her vocabulary and develop a sense for the feeling of words. "I had a real journeyman's experience through writing—I didn't first learn about the way a sentence should push and swerve in school, I learned that when I hung out with rappers," she said. She worked for the Roots for a couple years before moving to New York City.

Ghansah enrolled in the Eugene Lang College of Liberal Arts at the New School, where she studied with professors such as media theorist McKenzie "Ken" Wark and writer Ferentz LaFargue. She briefly worked as an assistant to writer dream hampton and, with the encouragement of *Harper's Magazine* editor Lewis Lapham, applied for and obtained an unpaid internship at the long-running magazine. She wrote about that experience in "The Weight," an essay about the influence of African American novelist James Baldwin that was later collected in the anthology *The Fire This Time: A New Generation Speaks about Race* (2016). Ghansah was the first African American intern in the magazine's 150-plus-year history.

Ghansah graduated from the New School with a degree in culture and media in 2006. For a time, she worked as a public school teacher in New York. She went on to study with novelist Zadie Smith at Columbia University and earned a master's degree in 2011.

"IF HE HOLLERS LET HIM GO" AND OTHER ESSAYS

"Profiles are these deeply intimate pieces of writing where hopefully you are working towards an empathetic study of someone," Ghansah told Kameelah Janan Rasheed in an interview for the now-defunct website *Gawker* (7 June 2014). "This doesn't mean you hold their hand or that it becomes hagiography, but that you definitely get to say, 'This is what I see about you.' It is very empathetic work." Ghansah's essays, most of them profiles, have garnered praise.

In 2013, Ghansah's writing career began to take off. While living in New Orleans, Ghansah published a profile of rapper Kendrick Lamar, who went on to win a Pulitzer Prize alongside Ghansah in 2018. "When the Lights Shut Off: Kendrick Lamar and the Decline of the Black Blues Narrative," was first published in the *Los Angeles Review of Books* in January 2013. In it, Ghansah situates Lamar in a larger history of black memoir and the blues.

Later that same year, she wrote a profile of comedian Dave Chappelle for the *Believer* called "If He Hollers Let Him Go." The piece is among her best known. Chappelle refused to meet with Ghansah, so the profile is more of an exploration of Chappelle's departure from his wildly popular television show. For Ghansah, context is the key to understanding; the piece begins with a short history of Yellow Springs, the small Ohio town where the fiercely private comedian lives. "If He Hollers Let Him Go"—the title of which refers to the Chester Himes novel of the same name, not the nursery rhyme—was a finalist for a 2014 National Magazine Award for Essays and Criticism. It was also anthologized in two books that

year: *Read Harder* and *The Best American Nonrequired Reading*.

In 2014, Ghansah broadened her scope, writing an essay in March for NPR called "How Sweet It Is to Be Loved by You: The Beyhive," about singer Beyoncé's fiercely loyal fan base. A personal essay about her grandparents, "We a Baddd People," was published in the *Virginia Quarterly Review*, a prestigious literary journal, that June. In 2015, she wrote about Nobel Prize–winning novelist Toni Morrison ("The Radical Vision of Toni Morrison") and Jimi Hendrix's Electric Lady Studios ("A River Runs through It"). Ghansah has also profiled New York City's First Lady Chirlane McCray ("Chirlane McCray and the Limits of First-Ladyship," 2016) and rapper Missy Elliott ("Her Eyes Were Watching the Stars," 2017).

"A MOST AMERICAN TERRORIST: THE MAKING OF DYLANN ROOF"

In late 2016, Ghansah traveled to Charleston to cover the trial of Dylann Roof, the white man who was convicted of murdering nine at Mother Emanuel AME Church on June 17, 2015; Roof became the first person in United States history to be sentenced to death for a federal hate crime. Ghansah had intended to write a story about the lives of the victims—Reverend Clementa C. Pinckney, Cynthia Hurd, Susie Jackson, Ethel Lance, DePayne Middleton-Doctor, Tywanza Sanders, Daniel Simmons, Sharonda Coleman-Singleton, and Myra Thompson; the three survivors; and their families.

The experience of watching the trial pushed Ghansah to take a different approach, however. She was disturbed and angered by Roof's silence. He refused to answer for his crimes or express remorse. He guarded his own history, while the families of the victims got up one by one to testify to the character of their dead relatives. Ghansah became determined to tell Roof's story after a comment he made at the end of the trial. "And at the moment that he said, you don't know me; you don't know what hatred is, I said, no, I'm going to find out who you are, and I'm going to know you because you are hatred," she recalled to Kelly McEvers for the NPR program *All Things Considered* (4 Sept. 2017).

Ghansah interviewed Roof's family members and acquaintances in an effort to better understand Roof's background and motive. The resulting essay, "A Most American Terrorist: The Making of Dylann Roof," was published in *GQ Magazine* in August 2017. Ghansah pulled the article hours before it was printed because editors wanted to call it "The Making and Unmaking of Dylann Roof." "Obviously, there is no unmaking to a racist terrorist," she told Sultan. "But they were so committed to this absurd and offensive title that they sent it to the printers without my permission. I had to actually pull it to stop them." The title was changed, and the piece ran. It won the 2018 National Magazine Award for Feature Writing and later the Pulitzer Prize. The Pulitzer committee praised Ghansah for her "unforgettable portrait . . . using a unique and powerful mix of reportage, first-person reflection and analysis of the historical and cultural forces" behind Roof's heinous crime.

PERSONAL LIFE

In addition to her writing, Ghansah is also an adjunct assistant professor of writing at the Columbia Journalism School. She is married to film producer Eli Cane and lives in Brooklyn, New York.

SUGGESTED READING

"Brief but Spectacular: Rachel Kaadzi Ghansah, Essayist and Critic." *PBS NewsHour*, 4 Feb. 2016, www.pbs.org/newshour/brief/170671/rachel-kaadzi-ghansah. Accessed 5 June 2018.

McEvers, Kelly. "How One Reporter Found Herself Writing about the Charleston Church Shooter, Dylann Roof." *All Things Considered*, NPR, 4 Sept. 2017, www.npr.org/2017/09/04/548505825/how-one-reporter-found-herself-writing-about-the-charleston-church-shooter-dylan. Accessed 9 June 2018.

Rasheed, Kameelah Janan. "Stakes Is High—and Black Lives Are Worthy of Elaboration." *Gawker*, 7 June 2014, gawker.com/stakes-is-high-and-black-lives-are-worthy-of-elaboratio-1587471910. Accessed 10 June 2018.

Smith, Zadie, and Rachel Kaadzi Ghansah. "Zadie Smith on the Young Writer Who Teachers Her Everything." *Elle UK*, 6 Dec. 2016, www.elle.com/uk/life-and-culture/culture/articles/a30848/zadie-smith-introduces-rachel-kaadzi-hhansah. Accessed 6 June 2018.

Sultan, Chloe Wayne. "Rachel Kaadzi Ghansah." *Creative New York*, Museum of Modern Art, 27 Apr. 2018, nyc.moma.org/rachel-kaadzi-ghansah-f29547459bee. Accessed 5 June 2018.

SELECTED WORKS

"Don't Let the Green Grass Fool You: The Roots Are One of the Most Respected Hip-Hop Groups in the World; Why Can't They Leave the Sad Stuff Alone?," 14 Dec. 2011; "When the Lights Shut Off: Kendrick Lamar and the Decline of the Black Blues Narrative," 31 Jan. 2013; "If He Hollers Lets Him Go," Oct. 2013; "A Most American Terrorist: The Making of Dylann Roof," 21 Aug. 2017

—*Molly Hagan*

Rudy Gobert

Date of birth: June 26, 1992
Occupation: Basketball player

Rudy Gobert, a center for the Utah Jazz, is one of the best defensive players in the National Basketball Association (NBA). The "Stifle Tower," as he is affectionately known, stands seven feet, two inches tall and boasts a wingspan of seven feet, nine inches. In the 2016–17 season, he led the league in blocks per game and tied with Washington Wizards center Marcin Gortat for the most per-game screen assists, or blocks that directly enable a teammate to score a field goal. "Screening is more of an art and a skill than people realize," Jazz coach Quin Snyder said to Kyle Goon for the *Salt Lake Tribune* (8 Mar. 2018). "We assume screening is you just get there and get in the way." This is perhaps the best way to describe the twenty-five-year-old Frenchman: in his brief NBA career thus far, he has made an art of getting in the way.

Born in a small town in France, Gobert, like his father, who had played college basketball in New York, dreamed of playing for the NBA. As a gangly teen, he failed to win entrance to France's most elite training program. The rejection fueled his competitive drive, eventually making him a draft prospect in 2013. Gobert was selected in the first round, twenty-seventh overall, by the Denver Nuggets and was traded to the Utah Jazz the same night. He saw his draft number as a poor estimation of his talent, and after a rookie year in the NBA Development League, or

Photo by Stacy Revere/Getty Images

D-League, he was primed to prove himself again, this time with a jaw-dropping performance for France's International Basketball Federation (Fédération Internationale de Basket-ball, or FIBA) team in the summer of 2014.

Gobert has always had big plans for himself. Having shown the world what he can do defensively, he is working on other aspects of his game, and off the court he has voiced a desire to venture into music, specifically rap. "I wouldn't put a ceiling on him," Snyder said to Tim Mac-Mahon for *ESPN* (16 Mar. 2017). "His game's going to take its own direction."

EARLY LIFE AND CAREER

Rudy Gobert-Bourgarel was born on June 26, 1992, in Saint-Quentin, a town in the Aisne department of northern France. His father, Rudy Bourgarel, born on the French Caribbean island of Guadeloupe, was a backup center at Marist College in Poughkeepsie, New York, in the 1980s; he met Gobert's mother, cosmetologist Corinne Gobert, when he was playing for the Ligue Nationale de Basket (LNB) team in Saint-Quentin. Gobert has two much older stepsiblings from his mother's previous relationship.

Gobert's parents split up a few years after he was born, and his father moved back to Guadeloupe, where Gobert and his mother could only afford to visit every few years. Despite his father's absence, Gobert aspired to be like him. "Even if he wasn't there much of the time to teach me stuff, I think I was trying to be a basketball player too, like him," he said to Ben Reiter for *Sports Illustrated* (31 Jan. 2016).

Though Gobert was a good student, he often got into fights at school, so his mother encouraged him to put his excess energy into sports. He tried track and field, boxing, karate, and ping-pong, but basketball was the sport that stuck. When he was thirteen, he trained at a basketball academy about an hour from Saint-Quentin, returning home on weekends. During this time, while at a tournament, he met fellow Frenchman Evan Fournier, who would later play for the Orlando Magic. "As a kid, he was not necessarily confident," Fournier recalled to MacMahon. "But he was always competitive."

Two years later, at age fifteen, Gobert tried out for a number of French youth teams, including a prestigious program offered by the National Institute of Sport, Expertise, and Performance (Institut National du Sport, de l'Expertise et de la Performance, or INSEP), France's national sports academy. "Supposedly the best of a generation go there," Gobert said to Aaron Falk for the *Salt Lake Tribune* (25 Oct. 2015). "They didn't take me." Gobert was only accepted by one team, and it was in Cholet, five hours away.

Between the ages of fifteen and eighteen, Gobert grew a whopping seven inches, reaching his full height of seven feet two inches with a seven feet nine inch wingspan. As an adult, Gobert finds his size to be an asset, but early on, he had trouble controlling his growing limbs. "He could not stand on his legs," coach Philippe Urie recalled to Reiter. "He could not grab the ball. It was a very tough time for him."

In 2010, when Gobert was eighteen, he joined Cholet's Pro A team (Pro A is the top division in the LNB). He only played in two games during the 2010–11 season, but he played an average of 13.3 minutes per game the next season and was named best center in the *Eurobasket. com* All-European Championships Under-20 (U20) Awards 2012. He subsequently attended the 2012 Adidas Eurocamp, where he impressed scouts enough that respected basketball website *DraftExpress* bumped him into the top five of its 2013 mock draft. Gobert could have opted to declare for the NBA draft that year, but instead he elected to remain in Cholet through the 2012–13 season, during which he averaged 8.5 points, 5.4 rebounds, and 1.8 blocks in an average of 22.4 minutes per game. He was selected as a reserve for the 2012 LNB All-Star Game and was named to the 2012 FIBA Europe U20 Championship All-Tournament Team.

NBA DRAFT

At a predraft event in 2013, Gobert set an NBA record just by showing up: he was the longest player in history to attend the NBA Draft Combine in Chicago, with a standing reach of nine feet, seven inches, enabling him to reach within five inches of the hoop without jumping. Still, he fared poorly in the workouts leading up to the draft. Most teams saw a weak version of Gobert, except, notably, the Utah Jazz, whose workout proved to be an ideal showcase for his defensive range and instincts. His performance impressed Jazz executives, particularly general manager Dennis Lindsey, who had caught him practicing late in the gym the night before. "He likes to play. Like, he enjoys playing," Jazz assistant coach Alex Jensen said to MacMahon, speaking of Gobert's unusual dedication to the game. "I think a lot of big guys kind of fall into [basketball] because of just being big, but he likes to play and he wants to be good. It sounds simple, but it's rare. It's not the norm."

Gobert was chosen by the Denver Nuggets in the first round of the 2013 draft, twenty-seventh overall. That same night, the Jazz made a trade deal to put him on their team. Gobert was pleased to join the Jazz but displeased by his draft number, feeling he should have been picked sooner. He subsequently adopted the jersey number 27 as a reminder to keep pushing himself.

The Jazz kept Gobert on the bench for most of his rookie season, giving him similar displeasure. He poured himself, at his team's behest, into strength training. "The fact that I wasn't playing, I had a lot of energy going to the weight room," Gobert said to MacMahon. "I was kind of putting my anger into the weight room." He also spent part of his first NBA season playing with the Bakersfield Jam, a D-League team based in Bakersfield, California.

RISE OF THE STIFLE TOWER

In the summer of 2014, Gobert made his debut with France's FIBA Basketball World Cup team. Playing without French powerhouses Tony Parker and Joakim Noah, Gobert seized the opportunity to prove himself. "FIBA was really a challenge for me because, in France, people didn't really know me," he said to Leo Sepkowitz for *Slam* magazine (22 Oct. 2015). "They thought I was an NBA bench player and wasn't supposed to be good, or maybe at best a good rotation player. At best." Gobert's performance successfully silenced his naysayers; Sean Deveney, writing for *Sporting News* (10 Sept. 2014), called him "the driving force behind a shocking upset at the tournament"—namely, France's narrow victory over Spain in the quarterfinals. Gobert scored only five points, but with thirteen rebounds, it was the points he prevented Spain from scoring that really counted.

Coming in to the 2014–15 season, Gobert was armed with an effective argument for more playing time. Snyder began playing him, and his defensive play earned him more minutes. Midseason, the Jazz traded center Enes Kanter to the Oklahoma City Thunder, clearing the way for Gobert to become the team's starting center.

In January 2015, Gobert sent a direct message to the NBA's Twitter account, scolding the league for counting one clean block in a game when they should have counted two. In March, he scored a double-double: fifteen points and a career-high twenty-four rebounds in a win against the Memphis Grizzlies. "Rudy is a presence," Snyder said after the game, speaking to Clay Bailey for the Associated Press (3 Mar. 2015). "He gets a lot of second-chance points, which is important. He dominated the glass, and he contests." Gobert ended the season with twenty-five double-doubles and finished third in voting for the 2014–15 NBA Most Improved Player Award.

Although Gobert missed several weeks of the 2015–16 season after injuring his left knee, he signed a four-year, $102 million contract extension with the Jazz in 2016. In January 2017, he set a franchise record, recording twenty-five consecutive games with ten or more rebounds. In the twenty-fifth game, a win against the Cleveland Cavaliers, Gobert recorded his twenty-seventh double-double of the season. Less than two weeks later, in a win against the

Dallas Mavericks, Gobert scored career highs with twenty-seven points and twenty-five rebounds. (The win marked his twenty-ninth consecutive ten-plus rebound game; the streak would end at thirty.) "What I love about Rudy, is he's trying to win the basketball game and he doesn't like to lose," teammate Gordon Hayward said to Stephen Hawkins for the Associated Press (21 Jan. 2017). "He's got a fire inside of him and it's definitely something that you can feel when you're out there."

Gobert helped the Jazz reach the first round of the 2017 NBA Playoffs, where the Jazz faced off against the Los Angeles Clippers. He injured his left knee again in game one but returned in time for game four, and though he struggled through game seven, he helped the Jazz earn their first postseason victory since 2010. Although the Jazz subsequently lost four straight games to the dominant Golden State Warriors in the conference semifinals, at the end of the season Gobert was named to the first NBA All-Defensive Team and the second All-NBA Team.

INJURIES AND COMEBACK

At the beginning of the 2017–18 season, Gobert was leading the league in blocks per game before two successive knee injuries sidelined him again. He returned in January 2018 with a vengeance, recording twenty-three points, fourteen rebounds, and three blocks in a close-fought game against the New York Knicks, which the Jazz ultimately lost 115–117. Less than two months later, in a home game against the Minnesota Timberwolves, Gobert bested his previous performances that season with twenty-six points, sixteen rebounds, and four shots, helping lead the Jazz to a 116–108 victory.

As of mid-March 2018, despite having missed twenty-six games of the season thus far—close to one-third of the entire season—Gobert was still ranked tenth in the league in total blocks per season (96, working out to an average of 2.3 per game) and was leading the league in screen assists per game (5.9) for the second season in a row. "You don't see it on the stats, but it makes me happy when I set a screen and my guy gets a shot or we end up scoring," he said to Goon. "It makes you feel like you contribute."

SUGGESTED READING

Deveney, Sean. "Rudy Gobert Leads France in FIBA Stunner over Spain." *Sporting News*, 10 Sept. 2014, www.sportingnews.com/nba/news/rudy-gobert-utah-jazz-fiba-world-cup-france-spain-tony-parker-pau-gasol/lrg5huaapxnt17dyspk4xe7vd. Accessed 10 Mar. 2018.

Falk, Aaron. "Utah Jazz: Rudy Gobert, Leader of the Jazz's Unwelcome Committee." *The Salt Lake Tribune*, 25 Oct. 2015, archive.sltrib.com/

article.php?id=3090673&itype=CMSID. Accessed 10 Mar. 2018.

Goon, Kyle. "Rudy Gobert Quietly Has Become a Master at Screens, Powering the Jazz Offense." *The Salt Lake Tribune*, 8 Mar. 2018, www.sltrib.com/sports/jazz/2018/03/08/rudy-gobert-quietly-has-become-a-master-at-screens-powering-the-jazz-offense/. Accessed 10 Mar. 2018.

Hawkins, Stephen. "Gobert 27 Points, 25 Rebounds in Jazz 112–107 OT Win at Mavs." *AP News*, Associated Press, 21 Jan. 2017, apnews.com/ff074a2dbdbf4db8952ea7d2589e0407. Accessed 10 Mar. 2018.

MacMahon, Tim. "The Making of Rudy Gobert." *ESPN*, 16 Mar. 2017, www.espn.com/nba/story/_/page/presents170316b/how-utah-jazz-turned-rudy-gobert-next-bill-russell. Accessed 10 Mar. 2018.

Reiter, Ben. "Standing Tall: Rudy Gobert Altering Shots, Perceptions of French Players." *Sports Illustrated*, 31 Jan. 2016, www.si.com/nba/2016/02/03/rudy-gobert-utah-jazz-france-stifle-tower. Accessed 10 Mar. 2018.

Sepkowitz, Leo. "Tower of Power." *SLAMonline*, Slam Media, 22 Oct. 2015, www.slamonline.com/the-magazine/features/rudy-gobert-interview-jazz/. Accessed 10 Mar. 2018.

—*Molly Hagan*

Dominique Goblet

Date of birth: July 8, 1967
Occupation: Artist, graphic novelist

Since the 1990s, the Belgian sculptor and artist Dominique Goblet has been one of the leading lights of the European graphic novel scene, best known for her riveting experimental work, which varies in postmodern styles and mediums. Her work was introduced to the United States for the first time with the 2017 publication of *Pretending Is Lying*, the English translation of her biographical graphic novel *Faire semblant c'est mentir* (2007), which she began in 1995.

Pretending Is Lying, which recounts Goblet's visit to her estranged father with her three-year-old daughter in tow and her simultaneous contemplation of the next steps to take with her boyfriend, impressed critics on both sides of the Atlantic with its searing honesty and humor as well as its artistic dexterity. In a review of the translated work for *Tank* magazine (16 Aug. 2017), James Baty wrote, "Goblet forgoes a strict sense of chronology, giving scenes and moments in her life rather than an overarching story, and thereby captures far more of its overall tone than could be brought across in a typical

By R.J.W. Usher [CC BY-SA 4.0], via Wikimedia Commons

autobiography. The memoir is left open-ended and largely avoids passing judgment on her characters, despite the frequent wrongs they do to each other—just part of what lends the book its astonishing sense of tenderness and humanity."

EARLY LIFE AND CAREER
Dominique Goblet was born in Brussels, Belgium, on July 8, 1967. Her father, Jean Lieve Goblet, was a firefighter prior to his death in 1998. He spoke French, and Goblet's mother, who was Flemish, spoke Dutch; Goblet herself grew up fluent in both languages.

Goblet studied for six years at the Institut Saint-Luc in Brussels, where many young art students hone their skills and go on to work in the comics industry, first receiving higher secondary education in the visual arts (1984–87) and then pursuing specialized training in illustration (1987–90). After graduating in 1990, she began her career as an early contributor to the magazine *Frigorevue*, founded by fellow Institut Saint-Luc alumni, in addition to working on joint projects with the artists behind the magazine. "We were very active," Goblet recalled in an interview for the website *I Love Belgium* (Mar. 2016). "We did exhibitions, created narrative objects, collected experimental comics and reflected upon the limits of the genre. We wanted to find new ways of expression both graphic and narrative. That's why we founded our own publishing house, to publish things that at the time didn't fit into the norm."

That publishing house was Fréon, established in 1994; Goblet's first graphic novel,

Portraits crachés (Spitting images), a collection of stories and illustrations that had previously appeared in *Frigorevue* and other magazines, was published by Fréon in 1997. She followed this in 2001 with *Souvenir d'une journée parfait* (Memory of a perfect day), also from Fréon, about a woman who, while searching for her missing father, discovers a notebook through which she comes to know a stranger named Matthias Khan.

In 2001, Goblet returned to school, receiving her teaching certificate the following year. She then took a second year-long course, at the end of which she received certification in the English language.

L'ASSOCIATION

Goblet began her fruitful relationship with famed French publisher L'Association, best known for publishing such critically acclaimed graphic novels as Marjane Satrapi's *Persepolis* (2000; English translation, 2003–4) and David Beauchard's *L'ascension du haut mal* (1996–2003; *Epileptic*, 2005), in 2007. Her first graphic novel with L'Association was *Pastrami* (2007), a travel diary about her experiences in New York, Mexico, Guatemala, and Belize, published in the same year as *Faire semblant c'est mentir*.

In 2010, Goblet published two more books: *Les hommes-loups* (The wolfmen), through the publishing house Frémok (FRMK), formed by the merger of Fréon and French publisher Amok; and *Chronographie* (Chronography), again through L'Association, on which she collaborated with her daughter, Nikita Fossoul. *Chronographie* was built on a pact between mother and daughter: in 1998, when Fossoul was just seven years old, the pair promised to draw portraits of one another once a week for ten years. In the book's afterword, Goblet explains that the idea was to capture, not so much their likenesses, but their bond. Over the course of this effort, they used a variety of mediums to depict each other, including paint, pencil, and even collage. The book was praised both for its intimacy and for how it demonstrates the artistic development of mother and daughter over the same period. Bart Beaty, in a rave review for the *Comics Reporter* (14 June 2010), wrote, "By far the most extraordinary comic book I have read this year is *Chronographie*. . . . Many readers will dismiss it as something 'other than a comic book.' They'd be wrong, and they'd miss out on a once-in-a-lifetime aesthetic experience." He concluded, "There is a story here, and it's a profound one. It's a story of struggle, of growth, of understanding, and of seeking to understand the ones we love. *Chronographie* is one of the towering achievements of recent comics."

Goblet's next graphic novel was *Plus si entente* (More if it clicks, 2014), a graphic novel about a middle-aged woman with a lively imagination, which she cowrote and co-illustrated with German artist Kai Pfeiffer and published through FRMK. Her work has also appeared in several anthologies. Since the early 1990s, she has been published in numerous French-language magazines, and her work has been exhibited widely across Europe.

SAINT PETERSBURG EXHIBITION CONTROVERSY

Among the exhibitions in which Goblet's work was displayed was a 2015 installation at a festival called Boomfest, which is held annually at the Nabokov Museum in Saint Petersburg, Russia. The exhibition featured some of the work Goblet and Pfeiffer did for *Plus si entente*, including depictions of a nude fifty-year-old woman and her fantasies of naked men in her garden. When the figures' nudity was raised as an issue, the artists decided to cover them up in a humorous way—first with bright pink and orange undergarments, then with black dots, grape leaves, and other "censor boxes" covering the figures' genitals. But the University of Saint Petersburg, which runs the museum, objected and asked that the exhibition be closed, almost two weeks before its scheduled ending.

Both artists were flabbergasted by the abrupt cancellation, noting how nude figures were seen in museums across the world, including Saint Petersburg's famous Hermitage Museum. Some observers speculated that extremists in the Russian Orthodox Church were involved; others suggested the Russian government wanted it shuttered because of a perceived idea that it promoted homosexuality. Speaking to Aliide Naylor for the *Moscow Times* (12 Oct. 2015), Sasha Obukhova, a curator at the Garage Museum of Contemporary Art in Moscow, proposed a different explanation. "Small museums are very uncertain of their exhibitions in general," she said. "The Nabokov Museum is small, it is not protected by city government, and the exhibition they were showing didn't belong to them."

PRETENDING IS LYING

Faire semblant c'est mentir, Goblet's most widely known work to date, was published by L'Association in 2007 but did not appear in English until 2017, when it was released by New York Review Comics, the comics imprint of New York Review Books, under the title *Pretending Is Lying*. Goblet worked on the graphic novel over the course of a dozen years, from 1995 until its initial publication in 2007. Postmodern in its approach, *Pretending Is Lying* is both a memoir and something of an artistic exhibition. Throughout the work, Goblet uses a wide variety of styles and mediums, including charcoal, pencil, and ink, to depict Dom and her young daughter, Nikita—fictionalized versions of Goblet and

Fossoul—making a visit to Dom's father, dubbed Grandpa Mustache, whom she has not seen in several years because of his excessive drinking. While there, Dom and her daughter are also confronted with Grandpa's partner, Blandine. The pair is depicted in an exaggerated way— Grandpa with dark mustache and eyebrows, a large paunch, and splayed legs; Blandine, hairless and almost featureless, with circles for her nose and eyes.

At the time of this visit, Dom is seeking to work on her relationship with her lover, GM, who is still quite literally haunted by an ex-girl-friend, portrayed as a hovering white ghostlike figure. The story also incorporates flashbacks to Dom's childhood in Belgium, in particular her relationship with her mother. Characters visually morph throughout the book, as their appearances vary based on their moods and the mood of the author herself, and Goblet demonstrates her ability to adapt her drawing to photographic forms, producing impressive urban illustrations. For the English-language publication, she relettered each page, since the style of the lettering in the original was designed to be indicative of each character's speaking style. The graphic novel ends with a telephone conversation between Dom and GM, with an ambiguous sense of possibility between them.

Upon its publication in the United States, *Pretending Is Lying* received rave reviews from major media outlets. Sheila Heti wrote for the *New York Times* (24 Feb. 2017), "It is a rare gift to come across a book as tender, affecting and complete as *Pretending Is Lying*. . . . One closes the book knowing that our deepest relationships both make time move forward and stand still." In a review for NPR (5 Feb. 2017), Etelka Lehoczky wrote, "Goblet's characters are incredibly alive, full-bodied and appealing even when they hurt one another. In the best tradition of Expressionism, she distorts people's bodies to reflect their impact on those around them." Writing for the *Los Angeles Review of Books*, Tahneer Oksman declared, "The true focus here, as in other groundbreaking graphic memoirs like Art Spiegelman's *Maus* (1980–91) or Alison Bechdel's *Fun Home* (2006), is on how our childhoods remain perpetually alive and visible to us, and how in adulthood we continue to navigate the past in the present—sometimes more self-consciously than others."

In addition to English, some of Goblet's books have been translated into Dutch, German, and Norwegian. She has received numerous nominations and awards for her work, including the 2007 Prix Töpffer International, for *Faire semblant c'est mentir*, and the 2011 École Européenne Supérieure de l'Image (ÉESI) Prize at the Angoulême International Comics Festival.

PERSONAL LIFE

Goblet lives and works in Brussels. Her boyfriend, music producer Guy Marc Hinant, was the basis for GM, the haunted boyfriend character in *Pretending Is Lying*.

SUGGESTED READING

Baty, James. "The Graphic Novel's Tender Humanity." Review of *Pretending Is Lying*, by Dominique Goblet, translated by Sophie Yanow. *Tank*, 16 Aug. 2017, tankmagazine.com/tank/2017/08/pretending-is-lying/. Accessed 6 Feb. 2018.

Beaty, Bart. "Conversational Euro-Comics: Bart Beaty on *Chronographie* by Dominique Goblet and Nikita Fossoul." Review of *Chronographie*, by Dominique Goblet and Nikita Fossoul. *The Comics Reporter*, 14 June 2010, www.comicsreporter.com/index.php/briefings/eurocomics/26438/. Accessed 6 Feb. 2018.

Goblet, Dominique. "The Goblet Way." *I Love Belgium*, Mar. 2016, www.ilovebelgium.be/goblet-way. Accessed 6 Feb. 2018.

Heti, Sheila. "A Belgian Artist's Graphic Memoir Looks at the Sometimes Tortured Course of Love." Review of *Pretending Is Lying*, by Dominique Goblet, translated by Sophie Yanow. *The New York Times*, 24 Feb. 2017, www.nytimes.com/2017/02/24/books/review/pretending-is-lying-dominique-goblet.html. Accessed 6 Feb. 2018.

Lehoczky, Etelka. "With a Photographer's Eye, a French Cartoonist Interrogates Truth." Review of *Pretending Is Lying*, by Dominique Goblet, translated by Sophie Yanow. *NPR*, 5 Feb. 2017, www.npr.org/2017/02/05/512043013/with-a-photographers-eye-a-french-cartoonist-interrogates-truth. Accessed 6 Feb. 2018.

Naylor, Aliide. "St. Petersburg Exhibition Censored and Closed." *The Moscow Times*, 12 Oct. 2015, themoscowtimes.com/articles/st-petersburg-exhibition-censored-and-closed-50223. Accessed 6 Feb. 2018.

Oksman, Tahneer. "'The Things That Scare You': Dominique Goblet's *Pretending Is Lying*." Review of *Pretending Is Lying*, by Dominique Goblet, translated by Sophie Yanow. *Los Angeles Review of Books*, 8 June 2017, lareviewofbooks.org/article/the-things-that-scare-you-dominique-goblets-pretending-is-lying/. Accessed 6 Feb. 2018.

SELECTED WORKS

Portraits crachés, 1997; *Souvenir d'une journée parfait*, 2001; *Faire semblant c'est mentir* (*Pretending Is Lying*), 2007; *Pastrami*, 2007; *Chronographie* (with Nikita Fossoul), 2010; *Les hommes-loups*, 2010; *Plus si entente* (with Kai Pfeiffer), 2014

—*Christopher Mari*

GoldLink

Date of birth: May 17, 1993
Occupation: Rapper

Rapper GoldLink is best known as the purveyor of a kind of club-rap that combines such disparate genres as bachata, go-go, and house. He calls it "future bounce." Born in Washington, DC, he grew up in various places within the region accessible by the DC Metro, referred to by locals as the DMV—DC, Maryland, and Virginia. He is thoroughly of the DMV, drawing significant inspiration from the region's distinct and exuberant variety of funk music called go-go. The godfather of go-go, the late Chuck Brown, began throwing go-go parties in the 1970s, in which live bands played continuous grooves through the night. GoldLink attended his first go-go party when he was in the sixth grade.

He pays homage to that period of his young life on his debut album. "With *At What Cost*, I was basically reliving a time in my life during the go-go era," he told Lawrence Burney for *Noisey* (26 Jan. 2018). "I remember when it was popping for my generation and how that felt and what it looked like." One of the songs from that album, the smash-hit "Crew," featuring local talents Brent Faiyaz and Shy Glizzy, was nominated for a Grammy Award for Best Rap Performance. Writer Nazuk Kochhar, a DMV native, saw the nomination as a sign that the region's sound was finally getting its due. For the *Fader* (4 Dec. 2017), he wrote, "Hearing three young, rising stars from the area coming together to support one another while collectively putting on for their home on a national level was like watching a hometown dream unfold." In 2018, GoldLink appeared on the Anderson.Paak-produced Christina Aguilera single "Like I Do."

EARLY LIFE

GoldLink was born D'Anthony Carlos in Washington, DC, on May 17, 1993. His father was a parks and recreation worker, and his mother was a secretary at a law firm. He has a brother who is nearly ten years older. When he was two years old, his family's house burned down, and for the next several years, he and his family lived in various motels. He then spent most of his childhood in Landover, Maryland. His parents divorced when he was sixteen; after that, he and his mother moved to Bowie, Maryland, and then to Northern Virginia. He did not speak to his father for years, and his relationship with his mother was strained. "My mom and I weren't that close when I was growing up because she was gone seven days of the week; she was always in church," he recalled to Lauren Nostro for *Complex* magazine (9 July 2014).

By Mac Downey, via Wikimedia Commons

GoldLink graduated from Hayfield Secondary School in 2011. A smart teenager with mediocre grades, he was not interested in college and had difficulty finding a job. He decided that he wanted a career in rap music and pursued this aim with a singular focus, studying his favorite artists with an academic fervor. "It was a lot of research as opposed to influences," he told Julian Kimble for the *Washington City Paper* (6 Aug. 2015). "It was more like, how can I take that and say [certain things] in a different way with a unique sound?" He studied rappers such as the late Big L from New York and early hip-hop great KRS-One. He also read Edgar Allan Poe and watched the popular spoken-word television series *Def Poetry Jam*. Electronic artists such as Grimes and Lykke Li rounded out his curriculum. He saw himself as the vanguard of a new "wave" of rap music, he told Kimble. "I was like, 'I think this is the sound that's going to happen,'" he said. "It was all work, research, prediction, and prayer."

EARLY RECORDING CAREER

In 2012, GoldLink met a concert promoter named Henny Yegezu. Yegezu ran a recording studio in Falls Church, Virginia, called Indie Media Lab. He began a program called the Movement, in which he allowed a talented few young rappers to record at the studio for free. Yegezu, who is now GoldLink's manager, told Kimble, "That stuff"—what GoldLink was recording at nineteen—"was super raw compared to what he's making now. But even from the jump, he naturally leaned into the production and had a lot of character in his flow." Yegezu was impressed enough to let the rapper continue to record for free, even after the program was over.

However, GoldLink, whom Yegezu described to Nostro as "hard-headed and stubborn," spent a year recording elsewhere before returning in the spring of 2013. The two spent hours looking for beats on the music website *SoundCloud*, where they found producers such as Sango and Canadian DJ Kaytranada. GoldLink released his first mixtape, *The God Complex*, in 2014. It was a debut in more ways than one: it marked the first time that GoldLink revealed his face to his fans. Jayson Greene, writing for *Pitchfork* (9 May 2014), rated the tape a 7.9 out of 10—a very impressive showing for an almost totally unknown artist with only a handful of songs to his name. Greene wrote that GoldLink, with his playful samples, upbeat tempo, and hard rhymes, "skips through the minefield separating rap's ideas of 'hard' and 'soft.'" By the time of the review, GoldLink had garnered a small fanbase on *SoundCloud* and locally in the DMV. Noting this success, Greene wrote, "He's struck a nerve, even if no one knows exactly where that nerve is just yet."

The God Complex caught the attention of Rick Rubin, a famed producer and cofounder of Def Jam Records, who became a mentor to GoldLink as he developed his next mixtape. "GoldLink connects progressive rap styles with cutting edge dance music," Rubin told Emmanuel C. M. for *XXL* magazine (17 Feb. 2015). "He bridges the electronic DJ culture with hip hop in a way we haven't heard before." The hip hop magazine went on to name GoldLink in their coveted "Freshman Class" list of rappers on the rise in 2015. The same year, he released a single called "Spectrum." In the song, he raps candidly about a past relationship over production from Louie Lastic and a Missy Elliott sample. "GoldLink's skilled tongue can mask the vulnerability, but his precision ensures that no line is lost," Matthew Strauss wrote for *Pitchfork* (15 Oct. 2015). "With GoldLink, a personally revealing song never feels heavy, just thorough, compelling, and insightful."

GoldLink released *And After That, We Didn't Talk*, an ode to past relationships including the teenage breakup discussed in "Spectrum," in 2016. Sheldon Pearce, who reviewed the tape for *Spin* (11 Nov. 2015), described it as a more mature record than *The God Complex* and one that revealed more about GoldLink as a person. "*Talk* is brimming with personality, trickier flows, crisper textures, and the same careful curator's touch GoldLink has used to manage his public identity thus far," Pearce wrote.

AT WHAT COST

For his major label debut album, *At What Cost*, GoldLink returned to his roots in the DMV. Drawing inspiration from go-go and local artists, he told Lakin Starling for the *Fader* (24 Mar. 2017) that he felt an urgent need to tell the story of his hometown. "I felt like if it wasn't me, it would . . . be a kid that was coming after me, but it may be too late," he said later. "I just felt it was my job." Alongside go-go there was also terrible grief. Go-go parties, which all but disappeared after 2011, were often cut short by fights between rival neighborhoods. The violence of this era finds its way onto the record as well. "I was losing my homies so quick that I appreciated life more. I cried on my eighteenth birthday because my friend had just got smoked that year before. But, there are a lot of good things that came out of go-go," he told Starling. "I don't want to just talk about the violence, I'm trying to talk about everything." This bittersweet view of his world is exemplified on the upbeat jam "Crew."

In 2017, GoldLink released the singles "Crew" and "Meditation," and he became the first DC rapper to perform at the music festival Coachella. He released his debut album, *At What Cost*, in March. Mehan Jayasuriya described the sound of the album for *Pitchfork* (11 Apr. 2017) as "quintessentially that of GoldLink's hometown: loose, organic, as humid as a D.C. summer." The album's first track, a song produced by Kaytranada called "Hands on Your Knees," is a "straight-up go-go number" featuring DC performer Kokayi emceeing a party. Meanwhile, "Meditation" ends with the sound of "gunfire erupting outside of a party." The album also features a host of local artists, including DC's best-known rapper Wale and the R&B singer Mýa, as well as relative unknowns such as the rapper Cisero. "*At What Cost* is clearly guided by GoldLink's vision from start to finish," Jayasuriya wrote. "He's leveraging the music that shaped him, working with producers with whom he has real chemistry, and putting on as many DMV artists as he can . . . [it] feels like an album only GoldLink could make, one that's forward-thinking yet firmly rooted in D.C. tradition."

PERSONAL LIFE

Though people around him have suggested that he move to Los Angeles to further his career, GoldLink has resisted. He still lives in the Washington, DC, area.

SUGGESTED READING

Burney, Lawrence. "What a Time, What a Year It's Been for GoldLink." *Noisey*, 26 Jan. 2018, noisey.vice.com/en_us/article/yw58wg/what-a-time-what-a-year-its-been-for-goldlink. Accessed 10 June 2018.

GoldLink. "GoldLink's New Album *At What Cost* Is a Vivid Love Letter to D.C."" Interview by Lakin Starling. *The Fader*, 24 Mar. 2017, www.thefader.com/2017/03/24/goldlinks-new-album-iat-what-costi-is-a-vivid-love-letter-to-dc. Accessed 11 June 2018.

Greene, Jayson. Review of *The God Complex*, by GoldLink. *Pitchfork*, 9 May 2014, pitchfork.com/reviews/albums/19325-goldlink-the-god-complex/. Accessed 11 June 2018.

Jayasuriya, Mehan. Review of *At What Cost*, by GoldLink. *Pitchfork*, 11 Apr. 2017, pitchfork.com/reviews/albums/23109-at-what-cost/. Accessed 11 June 2018.

Kimble, Julian. "GoldLink's Past, Present and Future Bounce." *Washington City Paper*, 6 Aug. 2015, www.washingtoncitypaper.com/arts/music/blog/13082183/goldlinks-past-present-and-future-bounce. Accessed 10 June 2018.

Nostro, Lauren. "Who is GoldLink? The DMV Rapper Talks the Allure of Anonymity, Finding Success and *The God Complex*." *Complex*, 9 July 2014, www.complex.com/music/2014/07/who-is-goldlink. Accessed 10 June 2018.

Pearce, Sheldon. "Review: GoldLink Explains It All on *And After That, We Didn't Talk*." Review of *And After That, We Didn't Talk*, by GoldLink. *Spin*, 10 Nov. 2015, www.spin.com/2015/11/review-goldlink-explains-it-all-on-and-after-that-we-didnt-talk/. Accessed 11 June 2018.

—*Molly Hagan*

Robert J. Gordon

Date of birth: September 3, 1940
Occupation: Economist

Leading American macroeconomist Robert J. Gordon has earned a reputation as "the scourge of the techno-optimists," as Chris Wellisz called him in *Finance & Development* (June 2017), for his pessimistic views about future US growth and productivity. Known particularly for his expertise on inflation, unemployment, and long-term economic growth, Gordon has taught economics at Northwestern University for over four decades.

Gordon has also authored five books, the most recent of which, *The Rise and Fall of American Growth: The U.S. Standard of Living since the Civil War*, was published in 2016. The book, which was met with popular and critical success, exemplifies his life's work on economic growth in America. Among his most controversial assertions is that twenty-first-century innovations in computer technology will not spur the same kind of economic growth that inventions from the late nineteenth and early twentieth centuries did. As he put it to Wellisz, "I'm here as the prophet of pessimism."

EARLY LIFE AND EDUCATION

Robert James Gordon was born on September 3, 1940, and raised in Berkeley, California. He comes from a prominent family of economists. Both of his parents were longtime, well-regarded professors of economics at the University of California, Berkeley, and served on presidential commissions. Gordon's father, Robert Aaron Gordon (1909–78), was a leading expert on business cycles, manpower policy, and unemployment, while his mother, Margaret Shaughnessy Gordon (1911–94), was well known for her many studies on health, welfare, employment, and higher education. His younger brother, David (1944–96), became a trailblazer in radical political economics and taught at the New School for Social Research in New York.

Growing up, Gordon engaged in spirited debates with his family over economic theory. In an interview with Brian Lamb for his C-SPAN series *Q&A* (10 Mar. 2016), he described his parents as "knee-jerk New Deal liberals" and said that his brother was a "self-avowed radical Marxist." Gordon himself developed liberal conservative economic views, but upon entering Harvard University in the late 1950s, he initially planned to major in history. After receiving a B in a history course, however, he switched to economics. He earned his bachelor's degree in that subject, graduating magna cum laude in 1962. He then received a Marshall Scholarship to study at Oxford University, where he obtained a master's degree with honors in 1969.

Instead of following in his parents' footsteps, both of whom earned PhDs in economics from Harvard, Gordon pursued his doctorate at the Massachusetts Institute of Technology (MIT), which made him "the black sheep of the family," as he quipped to Lamb. He earned his PhD in economics from MIT in 1967. Nevertheless, Gordon's brother earned a PhD from Harvard in 1971. This prompted *Businessweek* to label the Gordon clan the Flying Wallendas of Economics, referring to the family of circus performers.

EARLY CAREER

It was at MIT where Gordon first formulated his ideas on economic growth. Influenced by such Nobel laureates as Paul Samuelson and Robert Solow, both neo-Keynesian economists, Gordon became intrigued by the unprecedented production of goods and services that occurred in the United States between the 1920s and 1950s. Though the country's output doubled during that time, the capital it used to produce its goods and services did not increase, which ran counter to conventional economic wisdom. This led to Gordon's PhD dissertation exploring flaws in the measurement of capital, with Solow as his adviser.

Gordon soon settled into a career in academia. In 1968, he was appointed a research associate for the National Bureau of Economic Research, a position he still holds. In 1973, following teaching stints at Harvard University and the University of Chicago, he became a professor of economics at Northwestern University in Evanston, Illinois. There, he has taught elementary and intermediate economics courses. In 1987, he was appointed the Stanley G. Harris Professor of the Social Sciences and, from 1992 to 1996, served as chair of his department.

Over the course of his career, Gordon has published more than a hundred academic journal articles on various economic issues. He has also written five books, the first of which was *Macroeconomics* (1978), a textbook widely used in American universities and now in its twelfth edition. The book was the first to present a version of the Phillips curve—which reflects the supposed inverse relationship between unemployment and inflation—that factored in the rational expectations theory. Often used in the analysis of inflation rates, rational expectations theory considers past events and experiences in explaining how producers and suppliers make choices.

EXPERT ON ECONOMIC GROWTH AND INFLATION

Gordon's research has concentrated heavily on long-term growth trends and problems associated with measuring capital. His third book, *The Measurement of Durable Goods Prices* (1990), reflects this area of focus. It expands on ideas Gordon first developed in his dissertation, in which he created a model for estimating construction costs. Chronicling the impact of modern technological innovations on the US economy, the book illustrates how such innovations, from automobiles and airplanes to televisions and computers, improved the quality of people's lives. It is noted for taking this improved quality into account when examining official measures of capital, which was "a very, very important contribution and changed the way people think about growth," as Lawrence Christiano, the chair of Northwestern's economics department, told Chris Wellisz.

Gordon has also been known for his work on inflation. He is credited with developing what is known as the "triangle model of inflation," which incorporates such factors as inertia and shifts in supply and demand in explaining the inflation rate. The model helped explain the simultaneously low rates of unemployment and

inflation that occurred in the United States during the 1990s, a phenomenon that is referred to as a "Goldilocks economy." According to Wellisz, Gordon's triangle model has highlighted the significance of core inflation, which excludes volatile commodities from the food and energy sectors.

In 1995, thanks to his reputation in economic circles, Gordon was appointed to serve on the Boskin Commission, which was formed by the US Senate Finance Committee to evaluate the consumer price index (CPI) in the context of government-funded benefit programs. Headed by Stanford University economist Michael J. Boskin, the five-member panel of economic experts found that the CPI overstated inflation by 1.1 percent. This ultimately influenced the US Bureau of Labor Statistics to change the way it calculated the CPI.

In 2003, Gordon was named to the US Bureau of Economic Analysis Advisory Committee.

ECONOMIC PESSIMIST

Gordon's pessimism about US economic growth began to materialize in 2000, when he published a controversial working paper titled "Does the 'New Economy' Measure Up to the Great Inventions of the Past?", focusing on the long-term impact of computers and the Internet. In it, he argued that computer technology, despite revolutionizing the way people work and communicate, would not have the same sweeping effects on the US economy as past inventions had. In 2012, he took that view even further with the publication of "Is U.S. Economic Growth Over? Faltering Innovation and the Six Headwinds," a working paper that predicted that the economy would grow half as fast, or less, than it did between 1860 and 2007, when it grew at a rate of 1.9 percent per year.

In a February 2013 TED Conference talk, called "The Death of Innovation, the End of Growth," Gordon discussed the threat of headwinds—namely, demographics, education, debt, and inequality—to US economic growth. "Because of the headwinds, if innovation continues to be as powerful as it has been in the last 150 years, growth is cut in half," he explained. "If innovation is less powerful, invents less great, wonderful things, then growth is going to be even lower than half of history." He cited such revolutionary late-nineteenth-century innovations as the electrification of tools and the internal combustion engine and opined that because future innovations will fail to measure up to them, US growth will stagnate.

Such arguments were given in-depth treatment in Gordon's best-selling 2016 book *The Rise and Fall of American Growth*, which took four years to write and was published to wide acclaim. On a visit to a bed and breakfast in Michigan, Gordon gained inspiration when he came across a book by Otto Bettmann, titled *The Good Old Days: They Were Terrible!* (1974), which depicts slum life in America during the late nineteenth century. Gordon recalled to Wellisz that the photos helped him "see how enormously things have improved since then."

THE RISE AND FALL OF AMERICAN GROWTH

Filled with rich and vivid historical detail, *Rise and Fall* represents more than four decades of research on US economic growth. The 784-page tome centers around the idea that US productivity growth, which has slowed considerably since the 2008–9 global financial crisis, will languish for the foreseeable future. Covering the preceding 150 years of US economic history, the book focuses on the period between 1870 and 1970, which Gordon deems the "special century." It was during that hundred-year period when the modern world began to take shape, starting with what Gordon refers to as the "great inventions," among them electric lighting and machinery, the internal combustion engine, urban sanitation and indoor plumbing, vaccines and antibiotics, telephones, automobiles, and airplanes.

These inventions transformed life around the world and fostered levels of growth and progress that were unprecedented in human history. As Gordon points out, however, US productivity growth began to slow sharply around 1970, and save for the economic boost the country experienced during the 1990s internet boom, it has remained that way ever since. Gordon cites two main reasons for his pessimism: first, the social and economic changes that occurred during the "special century" were unique because they cannot be repeated, and second, the aforementioned headwinds will ultimately impede future technological innovation.

At the center of *Rise and Fall* is Gordon's argument that simply "some inventions are more important than others," as he states in its introduction. Though computers and twenty-first-century innovations like the smartphone and social media have become ubiquitous in American life, he argues, they pale in comparison to the transformative inventions of the past. According to Gordon, most, if not all, of these newer technological inventions have only brought about incremental advances, such as cellphones and smartphones, which are but refinements on the telephone. Citing another example, he told Wellisz, "We moved from the speed of the horse and the sail to the Boeing 707, and we have not gone any faster since."

CRITICAL RECEPTION

Rise and Fall brought Gordon national attention and earned him a place on Bloomberg's 2016 list of the world's fifty most influential people in finance. The book was widely reviewed and earned a generally positive response from critics, most of whom praised its meticulous attention to detail and well-informed economic scholarship. In a representative review for the *New York Times* (25 Jan. 2016), the Nobel Prize–winning economist Paul Krugman called the book "a magisterial combination of deep technological history, vivid portraits of daily life over the past six generations and careful economic analysis."

Some critics, such as economist Tyler Cowen, faulted Gordon for dismissing positive factors in the US economy and past periods of uneven progress in his forecast of future economic and productivity growth rates, which Gordon predicts will remain low for the next twenty-five years. Gordon, however, has remained obstinate in his pessimistic beliefs and has shot down the idea that ever-evolving, cutting-edge technologies like robots and artificial intelligence will have the same impact on the economy as earlier inventions. As he told Timothy Aeppel for the *Wall Street Journal* (15 June 2014), "The rapid progress made over the past 250 years could well turn out to be a unique episode in human history."

ACCLAIM

Over the course of his career, Gordon has received numerous honors for his contributions to economics. He was elected to the Econometric Society in 1977 and received a Guggenheim Fellowship in 1980. Gordon was inducted into the American Academy of Arts and Sciences in 1997 and, in 2014, was named a distinguished fellow of the American Economic Association in 2014.

PERSONAL LIFE

Gordon married Julie S. Peyton, an artist and fellow Northwestern professor, in June 1963. The couple reside in Evanston, Illinois, with their dog. Gordon enjoys the arts and has collected photographs of economists.

SUGGESTED READING

Aeppel, Timothy. "Economists Debate: Has All the Important Stuff Already Been Invented?" *The Wall Street Journal*, 15 June 2014, www.wsj.com/articles/economists-duel-over-idea-that-technology-will-save-the-world-1402886301. Accessed 2 June 2018.

Cowen, Tyler. "Is Innovation Open?" *Foreign Affairs*, Mar.–Apr. 2016, www.foreignaffairs.com/reviews/review-essay/2016-02-15/innovation-over. Accessed 2 June 2018.

Gordon, Robert. "Q&A with Robert Gordon." Interview by Brian Lamb. *C-SPAN*, 10 Mar. 2016, www.c-span.org/video/?406230-1/qa-robert-gordon. Accessed 2 June 2018.

Gordon, Robert. "The Death of Innovation, the End of Growth." *TED*, TED Conferences, Feb. 2013, www.ted.com/talks/

robert_gordon_the_death_of_innovation_
the_end_of_growth/transcript. Accessed 2
June 2018.

Krugman, Paul. Review of *The Rise and Fall of American Growth*, by Robert J. Gordon. *The New York Times*, 25 Jan. 2016, www.nytimes.com/2016/01/31/books/review/the-powers-that-were.html. Accessed 2 June 2018.

Nordhaus, William D. "Why Growth Will Fail." Review of *The Rise and Fall of American Growth*, by Robert J. Gordon. *The New York Review of Books*, 18 Aug. 2016, www.nybooks.com/articles/2016/08/18/why-economic-growth-will-fall. Accessed 2 June 2018.

Wellisz, Chris. "Prophet of Pessimism." *Finance & Development*, June 2017, economics.weinberg.northwestern.edu/robert-gordon/files/ROBERTGORDONPROFILE.pdf. Accessed 2 June 2018.

SELECTED WORKS

Macroeconomics, 1978; *The Measurement of Durable Goods Prices*, 1990; *The Rise and Fall of American Growth*, 2016

—*Chris Cullen*

By Mwinog2777 via Wikimedia Commons

Marcin Gortat

Date of birth: February 17, 1984
Occupation: Basketball player

Veteran National Basketball Association (NBA) center Marcin Gortat, the self-dubbed Polish Machine, has played eleven seasons in the league, including five years with the Washington Wizards. Chris Barnewell, writing for *CBS Sports* (12 Jan. 2018), described Gortat's workhorse utility this way: "He won't be going to the Hall of Fame, but he found a role that worked for him and made a career out of it." Gortat, who played for professional teams in Poland and Germany, was the fifty-seventh pick of the 2005 NBA Draft. He spent two more years in Europe before officially signing with the Orlando Magic in 2007. After spending several years playing backup center to superstar Dwight Howard, Gortat went to the Phoenix Suns in 2010 and then, in 2013, to the Washington Wizards. At the beginning of Gortat's tenure with the Wizards, Mike Wise, writing for the *Washington Post* (11 Dec. 2014) described him as the "smiling soul" of the team. "The aura that's around me, the positive energy around me, I guess, has influence on different people," Gortat told Wise.

Gortat has expressed gratitude for his extraordinary rise. Eight years after first picking up a basketball, he told Wise for the *Post* (5 Dec. 2013), "I was playing in the NBA Finals. Ten years later, I have a check coming with seven digits." This blithe summation does not account for all of Gortat's hard work—he doesn't call himself a machine for nothing—but it emphasizes how unusual it was, and is, for a Polish player to make it in the NBA. Poland enjoyed a strong national team in the 1960s and 1970s but has not qualified for the Olympic Games since 1984. Gortat himself grew up watching NBA stars like Michael Jordan and Shaquille O'Neal, but a parliamentary act in 1992 saw the disappearance of American basketball games from public television. "That's when everything started to really fall apart," Gortat wrote for the *Players Tribune* (9 Nov. 2016).

Gortat, who is the fourth Polish player to ever play in the NBA, hopes to use his popularity to rekindle enthusiasm for the sport in his country. Gortat has organized basketball camps for young Polish players and in 2009 founded a fee-free sports academy in his hometown.

EARLY LIFE

Marcin Janusz Gortat was born in Łódź, Poland, on February 17, 1984. His mother, Alicja, played volleyball for the Polish national team and later worked as a physical education teacher. His father, Janusz, is a former army captain and light-heavyweight boxer who won bronze medals for Poland at the 1972 and 1976 Olympics. With his family pedigree came the weight of expectation. "Being Mr. Gortat's son, the Gortat Jr., wasn't easy," he told Wise. "There was a lot of expectation. Everybody knew I am going to one day be an athlete. A lot of people obviously tried to take a shot at me." Gortat and his brother, Phillip, were raised in the Bałuty district of Łódź mostly by their mother; their father lived in Warsaw.

Physically, the six-feet-eleven athlete grew quickly and began working out as a teenager to avoid becoming, as he told Donata Subbotko for the Warsaw newspaper *Wyborcza*, "skinny and fragile." Though his father tried to interest him in boxing, Gortat was drawn instead to soccer. "Tall and quick," he wrote, "I was a natural goalie." Off the field, Gortat enjoyed watching basketball on television. "I loved watching Dejan Bodiroga, a famous Serbian player who was just amazing," he wrote. "He won medals and championships all over Europe. Seeing him light up Europe was probably what planted the basketball seed in me in the first place." The way Gortat tells it, he wandered through his school's basketball court on the way to soccer practice one day when he was seventeen. He picked up a basketball and tried, but failed, to make a shot. "But it was too late," he recalled. "The ball had felt so good rolling off my fingertips. I was hooked."

EUROPEAN CAREER AND NBA DRAFT

Gortat quit his soccer team in 2001. His new basketball coaches were pleased with Gortat's height and agility. He soon began playing professionally for his hometown team, the ŁKS Łódź. Gortat joined the junior national team the same year. "How wild is that?" he wrote. "Just a year after I started playing basketball, I was already in the national-team system." But Gortat described that system as a "mess." The federation had little money. They hired unfit coaches who cultivated a lackadaisical approach to training and play. Gortat played for Łódź for a year before his coaches took him aside and encouraged him to pursue playing basketball outside of Poland.

In 2003, Gortat traveled to France with the under-twenty national team for a tournament, where he participated in his first dunk contest, winning with an elbow-deep, Vince Carter–inspired dunk. His prowess caught the attention of the German professional team RheinEnergie Köln. Gortat signed with the team, and though he played little that first year, he was encouraged to enter the 2005 NBA Draft.

Gortat did not know how the draft worked but agreed. His agent told him that he would likely be selected in the beginning of the second round. After many tense minutes, Gortat was drafted toward the end of the second round, number fifty-seven, by the Phoenix Suns. The Suns traded Gortat's drafting rights to the Orlando Magic within fifteen minutes. He played for the Magic's summer league, under head coach Brian Hill, in 2005, but Hill ultimately instructed Gortat to return to Cologne, Germany, for the regular season. The same thing—NBA summer league, European regular season—happened the next year. "I was devastated," he wrote. "I thought I was never going to make the NBA." He worked hard to make the cut, improving his shooting and rebounding in Euroleague and German League play, and after Stan Van Gundy was hired as head coach, the Magic officially signed him in 2007.

Still, Gortat felt he had something to prove. He recalled another player taunting him at the NBA rookie transition program in 2007. The player told him that he would be out of the league in two years; Gortat became determined to prove that prediction wrong.

EARLY NBA CAREER

Gortat began his NBA career on the D-League, playing for the Anaheim Arsenal. He made his debut with the Magic later that season. He distinguished himself as the backup to Dwight Howard, an All-Star, number-one draft pick and one of the best centers in the league. Gortat later told Scott Allen for the *Washington Post* (18 Apr. 2017) that Howard helped shape him as a player. "He made me bleed every day for my first four years in the NBA," Gortat said. He added, "Imagine the stuff that's going down here in the game, imagine the same stuff going three times harder in practice where you don't have whistles, fouls and stuff like that. It was pretty much for me about surviving practice, going to the weight room every day, lift hard, because otherwise I'm going to end up in the hospital or in a wheelchair."

Two years into his NBA career, Gortat was growing frustrated playing second fiddle to Howard. In 2009, he agreed to a five-year $34 million deal with the Dallas Mavericks as a restricted free agent. The Magic matched their offer, and he stayed. The team traded him to the Phoenix Suns in December 2010. Sports analyst Sebastian Hummels made a case in the *Bleacher Report* (20 Apr. 2011) for Gortat as the season's most improved player. In half a season with the Suns, Gortat averaged 12.9 points per game, 1.3 blocks, and 9.3 rebounds. "Compare those numbers to his stay in Orlando, and you see a completely different player," Hummels wrote. By the end of the season, Gortat was the team's starting center. He also acquired the nickname the Polish Hammer. Though considered among the best big men in the league, the rest of Gortat's tenure with the Suns was marked by the 2011 NBA lockout, conflicts with head coach Alvin Gentry, and a foot sprain that sidelined him for twenty-one games at the end of the 2012–13 season.

WASHINGTON WIZARDS

Gortat was traded to the Washington Wizards in October 2013. Wise described Gortat as a "godsend" for the struggling franchise. During the 2013–14 season, he led the team with thirty-seven double-doubles, averaged 13.2 points a game (placing him among the top ten scoring centers in the league), and led the team in rebounds, averaging 9.5 per game. In the Eastern Conference Semifinals in 2014, he scored 31 points and made 16 rebounds in game 5 against the Indiana Pacers. He signed again with the Wizards, inking a five-year $60 million deal, in July.

Alongside players such as John Wall and Bradley Beal, Gortat helped make the team competitive again, if not yet championship material. He hit a career high in double-doubles, with forty-one during the 2015–16 season, but the team missed the playoffs in 2016. Over the 2016–17 season, Gortat averaged 10.8 points and 10.4 rebounds per game; however, his 2017–18 season was less stellar, with an average of 8.4 points and 7.6 rebounds per game. Friction grew between him and Wall, and Gortat loudly resisted a new system of play. His displeasure with the team was clear.

In January 2018, Gortat expressed a wish to retire with the Magic, the team where his NBA career began. Gortat was traded to the Los Angeles Clippers that June. He was expected to enter free agency at the end of the 2018–19 season.

PERSONAL LIFE

In the offseason, Gortat lives in Florida; he also owns an apartment in Łódź near his mother's home. When off the court, he enjoys spending time at the gym, learning Spanish, watching television, videogaming, and practicing at the shooting range. In addition to establishing basketball camps, Gortat cares deeply about veterans and military families and has visited active-duty personnel in the United States and Afghanistan.

SUGGESTED READING

Allen, Scott. "Marcin Gortat on Former Teammate Dwight Howard: 'He's Going to Be Really Furious.'" *DC Sports Bog*, The Washington Post, 18 Apr. 2017, www.washingtonpost.com/news/dc-sports-bog/wp/2017/04/18/marcin-gortat-on-former-teammate-dwight-howard-hes-going-to-be-really-furious. Accessed 17 Sept. 2018.

Barnewell, Chris. "Veteran Big Marcin Gortat Plans to Retire Soon, Hopes to Finish Career with Magic." *CBS Sports*, 12 Jan. 2018. Accessed 17 Sept. 2018.

Gortat, Marcin. "How We Play Basketball in Poland." *The Players' Tribune*, 9 Nov. 2016, www.theplayerstribune.com/en-us/articles/marcin-gortat-washington-wizards-poland. Accessed 17 Sept. 2018.

Gortat, Marcin. "Marcin Gortat on Love, Loneliness, and the Polish Struggle." Interview by Donata Subbotko, translated and edited by Bartosz Bielecki. *TruthAboutIt.net*, ESPN TrueHoop Network, 31 July 2014, www.truthaboutit.net/2014/07/marcin-gortat-on-love-loneliness-and-the-polish-struggle.html. Originally published as "Marcin Gortat, Bałuty Boy," *Wyborcza.pl*, 4 July 2014, wyborcza.pl/magazyn/1,124059,16274402,Marcin_Gortat__Baluty_Boy.html.

Hummels, Sebastian. "2011 NBA Awards: Marcin Gortat's Case for Most Improved Player of the Year." *Bleacher Report*, 20 Apr. 2011, bleacherreport.com/articles/672032-2011-nba-awards-the-case-for-marcin-gortat-as-most-improved-player-of-the-year. Accessed 17 Sept. 2018.

Wise, Mike. "Marcin Gortat Is the Smiling Soul of the Washington Wizards." *The Washington Post*, 11 Dec. 2014, www.washingtonpost.com/sports/wizards/marcin-gortat-is-the-smiling-soul-of-the-washington-wizards/2014/12/11/3f615b10-817d-11e4-9f38-95a187e4c1f7_story.html. Accessed 17 Sept. 2018.

Wise, Mike. "Marcin Gortat, Washington Wizards Big Man, Is the 'Polish Machine' to New Teammates." *The Washington Post*, 5 Dec. 2013, www.washingtonpost.com/sports/wizards/marcin-gortat-washington-wizards-big-man-is-the-polish-machine-to-new-teammates/2013/12/05/fbc52c84-5e04-11e3-bc56-c6ca94801fac_story.html. Accessed 17 Sept. 2018.

—*Molly Hagan*

Shayne Gostisbehere

Date of birth: April 20, 1993
Occupation: Hockey player

Philadelphia Flyers defenseman Shayne Gostisbehere firmly believes that his team's fans are "the best in the league," he told Michelle Mass in an interview for *Philadelphia Style* (2 Mar. 2016). "They are so passionate," he said. "They'll let you know if you're doing bad, and they'll definitely let you know when you're doing well." Gostisbehere—widely known to fans as Ghost Bear (a modified pronunciation of his last name) or simply Ghost—officially joined the Flyers in the fall of 2015, and since then he has been doing quite well indeed. He achieved an impressive performance during his debut season with the team and was a finalist for the prestigious Calder Memorial Trophy as well as a member of the National Hockey League (NHL) All-Rookie Team. Although a hip injury and subsequent surgery contributed to a lackluster second season,

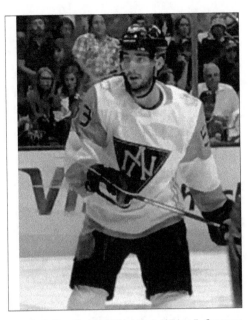

By Paperfire [CC BY-SA 4.0], via Wikimedia Commons

Gostisbehere rebounded in the fall of 2017, exceeding his previous season's number of goals and points scored within the first several months.

A hockey player since early childhood, Gostisbehere began his career in the sport playing with youth teams in South Florida. After three successful collegiate seasons at Union College in upstate New York, he joined the Flyers organization in 2014 as a member of the minor-league Adirondack Phantoms and Lehigh Valley Phantoms, before getting called up in late 2015. Although he spent much of his life on the ice, Gostisbehere remains astonished by his success. "I'm absolutely blown away," he told Dave Caldwell for the *New York Times* (26 Feb. 2016). "If you would have told me I'd be doing this, I'd say, What kind of drugs are you taking?"

EARLY LIFE AND EDUCATION

Shayne Gostisbehere was born on April 20, 1993, in Pembroke Pines, Florida. He spent his early years in the city of Margate, where he lived with his parents, Christine and Regis, and older sister, Felicia. Athletic pursuits were a major part of the family's life during Gostisbehere's childhood. His father immigrated to the United States from the Basque region of southern France to play professional jai alai (a Basque sport), and his sister was a talented figure skater who skated in national competitions.

As a child, Gostisbehere often accompanied his sister to her practices, and he soon learned to skate himself. His Canadian-born maternal grandfather, Denis Brodeur, introduced him to the sport of ice hockey, and Gostisbehere went

on to play for local youth teams such as the Red Raiders and Coral Springs Coyotes. He later played for the Junior Panthers, a youth team affiliated with the NHL's Florida Panthers, of which he was an avid fan. Gostisbehere dedicated himself further to hockey after his sister suffered an injury that ended her figure skating career while she was still only in her teens. "After her injury she told me something that still sticks with me: Go as far as you can with this because you don't know when it will stop," he wrote in an essay for the *Players' Tribune* (6 Dec. 2017).

Gostisbehere attended Coral Springs High School in Florida for two years before transferring to the South Kent School, a boarding school in western Connecticut with a strong hockey program. While attending South Kent, he was roommates with basketball player Nik Stauskas, who would go on to play professionally for teams such as the Brooklyn Nets. During his two years at the school, Gostisbehere made significant contributions to the boys' hockey team and was named most valuable player (MVP) during his senior season. He graduated in 2011. Although eligible to be drafted by an NHL team during his senior year, he was not selected and opted instead to attend college.

COLLEGE CAREER

During his junior year of high school, Gostisbehere was recruited to play hockey for Union College, a small liberal arts school in Schenectady, New York. The school's small size was particularly appealing to Gostisbehere. "I liked the small-school atmosphere," he told Caldwell. "I didn't want to go to a humongous school with all of these students." Despite its size, Union had a successful athletics program in the Division I level of National Collegiate Athletic Association (NCAA) competition. Gostisbehere decided to commit to Union College, and he enrolled in the school as an engineering major (he later switched to history) in the fall of 2011.

During his first season with the Union Dutchmen, Gostisbehere immediately established himself as a valuable member of the team, scoring five goals and seventeen assists over the course of the season. He accompanied the team to his first NCAA hockey tournament, where the Dutchmen were ultimately eliminated during the semifinals. Gostisbehere returned to the team the following season, during which he tallied eight goals and eighteen assists. He also played in the International Ice Hockey Federation's 2013 World Junior Championships, helping claim a gold medal for the United States. During the 2013–14 season, his last with the Dutchmen, Gostisbehere achieved nine goals and twenty-five assists. He went on to compete in the NCAA tournament, leading the Dutchmen to the team's first-ever championship. In recognition of his contributions, Gostisbehere was named the most outstanding player of the Frozen Four, the final stages of the competition.

PROFESSIONAL HOCKEY

In June 2012, between his freshman and sophomore seasons with the Dutchmen, Gostisbehere was selected by the Philadelphia Flyers as the seventy-eighth overall pick in the third round of that year's NHL Entry Draft. Having been told that he would likely be chosen in the sixth or seventh round of the seven-round draft, if at all, his relatively early selection came as a surprise. "I was eating breakfast with my family in Florida during the third round—and I really wasn't paying attention to the TV. The draft was on in the background and muted," he recalled for the *Players' Tribune*. "I saw the Flyers logo on the big board, then . . . GOSTISBEHERE popped up. . . . I was like, 'Uh, Mom?'" Although drafted by the Flyers, Gostisbehere spent two more seasons at Union College before leaving at the end of his junior year. In April 2014, he signed a contract with the Flyers and was assigned to the Adirondack Phantoms, an American Hockey League (AHL) affiliate team. Gostisbehere played two games with the Phantoms before the end of the 2013 AHL season.

For the 2014–15 season, Gostisbehere continued with what was now the Lehigh Valley Phantoms (the team having moved from Glens Falls, New York, to Allentown, Pennsylvania). He also played two games with the Flyers themselves at the beginning of the season, making his debut with the team on October 25, 2014, in a winning game against the Detroit Red Wings. Gostisbehere's season came to an end, however, five games into his tenure with the Phantoms, when he tore the anterior cruciate ligament in his knee in a game against the Manchester Monarchs. The injury required him to undergo surgery, and he was unable to play for the rest of the season while recuperating. Although unhappy about that turn of events, Gostisbehere made the best of his time off the ice, often watching his teammates play from the press box. "You get to see things up in the press box you've never seen before," he told Randy Miller for *NJ.com* (14 Feb. 2015). "You see how plays develop. You see how guys skate, what guys do without the puck that you can't see from the ice level when you're playing. I wouldn't call it a lost year. I would say it's more an educational year." During the following season, Gostisbehere played in fourteen games with the Phantoms, scoring two goals.

PHILADELPHIA FLYERS

Gostisbehere was called up to the Philadelphia Flyers in November of 2015 and made his first appearance as a member of the major-league team in a winning game against the Carolina Hurricanes on November 14. Widely cited as the first hockey player born and raised in Florida to join the NHL, Gostisbehere quickly established himself as a key member of the team, playing in sixty-four games over the course of the season. He soon became a favorite among Flyers fans, who gave him the nicknames of Ghost and Ghost Bear and began to form strong bonds with his teammates. "The team has been so welcoming even since day one—since I've been called up," he told Mass. "It's been awesome. It's brotherhood here."

Throughout the regular season, Gostisbehere offered up a strong performance, scoring seventeen goals and earning a total of forty-six points in 1,286 minutes on the ice. In the postseason, he accompanied the Flyers into the 2016 Stanley Cup playoffs, where the team was defeated by the Washington Capitals in the first round. In recognition of his achievements during his first season, Gostisbehere was named a finalist for the Calder Memorial Trophy, which is awarded annually to one outstanding rookie player. He was also named to the NHL All-Rookie Team.

OVERCOMING INJURY

Although the 2015–16 season was largely a success for Gostisbehere, his success on the ice came at the expense of his physical well-being. Following the end of the season, Flyers leadership announced that he had suffered a serious hip injury during the season and would undergo hip and abdominal surgery during the off-season. The injury was particularly frightening for Gostisbehere, as it was the same type of injury that had ended his sister's figure skating career a decade before. Despite worries that his own career might suffer the same fate, Gostisbehere underwent successful surgery in May of 2016 and returned to the Flyers in October 2016, at the start of a new season.

Gostisbehere struggled during his second season with the Flyers, playing in seventy-six games but scoring only seven goals and thirty-nine points, less than in the previous season. Although some commentators speculated that his performance was being affected by his recovering hip, Gostisbehere rejected that idea and instead worked to improve himself. "I mean, you could always say, 'Oh yeah, it's the injury. That's it,'" he explained to Wayne Fish for the *Burlington County Times* (29 Mar. 2017). "For me, it's just looking in the mirror and go put the work in." Despite such challenges, Gostisbehere remained a key member of the team during the season, and in the summer of 2017, he signed a $27 million contract extension that would keep him with the Flyers for an additional six years.

The 2017–18 season started off strong for Gostisbehere, as the Flyers won the season opener against the San Jose Sharks. He scored ten goals and forty points during his first fifty games of the season and contributed thirty assists. In addition to performing well during the regular season, Gostisbehere hoped to help his team achieve further triumphs in the postseason and perhaps even win the Stanley Cup, which the Flyers last won in 1975. "We know our division is tough, but we've got confidence in our room that the sky's the limit for us," he wrote for the *Players' Tribune*. "We want to make the Philly fans proud. We don't take their support for granted."

PERSONAL LIFE

Gostisbehere lives in Philadelphia with his girlfriend, Gina Valentine. In addition to playing hockey with the Flyers, he is active in a variety of philanthropic causes and in 2017 launched the GhostBear Foundation, dedicated to providing charitable assistance in several areas, including the protection of endangered animals and the promotion of hockey among young athletes. "I feel very fortunate to have the opportunity to use my platform as a professional athlete to advocate and raise awareness for causes I'm most passionate about," Gostisbehere said following the foundation's launch, as quoted by Steph Driver for *Broad Street Hockey* (2 Dec. 2017). "It's a privilege to have created The GhostBear Foundation with the help of family and friends. We're excited to start making a difference." Gostisbehere's sister is president of the foundation, while his mother serves as secretary.

SUGGESTED READING

Caldwell, Dave. "A Top NHL Rookie Skates In from the Heat." *The New York Times*, 26 Feb. 2016, www.nytimes.com/2016/02/28/sports/hockey/a-top-nhl-rookie-skates-in-from-the-heat.html. Accessed 9 Feb. 2018.

Driver, Steph. "Shayne Gostisbehere Launches the GhostBear Foundation." *Broad Street Hockey*, 2 Dec. 2017, www.broadstreethockey.com/2017/12/2/16726090/shayne-gostisbehere-launches-ghostbear-foundation-philadelphia-flyers. Accessed 9 Feb. 2018.

Fialkov, Harvey. "Flyers Defenseman Shayne Gostisbehere Returns to South Florida Roots." *Sun Sentinel*, 31 Oct. 2014, www.sun-sentinel.com/sports/florida-panthers/fl-florida-panthers-shanye-gostisbehere-1101-20141031-story.html. Accessed 9 Feb. 2018.

Fish, Wayne. "Confident, Healthier 'Ghost' Returning to Form for Flyers." *Burlington County Times*, 29 Mar. 2017, www.burlingtoncountytimes.com/e6d6fc14-14ac-11e7-bbe0-d710f0fd4ba3.html. Accessed 9 Feb. 2018.

Gostisbehere, Shayne. "Shayne Gostisbehere on Playing for the Philadelphia Flyers, the Stanley Cup & More." Interview by Michelle Mass. *Philadelphia Style*, 2 Mar. 2016, phillystylemag.com/shayne-gostisbehere-talks-stanley-cup-philadelphia-flyers-and-more. Accessed 9 Feb. 2018.

Gostisbehere, Shayne. "You Might Know Me as Ghost." *The Players' Tribune*, 6 Dec. 2017, www.theplayerstribune.com/shayne-gostisbehere-philadelphia-flyers-nhl/. Accessed 9 Feb. 2018.

Miller, Randy. "Flyers Prospect Shayne Gostisbehere Details 'Scary' ACL Tear, Getting Close to Return." *NJ.com*, 14 Feb. 2015. www.nj.com/flyers/index.ssf/2015/02/flyers_prospect_shayne_gostisbehere_details_scary.html. Accessed 9 Feb. 2018.

—*Joy Crelin*

Emily Graslie

Date of birth: June 14, 1989
Occupation: Educator

Emily Graslie arguably has the most unique job in the United States: she is the chief curiosity correspondent at the Field Museum of Natural History in Chicago, Illinois. Her job is to educate people in the sciences, both online and in person, with new media and with old-fashioned public appearances—and, specifically, to show just how much the Field Museum has to offer to both the scientist and the public.

An involvement in science museums that began as volunteer work while she was studying art as an undergraduate has enabled Graslie to develop a devoted online following, thanks to her show *The Brain Scoop* on YouTube. Part of her success, Graslie admits, is that she can make complicated scientific ideas and concepts accessible because she herself has no degree or formal background in any scientific field. Graslie told Chau Tu for *Science Friday* (20 Nov. 2014): "I'm learning all of this on the fly, too. . . . I document how I'm learning it—the points and the relevant words and phrases and connections and narrative contextualization that make sense to me. I kind of cut it up, distill it, break it down, and feed it back. It's worked well so far."

EARLY LIFE AND EDUCATION

Emily Graslie was born on June 14, 1989, and grew up in Rapid City, South Dakota. The natural world was part of the background of her early life: her father maintained a ranch located about

By Keilana via Wikimedia Commons

two hours northeast of Rapid City. In an interview with Andrea Appleton for *Dimensions* (July/Aug. 2017), Graslie recalled, "My parents really fostered my curiosity. I was totally an outside kid. I loved things that move. I've always been fascinated by animals and the great outdoors. . . . Even before I was really involved in science, I liked observing the natural world."

Because of her early love of animals, as a young girl she wanted to become a veterinarian. Throughout middle school she maintained an interest in science, but that changed when she entered high school. Graslie explained to Jill Filipovic for *Cosmopolitan* (28 July 2014): "In middle school you still do experiments, you go on field trips, you go to nature parks. Then in high school the system changes—it's more focused on performing well on standardized tests, and biology becomes more about understanding textbooks and diagrams than interacting with the natural world. So I lost my love of science and took up an interest in art." A high school art teacher, Mr. Gulbrandsen, allowed her to take "independent study painting," for which he supervised her while she painted whatever she wanted to paint.

After graduating from Central High School in Rapid City in June 2007, Graslie studied art at the University of Montana in Missoula, where she earned her bachelor's degree in fine arts in June 2011. But it was during this time, while still pursuing her art degree, that she lucked into an experience that would not only reconnect her to her love of the natural world, but also take her into an unexpected career.

DISCOVERING THE ZOOLOGICAL MUSEUM

In the fall of 2010, as an undergraduate, Graslie learned something unexpected from a couple of classmates: the University of Montana had a zoological museum on campus. The Philip L. Wright Zoological Museum is not very large; it has just twenty-four thousand specimens, including seventy grizzly bear skulls and a giraffe skeleton, inside a space the size of a classroom. Yet it was love at first sight for Graslie. "It was breathtaking," she recalled to Janet Potter for the *Chicago Reader* (27 Jan. 2014). "Every square inch of the place was packed, full of specimen boxes, skeletons, taxidermy mounts, taxidermied birds hanging from the ceiling. It was absolutely overwhelming the amount of things in there. I knew as soon as I went in that I wanted to work in the space."

She asked the curator if she could do an independent study at the museum, drawing specimens. The curator said it would be fine, if her art supervisor agreed that such a study would fulfill the last three credits Graslie needed to graduate. With all the approvals in hand, she returned to the museum as a volunteer. She earned her credits and graduated on time but continued to volunteer at the museum afterward. She supported herself with various odd jobs—baker, barista, prep chef—to spend as much time as she could with the specimens. She eventually created a blog, *UMZoology*, to document her work at the museum.

THE BRAIN SCOOP

Graslie began working on an MA in museum studies at Johns Hopkins University via distance learning. While working toward her advanced degree, she met Hank Green of the educational YouTube channel VlogBrothers, who wanted to come to the university museum to film an episode of a series on the vertebrate skeleton.

Graslie had known of and admired Green's work on VlogBrothers for a number of years. After he filmed at the museum, he told her he hoped they could work together again sometime. She loved the idea and sent him script ideas for about six months, with no response. Then, in November 2011, he asked if he could return and film again, this time recording her giving a tour. She readily agreed. After the video garnered more than 150,000 views on YouTube, Green asked her, based on the overwhelmingly positive response, if she would like to have her own show on her own channel.

On January 14, 2013, the first episode of *The Brain Scoop*, featuring Graslie, debuted. The channel created for the show had twenty thousand subscribers before its first upload. Viewers were immediately drawn to how Graslie presented her scientific subjects in a well-researched and knowledgeable way while also seeming humorous and spontaneous. She was a likeable presence, in part because she had no academic background in the sciences but was an enthusiastic learner, with a willingness to make the natural world comprehensible to a general audience. Some episodes involved discussing the various specimens the museum had collected. Others detailed how to prepare them and perform dissections. Six episodes about the museum's acquisition of a wolf that had been hit by a car proved to be among the most popular of the early episodes, as viewers were taken on the fascinating—and occasionally graphic—journey of preparing the wolf for exhibition.

CHIEF CURIOSITY CORRESPONDENT AT THE FIELD MUSEUM

The Brain Scoop earned early attention from *Scientific American* magazine and *Radiolab* podcast host Robert Krulwich, who praised Graslie's work as host. Then, in February 2013, Graslie made a fateful call to the Field Museum in Chicago, asking permission to film the museum's annual members' night in April. The members' night allows the museum's financial contributors access to parts of the collection usually reserved for scientists and curators. The museum agreed, and Graslie went to Chicago to film.

At the end of her visit, the collections curator, Bill Stanley, approached her with a proposal. Graslie told Jill Filipovic for *Cosmopolitan* that Stanley said that he thought the Field Museum could benefit from having a show like *The Brain Scoop* to drive interest in the museum. "I said, 'That would be awesome, you could find someone so easily,'" Graslie recalled. "He said, 'It should be you. We would like you to come to the Field Museum and bring your show with you.' I was floored."

Graslie immediately said yes. In July 2013, she became the Field Museum's first-ever chief curiosity correspondent, which, in addition to filming *The Brain Scoop*, allows her to conduct outreach and education, advocating for the museum and the type of scientific inquiry it provides. Sometimes her work entails promoting the Field online; other times it means fielding questions about the museum both inside and outside of it, often from young audiences. She particularly enjoys the outreach that both *The Brain Scoop* and her other museum work provide to young girls and women. She told Potter that her largest audience is "young women who have always had an interest in science and are starting to wonder if they should take it more seriously. If I was that age watching my show, I would want that reassurance—that what I was interested in was cool, that people would still like me and think I'm funny even if I'm into weird gross stuff that nobody else was talking about."

RECEPTION

The most famous video Graslie has ever done on *The Brain Scoop* is "Where My Ladies At?," in which she directly confronts the sexist comments that many of her videos have received. Sexist comments are prevalent on YouTube, particularly when it comes to female hosts covering science, technology, engineering, and mathematics (STEM) topics. Graslie has expressed frustration that this video is better known than any of those covering her usual science topics. "We're still talking about women struggling to be successful on a platform, and yet I'm still only asked about something I made five years ago," she said to Adrianne Jeffries for the *New York Times* (13 July 2018). "I wish I got more recognition for the other 200 videos that I've made."

Despite the online criticisms, Graslie has received numerous accolades for her work. She has been nominated for Webby Awards six times and received the American Alliance of Museums' Nancy Hanks Award for Professional Excellence. She was also named a Chicagoan of the Year 2017 by the *Chicago Tribune* and among *Forbes* magazine's 30 Under 30 list in education in 2018.

PERSONAL LIFE

Graslie lives in Chicago and travels broadly for her work. She continues to draw and paint in her spare time and enjoys reading books about museum history and taxidermy.

SUGGESTED READING

"CV." *Emily Graslie*, www.emilygraslie.com/curriculum-vitae. Accessed 24 Aug. 2018.

Graslie, Emily. "Get That Life: How I Became a Museum's Chief Curiosity Correspondent." Interview by Jill Filipovic. *Cosmopolitan*, 28 July 2014, www.cosmopolitan.com/career/news/a29534/get-that-life-emily-graslie-science. Accessed 24 Aug. 2018.

Graslie, Emily. "Q&A with Emily Graslie." Interview by Chau Tu. *Science Friday*, 20 Nov. 2014, www.sciencefriday.com/articles/qa-with-emily-graslie. Accessed 24 Aug. 2018.

Graslie, Emily. "Q&A with Emily Graslie: Science, Art, Curiosity, and *The Brain Scoop*." Interview by Andrea Appleton. *Dimensions*, July–Aug. 2017, www.astc.org/astc-dimensions/qa-emily-graslie-science-art-curiosity-brain-scoop. Accessed 24 Aug. 2018.

Jeffries, Adrianne. "Women Making Science Videos on YouTube Face Hostile Comments." *The New York Times*, 13 July 2018, www.nytimes.com/2018/07/13/science/youtube-science-women.html. Accessed 24 Aug. 2018.

Potter, Janet. "How Emily Graslie Went from YouTube Science Star to Full-Time at the Field Museum." *Chicago Reader*, 27 Jan. 2014, www.chicagoreader.com/chicago/

field-museum-emily-graslie-brain-scoop-you-tube/Content?oid=12236428. Accessed 24 Aug. 2018.

—*Christopher Mari*

Bryshere Y. Gray

Date of birth: November 28, 1993
Occupation: Actor

Actor Bryshere Y. Gray is best known for his role as Hakeem Lyon, the aspiring-rapper son of Lucious Lyon (Terrence Howard) and Cookie Lyon (Taraji P. Henderson) on the hit FOX television drama *Empire*, but Gray, also known as Yazz the Greatest, is a rapper in his own right. He landed a record deal with Columbia Records in 2016 and hopes to release his first album in the next couple of years. Born and raised in Philadelphia, Gray's first passion was rapping. His talent as a performer landed him a role on *Empire*, his first-ever acting gig, in 2014. The show, featuring award-winning actors Howard and Henderson, became a national phenomenon when it premiered in 2015.

In 2017, Gray played Michael Bivins of the 1980s R & B group New Edition for the popular Black Entertainment Television (BET) miniseries *The New Edition Story*. He reprised his role as Bivins in *The Bobby Brown Story*, a 2018 miniseries about the group's most notorious member. Gray has been nominated for a Black Entertainment Television (BET) Award, two National Association for the Advancement of Colored People (NAACP) Image Awards, and three Teen Choice Awards. Of late, he has been already garnering attention for his starring role in the film *Canal Street*, about a young man who is wrongfully accused of murder. The film is slated to premiere in fall 2018.

EARLY LIFE AND EDUCATION

Bryshere Yazuan Gray was born in the West Philadelphia section of Philadelphia, Pennsylvania, in 1993. He and his sister, Brianna, were raised by their mother, Andria Mayberry, who separated from Gray's father because he was abusive. Mayberry, who worked three jobs to support her children and currently works as a nurse, wrote a 2017 book, *Before Empire: Raising Bryshere "Yazz the Greatest" Gray*, about her experiences as a single mother and her son's manager. In the book, Mayberry writes that Gray was diagnosed with attention deficit hyperactivity disorder (ADHD) when he was five years old. For both mother and son, learning to manage the disorder was a struggle.

By iDominick via Wikimedia Commons

Gray attended Overbrook High School, where he played football. Sidelined by a broken arm, Gray discovered his passion for music. He started rapping seriously when he was sixteen. "I was working at Pizza Hut. . . . I was just tired. I was like 'Is this life?'" he recalled to a reporter for *Vibe* magazine (21 Jan. 2015). "I just graduated and I started rhyming and really fell in love with it. When I did my first performance, I was like 'This is what I really want to do.'" Gray used his first paycheck to finance a music video. He got fired after he got caught writing rap lyrics at work.

After that, Gray told *Vibe*, he "just really committed" to his ambition. He and his two back-up dancers performed in basements and local street shows, which he described to John Morrison for the *Philly Voice* (13 May 2016) as "one speaker, one mic and like a hundred artists there waiting to perform." Still, Gray made inroads with influential local deejays such as DJ Diamond Kuts, and landed his current manager, Charles Alston (better known as Charlie Mack), who has worked with Will Smith and Meek Mill. On September 1, 2013, Gray performed as Yazz the Greatest at the Budweiser Made in America Festival in Philadelphia.

EMPIRE

Gray was focused on making music, but Mack had other ideas. Longtime friends with Leah Daniels Butler, the sister of and casting director for producer Lee Daniels, Mack secured Gray an audition for Daniels's new television show, *Empire*. Although Gray had never acted before, he agreed to audition. He recorded a video, and Daniels liked it so much that he invited Gray to Los Angeles to audition in person. According to Mack, Gray initially missed his flight. They rescheduled the audition, and when Gray walked into the room he was awestruck by who he saw. "I'm expecting to just walk in to the director, Danny Strong, and a camera [but] I see Terrence and Taraji," he recalled to *Vibe*. "I was kind of blown away because they're like gods where I'm from. They're so respected. So it was cool I kept it together." He completed his audition scene with Howard; soon after that, he was told he had won the role.

Gray plays Hakeem Lyon, the swaggering, youngest son of Lucious Lyon (Howard). Set in New York, the show centers on Empire Entertainment, a fictional record company. Patriarch Lucious is diagnosed with amyotrophic lateral sclerosis (ALS, also known as Lou Gehrig's disease) and pits his family members against one another to find the right heir to his throne. (In the pilot episode, the middle brother, Jamal, asks his father, incredulous, "What is this, we *King Lear* now?" referencing the Shakespearean tragedy from which *Empire* pulls its premise.) Among the family members is Lucious's ex-wife, Cookie (Henderson), who has just completed a seventeen-year prison sentence for the family's first business, drug dealing. She helped build Empire, and now she wants a piece of it. The brothers have their own strengths and challenges. The eldest, Andre (Trai Byers), is a businessman without musical talent; Jamal (Jussie Smollett) is a sensitive singer-songwriter who Lucious cannot accept as gay. Hakeem, Lucious's favorite, is a rising star in the rap world but is also hot-headed, lazy, and selfish. A month after the show began, Jozen Cummings, writing for *Billboard* magazine (18 Feb. 2015), ranked Hakeem last among the show's "deplorable" characters in terms of likeability. "The hate for Hakeem knows no bounds. . . . He may be a fictional character, but my disgust for him is very real."

CRITICAL RECEPTION OF *EMPIRE*

Empire premiered on FOX in 2015 and quickly became the highest-rated new television series that season. Fans relished the villainy of the characters as well as the show's original music. Gray cowrote a song in season 2 called "Bout 2 Blow" with Timbaland, who also serves as an executive music producer for the show. *Empire* has enjoyed reservedly positive reviews. Critic Alessandra Stanley, writing for the *New York Times* (6 Jan. 2015), lamented its soapy, formulaic plot but found it compulsively watchable thanks to its "stellar cast." Stanley compared *Empire* to the classic primetime soap opera *Dynasty*, as well as another television drama about the music industry, *Nashville*. Like those shows, "*Empire* is a rollicking family drama that has glints of wit and self-awareness behind the brio." Lori Adelman, a *Feministing* editor who contributed to a piece about *Empire* for the *New York Times* (18 Mar. 2015), was drawn to the show's portrayal of African American ambition. Lucious and Cookie scrapped to build their empire; their children have similarly large dreams. "Like its characters, 'Empire' aims high. It stands to become a major network television hit that black audiences not only enjoy but also feel a part of in its success. To be triumphantly, unapologetically successful and black—this is perhaps the show's most lofty ambition," Adelman wrote.

THE NEW EDITION STORY

In 2017, Gray played Michael Bivins, a founding member of the R & B group New Edition, in *The New Edition Story*, a limited series on BET. Gray's manager Mack knew the singing group from when they got their start in the late 1970s and early 1980s. Gray was originally considered for the role of Ronnie DeVoe but was ultimately cast as Bivins. The series was a long time in the making, and fans—and the band members themselves—were excited. Gray told Emma Sarran Webster for the Chicago-based *Michigan Avenue* magazine (16 May 2017) that Bivins called him every morning before shooting, saying, "'Heyo, B, are you like me or what? Look in the mirror. Are you like me or what?' I'm like, 'I'm like you, Mike, I'm like you!'" Gray recalled. "I think that was the most fun part of playing Michael Bivins. And I was just honored."

After it premiered in January 2017, *The New Edition Story* became an overwhelming success. It was one of BET's highest-rated and most-watched shows ever. It received positive reviews, including one from Mikael Wood for the *Los Angeles Times* (24 Jan. 2017), who argued that the "painstaking" three-part series gives the groundbreaking group the recognition they deserve as the first boy band of the modern era. "What makes 'The New Edition Story' such a pleasure—and it is one—is how lightly it wears that purpose," Wood wrote. "Even as it stretches toward the six-hour mark, the film maintains a crisp forward momentum." He reprises his role as Bivins in *The Bobby Brown Story*.

Gray's most recent project, a film called *Canal Street*, is due to premiere in fall 2018. Inspired by real stories of wrongful imprisonment like the Central Park 5, John Bunn, or the late Kalief Browder, *Canal Street* tells the story of a young black man who is wrongfully accused of murder. Gray plays protagonist Kholi Styles. "Bryshere Gray is growing as an actor, making you forget that he is the spoiled Hakeem Lyons," critic N. D. Smith, who saw an early screening of the film, wrote for the *Source* (1 July 2018). "He jumps all the way in and almost is unrecognizable as the stripped-down teen (even going as far as getting braces to bring the character to life). You instantly relate his character to the many boys that you know that could by a fluke of circumstance could be in the same wrongfully accused/wrongfully convicted position."

PERSONAL LIFE

Gray lives in Los Angeles, but as he told Tamara Best for the *New York Times* (25 Mar. 2016), "Philly will always be my home."

SUGGESTED READING

Adelman, Lori, et al. "Why Can't We Stop Watching Empire?" *The New York Times*, 18 Mar. 2015, www.nytimes.com/2015/03/18/magazine/why-cant-we-stop-watching-empire.html. Accessed 12 Aug. 2018.

Cummings, Jozen. "Every 'Empire' Character Ranked by Likeability." *Billboard*, 18 Feb. 2018, www.billboard.com/articles/columns/the-juice/6473163/empire-characters-ranked. Accessed 11 Aug. 2018.

Gray, Bryshere Y. "From West Philly to 'Empire': Rapper/Actor Bryshere Y. Gray." Interview by John Morrison. *Philly Voice*, 13 May 2016, www.phillyvoice.com/west-philly-empire-rapper-actor-bryshere-y-gray/. Accessed 10 Aug. 2018.

Gray, Bryshere Y. "Meet Bryshere Gray, the Bad Boy Doing Better on 'Empire.'" Interview. *Vibe*, 21 Jan. 2015, www.vibe.com/2015/01/bryshere-gray-yazz-the-greatest-empire-interview/. Accessed 10 Aug. 2018.

Gray, Bryshere Y. "Q & A: Bryshere Y. Gray on 'Empire' and Navigating Hollywood." Interview by Tamara Best. *The New York Times*, 25 Mar. 2016, www.nytimes.com/2016/03/27/arts/television/q-and-a-bryshere-y-gray-on-empire-and-navigating-hollywood.html. Accessed 10 Aug. 2018.

Smith, N. D. "Bryshere Gray's New Film Canal Street Tackles Wrongful Imprisonment." Review of *Canal Street*, written and directed by Rhyan LaMarr. *The Source*, 1 July 2018, the-source.com/2018/07/01/bryshere-gray-canal-street-wrongful-imprisonment. Accessed 12 Aug. 2018.

Stanley, Alessandra. "Dynastic, in a Hip-Hop Sort of Way." Review of *Empire*, created by Lee Daniels and Danny Strong. *The New York Times*, 6 Jan. 2015, www.nytimes.com/2015/01/07/arts/television/empire-a-terrence-howard-drama-on-fox.html Accessed 12 Aug. 2018.

SELECTED WORKS

Empire, 2015– ; *The New Edition Story*, 2017; *Canal Street*, 2018

—Molly Hagan

Maggie Haberman

Date of birth: October 30, 1973
Occupation: Journalist

"One of the saving graces of the [President Donald] Trump era is the journalism it has inspired," David Remnick wrote for the *New Yorker* (21 July 2017). "Maggie Haberman is a tireless, keen-eyed example." In 2015 Haberman—whose background includes reporting jobs at such media outlets as the *New York Post*, *New York Daily News*, and *Politico*—was hired by the *New York Times* in 2015 to provide coverage of the presidential campaign that resulted in real-estate mogul and reality-television star Donald Trump's election to the nation's highest office. Since then, she has been a key player in a nonstop rollercoaster of news that is riveting the world. "Many of the juiciest Trump pieces have been broken by her," Rachel Combe wrote for *Elle* (24 May 2017). "That story about him spending his evenings alone in a bathrobe, watching cable news? Haberman reported and wrote it with her frequent collaborator, Glenn Thrush. The time Trump called the *Times* to blame the collapse of the Obamacare repeal on the Democrats? It was Haberman he dialed. When he accused former national security adviser Susan Rice of committing crimes, and defended Fox News' Bill O'Reilly against the sexual harassment claims that would soon end his career at the network? Haberman and Thrush again."

Photo by Bryan Bedder/Getty Images for *New York Magazine*

Haberman, who has earned a reputation as a tough but fair journalist, believes that one of her main missions is to hold accountable to the truth a president who is regularly documented telling outright falsehoods. "When we as a culture can't agree on a simple, basic fact set—that is very scary," Haberman explained to Combe. "That [Trump] is unconcerned by that, I think, is the big issue. This is a very precarious moment, in terms of what anyone can believe in. What erodes that is very dangerous."

Like many members of the media, Haberman regularly finds herself on the receiving end of Trump's verbal vitriol and Twitter attacks. "It's all part of the business," she said to Marisa Guthrie for the *Hollywood Reporter* (14 Apr. 2017). "Elected officials have been yelling at reporters for a very long time. . . . There really is very little that's actually new under the sun. The medium [Twitter] is just new. This is the business, this is what happens. It's not personal."

EARLY LIFE AND EDUCATION
Maggie Lindsy Haberman was born on October 30, 1973, in New York City. Her mother, Nancy Haberman, is an executive vice president at the New York public relations firm Rubenstein. (Trump has used the firm's services, but never met Nancy.) Her father, Clyde Haberman, was a Pulitzer Prize–winning writer for the *New York Times* from 1977 to 2013, retiring shortly before his daughter's arrival at the paper (he was also a reporter at the *New York Post*, and met his wife there). He told Combe that reporting was "hardwired" into his daughter at an early age, asserting, "She grew up in an environment where journalism that was as accurate as humanly possible was practically a religion." Maggie Haberman's brother, Zach, is also a journalist, serving as an editor at the *New York Daily News*.

The family lived on the Upper West Side of Manhattan, and Haberman attended the Ethical Culture Fieldston School, an elite private school known for its intellectual rigor and emphasis on the social good. In 1980, when she was seven years old, Haberman interviewed Mayor Ed Koch for a children's section of the *New York Daily News*; the article marked the first time her name appeared in a byline.

Trump was a storied figure in the city during Haberman's youth. As Combe described it, "The 1980s and '90s New York in which Haberman was raised is the same milieu in which Trump began his crusade to sand down his Queens edges and gild the Manhattan skyline."

After graduating from high school in 1991, Haberman attended Sarah Lawrence College, a private liberal arts college just north of the city. There she studied creative writing and psychology, with the goal of working in the magazine business. When she earned her bachelor's degree in 1996, however, magazine jobs were hard to come by, even for recent graduates as well-connected as Haberman, and she ended up taking a temporary bartending job at an Upper West Side jazz club called Cleopatra's Needle.

JOURNALISM CAREER
After a short stint serving drinks, Haberman accepted an entry-level job at the *New York Post*. While her duties included administrative work and errands, once a week, the *Post's* youngest employees were sent out with veteran reporters to learn the ropes. She greatly impressed Stu Marques, then the metro editor of the paper, with her ability to extract memorable quotes from her subjects and craft a story quickly and concisely. By 1999 she had been placed on the City Hall beat, covering New York's brash mayor Rudy Giuliani. Thanks, in part, to Giuliani's larger-than-life personality, City Hall was a fun and exciting place from which to report, and Haberman became hooked on political journalism. (Trump, when he was covered in the paper, appeared most often in the popular gossip section known as Page Six; he was something of a fixture during his second marriage to beauty queen and actor Marla Maples—and during his subsequent divorce from her.)

In the early 2000s Haberman moved to New York City's other tabloid newspaper, the *Daily News*, where she covered Michael Bloomberg's early tenure as mayor and Hillary Clinton's Senate campaign, as well as her first presidential run. In 2006 Haberman quoted Trump for the first time in a bylined article, writing: "Real-estate mogul Donald Trump talked up Clinton as the next president in Florida on Friday night, reportedly saying at a state GOP fund raiser, 'She's a brilliant woman and she's going to be a very, very formidable candidate.'" She had occasion to contact him from time to time after that, and, as Combe explained, "In hindsight, Haberman was building a reservoir of knowledge and contacts that would make her probably the best-sourced reporter of the 2016 campaign. Significantly, she was accumulating sources who were close to Trump, who knew when he was angry and what he watched on TV and how he could only sleep well in his own bed. Her expertise wasn't just Trump—it was the Trump psyche."

Haberman returned to the *Post* to cover the 2008 presidential campaign and remained there until 2010, when she was hired as a senior reporter at *Politico*, an online media outlet that had been launched just a few years earlier by veteran *Washington Post* reporters. There she frequently covered Trump, who was dipping a toe into politics, intimating that he might become a candidate in the 2012 Republican primary and spreading the debunked theory that Barack Obama had not been born in the United States.

"In New York politics, the *Post* is completely dominant and it sets the agenda," Haberman told Joel Meares for the *Columbia Journalism Review* (2 Sept. 2010), comparing her new employer with her old. "It's sort of apples and oranges, though. *Politico* is also very dominant and it sets the agenda in Washington. It's been about adapting a New York flavor to a broader audience."

Concurrently, in 2014 Haberman began working for CNN as a political analyst, a post she still holds. In 2015—as the *New York Times* began expanding and strengthening its political-reporting team in preparation for the 2016 presidential campaign—it recruited Haberman. In June 2015, when Trump formally announced his candidacy with a now infamous speech in which he characterized Mexican immigrants as criminals and rapists, Haberman was assigned to cover him.

THE AGE OF TRUMP

Haberman quickly noted that among the biggest challenges of covering Trump, both as a candidate and as president, is his willingness to contradict proven facts—and his supporters' willingness to overlook that characteristic. "He was seen as presidential [on the reality show *The Apprentice*], sitting in this leather-bound, high-backed chair at a boardroom table, seeming decisive," she said to Remnick. "The line between news and entertainment has blurred dramatically, and so viewers don't make the same distinction that we [as journalists] do. And so I think his supporters . . . choose either to see him as they saw him on TV or they are very mistrustful of the media."

Because she readily points out his misstatements, Trump just as readily targets Haberman, tweeting that she is "third-rate" "sad," and "biased," and tarring the *Times* as a "failing" purveyor of "fake news." Still, he continues to agree to speak to her, leading Remnick to characterize him as Haberman's "ardent, twisted suitor." Although she has objected to that particular metaphor, she readily acknowledges that Trump, as much as he rails against the *Times*, craves validation from his hometown newspaper. Like other journalists who have raised Trump's ire, she is also a regular recipient of death threats and anti-Semitic harassment, both online and through the mail. She shrugged this off to Remnick: "It is what it is. Short of moving, there's not much I can do."

On the other hand, Haberman is sometimes also berated by Trump's opponents, who accuse her of "normalizing" the president by treating him as she would any other politician. "There has been a very protracted shocked stage in Washington, and I think people have to move past that. Because otherwise you're just never going to be able to cover him," she argued to Combe. "Every moment cannot be, 'Wow! Can you believe what he just did?' Yes, I can! Because he is the same person he was during the campaign." She has explained that she views Trump's presidency through the lens of New York City's rough-and-tumble political scene, reminiscent in certain ways of the take-no-prisoners style of Ed Koch and Rudy Giuliani.

PERSONAL LIFE

Haberman has been married since 2003 to fellow journalist Dareh Gregorian. They have three children and live in the New York City borough of Brooklyn.

She is a furious multitasker, and her colleagues often characterize her as "intense," marveling at her ability to talk to multiple sources, text, and conduct online research all at the same time. She reportedly received word that Trump campaign manager Corey Lewandowski had been fired during her child's kindergarten graduation; she confirmed the news and wrote the story for the *Times* on her cell phone during the ceremony.

SUGGESTED READING

Byers, Dylan. "Maggie Haberman: The *New York Times* Reporter Trump Can't Quit." *CNN*, 7 Apr. 2017, money.cnn.com/2017/04/07/media/maggie-haberman-trump/index.html. Accessed 5 Dec. 2017.

Calderone, Michael. "*New York Times* Staffing Up For 2016 Election with Maggie Haberman Hire." *HuffPost*, 1 Sept. 2015, www.huffingtonpost.com/2015/01/09/politico-maggie-haberman_n_6443442.html. Accessed 5 Dec. 2017.

Combe, Rachel. "Wanna Know What Donald Trump Is Really Thinking? Read Maggie Haberman." *Elle*, 24 May 2017, www.elle.com/culture/career-politics/a45485/maggie-haberman-new-york-times-trump-profile/. Accessed 5 Dec. 2017.

Guthrie, Marisa. "*New York Times*' Maggie Haberman: Trump 'Is a Whirlwind of One.'" *Hollywood Reporter*, 14 Apr. 2017, www.hollywoodreporter.com/news/new-york-times-maggie-haberman-trump-is-a-whirlwind-one-993809. Accessed 5 Dec. 2017.

Meares, Joel. "Q & A: *Politico*'s Maggie Haberman." *Columbia Journalism Review*, 2 Sept. 2010, archives.cjr.org/campaign_desk/q_a_politicos_maggie_haberman.php. Accessed 5 Dec. 2017.

Remnick, David. "A Conversation with Maggie Haberman, Trump's Favorite Foe." *The New Yorker*, 21 July 2017, www.newyorker.com/

news/news-desk/a-conversation-with-maggie-haberman-trumps-favorite-foe. Accessed 5 Dec. 2017.

—*Mari Rich*

Haim

Occupation: Band

ESTE HAIM
Date of birth: March 14, 1986
Occupation: Bass guitar, vocals

DANIELLE HAIM
Date of birth: February 16, 1989
Occupation: Lead guitar, vocals

ALANA HAIM
Date of birth: December 15, 1991
Occupation: Percussion, vocals

The pop rock band Haim rose to fame in 2013 with their critically lauded debut album *Days Are Gone*. In 2017, they released their much-anticipated follow-up album, *Something to Tell You*. The core members of Haim are Este Haim on bass guitar and vocals, Danielle Haim on lead guitar and vocals, and Alana Haim on percussion and vocals. (The band has employed a succession of drummers to round out the quartet.) Music has always been a family business for the three sisters, who were born and raised in Los Angeles, California. They got their start playing classic rock and folk covers with their parents when they were in elementary school. After graduating from the Los Angeles County High School for the Arts, the sisters began writing songs together and performing using their last name as a band name. Haim, the Hebrew word for "life," is pronounced "high-im," though according to the sisters, a pronunciation that rhymes with "time" is also acceptable. Musically and visually, the sisters evoke a different era. They wear their hair long and straight and dress in vintage clothes. Their songs sound more like the 1970s pop group Fleetwood Mac—and recently, a little like the 1990s trio Wilson Phillips—than their current pop contemporaries. As Melena Ryzik of the *New York Times* (6 July 2017) put it, Haim's "organic guitar-bass-drums-keys sound is anachronistic, and proudly so." Their infectious songs have won them a diverse coterie of fans including rapper Kid Cudi (Haim recorded a duet with Cudi called "Red Eye" in 2013) and pop star Taylor Swift, who befriended the sisters on tour in 2015. Academy Award–nominated director Paul Thomas Anderson, best known for the gothic drama *There Will Be Blood* (2007), is also a fan. He directed a video for Haim's plaintive 2017 single "Right Now," that captured the band in their element, jamming in the studio.

ROCKINHAIM AND THE VALLI GIRLS

The Haim sisters were born to parents Donna and Moti Haim, both of whom have musical talent. Their mother, an art teacher turned real estate agent, was a folk singer in the 1970s. Their father, who was born and raised in Israel, was a professional soccer player who played the drums. He also worked in real estate. In lieu of a first dance at the couple's wedding, they sang a first duet. Este, the eldest of the three sisters, was born on March 14, 1986. Danielle was born on February 16, 1989, and Alana was born on December 15, 1991. They were raised in the Studio City neighborhood of Los Angeles, where

By Kim Metso, via Wikimedia Commons

their parents guided them towards instruments befitting their various personalities. Alana was suited for the wildness of the drums, while the more mellow Este and Danielle thrived learning the melodic folk songs of Joni Mitchell on guitar. Danielle proved the better student of the instrument, so therefore, Moti decided, Este would do well learning to play bass, an instrument with fewer strings. The family formed a band called Rockinhaim when the sisters were children. They played their first show at Canter's Deli, a popular eatery near West Hollywood. They were paid in matzo ball soup. They continued to play shows—at street fairs and local fundraisers—every few months for the next fifteen years. Rockinhaim played covers of popular rock songs from the 1970s and 1980s. Despite the seemingly casual nature of their union, the sisters say that the family rehearsed constantly. Their dedication showed.

After a show in 2004, a woman approached the family, asking if Este and Danielle, the two older sisters, would be interested in joining a girl group called the Valli Girls. The appeal of the pop-punk Valli Girls, Danielle told Duncan Cooper for *Fader* (25 June 2013), was multifold. For one, "there was a deal on the table from Columbia," she recalled. "We were like, 'We want to play music, we want to be signed.' We had never played without our parents before." Este and Danielle joined the group after the Valli Girls had already recorded their first album, but the girls appeared in a few music videos for the group, including "It's a Hair Thing," the theme for the short-lived animated series *Trollz* (2005), based on the toy dolls of the same name. They also appeared in the video for the empowerment anthem "Born to Lead," sponsored by the teen magazine *CosmoGirl*. They sang a ballad called "Always There in You" for the *Sisterhood of the Traveling Pants* soundtrack, and they attended the Nickelodeon Kid's Choice Awards with the Valli Girls in 2005. It was their last public appearance with the group; they ended their contracts soon after.

FORMING THE BAND

All three sisters attended the Los Angeles County High School for the Arts, though Este was the only one who gravitated toward theater. She won a citywide monologue competition at sixteen and dreamed of performing on the long-running sketch comedy show *Saturday Night Live*. But after graduation, she and Danielle opted to stay in Los Angeles and write songs with Alana. They had learned to write music, Alana told Ryzik, while analyzing the classic rock songs they played with their parents in Rockinhaim. They played their first official show as Haim, at a museum in the San Fernando Valley, in 2007. Meanwhile, Este worked as a host at the chain restaurant The Cheesecake Factory and earned her real estate license. She began studying for a music degree. In 2009, Danielle entered the Los Angeles music scene after attending a jam session in Laurel Canyon with indie rocker Jenny Lewis. Lewis asked Danielle to join her touring band as a guitarist. Not too long after that, Julian Casablancas, the lead singer of the rock band The Strokes, saw one of Lewis's shows in New York and hired Danielle for his own solo backing band. Este was proud of her sister but also newly determined. "I was like: 'F—— this. My sister's going on tour with Julian Casablancas? Why am I here studying?' That really lit a fire up my a——, to make Haim happen," she recalled to Tom Lamont for the *Guardian* (21 Sept. 2013). Haim continued to play gigs when they could. Este slyly arranged for Haim to play at her college campus. The sisters used the money they earned from that performance to follow Casablancas on tour, opening for him every night. The veteran rock singer offered them some valuable advice. "Julian told us: disappear, come back in a year with stronger songs and hit the ground running," Danielle told Lamont.

The Haim sisters followed this advice. They stopped gigging for a year, instead gathering at Danielle's apartment in Venice, California, to write using a Yamaha drum machine and the music-making app GarageBand. This period marked a "turning point," Danielle told Jonah Weiner for *Rolling Stone* (12 Nov. 2013). During that time, Alana graduated from high school, and Haim got a new manager and a producer. In 2012, they posted their first single, "Forever," online. The song got radio play in the United Kingdom, landing the band a record deal with Columbia. Their music caught the attention of Florence Welch of Florence and the Machine; the English singer asked Haim to open for her in London. They made a similar connection to the British band Mumford and Sons, with whom they ended up touring cities across the world. The sisters worked on their debut album between performances.

DAYS ARE GONE AND *SOMETHING TO TELL YOU*

Haim released their debut album *Days Are Gone* in September 2013. Thanks to the early popularity of "Forever," it debuted at number one in the United Kingdom. Larry Fitzmaurice, who reviewed the album for *Pitchfork* (30 Sept. 2013), praised the ease with which the band played together, as well as their percussive precision, evident in Danielle's uniquely pleasing staccato vocals. He described *Days Are Gone* as an "outstanding" and "impeccably crafted" debut. This seamlessness—catchy hooks, exuberant synths—divided critics. Some felt that the debut lacked a true identity. Others, like Fitzmaurice, engaged with this argument but came out on the other side when describing their influences of 1990s R & B, California folk, 1980s pop, and contemporary indie rock. "When you hear about the influences and consider just how slick the record can be, you might imagine Haim coming over as faceless," Fitzmaurice wrote. "But the band's most unusual quality on *Days Are Gone* is their ability to absorb inputs and continue to sound distinct." He described Haim's persona as "affable, playing-to-the-rafters rock stars" and "studio pros." Haim was nominated for a Grammy Award for Best New Artist in 2015. The band spent the next four years touring, including a stint on Taylor Swift's massive *1989* tour in 2015. "We really felt on fire as a band," Danielle told Ryzik. When they returned to the studio to record their second album, they concentrated on songwriting and, as Danielle described it to Ryzik, creating a more "raw" sound. In these endeavors, they received guidance from rock royalty: Fleetwood Mac's Stevie Nicks. *Something to Tell You*, a pop album about heartbreak, was released in July 2017. Jenn Pelly of *Pitchfork* (7 July 2017) dubbed Haim "masters of rhythm," making an apt comparison between Haim's crisp percussive sound and the George Michael song "Faith." She noted the dissonance between the album's lyrics and its melodious hooks and harmonies. "Beat by beat, Haim are the classic sound of heartbreak alleviated, if only for a moment." Still, critics elsewhere complained that the album did not sound much different from their last. To paraphrase one critic at *Spin*, Haim, for some, is too much nostalgic sheen and not enough innovation.

PERSONAL LIVES

Este, the former aspiring actor, is the band's clown. She is also affectionately known among fans for her "bass face," a series of contorted facial expressions she makes while deep in the groove of performance. She is also diabetic; at one performance in Glastonbury, England, in 2013, she nearly had a seizure onstage because her blood sugar dropped too low. Danielle, according to Ryzik, is the most "serious-minded" of the group. She has been dating Grammy Award–winning producer Ariel Rechtshaid, who worked on both Haim records, for the past several years. She lives in the Silver Lake neighborhood of Los Angeles. The outspoken Alana, sometimes referred to as Baby Haim or Merlin, enjoys baking.

SUGGESTED READING

Cooper, Duncan. "Haim: Best Friends Forever." *Fader*, no. 86, 25 June/July 2013, www.thefader.com/2013/06/25/haim-best-friends-forever. Accessed 7 Mar. 2018.

Fitzmaurice, Larry. "Haim, *Days Are Gone*." *Pitchfork*, 30 Sept. 2013, www.pitchfork.com/reviews/albums/18574-haim-days-are-gone/. Accessed 7 Mar. 2018.

Lamont, Tom. "Haim: 'Dad Would Be Like, Let's Go and Jam in the Living Room.'" *The Guardian*, 21 Sept. 2013, www.theguardian.com/music/2013/sep/22/haim-sisters-days-gone-interview. Accessed 7 Mar. 2018.

Pelly, Jenn. "Haim, *Something to Tell You*." *Pitchfork*, 7 July 2017, www.pitchfork.com/reviews/albums/haim-something-to-tell-you/. Accessed 7 Mar. 2018.

Ryzik, Melena. "Haim Wants to Prove That Vintage Vibes Feel Just Fine for Now." *The New York Times*, 6 July 2017. www.nytimes.com/2017/07/06/arts/music/haim-something-to-tell-you-interview.html. Accessed 7 Mar. 2018.

Weiner, Jonah. "How Haim's Three Geeky Sisters Became the Year's Coolest New Band." *Rolling Stone*, 12 Nov. 2013, www.rollingstone.com/music/news/how-haims-three-geeky-sisters-became-the-years-coolest-new-band-20131112. Accessed 7 Mar. 2018.

—Molly Hagan

Lisa Halliday

Date of birth: ca. 1977
Occupation: Author

Lisa Halliday won the Whiting Award in Fiction in 2017 and published her debut novel, *Asymmetry*, to critical acclaim in February 2018. The Massachusetts native got her start as a literary agent for the prestigious Wylie Agency in New York City in the late 1990s. Working with famous writers, she told Alexandra Alter for the *New York Times* (2 Feb. 2018), inspired her to begin writing fiction herself. "Prior to that, I thought there was some sort of magic involved, and that I just didn't have that magic," she said. The example of the Pulitzer Prize–winning novelist Philip Roth in particular taught her that writing was less magic and more exhaustive application of craft. "A lot of it is showing up even when you feel it's not working. He [was] very good at that," she said to Alter.

Halliday published her first work, a short story titled "Stump Louie," in the *Paris Review* in 2005. It took her many more years to complete her first novel. True to its name, *Asymmetry* is comprised of three very loosely related stories exploring imbalance. The most talked about of the stories is based on Halliday's brief romance with Roth when she was in her twenties. The two remained close friends until Roth's death in May 2018. He reportedly read *Asymmetry* before it was published, writing in an email that the book was "a considerable achievement," Alter reported. Other reviewers seemed to agree; *Asymmetry* was lauded by critics, including Katy Waldman of the *New Yorker* (12 Apr. 2018), who described it as a "literary phenomenon." Halliday described the overwhelming response to *Asymmetry* as disorienting. "It almost feels like it's happening to someone else," she told Kate Tuttle for the *Boston Globe* (20 Apr. 2018). "And I must say I like that, because I'm a very private person. The geographical distance is a good thing; it creates a kind of psychological distance."

EARLY LIFE AND EDUCATION

Lisa Ann Halliday grew up in Medfield, Massachusetts. Her father, a mechanic-repairman, and her mother, a seamstress, divorced when she was five. Halliday and her sister, Andrea, moved in with their mother, Elizabeth, and their mother's boyfriend (and eventual husband), Ralph Godin. The Godins began a pest extermination business together.

The family lived near the Medfield Public Library, and Halliday recalls spending summer mornings sitting outside on the library steps, waiting for it to open. She read voraciously, working her way through *Charlotte's Web* by E. B. White and Laura Ingalls Wilder's *Little House of the Prairie* series, before tackling the works of Charles Dickens, F. Scott Fitzgerald, and Edith Wharton.

Halliday received an excellent public education in Medfield, she told Laura Drinan for Medfield's *Hometown Weekly* (2 May 2018), echoing an opinion she had also voiced in interviews with other publications: "The school system is just amazing. . . . It just set me on a track in life, and I almost feel sort of nervous to think when I think of how it might have gone another way." After graduating from high school, Halliday became the first person in her immediate family to attend college. She enrolled as an art history student at Harvard University.

EARLY CAREER

After graduating from Harvard in 1998, Halliday took a job as an assistant literary agent with the Wylie Agency in New York City. She soon became an agent herself and befriended some of the agency's illustrious clientele, including the National Book Award–winning fiction writer Louise Erdrich and the Pulitzer Prize–winning poet Louise Glück. Around the same time, she also met and began a romantic relationship with Roth.

Inspired, but also intimidated, by her famous friends, Halliday began to write fiction herself. She enjoyed many "encouraging rejections," she told Claire Armitstead for the *Observer* (14 Jan. 2018). One gatekeeper suggested that she had talent but had yet to find a story to tell, likening

her work to the anthropomorphic picture book "*Babar* written by EM Forster." She earned her first publication—a short story called "Stump Louie" in the *Paris Review*—in the summer of 2005. The interwar-era story follows a piano prodigy who becomes the star of a successful radio program called "Stump Louie," in which listeners call in and try to "stump Louie" by requesting songs that the young pianist might not know how to play.

Halliday left her job with the Wylie Agency, for which she had worked both in New York and in the United Kingdom, to focus on writing fiction in 2006. To make ends meet, she worked as a freelance editor, proofreader, translator, and ghostwriter. Halliday even interviewed Erdrich for the *Paris Review*—a literary magazine known for its in-depth interviews—in 2010. Armitstead described this period as Halliday's "second apprenticeship" in structure and storytelling.

ASYMMETRY

The epiphany for Halliday's three-part debut novel, *Asymmetry*, was to pair stories about two different people living during the Iraq War. In the first part, "Folly," Mary-Alice Dodge meets Pulitzer Prize–winning novelist Ezra Blazer on a park bench in New York City. He begins seducing her by buying her an ice cream cone, and the two enjoy a months-long spring-winter romance. Halliday insists that Alice's story is not entirely autobiographical. "Of course there are details of Alice's life that overlap with my own, but so much is invented for the sake of the narrative," she explained to Alter. Alice works as an editorial assistant and wants to be a writer but feels trapped in Blazer's shadow. "I wanted to write about an aspiring writer who was having trouble under what I think Harold Bloom called 'the anxiety of influence,' because I certainly felt that," Halliday added. Blazer's encouragement and advice provides a through line for exploring storytelling and life.

The second part of the novel, "Madness," features an Iraqi American economist named Amar Ala Jaafari, who ponders various moments from his life while being detained at Heathrow Airport in London. (Halliday has some experience with British immigration authorities: she was once detained at Heathrow on suspicion of taking advantage of the British health care system.)

The final story, "Ezra Blazer's Desert Island Discs," takes the form of a transcript for a BBC radio interview in which Ezra explains which albums he would take with him if he were stranded on a desert island. Critic Katy Waldman described this seemingly incongruous third act as "a slim, revelatory coda."

CRITICAL RECEPTION

It took Halliday a handful of years to write *Asymmetry* because of her various freelance gigs, but also because she needed to discover how best her material cohered. Early on, Halliday tried to force her disparate threads to intersect. She ultimately decided to let them play against one another thematically. Of her decision, Armitstead quoted a piece of advice from Ezra Blazer: "'Sometimes,' as Ezra says, 'you just have to let your characters get on with it, which is to say coexist.'" Halliday worked, she told Alter, following Erdrich's dictum to "write as though you're writing in secret, as though no one will actually read it."

Thus, she was surprised when, in 2016, her manuscript sparked a bidding war among seven different publishing companies. Publisher Granta Books billed the book as "an extraordinary study of the power plays between young and old, West and Middle East, luck and talent, fairness and injustice, and the personal and the political," as reported by Natasha Onwuemezi for the *Bookseller* (5 Aug. 2016). The initial enthusiasm may have had more to do with the book's connection to Roth, however. On the strength of her unpublished novel, Halliday won the prestigious Whiting Award in 2017. *Asymmetry* was published in February 2018.

Parul Sehgal, who reviewed the book for the *New York Times* (6 Feb. 2018), described *Asymmetry* as a "scorchingly intelligent first novel . . . which poses deep questions about free will, fate and freedom, the all-powerful accident of one's birth and how life is alchemized into fiction." She concluded, "You won't find one key that will unlock all its mysteries—this book is musical, not architectural in structure; themes don't build on each other as much as chime and rhyme, repeat and harmonize, so what we receive is less a series of thesis statements than a shimmering web of associations; in short, the world as we know it."

Christian Lorentzen, writing for *Vulture* (7 Feb. 2018), was somewhat critical of Halliday's short story but praised *Asymmetry*. He described it as an "experiment of a novel," concluding that by its end, Halliday pulls off a "stunt of transcendence." "As with a gymnast who's just stuck a perfect routine," he wrote, "your impulse is to ask her, what's next?"

As of 2018, Halliday was working on another novel, which is set partly in Italy. This next novel explores the evolution of conspiracy theories and the sometimes-murky boundary between truth and fiction.

PERSONAL LIFE

In 2011, Halliday moved to Milan, Italy, where her husband, Theo Collier, became the foreign rights director for the Italian publishing house Feltrinelli. It was in Italy that she began work on what would become her first novel. Halliday resides in Milan with her husband and their daughter.

SUGGESTED READING

Alter, Alexandra. "Lisa Halliday's Debut Novel Is Drawing Comparisons to Philip Roth. Though Not for the Reasons You Might Think." *The New York Times*, 2 Feb. 2018, www.nytimes.com/2018/02/02/books/in-lisa-hallidays-debut-novel-philip-roth.html. Accessed 4 Aug. 2018.

Armitstead, Claire, et al. "Meet the New Faces of Fiction for 2018." *The Observer*, 14 Jan. 2018, www.theguardian.com/books/2018/jan/14/debut-novelists-2018-donkor-halliday-gowar-bracht-kitson-libby-page-aj-pearce. Accessed 5 Aug. 2018.

Drinan, Laura. "Hometown Author Returns to Medfield." *Hometown Weekly*, 2 May 2018, www.hometownweekly.net/medfield/hometown-author-returns-medfield. Accessed 4 Aug. 2018.

Lorentzen, Christian. "Lisa Halliday's Tremendous New Experiment of a Novel." Review of *Asymmetry*, by Lisa Halliday. *Vulture*, 7 Feb. 2018, www.vulture.com/2018/02/lisa-hallidays-tremendous-new-experiment-of-a-novel.html. Accessed 5 Aug. 2018.

Onwuemezi, Natasha. "Granta Wins Halliday Debut in Seven-Way Auction." *The Bookseller*, 5 Aug. 2016, www.thebookseller.com/news/granta-win-two-halliday-seven-way-auction-371511. Accessed 5 Aug. 2018.

Sehgal, Parul. "Two Stories Harmonize in Lisa Halliday's Deft Debut Novel." Review of *Asymmetry*, by Lisa Halliday. *The New York Times*, 6 Feb. 2018, www.nytimes.com/2018/02/06/books/review-asymmetry-lisa-halliday.html. Accessed 5 Aug. 2018.

Waldman, Katy. "Why 'Asymmetry' Has Become a Literary Phenomenon." *The New Yorker*, 12 Apr. 2018, www.newyorker.com/books/page-turner/why-asymmetry-has-become-a-literary-phenomenon. Accessed 5 Aug. 2018.

—*Molly Hagan*

Liz Hannah

Date of birth: December 14, 1985
Occupation: Screenwriter, producer

In October 2016, screenwriter Liz Hannah received a phone call delivering unexpected news: film executive Amy Pascal wanted to purchase the rights to Hannah's script *The Post*, a screenplay that Hannah had written in an attempt to

Photo by Alberto E. Rodriguez/Getty Images

get an agent and thought would never be produced. "It's the greatest phone call you've ever gotten, and then it's the most horrifyingly terrifying phone call you've ever gotten," she recalled to Jenna Marotta for *IndieWire* (1 Dec. 2017). "You're like, 'Oh, they want to actually make this, and I've never made a movie before.'" Just over a year later, the film incarnation of *The Post*—directed by Steven Spielberg and starring Meryl Streep and Tom Hanks—premiered in theaters, and it went on to be nominated for the Academy Award for Best Picture, among other accolades.

Although Hannah's abrupt rise to fame as a screenwriter was unique, her background in the film industry aptly prepared her for the new world in which she found herself. A graduate of the Pratt Institute and the American Film Institute (AFI) Conservatory, she began her career in production, completing several internships before taking a position at Denver and Delilah Productions, the production company founded by actor and producer Charlize Theron. Despite her interest in production, Hannah was drawn to writing and, with the encouragement of her supervisors, quit her job to pursue opportunities in that field. Although she never expected to see *The Post* on screen, her compelling approach to the story of *Washington Post* publisher Katharine Graham ultimately attracted high-profile talent as well as the interest of audiences and critics worldwide. "I've learned that if you throw your passion into something, it makes other people care," she told Amy Nicholson for the *Washington Post* (21 Dec. 2017).

EARLY LIFE AND EDUCATION

Elizabeth Hannah was born on December 14, 1985, in New York City. Her father worked as an industrial designer, and her mother was a social worker. The family moved to Connecticut when she was four, and she attended school there. When her father later returned to New York, Hannah spent her weekends in the city with him and lived in Connecticut with her mother during the week.

As a child, Hannah was an avid reader. She likewise watched films with her parents, who had wide-ranging tastes. "We would just watch everything without, really, any specific genre or direction," she told Scott Myers for *Go into the Story* (8 Jan. 2018), a blog operated as part of the *Black List* screenwriting website. "We were constantly consuming. I think my love of storytelling came from them."

Hannah attended Westport's Staples High School, and after graduating in 2003, she enrolled in the Pratt Institute to study film. "I always knew I wanted to make movies," she told Myers of her aspirations. "I didn't really know what that meant, ever. Part of it helps that I wasn't really good at math, so I had to diverge and figure out what else I could be good at." Meanwhile, on her summer breaks, she began to receive real-world training and experience through production internships on films such as the 2006 comedy *Wedding Daze* and the 2007 drama *Reign over Me*. She also produced a short film that went on to play at a variety of film festivals.

Soon after earning her bachelor of fine arts in film from Pratt in 2007, she moved to Los Angeles, California, and enrolled in AFI to study producing, with the goal of becoming a creative producer for films. While there, she gained hands-on experience in a variety of areas of the filmmaking process by serving as a crew member for her classmates' thesis films. Perhaps the most significant moment in her budding career to that point, however, came when she secured an internship at Denver and Delilah Productions, a production company led by actor and producer Charlize Theron as well as producers Beth Kono and AJ Dix.

EARLY CAREER

After completing her internship while a student at AFI, from which she graduated in 2009, she was hired on as a development employee at Denver and Delilah Productions and spent nearly five years with the company. "I spent the entirety of my mid-20s there, learning," she told Carly Mallenbaum for *USA Today* (12 Jan. 2018). "One of the fortunate things about working with Charlize and Beth is that they felt so strongly about female voices." As a company dedicated to producing film and television content by and about women, Denver and Delilah Productions was a formative environment for Hannah, who came to recognize the extent to which the presence of women behind the scenes contributed to an increase in representation of women on-screen.

Although Hannah enjoyed her time at Denver and Delilah Productions, she found herself increasingly drawn to the writing side of the film industry. While she had written at various points throughout her life, she had doubted her abilities and had not attempted to find work in that field. Her outlook changed, however, after she completed a sample screenplay with the intent of seeking feedback from her supervisors. "I sent the script to my boss and the woman who is now my manager, and I said to them, 'If this is good, I will quit my job,'" she recalled to Joy Press for *Vulture* (20 Dec. 2017). "And they both were like, 'Quit your job!'" With that encouragement, she left her production job to focus on her writing. Over the next years, she wrote and directed the 2014 short film *Skin* and contributed a 2016 episode to the web series *Guidance*.

FROM SPEC SCRIPT TO THE SCREEN

While working to establish herself as a screenwriter, Hannah began work on a screenplay about Katharine Graham, who served as publisher of the *Washington Post* during the 1960s and 1970s. In addition to being the first woman to serve as publisher of a major newspaper in the United States, Graham was significant for her connection to the Pentagon Papers, a collection of government documents that, upon being leaked to the press in 1971, revealed many of the US government's lies and omissions regarding the Vietnam War. After a *New York Times* series of articles on the revelations presented in the Pentagon Papers was prevented from continuing, Graham and fellow leaders at the *Washington Post*, including executive editor Ben Bradlee, struggled to decide whether to publish stories about the papers themselves. For Hannah, the intertwining stories of Graham and the Pentagon Papers made for an intriguing narrative that not only presented a compelling period in American history but also told the story of a woman who came into her own in the face of adversity. While Graham's association with the *Washington Post* was lifelong, the Pentagon Papers era was "the moment where she came of age" and "the most interesting and relatable window into [her] life," as Hannah told Nicholson.

Despite Hannah's passion for Graham's story, she did not expect that the film would ever be made. Rather, she wrote the screenplay as a spec script—a screenplay that has not been purchased or commissioned by a film studio or other company—that she hoped would help her obtain an agent. After completing her first draft of the screenplay, titled *The Post*, in early

September 2016, she spent the next weeks revising the screenplay based on feedback from her managers and other readers. To her surprise, it made its way to a number of film studios in late October, and within a day, film executive Amy Pascal had purchased the rights to the script.

Following that acquisition, screenwriter Josh Singer was brought in to contribute to and rewrite portions of the screenplay. The cowriter of the Academy Award–winning screenplay for the 2015 film *Spotlight*, which focused on the *Boston Globe*'s investigation of child abuse in the Catholic Church, Singer had extensive experience that was directly relevant to Hannah's newspaper-focused narrative, and the two formed a positive working relationship during the rewrite process.

THE POST

In light of the production team's belief that the story of *The Post* was particularly relevant to the political climate in the United States as of late 2016, the film's development was fast-tracked, and shooting began early in 2017. Acclaimed filmmaker Steven Spielberg had joined the project as its director, and veteran actors Meryl Streep and Tom Hanks were cast as Graham and Bradlee, respectively. Thrilled that the project was moving forward, Hannah was particularly excited to have the opportunity to work alongside such well-regarded professionals. "I was on set every day saying, 'You guys, I have to quit after this because I'm never going to make a better movie. I have peaked,'" she told Press.

The Post premiered in December 2017 and opened in theaters throughout the United States the following month. The film met with largely positive reviews, and the screenplay's unusual journey to the screen made Hannah a figure of interest among many journalists. In addition to receiving widespread critical acclaim following its release, *The Post* was nominated for the Academy Award for best motion picture of the year, while Streep was nominated for the award for best actress for her portrayal of Graham. The film likewise was nominated for numerous other awards, including several Golden Globes. Although *The Post* did not claim many of the awards for which it was nominated, Hannah and Singer received significant accolades for their work, including the Paul Selvin Award from the Writers Guild of America West.

FUTURE PROJECTS

Following the success of *The Post*, Hannah became an in-demand screenwriter and signed on to several projects, including a miniseries about early female pioneers in the US space program and a feature film about George W. Bush's experiences during the September 11, 2001, terrorist attacks. She also wrote the 2018 short film *Hello*

Apartment, which was directed by actor Dakota Fanning. "I have decided I'm going to throw everything at the wall," Hannah told Press of her plans for the future. "I did a lot of meetings after the script sold, and people would ask, 'What is your dream project?' I'd answer, 'Oh, I just made it.'" In addition to her writing work, she is active in the Time's Up movement, which seeks to combat sexual harassment and promote gender equality in Hollywood.

PERSONAL LIFE

Hannah married Brian Millikin in November 2017. A fellow writer, Millikin has written for television shows such as *Haven* and *Time after Time*. They live in Los Angeles.

SUGGESTED READING

Hannah, Liz. "*Go into the Story* Interview (Part 1): Liz Hannah." Interview by Scott Myers. *Go into the Story*, 8 Jan. 2018, gointothestory. blcklst.com/go-into-the-story-interview-part-1-liz-hannah-646540cba080. Accessed 9 June 2018.

Lynch, Matthew. "How *The Post* Became the Hottest Screenplay in Hollywood." *Vanity Fair*, 2017, www.vanityfair.com/hollywood/2017/12/how-the-post-became-the-hottest-screenplay-in-hollywood. Accessed 9 June 2018.

Mallenbaum, Carly. "*The Post* Writer Liz Hannah Shows What's Possible When Women Occupy Powerful Roles in Hollywood." *USA Today*, 12 Jan. 2018, www.usatoday.com/story/life/entertainthis/2018/01/12/post-liz-hannah-screenwriter/1018876001/. Accessed 9 June 2018.

Marotta, Jenna. "*The Post*: Screenwriters Liz Hannah and Josh Singer on Revisiting History with Meryl Streep and Steven Spielberg." *IndieWire*, 1 Dec. 2017, www.indiewire.com/2017/12/the-post-screenwriters-liz-hannah-josh-singer-meryl-streep-tom-hanks-steven-spielberg-1201902755/. Accessed 9 June 2018.

Nicholson, Amy. "How a Writer Defied 'One in a Million' Odds to Get Her First Movie Made by Steven Spielberg." *The Washington Post*, 21 Dec. 2017, www.washingtonpost.com/entertainment/how-a-writer-defied-one-in-a-million-odds-to-get-her-first-movie-made-by-steven-spielberg/2017/12/20/7 6131f9c-e424-11e7-a65d-1ac0fd7f097e_story.html?noredirect=on&utm_term=.16feb2bcd94b. Accessed 9 June 2018.

Press, Joy. "*The Post*'s Liz Hannah on How Her Spec Script Launched an Oscar Campaign." *Vulture*, 20 Dec. 2017, www.vulture.com/2017/12/liz-hannah-the-post-pentagon-papers-script.html. Accessed 9 June 2018.

—*Joy Crelin*

Laura Harrier

Date of birth: March 28, 1990
Occupation: Actor, model

Up-and-coming actor Laura Harrier got her proverbial "big break" relatively early in her career. She had modeled for such popular beauty and fashion brands as Urban Outfitters, Garnier, and L'Oréal and appeared in a short-lived online version of the soap opera *One Life to Live* in 2013 before getting cast in the 2017 big-budget Hollywood film *Spider-Man: Homecoming*. As Liz, a high school classmate of Peter Parker, she plays the love interest of the titular superhero. "What's cool about this movie and Peter and Liz's relationship is it's an interracial relationship, but it's not talked about. It's not a big deal and shouldn't be made into a big deal," Harrier told Darcel Rockett for the *Chicago Tribune* (5 July 2017). "It's not this romance where they needed arm candy for the superhero. . . . I'm really proud to be playing Liz, playing someone little girls can look at and identify with and understand that she is intelligent and beautiful and driven."

Though Harrier was not entirely confident during screen tests that she would get the role, the film received largely positive reviews upon its release that included praise of her performance and contribution to the authenticity of the cast. Amid increased attention that came with the role, she has admitted to still feeling star-struck herself and has expressed gratitude for what she learned on the set of her first major feature: "I'm a normal girl from Evanston, I don't know how

By Gage Skidmore [CC BY-SA 2.0], via Wikimedia Commons

I'm in this situation with these people. . . . Sitting on set doing a scene with Michael Keaton was nerve-wracking, and it going well was really incredible and eye-opening," she explained to Rockett.

EARLY LIFE

Laura Harrier was born on March 28, 1990, in Chicago, Illinois, and was raised in the suburban town of Evanston. Her father works in the field of insurance and her mother is a speech pathologist. She has described her parents as bright, creative people who nonetheless had no interest whatsoever in show business and told John Ortved for *Interview* magazine (5 June 2016) that she had a "very Midwestern, adorable childhood." She credits both parents with being wonderful role models and has characterized the women in her family as exceptionally strong. "My mom is also my favorite feminist," she asserted to Rockett. "She was one before it was cool to be one." In addition to perusing comic books, she loved the Harry Potter series; she read at least the first book several times and envisioned belonging to the academic house Ravenclaw, whose fictional students are known for their keen intelligence. At the same time, she was also interested in learning about outer space.

Even at a young age, Harrier, who is biracial, was conscious that her family, no matter how loving and solid, was different from those she saw in popular culture. "Growing up, there were no families on TV that looked like mine," she recalled to Ashley Weatherford for *New York* magazine's fashion blog and website *The Cut* (5 July 2017). Still, she remembers that Evanston was a comfortably diverse place in which to grow up, saying in her conversation with Weatherford, "It's such a bubble and I never thought about things in terms of racial identity. People are like, 'Was it hard growing up mixed?' 'Did you not fit in?' and I'm like 'No? What? That's the dumbest question ever.'"

MODELING AND TRANSITIONING TO ACTING

One day, when Harrier was a teen returning home from school, a family friend who worked as a location scout staged a shoot at her house and a photographer suggested that she try her hand at modeling, recommending an agent. After placing a call to the agent, she began to get catalog jobs—unglamorous, entry-level assignments modeling off-the-rack clothing.

Having graduated from Evanston Township High School in 2008, Harrier continued to work and book a variety of modeling gigs after moving to New York City to attend New York University's Gallatin School of Individualized Study, a liberal-arts college with a focus on self-directed learning and intellectual exploration. Although she appreciated many aspects of modeling, she quickly found herself discontented. "[Modeling] was just kind of this weird job I fell into that wasn't the plan at all," she recalled to Stephanie Eckardt for *W* magazine (15 June 2017). Deciding to make a drastic change, she gave in to her longtime interest in acting as a greater platform for expressing her creativity and withdrew from Gallatin (having already deferred entrance into the program) to undertake an intensive two-year acting program at the William Esper Studio, a prestigious facility whose students learn the Meisner technique, which emphasizes organic, truthful, expressive performances. (Among the studio's alumni are Kathy Bates and Jeff Goldblum.) While she enjoyed her studies, she was still unsure of her future path. "I thought I'd be doing weird, Off Broadway theater after I graduated," she joked to Weatherford.

BURGEONING ACTING CAREER

Those fears did not come to pass. In 2013, Harrier found work on the soap opera *One Life to Live*, which had aired on ABC for more than four decades, from 1968 to 2012, and was then picked up by the online streaming services Hulu and iTunes. She appeared on approximately forty episodes of the reboot, playing the part of a young mother named Destiny Evans, but the updated version of the iconic daytime drama did not draw the audience of the beloved original and was canceled after one season. Regardless, she considers the short-lived gig a valuable opportunity to learn. "It was such a weird experience, being thrown into something where everyone else has been there for, like, fifty years," she told Ortved. "I was replacing another actress, and soap fans are crazy; I would get hate mail. It was good because I can memorize anything now. They would throw you fifty pages a night and you would have to know them right away."

In 2014, Harrier made guest appearances on the CBS detective show *Unforgettable*, starring Poppy Montgomery, and later that year she had a small part in the Anna Kendrick–helmed musical *The Last Five Years*. Following an appearance in the science-fiction television movie *Galyntine* (2014), she took on a role in *4th Man Out* (2015), a comedy about a gay auto mechanic whose friends, after a period of adjustment, support him in his search for love.

Those television and film roles, although minor, caught the eye of British director Steve McQueen, who had won widespread acclaim for his 2013 film *12 Years a Slave*. He cast Harrier in his planned HBO project *Codes of Conduct*, about a newly wealthy software developer thrust into New York City's social scene. Pitched in the industry as *Six Degrees of Separation* meets *Shame*, the planned miniseries was ultimately passed on by HBO in early 2016 after only the pilot had been shot. Although the network's reasons were not made public, some insiders speculated that there were concerns over either projected budget or the director's iconoclastic vision.

BREAKOUT ROLE IN *SPIDER-MAN: HOMECOMING*

Refusing to let that disappointment get to her too much, at around that time she also starred in *The Realest Real* (2016), a film short by comedian and filmmaker Carrie Brownstein that also features Natasha Lyonne and Mahershala Ali. Additionally, she had auditioned for what would be her biggest role to date in the upcoming installment of the Spider-Man franchise, a nerve-wracking process entailing several auditions and screen tests shrouded in secrecy. She was excited, not only because of the high-profile nature of the film, but because her brother had always been a fan of Marvel's Spider-Man, and she herself had loved to read comics of all sorts as a child.

"It literally didn't cross my mind ever that I was going to get this role, ever," Harrier recalled to Eckardt. "I was living my normal life, obviously, but I also couldn't do anything. I couldn't talk about it or tell anybody." When the moment finally came, after six weeks of waiting, she had gone out for a massage in an attempt to ease her mind, and when she turned her phone back on, she discovered that she had missed numerous calls from her agent. Stunned, she sat on the floor and tried to absorb the news that she had won the part of Liz.

Spider-Man: Homecoming follows the superhero, also known as Peter Parker (played by Tom Holland), as a teenager in high school. Harrier's character, Liz, is a senior at the school, the captain of the academic decathlon team, and the subject of Parker's affections. Though Harrier was stressed about working with veteran actors like Michael Keaton and being required to perform many of her own stunts, she became friendly with some of her fellow younger actors. "Even though *Spider-Man* is a huge blockbuster, it really didn't feel like that," she told Eckardt of the filming. "It felt like we were making this weird, funny, high school movie. Like just hanging out with a group of friends."

The film was released in the summer of 2017 and garnered positive reviews for its talented stars and for its portrayal of the web-slinging crime fighter's early years. In interviews, director Jon Watts explained that he had purposely set out to cast diverse actors in the film to ensure that it would more truly represent its setting in multicultural New York City. As her character had been portrayed only minimally outside of the comics, Harrier was given more leeway to truly make the role her own, and she found it gratifying to play the part of a strong, self-possessed young woman. "There are a million things that are her focus: school, her career, college applications, all these things, but definitely not the boy," she stressed to Eckardt. "She's not there just to look pretty and hang out with Peter."

Following this breakout role, Harrier was cast in an HBO adaptation of Ray Bradbury's classic dystopian novel *Fahrenheit 451*, set to air sometime in 2018 and costarring Michael B. Jordan.

PERSONAL LIFE

Harrier lives in the Red Hook section of New York City's Brooklyn borough. As a hobby, she does ceramics at a studio in the nearby neighborhood of Greenpoint. She relied heavily upon this hobby during the downtime in between her auditions for *Spider-Man: Homecoming* and waiting to hear whether she had earned the role.

SUGGESTED READING

Chang, Mahalia. "Everything You Need to Know about *Spider-Man* Babe, Laura Harrier." *Elle*, 3 July 2017, www.elle.com.au/celebrity/laura-harrier-spiderman-facts-13641. Accessed 6 Nov. 2017.

Eckardt, Stephanie. "Laura Harrier Isn't in *Spider-Man: Homecoming* Just to Look Pretty for Peter Parker." *W*, 15 June 2017, www.wmagazine.com/story/laura-harrier-spider-man-homecoming-feminist-mary-jane. Accessed 6 Nov. 2017.

Harrier, Laura. "Laura Harrier." Interview by John Ortved. *Interview*, 5 June 2016, www.interviewmagazine.com/film/laura-harrier. Accessed 6 Nov. 2017.

Harrier, Laura. "Meet *Spider-Man*'s Laura Harrier, an Evanstonian in a Marvel Universe." Interview by Darcel Rockett. *Chicago Tribune*, 5 July 2017, www.chicagotribune.com/entertainment/movies/ct-laura-harrier-spiderman-mov-0707-20170705-story.html. Accessed 6 Nov. 2017.

Weatherford, Ashley. "Laughing and Crying with Laura Harrier, the New Star of *Spider-Man*." *The Cut*, New York Media, 5 July 2017. Accessed 6 Nov. 2017.

SELECTED WORKS

One Life to Live, 2013; *Unforgettable*, 2014; *The Last Five Years*, 2014; *4th Man Out*, 2015; *Spider-Man: Homecoming*, 2017

—*Mari Rich*

Patricia Harris

Date of Birth: September 1, 1956
Occupation: CEO of Bloomberg Philanthropies

Patricia Harris has often been cited as one of the most powerful women in New York City, and with good reason. The chief executive officer (CEO) of Bloomberg Philanthropies, Harris is responsible for donating much of politician and businessman Michael Bloomberg's personal wealth—an amount reportedly in excess of $40 billion as of 2017—to worthy causes through a variety of high-profile charitable initiatives. The responsibility is a daunting one, but for Harris, it is the culmination of decades of influential work. A former assistant in the administration of New York City mayor Ed Koch and public relations executive, she has worked with Bloomberg since joining the corporation Bloomberg LP in 1994. Following Bloomberg's election as mayor of New York in 2001, she established herself as a highly effective deputy mayor, rising to the high-ranking position of first deputy mayor in 2005. Although she is a notoriously private person who has long preferred to carry out her work in the background, those working closest to her have widely acknowledged the significance of her contributions. "There's no decision that I don't run by her. There is a reason she is my confidant. Her judgment is impeccable," Bloomberg told Heidi Evans for the *Daily News* (16 Nov. 2009).

EARLY LIFE AND EDUCATION

Patricia E. "Patti" Harris was raised in the Upper East Side neighborhood of New York's Manhattan borough. She was born to a social worker and an executive who worked for companies such as the department store Abraham & Straus and the luxury goods brand Alfred Dunhill before later cofounding the vitamin company Nature's Best. She was a lover of the arts from a young age, and she often accompanied her mother to the city's many museums. As a child and teenager, she attended the Ethical Culture Fieldston School, a system of affiliated private schools in Manhattan and the Bronx. She graduated from high school in 1973.

In addition to her interest in the arts, Harris demonstrated an affinity for politics early in life. As a teenager, she volunteered for politician Ed Koch, who, at the time, represented her district of New York in the US House of Representatives. Working in Koch's office, she assisted with making copies and other administrative tasks. After graduating from high school, she pursued studies in government at Franklin & Marshall College in Lancaster, Pennsylvania. She earned her bachelor's degree from the college in 1977.

DANIEL LEAL-OLIVAS/AFP/Getty Images

EARLY CAREER

That same year, Koch ran for mayor of New York City, and Harris decided to resume volunteering for the politician upon her return to New York. "I thought, 'Okay, I'll help out,'" she recalled to Evans. "I stood on the street and got petitions signed." Koch ultimately won the election, and Harris launched her career in city government following his ascension to the office of mayor in 1978. In addition to serving for a time as the liaison to the New York City Board of Estimate, she became an assistant first to the deputy mayor and later to Koch himself. She remained an assistant to the mayor throughout his 1981 reelection campaign and into his second term.

In 1983, Harris was appointed executive director of the Art Commission of the City of New York, which would later become known as the Public Design Commission. In that role, she oversaw a variety of projects relating to the design and appearance of city property and public spaces, including restoration projects within city hall. She remained head of the commission until 1991. That year, she transitioned into public relations, becoming vice president for public relations at the entertainment marketing agency Rogers & Cowan. She remained with the agency until 1993, when she took on a similar position at advertising agency Serino/Coyne. She left that agency, which specializes in advertising for theatrical and entertainment-related projects and organizations, the following year.

BLOOMBERG LP

A turning point in Harris's career came in 1994, when she took a new position at a company that would greatly shape her trajectory over the next decades: the software and media giant Bloomberg LP. Founded by Michael Bloomberg in 1981, Bloomberg LP initially existed to provide financial data and data terminals to investment firms but went on to expand into a variety of media and financial industries. By the time of Harris's tenure with the company, Bloomberg LP encompassed not only its original terminal business but also Bloomberg Radio, Bloomberg News, and the magazine *Bloomberg Markets*.

As head of Bloomberg LP's corporate communications department, Harris became responsible not only for the company's public relations efforts but also for its government affairs division and its philanthropic work. Over the course of her time with the company, she developed a close working relationship with its founder and namesake, becoming his adviser on philanthropic issues as well as many other areas. "I know what he expects from people and I try to anticipate what questions he'll want answers to or what concerns he'll raise," she later told Jennifer Steinhauer for the *New York Times* (6 Dec. 2005) of her work with Bloomberg. She remained with the company into 2001.

Throughout the late 1990s, Bloomberg had considered running for mayor of New York and discussed his political ambitions with Harris on numerous occasions. His tentative plans came to fruition in early 2001, when he announced that he would be running for mayor with the hope of succeeding Mayor Rudy Giuliani, whose second and final term was coming to an end. He stepped down as Bloomberg LP's chairman to run for mayor, and Harris left the company as well, returning to her career in politics as one of Bloomberg's primary advisers. She was responsible for hiring staff throughout the campaign and, following Bloomberg's election in November 2001, oversaw the hiring of members of his administration.

THE BLOOMBERG ADMINISTRATION

After Bloomberg was sworn in as mayor, Harris officially joined the Bloomberg administration as a deputy mayor. She advanced to the position of first deputy mayor in 2005, becoming the first woman to hold that position in New York's city government. In her role as first deputy mayor, she had a wide range of responsibilities, including supervising departments such as the parks department and serving as Bloomberg's chief of staff. She also oversaw the hiring of high-level administration officials, managed special events, and handled philanthropic efforts on behalf of the mayor. As head of the Mayor's Fund to Advance New York City, she worked to form connections between private donors and public programs and organizations. During her tenure with the fund, she helped raise more than $60 million for relief and recovery programs following 2012's devastating Hurricane Sandy, among other efforts.

While serving as first deputy mayor, Harris also began overseeing the Bloomberg Family Foundation, a charitable organization dedicated to distributing the majority of Bloomberg's personal wealth to causes that Bloomberg and his advisers—particularly Harris—considered to be of great importance. As her work with the foundation, later renamed Bloomberg Philanthropies, coincided with her tenure as first deputy mayor, Harris's involvement drew criticism from some in government and the media, who cautioned that conflicts of interest could arise. Harris and Bloomberg, however, argued that her concurrent work was acceptable and in 2008 gained approval for her unpaid work with the foundation from the New York City Conflicts of Interest Board.

Throughout her time as deputy mayor and first deputy mayor, Harris worked largely in the background, preferring to avoid the spotlight that surrounded Bloomberg himself. When asked about her influential role, she noted that her position as Bloomberg's primary confidant was the result of many years of collaboration and trust. "When you work with people, sometimes, as time goes on, you gain respect for them, you laugh, you take on a new challenge and it's successful," she told Evans. Perhaps the most significant recognition came in 2009, when Franklin & Marshall College announced that it would be naming a newly renovated building after Harris after receiving an anonymous donation of more than $1 million, later revealed to have been given by Bloomberg in honor of his longtime employee and friend. The Patricia E. Harris Center for Business, Government, and Public Policy at Franklin & Marshall College was dedicated in her honor in October of that year. "This is one of the supreme honors of my life," Harris said upon the center's dedication, as quoted in a report published on Franklin & Marshall's website (15 Oct. 2009). "I really want this building to become a center for inspiration and innovation."

BLOOMBERG PHILANTHROPIES

Harris was appointed chair and CEO of Bloomberg's charitable foundation in 2010, again prompting concerns from government watchdogs as she kept her position in city hall. She remained with the Bloomberg administration throughout not only the mayor's first two terms but also his third, secured after the term limit for New York mayors was temporarily extended from two to three consecutive terms. She left city hall at the end of 2013, when Bloomberg was succeeded as mayor by Bill de Blasio.

Following the end of Bloomberg's third term as mayor, Harris took on the role of CEO for Bloomberg Philanthropies full time. As head of the organization, which has come to encompass Bloomberg's foundational, personal, and corporate charitable giving, she is responsible for overseeing initiatives related to a selection of key areas, including education, the environment, and the arts. "We're entrepreneurial at heart and apply the best lessons from business and government to the management of our global philanthropic work," she explained in a 2015 letter posted on the Bloomberg Philanthropies (Bloomberg.org) website. "Ensuring better, longer lives for the greatest number of people is our mission, and it is inspiring to come to work each day knowing that we have an opportunity to advance that mission." Among other initiatives, Bloomberg Philanthropies has partnered with Johns Hopkins University to address public health issues such as opioid addiction and gun violence and has sought to continue efforts to address climate change in response to inaction on the federal level. According to the organization's annual reports, its philanthropic efforts have expanded to more than 120 countries and total donations have increased yearly, with the figure cited as $600 million for 2016.

In addition to her philanthropic work through the programs of Bloomberg Philanthropies, Harris has dedicated herself to promoting several causes and organizations in her private life. She serves as a trustee for both Franklin & Marshall College and Cornell University and is a member of the board of directors—chaired by Bloomberg—of the 9/11 Memorial and Museum. In keeping with her lifelong appreciation of the arts, she sits on the board of directors for the Public Art Fund, a nonprofit organization devoted to promoting contemporary art in New York and holding free exhibitions and other events. She has received extensive recognition over the course of her career in government and philanthropy, including being named one of the most powerful women in New York and in the world by publications such as Forbes and Crain's.

PERSONAL LIFE

Harris married lawyer Mark Lebow in 1988. They have two children together, and Lebow also has a son from his previous marriage. In addition to philanthropy and the arts, Harris enjoys scuba diving and skiing.

SUGGESTED READING

Barbaro, Michael, and David W. Chen. "Top Bloomberg Aide Will Lead His Charity Board." The New York Times, 31 Mar. 2010, www.nytimes.com/2010/04/01/nyregion/01harris.html. Accessed 14 Nov. 2017.

"College Raises Curtain on Harris Center." Franklin & Marshall College, 15 Oct. 2009, www.fandm.edu/news/latest-news/college-raises-curtain-on-harris-center. Accessed 14 Nov. 2017.

Evans, Heidi. "The Quiet Power of Patti Harris: Mayor Bloomberg's Confidant 'Can Do Anything.'" Daily News, 16 Nov. 2009, www.nydailynews.com/news/quiet-power-patti-harris-mayor-bloomberg-confidant-article-1.417178. Accessed 14 Nov. 2017.

Freedlander, David. "Mrs. Mayor: Patti Harris Is the Gatekeeper for a Bloomberg Empire That Extends Well Beyond Government." Observer, 8 Dec. 2010, observer.com/2010/12/mrs-mayor-patti-harris-is-the-gatekeeper-for-a-bloomberg-empire-that-extends-well-beyond-government/. Accessed 14 Nov. 2017.

Harris, Patricia. "Patti Harris' Letter on Philanthropy." Bloomberg Philanthropies, 2015, www.bloomberg.org/about/annual-update/patti-harris-letter-philanthropy-2/patti-harris-letter-philanthropy/. Accessed 14 Nov. 2017.

Steinhauer, Jennifer. "Bloomberg's New Deputy Has a Velvet Fist." The New York Times, 6 Dec. 2005, www.nytimes.com/2005/12/06/nyregion/bloombergs-new-deputy-has-a-velvet-fist.html. Accessed 14 Nov. 2017.

—Joy Crelin

David G. Haskell

Date of birth: March 1969
Occupation: Biologist

"Science deepens our intimacy with the world," biologist David G. Haskell told James Gorman for the New York Times (22 Oct. 2012). "But there is a danger in an exclusively scientific way of thinking. The forest is turned into a diagram; animals become mere mechanisms; nature's workings become clever graphs." Throughout his career, Haskell has rejected such an impersonal view of the natural world, instead calling attention to the complex connections between all organisms in nature through his scholarly research and writing. His publications also include books for more general audiences, such as the Pulitzer Prize finalist The Forest Unseen (2012), which documents a year of observations within a Tennessee old-growth forest.

Haskell studied zoology, ecology, and evolutionary biology at the University of Oxford and Cornell University prior to beginning his career as an award-winning teacher widely recognized for his creative teaching methods. He became a professor at the University of the South—also known as Sewanee—in 1996. Following the publication of *The Forest Unseen*, he likewise became well known as a nature writer, earning accolades for his poetic approach to his subject. Haskell further cemented his reputation as an insightful observer of the natural world in 2017 with the publication of *The Songs of Trees: Stories from Nature's Great Connectors*, a work that builds upon his observations of twelve different trees in order to explore the interconnected nature of the natural world. "Trees are such massive beings and so long-lived that they really are extraordinary examples of interconnection and of belonging within a place," Haskell told Diane Toomey for *Yale Environment 360* (24 Aug. 2017) about the book. "I wanted to use them as windows into these larger questions about ecology, evolution, and ethics."

EARLY LIFE AND EDUCATION

David George Haskell was born in London, England, in March of 1969. He was one of two children born to George Purkis Haskell, a physicist who spent many years with the European Space Agency, and Jean Boulton Haskell, a biologist. When Haskell was three years old, his family moved to Paris, France, for his father's work. He grew up in the city, where he attended the British School of Paris and developed a love of both science and poetry.

Following in his parents' footsteps, Haskell pursued further education in science after his time at the British School of Paris. He returned to England and enrolled in the University of Oxford to study zoology. During his time at the university, Haskell was greatly influenced by professor William D. Hamilton, a renowned evolutionary biologist who also served as his advisor for a thesis focused on parasites and blackberries. A strong student within the university's zoology program, he won the Gibbs Prize for his academic work in 1990. Haskell went on to earn his bachelor's degree with first honors that year.

After completing his undergraduate studies, Haskell moved to the United States to attend Cornell University in Ithaca, New York. He studied ecology and evolutionary biology at the university, where he worked under thesis advisor David W. Winkler. Haskell's doctoral research focused on the small birds known as wood warblers. He also began developing his teaching approach during that period, earning a 1995 Outstanding Teaching Assistant Award from the university's College of Agriculture and Life Sciences. Haskell earned his doctorate from Cornell University in 1996.

ACADEMIC CAREER

After completing his PhD, Haskell moved to Tennessee to join the faculty at the University of the South. Located in Sewanee, Tennessee, and often referred to simply by the name of that

town, the university owns a large tract of forested land that appealed greatly to Haskell, who focused on the fields of biology and environmental studies. He joined the institution initially as an assistant professor and was later promoted to the positions of associate professor and full professor over the course of his years at the university. In addition to teaching a variety of classes, Haskell served as chair of biology for a time. He also held several fellowships throughout his academic career, serving as an Associated Colleges of the South Environmental Fellow from 2000 to 2002 and a Contemplative Practice Fellow of the American Council of Learned Societies in 2005.

As a professor, Haskell taught a variety of subjects related to his areas of interest, which included biodiversity, evolution, conservation, and writing. Over his decades of work at the University of the South he became known for offbeat and creative teaching methods that encouraged students to form a more well-rounded view of nature. "I challenge my students: Okay, now that you've learned the songs of one hundred birds, your task is to learn the sounds of twenty trees," he told Ed Yong for the *Atlantic* (4 Apr. 2017). "Can you tell an oak from a maple by ear? I have them go out, pour their attention into their ears, and harvest sounds." In recognition of his work as a professor, Haskell received the 2007 Teacher of the Year Award from the Society of Sewanee Scholars. In 2009, the Carnegie Foundation and the Council for Advancement and Support of Education (CASE) named him the professor of the year for the state of Tennessee.

THE FOREST UNSEEN

For Haskell, the University of the South's large holdings of undeveloped land provided an excellent opportunity to carry out observations within the old-growth forest, a complex ecosystem that was home to a vast array of living creatures. His first book, 2012's *The Forest Unseen: A Year's Watch in Nature*, documents observations of the forest and its inhabitants gleaned over the course of a year. During that year, Haskell visited and observed the same spot in the forest on a regular basis. He did not carry out formal experiments but simply set out to observe the natural happenings within his chosen spot, a small area measuring one square meter (about ten square feet) that was located near a rock on which he would sit. "Usually, if you stay here for a while, something is going to happen," he told Gorman about the area. "There's a blue jay. There are the cicadas. There are the harvestmen crawling around."

Upon its publication, *The Forest Unseen* received overwhelmingly positive reviews from critics, who praised Haskell's insightful and poetic approach to documenting the interconnected elements of the natural world. He won the Reed Environmental Writing Award and the National Outdoor Book Award for natural history literature for his work. He gained even more attention in 2013, when *The Forest Unseen* was named a finalist for the Pulitzer Prize in the category of general nonfiction. "I was delighted by that recognition and was very happy," Haskell told John Shearer for the *Chattanoogan* (25 Apr. 2013). "I was also very surprised. There are a lot of great books out there, so it was an honor to have my work recognized from among all the great books that have come out." *The Forest Unseen* was also named runner-up for the 2013 PEN/E. O. Wilson Literary Science Writing Award. It went on to be translated into more than ten other language editions, and in 2016 Haskell received the Dapeng Nature Writing Award for the Chinese edition of his book.

THE SONGS OF TREES

For his next book, Haskell sought to tell the stories of specific trees located around the world. These included a pear tree in the Upper West Side of Manhattan, New York; a white pine bonsai at the National Arboretum; a ceibo in remote Ecuador; and charcoal fragments of a hazel tree discovered by archaeologists in Scotland. In keeping with his approach in *The Forest Unseen*, Haskell sought to focus on observation rather than experimentation. Perhaps surprising to some readers, however, was his focus on sound rather than sight. "I've come to realize that trees have all sorts of sounds within them and coming from them and sounds wrapped into their community life, sounds of both plants and animals, including the human animal. And I wanted to explore those sounds and see what sort of story those sounds would lead me to," Haskell explained to Toomey. "Part of the origin of the book came from literally just listening, opening my ears." To assist in his observations, he made use of a variety of listening devices, including stethoscopes and recording technology.

Published in 2017, *The Songs of Trees: Stories from Nature's Great Connectors* focuses not only on the audible sounds produced by trees but also on the specific trees' histories and connections to their surrounding ecosystems. Haskell highlights the various living creatures—including birds, insects, and plants such as moss, and algae—that coexist with the trees as well as the complex relationships between humans and the trees in question. In doing so, he calls attention to the connections that underlay the entire world and emphasizes the importance of understanding and acknowledging such connections both in nature and in society. "We need to listen to one another," he told Shannon L. Bowen for *Signature* (7 Apr. 2017) of the work's thematic message. "The birdwatchers need to listen to the loggers, who need to listen to the paper makers, who can listen to the kids playing in the forest—these are all different ways of knowing the forest within the human community, and we would be better off if we were listening to one another a little more." Much like *The Forest Unseen*, *The Songs of Trees* received widespread critical acclaim upon its publication. In 2018 Haskell received the John Burroughs Medal for natural history writing in recognition of his work.

OTHER WORK

In addition to his books, Haskell is a prolific writer of shorter articles, including essays and opinion pieces that have been published in venues such as *Scientific American*, the *New York Times*, and *Nature Woodlands*. He has also written and cowritten a variety of papers for journals such as *International Journal of Ecology*, *Conservation Genetics*, and *Conservation Biology*. Topics of interest have included animals such as birds, snails, and salamanders as well as the overall effects of human activity on the natural world. In recognition of his science writing, Haskell was named a Fellow of the John Simon Guggenheim Memorial Foundation in 2014.

PERSONAL LIFE

Haskell dated Katherine Lehman, who had served as a professor of music at the University of the South before becoming executive director of Colorado's Boulder Philharmonic Orchestra. He was formerly married to Sarah Vance, owner of a small farm in Sewanee. A lover of poetry since his early years, Haskell remained interested in the form and contributed his own poems to the 2010 anthology *Wildbranch: An Anthology of Nature, Environmental, and Place-Based Writing*.

SUGGESTED READING

Gorman, James. "Finding Zen in a Patch of Nature." *The New York Times*, 22 Oct. 2012, www.nytimes.com/2012/10/23/science/david-haskell-finds-biology-zen-in-a-patch-of-nature.html. Accessed 9 Mar. 2018.

Haskell, David G. "How Listening to Trees Can Help Reveal Nature's Connections." Interview by Diane Toomey. *Yale Environment 360*, Yale School of Forestry & Environmental Studies, 24 Aug. 2017, e360.yale.edu/features/how-listening-to-trees-can-help-reveal-natures-connections. Accessed 9 Mar. 2018.

Haskell, David G. "The Songs of Trees: On the Beauty, Wonder, and Balance of Nature." Interview by Shannon L. Bowen. *Signature*, 7 Apr. 2017, www.signature-reads.com/2017/04/the-songs-of-trees-on-the-beauty-wonder-and-balance-of-nature/. Accessed 9 Mar. 2018.

Kvinta, Paul. "David Haskell Speaks for the Trees." *Outside*, 23 Mar. 2017, www.outside-online.com/2167116/david-haskell-speaks-trees. Accessed 9 Mar. 2018.

Shearer, John. "University of the South Biology Professor David Haskell Named Pulitzer Finalist." *TheChattanoogan.com*, 25 Apr. 2013, www.chattanoogan.com/2013/4/25/249793/University-Of-The-South-Biology.aspx. Accessed 9. Mar. 2018.

Yong, Ed. "Trees Have Their Own Songs." *The Atlantic*, 4 Apr. 2017, www.theatlantic.com/science/archive/2017/04/trees-have-their-own-songs/521742/. Accessed 9 Mar. 2018.

—*Joy Crelin*

Matthew Henson

Occupation: Fashion stylist

Matthew Henson's personal style can often be "pretty all over the place," as he told Emely Grullon for *BET* (20 July 2016). A celebrity fashion stylist and a fashion influencer in his own right, he has long been known for an eclectic sense of style that draws from and mingles vintage and contemporary streetwear, luxury brands, and time-tested classic styles. "I love all different types of clothes and my closet definitely reflects that," he told Grullon. "It truly is driven by where I'm going." And Henson is undoubtedly going places. Since leaving his position as fashion editor at *Complex* magazine to begin an independent career, Henson has tapped further into his deep understanding of fashion to put together memorable looks for celebrities such as rapper A$AP Rocky and singer the Weeknd. His work with such influential public figures has extended to print advertisements for brands such as Dior Homme and Puma, among others, and Henson has become a sought-after stylist for a wide range of fashion brands.

A devotee of fashion and style since early childhood, Henson began his career in the industry with a series of internships before securing a full-time position at the fashion and lifestyle magazine *Flaunt*. He spent five years with that publication before moving on to *Complex*, where he served as market editor and later fashion editor. Throughout his career, Henson has worked to explore the possibilities of fashion while remaining a positive and productive force within the menswear community. "I'm most proud of being a representation of what you can achieve if you're a nice person, stay positive and truly want to offer something in a different perspective to what's going on in our industry," he told the fashion website the *Coveteur* (20 July 2016). "I love everybody that I work with. . . . It's like a little family."

EARLY LIFE AND CAREER

Matthew A. Henson was born in New Jersey and grew up in the city of Long Branch, on the Jersey shore. He was the only child of parents who both worked in the medical field, whom he described to the *Coveteur* as "very, very well put together people." Henson has credited his parents with fostering his interest in style during his early years. "But they also let me be free to express myself, free to go outside and be dirty and come back in and they would clean me up," he told the *Coveteur*. "It was a really great upbringing." Henson's early interest in fashion manifested in a devotion to specific items of clothing, including a toddler-sized outfit from the brand Izod that he tried to keep wearing long after he had outgrown it. He was similarly attached to his favorite pair of red Keds shoes, which he has cited as shaping his footwear preferences as an adult.

After graduating from college, Henson was unsure of his ideal career path; although he knew he wanted to work in fashion, he was not sure which area of the industry best suited him. To explore his options, he completed various internships with New York magazines and public relations firms, all the while maintaining a full-time job in the hospitality industry. "I would use all of my sick days, all of my vacation days, and also come up with outlandish excuses to intern at Seventh House PR," he recalled to Chioma Nnadi for *Vogue* (17 Apr. 2014) of that time in his life. When a friend told him about an internship opportunity with *Flaunt*, a Los Angeles–based fashion and culture magazine that had an office in New York, Henson applied for and won the position, beginning what would become a five-year tenure with the publication. Moving from intern to employee, he rose through the ranks at *Flaunt* under the guidance of style director and magazine cofounder Long Nguyen. He eventually took on the role of fashion editor for the magazine. He left the magazine to focus more on menswear, which had become his primary fashion interest.

COMPLEX

Following his departure from *Flaunt*, Henson took the position of market editor with the magazine *Complex*, which focused on popular culture, fashion, and lifestyle topics. In his role as market editor, Henson was responsible for curating lists of products to recommend to the publication's readers, particularly young men who might not yet have developed their personal styles. "More often than not, guys approach style in the opposite manner in which they should," Henson told the blog the *Motley* (17 Nov. 2011). "You see a trend, you go buy it, but it might not be the right thing for you. That's why what I try to do is present the best items in the market and let people choose what's right for them. That's ultimately what having great style is about." During his time as market editor, Henson compiled lists with titles such as "The Complex Guide to Essential Spring Footwear" and "The Ten Parka Jackets You Need This Winter," highlighting products from a variety of brands and available at a range of price points. Henson was later promoted to fashion editor for the magazine.

Over the course of his time at *Complex*, Henson was responsible for styling models and celebrities for the magazine's covers, fashion editorials, and fashion guides. His work gave him the opportunity to style many of the stars most popular among the magazine's readers. "I loved when we shot Beyoncé," Henson told the *Coveteur*. "Just to be in her presence. It was magical because she's so polite and professional, unlike most people—she was on time, she spoke to everyone. We did her shoot with about six looks in less than two hours; she was in and out." He also particularly enjoyed working with singer Nick Jonas, in part because the photoshoot involved the use of pyrotechnics. "That was my first shoot setting someone on fire, but hopefully not the last," he told the *Coveteur*.

The year 2012 saw Henson's first collaboration with rapper A$AP Rocky, who appeared on the cover of *Complex*'s February/March issue alongside designer Jeremy Scott. Henson was impressed by A$AP Rocky's knowledge of fashion and personal sense of style, and although the rapper was not entirely convinced by some of Henson's choices for that initial shoot, the two would go on to become frequent collaborators both during the remainder of Henson's tenure at *Complex* and afterward. Henson left *Complex* in June 2016, after nearly six years with the magazine.

INDEPENDENT STYLIST

In 2016, Henson moved away from magazine-based styling and launched a career as an independent stylist. Although he enjoyed working for *Complex*, he felt that that time was right to go in a different direction. "I knew if I waited any longer, the opportunity to do something on my own might not be there for me, he told" Max Berlinger for the *New York Times* (6 Apr. 2017). Since launching his business, he has worked on campaigns for a variety of brands. Notable advertising work has included a Nike campaign featuring football player Odell Beckham Jr.; campaigns for the denim brand DL 1961 featuring prominent models such as Emily Ratajkowski and Sofia Ritchie; and work for the streetwear company Stampd.

Perhaps Henson's best-known efforts, however, have been his frequent collaborations with A$AP Rocky, whom he has styled not only for advertising campaigns for Calvin Klein and Dior Homme but also for high-profile events such as New York's Met Gala and music videos such as "Fashion Killa" and "Jukebox Joints." He has also contributed to the work of the AWGE collective, a project headed by the A$AP Mob, of which A$AP Rocky is a member. Although Henson is generally referred to as the rapper's stylist, he has noted that their working relationship is far more collaborative than that title would suggest. "I don't dictate what he wears," he told Nnadi. "He actually hates the word stylist because I think in the general sense of the word it means you are dressing someone who does not know how to do so, and he is the opposite of that." In addition to A$AP Rocky, Henson has worked extensively with the Canadian-born singer the Weeknd, whom he styled for a fall 2017 campaign for Puma. He also lent his styling expertise to the music videos for several of the Weeknd's songs, including "Starboy," which also featured the electronic duo Daft Punk, and "Lust for Life," a collaboration with singer Lana del Rey.

STYLE

Although best known for his work with *Flaunt* and *Complex*, brand collaborations, and association with celebrities such as A$AP Rocky and the Weeknd, Henson has become somewhat of a fashion icon himself. He has amassed dedicated fans on the photo-sharing app Instagram and caught the attention of street-style photographers in New York. A fan of streetwear, denim statement pieces, and limited-edition clothing items, he owns a variety of pieces from popular brands such as Supreme, Loewe, and Raf Simons. In addition to accumulating clothing to wear in his day-to-day life, Henson has amassed a large collection of Vans shoes, which he identifies as particular favorites. "I probably have about sixty pairs in the house right now and a ton in storage," he told the *Coveteur*. "I am definitely Vans to death." Henson also collects hoodies from noted streetwear brands.

Despite spending much of his time deeply immersed in fashion, Henson has observed that he does not always dress the part of a celebrity stylist. "You've got to turn it on at fashion week," he told Berlinger. "But when I'm working, people are like, 'Are you a messenger?'"

PERSONAL LIFE

Henson lives in Brooklyn, New York. He has explained in interviews that he considers the city to be one of his major inspirations. "I love the grit, the bite, the attitude," he told the *Motley*, "but also New York is very nurturing in that artists, designers, truly creative people are the ones that make up the city and end up successful. It's full of culture and diversity."

SUGGESTED READING

Berlinger, Max. "The Man Who Dresses A$AP Rocky and the Weeknd." *The New York Times*, 6 Apr. 2017. www.nytimes.com/2017/04/06/fashion/mens-style/matthew-henson-stylist-asap-rocky-the-weeknd.html. Accessed 14 Dec. 2017.

Dool, Steve. "How to Make It in Menswear According to 5 Dudes Who Have Done It." *Fashionista*, 16 May 2017. fashionista.com/2017/05/menswear-mens-fashion-clothing-career-advice. Accessed 14 Dec. 2017.

Henson, Matthew. "Interview: Celebrity Stylist Matthew Henson on the Importance of Denim Statement Pieces." By Emely Grullon. *BET*, 20 July 2016. www.bet.com/shows/how-to-rock/denim/interviews/matthew-henson-celebrity-stylist-closet.html. Accessed 14 Dec. 2017.

Henson, Matthew. "Matthew Henson." *Coveteur*, 20 July 2016. coveteur.com/2016/07/20/matthew-henson-asap-rocky-stylist/. Accessed 14 Dec. 2017.

Henson, Matthew. "Men of Distinction: Matthew Henson, Market Editor at *Complex*." *The Motley*, 17 Nov. 2011. www.themotley.com/magazine/men-of-distinction-matthew-henson-market-editor-at-complex/. Accessed 14 Dec. 2017.

Nnadi, Chioma. "Fashion Beat: Meet A$AP Rocky's Stylist, Matthew Henson." *Vogue*, 17 Apr. 2014. www.vogue.com/article/asap-rocky-stylist-matthew-henson. Accessed 14 Dec. 2017.

—*Joy Crelin*

Juan Orlando Hernández

Date of birth: October 28, 1968
Occupation: President of Honduras

Juan Orlando Hernández, of the National Party of Honduras, became the president of Honduras in 2014 and has increasingly relied on the use of a militarized security force to control violence and suppress opposition to the government.

EARLY LIFE AND EDUCATION

Juan Orlando Hernández was born on October 28, 1968, in Gracias, in the department of Lempira, Honduras, to Juan Hernández Villanueva and Elvira Alvarado Castillo. He attended elementary and secondary schools in Gracias before graduating from the Military High School North with the rank of second lieutenant.

Hernández attended the National Autonomous University of Honduras, where he earned a law degree in 1990. While in college, he became active in politics and served as the president of the Association of Law Students from 1988 to 1989. He later studied in the United States at the State University of New York at Albany, graduating in 1995 with a master's degree in public administration with a specialization in legislative administration. From 1997 to 1999, he taught constitutional law at the Universidad Nacional Autónoma de Honduras. He qualified as a lawyer in 1999. Prior to entering politics, Hernández also worked in the radio, television, and hotel industries.

POLITICAL CAREER

Hernández entered politics in 1997 when he won a seat in the National Congress representing Lempira, taking office in 1998. He was re-elected in 2001 and 2005. In his second term, he was elected the first secretary of the National Congress, serving from 2002 to 2006. He served on several legislative committees, including the telecommunications, development, and budget committees. Rising rapidly through the ranks of the National Party, he served as the secretary-general of the party from 2005 to 2009.

As a member of the National Congress, Hernández was the chair of a congressional committee that endorsed the 2009 military coup that removed the democratically elected president, Manuel Zelaya, from office. Hernández played an active role in the presidential campaign of Porfirio Lobo in the general election held in 2009. Following Lobo's victory, Hernández was elected president of the National Congress in 2010, a position he held until 2014. As president of the National Congress, Hernández backed the creation of a temporary military police force to patrol the streets. He also helped to depose four of five judges from the Supreme Court in December 2012 after they ruled a proposed law was unconstitutional.

Hernández ran for president in the 2013 presidential election. The election was significant in that it was both the first election with candidates from parties other than the two that traditionally dominated Honduran politics and the first with a female candidate. All candidates faced formidable challenges. By the 2013 election, Honduras had the highest murder rate in the world, organized crime were using the country as a major transit point, unemployment and underemployment rates were increasing, much of the population lived in poverty, and state institutions were weak and corrupt. Honduras also had a huge budget deficit.

Hernández and Xiomara Castro were the major contenders. Castro, the wife of the ousted president, Zelaya, ran as the candidate for the liberal Freedom and Refoundation Party (also known as LIBRE) and offered voters an alternative to the traditional parties that had done little to combat crime and poverty by pledging to create a new national constituent assembly to promote public participation. Hernández ran on an anticrime platform, promising to put "a soldier on every corner."

Despite polls showing Castro as the favored winner, Hernández won the election with 36 percent of the vote, while Castro captured 29 percent. Castro claimed voter fraud and unsuccessfully appealed to the Honduran electoral tribunal to disqualify the results. Hernández was sworn in on January 27, 2014. In the first two years of his four-year term, he expanded the Military Police for Public Order, a military security force that patrols the streets in place of the police. As a result, the crime rate declined, although it remained high. However, the improved security came at the expense of human rights abuses committed by the military police force. There have been several reported incidents of military police kidnapping, beating, and murdering journalists and other civilians. Hernández attempted to make the Military Police for Public Order a permanent security force, requesting Congress to give it constitutional status. After the National Assembly denied his request in January 2015, Hernández announced his plan to ask voters to decide the issue in a 2017 plebiscite.

IMPACT

The improved security situation in Honduras resonates with many Hondurans. It also resonates with the United States government, a key supporter of Juan Orlando Hernández's government. Other international bodies are not as supportive. The United Nations and human rights organizations have called for an end to the use of military troops to provide security, saying they are responsible for human rights abuses, particularly of activists, journalists, and political opponents. They also fear that Hernández is increasingly amassing control over the judicial and National Congress, and this control weakens state institutions and threatens Honduras's democracy.

PERSONAL LIFE

Hernández is married to Ana Rosalinda García. They have four children: Ivonne María, Juan Orlando, Ana Daniela, and Isabela.

SUGGESTED READING

Cabrera, Jorge. "Military Helps Cut Honduras Murder Rate, but Abuses Spike." *Reuters*, 9 July 2015, www.reuters.com/article/us-honduras-military-insight/military-helps-cut-honduras-murder-rate-but-abuses-spike-idUSKCN0PJ0E920150709. Accessed 23 Aug. 2018.

Frank, Dana. "Just Like Old Times in Central America." *Foreign Policy*, 9 Mar. 2015, foreignpolicy.com/2015/03/09/just-like-old-times-in-central-america-honduras-juan-orlando-hernandez. Accessed 23 Aug. 2018.

Gagne, David, and Steven Dudley. "Honduras Appoints Army General to Run Police Force amid Crime Spike." *The Christian Science Monitor*, 23 Dec. 2014, www.csmonitor.com/World/Americas/Latin-America-Monitor/2014/1223/Honduras-appoints-Army-general-to-run-police-force-amid-crime-spike. Accessed 23 Aug. 2018.

"Honduras Candidates: Right-Wing Man vs Leftist Woman." *Agence France-Presse*, 24 Nov. 2013, www.bbc.com/news/world-latin-america-25346676. Accessed 23 Aug. 2018.

"Honduras: Juan Orlando Hernandez Confirmed as President." *BBC News*. BBC, 12 Dec. 2013. Web. 19 Apr. 2016.

Lakhani, Nina. "Honduras President Announces International Body to Tackle Corruption." *The Guardian*, 19 Jan. 2016, www.theguardian.com/world/2016/jan/19/honduras-juan-orlando-hernandez-oas-international-corruption-maccih. Accessed 23 Aug. 2018.

—*Barb Lightner*

Sheila Heti

Date of birth: December 25, 1976
Occupation: Author

Sheila Heti is a Canadian author whose writing has found international success and has been translated into a dozen languages. Her best-known works include the autobiographical novels *How Should a Person Be?* (2012) and *Motherhood* (2018), and the nonfiction work *Women in Clothes* (2014). Her writing has been featured in the *Guardian* and the *New York Times*. She also had a role in *Teenager Hamlet* (2010), a movie directed by painter Margaux Williamson.

Her goal in writing, as she told Alec Niedenthal for *Brooklyn Rail* (5 June 2018), is to get her readers to complete the entire book. "I'm the kind of reader who can't bring myself to finish a book. So to me the real achievement is getting someone to finish the book." Having never studied book writing formally, Heti set herself a different writing-related challenge to master with each new work. *Motherhood* was the first work in which she felt she had completed the challenges of plot, character, style, and relevance to society. Speaking with Claudia Dey for the *Paris Review* (28 April 2018) about her writing process for *Motherhood*, Heti said, "I wanted every sentence to be a sentence I liked and to be a sentence I could stand behind."

Infrogmation of New Orleans, via Wikimedia Commons

Glouberman was the emcee of the lecture series. The premise was that three people spoke for eight minutes on an area that interested them, but was not their specialty, and then took questions from the audience. Heti, until she left the show in the mid-2000s, selected lecturers who preferred not to lecture publicly to keep the show unpredictable.

Heti graduated from Trinity College with a bachelor's degree in philosophy and art history in 2002.

TICKNOR AND MORE

Heti's historical novella *Ticknor* (2005), set in nineteenth-century Boston, focused on academician George Ticknor's friendship with the historian William H. Prescott. Ticknor was Prescott's biographer. James Wood, writing for *New Yorker* (25 June 2012) described *Ticknor* as "a gently compassionate portrait, a dramatic monologue, delivered by a man who considers himself a failure, about his unequal relations (imagined or true), with an old friend, who is now a famous man of letters."

Heti admitted that the unhappiness of the protagonist mirrored her own unhappiness at the time. As she told Niedenthal, "When I read *Ticknor*, I think, oh, there's that terrible envy and isolation and internal near-madness and obsession. . . . Even that modernist form, and writing about a character so far from my lived reality, felt like a perfect expression of my reality. Being in a marriage that was inappropriate. The book's sense of being trapped and alien in one's life. I feel all that when I read the book."

In 2007, Heti began working as the interviews editor for the *Believer*, a position she held until 2014. During that time, she transcribed and edited *The Chairs Are Where the People Go* (2011), a compilation of seventy-two essays spoken by Glouberman. She also wrote the children's book *We Need a Horse*, which McSweeney's published that same year.

ALL OUR HAPPY DAYS ARE STUPID

In 2012, Heti wrote the autobiographical novel *How Should a Person Be?*, which was named a *New York Times* Book Review Notable Book. The novel's protagonist, Sheila, attempts to write a play, but fails. Other characters in the book reflect her friendships at the time she was writing. When writing the novel, Heti told Niedenthal, "The aesthetic agenda would be like, make art in the midst of living, rather than art as a process separate from living—and separate from being with other people."

A significant portion of *How Should a Person Be?* is devoted to the difficulties Heti had had producing her 2001 play *All Our Happy Days Are Stupid*, which was commissioned by the Nightwood Theatre. She abandoned the absurdist

EDUCATION AND EARLY CAREER

Heti grew up in Toronto, Ontario, in an upper-middle-class Jewish neighborhood and attended North Toronto High School. Heti knew from a young age that she wanted to become a writer. As a teenager, she was interested in the works by twentieth-century gay male writers—who attracted her because they were outside societal norms—including Christopher Isherwood and Edmund White, as well as works by playwrights such as Harold Pinter and Oscar Wilde.

Following high school, Heti studied playwriting at the National Theatre School of Canada in Montreal. Although she left the school after her first year, Heti's time in the program informed her later writing. As she explained to Niedenthal, "I remember reading Aristotle's *Poetics*, and there was something that stuck with me, which was—anything you can take out of a play that doesn't alter the whole, should be taken out, so a narrative is the least amount you need in order to tell it. If something can be taken out without alteration to the whole, it should be. That stuck with me."

Heti spent two years in the editorial department at the Canadian magazine *Shift*. In 2000, she published five stories in *McSweeney's*—a quarterly literary journal founded by writer and editor Dave Eggers—while studying at Trinity College at the University of Toronto. Her short-story collection *The Middle Stories* was published in 2001.

Also in 2001, Heti cofounded Trampoline Hall, a monthly lecture series held in Toronto bars, with friend and author Misha Glouberman.

script in the spring of 2006 after three different directors failed in their attempts to stage it. As she told Simon Houpt for *Globe and Mail* (23 Oct. 2013), "It wasn't good, somehow, and I didn't know if it was the fault of the play or the fault of the production. I kept trying to rewrite it, and it didn't get any better."

After the success of *How Should a Person Be?*, however, director Jordan Tannahill contacted Heti in 2012 to ask whether a script for *All Our Happy Days Are Stupid* existed, and whether she would allow him to produce it at his storefront performance space in downtown Toronto. Heti accepted, and the play, directed by Erin Brubacher and Tannahill and staged by his Suburban Beast theater company, opened in October 2013. Both professional actors and friends of Heti's played the thirteen roles, and singer-songwriter Dan Bejar wrote eight original songs for the play. After its brief run in Toronto, *All Our Happy Days Are Stupid* debuted in New York at The Kitchen in 2015, with Tannahill and Brubacher directing the same cast. The play drew mixed reviews from critics but received multiple nominations for Canada's 2014 Dora Mavor Moore Awards, including the nomination for outstanding new play.

WOMEN IN CLOTHES

In 2014, Heti published the coedited the nonfiction work *Women in Clothes* with author Heidi Julavits and artist Leanne Shapton. The book features a collection of writing and visual art about clothing by 639 women from around the globe. For the creation of the book, the editors devised and distributed an eighty-three-item questionnaire and asked women to design creative projects related to clothing.

The genesis of the work began with Heti, as she told Maya Dukmasova for *Harper's Magazine* (17 Sept. 2014): "I was looking for a book that would tell me what women thought about as they got dressed, how they put their style together and what the meanings were for them in dressing. It wasn't an area of my life that I had given that much thought to. I literally went to a store to look and there was no such book." She sent a few questions to friends via email; it was Julavits who thought the material might form a book and suggested they work on it together. She then approached Shapton—who produced the cover of one of Heti's previous books—about being part of the project.

The trio used their own contacts, as well as journalists, to reach out to women of different backgrounds from all around the world. In addition, Shapton made business cards to be handed when they saw a woman whose clothes or style interested them. They also considered women who wore uniforms from a variety of professions.

In selecting which responses to use, Heti, Julavits, and Shapton looked for candid answers. Heti told Dukmasova, "The more original answers to us were when women were not trying to impress, were being vulnerable, were being private, were going a little bit deeper and not disguising, or concealing, or fixing, or being prescriptive." *Women in Clothes* became a *New York Times* Best Seller shortly after its publication.

MOTHERHOOD

Although Heti began writing her novel *Motherhood* in 2010, she did not seriously work on it until 2015. After several revisions and severe editing of the original seven-hundred-page manuscript, *Motherhood* was published in 2018.

Heti's original conception of the novel was as a nonfiction work made up of a series of interviews and conversations. However, she ultimately decided against using that structure since she had already done so in *Women in Clothes*. She opted instead to write a novel. In an interview with Dey, Heti explained why she considered *Motherhood* to be a novel, rather than a memoir, saying, "For me, a memoir is supposed to be understood as a representation of your life. Whereas a novel is self-consciously symbolic. I want this book to be read with an openness toward symbolic associations."

The work fictionally depicts Heti's struggle with the question of whether to have a child. One of the stories that informs her own is that of the biblical character of Jacob, who wrestles with an angel, alone, having sent his family to the other side of the river. Jacob became a symbol for Heti's own loneliness and struggle, as her friends had children and she did not.

In an interview with Kate Wolf for the *Los Angeles Review of Books* (7 May 2018) discussing the question of choosing motherhood, Heti said, "There is no history showing how women have struggled with this decision that a contemporary person can consult. We don't have a common language or a language that goes far back enough in time for how one is supposed to decide something of this nature. So I think my book is also about the *absence* of a language for thinking and how you think through something when that is the case."

PERSONAL LIFE

Heti was briefly married to music columnist Carl Wilson. She lives with her boyfriend and her Rottweiler, Feldman, in Toronto. She has a brother who is a stand-up comedian.

SUGGESTED READING

Dew, Spencer. Review of *How Should a Person Be?: A Novel from Life*, by Sheila Heti. *Religious Studies Review*, vol. 39, no. 2, 2013,

p. 94. *ATLA Religion Database*, search.eb-scohost.com/login.aspx?direct=true&db=rfh&AN=ATLA0001946535&site=ehost-live&scope=site. Accessed 5 June 2018.

Haglund, David. "Her Ideal Self." Review of *How Should a Person Be?: A Novel from Life*, by Sheila Heti. *New York Times*, 5 July 2012, www.nytimes.com/2012/07/08/books/review/how-should-a-person-be-by-sheila-heti.html. Accessed 9 July 2018.

Heti, Sheila. "A Fundamentally Absurd Question: Talking with 'Motherhood' author Sheila Heti." Interview by Kate Wolf. *Los Angeles Review of Books*, 7 May 2018, lareviewofbooks.org/article/a-fundamentally-absurd-question-talking-with-motherhood-author-sheila-heti/. Accessed 12 June 2018.

Heti, Sheila, et al. "Sheila Heti, Heidi Julavits, and Leanne Shapton on *Women in Clothes*." Interview by Maya Dukmasova. *Harper's Magazine*, 17 Sept. 2014, harpers.org/blog/2014/09/sheila-heti-heidi-julavits-and-leanne-shapton-on-women-in-clothes/. Accessed 3 July 2018.

Heti, Sheila. Interview. By Jonathan Derbyshire. *New Statesman*, vol. 142, no. 5142, 2013, p. 47. *Literary Reference Center Plus*, search.ebscohost.com/login.aspx?direct=true&db=lkh&AN=85107542&site=lrc-plus. Accessed 5 June 2018.

Heti, Sheila. "New Routes in Fiction: Sheila Heti with Alec Niedenthal." Interview by Alec Niedenthal. *Brooklyn Rail*, 5 June 2018, brooklynrail.org/2018/06/fiction/SHEILA-HETI-with-Alec-Niedenthal. Accessed 2 July 2018.

Heti, Sheila. "The Child Thing: An Interview with Sheila Heti." Interview by Claudia Dey. *The Paris Review*, 26 Apr. 2018, www.theparisreview.org/blog/2018/04/26/the-child-thing-an-interview-with-sheila-heti/. Accessed 12 June 2018.

SELECTED WORKS

The Middle Stories, 2001; *Ticknor*, 2005; *How Should a Person Be?*, 2010; *All Our Happy Days Are Stupid*, 2013; *Women in Clothes* (with Heidi Julavits and Leanne Shapton), 2014; *Motherhood*, 2018

—*Judy Johnson*

Photo by Monica Schipper/Getty Images

Freddie Highmore

Date of birth: February 14, 1992
Occupation: Actor

British actor Freddie Highmore first charmed US audiences in 2004, when, at the age of twelve, he costarred in the Academy Award–winning film *Finding Neverland* alongside Johnny Depp. A year later, the pair reunited for *Charlie and the Chocolate Factory*, Tim Burton's 2005 adaptation of Roald Dahl's 1964 children's novel by the same name. After portraying an orphan in 2007's *August Rush* and voicing a series of animated film characters, Highmore made the transition to adult roles with the quirky coming-of-age romance *The Art of Getting By* (2011). But it was Highmore's portrayal of a teenage Norman Bates in A&E's *Bates Motel* that transformed him into a household name. During its five seasons (2013–17), the critically acclaimed drama became the network's longest-running—and last—original scripted show, earning Highmore consecutive nods from the Critics' Choice Television Awards in 2014 and 2015.

Although other young British actors such as Tom Holland and Taron Egerton are forging successful film careers, Highmore has concentrated on the small screen, taking on the role of an autistic surgeon in ABC's *The Good Doctor* in 2017. "Instead of being a smaller part of more things, I've really enjoyed being a bigger part of something that goes on for a long time," he told Nancy Mills for the *Columbus Dispatch* (25 Sept. 2017). That decision has paid off; *The Good Doctor* not only ended its first season as the network's most-watched freshman drama in more than a decade but also earned Highmore his first-ever Golden Globe Award nomination.

EARLY LIFE

Alfred "Freddie" Thomas Highmore was born to Sue Latimer and Edward Highmore on Valentine's Day 1992 in Camden Town, a northwestern district of London, England. Highmore and his younger brother, Albert, were primarily raised by their father, an actor, while their mother worked as a talent agent, representing her husband as well as such high-profile clients as Imelda Staunton and Daniel Radcliffe. Growing up, Highmore attended a primary school in North London's Hampstead Garden suburb.

At age seven, Highmore followed in his father's footsteps and entered the acting world. He was first cast in the drama *Walking on the Moon* (1999), but his scenes in that film ended up on the cutting room floor. He then made his official film debut alongside his brother—and Helena Bonham Carter—in *Women Talking Dirty*, a film adaptation of the Isla Dewar best seller by the same title. That film premiered at the 1999 Toronto International Film Festival (TIFF). After appearing as a bus driver's son in the BBC film *Happy Birthday Shakespeare* (2000), Highmore portrayed a young King Arthur of Camelot in the two-part TNT miniseries *The Mists of Avalon* (2001). He then appeared alongside his father in the 2001 CBS miniseries *Jack and the Beanstalk: The Real Story*, followed by a minor role in the British television drama *I Saw You* (2002).

CHILDHOOD ACTING CAREER

Highmore resurfaced two years later, in the summer flick *Two Brothers* (2004), Jean-Jacques Annaud's live-action adventure about two young tigers separated for a year before eventually being reunited. Highmore received top billing for his next film, an adaptation of E. Nesbit's 1902 fantasy-adventure novel *Five Children and It*. The film, in which Highmore starred as one of five siblings who unearth an ancient wish-granting sand fairy, debuted at TIFF in September 2004.

Highmore's big break came in November 2004 with his well-received performance in *Finding Neverland*, which he filmed at age nine. Legendary film critic Roger Ebert hailed Highmore's portrayal of emotionally troubled Peter Llewelyn Davies as "remarkable" (18 Nov. 2004), while William Arnold described him as "eerily right" in his review for the *Seattle Post-Intelligencer* (18 Nov. 2004). For his effort, Highmore claimed the Young Artist Awards' ensemble prize; outstanding new talent at the Satellite Awards; and nods from the Screen Actors Guild (SAG) Awards, London Critics' Circle Film Awards, and Broadcast Film Critics Association Awards (BFCAA), among others.

Depp was equally captivated by Highmore's mature acting chops. "When there were scenes with Freddie," Depp recalled to Dave Karger for *Entertainment Weekly* (10 Jan. 2005), "Kate and

I just stood back and let him go. It's unbelievably compelling." On Depp's recommendation, Highmore, then twelve, was cast opposite him in Tim Burton's *Charlie and the Chocolate Factory* (2005). Highmore filmed at Pinewood Studios in Buckinghamshire while attending school in North London. The film was released to audiences in July 2005, amassing $475 million globally and earning Highmore his second straight BFCAA. (Highmore also voiced the title character for the companion video game.)

After playing a younger version of Russell Crowe's character in Ridley Scott's *A Good Year* (2006), Highmore appeared in his first animated film, *Arthur and the Invisibles* (2006), and also lent his voice to the accompanying video game, released in January 2007. That fall, he starred alongside Robin Williams in the feel-good drama *August Rush* as an orphaned musical prodigy in search of his birth parents. Highmore subsequently earned acting credits in the fantasy-adventure films *The Golden Compass* (2007) and *The Spiderwick Chronicles* (2008); in the latter, he portrayed identical twins. He followed that up with voice roles in *A Fox's Tale* (2008) and *Astro Boy* (2009), as well as the latter's tie-in video game, before starring in the CGI-animated films *Arthur and the Revenge of Maltazard* (2009) and *Arthur 3: The War of the Two Worlds* (2010), sequels to *Arthur and the Invisibles*.

ADULT ROLES AND BEGINNING OF TELEVISION CAREER

Highmore graduated to teen roles in 2010, portraying British chef Nigel Slater in *Toast*, a BBC biopic that reunited him with Bonham Carter. He also played the seventeen-year-old title character, Harold "Hally" Ballard, in the film adaptation of Athol Fugard's 1982 play *"Master Harold" . . . and the Boys*, which deals with apartheid in South Africa. The film was screened at the 2010 Cape Winelands Film Festival in South Africa and the 2011 New York International Independent Film and Video Festival. Highmore tackled his first romantic role opposite Emma Roberts in the coming-of-age tale *The Art of Getting By*, which premiered at the 2011 Sundance Film Festival in January before being widely released that June.

In 2012, Highmore was cast as a teenage Norman Bates in the A&E scripted drama *Bates Motel*, a prequel to *Psycho*, Alfred Hitchcock's classic 1960 thriller. When the first episode debuted the following March, it attracted around 3 million viewers, including a record 1.6 million viewers in the coveted demographic of adults from age eighteen to forty-nine. Within a month, the series had been greenlit for a second ten-episode season. The first season wrapped in late May 2013, with *Bates Motel* averaging 2.7 million viewers and finishing second among top new cable dramas. Following a July appearance at San Diego's Comic-Con convention, Highmore voiced the lead role in the animated adventure *Justin and the Knights of Valour* (2013).

Season two of *Bates Motel* premiered in March 2014, attracting more than three million viewers. A month later the series, which then averaged more than two million viewers, was renewed for a third season. Highmore's performance earned him a first-time nod for Best Actor in a Drama Series from the Critics' Choice Television Awards. He also partnered with one of the series' cocreators and show runner Kerry Ehrin to pitch a half-hour comedy to NBC; the network ordered a pilot but did not pick up the show.

When *Bates Motel* returned for season three in March 2015, it drew over 2 million viewers—its lowest debut—and went on to average 1.8 million viewers. Despite this, A&E renewed the series for two additional seasons in mid-June, less than a month after Highmore's second consecutive Critics' Choice Television Award nod. During the series' fourth season, which debuted in March 2016, Highmore tried his hand at writing with the episode "Unfaithful," which aired in May. That fall, he starred in two independent films making the festival-circuit rounds—*The Journey* (2016) and *Almost Friends* (2016)—before capping off the year with a starring role in the BBC miniseries *Close to the Enemy*.

Bates Motel's fifth—and final—season, which ended in April 2017, was highlighted by Highmore's directing debut and a Critics' Choice Award nod. In an interview with Debra Birnbaum for *Variety* (24 Apr. 2017), he expressed his pride regarding the show and his sadness over leaving the cast he had worked with for so many years: "I know everyone will talk about their family and how hard it was to say goodbye to everyone. But genuinely on this, this was the case. This was the most special group of people I've been lucky enough to work with." His lone 2017 film credit was a supporting role in the HBO mockumentary *Tour de Pharmacy*.

THE GOOD DOCTOR

Three days after wrapping up *Bates Motel*, Highmore met with David Shore, who tapped him to play Shaun Murphy, a surgical resident with autism, in his new medical drama, *The Good Doctor*. "With Freddie, there's something captivating about those eyes," Shore told Michael Schneider for *Indiewire* (6 Nov. 2017). "He's able to project so much emotion into what he's going through when in reality he's not always telling you."

Though reception of the show was mixed, Highmore's performance was well received by critics. In a review for *Variety* (25 Sept. 2017), Maureen Ryan criticized the show's writing but described Highmore as "an immensely talented actor" who "brings intelligence and depth to his portrayal," adding that he "makes the viewer care, thanks to his intense presence and precise portrayal." Kelly Lawler, for *USA Today* (22 Sept. 2017), felt similarly, criticizing the show as a whole but writing that "Highmore remains an appealing young actor, and his interpretation of Shaun gives him room to grow."

Highmore's portrayal also resonated with the viewers. When *The Good Doctor* premiered in September 2017, it was an instant hit, with its first episode attracting over 11 million viewers. The drama became ABC's most-watched Monday show in more than two decades and the network's most-watched first-year series in thirteen years, and it was renewed for a second season in March 2018. For his efforts, Highmore, who also serves as a series producer, was recognized with his first Golden Globe nomination.

PERSONAL LIFE

Highmore, who lives in London, is fluent in Spanish and Arabic, which he studied at Emmanuel College, part of the University of Cambridge. He is also a fan of the Arsenal Football Club.

SUGGESTED READING

Arnold, William. "Depp Leads Us on a Magical Journey to Barrie's *Neverland*." *Seattle Post-Intelligencer*, 18 Nov. 2004, www.seattlepi.com/ae/movies/article/Depp-leads-us-on-a-magical-journey-to-Barrie-s-1159890.php. Accessed 9 June 2018.

Ebert, Roger. Review of *Finding Neverland*, directed by Marc Forster. *RogerEbert.com*, 18 Nov. 2004, www.rogerebert.com/reviews/finding-neverland-2004. Accessed 9 June 2018.

Karger, Dave. "Young Freddie Highmore Steals the Screen in *Finding Neverland*." *Entertainment Weekly*, 10 Jan. 2005, ew.com/article/2005/01/10/young-freddie-highmore-steals-screen-finding-neverland/. Accessed 9 June 2018.

Lawler, Kelly. "Review: *The Good Doctor* Is a Too-Sentimental Portrait of a Doctor with Autism." Review of *The Good Doctor*, created by David Shore. *USA Today*, 22 Sept. 2017, www.usatoday.com/story/life/tv/2017/09/22/review-the-good-doctor-too-sentimental-portrait-doctor-with-autism/688744001/. Accessed 9 June 2018.

Mills, Nancy. "Freddie Highmore Gets a Shot at 'Good Guy' for a Change." *The Columbus Dispatch*, 25 Sept. 2017, www.dispatch.com/entertainmentlife/20170925/freddie-highmore-gets-shot-at-good-guy-for-change. Accessed 9 June 2018.

Ryan, Maureen. Review of *The Good Doctor*, created by David Shore. *Variety*, 25 Sept. 2017, variety.com/2017/tv/reviews/

good-doctor-review-freddie-highmore-abc-1202569866/. Accessed 9 June 2018.

Schneider, Michael. "*The Good Doctor* Phenomenon: Creator David Shore Says He Couldn't Have Made This Show a Decade Ago, but Now It's a Hit." *Indiewire*, 6 Nov. 2017, www.indiewire.com/2017/11/the-good-doctor-david-shore-freddie-highmore-abc-ratings-1201894796/. Accessed 9 June 2018.

SELECTED WORKS

Finding Neverland, 2004; *Charlie and the Chocolate Factory*, 2005; *The Art of Getting By*, 2011; *Bates Motel*, 2013–17; *The Good Doctor*, 2017–

—Bertha Muteba

Jazmine Hughes

Date of birth: October 25, 1991
Occupation: Journalist

In 2016, *Brooklyn* magazine named journalist Jazmine Hughes fortieth in their list of 100 influential people in Brooklyn. As a special section editor for the *New York Times Magazine*, she was also named as one of *Forbes*'s "30 Under 30" figures to watch in 2018. The recognition capped Hughes's rapid ascent in the publishing world, fueled by her engaging humor and her command of online platforms. She herself noted the unlikelihood of such success at such a young age: "I love my job, and it's a peculiar, humbling honor to show up to work every day, but getting that job felt less like a victory and more like a successful scam," she stated in her 2018 keynote address at Connecticut College, her alma mater. Hughes, whose other credits include cofounding the *Writers of Color* database, also received an honorary doctorate of letters from the college at that ceremony, becoming the youngest person ever to be so honored.

EARLY LIFE AND EDUCATION

Jazmine Siné Hughes grew up in Connecticut as the oldest of five sisters, all with first names beginning with the letter *J* and rhyming middle names. Until fifth grade, which she began at age eight, she was home schooled. She was an avid reader, going through several books a week. She and her sisters were enrolled in ballet and tap dance lessons. Hughes was an award-winning tap dancer as a preteen and continued to dance as she got older.

Hughes's parents' marriage was not happy, and she was frequently witness to their arguments. At times, the children themselves attempted to stop the verbal battles. Her parents divorced in 2012, after Hughes had gone to college. About her sisters and her desire to protect them, Hughes wrote for the *Hairpin* (15 Dec. 2014), "I'd known for a while that the world was a terrible place, and figured out ways to protect myself from it, but I had no idea how I'd protect *them*. I was terrified. I was overwhelmed. I understood my parents a lot more."

Although Hughes did not consider writing as her career path, she took so many English classes in college many thought she was an English major. Instead, she majored in government at Connecticut College. She explained her choice to Marissa Miller for *Teen Vogue* (21 Jan. 2015), "When you grow up, you want to model yourself after people on TV that you think are pretty and seem cool, and everyone I idolized became a lawyer." She also told Kristin Iversen for *Brooklyn* (3 Dec. 2014), "Majoring in government was actually a very screwed up blessing in disguise—I realized too late, to the downfall of both my sanity and my GPA, that government wasn't a field I wanted to go into, but it was such a writing-heavy concentration that I was constantly exercising that muscle."

EARLY CAREER AND *THE HAIRPIN*

Hughes interned at *New York* magazine the summer following her junior year of college, which sparked her desire to work in New York City. During her senior year, Hughes became editor-in-chief of the college newspaper and there found delight in writing nonfiction. She graduated from Connecticut College in 2012 at age twenty, and then took a six-week publishing course at Columbia University.

Hughes had already begun emailing her former boss at *New York* every three months to keep herself in their sights. Offered a job as a fact-checker in August 2012, she accepted despite envisioning herself in a higher-profile role writing cover stories. After a year, she moved to a position as editorial producer for the magazine's website, where she managed video content and wrote listings. "I learned a lot," Hughes told Iversen of her time in these roles. "Especially that 'not everyone who works at a magazine writes for that magazine.'"

After living at home and commuting to the city for a time to save money, Hughes moved back to New York. To better afford living in the city, and to fulfill her desire to write more, she began writing freelance for various outlets. One of her first pieces to get significant recognition was a 2013 article for the website *Jezebel* about her interracial relationship. She also landed an article in the Shouts & Murmurs section of the *New Yorker* in 2014. Meanwhile, Hughes established a social media presence to both build her "brand" and serve as another outlet for her creativity. At first this largely consisted of jokes posted to Twitter, and her following grew steadily.

One of the outlets Hughes began freelancing for was the women-focused general interest blog *The Hairpin*. When she found out the site's editorial leadership was changing in 2014, she got in touch to ask for a job and befriended new editor Hayley Mlotek. By early 2015 Hughes had left *New York* magazine to become a full-time contributing editor for *The Hairpin*.

In her new role Hughes wrote at least one post daily, even if it was simply a link to other content. Her pieces were consistently popular, and she drew more and more attention in the publishing community. She also continued freelancing, with articles appearing in magazines such as *New Republic*, *Cosmopolitan*, and *Elle*. Yet she had to overcome a sense of guilt at finding such success at such a young age. "I find myself using my age as motivator but also as a shield to keep myself from doing things that I am too afraid to do," she told Iversen. "It's easy to postpone goals when you've convinced yourself you have an extra two years to do them. But that's such limiting, poisonous thinking, and I have to try really hard to get myself out of it. There's no excuse not to do anything right now."

THE NEW YORK TIMES

Hughes had barely begun her full-time role at *The Hairpin* when she was contacted by a hiring editor for the *New York Times Magazine*, setting off a lengthy process of interviews and tests. Although the publication had contacted her, she did not expect to get the job. "Most of this anxiety was rooted in not looking and feeling the part," she wrote for *Cosmopolitan* (22 Oct. 2015). "For one, I'm not a white dude. My career is relatively inchoate; my editing experience meager. I don't speak any other languages. I didn't go to an Ivy League . . . I can barely spell the word 'February.'" Yet despite her fears, she was offered the position of associate digital editor in March 2015 and accepted the job.

After her first months of working at the prestigious *New York Times*, Hughes realized she had a serious case of imposter syndrome: the expectation of being discovered as an undeserving fraud and fired. She found herself dismissing any accomplishments as either mistakes or mere luck. Characteristically, she decided to write an article on the subject (freelancing for *Cosmopolitan* rather than for her everyday employer), combining her trademark humor with real social insight. The resulting piece documented her experience trying to overcome her imposter syndrome by dressing in the over-the-top manner of the character Cookie from the hit television show *Empire*. "One of the first steps to solving a problem is to figure out who is causing it—and sometimes that person is you," she wrote (22 Oct. 2015). "No one can improve the situation at hand more than you."

Among Hughes's early responsibilities at the *New York Times* was editing a column called Talk, which she handled for two years. In addition to editing, Hughes also wrote occasional articles for the *New York Times*. Her topics ranged from a profile of pothos, the houseplant she cannot kill, to interviews with figures such as actor and political candidate Cynthia Nixon and radio host Charlemagne Tha God. Of her work, she told Thora Siemsen for the *Creative Independent* (12 July 2018), "I'm laser focused. I just want to know how a magazine comes together. I am interested in book stuff, and writing screenplays and so on. But I have this project before me, and it's all I can see."

WRITERS OF COLOR AND OTHER ADVOCACY

As a result of a conversation over lunch, in 2015 Hughes and freelance writer Durga Chew-Bose set out to improve the diversity of the publishing industry. Working with Hughes's *New York Times* colleague Vijith Assar, a software engineer, they developed a database to help assignment editors find a more diverse pool of writers. Soon the project evolved into a complete website and began attracting attention.

As the *Writers of Color* site proclaims, "We aim to create more visibility for writers of color, ease their access to publications, and build a platform that is both easy for editors to use and accurately represents the writers." The project gained additional attention when the *Huffington Post* featured the site in an article.

As Hughes became more and more visible in the publishing industry, she was increasingly asked for advice about her profession. She told Hallie Bateman for the *Daily Dot* (12 Jan. 2015) that she advises young writers, "Treat writing as a sport, as a talent you have to develop and exercise. Think of a way to frame a story every day (or every other day), even if you don't end up writing it—just get in the habit of discerning what's a story and why." She also recommended having a job besides full-time writing, as it allows one the freedom to write whatever one chooses. For example, being an editor gave her time and space to develop her writing on her own time, selecting her own subjects. Although she claimed to prefer talking to writing, she also continued to hone her own writing skills. "I don't write for writing," she told Bateman. "I do it so it's done and I can be like, 'Look what I made!'"

Hughes particularly encourages young women writers, calling on them to draw inspiration from each other. "Find women you like and just talk to them. Be in their presence. Women are magic and we should share it amongst each other," she advised to Sarah Galo for the *Guardian* (6 Jan. 2015). "I think there's power in surrounding yourself with women you admire." Hughes also appeared as one of the guest speakers at a

Girls Write Now conference held at the New York Historical Society in June 2018. The event focused on adolescents' projects in digital media platforms, and Hughes expressed her belief that these young women can serve as an important force for social change.

PERSONAL LIFE

Hughes has described how her friendships helped her develop as a person. "I realized the value of surrounding yourself with people who are doing what they want to do," she told Bateman. "Becoming friends with smart people just pushed me." She has also been open about her romantic relationships in various writings, including the fact that dating white men as a black woman still often attracts prejudice. Meanwhile, she maintains close relationships with her sisters.

Hughes's favorite comfort food is mashed potatoes, and her favorite writer is Norah Ephron. In fact, she told Bateman, "My goal in life is to be the black Nora Ephron. Which is, really, just to be Nora Ephron but still me, to be able to have this [product] in my hair."

SUGGESTED READING

Hughes, Jazmine. "How to Make It as a Freelance Writer on the Internet." Interview by Hallie Bateman. *The Daily Dot*, 12 Jan. 2015, www.dailydot.com/irl/jazmine-hughes-interview/. Accessed 7 Aug. 2018.

Hughes, Jazmine. "I Dressed Like Cookie for a Week to Get Over My Imposter Syndrome." *Cosmopolitan*, 22 Oct. 2015, www.cosmopolitan.com/entertainment/tv/a48078/dressed-like-cookie-from-empire-for-a-week-essay/. Accessed 7 Aug. 2018.

Hughes, Jazmine. "Jazmine Hughes: Women Are Magic." Interview by Sarah Galo. *The Guardian*, 6 Jan. 2015, www.theguardian.com/books/2015/jan/06/jazmine-hughes-women-are-magic. Accessed 7 Aug. 2018.

Hughes, Jazmine. "On Learning to Write Professionally." Interview by Thora Siemsen. *The Creative Independent*, 12 July 2018, thecreativeindependent.com/people/writer-and-editor-jazmine-hughes-on-learning-to-write-professionally/. Accessed 7 Aug. 2018.

Hughes, Jazmine. "Sisters, Ranked." *The Hairpin*, 15 Dec. 2014, www.thehairpin.com/2014/12/sisters-ranked/. Accessed 7 Aug. 2018.

Hughes, Jazmine. "30 Under 30: Jazmine Hughes, Writer/Editor at The Hairpin." Interview by Kristin Iversen. *Brooklyn*, 3 Dec. 2014, www.bkmag.com/2014/12/03/30-under-30-jazmine-hughes-writereditor-at-the-hairpin/. Accessed 7 Aug. 2018.

Miller, Marissa. "Dream Jobs: Get to Know Jazmine Hughes of The Hairpin." *Teen Vogue*, 21 Jan. 2015, www.teenvogue.com/story/jazmine-hughes-dream-jobs-the-hairpin. Accessed 7 Aug. 2018.

—*Judy Johnson*

Sandra Hüller

Date of birth: April 30, 1978
Occupation: Actor

Sandra Hüller is a German actor best known as a star of the hit indie comedy *Toni Erdmann*, which was nominated for Best Foreign Language Film at the 2016 Academy Awards. The film premiered to wide critical acclaim at the Cannes Film Festival and swept the major categories at the European Film Awards, placing Hüller—and more largely, German cinema—firmly in the international limelight. Still mostly a theater and indie film actor, Hüller is hesitant to make the leap into mainstream Hollywood movies. "To go big in America, I would have to change a lot of things about my body and my face," she speculated to Catherine Shoard for the *Guardian* (26 Jan. 2017). "I would, at least from the outside, become another person."

Ironically, chief among Hüller's talents is her ability to become another person. Before *Toni Erdmann*, Hüller starred in the 2006 Hans-Christian Schmid drama *Requiem*. The film was based on the true story of Anneliese Michel, a young woman who believed that she was

Photo by Franziska Krug/Getty Images

possessed by the devil and died after a series of exorcisms in 1976. (A more sensationalized version of the story is told the 2005 film *The Exorcism of Emily Rose*.)

EARLY LIFE AND THEATER CAREER

Hüller was born in eastern Germany, then the German Democratic Republic (GDR), in 1978. She found life in the former Soviet bloc comforting, she told Shoard. "People told me I would definitely have a job later: 'Nobody needs to starve here or live in the streets.' There were no drug issues. Maybe it wasn't the truth, but as a child there was not so much fear," she said, referring to the current climate in Germany surrounding the influx of refugees from other countries. Hüller, who grew up in Suhl, a forest town of Thuringia, was eleven years old when the Berlin Wall fell. The change was disorienting; she said later in an interview that it reinforced for her the profound uncertainty of the world.

As a child, Hüller loved acting in school plays but never considered that she might pursue theater as a profession. Still, she applied and was accepted to the competitive Ernst Busch Academy of Dramatic Art in Berlin in 1996. She graduated in 2000 and went on to perform with theaters across Germany, particularly in Leipzig and Jena. She joined the ensemble at Theater Basel in Switzerland, where she won accolades for playing Gretchen in Johann Wolfgang von Goethe's *Faust* in 2002. In 2003 the German magazine *Theater heute* (*Theater today*) named her the best up-and-coming actress of the year. Over the years she has been affiliated with Munich Kammerspiele (intimate theatre), the Ruhrtriennale (Ruhr festival), Staatsschauspiel Hannover (Hanover State Theatre), the Theater Freiburg, and Volksbühne (People's stage) Berlin.

REQUIEM

Hüller has acted in films since her theater school days. In 2004 she received the script for *Requiem* and signed on to play Michaela Klinger, a German college student in the 1970s who has seizures and experiences mental illness. Based on a true story, Michaela eschews medical treatment for religious intervention, with the consent and blessing of her World War II–generation parents, in the form of exorcism to cure her ailments. In the film, Hans-Christian Schmid explores both religious extremism and familial relationships. In real life, the young woman, Anneliese Michel, died of starvation and pneumonia at twenty-three. Her case famously went to trial, and her parents and two priests who performed the exorcisms were convicted of negligent manslaughter. Schmid's film, which does not include the trial, is more interested in the subtle psychological unraveling of his protagonist, Michaela.

Requiem was notable for its refusal to sensationalize Michaela's story or the lurid details of her exorcisms. The film was critically praised in large part thanks to Hüller's skill as an actor. Jeannette Catsoulis, who reviewed it for the *New York Times* (20 Oct. 2006), described Hüller's performance as "devastating." "Balancing Ms. Hüller's astonishingly physical performance with an intimate, naturalistic style, 'Requiem' is a moving study of a tortured young woman more at peace with medieval ritual than with modern medicine," Catsoulis wrote. The film was a surprise hit in Europe. Hüller, who won the Silver Bear for Best Actress at the prestigious Berlinale, or Berlin International Film Festival, became a star overnight. "I didn't know what to do," she recalled to Kaleem Aftab for the *Independent* (16 May 2017). "I had been doing theatre for seven years and I didn't even know what the Berlinale [Berlin Film Festival] was, then from one day to the next everything changed. I was overwhelmed."

LATER FILMS

For writer-director Nanouk Leopold's *Brownian Movement*, Hüller plays Charlotte, a German-born doctor whose sexual addiction threatens her marriage and who tries to start over with him by moving abroad. *Brownian Movement*, which premiered at the Toronto International Film Festival in 2010, was screened at the Berlinale.

Hüller went on to star in *Über Uns Das All* (*Above Us Only Sky*), a drama about a schoolteacher named Martha whose husband suddenly kills himself. After his shocking death, Martha discovers that he had been leading a secret life. Martha learns more as the film progresses, but the story takes a turn when she begins a new relationship with a history professor. *Above Us Only Sky* played at the Canberra International Film Festival in 2009. Lynden Barber, who reviewed the film for Australia's SBS television network (1 Jan. 2009), noted the dearth of "juicy" roles for Hüller since her debut and hailed *Above Us Only Sky* as worthy of her considerable talent. "Hüller's handling of her character's challenging emotional journey is never less than subtle, commanding, utterly authentic and unpredictable," Barber wrote. *Above Us Only Sky* was released in 2011.

In 2013 Hüller appeared in an ensemble film called *Finsterworld*, the fiction debut of documentary filmmaker Frauke Finsterwalder. The modern-day fairy tale features several interconnected stories about German identity and frustrated human connection. Hüller plays a documentary filmmaker with a police officer boyfriend. The well-received film premiered at the Montreal Film Festival, where it won the Bronze Zenith for the First Fiction Feature

Film, and enjoyed accolades on the European festival circuit.

Her next venture was the historical romance *Amour Fou* (*Crazy Love*) (2014), for which she played Marie, the cousin and love interest of suicidal writer Heinrich von Kleist. The film was screened at Cannes but received mixed reviews from critics.

TONI ERDMANN

When Hüller first read the script for an un-usual—and unusually long—film called *Toni Erdmann*, she was skeptical. "To be honest at first I didn't get it," she told Carlos Aguilar for *MovieMaker Magazine* (29 Dec. 2016). Hüller's character, Ines Conradi, "was so strange to me, unlike any character that I've never read before. I also can't say that I really liked her." Writer and director Maren Ade spent years honing the script, continuing to edit it over the year during which Hüller and her costar Peter Simonischek rehearsed the film—any rehearsal, much less a yearlong rehearsal, is basically unheard of in American film—and through the fifty days of shooting. Ade, known for her award-winning 2009 romantic drama *Alle Anderen* (*Everyone Else*), did not set out to write a comedy, per se, though reviewers have noted its similarities to American television shows that bask in awk-wardness like *Seinfeld*, *The Office*, and *Curb Your Enthusiasm*. "It's always important that it happens in a certain context and it's not pure comedy—that's something I'm not interested in," Ade told Aguilar. "It was what came out of the story, but the story is a drama. For me the foundation of the film is a drama."

Hüller plays a high-powered corporate con-sultant living in Bucharest, Romania. She is all hard edges, impatient, and work-obsessed, un-like her goofy practical joker of a father, Win-fried (Simonischek). After his beloved dog dies, the retiree Winfried visits his daughter but grows concerned about her toxic work culture and her seeming inability to enjoy her-self. To remedy this, Winfried reappears in Bucharest, wearing false teeth and a flowing black wig, in the guise of a life coach named Toni Erdmann. Ironically, Toni makes Ines's life more difficult, causing her to humiliate herself in front of colleagues and clients, but Ade's film hovers tonally between the real and surreal. *Toni Erdmann* is about the fractured relationship between a father and a daughter, but it is also about the deadening effects of corporate culture.

The strangeness of the film—highlights in-clude a naked birthday party and a karaoke scene featuring a rollickingly hateful version of the Whitney Houston ballad "The Greatest Love of All"—captivated audiences across Europe and in the United States. *Sight & Sound*, the magazine of the prestigious British Film Institute, polled 163 critics who named it their favorite film of 2016. Mark Kermode, who reviewed the film for the *Guardian* (5 Feb. 2017) gave it five out of five stars, describing it as "something utterly unique and wholly indefinable." *Toni Erdmann*, A. O. Scott wrote for the *New York Times* (22 Dec. 2016), "is its own kind of rebellion, a thrill-ing act of defiance against the toxicity of doing what is expected, on film, at work and out in the world."

Hüller won the European Film Award for Best European Actress for her role in *Toni Erd-mann* in 2016.

GÖHTE FRANCHISE AND OTHER PROJECTS

In 2017 Hüller appeared in the third and final installment of the popular German franchise Fack Ju Göhte, her first true comedy. The first film in the franchise follows the story of a former convict who takes a job at a high school where he has stashed money from an old robbery. The films, which follow his teaching exploits, are wildly popular in Germany. In *Fack Ju Göhte 3*, Hüller plays a teacher dealing with problem students. The film, which opened in October, made $18 million during its opening week-end—far and away the best opening of the year in Germany.

Upcoming projects for Hüller include a ro-mance called *In Den Gängen* (In the aisles). Directed by Thomas Stuber, the film is an adaption of a short story by the German writer Clemens Meyer, about the lives and loves of supermarket employees.

PERSONAL LIFE

Hüller and her daughter, who was born in 2013, live in Leipzig.

SUGGESTED READING

Ade, Maren, and Sandra Hüller. "Laughing with Pain: Director Maren Ade and Sandra Hüller on Their Hilarious Father-Daughter Dramedy *Toni Erdmann*." Interview by Carlos Aguilar. *MovieMaker Magazine*, 29 Dec. 2016, www.moviemaker.com/archives/interviews/maren-ade-sandra-huller-toni-erdmann. Accessed 14 Dec. 2017.

Aftab, Kaleem. "Sandra Hüller Interview: Actor Talks Toni Erdmann Remake, In the Aisles and Being the Face of German Cinema." *The Independent*, 16 May 2017, www.indepen-dent.co.uk/arts-entertainment/films/features/sandra-heller-interview-toni-erdmann-in-the-aisles-requiem-german-cinema-cannes-film-festival-a7738081.html. Accessed 14 Dec. 2017.

Barber, Lynden. "Above Us Only Sky Review: Identity Crisis Carried by Hüller's Superb Performance." Review of *Above Us Only Sky*, directed by Jan Schomburg. *SBS Movies*, SBS, 1 Jan. 2009, www.sbs.com.au/movies/review/above-us-only-sky-review. Accessed 14 Dec. 2017.

Catsoulis, Jeannette. "A Mind in Torment Faces a Terrible Decline." *The New York Times*, 20 Oct. 2006, www.nytimes.com/2006/10/20/movies/a-mind-in-torment-faces-a-terrible-decline.html. Accessed 14 Dec. 2017.

Kermode, Mark. "Toni Erdmann Review—Talk about Embarrassing Parents . . ." *The Guardian*, 5 Feb. 2017, www.theguardian.com/film/2017/feb/05/toni-erdmann-observer-film-review. Accessed 14 Dec. 2017.

Scott, A. O. "Review: In 'Toni Erdmann,' Dad's a Prankster Trying to Jolt His Conformist Daughter." Review of *Toni Erdmann*, directed by Maren Ade. *The New York Times*, 22 Dec. 2016, mwr.nytimes.com/2016/12/22/movies/toni-erdmann-review.html. Accessed 14 Dec. 2017.

Shoard, Catherine. "Toni Erdmann's Sandra Hüller: 'Everybody Knows the German Clichés. Maybe They're True." *The Guardian*, 26 Jan. 2017, www.theguardian.com/film/2017/jan/26/toni-erdmanns-sandra-huller-interview-east-germany-gdr. Accessed 14 Dec. 2017.z

SELECTED WORKS

Requiem, 2006; *Brownian Movement*, 2010; *Über Uns Das All* (*Above Us Only Sky*), 2011; *Finsterworld*, 2013; *Toni Erdmann*, 2016

—*Molly Hagan*

Kareem Hunt

Date of birth: August 6, 1995
Occupation: Football player

On September 7, 2017, in Foxborough, Massachusetts's Gillette Stadium, the first game of the official National Football League (NFL) season took place, with the New England Patriots, the defending Super Bowl champions, facing off against the Kansas City Chiefs. Many pundits believed that the Patriots would rack up an easy win to kick off their season. Kansas City's starting running back, Spencer Ware, was injured during the preseason and Kareem Hunt, a rookie who was a third-round draft pick from the University of Toledo, took his place. On Hunt's first carry, he fumbled the ball and forced a turnover. That play shook some people's confidence, including Hunt himself. "I just had to keep playing through it, not get down on myself and keep making plays," he told Josh Alper for *NBCSports.com* (8 Sept. 2017). "Honestly, that's

Photo by Peter G. Aiken/Getty Images

not the way I wanted to start. It was a rough one because I don't remember the last time I fumbled."

Hunt rebounded quickly, however, racking up 246 total yards, both rushing and receiving, the most ever for an NFL rookie in his debut game. He also scored three touchdowns, including a 78-yard touchdown pass. All told, Hunt's performance helped propel Kansas City to a stunning 42–27 upset over the Patriots.

Before his explosive debut, Hunt had been a player who had largely flown under the radar. However, those who knew him and had seen him play knew that this was the level of performance one could expect from him. A star in high school and college, Hunt broke records at Toledo and was the offensive most valuable player (MVP) of the 2015 GoDaddy Bowl against Arkansas State. In that game, he rushed for 271 yards and five touchdowns, tying a record set by his boyhood idol, Barry Sanders. "He had an amazing college career, and that carried over," Charcandrick West, a veteran backup running back for Kansas City, told Tim Rohan for *Sports Illustrated* (8 Sept. 2017). "You don't wake up and forget how to play football. That's what we expect from him. That's why we drafted him."

EARLY LIFE AND EDUCATION

Kareem A. J. Hunt was born on August 6, 1995, in Willoughby, Ohio, to parents Stephanie Riggins and Kareem Abdul-Jabbar Hunt. Hunt's father, who was named after the famous basketball player Kareem Abdul-Jabbar, wanted to pass his full name on to his son, but Riggins would only allow the initials.

Hunt's father was a star basketball and football player. Like his father, Hunt was also interested in football. His favorite player was Barry Sanders, a running back for the Detroit Lions from 1989 to 1998. "When I was growing up I definitely had a Barry Sanders poster right on my wall," he told Mike Herndon for *AL.com* (5 Jan. 2015). "I always used to look up to that man."

Riggins raised Hunt and his brother, Clarence, on her own, and money was often tight. "Sometimes it was hard to buy enough groceries," Riggins told Dan Pompei for *Bleacher Report* (2 Oct. 2017). "They didn't have the name-brand clothes like the other kids. But all [Kareem] really cared about is if he could go outside and play sports."

As a child, Hunt played peewee football. One of the players on an opposing team was Mitch Trubisky, who is now a quarterback for the Chicago Bears. As time went on, Hunt became more and more obsessed with the sport, to the point that it was all he focused on. His peewee coach, Ray Wank, knew that Hunt was destined for the NFL and even held on to the young Hunt's shoes, describing them as his "most guarded possession" to Jacob Feldman for *Sports Illustrated* (13 Sept. 2017). "People always laughed at me, making fun of me," Wank said. "But I told them, 'I know what's coming.'"

As a teenager, Hunt became one of the standout athletes at Willoughby South High School, running track and playing tailback on the football team. In his senior year, he rushed for 2,685 yards (a record for Lake County) and 44 touchdowns. "The most important thing I learned at South was to never give up," Hunt told Jeff Schudel for Willoughby's *News-Herald* (11 May 2017). "You don't always see the light at the end of the tunnel. In high school, you're always thinking about the now. The future came fast. I worked hard every day, knowing I wanted to go to the NFL. Every day I had to do something to help myself get to the next level."

A lifelong fan of Ohio State football, Hunt hoped to be able to play for the school. He had some initial talks with Ohio State, but they did not materialize into an offer. Additionally, other schools failed to show much interest in the young prospect, despite his impressive numbers. The feeling among some of the larger schools was that Willoughby South's comparatively small size and lack of competition somewhat diminished the impact of those numbers. One person who was interested, however, was the University of Toledo football coach Mike Campbell. Toledo made Hunt an offer and, impressed with the program, the young player decided to sign on as a running back for the Rockets.

COLLEGE CAREER

Midway through Hunt's freshman season, the starting running back was injured and Hunt was put into the game. In that first game, he racked up 127 yards and a touchdown. He continued in that vein for the remainder of the season, rushing for a total of 866 yards and 6 touchdowns on 137 carries (an average of 6.3 yards per carry). His sophomore year was similarly impressive, rushing for 1,631 yards on 205 carryings, averaging nearly 8 yards per carry. Hunt's achievements in his sophomore season put him in the top five college players in the country. In his junior year, however, Hunt's momentum was halted when he was suspended for two games due to an unspecified violation of the team's policies. When he returned, he managed to still play well, rushing for 973 yards, but some observed that he had lost a step, possibly from the suspension, but also due to injuries he suffered to his hamstring and ankle. "I'm sure he was down," Terry Swanson, one of Hunt's teammates at Toledo, told Sam Mellinger for the *Kansas City Star* (15 Sept. 2017). "I mean, he had to be. But you could ask anybody in the locker room. We never saw it. He never showed it."

Hunt finished his college career with 4,945 rushing yards, breaking the school record set by Chester Taylor, who became an NFL running back on such teams as the Baltimore Ravens, the Minnesota Vikings, and the Arizona Cardinals. His career yardage while playing for the Rockets placed him third all-time in Mid-American Conference history. "Recruiting in general is an art, not necessarily a science," Toledo head coach Jason Candle, an assistant during Hunt's recruitment, told *ESPN.com*. "You sign 20 [to] 25 kids every year and hope just one turns out to be what Kareem's become. You've got to be emotionally stable, physically able, ready to handle the playbook, and Kareem was all of those things for us."

NFL CAREER

On April 28, 2017, Hunt was selected by Kansas City in the third round of the 2017 NFL Draft. He was the eighty-sixth pick overall and the first Toledo Rocket to be drafted that year. "It'll be a very emotional day," Hunt told Mark Podolski for the *News-Herald* (28 Apr. 2017) shortly before being selected. "I've always dreamed of playing in the NFL, and when I told people that when I was growing up they didn't believe me. But it now it's almost here."

Initially, Hunt was relegated to a second-string position, but after starting running back Spencer Ware suffered a season-ending knee injury during a preseason game against the Seattle Seahawks, he was moved to the starting position. Following his debut against the Patriots, expectations were high for Hunt, and he continued to play well for Kansas City. In his second start for the team, playing against the Philadelphia Eagles, Hunt rushed for 81 yards on 13 carries and 2 rushing touchdowns to help Kansas City to a 27–20 victory. With 5 touchdowns under his belt, Hunt tied the record for NFL touchdowns through a player's first two games since 1921. The only other players to accomplish this feat are Jahvid Best in 2010 and Billy Sims in 1980, both for the Detroit Lions.

At the end of September, Hunt was named the AFC Offensive Player of the Month, having led the NFL in rushing yards with 401 yards from scrimmage with 538 and yards per carry with 8.53. Records showed that, since 1950, only Jim Brown averaged more yards per carry through the first three games of an NFL season. He was also the first player in NFL history to record a touchdown of 50 yards or longer in his first three games. In addition, Hunt was also featured on the cover of *Sports Illustrated*, and his jersey was put on display in the Pro Football Hall of Fame in Canton, Ohio.

October 2017 proved to be another strong month for Hunt. Playing against the Houston Texans, Hunt rushed for 107 yards, his fourth consecutive 100-yard game. The feat brought his career total to 609 rushing yards, making him the first Kansas City rookie to break 600 yards since Christian Okoye thirty years earlier. In his next two games, he had fewer rushing yards but together with receptions, notched 110 and 117 total scrimmage yards, respectively, the seventh game in a row in which he had 100 or more scrimmage yards. On October 30, playing against the Denver Broncos, Hunt's streak was snapped, with the Broncos holding him to just 68 yards. Nevertheless, Kansas City still managed to win, keeping the team in first place in the American Football Conference West. In his last game before the team's bye week, Hunt was held to 37 rushing yards on 9 carries by the Dallas Cowboys, with Kansas City taking a 17–28 loss. Still, Hunt found reason to be excited, as he was able to play against Cowboys running back Ezekiel Elliot, whom he had known during his years at Toledo (Elliot had played football for Ohio State). Hunt knew that, going into the game, he was going to be facing a difficult challenge. "I was like no excuses, those guys are going to be ready to run the football," Hunt told the *Dallas Morning News* (6 Nov. 2017). "It was good to see a back like Zeke get to play tonight. I'm actually happy for him. . . . I like watching guys run the ball, do it all, jump over you and run hard."

PERSONAL LIFE

When he is not setting or breaking records on the field, Hunt leads a relatively simple life. As of October 2017, he was dating Julianne Oser, whom he met while they were students at Toledo. He is also an avid video gamer and a big fan of the *Call of Duty* game series. Despite the accolades and adulation he's received, Hunt has not let the fame go to his head. Every Friday, he still gets coffee and breakfast for his teammates and helps carry their helmets and shoulder pads into the locker room. This, says people who know Hunt, is in keeping with his levelheaded personality. "The fame won't bother him," his brother, Clarence Riggins, a welder in Lorain, Ohio, told Mark Podolski for the *News-Herald* (10 Oct. 2017). "Kareem loves talking to people. Plus, Kareem's a humble kid. This won't change him. The people around him won't allow it. He's got a lot of positive people around him."

SUGGESTED READING

Alper, Josh. "Kareem Hunt: I Couldn't Get Down on Myself after Fumble." *NBC Sports*, 8 Sept. 2017, profootballtalk.nbcsports.com/2017/09/08/kareem-hunt-i-couldnt-get-down-on-myself-after-fumble/. Accessed 21 Oct. 2017.

Herndon, Mike. "Toledo's Kareem Hunt Joins Boyhood Idol Barry Sanders with Record-Tying GoDaddy Bowl Performance." *AL.com*, 5 Jan. 2015, www.al.com/sports/index.ssf/2015/01/toledos_kareem_hunt_joins_boyh.html. Accessed 21 Oct. 2017.

Lyles, Harry, Jr. "Who Is Kareem Hunt, and How Did He Run All over the Patriots?" *SBNation*, 8 Sept. 2017, www.sbnation.com/2017/9/8/16272494/kareem-hunt-who-is-the-chiefs-rookie-running-back. Accessed 21 Oct. 2017.

Mellinger, Sam. "The Making of Kareem Hunt, from His First Pee Wee Game to the NFL's Newest Star." *The Kansas City Star*, 15 Sept. 2017, www.kansascity.com/sports/spt-columns-blogs/sam-mellinger/article173491466.html. Accessed 21 Oct. 2017.

Podolski, Mark. "Kareem Hunt's Immediate NFL Success Has Been a 'Life Changer.'" *The News-Herald*, 10 Oct. 2017, www.news-herald.com/sports/20171010/kareem-hunts-immediate-nfl-success-has-been-a-life-changer. Accessed 23 Oct. 2017.

Schudel, Jeff. "Chiefs Running Back Kareem Hunt Says Willoughby 'Will Always Be Part of Me.'" *The News-Herald*, 11 May 2017, www.news-herald.com/sports/20170511/chiefs-running-back-kareem-hunt-says-willoughby-will-always-be-part-of-me. Accessed 21 Oct. 2017.

Teicher, Adam. "Chiefs RB Kareem Hunt Seems to Find a Way to Handle Any Situation." *ESPN*, 15 Sept. 2017, www.espn.com/blog/afcwest/post/_/id/79301/chiefs-rb-kareem-hunt-seems-to-find-a-way-to-handle-any-situation. Accessed 21 Oct. 2017.

—*Jeremy Brown*

Sam Hunt

Date of birth: December 8, 1984
Occupation: Singer-songwriter

"He looks like Captain America in a baseball cap, and if he isn't here to save country music, he's at least here to change it," Chris Richards wrote of country musician Sam Hunt for the *Washington Post* (4 Nov. 2014). Following the 2014 release of Hunt's major-label debut album, *Montevallo*, which hit number one on the country music charts and would eventually be certified triple platinum, many critics agreed that the singer-songwriter was poised to be a breakthrough star with his modern, hybrid sound blending country with R&B, hip-hop, and pop. "Country music has always evolved," Hunt told Nick Murray for *Rolling Stone* (26 Feb. 2015), "I've just stepped into that evolution."

A serious college football quarterback, Hunt's path to musical success was somewhat unusual. And his defiance of country music's conventions raised the ire of some traditionalists, while other critics raised eyebrows at his seemingly perfect commercial appeal. "In a way, Hunt is almost like a male Taylor Swift. Tall. Attractive. Charming. Talented. In short, the total package, a marketing machine come to life," Clint Hale wrote for the *Houston Press* (13 Mar. 2017). Yet Hunt, who made chart history in 2017 when his single "Body Like a Back Road" topped Billboard's hot country songs chart for a record-breaking thirty-four weeks in a row, takes such perceptions in stride. "It was never my intention to be controversial, but I like the idea that [my work] may stir up conversation about music, and genres, and what's what," he told Richards. "I like disagreement, because it forces both sides to question their own opinions and why they feel that way."

EARLY LIFE AND EDUCATION

Sam Lowry Hunt was born on December 8, 1984, in Cedartown, Georgia—a town mentioned in an early murder ballad by country music legend Waylon Jennings. His mother, Joan, was an elementary school teacher, and his father, Allen, was an insurance agent. The eldest of three siblings, Hunt focused more on sports as a youngster than on music. "I had a couple CDs," he recalled to Richards. "But I never had that first concert experience, that first record thing." According to his mother, it never even occurred to her to suggest that he learn to play an instrument, because he seemed happiest when outside, throwing around a ball. His main exposure to music came during church suppers, when he would escape to sit in the car and listen to the radio. He absorbed plenty of 1990s-era country

By Jessxtn [CC BY-SA 4.0], via Wikimedia Commons

music, but also became a fan of hip-hop acts such as Boyz II Men and Usher.

Hunt attended Cedartown High School, where he lettered in basketball and baseball but particularly distinguished himself on the football field. Among other honors, he was named Georgia's 2002 Co-Offensive Player of the Year, picked for the All-State Class AAA first team by the Georgia Sportswriters Association, and nominated for the Wendy's High School Heisman Award. After graduating high school, he was recruited and decided to seriously pursue football in college, but also bought a cheap acoustic guitar to take with him to school after trying out a friend's instrument. He learned a few simple chords in order to play songs by artists such as Kenny Chesney and Lynyrd Skynyrd and soon began spending much of his free time practicing and playing music.

COLLEGE FOOTBALL AND MUSICAL BEGINNINGS

Hunt began his college career at Middle Tennessee State University, where he played as quarterback in a few games from 2003 to 2004. He transferred to the University of Alabama at Birmingham (UAB) in 2005, redshirting his first season there. Hunt started at quarterback for the UAB Blazers in 2006 and 2007. A strong athlete, he performed well in both passing and running.

When not on the field or in classes, Hunt began to get more serious about music, despite having little guidance. "I never saw myself as a musician or having any musical talent," he explained to Murray. "I didn't know anybody else who I played ball with who also played music. It took me a while to get over that." Yet his personal enjoyment led him to experiment with writing his own songs, and he eventually performed some for his roommates. Suitably impressed, his friends encouraged him to play open mic nights and gigs at local bars.

Although Hunt had started off as a philosophy major, he ultimately earned a degree in economics. After graduating in 2007, he flirted with the idea of a career in pro sports. He earned a tryout with the National Football League's Kansas City Chiefs, sticking with the club for two months. Only when that attempt proved unsuccessful did he begin to seriously consider forging a career as a musician. Much to the surprise of his family and friends, in 2008 Hunt borrowed his mother's minivan, loaded it with a mattress and some food, and made the move to Nashville, the epicenter of the country-music industry.

Hunt faced steep challenges in trying to make a living in music, beginning with his total lack of experience. "I was very new to songwriting, according to the Nashville paradigm," he admitted to Marissa R. Moss for *Rolling Stone* (28 Oct. 2014). "I experimented and explored ways to find my own niche in Nashville, and I was having trouble with it for a while because stylistically I didn't feel like I necessarily fit in." He earned money initially by working as a parking lot valet while attempting to make connections in the music industry.

NASHVILLE SONGWRITER

Hunt made his most important connection when he met Shane McAnally and Josh Osborne, two songwriters also interested in breaking new ground in country music. "They really embraced and encouraged what I wanted to do," Hunt told Murray. "I felt like, 'Finally, maybe I do have something to offer here; maybe I do have something unique.'" He began to have some success selling his songs to other artists. In 2012, for example, he cowrote "Come Over," which became a massive hit for country star Kenny Chesney and earned Hunt an award from the American Society of Composers, Authors and Publishers (ASCAP).

Despite rising from an unknown to a successful songwriter relatively quickly, Hunt longed to record his songs himself and make an impact as a performer. In response to the industry's slowness to develop new talent, Hunt decided to record a mixtape and release it for free online—a strategy common in hip-hop but virtually unheard of in the Nashville scene. Working with producer Zach Crowell, he released *Between the Pines* in October 2013. Though it attracted little attention, the track "We Are Tonight" was quickly covered by artist Billy Currington and that version eventually made it to number one on the country

radio charts. Meanwhile, Hunt began working on a debut album, realizing that country was beginning to accept more varied sounds. "I felt like there was a place for me within the genre," he told Moss. "It was good for the direction I was going in."

Before Hunt could finish making his record, another song from *Between the Pines* was turned into a hit by another artist. "Cop Car," whose lyrics tell the tale of a young couple in love and under arrest, was released by popular singer Keith Urban, who also performed it at the Grammy Awards ceremony in January 2014. However, Hunt was less than happy about this high-profile development—even taking to social media to complain about it—as he had planned to release a new version of the song himself. "The way that song made it out into the world—it happened through a series of unfortunate circumstances that ended up being out of my control," Hunt told Richards. "I just felt like I was putting this movie together and this was a pivotal scene that was unfortunately taken out early and put in a different context."

MONTEVALLO

In early 2014 Hunt signed a recording contract with MCA Nashville, and he continued to slowly work on the recording of his album with Crowell, McAnally, and others. Crowell described Hunt's working process to Murray: "He's super-duper slow. Most people try to write a song in a day, but he doesn't think that way." Developing each track involved much experimentation, as Hunt sought new sounds that would complement his progressive vision of country.

In the summer of 2014 Hunt's label released *X2C*, a four-song extended play (EP) meant to build anticipation for the full-length record. It debuted at number five on the Billboard top country albums chart, powered by the debut single, "Leave the Night On." That track quickly went to number one on the country singles chart, and garnered Hunt several honors, including CMT's breakthrough video of the year. The album itself, titled *Montevallo*, was released in October 2014. By November it had landed at the top of the Billboard country album chart, and successive singles, including "Take Your Time," "House Party," "Break Up in a Small Town," and "Make You Miss Me," continued his streak of success. The record also included Hunt's version of "Cop Car."

Montevallo ultimately reached number three on the Billboard 200 chart and was certified triple platinum, showing Hunt's appeal beyond traditional country audiences. Four of its singles broke the Top 40 charts, four were certified platinum, three topped the Billboard Hot Country Songs chart, and four topped the country airplay category. Hunt became the first solo male artist ever to land four country airplay chart-toppers from a debut album. Reviews were also largely positive, if not as strong as the commercial performance. Many critics appreciated Hunt's blend of country with hip-hop and R&B, though some questioned if he could truly be considered a country artist and a few derided him as overly commercial "bro-country." *Montevallo* brought Hunt Grammy nominations for best country album and best new artist, though he won neither.

"BODY LIKE A BACK ROAD"

To commemorate the one-year anniversary of *Montevallo*'s release, Hunt's label reissued *Between the Pines* in October 2015. The following month Hunt won an American Music Award as new artist of the year. While the final single from *Montevallo* came out in 2016, Hunt was already working on new material.

In February 2017, Hunt released "Body Like a Back Road," the lead single from his still-unfinished sophomore studio album. Within two weeks the song had landed atop the Hot Country Songs chart, where it remained for months, shattering the band Florida Georgia Line's record of twenty-four weeks. The song also made inroads onto the Hot 100 singles chart, inciting new discussion about how to categorize Hunt's music. "I'm not trying to become a pop artist, and I'm not trying to make sure I stay a country artist. I'm just trying to make sure I make the best music I can, according to my way," the singer explained to Moss. "Hopefully all those walls break down, and music is just music."

PERSONAL LIFE

Many of Hunt's fans avidly followed his on-again, off-again relationship with Alabama native Hannah Lee Fowler, who he began dating in 2008. *Montevallo* was reportedly named after Fowler's hometown, and she inspired many of Hunt's hits, including "Body Like a Back Road" and "Drinkin' Too Much." The couple's engagement was made public in January 2017, and they married on April 15, 2017, in Hunt's native Cedartown.

SUGGESTED READING

Hale, Clint. "The Jury Is Still Out on Sam Hunt." *Houston Press*, 13 Mar. 2017, www.houstonpress.com/music/is-sam-hunt-good-9262790. Accessed 2 Feb. 2018.

Hunt, Sam. "Sam Hunt Interview: The Singer Looks Back on His Insane Debut Year." Interview by Madison Vain. *Entertainment Weekly*, 27 Oct. 2015, ew.com/article/2015/10/27/sam-hunt-interview-debut-year/. Accessed 2 Feb. 2018.

Moss, Marissa R. "Sam Hunt Defends His Country Cred on New Album Montevallo." *Rolling Stone*, 28 Oct. 2014, www.rollingstone.com/music/features/sam-hunt-montevallo-album-interview-20141028. Accessed 2 Feb. 2018.

Murray, Nick. "Sam Hunt: How a Former College Football Star Is Making Over Country Music." *Rolling Stone*, 26 Feb. 2015, www.rollingstone.com/music/features/sam-hunt-how-a-former-college-football-star-is-making-over-country-music-20150226. Accessed 2 Feb. 2018.

Richards, Chris. "Another Country: Sam Hunt Maps out Nashville's Bold New Future." *The Washington Post*, 4 Nov. 2014, www.washingtonpost.com/lifestyle/style/another-country-sam-hunt-maps-out-nashvilles-bold-new-future/2014/11/04/bd37cf86-643d-11e4-bb14-4cfea1e742d5_story.html. Accessed 2 Feb. 2018.

Stutz, Colin. "Sam Hunt Talks 'Body Like a Back Road,' Fashion, Not Getting Star-Struck at CMT Music Awards." *Billboard*, 8 May 2017, www.billboard.com/articles/columns/country/7825566/sam-hunt-body-like-a-back-road-cmt-music-awards-interview. Accessed 2 Feb. 2018.

Willman, Chris. "With Second Album Not Yet in Sight, Sam Hunt Embraces Being a Singles Guy." *Billboard*, 14 Apr. 2017, www.billboard.com/articles/news/7759609/sam-hunt-embraces-singles-approach-sophomore-album. Accessed 2 Feb. 2018.

—*Mari Rich*

Kyrie Irving

Date of birth: March 23, 1992
Occupation: Basketball player

In 2017, All-Star point guard Kyrie Irving left the Cleveland Cavaliers, the 2016 National Basketball Association (NBA) champions, to play for the Boston Celtics. Irving was the number one pick of the draft in 2011, when he joined the Cavs. He was named Rookie of the Year in 2012, and in 2013, he played in his first All-Star Game. Still, after superstar LeBron James's return to his hometown and home team in 2014, Irving became the Cavs' beloved second fiddle. His abrupt move to a rival team signals a new era in his career. Irving is ready to become a leader in his own right, and so far, he has proved successful in this role. After the season opener in October 2017, during which another Celtics newcomer, Gordon Hayward, ended his season by dislocating his left ankle and fracturing his left tibia, critics predicted a poor year for the team. But Irving went on to lead the Celtics—despite a facial injury—on a sixteen-game winning streak that fall, the fourth-longest streak in

By TonyTheTiger [CC BY-SA 4.0], via Wikimedia Commons

the storied franchise's history. As of the spring of 2018, the Celtics have one of the best records in the Eastern Conference. They stand poised to give the dominant Cavs a run for their money in the Eastern Conference Finals.

Irving's new position comes with a platform, and the player has used it to reveal some peculiar ideas about the world. He has, for instance, offered numerous endorsements of the long-disproven theory that the Earth is flat and questioned if astronauts really landed on the moon. In February 2018, Irving announced the release date for *Uncle Drew*, a movie that features him as an elderly man who challenges young people to pick-up games on the street. The comedy is based on a character that Irving first played in a viral Pepsi Max commercial in 2012.

EARLY LIFE

Irving's parents met at Boston University, where his father, Drederick "Dred" Irving, was a college basketball star and economics major who had led the Boston University Terriers to the 1988 National Collegiate Athletic Association (NCAA) Championship. The Irvings married after graduation. When Dred accepted an offer to play professional basketball with the Bulleen Boomers, the family moved to Melbourne, Australia, where, on March 23, 1992, their son, Kyrie Andrew Irving, was born. Dred's childhood best friend, former NBA star Rod Strickland, is Irving's godfather.

When Irving was less than a year old, his mother, Elizabeth (Larson) Irving, left the family and returned to Washington State. She died

from an illness when Irving was four years old. He and his older sister, Asia, were subsequently raised by his father and four aunts.

The Irvings returned to the United States in 1994, settling first in New York and then in Newark, New Jersey, after Dred got a job at a brokerage firm on Wall Street. Irving's father, a senior bond analyst for Thomson Reuters in 2011, recalls taking the children to his professional-amateur and adult league basketball games. "I would have them in a stroller at the end of the bench," Dred told Marc J. Spears for *Yahoo Sports* (17 June 2011). "As they got older, I would take them from the babysitter after work and bring them to my game. They would sit at the end of the bench and watch. They were well-behaved kids. If they needed something, I'd call a timeout and tend to the kids, but very rarely." Dred later remarried; Irving has a stepmother named Shetellia Riley Irving and a young half-sister named London.

HIGH SCHOOL AND COLLEGE CAREER

Inspired by his father, Irving fell in love with basketball at an early age. When Irving was in the fourth grade, his youth team played on the old New Jersey Nets basketball court in Newark. The experience was so transformative, Irving told Spears, that he scrawled a promise to himself on the wall of his closet: "I will play in the NBA, I promise," it said. But Irving would have to work on his confidence first. His father once drove him into the city to play street ball with the kids in New York. Young Irving was rattled by their skill and their trash talk. His father spent the ninety-minute car ride home telling Irving that he should not be afraid of anyone, and Irving internalized the advice.

As a fourteen-year-old freshman at Montclair Kimberley Academy in Montclair, New Jersey, Irvin studied game films during his free period, while his teammates were hanging out. Athletic director Todd Smith recalled to Mary Schmitt Boyer for the Cleveland *Plain Dealer* (25 June 2011), "You knew right away. . . you were dealing with something special," he said. By Irving's sophomore year, he had scored 1,000 points and led the team to a state prep championship. Just before his junior year, Irving transferred to St. Patrick High School in Elizabeth, a nationally known training ground for basketball players. He was a good student and well-liked among his classmates. A singer like his mother, he even performed in the school's production of "High School Musical." He blossomed during the summer before his senior year, coming into the season as a top-five recruit. He averaged 24.5 points, 5 rebounds, 6.5 assists and 1.6 steals. In 2010, the year he graduated, he was named New Jersey Player of the Year by the Newark-based

Star-Ledger and New Jersey Gatorade Player of the Year.

Irving signed with coach Mike Krzyzewski at Duke University after the legendary coach sent a handwritten note to Irving's house. In 1988, Irving's father had led his Boston University team to the NCAA championship, only to lose in the first round to Duke. Thus, Irving's ascension to the famed team was a kind of family redemption. Irving planned to play only one or two seasons with the Blue Devils—he was already a top NBA draft prospect—but those plans were complicated by a toe injury. Eight games into his freshman season, Irving twisted the ligaments in his right big toe. He sat out the rest of the season, returning only for three games in the NCAA tournament. He explained his decision to Boyer. "No. 1, I came back to prove to everyone that I was ready [for the NBA]," he said. "And No. 2, I wanted to stop all the questions whether I was healthy enough, whether this toe injury would have a lingering effect on my career. If I didn't play in the NCAA tournament, I wouldn't have come out [for the draft]." Duke was upset in the Sweet Sixteen, but Irving proved his bona fides, scoring 28 points in his final game. During his 11-game tenure with Duke, Irving averaged 17.5 points, 4.3 assists, and 3.4 rebounds.

CLEVELAND CAVALIERS

After his freshman season at Duke, Irving decided to declare for the 2011 NBA draft. "I'm only 19 years old, but I feel I was ready to go on to the NBA, and I'm going to make a difference once I get there," Irving told Spears at the time. In June, he was chosen first overall by the Cleveland Cavaliers. The Cavs had recently (and painfully) lost their star and hometown hero, LeBron James, to the Miami Heat. Irving's rookie season was a rebuilding year for the Cavs, and Irving's undisputed skill gave the team's fans hope. Irving quickly established himself as one of the best offensive players in the league. Michael Keefe, writing for *Bleacher Report* (8 Feb. 2012), described Irving's debut as "one of the greatest seasons ever played by a rookie point guard." He added, "Irving is faster, stronger and more athletic than any NBA analyst or player predictor indicated before the draft." In January 2012, Irving scored 34 points in the Rising Stars Challenge during All-Star weekend and was named the game's most valuable player (MVP). At the end of the season, he led all rookies in scoring, averaging 18.5 points a game—a significant achievement, considering that his closest competitor, Brandon Knight, averaged only 12.8 points per game. Irving's shooting percentage was 46.9 percent; this combination of stats placed him in the company of only three NBA players that season, league superstars Kevin Durant, Chris Paul, and

LeBron James. At the end of the 2012 season, Irving was named Kia NBA Rookie of the Year.

In the summer of 2012, Irving broke a bone in his right hand during a practice. It healed by the start of the season, though, and in December, he scored 41 points in a losing game against the New York Knicks at Madison Square Garden. In January, he was invited to play in the 2013 All-Star game. That weekend, he upset six shooters, including Steph Curry, to win the ultra-competitive Foot Locker Three-Point Contest. The following year, Irving was invited to the All-Star game again and was named MVP.

In July 2014, James announced his return to the Cavs. That season, 2014–15, marked the first in Irving's NBA tenure that the Cavs were a serious contender for the NBA championship. Highlights from the season include a March game against the San Antonio Spurs in which Irving scored 57 points. Playing alongside James and Kevin Love, Irving made it to his first championship final in 2015. He sustained a fractured kneecap in game 1, though, cutting his series short. The Cavs ultimately lost to the Golden State Warriors in six games. Due to his knee injury, Irving did not make his 2015–16 season debut until December. The Cavs returned to the finals, again facing off against the Warriors, who were hot on the heels of the winningest season in NBA history. Irving scored 17 points in the final half of the series' game 7, and with 53 seconds left and a tied score, he sunk a 25-foot three-pointer. The final moments of the game played out in agonizing slow motion, but ultimately led to the Cavs' first championship title. Of his miraculous play, Irving told Jeff Zillgitt for *USA Today* (20 June 2016), "It was a shot I've been practicing for a while. . . . It was really just the trust from my teammates and just being in that moment."

During Irving's last season with the Cavs, he averaged 25.2 points a game. In game 4 of the Eastern Conference Finals against the Boston Celtics, he scored 42 points to win the game. After winning game 5 against the Celtics in the conference finals, the Cavs returned to the NBA Finals in 2017 to face the Warriors for a third year in a row. They pulled out a win in game 4, with Irving scoring 40 points, but the team ultimately lost the series and the title in game 5. After game 4, James praised Irving's ability to perform in the clutch. "He's just been built for that moment," James told Zillgitt for *USA Today* (10 June 2017). "I said that over and over again—that he's always been built for the biggest moments, and tonight he showed that once again. It's not surprising. He's just that special."

PERSONAL LIFE

Irving has dual citizenship in the United States and Australia. A reader and journal keeper, his favorite book is *Catcher in the Rye*, by J. D. Salinger.

SUGGESTED READING

Boyer, Mary Schmitt. "For Kyrie and Dred Irving, a Long, Winding Road Took Them to a Magical Draft Night (and the Cleveland Cavaliers)." *The Plain Dealer* [Cleveland], 25 June 2011, www.cleveland.com/cavs/index.ssf/2011/06/for_kyrie_and_dred_irving_a_lo.html. Accessed 10 Feb. 2018.

Keefe, Michael. "5 Reasons Kyrie Irving Is Having Historic Rookie Season for Cleveland Cavaliers." *Bleacher Report*, 8 Feb. 2012, bleacherreport.com/articles/1057931-5-reasons-why-kyrie-irving-is-having-historic-rookie-season-for-cavaliers. Accessed 13 Feb. 2018.

"Kyrie Irving." *NBA.com*, 2018, www.nba.com/players/kyrie/irving/202681. Accessed 14 Feb. 2018.

Spears, Marc J. "Irving Rewards Father's Perseverance." *Yahoo Sports*, 17 June 2011, www.yahoo.com/news/irving-rewards-fathers-perseverance-183900010--nba.html. Accessed 10 Feb. 2018.

Zillgitt, Jeff. "Cavs' Kyrie Irving 'Built' for Moments like Finals Game 4 Performance." *USA Today*, 20 June 2017, www.usatoday.com/story/sports/nba/playoffs/2017/06/10/cavs-kyrie-irving-nba-finals-lebron-james-golden-state-warriors/102699586/. Accessed 13 Feb. 2018.

Zillgitt, Jeff. "How the NBA Finals Validated Kyrie Irving." *USA Today*, 20 June 2016, www.usatoday.com/story/sports/nba/playoffs/2016/06/20/kyrie-irving/86138456/. Accessed 13 Feb. 2018.

—*Molly Hagan*

Roy Jacobsen

Date of birth: December 26, 1954
Occupation: Writer

Although Roy Jacobsen is not well-known in the United States, he is a major literary figure in his native Norway, a country with a rich literary tradition that dates to the great Norse sagas of the medieval period—which is relevant because of Jacobsen's own wide-ranging interests in family, history, and the interplay of the traditional and modern. His novels have historical settings ranging from the middle ages to the contemporary world, with the portentous developments of the twentieth century—during which Norway underwent extensive social and political development due, in part, to the discovery of oil, and

By Bjarne Thune, via Wikimedia Commons

weathering two world wars—being Jacobsen's main area of focus.

Asked by Thea Lenarduzzi for the online interview series *Five Books* whether Norway is currently enjoying something of a golden age of literature, Jacobsen replied, "We have a lot of contemporary authors who are quite successful both at home and abroad. These are also very different voices, not one of them can easily be put in a category with the other. We also have an interested and well-informed readership, as well as good and organised systems for supporting and spreading literature. But I am not sure there is a simple reason for this contemporary well-being—I have always been a little bit sceptical towards sociological or historical explanations for this or that in such an individual profession as ours."

Norway's forbidding geography, exceedingly cold climate, and sparsely populated regions are widely thought to contribute to the thoughtful and brooding quality of much of its literature, past and present. Famed Norwegian playwright Henrik Ibsen once asserted: "The magnificent, but severe, natural environment surrounding people up there in the north, the lonely, secluded life—the farms are miles apart—forces them to . . . become introspective and serious. . . . At home every other person is a philosopher!" Perhaps as a result, as Jacobsen, whose laurels include the prestigious Norwegian Critics Prize for Literature, told Lenarduzzi, "We tend not to stay away from anything human, no matter how awkward, grandiose, sentimental, nostalgic, embarrassing, hyperbolic, stupid, hilarious, or dangerous it may be."

EARLY YEARS

Roy Jacobsen was born in Oslo on December 26, 1954. His father, Rolf, was a machinist, and his mother, the former Ingeborg Margrete Strand, was a factory worker. He was raised in Oslo's Årvoll neighborhood. Despite being raised in a blue-collar household, Jacobsen loved literature, and as a child, if he read a book that concluded on a sad note, he wrote out new, more positive endings. Although he enjoyed books by native Norwegian writers, he also came to appreciate such foreign writers as the Russian Fyodor Dostoyevsky and the Britons Joseph Conrad and Graham Greene.

As a teen, Jacobsen fell in with a street gang that roamed Årvoll taking drugs, vandalizing property, and stealing. At sixteen years old, he was arrested for possession of illegal weapons and theft. He was jailed and placed in solitary confinement for over a month in an Oslo prison. The punishment allowed for a lengthy period of introspection, and Jacobsen has described his time in confinement as brutal and formative, coming as it did during his adolescence, a time when he was still forming a sense of self-identity and purpose.

Norway, too, was undergoing changes in the 1970s. Much of the nation's economy had previously been centered on the fishing and lumber industries, but in 1969 Phillips Petroleum discovered oil in the North Sea at a site called Ekofisk, which ultimately proved to be one of the most important oil fields in the North Sea. Over the subsequent decade, Norway's economy burgeoned. In a YouTube interview conducted with MacLehose Press to celebrate the company's publication of his novel *Child Wonder* in English translation in 2011, Jacobsen recalls that his father, Rolf, was pessimistic about the nation's newfound wealth, believing it would cause irreparable harm to the Norwegian character, but the author found those fears to be baseless. "We lost our innocence, but not our souls," he opined.

In the mid-1970s Jacobsen moved to the town of Solfjellsjøen in the northern Norwegian municipality of Dønna, where his mother had been raised. Jacobsen has said that her homestead was so primitive that until she moved away as a young woman she had no idea what electricity was. He supported himself variously as a fisherman, carpenter, and stevedore before deciding to forge a writing career.

WRITING CAREER

In 1982, Jacobsen published his first book, *Fangeliv*, a volume of short stories whose name translates as "Prison Life." *Fangeliv* attracted comparisons to works by Ernest Hemingway and garnered a Tarjei Vesaas *debutantpris*, a prize awarded by the Norwegian Authors' Union for a first piece of fiction in Norwegian. After that, Jacobsen has told interviewers, he could not conceive of being anything besides a writer. He followed up with the novels *Hjertetrøbbel* (*Heart Trouble* 1984) and *Tommy* (1985), but it was not until 1987 that he published a book that would be translated into English. *Det nye vannet*, released in the United States in 1997 as *The New Water*, tells the tale of a withdrawn loner who is prone to having visions. One day he sees what he believes to be two men dumping a body into a lake, and tensions ensue in his small island community. A critic for *Kirkus Reviews* (1 May 1997) called it "a claustrophobic and riveting psychological novel" and wrote, "a memorable characterization of a man who scarcely knows himself whether he's hero, villain, or victim."

In 1991 Jacobsen published what many critics consider his breakthrough, the multigenerational novel *Seierherrene* ("The Conquerors"), which drew upon his own family history and marked his masterful move into historical fiction. The book (which has not appeared in English) traces, through three generations of one family, the upward social mobility and postindustrial advancement that marked life in Norway during the twentieth century; the book was nominated for the Nordic Council Literature Prize. He received another nomination in 2004 for this prize, awarded each year for a work of literature from one of the Nordic countries, for the novel *Frost*, which takes place against the backdrop of the Norse conquest of England in the early eleventh century. Between these two books, he published novels, short story collections, and a biography of Trygve Bratteli, who was prime minister of Norway in the 1970s; the biography caused some controversy when it was published in 1995, for being partly fictionalized.

Although he continued to write prolifically, English-language readers did not have the opportunity to read another work by Jacobsen until 2007, when his 2005 novel *Hoggerne* was published in Britain as *The Burnt-Out Town of Miracles*—translated, as his next three English translations would be too, by Don Bartlett and Donald Shaw. The novel tells a story set during the Winter War, a conflict in which the Soviet Union invaded Finland at the start of World War II. In particular, Jacobsen fictionalizes the historical Battle of Suomussalmi, when some 1,500 Finns defeated 50,000 Russian soldiers advancing on a tiny border town in the frigid Finnish winter. In Jacobsen's story, the residents of Suomussalmi abandon the town and take to the forests to resist the Soviet advance—all except for one resident, who stays behind because he cannot imagine leaving his home or doing anything but logging, and he ends up helping the Russian soldiers. "An inventive wordsmith and a great storyteller, [Jacobsen] never sacrifices substance for style," Tone Sutterud wrote in a review for the London *Independent* (14 Feb. 2008). "His research is meticulous; he knows when to hold back and let the unspoken speak for itself, the hallmark of an author so familiar with his subject that he knows precisely where to let the reader fill in the gaps."

Jacobsen's next book to appear in English translation was *Child Wonder* (2011; *Vidunderbarn*, 2009), the story of a working-class boy named Finn who finds out in 1961 that a previously unacknowledged half-sister will be coming to live in the family's cramped Oslo apartment. Calling it an "intricately worked novel, as rich in detail and implication as it is classical in construction and stylistic restraint," Paul Binding wrote for the London *Independent* (9 June 2011), "Jacobsen tells us in his foreword that *Child Wonder* is about an Oslo of 'rather rough experimentation. Before oil. Before anybody had any money at all.' This book is, even more, about the perennial sad irregularities of the human heart."

Borders (2015; *Grenser*, 1999) received similarly positive reviews for its tale of literal and emotional bridge-building, set in World War II–era Germany and Luxembourg. However, his next novel, *The Unseen* (2016; *De Usynlige*, 2013), has brought Jacobsen the most attention to date in the English-speaking world. Another intergenerational novel that explores the interplay of traditional lifeways and modernization at the dawn of the twentieth century, *The Unseen* offers the story of a family living on a small, rocky island off Norway's coast. "Stoical, intense, gruffly matter-of-fact," Justine Jordan wrote of the novel's characters in a review for the *Guardian* (12 May 2017). They "endure physical and existential hardship. They also revel in occasional wonders: the softness of eider down, the miracle of a sea frozen for skating, one's own chair to sit on. Yet wider society encroaches, even as their own dreams and ambitions run up against the limits of the land and weather." In an opinion widely shared by other critics, Jordan wrote: "This is a profound interrogation of freedom and fate, as well as a fascinating portrait of a vanished time, written in prose as clear and washed clean as the world after a storm." *The Unseen* was shortlisted for the 2017 Man Booker International Prize, awarded to authors of any nationality for works available in English.

Of his longtime translator Don Bartlett, Jacobsen told Lenarduzzi, "Don has been my protecting angel for years. He says himself that I am the most challenging one of his Scandinavian clients, but I have, to this day, not read a single review without the critic praising the translation—it looks like the book is written originally in English, they say."

Jacobsen also cowrote the screenplay for a little-seen film, *Valhalla Rising* (2009), a bloody epic about a Norse warrior named One-Eye who joins a band of Christian crusaders, lost on their way to the Holy Land.

PERSONAL LIFE

Jacobsen, a member of the Norwegian Academy for Language and Literature, has been married since 1979 to university professor Anneliese Pauline Pitz.

SUGGESTED READING

Binding, Paul. Review of *Child Wonder*, by Roy Jacobsen. *Independent* [London], 9 June 2011, www.independent.co.uk/arts-entertainment/books/reviews/child-wonder-by-roy-jacobsen-trans-don-bartlett-with-don-shaw-2295271.html. Accessed 28 Jan. 2018.

Graham, Tom. "*The Unseen* by Roy Jacobsen—Blunt and Brilliant." *Financial Times*, 12 May 2017, www.ft.com/content/49b39e8e-34c7-11e7-bce4-9023f8c0fd2e. Accessed 28 Jan. 2018.

Jacobsen, Roy. "Essential Norwegian Fiction." Interview by Thea Lenarduzzi. *Five Books*, fivebooks.com/best-books/essential-norwegian-fiction-roy-jacobsen-man-booker/. Accessed 28 Jan. 2018.

Jordan, Justine. "A Profound Interrogation of Freedom and Fate." Review of *The Unseen*, by Roy Jacobsen. *The Guardian*, 12 May 2017, www.theguardian.com/books/2017/may/12/unseen-roy-jacobsen-review-norway. Accessed 28 Jan. 2018.

Sutterud, Tone. Review of *The Burnt-Out Town of Miracles*, by Roy Jacobsen. *Independent* [London], 14 Feb. 2008, www.independent.co.uk/arts-entertainment/books/reviews/the-burnt-out-town-of-miracles-by-roy-jacobsen-trans-don-bartlett-don-shaw-781937.html. Accessed 28 Jan. 2018.

Tankard, Lanie. Review of *Borders*, by Roy Jacobsen. *World Literature Today*, Jan. 2017, www.worldliteraturetoday.org/2017/january/borders-roy-jacobsen. Accessed 28 Jan. 2018.

SELECTED WORKS

The New Water, 1987; *The Burnt-Out Town of Miracles*, 2008; *Child Wonder*, 2011; *Borders*, 2016; *The Unseen*, 2017

—*Mari Rich*

Katrín Jakobsdóttir

Date of birth: February 1, 1976
Occupation: Prime minister of Iceland

In a country where politicians are distrusted and political scandals have resulted in multiple government collapses in recent years, Prime Minister Katrín Jakobsdóttir of Iceland holds a rare distinction: she had been named in numerous polls as her nation's most trusted politician. Jakobsdóttir, who assumed office in late 2017, has wasted no time in putting forth an optimistic, progressive-minded government agenda that includes tackling climate change and gender inequality and further shoring up the national economy, which suffered greatly during the Great Recession of 2008–10.

Although she heads a coalition government comprising three political parties with vastly different viewpoints, Jakobsdóttir believes her fellow citizens will give her government the time it needs to bring about political stability after a decade of economic uncertainty and political scandals. "She is the party leader who can best unite voters from the left and right," Eva H. Önnudóttir, a political scientist at the University of Iceland, said to Richard Martyn-Hemphill for the *New York Times* (30 Nov. 2017). "Because this coalition includes parties from the left to the right, their work will be more about managing the system instead of making 'revolutionary' changes. This could work quite well as long as the economy is stable and prosperous."

EARLY LIFE AND EDUCATION

Hailing from a family of poets and professors, Katrín Jakobsdóttir was born in 1976, in Reykjavík, to parents Jakob Ármannsson and Signý Thoroddsen. She has two older brothers, twins Armann and Sverrir Jakobsson, both of whom are humanities professors at the University of Iceland. Her parents, like her brothers, were literary minded but not members of any political party.

Jakobsdóttir earned her undergraduate degree in Icelandic, with a minor in French, from the University of Iceland in 1999. She then continued her education there, pursuing a master's degree in Icelandic literature, which she received in 2004. Her master's thesis was on the work of Arnaldur Indriðason, the noted Icelandic crime writer.

Prior to her political career, Jakobsdóttir worked for Ríkisútvarpið (RÚV), Iceland's national broadcasting service. She also appeared in the music video "Listen Baby," by the Icelandic band Bang Gang, an episode in her life that continues to amuse political pundits. In an interview with Traci Tong for Public Radio International (PRI) (19 Dec. 2017), she, perhaps facetiously, attributed her diverse professional

By Magnus Fröderberg, via Wikimedia Commons

interests—including literary theory of crime fiction and past appearances in several "pop music videos"—to her country's small population (just under 340,000 as of 2017), noting, "We all have to play a lot of different parts, not least [of all] in a small society like Iceland."

EARLY POLITICAL CAREER

In an interview with Valur Gunnarsson for the *Reykjavík Grapevine* (1 Feb. 2018), Jakobsdóttir explained that while she was not always political, she is "a person of strong opinions" and "was always very socially engaged and wound up in committees, be it at school or in [her] apartment building. . . . When social engagement and strong opinions go together, politics is a natural place to wind up." She joined the Left-Green Movement political party in 2002 because its members, like her, were opposed to the controversial Kárahnjúkar Hydropower Plant project due to the negative environmental impact of its associated dams. During the 2003 election she served as the Left-Greens' election manager in Reykjavík, in charge of getting out the youth vote. She was subsequently asked to become the vice-chair of the party as a representative of young people. The Left-Greens improved their standing in the polls during the 2006 municipal elections.

During the 2007 general elections, Jakobsdóttir ran for and won a seat as a member of the Althingi, Iceland's national parliament. The Althingi consists of sixty-three seats and is headed by the prime minister, who achieves the position by being the leader of the majority party or, when no single party holds a majority of seats, a majority coalition of two or more parties.

Shortly after Jakobsdóttir took her seat as a member of parliament, Iceland—along with the rest of the world—was faced with the economic fallout of the Great Recession, which pushed the nation nearly to the point of bankruptcy. In response, Iceland's government sought to stabilize the economy while tackling issues such as wealth inequality. A tourism boom helped bring about an economic recovery and shrink unemployment, as well as fuel the country's long-term goal to become completely carbon neutral by 2040, which has been aided, in part, by the national reliance on geothermal energy.

The lessons Jakobsdóttir learned in those early days in the Althingi have remained with her. "[The recession] was a great shock to the nation," she recalled to Tong. "And I should say that even though we have recovered quite well economically, we haven't quite recovered when it comes to the political situation, trust in politics, our confidence in politicians, it's been very low. I've gone through five elections so you can imagine the turbulence that's been here."

CABINET MINISTER

During this period of turbulence, from 2009 to 2013, Jakobsdóttir served as the minister of education, science, and culture in the cabinet of Jóhanna Sigurðardóttir, Iceland's first female prime minister, who presided over a coalition government between the Social Democratic Alliance and the Left-Greens. Because of the economic uncertainty of the period, she found herself having to make cuts to educational programs that she personally supported. "It was a strange position to be in," she said to Gunnarsson. "I am very passionate about these issues and yet I had to make budget cuts. I tried to be in good contact with all interested parties to find out how best to go about this. I think on the whole, the education system performed admirably in those trying times, for example by allowing people to study who had lost their jobs."

Shortly before the 2013 parliamentary election, Left-Green founding member Steingrímur J. Sigfússon announced that he would be stepping down from the position of party chair, which he had held since the Left-Green Movement's formation in 1999. Jakobsdóttir, then the vice-chair, decided to run for the position and was elected in February 2013. Two months later, in the parliamentary election, Sigurðardóttir's coalition government was voted out of office, and Jakobsdóttir again found herself as a member of the opposition in the Althingi. She did not see this as a defeat, however, or as a reason to potentially reassess her career choice. "I often feel I do better in adversity," she explained to Gunnarsson. "We felt we could learn a lot from our

cabinet experience and did a lot of work within our party. . . . I felt it was a worthwhile challenge. But at the same time, it must be said that it can be challenging to turn being in opposition into a creative endeavor. Even if we try to be effective, the goal is to always be able to affect policy changes, and the best way to do this is to be in government."

BECOMING PRIME MINISTER

Snap elections have become more frequent in Iceland since 2009, shortly after the financial crisis rocked the country, but the successive elections in 2016 and 2017 were prompted by scandals of a political nature. In 2016 the government headed by Prime Minister Sigmundur Davíð Gunnlaugsson, Sigurðardóttir's successor and the leader of the center-right Independence Party–Progressive Party coalition government, was brought down by the public outcry following the revelation that his family had sheltered a fortune in offshore accounts to keep it safe from taxation. Then, in 2017, the new three-party coalition government, headed by Independence Party leader Bjarni Benediktsson, lost its majority after just ten months in office when the Bright Future political party left the coalition following the revelation that Benediktsson had attempted to cover up his father's efforts to restore the reputation of a convicted child sex offender. Despite the scandal surrounding Benediktsson, his Independence Party won a narrow majority in the October 2017 elections, but they had lost so many seats that the two runner-up parties, the Left-Greens and the Progressive Party, were tapped to form a coalition government. The Left-Greens agreed on the condition, supported by the Progressives, that Jakobsdóttir become prime minister; in exchange, Benediktsson would be appointed finance minister.

The new coalition government formed under Jakobsdóttir's premiership, which took power on November 30, 2017, comprised three very different political parties: her own Left-Green Movement, which would have the prime minister's office as well as the ministries of health and the environment; the center-right Independence Party, which would control the ministries of finance, foreign affairs, fishing, and business; and the Progressive Party, a center-right agrarian party, which would be in charge of the ministries of transportation, education, and welfare. Many political pundits contended that a coalition government of such different political leanings would not last long, as no three-party coalition had lasted for a full term since Iceland proclaimed itself a republic in 1944. The new prime minister, however, remained optimistic at the outset of her term. "We have seen great changes in the party structure and many new parties running," she said to Gunnarsson shortly after taking office. "I think this coalition government is an attempt to shake up old ideas about the party structure. It may be taking a risk, but so is being alive."

PRIORITIES AS PRIME MINISTER

At the start of her government's term in office, Jakobsdóttir outlined her priorities as prime minister: continuing to add stability to Iceland's economic recovery; investing more in education, health care, and green technologies; and improving the country's civil rights record, particularly in gender equality. One of her government's first efforts was the implementation of a law designed to shame companies with more than twenty-four employees into shrinking the pay gap between men and women by forcing them to obtain government certification that employees are paid equally for doing the same job regardless of sex. Failure to obtain certification could result in fines.

Another focus was ensuring the stability of the Icelandic currency, the krona, the value of which had been in flux for some time. A panel of economists had been empowered by the previous government to investigate the options, among them whether the krona should be pegged to another currency, such as the US dollar, or whether it should have a floating or a fixed exchange rate. Jakobsdóttir said to Ragnhildur Sigurdardottir for *Bloomberg* (29 Jan. 2018) that her government would explore the panel's proposals, such as "whether connecting the krona to another currency is a viable option." She added, "My personal view is that we should continue with the Icelandic krona, but with a stricter framework."

Other issues facing Jakobsdóttir's fledgling government include whether to remain in the North Atlantic Treaty Organization (NATO), involvement in which her party has long been opposed to; additional efforts to promote a lifestyle that will curb the country's contributions to anthropogenic climate change; and absorbing more refugees from war-torn nations.

PERSONAL LIFE

Katrín Jakobsdóttir is married to Gunnar Örn Sigvaldason, with whom she has three sons. Although she enjoys her life in politics, she also sees a life for herself outside of it—possibility involving literature again, or perhaps writing a novel herself—but she has no definite personal plans. "I am a great believer in planning for the long-term in politics, but I never make long-term plans for myself," she said to Gunnarsson. "In politics, you are never quite in control of what happens—you can only try to deal with the tasks before you and then events take their course."

SUGGESTED READING

Carlin, John. "A Nordic Revolution: The Heroines of Reykjavik." *The Independent*, 20 Apr. 2012, www.independent.co.uk/news/world/europe/a-nordic-revolution-the-heroines-of-reykjavik-7658212.html. Accessed 2 Mar. 2018.

Henley, Jon. "Iceland Seeks Return to Political Stability with New Prime Minister." *The Guardian*, 30 Nov. 2017, www.theguardian.com/world/2017/nov/30/iceland-prime-minister-katrin-jakobsdottir-left-green-movement. Accessed 2 Mar. 2018.

Jakobsdóttir, Katrín. "From Crime Fiction to Running the Government: Meet Iceland's New Prime Minister." Interview by Valur Gunnarsson. *The Reykjavik Grapevine*, 1 Feb. 2018, grapevine.is/mag/feature/2018/02/01/from-crime-fiction-to-running-the-government-we-meet-with-icelands-new-pm/. Accessed 2 Mar. 2018.

Jakobsdóttir, Katrín. "Iceland's Most Trusted Politician Is a Feminist Environmentalist Who Is the 'AntiTrump.'" Interview by Traci Tong. *PRI*, Public Radio International, 19 Dec. 2017, www.pri.org/stories/2017-12-19/icelands-most-trusted-politician-feminist-environmentalist-who-antitrump. Accessed 2 Mar. 2018.

Martyn-Hemphill, Richard. "An Environmentalist Is Iceland's New Prime Minister." *The New York Times*, 30 Nov. 2017, www.nytimes.com/2017/11/30/world/europe/iceland-prime-minister-katrin-jakobsdottir.html. Accessed 2 Mar. 2018.

Sigurdardottir, Ragnhildur. "Iceland's New Leader Wants 'Strict' New Currency Regime." *Bloomberg*, 29 Jan. 2018, www.bloomberg.com/news/articles/2018-01-30/iceland-s-new-leader-wants-strict-new-currency-regime. Accessed 2 Mar. 2018.

Stone, Jon. "Left-Greens' Katrin Jakobsdottir Becomes Iceland's New Prime Minister at Head of Coalition Government." *The Independent*, 1 Dec. 2017, www.independent.co.uk/news/world/europe/iceland-new-government-katrin-jakobsdottir-coalition-prime-minister-left-green-independence-party-a8086281.html. Accessed 2 Mar. 2018.

—*Christopher Mari*

Patty Jenkins

Date of birth: July 24, 1971
Occupation: Director

Throughout her career, director Patty Jenkins has been proving the conventional wisdom of the film industry wrong, perhaps nowhere more notably than with the success of her blockbuster 2017 film *Wonder Woman*. The film, the first live-action feature to center on the famed DC Comics superhero, proved tremendously popular upon its release, grossing more than $800 million worldwide and making Jenkins the first female director to achieve such financial success with a single film. For Jenkins, the success of the film was a sign that many decision makers in the film industry had a poor understanding of American and global audiences. "People really thought that only men loved action movies and only men would go see a superhero movie," she told Hermione Hoby for the *Guardian* (26 May 2017). With its financial and critical success, *Wonder Woman* demonstrated that such stereotypes about fans of superhero films were entirely wrong.

Educated at New York's Cooper Union and California's American Film Institute, Jenkins began her career as a camera operator for commercials and music videos but established herself as a talented director to watch with her 2003 film *Monster*, a crime film about the real-life serial killer Aileen Wuornos. Jenkins defied conventional wisdom for that early film as well, making it on a very low budget and casting actor Charlize Theron, who was not yet known for her dramatic work but would win an Academy Award for her portrayal of Wuornos, in the lead role. Following the success of *Monster*, she directed a variety of well-received television projects before moving on to *Wonder Woman*, a project that she notes has become much more than just a film. "To have such pure response come back from people talking about heroes, talking about the future, talking about love—that blows my mind," she told Gina McIntyre for *Rolling Stone* (2 June 2017). "It's so powerful that what I wanted to talk about is also what everybody wanted to talk about. That's a beautiful, uniting experience to make a film that does that."

EARLY LIFE

Patricia Lea Jenkins was born on July 24, 1971, at George Air Force Base in Victorville, California. Her father, William T. Jenkins, was an officer and fighter pilot in the US Air Force, and her mother, Emily Roth, was an environmental scientist. Jenkins has two sisters, one of whom, older sister Elaine Roth, went on to become a film professor. Her family moved frequently during her early years due to the demands of her father's

By Gage Skidmore [CC BY-SA 2.0], via Wikimedia Commons

career, and they spent time in countries such as Thailand, Germany, and Cambodia. When she was seven, her father died in a plane crash during a training exercise. The family then settled in Kansas, and she spent much of the remainder of her early years in the city of Lawrence.

Jenkins's interest in the arts, and especially film, began early in life. She has noted often in interviews that she was particularly inspired by the 1978 film *Superman*, directed by Richard Donner and starring actor Christopher Reeve in the title role. "In 1978, when *Superman* came out, that movie made me have an experience that I had never [had] before. I cried for Superman, I wanted to be Superman. That's the most powerful artistic experience I had as a child," she said of the film, as quoted by Borys Kit and Mia Galuppo in the *Hollywood Reporter* (23 July 2016). While in junior high school, she had her first experience with the behind-the-scenes aspects of filmmaking, serving as a production assistant for a documentary about the Beat poets. As a teenager attending a high school with a strong arts program, she often visited the Lawrence campus of the University of Kansas to attend screenings of art house films. She left the city after her junior year of high school and spent her senior year in the Washington, DC, area.

EDUCATION AND EARLY CAREER

After graduating from high school, Jenkins moved to New York City. She enrolled in the Cooper Union to study painting and photography, which, at the time, were her preferred art forms. During her first year at the college, however, she took a film course that instantly changed her path as an artist. "The second I sat down putting pictures to music, it was the most authentic relationship I had ever had to art," she recalled in an interview for the Cooper Union's website (27 July 2017). "I was like, 'I can't stop doing this. I have to figure this out.'" Following that experience, she changed her focus to film studies, eventually graduating from the Cooper Union in 1993.

Jenkins began her career as a camera operator for a variety of short-form projects, including hundreds of commercials and music videos. She turned her attention primarily to directing, however, after moving to California to study directing at the American Film Institute, from which she earned her master's degree in 2000. During her early years as a director, she observed and was perplexed by a major gender disparity in her chosen field, which was largely male dominated. "I'm sure there's a long history of belief that certain jobs are masculine," she later explained to Tatiana Siegel for the *Hollywood Reporter* (31 May 2017). "But why a director would fall into that [category] makes me very confused. Because it feels like a very natural job for a woman. It's incredibly maternal in a way. You're caretaking all of these sorts of things." Following her graduation from the American Film Institute, she began gaining experience as a director with work such as the 2001 short films *Just Drive* and *Velocity Rules*, which she also wrote.

MONSTER

During her early years in the film industry, Jenkins began to think about writing and directing a film focused on Aileen Wuornos, a serial killer who murdered several men in the late 1980s and early 1990s. To gain a better understanding of Wuornos, Jenkins reached out to her and, just prior to Wuornos's execution in 2002, was granted access to letters she wrote while in prison. Having gained Wuornos's trust, Jenkins was adamant that she was the only filmmaker who should handle her story. "There was no negotiation, it was going to be me or no one," she recalled to Lisa Rosen for *DGA Quarterly* (2013). "I had been given the responsibility to see it through, and that's what was going to have to happen."

Produced on a low budget, Jenkins's debut feature film, *Monster*, was released in a limited number of theaters in December 2003 and had a subsequent wide release in January 2004. Prior to the release of the film, *Monster* gained attention in the media for Jenkins's decision to cast South African–born actor and former model Theron, who was not known for her dramatic work, in the lead role. "Nobody else would have done that," Theron told Siegel, regarding Jenkins's choice. "It was very, very unusual. She

looked at me in a way that nobody has ever looked at me." Jenkins's dedication to her film's subject and seemingly risky casting choice paid off: *Monster* received extensive critical acclaim and was nominated for numerous awards, claiming the award for best first feature at the Film Independent Spirit Awards and the Academy Award for best actress for Theron.

TELEVISION WORK

Following her work on *Monster*, Jenkins primarily took on opportunities in television, directing episodes of series in a variety of genres. Although she first became widely known for directing projects that she had developed and written, she enjoyed having the opportunity to work on other professionals' television projects. "If you love the show and respect the people involved, living up to somebody else's vision is a great learning ground," she told Rosen. She directed a 2004 episode of the comedy *Arrested Development* and in 2006 directed two episodes of the HBO series *Entourage*. She went on to win acclaim for the 2011 pilot and 2012 finale episode of the series *The Killing*, earning an Emmy Award nomination and a Directors Guild of America Award for her work on the pilot. She later directed the pilot episode of the 2013 series *Betrayal*.

Although Jenkins was involved in the developmental stages of several film projects during that period, a Jenkins-directed film was not released for more than a decade after the premiere of *Monster*, despite her success with that film. In some cases, her projects languished in the developmental stage, whereas in others, she opted to walk away from projects that she considered to be troubled. "I thought, 'If I take this, it'll be a big disservice to women. If I take this knowing it's going to be trouble and then it looks like it was me, that's going to be a problem,'" she told Siegel of one project, which Siegel identified as most likely the 2013 Marvel superhero film *Thor: The Dark World*. "'If they do it with a man, it will just be yet another mistake that the studio made. But with me, it's going to look like I dropped the ball, and it's going to send a very bad message.'"

WONDER WOMAN

Long intrigued by superheroes, Jenkins reportedly first pitched her idea for a film based on the DC Comics character Wonder Woman in 2010. Created by psychologist William Moulton Marston and debuted in DC's *All Star Comics* in 1941, Wonder Woman was among the most iconic of DC's superheroes and was featured in a variety of media adaptations, including a television show that aired during Jenkins's childhood. However, the character had not yet headlined a live-action feature film, and Jenkins saw an opportunity to create a compelling action-filled film focusing on a female superhero. In April 2015, five years after she had first pitched a Wonder Woman film, she was hired to direct a film featuring the character, who would first appear in 2016's *Batman v Superman: Dawn of Justice.*

In directing *Wonder Woman*, Jenkins focused on the character's status as an iconic figure who in some ways represents the fantasies of her female fans, much in the same way as DC's male superheroes reflect the fantasies of their male fans. "It would be more practical if Batman were built like a very small rock climber, it would be much easier to get into spaces, to do all kinds of things. Well, that's not your fantasy. Your fantasy is he's unreasonably big and built," she explained to Hoby. "Good. My fantasy is that I could wake up looking amazing, that I could be strong and stop the bully but that everybody would love me too. I think that's intrinsic to fantasy." Overall, Jenkins emphasized her goal to represent the complexity of Wonder Woman's character, balancing her strength with her iconic spirit and compassion. Starring Israeli actor Gal Gadot in the title role, the film follows Wonder Woman—also known as Diana—as she leaves her island home and fellow Amazon warriors to defeat the war god Ares and help American pilot and spy Steve Trevor (Chris Pine) prevent the development of a deadly chemical weapon during World War I.

With an estimated budget of nearly $150 million and worldwide grosses of more than $800 million, *Wonder Woman* was the most expensive film to be directed by a woman and became the highest-grossing live-action film by a female director following its release in the summer of 2017. The film received a positive response from superhero fans (both male and female) as well as the general public, and critics widely regarded it to be the best of the ongoing series of DC superhero films released to date. In September 2017, it was announced that Jenkins would return to direct a Wonder Woman sequel, scheduled for release in December 2019. She also announced that she would reunite with the film's costar, Pine, for the TNT miniseries *One Day She'll Darken.*

PERSONAL LIFE

Jenkins married writer Sam Sheridan in 2007. They live in Santa Monica, California, with their son. In addition to her artistic pursuits, she enjoys rollerblading and skiing.

SUGGESTED READING

Hoby, Hermione. "*Wonder Woman* Director Patty Jenkins: 'People Really Thought That Only Men Loved Action Movies.'" *The Guardian*, 26 May 2017, www.theguardian.com/film/2017/may/26/wonder-woman-director-patty-jenkins-people-really-thought-that-only-men-loved-action-movies. Accessed 14 Dec. 2017.

Jenkins, Patty. "Art School Superhero." *The Cooper Union*, 27 July 2017, cooper.edu/art/news/art-school-superhero. Accessed 14 Dec. 2017.

Jenkins, Patty. "*Wonder Woman* Director Patty Jenkins: 'We Need a New Kind of Hero.'" Interview by Gina McIntyre. *Rolling Stone*, 2 June 2017, www.rollingstone.com/movies/features/wonder-woman-director-we-need-a-new-kind-of-hero-w485183. Accessed 14 Dec. 2017.

Niccum, Jon. "How to Build a 'Monster.'" *Lawrence Journal-World*, 16 Jan. 2004, ljworld.com/news/2004/jan/16/how_to_build/. Accessed 14 Dec. 2017.

Rosen, Lisa. "Natural-Born Director." *DGA Quarterly*, 2013, www.dga.org/Craft/DGAQ/All-Articles/1301-Winter-2013/Director-Patty-Jenkins.aspx. Accessed 14 Dec. 2017.

Siegel, Tatiana. "The Complex Gender Politics of the *Wonder Woman* Movie." *The Hollywood Reporter*, 31 May 2017, www.hollywoodreporter.com/features/complex-gender-politics-wonder-woman-movie-1008259. Accessed 14 Dec. 2017.

SELECTED WORKS

Monster, 2003; *The Killing*, 2011–12; *Wonder Woman*, 2017

—*Joy Crelin*

Clifford V. Johnson

Date of birth: March 5, 1968
Occupation: Physicist

"Science belongs to everyone," theoretical physicist Clifford V. Johnson declared to Greg Bernhardt for *Physics Forums Insights* (26 Feb. 2018). Indeed, Johnson's career itself has aptly demonstrated the truth of that assertion. An award-winning physics professor and an accomplished researcher in theoretical physics, he first became interested in scientific experimentation and asking questions about the world long before learning that science was a viable career. Johnson eventually earned his doctorate from the University of Southampton and found work at a series of universities before joining the faculty of the University of Southern California (USC) in 2003.

In the decades since, Johnson has established himself as a valuable contributor to the public understanding of science, rendering complex physics concepts understandable by a general audience through his appearances in

Photo by Sonia Recchia/Getty Images for Sundance Film Festival

science documentaries and his 2017 graphic novel, *The Dialogues: Conversations about the Nature of the Universe*. He has notably served as a consultant for major film and television companies such as Marvel Studios, contributing elements of scientific fact to blockbuster superhero films and other projects. For Johnson, scientific outreach is among the most significant aspects of his work as a physics educator. "I get to drive home the idea that science is in the mouths of everyday people, and out there in the world, as opposed to specialists in a lab or seminar room," he told Adam Frank for NPR's *13.7: Cosmos & Culture* blog (23 Feb. 2018).

EARLY LIFE AND EDUCATION

Clifford Victor Johnson was born on March 5, 1968, in London, England. The youngest of three children born to Delia O'Garro and Victor Johnson, he has a brother named Robert and a sister named Carol. In 1972, the family moved from the United Kingdom to Montserrat, a British territory in the Caribbean, where Johnson's father had been born. Johnson spent much of his early life in Montserrat, where he lived with his mother following his father and siblings' successive returns to England. When Johnson was fourteen, he and his mother returned to England as well, settling in the city of Preston. His father later rejoined them there.

As a youth, Johnson enjoyed reading comic books and playing guitar. He exhibited a curious nature early in life and soon found himself drawn to science. "I just asked lots of questions about the world, and found ways to get them answered, either by experimenting, or taking things apart and putting them back together, or reading about things. I got hooked on that, and I guess people left me alone to just get on with that," he told Bernhardt. He added, "I later learned that there was this career where you could just continue asking questions and figuring out how stuff worked, which is what I liked to do anyway."

After completing secondary school, Johnson enrolled in Imperial College, then part of the University of London. He earned his Bachelor of Science degree in physics there in 1989. Although he enjoyed the experimental side of physics, Johnson found himself particularly drawn to theoretical physics as a discipline. "As I learned more about how careers worked it seemed that more and more you had to choose either experiment or theory, and theory seemed to allow me to go as deep or as wide as I wanted," he explained to Bernhardt. Johnson went on to pursue a doctorate in theoretical physics at the University of Southampton, earning his PhD in 1992. His doctoral thesis focused on string theory.

TEACHING CAREER

Following his time at the University of Southampton, Johnson traveled to the United States to take a position at Princeton University's prestigious Institute for Advanced Study School of Natural Sciences. He remained at that institution until mid-1994, at which time he received several fellowships, including a NATO Fellowship from the UK's Science and Engineering Research Council (now the Engineering and Physical Sciences Research Council). He served as a lecturer and postdoctoral researcher at Princeton for a time before moving on to the University of California (UC), Santa Barbara, in September 1995. Serving as a postdoctoral research associate within the university's Institute for Theoretical Physics, Johnson remained in Santa Barbara into 1997.

In 1997, Johnson took an assistant professorship at the University of Kentucky. While there, Johnson received a National Science Foundation (NSF) grant that supported his research and enabled the university to bring in additional visiting researchers. He returned to England in 2000 to serve as a professor at Durham University. Although he enjoyed working at the university, where he was considered a member of the Department of Mathematical Sciences rather than the Department of Physics, he returned to California in 2003 to take a full-time position at USC; until the 2006–7 academic year, Johnson also maintained a visiting professorship at Durham. "Once you've been to California, southern California, you tend to find your way back eventually," he explained to Larry Crowe in an oral history interview for the *HistoryMakers* website (26 Apr. 2011).

RESEARCH

In August 2003, Johnson joined the faculty of USC as a professor within the Department of Physics and Astronomy. A member of the USC Theoretical High Energy Physics Group, Johnson has focused his research efforts on gaining a greater understanding of the universe through the study of string theory, quantum field theory, and gravity, among other areas. "I like to say I work on origins questions," he told Deborah Netburn for the *Los Angeles Times* (9 Jan. 2018). "So, what's everything made of? Where does it come from? What is the origin of space and time?" Johnson was later awarded the university's Albert S. Raubenheimer Award in 2005 for his work as both a teacher and a researcher. Around this same time, Johnson helped organize the short-lived African Summer Theory Institute, intended to foster the sharing of scientific findings and encourage collaboration among different universities and career stages.

Over the course of his career, Johnson has published numerous works on his findings. He gained significant attention for "Notes on D-Branes," coauthored with fellow postdoctoral researcher Shyamoli Chaudhuri and established researcher Joseph Polchinski, which popularized Polchinski's approach to a particular area of string theory. "Suddenly everybody was on the same page literally. They had the same techniques in the same notation in the same normalization in a nice, handy set of notes that Joe had given, and we'd sort of expanded and helped him write into this nice form," Johnson recalled to Crowe. "And so those notes became super famous. Everybody had a copy of those notes in the field." Johnson continued to work on D-branes over the next years and in 2003 published the monograph *D-Branes*. He likewise authored and coauthored dozens of papers on a variety of topics over the following decades, publishing his work in journals such as *Physics Letters*, *Physical Review*, and the *Journal of High Energy Physics*. In recognition of his contributions as a researcher, Johnson received the James Clerk Maxwell Medal and Prize from the United Kingdom's Institute of Physics in 2005.

SCIENTIFIC OUTREACH

Throughout his career, Johnson has focused extensively on making physics more accessible to the public, and particularly to women and minorities who are underrepresented in the sciences. Among his projects have been multiple efforts to convey scientific concepts through mediums other than scholarly publications. "I see physics as storytelling," he opined to April Wolfe for *LA Weekly* (18 May 2017). "To some

extent, all of science is. Not just in communicating the idea but the whole business of finding out why a thing is the way it is and how that thing gets to be the way it is. These are the same sets of questions we ask when we're telling stories." A prolific blogger, Johnson has discussed topics related to his work on his own blog, *Asymptotia*, and contributed to various other blogs and websites.

In 2017, Johnson took a new approach to scientific outreach, publishing the graphic novel *The Dialogues: Conversations about the Nature of the Universe*. Presenting a series of eleven conversations between different characters, the work explores scientific concepts in a manner that is accessible to nonscientists yet does not neglect to address complex issues. A fan of comic books since childhood, Johnson chose to write a graphic novel, in part, because of a dearth of science-related material in that medium. "I'd love to read more graphic books for grown-ups that are primarily about science ideas (as opposed to biographical accounts of scientists, or adventure stories that include science)," he told Frank. "Surprisingly, there just aren't many, so that's a reason I made mine." Rather than working with an established illustrator, Johnson taught himself to draw so that he could complete the artwork for the book himself. "I succeeded through gradually figuring out what my strengths and weaknesses were and then practicing. A lot. Which is really the only way to learn to draw," he told Frank.

In addition to his written works, Johnson contributes frequently to television programs, podcasts, and other media dealing with theoretical physics. Among other programs, he has appeared in documentary series such as *Nova*, *The Universe*, and *Horizon*. He likewise served as a scientific consultant for the play *Dark Matters* by Oliver Mayer, associate dean of the USC School of Dramatic Arts. In 2018, the American Association of Physics Teachers recognized Johnson's contributions to the public as a physics educator with the Klopsteg Memorial Lecture Award.

SCIENCE IN FILM

Although Johnson has long consulted for creators of a variety of media, he gained attention in the 2010s for his contributions to major film and television projects. He is perhaps best known as a frequent consultant for Marvel Studios, having provided scientific input for superhero-related projects such as the television series *Agent Carter* and the blockbuster film *Thor: Ragnarok*. "What I spend most of my time doing involves scientific believability and consistency," Johnson explained to Wolfe. "I study how our existing universe works, and my job is to study those rules so I can help [creators] build a different universe with its own rules, where all your crazy stuff can happen. But then they have to allow me to help make it consistent." In addition to his work for Marvel Studios, Johnson has consulted on projects such as *Star Trek: Discovery*, an installment in the long-running Star Trek television franchise, and the first season of the television series *Genius*, which focuses on the life of physicist Albert Einstein.

PERSONAL LIFE

Johnson lives in Southern California with his second wife and son (b. 2014). In addition to sketching and blogging, he gardens, cycles, and bakes in his free time.

SUGGESTED READING

"Clifford Johnson." *HistoryMakers*, 26 Apr. 2011, www.idvl.org/sciencemakers/Bio39.html. Accessed 13 Apr. 2018.

"Clifford V. Johnson Named as Recipient of the 2018 Klopsteg Memorial Lecture Award." *American Association of Physics Teachers*, 8 Mar. 2018, www.aapt.org/aboutaapt/Clifford-Johnson-2018-Klopsteg.cfm. Accessed 13 Apr. 2018.

Johnson, Clifford V. "Clifford Johnson." Interview by Larry Crowe. *The ScienceMakers*, The HistoryMakers, 26 Apr. 2011, smdigital.the-historymakers.org/storiesForBio;ID=A2011.0 34;sID=31083. Accessed 13 Apr. 2018.

Johnson, Clifford V. "'The Dialogues' Takes on Physics and Reality in Words and Pictures." Interview by Adam Frank. *13.7: Cosmos & Culture*, NPR, 23 Feb. 2018, www.npr.org/sections/13.7/2018/02/23/588243747/the-dialogues-takes-on-physics-and-reality-in-words-and-pictures. Accessed 13 Apr. 2018.

Johnson, Clifford V. "Interview with Theoretical Physicist Clifford V. Johnson." By Greg Bernhardt. *Physics Forums Insights*, Bernhardt, 26 Feb. 2018, www.physicsforums.com/insights/interview-theoretical-physicist-clifford-johnson. Accessed 13 Apr. 2018.

Netburn, Deborah. "This USC Physicist Wants You to Talk about Science. His New Graphic Novel Can Get You Started." *Los Angeles Times*, 9 Jan. 2018, www.latimes.com/science/la-sci-sn-talking-about-science-20180109-htmlstory.html. Accessed 13 Apr. 2018.

Wolfe, April. "Meet the Physicist Marvel Calls to Consult on Superhero Movies." *LA Weekly*, 18 May 2017, www.laweekly.com/film/physicist-dr-clifford-v-johnson-is-a-consultant-on-superhero-movies-8232890. Accessed 13 Apr. 2018.

—*Joy Crelin*

Leslie Jones

Date of birth: September 7, 1967
Occupation: Comedian, actor

Comedian and actor Leslie Jones's life changed forever after she won a college comedy competition. "As soon as I touched the mic I knew that's what I would do for the rest of my life," she shared with Emily Strohm for *People* (14 July 2016). After around twenty-five years on the comedy circuit, managing the highs and lows of the stand-up world, she landed her big break in 2013, when she first auditioned to join the cast of the long-running NBC sketch-comedy series *Saturday Night Live* (*SNL*). Despite not making the initial cut, she was hired as a staff writer before graduating to the cast in 2014.

Though, like many comedians, some of Jones's blunt material has generated backlash on social media, such as her *SNL* debut in front of the camera—a "Weekend Update" monologue about slavery—overall, her comedic talent has been praised, and she has earned the greater exposure and opportunities that she craved as an often-struggling stand-up comic. In addition to landing a lead role in the all-female *Ghostbusters* (2016) reboot, as a longtime enthusiast she served as a contributor for NBC's coverage of the Olympics in both 2016 Summer Games and 2018 Winter Games. Speaking to Andrew Marantz for the *New Yorker* (4 Jan. 2016), Jones's *SNL* castmate Michael Che summed up her raw comedic appeal: "It's not that Leslie yells and screams and jumps around. It's that she's

Photo by Mark Sagliocco/WireImage, via Getty Images

brutally honest, and she knows how to sell material more convincingly than anyone I can think of. As soon as she walks onstage, you know she's the boss."

EARLY LIFE AND EDUCATION

Jones was born on September 7, 1967, in Memphis, Tennessee. Her family relocated to Lynwood, California, around 1979, when her father accepted a position at KJLH, Stevie Wonder's newly acquired R & B radio station. She grew up listening to her father's comedy albums and remembers being inspired by comics such as Whoopi Goldberg and Richard Pryor. "It was just that feeling from laughing really, really hard and getting that tickling feeling in your stomach," she recalled to Sylvia Obell for *BuzzFeed* (24 June 2017). "I wanted to make people feel like that."

Jones's involvement in sports also began early. Recruited to join the girls' basketball team after a coach spotted her walking to class, Jones, who grew to be six feet tall, subsequently honed her skills playing for Lynwood High School.

Upon graduating from high school, Jones attended Chapman University on a basketball scholarship. By her sophomore year, she had transferred to Colorado State University (CSU) at the invitation of her former Chapman coach, who had just been hired at CSU. "The plan was to get an education and then maybe play for the U.S. Olympic team," she told Tony Phifer for *Colorado State: The Magazine for Alumni and Friends* (Fall 2015). However, her life officially went in a different direction in November 1987, when a friend secretly entered her in a "Funniest Person on Campus" contest. Jones easily won the title—and confirmed her calling. "The stage felt like home, and I felt that mic (microphone) had been part of my life forever," she shared with Phifer. "It all came together the first time I heard that laughter."

COMEDY FULL TIME

Determined to become "the next Eddie Murphy," as Jones noted to Nosheen Iqbal for the *Guardian* (7 July 2016), she left basketball and CSU, returning to California to pursue comedy full time. After only a month, she booked a promising gig opening for Jamie Foxx, but she struggled. "I wasn't good. I didn't have anything to talk about," she admitted to Erin Udell for the *Coloradoan* (18 Apr. 2016). While consoling Jones over a meal following the show, Foxx suggested that, as she was still young, she should go out and gain some valuable real-life experience that would provide much-needed material for her stand-up routine.

Over the next several years, Jones honed her chops on the local comedy scene and supported herself with various part-time jobs, ranging from UPS worker, cook, and cashier to fragrance sales

associate and justice of the peace. Her perseverance paid off. In 1994, Jones, then a server at soul-food chain Roscoe's Chicken and Waffles, made her small-screen debut on the BET (Black Entertainment Television) showcase *ComicView* before appearing in the comedy shorts *Sploosh* (1998) and *Does That Make Me a Bad Person?* (1998). Next came bit parts in the dramatic short *A Feeling Called Glory* (2000) and the made-for-television movie *Mermaid* (2000).

Jones began making headway on the comedy circuit during the first decade of the 2000s, competing on NBC's *It's Showtime at the Apollo* and performing on several showcase series, including the Starz original program *Martin Lawrence Presents: 1st Amendment Stand Up* (2005) and HBO's long-running *Def Comedy Jam*. At the same time, she appeared in the big-screen comedies *A Guy Thing* (2003) and *National Security* (2003), the UPN sitcom *Girlfriends* (2004), and Master P's straight-to-DVD feature *Repos* (2006). Her 2007 credits included *Gangsta Rap: The Glockumentary* and the short-lived Comedy Central sitcom *American Body Shop*.

SNL WRITER

Jones's next big break on the comedy circuit came when she opened for Katt Williams on his six-month comedy tour, which kicked off in January 2008 and hit more than one hundred cities. A year later, she taped her very first stand-up special in front of a live audience at a theater in Hollywood; *Problem Child* premiered on the Showtime cable network in February 2010. Around that time, she also made a fateful decision regarding her stand-up career. "I stopped only doing black clubs," she recounted to Marantz. "I knew how to relate to that audience, and I was winning where I was, but I wasn't moving forward."

Jones secured a regular prime-time slot at Los Angeles's Comedy Store, where she started experimenting more with crowd work and less with just telling jokes. There, she had a memorable run-in with Chris Rock, whom she had first met on the male-dominated circuit during the late 1980s. "I remember being at a comedy gig and saying to him: 'I'm not going to make it unless someone like you puts me on,'" she recalled to Iqbal. "Then he saw me at the Comedy Store . . . and he was like: 'That's next level. You've next-levelled.'" Her breakthrough finally came in December 2013. On Rock's recommendation, she was among several comedians auditioning for *SNL* following comments about the show's lack of racial diversity. She was not the least bit intimidated by *SNL*'s producers, including the show's legendary creator, Lorne Michaels. "I got onstage, took the mike out of the stand, and went, 'Nope. Y'all are gonna have to move up to where I can see you.' And Lorne got . . . up and moved," she explained to Marantz.

Despite losing out to Sasheer Zamata, Jones impressed Michaels, who offered her a staff writer position. On May 3, 2014, months into her new gig, she debuted on-camera during SNL's "Weekend Update." The monologue, during which she joked about women in slavery and breeding, proved controversial, and its sensitive nature prompted significant Twitter backlash from the African American community. In response, Jones questioned whether any of her male counterparts would have been similarly treated and remained unapologetic about the joke.

SNL CAST AND *GHOSTBUSTERS*

In the fall of 2014, Jones took on a role in Rock's semiautobiographical feature *Top Five* before returning to SNL, where, despite not considering herself much of an impressionist and having not watched the show regularly herself, she was promoted to featured player, an opportunity that she has not taken for granted following years of hard work. (She performed double duty until the following May.) In another breakout opportunity, her appearance on the show had also convinced writer-director Paul Feig to cast her in his all-female reboot of the 1984 science-fiction box-office hit *Ghostbusters*. "I don't normally like when actors are big and loud," Feig told Marantz. "But she was able to do it with this grounded, relatable sort of energy." Additionally, her *Top Five* performance led director Judd Apatow to write a cameo for her in the Amy Schumer summer hit *Trainwreck* (2015). Later that year, she voiced a character in *The Awesomes*, SNL alum Seth Meyers's animated series, and as part of the SNL writing team, she received a nod from the Writers Guild of America (WGA) in the comedy/variety series category.

After the *Ghostbusters* trailer was released in March 2016, it garnered negative Twitter comments for its largely female cast and for its depiction of Jones's Patty Tolan character—the quartet's only nonscientist and nonwhite character. Jones denied that her role—a street-savvy New York City transit employee—was stereotypical and insisted the focus should not be on gender or class. Upon its release to theaters, the film received mixed reviews from both critics and audiences, but it succeeded in familiarizing a wider viewership with Jones's comedic presence.

OLYMPICS AND OTHER PROJECTS

Barrages of hateful tweets prompted by the film led Jones to take a brief hiatus from the social media platform. Despite this, upon her return to Twitter, Jones began offering witty real-time observations of the 2016 Summer Olympics in Rio de Janeiro, Brazil. Former SNL producer Mike Shoemaker eventually persuaded Jim Bell, president of NBC's Olympics production and programming, to offer the comedian a correspondent gig. Jones attended various events, including beach volleyball, gymnastics, and swimming, and interacted with several US athletes and celebrities while posting behind-the-scenes videos and commentary on Twitter.

After she attended the Primetime Emmy Awards, and as the heist film *Masterminds* (2016), in which she portrays an FBI agent, premiered, she returned to SNL. She had also lent her voice to the computer-animated big-screen musical *Sing* (2016). Regardless of the project she is involved in, she has continued to emphasize the essential importance of comic relief: "People don't really understand how important comedians are, comedy is part of what we need in our life, like movies and art and water and air. We have to have the release of laughter," she explained to Iqbal.

The year 2017 brought Jones critical and popular recognition for her work. When Jones was announced in March as emcee of the 2017 BET Awards, it marked her first time hosting a high-profile awards show. Weeks later, she achieved another first: a spot on *Time*'s annual list of the world's hundred most-influential people. After making her highly anticipated BET Awards hosting debut in June, she received a first-time Emmy Award nomination for Outstanding Supporting Actress in a Comedy Series and made a special guest appearance during Dave Chappelle's residency at New York City's Radio City Music Hall. That fall, Jones kicked off another SNL season, garnering attention for her impersonations of former White House staffer Omarosa Manigault.

In February 2018, Jones reprised her role as Olympics contributor, traveling to the Winter Games in Pyeongchang, South Korea. That same month, she also guest-starred on an episode of the ABC comedy *Kevin (Probably) Saves the World*.

PERSONAL LIFE

Not long after the controversy over her *Ghostbusters* role, Jones faced another challenge: finding designers volunteering to dress her for the film's July premiere. This difficulty sparked public discussion about the necessity of size-inclusive clothing in Hollywood. Christian Siriano quickly responded to Jones's tweet, collaborating with her on a shoulder-baring, high-slit red gown. Siriano later designed the custom blue jumpsuit Jones wore to the 2016 Primetime Emmys and her outfit for the 2017 Emmys.

Jones, a Harlem resident, has said in interviews that the deaths of her father, mother, and brother have inspired her to be more comfortable with herself and to not take life for granted.

SUGGESTED READING

Iqbal, Nosheen. *"Ghostbusters'* Leslie Jones: 'The US Is the Most Depressed Nation in the World and I Blame Comedians.'" *The Guardian*, 7 July 2016, www.theguardian.com/film/2016/jul/07/leslie-jones-ghostbusters-us-most-depressed-nation-blame-comedians. Accessed 15 May 2018.

Marantz, Andrew. "Ready for Prime Time." *The New Yorker*, 4 Jan. 2016, www.newyorker.com/magazine/2016/01/04/ready-for-prime-time. Accessed 15 May 2018.

Obell, Sylvia. "The Unbreakable Leslie Jones." *BuzzFeed*, 24 June 2017, www.buzzfeed.com/sylviaobell/nothing-can-stop-leslie-jones. Accessed 15 May 2018.

Phifer, Tony. "Leslie Jones Found Her Funny at CSU." *The Magazine*, Fall 2015, magazine.colostate.edu/issues/fall-2015/leslie-jones-found-her-funny-at-csu. Accessed 15 May 2018.

Strohm, Emily. "Leslie Jones Talks Childhood Insecurities about Her Looks—And How She Found Her Confidence." *People*, 14 July 2016, people.com/movies/leslie-jones-talks-childhood-insecurities-about-her-looks. Accessed 15 May 2018.

Udell, Erin. "Leslie Jones: From Colorado State to *Saturday Night Live*." *Coloradoan*, 18 Apr. 2016, www.coloradoan.com/story/entertainment/2016/04/18/leslie-jones-colorado-state-saturday-night-live/82916122. Accessed 15 May 2018.

SELECTED WORKS

Top Five, 2014; *Saturday Night Live*, 2014– ; *Ghostbusters*, 2016; *Masterminds*, 2016

—Bertha Muteba

Radhika Jones

Date of birth: 1973
Occupation: Editor in chief of *Vanity Fair*

When, in November 2017, the media corporation Condé Nast announced that Radhika Jones would be taking over as editor of the magazine *Vanity Fair* following the departure of longtime editor Graydon Carter, the news came as a surprise to some in the media—particularly those unfamiliar with Jones's impressive career in publishing. Serving as editorial director of the Books section of the *New York Times* at the time of the announcement, she had previously spent eight years at *Time* magazine, where she

Photo by Larry Busacca/Getty Images for TIME

oversaw notable features such as the *Time* 100 list. While some publishing industry observers expressed concerns about what Carter's departure would mean for *Vanity Fair*, Condé Nast leadership was confident in Jones's abilities as an editor. "Radhika is an exceptionally talented editor who has the experience and insight to drive the cultural conversation—balancing distinctive journalism with culture and humor," Condé Nast chief executive Bob Sauerberg was quoted as saying in the company's press release announcing Jones's hiring (13 Nov. 2017). "With her expansive worldview, I know she will guide *Vanity Fair*'s history of provocative and enduring storytelling well into its future."

The child of a folk musician turned music festival producer, Jones grew up in the world of arts and culture and turned her focus to literature while in college, eventually earning a doctorate in English and comparative literature from Columbia University. She worked for a variety of publications throughout her early career, including the *Moscow Times*, and spent three years at the *Paris Review* before joining *Time*. Encompassing a wide range of subject matter and literary mediums, Jones's career reflects her personal appreciation of the broad field of contemporary culture. "I'm an omnivore, culturally speaking, and story-wise too," she told Joe Pompeo for *Vanity Fair* (13 Nov. 2017). "I'm always ready to be interested in something."

EARLY LIFE AND EDUCATION

Radhika Jones was born in New York. Her parents, Robert and Marguerite, had met in Paris several years before, when her father, a former folk musician and music festival producer, was working as a road manager for the jazz bandleader Duke Ellington and her mother was working for Air India. The family later settled in Cincinnati, Ohio, where Jones and her siblings, Nalini and Christopher, spent their early years. Each summer, she and her family would take a trip to New York City. As a teenager, she became involved in some of the music events her father produced, selling tickets and carrying out other behind-the-scenes work at events such as the Rhode Island–based Newport Jazz Festival. Although she would not go on to pursue a career in music, her exposure to such events would prove key to the development of her editorial perspective. "One thing I really learned from my father . . . was the kind of excitement and rush of discovering new talent and keeping an open mind to new voices and bringing artists together," she explained to Sydney Ember for the *New York Times* (13 Nov. 2017).

In 1985, the Jones family moved to Ridgefield, a Connecticut town bordering New York. Jones spent the remainder of her childhood in Connecticut, where she attended the preparatory school Greenwich Academy. After graduating from high school, she enrolled in Harvard University to study English and American literature.

CAREER

Following her graduation from Harvard with a bachelor's degree, Jones began her career in publishing as a copy editor for the *Moscow Times*, an English-language paper based in Russia. She later served as arts editor for the publication. Upon her return to the United States, she worked for several different publications, including *Grand Street*, *Colors*, and *Artforum*. In 2005, she took on the role of managing editor for the *Paris Review*, a long-running New York–based literary magazine that features essays, fiction, and poetry. She remained with the *Paris Review* into 2008 and would later contribute writing to the magazine, including entries in the publication's column A Week in Culture. She also contributed writing to a variety of other publications, including *Bookforum*. Meanwhile, she furthered her education by pursuing graduate studies at Columbia University, focusing on English and comparative literature. In addition to working for a variety of publications throughout that period, she taught writing and literature courses at Columbia and contributed introductions and notes to volumes in the Barnes & Noble Classics series, including editions of Charles Dickens's *Great Expectations* (1861) and *David Copperfield* (1850). Her doctoral dissertation was titled "Required Rereading, or How Contemporary Novels Respond to the Canon."

After earning her PhD from Columbia, in 2008, Jones accepted the position of arts editor at *Time* magazine, where she would remain for the better part of a decade. In addition to representing a new step in her career, her move to *Time* came amid what she would later identify as a crucial period of cultural evolution. "It felt like this moment where entertainment and celebrity were really starting to change," she recalled to Pompeo. "Reality TV was gaining momentum, and the ways that people watched TV and watched movies and read about them and participated in the voyeurism of celebrity life, all of those things seemed to be changing. It's the kind of thing you can look back on, years later, and think, wow, something fundamental shifted in the culture." As an editor for one of the United States' most widely read magazines, she had the opportunity not only to observe such cultural shifts up close but also to document and at times help to shape them. After working as arts editor, assistant managing editor, and executive editor, she was named deputy managing editor of *Time* in 2013.

DEFINING INFLUENCE

During her tenure at *Time*, Jones was one of the publication's employees responsible for the daunting task of choosing the one hundred people to include in the yearly *Time* 100 list of the world's most influential people. "The list is about influence, and it doesn't really bow to any particular metrics. It's not about wealth or necessarily a number of fans or Box Office or any of the usual . . . metrics we count on to tell us who's on top," Jones explained to Charlie Rose in an interview for his self-titled television program (22 Apr. 2016). "We just try to think very broadly about who is sort of owning their field? Who is rising, who is having influence, not just perhaps in a single lane but sort of across boundaries." Individuals on the lists during her years at *Time* included politicians, media figures, athletes, technology leaders, and activists, among others. In addition to that task, she also oversaw the creation of many of the magazine's Person of the Year special issues, which highlighted a single individual or group considered to be the most influential in that year.

After eight years with *Time*, Jones left the magazine in November 2016 to join the *New York Times* as editorial director for the Books section. Although different in nature from her work for *Time*, her responsibilities at the *New York Times* likewise dealt with the concepts of influence and notability, as she and her colleagues sought to revamp the publication's books coverage while highlighting emerging writers. "Sometimes it may seem like, 'Well, what is the point of reviewing this small, charming debut novel that doesn't seem to have anything to do with anything that anyone is thinking of at this particular moment? But it's a lovely novel and we're going to review it,'" she explained to John Maher for *Publishers Weekly* (20 Aug. 2017). "Twelve years from now, when that writer wins the Pulitzer Prize, we're on the record as having reviewed that novel, and we can bring that knowledge to bear." During her year at the *New York Times*, Jones and her fellow editors sought to promote literature further among the publication's readers by "provid[ing] some different entry points into the whole landscape of books," as she told Maher.

VANITY FAIR

In September 2017, longtime *Vanity Fair* editor Graydon Carter announced that he would be stepping down from the position, which he had held since 1992. First issued in 1913 as *Dress and Vanity Fair* before being rebranded the following year, *Vanity Fair* was one of the first magazines operated by the Condé Nast publishing empire. Although the original incarnation of the publication was shut down in 1936, the magazine relaunched in 1983 and experienced significant success under the leadership of Tina Brown and her successor, Carter. Due in large part to his long tenure with the magazine, Carter came to be considered by some to be synonymous with *Vanity Fair*, and his announced departure prompted intense discussion within the magazine industry regarding his replacement.

In November 2017, Condé Nast leadership announced that Jones had been hired to take over from Carter as *Vanity Fair*'s editor. The decision came as a surprise to many in the industry, including, to a certain extent, Jones herself. "I've worked at a number of different places, and the more I thought about it, the more I thought that I could draw on different parts of my experience in a way that would be meaningful. But I always thought I was a long shot, so maybe that took a bit of the pressure off," she told Pompeo. Officially joining the magazine in mid-December, she became the fifth editor to head the publication since its revival.

As editor of *Vanity Fair*, which focuses heavily on topics such as current events, culture, and style, Jones was tasked with finding new ways for the magazine to flourish in an era in which many publications have struggled financially and with finding readers. Among other areas, she has expressed interest in exploring further opportunities in online publishing as well as in the live events hosted by the magazine, which notably include an annual party after each year's Academy Awards ceremony. "They're both areas where *Vanity Fair* is already strong and it would be incredible to build on that," she told Pompeo. However, Jones was adamant upon taking the position that she did not intend to begin her tenure as editor by making immediate sweeping changes. "I need to get oriented first," she told Ember. "There's a lot to take in."

PERSONAL LIFE

Jones lives in New York City's Brooklyn borough with her husband and son. In addition to working in magazine publishing, she enjoys reading travel and food magazines and "aspire[s] to watch more television," as she told Pompeo.

SUGGESTED READING

"Condé Nast Names Radhika Jones as Editor-in-Chief of *Vanity Fair*." *Condé Nast*, 13 Nov. 2017, www.condenast.com/press/conde-nast-names-radhika-jones-as-editor-in-chief-of-vanity-fair/. Accessed 9 Feb. 2018.

Driscoll, Eugene. "'Living Legend' Battles Rare Disease." *The News-Times*, 26 Apr. 2005, www.newstimes.com/news/article/Living-legend-battles-rare-disease-119646.php. Accessed 9 Feb. 2018.

Ember, Sydney. "Radhika Jones, *Vanity Fair*'s Surprise Choice, Is Ready to Go." *The New York Times*, 13 Nov. 2017, www.nytimes.com/2017/11/13/business/radhika-jones-vanity-fair.html. Accessed 9 Feb. 2018.

Jones, Radhika. Interview. By Charlie Rose. *Charlie Rose*, 22 Apr. 2016, charlierose.com/videos/27060. Accessed 9 Feb. 2018.

Jones, Radhika. "Meet Radhika Jones, *Vanity Fair*'s Next Editor-in-Chief." Interview by Joe Pompeo. *Vanity Fair*, 13 Nov. 2017, www.vanityfair.com/news/2017/11/meet-radhika-jones-vanity-fair-next-editor-in-chief. Accessed 9 Feb. 2018.

Maher, John. "The *New York Times* Books Desk Will Make You Read Again." *Publishers Weekly*, 20 Aug. 2017, www.publishersweekly.com/pw/by-topic/industry-news/publisher-news/article/74530-the-new-york-times-books-desk-will-make-you-read-again.html. Accessed 9 Feb. 2018.

Silverman, Rosa. "Who Is Radhika Jones, the Unexpected New Editor-in-Chief of *Vanity Fair*?" *The Telegraph*, 15 Nov. 2017, www.telegraph.co.uk/women/life/radhika-jones-unexpected-new-editor-in-chief-vanity-fair/. Accessed 9 Feb. 2018.

—*Joy Crelin*

Lindsey Jordan

Date of birth: June 16, 1999
Occupation: Musician

Singer-songwriter and guitarist Lindsey Jordan is the primary creative force and core member

Lhcollins, via Wikimedia Commons

of the indie-rock project Snail Mail, which she founded in 2015, while she was still in high school. Lauren O'Neill, writing for *Noisey* (23 Jan. 2018), described Jordan thus: "I could say that Lindsey Jordan is an 18-year-old musical prodigy. . . . Or I could tell you that Lindsey Jordan is blazing a trail for young women in music. But if I went with either of those things, I think I would be doing Lindsey Jordan a disservice. Not because they aren't true—they very much are—but just because they feel like lazy ways to describe someone so interesting. So instead, I will simply say this: Lindsey Jordan is f——ing cool."

Indie fame has come quick and early for Jordan, but her youth has been central to her rise. Snail Mail's critically acclaimed first EP, *Habit* (2016), paired classic-sounding rock riffs with lyrics of teenage angst. Jordan's self-awareness makes the combination arresting. Singing about a crush on the song "Dirt," Jordan writes, "Baby when I'm 30 I'll laugh about how dumb it felt." Snail Mail released its debut full-length album, *Lush*, in 2018. Critics praised the album as engaging, interesting, and sincere. *Pitchfork* reviewer Ryan Dombal gave the album high marks and hailed Jordan as a leader of the next generation of indie rockers.

EARLY LIFE AND EDUCATION

Jordan was born on June 16, 1999, and grew up in Ellicott City, Maryland, a suburb outside of Baltimore. Her mother owns a lingerie store in Fulton, Maryland, called Bra-la-la. Her father works for a company that provides

materials to home-schooled children. She has one older sister.

As a small child, Jordan was influenced by her mother and sister's musical tastes, an eclectic mix of rock artists like Coldplay and the harder Warped Tour bands. Until she heard the emo pop-punk band Paramore, with frontwoman Hayley Williams, she told Caryn Ganz for the *New York Times* (16 May 2018), "I actually didn't know women were allowed in bands."

Jordan asked her parents for a guitar when she was five years old. She began classical guitar lessons and forced herself to practice for two hours every day. She went to rock-n-roll camp but disliked its competitive nature. When she was nine, she joined her parents friend's cover band, the Eight Balls, and began playing at local bars. At eleven, she began writing songs and booking her own gigs at coffee shops and restaurants. And at fourteen, she started working as a security employee at Merriweather Post Pavilion, described as "Maryland's music megafortress" by James Callahan for *City Paper* (16 May 2017).

Jordan attended Patapsco Middle School and Mount Hebron High School, where she joined the jazz band. She also played left wing on the high school's ice hockey team. Jordan was passionate about the sport; the music video for "Heat Wave" the first single from her debut album, *Lush* (2018), features her in full gear getting checked by a horde of male players on the ice. Jordan has compared playing indie rock music to playing hockey, having been the only girl on her high school team. Even though she was a better player than many of her teammates, the boys were always putting her down, and eventually she quit the team in 2016 due to their harassment. "I've experienced the worst from music and from sports. I feel like that's the reason I'm really confident now," Jordan told Jenn Pelly for *Pitchfork* (1 Mar. 2017). "There's this thing where it seems like to be a girl in a field that's all boys, you have to be better than everyone else. But I want there to be a situation where girls know—or anyone knows—that you don't have to prove yourself to those kinds of people."

SNAIL MAIL

Jordan, who graduated from Mount Hebron in 2017, was still a student when she decided to form a band called Snail Mail in the spring of 2015. Snail Mail's earliest members included Ryan Viera and Shawn Durham, students at Goucher College in Baltimore. Just two weeks after the formation of Snail Mail, the band was invited by Jordan's friend Angela Swiecicki, a local punk band member, to perform at a punk festival called Unregistered Nurse (U+NFest), held in Baltimore in early October 2015. Singing songs from their recent Garageband demo *Sticki*

EP, Snail Mail debuted alongside established punk acts like the Screaming Females and Sheer Mag. Another band, the DC–based Priests, were so impressed by Snail Mail that they offered to release a DIY tape of the band on their label, Sister Polygon Records.

Things continued to happen rather quickly for Jordan. As the band's popularity grew, Jordan began taking guitar lessons with legendary indie guitarist Mary Timony. "It was immediately obvious to me that she was really, really good on guitar," Timony told Jessica M. Goldstein for the *Washington Post* (19 Apr. 2018). "She's one of those people who is just a natural musician. . . . The way she plays guitar is her own sort of thing, which only happens when you really have music in your brain." Lessons with Timony proved invaluable to Jordan. Timony, she told Pelly, "helped me learn to shred."

HABIT EP

With new band members Alex Bass on bass and Ray Brown on drums, Snail Mail released a six-song EP called *Habit* through Sister Polygon in July 2016. The record's slow-burning success—*Pitchfork* published a review of the EP a full year after its release—led to tours with Priests and popular indie bands like Waxahatchee and Girlpool. (Katie Crutchfield of the former became a mentor to Jordan in 2017.) Callahan described *Habit* as featuring "27 minutes of Jordan's bright and lightly distorted guitar playing while she wistfully, and periodically explosively, sings about detachment, uncertainty, and yearning." *Pitchfork's* Quinn Moreland was more specific, echoing other descriptions of Jordan's nostalgic-for-the-present lyrics. "The six songs here wallow in the spiral of uncertainty and transition that feels both adolescent and eternal," Moreland wrote (27 July 2017). "There's no grandstanding here, no attempts at hiding how truly confusing it is to be young and feel like the world is simultaneously infinite and hopeless."

Standout songs include "Thinning" and "Slug." The sound of the former, according to Moreland, makes "ennui sound somewhat enjoyable." The upbeat song was written during an illness—Jordan was reportedly sick from exhaustion during the recording of the album itself. On it, Jordan sings, "I wanna spend the entire year / Just face down / And on my own time / I wanna waste mine." On "Slug," Jordan uses the titular mollusk as a metaphor for losing one's identity. She sings, "Oh useless thing / What does another useless day bring? / Did you just lie in place? / Emulated by the way I lie awake."

MATADOR AND SOUTH BY SOUTHWEST

Jordan had planned to attend St. Joseph's College in Brooklyn and even briefly moved to the New York City borough before returning home to Baltimore to pursue music full-time. After *Habit*, Snail Mail signed with the independent rock label Matador Records, home to artists like Kurt Vile, Sonic Youth and Pavement. Jordan told Patrick D. McDermott for the *Fader* (21 Mar. 2018) that she was "honored" to join the legendary outfit. "I don't feel like there are any bands on there that are trendy or riding out a hype cycle," she said. "It feels like everyone who owns that label, or works on it, are just super interested in things that will last." Snail Mail performed at South by Southwest in 2017 and, by many accounts, stole the show. "There was a push, an energy," Jordan told Goldstein of that time. "Sort of a real expectation for you to ride the wave." But Jordan is a slow writer and perfectionist. She wanted to take the necessary time to write and record her debut, *Lush*.

LUSH

In an interview with Stephanie Eckardt for *W Magazine* (16 May 2018), Jordan described the material for *Lush* as more intentional and "definitely more gay" than *Habit*; Jordan came out as a lesbian after the release of *Habit*. "I didn't really intend to make [*Lush*] a message or anything, but it's nice to be able to write about someone and say 'her' or 'she' and not be worried about what my friends or family would think," she said. Over the course of two years, Jordan amassed thirty songs for the record and kept only ten. She recorded with the band and an engineer on a farm in Woodstock, New York. It was a difficult process of rewriting and honing, she told Goldstein. "Even though I know we bettered [the music]," she said, "I've never felt worse in my life."

Lush was released on June 8, 2018. Steven Edelstone for *Consequence of Sound* (11 June 2018) called it one "of the most engaging and relatable indie rock debuts in quite some time." Edelstone praised her lyrics, adding, "Jordan never lets herself slip into the acoustic guitar-brandishing cliché of an emotional lyricist, rather creating some of the most interesting and melodic guitar lines in recent memory." Ryan Dombal, who reviewed the album for *Pitchfork* (8 June 2018), rated *Lush* an impressive 8.7 out of 10 and wrote that *Lush* solidified Jordan "as a leader in the next generation of indie rock." He (and several others) compared her to an early Liz Phair—*Pitchfork* published a conversation between Jordan and nineties legend Phair in May 2018—though he added, "there are details [on *Lush*] that separate it from the tried-and-true indie of yesteryear, that make it feel born into her era." Dombal singled out songs like "Pristine," "Heat Wave," and "Full Control." "Sincerity is Lindsey Jordan's superpower," Dombal wrote. "Throughout the record, each line is given its own story. Every vocal feels deeply considered and felt, yet nothing is over-rehearsed. She knows precisely when to dial in and when to dial back, when to fully commit to her longing and when to step back and shake her head at it."

SUGGESTED READING

Callahan, James. "Slow and Steady: Snail Mail Is Making Moves." *Baltimore City Paper*, 16 May 2017, www.citypaper.com/music/music-features/bcp-051717-music-snail-mail-20170516-story.html. Accessed 14 July 2018.

Dombal, Ryan. "Snail Mail, *Lush*." Review of *Lush*, by Snail Mail. *Pitchfork*, 8 June 2018, pitchfork.com/reviews/albums/snail-mail-lush. Accessed 15 July 2018.

Eckhardt, Stephanie. "Snail Mail's Lindsey Jordan Didn't Expect Sudden Stardom at 19, but She's Here to Stay." *W Magazine*, 16 May 2018, www.wmagazine.com/story/snail-mail-band-lindsey-jordan-lush-album. Accessed 15 July 2018.

Ganz, Caryn. "An Indie Rock Star at 18? Snail Mail Is Figuring It Out." *New York Times*, 16 May 2018, www.nytimes.com/2018/05/16/arts/music/snail-mail-lindsey-jordan-lush.html. Accessed 13 July 2018.

Goldstein, Jessica M. "High School's Done. Now Comes Indie Rock Stardom for Snail Mail." *Washington Post*, 19 Apr. 2018, www.washingtonpost.com/lifestyle/high-schools-done-now-comes-indie-rock-stardom-for-snail-mail/2018/04/18/ff6e2bd0-3814-11e8-9c0a-85d477d9a226_story.html. Accessed 14 July 2018.

Moreland, Quinn. "Snail Mail, *Habit EP*." Review of *Habit*, by Snail Mail. *Pitchfork*, 27 July 2017, pitchfork.com/reviews/albums/snail-mail-habit-ep. Accessed 14 July 2018.

Pelly, Jenn. "Snail Mail's Lindsey Jordan Is the Wisest Teenage Indie Rocker We Know." *Pitchfork*, 1 Mar. 2017, pitchfork.com/features/rising/10027-snail-mails-lindsey-jordan-is-the-wisest-teenage-indie-rocker-we-know. Accessed 14 July 2018.

—*Molly Hagan*

By Keith Allison [CC BY-SA 2.0], via Wikimedia Commons

Aaron Judge

Date of birth: April 26, 1992
Occupation: Baseball player

At the close of the 2017 season, twenty-five-year old rookie Aaron Judge of the New York Yankees was the biggest man in Major League Baseball—not just physically, which he is, at six foot seven inches and 282 pounds—but as a competitor, leading the American League (AL) with 52 home runs, 128 runs, 127 walks, and ranking second in both runs batted in (RBIs) with 114 and an on-base plus slugging (OPS) of 1.049. For his remarkable season, during which he set the American League home run record for rookies, he was unanimously named his league's Rookie of the Year and finished second behind Jose Altuve of the Houston Astros for the AL's Most Valuable Player Award.

Perhaps what is most remarkable about Judge is the genuine humility he displays both on and off the field, and the ease with which he interacts with fans, sportswriters, and fellow players in the fishbowl media environment of New York City. And despite his relatively young age, he seems keenly aware of the importance of taking things one day at a time. "You can't just enjoy the positives," Judge told Stephanie Apstein for *Sports Illustrated* (9 May 2017). "You gotta enjoy the negatives. I don't like going 0 for 7. I don't like striking out—no one does—but you can't have the good without the bad. The most important thing is when you have those bads, make sure you learn from them. Don't come in here and slam your helmet and start cussing. Because the game's not going to stop."

EARLY LIFE AND EDUCATION

The son of teachers, Aaron James Judge was born on April 26, 1992. He and his older brother, John—both of whom were adopted—were raised in Linden, California. A farming community with a population of under two thousand located about fifty miles southeast of Sacramento, Linden is home to just a pair of restaurants, another pair of grocery stories, and a single stop sign.

Aaron learned he was adopted around age ten. "I think it was like, 'I don't look like you, mom. I don't look like you, dad. Like, what's going on here?'" Judge told *MLB.com*, as quoted by Alvin Reid for the *St. Louis American* (15 June 2017). "Nothing really changed. I honestly can't even remember too much, because it wasn't that big of a deal. They just told me I was adopted, and I said, 'OK, can I go outside and play?'"

Judge took to sports early. Even when he was playing T-ball as a young boy, fellow players were intimidated by the power with which he hit the ball. Despite his athletic gifts, friends in Linden recalled him as being humble and soft-spoken and grounded by his Christian faith. He attended Linden High School, where he excelled at baseball, football, and basketball. He also proved to be an excellent student, holding a 3.5 grade point average while working as a member of both the student government and the school's anti-drunk-driving program. "We just keep waiting for them to name the high school Aaron Judge Field," James Lagorio, Judge's friend and high school teammate, told Zach Braziller for the *New York Post* (6 May 2017). "They had a play in basketball, [an] inbounds straight to him, he would jump over guys and dunk it. In football, they would just throw it up to him. Nobody had a chance to guard him. In baseball, he was putting balls on top of the buildings in deep center field."

Various college football scouts, including ones from Notre Dame, Stanford, and UCLA, sought to recruit Judge, but even in high school he had his heart set on baseball, where he excelled at hitting, pitching, and playing first base. During the 2010 Major League Baseball Draft, the Oakland Athletics selected him in the thirty-first round. He declined to join the Athletics franchise, instead opting to earn his college degree and hone his baseball skills at California State University, Fresno. There, as a member of the Fresno State Bulldogs, he would become a star player, leading the team in homers, doubles, and RBIs and winning the 2012 TD Ameritrade College Home Run Derby.

BECOMING A YANKEE SUPERSTAR

During the 2013 Major League Baseball Draft, the New York Yankees selected Judge in the first round. He earned a $1.8 million signing bonus with the Yankees and began working out with their minor-league farm system. An injury kept him on the sidelines for the duration of the 2013 season, but he reported for spring training in 2014 with the Charleston RiverDogs. Following a successful period in Charleston, the Yankees promoted him to the Tampa Yankees later in 2014. In 2015, the Yankees brought him over to the Trenton Thunder. Moving him out of Double-A, the Yankees brought him up to their Triple-A team at Scranton/Wilkes-Barre, where he struggled a bit with a knee injury, but the team's management was confident in his potential as the biggest hitting prospect in their minor-league system.

Judge was called up to the majors toward the end of the 2016 season, on August 13, when he made his debut as a New York Yankee facing off against the Tampa Bay Rays. He hit a home run in his first major league at bat, then hit a second homer in his second big-league game, the first Yankee player to do so since Joe Lefebvre in 1980. Despite this initial success, Judge struggled for the rest of the season, batting just .179 and striking out forty-two times in eighty-four at-bats. His season ended on September 13, when he was placed on the disabled list with an oblique strain.

Judge keeps that .179 batting average as a note on his phone, as motivation to do his best every day. And he has done just that, becoming the new face of the Yankees—and possibly all Major League Baseball—since the beginning of 2017, the first year he has played a full big-league season. Near the start of the regular season in April, Judge became the talk of the baseball world by becoming the youngest player to hit thirteen homers in his first twenty-six regular-season games. He would continue to hit baseballs and shatter records throughout the season. The exit velocity of his homers measured by Statcast reached 121.1 miles per hour on June 10. At the All-Star break, he became the second rookie, after Mark McGwire in 1987, to hit thirty homers by mid-season. By season's end, he also held the MLB record for most walks, with 127.

Although he ended the season with a staggering 52 home runs, the most ever by a rookie, he also struggled for parts of the season, now holding the MLB records for striking out in thirty-seven consecutive games and most strikeouts by a rookie with 208. Yet despite these struggles, the impression he left most baseball fans with was of a masterful young athlete with incredible power and potential. Writing for the *Atlantic* (10 July 2017), Robert O'Connell gave a vivid portrait of Judge in his spectacular rookie year: "Judge would be large by NBA or NFL standards, but within the context of his chosen sport he is a titan. At six feet seven inches tall and 282 pounds, everything he does is outsized. He stands statue-still at the plate and, when he gets a pitch he likes, sweeps his bat to it, sending it zooming skyward faster and farther than anyone else." He finished the season with a .284 batting average, 154 hits, and 114 RBIs.

POSTSEASON AND ROOKIE OF THE YEAR

Judge's tremendous offensive power, coupled with his great defensive playing in right field, helped to lift the Yankees into the postseason—an unanticipated outcome for a club that most observers considered to be at least another season from contention. After the Yankees clinched the Wild Card spot, they played against the Minnesota Twins on October 3; during the game Judge homered to help secure the Yankees' 8–4 victory. The Yanks then moved on to the American League Division Series (ALDS), in which they defeated the Cleveland Indians three games to two. Judge struggled at the plate in the series, striking out sixteen times, but made a spectacular catch in Game 3, robbing Francisco Lindor of a homer, which helped to preserve the tie and allow the Yankees to win the game.

The Yankees then faced the Houston Astros in the 2017 American League Championship Series (ALCS). The two teams would battle it out for a full seven games, with the Astros eventually emerging as the victors, but Judge demonstrated his ability as a clutch player throughout, homering three times in the series and robbing Yuli Gurriel of a homer in Game 7.

With the end of the season, it became clear that baseball was entering another era of power hitters, one that fans hoped had little connection to the "steroid era," during which records were set by players who had enhanced their natural talents with a variety of drugs. With performance-enhancing drugs banned and players regularly screened, a new generation of talented players has emerged, which MLB leadership hopes will remove the taint of the prior era. Among these new stars are Judge and Cody Bellinger of the Los Angeles Dodgers, both of whom earned their leagues' Rookie of the Year award. These two players are among those frequently considered to be the new faces of professional baseball. Judge, however, dismisses the idea that he has any more claim to that title than others. "There's a lot of young faces who could be the face of M.L.B.," he said to Tyler Kepner for the *New York Times* (13 Nov. 2017). "If you look around, from a lot of the rookies we had this year, a lot of the younger guys in their early to mid-20s, and how they've impacted the game—we've got a special group here in Major League Baseball." Indeed, major league players hit an unprecedented 6,105 homers during the regular season; in the World Series between the Dodgers and the Astros, players hit 25 homers.

In addition to winning the Rookie of the Year award, Judge came in second behind Jose Altuve for the American League's MVP award. Following the announcement, Judge tweeted out a picture of the pair of them along with the following caption: "M-V-P!!! Nobody more deserving than you!! Congrats on an unforgettable 2017!! @JoseAltuve27."

PERSONAL LIFE

If Judge does not believe himself to be one of the new faces of baseball, corporations certainly do. Sony put him on the cover of the 2018 edition of its video game *MLB The Show*, and he has also earned an endorsement deal with Pepsi. Despite the growing media attention, Judge remained humble about his achievements, living out of a hotel in Times Square for the 2017 season instead of buying his own place—in case things did not work out in the big leagues. He has also refrained from checking out New York City's nightlife. This humility and strong work ethic has earned him comparison to Yankee great Derek Jeter, who led the Yankees to five World Series championships. "I have a very short window to play this game," Judge told Stephanie Apstein. "The last thing I want to do is waste it being out on the town. I want to get every ounce I can out of my body."

SUGGESTED READING

"Aaron Judge Stats, Fantasy & News." *MLB.com*, 2017, m.mlb.com/player/592450/aaron-judge. Accessed 17 Nov. 2017.

Apstein, Stephanie. "Powerful Yankees Slugger Aaron Judge Stands Out, But All He Wants to Do Is Blend In." *Sports Illustrated*, 9 May 2017, www.si.com/mlb/2017/05/09/aaron-judge-new-york-yankees. Accessed 17 Nov. 2017.

Braziller, Zach. "Where Aaron Judge Comes from Explains Who He Is." *New York Post*, 6 May 2017, nypost.com/2017/05/06/where-aaron-judge-comes-from-explains-who-he-is/. Accessed 17 Nov. 2017.

Kepner, Tyler. "Aaron Judge and Cody Bellinger Unanimously Named Rookies of the Year." *The New York Times*, 13 Nov. 2017, www.nytimes.com/2017/11/13/sports/baseball/aaron-judge-cody-bellinger-rookie.html. Accessed 14 Nov. 2017.

Mazzeo, Mike. "Aaron Judge Finishes Second in AL MVP Voting to Jose Altuve." *New York Daily News*, 17 Nov. 2017, www.nydailynews.com/sports/baseball/yankees/aaron-judge-finishes-al-mvp-voting-jose-altuve-article-1.3638479. Accessed 17 Nov. 2017.

O'Connell, Robert. "Baseball's Eyes Are on Aaron Judge." *The Atlantic*, 10 July 2017, www.theatlantic.com/entertainment/archive/2017/07/aaron-judge-yankees-rookie/533037/. Accessed 17 Nov. 2017.

—*Christopher Mari*

Cush Jumbo

Date of birth: September 23, 1985
Occupation: Actor, writer

"I'm not interested in being in *Heat* magazine," Cush Jumbo told Elizabeth Day for the *Guardian* (24 Nov. 2012), referring to a popular celebrity-focused publication. "But I've got a lot of interest in playing someone else really, really well." That attitude has led Jumbo to become, in Day's words, "one of the most acclaimed stage actresses of her generation," with memorable roles in such productions as *Love's Labour's Lost*, *The Cherry Orchard*, *The Crucible*, *The Doll House*, *Pygmalion*, *She Stoops to Conquer*, *Julius Caesar*, and *As You Like It*, for which she earned the coveted 2012 Ian Charleson Award for classical actors under the age of thirty in the United Kingdom.

Although Jumbo belongs, as Day describes, "to a new wave of young women who have chosen to cut their teeth on classical repertoire rather than rushing headlong into the fame and fortune offered by the film business," the actor has not spurned screen roles. She has appeared in several well-regarded British television shows, including the detective series *Vera* and the *Doctor Who* spin-off *Torchwood*, and she is well known to US fans for her portrayal of savvy lawyer Lucca Quinn in the drama *The Good Wife* and its 2017 spin-off, *The Good Fight*.

Jumbo notes that there are commonalities between preparing for a classical stage role and getting ready to deliver the rapid-fire dialogue that has made those two legal dramas favorites with fans and critics. "You have to look up every inch of the dialogue and say it in a way that an audience would believe it," she explained to Rachel Ward for the *Telegraph* (31 Mar. 2017). "It's actually quite a theatre way of doing things when you have to investigate the text, like you would with Shakespeare."

Jumbo has credited her classical training for much of her success but bemoans the fact that actors of color are still often overlooked by the British television and film industry. In a widely quoted speech given during a 2017 evidence session for the Labour Party's inquiry into diversity in the arts, she asserted, "If there was work here, I would be working here. . . . I didn't run to America, I didn't even ask for America, I just took a play there and suddenly everyone was telling me 'you're so talented, would you like 52 jobs.'" She told the panel that her role in *The Good Wife* had marked "the first time [an offered script] hadn't specified black or mix race or exotic best friend" and concluded, "There's only so many years I can sit here, hitting that best friend ceiling before I go over to Amazon because they'll give me a role and they'll pay me for it."

Photo by Jamie McCarthy/Getty Images

EARLY LIFE AND EDUCATION

Jumbo was born in 1985 in South London, the second of six children. Her father, Marx Jumbo, had fled his native Nigeria in the late 1960s to escape the civil war then ravaging the country. Granted asylum in the United Kingsom (UK), he married Angela Hall, a British-born psychiatric nurse whom he had met at a party. Jumbo's first name, she has said, is derived from that of an ancient Egyptian king. "It's a name that took a few years to grow into, but now I feel it was meant to be," she told Kathy Henderson for *Broadway Buzz* (13 Nov. 2014). "It's absolutely who I am, and I love it."

As the family expanded, they moved to larger quarters, staying mostly in working-class areas of South London. Marx remained home to care for the brood, while Angela worked. "My view of the world has always been slightly different [because of that]," Jumbo recalled to Day. "My Dad is the first to say that Mum deals with the mortgage payments, the bills, the rota, things like that, while my Dad is the emotional one who keeps the home together."

Jumbo, who later found that she could win friends by doing comic impressions of her teachers, became interested in performing at an early age. As a young child, she began taking dance classes at a local dance studio. Even then, she loved watching old musicals on television, and she harbored a fondness for Fred Astaire, Ginger Rogers, and Gene Kelly. One Sunday afternoon when she was about seven or eight, she happened to catch a Channel 4 showing of the 1934 film *Zouzou*, starring Josephine Baker, the first African American woman to headline a major big-screen release. "She was the star of the movie, and the only time I'd seen anybody who looked like me in one of those old musicals, they were like a nurse or a maid or a dresser," she said to Ronda Racha Penrice for the *Root* (18 Oct. 2015). "They were never the star. They never had fur or diamonds on as she did, and the whole cast . . . were white, [but] nobody seemed to be making anything of the fact that she was brown, and I just thought it was mind-blowing."

Jumbo was deeply unhappy while attending a state secondary school in the Penge district of London. She frequently got into fights with the other girls, and halfway through one term the teacher of drama—the only class Jumbo truly enjoyed—quit. Fortuitously, while watching *Blue Peter*, a long-running British children's television show, she learned of the BRIT School, a tuition-free performing arts school for teens in Croyden. At age fourteen she was one of forty applicants accepted from a field of three thousand candidates. "It felt like somewhere different, like an escape route," she told Day. "If I hadn't left for there, I don't know what would have become of me. It was the first time I'd met gay kids, proper grungesters, kids who wanted to change gender. . . . It was like being put into the world."

Jumbo next entered the University of London's Royal Central School of Speech and Drama, where she earned an honors degree in acting.

ACTING CAREER

In 2007, soon after graduating, Jumbo was cast on an episode of the television comedy *My Family*, and a string of other television roles followed, including stints on *Harley Street* (2008), *Torchwood* (2009), *Lip Service* (2010), *Getting On* (2010–12), and *Vera* (2012–16). At the same time, she was gaining attention for her work on the British stage.

In 2010, she starred as Eliza Doolittle in *Pygmalion* (the play by George Bernard Shaw upon which *My Fair Lady* is based) at the Royal Exchange in Manchester, and the following year she returned to that venue to play Rosalind in a modern adaptation of Shakespeare's *As You Like It*. Her gender-bending performance led reviewers to deem her a rising star and garnered her the 2012 Ian Charleson Award, one of the most prestigious honors for young actors making their marks on the British stage.

In 2012 Jumbo wowed critics as the flirtatious Constance Neville in Oliver Goldsmith's eighteenth-century comedy *She Stoops to Conquer* at the National Theatre, and later that year she took on the role of Mark Antony in an all-female production of Shakespeare's *Julius Caesar*. Directed by Phyllida Lloyd, the show was set in a women's prison and starred Frances Barber,

whom Jumbo had long admired, in the title role. (In 2009, Jumbo had been late on her rent after spending money on an expensive ticket to see Barber in a West End production of *Madame de Sade*.) "Playing Mark Antony in *Julius Caesar* was the most thrilling thing I've done," Jumbo told Henderson. "You get these speeches that were written for men, and you're running around like an action hero, climbing scaffolding and beating people up. It was very freeing." The role earned her a nomination for an Olivier Award (the British equivalent of a Tony) as best supporting actress of the year. Jumbo reprised the role in 2013, when Lloyd's production traveled to St. Ann's Warehouse in New York.

JOSEPHINE AND I

Despite the steady stream of work and accolades, Jumbo remained creatively unfulfilled by her professional life. She longed to be offered lead roles instead of supporting ones and felt hampered by casting restraints related to race. She toyed with the idea of becoming a teacher but decided to do one final theater project, thinking that her family and friends might like to see her one more time on the stage before she abandoned it for the classroom.

Jumbo drew upon her childhood love for Josephine Baker to write *Josephine and I*, a cabaret-style look at the iconic performer's life. The show, which Lloyd agreed to direct and which featured Jumbo in twenty-five roles, played at London's Bush Theatre in 2013, earning her the Evening Standard Award for Emerging Talent. The show then moved to New York's highly regarded Public Theater in 2015, where Jumbo earned the Lucille Lortel Award for Best Solo Performance. Between productions of *Josephine and I*, Jumbo made her Broadway debut alongside Hugh Jackman and Laura Donnelly in Jez Butterworth's *The River*, a three-person drama set in a rural fishing cabin and mounted at the Circle in the Square Theater on Broadway in 2014.

THE GOOD WIFE AND THE GOOD FIGHT

Josephine and I won Jumbo an important group of fans: Christine Baranski, who starred in *The Good Wife* and whom Lloyd knew from past projects, and Robert and Michelle King, the husband-and-wife team who had created the hit series. They quickly offered her a part. "I once went for a TV job where I was told that I was the best person for the part but that I didn't work 'shade wise': I was too white; not quite black enough," Jumbo recalled to Ward. "So when I was offered *The Good Wife*, where the cast sheet didn't say black or bi-racial, it just said woman, age, and character, well, that doesn't often come up as a leading role in the UK so I couldn't say no."

So popular was Jumbo's character, the impeccably dressed and sharp-witted Lucca Quinn, that Jumbo was asked to star in the 2017 spin-off, *The Good Fight*, which takes place one year after the events of *The Good Wife*'s finale, with the female leads reunited at a new, high-powered law firm. *The Good Fight* is exclusively available on CBS All Access, a streaming service meant to compete with established players such as Netflix and Amazon Prime.

When not filming the legal drama, Jumbo takes on other roles. In the summer of 2017, for example, she returned to the stage of the National Theatre in London to star in *Common*, a new play set in 1809 and which Jumbo described to Rebecca Nicholson for the *Guardian* (24 May 2017) as "a mixture of Shakespeare, Harry Potter and some kind of Angelina Jolie movie." She is also preparing to star in a big-screen version of *Josephine and I* and is reportedly writing a script for a musical based on the true story of an all-female gang active in Georgian London.

PERSONAL LIFE

In 2014, following a matinee performance of *The River*, Jumbo married Sean Griffin, who works in digital media. The couple was married on a Broadway stage and Hugh Jackman served as one of their witnesses. In January 2018, Jumbo announced that she and Griffin were expecting their first child and also that her character, Lucca Quinn, will be pregnant on *The Good Fight*.

SUGGESTED READING

Jumbo, Cush. "Cush Jumbo: I'm Not Interested in Being in *Heat* Magazine." Interview by Elizabeth Day. *The Guardian*. 24 Nov. 2012, www.theguardian.com/stage/2012/nov/25/cush-jumbo-donmar-julius-caesar-interview. Accessed 8 Feb. 2018.

Jumbo, Cush. "Cush Jumbo on Her Unusual Name, Her New Buddy Hugh Jackman & Starring in the 'Shocking' Drama *The River*." Interview by Kathy Henderson. *Broadway Buzz*, www.broadway.com/buzz/178382/cush-jumbo-on-her-unusual-name-her-new-buddy-hugh-jackman-starring-in-the-shocking-drama-the-river/, 13 Nov. 2014. Accessed 8 Feb. 2018.

Jumbo, Cush. "Meet Cush Jumbo, the Brit Star Who Plays *The Good Wife*'s New BFF." Interview by Ronda Racha Penrice. *The Root*, 18 Oct. 2015, www.theroot.com/meet-cush-jumbo-the-brit-star-who-plays-the-good-wife-1790861437. Accessed 8 Feb. 2018.

Nicholson, Rebecca. "A Lover and a Fighter: Cush Jumbo on *The Good Wife*'s Spinoff and Her Raucous New Play." *The Guardian*, 24 May 2017, www.theguardian.com/stage/2017/may/24/cush-jumbo-the-good-fight-common-national-theatre. Accessed 8 Feb. 2018.

Shore, Robert. "Cush Jumbo: My Childhood Idol Josephine Baker Saved My Career." *Metro*, 11 July 2013, metro.co.uk/2013/07/11/cush-jumbo-my-childhood-idol-josephine-baker-saved-my-career-3877394/. Accessed 8 Feb. 2018.

Ward, Rachel. "*The Good Fight*'s Cush Jumbo: 'I Was Told I Was Too White, but Not Quite Black Enough.'" *The Telegraph*, 31 Mar. 2017, www.telegraph.co.uk/tv/2017/03/31/good-fights-cush-jumbo-told-white-not-quite-black-enough/. Accessed 8 Feb. 2018.

SELECTED WORKS

Torchwood, 2009; *Vera*, 2012–16; *Josephine & I*, 2013, 2015; *The Good Wife*, 2015–16; *The Good Fight*, 2017

—*Mari Rich*

Jodi Kantor

Date of birth: April 21, 1975
Occupation: Journalist

As the Washington correspondent for the *New York Times*, Jodi Kantor focused much of her career on politics. However, in 2017, she and colleague Megan Twohey broke the story of decades of allegations of sexual harassment and abuse against film producer Harvey Weinstein. The two women were among several reporters at the *New York Times* who reported on powerful men abusing women. Of the work they did, Kantor said to Brent Lang for *Variety* (13 Dec. 2017), "Sometimes it has felt as though we're standing in a river of pain, and I don't want to diminish that, but there have also been moments of recognition and hope and connection. The question now is whether or not private pain can be turned into collective strength."

Kantor and Twohey's work won the *New York Times* the 2018 Pulitzer Prize for public service, which the paper shared with the *New Yorker* for reporting done by Ronan Farrow on the same topic. The Pulitzer citation stated that the award was given "for explosive, impactful journalism that exposed powerful and wealthy sexual predators, including allegations against one of Hollywood's most influential producers, bringing them to account for long-suppressed allegations of coercion, brutality and victim silencing, thus spurring a worldwide reckoning about sexual abuse of women." All three were named to *Time* magazine's 2018 list of the one hundred most influential people, and Kantor and

By Miller Center, via Wikimedia Commons

Twohey also received the 2018 McGill Medal for Journalistic Courage from the University of Georgia's Grady College of Journalism and Mass Communication.

EARLY LIFE AND EDUCATION

Growing up in the Queens and Staten Island boroughs of New York City, and later in Holmdel Township, New Jersey, Jodi Michelle Kantor knew no writers or journalists. "I didn't think that being a journalist was something I could actually do, because I didn't know anybody who did it," she said to Alexis Tonti for *Columbia College Today* (Summer 2012). However, her parents subscribed to *New York Times*, and, as Kantor recalled to Mikayla Harris for the *Politic* (25 Nov. 2013), "I absolutely gobbled the paper everyday. I read it from a really young age, like when I was 12 or 13 years old. I would sit with the newspaper after school. It had a huge impression on me."

Kantor's Jewish heritage shaped her life and career. "I grew up around people with numbers on their arms—my grandparents are Holocaust survivors," she explained to Rose Minutaglio for *Marie Claire* (23 Oct. 2017). "It led me to think about the big questions we often ask in investigative journalism: 'How could something like this have gone on? What allowed this to happen?'"

After graduating from Columbia College, an undergraduate college of Columbia University, in 1996, Kantor spent a year in Israel on a Dorot Fellowship, followed by a year in the New York City Urban Fellows Program. She began attending Harvard Law School in 1998 but found herself unenthusiastic about the work. In a December 2012 speech at Columbia University's Robert K. Kraft Family Center for Jewish Student Life, Kantor recalled looking through eight hundred pages of summer internships and finding nothing that interested her. "That's the question to ask yourself," she said to the audience, as reported for the *Columbia College* website (5 Dec. 2012). "What do you do as a lawyer, or as a journalist, at 10 a.m. on a Tuesday? And is *that* what you want to be doing with your life?"

After just one semester of law school, Kantor dropped out and joined the staff of *Slate*, then a start-up online publication, as an editorial assistant. While there, she coedited *The Slate Diaries* (2000), a collection of several dozen diaries that the magazine had originally solicited to be published in real time, and ultimately rose to become *Slate*'s New York editor.

THE NEW YORK TIMES

When Kantor left *Slate* to become editor of the *New York Times'* Arts & Leisure section in 2003, she was, at twenty-seven, the youngest section editor anyone there could recall. She soon made her mark on the cultural landscape; her 2006 article about the class issues surrounding breastfeeding and the need of women for places to pump breast milk while working, for example, sparked the movement for freestanding lactation suites, common now in public spaces such as stadiums and airports.

Kantor began covering politics for the *New York Times* in 2007, with a focus on then presidential candidate Barack Obama and his family, and was among the first to write about future First Lady Michelle Obama. Following Obama's election in 2008, she continued her close coverage of the president and First Lady, eventually developing something of a relationship with them. "I've been covering the Obamas since 2007, and the second story I ever wrote was one in which I broke the news of the tension between Barack Obama and his pastor, Jeremiah Wright," she later recounted to Noreen Malone for *New York* magazine's *Daily Intelligencer* (13 Jan. 2012). "And from then until now, I've written a series of stories that are really close to home about them. I've written about race; I've written about their children, about their marriage; I've written about their family. I interviewed them for 40 minutes in the Oval Office about their marriage. Rachel Swarns and I traced Michelle Obama's roots back to slavery." She added, "Nobody has a lot of access to them. There is no journalist with whom they spend a tremendous amount of time. But . . . sometimes when I do see them at media speeches and even briefly at the White House Christmas parties, the moment feels very intense. What feels more intense than even that is just writing so personally about a president and first lady and having done it for so long."

THE OBAMAS

Kantor's interest in the first family ultimately led her to write the book *The Obamas* (2012), a broad, sweeping view of the Obama White House with a heavy focus on the relationship between the president and First Lady. She used their marriage to highlight the political dynamic of the couple, for whom the personal and the political were clearly interrelated. "The Obamas' marriage in particular fascinated me because it was a real back-and-forth and a real debate," Kantor explained to Harris. "If you look at the Obamas before they get to the White House, they basically spent their entire marriage arguing—and I mean arguing in a robust way, not arguing in a nasty way—about many political questions. They wondered, is politics the best means through which to achieve social change? And is political life really livable? They knew that, in the White House, they were going to have to tackle those questions like never before."

The Obamas became a *New York Times* Best Seller and was well received by critics. However, it also drew an unexpected amount of largely unfounded media criticism due to widely publicized misrepresentations of its contents. Some of the pushback stemmed from a televised interview in which Michelle Obama, who admitted to not having yet read the book, nevertheless objected to its reputed portrayal of her. "There's a really strange thing going on with this book, which is that the book that's being discussed on TV is not the book that I actually published," Kantor said to Malone just days after its release. Later, speaking to Tonti, she elaborated, "It was a strange situation, with people opining with great certainty on cable TV about a book they hadn't read; once they started reading it, the conversation really changed. I think it goes to the challenges of publishing a book about a sitting President and First Lady. The political atmosphere is so polarized, everything gets put into positive and negative categories."

CORPORATE CONCERNS

One of the important stories Kantor covered in 2014 was that of working conditions for the more than 130,000 baristas employed by Starbucks. She followed a Starbucks employee through a single day, reporting on the ways that low-wage employers arrange schedules of part-timers to the company's advantage, making it difficult for their employees to manage child care or a second job. Kantor spoke with a Starbucks executive two days before the article went to press; the day after the story broke, Starbucks changed their policy, mandating a greater lead time in schedule changes and ending the practice known as "clopening," in which an employee who closes the stores also opens the next day.

In 2015, Kantor and fellow reporter David Streitfeld examined Amazon's work culture. The company boasted of its very high expectations for workers, which included regularly sending emails to employees after midnight and demanding immediate replies. The company requires employees at all levels to sign confidentiality agreements; Kantor and Streitfeld spoke only to a few senior-level managers. Still, they gathered enough information to describe CEO Jeff Bezos's success in building Amazon, which he founded in 1994, into a retail behemoth as based on an "eagerness to tell others how to behave; an instinct for bluntness bordering on confrontation; and an overarching confidence in the power of metrics," and to report that the company's unusually high rates of employee burnout and subsequent turnover were intentional products of a strategy that one former high-level human resources executive described as "purposeful Darwinism." Ultimately, Kantor and Streitfeld provided an eye-opening account of what working at the retail giant required and the human toll it took. Their article received the most feedback of any *New York Times* piece to date.

TAKING ON HOLLYWOOD

In spring 2017, Kantor and Megan Twohey began investigating claims of sexual harassment against movie mogul Harvey Weinstein. Initially, they thought they were dealing with an issue from earlier years, but they soon discovered that some of the allegations were as recent as 2015. "When we started, we said to ourselves, 'This is a story about stuff that happened a very long time ago, so it's about correcting a record,'" Kantor recalled to Minutaglio. "But when we found out about the 2015 incidents, it shifted the moral gravity of the piece. We began to see a serial pattern that had gone on for years."

Kantor and Twohey's article appeared on the front page of the *New York Times* print edition on October 6, 2017, under the headline "Sexual Misconduct Claims Trail a Hollywood Mogul." (The title of the online article, published the day before, was far blunter: "Harvey Weinstein Paid Off Sexual Harassment Accusers for Decades.") It was a game changer, sparking what soon became the #MeToo and #TimesUp global movements. As the authors of the Weinstein story, Kantor and Twohey were seen as leading the charge, and for months afterward they continued to receive reports of abuse by prominent men from victims around the globe. "Sometimes they hope we write about them, but sometimes they just want to be heard," Kantor said to Zach Schonfeld for *Newsweek* (21 Dec. 2017). The response, she said, left her "staggered, energized, saddened, thunderstruck, moved, troubled and inspired. All of it—occasionally on the same phone call."

Kantor found working with Twohey valuable in ways beyond typical reporting. "One of the saving graces of this process has been the partnership with Megan because this was a responsibility that we each needed to share with another person," Kantor said to Lisa Ryan for the *Cut* (10 Jan. 2018). "We barely knew each other when we teamed up on this story. Not only were we in constant communication with each other and not only did we compare notes, check judgment, and plot strategy on those matters great and small, but the weight of this reporting is such that you just need somebody to share it with. A lot of the stories we heard are incredibly disturbing, and you don't want to carry those alone."

Weinstein, who met with Kantor and Twohey twice at the *New York Times* during their investigation, threatened legal action against the newspaper. Managing and executive editors—particularly Rebecca Corbett, with whom Kantor had worked for over a decade, and Dean Baquet—backed the two journalists. "The institution was willing to stand up to somebody powerful, willing to lose advertising to do this story," Kantor said to Minutaglio. "So if we didn't stand up for what is right and give this all we got, what were we doing with our careers? Why are we here?"

Soon, more victims came forward to accuse not only Weinstein but also several other high-profile men in a wide range of industries, including entertainment, business, journalism, and politics. Weinstein was fired from his film studio, the Weinstein Company, which subsequently declared bankruptcy in March 2018.

The project on the abuses of powerful men grew to such an extent that Kantor and Twohey decided to write a full-length treatment of the story. Their book will be published by Penguin Press in the United States and by Bloomsbury in the United Kingdom. In addition, production companies Plan B and Annapurna Pictures announced in April 2018 that they had jointly acquired the rights to produce a film based on Kantor and Twohey's story.

PERSONAL LIFE
Kantor married Ron Lieber, a personal finance columnist for the *New York Times*, in 2002. They live in Park Slope, Brooklyn, with their two daughters, Talia and Violet.

SUGGESTED READING
Kantor, Jodi. "How I Get It Done: Jodi Kantor, Investigative Reporter for the *New York Times*." Interview by Lisa Ryan. *The Cut*, New York Media, 10 Jan. 2018, www.thecut.com/2018/01/jodi-kantor-new-york-times-interview.html. Accessed 2 May 2018.

Kantor, Jodi. "An Interview with Jodi Kantor." Interview by Mikayla Harris. *The Politic*, 25 Nov. 2013, thepolitic.org/harvard-yale-and-everything-in-between/. Accessed 2 May 2018.

Kantor, Jodi. "Jodi Kantor Talks about White House Blowback on Her Book, *The Obamas*." *Daily Intelligencer*, New York Media, 13 Jan. 2012, nymag.com/daily/intelligencer/2012/01/jodi-kantor-on-white-house-the-obamas-blowback.html. Accessed 2 May 2018.

Kantor, Jodi. "Jodi Kantor, the Reporter Who Helped Bring Down Harvey Weinstein, Reflects on Two Months of the #MeToo Revolution." Interview by Zach Schonfeld. *Newsweek*, 21 Dec. 2017, www.newsweek.com/2017/12/29/harvey-weinstein-jodi-kantor-sexual-assault-journalism-754641.html. Accessed 2 May 2018.

Kantor, Jodi, and Megan Twohey. "How *New York Times* Reporters Broke Hollywood's Biggest Sexual Harassment Story." Interview by Brent Lang. *Variety*, 13 Dec. 2017, variety.com/2017/biz/features/new-york-times-harvey-weinstein-report-megan-twohey-jodi-kantor-1202637948/. Accessed 2 May 2018.

Minutaglio, Rose. "How These Two Women Finally Exposed Harvey Weinstein." *Marie Claire*, 23 Oct. 2017, www.marieclaire.com/career-advice/a13051614/harvey-weinstein-jodi-kantor-megan-twohey/. Accessed 2 May 2018.

Tonti, Alexis. "Jodi Kantor '96 Offers Revealing Portrait of the First Couple." *Columbia College Today*, Summer 2012, www.college.columbia.edu/cct/archive/summer12/cover_story. Accessed 2 May 2018.

—*Judy Johnson*

Kapka Kassabova

Date of birth: 1973
Occupation: Writer

Kapka Kassabova is a European poet, novelist, and nonfiction writer. She was born in Sofia, Bulgaria, when it was still under Communist rule. Despite the concrete monotony of her surroundings—richly described in her 2008 memoir *A Street Without a Name*—Kassabova found an intellectual and imaginative escape in books, gorging herself on the works of various international authors. This background would play a major part in her own development into an author. As she told Nick Major for the *Scottish Review of Books* (10 Feb. 2018), "It is hard for me to draw a line between being a reader and a

By slowking4, via Wikimedia Commons

writer, because books were always such a huge part of my life."

After the fall of the Soviet Union and the Berlin Wall, Kassabova and her family immigrated to New Zealand. She studied languages and writing, and became a poet, novelist, and an avid traveler, eventually settling in Scotland. Her work has received much critical praise and won several awards. Her nonfiction book *Border: A Journey to the Edge of Europe* (2017) won the Stanford Dolman Travel Book of the Year Award and the Saltire Society Scottish Book of the Year Award, further raising her international profile. The book, in which Kassabova recounts her travels along the border zone between Bulgaria, Turkey, and Greece, highlights persistent themes in her work, including migration and a longing for home.

EARLY LIFE BEHIND THE IRON CURTAIN

Kapka Kassabova was born in Sofia, Bulgaria, in 1973, when Bulgaria was a Soviet satellite state. Her father was a mathematician and her mother was an engineer. As she would later relate in her memoir, the family lived in a two-bedroom apartment in a nondescript building like thousands of others. The concrete conformity of the landscape around her and the general monotonous oppression of Communist society fueled her dreams of escaping elsewhere. From an early age, she enjoyed adventure stories such as the work of Jack London. "I was instinctively drawn to stories of escape, adventure and the high seas," she told Major. "It wasn't just that I was

living in a society where I felt trapped, it was also because I was a reader and a dreamer."

The variety of Kassabova's reading material increased as the Communist regime's censorship gradually grew less strict in the 1980s. Though many major Western books were still banned, she was able to read science fiction and other works that would never have previously been available in Bulgaria. Kassabova was enrolled at a French-speaking school at the age of thirteen, and read the work of French authors such as Albert Camus and Jean-Paul Sartre, becoming fluent in French. She also enjoyed Russian and Italian books, films, and music, but English-language media was more strictly controlled. Kassabova began writing her own poetry, and as a teenager worked for a literary magazine at her school, but she did not decide to pursue writing as a career until she was in her twenties.

The Berlin Wall fell when Kassabova was sixteen years old, bringing major changes for many people living in Communist states. "I was not aware of the adults seeing it coming," she told Major, though there was an air of social unrest and rebellion in Bulgaria. "The regime was so repressive until the last moment that people almost didn't dare hope for change." In Bulgaria, reforms were eventually brought about by a coup within the Communist Party itself, not a revolution. When Kassabova was eighteen, she and her family immigrated to Dunedin on the South Island of New Zealand. (They had first attempted to move to Great Britain but were forced to change their plans due to visa issues.) It was a profound cultural change for Kassabova, as she told Major: "New Zealand was another world. I was stuck between cultures and languages. . . . It was a rough transition."

FIRST PUBLICATIONS

In New Zealand, Kassabova studied French and linguistics at Victoria University of Wellington and went on to receive her master's degree in creative writing from the school's International Institute of Modern Letters. During this time, as she struggled to adapt to the English language, she came to focus on poetry. In 1997 she published her first book, the poetry collection *All Roads Lead to the Sea*. It received positive attention locally and won both the Jessie Mackay Best First Book Award for Poetry and the Montana Book Award in 1998. She followed this up with a second collection called *Dismemberment* (1998).

In 1999, Kassabova published her debut as a novelist, *Reconnaissance*, about a young Bulgarian woman backpacking across New Zealand. It won the 2000 Commonwealth Writer's Prize Best First Book Award for the South East Asia and South Pacific region. She published another novel, *Love in the Land of Midas*, in 2001. The story, told from multiple perspectives, revolves around the Greek Civil War, after World War II. However, Kassabova mostly made her living as a travel writer. In 2002, she won the Cathay Pacific Travel Writer of the Year Award for New Zealand.

Kassabova left New Zealand for Berlin in 2002 after she was awarded a creative residency. She also lived briefly in France before settling in Scotland when she was thirty years old. There she had to essentially begin her career anew, as the world of New Zealand literature was barely recognized in the United Kingdom. However, her new homeland quickly proved inspiring. "My writing comes out of physical places," she told Major. "I become obsessed with a particular place, then stories and characters and themes begin to emerge from that place as if by osmosis. It's the same for me as a living being. I am sensitive to the place where I'm living."

EUROPEAN CAREER AND *A STREET WITHOUT A NAME*

Kassabova's European publication career began in 2003 with a poetry collection called *Someone Else's Life*. The book included poems from *All Roads Lead to the Sea* and *Dismemberment*, but also new poems. She published another poetry collection, *Geography for the Lost*, in 2007. Many of her poems drew on her experience of living as something like a migrant, with no permanent home. However, she much preferred her new rooted existence in Scotland. "I was looking for a place that I felt was right," she told Teddy Jamieson for Scotland's *Herald* (3 Feb. 2017). "You can't always rationalize that feeling. The relationship between an individual and a place, there's something mysterious about it."

Kassabova published her memoir *A Street Without a Name: Childhood and Other Misadventures in Bulgaria* in 2008. As the subtitle suggests, it recounts her childhood in Sofia, framed by her return to the same city twenty years later. Key to the narrative is the stark difference between the Bulgaria she knew in the twilight of Communism in the 1970s and 1980s and the one she finds as an adult. The book was widely reviewed to much acclaim and launched her to a new level of recognition in the European literary scene. Carmen Bugan, writing for the *Harvard Review* (20 Jan. 2011), described it as both "a travel guide" and "a personal search for a lost childhood in a lost country," noting that Kassabova's "lucid narrative, conversational tone, and outbursts of poetic description bring a fresh voice to contemporary European literature." Other critics were similarly taken in by *A Street Without a Name*, remarking on how the book works on both personal and broader cultural levels. It was subsequently shortlisted for the

Stanford Dolman Travel Book of the Year Award and the Prix du Livre Européen.

Kassabova built on her success by returning to fiction, releasing the novel *Villa Pacifica* in 2010. The plot concerns a Finnish travel writer named Ute visiting an unnamed country in South America. She and her husband Jerry stay at an off-the-beaten-path animal sanctuary called Villa Pacifica, where many things begin to go wrong. Though fairly well reviewed, the novel did not attract as much attention as Kassabova's breakthrough work of nonfiction.

TWELVE MINUTES OF LOVE AND *BORDER*

Kassabova's next book brought her back to nonfiction, through *Twelve Minutes of Love: A Tango Story* (2011) would prove difficult to classify. In a review for the *Independent* (6 Nov. 2011), Doug Johnstone described the work as a "travelogue, memoir, dance history and some seriously good writing on the human condition," further praising it as "sharp, clever and engaging, a wonderful mix of self-deprecating humor and genuine insight." At the most basic level, *Twelve Minutes of Love* is a book about the form of dance known as tango. Kassabova first fell in love with the tango in New Zealand, later traveling to Argentina (where the dance was born) and other locations around the globe to research it. She weaves her own experience in with the complex history of the dance, creating a rich narrative that was praised for its insight and humor.

Kassabova continued her success in narrative nonfiction with *Border: A Journey to the Edge of Europe* (2017). In it, she writes about the people she met on a journey crossing through the border region of Bulgaria, Greece, and Turkey. "I started from a position of relative emptiness and ignorance, with a gut sense that there was something rich to tell," she told Jeffery Gleaves for the *Paris Review* (12 Sept. 2017). "As soon as I started hearing people's stories, it became obvious to me that this book was also going to be about how people narrate their lives, about how we all narrate our lives." Those profiled include everyone from shepherds to human traffickers, former border guards to refugees, all shaped by the region's political and cultural borders. Building on their oral stories, Kassabova creates a narrative that, in her signature style, serves multiple ends. The book is a travelogue, a history, and a reflection on identity. Of course, as a Bulgarian, part of that reflection is inward, incorporating her own family background. "It ended up feeling a little bit like an attempt at exorcism, as if I needed to name the bones," Kassabova told Jamieson of the research and writing process.

Border brought Kassabova some of the best reviews of her career. Jacob Mikanowski, who reviewed the book for the *Los Angeles Review of Books* (1 Oct. 2017), called it "that rarest of things: a travel book with a conscience that is also a compendium of wonders." Many critics noted the skillful way in which the book balances exploration of the past with discussion of the contemporary mass migration of refugees into the region and Europe as a whole, showing how borders are continually relevant, even as they change in substance and meaning. *Border* again pushed Kassabova to a new level of recognition, winning several notable awards.

PERSONAL LIFE

After coming to Scotland, Kassabova lived in Edinburgh for some time before moving to a rural cottage near Inverness. There her partner owned an art gallery in a former church. Despite her love of travel, Kassabova has also discussed her need to establish roots. "I don't think I'm a nomad," she told Jamieson. "I guess I feel quite settled in Scotland rather than looking beyond the horizon. I really think I've arrived home in Scotland."

SUGGESTED READING

Bugan, Carmen. Review of *Street Without a Name: Childhood and Other Misadventures in Bulgaria*, by Kapka Kassabova. *Harvard Review*, 20 Jan. 2011, www.harvardreview.org/?q=features/book-review/street-without-name-childhood-and-other-misadventures-bulgaria. Accessed 3 May 2018.

Jamieson, Teddy. "Author Kapka Kassabova on Borders, Brexit and Her Life in Scotland." *The Herald* [Scotland], 3 Feb. 2017, www.heraldscotland.com/news/15070379.Author_Kapka_Kassabova_on_Borders__Brexit_and_her_life_in_Scotland/. Accessed 7 May 2018.

Johnstone, Doug. Review of *Twelve Minutes of Love: A Tango Story*, by Kapka Kassabova. *Independent*, 6 Nov. 2011, www.independent.co.uk/arts-entertainment/books/reviews/twelve-minutes-of-love-a-tango-story-by-kapka-kassabova-6257716.html. Accessed 3 May 2018.

"Kapka Kassabova." *British Council Literature*, 2018, literature.britishcouncil.org/writer/kapka-kassabova. Accessed 7 May 2018.

Kassabova, Kapka. "Mouths Full of Earth: An Interview with Kapka Kassabova." Interview by Jeffery Gleaves. *The Paris Review*, 12 Sept. 2017. www.theparisreview.org/blog/2017/09/12/mouths-full-of-earth-an-interview-with-kapka-kassabova/. Accessed 3 May 2018.

Kassabova, Kapka. "The SRB Interview: Kapka Kassabova." Interview by Nick Major. *Scottish Review of Books*, 10 Feb. 2018, www.scottishreviewofbooks.org/free-content/the-srb-interview-kapka-kassabova/. Accessed 3 May 2018.

Mikanowski, Jacob. "The Southern Curtain: Kapka Kassabova's 'Border.'" Review of *Border: A Journey to the Edge of Europe*, by Kapka Kassabova. *Los Angeles Review of Books*, 1 Oct. 2017, lareviewofbooks.org/article/the-southern-curtain-kapka-kassabovas-border. Accessed 3 May 2018.

SELECTED WORKS

All Roads Lead to the Sea, 1997; *Dismemberment*, 1998; *Reconnaissance*, 1999; *Someone Else's Life*, 2003; *Geography for the Lost*, 2007; *A Street Without a Name: Childhood and Other Misadventures in Bulgaria*, 2008; *Villa Pacifica*, 2010; *Twelve Minutes of Love: A Tango Story*, 2011; *Border: A Journey to the Edge of Europe*, 2017

—*Molly Hagan*

Case Keenum

Date of birth: February 17, 1988
Occupation: Football player

Quarterback Case Keenum's road to success in the National Football League (NFL) has been perhaps a more circuitous route than most. A high school football star who went on to play four full seasons of football for the University of Houston over the course of six years, he was not selected by a professional team during the 2012 NFL Draft and instead signed with the Houston Texans as a free agent. Over the next several years, Keenum bounced between the Texans and the St. Louis Rams, between the teams themselves and their practice squads, and between cities as the Rams franchise moved from Missouri to California. Although that itinerant lifestyle could be draining for many athletes, Keenum made the best of the learning opportunities it offered. "You're almost lucky in a way. Sure, there's less job security. And sure, the paycheck is smaller. And sure, you could be packing your bags at a moment's notice," he wrote in a personal essay for the *Players' Tribune* (11 Jan. 2018). "But still, I'm telling you—there's something about that life. . . . You learn things on the fringes." After accompanying the Minnesota Vikings into the playoffs following the 2017 season and signing a new two-year contract with the Denver Broncos in March 2018, however, Keenum's time confined to the fringes of the NFL seems poised to come to an end.

EARLY LIFE AND EDUCATION

Casey Austin Keenum was born on February 17, 1988, in Brownwood, Texas. One of three children born to Steve and Susan Keenum, he grew

Kevin B Long, via Wikimedia Commons

up in Abilene, Texas. Keenum's family was heavily involved in sports throughout his childhood: his father coached high school and college football and would later become an area director for the Fellowship of Christian Athletes, while his mother taught physical education in the Abilene school system. Keenum has credited his father with teaching him to play football. "He taught me the game, taught me the basics of what it means to be a football player and a quarterback," he told Sid Hartman for the *StarTribune* (5 Oct. 2017). "I'd say my dad has been the most influential person."

As a teenager, Keenum was active in a variety of sports and competed on the varsity baseball and track teams while attending Wylie High School in Abilene. However, he focused primarily on football, playing quarterback for the Wylie Bulldogs, and aspired to play professionally one day. As in many high schools in the area, football was an overwhelming passion in Keenum's school, as he recalled in his piece for the *Players' Tribune*. "It was traditions and superstitions," he wrote. "It was pep rallies and cheerleaders and letter jackets. It was having a decal with your name and number on the back of your truck, so that everybody knew whose truck it was." As quarterback, Keenum played a major role in helping the Bulldogs win the Texas Class 3A Division 1 State Championship in 2004, the first state championship ever won by the team. Keenum graduated from Wylie in 2006.

COLLEGE CAREER

As a talented high school player and the member of a state championship–winning team, Keenum attracted significant attention from colleges and universities and was scouted seriously by several institutions. Following his graduation, he enrolled in the University of Houston, which had offered him a scholarship. Given his longtime interest in sports, he chose to major in kinesiology and sports administration and minored in business administration.

Keenum initially hoped to play football for the Houston Cougars beginning in his freshman year. However, team leadership held off on having Keenum compete with the team in a process known as redshirting, in which an athlete is allowed more time to develop skills and strength before joining a team. The process enabled Keenum to begin his four years of college football eligibility as a so-called redshirt freshman, in what was technically his second year of college. He joined the team as a quarterback in 2007 and continued to play for the Cougars in 2008 and 2009. The 2010 season, however, brought a major setback that altered the course of Keenum's college career. Three games into what would have been his last season, Keenum tore the anterior cruciate ligament (ACL) in one of his knees. The injury instantly ended his season, forcing Keenum to sit out while his team competed without him.

For Keenum, the injury provided a degree of perspective about the sport of football that he had previously been lacking. "I've learned that football is not the most important thing in my life and really it shouldn't be the most important thing in anybody's life," he told Don Leypoldt for the University of Houston's football website (13 Oct. 2011). "I learned really quickly that it can be taken away." Not content to allow his final season at the University of Houston be taken away from him, Keenum again made use of established redshirting procedures, obtaining permission to return to the Cougars for a final season in his sixth year of college after sitting out the 2010 season for medical reasons. To that end, Keenum enrolled in the university's graduate school to pursue further studies in physical education with a concentration in sports administration after completing his bachelor's degree in December 2010. Over the course of his final season, Keenum achieved a pass-completion percentage of 71.0 percent, 5,631 passing yards, and forty-eight passing touchdowns. In November 2011, he was named a finalist for the Davey O'Brien Trophy, which recognizes excellence among college and university quarterbacks.

HOUSTON TEXANS

In April 2012, Keenum entered that year's NFL Draft in the hope of being selected to play for a professional football team. He particularly hoped to be chosen by the Houston Texans, a team he had long admired and that was also close to home. However, by the final round of the draft, Keenum had not been chosen by any team. "At that point, I was just hoping that nobody would draft me and that I would be able to do something with the Texans afterward," he recalled to Joseph Duarte for the *Houston Chronicle* (28 Apr. 2012). Keenum's dream came true following the draft, when the Texans signed him as an undrafted free agent. "I'm really glad it happened," Keenum told Duarte following the announcement. "I truly believe it's a first-class championship franchise and look forward to being part of a whole lot of championships in the years to come."

Despite Keenum's high hopes for his time with the Texans, he did not have the opportunity to play for the main Texans team in 2012, instead spending the season honing his skills as a member of the franchise's practice team. He made his official regular-season debut with the team on October 20, 2013, in a game against the Kansas City Chiefs. Keenum's brief tenure with the Texans was largely unsuccessful, as the team lost every game in which he played, and he was later removed from the team's lineup. In the fall of 2014, the St. Louis Rams acquired Keenum and assigned him to their practice squad, where he remained for less than two months. Keenum again signed with the Houston Texans in December 2014 and played two games with the team late in the 2014 season, both of which the Texans won.

ON THE MOVE

Following his brief season with the Texans, Keenum was traded to the Rams, rejoining that team in March 2015. He was named a starting quarterback for the Rams for the 2015 season and played in six games over the course of the regular season, achieving a pass-completion percentage of 60.8 percent, 828 passing yards, and four passing touchdowns. In early 2016, the Rams organization moved to Los Angeles, California, and Keenum signed a one-year contract with the team. He began the 2016 season as starting quarterback for the newly minted Los Angeles Rams and went on to play in a total of ten games over the regular season.

Since joining the NFL in 2012, Keenum had undergone a great deal of movement between teams, an experience that some players may have found disheartening. For Keenum, however, the experience both provided him with numerous opportunities and underscored his commitment to his sport. "You learn how to put your head down and go to work," he wrote for the *Players' Tribune*. "You learn the value of having people who believe in you—and the value of

proving them right. . . . You learn how to cherish every opportunity, right down to the last one . . . because you never know how many you're gonna get."

Keenum was on the move again in March 2017, when he signed a one-year contract with the Minnesota Vikings. Over the course of the regular season, Keenum played in fifteen games and achieved a pass-completion percentage of 67.6 percent, 3,547 passing yards, and twenty-two passing touchdowns, the best statistics he had put forth to date in the NFL. The Vikings had a strong season overall, winning thirteen of the sixteen games played during the season. Thanks to the strong performance of Keenum and his teammates, the Vikings earned a spot in the playoffs during the postseason and competed against the New Orleans Saints in the National Football Conference (NFC) divisional playoffs. The Vikings beat the Saints 29–24 and went on to the NFC Championship, where they were defeated by the Philadelphia Eagles, the eventual Super Bowl champions.

DENVER BRONCOS

After the 2017 football season concluded, Keenum was again set to become a free agent, eligible to sign with any team that made him an offer. In March 2018, he signed a two-year, $36 million contract with the Denver Broncos, his longest contract to that point. Although he had experienced some success with the Vikings, Keenum hoped to take his career to new heights in Denver. "It's nice to have the freedom to come out here and compete and really pursue just excellence that I want out of the quarterback position and out of my craft," he told Lindsay H. Jones for *USA Today* (1 June 2018). "It's not just X's and O's and getting the ball down the field, it's the leadership part of that that helps." The Broncos' preseason was scheduled to begin in August 2018, and the team is set to play its first regular-season game, a bout against the Seattle Seahawks, on September 9.

PERSONAL LIFE

Keenum met his wife, Kimberly (Caddell) Keenum, while they were both attending high school in Texas. They married in 2011. In addition to focusing on football, Keenum wrote a memoir, *Playing for More*, that is scheduled for publication in September 2018. "It's kind of the story of me off the field, not just on the field, but why I play, why I do what I do and why I get to stand up here and talk to you guys—be the Denver Broncos' quarterback," he told journalists, as reported by Aric DiLalla for the website of the Denver Broncos (12 June 2018). "If it encourages and challenges somebody, then I've accomplished something with it."

SUGGESTED READING

DiLalla, Aric. "A New Chapter: Author (and Quarterback) Case Keenum Pens Memoir, 'Playing for More.'" *Denver Broncos*, 12 June 2018, www.denverbroncos.com/news/a-new-chapter-author-and-quarterback-case-keenum-pens-memoir-playing-for-more. Accessed 13 July 2018.

Duarte, Joseph. "Keenum Goes Undrafted but Joins Texans as Free Agent." *Houston Chronicle*, 28 Apr. 2012, www.houstonchronicle.com/sports/texans/article/Keenum-goes-un-drafted-but-joins-Texans-as-free-3518857.php. Accessed 13 July 2018.

Hartman, Sid. "Case Keenum's College Coaches Believe in His Ability to Lead Vikings." *Star-Tribune*, 5 Oct. 2017, www.startribune.com/case-keenum-s-college-coaches-believe-in-his-ability-to-lead-vikings/449510973/. Accessed 13 July 2018.

Jones, Lindsay H. "With Broncos, Case Keenum Gets First Turn as Offensive Centerpiece." *USA Today*, 1 June 2018, www.usatoday.com/story/sports/nfl/broncos/2018/06/01/case-keenum-denver-broncos-of-fense/662148002/. Accessed 13 July 2018.

Keenum, Case. "Interview with Keenum." By Don Leypoldt. *University of Houston Football*, 13 Oct. 2011, www.uhcougars.com/sports/m-footbl/spec-rel/101311aab.html. Accessed 13 July 2018.

Keenum, Case. "Right Team, Right Time." *Players' Tribune*, 11 Jan. 2018, www.theplayers-tribune.com/en-us/articles/case-keenum-vikings-playoffs. Accessed 13 July 2018.

Trapasso, Chris. "'Who the Heck Is Case Keenum Again?" *Bleacher Report*, 18 Oct. 2013, bleacherreport.com/articles/1816003-who-the-heck-is-case-keenum-again. Accessed 13 July 2018.

—*Joy Crelin*

Kelela

Date of birth: June 6, 1983
Occupation: Singer

Kelela is an experimental R & B singer whose debut album, *Take Me Apart* (2017), has won her both critical and popular success, featuring in numerous media outlets' year-end lists—including that of the music website *Pitchfork*, which ranked it number four on its list of the fifty best albums of 2017—and a nomination for the 2018 GLAAD (Gay & Lesbian Alliance Against Defamation) Media Award for outstanding music artist. In November 2017, she was one of a handful of musical artists selected by her close

By Valentinostarz, via Wikimedia Commons

friend and fellow R & B artist Solange to feature in Calvin Klein's spring 2018 "Our Family" campaign, for which she and Solange also recorded a brief duet.

Kelela was born in Washington, DC, and raised in a nearby Maryland suburb. She was a musician and a singer from an early age, though it took her years of singing jazz standards in clubs and fronting rock bands to find her true artistic voice. Critics often say that Kelela's music defies genre; for the artist, this is a conscious, political choice. She claims all genres because no genre can fully define her. "When I'm thinking about lyrics and when I'm thinking about sonics, I'm thinking about the black women who have never really felt perfectly shaped for the spaces that have been made for them," she said to Hunter Harris for *Vulture* (6 Oct. 2017). "Or the black women who are trying to fit into something. I wanted to create a space for us to not be subject to any confines, especially when it comes to sound."

Kelela's sound combines electronica and classic R & B, while her lyrics express power in vulnerability and radically assert the complexity of black womanhood. After moving to Los Angeles in 2010, she teamed up with various producers from the LA–based electronic music label Fade to Mind and its British sister label Night Slugs to record her first mixtape, *Cut 4 Me*, released in 2013. The mixtape was well received, establishing Kelela as an artist adept at combining mainstream and avant-garde sounds into an enticing, futuristic-sounding package that, as Anupa Mistry wrote in a review of her 2015 extended-play album (EP) *Hallucinogen* for *Pitchfork* (7 Oct. 2015), "feels like there is blood flowing through it" and "looks to a future with a decidedly human shape."

EARLY LIFE

Kelela Mizanekristos was born in Washington, DC, on June 6, 1983. Her parents, who had both immigrated to the United States from Ethiopia in the 1970s to attend college on full scholarships, met while at school "through a radical student movement that was interested in reform," Kelela said to Lakin Starling for the *Fader* (3 Oct. 2017). "They were about social justice." Following in their footsteps, Kelela became interested in social justice, and particularly issues of institutionalized racism, at an early age. "*How did white people take over the world?* I could not get off of this question," she recalled to Starling. "It consumed me."

Music was another early interest of Kelela's. Growing up in Gaithersburg, Maryland, a suburb of DC, she was exposed to a variety of musical genres by both of her parents, who never married and lived on different floors in the same apartment building. Her mother was a singer herself, and in her apartment, Kelela listened to classic records by the South African singer Miriam Makeba, jazz singer Sarah Vaughan, and soul singer Bobby Womack. In her father's apartment, she heard for the first time the rich tones of blues singer Tracy Chapman.

As a child, Kelela played the violin and sang in the school choir. In the eighth grade, she auditioned and won admission to the prestigious Duke Ellington School of the Arts, but her parents could not afford the tuition. Kelela was deeply disappointed. She broadened her artistic scope as a teenager, listening to electronic music and experimental jazz as a student at Magruder High School in Rockville, Maryland. A boyfriend encouraged her to pursue a singing career, but Kelela was unsure, feeling that she had missed her chance at such a career when she was forced to turn down her admission to Duke Ellington.

EARLY CAREER

After graduating from high school in 2001, Kelela briefly attended Montgomery College in Rockville, where she met and drew inspiration from her classmate Amir Mohamed el Khalifa, a rapper who performs under the stage name Oddisee. She later transferred to American University in DC and began studying sociology, less to pursue a career in the field than to try to understand the various forms of institutionalized discrimination against which she fought. "Every time I experience racism and sexism, the intersection of both, or misogynoir, it's almost like I go back to the drawing board. . . . I feel so crushed and hurt every time," she said to

Starling. Feeling stifled by her university experience, Kelela never finished her degree, instead dropping out to return to music. In 2007 she began singing jazz standards at open-mic events at Café Nema, a now-shuttered Somali café and jazz venue in DC's U Street Corridor.

While Kelela worked on challenging herself as a singer by tackling different genres of music—including songs in Arabic and Urdu, which she taught herself to sing—she had yet to try writing her own songs. She received encouragement from Yukimi Nagano, lead singer of the Swedish electronic band Little Dragon, whom she met in 2008 after attending one of the group's concerts in DC. Nagano gave her some simple but ultimately transformative career advice, Kelela recalled to Starling: "Be with people you like. And just jam out."

With this directive in mind, Kelela further explored various music genres, joining an indie band called Dizzy Spells and singing for a while with the progressive metal band Animals as Leaders after meeting the group's guitarist, Tosin Abasi, outside a DC café. She and Abasi dated for a time and began writing songs together, but Kelela remained reluctant to attempt solo songwriting. Only after attending an inspiring workshop in 2009—where, she told Starling, she was "taught . . . that if you want something to happen, it's not by chance," and that "the greater the risks and the more uncomfortable you feel, the greater the outcome and the potential gain"— and learning how to record music on her laptop computer, which afforded her a much-needed sense of creative privacy, did she begin to see herself as individual artist rather than a member of a band. "That's literally when I started writing my own music," she recalled to Chris Richards for the *Washington Post* (14 Apr. 2014). "Being able to pursue it and [mess] it up? I couldn't *get it* with other people like that."

CUT 4 ME (2013) AND *HALLUCINOGEN* (2015)

In 2010, Kelela moved to Los Angeles, where she entered into a fruitful collaboration with producers from the record labels Fade to Mind and Night Slugs. For the next three years, she plugged away at writing and recording her debut mixtape, *Cut 4 Me*, which she finally released in October 2013 and which features in-demand electronic music producers such as Bok Bok and the production duo Nguzunguzu. Miles Raymer, in a review for *Pitchfork* (18 Oct. 2013), marveled at Kelela's singular vision, writing, "*Cut 4 Me* is an ambitiously catchy record as well as being an aesthetically ambitious one. . . . The more important things that *Cut 4 Me* teaches us about Kelela are that she has the taste to pick out a fantasy all-star team of collaborators, the talent to make herself heard over their beats, and the intelligence to get it all together at the exact right moment."

Despite the mixtape's positive reception, Kelela was perturbed by the tone of much of the praise she received—specifically, by the tendency of predominantly white music critics to emphasize the "innovative" nature of her work. "There was a rhetoric around [*Cut 4 Me*] being the first time that R & B got innovative," she later recalled in a question-and-answer session at the University of London's School of Oriental and African Studies (SOAS), as reported by Charlie Brinkhurst-Cuff for *Dazed* (14 Oct. 2017). "It implies we have such a low expectation of this genre that 'now it is palatable and now it is worthy of praise.' It felt like there was a moment where white people got the R & B memo." Kelela views her music as part of a long, specifically black tradition of innovation. "It's fine to be introduced to a genre of music but there's a way that whiteness usurps and snatches," she explained. "I use that word because it feels quite violent. Every seeming triumph, it's still tainted by that weird thing. The world still has it out for you, even when you're getting praised."

Two years later, in 2015, Kelela released *Hallucinogen*, which she recorded with electronic producers such as Arca, who has worked with Björk, Kanye West, and Frank Ocean, as well as hip-hop producer DJ Dahi. The EP was included in *Rolling Stone* magazine's list of the twenty best R & B albums of 2015. Kelela was also featured on "Scales," a song from Solange's critically acclaimed album *A Seat at the Table* (2016).

TAKE ME APART (2017)

Like *Cut 4 Me* and *Hallucinogen*, Kelela's debut studio album, *Take Me Apart*, was a long time in the making. The notoriously perfectionist artist began fleshing it out when she began working on *Cut 4 Me* seven years before. She worked with a host of diverse collaborators, including Romy Madley Croft of the XX and Sabina Sciubba of the Brazilian Girls.

Thematically, the album chronicles a painful break-up, a return to single life, and the euphoria of a new romantic relationship. The lead single, "LMK" (an abbreviation of the phrase "let me know"), is a sexy and playful groove that evokes 1990s-era R & B singers such as Aaliyah. The sonically layered break-up groove "Frontline," which premiered on a September 2017 episode of the HBO television show *Insecure* (2016–), is "completely transportive" and "a cinematic document in and of itself," according to Julianne Escobedo Shepherd for *Pitchfork* (6 Oct. 2017). "Frontline" drew widespread media attention in February 2018 with an animated music video that deliberately mimics the visuals of the Sims computer game franchise, featuring a Sims-style

Kelela breaking up with her boyfriend and then driving away with her friends.

Take Me Apart was highly praised by critics. "It's a digital phantasm, a matrix of synthetic sounds enfolding countless tracks of Kelela's vocals," Jon Pareles wrote in a review for the *New York Times* (4 Oct. 2017). "Yet for all its electronic metamorphoses, the goal it achieves is intimacy. . . . [Kelela] makes sure that virtuality leads back to physicality." Karas Lamb, reviewing the album for *Consequence of Sound* (6 Oct. 2017), called it "a graduation of sorts that finds her in lockstep with production that would have swallowed her in the past," as well as "a multi-faceted sidewinder of a release that refines the aesthetics of Kelela's previous projects and painstakingly marries them to exemplary result." Katherine St. Asaph wrote for *Pitchfork* (12 Dec. 2017), in a brief review for the website's list of the fifty best albums of 2017 (on which *Take Me Apart* was ranked fourth), "Vulnerability is often expressed through smallness, but for Kelela, it's a magnifying force."

PERSONAL LIFE

Kelela, who identifies as queer, has said that her frank treatment of intimacy in her music is a way of defining her own sexuality, rather than allowing others to define it for her, and empowering others to do the same. "As a queer black woman, [that] means the world to me, because I've experienced what it feels like to be a queer black girl growing up in the US," she said to Tara Joshi for the *Quietus* (10 Oct. 2017). "So all I'm thinking about when I write is—is it gonna be a safe thing for them to sing? Can they get in their car on a s—— day and sing this song and feel really good about it? That is basically what I'm trying to make sure of—that even when it's sad, it's really empowering somehow."

SUGGESTED READING

Bin Shikhan, Amani. "How Kelela Found Her Voice." *The Ringer*, Vox Media, 14 July 2017, www.theringer.com/2017/7/14/16078134/kelela-r-b-debut-album-take-me-apart-59da526e1985. Accessed 18 Apr. 2017.

Brinkhurst-Cuff, Charlie. "Kelela on the Joy and Pain of Being a Black, Queer Musician." *Dazed*, 14 Oct. 2017, www.dazeddigital.com/music/article/37763/1/kelela-on-the-joy-and-pain-of-being-a-black-queer-musician. Accessed 17 Apr. 2018.

Kelela. "Kelela Is R&B's Futurist." Interview by Hunter Harris. *Vulture*, New York Media, 6 Oct. 2017, www.vulture.com/2017/10/interview-kelela.html. Accessed 17 Apr. 2018.

Kelela. "Kelela on the Intersections of Identity, Gender, Sexuality & Ethnicity for *Oyster* #108." Interview by Lucy Jones. *Oyster*, 13 May 2016, new.oystermag.com/

kelela-mizanekristos-on-hallucinogen-gen-der-sexuality-ethnicity-and-identity-for-oyster-108. Accessed 18 Apr. 2018.

Kelela. "Power in Vulnerability: An Interview with Kelela." By Tara Joshi. *The Quietus*, 10 Oct. 2017, thequietus.com/articles/23351-kelela-interview. Accessed 20 Apr. 2018.

Richards, Chris. "Kelela: An R&B Star-to-Be." *The Washington Post*, 14 Apr. 2014, www.washingtonpost.com/lifestyle/style/kelela-an-randb-star-to-be/2014/04/14/f4681b6a-bb4a-11e3-96ae-f2c36d2b1245_story.html. Accessed 16 Apr. 2018.

Starling, Lakin. "Kelela Is Ready for You Now." *The Fader*, 3 Oct. 2017, www.thefader.com/2017/10/03/kelela-cover-story-take-me-apart-interview. Accessed 16 Apr. 2018.

SELECTED WORKS

Cut 4 Me, 2013; *Hallucinogen*, 2015; *Take Me Apart*, 2017

—*Molly Hagan*

Erin Entrada Kelly

Occupation: Author, educator

A broad theme of American literature—and of children's literature in particular—is the exploration of the individual in American society, how one fits into it and makes one's way through it. This theme is explored in detail in the young-adult novels of Erin Entrada Kelly, an American novelist of Filipina ancestry who has won a number of awards for her work, including the Newbery Medal in 2018 for her third novel, *Hello, Universe* (2017).

Her other novels, *Blackbird Fly* (2015) and *The Land of Forgotten Girls* (2016), have also been award winners. Each of those has addressed the theme of Filipina identity in American life. Her book *You Go First*, published in 2018, delves into the budding online friendship of a pair of preteens who feel isolated from their peers. "Loneliness is a common theme in all of my books because I was a lonely kid," Kelly said in an interview with James McDonald for *Kirkus Reviews* (13 Apr. 2018). "I like to write for kids who are also lonely. . . . You can feel alone in your family, in school, and sometimes even with your friends. Loneliness is such an incredibly weighty emotion, such an experience."

EARLY LIFE AND CAREER

Erin Entrada Kelly was born in the United States and raised in Lake Charles, Louisiana. Her mother, who was an immigrant from the Philippines, loved to read to Kelly throughout childhood. In an interview with Brett Downer for *Thrive Magazine* (18 Mar. 2015), Kelly recalled, "When I was a little girl, my mother read to me at night ('The Cat in the Hat' was one of our favorites) and I would ask if I could read to her instead. She usually fell asleep to me reading, instead of the other way around. Around that time, I started writing my own stories. My father showed me how to staple the loose-leaf pages together to make them look like 'real books.' Once he even taped two pieces of cardboard together to make a hardcover."

Young Kelly dreamed of becoming a writer. She remembers promising to write her mother a best seller someday. But high-quality young-adult novels were rare when she was growing up, and few of them were populated by characters with ethnic backgrounds similar to hers. She told Downer, "In the 1980s, there wasn't much to choose from—so I was just starting to read grown-up novels. If you had asked me what my favorite book was, I probably would have said 'Cujo' or 'Pet Sematary' by Stephen King."

In school, Kelly was lonely and felt set apart from her fellow classmates. She was the only one in her classes with Filipino ancestry. She has admitted in interviews that she hated school. After attending LaGrange High School, where she took creative writing and became interested in journalism following a visit by a reporter from the *American Press*, she earned a bachelor's degree in women's studies and liberal arts from McNeese State University in Lake Charles. Later on, she would earn a master of fine arts (MFA) degree from Rosemont College in Rosemont, Pennsylvania.

For about a decade, Kelly worked as a reporter for the *American Press* and later at *Thrive Magazine* as a writer and editor. During this time, she also wrote short fiction, which was nominated for the Pushcart Prize and a Philippines Free Press Literary Award. While earning her MFA, she moved to Pennsylvania and eventually settled in Philadelphia.

BLACKBIRD FLY

Kelly has described her first young-adult novel, *Blackbird Fly* (2015), as being somewhat autobiographical. In it, she tells the story of Analyn "Apple" Yengko, a young Filipina who has moved to the United States following the death of her father. At twelve, all she has to remember her father by is a Beatles cassette tape with his name on it. She loves music and is determined to buy her own guitar, despite what her mother says. And she is just as determined to keep up her self-esteem, despite the taunts and bullying she endures from her classmates in the small town in Louisiana she has moved to. As the novel unfolds, Apple comes to respect the things that make her different and develops friendships with classmates who are not cruel to her.

The novel was named a 2016 Golden Kite Honor Book and would be met favorably by most critics. "Each character in Kelly's debut novel—the mean kids, the misfits, the adults and Apple herself—is portrayed with remarkable authenticity. The awkwardness and intense feelings inherent to middle school are palpable," noted a critic for *Kirkus Reviews* (22 Dec. 2014). "Children's literature has been waiting for Apple Yengko—a strong, Asian-American girl whose ethnic identity simultaneously complicates and enriches her life."

THE LAND OF FORGOTTEN GIRLS

Kelly's second novel, *The Land of Forgotten Girls*, which was first published in 2016, explores the lives of two Filipina American sisters, Soledad and Ming, who are forced to live in Louisiana with their stepmother, Vea. They try to escape the grief Vea gives them by recalling the magic-filled stories that their mother, Mei-Mei, told them about her sister, their Aunt Jove, who supposedly traveled all over the world. When Ming, the younger of the two sisters, begins to believe that Aunt Jove's magical adventures were real, as a way to escape their lives with Vea, Soledad looks for ways to help her—as well as ways to bridge their differences with their stepmother.

Like Kelly's debut novel, *The Land of Forgotten Girls* was met with warm praise. Writing for *School Library Journal* (21 Dec. 2015), Tiffany Davis declared, "This book will appeal to a broad array of readers, as it has a little bit of everything—fantasy, realism, sisterhood, friendship, suspense, and humor." *The Land of Forgotten Girls* earned a 2016–17 Asian Pacific American Librarians Association (APALA) Award.

WINNING THE NEWBERY MEDAL FOR *HELLO, UNIVERSE*

Kelly's most successful young-adult novel to date has been *Hello, Universe*, which was published in 2017. The novel explores the relationship of three sixth graders, Virgil Salinas, Kaori Tanaka, and Valencia Somerset, who come together when a bully named Chet Bullens does something awful. Each of the three friends is dealing with personal issues: Virgil would prefer to spend time with his guinea pig, Gulliver, than spend time with other people; Kaori believes herself to be psychic and wants to put some distance between herself and her younger sister; and Valencia is deaf and shunned by most of her classmates. But when Chet pulls a prank that ends with Virgil and Gulliver trapped in an old well, the group comes together to find him.

The novel found almost universal praise among critics. A reviewer for *Publishers Weekly* (19 Dec. 2016) wrote, "Kelly rotates among the viewpoints of Kaori, Virgil, Valencia, and neighborhood bully Chet, who contribute their own distinct stories, voices, and challenges. Infused with humor and hope, this book deftly conveys messages of resilience and self-acceptance through simple acts of everyday courage. Readers will be left inspired to tackle life's fears head-on."

In February 2018, Kelly learned that *Hello, Universe* had won the John Newbery Medal, one of the most prestigious awards presented to works of children's literature. Since 1922, it has been presented by the Association for Library Service to Children (formerly the Children's Librarians' Section), a division of the American Library Association (ALA). Past winners include such famed authors as Madeleine L'Engle, Scott O'Dell, and Lois Lowry. Kelly was stunned to hear that she had won the award and had even started driving into work the day the award was announced because she had not received a call from the medal committee early that morning. As it turns out, the committee had been trying to reach her but had her old phone number and had not been able to let her know that she had won. Of the experience, Kelly told Bethany Ao for the *Philadelphia Inquirer* (12 Feb. 2018), "I was floored, amazed, it was a tremendous honor. . . . You never actually think you're going to win something this big."

YOU GO FIRST AND FUTURE PLANS

After the Newbery announcement, Kelly was out publicizing her fourth novel, *You Go First*, which debuted in April 2018. In it, she employs alternating first-person points of view to explore the mindsets of Charlotte Lockard and Ben Boxer, a pair of preteens who enjoy playing the word game Scrabble online. Charlotte lives in Pennsylvania; Ben in Louisiana. They are both extremely bright for their ages but are very lonely and isolated from their fellow classmates, which helps to bring them closer together online. After a time, they each begin to confide in the other about the problems they face in their individual schools and in their home lives. Charlotte is having trouble with a best friend who has suddenly turned on her and at the same time is dealing with the fact that her father has just suffered a heart attack. Ben, on the other hand, is being publicly mocked for running for student council and is also dealing with his parents contemplating divorce.

"The idea behind the book is we never struggle alone," Kelly explained to McDonald, "even if we don't know it. Even if Charlotte and Ben are going through their struggles without much support, the reader knows that they are not alone, and hopefully, when the reader knows that, the reader will then say, 'Ok, well I know that I'm not struggling alone either.'"

Like its predecessors, *You Go First* received a lot of critical acclaim. A critic for *Kirkus Reviews* (22 Jan. 2018) called Kelly's latest a "well-crafted, entertaining call for middle schoolers to find their voices and remain accountable in shaping their own social spheres."

Even with the accolades and awards that have come to her, Kelly has little interest in slowing down. As of early 2018, she was in the middle of editing her first book of fantasy, which was inspired by her interest in and knowledge of Filipino folklore. That book is due out in 2019. "I love to write, it's my life," she said to Shannon Maughan for *Publishers Weekly* (13 Feb. 2018). "I've been trying to hone my illustrating skills as well, so I've been doing lots of doodles. I'm slightly obsessed with productivity, I think. At some point I'm just going to collapse. But not yet, though! Not anytime soon!"

PERSONAL LIFE

Kelly now teaches children's literature in the graduate fiction and publishing programs at Rosemont College.

SUGGESTED READING

Ao, Bethany. "Philadelphia Author Erin Entrada Kelly Wins Prestigious Newbery Medal." *The Inquirer*, 12 Feb. 2018, www.philly.com/philly/entertainment/literature/erin-entrada-kelly-newbery-medal-philadelphia-20180212.html. Accessed 21 May 2018.

Davis, Tiffany. Review of *The Land of Forgotten Girls*, by Erin Entrada Kelly. *School Library Journal*, 21 Nov. 2015, www.slj.com/2015/12/reviews/the-land-of-forgotten-girls-by-erin-entrada-kelly-slj-review/#_. Accessed 21 May 2018.

Kelly, Erin Entrada. "First Person with Erin Kelly." Interview by Brett Downer. *Thrive Magazine*, 18 Mar. 2015, www.thriveswla.com/places-faces/first-person-with-erin-kelly. Accessed 21 May 2018.

Kelly, Erin Entrada. Interview. By James McDonald. *Kirkus Reviews*, 13 Apr. 2018, www.kirkusreviews.com/features/erin-entrada-kelly-2/. Accessed 21 May 2018.

Maughan, Shannon. "Housecleaning and 'Lots of Champagne': Erin Entrada Kelly Toasts Her Newbery Win." *Publishers Weekly*, 13 Feb. 2018, www.publishersweekly.com/pw/by-topic/childrens/childrens-authors/article/76054-housecleaning-and-lots-of-champagne-erin-entrada-kelly-toasts-her-newbery-win.html. Accessed 21 May 2018.

Review of *Blackbird Fly*, by Erin Entrada Kelly. *Kirkus Reviews*, 22 Dec. 2014, www.kirkusreviews.com/book-reviews/erin-entrada-kelly/blackbird-fly/. Accessed 21 May 2018.

Review of *Hello, Universe*, by Erin Entrada Kelly. *Publishers Weekly*, 19 Dec. 2016, www.

publishersweekly.com/978-0-06-241415-1. Accessed 21 May 2018.

SELECTED WORKS

Blackbird Fly, 2015; *The Land of Forgotten Girls*, 2016; *Hello, Universe*, 2017; *You Go First*, 2018

—*Christopher Mari*

Khalid

Date of birth: February 11, 1998
Occupation: Singer

Grammy-nominated R & B singer Khalid fits squarely into the category of artists who appeal to teens because he is one: he is not harkening back, like so many musicians, to the lived experience of a teenager, but instead channels it directly—on his first album, at least. "Are you still trying to understand that intense first love? Are you grounded from messing up your mom's car? Are you passionate about music that makes it all worthwhile? If so, then maybe you're a teenager looking for an anthem," host Michelle Martin said on the National Public Radio (NPR) show *All Things Considered* (27 May 2017). "Enter Khalid Robinson with his debut album, *American Teen*, which he wrote when he was a senior in high school."

Khalid—who, like Adele, Madonna, and Prince, is known by his first name—signed a major-label deal soon after uploading an early tune in the spring of 2016 to SoundCloud, a popular social network for listening to and sharing music, and he has been heaped with praise by such respected music publications as *Rolling Stone*. That early R & B–inflected track, "Location," was released as a single in February 2017 and was certified platinum by the end of May. Of his work's resonance with young fans, he told Nolan Feeney for *Entertainment Weekly* (2 Mar. 2017), "We forget that when you grow up, there are a lot of people who are in the same position as you. The reason we forget is because there's not really a true voice that talks from the perspective of youth."

In a review of *American Teen* for the *New York Times* (1 Mar. 2017), Jon Caramanica concurred, writing, "He's nailing the fitfulness of knowing the bright options the future might hold while still being stuck in school, or in his hometown, or in the frame of mind that tells you to do only what's expected of you. That's an almost universal teen conundrum. . . . He's sketching a generational mood." On NPR, however, Martin pointed out that the songs on Khalid's debut album possessed a broad appeal that easily crossed age lines: "While his lyrics are very much of the

Photo by Steve Jennings/WireImage

moment, the themes he explores—belonging, love, loneliness, loss—are timeless."

EARLY LIFE AND EDUCATION

Khalid Robinson was born on February 11, 1998, at Fort Stewart, Georgia, home of the US Army's Third Infantry Division. His mother, Linda Wolfe, served in the Army for more than two decades, starting as a supply technician and retiring in early 2017 as a sergeant first class. Wolfe had separated from Khalid's father early on, and raised Khalid and his younger sister as a single mother.

A skilled musical artist in her own right, Wolfe had harbored aspirations of becoming a professional R & B singer in her youth but ultimately chose the more reliable path of a military career because of family obligations. She did, however, train for a military occupational specialty at the US Army School of Music, and she spent the latter part of her time in the service performing in various ensembles, including the First Armored Division Band and the US Army Europe Band and Chorus.

When Khalid was in the second grade, his father was killed by a drunk driver. "I was very upset, mad—the stages of grief," he told Jonah Weiner for *Rolling Stone* (31 July 2017). "That's probably why I matured a lot faster than a lot of people my age, because I already lost something super-close to me."

Wolfe's career required frequent moves, and Khalid lived at various times in Kentucky, upstate New York, and Germany. "I felt a sense of loneliness," he admitted to Gerrick D. Kennedy

for the *Los Angeles Times* (3 Mar. 2017). "You move so much and you meet so many different people, you kind of meet the same people, in a sense. You build this relationship for a certain amount of years that you share with people and then boom, it's gone." Like Linda, he found solace and pleasure in music. "I feel like growing up with my mom was the foundation of my (interest in music)," he recalled to Dave Acosta for the *El Paso Times* (7 Feb. 2017). "In my home, we listened to music all the time. I was raised through music and I've been interested in it since I was three. I've been singing since I could talk correctly."

Khalid took part in school choirs and studied musical theater in whatever locale he found himself. He appeared in school productions, playing Cornelius in *Hello, Dolly* and Seaweed in *Hairspray*, to name just a few. At home, he watched video clips of favorite artists from across a wide variety of genres, including Frank Ocean, James Blake, Brandy, Usher, Fleetwood Mac, Adele, Bill Withers, Aaliyah, Andrea Bocelli, and Father John Misty, noting their stage technique and the ways in which they conveyed emotion. His interest in musical theater was something of a double-edged sword: while his unquestionable talent gave him a modest degree of popularity, it also attracted disparaging comments that he was not masculine enough. In response, he told Weiner, "I was like, 'OK, but I'm still gonna be successful, and you're not.'"

When Khalid's mother was transferred to Fort Bliss, adjacent to El Paso, Texas, Khalid moved yet again, this time shortly before the start of his senior year. He enrolled in El Paso's Americas High School, a large, diverse institution located on the east side of the border city. Although he assumed that he would probably become a music teacher one day, he had bigger dreams of writing and recording his own songs, and he channeled his sorrow at leaving his last group of friends into a growing portfolio of lyrics. He recalled to Kennedy, "I just turned all the negativity into a creative." His output surprised and impressed his mother. "I knew that he was very gifted, vocally. I knew that he was a very smart, bright kid. But the writing skills—I didn't know he had that," she told Martin. "DNA's a powerful thing!"

Luckily, at Americas Khalid soon found a new and accepting group of friends, as well as teachers who were supportive of his musical aspirations. As an experiment, he recorded two songs, "Saved" and "Stuck on You," and uploaded them to a SoundCloud page. The experience convinced him that he wanted to record professionally. As his senior year drew to a close, he uploaded what would become his first massive hit, "Location." He had rushed to complete the song, he has told journalists, because he wanted it to be available to his classmates before the senior prom, in hopes that he would be elected prom king. The strategy worked, and he won.

Khalid graduated on May 28, 2016, and fans can still watch the ceremony, which was filmed and is now archived on his school district's YouTube channel. In it, he does a small dance before walking across the stage to get his diploma. He told his mother he wanted to skip college and become a recording artist instead; knowing his talent well, she agreed.

MUSIC CAREER

On the strength of his SoundCloud efforts, Khalid found a manager and began working with the producer Joshua "Syk Sense" Scruggs, who had also produced tracks for Drake and Travis Scott. He soon caught the ear of Tunji Balogun, the vice president of artists and repertoire (A&R) for RCA Records, who listened with fascination as Khalid sent him a series of tracks exhibiting increasing maturity and musical skill. Balogun recalled to Acosta that when he heard "Location," he thought, "Oh, my God, this kid knows how to make a hit, in addition to being a talented vocalist and being ahead of his age. . . . The stars aligned."

Some stars were apparently also listening. Reality television star Kylie Jenner posted a video on Snapchat of herself and a group of friends listening to "Location," and the song quickly went viral. Streamed millions of times in a matter of just weeks, the track peaked at number sixteen on the Billboard Hot 100 chart, cracked the top ten Hot R & B/Hip-Hop Songs, and was quickly certified platinum. It was included on Khalid's debut album, *American Teen*, along with "Young Dumb & Broke," "8Teen," "Let's Go," "Coaster," and "Hopeless," among other tunes.

The album garnered largely positive reviews, with most critics mentioning the astuteness and sensitivity with which Khalid examines the issue of love in an age of cell phones, ride-sharing apps, and GPS pins—all of which can sometimes enable connection and sometimes thwart it. ("I'll keep your number saved, 'cause I hope one day you'll get the sense to call me," he sings on "Saved.")

Naming *American Teen* one of the top albums of 2017, the editors of *Rolling Stone* (20 June 2017) wrote: "[This is] the sound of the world opening up wide, one Uber ride and lovelorn text at a time. . . . At 19, Khalid is one of the most original voices in both R & B and pop, creating a late-night music full of warmth and flickering light."

Since working on the album—whose title, he has explained, is meant to provoke discussion about the current political climate, race, patriotism, and other hot-button issues—Khalid

has been featured as a guest singer on a track by Alina Baraz, had his single "Angels" used on the ABC drama *Grey's Anatomy*, and won best new artist honors at the 2017 MTV Video Music Awards. He has a six-month tour of North America and Europe planned for 2018, and he closed out 2017 with five nominations for the 2018 Grammy Awards, including nominations for best new artist and best R & B song (for "Location").

PERSONAL LIFE

Khalid has admitted that sudden fame has its drawbacks. He can no longer shop unrecognized, for example. Still, he appreciates the fact that other lonely people and outsiders find value in his work and relate to his lyrics.

Although Khalid has moved out of his mother's home and currently lives in Los Angeles, he envisions one day buying a large property in El Paso, a city he has grown to love. "I want kids to drive by and say, 'That's Khalid's house,'" he explained to Weiner. "It'll inspire them. That's how dreamers are born."

SUGGESTED READING

Acosta, Dave. "Khalid Finds His 'Location' in El Paso." *El Paso Times*, 7 Feb. 2017, www.elpasotimes.com/story/entertainment/2017/02/07/khalid-finds-his-location-el-paso/97422304/. Accessed 13 Nov. 2017.

Caramanica, Jon. "On Khalid's 'American Teen', Songs of Young Love and Technology." Review of *American Teen*, by Khalid. *The New York Times*, 1 Mar. 2017, www.nytimes.com/2017/03/01/arts/music/on-khalids-american-teen-songs-of-young-love-and-technology.html. Accessed 13 Nov. 2017.

Feeney, Nolan. "How 'Location' Singer Khalid Is Becoming a Voice for Young People." *Entertainment Weekly*, 2 Mar. 2017, ew.com/music/2017/03/02/khalid-location-american-teen-interview/. Accessed 13 Nov. 2017.

Kennedy, Gerrick D. "Khalid Had Many a 'Location' Growing Up: Now He's Standing Squarely in the Spotlight." *Los Angeles Times*, 3 Mar. 2017, www.latimes.com/entertainment/music/la-et-ms-khalid-20170303-story.html. Accessed 13 Nov. 2017.

Khalid. "Khalid's Timeless Pop Anthems for American Teens." Interview by Michelle Martin. *All Things Considered*. NPR, 27 May 2017, www.npr.org/2017/05/27/530085465/khalids-timeless-pop-anthems-for-american-teens. Radio Transcript.

O'Connor, Roisin. "American Teen Talks Early Fame, Touring with Lorde and Celebrating Youth." *Independent*, 16 June 2017, www.independent.co.uk/arts-entertainment/music/features/khalid-interview-american-teen-tour-dates-lorde-melodrama-calvin-harris-rollin-kendrick-lamar-a7792916.html. Accessed 13 Nov. 2017.

Weiner, Jonah. "Khalid: How a Lonely Teenager Made the Year's Freshest, Most Surprising Debut." *Rolling Stone*, 31 July 2017, www.rollingstone.com/music/features/khalid-american-teen-is-freshest-surprising-debut-album-w494814. Accessed 13 Nov. 2017.

—*Mari Rich*

By Georges Biard, via Wikimedia Commons

So Yong Kim

Date of birth: August 16 1961
Occupation: Filmmaker

"I don't see myself making big-statement films, because I don't think that's something I can do," award-winning Korean American filmmaker So Yong Kim told S. T. VanAirsdale for *Filmmaker* (Summer 2006). "I just try to find some sort of honesty in what I make, have that come from personal experience and try to relate that to the audience." Kim's films—among them the semi-autobiographical *In Between Days* (2006) and *Treeless Mountain* (2008)—explore the complexities of family, particularly the confusing, imperfect relationships between parents and children. Originally an experimental filmmaker, Kim creates films that are intimate and non-linear, embracing only the loosest definition of narrative film. Instead of plot, her films are defined by arresting moments—the teenage girl in *In Between Days* quietly remembering a sexual encounter; the deadbeat dad in *For Ellen* (2012) trying to buy his estranged daughter a new doll at the mall—and close camera angles.

Kim, who was born in South Korea, spent her teenage years in Los Angeles and earned her master of fine arts (MFA) degree from the School of the Art Institute of Chicago, where she met fellow filmmaker Bradley Rust Gray. The two, now married and cofounders of a production company, are close collaborators. Kim's debut, *In Between Days*, about a teenage Korean immigrant adjusting to life in North America, won a Dramatic Special Jury Prize at the Sundance Film Festival in 2006. Her 2016 film *Lovesong*, about love and reconnection, premiered at Sundance and likewise won strong praise from critics. She has also directed episodes of television shows such as *Queen Sugar* (2016), *Transparent* (2016), and *The Good Fight* (2017).

EARLY LIFE AND COLLABORATION

Kim was born on August 16, 1961 in Pusan, South Korea. Her parents divorced when she was young. After her mother moved to the United States, she lived for a time with her grandparents on a rice farm. She joined her mother in the United States when she was around twelve years old, growing up in and around Los Angeles.

In order to study the subjects she was really interested in and have her mother's assistance with paying for her education, Kim appeased her mother's one demand and first spent four years obtaining a business degree. "My mother told me to study business in college so I can learn how to support myself," she said in an interview for *IndieWire* (20 May 2007). Once she had met that requirement, she went on to study painting and performance art at the School of the Art Institute of Chicago (SAIC), but she would later become interested in film after she sought to include projections in her performance productions. While at SAIC, she had also met and begun dating a film student named Bradley Rust Gray. For their first date, she accompanied Gray on an early-morning run delivering muffins on Chicago's West Side.

At first, the two were interested only in experimental film, but when Gray later studied at the British Film Institute in London, both he and Kim began to gravitate toward narrative film. After earning her MFA from SAIC in 1996 and marrying Gray, Kim worked on his writing and directorial debut, a film titled *Salt*, which was shot in Iceland and premiered in 2003. Kim was officially listed as a producer, though, as another producer named Ben Howe told Dennis Lim for the *New York Times* (15 Apr. 2009), her involvement has historically gone far deeper. "It's almost as if they think together," he said of Kim and Gray. "It's definitely one or the other's film, but every decision is made with the other one close at hand." Their continued artistic collaboration, which included the creation of their shared production company, has been an important part of Kim's story.

IN BETWEEN DAYS

Salt is a coming-of-age story set in Iceland. Kim's first film, *In Between Days* (2006), is also a coming-of-age story, and it draws on elements of her own life. "With your first films you want them to be personal, even if it seems self-involved," she told Lim. Cowritten and produced by Gray, *In Between Days* is informed by Kim's teenage years in Los Angeles. In her original vision, she told Scott Macaulay for *Filmmaker* (17 Feb. 2017), the film was set in Los Angeles and featured "street gangs and stolen car chases." But when she decided to make the film herself, she and Gray worked to make adjustments: they set the film in Toronto; they cast a nonactor, a girl the couple had met at a bakery in New Jersey, as the lead; and a stolen car became a stolen car radio. The film follows a young Korean immigrant named Aimie (played by Jiseon Kim) and her unrequited love for her best friend, Tran (Taegu Andy Kang). *In Between Days* won the Dramatic Special Jury Prize for Independent Vision when it premiered at the Sundance Film Festival in 2006. Critics praised the film, though some were frustrated by its lack of plot and concordant pace.

Thematically, the film compares the frustrations associated with young love, growing up, and cultural assimilation—or, as Noel Murray put it in his review for the *A.V. Club* (6 July 2007), "the queasy uncertainty of pre-adulthood and the narrow confusion of pre-citizenship." Murray went on to say that *In Between Days* "plays like a teen movie with all the narration removed." Kim favors handheld close-ups to emphasize Aimie's loneliness as a new immigrant as well as her singular fixation on Tran. Critic A. O. Scott was more fervent in his praise in his review for the *New York Times* (27 Jan. 2006), writing that Kim "generates an extraordinary sense of intimacy without seeming invasive or prurient, and without insulting the audience or the character with too much explanation." Kim was grateful for the opportunity to screen her work at the festival for the first time and considered it a valuable learning experience.

TREELESS MOUNTAIN

The critical success of *In Between Days* helped Kim raise funds and garner support for her next film, *Treeless Mountain*, which Gray once again helped produce. Because the subject of the film was so personal, as it was inspired by her early years growing up in South Korea, it took her quite a long time to finish the script. She described the difficult process to fellow director Ryan Fleck for *BOMB* magazine (1 July 2009): "I had to go through this process of growing up and letting go; I was too attached to actual past events," she said. "I had to go back and write it from scratch. It wasn't so much about finding a formula to transform a personal story into a good film, but about figuring out what wasn't working in the script."

The film, which premiered at the Toronto International Film Festival in 2008, follows six-year-old Jin and her younger sister, Bin, as they are growing up in Seoul. One day, their mother decides to find the girls' absent father—why he left is a question left unanswered—and leaves them with her alcoholic sister-in-law, whom the girls call Big Aunt. Big Aunt soon brings the girls to their grandparents' farm. The film chronicles these upheavals as experienced by the young girls. Kim shot much of the film in her hometown of Hunghae. Manohla Dargis, who reviewed the film for the *New York Times* (21 Apr. 2009), described it as "more accessible" and "more approachable" than *In Between Days*. Still, like *In Between Days*, *Treeless Mountain* does not have a plot in any traditional sense. Kim, Dargis wrote, captures the children's world "with a low-placed camera and hushed sense of intimacy." Dargis compared Kim to Yasujiro Ozu, a twentieth-century Japanese filmmaker. Ozu, like Kim, favored low-placed shots and slow, lifelike pacing.

The following year, Kim worked with Gray to edit his second directed full-length film, *The Exploding Girl* (2009). In an interaction characteristic of their work together, she was adamant that he keep a scene rather than look for an alternative, while he had similarly pushed her to retain a certain scene in *Treeless Mountain*. She also served as a producer for this project.

FOR ELLEN

Kim's next film, *For Ellen*, was released in 2012. *For Ellen* is also about family and parent-child relationships, but unlike her first two films, it does not draw (at least overtly) on elements from her own life. Although she did formulate the initial idea of the story from ruminations about a time when her absent father had briefly introduced himself when she was a girl, only to disappear again, she largely created the main character and his conflict from the emotional state of her life at the time: "We have a lot of musician friends, and they are struggling like we are: the script just wrote itself after that. I ended up putting all my own anxieties as a film-maker into him, my hang-ups, and what I want to achieve in life," she explained to Andrew Pulver for the *Guardian* (11 Feb. 2013).

The film, which premiered at the Sundance Film Festival in 2012, follows the story of a heavy-metal singer named Joby Taylor (Paul

Dano), who is trying to reconnect with his estranged young daughter. In a further break from Kim's previous efforts, other stars include Jon Heder and Dakota Johnson. Joby is a quiet cipher, and his bumbling efforts to forge a bond with his daughter, Ellen (Shaylena Mandigo), provide the "softly beating dramatic heart of the film," Scott wrote for the *New York Times* (4 Sept. 2012). Scott gave *For Ellen* a moderately positive review, noting that the film focused too closely on Joby at the expense of a fuller picture of his life and the people in it. Roger Ebert, who reviewed the film for the *Chicago Sun-Times* (17 Oct. 2012), was more enthusiastic and reserved particular praise for Dano for turning in a brave performance.

LOVESONG

In addition to teaching screenwriting at New York's Bard College, Kim premiered her fourth feature-length project, *Lovesong*, at the Sundance Film Festival in 2016. Cowritten with Gray, the film follows a young mother named Sarah (Riley Keough), who reconnects with her childhood best friend Mindy (Jena Malone). Stephen Holden, who reviewed the film for the *New York Times* (16 Feb. 2017), described it as an "exquisite, beautifully shot meditation on love clouded by fear and doubt." In it, Sarah, her small daughter, and Mindy embark on a spontaneous road trip through Pennsylvania. Moments of romance and emotional intimacy provide the film's tension—what exactly is the relationship between these women, and which one will be the first to name it? Like Kim's other films, this question remains unresolved. Kim's natural tendency toward ambiguity is the film's greatest asset, Justin Chang wrote in his enthusiastic review for *Variety* (25 Jan. 2016). "As is often the case with Kim's films, it's what she chooses to leave unspoken and undramatized that matters most," he wrote. The film was released to theaters in the United States in 2017, at which point Kim had also continued experimenting with directing for television.

PERSONAL LIFE

Kim gave birth to a daughter, Sky, in 2007, and she had a second daughter, Jessie, in 2011; both appeared in *Lovesong*. Along with her husband, Gray, she and her daughters lived for a time in Lackawaxen, in rural Pennsylvania, before moving to South Pasadena, California.

SUGGESTED READING

Dargis, Manohla. "Two Children Are Cast Adrift in a World Without Anchors." Review of *Treeless Mountain* directed by So Yong Kim. *The New York Times*, 21 Apr. 2009, www.nytimes.com/2009/04/22/movies/22tree.html. Accessed 9 Apr. 2018.

Kim, So Yong. "5 Questions for *Lovesong* Writer/Director So Yong Kim." Interview by Scott Macaulay. *Filmmaker*, 17 Feb. 2017, filmmakermagazine.com/97178-5-questions-for-livelong-writerdirector-so-yong-kim. Accessed 9 Apr. 2018.

Kim, So Yong. Interview. By Ryan Fleck. *BOMB*, 1 July 2009, old.bombmagazine.org/issues/999/articles/3324. Accessed 9 Apr. 2018.

Lim, Dennis. "Independently Intimate Directors." *The New York Times*, 15 Apr. 2009, www.nytimes.com/2009/04/19/movies/19lim.html. Accessed 1 Apr. 2018.

Murray, Noel. Review of *In Between Days* directed by So Yong Kim. *The A.V. Club*, 6 July 2007, film.avclub.com/in-between-days-1798202803. Accessed 9 Apr. 2018.

Scott, A. O. "Caught Between Rock Music and a Hard, Lonely Place." Review of *For Ellen*, directed by So Yong Kim. *The New York Times*, 4 Sept. 2012, www.nytimes.com/2012/09/05/movies/for-ellen-directed-by-so-yong-kim.html. Accessed 9 Apr. 2018.

VanAirsdale, S. T. "25 New Faces of Independent Film 2006." *Filmmaker*, Summer 2006, filmmakermagazine.com/archives/issues/summer2006/features/25_faces1-5.php. Accessed 9 Apr. 2018.

SELECTED WORKS

In Between Days, 2006; *Treeless Mountain*, 2008; *For Ellen*, 2012; *Lovesong*, 2016

—*Molly Hagan*

John Kitzhaber

Date of birth: March 5, 1947
Occupation: Politician

John Kitzhaber served the people of Oregon as a state representative, state senator, and governor. Shortly after winning an unprecedented fourth term as governor, Kitzhaber resigned on February 18, 2015.

EARLY LIFE AND EDUCATION

John Kitzhaber was born on March 5, 1947, in Colfax, Washington, to Albert Raymond Kitzhaber and Annabel Reed Wetzel. His family moved to Oregon in 1958. Kitzhaber graduated from South Eugene High School in 1965 and then attended Dartmouth College. Following his graduation from Dartmouth in 1969, he enrolled in the University of Oregon Medical School, now the Oregon Health and Science University (OHSU). He earned his medical degree in 1973 and worked as an emergency room doctor in Roseburg, Oregon, from 1974 to 1988.

Kitzhaber has cited Robert F. Kennedy as his inspiration for pursuing a career in politics. Kennedy was killed during his 1968 presidential campaign, while Kitzhaber was an undergraduate student, and his campaign so moved Kitzhaber that he decided he wanted to dedicate his life to public service. He became a physician to help improve people's lives. After fourteen years working in the health care field, Kitzhaber entered politics with the same goal: to help improve the lives of the people of Oregon.

POLITICAL CAREER

Kitzhaber is a member of the Democratic Party. His first foray into politics was as a representative in the Oregon House of Representatives. Elected in 1978, he served one two-year term before being elected to the Oregon State Senate in 1980. Kitzhaber served three terms as a state senator, serving as the president of the Oregon State Senate from 1985 to 1993. As president of the state senate, Kitzhaber helped pass the Oregon Health Plan, which expanded health care coverage for Oregonians. He not only authored the plan but helped foster dialogue between members of diverse groups to gain support for the legislation.

In 1994, Kitzhaber successfully ran for governor of Oregon. He took the oath of office on January 9, 1995, becoming Oregon's thirty-fifth governor and succeeding Barbara Roberts. As governor, Kitzhaber continued to focus on health care issues and worked to improve the state's economy. He expanded the Oregon Health Plan and introduced the Oregon Option, a welfare reform plan that streamlined government services and increased accountability. He also focused on the environment, creating the Oregon Plan for Salmon and Watersheds, which seeks to restore Oregon's native fish populations and improve the water quality of their environments. In 1998 he was reelected to a second term with 64 percent of the vote.

Oregon law prohibits a governor from serving more than two consecutive terms, so when his second term expired, Kitzhaber left his elected office. For a time, he worked in a variety of nongovernmental jobs, including stints as a clinical professor at OHSU and as the president of the Estes Park Institute, which provides continuing education conferences to hospital executives and other health care leaders.

Kitzhaber ran for governor again in 2010. He narrowly defeated Republican candidate Chris Dudley and was sworn in on January 10, 2011, as the thirty-seventh governor of Oregon. He and his fiancé, Cylvia Hayes, moved into Mahonia Hall, the governor's mansion in Salem. During his third term as governor, Kitzhaber's primary goals were education, health care reform, and job creation. He helped implement the

Oregon Business Plan, a blueprint for the state's economic recovery; passed legislation making economic development easier for companies; and formed a special fund to promote job hiring and training. He also created several programs to increase jobs and economic development in rural areas. Although focusing on health care, economic development, and the environment, he also pushed for increased educational funding and reforms.

In 2014, Kitzhaber campaigned for a fourth term. By this time, questions had been raised about Hayes and work she had conducted for businesses that had contracts with the state. Investigations into these questions uncovered other revelations, including that she had previously married someone so he could obtain a green card, or residency status and immigration benefits. Despite the growing allegations and resulting scandal, Kitzhaber won the election and was sworn in as governor for an unprecedented fourth term on January 12, 2015. One month later, however, Kitzhaber announced his plan to resign. He stated that despite his desire to remain governor and serve the people of Oregon, he realized he had become a liability and it was in the state's best interest that he resign. He also asked the attorney general and an ethics committee to investigate his actions, stating that he was certain he had not broken the law or violated any ethical rules. His resignation became effective on February 18, 2015.

After leaving office, Kitzhaber initially kept a low profile. In his first public appearance following his resignation, he vowed to return to a life of public service, but as a private citizen rather than an elected official.

IMPACT

Although the controversy surrounding Kitzhaber's resignation threatened to tarnish his image, he nonetheless has left behind a legacy of reforms in health care, the environment, education, and business in Oregon. In 2015, Republicans threatened to use Kitzhaber's removal from office as an opportunity to investigate and reform the health care system he created.

PERSONAL LIFE

Kitzhaber has married and divorced twice. His first marriage, to Rosemary Linehan, ended in 1974. He married Sharon LaCroix in 1995. Together, they had one child, Logan, who was born in October 1997. He and LaCroix divorced in 2003. Kitzhaber then became engaged to Cylvia Hayes, whom he campaigned for during her failed bid for a seat in the Oregon House of Representatives in 2002. They live in Cedar Hills, Oregon.

SUGGESTED READING

Buntin, John. "Kitzhaber: Three-Time Governor Turning Oregon's Tide." *Governing*. e.Republic, May 2012. Web. 9 Nov. 2015.

Carson, Teresa. "John Kitzhaber Says He'll Be Back." *KOIN 6*. LIN Television, 17 Mar. 2015. Web. 9 Nov. 2015.

Chokshi, Niraj. "The Reporting That Led Oregon Gov. Kitzhaber to Resign." *Washington Post*. Washington Post, 5 Feb. 2015. Web. 9 Nov. 2015.

"Governor John A. Kitzhaber's Administration: January 9, 1995 to January 13, 2003." *Oregon State Archives*. Oregon.gov, n.d. Web. 9 Nov. 2015.

Manning, Jeff. "John Kitzhaber's Final Days: The Inside Story of Ambition, Love and Loyalty." *Oregon Live*. Oregon Live, 20 Mar. 2015. Web. 9 Nov. 2015.

Rosman, John. "Oregon Governor John Kitzhaber's Legacy." *OPB*. Oregon Public Broadcasting, 13 Feb. 2015. Web. 9 Nov. 2015.

Tims, Dana. "Under Gov. Kitzhaber, Has Oregon's Unemployment Rate Dropped to Its Lowest Point in Three Years? PolitiFact Oregon." *Oregon Live*. Oregon Live, 3 July 2014. Web. 9 Nov. 2015.

—*Barb Lightner*

Photo by Gary Gershoff/WireImage

Lisa Ko

Date of Birth: 1974
Occupation: Author

"Internalized oppression runs deep," Lisa Ko explained in an essay posted on her official website. "When you're a girl from an immigrant family where financial anxiety is paramount, and your grandparents had third-grade educations, becoming a writer was not encouraged." Ko—the daughter of parents of Chinese descent who came to America from the Philippines—not only pursued a career as a writer, she became an award-winning one. Her 2017 debut novel, *The Leavers*, which she wrote over a period of more than eight years after being inspired in large part by real-life immigrant stories, garnered the PEN/Bellwether Prize for Socially Engaged Fiction and became a National Book Award finalist.

The book—a tale of an undocumented Chinese immigrant who sets off to work one day only to vanish, leaving her American-born child to be adopted by a white couple—was praised by many critics for its timeliness, given the political climate in the United States. At the same time, some critics noted that *The Leavers* was actually following a long literary tradition. "The immigrant novel is a staple of American literature—after all, the American immigrant story is as old as the country itself," Steph Cha wrote for the *Los Angeles Times* (8 June 2017). "Ko is part of an active subgenre shining a light on an ugly truth about our country—that it is possible to come to America and be worse off as a result."

EARLY LIFE

Lisa Ko was born in New York City and grew up in a nearby suburb of northern New Jersey. Hers was among the only Asian families in their predominantly white town. Her parents were of Chinese descent and had been born and raised in the Philippines. They came to the United States soon after the signing of the 1965 Immigration and Nationality Act, which abolished the discriminatory quota system based on national origin that had been in place for decades. They earned their living running stands at local craft fairs and flea markets, where they sold toys and assorted bric-a-brac. The family made the thirty-minute trip into Manhattan's Chinatown frequently to buy groceries and visit friends; Ko has written that even in that milieu, where the majority of passersby shared similar physical features, she generally felt out of place.

Ko delighted in hearing tales of distant (and often eccentric) relatives from the adults in the family. "I was always really aware that my family's history ended with me 'cause I was the only grandchild on one side," she told Melissa Hung for *NBC News* (1 May 2017). "So there was a lot of anxiety about being the receptacle of all of my family's story and not wanting to forget from a very young age." An only child, she was frequently lonely, and in addition to reading avidly, she began writing her own stories at about age five. "I wrote the community I craved into existence, filling our house up with fictional families, writing their letters, sketching their pictures, and scribbling their lives," she recalled in her essay on her official website. The heroine of her first serious effort was named after her favorite color of crayon. Her tastes did little to endear her to her classmates; she has remembered, for example, that one favorite book from her elementary school years was about the bubonic plague. She was particularly fascinated and grateful when, in middle school, she discovered a book with an Asian American protagonist: *In the Year of the Boar and Jackie Robinson* (1984), by Bette Bao Lord.

EDUCATION AND EARLY CAREER

In high school, increasingly confident and more secure in her own identity, Ko began sharing some of her writing with supportive teachers, and she found a small group of like-minded outsiders while hanging around at record shops. Upon graduating, she enrolled at Wesleyan University, a well-regarded liberal-arts college in Middletown, Connecticut, where she majored in English and minored in women's studies. Though she did participate in writing workshops, she found them discouraging and did not find true inspiration until interning for the Asian American Writers Workshop. She graduated with a bachelor's degree in 1998 and moved to New York City, finding it something of a relief to be among so many others with artistic and literary aspirations. Soon, she began editing, managing, and writing for a periodical published by the Asian American Writers Workshop, discovering, in the process, that initiatives aimed at minority authors or those from other disenfranchised groups provided a strong pool of role models and a sense of community. To earn extra income, she also took on such jobs as coordinating promotions for *Columbia University Press*, writing discussion guides for Penguin Putnam, and serving as an assistant editor for the magazine *Yahoo! Internet Life*.

In 2002, Ko moved to the West Coast and helped launch *Hyphen*, a nationally distributed magazine for Asian Americans, for which she also held a position as books and web editor. Concurrently, she served as a web writer for the PBS series *Independent Lens*, which showcases original documentary films each week. While in California, she also earned a master's degree from San José State University. She explained that educational decision in an essay for *Literary Hub* (3 May 2017), writing, "In my twenties, I took writing classes after work and read voraciously, piecing together paragraphs like puzzles,

trying to figure out how my favorite authors did it. I published a couple of stories. I sent away for MFA program catalogs and threw them out, because what kind of career was that? Instead, I got a master's degree in library science." Despite her decision to focus on library science, she continued to write in her spare time.

In 2005, when she was turning thirty years old, Ko moved back to New York City to make a serious attempt at writing a novel. Yet, she still struggled with doubt. "I should concentrate on my real career, settle down, do what's expected of me. Stop being such a disappointment," she lamented in the personal essay published on her website. As she was writing, mainly short stories, she did indeed devote much energy to a string of conventional jobs, including working in the archives at the World Monuments Fund and the Brooklyn Navy Yard.

WRITING A NOVEL

In 2009, Ko read an article in the *New York Times* about Xiu Ping Jiang, an undocumented immigrant from Fuzhou, China, who had been detained by immigration agents while taking a bus from New York City to Florida to start a new waitressing job. Held in jail for more than a year, she had already lost custody of her young son, who had been adopted by a Canadian family after trying to get to the United States through Canada and being caught by officials. This story, and other cases she found involving the deportation or imprisonment of immigrant parents whose US–born children were taken from them, inspired Ko to really begin writing what would eventually become her first novel. That same year, she enrolled in a master's program at the City College of New York (CCNY).

Finding time between working and school as well as continuing to learn more about herself as a writer and the craft itself would mean that the manuscript would eventually go through several drafts. From 2010 to 2012, Ko worked as an adjunct professor at CCNY, teaching writing to undergraduates (while finally earning her long-desired master of fine arts degree), and worked as a project manager for the American Council on the Teaching of Foreign Languages. After a stint as a development writer creating content for a medical center affiliated with New York University (NYU), from 2013 to 2016 she took on a full-time job as a web writer and content specialist at NYU.

Throughout all that, Ko doggedly worked on her own fiction. "So what if I wasn't going to publish a book by thirty, or thirty-five, or even forty? I'd worked too long to give up now (though I thought of giving up all the time)," she wrote on her website. As part of that effort, she took time off from her day job and earned a steady stream of fellowships and residencies from such organizations as the Blue Mountain Center, MacDowell Colony, the Lower Manhattan Cultural Council, and Hawthornden Castle (an actual medieval castle in rural Scotland that hosts retreats for select groups of writers). Ultimately, her work appeared in such outlets as *Apogee*; one piece, published in the literary journal *Copper Nickel* after being rejected more than twenty times by other editors, ended up being selected by guest editor Junot Díaz for the volume *The Best American Short Stories 2016* (2016). "I started this goal to get fifty rejections a year," she explained of her approach to submitting her writing to Hung for *Hyphen* (28 May 2017). "I never hit fifty. But it always works. 'Cause the more you send out, the more you put yourself out there and the more chances there are of you getting stuff accepted."

THE LEAVERS

In the spirit of reaching her rejection goal, Ko submitted her manuscript for her first novel, *The Leavers*, despite it still feeling unfinished, as a contender for the 2016 PEN/Bellwether Prize for Socially Engaged Fiction, a $25,000 award established by the novelist Barbara Kingsolver to promote fiction that addresses issues of social justice. She was honored to learn that her book had won the prize and, subsequently, a publishing contract. After several years and much workshopping, she had molded her story into the most complete draft yet: "I ended up writing many versions of the novel before cutting it down and finding the characters' journeys," she explained to Stuart Miller for *Paste* (12 May 2017).

The novel, published in May 2017, examines themes of immigration, abandonment, prejudice, and family ties as the protagonist, Polly, vanishes one day on her way to work in a Bronx nail salon, leaving her eleven-year-old son, Deming, with no one to care for him. He is eventually adopted by two white college professors who rename him Daniel, forcing him to adjust to a new life as he wrestles with complex feelings about his mother and his Chinese heritage. Largely well received by critics, it was also a finalist for the 2017 National Book Award, in the category of fiction.

After her story was covered by the *New York Times*, Jiang was released and received asylum, but Ko has pointed out that she was one of the few lucky ones, with thousands of families suffering much less favorable outcomes. "*The Leavers* is my effort to go beyond the news articles," she wrote for the *Algonquin Reader* (Spring 2017). "It's the story behind the story, a tribute to sweat, heart, and grind. But it's really the story of one mother and her son—what brings them together and takes them apart."

PERSONAL LIFE

Ko and her partner live in the New York City borough of Brooklyn, where they enjoy cooking together and tending flowers on their apartment's roof garden. She prefers to write in the morning, at a desk she has used since childhood.

SUGGESTED READING

Cha, Steph. "The Immigrant Novel, 2017: Lisa Ko's *The Leavers* Shines a Light on Ugly Truths." Review of *The Leavers*, by Lisa Ko. *Los Angeles Times*, 8 June 2017, www.latimes.com/books/jacketcopy/la-ca-jc-leavers-lisa-ko-20170608-story.html. Accessed 3 Jan. 2018.

Hung, Melissa. "*The Leavers* Novelist Lisa Ko Found Success through Massive Failure." *NBC News*, 1 May 2017, www.nbcnews.com/news/asian-america/leavers-novelist-lisa-ko-found-success-through-massive-failure-n750811. Accessed 3 Jan. 2018.

Ko, Lisa. "About Me." *Lisa Ko*, lisa-ko.com/about/. Accessed 3 Jan. 2018.

Ko, Lisa. "Interview with *The Leavers* Author Lisa Ko." Interview by Melissa Hung. *Hyphen*, 28 May 2017, hyphenmagazine.com/blog/2017/05/interview-leavers-author-lisa-ko. Accessed 3 Jan. 2018.

Ko, Lisa. "Not Finishing My Novel Would Have Ruined My Life." *Literary Hub*, 3 May 2017, lithub.com/not-finishing-my-novel-would-have-ruined-my-life/. Accessed 8 Jan. 2018.

SELECTED WORKS

"The Night Suzy Link Goes Missing," *Apogee*, Spring 2015; "Pat + Sam," *Copper Nickel*, Fall 2015; *The Leavers*, 2017

—Mari Rich

Ewa Kopacz

Date of birth: December 3, 1956
Occupation: Former Prime Minister of Poland

Ewa Kopacz is a Polish physician and politician. She was a health minister and the first female speaker of parliament before serving as the prime minister of Poland from September 2014 to November 2015.

EARLY LIFE AND EDUCATION

Ewa Kopacz was born Ewa Lis on December 3, 1956, in Skaryszew, Poland. Her mother was a tailor, and her father was a locksmith. She attended the Medical University of Lublin, graduating with a medical degree specializing in pediatrics and family medicine.

She began her medical career in the 1970s working as a court-appointed doctor in the small town of Szydłowiec, which is approximately eighty miles south of Warsaw. She became director of a health care center in the town in the 1990s and held that position until the early 2000s.

POLITICAL CAREER

Kopacz entered politics after running her husband's unsuccessful 1997 bid for parliament as the Freedom Union's candidate. She joined the party and was named the head of the Radom branch. She served as councilor for the regional council in Mazowiecki from 1998 to 2001.

A power struggle within the Freedom Union resulted in party leader Donald Tusk leaving the party and forming the Civic Platform Party in 2001. Kopacz followed and was elected to parliament as the Radom representative. She was then named chairperson of parliament's Committee on Health in 2007.

Tusk became Kopacz's political mentor, and they remained close associates. When Tusk became Poland's prime minister in 2007, he appointed Kopacz to his first cabinet as the minister of health where she helped enact several health care reforms, including restructuring drug reimbursements and commercialization of hospitals. Health care reform was a contentious issue, however, and opponents were often critical of Kopacz's proposals and actions. She survived two votes of no confidence (2008, 2011), which were both brought by the Law and Justice Party.

Kopacz's term as health minister was marred by controversy. First, she refused to purchase extra swine flu vaccine in 2009 despite worldwide concern of a swine flu pandemic. Kopacz claimed that Poland had sufficient vaccine and that it was her responsibility to make decisions in the best interest of the people of Poland not the pharmaceutical companies. Second, in April 2010, she assisted in the identification of bodies after a presidential plane crashed in Smolensk, Russia, that killed all ninety-six people aboard, including President Lech Kaczynski. She later received criticism for her handling of the situation when it was discovered that many of the bodies had been wrongly identified. Moreover, she was also accused of covering up claims that Russian officials on the scene had desecrated many of the bodies.

In 2009, the European Healthcare Fraud and Corruption Network awarded Kopacz its first Excellence Award in recognition of her work as finance minister to regulate the pharmaceutical industry's advertising and promotion practices. Kopacz became the deputy chairperson of the Civic Platform in 2010. In November 2011, she was elected the marshal, or speaker, of the parliament, gaining votes of support from all political parties except the Justice and Law party. Her responsibilities as speaker were largely supervisory and included presiding over parliamentary debates, appointing the chief labor inspector, submitting passed bills to the president, and being a representative of the parliament during nonparliamentary events.

In 2014, Prime Minister Tusk resigned to take a seat on the European Council and handpicked Kopacz as his successor. Leaders from the governing coalition made up of the Civic Platform and Polish People's Party also nominated her as their candidate for prime minister. While Kopacz had proved to be an adept speaker of parliament, many political observers noted that she lacked political clout. Nicknamed the "Iron Lady" for her firm support of Tusk, she was known more for her loyalty to the former prime minister than she was for her political expertise or vision.

President Bronisław Komorowski named Kopacz prime minister in September 2014, and she was sworn in later that month. She quickly formed her new cabinet, naming several new ministers and notably adding her chief rival, Grzegorz Schetyna, as minister of foreign affairs. Kopacz announced her intent to continue the policies of her predecessor and provide governmental continuity. Her inclusion of Schetyna was interpreted as an attempt to minimize party conflicts and challenges to her authority. The new government received a vote of confidence on October 1, 2014, and Kopacz delivered her inauguration speech and laid out modest governmental proposals prior to the parliamentary elections scheduled for November 2015. She stressed cooperation and called on government agencies to work together. She announced her plan to increase the defense budget to meet security issues and discussed the conflict in the Ukraine as well as ways to reduce Poland's energy dependence. She also pledged to consider joining the euro zone after it emerged from its crisis. During the 2015 elections, however, Kopacz and the Civic Platform lost to Beata Szydło of the Law and Justice Party.

IMPACT

Internal power struggles within the Civic Platform Party worsened during Ewa Kopacz's time in office. She was unable to overcome them, and the party suffered during both the 2015 presidential and the parliamentary elections. Kopacz lost the opportunity to run for leader of the party when her rival, Schetyna, acquired that position. After stepping down as prime minister, Kopacz's future in politics remains uncertain.

PERSONAL LIFE

Kopacz was married to lawyer Marek Kopacz, and they divorced in 2008. She has one child, a daughter, Katarzyna, who is a physician.

SUGGESTED READING

Chapman, Annabelle. "Ewa Kopacz—Reasonable Woman." *Politico*. Politico SPRL, 25 Sept. 2014. Web. 23 May 2016.

Chapman, Annabelle. "Poland's PM in Waiting: Few Have Heard of Ewa Kopacz but She's Bound for the Top." *Newsweek*. IBT Media, 11 Sept. 2014. Web. 27 Apr. 2016.

"Ewa Kopacz, Poland's Next Prime Minister?" *Smolensk Crash News*. DoomedSoldiers, 10 Sept. 2014. Web. 23 May 2016.

"Ewa Kopacz." *Chancellery of the Prime Minister*. Chancellery of the Prime Minister, n.d. Web. 27 Apr. 2016.

"Exposé of Prime Minister Ewa Kopacz." *Chancellery of the Prime Minister*. Chancellery of the Prime Minister, 1 Oct. 2014. Web. 27 Apr. 2016.

"Reconstruction of a Mass Hysteria: The Swine Flu Panic of 2009." *Coto Report*. COTO Report, 15 Mar. 2010. Web. 23 May 2016.

—*Barb Lightner*

King Krule

Date of birth: August 24, 1994
Occupation: Singer-songwriter

King Krule, born Archy Ivan Marshall, is a British rock singer known for his rich, deep baritone and haunting and melancholy lyrics. His King Krule persona—which Joe Coscarelli for the *New York Times* (4 Oct. 2017) described variously as "a child of bohemia with a sharp proletarian edge" and "a zonked-out lounge crooner"—is as unquantifiable as his music. The name, King Krule, offers few clues. It comes from the 1958 Elvis Presley film *King Creole*, but also, Marshall explained to Rob Fitzpatrick for the *Guardian* (24 Aug. 2013), the image of "a king crawling through the city on his hands and knees." Marshall is influenced by jazz, punk rock, Afrobeat, and hip-hop, and incorporates elements from these genres into his work. In this way, he is an emblem of the Internet era. The web taught him how to play guitar and introduced him to his favorite bands; it also provided the launching pad for his career. Marshall began recording music as a child and posted his first songs online at the age of fourteen. He released his first album as King Krule—other personas include Zoo Kid, DJ JD Sports, and Edgar the Beatmaker—at the age of nineteen in 2013. That album, *Six Feet*

Photo by Scott Dudelson/WireImage

Beneath the Moon, won him famous fans including Beyoncé, Frank Ocean, and Kanye West. (He reportedly turned down a collaboration with West because he feared that being made to create on demand would result in mediocre art; Marshall and Ocean meanwhile, engaged in an epic jam session at Marshall's mother's house in London, though no song came out of it.) His critically lauded 2017 album, *The OOZ*, was several years in the making. Marshall is taking his time. "You see kids, they make one good track, they do one great feature and then they're everywhere, they've got a million people watching them," he told Coscarelli. "I wanted to develop and preserve my art."

EARLY LIFE AND EDUCATION

Marshall was born in London on August 24, 1994. His parents are divorced; his mother, a costume designer, lived in London's working-class East Dulwich, and his father, an art director and musician, lived in middle-class Peckham. The young Marshall traveled back and forth between the two. Marshall's older brother, Jack, is an artist and frequent collaborator of Marshall's who sometimes goes by the name Mistr Gone.

Marshall wrote and recorded his first song when he was eight years old. "I wrote about escaping the city [and] living in the countryside, on a farm," he recalled to Melena Ryzik for the *New York Times* (13 Sept. 2013). Those early songs about animals inspired his first stage name: Zoo Kid. An early influence was Fela Kuti, the famed Nigerian musician and Afrobeat pioneer; his mother had a picture of Kuti hanging in her house. Inspired by his father, Marshall picked up a guitar and taught himself to play, practicing by looking up the guitar tabs for various songs on the Internet. He performed his first show at a pub when he was twelve. At thirteen, Marshall refused to continue attending school. His parents found him a home tutor, but eventually, Marshall was placed in an education center for children excluded from mainstream education; he was subsequently moved to a different center. His persistent refusal to attend nearly landed his parents in jail; his father often physically dragged him to class. At the same time, Marshall was undergoing tests for mental illness at Maudsley Hospital in London. It was a difficult time for Marshall in what he characterizes as an already difficult childhood. "Basically, I hated everyone," he told Fitzpatrick of his feelings at the time. Through this period, Marshall's love of music remained a constant. Plagued by insomnia, Marshall listened to such bands as the Pixies and the Libertines on his headphones through the night. The sensory experience inspired him. "That was when I began to think about creating soundscapes," he told Fitzpatrick. This interest led Marshall to carry around a pocket-sized recorder, capturing sounds from his everyday life with the aim of incorporating them into his music.

EARLY CAREER

Marshall's desire to learn more about music pushed him, improbably given his spotty educational history, to win a place at the BRIT School for Performing Arts and Technology in London. (Alums include pop singer Adele and the late singer Amy Winehouse.) Around the same time, his brother formed a band, and Marshall, as Zoo Kid, began performing as its supporting act. He began releasing music on the Internet as well. In 2009, Marshall released a nine-track EP called *$quality*. He continued to post tracks online, eventually collecting them under the title *U.F.O. W.A.V.E.* in 2010. The completion of the EP was a turning point in Marshall's career because it proved what he could achieve as a musician. "It started to get real good when I completed the *U.F.O.* mixtape," he told Jeremy Abbott for *i-D* magazine (19 Nov. 2013). "Then I realized I'd created something, a nice collection of music. That was where I really found my desire and style." His efforts attracted the attention of those in the music business. In 2010, when Marshall was sixteen years old, he released his first single through the independent label House Anxiety. The song, "Out Getting Ribs," takes its name from a 1982 pencil drawing from artist Jean-Michel Basquiat. The music website *Pitchfork* endorsed the song; writer Brandon Soderberg (4 Jan. 2011) described it as "oddly intimate and irrevocably bleak." The surprise success of the

song led Marshall to reconsider his Zoo Kid persona. He did not want to be a "kid" forever, he told Fitzpatrick. "I want to get more and more sophisticated. I'm ready to go from being a kid to being a king." In 2011, Marshall christened his new persona by releasing a self-titled EP, *King Krule*. The EP was successful, and Marshall, who had already dropped out of school to pursue music full-time, launched a tour across Europe and the United States.

SIX FEET BENEATH THE MOON

Marshall released his debut album, *Six Feet Beneath the Moon*, in 2013. The album incorporates several tracks from *U.F.O. W.A.V.E.*, including "A Lizard State," "Ocean Bed," and "Out Getting Ribs." The album's general vibe positioned him as a kind of punk Chet Baker, a 1950s jazz trumpeter with a heartbreaking and soulful voice. Jayson Greene, who reviewed the album for *Pitchfork* (29 Aug. 2013), described Marshall's voice as "blood-freezing." Kitty Empire, for the *Guardian* (17 Aug. 2013), observed, "The longer you listen, the more these disparate influences and structured elements coalesce into a very cogent record." In a nod to Marshall's appreciation of soundscapes, she added, "It helps to stop expecting *songs* from King Krule, and instead lay yourself open to his drawling, sprawling atmospheres and just let the tunes blindside you when they come." The same year, Marshall, as his hip-hop persona, Edgar the Beatmaker, released two EPs: *Darkest Shades of Blue* and *Baby London*. (The name comes from Edgar the Peacemaker, the early English king who created Dulwich in 967.) For another, more mysterious, side project, Marshall released a handful of unnamed tracks of dreamy, ambient beats under the name DJ JD Sports. In 2015, Marshall took a break from King Krule to collaborate on a project with his brother. The two made a book of paintings, photographs, and poems with an accompanying short film and soundtrack devoted to their mother's home (where Marshall was born) and the surrounding town of East Dulwich. The project, which Marshall released under his given name, is called *A New Place 2 Drown*. *Pitchfork*'s Greene, who was more enthusiastic about the project than about Marshall's debut, praised Marshall's skills as a producer, writing (11 Dec. 2015) that he had made "tremendous strides" in the role, "gorgeously reproducing the gloom and loneliness of early '90s hip-hop and finding a way to integrate it into his own style."

THE OOZ

Marshall released his second album, *The OOZ*, in 2017. The album, four years in the making, represents a new height for Marshall. Greene, who reviewed it for *Pitchfork* (13 Oct. 2017), called it "the richest and most immersive album he's made yet, under any name, by some distance." The title is a metaphor that represents excess emotion being discharged in the way that human bodies discharge "excess crud," as Coscarelli put it. Marshall struggled to make the album at first, but a chance encounter with a new artist helped recharge and inspire him. Marshall met Spanish saxophonist Ignacio Salvadores after he sent Marshall a video of himself playing under a London bridge. The two met and jammed; Salvadores, who is now a member of Marshall's band, appears on a number of songs on *The OOZ*. Marshall's characteristically confessional lyrics discuss heartbreak and artistic frustration. Tyler Clark, who reviewed the album for *Consequence of Sound* (10 Oct. 2017), found some of the tracks excessive, but wrote "the album is still an essential listen; disorienting but never dull, heartsick but never maudlin, the rambling melancholy of *The Ooz* seems destined to soundtrack thousands of lonesome nights." Clark's assessment echoes Marshall's own description of the project, and his larger artistic intent. "[It's about] creating this world that you're only getting snippets of," he told Jack Mills for *Dazed* magazine (28 Nov. 2017), "somewhere in-between dreaming and reality."

SUGGESTED READING

Abbott, Jeremy. "King Krule, if the Crown Fits, Wear It." *i-D*, 19 Nov. 2013, i-d.vice.com/en_us/article/9kybwy/if-the-crown-fits-wear-it. Accessed 14 Feb. 2018.

Coscarelli, Joe. "King Krule, a Cult Singer in the Making, Is Setting the Terms Himself." *The New York Times*, 4 Oct. 2017, www.nytimes.com/2017/10/04/arts/music/king-krule-the-ooz-interview.html. Accessed 13 Feb. 2018.

Empire, Kitty. Review of *Six Feet Beneath the Moon*, by King Krule. *The Guardian*, 17 Aug. 2013, www.theguardian.com/music/2013/aug/18/king-krule-6-feet-moon. Accessed 14 Feb. 2018.

Fitzpatrick, Rob. "King Krule: 'Basically, I Hated Everyone.'" *The Guardian*, 24 Aug. 2013, www.theguardian.com/music/2013/aug/24/king-krule-interview. Accessed 13 Feb. 2018.

Greene, Jayson. Review of *The OOZ*, by King Krule. *Pitchfork*, 13 Oct. 2017, pitchfork.com/reviews/albums/king-krule-the-ooz/. Accessed 14 Feb. 2018.

King Krule. "From Zoo Kid to Heartthrob." Interview by Melena Ryzik. *The New York Times*, 13 Sept. 2013, www.nytimes.com/2013/09/15/arts/music/king-krule-on-his-debut-album-6-feet-beneath-the-moon.html. Accessed 13 Feb. 2018.

Soderberg, Brandon. Review of *Out Getting Ribs*, by Zoo Kid. *Pitchfork*, 4 Jan. 2011, pitchfork.com/reviews/tracks/12072-zoo-kid-out-getting-ribs/. Accessed 14 Feb. 2018.

—*Molly Hagan*

Greg Kurstin

Date of birth: May 14, 1969
Occupation: Record producer, songwriter, and musician

Greg Kurstin has been described by Paul Tingen of *AudioTechnology Magazine* (20 Mar. 2015) as "the consummate DIY writer and producer," who has had a hand in creating some of the biggest pop music of the 2010s. After more than a decade doing production work with everyone from Adele, Lily Allen, and Sia to Beck, the Shins, and Foo Fighters, Kurstin won five Grammy Awards in 2017 and 2018, including Producer of the Year, Non-Classical, both years; as producer he also shared 2017 Grammys with Adele for her blockbuster album *25* and its single "Hello."

A prolific musician in his own right, Kurstin has attributed much of his success to understanding the goals and wishes of his artists and respecting their vision. "I try not to force my sound on everybody," he told Mesfin Fekadu for the *Lowell Sun* (3 Feb. 2015). "I try to yield unto each artist and . . . I try to just support that sound rather than force a sound that might not fit." Of his current level of fame, he quipped in *Pop Dust* (8 Feb. 2013): "One little thing hit here, one thing hit there, and it just kinda snowballed into where I'm at now."

EARLY YEARS AND EDUCATION

Gregory Allen Kurstin was born on May 14, 1969, into a family of Jewish descent. His

By Peter Hill, via Wikimedia Commons

mother was a school administrator, and his father was a distributor of steel products. He grew up in Los Angeles, California, not far from the well-known Getty Center arts complex.

At the age of five he began taking piano lessons, and not long after that he took up the guitar and bass. In what he has described as an "only in L.A." turn of events, he attended middle school with Dweezil Zappa, son of the iconic experimental musician Frank Zappa. Forming a band, the pair noodled around in Zappa's home recording studio, and in 1982 they released a single, "My Mother Is a Space Cadet," which had as its B-side the tune "Crunchy Water," cowritten by Kurstin. Adding to the surreal nature of the experience was that Frank Zappa had asked famed rocker Eddie Van Halen to produce the record for the two twelve-year-olds. "My life was not always insane like that," Kurstin told Michael Tedder for *Billboard* (8 Feb. 2017). "Once it was over, nothing like that happened again for a long, long, long time. I went back to high school bands and playing in garages."

During his teens, Kurstin developed a deep love of jazz that took him to New York City to study at the New School with the pianist Jaki Byard, who had played with jazz great Charles Mingus. Accustomed to California's more laid-back atmosphere, he disliked the high-pressure world of the New School and the intensity of his classmates. "Every time you played in a jam session you had to be great or they'd just write you off," Kurstin recalled to Mikael Wood for the *Los Angeles Times* (4 Dec. 2012). "It almost pushed me away from jazz." He subsequently returned to the West Coast, and in 1992 he earned a bachelor of fine arts degree at the California Institute of the Arts.

THE START OF A MUSIC CAREER

Together with his friend Tommy Jordan, Kurstin formed the band Geggy Tah. The name originated because each had a younger sister who had not been able to properly pronounce her brother's name as a child: Greg became "Geggy," and Tommy was "Tah." When the musician David Byrne of the Talking Heads heard their sound, he offered to release their music on his own label, Luaka Bop. Although he still wanted to focus on jazz, Kurstin realized that an amazing opportunity was presenting itself. "We were like, 'Oh my God—how could we pass this up?'" he recalled to Wood. Geggy Tah ultimately released a handful of albums: *Grand Opening* (1994), *Sacred Cow* (1996), and *Into the Oh* (2001). *Sacred Cow* included a quirky single, "Whoever You Are," which became a surprise radio hit and was later used in a television commercial for Mercedes-Benz. "I was struggling between playing jazz gigs and playing with Geggy Tah in my twenties," he told Tedder. "We were doing a

lot of radio shows when that song broke. People started showing up and we would play our song and there were screaming fans. It was a very brief moment, and then a reality check," the latter because the band failed to capitalize on this momentary success.

Kurstin also earned much of his living as a session musician—a freelancer, often uncredited, who plays during recording sessions for other artists. He was the keyboardist, for example, on the Red Hot Chili Peppers' 1999 hit album, *Californication*, and that high-profile gig led to a steady stream of others, including work with Beck and the Flaming Lips. Well-liked, he was often asked to tour with his clients, but eventually, the appeal of that way of life faded. By then a father of two, he disliked being on the road, and he began resenting having to devote all his time to someone else's music. "I thought I still had something creative to say," he asserted to Wood.

In the mid-2000s, he often worked with singer Inara George, the daughter of Lowell George, the late frontman of the 1970s-era band Little Feat. He played keyboard and drum machine on a solo album she was recording and accompanied her at her live shows around LA. At the end of the evening, to entertain themselves, they began playing jazz standards, putting an indie spin on the familiar tunes. Calling themselves the Bird and the Bee, they recorded an eponymous album in 2007, followed by *Ray Guns Are Not Just the Future* (2009), *Interpreting the Masters, Vol. 1: A Tribute to Daryl Hall and John Oates* (2010), and *Recreational Love* (2015). "Inara George . . . and Greg Kurstin are eager to claim themselves as the present face of jazz: They started out covering standards and have since dropped the j-word all over their MySpace and promo materials," Rob Mitchum wrote in a review of their debut for *Pitchfork* (13 Feb. 2007). "The group throws back to mixed-doubles teams like Stan Getz and Astrud Gilberto, with Kurstin whipping up the instrumental backdrops to buttress George's vocal talents. But as far as following the classic rules of jazz, the Bird and the Bee are loose interpreters."

A NEW CAREER PHASE

Kurstin was interested in sound engineering, so before the Bird and the Bee recorded their first album, he had a friend show him how to use Logic, a digital workstation used to record, edit, and produce audio files: he ended up engineering the entire album himself, developing a valuable set of skills. "For a long time I didn't really know what I was doing with respect to engineering, and as a result I did everything in-the-box in Logic," he admitted to Tingen. "Over the years I have progressed a lot and my engineering skills are much better now." (The Bird and the Bee's

Recreational Love, in fact, earned a 2016 Grammy nomination for best engineered non-classical album of the year.)

In addition, thanks to an introduction by a mutual friend, a music-publishing executive signed him to a deal, and he began writing tunes for several other artists. His first major break came in 2009, when he cowrote and produced *It's Not Me, It's You*, a well-received electro-pop album by British singer Lily Allen. His efforts were rewarded at Grammy time, when in 2010 he received his first nomination for non-classical producer of the year, for the Allen record and the Bird and the Bee's second effort. The first single from *It's Not Me, It's You*, "The Fear," spent four weeks atop the UK Singles Chart, and the album itself debuted at number five on the Billboard 100 album chart, eventually going triple platinum in the United Kingdom. For "The Fear," Allen and Kurstin won three 2010 Ivor Novello Awards from the British Academy of Songwriters, Composers and Authors, including for best song and best songwriters. Kurstin has since written and produced albums for some of the biggest names in pop music. "A lot of producers right now, they think they're the big name, which artists hate," one industry insider told Wood. "Greg knows his place in the room."

Among those big names have been Kelly Clarkson, with whom he wrote and produced the 2012 hit single "Stronger (What Doesn't Kill You)"; Pink, who credits him with helping her create her first number-one album in the US, *The Truth about Love* (2012); and Adele, with whom he cowrote and produced the juggernaut hit "Hello." "Hello" racked up several impressive stats, including hitting number one in some thirty countries, becoming the first record to exceed a million digital sales in a single week, spending ten consecutive weeks atop the Billboard 100, and reaching a billion YouTube views in under three months. He also works frequently with Sia and was, by all accounts, vital to the success of her best-known album to date, *1000 Forms of Fear* (2014), which spawned the ubiquitously played single "Chandelier" and helped earn him a 2015 Grammy nomination as best producer.

Kurstin is known for the unusual practice of playing all the instruments during his artists' sessions. "It's just faster for me," he explained to Tingen. "Plus I enjoy it. I'm a musician, and the thrill for me is to play. I suppose that's the bottom line. . . . I grew up with four-track recorders and building up arrangements all by myself. It gives you that instant gratification."

PERSONAL LIFE

Kurstin, who as of late 2017 was working with rock legend Paul McCartney on an upcoming project, met his wife, Rachel, while he was touring with Beck and she was working at Warner Brothers Records. They live in Los Angeles and she now manages his songwriting and production career.

SUGGESTED READING

Fekadu, Mesfin. "Ladies' Man: Greg Kurstin on Producing for Clarkson, Sia." *Lowell Sun*, 3 Feb. 2015, www.lowellsun.com/ci_27449335/ladies-man-greg-kurstin-producing-clarkson-sia. 22 Apr. 2018.

Halperin, Shirley. "Grammys 2018: Greg Kurstin Wins Producer of the Year." *Variety*, 28 Jan. 2018, variety.com/2018/music/news/grammys-2018-greg-kurstin-wins-producer-of-the-year-1202679560/. Accessed 22 Apr. 2018.

Mitchum, Rob. Review of *The Bird and the Bee*, by The Bird and the Bee. *Pitchfork*, 13 Feb. 2007, pitchfork.com/reviews/albums/9868-the-bird-and-the-bee/. Accessed 22 Apr. 2018.

Tedder, Michael. "Grammy-Nominated Adele Producer Greg Kurstin on His Long Road to 'Hello.'" *Billboard*, 8 Feb. 2017, www.billboard.com/articles/news/grammys/7685216/grammy-greg-kurstin-hello. Accessed 22 Apr. 2018.

Tingen, Paul. "Wigging Out." *AudioTechnology Magazine*, 20 Mar. 2015, www.audiotechnology.com.au/wp/index.php/wigging-out/. Accessed 22 Apr. 2018.

Weiss, David. "Writing and Recording a Huge #1: Inside Adele's "Hello" with Producer Greg Kurstin." *Sonic Scoop*, 28 Mar. 2016, sonicscoop.com/2016/03/28/writing-recording-1-hit-inside-adeles-hello-producer-greg-kurstin/2/. Accessed 22 Apr. 2018.

Wood, Mikael. "Greg Kurstin Is an In-Demand Songwriter-Producer—and Not Crazy." *Los Angeles Times*, 4 Dec. 2012, articles.latimes.com/2012/dec/04/entertainment/la-et-ms-greg-kurstin-20121204. Accessed 22 Apr. 2018.

—*Mari Rich*

Evgeny Kuznetsov

Date of birth: May 19, 1992
Occupation: Hockey player

One of the most dynamic players in the National Hockey League (NHL), the Washington Capitals' center Evgeny Kuznetsov wowed coaches, teammates, opponents, and fans with his dazzling array of skills. He is particularly known for his improvisational on-ice creativity and for his blazing speed, which has been said to give the effect of an optical illusion. As the Capitals' defenseman Matt Niskanen explained to Kristina

Rutherford for *Sportsnet* (13 May 2018), "He's really creative at finding teammates, at getting them the puck in unusual ways. He's unconventional in that way."

Kuznetsov, who is nicknamed "Kuzy," made his NHL debut with the Capitals in 2014 after spending five seasons in the Kontinental Hockey League (KHL), the top professional hockey league in Russia. After making the necessary adjustments to the NHL game, he emerged as one of the linchpins of the Capitals, completing a "transition from uncertain import to borderline NHL superstar," as Barry Svrluga wrote for the *Washington Post* (25 May 2018). Selected to the NHL All-Star Game in the 2015–16 season, he truly captured the attention of the hockey world with his electrifying performance during the 2018 Stanley Cup play-offs. He led all NHL players in postseason points, with thirty-two, en route to leading the Capitals to their first Stanley Cup championship in the franchise's forty-four-year history.

EARLY LIFE

Evgeny Kuznetsov was born on May 19, 1992, in Chelyabinsk, an industrial city located near the Ural Mountains in western Russia. In his hometown, "hockey is religion," as Kuznetsov wrote in an essay for the *Players' Tribune* (28 Dec. 2015). Unsurprisingly, he developed a fervent passion for the sport at an early age. His family's apartment was situated just across the street from a local indoor hockey rink, where he first learned how to skate. He eagerly ventured there every day after school to practice, and when it was occupied, he would play pickup street hockey games with other neighborhood children.

Growing up, Kuznetsov learned the importance of mastering fundamental skills such as skating, puck handling, and passing, which are considered hallmarks of the so-called Russian style of hockey. He has credited his father, a former player himself, with being the biggest influence on his hockey development. Kuznetsov's father taught him to handle the puck without looking at it, which increased his on-ice awareness, and encouraged unselfish play, emphasizing the value of creating scoring opportunities for his teammates.

Kuznetsov's effortless skating ability and creativity were apparent from the time he started playing hockey competitively. However, he always worked diligently on his skills, which were bolstered by practicing with players much older than him. At age nine, Kuznetsov started skating with the then-seventeen-year-old Alexander Semin, who would himself eventually turn professional and reach the NHL. The two were eager to train even when their local rink was closed and developed a solution: "We would save some money and go buy some Coca-Cola and take it to the security guard as a little gift, and he would open the gate for us," Kuznetsov recalled in his *Players' Tribune* essay. "This was important time. After 15, 16 years old, no one can teach you skill anymore. When you are young, it's automatic. That's when you need to learn skill."

Kuznetsov's unquenchable zeal for hockey was nevertheless tempered by tragedy: when he was eleven years old, his older brother was killed during violent May Day celebrations in Chelyabinsk. Though by his own admission too young at the time to truly process his grief, Kuznetsov would later remark that his brother's death left an irrevocable mark on his family. Still, his working-class parents kept a positive attitude, and when he was twelve, they moved from their hometown to Omsk, Russia, located more than 550 miles away, so he could play for a team there that had recruited him.

ROAD TO THE NHL

By the time he reached his teens, Kuznetsov had established himself as one of the best young players in Russia. He appeared, along with other Russian hockey luminaries, in Canadian filmmaker Dave Bidini's 2005 documentary *The Hockey Nomad Goes to Russia*, which, in addition to showcasing his already prodigious skills, features him discussing his late brother and his future professional hockey aspirations. However, it was not the NHL that he dreamed of, mainly because he knew very little about the league at the time.

Kuznetsov's introduction to the NHL and its marquee players largely came through the video-sharing website YouTube, which he first discovered after a friend got a computer. (According to Kuznetsov, he did not even see a computer for the first time until he was around fourteen years old.) With his friends, he would spend hours watching videos of past and present NHL stars such as Wayne Gretzky, Alexei Kovalev, and future Capitals teammate Alexander Ovechkin; they would then try to emulate the older players' moves on the ice.

At age seventeen, thanks to his already abundant abilities, Kuznetsov earned a spot on his hometown KHL team, Traktor Chelyabinsk. He made his professional hockey debut with Traktor during the 2009–10 season and continued to find success. Indeed, he impressed enough to be drafted by the Capitals with the twenty-sixth overall pick in the 2010 NHL Draft. However, Kuznetsov opted to continue developing his game in Russia. "I didn't think I was ready," he told Svrluga. "I needed time."

Kuznetsov spent the next four seasons playing with Traktor, during which he also represented Russia in international tournaments. He displayed flashes of his superstar potential at the 2011 World Junior Ice Hockey Championships, held in Buffalo, New York. There, he led Russia to an improbable come-from-behind victory over Canada in the decisive gold medal game after recording three pivotal third-period assists. Capitals forward Brett Connolly, who was a member of that Canadian team, noted to Svrluga, "You see it when he gets the puck. He's such a confident guy. . . . You know he's not afraid to take guys one-on-one. He believes he's better than anybody he plays against."

Kuznetsov continued playing with Chelyabinsk before finally agreeing to terms on an entry-level contract with the Capitals toward the end of the 2013–14 season. He made his NHL debut against the Pittsburgh Penguins on March 10, 2014, and appeared in seventeen games overall for the Capitals, who missed the play-offs that year.

TRANSFORMATION INTO A STAR PLAYER

Adjusting to life in the United States initially proved difficult for Kuznetsov, who reportedly trembled with fear at his introductory Capitals press conference due to his unfamiliarity with the English language. Overwhelmed by feelings of loneliness and isolation, he barely left his hotel room during his first month in Washington. He gradually picked up English over the ensuing months by listening and talking to people and watching television, and eventually he grew much more comfortable.

Further complicating matters, though, was Kuznetsov's uneasy transition to the NHL game, which unlike Russian hockey, is played on a smaller ice surface and characterized by a more physical style of play. Upon joining the Capitals, he was moved from wing to the center position, which coaches felt would maximize his speed and skills. By the midway point of his first full NHL season in 2014–15, however, he had made little impact on the Capitals. Despite exhibiting his characteristic flair, he struggled with inconsistency, which was marked by a tendency to give up on plays after they had failed to materialize.

A turning point for Kuznetsov came prior to a midseason game against the Detroit Red Wings, when the Capitals' then first-year head coach, Barry Trotz, asked the Red Wings' Russian-born, perennial All-Star center Pavel Datsyuk to talk to the younger player. Datsyuk counseled Kuznetsov to start "dogging the puck"—that is, trying to keep a play alive with multiple efforts—and to embrace the North American–style dump-and-chase strategy of hitting the puck into the opponent's end before aggressively trying to retrieve it. Following the advice, Kuznetsov modified his game and enjoyed a breakthrough performance during the 2015 Stanley Cup play-offs. Most notably, he scored the winning goal in game seven of the Capitals' first-round play-off series against the New York Islanders.

Kuznetsov went on to double his offensive production during the 2015–16 campaign. He led the Capitals and finished tied for ninth in the NHL in scoring with seventy-seven points (twenty goals and fifty-seven assists) in eighty-two games. He ranked fourth in the league in assists and earned his first career All-Star Game selection, as an injury replacement for teammate Alexander Ovechkin. "Kuznetsov has an extremely high hockey IQ," Trotz told Thomas Boswell for the *Washington Post* (3 Mar. 2016). "He loves to study film. He sees what others don't."

STANLEY CUP CHAMPION

Kuznetsov's emergence as a star helped transform the Capitals into perennial title contenders. With Kuznetsov serving as their main facilitator, the Capitals finished the 2015–16 and 2016–17 seasons with the NHL's best record and secured the Presidents' Trophy in both instances after leading the league in points. The team, though, failed to carry their regular-season momentum into the play-offs, suffering consecutive second-round defeats to the Pittsburgh Penguins.

Kuznetsov's personal production dipped slightly in 2016–17, with fifty-nine points (nineteen goals and forty assists) in eighty-two games. Still, he proved himself to be a difference-maker on a talented Capitals team that boasted such superstar players and fellow forwards as Ovechkin and Nicklas Backstrom. Accordingly, the Capitals re-signed him to an eight-year, $62.4 million contract in July 2017.

Living up to his new contract, Kuznetsov further developed his game during the 2017–18 season, which saw him answer Trotz's challenge to score at least twenty-five goals. Normally a pass-first player, he explained to Rutherford, "I've never been the big scorer guy. I can trade couple nice passes [and an] unbelievable goal for zero points. That's how I enjoy the game." He finished that regular-season with a new career-high eighty-three points, after scoring twenty-seven goals and tallying fifty-six assists in seventy-nine games.

Kuznetsov played an even more pivotal role for the Capitals during the 2018 Stanley Cup play-offs, after the team won the Metropolitan Division for the third consecutive season. After defeating the Columbus Blue Jackets in the first round of the play-offs, the Capitals again faced the Penguins, then the two-time defending Stanley Cup champions, in the second round. In game six of that series, Kuznetsov scored a dramatic game-winning goal in overtime to eliminate the Penguins and send the Capitals to their first Eastern Conference Final since 1998.

In that series, the Capitals dispatched the Tampa Bay Lightning in seven games after overcoming a three games-to-two deficit. The Capitals then defeated the expansion franchise Vegas Golden Knights in five games to win their first-ever Stanley Cup title. Kuznetsov led the NHL and set a Capitals franchise record with thirty-two points (twelve goals and twenty assists) in twenty-four play-off games. He recorded four assists in game four of the Stanley Cup Finals, becoming only the fourth player in NHL history to accomplish such a feat. Following the victory, Kuznetsov was considered a strong contender for the Conn Smythe Trophy, which is awarded to the most valuable player (MVP) in the playoffs. He ended up finishing second to Ovechkin, who led all NHL players with fifteen postseason goals, in voting for the award.

PERSONAL LIFE

Kuznetsov's flashy play on the ice is complemented by his colorful, fun-loving personality off it. Soon after entering the NHL, he earned a reputation as an inveterate jokester. During practices, he was known to entertain teammates with random English idioms, which prompted Capitals winger Tom Wilson to describe him to Svrluga as "the most interesting man in the world." This playful demeanor often carried over to games in the form of oddball goal celebrations, including flapping his arms like wings while prancing around the ice.

In 2011, Kuznetsov married Anastasia Zinov'yeva in a ceremony held at the Traktor Ice Arena in Chelyabinsk. They have a daughter, Esenia, who was born in 2015.

SUGGESTED READING

Boswell, Thomas. "What's Russian for 'Brilliant'? Evgeny Kuznetsov." *The Washington Post*, 3 Mar. 2016, www.washingtonpost.com/sports/capitals/whats-russian-for-brilliant-evgeny-kuznetsov/2016/03/03/eb88cfea-e171-11e5-846c-10191d1fc4ec_story.html. Accessed 23 July 2018.

Khurshudyan, Isabelle. "Evgeny Kuznetsov May Be the Key to the Capitals' Postseason." *The Washington Post*, 12 Apr. 2017, www.washingtonpost.com/sports/capitals/evgeny-kuznetsov-may-be-the-key-to-the-capitals-postseason/2017/04/12/a7de8dee-1fa9-11e7-a0a7-8b2a45e3dc84_story.html. Accessed 23 July 2018.

Kuznetsov, Evgeny. "How We Play Hockey in Russia." *The Players' Tribune*, 28 Dec. 2015, www.theplayerstribune.com/en-us/articles/evgeny-kuznetsov-capitals-russia-hockey. Accessed 23 July 2018.

Kuznetsov, Evgeny. "From Smokestacks to Stardom: Evgeny Kuznetsov's Roots Beyond the Urals." Interview by David Kerans. *Pucks and Recreation*, 21 Mar. 2017, pucksandrecreation.com/evgeny-kuznetsov-interview/. Accessed 23 July 2018.

Rutherford, Kristina. "The Artist." *Sportsnet*, 13 May 2018, www.sportsnet.ca/hockey/nhl/evgeny-kuznetsov-washington-capitals-creative-genius/. Accessed 23 July 2018.

Shpigel, Ben. "The Washington Capitals, After Years of Frustration, Win the Stanley Cup." *The New York Times*, 7 June 2018, www.nytimes.com/2018/06/07/sports/stanley-cup-washington-capitals-vegas-golden-knights.html. Accessed 23 July 2018.

Svrluga, Barry. "Evgeny Kuznetsov's Transition to Borderline NHL Superstar." *The Washington Post*, 25 May 2018, www.washingtonpost.com/sports/capitals/evgeny-kuznetsovs-transition-to-borderline-nhl-superstar/2018/05/25/92a21ff6-6051-11e8-b2b8-08a538d9dbd6_story.html. Accessed 23 July 2018.

—*Chris Cullen*

Jeanne Marie Laskas

Date of birth: September 22, 1958
Occupation: Writer, professor

Jeanne Marie Laskas, writing professor and director of the writing program at the University of Pittsburgh, never intended to go into academia. "I love being a part of a community of writers," she said to JoAnn Greco for *Saint Joseph's University Magazine* (Spring 2017), speaking of her unexpected career shift. "I was initially worried that I wouldn't have enough time to write, but I'm even more productive. The students fire me up with their energy and ideas." She is also the founding director of the university's Center for Creativity.

Laskas began her career in journalism. She has written several regular columns over the years, including Animal Affairs and My Life as a Mom for *Ladies' Home Journal*, the syndicated column Significant Others for the *Washington Post Magazine*, and the advice column Ask Laskas for *Reader's Digest*. She has also been a contributing editor for *Esquire* and remains a regular contributor to the *New Yorker* and *GQ*, among others. She has twice been a finalist for the American Society of Magazine Editors' National Magazine Award for feature writing: first in 2008, for her *GQ* article "Underworld," about coal mining; and then again in 2018 for her *New York Times Magazine* article "The Mailroom," about the work of President Barack Obama's mailroom staff, which handled some ten thousand pieces of mail, both print and electronic,

Photo by Vincent Sandoval/WireImage

daily. She has received more than a dozen Golden Quill Awards for journalistic excellence from the Press Club of Western Pennsylvania (formerly the Pittsburgh Press Club), as well as what she described to Greco as a "breathtaking note" of commendation from Obama himself following the publication of "The Mailroom."

EARLY LIFE

Laskas was born on September 22, 1958, in Philadelphia, Pennsylvania, to parents John Laskas, a dermatologist, and Claire Willette, a painter. She and her three older siblings, a brother and two sisters, were raised in the Philadelphia suburb of Media. "She didn't let us play with Barbie dolls," Laskas wrote of her mother in her memoir *Fifty Acres and a Poodle: A Story of Love, Livestock, and Finding Myself on a Farm* (2000). "That was no role model for a little girl. She didn't let us watch the Miss America pageant. . . . And she talked over and over again to me about independence, about being independent."

Rather than receive the private Catholic education of her siblings, Laskas was permitted to attend public school, an experience she described in *Fifty Acres and a Poodle* as "[her] mother's public school experiment." Though she was shy as a child, Laskas became more outgoing in junior high school, eschewing schoolwork for a more active social life and more typical teenage pursuits. "My mother yanked me out of that school, dressed me in a uniform, and whisked me away for ninth grade to a private allgirls school," she wrote. The "experiment" was deemed a failure.

The change took a toll on Laskas, who reverted to her formerly shy ways. "By the time I got to college, I felt like the only place I really belonged was in my own head," she wrote. "I discovered writing. Thank God for writing. It was a way of getting all the inward stuff out. It was like installing a ventilation system, a line of fans blowing through ductwork, releasing emotion and thought to the wind."

EDUCATION

Laskas attended Saint Joseph's University in Philadelphia. She majored in English and sought out additional opportunities to pursue writing, including an internship at *Philadelphia* magazine that sparked her interest in journalism. "I learned that there could be great adventures in writing for magazines," she said to Greco. "You could give in to your curiosity and see where it led you."

After graduating in 1980 with a degree in English, Laskas returned to her parents' home and created an office in the basement. "I learned how to put up drywall, I bought a thesaurus and a typewriter, and I said, 'Ok, I'm a writer,'" she recalled to Greco. On the recommendation of her best friend from college, she took a job as a writer for the *Hint*, a newspaper for teenagers published by the Archdiocese of Philadelphia.

Soon, seeking further direction in her goal of becoming a writer, Laskas applied to the University of Pittsburgh's graduate writing program. The works she submitted were read by Lee Gutkind—founder of the university's newly established MFA program for creative nonfiction, the first of its kind in the nation—who awarded Laskas a teaching fellowship on the strength of her submissions. "She was the first and has always been the best student we had," Gutkind said of Laskas to Mackenzie Carpenter for the *Pittsburgh Post-Gazette* (12 Sept. 2012). He added, "She has great energy in her work, smart prose that's lively and has personality and reaches out and touches other readers." Laskas earned her MFA from Pittsburgh in 1985.

EARLY CAREER

After graduate school, Laskas began working for *Pittsburgh* magazine, where she was permitted to explore her curiosity about river barges, tap dancers, and Mr. Rogers. She began submitting her work to other publications as well, eventually catching the attention of the *Washington Post*, which offered her a contract. Laskas accepted—on her own terms, which included not living in Washington, DC, or reporting in at the *Post* newsroom.

"Honestly, it was a very strong reaction," Laskas said to Carpenter of her response. "No way could I get any writing done in that environment." She envisioned the newsroom as "a giant high school cafeteria filled with cool people. And you're supposed to go in there and sit down and *eat*? Like, I would run to the nurse and fake illness so I could be sent home. Or I would find a janitor and ask if he would share his mac 'n' cheese with me by the sink." Instead, Laskas remained in the Pittsburgh area, and from 1994 until 2008 the newspaper ran her weekly column Significant Others, focused on her rural life, in the *Washington Post Magazine*.

During the early 1990s, Laskas went to the Soviet Union to report on its collapse for *Life* magazine. Her first book, *The Balloon Lady and Other People I Know*, was published in 1996. Three years later, Laskas published *We Remember* (1999), a compilation of interviews she conducted with twenty-five women whose lives spanned the twentieth century.

MEMOIR TRILOGY
Laskas published three memoirs that grew out of her *Washington Post* columns: *Fifty Acres and a Poodle*; *The Exact Same Moon: Fifty Acres and a Family* (2003); and *Growing Girls: The Mother of All Adventures* (2006). The first book details her falling in love in her late thirties and, together with the man who would become her husband, buying land near Pittsburgh. The epilogue of the book lets the reader know that they are adopting a daughter from China.

In *The Exact Same Moon*, Laskas tells the story of her mother's sudden illness and her own desire to become a mother. She and her husband dance delicately around their ages—thirty-nine and fifty-four, respectively—and whether they should become parents. They attend a meeting about adopting a Chinese daughter; due to China's one-child policy, girls are routinely abandoned and then cared for in state-run agencies. The meeting made everything clear, and Laskas and her husband traveled to China to meet their daughter, Anna, and bring her home.

Growing Girls continues Laskas's narrative about life on the farm with her husband and their two daughters, Anna and Sasha, the latter adopted from China two years after the former. The work includes Laskas's musings about motherhood and adoption, especially transnational adoption.

GQ ARTICLES
Laskas has also written numerous articles for various publications, perhaps most notably *GQ*. She spent time with underground miners for the Hopewell Mining Company in Cadiz, Ohio, to better understand their work and the culture surrounding coal miners. Her subsequent article on coal mining, "Underworld," was published in *GQ* in 2007 and was a finalist in the category of feature writing at the 2008 National Magazine Awards. It later became a chapter in her book

Hidden America: From Coal Miners to Cowboys, an Extraordinary Exploration of the Unseen People Who Make This Country Work (2012).

Of her writing process, Laskas said to Greco, "I'm watching and watching, I'm talking with [the subjects] and following them home. I don't know what's going to work, I just take notes, notes, notes." She added, "Writing is shockingly hard. The only thing that gets easier is that you learn to say, 'Oh this is the part where I start to take naps,' instead of thinking you're a terrible, lazy person. Pulling out that first draft is agonizing, but after that, it gets to be so much fun. That's the payoff."

One of Laskas's subjects was Bennet Omalu, a Nigerian-born Pittsburgh neuropathologist who was the first to make the link between head injuries and chronic traumatic encephalopathy (CTE) in professional athletes. Omalu first published his findings in the journal *Neurosurgery* in 2005, based on his autopsy of former Pittsburgh Steelers center Mike Webster three years earlier. In response, National Football League (NFL) demanded his paper be retracted, a serious action denoting fraudulent findings. The NFL had conducted its own research via a committee of fourteen medical personnel—all paid by the NFL, none of them neuropathologists—whose findings disagreed with Omalu's. The journal stood by Omalu and did not retract the article, but the controversy and the attempts to discredit Omalu continued.

Laskas's resulting piece, originally published in *GQ* in 2009, won a spot in the 2010 edition of Houghton Mifflin's *Best American Sports Writing* anthology. The article—in combination with further research done in 2009 among a thousand retired football players, which found that those athletes displayed Alzheimer's-like symptoms at a rate nineteen times higher than that of the general population—prompted an inquiry by the US House of Representatives Judiciary Committee. Omalu was not invited to participate.

Laskas's 2011 follow-up story in *GQ*, which centered on football player Fred McNeill adjusting to life after leaving the game, sparked litigation by 2,400 players against the NFL and the company that produced their helmets. It, too, was collected in *The Best American Sports Writing*, in 2012.

HIDDEN AMERICA AND CONCUSSION
Air-traffic controllers, coal miners, and truck drivers were among the people profiled for Laskas's sixth book, *Hidden America*, which Oprah Winfrey decreed a must-read work. The book, several chapters of which were originally published as *GQ* articles, examines the lives of people on whom the nation depends, but whose jobs are neither glamorous nor often profiled in the news.

Laskas took a ground-up approach to writing about these hidden jobs. "When I wrote about immigration, I didn't start broad. I started tiny with someone picking blueberries in a field," she explained to Matt Tullis for *Neiman Storyboard* (9 June 2015), referring to the chapter on migrant workers. "Those little tiny moments—we rarely start from them. We start broad and then go small. I wanted to start small and go broad. That was just, in general, my way of thinking about any issue. The issue is not as interesting as the people and the transaction."

Laskas's next book was *Concussion* (2015), an expansion of her previous work on head injuries in sports. The book was adapted into a movie of the same name starring Will Smith and Alec Baldwin, which premiered in late 2015. The film earned Smith a nomination for that year's Golden Globe Award for best actor in a drama, among other accolades.

More important for Laskas was the resulting conversation with the NFL, which finally acknowledged the link between on-field head injuries and CTE. "Mostly, I was happy for Bennet and for the players and their wives who were suffering in silence for so long," she said to Greco. "Lightbulbs were going off everywhere, and people started getting together to talk about their experiences. Writing is more than writing at that point; it becomes a move to community."

PERSONAL LIFE

Laskas married psychologist Alexander Levy in 1997. They live on Sweetwater Farm in Scenery Hill, about forty miles from Pittsburgh, with their two daughters, Anna and Sasha. They keep numerous animals on their farm, including horses, donkeys, sheep, cats, dogs, and a parrot. "It's a choice," Laskas said to Greco of her rural lifestyle. "I go to New York to meet with editors, and we have great dinners, and it's all a lot of fun. But I could never get any writing done if I had to live that life daily. I need solitude, I need to be on the outskirts."

SUGGESTED READING

Carpenter, Mackenzie. "Pittsburgh Author Jeanne Marie Laskas Has Carved Her Own Path to Journalistic Excellence." *Pittsburgh Post-Gazette*, 12 Sept. 2012, www.post-gazette.com/ae/books/2012/09/12/Pittsburgh-author-Jeanne-Marie-Laskas-has-carved-her-own-path-to-journalistic-excellence/stories/201209120193. Accessed 7 June 2018.

Greco, JoAnn. "Stories to Tell." *Saint Joseph's University Magazine*, Spring 2017, sites.sju.edu/magazine/2017/03/stories-to-tell/. Accessed 7 June 2018.

Krasny, Jill. "What One Woman Learned after Spending Months with the 'Unseen People'

of America." *Business Insider*, 7 Sept. 2012, www.businessinsider.com/jeanne-marie-laskas-goes-to-hidden-america-2012-9. Accessed 7 June 2018.

Laskas, Jeanne Marie. "Annotation Tuesday: Jeanne Marie Laskas and Guns 'R Us." Interview by Matt Tullis. *Nieman Storyboard*, 9 June 2015, niemanstoryboard.org/stories/annotation-tuesday-jeanne-marie-laskas-and-guns-r-us/. Accessed 7 June 2018.

Laskas, Jeanne Marie. "The Doctor the NFL Tried to Silence." *The Wall Street Journal*, 24 Nov. 2015, www.wsj.com/articles/the-doctor-the-nfl-tried-to-silence-1448399061. Accessed 7 June 2018.

Laskas, Jeanne Marie. *Fifty Acres and a Poodle: A Story of Love, Livestock, and Finding Myself on a Farm*. Bantam Books, 2000.

SELECTED WORKS

The Balloon Lady and Other People I Know, 1996; *We Remember: Women Born at the Turn of the Century Tell the Stories of Their Lives in Words and Pictures*, 1999; *Fifty Acres and a Poodle: A Story of Love, Livestock, and Finding Myself on a Farm*, 2000; *The Exact Same Moon: Fifty Acres and a Family*, 2003; *Growing Girls: The Mother of All Adventures*, 2006; *Hidden America: From Coal Miners to Cowboys, and Extraordinary Exploration of the Unseen People Who Make This Country Work*, 2012; *Concussion*, 2015

—*Judy Johnson*

Francisco Lindor

Date of birth: November 14, 1993
Occupation: Baseball player

Shortstop Francisco Lindor is widely known for his positive attitude both on and off the baseball field, and for good reason. In addition to the smile he often sports during games, he has demonstrated a relentless commitment to being the best he can be, regardless of the challenges he faces in bouts against other Major League Baseball (MLB) teams. "When it's cold and raining, you need to know you can do it, that you will do it. Stay positive," Lindor told Jorge L. Ortiz for *USA Today* (11 May 2016) of his mindset. "When it's hot and you've already had 700 at-bats, and it's the 161st game of the season and you're hitting .301, are you going to sit on it? Or are you going to want to play the last two games, regardless of whether you hit .299 or .305?"

As Lindor's record suggests, his positivity and dedication to the sport of baseball have paid off. A baseball player since early childhood, he spent several seasons in the minor leagues

By Arturo Pardavila III [CC BY 2.0], via Wikimedia Commons

before being called up to the Cleveland Indians in 2015. He accompanied the team to his first World Series during his second season in the majors, and in 2017, Lindor contributed to a twenty-two–game winning streak that rivaled nearly all that had come before. Lindor, however, prefers to focus on future games rather than past achievements. "If you stay focused on winning and stay focused on doing your job, things are going to happen," he told Marly Rivera for *ESPN* (8 July 2017).

EARLY LIFE AND EDUCATION

Francisco Miguel Lindor was born on November 14, 1993, in Caguas, Puerto Rico. He began playing baseball at the age of four, learning from his father and other relatives who enjoyed the game, and soon demonstrated a talent for the sport. As a child, he played baseball in local competitions and met and befriended fellow young shortstop Javier Baez, who would go on to play for the Chicago Cubs. Lindor's parents, Maria and Miguel, divorced when he was a child, and he later lived primarily with his mother.

When he was twelve years old, Lindor traveled alone to Florida, where he joined his father, stepmother, and stepsisters, who had moved to that state to pursue medical treatment for one of the children. Lindor enrolled in Montverde Academy, a preparatory school in Montverde, Florida, known for its athletic programs. He lived at the school for much of his time there and initially struggled to adjust to both the school and life in Florida. "At first I would cry and call my mom, tell her I couldn't do it," he

told Ortiz. "I couldn't get used to sleeping in the same quarters with a classmate I didn't know and who didn't speak my language." Lindor later acclimated to his new life, and as a young adult, he would help his mother and siblings join him in Florida.

At Montverde Academy, Lindor played varsity baseball beginning in eighth grade and established himself as a valuable member of the team the following year, achieving a batting average of .364 and a fielding percentage of .944, the latter through his work as a shortstop. He continued to excel over the remainder of his time with the Montverde Eagles, amassing consistently impressive statistics and scoring numerous runs. In his final season with the Montverde Eagles, he achieved a batting average of .528. Lindor graduated from Montverde Academy in 2011. He considered attending Florida State University following his graduation but ultimately decided to focus on his professional career.

MINOR LEAGUES

In June 2011, Lindor was selected by the Cleveland Indians as the eighth overall pick in the first round of the 2011 Major League Baseball (MLB) draft. He officially joined the organization in August of that year, signing a contract that included a $2.9 million signing bonus. The team's leaders were confident that Lindor's skills as a shortstop and batter made him a valuable investment. "It's not often that we go and scout high school players that we have the ability to say, 'This guy can play shortstop at the Major League side of things,'" Brad Grant, the Indians' director of amateur scouting, told Joe Williams for the *Orlando Sentinel* (16 Aug. 2011) "It's the intangibles. The instincts and the way he plays the game are pretty special."

After signing with the Cleveland Indians organization, Lindor was first assigned to the Mahoning Valley Scrappers, a Short-Season A–level developmental team affiliated with the Indians. He played in five games for the team during the regular season, earning four runs, a batting average of .316, and a fielding percentage of .950. Lindor moved to the Lake County Captains for the 2012 season and split 2013 between the Carolina Mudcats and the Akron Aeros, later renamed the Akron RubberDucks. After playing eighty-eight games with Akron during the 2014 season, Lindor was transferred to the Triple-A affiliate Columbus Clippers, the highest-level minor-league team in the Cleveland Indians organization. He played the remainder of the 2014 season with the Clippers and returned to the team for the first months of the 2015 season, playing in fifty-nine games during that time.

Lindor participated in spring training with the Indians on two occasions prior to being called up to that team, attending the camp in

2014 and 2015. In addition to excelling during games, he was recognized with a variety of honors during his years in the minor leagues, including being named a midseason all-star for his play with the Captains, the Mudcats, and the RubberDucks. He was also named the *MILB.com* Organization All-Star on several occasions and selected for the All-Star Futures Game in 2012, 2013, and 2014.

CLEVELAND INDIANS

After several years in the minor leagues, Lindor made his major-league debut with the Indians in the middle of the 2015 season, in a June 14 away game against the Detroit Tigers. Although that first game was not successful for the Indians, Lindor became a valuable contributor to the team during the remainder of the season. Over ninety-nine games, he scored fifty runs, achieved a batting average of .313 and fielding percentage of .974, and led the league in sacrifice hits and sacrifice flies. He also gained notice for his positive attitude during games, which became something of a trademark for Lindor. "I'm not out there running around telling everyone to smile, like 'hey guy, enjoy the game' but when you go out there, play hard, respecting the game and have fun doing it, I think guys feed off that," he explained to Andy Frye for *Rolling Stone* (4 Oct. 2016). "There's not a better way to play." The Indians ultimately placed third in their division and did not participate in the 2015 playoffs.

Lindor continued to showcase his skills as both a fielder during his second season with the Indians, achieving a fielding percentage of .982 over the course of the season. His fielding percentage was the fourth-highest among shortstops in the American League. In recognition of his work as a shortstop, Lindor received the American League Gold Glove Award and the Rawlings Platinum Glove Award for 2016. He likewise displayed his skills as a batter throughout the season, achieving a batting average of .301. In addition to scoring ninety-nine runs as well as 182 hits in 604 at-bats, Lindor placed fifth in the American League in singles hit and fourth in doubles. The season was a successful one for the Indians overall, and the team ranked first in the American League Central Division by the end of the season, with a record of ninety-four games to sixty-seven.

During the 2016 postseason, the Indians defeated the Boston Red Sox three games to zero to claim the American League Central Division title and proceeded to the American League Championship Series, where Lindor and his teammates beat the Toronto Blue Jays four games to one. That win was a major milestone for the team, qualifying them to play in the World Series for the first time since 1997 and presenting the possibility of a World Series win, which would be the franchise's first since 1948. In the World Series, the Indians faced off against the Chicago Cubs in a tight competition. The Cubs ultimately won the series, four games to three, breaking that franchise's 108-year streak without a World Series title.

2017 SEASON

In March 2017, shortly before opening of the MLB season, Lindor played in the 2017 World Baseball Classic as a member of the Puerto Rican team. The team ultimately claimed second place in the competition. Following the beginning of the MLB season, Lindor reconfirmed his status as a key contributor to the Indians. He hit his first career grand slam—a home run hit while players are on first, second, and third base, thus allowing four runs to be scored at once—only three games into the season. Despite such milestones, Lindor remained aware of the need to give each individual game his full attention. "Playing baseball has many ups and downs," he told Rivera. "Baseball makes you humble in a snap."

Over the course of the season, Lindor played in 159 games and scored ninety-nine runs, with a batting average of .273. He led the league in at-bats and plate appearances, placed ninth in runs scored, and had the second-highest fielding percentage—a career-high .984— among all shortstops in the American League. In the fall, he helped the team hit a twenty-two–game win streak, one of the longest such streaks in MLB history. During the postseason, the Indians placed first in the Central Division and moved on to the American League Division Series. The team ultimately lost to the New York Yankees, two games to three. Nevertheless, the season was an overall success for Lindor, who won his first Silver Slugger Award in recognition of his offensive play in November 2017.

PERSONAL LIFE

Lindor lives in Cleveland during the baseball season and spends much of the off-season in Florida, where much of his family still lives. In addition to playing for the Indians, he coaches children in baseball through the MLB's Reviving Baseball in Inner Cities program. "When I was growing up, I had a lot of people who helped me," he told Frye. "The only way, and the best way for me to give back for the help I received was my time. Not with material things, but talking with the kids, showing them the game, and telling them it's possible."

SUGGESTED READING

Frye, Andy. "Francisco Lindor and Cleveland Indians Look to Overcome Baseball's Other Title Drought." *Rolling Stone*, 4 Oct. 2016, www.rollingstone.com/sports/

francisco-lindor-is-key-to-cleveland-indians-playoff-success-w443179. Accessed 9 Feb. 2018.

Noga, Joe. "Cleveland Indian's Francisco Lindor, Jose Ramirez Win First Career Silver Slugger Awards." *Cleveland.com*, 9 Nov. 2017, www.cleveland.com/tribe/index.ssf/2017/11/cleveland_indians_francisco_li_34.html. Accessed 9 Feb. 2018.

O'Connell, Robert. "Francisco Lindor Is Baseball's Future." *The Atlantic*, 12 Apr. 2017, www.theatlantic.com/entertainment/archive/2017/04/francisco-lindor-is-baseballs-future/522693/. Accessed 9 Feb. 2018.

Ortiz, Jorge L. "The Indians' Better Man: Francisco Lindor Appreciates Game after Childhood Journey." *USA Today*, 11 May 2016, www.usatoday.com/story/sports/mlb/2016/05/10/mlb-francisco-lindor-indians-carlos-correa-puerto-rico/84207642/. Accessed 9 Feb. 2018.

Ortiz, Jorge L. "Parallel Lives Lead Indians' Francisco Lindor, Cubs' Javier Baez to Same World Series." *USA Today*, 24 Oct. 2016, www.usatoday.com/story/sports/mlb/playoffs/2016/10/24/francisco-lindor-javier-baez-world-series-cubs-indians/92707240/. Accessed 9 Feb. 2018.

Rivera, Marly. "Lindor: 'This Will Be an Out-of-This-World Experience.'" *ESPN*, 8 July 2017, www.espn.com/mlb/story/_/id/19937350/cleveland-indians-shortstop-francisco-lindor-sharing-all-star-festivities-father. Accessed 9 Feb. 2018.

Williams, Joe. "Former Montverde Shortstop Francisco Lindor Signs with Indians." *Orlando Sentinel*, 16 Aug. 2011, articles.orlandosentinel.com/2011-08-16/sports/os-hs-baseball-deadline-lindor-20110815_1_montverde-academy-shortstop-francisco-lindor-lake-brantley-s-felipe-lopez. Accessed 9 Feb. 2018.

—*Joy Crelin*

Dua Lipa

Date of birth: August 22, 1995
Occupation: Singer-songwriter

English pop star Dua Lipa is best known for her 2017 hit single "New Rules," a song about staying strong after a breakup. "New Rules," from Lipa's self-titled debut album, helped skyrocket the twenty-two-year-old artist to fame in the United States. Lipa has won comparisons to the brooding pop singer Lana Del Rey (the two share a manager) but Lipa's style is more closely aligned with that of one of her idols, the brash and banging pop singer Pink. Lipa has

By Daniel Åhs Karlsson [CC BY 3.0], via Wikimedia Commons

a recognizably deep voice, and like Pink, she aims for arresting honesty in her songs, most of which she writes herself. Her lyrics rebuke bad boyfriends—"IDGAF"—and describe the exhilarating anguish of new love—"Lost in Your Light." But sonically, Lipa's songs are pure pop. Talking to Jon Pareles for the *New York Times* (31 May 2017), Lipa applied humorous descriptors to her music, calling it "dark pop" and "dance-crying." Born to Kosovar parents in London, Lipa lived for a time in Pristina, Kosovo, before returning to London to pursue a career in music. For several years, she doggedly recorded cover songs, posting the videos on YouTube, and sang demos. She was signed to Warner Brothers Records in 2015, and the same year released the unexpectedly popular single, "Be the One." The success of the song buoyed her budding career; she worked on her debut album with a number of coveted musicians and producers, including Chris Martin of Coldplay, with whom she wrote the song "Homesick." *Dua Lipa* was released in June 2017.

EARLY LIFE AND EDUCATION

Lipa was born in London on August 22, 1995. Both of her parents are ethnic Albanians who had emigrated from Kosovo a few years before. Lipa's first name means "love" in Albanian. Her father, Dukagjin Lipa, is a rock musician who works in marketing. He introduced Lipa to the music of rock greats like Bob Dylan and Sting when she was a child. The rest of Lipa's family includes her mother, Anesa Lipa, and a younger brother and a younger sister. Lipa loved singing from an early age. By the first grade, she knew all of the lyrics to Canadian pop singer Nelly Furtado's debut album *Whoa, Nelly!* (2000). She briefly tried her hand at playing the cello but gave it up because she was too small to carry the massive instrument on her back. Lipa auditioned for her elementary school choir but was rejected because she could not hit the high notes. The choir director told her she could not sing at all, Lipa recalled. She was devastated. Her parents enrolled her in classes at the Sylvia Young Theatre School on weekends, and Lipa thrived. (Soul singer Amy Winehouse and pop star Rita Ora are among the school's alums.) Most of the students there were interested in musical theater. "It was very cliché—kids singing around in halls practicing their lines and people just tap dancing in the f—king corridors," Lipa told Amy Davidson for the British entertainment magazine *Digital Spy* (11 Dec. 2015). "But it was great. I made some of my closest friends there. It was really good confidence-wise, especially after the whole choir thing." When Lipa was eleven, her father got a job in Pristina, the capital of Kosovo, and the family decided to move. It was not, Lipa told David Smyth for the London *Standard* (29 July 2016), a "massive culture shock." "It's much safer than London so I was allowed to do a lot more things," she recalled. "I could go to the city center with my friends." Lipa saw her first concert—rappers Method Man and Redman—in Pristina. A huge hip-hop fan, she later saw 50 Cent, Chamillionaire, Snoop Dogg, and Busta Rhymes there as well.

EARLY CAREER

But Lipa grew restless in Pristina. When she returned to London at fifteen to complete her General Certificate of Secondary Education (GCSE) exams, Lipa convinced her parents to let her stay in the city and pursue a music career. At first, the teenager lived with a friend who was studying for her master's degree. Later, Lipa lived with friends from Sylvia Young. Living on her own was a challenge. "When it suddenly hit me that no one was going to clean up after me, that's when I was like, 'Oh no! What have I done?'" Lipa recalled to Smyth. "But as long as I stayed in school, [my parents] let me be here." Lipa attended Parliament Hill girl's school, where she completed her A-level exams (required in the United Kingdom to graduate from secondary school) in politics, psychology, English, and media. To support herself, Lipa worked in retail, and as a hostess at a nightclub and then a Mexican restaurant. She also enjoyed a brief modeling career, posing for online catalogues for brands like ASOS, a British online fashion retailer. But when her agents pressured the sixteen-year-old to lose weight to walk the runway, she quit. At home, Lipa recorded cover songs from artists like Furtado and Christina Aguilera. In 2012, Lipa posted a song she wrote herself called "Lions & Tigers & Bears" on the music-sharing website *SoundCloud*. The moody ballad caught the attention of Ben Mawson, Lana Del Rey's manager. Mawson helped get Lipa signed to Warner Brothers records in 2015.

Later that year, Lipa released her first single, a promotional track called "New Love," produced by Andrew Wyatt and Emile Haynie, known for his collaborations with Lana Del Rey and FKA Twigs. The song is about unrequited love, Lipa told Aimee Cliff for the *Fader* (20 Aug. 2015), though the inspiration was not romantic. "At the time I was writing this song it was about finding my place in an industry that often seems to neither want nor need you," Lipa said. "This is a song about facing the fear of losing the only thing that matters to you." Just a couple months later, in October 2015, Lipa released a synth-pop tune called "Be the One," written by songwriters Lucy Taylor and Nicholas James Gale. "As much as I loved the song, at first I wasn't sure I wanted to record it because I hadn't written it," she told Nick Levine for the British music magazine *NME* (19 May 2017). "It was a pride thing, but it was also like, 'I can't take a song I haven't written because then no one will believe I write any of my own stuff.' But I just had to get over it. And now that song has helped me to get the stuff that I did write out there." The song was an unexpected smash; Lipa released it online, but it was quickly picked up by radio stations in Germany and then across Europe. Lipa recalled the first time she heard it on the radio. She knew the song was set to make its UK premiere on DJ Annie Mac's show on BBC Radio 1. She had hoped the song would play as she was making her way home in a cab, but it did not. The song came on after she opened the door to her apartment. "I collapsed on the floor and I was in tears, and I just couldn't believe what was happening," Lipa told Brennan Carley for *GQ* (24 Jan. 2018).

DUA LIPA (2017)

Lipa's debut album, *Dua Lipa*, was slated for release in 2016, but the release was postponed twice because Lipa was unsatisfied with the finished product. She began touring in 2016, and released a song called "Last Dance," a trippy pop tune about homesickness. The music video was shot in the California rainforest in the winter. In the video, Lipa rises out of a lake; the memorably frigid shoot was her first taste of the less-than-glamorous aspects of the music business. "Last Dance" was followed by the electronic dance music (EDM)–inflected single "Hotter than Hell," about a toxic relationship. Her next single, "Blow Your Mind (Mwah)," was Lipa's first major hit in the United States, peaking at number seventy-two on the Billboard Hot 100 chart in November. Around the same time, her album's lead single, "Be the One," reached the top ten on the UK Singles Chart, peaking at number nine. In November, Lipa teamed up with Jamaican rapper Sean Paul on the song "No Lie," and early 2017, she joined forces with Dutch DJ Martin Garrix on the song "Scared to Be Lonely," which reached number seventy-six Billboard Hot 100 in March of 2017. Lipa's album, *Dua Lipa*, was released in June, and with it, another single, "New Rules." The song, about female friendship and bad exes, hit number one in the UK—it peaked at number seven in the US—but perhaps more impressively, has garnered nearly one billion views on YouTube.

Lipa's album performed well with both audiences and critics. *Rolling Stone* rated it number nine on their year-end list of the twenty best pop albums of 2017. It also made the same list on the *Pitchfork* website, at number twenty. The notoriously snobbish music website declared Lipa the "winner of the battle royale of alt-pop newcomers," Katherine St. Asaph wrote (19 Dec. 2017). Jamie Milton, writing for *NME* (1 June 2017), gave the album four out of five stars, called it a "sass-packed, honest uncompromising storm." "No dull moments," he added, "not a whiff of boring, just bangers." Lipa released another single from the album, "IDGAF" (an abbreviation for "I Don't Give a F—k"), in January 2018. Lipa is working on her second album.

SUGGESTED READING

Cliff, Aimee. "Dua Lipa Is Our 'New Love.'" *The Fader*, 20 Aug. 2015, www.thefader.com/2015/08/20/dua-lipa-new-love-video. Accessed 7 Feb. 2018.

Levine, Nick. "Dua Lipa: How the Rising Star Put Herself on the Path to Pop's Premiere League." *NME*, 19 May 2017, www.nme.com/features/dua-lipa-be-the-one-interview-2017-2073065. Accessed 7 Feb. 2018.

Lipa, Dua. "Dua Lipa Is Changing the Rules of Pop Music." Interview by Brennan Carley. *GQ*, 24 Jan. 2018, www.gq.com/story/dua-lipa-is-changing-the-rules-of-pop-music. Accessed 7 Feb. 2018.

Lipa, Dua. "Meet Your New Favorite Popstar Dua Lipa—Just Don't Call Her the New Lana Del Rey." Interview by Amy Davidson. *Digital Spy* (UK), 11 Dec. 2015, www.digitalspy.com/music/new-music/interviews/a776876/meet-your-new-favourite-popstar-dua-lipa-just-dont-call-her-the-new-lana-del-rey/. Accessed 7 Feb. 2018.

Milton, Jamie. "The Next Pop Superstar? Dua Lipa's Debut Does Everything to Prove It." Review of *Dua Lipa*, by Dua Lipa. *NME*, 1 June 2017, www.nme.com/reviews/album/dua-lipa-review. Accessed 8 Feb. 2018.

Pareles, Jon. "Dua Lipa Was Raised on Pop Bangers, Now She Writes Them." *The New York Times*, 31 May 2017, www.nytimes.com/2017/05/31/arts/music/dua-lipa-interview.html. Accessed 7 Feb. 2018.

Smyth, David. "Dua Lipa Talks about Her Teen Years in Kosovo and Why It's Tough for New Music Artists to Break Through." *Evening Standard*, 29 July 2016, www.standard.co.uk/go/london/music/dua-lipa-talks-about-her-teen-years-in-kosovo-and-why-its-tough-for-new-music-artists-to-break-a3307341.html. Accessed 7 Feb. 2018.

—*Molly Hagan*

Olivia Locher

Date of birth: 1990
Occupation: Photographer

A friend once offhandedly commented to photographer Olivia Locher that in the state of Alabama, it is illegal for one to carry an ice cream cone in one's back pocket. For some, that odd statement (which ultimately turned out to be incorrect, at least in Alabama's case) might just have been an interesting bit of trivia, but for Locher, it became a source of creative inspiration. Over several years, she created photographs based on unusual laws from all fifty states, some legitimate and some of dubious origin. "There are some that are just totally random, like you can't disguise a bird to look like a parakeet. That's just weird," she told Lilah Ramzi for *Vogue* (22 Aug. 2017). "I found that it's really expensive to remove a law, so sometimes the mundane ones just stay in effect. For the laws that are myths, you wonder, Why did someone make that up and why did it go viral?" Known as the *I Fought the Law* series, the fifty photographs earned her significant attention from the media and the public, and they went on to be published in book form in 2017.

A photographer since her teen years, Locher honed her skills first at her childhood home in Pennsylvania and later at New York's School of Visual Arts (SVA), from which she earned her bachelor of fine arts degree in 2013. She went on to make a name for herself with work such as her *How To* series as well as her fashion photography, which appeared in venues such as *W* magazine. With her much-imitated *I Fought the Law* series, she demonstrated not only her talent as an artist and pop art influences but also a commitment to exploring familiar concepts in offbeat ways. "I have learnt to trust my ideas and act on them, sometimes impulsively," she said in an interview for *Autre* (22 Jan. 2015). Her approach garnered her a large online following as well as recognition from magazines such as *Forbes*, which in 2018

By Olivia Locher via Wikimedia Commons

and Cindy Sherman, whose *Untitled Film Stills* series heavily influenced her as a teenager.

EDUCATION AND EARLY CAREER

Locher attended public schools until high school, which she completed through an online homeschooling program. She went on to enroll in SVA in New York City to pursue a BFA in photography. Although she initially found that SVA's photography program deemphasized fashion photography, she made her own opportunities to explore that field, including by sneaking into fashion shows during the prestigious New York Fashion Week. "I would hide in the [venue's] bathroom for like 12 hours," she told Libby Peterson for *Rangefinder* (17 Nov. 2017). "And then I'd come out and be like, 'Here I am, at Marc Jacobs!' And they didn't know, at that point they were like, 'OK, this girl's inside.' Back then it was a lot more lax—in 2009, they really didn't care who got in."

In addition to making unauthorized appearances at fashion events, Locher began to exhibit her photographs while in college, participating in group exhibitions in New York, Pennsylvania, and elsewhere. She self-published the book *In Dreams* in 2012 and went on to self-publish a variety of additional books and zines. She also began publishing photographs in a variety of print publications. She earned her bachelor's degree from SVA in 2013.

HOW TO

One of Locher's well-known photography projects is her *How To* series, which she began as her thesis project in her final year at SVA. "Around the time I started the project I was looking through a lot of cookbooks," she told Lauren Poggi for *T Magazine* (23 Oct. 2014). "After a few cooking disasters, I got inspired by how directions could be easily lost in translation. I started illustrating simple tasks that were a little off." Among the earliest photographs in the series were "How to Get an Idea," which features a man wearing a hat with a lightbulb attached to it, and "How to See North America," in which a globe has been painted completely blue, aside from the United States.

Locher continued to create new installments in the *How To* series over the years following her graduation from SVA, producing brightly colored, distinctive artwork that reflects many of the artist's influences, including fashion photography and pop art. Later photographs in the series included "How to Apply Lipstick," which shows lipstick being applied to a mouth surrounded by painter's tape; "How to Beat a Rubik's Cube," in which the sides of the cube are painted the correct colors; and "How to Be Taller," which shows a model standing on makeshift stilts fashioned out of books and blue tape. The

named her to its 30 Under 30 list in the field of art and style.

EARLY LIFE

Olivia Locher was born in 1990 in Johnstown, Pennsylvania, to William and Marianne Locher. Local art and music thrived in Johnstown during her early years, and she developed an interest in the arts at a young age. She was particularly influenced by her older brother, Brandon, who put on art shows with his friends and went on to become a multimedia artist. Her involvement in photography began when she was a teenager, and she later noted that the original motivation for her work was her desire to have unique and impressive photographs of herself to post on the social networking website *MySpace*. She soon amassed a small following on the website *LiveJournal*, and one follower sent her a more advanced camera than the one she had previously been using.

Throughout Locher's early years, she was particularly drawn to the fields of fashion and fashion photography. "As a young girl, I found my way to the bookstore and slowly started subscribing to all of the fashion magazines," she recalled to Alexandria Deters for *Gallery Gurls* (24 Sept. 2017). "*W* was one of those first magazines I got my hands onto. I loved the fantasy world that was being presented to me within the pages of the editorials." As Locher expanded her knowledge of photography, she was inspired by artists such as Juergen Teller, whose fashion work she attempted to replicate with friends, project continued into 2018 with photographs such as "How to Clean Your Pores," which shows a woman using a vacuum cleaner on her face. Many of the photographs in the *How To* series deal with health and beauty.

I FOUGHT THE LAW

Amid her work on the *How To* series and other projects, Locher began an ambitious project known as *I Fought the Law*. The project originated when a friend informed Locher that it was allegedly illegal to carry an ice cream cone in one's back pocket in the state of Alabama. Fascinated by that supposed law, she began to research unusual laws either still in place, enforced at one time, considered for legislation, or fabricated throughout the United States and create a series of photographs dealing with one law found in each of the fifty states. The first photograph was based on the Alabama "law" (which turned out was a myth at least in Alabama; Georgia and Kentucky once had laws to this effect) and featured an ice cream cone melting while tucked into the back pocket of a pair of white shorts. The eye-catching photograph drew significant attention to the project, which took several years to complete. In addition to posting her work online, where it at times went viral, Locher displayed some of the photographs from the *I Fought the Law* series at *Pheromone Hotbox*, a group exhibition of work by female photographers at the Steven Kasher Gallery in New York, in 2015. A solo exhibition dedicated to the series took place at that gallery in 2017.

Following the completion of the *I Fought the Law* series, the photographs in the series were collected and published in 2017 by Chronicle Books. Concerned about losing creative control over her work, Locher initially delayed publication by not signing the contract but ultimately decided to move forward with the book, her first to be published by an entity other than herself. The delay proved fortuitous, as the book's blending of real laws and urban legends suited 2017, a year marked by concerns about so-called alternative facts. "It's almost magic that I took forever to sign it, because now it feels so much more appropriate," she told Ramzi. In interviews, she refused to tell which of the laws were real and which were not, noting to Ramzi that doing so would "suck the fun out of it."

Although the overall response to the *I Fought the Law* series was positive, Locher noted that the viral nature of her photographs led to issues of copyright infringement and creative dishonesty. "They started popping up everywhere, it got kind of out of control," she told Peterson. "At this point, it almost feels like it's sort of everyone's property, where everyone feels fine sharing it." Although she appreciated the "funny little life force that [her work] took on," as

she described it to Peterson, she was troubled by the tendency of commercial businesses to copy the imagery from some of her most iconic photographs without crediting her or commissioning her to create new artwork. The Alabama photograph from the *I Fought the Law* series proved a particularly popular source image for fashion brands.

RECOGNITION

In addition to working on series such as *How To* and *I Fought the Law*, Locher contributes fashion photographs to publications such as *W* magazine and has also had work featured in periodicals such as the *New York Times Magazine*, *Interview*, *Neon*, and *Glamour*. She has credited much of her success to her online presence, particularly her regular posts to the image-sharing site Instagram. "When editors approach me for commissions I find most of them discovered my work on Instagram," she explained to Wendy Syfret for *i-D* (24 Aug. 2016). "These digital platforms have completely replaced my printed portfolio. I haven't updated my physical book since 2013; no one wants to look at it. I think Instagram is so powerful and enjoyable because it gives you insight into someone's personal life and practice." In recognition of her work, she was named to *Forbes* magazine's 30 Under 30—Art & Style list for 2018.

PERSONAL LIFE

Locher resides in New York, where she shares a living and work space with her brother. "New York City inspires me because of how much content there is to take in," she said to Patricia Sprouse for *Plastik* (Spring 2017) of her home. "It's an amazing city, because any artist you'd have a desire to see generally shows with very little wait time. One of my favorite things to do is make a huge list of current shows in Chelsea and spend the entire day paralyzing myself with work. I also watch at least one film per day. I love overwhelming myself with content." She is also an avid practitioner of transcendental meditation.

SUGGESTED READING

Locher, Olivia. "In Conversation with Olivia Locher: A Photographer Breaking the Law with a Fashionable Twist." Interview by Alexandria Deters. *Gallery Gurls*, 24 Sept. 2017, gallerygurls.net/interviews/2017/9/24/in-conversation-with-olivia-locher. Accessed 14 Sept. 2018.

Locher, Olivia. "Interview: Olivia Locher Fighting the Law." Interview by Patricia Sprouse. *Plastik*, Spring 2017, eli-rezkallah-o4kr.squarespace.com/olivialocher. Accessed 14 Sept. 2018.

Locher, Olivia. "Meet the Photographer Turning Alternative Facts into Art." Interview by Lilah Ramzi. *Vogue*, 22 Aug. 2017, www.vogue.com/article/olivia-locher-i-fought-the-law. Accessed 14 Sept. 2018.

Locher, Olivia. "Olivia Locher on Her Group Show 'Pheromone Hotbox.'" *Autre*, 22 Jan. 2015, autre.love/interviewsmain/2015/1/21/olivia-locher-on-her-group-show-pheromone-hotbox. Accessed 14 Sept. 2018.

Locher, Olivia. "Olivia Locher Is Your Favourite Artist, You Just Didn't Know Her Name." Interview by Wendy Syfret. *i-D*, Vice, 24 Aug. 2016, i-d.vice.com/en_au/article/zmnzga/olivia-locher-is-your-favourite-artist-you-just-didnt-know-her-name. Accessed 14 Sept. 2018.

Peterson, Libby. "The Ever-Clever Olivia Locher's Interesting Dance with Virality." *Rangefinder*, 17 Nov. 2017, www.rangefinderonline.com/news-features/profiles/ever-clever-olivia-lochers-interesting-dance-virality/. Accessed 14 Sept. 2018.

Poggi, Lauren. "Olivia Locher's Tongue-in-Cheek Photographs of How-Tos." *T Magazine: The New York Times Style Magazine*, 23 Oct. 2014, www.nytimes.com/2014/10/23/t-magazine/olivia-locher-how-to-photo.html. Accessed 14 Sept. 2018.

—*Joy Crelin*

Logic

Date of birth: January 22, 1990
Occupation: Rapper

Inspired by such hip-hop acts as the Wu-Tang Clan, A Tribe Called Quest, Kendrick Lamar, and J. Cole, the rapper Logic made a name for himself as an original artist who is willing to explore his troubled upbringing in his lyrics and able to do so using a variety of conceptual approaches. Before putting out his studio album debut, *Under Pressure* (2014), he had already released several mixtapes, including the Young Sinatra series, which earned critical acclaim and built his following. He continued to expand his explorations of science fiction and other themes in his second and third albums, *The Incredible True Story* (2015) and *Everybody* (2017), which launched him to mainstream success.

Logic's rise to prominence allowed his signature messages of positive empowerment to reach a wide audience. Notably, his song "1-800-273-8255," released as a single from *Everybody*, featured the number of the National Suicide Prevention Lifeline as its title and drew attention for its focus on suicidal people getting help. The

By Nick Mahar [CC BY-SA 3.0], via Wikimedia Commons

song was quickly certified triple platinum and nominated for a Grammy Award for song of the year. "I wanted to tell the stories of other people who may not have the voice I do," Logic told Steven J. Horowitz for *Billboard* (4 May 2017). "I felt the necessity to discuss these things, because I am proud to be me, I am proud of where I come from, and at the same time, it's also bigger than me."

EARLY LIFE AND EDUCATION
The rapper known as Logic was born Sir Robert Bryson Hall II on January 22, 1990, in Gaithersburg, Maryland. The son of an African American father and a white mother, his mixed heritage would shape his self-identity and eventually inform his music. Both his parents had substance abuse issues, and he was raised by his mother alone, though various siblings came and went from the household. His mother was abusive in many ways, calling him by various racial slurs and otherwise providing an emotionally unstable environment. "My mother took me out of school in the fifth grade because they said I had emotional problems," Logic told Greer Smith for the *Churchill Observer* (25 May 2012). "In actuality, my mother had a lot of problems, mental and life problems, and would put her business out there to people, and so they thought I had problems too."

Logic went back to school for eighth grade, but his high school experience was short-lived. Despite initially doing well academically, the troubles at home and the subsequent trauma he carried led him to skip school and perform poorly in most classes. Expelled from several schools, he dropped out in the tenth grade. His family environment remained challenging, to say the least. "Between my brothers dealing crack, my father smoking it, my mother drinking, seeing my sister get pregnant at a young age, and dealing with all these things, it was almost an example of what not to do," Logic told Michael Nguyen for *HipHopDX* (17 May 2013). Around the age of seventeen he moved out on his own, no longer able to deal with life at home.

Taking on multiple jobs to support himself, Logic began writing and producing music. From an early age, he had been deeply inspired by hip-hop, particularly after watching the Quentin Tarantino movie *Kill Bill: Volume 1* (2003) and hearing its score, produced by the artist RZA of the legendary hip-hop group the Wu-Tang Clan. He often composed his own raps, eventually drawing on soundtracks and other instrumental hip-hop to put his lyrics to beats. In addition to the Wu-Tang Clan, his influences came to include A Tribe Called Quest, Jay-Z, and Nas, among others. He devoted himself to his music, later noting how it took the place of the drugs he saw so many people around him succumb to.

MIXTAPES

Logic, then using the name Psychological, released his first mixtape in 2009. Completely independent, he self-promoted on social media sites like YouTube and Facebook. He then joined the independent label Visionary Music Group after the release of *Young, Broke, & Infamous* (2010), his first official mixtape under the name Logic. He continued to develop his image and brand along with his music, and began to earn an online following.

His next work was the so-called Young Sinatra trilogy—three more mixtapes, in part inspired by his love of the singer, actor, and popular culture personality Frank Sinatra. He identified with Sinatra in part because they both had blue eyes—unlike everyone in his own family—and partly due to the famous singer's trademark debonair style, which he wished to emulate in a hip-hop setting. The first mixtape in the series, *Young Sinatra* (2011), earned positive attention and led to the even more successful *Young Sinatra: Undeniable* (2012). The latter tape's musicality and gravitas in exploring serious themes from Logic's personal life led the hip-hop magazine *XXL* to select the rapper for its "Freshman Class of 2013" list of up-and-coming artists. He also headlined his first tour in support of the recording.

Logic followed this progress with *Young Sinatra: Welcome to Forever* (2013), which also earned critical acclaim. Even before that tape was officially released, he was signed by the Def Jam record label and announced plans for his first full-length album. He embarked on another headlining tour and toured as a supporting act for high-profile hip-hop acts.

UNDER PRESSURE

Logic's debut album, *Under Pressure*, appeared in 2014, with executive production by notable producer No I.D. Like his previous mixtapes, it focused on themes and issues drawn directly from his own life. This personal touch was emphasized by the decision not to include featured artists on any of the tracks, a somewhat unusual move in hip-hop, especially for a largely unproven artist. On the song "Gang Related," he raps from the perspectives of both himself as a boy and his brothers about the trials and tribulations of growing up in challenging conditions. "Nikki" is about his main vice, cigarettes (which he eventually gave up). On the long title track, "Under Pressure," he addresses the various pressures he experiences, both personal and professional. Family is, indeed, one of the conceptual threads holding the album together: phone messages from various family members are sprinkled throughout the record.

Under Pressure was lauded by many fans and music critics alike. Some reviewers compared Logic's use of his adolescent autobiography to other successful contemporary rappers' debuts, such as Kendrick Lamar's critically acclaimed album *Good Kid, M.A.A.D. City* (2012). Similar praise came from Eric Diep in a review for *XXL* (21 Dec. 2014), who called this Logic album "darker than his previous work, yet invigorating to hear a 24-year-old willing to be so open about his life. Shades of Drake, Kendrick Lamar, and J. Cole's free expression come to mind, but Logic's subject matter is just as eye-opening." Although a few critics were less wholly impressed, most agreed that the album represented a strong first foray into the mainstream. More pressure would follow Logic as he began to make his next album.

THE INCREDIBLE TRUE STORY

Already earning attention for being a highly dexterous, quick rapper, Logic stepped up the lyrical speed even more on his second album, *The Incredible True Story* (2015). It is very much a concept album, a kind of science-fiction-meets-hip-hop adventure set in the future. The broader story is narrated by two central characters, Quentin Thomas and William Kai, who are traveling on a spaceship called Aquarius III and ostensibly listening to the album during the trip. After the Earth has been rendered uninhabitable, the two are looking for a new planet, which happens to be called Paradise.

The album, like much of Logic's oeuvre, is inspired by a variety of media, from classic and contemporary hip-hop to Tarantino films and science fiction epics. A few guest artists appear, including in "cameo" appearances through the spaceship's computer program, Thalia (who also appeared as a character on *Under Pressure*), but the work remains a highly personal record. For instance, several lyrics appear to confront the wide-ranging reactions to the artist and his music that have appeared online. He raps about how discussion of his racial heritage often took over commentary on his previous album despite his never mentioning the issue on that work. An overall uplifting tone continued his tendency to incorporate positive messages into his works.

Perhaps due to its ambitious concept, *The Incredible True Story* was somewhat divisive among critics. Although it was well-received overall, with praise for Logic's technical skills as a rapper, some reviewers criticized it for over-relying on concepts and styles of other artists. In a review for the influential music site *Pitchfork* (18 Nov. 2015), Julian Kamble concluded, "Logic has the tools to create music that has longevity, but has yet to unlock the characteristics that truly set him apart. If he's able to tap into that, his subsequent releases will have the impact he aspires for." However, David Jeffries, writing for the website *AllMusic*, offered serious praise, noting that "this is the album where it all changed, as the one they call Young Sinatra comes into his own and proves his nearly perfect debut was no isolated fluke." Indeed, the record outperformed his previous one, launching at number three on the Billboard 200 chart and topping the hip-hop/R & B chart.

EVERYBODY

After releasing yet another mixtape, *Bobby Tarantino* (2016), Logic put out his third official studio album, *Everybody*, in 2017. Continuing his ambitious reach, the work—reportedly inspired by a short story titled "The Egg" by Andy Weir—is a sort of science fiction take on reality, examining everything and, as the title indicates, everybody. The universe, identity, social media, race, religion, kindness, and the meaning of how we treat others and ourselves are all themes in play. They are examined both through the raps and in an interwoven dialogue between God (or a god-like being, voiced by the famous astrophysicist Neil deGrasse Tyson) and a black man who has recently died. However, the deep messages of the lyrics and narration are counterbalanced by generally up-tempo beats and otherwise snappy production.

Most critics enthusiastically praised the album. Many reviewers felt Logic's explorations of his biracial identity, a recurring theme in his works, were deeply heartfelt and insightful, showcasing his trademark personal touch. Yet at the same time, unlike the rapper's previous albums, *Everybody* was also full of feature appearances by hip-hop heavyweights, including Killer Mike, Black Thought, and Chuck D of Public Enemy. These strengths helped propel the album to a number-one debut on the Billboard 200, solidifying Logic's transition from an up-and-coming name to a bona fide star.

The album also won attention for directly and soberly tackling mental health issues, particularly on the tracks "Anziety" and "1-800-273-8255." The latter song's promotion of the actual phone number of the National Suicide Prevention Lifeline was said to cause a significant increase in traffic on the support network. Logic discussed his intent to use his profile to help society with Janice Williams for *Newsweek* (31 Aug. 2017), as well as the challenges that come with such a role: "I want to use my voice to promote positivity. I want to use my voice to discuss the things that are going on in the world. However, I refuse to also let it consume me."

PERSONAL LIFE

Logic married the singer Jessica Andrea in 2015. He maintains relationships with both his parents and his siblings despite his troubled upbringing. Since quitting cigarettes, he has noted that he does not smoke or use drugs and rarely drinks. Logic has referred to himself as a nerd, with interests in video games, anime, and movies.

SUGGESTED READING

Horowitz, Steven J. "How Logic Found Happiness: Marriage, Therapy and Addressing His Biracialism on 'Everybody.'" *Billboard*, 4 May 2017, www.billboard.com/articles/news/magazine-feature/7783971/logic-marriage-therapy-biracialism-new-album-everybody. Accessed 5 Jan. 2018.

Logic. "Logic Details Aligning with No I.D. & Def Jam While Maintaining His Lyrical Approach." Interview by Michael Nguyen. *HipHopDX*, 17 May 2013, hiphopdx.com/interviews/id.2108/title.logic-details-aligning-with-no-i-d-def-jam-while-maintaining-his-lyrical-approach. Accessed 5 Jan. 2018.

Logic. "Logic: 'Do Something for Yourself.'" Interview by Ali Shaheed Muhammad and Frannie Kelley. *NPR Music*, 12 Nov. 2015, www.npr.org/sections/microphone-check/2015/11/12/455768224/logic-do-something-for-yourself. Accessed 5 Jan. 2018.

Logic. "Who Is Logic? Breakout Rapper behind '1-800-273-8255' on Why He's Not Always the 'Dude with the Message.'" Interview by Janice Williams. *Newsweek*, 31 Aug. 2017, www.newsweek.com/logic-rapper-everybody-vmas-suicide-prevention-658019. Accessed 5 Jan. 2018.

Preezy. "Logic Presents the Man in the Middle on 'Everybody' Album." *XXL*, 12 May 2017, www.xxlmag.com/rap-music/reviews/2017/05/logic-represents-the-man-in-the-middle-on-everybody-album/. Accessed 5 Jan. 2018.

Smith, Greer. "Montgomery County Rapper Rises to Fame." *The Churchill Observer*, 25 May 2012, www.thechurchillobserver.com/top-stories/2012/05/25/montgomery-county-rapper-rises-to-fame/. Accessed 5 Jan. 2018.

SELECTED WORKS

Under Pressure, 2014; *The Incredible True Story*, 2015; *Everybody*, 2017

—*Michael Tillman*

London Grammar

Occupation: Band

DOMINIC MAJOR
Date of birth: February 23, 1991
Occupation: Musician

HANNAH REID
Date of birth: December 30, 1989
Occupation: Singer-songwriter

DAN ROTHMAN
Date of birth: September 23, 1989
Occupation: Guitarist

The electronic indie-pop band London Grammar—who at times have been compared to the xx, Alt-J, Portishead, and Florence and the Machine—quickly earned a reputation as an exciting young trio while its members were still in college. A few years after getting signed to a record label, the band released its debut album, *If You Wait* (2013); the first single from the album, "Hey Now," had been out since the previous year, gaining fans and generating buzz. *If You Wait* would go on to sell two million records and earn the young trio a respectable reputation as an exciting live act and a detail-obsessed studio band. After touring relentlessly, the band released its second album, *Truth Is a Beautiful Thing*, in June 2017.

EARLY LIVES
Dominic Major, better known as Dot, grew up in Northampton in England's East Midlands, the son of a machinery dealer. An evident musical prodigy, he began playing piano at age four. He has an older brother, Bruno, also a musician.

Hannah Reid grew up in the Acton area of West London, England. She was praised in school for her singing voice—"There was a teacher at school who let me record all my music and he said I was brilliant," she recalled to Craig McLean for the *London Evening Standard* (7 Feb. 2014), later adding, "When I auditioned for the choir my teacher said, 'I almost fell off my stool'"—but, she said, she "just didn't think much of it." Before meeting her future bandmates, she had earned a drama scholarship and intended to be an actor, but this ambition was

Photo by Frank Hoensch/Redferns

thwarted by both her stage fright and, as she told McLean, the fact that she "was an awful actress." (Dan Rothman, she said, eventually "forced [her] to get over" her fear of performing.)

Dan Rothman grew up in the London suburb of Hendon and attended the Jewish Free School in the Kenton area of North London. Although Reid held no musical aspirations as a child, Rothman joined a series of ultimately unsuccessful bands as a teenager, encouraged by his stepfather, an antique silverware dealer. His stepfather, himself "quite musical," was "very supportive from the beginning" regarding his musical career, Rothman told Francine Wolfisz for the *Jewish News* (19 June 2014), whereas his mother was initially "concerned, in a really typical Jewish mother sense, for me to get a proper job."

BAND FORMATION

Major, Reid, and Rothman first met while they were students at the University of Nottingham, where Major studied English, Reid studied English and art history, and Rothman studied economics and philosophy. Reid and Rothman met first, in 2009, during their first year at the school; after seeing a photo of Reid with a guitar on Facebook, Rothman sent her a message asking her if she wrote songs, and the two began to play music together. Later, through Rothman's girlfriend, they were introduced to Major, a multi-instrumentalist who plays both keyboard and drums, including the djembe, a skin-covered African drum that is played with bare hands.

The newly formed trio started playing small venues together, mostly bars. One night in late 2010, while playing a gig at a pub in the hip, music-filled Camden neighborhood of London, they were spotted by an employee of the Ministry of Sound record label; the label signed them the following year, soon after Reid and Rothman graduated. (Major, a year below the other two, graduated in 2012.)

In 2012 London Grammar uploaded its first single online, the heartfelt and ethereal "Hey Now," and quickly found a following. A year later, the band released its debut EP, *Metal & Dust* (2013), a short collection of songs that would go on to climb the digital charts. That year the group also played some very important live shows, namely at the Great Escape Festival in Brighton, England, and at the Islington Assembly Hall in London.

IF YOU WAIT

London Grammar's debut album, the aptly titled *If You Wait*, took a year and a half to complete. The fact that the album was already highly anticipated before its 2013 release certainly helped spread awareness of the band, but it also may have made some critics (and fans) more skeptical.

Luckily for the band, their ethereal, quietly emotional brand of electro-indie pop won out. In a review of the album for the music website *Pitchfork.com* (17 Sept. 2013), Renato Pagnani lauded Reid's vocals as "an elemental power that can clear entire fields, displaying an outward composure that always provides glimpses of a staggering vulnerability lurking just below the surface," and praised Major and Rothman for "wisely stay[ing] out of Reid's way when she locks her sights on a target" and "us[ing] their knack for dynamics to support her in subtle ways." Similarly, Scott Kerr's review for the *AllMusic* website noted that "Reid's beautiful, emotive vocal ability . . . rises and falls with an alarmingly disarming effect" and that while at times her vocals "come close to overshadowing the subtle instrumentation provided by Major and Dan Rothman, it's actually the intrinsic balance between the contributions of all three that defines their sound."

If You Wait debuted at number 2 on the UK's Official Albums Chart Top 100 and peaked at number 1 on the Official Independent Albums Chart Top 50. In the United States, the album peaked at number 91 on the Billboard 200 chart, number 20 on the Billboard Top Rock Albums chart, and number 16 on the Billboard Alternative Albums chart.

A BRIEF CRASH

In July 2014, following a solid twelve months of touring, the band was scheduled to fly to Australia for a music festival. Their original flight, scheduled for the day after Malaysia Airlines Flight 17 was shot down over Ukraine, was canceled. In order to arrive at the festival in time, Rothman recalled to Craig McLean for *GO London* (5 Apr. 2017), "the flight we'd have to get would mean we'd land, do a gig that same evening, then go to Japan for 12 hours. Bearing in mind this was after 12 months of touring . . . . We were close to being destroyed, physically and mentally."

For Reid, at the time suffering from exhaustion and various related health problems that exacerbated her previously manageable stage fright, the newly tightened schedule was the last straw. "I was so exhausted by then, I didn't even turn up at the airport," she confessed to Bronwyn Thompson for the *Sydney Morning Herald* (20 Aug. 2017). "I was like, 'I just can't. I can't. I actually cannot get out of bed.'" She called Rothman in tears, and they decided to cancel the trip. The band postponed its future tour dates, citing "illness" and "vocal fatigue."

In retrospect, Reid said to Hannah J. Davies for the *Guardian* (8 June 2017), "The thing about touring is that young artists don't always have much say or control. You're quite naive. You say: 'Yeah, I want to do everything.' And you want to please everyone. You're so grateful, but you get sick at some point because everyone does. You have to cancel stuff, and then that has to get rescheduled. It can very quickly go from being manageable to snowballing into the kind of schedule that can end up wrecking your voice. The worst thing about it is disappointing the fans," she added. "We're going to do things differently this time."

After rescheduling the canceled performances and recovering from the physical and emotional crash, the band developed a schedule in which they take a day off for every two days they perform. "It will never go away—and I understand that now—but as long as I know that I've got that time to kind of recover, then my stage fright isn't actually as bad," Reid said to Davies. "I think that's made a huge difference." Finally, in early 2015, the band returned to the studio to work on a follow-up album.

TRUTH IS A BEAUTIFUL THING

London Grammar's sophomore studio effort, *Truth Is a Beautiful Thing*, continued the group's exploration of expressive, meditative soundscapes. Of the recording process, Reid said to Thompson, "It took us about 18 months and it was really hard. There was a lot of pressure—I think naturally there always is, for a lot of artists that have successful first albums and want to make a second. . . . By the end of it we realized, 'You know what? You can't think about it or you're not going to do your best work.'"

Like the band's first studio album, *Truth Is a Beautiful Thing* was well reviewed by most critics and highly praised by many. Neil Z. Yeung wrote of the album for *AllMusic*, "Once again, vocalist Hannah Reid takes center stage with her powerful, angelic instrument, which can stir the soul at the smokiest depths before jolting everything to the heavens. . . . Dan Rothman and Dominic Major provide lush accompaniment to Reid's voice, creating a gorgeous cinematic landscape that ranges from dreamlike wisps to fully enveloping grandeur." In a review for *NME* (7 June 2017), Larry Bartleet observed that though the album is more professionally produced than *If You Wait*, it has "a refreshing amount of stylistic variation" in comparison to that previous offering; he commended in particular "a weird sample of Reid's voice" in the song "Bones of Ribbon," Major's "swaggering, two-beat drum line" on "Non Believer," and the "gorgeous, reverb-heavy guitar against skittering beats" of "Leave the War with Me." Some reviewers, however, were less impressed; Harriet Gibsone wrote for the *Guardian* (8 June 2017) that "musically . . . the album is one note" and that while *If You Wait* "had moments of heft," the group's second album "drowns in its own despair."

Reid herself, though not unhappy with the album, does not consider it to be the group's best work. "I think I both grew as a writer and also shrunk away," she admitted to Thompson. "I think there are some amazing songs on the second album that I really love, but I view this second album as the stepping stone to our third one. We wanted to find a new sound and there is a new sound in it, but it has the potential to be really, really amazing but it's not quite there yet. That's how I view it."

Truth Is a Beautiful Thing peaked at number 129 on the Billboard 200 chart, number 29 on the Billboard Top Rock Albums chart, and number 16 on the Billboard Alternative Albums chart.

SUGGESTED READING

Davies, Hannah J. "London Grammar: 'We Were Hanging by a Thread.'" *The Guardian*, 8 June 2017, www.theguardian.com/music/2017/jun/08/london-grammar-we-were-hanging-by-a-thread. Accessed 8 Jan. 2017.

Duerden, Nick. "London Grammar Interview: Will They Overcome Their Morbid Fear of the Spotlight?" *The Independent*, 29 Aug. 2014, www.independent.co.uk/arts-entertainment/music/features/london-grammar-interview-can-they-overcome-their-morbid-fear-of-the-spotlight-9698660.html. Accessed 8 Jan. 2017.

McLean, Craig. "London Grammar: How the Capital's Hottest Trio Won Over the Big Apple (Anna Wintour Included)." *London Evening Standard*, 7 Feb. 2014, www.standard.co.uk/lifestyle/esmagazine/london-grammar-how-the-capitals-hottest-trio-won-over-the-big-apple-anna-wintour-included-9109605.html. Accessed 8 Jan. 2017.

McLean, Craig. "London Grammar, Interview: 'We Were Close to Being Destroyed, Physically and Mentally.'" *GO London*, Evening Standard, 5 Apr. 2017, www.standard.co.uk/go/london/music/london-grammar-interview-we-were-close-to-being-destroyed-physically-and-mentally-a3507871.html. Accessed 8 Jan. 2017.

Thompson, Bronwyn. "'I Was Terrified': How London Grammar's Hannah Reid Came Back from the Brink." *The Sydney Morning Herald*, 20 Aug. 2017, www.smh.com.au/entertainment/music/how-london-grammar-came-back-from-the-brink-and-hannah-reids-missed-flight-20170814-gxw46o.html. Accessed 8 Jan. 2017.

Wolfisz, Francine. "London Grammar's Dan Rothman: 'My Hendon Home Was Our Creative Hub.'" *Jewish News*, 19 June 2014, jewishnews.timesofisrael.com/

london-grammar-dan-rothman/. Accessed 8 Jan. 2017.

Wolfson, Sam. "London's Perfect Grammar." *The Guardian*, 30 Nov. 2013, www.theguardian.com/music/2013/nov/30/london-grammar-nightcall-if-you-wait. Accessed 8 Jan. 2017.

—*Michael Tillman*

Layli Long Soldier

Occupation: Poet

Layli Long Soldier's debut collection of poems, *Whereas* (2017), was a finalist for the National Book Award for Poetry in 2017. A United States citizen as well as a member of the Oglala Sioux Tribe and a citizen of the Oglala Lakota Nation, Long Soldier's work explores the fissures of her cultural identity. As a dual citizen, Long Soldier lives in the divide. There, she writes in her introduction to *Whereas*, "I must work, I must eat, I must art, I must mother, I must friend, I must listen, I must observe, constantly I must live." Very few poetry collections enjoy mainstream success, but Long Soldier's singular work was quickly embraced by readers and mainstream press outlets such as the *New York Times*, which published an excerpt of the book and named it one of their 100 Notable Books of 2017. Toggling between the English and Lakota languages, the centerpiece of Long Soldier's book, a poem entitled "Whereas," reckons with a 2009 resolution on behalf of the United States government, apologizing to Native Americans for pain and suffering, while absolving itself of guilt in any legal sense. In the apology, each line admitting wrongdoing, but shirking responsibility, begins with the word "whereas." Experimental in form, Long Soldier's poems explore the multitudes contained in each "whereas." In his review for the *Los Angeles Times* (5 May 2017), John Freeman wrote that Long Soldier "has rubbed two languages together and made their shared silences into gravel—paving a perch from which a reader can see clearly." Long Soldier earned a Lannan Literary Fellowship in 2015, and in 2016, she received a prestigious Whiting Award in poetry.

EARLY LIFE AND EDUCATION

Long Soldier's mother was a white woman from Idaho. Her father was from the Pine Ridge Indian Reservation in South Dakota. Her parents separated when Long Soldier was a child. She grew up in the care of her mother, and when she was eleven years old, the two moved to the Four Corners regions of Arizona after her mother took a job with the Navajo Nation. As a child, Long Soldier dreamed of being a singer and musician. She studied the violin and piano—her mother was a trained pianist—and later learned to play the electric guitar and bass. After high school, Long Soldier moved to Santa Fe, New Mexico, where she played in a band called Hunska. Her love of music led her to a love for writing. "There was an articulation in writing that I couldn't achieve through music, so for me, the two disciplines were almost like left and right hands," she told Jillian Mukavetz for the blog *womens quarterly conversation* (6 Mar. 2013). "My right hand was music, what I reached out with the most. But writing, on the left, was the silent doer; picking up little words and phrases, tinkering, twirling, investigating." She took her first writing class at the Institute of American Indian Arts (IAIA) in Santa Fe in 2005, and graduated with a bachelor of fine arts degree in creative writing in 2009. In college, Long Soldier studied the work of Native American writers like poet Joy Harjo; Luci Tapahonso, the first poet laureate of the Navajo Nation; and Susan Power, author of the award-winning novel *The Grass Dancer* (1995). These women later became Long Soldier's colleagues and supporters. She is also inspired by the work of avant-garde icon, Gertrude Stein. Stein's influence is evident in Long Soldier's interest in language and experimental forms. Long Soldier earned her master of fine arts degree from Bard College in New York.

EARLY WORK

As Long Soldier continued to write, her poems were published in various literary magazines. She worked as a contributing editor of a journal called *Drunken Boat* (now known as *Anomaly*) and as a poetry editor at the Arizona-based Kore Press. She is currently an adjunct professor at Diné College, a tribal college in Tsaile, Arizona. Long Soldier published a chapbook called *Chromosomory* in 2010. She wrote and took classes, continuing to hone her style, and began her best-known project, the collection *Whereas*, in 2011. The book began as a response to a congressional resolution of apology to Native Americans issued on behalf of the United States government. President Barack Obama signed the resolution in late 2009, but Long Soldier was not made aware of it until the spring of 2010. In hindsight, Long Soldier acknowledges, her ignorance of the resolution is not surprising. The government did not announce the apology or otherwise deliver it to Native American leaders. It was quietly tucked into and enacted as a part of the Defense Appropriations Act of 2009. Long Soldier's initial reaction was directed at the delivery, or more accurately the "non-delivery," as she put it in an interview with Krista Tippett for the award-winning podcast *On Being* (30 Mar. 2017), of the document itself. As Rob Capriccioso wrote for

Indian Country Today (13 Jan. 2010), "Is an apology that's not said out loud really an apology?" Long Soldier went further. "Were Native people considered important enough to deliver this Apology face-to-face, as a sincere gesture?" she asked Molly Boyle for the *Santa Fe New Mexican* (14 Nov. 2017). "In my gut, the answer was 'no.' And in my gut, I felt a desire to kick back. It was motor reflex."

WHEREAS (2017)

Upon closer examination, Long Soldier was similarly offended by the careful wording of the apology. The document acknowledges the "official depredations and ill-conceived policies" of the federal government against a group of people that had inhabited the land now called the United States for "thousands of years" prior to European settlers. The apology continues with a series of statements beginning with the word "whereas." The first reads: "Whereas the arrival of Europeans in North America opened a new chapter in the history of the Native Peoples." The sentence, indicative of the ones that follow, made Long Soldier angry—where for instance, was the word "genocide," she wonders in the collection's first poem—as did the assertion that the crimes of the US government against Native American people were not actionable in court. In 2011, Long Soldier began her response to both the language and content of the apology. That response grew into a larger meditation on deceitful language and attempts to rewrite history. Long Soldier's debut collection, *Whereas*, is divided into two parts. The first part, "These Being the Concerns," contains poems that explore the fusty strictures of the English language, and others that seek to convey the untranslatable meanings of the Lakota language. Take for instance, the collection's first poem, "H̆e Sápa," about the multitudes contained in the two words that do not quite mean "black hill."

Another poem, "38," recalls the hanging of thirty-eight Dakota men in 1862. The mass execution was approved by President Abraham Lincoln the same week that he signed the Emancipation Proclamation, freeing every enslaved person in the United States. The poem is a good illustration of Long Soldier's larger point about the ways in which the English language can be contorted to obscure truth and commit violence. The poem begins, "Here, the sentence will be respected. / I will compose each sentence with care, by minding what the rules of writing dictate." She goes on to reaffirm her thesis, adding, "Also, historical events will not be dramatized for an 'interesting' read." Her only allegiance, she asserts, is to the grammatical structure of the sentence itself. Her theme thus laid out, Long Soldier describes in dispassionate detail the events that led to the execution of the "Dakota 38," as they are known. Long Soldier tells the story while continuously drawing attention to how she tells it. For example, she writes: "[Y]ou might be asking, 'Why were thirty-eight Dakota men hung? / As a side note, the past tense of hang is *hung*, but when referring to the capital punishment of hanging, the correct tense is *hanged*. / So it's possible that you're asking, 'Why were thirty-eight Dakota men hanged?'" Long Soldier writes about the broken treaties that resulted in the purposeful starvation of the Dakota people. Those same starving people organized the Dakota Uprising in protest, and in punishment for this, thirty-eight men were killed. The end of the poem relays an anecdote that Long Soldier references in the book's first poem. One trader, refusing to sell food to the Dakotas, suggested that if the Dakota people were starving, "let them eat grass." During the uprising, that trader was murdered. His body was found with a mouthful of grass. "I am inclined to call this act by the Dakota warriors a poem. / There's irony in their poem. / There was no text." Long Soldier writes. In this way, Long Soldier drives her point home. The sentence, correctly constructed, does not allow for the depth of misery, rage, and grief that Long Soldier seeks to express.

The second section of the book, "Whereas," begins with a short introduction explaining the US government's 2009 apology. In Long Soldier's poetic response, each line or section begins with the word "whereas." Most of the poems in this section look like prose poems, with free verse spilling into each line. She writes about uncaring strangers, but more movingly, about her own young daughter, and the legacy of power and pain that she will inherit.

PERSONAL LIFE

Long Soldier is married to poet Orlando White. The couple met when Long Soldier was playing in her band; Hunska often opened for White's punk band, Unofficial. White also attended IAIA and is a faculty member at Diné College. They have a daughter named Chance, and live in Santa Fe, New Mexico.

SUGGESTED READING

Boyle, Molly. "IAIA Grad Up for Prestigious Poetry Prize." *Santa Fe New Mexican*, 14 Nov. 2017, www.santafenewmexican.com/life/features/iaia-grad-up-for-prestigious-poetry-prize/article_442f1903-2b5f-528e-9d59-bfaee6ca6068.html. Accessed 5 Feb. 2018.

Capriccioso, Rob. "A Sorry Saga: Obama Signs Native American Apology Resolution; Fails to Draw Attention to It." *Indian Country Today*, 13 Jan. 2010, www.indianlaw.org/node/529. Accessed 5 Feb. 2018.

Long Soldier, Layli. "Layli Long Soldier: The Freedom of Real Apologies." Interview by

Krista Tippett. *On Being*, 30 Mar. 2017, www. onbeing.org/programs/layli-long-soldier-the-freedom-of-real-apologies-mar2017/. Accessed 5 Feb. 2018.

Long Soldier, Layli. "Profiles in Poetics: Layli Long Soldier." Interview by Jillian Muka- vetz. *womens quarterly conversation*, 6 Mar. 2013, www.womensquarterlyconversation. com/2013/03/06/profiles-in-poetics-layli- long-soldier/. Accessed 5 Feb. 2018.

—*Molly Hagan*

Robert Lopez

Date of birth: February 23, 1975
Occupation: Songwriter

The so-called EGOT is a holy grail among per- formers; the acronym stands for the four major awards in entertainment: an Emmy Award; a Grammy Award; an Oscar, or Academy Award; and a Tony Award. To achieve an EGOT—to win all four of these awards—is a rare feat. Only twelve people, among them actor Rita Moreno, director Mel Brooks, and composer Richard Rodgers, have ever done it.

This fact makes it all the more remarkable that in 2018, songwriter Robert Lopez became the first person in history to achieve the EGOT twice. Born and raised in New York City, he wrote his first song when he was around seven years old. Though he studied English at Yale University, he harbored dreams of writing mu- sicals. His first musical creation, written with Jeff Marx, was the raunchy, smash-hit musical comedy *Avenue Q*, which first opened in 2003. He went on to develop and write for the equally lauded (and equally profane) Broadway musical *The Book of Mormon* (2011) with Matt Stone and Trey Parker, the creators of the long-running animated television show *South Park*.

Although he might not be as well-known as his fellow EGOT achievers, Lopez is responsible for some of the most ubiquitous songs in the contemporary musical canon. He and his wife, lyricist Kristen Anderson-Lopez, won an Oscar— Lopez's first—for writing the explosively popu- lar song "Let It Go," for the Disney film *Frozen* (2013). They also wrote, and won an Oscar for, "Remember Me," the touching anthem from the Disney film *Coco* (2017). The couple have con- tinuously expressed gratitude for the opportuni- ties that they have had to contribute to so many significant projects, and in reflecting on their building successes, particularly at the point of the overwhelmingly positive reception of *Frozen*, Lopez told Greg Ehrbar for *IndieWire* (27 Nov. 2013), "I really have no idea how it happened

Photo by Kevork Djansezian/Getty Images

that we're here and we're doing it, so we're not taking a lot of time to look around, but we are really enjoying the ride."

EARLY LIFE AND EDUCATION

Lopez was born in New York City to parents Katherine and Frank Lopez on February 23, 1975. His brother, Billy, is an Emmy Award–win- ning writer for children's television, and Lopez has won two Emmy Awards himself for work on the show *Wonder Pets!* While he began playing the piano when he was six years old, his mother told Julie Salamon for the *New York Times* (22 June 2005) that it was a "fluke" that he picked up the instrument at all. The family, lifelong New Yorkers, had recently returned to the city after spending a year in Massachusetts, where Lopez's father was working for Clark Univer- sity. When they returned, the sublet where the family was living had a piano, and Lopez began taking lessons.

His parents were wary of his devotion, but the next year, they bought him a piano of his own. "If you quit, we'll make you eat it," his parents told him, as he recalled to Salamon. Whether or not he would be forced to consume the instru- ment soon became a moot point, however, as he got more serious about music. On the encour- agement of his piano teacher, Bennett Lerner, he even wrote his first song, "Oy Vey, What a Day," when he was around seven years old.

Lopez took classes at the Greenwich House music school in his own Greenwich Village neighborhood. Though at one point he began to grow restless and briefly took up the saxophone, he ultimately returned to the piano. In 1991, he won a national competition for a song he wrote. Though he tried to give half of his prize to the school as a gift, the director sent the money back, telling him that he could give a donation after he had made more money. Nearly fifteen years later, after the unexpected success of *Avenue Q*, Lopez would throw a fundraiser for the school, making good on that wish.

Lopez attended Hunter College High School, where he acquired a greater taste for writing by composing musicals for the school's drama group. After graduating from Hunter College High School in 1993, Lopez went on to study English at Yale, where he took a class on William Shakespeare from the celebrated literary critic Harold Bloom. He wrote three plays as an undergraduate: a musical featuring adults playing children called *All Grown Up*; a play about early twentieth-century New York intellectuals called *Down Bleecker Street*; and a musical that he described to a reporter for *Yale News* (25 Feb. 2011) as sort of like Edward Albee's acidic drama *Who's Afraid of Virginia Woolf?*: "We didn't really understand what being in your forties and drunk was like," he joked of the interpretation.

EARLY CAREER AND *AVENUE Q*

After graduation in 1997, hoping to write musicals for a living, Lopez moved back in with his parents. "I didn't have another plan," he admitted to Salamon. In addition to working several temp jobs and holding a part-time job as a weekend receptionist at Greenwich House, he also studied musical theater at the BMI Lehman Engel Musical Theatre Workshop. There, he met his writing partner, Marx, as well as his future wife, Anderson-Lopez. Lopez and Marx achieved their first earnings after writing the music for two children's musicals, *Ferdinand the Bull* and *Reading Rainbow*. "We really clicked. We wanted to write shows that were relevant and funny for people our age. We wanted to write for people who didn't necessarily go to Broadway for their entertainment," Lopez said of the strength of their collaborative relationship to Richard Ouzounian for the *Toronto Star* (14 Sept. 2014).

With his earnings, Lopez was able to afford his own place. At the same time, he and Marx were also working on a larger, much more adult project that would later become *Avenue Q*, a coming-of-age musical involving foul-mouthed puppets. Lopez and Marx developed the musical at the Eugene O'Neill Theater Center in Waterford, Connecticut, in 2002. After a poor first reading, Lopez and Anderson-Lopez, stayed up all night reworking the script. The show premiered Off-Broadway at the Vineyard Theatre in March 2003 and won the Lucille Lortel Award for Outstanding Musical before premiering on Broadway, at the John Golden Theatre, in July 2003.

In his review for the *New York Times* (1 Aug. 2003), Ben Brantley described the musical as "savvy, sassy and eminently likable," and Lopez and Marx's songs as "unfailingly tuneful and disgustingly irresistible"—even with titles like "Everyone's a Little Bit Racist" and "The Internet Is for Porn." In 2004, *Avenue Q* won a Tony Award for Best Musical—beating out the popular *Wicked*—as well as for Best Book (Musical) and Best Original Musical Score. The show closed, after six years and 2,534 performances, in September 2009. In the meantime, in 2006, Lopez and Anderson-Lopez had their first experience working together full time and with Disney when they converted the beloved film *Finding Nemo* (2003) into a live musical performed at the company's Animal Kingdom theme park.

THE BOOK OF MORMON

At an early performance of *Avenue Q*, Lopez met Stone and Parker, the creators of the animated adult television show *South Park*. A huge fan of the show, he told them that he was interested in writing a musical about Joseph Smith, the founder of Mormonism. As Lopez recalled to *Yale News*, "They said, 'That's coincidental. That's what we wanted to do for the past 10 years.'" The three began working on *The Book of Mormon* while *South Park* was on hiatus. The show follows two Salt Lake City missionaries to a tiny village in northern Uganda. "It's not meant to make fun of Mormonism," he told *Yale News*. "Ultimately, it's about faith and the value of faith. It's telling the story of a guy who loses faith and regains it in another way." At the same time, like *Avenue Q*—and *South Park*—the show is exuberantly profane.

Though Stone and Parker, used to working in the medium of television, initially envisioned the story potentially as a film, Lopez, who felt it was best suited for the stage, encouraged them to consider it as a musical and go through the process of workshopping. After years of the trio finding time to travel to meet each other and to research and rework, the musical enjoyed its first workshop in 2008 and premiered on Broadway, at the Eugene O'Neill Theatre, in March 2011. Brantley, writing for the *New York Times* (24 Mar. 2011), was an early evangelist for the show, describing it in his review as "heaven on Broadway." That same year, *The Book of Mormon* won the coveted trifecta of Tony Awards, snagging Best Musical, Best Book (Musical), and Best Original Musical Score, and Lopez shared his first Grammy Award for the original cast album. Seven years and thousands of performances later, the show was still running in 2018.

FROZEN **AND** *COCO*

Also in 2011, Disney approached Lopez and Anderson-Lopez, who had penned original songs for the animated musical film *Winnie the Pooh* (2011), once more to write the songs for a film called *Frozen*. The couple signed on, excited to tell the story of two sisters. "That really resonated for us, having two daughters. Our youngest just thinks our oldest is a superhero. And our oldest is often like 'Leave me alone,'" Anderson-Lopez explained to Bryan Alexander for *USA Today* (25 Nov. 2013). "We knew exactly what that older-younger dynamic is." One of the songs they wrote, a powerful anthem called "Let It Go," has become one of the most familiar and popular songs in the Disney canon since the film's release to theaters in 2013. It earned the couple their first Academy Award for best original song and, sung by actor and singer Idina Menzel, even made it to mainstream radio. Their work on the film also earned them two Grammy Awards in 2014.

In summing up their successful approach to composing for the film, Lopez told Ehrbar, "The kind of songs we wanted to write for *Frozen* were the kind that, if they were removed from the movie, nothing would make sense at all. Each song needed to bear it's storytelling weight." Also in 2014, Lopez and Anderson-Lopez appeared on *Time* magazine's list of the one hundred most influential people. In 2015, they collaborated on a musical romantic comedy called *Up Here*. The show premiered at La Jolla Playhouse to middling reviews.

Meanwhile, Lopez and Anderson-Lopez had also met with Lee Unkrich, the director and cowriter of Disney's *Coco* (2017). Unkrich told the couple that he wanted a song that could mean different things at different points in the film's plot. Attracted to this idea, the duo eventually wrote the song "Remember Me," which went on to earn the couple their second Oscar for best original song. In interviews, Anderson-Lopez has recalled that she wrote the lyrics for the song while riding the subway. That song, like others the couple have written for Disney, was inspired by their relationship with their daughters. "We knew a lot about the power of the lullaby to stay connected when you're far away," Anderson-Lopez told Julie Miller for *Vanity Fair* (16 Feb. 2018). Long business trips to Los Angeles, she said, are "the agony of our life, and we deal with it by writing songs that they could sing with their babysitters when we're gone." Only months after *Coco*'s release, a stage version of *Frozen* premiered on Broadway in early 2018; the duo wrote twelve new songs for the project.

PERSONAL LIFE

Lopez and Anderson-Lopez were married in 2003. They have two daughters and live in Brooklyn.

SUGGESTED READING

Alexander, Bryan. "*Frozen*: Family Affair for Married Songwriters." *USA Today*, 25 Nov. 2013, www.usatoday.com/story/life/movies/2013/11/25/robert-and-kristen-anderson-lopez/3652505/. Accessed 12 June 2018.

Anderson-Lopez, Kristen, and Robert Lopez. "Writing Songs for *Frozen*: An Interview with Kristen Anderson-Lopez and Robert Lopez." Interview by Greg Ehrbar. *IndieWire*, 27 Nov. 2013, www.indiewire.com/2013/11/writing-songs-for-frozen-an-interview-with-kristen-anderson-lopez-and-robert-lopez-124605/. Accessed 12 June 2018.

Brantley, Ben. "Theater Review; A Feeling You're Not on Sesame Street." Review of *Avenue Q*, directed by Jason Moore. *The New York Times*, 1 Aug. 2003, www.nytimes.com/2003/08/01/movies/theater-review-a-feeling-you-re-not-on-sesame-street.html. Accessed 12 June 2018.

Lopez, Robert. "Robert Lopez '97: Composer, Lyricist, Beatbox Enthusiast." *Yale News*, 25 Feb. 2011, yaledailynews.com/blog/2011/02/25/robert-lopez-97-composer-lyricist-beatbox-enthusiast/. Accessed 12 June 2018.

Miller, Julie. "For *Coco* Songwriters Robert Lopez and Kristen Anderson-Lopez, Oscar Season Is a Family Affair." *Vanity Fair*, 16 Feb. 2018, www.vanityfair.com/hollywood/2018/02/coco-songwriters-robert-lopez-and-kristen-anderson-lopez-on-remember-me. Accessed 12 June 2018.

Salamon, Julie. "Student Who Made Good on *Avenue Q* Gives Back." *The New York Times*, 22 June 2005, www.nytimes.com/2005/06/22/theater/newsandfeatures/student-who-made-good-on-avenue-q-gives-back.html. Accessed 12 June 2018.

SELECTED WORKS

Avenue Q, 2003; *The Book of Mormon*, 2011; *Frozen*, 2013; *Coco*, 2017

—*Molly Hagan*

Valeria Luiselli

Date of birth: August 16, 1983
Occupation: Author

When the National Book Critics Circle named *The Story of My Teeth* (2015), by Valeria Luiselli, a finalist for its fiction award, it marked only the third time in the history of the prize that a book originally written in a foreign language had been shortlisted. The volume ultimately garnered a *Los Angeles Times* Book Award and appeared on several lists of best books of the year, including

By Andrew Lih, via Wikimedia Commons

and outspoken and have really loud voices, so even within my family space, I've always been pretty silent—I always had to rush what I had to say, otherwise they would start speaking on top of me," she recalled to Wendy Smith for *Publishers Weekly* (25 Apr. 2014). "I found in writing the space to say things in the very slow and soft pace that I think in, with my particular rhythm and tone and volume, which is not very loud!"

Luiselli's father had worked as an adviser to Mexican president José López Portillo, and Portillo's successor, Carlos Salinas de Gortari, subsequently assigned him to diplomatic posts around the world. It was, as Luiselli recalled to Lauren Oyler for *Vice* (15 Sept. 2015), "a form of exiling someone that you don't want too near but you [do] want inside the umbrella of state supervision." The family lived for various periods of time in Wisconsin, Costa Rica, South Korea, and South Africa, among other locales. It was not until her teens that Luiselli returned to Mexico with her mother, who had by then separated from her father. "I couldn't quite adapt," she told Smith. "I had learned how to be a foreigner, but I didn't know how to be a Mexican."

Choosing not to settle down in Mexico, she applied for a scholarship to attend a boarding school in Maharashtra, India. She wrote long e-mails to her parents once a month, trusting the missives to the region's sporadic Internet service, but was otherwise independent of her family. She volunteered in a local old-age home and went on trips with friends to Mumbai's markets and museums.

After graduating from high school, she studied for a time in Madrid, Spain, but returned to her native country in her early twenties to attend the National Autonomous University of Mexico, where she received a bachelor's degree in philosophy in 2008. While there, she lived in the neighborhood of Colonia Roma, which had suffered severe damage in an earthquake in 1985. "I guess I'm part of the earthquake generation," Luiselli mused to Jennifer Kabat for *Bomb Magazine* (1 Oct. 2014). "When I read other Mexican writers my age, I realize that the earthquake is like a leitmotif in our writing, though most of us don't remember it. . . . There is, of course, a lyrical approach to things collapsing or disappearing that allows you to play with linguistic analogies—like stuttering and untranslatability, for example—but there's also the concrete fact that an earthquake can happen at any moment in Mexico City, and everything can just collapse again."

Luiselli next traveled to New York to conduct her graduate studies at Columbia University. She earned an MA in 2012, an MPhil in 2014, and a PhD in 2015.

those compiled by the *New York Times* and *National Public Radio* (*NPR*). Luiselli herself was named one of the twenty best Mexican writers under the age of forty (in celebration of a collaboration between the London Book Fair and Guadalajara Book Fair) and received similar recognition from the National Book Foundation, which included her on its "5 under 35" list.

Luiselli serves as an assistant professor of Romance languages and literatures at Hofstra University. She has written a handful of other books that have been published in the United States, including *Faces in the Crowd* (2014), a complex novel with multiple narrators, and *Tell Me How It Ends: An Essay in Forty Questions* (2017), which draws upon her experiences as a volunteer translator working with undocumented Latin American children facing deportation. "I feel very porous to the world around me," she told Jeffrey Zuckerman for the *Los Angeles Review of Books* (18 May 2014), explaining where she finds inspiration for her fiction and nonfiction. Commenting on Luiselli's famously peripatetic life, Zuckerman wrote: "The great beauty of her art is seeing all her contrasting stories collapse or blend or combine into an unexpected whole. . . . And maybe that, for her, is the closest thing to a true idea of home: not a single place, not a single language, but a single heart and mind, taking in the multitudes of the real world, pumping out a multiplicity of brilliant words."

EARLY YEARS AND EDUCATION

Valeria Luiselli was born in Mexico City, Mexico, on August 16, 1983. She was the youngest of three sisters. "My sisters are very eloquent

BEGINNING A WRITING CAREER

When she was just twenty-one and living in Madrid, Luiselli began writing her first book, *Papeles falsos* ("False papers"), which she described to Nicholas Guappone for *The Rumpus* (9 Nov. 2015) as "a kind of bibliographic autobiography, as much as it is a venture into urbanism from the viewpoint of literature [and it] deals with our relationship to spaces, books, and languages, among other things." She continued, "I taught myself to write while I wrote [it], so it is a book that has no pretense other than to find the most exact words for things I had never been able to articulate until that point." The Spanish-language edition of the book was published by Sexto Piso in 2010. Her next book, the novel *Los ingrávidos* ("The weightless") was released by the company the following year.

Luiselli's first two volumes were published simultaneously in 2014 in the United States by Coffee House Press. Translated by Christina MacSweeney, *Papeles falsos* was released as *Sidewalks*. Critics took note of how the book takes the reader from place to place. As Smith wrote, "These wanderings are unified by a distinctive narrative voice: pensive, questioning, always something of a stranger in a strange land." Among the most popular of the essays is "Other Rooms," in which Luiselli records her interactions with a philosophical doorman and ponders his advice to spend as many nights as possible away from home, in a journey of self-discovery.

Los ingrávidos, also translated by MacSweeney, appeared in American bookstores as *Faces in the Crowd*. It gained attention for its three narrators: a young translator in New York who is obsessed with the Mexican poet Gilberto Owen, Owen himself, and an older married woman in Mexico (who may or may not be the translator). Oyler described the book as "more wistful than *Sidewalks*, with narrators that bleed into each other and are thus a little confusing, but it's nothing too strenuous—a combination of Jenny Offill and Ali Smith, with a Bolaño-esque scattering of both explicit and hidden literary allusions and the dry surprise of Zadie Smith's sense of humor." "Very different preoccupations motivated the two books," Luiselli told Guappone. "*Faces in the Crowd* is sadder, deeper, more complex. . . . It is a book about not coming to terms with the life we have chosen, and the way that fiction may either redeem us or further our sense of disconnection from our lives."

THE STORY OF MY TEETH

Luiselli was next commissioned to write a new piece of fiction to accompany a show at a contemporary art museum in Mexico City funded by a juice factory. She chose to involve the factory workers, sending them each chapter as she wrote it and incorporating their feedback into the next installment. *La historia de mis dientes* (2012), published by Coffee House Press as *The Story of My Teeth* in 2015, tells the tale of Gustavo Sánchez Sánchez, an auctioneer born with terrible dental problems who collects the pulled teeth of such luminaries as Plato and Virginia Woolf. The work quickly garnered positive critical attention. "Luiselli's tale is a surreal allegory about the power of storytelling to recast the ordinary as extraordinary, to imbue objects with seemingly inherent value," Julia Felsenthal wrote for *Vogue* (3 Mar. 2016).

"Writing literature can be such a bourgeois and self-indulgent thing," Luiselli admitted to Guappone. "While writing this novel I had to both entertain tired factory workers after their long day's work, and be able to extract from them enough material to write the next installment. . . . It was like being a clown and a psychologist at the same time."

Luiselli followed *The Story of My Teeth* with 2017's *Tell Me How It Ends: An Essay in 40 Questions*. It was also critically acclaimed, and *Kirkus* (31 Mar. 2017) called it "a powerful call to action and to empathy." While waiting for her own green card, Luiselli volunteered as a translator for a pro bono legal service, administering a forty-question immigration survey to Latin American youths in danger of deportation. "Luiselli effectively humanizes the plights of those who have been demonized or who have been reduced to faceless numbers," *Kirkus* wrote. "Though [she] may not convince those adamantly opposed to loosening regulations, she hopes that those who have been willfully blind to the injustices will recognize how they 'haunt and shame us.'"

PERSONAL LIFE

Luiselli is married to fellow writer Álvaro Enrigue. They met when he was an editor at the Mexican magazine *Letras Libres* and she was an undergraduate whose instructor submitted one of her essays to him. Together, they have one daughter, Maia, and Enrigue has two sons, Miquel and Dylan, from a former relationship. They live in the northern Manhattan neighborhood of Hamilton Heights.

Although Luiselli frequently writes well into the middle of the night, and Enrigue wakes exceptionally early to work, Luiselli told Felsenthal that the two "contaminate each other to a degree. In a positive way."

SUGGESTED READING

Felsenthal, Julia. "Married Mexican Writers Álvaro Enrigue and Valeria Luiselli on Their Buzzy New Novels and New York Life." *Vogue*, 3 Mar. 2016, www.vogue.com/article/alvaro-enrigue-valeria-luiselli-profile. Accessed 17 Jan. 2018.

Luiselli, Valeria. "Interview: Valeria Luiselli." Interview by Jennifer Kabat. *Bomb Magazine*,

1 Oct. 2014, bombmagazine.org/articles/vale-ria-luiselli/. Accessed 17 Jan. 2018.

Luiselli, Valeria. "The Rumpus Interview with Valeria Luiselli." Interview by Nicholas Guappone. *The Rumpus*, 9 Nov. 2015, therumpus. net/2015/11/the-rumpus-interview-with-vale-ria-luiselli/. Accessed 17 Jan. 2018.

McArdle, Molly. "The Work of Translation." *Brooklyn Magazine*, 6 Apr. 2017, www.bkmag. com/2017/04/06/talking-valeria-luiselli-tell-me-how-it-ends-immigration/. Accessed 17 Jan. 2018.

Oyler, Lauren. "Valeria Luiselli: the Novelist All Your Smart Friends Are Talking About." *Vice*, 15 Sept. 2015, broadly.vice.com/en_us/ article/8qwjxx/valeria-luiselli-the-novelist-all-your-smart-friends-are-talking-about. Accessed 17 Jan. 2018.

Smith, Wendy. "An International Life in Essays and Fiction: Valeria Luiselli." *Publishers Weekly*, 25 Apr. 2014, www.publishersweekly.com/ pw/by-topic/authors/profiles/article/62009-an-international-life-in-essays-and-fiction-valeria-luiselli.html. Accessed 17 Jan. 2018.

Zuckerman, Jeffrey. "Porous to the World around Me: The Writing of Valeria Luiselli." *Los Angeles Review of Books*, 18 May 2014, lareviewofbooks.org/article/porous-world-writing-valeria-luiselli/. Accessed 17 Jan. 2018.

SELECTED WORKS

Faces in the Crowd, 2014; *Sidewalks*, 2014; *The Story of My Teeth*, 2015; *Tell Me How It Ends: An Essay in 40 Questions*, 2017

—Mari Rich

Mina Lux

Date of birth: August 10, 1968
Occupation: Entrepreneur

For some, the gulf between the fields of biochemistry and engineering and that of digital marketing may seem so wide as to be insurmountable. For entrepreneur and marketing expert Mina Lux, however, the two fields are truly not so different. "To me, biochemistry/engineering research and digital marketing have two things in common: 1) the ability to spot the trend and 2) to know which numbers matter and which do not," she told Kyle Bournes for the University of Ottawa online publication *Tabaret*. Indeed, Lux, a former biochemistry and chemical engineering student who turned down a full graduate school scholarship in the 1990s to join her brother's email company instead, has built her career on her ability to identify trends and meaningful data. The founder and chief executive officer of the big-data company Meelo

Logic, she works to bring that understanding to a variety of major companies with the goal of providing crucial insights using proprietary artificial intelligence technology.

Lux began her career in digital marketing as vice president of sales and marketing at FloNetwork, one of the early forces in email marketing. After leaving that company in 1998, she spent the better part of two decades bringing her marketing expertise to companies such as *USA Today*, *Scientific American*, and the website *The Frisky*. All the while, she has drawn on her scientific background while creating digital strategies that often increased not only the readership but also the profitability of the companies for which she worked. "Whereas some marketers may want to know as much as they can, I move to identify the variables that have the biggest impact for the brand towards meeting its goals," she explained to Bournes of her process. "This is not easy for many because there is always the fear that 'if I don't look at this, will I be missing out?' As an engineer, I learned that to be able to optimize, you must limit the number of variables that you are testing at any one time."

EARLY LIFE AND EDUCATION

Lux was born Mina Chen on August 10, 1968, in Taipei, Taiwan. When she was eleven years old, she immigrated to Canada with her parents, Agnes and Chih Yuan Chen, and her brother, Paul. The family settled in Nepean, Ontario.

As a teenager, Lux became deeply interested in science, inspired in part by articles she read in the magazine *Scientific American*. She aspired to become a biochemical engineer and, upon enrolling in the University of Ottawa, double-majored in biochemistry and chemical engineering to prepare herself for that role. During the summers, she worked at Chalk River Laboratories, a nuclear research facility in northern Ontario. She earned her bachelor of science from the University of Ottawa in 1990 and bachelor of applied science in chemical engineering in 1992.

After completing her undergraduate studies, Lux initially planned to pursue doctoral research focusing on the ways in which proteins are used to deliver pharmaceutical drugs within the body. However, despite winning a full scholarship to pursue her PhD, Lux was uncomfortable with the animal testing her research would require. She ultimately decided not to enroll in a doctoral program, instead beginning what would become a long and successful career in digital marketing.

EARLY CAREER

Upon leaving the academic world behind, Lux had the opportunity to join the Toronto-based company Media Synergy, which had been founded by her brother, Paul Chen. The company, which was later renamed FloNetwork, initially focused on integrating multimedia technology into email. "I thought, 'Why not? How hard can it be?' I knew it was going to be tough but thought 'Heck, it's going to be fun.' And it was," Lux told Bournes of her decision to join the company. "There was a lot of money being invested in this new information era and that created a lot more room for us to experiment. We made mistakes. We learned from them. We got back on the right track and kept going."

Taking on the role of vice president of sales and marketing, Lux was a dedicated proponent of the company's move into incorporating multimedia into email—a brand new development at that time. "If a picture's worth a thousand words, then animation is worth a billion," she told Jon Swartz for *SFGate* in 1996. "This sets a framework, a mood, for e-mail. And it jazzes up your message." FloNetwork went on to pioneer the use of direct email in marketing, specifically facilitating the creation of mass email campaigns. Lux moved on from FloNetwork in 1998, and in 2001 the company was sold to the advertising technology provider DoubleClick for $80 million.

In 1998, Lux joined the publication *USA Today* as director of marketing. In that role, she was tasked with promoting the publication's website, a relatively new venture that had not yet found a wide audience. "At that time, *USA Today* had more than 2 million daily readers, but research showed that most of them did not know that we had a Web site," she recalled to Melissa Campanelli for *Target Marketing* (21 Feb. 2008). "We needed to let the readers know that not only can they get the content they love from print on the site, but also even more." Under Lux's leadership, the company made various efforts to promote the *USA Today* website among the print publication's readers, including by featuring a banner-style advertisement in the print edition that directed readers to visit the site. Within four months of Lux's arrival at the company, the *USA Today* website had become the number-one general news site online, outpacing CNN and MSNBC.

DIGITAL MARKETING EXPERT

Having gained significant experience and achieved impressive results through her work at FloNetwork and *USA Today*, Lux established herself as an expert in the field of digital marketing and brought her skills to a variety of companies over the next nearly two decades. In mid-1999, after leaving *USA Today*, she was tasked with overseeing the marketing of the Doubleday Select book clubs as well as related online marketing and branding efforts. She joined the Working Woman Network the following year as senior vice president of marketing. In that role, Lux oversaw all advertising, marketing, and market research efforts as well as developing

business-to-business marketing initiatives, focusing particularly on women-owned businesses.

In 2001, Lux joined the publication *Scientific American* as head of its online magazine. Having been inspired by *Scientific American's* content as a teenager, she sought to make it available to new audiences online, often in forms other than traditional magazine articles. "We believed that in order for us to be effective, we must take advantage of the strength of the digital media," she told Campanelli. "With video, we are able to present complex ideas in an entertaining manner. With audio, we are able to deliver portable science with the wide MP3 install base. With blogs, we are able to have a young, hip voice reporting on complex ideas on all aspects of science while still making it a quick, entertaining read." Throughout Lux's time at *Scientific American*, she oversaw the publication's digital strategy, increased revenues and subscriber numbers, and advised other branches of the magazine's parent company.

Lux left *Scientific American* in 2008 to pursue independent consulting work, founding Mina Lux Consulting. Over the subsequent years, the firm was particularly active in the field of entertainment, consulting for television channels such as CNN, Cartoon Network, and truTV, as well as the film and television distributor Image Entertainment. In 2009, Lux also became general manager of the website *The Frisky*, which was owned by Turner Broadcasting at the time of her hiring. Over the course of several years, Lux led efforts to increase traffic and revenue for the site, which focused primarily on entertainment and women's lifestyle topics. In 2011, the site was sold to the company BuzzMedia, later renamed SpinMedia. Lux played a key role in the sale process and remained with the website for nearly two years after its acquisition, continuing her efforts to establish *The Frisky* as a popular and profitable brand.

MEELO LOGIC

After working for many years in marketing, Lux moved in a new, yet related direction beginning in 2013, when she began raising funds for her new startup, Meelo Logic, collecting $1.5 million of funding from angel investors. The following year, the company raised an additional $1.5 million from Centripetal Capital Partners in its seed-funding round. Lux serves as chief executive officer for the New York–based company, which uses artificial intelligence technology such as the proprietary Context in Time Artificial Intelligence (CIT AI) to interpret customer data for marketing purposes and other uses. "Most businesses need to continuously activate, engage and motivate their customers to grow revenue and foster loyalty," Lux explained in a press release published on *Newswire* (5 May 2016). "Meelo solves this challenge by assessing the best ways to fit your product into your consumers' habits or routines." Since its launch, Meelo Logic has worked with a variety of major brands, including Macy's, Viacom, and the Warner Music Group. In recognition of her work with the company, Lux was named entrepreneur of the year by the University of Ottawa Faculty of Engineering in 2016.

PERSONAL LIFE

In interviews and public statements, Lux has drawn connections between her success as an entrepreneur and her status as an immigrant, both from Taiwan to Canada and from Canada to the United States. "Immigrants take the risk because of a dream. It's the passion of making a better life and having that chance to actually carry it out," she said in a Meelo Logic press release published on *Newswire* (4 Nov. 2016). "Does risk come in to play? From time to time . . . , but then we flip right back to that dream of having an opportunity unavailable elsewhere. That's always been the root of my strength."

Lux lives in the Greater New York City area. She has a son, Derek, who was born in 2000.

SUGGESTED READING

Bournes, Kyle. "The Science of Marketing." *Tabaret*, University of Ottawa, www.uottawa. ca/tabaret/en/content/science-marketing. Accessed 14 Dec. 2017.

Campanelli, Melissa. "Q&A: Internet Marketing and Publishing Consultant Mina Lux." *Target Marketing*, 21 Feb. 2008, www.targetmarketingmag.com/article/qa-internet-marketing-and-publishing-consultant-mina/. Accessed 14 Dec. 2017.

"Mina Lux Overview." *Crunchbase*, 2017, www. crunchbase.com/person/mina-lux. Accessed 14 Dec. 2017.

"A New Power Rising: Female Immigrant-Owned Businesses." *Newswire*, 4 Nov. 2016, www.newswire.com/news/a-new-power-rising-female-immigrant-owned-businesses-16033285. Accessed 14 Dec. 2017.

Swartz, Jon. "The Multimedia Is the Message." *SFGate*, 12 Nov. 1996, www.sfgate.com/business/article/THE-MULTIMEDIA-IS-THE-MESSAGE-E-mail-is-2959083.php. Accessed 14 Dec. 2017.

"TiEcon 2016 Announces Meelo a 2016 TiE50 Top Start-Up." *Newswire*, 5 May 2016, www. newswire.com/news/tiecon-2016-announces-meelo-a-2016-tie50-top-start-up-10808166. Accessed 14 Dec. 2017.

—*Joy Crelin*

Danielle Macdonald

Date of birth: 1991
Occupation: Actor

Critics are hailing Danielle Macdonald as an up-and-coming star for her tour-de-force performance in the indie film *Patti Cake$*, which debuted to a standing ovation at the Sundance Film Festival in 2017. In the film, Macdonald portrays a plus-sized, working-class white woman seeking to make her name in the rap world. Her inspirational role has now opened up a world of opportunities in Hollywood for the young Australian who, prior to the filming, had had very few leading roles and was often relegated to supporting character roles. As further recognition of her burgeoning talent, the next gig she landed was starring alongside Jennifer Aniston in the title role in the film adaptation, set for release in 2018, of *Dumplin'*, the popular 2015 young-adult novel by Julie Murphy.

"If you make one person happy, there you go—you did your job," Macdonald said of her role in *Patti Cake$* in an interview with Matthew Jacobs for the *Huffington Post* (14 Aug. 2017). "With this movie, it was very weird because on set it felt very special always. Very magical. But at the same time, you're like, 'No one will see this, but this feels special.' When Sundance happened, it felt insane and not like reality at all. I was in this bubble with these same people. Now I'm just taking it one day at a time."

Photo by John Sciulli/Getty Images for G'Day USA

EARLY LIFE AND CAREER

Danielle Macdonald was born in Sydney, Australia. Her father is a shipping company manager and her mother is an accountant. During her childhood, she maintained an active interest in the world of fantasy, aided in part by her love of the Harry Potter series of novels by J. K. Rowling. She also discovered that she loved performing in front of crowds. In an interview with Dixie Limbachia for *Variety* (27 July 2017), she recalled, "My sister, myself and my cousins would put on shows for our parents and charge them to come and watch, apparently. That's what I'm told. My parents said I knew how to milk it." Though she was involved in swimming, water polo, and gymnastics, after years of watching as many films as she could, she had decided to turn her attention seriously to acting.

She attended the Australian Institute for Performing Arts, where she became passionate about improvisation and anticipated beginning an acting career in Australia. Yet despite her preparations and the studying she did at school, the work never materialized. Therefore, she decided, at around age eighteen, to try to break into Hollywood and chase her dreams in the film capital of the world. She said of shifting her focus to the United States to Steph Harmon in their interview for the *Guardian* (15 June 2017), "I'd had a couple of different agents over a couple years in Australia and I had never had an audition. I was like, 'Man, I can't even get an audition out here. How am I ever even meant to improve at auditions to get a job if I can't get an audition?'" She added, "I knew there was more opportunity in America. I saw it. You see it on TV. And it was a little more diverse, as well."

FINDING HER WAY IN FILM

Macdonald began her American sojourn by participating in workshops in Hollywood. Her very first audition in the United States won her the lead role on ABC Family's sitcom *Huge*, but she lost the part when she had trouble with securing her US visa in time. However, after finally successfully moving to Los Angeles, small parts filled the vacuum quickly, and in addition to making her first official debut on a set as a cashier in the short film *The Thief*, directed by Rachel Weisz, a role on the Fox series *Glee* in 2011 earned her a Screen Actors Guild (SAG) card. Other roles on television series and in films soon followed, including a part on *Newsreaders* (2013), her first appearance in a feature film in 2013's thriller *The East*, and roles in the series *Pretty Little Liars* (2013) and *Toolies* (2014) as well as the TV movie *The Valley* (2014). The roles might have been small, but the work was steady. "It was like, you'll be the best friend (or) you'll be the character (actor). And I was like 'OK, cool. I accept that,'" she said in an interview with Andrea Mandell for *USA Today* (14

Aug. 2017). "I like working. Honestly, a lot of the time the character roles are the best roles."

In 2014, after seeing a photo of Macdonald, despite her lack of experience, veteran music video director and musician Geremy Jasper asked the young actor to come to the Sundance Directors Lab in Utah. He was at work further developing his debut feature film, which he had already spent time workshopping with film industry greats such as Quentin Tarantino during the institution's Screenwriters Lab, about a young white girl from New Jersey who is eager to make it as a rapper in New York City—just across the Hudson River, but a galaxy away from her lower-middle-class life. Jasper discussed the character of Patti with Macdonald, who, though she was intrigued by the role, was convinced there was no possible way she could do it, both because the character was nothing like her and because she could—in no way, shape, or form—rap. "I was just like, 'What have you seen that makes you think I can do it? Because I really, truly don't think I can,'" she said to Katherine Cusumano for *W* magazine (17 Aug. 2017). "I'm also really different from this character."

But Jasper worked on Macdonald's reticence as Macdonald helped him define Patti's character: the stifling home life with her mother and grandmother, the dead-end jobs, and the confident mask she puts on for the world that hides her discontent with the world. As they worked, Jasper grew ever more convinced that he had found his star: "She does a little bit of everything. . . . She's able to handle comedy, she's vulnerable, she has incredible charisma, she can be sexy. She can look like a classic Hollywood star or the girl next door," he said to Mandell.

PATTI CAKE$

At the same time, Macdonald's first good notices came from her performance in the thriller *Every Secret Thing*, which was released to theaters in 2015 and starred Elizabeth Banks, Dakota Fanning, and Diane Lane. Although the film itself underwhelmed at the box office and did little to impress critics, Macdonald was singled out for her performance. In a review for the *New York Daily News* (13 May 2015), Katherine Pushkar declared, "The film actually belongs to Danielle Macdonald, effective as cruel, jealous Alice." Following that performance, she returned to television, where she again began receiving roles in such series as *2 Broke Girls* (2015), *The Middle* (2015), and *American Horror Story* (2016).

Meanwhile, after Macdonald had left the Sundance lab, she was convinced that Jasper's script was good enough that a studio would, indeed, pick it up and film it—but also that she would not be in the lead role, as the studio would want a famous actor cast. But then she got the call: the role was hers. Prior to filming, she needed to learn how to rap and did so by singing along with various singles, marking up the lyrics on paper to show where she needed to pause, and giving herself a tutorial in rap history. By the time filming began, she was able to record her character's songs and speak in a convincing New Jersey accent. "I had to get over my own fears or insecurities because learning a new skill is always difficult. . . . I think listening to a lot of different songs and just doing them alone in my car or my closet when no one could hear me really helped," she explained to Limbachia.

It would be her lead role in Jasper's film, titled *Patti Cake$*, that would make Macdonald one of the breakout performers of 2017. In the film, her character, Patti, teams with her friends (played by Siddharth Dhananjay and Mamoudou Athie) to make a record and become stars. When not working as a bartender, she must help her sickly grandmother (played by Cathy Moriarty) while locking horns with her mother (played by Bridget Everett), a hairdresser who drowns her own former dreams of stardom in alcohol. While Macdonald had experienced initial reservations about playing the character, she also found that her raw emotions and ultimate connection with the character helped her portray Patti authentically: "I think I understood her—understood her want for this dream she had, her goals, but kind of not being able to get there or people telling her she won't be able to. I've definitely experienced that, for sure," she told Gautam Balasundar for the *Last Magazine* (17 Aug. 2017).

The Sundance Film Festival has become the largest independent film festival in the United States, showcasing the works of independent filmmakers every January in Utah. *Patti Cake$* received a standing ovation following its premier at Sundance in January 2017 and was subsequently sold to Fox Searchlight for almost $10 million. Upon its theatrical release in August, it cemented Macdonald's place as a star on the rise. In describing her turn as Patti, Jacobs wrote for the *Huffington Post*, "Onscreen, she carries herself with the command of a veteran star, well aware of the winking humor inherent in a doughy white girl who can out-perform the best of them."

UPCOMING FILMS

Macdonald's new higher profile has enabled her to receive more offers for high quality roles. One role of particular note is the leading role in *Dumplin'*, the film adaptation of Julie Murphy's novel of the same name about an overweight teen named Willowdean who decides to enter a teen beauty pageant. The film, directed by Anne Fletcher, costars Jennifer Aniston as the mother of Macdonald's character—a former beauty queen herself. Macdonald loves the part, both because of the inspirational nature of the book and also the author's willingness to tackle body image issues. "I would have wanted to see this movie made when I was a teenager growing up," she said of *Dumplin'* in her interview with Cusumano. "That would have been really cathartic." *Dumplin'* is due out in 2018.

Also on the docket for Macdonald is the drama *Skin*, based on a true story about a white supremacist who falls in love with a mother of three (played by Macdonald) and turns away from racism and hatred. The film is also scheduled for release in 2018. "There is literally nothing mentioned about body image [in that film] at all," she said in her interview with Harmon about *Skin*. "I'm just a person in it. . . . It's so important to have conversations about [diversity], because equality is so important, in every aspect of life—but it feels amazing when you can do a project and just normalise it . . . so people don't think it's such a thing—because it *shouldn't* be a thing."

SUGGESTED READING

Cusumano, Katherine. "How *Patti Cake$* Turned Danielle Macdonald into a Battle-Rapping Underdog Hero—and a Star." *W*, 17 Aug. 2017, www.wmagazine.com/story/patti-cakes-movie-danielle-macdonald. Accessed 10 Jan. 2018.

Harmon, Steph. "Danielle Macdonald: Up-and-Coming Australian to Star with Jennifer Aniston in *Dumplin'*." *The Guardian*, 15 June 2017, www.theguardian.com/film/2017/jun/15/danielle-macdonald-up-and-coming-australian-to-star-with-jennifer-aniston-in-dumplin. Accessed 11 Jan. 2018.

Jacobs, Matthew. "Playing an Aspiring Rapper in *Patti Cake$*, Danielle Macdonald Is Summer's Breakout Star." *HuffPost*, 14 Aug. 2017, www.huffingtonpost.com/entry/patti-cake-danielle-macdonald_us_598b7db4e4b0d793738c7134. Accessed 11 Jan. 2018.

Macdonald, Danielle. "*Patti Cake$* Star Danielle Macdonald on Learning to Rap for Sundance Film." Interview by Dixie Limbachia. *Variety*, 27 July 2017, variety.com/2017/film/features/actress-danielle-macdonald-1202506523/. Accessed 11 Jan. 2018.

Mandell, Andrea. "Star Rising: Why You'll Know Danielle Macdonald's Name." *USA Today*, 14 Aug. 2017, www.usatoday.com/story/life/movies/2017/08/14/danielle-macdonald-patti-cakes/563581001/. Accessed 11 Jan. 2018.

SELECTED WORKS

The East, 2013; *Every Secret Thing*, 2015; *Patti Cake$*, 2017

—*Christopher Mari*

Zayn Malik

Date of birth: January 12, 1993
Occupation: Singer

When the British boy band One Direction burst onto the pop scene in 2010, they incited a frenzy among teenage fans. It was, in the words of Jane Mulkerrins, a reporter for the London *Evening Standard* (19 June 2017), like "Beatlemania with added iPhones." Among the group's original members was Zayn Malik, a seventeen-year-old of English and Pakistani descent who was not immediately attracted to the idea of celebrity. Under the direction of impresario Simon Cowell, he was marketed as "the mysterious one."

"A decade after *NSYNC broke up, One Direction invigorated the boy band model by injecting every calculated thing they did with a dose of genuine-seeming anarchy," Duncan Cooper wrote for the music magazine *Fader* (Dec. 2015/ Jan. 2016). The band, which became an international sensation, went on to make four platinum-selling albums, each of which debuted at number one on the Billboard 200 chart. It thus surprised and dismayed many of their fans, who call themselves "Directioners," when Malik left the group in early 2015, citing stress and exhaustion as factors. Free to express himself creatively in ways he felt he had not been able to as part of a five-member band, he has since forged a wildly successful solo career. Although fans regularly speculate online about the possibility that One Direction will reunite, they are supportive of his efforts as a solo artist—so supportive, in fact, that his first solo album, *Mind of Mine* (2016), debuted at number one in both the United Kingdom and the United States and had been downloaded more than one billion times on Spotify as of the summer of 2017.

EARLY YEARS AND EDUCATION

The singer was born Zain Javadd Malik on January 12, 1993, in Bradford, a working-class town in the northern England county of West Yorkshire. Of growing up in the neighborhood of East Bowling, he told Cooper, "It's not the most funded place, in terms of the government, but there's a lot of character there. . . . Everybody's very proud, and everybody's stuck in their ways. That rubbed off on me a little bit."

Malik's father, Yaser, whose family had immigrated to England from Pakistan, was a personal trainer. He later gave up his job to stay at home with Malik and his three sisters, Doniya, Waliyha, and Safaa. In his 2016 autobiography, *Zayn*, Malik wrote, "My dad's a hard worker and he has strong values. . . . He used to go on at me all the time about being a good student and getting the right education. He wanted the best for me, and I wanted to please him in return." He also credits his father with shaping his musical tastes

Eva Rinaldi [CC BY-SA 2.0], via Wikimedia Commons

by playing records from such artists as R. Kelly, Usher, Prince, and Tupac Shakur.

Malik's mother, Trisha, who worked in a local public school as a chef, cooking halal meals for the Muslim students, had been born into a family of British pub keepers. When she met and married Yaser, she converted to Islam. "I've always tried to learn as much as I can about my husband's religion and culture," she told Shabnam Mahmood for *BBC News* (19 Dec. 2013). "I made sure the children went to the mosque. Zayn has read the Koran three times." Malik has said that he enjoyed reading books of all types, a habit he developed by reading to his paternal grandfather, a first-generation immigrant from Pakistan who did not speak much English.

Malik attended Lower Fields Primary School and then went on to Tong High School, a large, diverse institution where he took performing arts classes and acted in school productions—even landing the role of Danny Zuko in the school's production of the famous musical *Grease*. He dreamed of appearing on a televised talent competition like X *Factor*, which he watched often and was then extremely popular in the United Kingdom. He got his chance in 2010, during the show's seventh season. Due in part to a struggle with confidence that has long plagued him, that fateful audition almost did not happen: "At the time, I was a lazy teen," he admitted to Cooper. "If I was in control of me going to audition for X *Factor*, I would have never gone because I would have never got up on the day of the audition at four in the morning. The reason I woke up is because my mom came in the room and was like,

'You have to go audition for this show.' I felt like I had to do it because I owed it to her."

CAREER IN ONE DIRECTION

During Malik's initial audition, held in Manchester, he sang the R & B song "Let Me Love You," by Mario, performing well enough to be put through to the next round. During that round, however, he was reluctant to take part in a dance routine, despite the entreaties of Cowell, who was serving as a judge. Although he did eventually participate, he was ultimately eliminated, along with four other male contestants: Harry Styles, Liam Payne, Niall Horan, and Louis Tomlinson.

In the wake of that failure, Cowell made what seemed to be an unexpected offer, suggesting that the five remain in the competition, not individually but as a group. They agreed, and One Direction, as they were dubbed, performed together in the next round, singing a cover version of the Natalie Imbruglia song "Torn." Although the five subsequently sang credible covers of Kelly Clarkson's "My Life Would Suck without You," Elton John's "Something about the Way You Look Tonight," and Bonnie Tyler's "Total Eclipse of the Heart" over the course of the rest of the season, they did not ultimately win the competition, coming in third. Still, within a few weeks of the finale, they had inked a deal with Cowell's record label, Syco.

In September 2011, One Direction released the single "What Makes You Beautiful," which was played in heavy rotation on the radio and won a Brit Award (the British equivalent of an American Grammy Award) for best British single. Their debut album, *Up All Night*, hit the market in November and quickly appeared in the number-one spot on the charts in several countries, including the United States, where it sold 176,000 copies in its first week alone. Within a year, it had been certified double platinum. Many critics argued that the group found such immediate success by serving as a fresh iteration of the boy bands that had been popular in the late 1990s and early 2000s but had largely disappeared. In a review whose sentiments were widely echoed by other critics, Adam Markovitz wrote for *Entertainment Weekly* (20 Mar. 2012), "They're the first viable next-gen boy band for a tween demographic that knows Backstreet Boys and *NSYNC only as golden oldies. . . . *Up All Night* marches to a new, postmillennial tiger beat: The irresistibly bouncy 'One Thing,' the Kelly Clarkson-co-penned 'Tell Me a Lie,' and the party-till-Mom-comes-home title track are all charmingly gimmick-free slices of white-bread wonder." He concluded, "If a tween-pop empire is what these boys are after, they're definitely headed in the right direction."

One Direction released one album per year after that—*Take Me Home* in 2012, *Midnight Memories* in 2013, and *Four* in 2014—each of which sold millions of copies worldwide. They were, up to that date, the only group in the history of the Billboard 200 chart to debut their first four albums at number one. When they were not in the recording studio, they toured the globe, performing to sold-out stadiums crammed with crowds of screaming fans.

FEELING RESTLESS

During their 2015 tour, however, Malik was frequently missing, and he dropped out of the tour officially in March of that year, citing stress and exhaustion. A few days after that announcement, he left the group altogether, writing on Facebook, "I'd like to apologize to the fans if I've let anyone down, but I have to do what feels right in my heart." He later admitted to having suffered from an eating disorder throughout much of his time with One Direction. "It was a control thing," he explained to Hermione Eyre for the London *Times* (19 Mar. 2017). "Every area of my life was so regimented and controlled . . . it was the one area where I could say, 'No, I'm not eating that.'" He has also explained that, while being in the band taught him a lot about performing and the music industry in general, lessons that he would always be grateful for, he was seeking more autonomy and control artistically. "There was never any room for me to experiment creatively in the band," he told Cooper. "There was just a general conception that the management already had of what they want for the band. . . . It was music that was already given to us, and we were told this is what is going to sell to these people. As much as we were the biggest, most famous boy band in the world, it felt weird."

By the summer of 2015, Malik had announced that he had signed a new deal to have RCA Records serve as his label for his burgeoning solo career. One Direction had continued to tour and record without Malik before announcing, at about the same time, that they would be taking a long-term hiatus after the release of their fifth album.

SOLO MUSIC CAREER

In March 2016, a rejuvenated Malik released his solo debut album, *Mind of Mine*, which spawned the hit single "Pillowtalk." The track debuted at number one on both the Billboard Hot 100 chart and the UK singles chart, and the album landed in the top spot on both sides of the Atlantic. Critics were cautiously impressed. In one representative review, Brittany Spanos wrote for *Rolling Stone* (25 Mar. 2016), "Malik's move into deep, freaky R & B is immersive, even if his DNA is still catchy, accessible pop." While bemoaning the occasional tepid ballad, she praised the album's more experimental tunes and concluded, "The welcome surprises not only take Malik off the Justin Timberlake-paved track of post-boy band R & B album tropes, they create unique possibilities of his own."

At the end of 2016, Malik collaborated with the hugely successful Taylor Swift for a song to be included on the soundtrack for the second installment of the popular Fifty Shades film franchise, *Fifty Shades Darker* (2017). The track, "I Don't Wanna Live Forever," earned the pair the Video Music Award for best collaboration in 2017.

PERSONAL LIFE

Outside of his musical pursuits, Malik is active in the world of fashion, and he has collaborated with the design house Versace on a capsule collection of clothing. He was engaged for two years to British singer Perrie Edwards, but their relationship ended in 2015. As of November 2017, he was in a relationship with American model Gigi Hadid, whom he had begun dating in late 2015. In addition to buying a home for his parents, he has reportedly owned homes in both London and Los Angeles.

SUGGESTED READING

Cooper, Duncan. "Zayn Malik's Next Direction." *Fader*, Dec. 2015/ Jan. 2016, www.thefader.com/2015/11/17/zayn-malik-fader-cover-story-interview-solo-album-one-direction. Accessed 2 Nov. 2017.

Eyre, Hermione. "Zayn Malik: 'Love Hurts . . . Love Is Hard.'" *The Times*, 19 Mar. 2017, www.thetimes.co.uk/article/zayn-malik-on-gigi-hadid-bradford-pillowtalk-one-direction-65kvx3d3v. Accessed 2 Nov. 2017.

Mahmood, Shabnam. "Mum Direction: Zayn Malik's Mother on Raising a Pop Star." *BBC News*, 19 Dec. 2013, www.bbc.com/news/entertainment-arts-25430560. Accessed 2 Nov. 2017.

Markovitz, Adam. Review of *Up All Night*, by One Direction. *Entertainment Weekly*, 20 Mar. 2012, ew.com/article/2012/03/20/all-night-review-one-direction/. Accessed 2 Nov. 2017.

Martins, Chris. "Zayn Malik Speaks Out in Revealing *Billboard* Cover Story: 'I'm Not Censoring Myself Anymore.'" *Billboard*, 7 Jan. 2016, www.billboard.com/articles/news/cover-story/6835305/zayn-malik-solo-career-one-direction-new-music. Accessed 2 Nov. 2017.

Ringen, Jonathan. "Zayn Opens Up about Conquering Anxiety, Prepping Album No. 2—and Why He's Been Living on a Farm." *Billboard*, 2 Nov. 2017, www.billboard.com/articles/news/magazine-feature/8022234/zayn-malik-interview-billboard-cover-story-2017. Accessed 2 Nov. 2017.

Spanos, Brittany. Review of *Mind of Mine*, by Zayn Malik. *Rolling Stone*, 25 Mar. 2016, www.rollingstone.com/music/albumreviews/zayn-malik-mind-of-mine-20160325. Accessed 2 Nov. 2017.

SELECTED WORKS

Up All Night, 2011; *Take Me Home*, 2012; *Midnight Memories*, 2013; *Four*, 2014; *Mind of Mine*, 2016

—*Mari Rich*

Samuel Maoz

Date of birth: May 23, 1962
Occupation: Filmmaker

Award-winning Israeli filmmaker Samuel Maoz's most recent film, *Foxtrot*, suggests the absurdity of war through the surrealist tale of one Tel Aviv family and their son, a soldier in the Israeli army. Condemned by Israel's minister of culture and sports, the film stirred controversy in Israel, though it also won a slew of Ophir Awards, Israel's answer to the Oscars, including best film and best director. *Foxtrot* was one of nine films shortlisted for an Academy Award for Foreign Language Film from among ninety-two films but ultimately was not nominated. Before *Foxtrot*, Maoz was best known for his debut, *Lebanon* (2009). The autobiographical film faithfully recounts his experiences as a tank gunner for the Israeli army in the First Lebanon War. It won the Golden Lion, the highest award given at La Biennale di Venezia (the Venice Film Festival),

By nicolas genin, via Wikimedia Commons

in 2009. Maoz spent a portion of his mandatory military service fighting in the First Lebanon War in 1982. The experience, which he felt compelled to write about after the onslaught of the Second Lebanon War in 2006, profoundly altered his worldview. His films express his ideas about grief, war, humanity, and multigenerational trauma. *Lebanon*, he told Neta Alexander for *Film Comment* (22 Dec. 2017), "helped me to try and understand what it means to kill other human beings, as I did during my military service at the IDF [Israel Defense Forces]. I had no other choice, and yet the notion of taking lives is an excruciating burden I am forced to live with." *Foxtrot* was born of Maoz's interactions with other former soldiers. "There are endless variations of my story and the kind of pain and guilt it germinates," he said.

EARLY LIFE AND MILITARY SERVICE

Maoz was born Samuel "Shmulik" Aziz in 1962, in Herzliya outside Tel Aviv, Israel. (His family changed their surname to the more Hebrew-sounding Maoz in the 1970s.) Maoz's father, who was of Turkish descent, drove a bus and played bass, and his Polish mother was a nurse. Maoz, the youngest of three children, always knew he wanted to make films. For his bar mitzvah, he was given an eight-millimeter camera and four minutes' worth of film.

Like all teenagers in Israel, Maoz was compelled to spend two years serving in the Israeli army. Twenty-year-old Maoz was still in the service in 1982, when Israel invaded Lebanon to attack the Palestinian Liberation Organization (PLO). The operation was meant to last three weeks, but vestiges of the original conflict continued for nearly eighteen years. Maoz was a gunner in the tank corps. On June 6, Maoz received orders to kill an Arab man in a small truck. Though Maoz could not tell if the man was an enemy, he obeyed the command, and his life was forever changed. In total, he spent forty-five days in Lebanon, of which he spent thirty cloistered in that tank with the driver, the loader, and their commander.

Despite his dangerous position, Maoz survived the war without serious injury. When he returned, his mother was so happy to see him that she hugged him and wept. But Maoz bore other, invisible scars. "She was embracing an empty shell," Maoz recalled to Rachel Cooke for the UK *Guardian* (1 May 2010). "I could not escape the fact that I had pulled the trigger, that I was a kind of executioner, that I was the last person in the death link." He did not express these thoughts at the time. Then, Maoz recalled, complaining about his service—to say nothing of seeking treatment for posttraumatic stress disorder (PTSD)—was considered a deep insult to his elders. "To complain afterwards that you felt bad inside was unforgivable," he told

Cooke. "The older generation told us, 'Say thank you that you are alive; we were in the [Nazi concentration] camps.' We hated them because they used the camps against us and this made us feel we had no right to complain."

A mere six months after fulfilling his mandatory service, Maoz was hit in the face by a rock while serving as a reservist in Rafah, Gaza. His eye socket was shattered. At first, Maoz thought he would lose his eye, but doctors managed to save it.

LEBANON

After his service, Maoz studied cinematography at the Beit Zvi School of the Performing Arts. He graduated in 1987 and began working as an art director for film and television. Later, he began to direct commercials and music videos. He made his first film, a fifty-five-minute art/documentary hybrid called *Total Eclipse* for ARTE (Association relative à la télévision européenne), in 2000. The film featured choreographer Ohad Naharin and award-winning Russian Israeli actor Evgenia Dodina.

Years before, in 1988, Maoz had attempted to develop a script based on his wartime experiences, but the trauma was too fresh. He put the script away. In 2006, Israel invaded Lebanon again, and Maoz was compelled to revisit his past. "I realised that this was no longer about me and my needs, my problems, my memories, my pain," he told Cooke. "Our boys were dealing with the same thing all over again. I suppose you could say it was a mission. I wanted to make a film that might save a life. I took a life; now I could save a life."

Maoz began writing *Lebanon*. He shot the film on a shoestring budget and released it in 2009. The film is drawn predominantly from Maoz's lived experience; the characters are even named after Maoz's real crew. It follows a young man named Shmulik (Yoav Donat) as he transforms into a killer. The entire film takes place inside Shmulik's tank; combat is viewed only through Shmulik's gun sight. Maoz has said that his artistic choices were meant to emphasize one of the wrenching conundrums of war: just because one must shoot to survive does not absolve one of the responsibility—and corresponding guilt and anguish—of having shot. "I'm trying to explain that war cannot open for you the option to be moral," he told Steven Erlanger for the *New York Times* (30 July 2010).

Cooke compared *Lebanon* to the 1981 film *Das Boot*, about the crew of a German submarine during World War II, but *Lebanon* is more closely associated with two other films about the First Lebanon War that were released around the same time: the Oscar-nominated *Beaufort* (2007), cowritten by journalist and Lebanon veteran Ron Leshem and director Joseph Cedar; and *Waltz with Bashir* (2008), Ari Folman's

Oscar-nominated autobiographical animated film. *Lebanon* enjoyed a rapturous reception at the Venice Film Festival in 2009. After the screening, the audience gave Maoz a twenty-minute standing ovation. *Lebanon* was awarded the festival's top prize, the Golden Lion. In Israel, the film won four Ophir Awards, including best cinematography and best art direction. Elsewhere, the film was more controversial for its focus on the war's perpetrators rather than its victims.

FOXTROT

Maoz's second film, *Foxtrot*, premiered eight years later, in September 2017. It was inspired by a harrowing incident in Maoz's life, but structurally, it more closely resembles a Greek tragedy than *Lebanon*. In the mid-1990s, when Maoz's oldest daughter was a young teenager, she once missed a Tel Aviv city bus to school and, in doing so, narrowly avoided being killed by a suicide bomber. In *Foxtrot*, Maoz explores the mechanisms of fate, particularly as they pertain to violence. When the film begins, Dafna (Sarah Adler) and Michael (Lior Ashkenazi) have just been informed that their son, a soldier, has been killed. The film is divided into three parts. The first takes place almost entirely in the family's Tel Aviv apartment as Dafna and Michael process this news. In the second section of the film, Maoz reveals that the son, Jonathan (Yonatan Shiray), is really alive. This part of the film follows him and his fellow soldiers as they guard a military checkpoint. The third part of the film returns to Dafna and Michael for a twist ending. *Foxtrot* is not a realist film, elements of it could even be defined as surreal. "Each scene feels strangely off-kilter," David Sims wrote for the *Atlantic* (27 Feb. 2018), "presented like a hopeless fairy tale." The film's trifold structure, its tone, and it visual style, Sims wrote, are meant to convey "the limits of living a blinkered existence" as well as the sheer absurdity of militarism and war.

Foxtrot was named Israel's official submission to the Academy Award for Best Foreign Language Film—despite the controversy it generated in the country. Israel's minister of culture and sport, Miri Regev, condemned the film before it was released. Without having seen it, Regev accused Maoz of promoting an anti-Israel narrative and called him a traitor. She referred specifically to a scene in which Israeli soldiers commit a war crime and then try to cover it up. Regev tried to organize a boycott of the film. Her rage largely backfired, however, as it generated so much publicity. *Foxtrot* won eight Ophir Awards, though Regev's opinion gained some traction with right-wing Israelis. Maoz received death threats but mainly felt frustrated that his critics failed to see the difference between documentary realism and artistic license in a work of fiction and that they were equating social criticism with disloyalty. Elsewhere, the film enjoyed a more enthusiastic reception. *Foxtrot* won the Silver Lion Grand Jury Prize at Venice in 2017. American critics praised the film. *Foxtrot*, Manohla Dargis wrote for the *New York Times* (7 Dec. 2017), "builds into a devastating indictment of a nation, shock by shock, brutal moment by brutal moment." David Edelstein, writing in *Vulture* (27 Feb. 2018), called Maoz "a rare kind of artist: a director-poet."

SUGGESTED READING

Cooke, Rachel. "Samuel Maoz: My Life at War and My Hopes for Peace." *The Guardian*, 1 May 2010, www.theguardian.com/film/2010/may/02/israel-lebanon-samuel-maoz-tanks. Accessed 15 Apr. 2018.

Dargis, Manohla. "Review: The Architecture of Grief and Dread in 'Foxtrot.'" Review of *Foxtrot*, by Samuel Maoz. *The New York Times*, 7 Dec. 2017, www.nytimes.com/2017/12/07/movies/foxtrot-review-samuel-maoz.html. Accessed 16 Apr. 2018.

Edelstein, David. "*Foxtrot* Is a Punishing Drama That Toes the Line of Black Comedy." Review of *Foxtrot*, by Samuel Maoz. *Vulture*, 27 Feb. 2018, www.vulture.com/2018/02/foxtrot-movie-review.html. Accessed 16 Apr. 2018.

Erlanger, Steven. "A Tank's Eye View of an Unpopular War." Review of *Lebanon*, by Samuel Maoz. *The New York Times*, 30 July 2010, www.nytimes.com/2010/08/01/movies/01lebanon.html. Accessed 15 Apr. 2018.

Maoz, Samuel. "Interview: Samuel Maoz." Interview by Neta Alexander. *Film Comment*, 22 Dec. 2017, www.filmcomment.com/blog/interview-samuel-maoz. Accessed 16 Apr. 2018.

Sims, David. "*Foxtrot* Is a Dreamlike Interrogation of War." Review of *Foxtrot*, by Samuel Maoz. *The Atlantic*, 27 Feb. 2018, www.theatlantic.com/entertainment/archive/2018/02/foxtrot-review/554393. Accessed 17 Apr. 2018.

SELECTED WORKS

Total Eclipse, 2000; *Lebanon*, 2009; *Foxtrot*, 2017

—*Molly Hagan*

Hideki Matsuyama

Date of birth: February 25, 1992
Occupation: Golfer

Hideki Matsuyama is a top-ranked professional golfer from Japan. In 2017 he reached the world number two ranking following the US Open tournament, making him the highest-ranked Japanese golfer of all time. Just twenty-five years

Photo by Scott Halleran/Getty Images

old at the time, he earned comparisons to golf superstar Tiger Woods and was considered one of the sport's brightest young stars. By the beginning of 2018, Matsuyama had five PGA (Professional Golf Association) Tour victories and eight international victories as a professional golfer.

Matsuyama was the first amateur golfer from Japan to earn an invitation to the Masters Golf Tournament, in 2011. The two-time Asia-Pacific Amateur champion joined the PGA Tour in 2013. Already a media sensation in his home country, he quickly made a name for himself internationally as a talent to watch, known for the very distinctive pause in his backswing. Matsuyama is also known in the golf press for his quiet sense of humor—partly a product of the fact that he speaks little English—and his tireless work ethic. Many considered him a strong contender to become the first Japanese golfer to win a major tournament. At the 2017 PGA Championship, Jason Day, who won the event in 2015 and played with Matsuyama at the Presidents Cup, told Brian Wacker for *Golfworld* (11 Aug. 2017), "He's on the range and he's the last guy to leave. He's always putting. He's always doing something. He's working hard. And I feel like he's the hardest worker out here right now, just because he wants to win."

EARLY LIFE AND AMATEUR CAREER

Hideki Matsuyama was born in Ehime, Japan, on February 25, 1992. He was raised in Sendai, northeast of Tokyo. His father, Mikio, a club champion, introduced him to golf, and served as Matsuyama's first coach. When asked to name the moment he fell in love with the game,

Matsuyama told Sean Martin for *PGATour. com* (13 Jan. 2015), "Golf has been fun for me from the first time I picked up a club." Growing up, Matsuyama idolized American golfer Tiger Woods. He has recalled first seeing Woods on television, winning the 1997 Masters Tournament. Unable to view the event live, he taped the replay and watched the video over and over, working to emulate Woods's swing.

Matsuyama attended Tohoku Fukushi University in Sendai, where he golfed for coach Abe Yasuhiro. By 2008 he was representing Japan in international amateur competition. As an eighteen-year-old college student, Matsuyama was invited to play in the second-ever Asia-Pacific Amateur Championship at the Kasumigaseki Country Club in Kawagoe, Japan, in October 2010. Though he was already a promising player, he was only invited because as the host country, Japan was able to have ten golfers compete; he was not seen as a contender. Yet in a five-shot victory over Australian Tarquin MacManus, Matsuyama won the tournament. The win earned him an invitation to the 2011 Masters—the same tournament he had watched Woods win in 1997. He was the first Japanese amateur to receive the honor.

Just before Matsuyama's major debut, on March 11, 2011, Sendai was hit with a magnitude 9.0 earthquake, the strongest to hit the region on record, and a tsunami. Matsuyama was not there at the time, but inevitably, people he knew were among the 18,000 dead.

MASTERS DEBUT

Devastated by the destruction of his hometown, Matsuyama considered skipping the Masters. Ultimately, however, he decided to play, wearing the colors of Tohoku Fukushi University, where he was still a student. "Because of the encouragement I received from those close to me in Sendai and the other people in Sendai, I feel I should play," he said at the time through a translator, as quoted by Robin Barwick for the quarterly golf magazine *Kingdom* (2018). "All the people who have supported my golf—they all pushed for me to play. So I have decided I will, not just for myself but for the people who made me who I am. I hope I can play my best to lift the spirits of those who are rooting for me back home, supporting me even though they are suffering. . . . Doing my best is my obligation to them."

Matsuyama fared well in his first Masters. He was the only amateur to make the two-day cut to play the full four-day tournament. He scored one under par and tied with three-time Masters champion Phil Mickelson and others for twenty-seventh place. His performance earned him the Silver Cup for low amateur, meaning that he was the lowest-scoring amateur player in the tournament. He was the first Asian golfer to win the award. "Being low amateur was a direct result of the people of Japan and of Sendai encouraging me," said Matsuyama, as quoted by Barwick. "I felt their spirits throughout the event."

Matsuyama continued his strong play throughout 2011. He won the Japan Collegiate Championship, as well as individual and team gold medals at the World University Games. That October, Matsuyama returned to the Asia-Pacific Championship in Singapore as defending champion. He won the tournament again, setting a scoring record at eighteen under par. Again, his victory qualified him to play in the Masters. He also won the Taiheiyo Masters on the Japan Golf Tour, beating a field that included Charl Schwartzel, the reigning Masters champion. Matsuyama was only the third amateur to win on Japan's pro tour.

Though he made the cut again, Matsuyama did not fare as well in the 2012 Masters. He finished nine over par, tying for fifty-fourth place. Still, by August 2012 he was the top-ranked amateur in the world.

TURNING PROFESSIONAL

Matsuyama finished his degree in social welfare at Tohoku Fukushi University before turning pro in April 2013. Shortly after that, he won his second professional tournament, the 2013 Tsuruya Open, on the Japan Golf Tour. It would prove to be a banner year for Matsuyama. After the Tsuruya Open, he won three more tournaments on the Japan Tour: the Diamond Cup Golf, the Fujisankei Classic, and the Casio World Open. He also turned in top-ten appearances in both the US Open and the Open Championship (British Open).

Matsuyama participated in his first Presidents Cup in 2013, held that year in Muirfield Village in Dublin, Ohio. A particularly attention-grabbing shot in that tournament prompted Jack Nicklaus, one of the greatest golfers of all time, to comment during the television broadcast, as quoted by Tim Rosaforte for *Golf Digest* (7 Oct. 2013): "We're going to hear a lot more out of this young man before his career is done." Also notable was Matsuyama's twenty-first-place finish at the World Golf Championships (WGC)-Bridgestone Invitational, where he was paired for the first two rounds with his idol, Woods. Matsuyama's stellar 2013 season made him a huge star in Japan, and a rising one in the larger world of golf. As Karen Crouse wrote for the *New York Times* (5 Dec. 2016), Matsuyama began being "trailed by journalists from his homeland as if he were a Woods-in-waiting."

Matsuyama's success allowed him to officially join the PGA Tour for the 2013–14 season. He recorded his first PGA victory soon after. At twenty-two years and three months old, he became the youngest player to win the 2014 Memorial Tournament at Muirfield Village. The win

rocketed him to number thirteen in the world rankings. That year he also earned top-ten finishes at the *Frys.com* Open and the Waste Management Phoenix Open and won the Dunlop Phoenix and the Casio World Open on the Japan Tour. In 2015, Matsuyama finished fifth at the Masters, his best showing at the storied tournament to that point. He also tied for fifth at the Memorial Tournament and played again for the International Team in the Presidents Cup.

In February 2016, Matsuyama recorded his second PGA victory at the Waste Management Phoenix Open, after a sudden-death round against former top-ranked golfer Rickie Fowler. The same year, he tied for seventh at the Masters. He won the Japan Open Golf Championship—his first Japan Golf Tour major title—with a one under par in October 2016, and later that month won the WGC-HSBC Champions by a record seven-stroke margin at Sheshan International Golf Club in Shanghai. He won his second Taiheiyo Masters in November, and in December he won the Hero World Challenge, a tournament hosted by the Tiger Woods Foundation. Of Matsuyama's hot streak, Woods told Crouse, "It's going to give him a boatload of confidence going into next year, and he's going to be one of the top guys to beat for a very long time."

HIGH-RANKING SUCCESS

Matsuyama's run of strong performances continued through 2017. In February, Matsuyama defended his title at the Waste Management Phoenix Open, becoming the first back-to-back winner of the event since the 1970s. In June, he tied for second at the US Open at Erin Hills in Wisconsin. It was a stellar performance, and it helped boost him to number two in the world rankings, setting a record for Japanese golfers. After this achievement, many commentators opined that Matsuyama was the best golfer currently playing who had yet to secure a win in a major tournament.

In August 2017, Matsuyama earned his second WGC victory (and fifth overall PGA Tour win) at the WGC-Bridgestone Invitational. After a poor practice showing, he went on to tie the course record of 61. Only Sergio García Fernández, José María Olazábal, and Woods (twice) had ever posted such a score at Firestone Country Club in Akron, Ohio. Matsuyama's performance, Kyle Porter wrote for *CBS Sports* (6 Aug. 2017), "was a reminder that he has a gear few others on the planet possess." A week later, Matsuyama turned in a strong showing at the PGA Championship at Quail Hollow in Charlotte, North Carolina, yet failed to win his first major, finishing tied for fifth. It was not what he wanted, but Matsuyama remained determined.

In late 2017, Matsuyama turned in top-five finishes at the CIMB Classic in Kuala Lumpur, Malaysia, the Dunlop Phoenix, and the Hero

World Challenge. In January 2018 he was top-four at the Sentry Tournament of Champions at the Plantation Course in Kapalua, Hawaii. In February 2018, Matsuyama announced that he was withdrawing from the Waste Management Phoenix Open, preventing any chance of a three-peat. He cited a wrist injury as the cause.

PERSONAL LIFE

Matsuyama was married in January 2017. His wife gave birth to a baby girl in July of the same year. He has acknowledged interests outside of golf including baseball, fishing, photography, and unwinding by playing games on his phone.

SUGGESTED READING

Barwick, Robin. "Rising Son: Hideki Matsuyama." *Kingdom*, 2018, kingdom.golf/golf/rising-son/. Accessed 29 Mar. 2018.

Crouse, Karen. "Japan's Best Golfer? With a Smile, Hideki Matsuyama Begs to Differ." *The New York Times*, 5 Dec. 2016, www.nytimes.com/2016/12/05/sports/golf/golf-hideki-matsuyama-hero-world-challenge.html. Accessed 30 Mar. 2018.

"Get to Know Japan's Rising Son." *Today's Golfer*, 6 Feb. 2017, www.todaysgolfer.co.uk/news-and-events/tour-news/20171/february/get-to-know-japans-rising-son/. Accessed 3 Apr. 2018.

Kaspriske, Ron. "Swing Sequence: Hideki Matsuyama." *Golf Digest*, 2014, www.golfdigest.com/gallery/hideki-matsuyama-photos. Accessed 30 Mar. 2018.

Martin, Sean. "It's All on Matsuyama." *PGA Tour*, 13 Jan. 2015, www.pgatour.com/news/2015/01/13/hideki-matasuyama.html. Accessed 29 Mar. 2018.

Porter, Kyle. "WGC-Bridgestone Invitational: Hideki Matsuyama Claims Fifth Win with Superb 61." *CBS Sports*, 6 Aug. 2017, www.cbssports.com/golf/news/wgc-bridgestone-invitational-hideki-matsuyama-claims-fifth-win-with-superb-61/. Accessed 1 Apr. 2018.

Rosaforte, Tim. "Japan's Next Big Thing." *Golf Digest*, 7 Oct. 2013, www.golfdigest.com/story/gwar-hideki-matsuyama-rosaforte-report-1014. Accessed 30 Mar. 2018.

—*Molly Hagan*

Auston Matthews

Date of birth: September 17, 1997
Occupation: Hockey player

Auston Matthews is a hockey prodigy from Arizona who scored a history-making four goals in his National Hockey League (NHL) debut with the Toronto Maple Leafs in 2016, when he was

By Michael Miller, via Wikimedia Commons

eighteen years old. His performance that evening was so masterful that the rapper SVDVM (Samuel Siboko), was inspired to write a song about it—called, appropriately, "Auston Matthews." With 40 goals and 69 points, Matthews enjoyed the best rookie season in the Maple Leafs' history. The center led the team, formerly ranked last in the NHL, to the playoffs and its winningest season in a decade. Matthews was awarded the Calder Memorial Trophy for rookie of the year in 2017. Now in his second season, a lot of hopes are riding on Matthews. Toronto has not won a Stanley Cup since 1967, but as the NHL continues to seek to expand the sport beyond its fervid fan base in Canada, he is poised to become hockey's first twenty-first century superstar. Emily Kaplan of *ESPN* (16 Oct. 2017) expressed concern that the league, bound by conservative tradition, would not give their star the opportunity to shine. The NHL, Kaplan wrote, discourages the individuality that flourishes (and wins fans) in other sports. Take for instance, the activism of LeBron James, or even Russell Westbrook's wardrobe. Contrast these examples from the National Basketball Association (NBA) with the policies of Leafs' general manager Lou Lamoriello, who stipulates that all players on the team must have short hair and a clean-shaven face. "Matthews could be a once-in-a-generation star, pushing hockey toward a new—and diverse—fan base. But only if hockey lets him," she wrote. Evan Sporer for the *Ringer* (13 Apr. 2017) had a more optimistic take. Citing SVDVM's musical tribute and Matthews's social media accounts—his Instagram has over 400,000 followers—Sporer contends that Matthews and a new crop of young and talented NHL players are unwittingly taking the fate of the league into their hands by engaging with people their own age. In December 2016, Matthews delighted followers by posting a photograph of himself wearing a sweater featuring the deceased gorilla Harambe. Sporer thinks Matthews's social media presence is representative of a new era. "Call it memes on ice," he wrote.

EARLY LIFE

Matthews was born in Northern California on September 17, 1997, though he grew up in Scottsdale, Arizona. He is the second of three children; he has an older sister, Alexandria, and a younger sister, Breyana, who is one of the top teenaged golf players in Arizona. Athletic talent runs in his family. His father, Brian, was a pitcher for Loyola Marymount University, and his grandfather, Bobby, played for Pepperdine University. His great-uncle, Wes Matthews, played in the NFL for the Miami Dolphins in 1966. No one in his family, however, had ever played hockey. His mother, Ema, who was born and raised in Hermosillo, Mexico, had never even seen a hockey game until she moved to the United States. (Ema taught her son Spanish and refers to him by the affectionate nickname Papi.) Fortuitously, in 1996, the year before Matthews was born, the Jets, an NHL team from Winnipeg, moved to Arizona and became the Coyotes. Matthew's uncle, Billy, held season tickets. Were it not for this southward expansion, and perhaps his late uncle's interest in the sport, Matthews might not have seen his first professional hockey game as a toddler or expressed a desire to play hockey himself at the age of six. His parents were surprised. Hockey was not, at the time, a particularly popular sport in Arizona. It also cost quite a bit of money to play. His father recalled watching his beaming son set foot on the ice for the first time. "He had a very big grin on his face," Brian Matthews told Karen Crouse for the *New York Times* (26 Nov. 2014). "I remember seeing that smile and thinking, Dang, this is going to be an expensive sport." (Brian's hunch was not wrong. Later, when Matthews had reached an elite level, Ema Matthews worked two jobs to raise the money needed to keep him in the sport, which in some years was more than $20,000.)

RISE TO THE NHL

As a child, Matthews also played baseball, usually in the position of catcher, but when he was a teenager, Matthews told Crouse, hockey "kind of took over." "I was missing a lot of baseball practices because I always wanted to be on the rink shooting pucks," he said. The first rink he played on, Ozzie Ice in Phoenix, was only large enough for three-on-three games. This disadvantage worked out in Matthews's favor. "He

learned how to stickhandle in a phone booth, then all of a sudden he was put out in a full sheet of ice," his father joked to Sporer. He graduated to the Arizona Bobcats minor hockey program. Thanks to years of training with skating coach Boris Dorozhenko, Matthews is an extremely proficient skater; Dorozhenko emphasized that this was the result of hard work, not inborn talent. "Auston's talent was increasing every year," he told Sarah McLellan for the *Arizona Republic* (26 June 2016). In Matthews's last season with the Bobcats, when he was fifteen, he scored 55 goals and 100 points in 48 games. The next year, Matthews, who was homeschooled, moved to Ann Arbor, Michigan, to train with the elite United States National Team Development Program. That first year, 2013, he broke his left femur, missing three months of play.

When Matthews returned to the ice, the program bumped him up an age group. The team's youngest player, he led the US National Under-18 Team to a gold medal at the world championships in Finland 2014. In the final game against the Czech Republic, he scored five goals. The next season, at the age of seventeen, he broke the program's single-season goal record. In the 60 games he played in 2015, he made 55 goals and 62 assists for a total of 117 points. At the season's end, he led the U-18 team to another world championship gold medal against the Finnish team in Switzerland. He led the tournament in scoring and was named its most valuable player (MVP). That season he also played an exhibition game with the adult Team USA at the world championships in Austria, making him the first player to play with Team USA before reaching draft eligibility. By this time, buzz had been building around Matthews for some time. (He was the subject of a *New York Times* profile the year before in 2014.) He was ineligible for the 2015 draft—the age cutoff was a mere two days before he was born, September 15, 1997—and insiders expected him to join the Canadian Hockey League (CHL), for players ages sixteen to twenty. In that case, he would go to the Everett Silvertips in the Western Hockey League because the team had drafted him fifty-seventh in the WHL Bantam draft in 2012. (The rules of this procedure are rooted in age and scouting restrictions.) But Matthews also expressed an interested in playing for a college team, such as Boston University, Boston College, Michigan, North Dakota, Wisconsin, or the University of Denver. In the end, Matthews surprised everyone by doing neither.

Instead, Matthews chose to go pro in Europe, reasoning that he needed all the professional experience he could get before entering the NHL. Other factors, including his young age and mature talent, also came into play. "This was one of the very few times you'll ever see (that); when going to Europe was the right choice for a kid," an NHL scout told Stephen Harris for the *Boston Herald* (22 Nov. 2015). "But he was that good. He was good enough to do it." Matthews joined the Zurich Lions in the Swiss League National League A (NLA). His mother and older sister moved with him, though the cultural adjustments his new life required remained challenging. He claimed that the greatest challenge he faced was figuring out the country's elaborate rules surrounding recycling. "If you don't have it right . . . they yell at you," he told Sam Borden for the *New York Times* (12 Dec. 2015). "They take it very, very seriously." He was more at home on the ice. The top-seeded Lions were unexpectedly knocked out of the national finals, but during the regular season, Matthews managed to score 24 goals and 46 points in 36 games. Playing against adult pros and former NHL players, Matthews finished second in the NLA MVP voting.

TORONTO MAPLE LEAFS

As expected, Matthews was selected first overall in the 2016 NHL draft. He was only the seventh American to be drafted number one, and the first since 2007. No matter his origin, his new team, the last-ranked Toronto Maple Leafs, was certainly happy to have him. Having planned for his arrival, they made him the center of their rebuilding efforts. When asked if he felt this pressure, Matthews told Kevin Allen for *USA Today* (24 June 2016), "Hockey is a team sport, there is no savior. I want to be an impact player. I believe I can be a franchise centerman." It was a careful answer, and one that did not prepare fans for his history-making debut in October against the Ottawa Senators. His unprecedented four-goal rookie game drew social media applause from nearly every player in the league. Former Kings winger Marian Gaborik, as quoted by Kaplan, quipped on Twitter: "Since the start of this game I didn't even have a chance to drink 4 beers. And he's got 4 goals." Better still, his performance was no fluke. By the season's end, Matthews had scored 40 goals, making him just the second teenage rookie in thirty years—and the fourth in NHL history—to hit the 40-goal mark. He led all rookies with a total of 69 points, a statistic that tied him for second in scoring in the league. He received the Calder Memorial Trophy for rookie of the year. During his second year, Matthews expressed disappointment with the NHL's decision to skip the 2018 Olympic Winter Games in Pyeongchang, South Korea. He suffered a shoulder injury midseason but had previously led the team with 28 goals and 50 points.

SUGGESTED READING

Allen, Kevin. "Auston Matthews Taken by Maple Leafs with No. 1 Pick in 2016 NHL Draft." *USA Today*, 24 June 2016, www.usatoday.com/story/sports/nhl/2016/06/24/auston-matthews-toronto-maple-leafs-nhl-draft/86349764/. Accessed 8 Mar. 2018.

Crouse, Karen. "Though Ice Is in Short Supply, Arizona Warms Up to Hockey." *The New York Times*, 26 Dec. 2014, www.nytimes.com/2014/12/27/sports/though-ice-is-in-short-supply-arizona-warms-up-to-hockey.html. Accessed 8 Mar. 2018.

Harris, Stephen. "Matthews a Ringer." *Boston Herald*, 22 Nov. 2015, www.pressreader.com/usa/boston-herald/20151122/282325383878642. Accessed 8 Mar. 2018.

Kaplan, Emily. "Is Auston Matthews Ready to Be the New Face of the NHL?" *ESPN*, 16 Oct. 2017, www.espn.com/nhl/story/_/id/21007255/why-toronto-maple-leafs-auston-matthews-bigger-star-nhl. Accessed 8 Mar. 2018.

McClellan, Sarah. "Scottsdale's Auston Matthews Crowned NHL's Next Star." *Arizona Republic*, 26 June 2016, www.azcentral.com/story/sports/nhl/coyotes/2016/06/26/scottsdales-auston-matthews-crowned-nhls-next-star/86389590/. Accessed 8 Mar. 2018.

Sporer, Evan. "The Snapchat Generation Saved the Toronto Maple Leafs." *Ringer*, 13 Apr. 2017, www.theringer.com/2017/4/13/16041868/2017-nhl-playoffs-auston-matthews-toronto-maple-leafs-mitch-marner-william-nylander-5c16e6757863. Accessed 8 Mar. 2018.

—*Molly Hagan*

Aaron Maybin

Date of birth: April 6, 1988
Occupation: Artist, activist

Aaron Maybin is an artist, activist, and teacher who has used his platform as a former professional football player to raise awareness about pressing social issues. A native of Baltimore, Maryland, he was an All-American defensive end at Penn State University before being drafted by the Buffalo Bills in the first round of the 2009 National Football League (NFL) Draft. He failed to live up to his lofty draft status, however, and spent just five seasons in professional football before retiring in 2014.

Notwithstanding his disappointing NFL career, Maybin, buoyed by millions in earnings, embarked on a second career as an artist. He has since produced provocative works that confront and challenge injustice. In 2017, he began teaching art part-time at a Baltimore elementary school and released a collection of his art and poetry, titled *Art Activism: The Revolutionary Art, Poetry, & Reflections of Aaron M. Maybin*. He unintentionally became an advocate for education

Photo by Shareif Ziyadat, via Getty Images

funding in the winter of 2018, when he posted a viral video on Twitter that showed him teaching in a frigid classroom. As Maybin told Ryan Jones for *Baltimore Magazine* (Mar. 2018), "I'm not a politician, I'm not a preacher. I'm one of the people. I don't want to be a leader. I just want to be an example that we should all be *doing* something."

EARLY LIFE

Aaron M. Maybin was born on April 6, 1988, in Baltimore, Maryland, to Michael and Constance Maybin. He has a younger sister, Connie. Hyperactive as a child, Maybin used art early in life as an outlet for his energies. His parents bought him reams of oversize drawing paper and other supplies to make creations with. "You couldn't even keep aluminum foil in the house, because he would take it and make sculptures," his father recalled to Jones.

Art also helped Maybin channel his emotions. In January 1995, his mother died while giving birth to his sister, who was revived by doctors after being delivered stillborn. To honor his mother, who had developed late-term preeclampsia, a condition marked by high blood pressure, Maybin wrote a poem that he recited at her funeral. He has credited his mother, a former standout collegiate lacrosse player who enjoyed painting, with partly shaping his artistic sensibility. The family moved to Ellicott City, Maryland, shortly after her death.

About two years after Maybin's mother died, his father, then a fire inspector, remarried an English missionary named Violette Grant, whom he had met in church. Maybin quickly became close to his stepmother, who encouraged his artistic endeavors and fostered his love of reading. At age eleven, he painted a fifty-by-forty-foot wall mural—one that depicted three different-colored hands placing bricks in a wall—as part of a neighborhood revitalization project. He went on to win several art competitions during his youth.

ATYPICAL ATHLETE

Maybin's talent and passion for art was rivaled only by his innate athletic gifts. Growing up, he excelled not only in football but also in baseball, basketball, track, and wrestling. He became a multisport star at Ellicott City's Mount Hebron High School. By the time he entered his first year there, he had already begun to grow into what would become a six-feet-four, 240-pound frame.

Maybin's interests were not limited to sports, however. In addition to the art that remained a constant throughout his life, he also acted, played saxophone, and sang in the choir, which were activities that did not initially endear him to his peers. As Maybin put it to Childs Walker for the *Baltimore Sun* (8 Nov. 2015), "Art is not the typical passion for an African-American kid growing up in Baltimore, especially not for a boy. I was an awkward, outcast, goofy kid." That outcast status changed, though, once he started to distinguish himself as an athlete.

Shining particularly on the gridiron, Maybin resolved to play in the NFL before becoming a professional artist. Those aspirations began to crystallize his senior year at Mount Hebron, by which time he had developed into one of the top defensive end prospects in Maryland. Recruited by football powerhouses all over the country, Maybin accepted a scholarship to Penn State University, which his father had briefly attended years earlier. His football development was bolstered by an unparalleled work ethic: he routinely rose before dawn each day and ran to Mount Hebron with a weighted backpack before doing the same after school.

At Penn State, Maybin played under Joe Paterno, a legendary coach who fell from grace when it emerged that his longtime defensive coordinator, Jerry Sandusky, had been sexually abusing children. Maybin initially butted heads with Paterno over his lack of playing time and his involvement in Greek life but asserted to Walker that the old-school coach "helped make me who I am." Maybin and many other alumni stood by Paterno during the Sandusky scandal.

Nicknamed Mayhem, Maybin eventually became a starter for the Nittany Lions during his junior year, in 2008. That season he earned first-team All-America honors after tallying a conference-best three forced fumbles, twelve sacks, and twenty tackles for losses. He then decided to enter the 2009 NFL Draft.

DISAPPOINTMENT IN BUFFALO

Many football observers questioned whether Maybin's one All-American season would translate to NFL success. Still, draft experts projected him to be an early first-round selection. Enamored with his speed and explosiveness off the edge, the Buffalo Bills, who had just missed the playoffs for the ninth consecutive season, selected Maybin with the eleventh overall pick in the draft. A contract dispute forced Maybin to miss his rookie training camp, however, souring his relationship with the team. In August 2009, he agreed to a five-year deal that included approximately $15 million in guaranteed money and a $7 million signing bonus.

Maybin did not live up to his high expectations in Buffalo, however. He spent only two seasons with the Bills, during which he played for two different coaches and recorded zero sacks and a paltry twenty-six tackles in twenty-seven games. Maybin's second season with the team was particularly tumultuous. One month before 2010 training camp, his son David was stillborn on the same day that Tacori, his oldest daughter by a different mother, was born. The personal tragedy left Maybin scarred and cast a pall over his 2010 season, which saw him quickly fall out of favor with the Bills' first-year head coach Chan Gailey.

Maybin played sparingly under Gailey, who implemented a 3–4 defense, a scheme that he had never previously played in. This unfamiliarity, combined with an extremely fast metabolism that prevented him from putting on the weight necessary to be an every-down defender, contributed to his limited action. Maybin's colorful locker-room personality often left him subject to ridicule, especially because of his ineffective play. The Bills eventually cut Maybin during 2011 training camp, after which many people viewed him as "one of the worst draft picks in Buffalo Bills history," as Tim Graham noted in a profile of Maybin for BN Blitz (26 June 2015).

SHORT-LIVED NFL RESURRECTION

After being waived by the Bills, Maybin was signed by the New York Jets. The team released him, however, after the 2011 preseason. While waiting for another NFL opportunity, his life was again struck by loss. In September of that year, his aunt Dolores Maybin, who had often served as his personal chef, died of leukemia. During this time Maybin fell into a depression, putting a halt to his workout and diet regimen.

Maybin's spirits were lifted after the Jets' then head coach, Rex Ryan, offered him another chance with the team. Rejuvenated, Maybin went on to appear in thirteen games for the Jets during the 2011 season, showing flashes of his potential after six sacks and four forced fumbles. That off-season he signed a million-dollar deal to return to the team and entered the 2012 campaign hoping to become a better all-around player. Maybin's resurgence was short-lived, though, and after seeing limited playing time in eight games that season, he was released by the Jets a second time.

During 2013 training camp, Maybin received an opportunity to earn a roster spot with the Cincinnati Bengals but was cut again in August. He nonetheless appeared prominently in an episode of the HBO series Hard Knocks, in which the Bengals were featured that preseason. In the episode, he showcased his art and offered a glimpse of his post-football ambitions.

In October 2013, Maybin signed with the Toronto Argonauts in the Canadian Football League. He appeared in two games for the Argonauts but ultimately decided to retire from professional football in May 2014, one month after he turned twenty-six. Unfulfilled and unwilling to play the role of an NFL journeyman, Maybin, who had spurned a tryout offer from the Indianapolis Colts, explained to Graham, "I never wanted to be the guy, scraping to stay in the league and keep playing." His sister, Connie, added, "He's not just a guy in a jersey. He's a brother, a father, a son, a man who's been through something. He has a story."

ARTIST WITH A PURPOSE

After retiring from football, Maybin, who had studied communications and integrative arts at Penn State, relocated to his hometown of Baltimore to realize his dream of becoming a professional artist. He set up shop at his home studio in the city and took on a more active role with Project Mayhem, the arts-education foundation he founded upon entering the league in 2009. By then, Maybin had already sold pieces of his artwork to college and professional teammates and to private buyers through a website of the same name, with some paintings selling for thousands of dollars.

Maybin has cited the groundbreaking pop-culture artists Andy Warhol and Jean-Michel Basquiat as artistic influences, as well as the Baltimore painter Larry "Poncho" Brown, a longtime family friend and childhood mentor. Brown described Maybin's work to Walker as "a mix of good technical ability, 'hip-hop flair' and a probing desire to depict modern black consciousness." Maybin has painted portraits of African American cultural icons like boxer Muhammad Ali and rapper Tupac Shakur, as well as scenes depicting the symbolic struggles of everyday life in Baltimore. He explained to Walker, "I try to, in an eloquent way, paint terrible truths. . . . That's what I want my work to be, a reflection of the times."

In April 2015, Maybin found inspiration when Freddie Gray, a twenty-five-year-old African American man, died from spinal cord injuries sustained after his arrest by Baltimore police. Gray's death provoked riots across Baltimore, which Maybin recorded in hundreds of photos that he uploaded to Instagram. Maybin also produced art and writings inspired by what he witnessed, including a painting of eight fists raised in the air at a Baltimore intersection that was the scene of heavy rioting. These works eventually culminated in a book, titled *Art Activism*, which Maybin self-published in November 2017. The book features a collection of Maybin's paintings, drawings, poetry, and essays, which are geared toward raising awareness about social injustice.

TEACHING AND ADVOCACY

The same year *Art Activism* was published, Maybin added teaching to his list of endeavors. He began teaching art classes three days a week at Baltimore's Matthew A. Henson Elementary School (which Gray had attended), through an organization called Leaders of Tomorrow Youth Center. Maybin received national attention when, in January 2018, he tweeted a video of himself and some of his students discussing the frigid temperature in their classroom, which, like many throughout Baltimore, had no heat. The video quickly went viral, and Maybin unexpectedly became the face of advocacy efforts on behalf of Baltimore's notoriously underfunded schools.

In response to the video, a GoFundMe crowdfunding page was launched and more than $84,000 was raised to purchase space heaters and cold-weather clothing for students, which Maybin collected and distributed to schools. Maybin has expressed his desire to fight for other issues pertaining to Baltimore schoolchildren and hopes to continue using his art as a form of provocative social commentary. Football has "always been a game to me," he explained to Tyler Tynes for the sports news site *SB Nation* (10 Jan. 2018). "It was a kids' game I happened to be good at. What I'm doing now is fighting for kids to fight for the same opportunities I was blessed to do. This is now where my heart is at."

In addition to teaching at Henson Elementary, he leads art therapy classes for young women at the Children's Home, a residential youth facility in Catonsville, Maryland.

PERSONAL LIFE

A father of four, Maybin lives in Baltimore's Reservoir Hill neighborhood. With money from his rookie contract, he designed and built a dream house for his father and stepmother in Hilton Head, South Carolina.

SUGGESTED READING

Graham, Tim. "Aaron Maybin, a First-Round Draft Pick for Bills in 2009, Finds Peace through Art." *BN Blitz*, Buffalo News, 26 June 2015, buffalonews.com/2015/06/26/aaron-maybin-a-first-round-draft-pick-for-bills-in-2009-finds-peace-through-art-2. Accessed 3 May 2018.

Jones, Ryan. "In the Clutch." *Baltimore Magazine*, Mar. 2018, www.baltimoremagazine.com/2018/2/27/former-nfl-linebacker-aaron-maybin-tackles-injustice-through-art-and-activism. Accessed 3 May 2018.

Maybin, Aaron. "An Interview with Aaron Maybin." Interview by Dave Zirin. *The Nation*, 21 Feb. 2018, www.thenation.com/article/an-interview-with-aaron-maybin. Accessed 3 May 2018.

Tynes, Tyler. "Aaron Maybin's Fight for Baltimore Schools Won't End with Turning the Heat Back On." *SB Nation*, 10 Jan. 2018, www.sbnation.com/2018/1/10/16858844/aaron-maybins-baltimore-schools-heating-tweet. Accessed 3 May 2018.

Walker, Childs. "Former 1st-Round NFL Draft Pick Aaron Maybin Trades Helmet and Pads for Brush and Canvas." *The Baltimore Sun*, 8 Nov. 2015, www.baltimoresun.com/sports/nfl/bs-sp-aaron-maybin-nfl-artist-20151106-story.html. Accessed 3 May 2018.

—*Chris Cullen*

Danilo Medina

Date of birth: November 10, 1951
Occupation: President of the Dominican Republic

Danilo Medina became the president of the Dominican Republic in 2012. He is a technocrat, free-market advocate, and a populist committed to social inclusion and equality.

EARLY LIFE AND EDUCATION

Danilo Medina was born on November 10, 1951, in Arroyo Cano, Dominican Republic, to Juan Pablo Medina and Amelia Sánchez. He has seven younger siblings. He attended public schools in the rural town of Arroyo Cano for the first five grades and then moved to the city of San Juan de la Maguana to live with his uncle and continue his studies. After graduating high school, he studied chemical engineering at the Autonomous University of Santo Domingo. He later studied at the Technological Institute of Santo Domingo, graduating magna cum laude and earning a degree in economics in 1984.

During his youth, Medina developed a strong social awareness and interest in creating a more equitable society. While in college, he became active in politics and joined the Socialist Democratic University Front. He met Juan Bosch, a scholar and former Dominican Republic president who had been ousted by the military. Bosch became his mentor, and Medina assisted him when he formed the Dominican Liberation Party (PLD) in 1973. The next year, Medina became involved in the newly created Student Liberation Front and later served as its deputy secretary or organization and a member of its central and political committees.

POLITICAL CAREER

Medina was first elected to national office in 1986 when he won a seat as a deputy in the National Congress. Reelected in 1990 and 1994, he served as the president of the Chamber of Deputies from 1994 to 1995.

Medina worked on the PLD candidates' campaigns in the elections of 1994 and 1996. While Juan Bosch lost the 1994 election, Leonel Fernández Reyna won the latter. Following Fernández's victory, Medina resigned from congress and was appointed as the secretary of the presidency, a position comparable to chief of staff, and became a close advisor to President Fernández.

In 1998, Medina announced his own presidential ambitions. Fernández was constitutionally barred from a second consecutive term, and Medina won the PLD's nomination for the 2000 presidential election. He came in second, narrowly beating out former president Joaquín Balaguer with nearly 25 percent of the vote but earning only half the votes as Hipólito Mejía Domínguez of the Dominican Revolutionary Party. Balaguer and Medina declined a runoff election due to its cost and uncertain outcome, and Mejía was declared the winner.

In 2004, after Fernández regained the presidency and the PLD returned to power, Medina once again became the secretary of the presidency. His presidential ambitions still burned bright, and in 2006 he resigned as secretary to seek the PLD's nomination for the 2008 presidential election. By this time, the constitution had been revised to allow Fernández to hold two consecutive terms, and the PLD chose Fernández instead of Medina as its candidate.

With Fernández unable to seek a third consecutive term as president, Medina secured the PLD's nomination for the 2012 presidential election and selected Margarita Cedeño de Fernández, the incumbent president's wife, as his running mate. His opponents included former president Hipólito Mejía. Medina won over 51 percent of the votes in the first round of the elections, eliminating the need for a runoff. He was sworn in as president on August 16, 2012.

During his campaign, Medina had pledged to continue and expand upon Fernández's policies to improve the economy and infrastructure, combat corruption, increase spending for education, create jobs, reduce poverty, and create greater income equality. Medina has met many of his campaign promises. Economic

growth continued and the government deficit decreased. Increased funding for public works programs resulted in the construction of airport terminals, a subway system, roads, dams, and dozens of schools. The government created a national emergency system and invested 4 percent of the country's gross domestic product (GDP) in education. Medina also implemented anticorruption reform.

Despite these achievements, many poor and working-class Dominicans have failed to realize a significant change in their standard of living. Crime and corruption remain high, with the country a major stop of drug traffickers. Energy problems continue to plague the country, and power outages are common.

Medina was hugely popular with voters throughout his first term in office. Opinion polls throughout his term showed ratings as high as 90 percent. In his first year of office, he demonstrated his commitment to greater income equality when he renegotiated a contract with the Canadian-based operators of the Pueblo Viejo mine to gain more favorable terms for the Dominican Republic. Following a 2013 constitutional ruling that challenged the citizenship status of children born in the Dominican Republic to parents who were illegal immigrants from Haiti, he created an immigration plan that allowed illegal immigrants who had been in the country since 2011 to apply for legal residency status and prevented their deportation.

In 2015 the country's constitution was amended to allow a president to serve two consecutive terms, and Medina announced his plan to run for reelection in the 2016 presidential elections.

IMPACT

Danilo Medina's business-friendly policies have promoted strong economic growth and political stability, allowing the country to implement reforms that have resulted in a modest decline in income inequality and reduced the percentage of people living in poverty. These favorable conditions have resulted in high support for both Medina and the Dominican Liberation Party, indicating a high likelihood of political continuity.

PERSONAL LIFE

Medina married Cándida Montilla de Medina, a psychologist, in 1987. They have three daughters: Candy Sibely, Vanessa Daniela, and Ana Paula.

SUGGESTED READING

"A Popular President." *Economist*. Economist Newspaper, 19 Aug. 2014. Web. 13 Apr. 2016.

"Danilo Medina on Route to See His Dream of Being President Become Reality." *Diario*

Libre. Groupo Diario Libre, 16 May 2012. Web. 13 Apr. 2016.

"Dominican Republic's President Danilo Medina Sworn In." *BBC News*. BBC, 16 Aug. 2012. Web. 13 Apr. 2016.

Fieser, Ezra. "Dominican Republic Approves Law Allowing Medina to Run in 2016." *Bloomberg*. Bloomberg, 2 June 2015. Web. 13 Apr. 2016.

"His Excellency Mr. Danilo Medina, President of the Dominican Republic." *Permanent Mission of the Dominican Republic to the United Nations*. United Nations, n.d. Web. 13 Apr. 2016.

"One for All." *Business Year*. Business Year, 2015. Web. 13 Apr. 2016.

—*Barb Lightner*

By Dilma Rousseff [CC BY 2.0], via Wikimedia Commons

Kleber Mendonça Filho

Date of birth: 1968
Occupation: Director, writer

Kleber Mendonça Filho is an award-winning Brazilian filmmaker whose "command of the medium is both formidable and subtle," according to *New York Times* critic A. O. Scott (23 Aug. 2012). A former film critic himself, Mendonça Filho is best known for his 2016 film *Aquarius*, starring the acclaimed actor Sônia Braga. *Aquarius*, which, like most of Mendonça Filho's films, takes place in his hometown of Recife, Brazil, swept the film festival circuit and delighted critics across the globe. The film's political themes also resonated strongly with the unstable Brazilian political situation at the time. Mendonça Filho's public protests of the impeachment of Brazilian president Dilma Rousseff, however, meant that Brazil conspicuously declined to submit the film for consideration at the Academy Awards. Even despite this controversy, the film was well-received in Brazil as it was abroad, leading many publications to list the director as a major talent to watch.

Mendonça Filho's other works include his award-winning first feature film, *Neighboring Sounds* (2012), and several shorts. As part of a burgeoning filmmaking community in Recife, the capital of the state of Pernambuco, his films are rooted in the region's complicated history. Critics have consistently praised the way his works capture the lives of the people across racial and socioeconomic divides, living in his home city. He has also served as the film programmer at the Cinema da Fundação Joaquim Nabuco, a major alternative theater in Recife, promoting independent and art films in the community.

EARLY LIFE AND CAREER AS A CRITIC

Kleber Mendonça Filho was born into a middle-class family in Recife, an old coastal city in northeastern Brazil, in 1968. He grew up in the city, though he moved to England, where his mother was earning her PhD, with his family in 1982. He returned to Recife in 1987, and studied journalism at the Federal University of Pernambuco.

Combining journalism with his love of cinema, Mendonça Filho became a film critic, but he always harbored a desire to become a filmmaker. Although his earliest memories of films, such as seeing Steven Spielberg's *Raiders of the Lost Ark* (1981) when he was thirteen years old, were simply pleasurable experiences, it was not long before this turned into something more. It was John Carpenter's 1976 crime drama, *Assault on Precinct 13*, that first inspired him to make films himself. "It's very well made and very precise, but the scale is modest. It looks doable," he said of that film in an interview with David Jenkins for the film *Little White Lies* (*lwlies.com*) website in 2016. Similarly, he noted that although expansive, epic films, such as *Star Wars* (1977), were entertaining and impressive, it was relatively contained films that played a deeper role in convincing him that he could be a filmmaker, and therefore had a greater impact on his style. "I appreciate scope, but I also appreciate craft," he told Jenkins.

As a film lover, Mendonça Filho found film criticism to be a dream job at first, but eventually he grew fatigued with having to keep up with every latest movie, regardless of quality. Yet even when he struggled with being forced to watch bad films, he used the experience to learn. Speaking of reviewing films that he had no interest in, he told Jonathan Robbins for *Film Comment* (24 Aug. 2012), "Some of my best reviews, they came out of situations like that. . . . It wasn't about cruelly dismissing them, but using them as a means to think about some other ideas related to cinema. It's possible to make something good out of what initially feels like a negative situation."

BREAKING IN WITH SHORT FILMS

Mendonça Filho began making short films in the late 1990s while still working as a critic. Among his early releases were a 1997 thriller called *Enjaulado* (Caged in) and a 2002 horror film called *A Menina do Algodão* (The little cotton girl). As his reputation grew, he earned attention for a short called *Vinil Verde* (Green Vinyl), which premiered in 2004 at the Cannes Film Festival. Like many of his earlier works, *Green Vinyl* is set in Recife. A horror story based on a Russian fairytale, it involves a woman who gives her daughter a box of gramophone records but warns her: she may listen to any record, except the green one. The film is composed entirely of still photos with voiceover narration.

Following the success of *Green Vinyl*, Mendonça Filho released other shorts including *Eletrodoméstica* in 2005 and *Noite de sexta manhã de sábado* (Friday night Saturday morning) in 2006. In 2007, Mendonça Filho was featured in a profile at the International Film Festival Rotterdam (IFFR) that screened five of his works. In 2008, he directed a full-length documentary called *Crítico* (Critical), about the tension between artists and critics. For the film, Mendonça Filho interviewed over seventy critics and filmmakers between 1998 and 2007. He then returned to the short-film format with the mockumentary *Recife Frio* (Cold tropics) (2009).

This period of productive and award-winning filmmaking saw a corresponding decline in Mendonça Filho's work as a film critic. Around 2010, as he began work on his first feature film, he stopped his critical writing altogether due to his busy schedule and other conflicts. "I stopped writing as a critic because I just couldn't do it anymore, it got to be too much," he told Paul Sbrizzi for the film website *hammertonail.com* (6 Apr. 2013). "I was also finding myself in situations where I would rather not write about certain films because I was already a filmmaker and that created a situation where—I can't be writing about films by friends or colleagues."

NEIGHBORING SOUNDS (2012)

Mendonça Filho's debut feature film, *Neighboring Sounds* (O Som ao Redor), premiered in 2012 at the IFFR, where it won the FIPRESCI Award. The film is inspired by, and draws on elements of, his earlier short *Eletrodoméstica*, taking place

on a street in suburban Recife in the 1990s and exploring the lives of people that live there. "I wrote it in 1994," Mendonça Filho told Robbins of *Neighboring Sounds*, "but it took so long to get financing that it became a period piece." The film subtly examines the class tensions of the upper-middle-class neighborhood residents and their domestic help. In a series of vignettes, Mendonça Filho shows relatable characters like a lonely housewife, a maid who is having an affair with a security guard, and a doorman who keeps falling asleep on the job, but their stories are suffused with a sense of foreboding. The film's ambient music and other sound design contributes to the feeling of unease.

Mendonça Filho uses his character's lives to explore themes of security and paranoia, issues he also probed in *Green Vinyl*. Among the Brazilian middle class, he told Sbrizzi, "everybody's terrified of invasion, of trespassing, of having somebody coming into your home," leading many to move into high-rises, which they deem safer than ground-level houses. *Neighboring Sounds* captures this urban existence while also referring to Brazil's cultural and political history. For example, the film begins with still black and white photographs from a time when Recife was known for its sugarcane plantations. Mendonça Filho demonstrates how power dynamics from that era persist in modern Brazil.

Neighboring Sounds performed exceedingly well with critics. Describing the film in the *New York Times* as a "revelatory debut," A. O. Scott named it one of his top ten favorite films of the year. "The scope of [the] movie is narrow, but its ambitions are enormous, and it accomplishes nothing less than the illumination of the peculiar state of Brazilian (and not only Brazilian) society," Scott wrote. Similarly, Robert Abele for the *Los Angeles Times* (4 Apr. 2013) called it "one of the strongest feature debuts of the last decade," noting the skill with which Mendonça Filho depicts the spatial and sensory aspects of class divisions. Brazil submitted the film for consideration as best foreign film at the Academy Awards, though it ultimately did not receive a nomination.

AQUARIUS (2016)

Mendonça Filho's next feature, the 2016 film *Aquarius*, continued the director's exploration of themes of Brazilian society that he began in *Neighboring Sounds* and earlier works. It, too, is set in Recife, in an old apartment building called the Aquarius. The protagonist, Clara, is a sixty-five-year-old music critic and widow. She has inhabited a big, sunny apartment overlooking the ocean in the Aquarius for most of her adult life. But the owners of the building want to sell to real estate developers—and Clara is the last holdout. Throughout the film, Clara does battle with the forces that seek to oust her from her home.

With that simple premise, *Aquarius* develops more fully as a character study of Clara, played by Sônia Braga, a legend of Brazilian cinema. As Scott wrote in his *New York Times* review (13 Oct. 2016), the film unfolds as "a marvelous and surprising act of portraiture, a long, unhurried encounter with a single, complicated person." In a larger sense, Clara is representative of the idiosyncratic, cultural forces that new Brazil—personified by greedy real estate developers and gentrification—seeks to wipe out. The film premiered at the Cannes Film Festival in 2016 and was lauded by critics.

Despite immediate international accolades, *Aquarius* also brought Mendonça Filho a level of controversy. Critics noted the film's elements of political satire that paralleled developments in Brazilian politics at the time of its release. Days before it premiered, Brazil's president, Dilma Rousseff, was impeached in what some considered to be a right-wing coup. Mendonça Filho and members of the film's cast protested Rousseff's impeachment at Cannes, a move that outraged some Brazilians. Brazilian film critic Marcos Petrucelli suggested that Mendonça Filho was in league with Rousseff, and when the new Brazilian government placed Petrucelli on the country's Oscar selection committee, he barred consideration of *Aquarius*.

Yet despite the Oscars snub—and the calculated 18+ rating imposed by Brazilian censors—the film was well-received domestically. "The film seemed to hit a nerve in Brazilian society," Mendonça Filho told Tom Graham for *Sight & Sound* (22 Mar. 2017). "Sometimes this happens, and I think it's a beautiful thing because films are organic: you make them and then they develop their own lives, out of your control."

PERSONAL LIFE

Mendonça Filho is married to Emilie Lesclaux, a French film producer. The couple has two children.

SUGGESTED READING

Abele, Robert. "Review: Breathtaking 'Neighboring Sounds.'" Review of *Neighboring Sounds*, directed by Kleber Mendonça Filho. *Los Angeles Times*, 4 Apr. 2013, articles.latimes.com/2013/apr/04/entertainment/la-et-mn-neighboring-sounds-capsule-20130405. Accessed 6 Nov. 2017.

Jenkins, David. "Kleber Mendonça Filho: 'John Carpenter Is Always a Reference Point for Me.'" *Little White Lies*, 2016, lwlies.com/interviews/kleber-mendoncca-filho-aquarius/. Accessed 3 Nov. 2017.

Mendonça Filho, Kleber, and Emilie Lesclaux. "Interview: Kleber Mendonça Filho and Emilie Lesclaux." Interview by Jonathan Robbins. *Film Comment*, 24 Aug. 2012, www.filmcomment.com/blog/interview-kleber-mendonca-filho-neighboring-sounds/. Accessed 5 Nov. 2017.

Mendonça Filho, Kleber. "A Conversation with Kleber Mendonça Filho (*Neighboring Sounds*)." Interview by Paul Sbrizzi. *Hammer to Nail*, 6 Apr. 2013, www.hammertonail.com/interviews/a-conversation-with-kleber-mendonca-filho-neighboring-sounds/. Accessed 6 Nov. 2017.

Mendonça Filho, Kleber. "Kleber Mendonça Filho: '*Aquarius* Seemed to Hit a Nerve in Brazil.'" Interview by Tom Graham. *Sight & Sound*, 22 Mar. 2017, www.bfi.org.uk/news-opinion/sight-sound-magazine/interviews/kleber-mendonca-filho-aquarius-brazil-nerve. Accessed 8 Nov. 2017.

Scott, A. O. "In 'Aquarius,' a Widow Fights to Keep Her Home." Review of *Aquarius*, directed by Kleber Mendonça Filho. *The New York Times*, 13 Oct. 2016, www.nytimes.com/2016/10/14/movies/aquarius-review.html. Accessed 8 Nov. 2017.

Scott, A. O. "The Leisure Class Bears Its Burden." Review of *Neighboring Sounds*, directed by Kleber Mendonça Filho. *The New York Times*, 23 Aug. 2012, www.nytimes.com/2012/08/24/movies/neighboring-sounds-directed-by-kleber-mendonca-filho.html. Accessed 6 Nov. 2017.

SELECTED WORKS

Green Vinyl, 2004; *Crítico*, 2008; *Neighboring Sounds*, 2012; *Aquarius*, 2016

—*Molly Hagan*

Yves Meyer

Date of birth: July 19, 1939
Occupation: Mathematician

When French mathematician Yves Meyer received the prestigious Abel Prize from the Norwegian Academy of Science and Letters in 2017, the award was in many ways a recognition of his several decades of work in his field. The citation specifically highlighted Meyer's research into the oscillations known as wavelets, which have been his chief mathematical preoccupation since he first learned about the subject in the mid-1980s. As one of the leading figures in the study of wavelets, he has been credited with enhancing the overall understanding of the oscillations, which have been put to extensive use in the field of signal processing.

A talented mathematician since his teen years, Meyer began his academic career as a teaching assistant at the Université de

Strasbourg (University of Strasbourg) while working to complete his doctorate, after which he went on to teach at several of France's best-known institutions of higher education. He retired from the École Normale Supérieure Paris-Saclay in 2008. Over the course of his career, his areas of interest have varied greatly, encompassing broad fields such as harmonic analysis and number theory as well as specific mathematical problems such as the Navier-Stokes equations. Although Meyer has received significant recognition for his work, including the Abel Prize and the 2010 Carl Friedrich Gauss Prize, he takes a highly collaborative approach to mathematical research and has particularly sought to encourage his students to carry out challenging and innovative work. "It is clear to me that the progress of mathematics is a collective enterprise," he said to Ulf Persson in an interview for the *Newsletter of the European Mathematical Society* (June 2011), commonly known as the *EMS Newsletter*. "All of us are needed."

EARLY LIFE AND EDUCATION

Yves François Meyer was born in Paris, France, on July 19, 1939. His family moved to Tunisia during World War II, and he and his older sister grew up in the city of Tunis. Throughout his childhood, Meyer was intrigued by the city, which he described to Persson as "a melting pot where people from all over the Mediterranean had found sanctuary." Although "obsessed by the desire of crossing the frontiers between these distinct ethnic groups," as he told Persson, he "was limited by [his] ignorance of the languages which were spoken in the streets of Tunis."

Meyer attended the Lycée Carnot de Tunis, where he excelled in the humanities, particularly Latin and Greek, and enjoyed reading works by classical philosophers Socrates and Plato in the original Greek. At the same time, Meyer also demonstrated a noteworthy talent for mathematics. "I understood mathematics from the inside in a very natural way," he said to Bjørn Ian Dundas and Christian Skau in another interview for the *EMS Newsletter* (Sept. 2017). "When I was in high school, I understood mathematics by myself and not by listening to my teachers." His interest in math was stoked further when he had the opportunity to attend a talk by French mathematician Jean-Pierre Kahane, a significant contributor in harmonic analysis.

At the age of seventeen, Meyer returned to France, where he spent a year preparing to take the entrance examination for the École Normale Supérieure (ENS), an elite and highly competitive institute of higher education in Paris. He succeeded in securing a place in the school and began his studies there in 1957.

EARLY CAREER

After completing his education at the ENS in 1960, Meyer was required to complete a period of military service. As a Frenchman who had spent his early years in North Africa, he did not want to participate in French military action in Algeria, which at the time was fighting for independence from France. Instead, he arranged to complete his service by teaching at the Prytanée National Militaire, a military school in La Flèche, in western France. During the course of his time as a teacher, he found that he did not particularly enjoy teaching high-school-age students, nor was he particularly good at it. "My way of teaching was evaluated twice by truly experienced specialists. They told me that I was not a good teacher," Meyer recalled to Persson. "A good teacher at high school level needs to be much more methodical and organized than I was." He later determined that he much preferred mathematical research. "I eventually felt guilty to be the one who is always right while the pupils are wrong most of the time," he explained. "To do research is to be ignorant most of the time and often to make the mistakes I corrected in my students' homework." He ultimately completed his two years of military service at the Prytanée and remained at the school for a third year before leaving in 1963 to pursue further studies in mathematics.

Meyer applied for and was granted a teaching assistant position at the University of Strasbourg. The mathematics department at the university was small, and Meyer was one of fourteen assistants who worked together in a large office in which, as he told Dundas and Skau, "everyone was smoking" and "it was impossible to work." The teaching assistants, all of whom were pursuing doctoral studies, were granted a great deal of academic freedom and were permitted to choose their own thesis topics without supervision. When devising his own thesis topic, Meyer was inspired by the book *Trigonometric Series* (1935) by mathematician Antoni Zygmund. "I found the book fascinating and I asked myself what were the important problems in this subject?" he recalled to Dundas and Skau. "So I decided what were the important problems and I tried to solve the problems." Meyer's approach to his thesis proved successful, and he earned his PhD from the University of Strasbourg in 1966.

ACADEMIC CAREER

After completing his doctorate, Meyer began his academic career at what is now the Université Paris-Sud (University of Paris-Sud) in 1966. He remained with the institution until 1980, when he moved to the École Polytechnique, located in the suburbs of Paris. After six years, he again moved to the Université Paris-Dauphine (Paris Dauphine University), where he remained for nearly a decade. The year 1995 saw the final move in Meyer's academic career as he joined the École Normale Supérieure Cachan, later renamed the École Normale Supérieure Paris-Saclay. He remained at the institution until his retirement in 2008 but subsequently maintained his affiliation with the school as a professor emeritus.

Meyer supervised numerous doctoral students over the course of his career; at one point, while teaching at Paris Dauphine, he oversaw the work of nineteen PhD students at the same time. Although the work was often exhausting, Meyer found the process of supervising theses rewarding and enjoyed introducing students to areas of study that interested him. "I love transmitting the fire to the students and then doing something else. . . . It is a way of cheating because it means that it will be their responsibility to make a building from my ideas, while I can escape," he said to Dundas and Skau. "Like people who invite their friends and then disappear." A number of Meyer's doctoral students went on to become successful mathematicians and have made a variety of breakthroughs in areas such as singular integral operators and wavelets.

RESEARCH

Much as Meyer often changed his university affiliation during his lengthy career, he likewise became known for exploring a vast array of mathematical topics, often collaborating with colleagues and students to explore new areas of interest. Among Meyer's focuses during his career were Meyer sets, which are sets of points in space that can describe ordered but aperiodic structures known as quasicrystals. He was also interested in the mathematical findings of Argentinian mathematician Alberto Calderón and Polish mathematician Antoni Zygmund, the latter of whom wrote the book on trigonometric series that inspired Meyer's doctoral thesis. In addition to those topics, Meyer also explored the Navier-Stokes equations, mathematical equations named for physicists Claude-Louis Navier and George Gabriel Stokes, but ultimately made little progress addressing the mathematical questions surrounding the equations.

Among Meyer's best-known research is his work on wavelets, which he began in the mid-1980s, after being introduced to the topic while working at the École Polytechnique. While physicist Jean Lascoux was finishing making copies using the one copy machine shared by the physics and mathematics departments, he showed a paper on wavelets to Meyer, who was instantly fascinated. "I recognized Calderón's reproducing identity and I could not believe that it had something to do with signal processing," he recalled to Persson. The encounter sparked a new interest for him. "I fell in love with signal processing," he continued. "I felt I had finally found my home."

Known in French as *ondelettes*, wavelets are oscillations that, as their name suggests, somewhat resemble waves when represented visually. Wavelets can be described by mathematical functions and have a variety of practical uses, especially in signal processing, in which they are particularly useful for analyzing unknown signals. Over the course of his exploration of wavelets, Meyer provided the name for a distinct type, the Meyer wavelet, and published a variety of books and papers on the subject. In recognition of his work, Meyer was awarded the 2010 Carl Friedrich Gauss Prize for applications of mathematics for his research in areas such as wavelets, number theory, and harmonic analysis.

ABEL PRIZE

On March 21, 2017, the Norwegian Academy of Science and Letters announced that Meyer had been selected to receive the prestigious Abel Prize, which recognizes influential contributions to mathematics. Named after nineteenth-century Norwegian mathematician Niels Henrik Abel, the award has often been described as the mathematics equivalent of the Nobel Prize, which is awarded to major contributors to fields such as chemistry and physics but does not recognize achievements in mathematics. The Abel Prize Committee specifically sought to recognize Meyer "for his pivotal role in the development of the mathematical theory of wavelets," as noted on the award's official website. Upon learning that he was to receive the prize, Meyer said to Davide Castelvecchi for *Nature* (21 Mar. 2017), "I am at the same time happy, surprised, and slightly guilty."

The Abel Prize award ceremony was held in May 2017, and Meyer traveled to Norway to receive the prize from Norwegian king Harald V. In addition to widespread recognition, the prize is accompanied by an award of six million Norwegian kroner, equivalent to approximately $710,000 at the time.

PERSONAL LIFE

Meyer is married and has two children. An avid reader, he still enjoys reading the works of Plato, although he no longer reads them in Greek. Meyer is also a fan of Russian literature. In addition to his affiliation with the institutions at which he taught, he is a member of the French Academy of Sciences and a fellow of the American Mathematical Society (AMS).

SUGGESTED READING

Bellos, Alex. "Abel Prize 2017: Yves Meyer Wins 'Maths Nobel' for Work on Wavelets." *The Guardian*, 21 Mar. 2017, www.theguardian.com/science/alexs-adventures-in-numberland/2017/mar/21/abel-prize-2017-yves-meyer-wins-maths-nobel-for-work-on-wavelets. Accessed 14 Dec. 2017.

Castelvecchi, Davide. "'Wavelet Revolution' Pioneer Scoops Top Maths Award." *Nature*, vol. 543, no. 7646, 21 Mar. 2017, doi:10.1038/543476a. Accessed 14 Dec. 2017.

Daubechies, Ingrid. "The Work of Yves Meyer." *Proceedings of the International Congress of Mathematicians: Hyderabad, August 19–27, 2010*, edited by Rajendra Bhatia, vol. 1, Hindustan Book Agency, 2010, pp. 115–24. *Weierstrass Institute*, www.wias-berlin.de/imu/archive/ICM2010/www.icm2010.in/wp-content/icmfiles/laudaions/gauss.pdf. Accessed 15 Dec. 2017.

Meyer, Yves. "Interview with Abel Laureate Yves Meyer." Interview by Bjørn Ian Dundas and Christian Skau. *Newsletter of the European Mathematical Society*, Sept. 2017, pp. 14–22, doi:10.4171/news/105/5. Accessed 15 Dec. 2017.

Meyer, Yves. "Interview with Yves Meyer." Interview by Ulf Persson. *Newsletter of the European Mathematical Society*, June 2011, pp. 25–28, www.ems-ph.org/journals/newsletter/pdf/2011-06-80.pdf. Accessed 15 Dec. 2017.

"Yves Meyer Receives the Abel Prize." *The Abel Prize*, Norwegian Academy of Science and Letters, 21 Mar. 2017, www.abelprize.no/nyheter/vis.html?tid=69588. Accessed 14 Dec. 2017.

—*Joy Crelin*

Photo by Marcus Ingram/Getty Images for iHeartMedia

Julia Michaels

Date of birth: November 13,1993
Occupation: Singer-songwriter

Julia Michaels's hit song "Issues" was nominated for a 2018 Grammy Award for song of the year, and the singer-songwriter herself was nominated for best new artist after releasing her debut EP (extended play record) *Nervous System* in 2017. Michaels, however, is anything but new to the music industry. Only in her early twenties, she had already penned (with writing partner Justin Tranter) several top-forty hits, including Justin Bieber's chart-topping "Sorry" and Selena Gomez's "Good for You," before singing one of her own. Artists she has worked with include Nick Jonas, Gwen Stefani, Fifth Harmony, Kelly Clarkson, Ed Sheeran, and Britney Spears. She was a shy poet when she caught the attention of a professional songwriter when she was fifteen. Two years later, she cowrote her first television theme song, for the Disney Channel's *Austin & Ally*.

Over time, she has learned to trust her instincts, siphoning her innate emotional honesty into her work without overthinking it. She wrote "Issues" on the day that "Sorry" hit number one on the Billboard Hot 100 chart and following a fight with her boyfriend. Though she was still reluctant to put her own voice to her lyrics at first, she has since expressed gratitude for the ability to fully represent her own work as well as the largely positive reception of her efforts. In the end, no matter who sings her songs, she has consistently emphasized the importance of writing in her life: "I have to write. I physically, for my being, for my sanity, have to write songs. I don't feel like myself if I don't," she explained to Myles Tanzer for *Fader* (17 Aug. 2017).

EARLY LIFE

Julia Michaels was born Julia Cavazos in Davenport, Iowa, in 1993. Her Puerto Rican–born father adopted the stage name John Michaels when he was pursuing acting roles. She moved to Santa Clarita, California, with her family when she was six years old. When she was a child, her mother encouraged her to act as well, so she adopted her father's stage name. But becoming an actor, she conceded to Mark Savage for the BBC (30 July 2017), was not meant to be: "Writing was the thing I always wanted to do."

Always loving words and often penning lines of poetry, she has recalled winning a poetry contest in the fourth grade; for her, however, writing was more than something she was merely good at. Michaels was largely homeschooled, her parents divorced when she was young, and she did not have especially close relationships with her siblings. "Growing up, it was my way of feeling less alone," she explained to Savage. Her older sister was an aspiring singer, and a young Michaels would often tag along with her while she recorded demos for various songwriters to use as guides for artists. She was drawn to the emotional power of music and singing, and though she sang in secret, did not consider herself a singer. Without receiving formal instruction, she began turning her poems into songs using the piano but ultimately gave them to her sister to sing.

When Michaels was fifteen, she accompanied her sister to yet another demo recording. Her mother encouraged her to sing something for the songwriter, a woman named Joleen Belle. She sat down at the piano, playing a few chords and singing along. Her performance prompted Belle to ask if she also wrote music. "She must have seen something in me that I didn't see in myself," Michaels recalled to Heather Wood Rudulph for *Cosmopolitan* (2 Nov. 2015) of the serendipitous moment. After that, she began working with Belle, who became a mentor. The duo submitted songs for commercials and television promos, with some of their songs used on the MTV reality television show *The Hills* and in promotional advertisements for the daytime talk show *The View*. Two years into their partnership, they submitted their first television theme song, and got the gig. It was a song for the Disney Channel comedy series *Austin & Ally*, and its success boosted her confidence in her potential as a professional songwriter.

EARLY WRITING CAREER

Soon after Michaels landed the theme song for *Austin & Ally*, she met another songwriter, Lindy Robbins, who has been writing hit songs for pop acts since the late 1990s. She and Robbins began writing together, and their first few collaborations found big-name artists right away. They wrote the synth-pop songs "Fire Starter" for Demi Lovato's 2013 album *Demi* and "Slow Down," the second single on Selena Gomez's album *Star Dance*, also released in 2013. The fifth song they wrote together became the group Fifth Harmony's first single, "Miss Movin' On." The speed of Michaels's success was disorienting, but she knew songwriting was what she wanted to do. Her parents, who had hoped that she would apply to college, reluctantly supported her choice. Still, she acknowledged the precariousness of a songwriter's life. "I had all these singles come out within a two-month period, and then nothing for almost two years," she told Rudulph.

During that time, Michaels doubled down on her work ethic, writing more songs and working with more writers. It was a difficult period for her, as she was sometimes scheduled to work three songwriting sessions a day. Some sessions, she told Rudulph, are like blind dates because one does not always know their writing partner.

"You walk in there and you're practically getting naked for someone you just met," she said. The back-to-back-to-back sessions began to take their toll, and she suffered regular panic attacks from the stress. Finally, through Robbins, she found a new manager who encouraged her to take some time off when she needed it. She also began to find people she felt more comfortable and creative with, like her now-regular collaborator Tranter. Furthermore, she learned to trust in her own instincts, letting the song find her, as she explained to Rudulph. "If you doubt yourself and you have to work it out too much, it gets over-complicated and then you don't feel it anymore."

WORKING ON GOMEZ'S *REVIVAL* AND FURTHER HITS

By 2015, Michaels and Tranter had begun collaborating with Gomez on her second album, *Revival* (2015). It was the first time Michaels had worked directly with an artist, and she grew close to Gomez, helping her to continue finding a more mature style and contributing to several of the songs on the record, including "Hands to Myself," which was inspired by pop icon Prince, and "Good for You," featuring A$AP Rocky. *Revival* debuted at number one on the Billboard 200 album chart. Also in 2015, she, along with Tranter, wrote Bieber's "Sorry" and helped provide lyrics to many of the tracks on Gwen Stefani's 2016 album *This Is What the Truth Feels Like*. She told Rudulph that she arranged the single "Used to Love You" around a note Stefani had written herself after her divorce from Bush musician Gavin Rossdale: "There was this one phrase that read, 'I don't know why I cry but I think it's because I remembered for the first time since I hated you that I used to love you.' I said, 'Whoa, what a crazy line that is.' She just goes, 'Cool, make it a melody.'"

Increasingly recognized by the media as a hit songwriting duo, Michaels and Tranter worked with actor Hailee Steinfeld on her debut EP, *Haiz* (2015), as well. Michaels was recording demos for songs such as "Love Myself," which she co wrote, when Charlie Walk, who was then the executive vice president of Republic Records and would soon become president of the Republic Group, happened to be around. He was impressed by her voice and suggested she try breaking out on her own as a singer: "There was like a force of nature attracting me to this type of artist. I went up to her in the studio and I said, you're not a writer—you're an artist," he stated to KC Ifeanyi for *Fast Company* (25 July 2017). Michaels, however, politely declined.

At the same time, Michaels also cowrote the song "Trade Hearts" for Jason Derulo in 2015. He wanted to make the song a duet, and she recorded a demo for the female vocal track. A few days later, Derulo reached out to her, asking her to appear on the track. It was her first feature as a singer, and the credit served as a testament to her singing abilities.

In the following year, partnering with Tranter once more, she cowrote the popular song "Close" for Nick Jonas and Tove Lo, and the pair also worked closely with Britney Spears, writing a handful of songs on the singer's album *Glory* (2016), including "Slumber Party." Additionally, she cowrote a song for the Norwegian DJ Kygo titled "Carry Me," eventually performing it with him in August at the closing ceremony of the 2016 Olympic Games in Rio de Janeiro, Brazil. Not yet used to performing in public, she described the experience to Rebecca Milzoff for *Billboard* (6 Jan. 2017): "I remember the countdown, and then, after that, I feel like I blacked out and I woke up eating pizza."

"ISSUES" AND *NERVOUS SYSTEM*

Although she was growing somewhat more comfortable in the role of singer, it was writing that ultimately pushed Michaels to take the plunge into a solo career. At one point, she thought about giving away the song "Issues," written with Tranter and inspired by a fight she had had with her boyfriend, but soon realized, for the first time, that she had written a song that she did not want anyone else to sing. "I'm uncomfortable with the idea of someone singing such a personal song of mine," she told Erica Gonzales for *Harper's Bazaar* (26 May 2017). "When I wrote 'Issues,' I felt like I had found my voice and I had felt like I had found a song like me. It was the first time I had written a song that felt like me." Based on those feelings, she signed on with Republic Records in October, and released her debut EP in 2017.

"Issues," a song about sharing one's vulnerabilities with one's partner, was released in early 2017 and peaked at number eleven on the Billboard Hot 100 chart in June. Appearing for the first time on stage at a music industry awards show, Michaels performed the song at the Billboard Music Awards in May. Continuing to work with Gomez, she also cowrote the song "Bad Liar," which was released around that time. Numerous music publications went on to name the minimalist pop tune one of the best songs of the year. Meanwhile, Michaels's second single, the breathless, acoustic "Uh Huh," about the excitement of a crush, was released in the summer, and her debut EP, *Nervous System*, consisting of seven songs, subsequently appeared weeks later.

Writing for herself, Michaels tends toward a confessional tone and minimal production. Katherine St. Asaph, who reviewed *Nervous System* for *Pitchfork* (4 Aug. 2017), distilled Michaels's larger appeal—and why she has the potential to be a lasting star—writing that her singles "have bucked all the radio trends except the ones she started." The album, she added, might

be uneven, but Michaels's "unapologetic, relatable messiness" makes her a unique and "promising" artist. In addition to joining singer Shawn Mendes on his world tour later in 2017, it was also announced that she would be an opening act for Niall Horan as well as for the band Maroon 5 in 2018.

PERSONAL LIFE

Michaels, who has talked openly about her struggles with anxiety, exercises often and focuses on her dog to reduce some of the stress, particularly of transitioning to being in the forefront as an artist.

SUGGESTED READING

Michaels, Julia. "Get That Life: How I Became a Hit Songwriter by Age 21." Interview by Heather Wood Rudulph. *Cosmopolitan*, 2 Nov. 2015, www.cosmopolitan.com/career/interviews/a48541/get-that-life-julia-michaels-songwriter/. Accessed 15 Dec. 2017.

Michaels, Julia. "Julia Michaels: Songwriting Is Like 'Getting Naked to People You Don't Know.'" Interview by Erica Gonzales. *Harper's Bazaar*, 26 May 2017, www.harpersbazaar.com/culture/art-books-music/a9935485/julia-michaels-issues-interview/. Accessed 15 Dec. 2017.

Savage, Mark. "Julia Michaels: 'Dare to Suck.'" *BBC*, 30 July 2017, www.bbc.com/news/entertainment-arts-40704643. Accessed 15 Dec. 2017.

St. Asaph, Katherine. Review of *Nervous System*, by Julia Michaels. *Pitchfork*, 4 Aug. 2017, pitchfork.com/reviews/albums/julia-michaels-nervous-system-ep/. Accessed 15 Dec. 2017.

Tanzer, Myles. "Julia Michaels Wrote All the Songs You Know on the Radio. Now She's Singing Her Own." *Fader*, 17 Aug. 2017, www.thefader.com/2017/08/17/julia-michaels-genf-interview-issues. Accessed 15 Dec. 2017.

—*Molly Hagan*

Simone Missick

Date of birth: January 19, 1982
Occupation: Actor

After more than a decade as a working actor—mostly in minor walk-on roles on television series—Simone Missick had a breakout role in 2016 on *Luke Cage*, one of several interconnected shows on the online streaming service Netflix featuring superheroes from Marvel Comics. While the so-called Marvel Cinematic Universe (MCU) had proven hugely successful since 2008, the television format of the various Netflix

WikiGusta, via Wikimedia Commons

series starting in 2015 allowed depictions of more obscure yet fan-favorite characters, especially those who operate at a local rather than global or cosmic scale. One such character is Missick's Misty Knight, a popular supporting figure to many avid comic book readers but mostly unknown to the general public. Missick's portrayal pleased many devoted fans as well as general viewers, helping to make *Luke Cage* a critical and commercial success. She reprised the role for the connected miniseries *The Defenders* (2017) and the second season of *Luke Cage* in 2018 and was set to also appear in season two of Marvel's *Iron Fist*.

Playing Misty Knight put Missick in a lead role for the first time and pushed her career to a new level. She embraced the opportunity to demonstrate her range through such a well rounded, intriguing character with a built-in fanbase, but she also remained attuned to the value of even the smallest roles. "I know what it's like to be an extra. I know what it's like to be considered a 'human prop.'" I think that they help our shows be what they are. They make the world real," Missick recalled in an interview with Victoria Johnson for *Complex* (17 Aug. 2017). "I think that just living graciously and being grateful for everything just really helps to not take anything for granted and not take anything too seriously."

EARLY LIFE AND EDUCATION
Simone Missick was born Simone Cook on January 19, 1982, the youngest of Cassandra and Duane Cook's three children. Simone and her brother and sister were raised in

Detroit, Michigan, where her mother worked as a social worker and her father as a teacher. In fact, Duane Cook worked two jobs—as a high school math and government teacher and as an adult education teacher—to make sure the family was provided for. Despite their very busy schedules, both parents made sure their children received proper guidance. "They were always there to make sure that we were just good people," Missick recalled in her interview with Johnson.

Missick was a gifted student at Renaissance High School, where she was a violinist in national orchestras and was an all-around athlete, competing in track, basketball, and tennis. (Missick's love of basketball, in fact, would help to flesh out Misty Knight's backstory on *Luke Cage*.) She first developed an interest in acting when her older sister began acting in her teens, and she soon began to pursue it with serious interest. She continued to hone her craft as an undergraduate at Howard University in Washington, DC, from which she earned her BA in 2003.

Missick then studied at the British American Drama Academy at Oxford University in England under the respected British actor Alan Rickman, who died in 2016. While there she became friends with a fellow student, Nelsan Ellis, who would go on to fame on the cult vampire series *True Blood*. (Ellis died in 2017.) Missick recounted to Johnson a piece of advice given to her class by Rickman: "Nobody cares what you think about, you just better get that emotion out there."

EARLY ACTING CAREER
From the time she graduated from Howard, Missick worked as a professional actor, originally under her maiden name, Simone Cook. After returning from England she was initially based out of Detroit, where she participated in regional theater productions. Eventually she moved to Los Angeles in search of more acting gigs. She worked as an extra on various productions while gradually landing a few minor named roles. Among the more notable television shows in which she appeared in small parts were *Ray Donovan* in 2014, *Scandal* in 2015, and *Wayward Pines* in 2016.

Missick was also featured in the HBO comedy short *The Big Chop* (2016), in which she plays a woman who is forced to cut off her hair and is left with a very short natural afro. The previous year, however, she had already been cast in the role that would take her career to new heights. In September 2015 it was announced that she would fill the role of Misty Knight in the third Marvel Netflix series, *Luke Cage*, to air in 2016.

BECOMING MISTY KNIGHT
The comic book character of Misty Knight was inspired by the blaxploitation films of the 1970s.

Though generally portraying stereotypes, such films were written for and inspired by black audiences with the idea of portraying African Americans as the central characters, rather than as merely sidekicks or victims. Knight was developed by comic book creators Arvell Jones (like Missick, a Detroit native) and Tony Isabella for Marvel Comics in 1975, about three years after the successful debut of Luke Cage, the first African-American superhero who was also the titular character of his own comic book, *Luke Cage, Hero for Hire*.

In the comics, Misty Knight was a budding star in the New York City Police Department when a bomb exploded and blew off her right arm. Tony Stark, the billionaire inventor also known as the superhero Iron Man, developed a superpowered bionic arm for Knight, which she used with her detective and martial arts skills to fight crime. She generally appeared as a supporting character, often paired with friend and fellow martial artist Colleen Wing and became a fan favorite to many close followers of the expansive Marvel universe. Through the years Knight has been involved with such superheroes as Luke Cage and Danny Rand, also known as the Iron Fist, with whom she has had a longtime romantic relationship.

After Marvel found enormous success with interconnected film adaptations of characters such as Iron Man, plans were made to develop a number of television dramas about the company's "street level" superheroes. The first such series was *Daredevil*, released on Netflix in 2015 to much success and laying the groundwork for further shows, interconnected in the same manner as the Marvel films. When production began on *Luke Cage*, Misty Knight was set to be included as a major figure. "As soon as I read the description, I was drawn to this character because this is unlike any role I've ever auditioned for or read," Missick said in an interview with Mekeisha Madden Toby for the *Detroit News* (27 Oct. 2016). "Misty is so smart and strong and sexy and funny, but she's also a little vulnerable."

In the first season of *Luke Cage*, Missick's character is somewhat different from the comic book version—she has not yet lost her arm, let alone received a bionic one. As a police detective in Harlem, New York City, she maintains an evolving relationship with the bulletproof, superstrong Cage (played by Mike Colter), going from lovers to distrusting him to eventually realizing he might be able to help with Harlem's crime wave. She also has to confront the fact that her longtime partner was actually in the pocket of organized crime.

The thirteen-episode first season of *Luke Cage* debuted in 2016 to general critical acclaim, with many reviewers praising Missick along with other cast members. Though Netflix does not release official viewership numbers for its original programming, the show was estimated to have reached 3.5 million viewers, making it Netflix's fifth-highest rated original program. Missick herself praised the show for letting women shine. "I love how Marvel positions women in powerful roles and allow for us to do what women all across the world do every day, which is lead," she told Michael Rothman and Joi-Marie McKenzie for *ABC News* (22 June 2018).

MORE MARVEL SERIES

Missick reprised her role as Misty Knight in the miniseries *The Defenders* (2017), a crossover of the four previous Marvel Netflix series. The plot brought together the superheroes Daredevil (Charlie Cox), Luke Cage, Jessica Jones (Krysten Ritter), and Iron Fist (Finn Jones), along with supporting characters such as Knight and Colleen Wing (Jessica Henwick), to face an ancient criminal organization known as The Hand, headed by the mysterious Alexandra (Sigourney Weaver). Though the series received some mixed reviews, the acting was widely praised, including that of Missick, who appears in five of the eight episodes. Notably, Knight loses her right arm in a climactic battle, pushing her closer to her comic book portrayal.

Missick again returned as Misty in the second season of *Luke Cage*, which debuted in 2018. It depicts the character still dealing with the aftermath of her injury while at the same time attempting to get her career back into shape. Throughout the season Knight's relationship with Luke Cage continues to evolve as he faces new threats to maintaining the peace in Harlem. Meanwhile, her friendship with Colleen Wing is also further developed. "You see this wonderful relationship between Misty and Colleen onscreen," Missick explained to Rothman and McKenzie. "Again, you have two strong women, Misty is dealing with what she's dealing with and Colleen is like, 'Get it together! Pick yourself up off the ground.' To have her actions being motivated by another strong woman is important to see played out onscreen."

Perhaps the most significant development for fans of Misty Knight in *Luke Cage* season two is that she gets her iconic bionic arm, courtesy not of Tony Stark but of Danny Rand and his Rand Corporation. Missick's Knight uses the arm to considerable effect fighting alongside Cage. With the television version of Knight very close to her comic book counterpart by the end of the season, many fans—as well as Missick herself—expressed hopes that Knight and Wing might star in their own television series, based on their comic book adventures as the duo known as the Daughters of the Dragon.

OTHER ROLES

Following the second season of *Luke Cage*, Missick was scheduled to reprise her Misty Knight role in the second season of *Iron Fist.* Despite her busy schedule as a central figure in the Netflix branch of the Marvel Cinematic Universe, Missick also found time to explore other roles. In 2017 she appeared on the ABC online streaming comedy series *American Koko*, about a group of characters who run the Everybody's a Little Bit Racist Agency to help well-meaning people get out of difficult racial situations. She also starred alongside her real-life husband, Dorian Missick, in the film *Jinn* (2018), in which she plays a young mother who converts to Islam. Missick's collaboration with her husband can also been seen in *Luke Cage*, in which he played a wife-beating ex-con named Dontrell "Cockroach" Hamilton.

SUGGESTED READING

Johnson, Victoria. "Simone Missick Is the Heart of Netflix's Marvel Universe." *Complex*, 17 Aug. 2017, www.complex.com/pop-culture/2017/08/simone-missick-netflix-the-defenders-profile. Accessed 30 June 2018.

Missick, Simone. "Simone Missick on Luke Cage Season Two, Misty's Bionic Arm, and the Rise of Black Superheroes." Interview by Angelica Jade Bastién. *Vulture*, 2 July 2018, www.vulture.com/2018/07/luke-cage-season-2-simone-missick-interview.html. Accessed 13 July 2018.

Missick, Simone. "Simone Missick on 'Luke Cage' Season 2, Misty's New Arm & Her Role in 'Iron Fist' Season 2." Interview by Christina Radish. *Collider*, 23 June 2018, collider.com/simone-missick-interview-luke-cage-season-2/. Accessed 30 June 2018.

Rothman, Michael, and Joi-Marie McKenzie. "'Luke Cage' Star Simone Missick on the Power of Being a Man's Equal in Marvel series." *ABC News*, 22 June 2018, abcnews.go.com/GMA/Culture/luke-cage-star-simone-missick-power-mans-equal/story?id=56067410. Accessed 30 June 2018.

Toby, Mekeisha Madden. "Detroit Native Is a Hit in 'Luke Cage'." *The Detroit News*, 27 Oct. 2016, www.detroitnews.com/story/entertainment/television/2016/10/27/detroit-native-simone-missick-netflix-luke-cage/92856682/. Accessed 30 June 2018.

SELECTED WORKS

Luke Cage, 2016– ; *The Defenders*, 2017; *American Koko*, 2017

—Christopher Mari

Reed Morano

Date of birth: April 15, 1977
Occupation: Cinematographer, director

In 2017 Reed Morano became the first woman in twenty-two years to win an Emmy Award for directing a drama series. Morano directed the first three episodes of the award-winning Hulu original series *The Handmaid's Tale*, based on Margaret Atwood's classic 1986 novel of the same name. Before her win, Morano was best known for filming *Frozen River* (2008), which won a Grand Jury Prize at the Sundance Film Festival, and directing *Meadowland* (2015).

In 2011 Morano received a Kodak Vision Award at the Women in Film Crystal + Lucy Awards. Two years later, in 2013, she was invited to join the American Academy of Cinematographers; at the time, she was the organization's youngest member and one of only fourteen female members out of more than three hundred. The Fusion Film Festival named her their Woman of the Year in 2015, and in 2017 Morano received the Distinguished Vanguard Filmmaker Award at University of California, Los Angeles (UCLA) School of Theater, Film and Television (TFT) Festival.

As a cinematographer, Morano draws inspiration from various sources, including literature. She cites the magical realism of Gabriel García Márquez and the hard-edged realism of Charles Bukowski and Joan Didion as influences in her work. She prefers natural lighting and the movements of a hand-held camera. Her

Photo by Gregg DeGuire/Getty Images

favorite directors of photography (DPs) include Academy Award winner Conrad Hall (*American Beauty*; *Butch Cassidy and the Sundance Kid*; *Road to Perdition*), cinematographer Ellen Kuras (*Eternal Sunshine of the Spotless Mind*), and Academy Award winner Emmanuel Lubezki (*Gravity*; *Birdman*; *The Revenant*).

EARLY LIFE AND EDUCATION

Reed Dawson Morano was born in Omaha, Nebraska, on April 15, 1977, to Winslow and Lyn Mankin. After her parents divorced, Morano and her brother, Justin, moved to Long Island with their mother. There, their mother married Casey Morano, an entrepreneur who opened various businesses, including a seafood restaurant on Fire Island that members of Morano's family still run. Morano gained two stepsiblings and three younger siblings. The family moved often, living in Long Island, New Mexico, New Hampshire, and Vermont. "It was great because it taught me about all kinds of people and taught me to be adaptable as well as open to new things," Morano told author Sharon Pendana for *Pendulum* (7 June 2011). "If I had grown up in the same house all my life, I wouldn't have nearly as much material in my brain for storytelling."

Morano went to Beach Street Middle School on Long Island but attended high school in New Hampshire and Vermont. A creative child, she dreamed of becoming a writer until her stepfather gave her a video camera. She loved shooting footage of her family, and when the time came for her to apply for college, her stepfather suggested she consider film school. She enrolled at the New York University (NYU) Tisch School of the Arts to study film in the late 1990s. She began working as a production assistant and, on her first film shoot, was drawn to the role of director of photography. "To me, the DP was seeing the most action and had the most exciting job," she explained for the website *musicbed.com* (26 Apr. 2015). "Everything the audience would see, they would see through the DP's eyes." In what Morano considers a spiritually meaningful connection, she returned to her dorm room from that same shoot to receive word that her stepfather had suffered a heart attack. He died the next day. "He had been so obsessed with what I would do and what path I would take in life and I still find it interesting that right before he passed was the moment I knew what I wanted to do with my life," she told Pendana.

BREAKTHROUGH

At NYU, Morano recalled, every student seemed to want to be a director. By extension, being a DP was easy; one only had to join a project. "I felt like directing took life experience, and I didn't think I had any," she explained for *Musicbed*. Because she did not know what stories she wanted to tell, she decided to "go on other

people's adventures until [she] figured out what [her] own voice was," she said. Morano earned her bachelor of fine arts degree from NYU in 2001. (She later cotaught the school's first advanced television class as an adjunct professor of cinematography.)

For the next seven years, Morano attached herself to the adventures of others, taking every job she was offered. In 2006, she landed a DP gig on the TLC reality television show *Cover Shot*. It was the first time Morano was paid a wage that allowed her to live off her cinematography. In 2007, she was asked to work on an independent film, *Frozen River* (2008). It was the first project, she told *Musicbed*, "that felt representative of who I want to be as a filmmaker."

Frozen River, written and directed by Courtney Hunt, follows two working-class women who smuggle immigrants across the Canadian border into the United States. Several critics compared the film to a short story, with its spare, evocative details. In his review of the film for *Time* (31 July 2008), Richard Schickel lauded *Frozen River* for being "all show, no tell." The film premiered at the Sundance Film Festival—and took home the coveted Grand Jury Prize for best drama. Critics embraced the film, which was nominated for two Academy Awards: one for Hunt's original screenplay and another for lead actress Melissa Leo.

MEADOWLAND

After *Frozen River* premiered, Morano found work on a number of independent features including *Little Birds* (2011), written and directed by Elgin James, and *Yelling to the Sky* (2011), written and directed by Victoria Mahoney. In 2012, Morano worked on Korean director So Yong Kim's family drama *For Ellen* and, in 2013, John Krokidas's film *Kill Your Darlings*, starring British actor Daniel Radcliffe as Beat poet Allen Ginsberg. The latter film, set in the 1940s, tells the true story of the murder of David Kammerer. The film was moderately well received and featured some visual experimentation in homage to the defiant spirit of the Beats. In 2014, Morano served as the DP on the dramedy *The Skeleton Twins*, starring *Saturday Night Live* veterans Kristen Wiig and Bill Hader. That year Morano also returned to television, working as a DP on the pilot and first season of the dramedy *Looking*. She then served as DP for season 1 of legendary director Martin Scorsese's 1970s-era drama *Vinyl*, which aired on HBO in 2016. Later Morano worked as a cinematographer on Beyoncé's Emmy Award–nominated visual album, *Lemonade* (2016).

Morano made her directorial debut with the drama *Meadowland* (2015), starring Olivia Wilde and Luke Wilson as the parents of a missing child. The film, which Morano filmed herself, made its world premiere at the Tribeca Film

Festival and received positive reviews. *Meadowland* was also nominated for an Independent Spirit Award for best cinematography. Of Morano, Jordan Hoffman for the *Guardian* (24 Apr. 2015) wrote, "She makes terrific use of negative space in the frame . . . and avoids cliché when shooting New York. Even heartbreaking, music-drenched wanderings and searches in Times Square are filmed in shallow focus, making the familiar feel a little alien."

THE HANDMAID'S TALE

Around 2016, Morano read the pilot script for *The Handmaid's Tale*, a television adaptation of Margaret Atwood's dystopian novel about a future in which fertile women are forced to live as sex slaves. Morano was intrigued by the script but was told that she could not pitch it (bid to direct it) because Hulu had reached out to a top male director. Cunningly, Morano instead reached out to her friend Elisabeth Moss, who was cast as the protagonist, Offred, and secured a pitch meeting. In just seventy-two hours, Morano created a sixty-four-page pitch deck that demonstrated her vision for the series. Among her initial ideas, she told Jennifer Vineyard for the *New York Times* (3 May 2017), was to combine "intimate, hand-held shots" and "formal compositions" to convey extremes; she applied this unconventional idea to shifts in time as a visual cue indicating when the action is taking place. She also envisioned how the show's sound design could help create an ominous mood. The producers hired her to direct the show's first three episodes and, in doing so, gave Morano control over the series' tone. The series, premiering several months after the election of US president Donald Trump, struck a chord with both critics and audiences. The new administration's regressive attitudes toward women haunted the show's vision of a United States after a theocratic coup. *New York Times* critic James Poniewozik wrote (24 Apr. 2017) that Morano's direction "gives this nightmare a kind of serene, back-to-the-land wholesomeness that makes it all the more eerie." His reaction was echoed by renowned television critic Emily Nussbaum, who wrote in the *New Yorker* (22 May 2017) that the show dramatizes Offred's inner life by creating "gorgeous tableaux of repression." For her work, Morano received the 2017 Emmy Award for outstanding direction for a drama series.

That same year, Morano served as DP for the pilot of the HBO show *Divorce* and was nominated for the inaugural Emmy Award for outstanding cinematography for a single camera series (half hour).

In 2017 Morano directed *I Think We're Alone Now*, a postapocalyptic science-fiction film starring Peter Dinklage and Elle Fanning and slated for release in 2018. She then helmed an untitled film project about an ailing violinist, played by Jeff Bridges, and his wife, played by Diane Lane.

PERSONAL LIFE

In September 2008, Morano married Matt Walker. The couple has two sons, Casey and Fletcher. The elder, Casey, performed in *Meadowland*. Morano underwent treatment for squamous cell carcinoma in 2015 prior to filming *Meadowland*.

SUGGESTED READING

Hoffman, Jordan. "*Meadowland* Review—Every Parent's Nightmare." Review of *Meadowland*, directed by Reed Morano. *The Guardian*, 24 Apr. 2015, www.theguardian.com/film/2015/apr/24/meadowland-olivia-wilde-luke-wilson-first-look-film-review-tribeca. Accessed 2 Nov. 2017.

Morano, Reed. "Reed Morano on Directing the First Three Episodes of 'The Handmaid's Tale.'" Interview by Jennifer Vineyard. *The New York Times*, 3 May 2017, www.nytimes.com/2017/05/03/arts/handmaids-tale-director-reed-morano-interview-ofglen.html. Accessed 2 Nov. 2017.

Morano, Reed. "The Long Haul: A Conversation with Reed Morano." Interview. *Musicbed*, 26 Apr. 2015, blog.musicbed.com/articles/the-long-haul-a-conversation-with-reed-morano/49. Accessed 2 Nov. 2017.

Nussbaum, Emily. "A Cunning Adaptation of 'The Handmaid's Tale.'" Review of *The Handmaid's Tale*, directed by Reed Morano. *The New Yorker*, 22 May 2017, www.newyorker.com/magazine/2017/05/22/a-cunning-adaptation-of-the-handmaids-tale. Accessed 2 Nov. 2017.

Pendana, Sharon. "The Trove: Reed Morano Walker." *Pendulum*, 7 June 2011, pendulum-swing.wordpress.com/2011/06/07/the-trove-reed-morano-walker/. Accessed 2 Nov. 2017.

Poniewozik, James. "Review: 'The Handmaid's Tale' Creates a Chilling Man's World." Review of *The Handmaid's Tale*, directed by Reed Morano. *The New York Times*, 24 Apr. 2017, www.nytimes.com/2017/04/24/arts/television/review-the-handmaids-tale-creates-a-chilling-mans-world.html. Accessed 2 Nov. 2017.

Schickel, Richard. "The Grim Appeal of *Frozen River*." Review of *Frozen River*, directed by Courtney Hunt. *Time*, 31 July 2008, content.time.com/time/arts/article/0,8599,1828471,00.html. Accessed 2 Nov. 2017.

SELECTED WORKS

Frozen River, 2008; *Kill Your Darlings*, 2013; *Meadowland*, 2015; *The Handmaid's Tale*, 2017

—*Molly Hagan*

Maren Morris

Date of birth: April 10, 1990
Occupation: Musician

Singer-songwriter Maren Morris took Nashville by storm in 2015, when she released her self-titled EP, which fused elements of traditional or classic country music with pop, rock, R & B, and blues. The Texas native first established herself on the local music circuit as an eleven-year-old, honing her performance skills and cultivating a loyal following, thanks to years of constant touring and the release of three independent albums. In 2013, after a decade performing on-stage, a weary Morris briefly changed course by moving to Nashville, determined to reinvent herself as a professional songwriter—a decision that paid immediate dividends, with Morris landing a publishing deal in less than a year.

However, penning tracks for such well-known artists as Tim McGraw and Kelly Clarkson only served to rekindle Morris's interest in performing her own music. "At the end of the day, when I feel most at home is when I'm on-stage singing. It's transcendent, really cathartic," she told Jeff Gage for the *Dallas Observer* (11 Apr. 2017). "Whether I wrote the song or not, I just love to sing. . . . That's the most pure form of creation that I have to give to the world." A songwriting session in 2015 helped produce the soulful "My Church," which eventually became the centerpiece of her five-song EP and lead single on her critically acclaimed major-label debut in 2016. Response has been overwhelmingly positive for Morris's breakout hit, which was certified platinum and culminated in her first-ever Grammy win.

EARLY YEARS

Maren Larae Morris was born on April 10, 1990, to Scott and Kellie Morris, who named their older daughter after Maren Jensen, an actor in the 1970s sci-fi series *Battlestar Galactica*. Growing up in Arlington, Texas, Morris's interest in music began at an early age, thanks to her parents' eclectic tastes. "They had the biggest CD collection . . . from Led Zeppelin to Nirvana to Sheryl Crow to Journey to Motown," she said in an interview with Jonathan Bernstein for *Entertainment Weekly* (26 May 2016). When she was about nine or ten, she and her family embraced another musical genre. "I really started listening to Johnny Cash and Hank Williams and Patsy Cline, and that was when I realized I loved to sing." Morris's parents became aware of their daughter's talent, after hearing her serenade guests at a party with an impressive karaoke version of LeAnn Rimes's "Blue." "At one point, they were like, 'Did somebody turn the radio on?' and walked into the other room where I was," Morris recalled to Gage.

Photo by Rob Kim/Getty Images

Her parents encouraged her to develop her talent. When she was about eleven years old, she auditioned for Johnnie High's Country Music Revue, a weekly variety show at the Arlington Music Hall. The venue was located across from their family-owned, full-service salon, Maren Karsen, named after Morris and her sister. The try-out would prove life changing for Morris. "That was my first time being on stage in front of an audience with people behind me," she told Gage. "It was like, 'Oh my goodness, this is what I'm supposed to be doing.'" Bitten by the performing bug, she became a regular on the local music circuit, appearing at chili cook-offs and county fairs while singing along to prerecorded tracks.

LOCAL FOLLOWING

Morris was writing song lyrics even before her father gave her an acoustic guitar and taught her some chords at age twelve. "I loved creative writing and loved writing poems and short stories," she told Michael Bialas for the *Huffington Post* (3 June 2016). "But when I picked up the guitar, it just seemed so natural to put music to lyrics." Morris's family accompanied her to weekend gigs at local honky-tonks, including Poor David's Pub in Dallas, the White Elephant Saloon in Fort Worth, and Arlington's Grease Monkey Burger Shop & Social Club. Her father served as her roadie, booker, and manager, while her younger sister sold merchandise.

By 2005, Morris was attending James Bowie High School during the week and playing keyboard and singing harmonies for the rock band They Were Stars. That same year she released her debut record, *Walk On*, penning eight of the album's tracks, including the title tune—and theme song for the independent flick *Sweetwater* (2005). The following summer Morris was crowned Fort Worth Weekly's (FWW) Best Female Vocalist and attended the inaugural GRAMMY Camp in Los Angeles. She also played several clubs and festivals, as part of a UK tour sponsored by *Maverick Magazine*. However, failed auditions for *American Idol*, *The Voice*, *America's Got Talent*, and *Nashville Star* left her frustrated—but undeterred.

In 2007, after deciding to seriously pursue music, Morris signed with the Fort Worth–based Smith Music Group, a distribution and promotional label. She subsequently released *All That It Takes*. Her largely self-penned sophomore album yield two hits on the Texas Music Chart (the chart-topping title tune and top-five single "Dangerous"). Morris spent the next two years performing on the local music circuit while also appearing at South by Southwest (SXSW) 2008 and France's 2008 Equiblues Festival.

SONGWRITER

In the early 2010s, Morris was attending the University of North Texas and still performing locally. After one semester in college, Morris made a fateful visit to Nashville to see fellow Texan and aspiring singer-songwriter Kacey Musgraves, whom she had met on the music circuit. "I was . . . just getting into this cyclical touring, never really writing, and I just wanted to get out," Morris confided to Gage. "[Kacey] opened that door and was like, 'You should just come up here, you'll love it. You love to write, you'll learn so much from the songwriters up here.'" Morris released her third full-length album, *Live Wire* (2011). In June 2012, Morris was named New Music Seminar's Artist on the Verge, winning music equipment, as well as marketing, promotion, and consultations from several industry leaders.

In January 2013 Morris packed up her belongings in a U-Haul truck and drove to Nashville with her mom. Once there, Morris networked by attending writer nights and participating in writing rounds. Although Morris had given herself a year to land a songwriting deal, she would not have to wait that long. By September 2013, Big Yellow Dog Music had signed her to a four-year publishing deal. One of Morris's first assignments was a session with fellow singer-songwriters Ryan Hurd and Eric Arjes, resulting in the ballad "Last Turn Home," about a man finding comfort in his wife and family after being away from home. The next day her publisher sent the song to Tim McGraw, who recorded it for his 2014 disc, *Sundown Heaven Town*. In 2015 she scored a songwriting credit for "Second Wind," a track on the deluxe version of Kelly Clarkson's *Piece by Piece* (2015) album.

"MY CHURCH"

As Morris cultivated her songwriting chops, she saw a frustrating pattern developing: many of the songs she turned in were being passed over. "I started to notice publishers and my publisher telling me, 'Maren, this song is great you wrote yesterday, but I don't even know who to play it for. It sounds so you,'" she shared with *NPR* (3 Nov. 2016). "It took me a minute to realize, 'Maybe they're right.'" Morris's renewed confidence was on full display in March 2015, while attending a songwriting session in Los Angeles. The day before her meeting, Morris, still reeling from a recent breakup, took a memorable drive to the beach. "I just remember my windows were rolled down, and I saw the ocean come into view, and I remember whatever song was on the radio really moved me emotionally, and I just thought to myself, 'This is like church to me,'" she shared with Heather Stas and Brian Ives for *Radio.com* (3 June 2016). "I thought it would be a great song title, because it just sort of encapsulated all those feelings you get when you're really emotional over music." "My Church" took Morris and songwriter-producer Mike Busbee (a.k.a. busbee) less than an hour to write. They also penned the catchy pop-driven "80s Mercedes," which was inspired by friend and fellow songwriter Audra Mae's remarks about a potential love interest's well-kept car.

After becoming attached to "My Church," Morris made the decision to keep the song. In August 2015, she quietly uploaded her self-titled five-song EP to the streaming service Spotify. Within a month, "My Church" had generated more than 2.5 million streams, sparking a record label bidding war that ended in early September, when Morris joined Sony Music Nashville's Columbia Nashville imprint. Morris's label re-released her EP two months later, following her appearance at CMT's annual Next Women of Country showcase. Country audiences quickly embraced the album, which closed out November atop Billboard's Top Heatseekers chart.

ACCOLADES

Morris's EP also made an impression on country superstar Keith Urban, who invited her to join his summer tour. She kicked off 2016 with the January release of "My Church." In February Morris performed her new material while opening for Chris Stapleton during a sold-out performance at Nashville's Ryman Auditorium, once the home of the Grand Ole Opry. She then appeared at the UK's Country to Country (C2C) and SXSW in March, as "My Church" peaked at number 17 on Billboard's Digital Song Sales chart and reached the Hot Country Songs top-five. By late May Morris had made her Opry debut; the single had also cracked the top ten of the Country Streaming Songs and Country Airplay charts.

On June 3, a day after Morris had embarked on the five-month North American leg of Urban's RipCORD 2016 World Tour, her highly anticipated record debuted to critical raves. "*Hero* is destined to be recalled as one of the formidable first albums of the decade," Barry Mazor wrote for the *Wall Street Journal* (14 June 2016), while Jon Caramanica's *New York Times* review (1 June 2016) hailed it as an "outstanding major label debut . . . and perhaps the canniest country record in recent memory." *Hero* was equally embraced by fans, claiming the number-one spot on the Top Country Albums chart and reaching the Billboard 200 top five.

Morris also became a celebrated fixture at music awards shows. Her video for "My Church" was nominated for two awards—female video of the year and breakthrough video of the year—at the 2016 CMT Music Awards, where she joined Urban and Brett Eldredge for a live performance of Urban's "Wasted Time." She was also among the list of performers at the Academy of Country Music (ACM) Honors ceremony in August 2016, as well as the Fiftieth Annual Country Music Association (CMA) Awards, where she was one of the top nominees (with five nods) and new artist of the year winner. Morris's whirlwind 2016 ended with four Grammy Award nominations, the Breakthrough Artist Award at the Billboard Women in Music event, a *CMT Crossroads* special with R & B singer Alicia Keys, as well as her *Saturday Night Live* debut.

HEADLINING TOUR

By late January 2017, "80s Mercedes" had become Morris's second hit single, reaching the top 20 of the Billboard Hot Country Songs and Country Airplay charts. In February Morris bested Urban, Carrie Underwood, Miranda Lambert, and Brandy Clark to claim her first Grammy Award, for best country solo performance. Morris's duet with Keys was among the evening's highlights. That month Morris achieved another milestone, when she embarked on the winter/spring leg of her first headlining tour, the HERO Tour 2017, which lasted nearly two months; Hurd served as her opening act. She followed that up with release of the raw, emotional breakup ballad "I Could Use a Love Song" in late March and an appearance on the Thomas Rhett duet "Craving You," which they debuted at April's ACM Awards, where Maren was crowned new female vocalist of the year.

After receiving the Music Business Association's prestigious Breakthrough Artist Award in May 2017, Morris performed at the CMA Music Festival in early June before heading out on the road again, as the opener for Sam Hunt's four-month 15 in a 30 Tour. She launched the fall leg of her tour in October—the same month Morris debuted the Vince Gill duet "Dear Hate," her tribute to victims of the 2017 Las Vegas

mass shootings that topped the Billboard Country Digital Song Sales. Morris returned to the CMA Music Awards in November, as a three-time nominee (in the female vocalist, music video, and musical event categories) and as a performer, duetting with One Direction's Niall Horan on his folk-pop song "Seeing Blind." She subsequently kicked off the UK and Ireland leg of her HERO Tour. Morris's year ended on a high note, with a Grammy nomination for best country solo performance for "I Could Use a Love Song," which went on to become Morris's first solo number-one hit on the Billboard Country Airplay chart in January 2018.

Along with cowriting all eleven tracks on her debut, Morris has penned tunes for Jessie James Decker, the Brothers Osborne, and the cast of ABC's *Nashville*. In 2017 she signed a modeling contract with the Wilhelmina agency and guest starred on an episode of the CBS drama *NCIS: New Orleans*.

PERSONAL LIFE

Morris, an East Nashville resident, has been dating Hurd since December 2015. The pair became engaged in 2017.

SUGGESTED READING

Bernstein, Jonathan. "Maren Morris Previews *Hero*, Keith Urban Tour," *Entertainment Weekly*, 26 May 2016, ew.com/article/2016/05/26/maren-morris-hero-keith-urban-tour/. Accessed 12 Jan. 2018.

Bialas, Michael. "Hero Worship: Maren Morris Can Begin Telling Her Musical Glory Story," *HuffPost*, 3 June 2016, www.huffingtonpost.com/michael-bialas/hero-worship-maren-morris_b_10273058.html. Accessed 12 Jan. 2018.

Caramanica, Jon. "Review: Why 'Hero' Is an Outstanding Country Debut," Review of *Hero*, by Maren Morris. *The New York Times*, 1 June 2016, www.nytimes.com/2016/06/02/arts/music/maren-morris-hero-review.html. Accessed 12 Jan. 2018.

Gage, Jeff. "'This Is Not Just Country': Maren Morris on Her Jump from DFW Bar Singer to Headlining Star," *Dallas Observer*, 11 Apr. 2017, www.dallasobserver.com/music/the-true-story-of-country-music-star-maren-morris-rise-from-dfw-bars-to-nashville-royalty-9348705. Accessed 12 Jan. 2018.

Ives, Brian, and Heather Stas. "Maren Morris Finds Her 'Church' at the Ryman,'" *Radio.com*, 3 June 2016, news.radio.com/2016/06/03/maren-morris-my-church-ryman/. Accessed 12 Jan. 2018.

SELECTED WORKS

Walk On, 2005; *All That It Takes*, 2007; *Live Wire*, 2011; *Maren Morris EP*, 2015; *Hero*, 2016
—*Bertha Muteba*

Carla Morrison

Date of birth: July 19, 1986
Occupation: Singer

Latin Grammy Award–winning indie singer Carla Morrison released her most recent album, the critically acclaimed *Amor supremo* (Supreme love) in 2015. Morrison got her musical start as the lead singer of the indie trio Babaluca. Her singular style combines such disparate influences as country singer Patsy Cline and English rock star Morrissey. She is classified as an indie singer, though she disputes the label. "Indie is not a genre," she told Randy Cordova for the *Arizona Republic* (21 May 2013). "It's an independent way of doing stuff. My music is pretty alternative, but it's ballads. It's very Mexican, but at the same time, it's very pop." Morrison's musical style has expanded since her 2012 album, *Déjenme llorar* (Let me cry). Her 2015 album, *Amor supremo*, ditches acoustic guitars for dramatic synthesizers and organs, but her commitment to her own independence remains the same. She releases her albums through the distribution label Cosmica in Los Angeles but has not yet signed with a major recording label. Morrison is a major figure in Mexico's thriving indie music scene, though she is known throughout the Latin music world.

EARLY LIFE AND BABALUCA

Carla Patricia Morrison Flores was born on July 19, 1986, in Tecate, Baja California, a small town on the US–Mexico border near San Diego, California, and home of Tecate Brewery. In an interview with Rachel Martin for NPR's *Weekend Edition* (22 Nov. 2015), Morrison described her father as a "surfer guy" who introduced her to the Beach Boys, Rocío Dúrcal, and Patsy Cline. "She's one of my main inspirations," Morrison told Martin, "because my dad used to play her all the time and I would think, 'Who is this lady and why is she so hurt?'" Another inspiration was her mother, who sang while completing household chores.

Morrison has been singing all her life, though she did not sing publicly until she performed in a school talent show when she was fifteen. When she was seventeen, she moved to Arizona. She attended Marcos de Niza High School in Tempe, and after graduation, began taking music classes at Mesa Community College, in Mesa. Morrison struggled in school. "I used to flunk my music classes," Morrison recalled to Yezmin Villarreal for the *Phoenix New Times* (22 May 2013). "I couldn't pass piano, music theory, or guitar. I just couldn't do it. I preferred to take the route of learning it by myself." Morrison taught herself keyboard and then guitar, the instrument for which she is best known.

By Diario de Madrid, via Wikimedia Commons

Morrison dropped out of college to join a Tempe-based indie band called Babaluca, with Niki Petta and Nick Kizer. During the three years Morrison was with Babaluca they enjoyed an enthusiastic and diverse following. Emma Breysse, who wrote about the band for the *Phoenix New Times* (4 Dec. 2008), suggested that this was because their sound was so unique, "a beguiling brand of sparse indie rock that's simultaneously cutesy and devious." Morrison was the group's lead singer and wrote most of their bilingual lyrics. "Sometimes I can explain myself better in English, but sometimes in Spanish," she told Breysse. In 2007 Babaluca released a self-titled EP. Despite the band's loyal following, Morrison grew discouraged. Her brother, who had studied computer science, encouraged her to keep pushing herself and to have faith. She left the band and moved to Mexico City to pursue a solo career.

MIENTRAS TÚ DORMÍAS AND *DÉJENME LLORAR*

Morrison built a following by posting songs on the Internet. In 2009, she released her debut EP, *Aprendiendo a aprender* (Learning to learn), which Cosmica released in a deluxe version a year later, along with her first full-length album, *Mientras tú dormías* (While you were sleeping). The latter included an acoustic duet with Mexican pop singer Natalia LaFourcade (who produced the album) called "Pajarito del amor" (Lovebird), as well as her breakout single, "Compartir" (Sharing). Jasmine Garsd, who wrote about the song for *NPR* (24 Aug. 2010), compared Morrison's voice on the record to Etta

James and Eartha Kitt. The song, Garsd wrote, is "a beautiful love ballad about wanting to share yourself with someone you love, but who is far away." *Mientras tú dormías* was nominated for a Latin Grammy Award for Best Alternative Album. In 2011, Morrison released an EP called *Jugando en serio (Seriously playing)*, which was re-released in 2013.

Morrison's fame was solidified with the release of her solo studio album, *Déjenme llorar* in 2012. "I was making music for the longest time and then all this happened very quickly," she later told Cordova. Like the title track, featuring Latin Grammy Award–winning singer-songwriter Leonel Garcia, the album is full of acoustic, heartfelt love songs. She sings on "Déjenme llorar," "Let me cry alone, I want to get this off my chest." Referring to Morrison's performance on the album, Joshua Rothman wrote for the *New Yorker* (10 Dec. 2015), "There's humility to her heartbreak—a lightness to her sadness that makes it magnetic." *Déjenme llorar* won a Latin Grammy Award for Best Alternative Music Album, and "Déjenme llorar" won for Best Alternative Song in 2012. When she went onstage to accept her award, Morrison famously blurted out, "Viva Mexico Ch——" (Viva f——ing Mexico) on live television.

AMOR SUPREMO

In 2014, Morrison sang a popular duet called "A donde van los muertos" (Where the dead go) with Kinky, a band from Monterrey, Mexico. She also appeared on the song "Moon Never Rises" from Calexico's 2015 album *Edge of the Sun*. Most of Morrison's 2015 full-length album *Amor supremo* was recorded over the course of eight months in a beach house in Playas de Tijuana. With brothers Alejandro (Jandro) and Damien Jiménez producing, Morrison went through a collection of nearly thirty songs she had written over the previous few years. "I felt like remaking myself and doing something completely different," she told Judy Cantor-Navas for *Billboard* (28 Sept. 2015). The secluded setting let Morrison disengage from the more cerebral aspects of making an album. "I . . . was very much guided by my emotions and feelings; [the Jiménez brothers] were like the mind of the project, I was the soul," she said in an interview for *Rictus* magazine (6 Nov. 2015). The album's tone, expansive and more electronic than acoustic, reflects inspirations such as the sounds of the nearby ocean and the 2014 science fiction film *Interstellar*. Morrison collaborated with two drummers, Esteban Vaquez and Omar Cordoba, and recorded some of her vocals at her mother's house in Tecate.

Amor supremo was released in November 2015. It received a slew of enthusiastic reviews. Stephen M. Deusner for *Pitchfork* (5 Nov. 2015), who described Morrison's voice as somewhere between Florence Welch of the English rock band Florence and the Machine and the late singer-songwriter Jeff Buckley, called *Amor supremo* "one of the most rewarding and genuinely moving pop albums of 2015." Deusner particularly appreciated a song called "No vuelvo jamás" (I'm never coming back), about how love can hurt more than a physical wound. A lush, reverb-laden anthem, the song is a stark sonic departure for Morrison. As Deusner wrote, "This is pop music with a healthy sense of grandeur." Ben Ratliff, in his review for the *New York Times* (4 Nov. 2015), wrote that the album exists in a state of "lucid dreaming." Ratliff tentatively compared Morrison to Lana del Rey "for the way both singers make words and phrases stretch and swoop, and how they perform romantic sadness as ritual," but he added that "Morrison's voice is lighter and stronger, far more subtle, and she's not playing with her public image nearly as much. These are reports from the inside of the head, love songs about the contents of one soul's being decanted into another." The songs on *Amor supremo* often describe, as Ratliff put it, "a kind of love in which there is no separation, no independent will." On the percussive "Un beso" (A kiss), which reminded Rothman of the English rock band Joy Division, Morrison imagines fusing herself to her lover; on "Mi secreto" (My secret) she describes her love as a secret that exists only for her. References to other artists are no accident; she told Rothman, "We, as Mexicans, or Latin Americans, are always being inspired by these international artists. I thought, 'Why shouldn't we try something like that, too?'"

In 2016, the song "Vez primera" (The first time) from *Amor supremo* won a Latin Grammy Award for Best Alternative Song. That same year, she won critical acclaim for her featured performance on "The Train," a song from the album *This Unruly Mess I've Made* by the hip-hop duo Macklemore.

PERSONAL LIFE

Morrison lives in Mexico City.

SUGGESTED READING

Cantor-Navas, Judy. "Carla Morrison Discusses Her 'Conceptual' and 'Emotional' New Album." *Billboard*, 28 Sept. 2015, www.billboard.com/articles/columns/latin/6708166/carla-morrison-discusses-album. Accessed 15 May 2018.

Cordova, Randy. "Carla Morrison Making Music on Her Terms." *The Arizona Republic*, 21 May 2013, www.pressreader.com/usa/the-arizona-republic/20130521/282389807008960. Accessed 15 May 2018.

Deusner, Stephen M. Review of *Amor supremo*, by Carla Morrison. *Pitchfork*, 5 Nov. 2015, pitchfork.com/reviews/albums/21243-amor-supremo/. Accessed 15 May 2018.

Martin, Rachel. "Carla Morrison Looks Hard at Love's Gray Areas." *Weekend Edition*, NPR, 22 Nov. 2015, www.npr.org/2015/11/22/456545222/carla-morisson-looks-hard-at-loves-gray-areas. Accessed 15 May 2018.

Morrison, Carla. "Rictus Interviews Indie Superstar Carla Morrison, Talk New Record, Getting Rid of Her Folky Guitar." Interview. *Rictus*, 6 Nov. 2015, rictus.co/carla-morrison-interview-1/. Accessed 15 May 2018.

Ratliff, Ben. "Review: In Carla Morrison's 'Amor Supremo,' Love and the Void." Review of *Amor supremo*, by Carla Morrison. *The New York Times*, 4 Nov. 2015, www.nytimes.com/2015/11/05/arts/music/review-in-carla-morrisons-amor-supremo-love-and-the-void.html. Accessed 15 May 2018.

Rothman, Joshua. "Listen to Carla Morrison." *The New Yorker*, 10 Dec. 2015, www.newyorker.com/culture/culture-desk/listen-to-carla-morrison. Accessed 15 May 2018.

SELECTED WORKS

Aprendiendo a aprender, 2009; *Mientras tú dormías*, 2010; *Déjenme Llorar*, 2012; *Amor Supremo*, 2015

—Molly Hagan

CHRIS J RATCLIFFE/AFP/Getty Images

Fiona Mozley

Date of birth: February 26, 1988
Occupation: Author

Fiona Mozley has been lauded as an up-and-coming literary light since her debut novel, *Elmet*, was long-listed for the 2017 Man Booker Prize, the prestigious literary honor presented annually for the year's best original English-language novel published in the United Kingdom. Yet perhaps the most remarkable aspect of Mozley's achievement is that *Elmet* made the long list prior to its publication and shortly thereafter became a finalist before losing to George Saunders's *Lincoln in the Bardo* (2017). At twenty-nine years old, Mozley has produced something remarkable: an almost mythic novel with considerable international appeal that simultaneously maintains a distinctively British tone about life in modern Yorkshire in the north of England—impressive stuff for someone who had not sought a life as an author. In an interview with Hayley Maitland for *Vogue* (16 Oct. 2017), Mozley reflected: "I never made a conscious decision to have writing be my profession. It was more that I was keen to write a novel, but I had no idea if I would be able to finish it, let alone get it published." Noting the instability of the writing profession, she added, "It's only after everything that's happened with the Man Booker Prize shortlist that I have reluctantly started describing myself as a novelist."

EARLY LIFE AND EDUCATION

The younger of two daughters, Mozley was born on February 26, 1988, in Hackney, London, and grew up in York. Her father, Harold, was a social worker; her mother, Caroline, became head of research and development at York Health Services NHS Trust. During her childhood, Mozley and her sister attended the Fulford School, where they became known for their habitual lateness. Mozley recalled in an article she wrote for the *Guardian* (30 Sept. 2017): "I was renowned for having the second to worst punctuality record in its forty-something-year history, eclipsed in that department only by my older sister. It's true that I wasn't always thrilled by the prospect of school, but it wasn't this that kept me away." She explained how, amid morning preparations like bathing or dressing herself, she "would fall into a daydream, a deep stupor, and would be entirely unable to pull myself out of it."

Despite her frequent lateness, Mozley excelled and in 2006 was accepted to King's College at the University of Cambridge. After graduating with a master's degree in history and philosophy of science in 2010, she lived for about six months in Buenos Aires, Argentina, where she taught English. She returned to the United Kingdom in 2011, first interning at a London literary agency, then working as a travel agent.

WRITING PROCESS

The inspiration for Mozley's acclaimed first novel came during a return train trip from a visit to her family in York. At the time, she was sharing a cramped house in Honor Oak Park, just south of London, with five friends. The living arrangement wasn't totally legitimate either, as she was an unauthorized sub-lessor. Mozley recalled to Susannah Butter for the *Evening Standard* (28 July 2017) how her situation was taking its toll: "I was finding London life difficult—the strain of the capital was taking hold. I was living for the next pay cheque and at a loose end. I didn't know what career I was going to have or where I was going to live in the next year." She soon found her vocation while watching the Yorkshire scenery pass by as she journeyed back to London from a weekend at home. She has said in several interviews that the view, and musings about the lives of the people in the homes she saw, inspired her to write the entire first chapter of her first novel, then and there.

The book would be titled *Elmet*, after the name of the ancient Celtic kingdom that flourished from the fifth to seventh centuries CE where Yorkshire now exists. She imagined a mountain of a man living there in the countryside, along with his two teenage children. As she worked in snatched moments of time, often writing sections of the book on her phone and while commuting, the detailed filled themselves in: the man would be named John Smythe and would squat on a piece of land where he teaches his children to forage, hunt, and plant. The story would be narrated by Daniel, the younger of the two, and would feature his resourceful sister, Cathy.

As Mozley worked diligently for three years on the book, she told almost no one that she was writing a novel, until after she had signed the contract with her publisher. "When I started, I didn't mention it to anyone. And it just became a secret project that I pursued in the evenings and weekends," she explained to Scott Simon in an interview for *NPR* (16 Sept. 2017). "And as I got closer and closer to finishing, I felt that if I did tell someone then, it would make it even less likely to happen. So I kept it quiet."

ELMET

What Mozley wanted most was to capture the nature of the land itself in northern England, which had shaped the people who had worked it for centuries, until it was no longer necessary for them to do so. "There's this community that, at one point, all lived on the land and worked the land, and then were dragged from the land and into the mines or the mills because of the Industrial Revolution," Mozley said in an interview with Richard Lea for the *Guardian* (17 Aug. 2017). "Then the mines and the mills were no longer profitable, so we spat all these people out. But we don't give them back the land, so what do they do?"

In Mozley's novel, the family of John, Cathy, and Daniel retreat to a house John had built himself in the woods of Yorkshire, on a piece of property he did not own. John decides to bring his teenagers there after his fifteen-year-old daughter is punished in school for fighting bullies. The family quickly learns how to live off the land, eating deer, doves, and skylarks they hunt with homemade bows and arrows, while at the same time foraging or growing whatever fruits and vegetables they need. John—often described as a giant of a man—earns his living in illegal fights or as hired muscle. He teaches his children to be self-sufficient, which Cathy takes to readily but gives fourteen-year-old Daniel more trouble, as he is sensitive, skinny, and pale, a foil to his enormous, powerful father. The differences between brother and sister are highlighted during their visits to Vivien, a family friend, who teaches Daniel about history, poetry and art, and travel as his sister roams the gardens, woodlands, and fields. Troubles enter their lives in the form of Price, a man with whom John has had a long and complicated history. Price owns the land on which John has built the family home, and he is also the boss of a number of workers and land tenants John has aided and helped to organize for better conditions.

MAN BOOKER AND CRITICAL RECEPTION

Two weeks before the book was to be published in early August 2017, Mozley, who by then was working weekends at Little Apple Bookshop, was having coffee in a café when she received a call from her editor. "I thought she'd managed to secure a good quote for the front cover," Mozley said to Lea. "It was obviously good news. I could tell from the tone of her voice." As it turned out, her editor at John Murray Originals informed her that *Elmet* had been longlisted for the prestigious Man Booker Prize. The novel subsequently made the shortlist for the prize, which carries a purse of £50,000.

Although Mozley did not win, critics on both sides of the Atlantic heaped on praise following the novel's publication. A reviewer for the *Economist* (5 Aug. 2017) called Elmet "a dark and delicate fairy-tale of contemporary Britain" and "a quiet explosion of a book, exquisite and unforgettable." They further note, "Each carefully chosen detail illuminates the novel's themes of violence and exploitation. Yet far from being bleak, 'Elmet' is beautiful. Ms Mozley writes with clarity and insight, and her descriptions of the natural world and human relationships are both specific and profound." A critic for *Kirkus Reviews* (31 Oct. 2017) declared: "Part fairy tale, part coming-of-age story, part revenge tragedy with literary connections, Mozley's first novel is a shape-shifting, lyrical, but dark parable of life off the grid in modern Britain." The *Kirkus* reviewer went on to conclude, "Mozley's instantaneous success . . . is a response to the stylish intensity of her work, which boldly winds multiple genres into a rich spinning top of a tale." Not all reviews glowed so unequivocally, however. Critics for the *New York Times* and *Publishers Weekly* tempered their commendations, noting that although Mozley's power of description is strong and her blend of literary allusion deft, the violence seems overwrought and the villains one-dimensional.

PERSONAL LIFE

Mozley resides with her partner, fellow doctoral student Megan Girdwood, and their dog, Stringer, in her native York. There Mozley is pursuing her doctorate at the University of York's Centre for Medieval Studies. Her PhD thesis is on the place of forests in the late Middle Ages in England. She continues to work part time in the Little Apple Bookshop, where she occasionally sells copies of her own critically acclaimed novel to customers. When not working on her PhD, she continues to write fiction—that is, whenever she can rouse herself out of the sort of daily daydreams that helped her craft *Elmet*. Mozley is reportedly planning a second novel.

Mozley enjoys science fiction and westerns, music by the Yorkshire band Pulp, electric guitars, vintage film cameras, and fantasy football. She hopes one day to incorporate her knowledge about these esoteric subjects into her fiction.

SUGGESTED READING

Butter, Susannah. "Fiona Mozley: I Wrote a Novel on My Commute—Now It Might Win the Booker Prize." *Evening Standard*, 28 July 2017, www.standard.co.uk/lifestyle/london-life/fiona-mozley-i-wrote-a-novel-on-my-commute-now-it-might-win-the-man-booker-prize-a3598686.html. Accessed 11 Jan. 2018.

"Elmet." *Kirkus Reviews*, 31 Oct. 2017, www.kirkusreviews.com/book-reviews/fiona-mozley/elmet. Accessed 30 Dec. 2017.

"Fiona Mozley Is a Rising Star of British Fiction." *The Economist*, 5 Aug. 2017, www.economist.com/news/books-and-arts/21725754-29-year-olds-debut-novel-has-just-been-longlisted-2017-man-booker-prize-fiona. Accessed 30 Dec. 2017.

Lea, Richard. "'I Already Feel Like I've Won': Fiona Mozley, the New Face on the Booker Longlist." *The Guardian*, 17 Aug. 2017, www.theguardian.com/books/2017/aug/17/fiona-mozley-debut-novel-elmet-booker-longlist Accessed 30 Dec. 2017.

Maitland, Hayley. "Fiona Mozley on Her Debut Novel Being Shortlisted for the Man Booker Prize." *Vogue*, 16 Oct. 2017, www.vogue.co.uk/article/fiona-mozley-elmet-man-booker-prize-2017-interview. Accessed 30 Dec. 2017.

Mozley, Fiona. "Fiona Mozley: I'm on the Man Booker Shortlist and Top of My Fantasy Football League." *The Guardian*, 17 Sept. 2017, www.theguardian.com/books/2017/sep/30/fiona-mozley-elmet-my-writing-day. Accessed 30 Dec. 2017.

Simon, Scott. "Debut Author Channeled Her 'Darker Bits' into a Man Booker Shortlist Novel." *Weekend Edition Saturday*, NPR, 2 Dec. 2017, ww.npr.org/2017/12/02/567465301/debut-author-channeled-her-darker-bits-into-a-man-booker-shortlist-novel. Accessed 30 Dec. 2017.

—*Christopher Mari*

Antonio Muñoz Molina

Date of birth: January 10, 1956
Occupation: Author

Antonio Muñoz Molina is one of Spain's most celebrated contemporary writers. Since launching his career in the 1980s, he has done extensive journalistic work and authored more than a dozen novels, most of which have been constructed from seminal moments in Spanish history. Often blending reality and fantasy, his novels, which are written in Spanish and have received numerous literary honors, are known for their originality and complexity. They combine modern and postmodern flourishes with "a sweeping narrative energy that devotes itself to large questions as well as to minute levels of feeling and examinations of motive," as the Irish writer Colm Tóibín wrote for the *New York Review of Books* (10 July 2014).

Muñoz Molina was not well known outside Spanish-language literary circles until his novels started being translated into English in the 2000s. The most notable of these include *Sefarad* (2001; *Sepharad*, 2003), which traces the persecution of Jews throughout history; *La noche de los tiempos* (2009; *In the Night of Time*, 2013), a sprawling examination of the Spanish Civil War; and *Como la sombra que se va* (2014; *Like a Fading Shadow*, 2017), which taps into the mind of James Earl Ray, the assassin of civil rights leader Martin Luther King Jr.

EARLY LIFE

Antonio Muñoz Molina was born on January 10, 1956, in Úbeda, a city in the Andalusia region in southern Spain. He has a sister who is five years his junior. His father was a small farm owner and his mother was a homemaker. Despite growing

Mariusz Kubik, via Wikimedia Commons

up in a peasant farming family, he has said that he enjoyed a privileged upbringing compared to his parents, both of whom were forced to drop out of school as young children during the Spanish Civil War.

An inquisitive child, Muñoz Molina reveled in stories of the war told by his father and maternal grandfather, the latter of whom spent nearly two years in a concentration camp during the war. Such stories, as well as other reminders of the war, from maimed veterans to defaced walls and statues, made an impression on his young mind.

The first member of his family to receive a formal education, Muñoz Molina identified early on with marginalized groups of people, developing a class consciousness that would later surface in his novels. He first desired to become an author at the age of twelve after discovering the works of French writer Jules Verne. "Before that, I didn't know there was such a thing as writers," he told Maya Sela for Haaretz (21 Jan. 2011), adding that "the moment I realized that the books I loved so much had authors, I wanted to be the person who wrote them."

In addition to Verne, Muñoz Molina started reading works by such authors as Alexandre Dumas, Agatha Christie, Henry James, and Mark Twain. Later, his literary influences came to include those from his own country, namely Miguel de Cervantes, Gustavo Adolfo Bécquer, and Federico García Lorca.

EARLY CAREER

After graduating from high school, Muñoz Molina briefly studied journalism in the Spanish capital of Madrid before enrolling in 1974 at the University of Granada, where he switched his focus to art history. He lived in Granada for roughly the next twenty years. For seven of those years, he worked in the city as a municipal employee. In 1982, he began publishing his first articles in the newspaper Diario de Granada. Writing for the newspaper, Muñoz Molina noted in an autobiographical profile posted on his website, "taught me to write with regularity and discipline, with fixed limits."

Muñoz Molina's first published book, El Robinson urbano (1984), features a collection of his articles for the paper. Though the self-published book received only limited distribution around Granada, it caught the attention of a mainstream editor who helped him land a contract for his first novel, Beatus Ille, which was published in Spain in 1986. That year the novel, which Muñoz Molina reportedly began in 1976, shortly after the death of Spanish dictator Francisco Franco, was awarded the Icaro Prize. The English-language version of the novel, A Manuscript of Ashes, translated by Edith Grossman, appeared in 2008.

Set against the backdrop of the Spanish Civil War and Franco's subsequent dictatorship, the novel follows a university student, Minaya, who in 1969 is arrested in Madrid for protesting. After being released from jail, Minaya flees to his uncle Manuel's house in Mágina, an imaginary Andalusian city modeled after Muñoz Molina's birthplace and which figures in several of his later books. He arrives there to investigate the life of his uncle's deceased best friend, the radical poet Jacinto Solana, who briefly lived with Manuel before being executed by Franco's troops. In the process, Minaya uncovers a dark mystery surrounding the 1937 death of Manuel's wife, Mariana, an artist's model who was also loved by Solana.

Part detective story, part psychological horror, A Manuscript of Ashes helped introduce the complex style that has come to characterize many of Muñoz Molina's novels, which often feature sweeping historical backdrops, labyrinthine plots, characters both real and imagined, long, complex sentences and paragraphs, and probing questions about memory and the nature of time. Reviewing the novel for the Los Angeles Times (27 Aug. 2008), Tim Rutten called Muñoz Molina "an important writer unafraid of ideas, emotions, and genuine beauty."

RISE TO INTERNATIONAL ACCLAIM

Muñoz Molina's next novel, El invierno en Lisboa (1987; The Winter in Lisbon, 1999), marked his literary breakthrough. Drawing inspiration from film noir and jazz music, the atmospheric novel centers on a jazz pianist, Santiago Biralbo, who finds himself embroiled in a web of crime and intrigue after becoming enchanted by the wife of an American art dealer. In 1988, it was honored with two of Spain's premier literary prizes, the Premio de la Crítica and the Premio Nacional de Literatura. An eponymous film version of the novel, directed by José A. Zorrilla and featuring music by jazz legend Dizzy Gillespie, was released in 1991.

The success of *El invierno en Lisboa* enabled Muñoz Molina to leave his job as a municipal employee and begin concentrating on his writing career full-time. He produced a steady stream of fiction over the next decade, during which he received many awards and honors. His 1991 novel *El jinete polaco* (The Polish horseman), which explores the relationship between memory and desire through the journey of a pair of Spanish expatriates, was awarded that year's Planeta Prize and earned the Premio Nacional de Literatura in 1992. In 1995, he became the youngest person to be elected to the Royal Spanish Academy.

Concurrently with his fiction, Muñoz Molina wrote extensively for Spanish newspapers, magazines, and journals. He contributed regular articles to the Spanish national daily *ABC*, and in 1990, began a longstanding relationship with *El País*, Spain's leading newspaper, for whom he has written a weekly column. He also contributed a monthly science column to the magazine *Muy Interesante* and wrote about music for the journal *Scherzo*. In his autobiographical profile, Muñoz Molina wrote that the article "can be a sovereign form of literature."

SEPHARAD AND IN HER ABSENCE

Despite his esteemed literary reputation at home, Muñoz Molina remained relatively unknown outside of Spain until 2003, when *Sepharad*, the English-language version of his highly acclaimed 2001 novel *Sefarad*, was published. Taking its title from the Judeo-Spanish, or Ladino, word for Spain, the wildly ambitious novel, which was translated by Margaret Sayers Peden, is comprised of seventeen interconnected stories, all of them connected to Jews who have been persecuted in and exiled from Spain across time. It is told by an elusive first-person narrator who relates intricately woven tales about fictional and real-life exiles, chronicling such major historical events as the expulsion of the Jews from Spain in 1492, the purges led by Soviet communist leader Joseph Stalin in the 1930s, the Spanish Civil War, and the Holocaust.

Described as a fictionalized memoir-cum-history, the novel, which includes appearances by such famous figures as Franz Kafka, Walter Benjamin, Jean Améry, and Primo Levi, offers a powerful commentary on the preservation of memory as it relates to horrors of the twentieth century. In a review of *Sepharad* for the *New York Times* (21 Dec. 2003), Michael Pye called Muñoz Molina "fearless" and "an intensely self-conscious writer," commenting that the novel "has all the onward rush and effortfulness of an epic."

Muñoz Molina continued to bolster his international profile with a diverse array of well-received translations. These included the short novel *En ausencia de Blanca* (1999; *In Her Absence*, 2006, translated by Esther Allen), which takes inspiration from Henry James's 1898 horror novella *The Turn of the Screw*. It tells the story of a Spanish provincial clerk, Mario, who comes to suspect that his pretentious, art-loving wife, Blanca, has vanished and left him with a mysterious doppelganger.

IN THE NIGHT OF TIME

For the novel *La noche de los tiempos* (2009; *In the Night of Time*, 2013), Muñoz Molina returned to the subject of exiles, again using the backdrop of the Spanish Civil War for an elaborate story about an emotionally conflicted Spanish architect, Ignacio Abel, who embarks on a life-changing journey to America after abandoning his wife and two children in war-torn Madrid. There, he hopes to be reunited with an American woman, Judith Biely, with whom he had a passionate extramarital affair in Madrid during the buildup to the war.

Echoing many of Muñoz Molina's other novels, *In the Night of Time* features a mix of real and imagined characters and delves deep into the nature of time, memory, and love, as Ignacio repeatedly revisits defining moments in his life. Praised for its meticulous attention to historical accuracy and detail, the 600-plus-page novel, which was translated into English by Edith Grossman, won the prestigious French literary prize the Prix Mediterranée Étranger in 2012, and was widely hailed as a masterpiece.

In a review for the *Washington Post* (2 Jan. 2014), Marie Arana called *In the Night of Time* "one of the most eloquent monuments to the Spanish Civil War ever to be raised in fiction." Meanwhile, Colm Tóibín, in his article for the *New York Review of Books*, commented that the novel, like all of Muñoz Molina's fiction, "has a sense of the past as a living force, darting, shifting, haunting, impossible to pin down."

LIKE A FADING SHADOW

Muñoz Molina's next major novel, *Como la sombra que se va* (2014; *Like a Fading Shadow*, 2017), similarly brought the past to vivid life, this time retracing the steps of James Earl Ray in the weeks following his assassination of Martin Luther King Jr. on April 4, 1968. Like *Sepharad*, the novel blurs the boundaries between fiction, memoir, and history. It focuses particularly on a ten-day stint Ray had in Lisbon, Portugal, during his two-month flight from the authorities. Ray's stay in Lisbon, however, makes up only one strand of the novel, which also includes parallel narratives chronicling Muñoz Molina's own real-life visits to the city as a young writer and his present-day musings on youth, love, life, and literature.

Containing a dizzying amount of detail, *Like a Fading Shadow* expertly probes the psychology of an assassin, in addition to offering an illuminating portrait of a writer and his craft. As Jacob Silverman wrote for the *New Republic* (16 Aug. 2017), it is ultimately "a book about its own creation that lays bare the mechanics of fiction, questioning whether they work at all while simultaneously arguing for the importance of fictionalizing history."

In 2018, *Like a Fading Shadow* was shortlisted for the Man Booker International Prize, which is awarded annually to a single literary work that has been translated into English and published in the United Kingdom. In an interview for the prize's official website (17 Apr. 2018), the novel's translator, Camilo A. Ramirez, called Muñoz Molina "one of the most creative writers working today—always willing to take risks and push the limits of what is possible within the novel form."

PERSONAL LIFE

Muñoz Molina resides in Madrid with his wife, Elvira Lindo, a Spanish journalist and writer. He has three children from his first marriage. He served as director of the Cervantes Institute in New York from 2004 to 2006 and has taught at such American institutions as the City University of New York (CUNY) and Bard College. In 2013, he received the Jerusalem Prize and the Prince of Asturias Award for Literature for his influential body of work.

SUGGESTED READING

Muñoz Molina, Antonio. "Antonio Munoz Molina: Self-Portrait." *Antoniomunozmolina.es*, xn--antoniomuozmolina-nxb.es/biografia/. Accessed 21 June 2018.

Muñoz Molina, Antonio, and Camillo Ramirez. "*Like a Fading Shadow* Interview." *The Man Booker Prize*, 17 Apr. 2018, themanbookerprize.com/news/fading-shadow-interview. Accessed 21 June 2018.

Sela, Maya. "Dreaming of Something Better." *Haaretz*, 21 Jan. 2011, www.haaretz.com/1.5111140. Accessed 21 June 2018.

Silverman, Jacob. "Can a Historical Novel Be Too Deeply Researched?" Review of *Like a Fading Shadow*, by Antonio Muñoz Molina. *New Republic*, 16 Aug. 2017, newrepublic.com/article/144356/can-historical-novel-deeply-researched. Accessed 21 June 2018.

Tóibín, Colm. "Lust and Loss in Madrid." Review of *The Infatuations*, by Javier Marías, and *In the Night of Time*, by Antonio Muñoz Molina. *The New York Review of Books*, 10 July 2014, www.nybooks.com/articles/2014/07/10/lust-and-loss-madrid/. Accessed 21 June 2018.

SELECTED WORKS

Beatus Ille (A Manuscript of Ashes), 1986; *El invierno en Lisboa (The Winter in Lisbon)*, 1987; *Sefarad (Sepharad)*, 2001; *En ausencia de Blanca (In Her Absence)*, 2001; *La noche de los tiempos (In the Night of Time)*, 2009; *Como la sombra que se va (Like a Fading Shadow)*, 2014

—*Chris Cullen*

Kacey Musgraves

Date of birth: August 21, 1988
Occupation: Singer-songwriter

Grammy Award winner Kacey Musgraves does not particularly care for the "rebel" label often hung around her neck—it is one that gets tossed around easily in the country music world. It is safe to say, however, that the music she produces is unlike much of what is coming out of Nashville, Tennessee, the nation's country music capital, these days, with its powerful descriptions of bleak prospects in small towns, celebrations of casual sex and marijuana, and, on her 2018 record *Golden Hour*, the transcendent joys of romantic love. By pressing hard against the more restrictive measures in country music, even if that means less airplay time on mainstream country radio, Musgraves has forged a place in the country music scene by being unlike anyone else; she is considered by fans and critics alike to be among the brightest lights shining out of Nashville. "She's a rarity in this business, someone who refuses to be anyone but herself," Shane McAnally, a major country songwriter and producer, told Skip Hollandsworth for *Texas Monthly* (Mar. 2018). "And believe me, it takes a lot of courage in Nashville not to do what other people say you should be doing."

EARLY LIFE

Kacey Musgraves, born on August 21, 1988, was raised in the small town of Golden, Texas. Her father, Craig, owns a small printing business located about seven miles away in Mineola, where her mother, Karen, sometimes helps out when not working on her own art, and where Musgraves also worked for a time. Growing up, she was also close to her grandmother, who lived nearby and provided additional support for her musical passion.

By BruceC007 via Wikimedia Commons

Music filled Musgraves's household when she was young. Not just country, but also Neil Young, the Beach Boys, and even the Spice Girls. Before long, Musgraves was writing her own music as well. "Kacey would listen to whatever we were playing, and then she'd go to her bedroom and write her own songs," Craig Musgraves told Hollandsworth. "She wrote one called 'Movin' On,' which was about someone moving off his farm because all the crops had died and there was no water for the cattle. . . . I listened to it and said to Karen, 'You know, there's something going on here.'"

Having also started singing at a young age, Musgraves was performing at local opry venues and talent shows around Texas, singing classic country tunes by performers like Patsy Cline and Roy Rogers. She and her younger sister, Kelly, also performed in the Cowtown Opry Buckaroos, a local children's country music group. She also did yodeling duets with her friend Alina Tatum under the name the Texas Two Bits. The pair proved so popular they were asked to perform at the Texas State Society's Black Tie & Boots ball for President George W. Bush's inauguration in 2001. Her sister later went on to become a photographer and assists Musgraves with her professional and album photos.

MAKING MUSIC

Musgraves's songwriting developed further around the age of twelve, when she began taking guitar lessons. Learning from veteran teacher John DeFoore, she was encouraged to write and have her songs critiqued regularly. As early as

2002, she even began recording her own albums independently. Such early records—*Movin' On* (2002), *Wanted: One Good Cowboy* (2003), and *Kacey Musgraves* (2007)—are hard to come by these days, which is fine by the artist herself. "In the beginning, I wrote OK songs, but they didn't have a unique perspective," she said in an interview with Tim Lewis for the *Guardian* (31 Aug. 2013). "I had songs that would have worked for a female country singer, but it was boring to me because it had already been done. Like the angry female song: you left me and I'm angry about it. People would probably like that and it's not a bad song but I'm not an angry female. I have moments where I am, but I feel like that's a shtick in country music."

After graduating from Mineola High School in 2006, Musgraves, who admits she was never the best student, declined to go to college to focus seriously on a career in music. She moved to Austin, Texas, and got some gigs in small clubs, typically playing a mix of her own material with works by famed recording artists like Young and Willie Nelson. She then tried out for *Nashville Star*, the USA network's country music competition. She was urged to audition by country music star Miranda Lambert, who had made her name on the show and who shared the same music teacher with Musgraves. Despite qualifying for *Nashville Star* in 2007, Musgraves came in a disappointing seventh. At the same time, she has recognized in later interviews that she had not quite found her musical identity by that point. "I prefer a more organic approach to music," she said to Patrick Doyle for *Rolling Stone* (9 June 2015). "Nobody even remembers I did that, so it's fine."

THE NASHVILLE COUNTRY SCENE

Musgraves then tried to make a name for herself in Nashville. "I mean there are other ways people will find you, but just for me jumping into the scene and really wanting to get better at songwriting, I just knew I had to be here," she explained to Michael Bialas for the *Huffington Post* (18 Mar. 2013) of her decision to leave Texas for Nashville. Breaking in was slow going at first. She supported herself initially with various jobs that included dressing as cartoon characters for birthday parties.

Before long, Musgraves was making inroads into the Nashville country scene. She found work as a backup and demo singer. Then, a big break came when the music publisher Warner/ Chappell offered her a job as a staff songwriter, a role in which she would be teamed up with another writer or a pair of writers to produce hits for established artists. Some of her coauthored works were successful: Lambert recorded "Mama's Broken Heart," Martina McBride recorded

"When You Love a Sinner," and Gretchen Wilson recorded "Get Outta My Yard."

Musgraves's songwriting helped to open doors for her around Nashville. In 2011, after she had already formed friendships and begun working on material with songwriters and producers McAnally and Luke Laird, she met with Stephanie Wright, an A&R executive for the Universal Music Group Nashville, who immediately saw Musgraves's talent and potential. She agreed to sign—first with the imprint Lost Highway before a company reorganization rendered the imprint defunct and she was transitioned to Mercury Nashville—but only if she could control her major-label debut's content. She also wanted her rawer song, "Merry Go 'Round," about the realities of life in a small town, to be the first single. The record company executives resisted that, concerned that the content would not prove popular, but she pressed them. "They said it was too down, too depressing for a new female country artist," she told Hollandsworth. It eventually rose to the top ten on Billboard's Country Airplay chart.

SAME TRAILER DIFFERENT PARK

When her debut, *Same Trailer Different Park*, was released in early 2013, it went straight to the top of Billboard's Top Country Albums chart, primarily on the strength of Musgraves's writing—which was generally more rebellious than the staid Nashville country music scene was used to. One song, "It Is What It Is," describes no-strings casual sex. Some of Musgraves's other songs were also considered risqué in the conservative country music world. Lewis noted that "mainstream country has never seen anyone quite like Musgraves. . . . The heartland is religious, monogamous and conservative. . . . Musgraves is certainly not the first to have rebelled against these traits . . . but her assault is particularly threatening. Not only does she believe you should have sex with who you want, when you want; another of her songs (Follow Your Arrow) approves of smoking joints and gay relationships." Musgraves earned two Grammy Awards in 2014: Best Country Song, for "Merry Go 'Round," and Best Country Album, for *Same Trailer Different Park*. Between the two categories, she was put up against the likes of Lambert and Taylor Swift.

Pageant Material, Musgraves's 2015 followup album, again had her battling with her record label over content. Initially, the label wanted her to push the release date back, which she resisted. Then they wanted her to change a line in her single, "Biscuits," from "Pissing in my yard ain't gonna make yours any greener" to "Spitting in my yard ain't gonna make yours any greener." Because the line got such a great response when she performed it live, she again resisted label interference and kept the lyric as it was. Part of the difficulty she faced, she admits, is that none of her writing was like what was selling across the country music world. "[Label executives will say], 'We need an uptempo for summer, and it needs to be this long.' It's like, 'What happened to just a good song?'" she said to Doyle. *Pageant Material*, like its predecessor, debuted at number one on Billboard's Top Country Albums chart.

GOLDEN HOUR

In keeping with her eclectic nature, Musgraves decided to make a Christmas album, *A Very Kacey Christmas* (2016), her next release. For that project, she recorded just a few holiday standards, like "Have Yourself a Merry Little Christmas" and "Let It Snow," and instead opted for more eccentric covers, such as the Chipmunks' "Christmas Don't Be Late" and Gayla Peevey's "I Want a Hippopotamus for Christmas." She also sang a duet with one of her heroes, Nelson, on "A Willie Nice Christmas."

Continuing to find success and attract even people who would not normally consider themselves country music fans, Musgraves then released her 2018 effort, *Golden Hour*, to stellar reviews; the album was her third to debut atop the Billboard Top Country Albums chart. Writing for *Billboard* (29 Mar. 2018), Natalie Weiner called *Golden Hour* "a lovely, unexpectedly romantic record with two early singles, 'Butterflies' and 'Space Cowboy,' already hailed as among 2018's best yet." Musgraves's songwriting had been inspired by the development of her relationship with the singer-songwriter Ruston Kelly, who is now her husband. She met Kelly in 2016 at a Nashville writers' "round"—in which country performers sit onstage and perform new songs they have composed—and was struck by the power of Kelly's work. *Golden Hour* chronicles the development of their romance and the joy it has brought to Musgraves's life. In an interview for *All Things Considered* (1 Apr. 2018), Musgraves told Sarah McCammon, "With this record I tried to change it up a little bit. This record to me is all about feeling. It's not about thinking as much. My prior records have been more about thinking—thinking about each line, thinking about the way that I'm flipping a phrase. And thinking is great, but if you have all thought no feeling . . . I think that's a mistake."

Although this record is far different from Musgraves's previous major studio releases, no one should expect her to continue to write solely in a romantic vein. She wants to continue to explore a wide variety of styles and bring them into her music, telling Myles Tanzer for the *Fader* (Mar. 2018), "I mean you won't find somebody who loves country music more than me, the bones of the genre, the traditional country music, but I don't want that to limit me also."

PERSONAL LIFE

Musgraves and Kelly began dating in 2016. After becoming engaged on Christmas Eve, the couple were married in Tennessee in October 2017. They live in Nashville.

SUGGESTED READING

Doyle, Patrick. "Unbreakable Kacey Musgraves: Nashville's Sharpest Rebel Walks the Line." *Rolling Stone*, 9 June 2015, www.rollingstone.com/music/music-country/unbreakable-kacey-musgraves-nashvilles-sharpest-rebel-walks-the-line-67448. Accessed 10 Sept. 2018.

Hollandsworth, Skip. "Kacey Musgraves Has a Surprise for Nashville." *Texas Monthly*, Mar. 2018, www.texasmonthly.com/the-culture/kacey-musgraves-surprise-nashville. Accessed 10 Sept. 2018.

Lewis, Tim. "Kacey Musgraves: 'I Don't Want to Be the McDonald's of Music.'" *The Guardian*, 31 Aug. 2013, www.theguardian.com/music/2013/sep/01/kacey-musgraves-interview-same-trailer. Accessed 10 Sept. 2018.

Musgraves, Kacey. "Kacey Musgraves Knows Love Makes the World Go Round." Interview by Myles Tanzer. *The Fader*, Mar. 2018, www.thefader.com/2018/03/22/kacey-mugraves-golden-hour-interview. Accessed 10 Sept. 2018.

Musgraves, Kacey. "Kacey Musgraves on Her Stunning New Album, Nashville Double Standards, and How Psychedelics Made a 'Giant Impression' on Her." Interview by Natalie Weiner. *Billboard*, 29 Mar. 2018, www.billboard.com/articles/news/magazine-feature/8265267/kacey-musgraves-interview-billboard-cover-story-2018. Accessed 10 Sept. 2018.

Musgraves, Kacey. "Kacey Musgraves on Trusting Emotion at the 'Golden Hour' of Her Life." Interview by Sarah McCammon. *All Things Considered*, NPR, 1 Apr. 2018, www.npr.org/2018/04/01/596131754/kacey-musgraves-on-trusting-emotion-at-the-golden-hour-of-her-life. Accessed 10 Sept. 2018.

SELECTED WORKS

Same Trailer Different Park, 2013; *Pageant Material*, 2015; *A Very Kacey Christmas*, 2016; *Golden Hour*, 2018

—Christopher Mari

James Nachtwey

Date of birth: March 14, 1948
Occupation: Photojournalist

One of the world's most respected and decorated photojournalists, James Nachtwey has poignantly captured through his camera lens some of the most chilling and iconic images of the last forty years. He has covered virtually every major global armed conflict and social crisis since 1980, the year he launched his career as a freelance magazine photographer. A longtime contract photographer with *Time* magazine, he is known for taking photographs, usually in black and white, that place the viewer in the same space as the subject. This intimate approach has led to many brushes with death, but he has nonetheless handled his work with a grace, reverence, and unflinching sense of purpose that has separated him from many of his contemporaries. As Nachtwey told Hilary Roberts for the website of *Canon Europe* (23 May 2018), "I work in the moment . . . . My pictures are not intended to confirm what I already know. The process of photography is a way of exploring reality in real time, and real space."

Among many other honors, Nachtwey has been awarded the Robert Capa Gold Medal, the Overseas Press Club of America (OPC)'s highest honor, on five occasions, and in 2007, won a coveted TED Prize for his contribution to photojournalism. He was the subject of the highly acclaimed documentary *War Photographer* (2001), has published several photography books, and

By Voice of America, via Wikimedia Commons

has had his work exhibited at institutions around the world.

EARLY LIFE AND EDUCATION

Nachtwey was born on March 14, 1948, in Syracuse, New York, and grew up in Massachusetts. He has spoken little of his upbringing and personal life in interviews, in an attempt to focus attention solely on his work. However, in his interview with Roberts, he admitted that there was "nothing in my background growing up that would have indicated any interest or aptitude in photography."

After graduating from high school, Nachtwey attended Dartmouth College in New Hampshire. There, he studied art history and political science, graduating cum laude in 1970. Heavily influenced by the antiwar and civil rights movements of the 1960s, Nachtwey became interested in pursuing a career as a photographer after viewing the works of influential British photojournalists Larry Burrows and Don McCullin. As Nachtwey explained to Anne Strainchamps for *Wisconsin Public Radio* (11 Sept. 2015), "I saw that pictures could not only record history, they could help change the course of history, by becoming an element in the process of change."

Diving headlong into the profession, following a six-month stint as a cook with the US Merchant Marine, Nachtwey began teaching himself photography by taking pictures on a borrowed camera. He read books on how to expose and develop film and printed his own photographs using rented darkroom spaces. He also created fake magazine assignments for himself to help build a professional portfolio. During this time, he worked as an apprentice news film editor and a truck driver.

EARLY CAREER

Yearning to contribute to the exciting, fast-paced daily news cycle, Nachtwey applied to newspapers all over the country, and in 1976 accepted a job from the *Albuquerque Journal* in New Mexico. He worked there for the next four years, during which he made "every mistake known to man," as he quipped to Roberts, while learning the ins and outs of photojournalism. Covering everything from local news to state-fair pumpkin-carving contests, he has credited several of the newspaper's staff photographers with taking him under their wing and mentoring him.

In 1980, Nachtwey quit his job at the *Journal* and drove to New York to begin a freelance career. That year he began a five-year association with the Black Star photo agency, which was then run by Howard Chapnick, a pioneering figure in contemporary photojournalism. Chapnick took an instant liking to Nachtwey, and in 1981, sent him, at his own request, to Belfast,

Northern Ireland, to cover the Irish Republican Army (IRA) hunger strikes. Speaking of his first foreign assignment, Nachtwey recalled to Tom Seymour for the *British Journal of Photography* (24 Apr. 2015), "I was greener than the grass. But I wasn't scared of the situation. I just circulated the city, looking for trouble—and I found plenty."

Nachtwey's images of the violence that erupted around Belfast in response to the strikes, in which ten IRA prisoners, led by Bobby Sands, starved themselves to death in protest over inhuman jail conditions, were soon featured in a six-page spread in *Newsweek*. Upon returning to New York, Nachtwey felt restless, so much so that he flew out to Lebanon to cover the civil war there just two weeks later. His work in that country resulted in the first of five OPC Robert Capa Gold Medal awards for best published photographic reporting in 1983. (He also won the award in 1984, 1986, 1994, and 1998.)

For the rest of the 1980s, Nachtwey concentrated almost exclusively on covering global armed conflicts, compiling extensive photographic essays that chronicled wars in Guatemala, Nicaragua, El Salvador, Afghanistan, and Sri Lanka. Many of his photos appeared in *Time* magazine, for whom he became a contract photographer in 1984. Earning the label of a war photographer, Nachtwey said during a TED Talk (Mar. 2007) that he became "driven by an inherent sense that a picture that revealed the true face of war would almost by definition be an anti-war photograph."

DESCENT INTO THE INFERNO

Nachtwey broadened his focus to include social crises after the fall of the Berlin Wall in November 1989, which set in motion the collapse of Communism throughout Eastern Europe. The overthrow of Communist leader Nicolae Ceauşescu in Romania prompted Nachtwey to travel to that country, in part because of its remoteness in relation to other Eastern European countries.

As he has done in many instances throughout his career, Nachtwey self-financed his trip there without an assignment. He soon discovered an orphanage filled with thousands of children, most of whom suffered from physical birth defects. Subjected to barbaric conditions, the children were deemed among the country's "incurables" under the Ceauşescu regime. "It was different from the kind of violence I had witnessed in wars," Nachtwey explained to Roberts. "It was state sanctioned, institutionalized cruelty to completely innocent human beings and it really shook me up."

Nachtwey's experience in Romania helped lay the groundwork for a decade-long project that became his second book, *Inferno* (1999).

(His first book, *Deeds of War*, was published in 1989 and has long been out of print.) The large-format coffee-table book features 382 of Nachtwey's most powerful and thought-provoking black-and-white photographs, which were taken in war-torn and crisis-plagued countries around the world during the 1990s.

Upon its publication, the book was described by Douglas Cruickshank for *Salon* (10 Apr. 2000) as "a guided tour of hell." That tour included Nachtwey's coverage of the wars that resulted from the breakup of Yugoslavia in the early 1990s; the famines that struck Somalia and Sudan, in 1992 and 1993, respectively; the 1994 genocide in Rwanda; the civil war in Afghanistan that occurred after the Taliban seized control of the country in 1996; and the poverty that afflicted Indonesia in the wake of the resignation of dictator Suharto in 1998.

Among the most unsettling photographs in *Inferno* are from the Rwandan genocide, in which approximately 800,000 people, mostly members of the Tutsi ethnic group, were massacred over a three-month period by Hutu extremists. Somberly summing up the violence that occurred, one Nachtwey photograph simply depicts a pile of thousands of discarded machetes near the border between Rwanda and Zaire (now the Democratic Republic of Congo).

SEPTEMBER 11 WORK AND *WAR PHOTOGRAPHER*

Most of Nachtwey's work has appeared in black and white, a stylistic preference because "it distills the essence of what's happening without competing with color," as the photographer told Luis Carballo for *Euronews* (21 Oct. 2016). However, some of the most iconic images of his career—those which chronicled the September 11, 2001, terrorist attacks on the World Trade Center's Twin Towers in New York City—were taken in color.

On the morning of the attacks, Nachtwey, who had arrived home to his New York apartment late the previous night from a trip to France, rushed to the site, located just blocks away from where he lived, and started taking photographs. Among the best-known of those photographs was one showing the south tower collapsing, with the cross of a church starkly placed in the foreground. Immediately after taking the photograph, which was the last on a roll of thirty-six exposures, Nachtwey leapt into a nearby building to avoid the impact of flying debris. In the Wisconsin Public Radio article, he said to Strainchamps, "For over twenty years, I'd been covering what I thought were separate events in the Islamic world. . . . At that moment, history crystallized and I realized they were all connected."

Two months after September 11, Nachtwey appeared in the documentary *War Photographer* (2001), directed by the Swiss filmmaker Christian Frei. The film chronicles Nachtwey's travels to hostile areas of Indonesia, Kosovo, and Palestine during the late 1990s and early 2000s, and features interviews with his close friends and colleagues. Shot mostly on a special micro-camera that was affixed to Nachtwey's still camera, it received widespread critical acclaim, including earning an Academy Award nomination for best documentary feature.

Screened at film festivals all over the world, *War Photographer* significantly raised Nachtwey's public profile. It did little, however, to distract him from his work. That relentless dedication nonetheless led to another close brush with death in 2003, when Nachtwey suffered shrapnel wounds in a grenade attack while covering a platoon in Baghdad during the Iraq War. Undaunted, he returned to Iraq in 2006 to document the experiences of wounded US military veterans.

TED AWARD AND *MEMORIA* EXHIBITION

Nachtwey's interests have also extended to global health issues, which he began documenting in 2000. It was while covering the AIDS crisis in Africa that he first encountered the ravages of tuberculosis (TB). In 2007, upon winning the TED Prize, which came with a $100,000 award to help fulfill one wish to spark global change, Nachtwey used his prize money to focus on the disease, which is "a vital story that needs to be told," as he said in his TED Talk. He photographed TB victims at a hospital in South Africa, as well as in other places like Cambodia and Siberia, to build awareness about an extremely deadly form of TB known as extreme or extensively drug-resistant tuberculosis (XDR-TB). A collection of those photos was featured as part of an exhibition, titled *Struggle to Live: The Fight against TB*, which opened at 401 Projects, a gallery in Manhattan, in 2010.

Throughout his career, Nachtwey has had his work showcased at other exhibitions held at institutions and galleries all over the world. A comprehensive and definitive retrospective of his work, *Memoria*, debuted at the Palazzo Reale in Milan, Italy, in 2017. The exhibition, which Nachtwey helped curate, is divided into seventeen sections and features two hundred of his most significant photos, including his more recent work covering the refugee and migrant crisis in Europe in 2015 and 2016. It will travel to other museums worldwide; a companion book, *Memoria*, is slated for publication in the United States in November 2018.

In 2017, Nachtwey, who has also been a longtime chronicler of drug addiction, was commissioned by *Time* to document the opioid crisis in

America, which is the worst addiction epidemic in the country's history. That work resulted in a photographic essay called "The Opioid Diaries," which *Time* published in a special edition issue in February 2018. It marked the first time in the magazine's ninety-five-year history that an issue was devoted entirely to one photographer's work.

PERSONAL LIFE

A. O. Scott described Nachtwey, who has never married or had children, as being "thin and soft-spoken" with "the manner of an ascetic who has subsumed all his ego and passion into his morally and physically demanding work." This unyielding commitment has resulted in numerous awards and honors. In addition to his five Robert Capa Gold Medal awards and a TED Prize, Nachtwey has won, among many others, seven Magazine Photographer of the Year awards, three International Center of Photography Infinity awards, and two World Press Photo awards.

Nachtwey has also been the recipient of a number of honorary degrees, including one from Dartmouth, his alma mater, in 2010. He donated his life's work—an archive of more than 500,000 images—to Dartmouth's Hood Museum of Art in 2016.

SUGGESTED READING

Nachtwey, James. "James Nachtwey's 'Inferno.'" Interview by Douglas Cruickshank. *Salon*, 10 Apr. 2000, www.salon.com/2000/04/10/inferno/. Accessed 31 May 2018.

Nachtwey, James. "Remembering 9/11 through Lens of a Photojournalist." Interview by Anne Strainchamps. *Wisconsin Public Radio*, 11 Sept. 2015, www.wpr.org/remembering-9-11-through-lens-photojournalist. Accessed 31 May 2018.

Nachtwey, James. "'I Believe in the Power of Information': James Nachtwey in Conversation with Hilary Roberts." Interview by Hilary Roberts. *Canon Europe*, 23 May 2018, www.canon-europe.com/pro/stories/james-nachtwey-memoria-interview/. Accessed 31 May 2018.

Scott, A. O. "Witnessing the Witness: Looking over a Shoulder at War's Deprivation." Review of *War Photographer*, directed by Christian Frei. *The New York Times*, 19 June 2002, www.nytimes.com/2002/06/19/movies/film-review-witnessing-the-witness-looking-over-a-shoulder-at-war-s-deprivation.html. Accessed 31 May 2018.

Seymour, Tom. "James Nachtwey—The Improviser." *British Journal of Photography*, 24 Apr. 2015, www.bjp-online.com/2015/04/james-nachtwey-war-reporter-photography/. Accessed 31 May 2018.

SELECTED WORKS

Deeds of War, 1989; *Inferno*, 1999; *Memoria*, 2018

—Chris Cullen

Tomislav Nikolić

Date of birth: February 15, 1952
Occupation: President of Serbia

Tomislav Nikolić, a former ultranationalist and associate of former Serbian president and indicted war criminal Slobodan Milošević, was elected to a five-year term as president of Serbia in 2012.

EARLY LIFE AND EDUCATION

Tomislav Nikolić was born on February 15, 1952, in Bajčetina, a village near Kragujevac, Serbia, then a republic of Yugoslavia. After graduating from Technical High School in Kragujevac, he studied at the Faculty of Economics and Engineering Management in Novi Sad (now a part of University Business Academy).

In 1971 Nikolić began working as a construction technician for a railway company and helped build several bridges on the Belgrade Bar railway line. He left that position in 1978 and joined a public utilities company in his hometown, where he was responsible for overseeing the town's cemeteries. This job later earned him the nickname of Undertaker.

POLITICAL CAREER

Nikolić became active in politics shortly after the Communist Party in Yugoslavia ended its monopoly on political parties. He was first active with the People's Radical Party and helped the party merge with the local chapter of the Serbian Chetnik Movement to form the Serbian Radical Party (SRS) in 1991. The SRS's founder and president, Vojislav Šešelj, became his mentor, and Nikolić was named the party's vice president.

Nikolić was elected to the National Assembly of Serbia in 1992 and was reelected to every subsequent term. From March 1998 to June 1999, he served as the deputy prime minister of Serbia. Two months later, he became the deputy prime minister of the Federal Republic of Yugoslavia and served until 2000.

Nikolić first ran for president in 2000 as the SRS candidate of the Federal Republic of Yugoslavia, which consisted of Serbia and Montenegro and were two of the former Yugoslavia's six republics. This election was a critical time in Serbia's history. A nationalist movement calling for the creation of a Greater Serbia, or one state for all Serbs, had gained strength since four republics broke away from Yugoslavia. Led by Slobodan Milošević, then president of the Federal Republic of Yugoslavia and a former president of Serbia, Serbians fought with ethnic Albanians, Croatians, and Muslim Slavs in pursuit of this goal. In 1999 war broke out between Serbia and ethnic Albanians in Kosovo, and NATO–led forces ended the fighting in 2000. By then, Serbia's economy was severely damaged, and voters were dissatisfied with the nationalist movement. Voters were also dissatisfied with the efforts of the International Criminal Tribunal for the former Yugoslavia (ICTY) at The Hague to bring individuals accused of war crimes to trial. Milošević had been indicted in 1999 and many Serbians objected to his trial being held outside of Serbia. Nikolić, who had been the deputy prime minister during Milošević's presidency, ran against Milošević and four other opponents. Both Nikolić and Milošević lost, with Nikolić gaining only 6 percent of the vote.

Nikolić continued to advocate for a Greater Serbia and to attend rallies in support of individuals indicted for war crimes. He ran again in the November 2003 Serbian presidential election on an ultranationalist platform that opposed cooperation with the ICTY. Although he won the largest share of votes, he was not elected president due to low voter turnout. One year later, Nikolić ran again, campaigning on an anti-extradition platform. He was defeated by Boris Tadić in the final round but obtained 45 percent of the vote to Tadić's 53 percent.

In 2008 Nikolić ran for president of Serbia, which had broken away from Montenegro in 2006. Once again, he lost to Tadić, and shortly after the election, he left the SRS and formed the Serbian Progressive Party (SNS). He was elected the party's president and then distanced himself from his ultranationalist past and close alliance with Milošević and other accused war criminals, such as his former mentor Šešelj. No longer calling for a Greater Serbia, Nikolić adopted a pro-Western stance and sought to strengthen ties with Europe and the United States.

At the time of the 2012 presidential election, Serbia was facing serious economic problems with unemployment at nearly 24 percent. Nikolić campaigned on pledges to revitalize the economy by creating jobs, attracting foreign investments, and increasing taxes for high wage earners. In the second round of the election, he narrowly defeated incumbent president Tadić and was sworn in on May 31, 2012.

Following his victory, Nikolić stepped down as president of the SNS. His predecessor had started Serbia on the path to joining the European Union (EU) and Nikolić promised to continue this goal. In April 2013, he helped overcome one of the major obstacles blocking this goal when he signed an agreement normalizing relations between Serbia and Kosovo. Formal accession negotiations began in January 2014.

IMPACT

Since taking office, Tomislav Nikolić has formed close relations with both Western and Eastern countries. He has increased foreign investments in Serbia and visited numerous countries to strengthen political relations. While continuing to profess a desire for Serbia to join the EU, he has continued a foreign policy at odds with the EU by maintaining close ties with Russia. He also has asserted that Serbia would never agree to recognize Kosovo as an independent country—a condition for joining the EU.

PERSONAL LIFE

Nikolić and his wife Dragica Nikolić have two adult sons, Radomir and Branislav, and several grandchildren.

SUGGESTED READING

Bideleux, Robert, and Ian Jeffries. *The Balkans: A Post-Communist History.* New York: Routledge, 2007. Print.

Bilefsky, Dan. "Newly Elected, Serb Affirms Commitment to Joining European Union." *New York Times.* New York Times, 21 May 2012. Web. 2 Apr. 2016.

Fortin, Jacey. "Tomislav Nikolic, Former Milosevic Ally, Wins Serbian Presidency over Incumbent Boris Tadic." *International Business Times.* IBT Media, 21 May 2012. Web. 2 Apr. 2016.

"Serbia Will Never Lose Kosovo, but in Pristina I'm Not President—Serbia's Leader to RT." *RT.* Autonomous Nonprofit Organization, 2 June 2013. Web. 2 Apr. 2016.

"Tomislav Nikolič, President: Biography." *Predsednik.rs.* General Secretariat of the President of the Republic of Serbia, n.d. Web. 20 Apr. 2016.

—Barb Lightner

Kei Nishikori

Date of birth: December 29, 1989
Occupation: Tennis player

When Japanese tennis player Kei Nishikori moved to the United States in 2003, his coaches at Florida's prestigious IMG Academy had big plans for him. Nicknaming the teenager Project 45, they hoped that he would not only become a successful tennis player but also rise to the rank of forty-five or higher in the world rankings for male tennis players. By doing so, he would achieve a new milestone for a Japanese player by surpassing a record previously set by retired

By Carine06 [CC BY-SA 2.0], via Wikimedia Commons

player Shuzo Matsuoka. The efforts of Nishikori and his training team paid off, with the player surpassing Matsuoka's record in 2011 and rising into the top ten in 2014. As he rose through the rankings, Nishikori experienced significant success as a player, amassing eleven titles on the elite Association of Tennis Professionals World Tour between 2008 and 2016. He also excelled beyond that tour, taking home a bronze medal in men's singles tennis at the 2016 Olympic Games. In addition to gaining a devoted following in his native Japan, Nishikori has continually impressed tennis professionals and commentators with his efforts on the court. "Kei is one of the few players that I'd pay money to see play," veteran tennis star Andre Agassi told Hannah Beech for *Time* (9 Jan. 2015). "He's one of the greatest shotmakers in the game."

EARLY LIFE AND TRAINING

Nishikori was born on December 29, 1989, in Matsue, Japan. His father, Kiyoshi, is an engineer, and his mother, Eri, teaches piano. He has a sister named Reina. Nishikori began playing tennis at the age of five thanks to his father, who gave him a children's racket that he purchased while traveling in the United States for business. He demonstrated a talent for the sport as a young child and went on to find success in junior tennis competitions in his home country, winning events such as the All-Japan Selected Junior Tennis Championship and the All-Japan Elementary School Tennis Championship.

In 2003, Nishikori moved to the United States to train at IMG Academy, a Florida boarding school that integrates academic studies with intensive athletic training. A major force in the development of successful tennis players, the tennis training program's alumni included major players such as Andre Agassi, Maria Sharapova, and Serena and Venus Williams. Nishikori was able to attend IMG Academy with financial support from the Masaaki Morita Tennis Fund, a fund founded by a former CEO of the Sony Corporation and established for the benefit of developing Japanese tennis players.

Although Nishikori was enthusiastic about the opportunity to train at IMG Academy, the move to Florida was a challenging one, as the young player sought to learn English and adjust to a new culture. "I didn't know how to express my opinions," he told Beech. "I was a bit afraid to say what I thought because I hadn't yet been influenced by American culture." He also had to learn how to play against older players. "Even if I really respected them, I had to learn to get angry and surpass these athletes in competition," he recalled to Beech. As he trained, he gained the nickname Project 45, a reference to the world ranking of forty-six previously set by Japanese tennis player Shuzo Matsuoka. Nishikori and his coaches sought to beat that record, and he would eventually achieve that goal in October 2011.

PROFESSIONAL TENNIS

Nishikori made significant strides in competition beginning in 2006. During that season, he played in a variety of developmental tournaments organized by the International Tennis Federation (ITF) and also began competing on the Association of Tennis Professionals (ATP) Challenger Tour, a tour ranked just below the prestigious ATP World Tour. He competed in both singles and doubles tournaments during that year and made it to the finals of the ITF Mexico F18 competition and the semifinals of several events, including the ITF Mexico F4 tournament and USA F24 competition.

In 2007 Nishikori officially went pro, making his first ATP World Tour appearance in April of that year as part of the qualifying round of the US Men's Clay Court Championship in Houston, Texas. During 2007 he also participated in a variety of ITF, ATP Challenger Tour, and ATP World Tour events and notably made his first appearance in a Grand Slam tournament, participating in the qualification round for the US Open. In addition to the US Open, the Grand Slam tournaments encompass the Australian Open, French Open, and Wimbledon, and are generally considered to be the premier tournaments in professional tennis.

Nishikori won his first ATP World Tour title in February 2008 at Florida's Delray Beach Open, defeating American player James Blake to win the title. For Nishikori, the win was both thrilling and unbelievable. "I tried to imagine winning this final, but couldn't," he told Sandra Harwitt for *ESPN* (19 Feb. 2008). "I was so nervous in the first set I can't believe I beat James Blake." The youngest player to win an ATP World Tour title in a decade, he won more than $68,000 in prize money and gained significant attention from tennis fans and the media for the first time in his career. Nishikori competed in several events during the following year, but was inactive for the majority of 2009 after an elbow injury required surgery. He won several ATP Challenger Tour titles the following year and in 2011 competed primarily on the ATP World Tour, advancing to the finals at the US Men's Clay Court Championship and the Swiss Indoors Basel event.

CAREER SUCCESS

Over the following years, Nishikori amassed a variety of major career victories, including a win at the 2012 Japan Open in Tokyo. That year also saw his best Grand Slam performance to date, with Nishikori proceeding to the quarterfinals at the Australian Open. He would later play in the quarterfinals in 2015 and 2016 as well. Nishikori also won the Memphis Open four years in a row beginning in 2013, and in 2014 he claimed a total of four titles in one year.

In May 2014, after winning the quarterfinals of the Madrid Open, Nishikori made headlines by becoming the first male Japanese tennis player to be ranked among the top ten players in the world tennis rankings. He was also the first male player from Asia to reach that rank in a decade. Although pleased about that development, Nishikori understood that his top-ten status could be fleeting. "My goal is not to get one time into the top ten," he said, as quoted by the Associated Press (AP) for *ESPN* (12 May 2014). "Hopefully I can keep this ranking." He went on to win additional titles in 2015 and 2016, including at the Citi Open in Washington, DC.

Among the most exciting achievements for Nishikori came in 2014, when he beat six other players to advance to the finals of the US Open. His defeat of Serbian player Novak Djokovic in the semifinals came as a surprise to observers, as Djokovic had previously competed in four consecutive US Open finals. Although Nishikori lost in the finals to Croatian player Marin Čilić, his success at the US Open further established him as a major competitor in addition to earning him more than $1.4 million in winnings. Although he was eliminated in the first round of the US Open the following year, Nishikori performed well in the 2016 competition, moving on to the semifinals before losing to Swiss player Stan Wawrinka, the eventual champion.

OLYMPIC COMPETITOR

Nishikori made his first appearance in the Olympic Games in 2008, having been selected by the International Tennis Federation to participate in the games in Beijing, China. He was ultimately eliminated from the singles competition during the round of sixty-four, losing to German player Rainer Schuettler. Nishikori returned to Olympic play at the 2012 Summer Olympics in London, which proved to be far more productive for the player than his debut Olympics. Nishikori defeated Australia's Bernard Tomic, Russia's Nikolay Davydenko, and Spain's David Ferrer to proceed to the singles quarterfinals, where he fell to Juan Martín del Potro of Argentina. He also partnered with fellow Japanese player Go Soeda in the doubles competition, but the pair was eliminated in the round of thirty-two, losing to Wawrinka and fellow Swiss player Roger Federer.

At the 2016 Olympic Games in Rio de Janeiro, Nishikori focused solely on the singles tournament, defeating players Albert Ramos-Viñolas of Spain, John Milman of Australia, Andrej Martin of Slovakia, and Gaël Monfils of France to proceed to the semifinals. Although he lost to the eventual gold medalist, United Kingdom's Andy Murray, he made a strong effort in the bronze medal match against Spanish former gold medalist Rafael Nadal. "I got a bit tired, and [Nadal] started playing better. For sure I was rushing to win in the last couple of points," Nishikori recalled following the match, as quoted by Kelly Fleck for *Nikkei Voice* (17 Aug. 2016). "I tried to refresh my mind in the third set. I knew that I wasn't stepping in. As soon as I got the break, I started to play aggressive, and I played with confidence." Nishikori's aggressive and confident play paid off, as he defeated Nadal to claim his first Olympic medal. The win represented a major milestone not only for Nishikori but also for the Japanese tennis community, as an athlete playing for that country had not won an Olympic medal in tennis since 1920.

2017 SEASON

During the 2017 tennis season, Nishikori achieved a record of thirty wins to thirteen losses in individual singles matches. He made it to the finals in the Brisbane International presented by Suncorp as well as the Argentina Open and also competed in three of the Grand Slam tournaments, making it to the quarterfinals of the French Open, the third round at Wimbledon, and fourth round of the Australian Open. Although he planned to compete in the US Open, in August 2017 Nishikori announced that he was withdrawing from the event due to a wrist injury caused by a torn tendon. He further announced that he would be missing the remainder of the season to have his wrist evaluated and potentially pursue treatment options.

PERSONAL LIFE

Nishikori lives in Bradenton, Florida, to which he first moved to attend IMG Academy. Although his family and many of his friends remain in Japan, he spends little time in his home country, as his fame brings him an uncomfortable amount of attention there. "It is difficult," he told Simon Briggs for the *Telegraph* (2 Mar. 2016). "I have to wear sunglasses, a hat, a mask, everything." He plans to remain in the United States until his retirement from tennis, at which point he hopes to return to Japan. In addition to his competitive tennis efforts, Nishikori has signed numerous endorsement deals with brands such as the clothing company Uniqlo and the instant noodle brand Nissin.

SUGGESTED READING

Beech, Hannah. "His Time Is Now." *Time*, 9 Jan. 2015, time.com/3659376/his-time-is-now/. Accessed 14 Dec. 2017.

Briggs, Simon. "Kei Nishikori: Japan's Sporting Superstar Who Avoids His Homeland Because the Adulation Is Too Intense." *The Telegraph*, 2 Mar. 2016, www.telegraph.co.uk/tennis/2016/03/02/kei-nishikori-japans-sporting-superstar-who-avoids-his-homeland/. Accessed 14 Dec. 2017.

Fleck, Kelly. "Nishikori Takes Home Bronze at Rio Olympics." *Nikkei Voice*, 17 Aug. 2016, nikkeivoice.ca/nishikori-takes-home-bronze-at-rio-olympics/. Accessed 14 Dec. 2017.

Harwitt, Sandra. "Breadth, Depth of Nishikori's Game Illuminating." *ESPN*, 19 Feb. 2008, www.espn.com/sports/tennis/news/story?id=3252891. Accessed 14 Dec. 2017.

"Kei Nishikori Achieves Milestone." *ESPN*, 12 May 2014, www.espn.com/tennis/story/_/id/10921365/kei-nishikori-1st-japan-atp-top-10-rankings. Accessed 14 Dec. 2017.

"Kei Nishikori to Miss Remainder of Season with Torn Tendon in Wrist." *Tennis*, 16 Aug. 2017, www.tennis.com/pro-game/2017/08/14-us-open-runner-up-kei-nishikori-latest-out-of-us-open/68567/. Accessed 14 Dec. 2017.

Kilgore, Adam. "Kei Nishikori Is Expanding Horizons for Tennis Players from Japan." *The Washington Post*, 5 Aug. 2015, www.washingtonpost.com/sports/tennis/kei-nishikori-is-expanding-horizons-for-tennis-players-from-japan/2015/08/05/dd5cba7a-3b73-11e5-9c2d-ed991d848c48_story.html. Accessed 14 Dec. 2017.

—*Joy Crelin*

Aaron Nola

Date of birth: June 4, 1993
Occupation: Baseball player

While being drafted by a Major League Baseball (MLB) organization is the dream for many talented young baseball players, pitcher Aaron Nola's selection by the Toronto Blue Jays in the 2011 MLB Draft presented him with a difficult choice: join the Blue Jays organization as a player just out of high school or turn down the Blue Jays and enroll at Louisiana State University (LSU) to play baseball alongside his older brother, Austin. Nola's decision to go with the latter option proved to be beneficial, both for the LSU Tigers baseball team and for Nola himself. Initially selected as the 679th overall draft pick in 2011, he demonstrated his skills extensively at LSU, increasing his standing as a prospect to such an extent that he was ultimately selected as the seventh overall pick in the MLB Draft in 2014. Joining the Philadelphia Phillies organization, Nola spent less than two years in the minor leagues before moving up to the major-league Phillies team in July of 2015. For Nola, joining the team presented the opportunity to learn from the Phillies' established team members and ideally to play a role in reversing the fortunes of the team, which had struggled for the past several seasons. "The Phillies have great players on this team, some veterans that have played a lot of baseball and really succeeded, and I feel like the team is getting better as the days go on," he said, as quoted by Randy Miller for *NJ.com* (20 July

By Arturo Pardavila III, via Wikimedia Commons

2015). "I'm just glad I'm here and I'm going to try to help as best as I can."

EARLY LIFE AND EDUCATION

Aaron Michael Nola was born on June 4, 1993, in Baton Rouge, Louisiana, to A. J. and Stacie Nola. He grew up in Baton Rouge with his older brother Austin, who, as an adult, would go on to play for various minor-league affiliates of the Miami Marlins. A fan of baseball from an early age, Nola grew up collecting baseball cards and particularly liked the major-league player Ken Griffey Jr. He attended Catholic High School in Baton Rouge, where he joined the school's freshman and varsity baseball teams as a pitcher and achieved impressive statistics that caught the eye of both professional and college scouts. In his senior season, Nola achieved a 1.00 earned run average (ERA) and sixty-one strikeouts in forty-five innings, which led him to be named the class 5A state player of the year. Nola graduated from Catholic High School in 2011.

In June of 2011, Nola was selected by the Toronto Blue Jays in the twenty-second round of that year's MLB Draft, becoming the 679th overall player to be selected in the draft. "It's an honor to be drafted," he told Tammy Nunez for the New Orleans *Times-Picayune* (8 June 2011). "To get that opportunity out of high school is a good thing." However, the opportunity also presented a dilemma for Nola, as he had already agreed to attend LSU and play for the LSU Tigers, for which his brother already played as a shortstop. Although intrigued by the possibility of beginning his professional career right out of high school, he appreciated the idea of playing baseball alongside his brother, as they had consistently played for separate teams in high school and earlier. After considering his options, Nola decided to turn down the Blue Jays and maintain his commitment to LSU.

LOUISIANA STATE UNIVERSITY

Upon enrolling in LSU as a sports administration major, Nola joined the Tigers alongside Austin, who had likewise been drafted by the Blue Jays organization but chose to complete his final year of college. The two were teammates for one season, which presented a valuable opportunity for their parents to see the brothers play together for the first time. "It was really good and special for my parents," Nola told Matt Breen for the *Philadelphia Inquirer* (19 July 2015). "When I was in high school, one would be at my game and one would be at Austin's game. This was the time that they could be together and watch us on the same field and travel with us. That was very special."

Following his brother's graduation, Nola played two additional seasons for the university, becoming an integral part of the Tigers and

gaining widespread notice for his skills on the pitcher's mound. In recognition of his work, he was named Southeastern Conference (SEC) pitcher of the year in both 2013 and 2014, becoming the first pitcher to receive that title twice. He was also the only member of the Tigers to be named to the All-SEC First Team in 2014. Over the course of his final season with the team, Nola achieved an ERA of 1.47 and tallied a total of 134 strikeouts, the most of any pitcher in the SEC and the third-most of all college pitchers in the United States. Considering his success at LSU, Nola attracted significant attention from professional baseball organizations, and he ultimately left the university to pursue his professional career following his junior year.

PROFESSIONAL BASEBALL

In June of 2014, Nola was drafted by a professional baseball organization for the second time, this time being chosen by the Philadelphia Phillies in the first round of the draft, as the seventh overall pick. Sent to the minor leagues to develop his skills further, Nola made his professional debut with the Clearwater Threshers, a Florida-based A+ affiliate of the Phillies. Although the team was a lower-level team in the Phillies organization, Nola was focused on becoming the best team member he could. "My head's not anywhere else," he told Ross Dellenger for the Baton Rouge *Advocate* (12 July 2014). "It's not in Double-A, Triple-A or whatever." After playing seven games with the Threshers, Nola moved on to the AA Reading Fightin Phils, spending the remainder of 2014 with that team. He started the 2015 season with the Fightin Phils before moving on to the AAA Lehigh Valley IronPigs.

After a little over a year in the minor leagues, Nola debuted with Philadelphia Phillies on July 21, 2015, pitching six innings in a game against the Tampa Bay Rays. Although the team lost that game, Nola was excited to acclimate himself to his new team. "I'm just ready to get things started around here," he said before the game, as quoted by Miller. "It's good to get in the clubhouse and meet all the guys in there." At the time of Nola's arrival, the Phillies were struggling with poor overall performance, having failed to win a spot in the playoffs during the previous three seasons. Nola's optimism, however, extended to the team as a whole, and he was intent on maintaining a positive attitude. "The Phillies have great players right now and I like to live in the present and take it day by day," he said, as quoted by Miller. "But I'm ready to go and see how these guys play and learn from them."

Nola appeared in thirteen games with the Phillies during the remainder of the season. As a pitcher, he had an ERA of 3.59 and a total of thirty-one runs allowed and sixty-eight strikeouts. He also appeared in twenty-three at bats as a batter but managed only two hits, for a batting average of .087. He would go on to make occasional plate appearances as a batter over the following seasons but focused primarily on pitching. The Phillies ended the season with the worst win-loss record both in the National League East and in the major leagues, with sixty-three wins to ninety-nine losses.

PHILADELPHIA PHILLIES

The 2016 season became Nola's first season played solely with the Phillies, and he played in twenty games over the course of the season. He allowed sixty-eight runs, struck out players 121 times, and achieved an ERA of 4.78 over the course of the season. He also scored his first major-league run that season during a rare appearance as a batter. Despite plans to play for the full season, Nola was forced to end his season early, in August, due to an elbow injury. Despite suggestions from Phillies leadership that he might have to undergo surgery, Nola ultimately underwent rehabilitation and recovered from his injury without a need for surgery, returning to regular play in the 2017 season.

In 2017, Nola played in twenty-seven games and showed improvement over his previous season, achieving his best ERA—3.54—to date in the major leagues. He allowed sixty-seven runs over the course of the season but achieved 184 strikeouts, ranking seventh in the National League for strikeouts per nine innings played. As a batter, he also contributed three runs to the team that season. Nola spent some time on the disabled list due to a strained back and in May of 2017 returned to the minor-league Lehigh Valley IronPigs to play a single rehab game, but his injury did not prevent him from finishing the season with the Phillies. Despite Nola's efforts, the team finished last in the National League East, failing to make the playoffs for the sixth year in a row.

During the first months of the 2018 season, Nola gained attention for the improvements he had made to his pitches, particularly the pitch known as the change-up, in which a pitcher appears to throw a fast pitch but truly throws a slower one that confuses the opposing team's batter. "The past several games, I feel like it's the best it's been in my career, especially since I've been up here," Nola told Breen for the *Philadelphia Inquirer* (8 May 2018). "As a starter, it's crucial to have three pitches. A lot of guys do. A change-up is one of the better pitches that a starter can have." Nola's performance on the pitcher's mound during early 2018 suggested that his efforts had paid off: in his first nine games of the season, he achieved an ERA of 1.99, allowed only thirteen runs, and completed fifty-one strikeouts.

PERSONAL LIFE

Nola lives in Philadelphia.

SUGGESTED READING

Breen, Matt. "Aaron Nola Dominates Giants with 12 Strikeouts, Showcases His Change-Up in Phillies Win." *The Philadelphia Inquirer*, 8 May 2018. www.philly.com/philly/sports/phillies/phillies-giants-recap-score-aaron-nola-strikeouts-aaron-altherr-carlos-santana-20180508.html. Accessed 12 May 2018.

Breen, Matt. "Aaron Nola and His Brother, Austin, Dream of Facing Each Other in Major Leagues." *The Philadelphia Inquirer*, 19 July 2015. www.philly.com/philly/sports/phillies/20150719_Aaron_Nola_and_his_brother__Austin__dream_of_facing_each_other_in_major_leagues.html. Accessed 12 May 2018.

Breen, Matt. "Aaron Nola to Make Major-League Debut Tuesday." *The Philadelphia Inquirer*, 17 July 2015. www.philly.com/philly/blogs/sports/phillies/Aaron-Nola-to-make-major-league-debut-on-Tuesday.html. Accessed 12 May 2018.

Dellenger, Ross. "It's Baseball and the Beach as Aaron Nola Begins His Pro Career." *The Advocate* [Baton Rouge], 12 July 2014. www.theadvocate.com/baton_rouge/sports/lsu/article_23be2b44-6f8f-5fd4-bcaf-434693f66d49.html. Accessed 12 May 2018.

Dellenger, Ross. "Nola Claims SEC Pitcher of the Year." *The Advocate* [Baton Rouge], 30 May 2014. www.theadvocate.com/baton_rouge/sports/lsu/article_5b795865-dfaf-58a3-b6b7-94a13bd8ae06.html. Accessed 12 May 2018.

Miller, Randy. "Watch: Aaron Nola on Joining Phillies in First Interview as Big Leaguer." *NJ.com*, 20 July 2015. www.nj.com/phillies/index.ssf/2015/07/phillies_aaron_nola.html. Accessed 12 May 2018.

Nunez, Tammy. "MLB Draft Pick Aaron Nola Weighs Joining Brother with LSU Tigers or Signing Pro Deal." *The Times-Picayune* [New Orleans], 8 June 2011. www.nola.com/lsu/index.ssf/2011/06/draft_pick_aaron_nola_weighs_j.html. Accessed 12 May 2018.

—*Joy Crelin*

Dorthe Nors

Date of birth: May 20, 1970
Occupation: Author

The celebrated Danish author Dorthe Nors started gathering a following in English-speaking countries in 2009, when selections from her

By Arild Vågen [CC BY-SA 4.0], via Wikimedia Commons

EARLY LIFE AND CAREER

Nors was born on May 20, 1970, in Herning, a city on Denmark's Jutland peninsula. Her mother was a teacher and painter, and her father was a carpenter. She and her two older brothers grew up in the nearby village of Sinding-Ørre, to which her family had moved when she was four years old. As a child, although her mother encouraged her to draw, Nors preferred making up stories that she had her mother write down, word for word, and then read back to her. She began writing her own stories, poems, and plays at age eleven.

In 1990 Nors began attending the University of Aarhus, where she studied first Danish and then theology before finally focusing on Nordic literature and art history. She graduated in 1999 with a *candidata magisterii*, equivalent to a master of arts degree, having written her thesis on Swedish novelist Kerstin Ekman.

After graduating, Nors worked as a translator of Swedish novels before embarking on her own literary career. Her first novel, *Soul*, was published in Denmark in 2001; it was followed by two more novels, *Stormesteren* (2003) and *Ann Lie* (2005). These works have not yet been translated into English.

Many of Nors's stories focus on women trying to understand their identities in society, whereas others focus on the relationship between parents and their children. "Don't we all remember that moment when our parents stopped being heroes? I do," she said to Dwyer Murphy for the *Paris Review* (18 Mar. 2014). "I love my parents but I figured out they were human beings and that not everyone in the world saw them as the wonderful people I perceived them to be."

KARATE CHOP

Nors's short-story collection *Kantslag* was first published in 2008 in Denmark, where short-story writing is not as prevalent as it is in the United States. "Without me realizing it, I found that the short story—this compact, intensive way of writing—suited my voice," she explained to Murphy. "The short story isn't really part of our tradition in Denmark. This is the country of Hans Christian Anders[e]n and Karen Blixen, but for some reason there's this sense that we don't want to dirty our hands with the short story." Even so, *Kantslag* proved popular among Danish readers—and, beginning in 2009, American readers as well, after individual stories from the collection started appearing in translation in several respected English-language magazines, including *Harper's*, the *Boston Review*, *AGNI*, *Guernica*, and the *New Yorker*. In 2011, Nors was awarded a three-year grant from the Danish Arts Council (now the Danish Arts Foundation) for her contributions to Danish literature.

short-story collection *Kantslag* (2008; *Karate Chop*, 2014) began appearing in translation in various well-respected magazines. When her story "The Heron" was published in the September 9, 2013, issue of the *New Yorker*, she became the first Danish writer to ever have a story appear in its pages. Her novellas *Dage* (2010; *Days*) and *Minna mangler et øvelokale* (2013; *Minna Needs Rehearsal Space*) were translated into English and published jointly under the title *So Much for That Winter* in 2016. Her novel *Spejl, skulder, blink* (2016), translated as *Mirror, Shoulder, Signal* in 2017, met with widespread critical acclaim in the United States and the United Kingdom and was a finalist for the Man Booker International Prize in 2017.

Nors, whose stories often explore the interior lives of middle-aged women who find themselves set apart from the societies in which they live, is admired both at home and abroad for the precision of her language, her insight into the human condition, and the ways in which she carefully explores her characters' psyches. "I write minimalism that is under attack from within," she explained to Susie Mesure for the *Independent* (28 Feb. 2015). "I was trained in the Swedish tradition where existential structures are very important. Swedish form is bigger than the Danish. But I combine these. There's always something bursting out of this very tight structure. It's like an elephant in a very cool Danish chair, a [Hans] Wegner, or an Arne Jacobsen."

Graywolf Press, in collaboration with the magazine *A Public Space*, purchased the complete collection of stories in 2012 and published them two years later under the title *Karate Chop*. The translation was met with considerable praise in the United States (and, the following year, in the United Kingdom), where critics applauded Nors's dark look at modern life, the droll way in which she wove her tales, and the considerable care and complexity with which she depicted her characters' pain. They also marveled at the way Nors could pack so much into so few words, some of the fifteen stories in the collection being no more than a page or two long.

Nors recalled to Murphy how the stories in *Karate Chop* flowed out of her over the course of a two-week vacation at a cottage on the west coast of Denmark. "At the time, I was in love," she said. "That's part of what brought those stories out of me like crazy—that energy and openness you have when you think you just met the love of your life. There was a joy in writing these stories, even though I was writing about battered women and such very bad things. You know, Johann Sebastian Bach, after his wife and kids died, wrote in his diary that he hoped their deaths wouldn't take away his joy. What he meant was the joy of creation. He could write the most dark and beautiful things, but there was a joy in being able to do it. I felt that during those two weeks. It was a creative happiness."

SO MUCH FOR THAT WINTER

So Much for That Winter (2016) collects two novellas in translation: *Days*, which was first published in 2010, and *Minna Needs Rehearsal Space*, first published in 2013. (Both novellas were republished in Danish in a single volume, *Det var så den vinter*—the Danish translation of the English title—in 2016.)

Minna Needs Rehearsal Space is written entirely in short sentences that read like declarative headlines, as if giving the reader real-time status updates on Minna's emotional state and activities. The story follows Minna, a young composer, after she has been dumped by text by her boyfriend Lars, a music reporter who has hooked up with a classically trained guitarist named Linda. Throughout the novella, the reader is confronted with Minna's needs and desires moment by moment as she seeks a rehearsal space of her own and reflects on the works of Ingmar Bergman. In *Days*, Nors switches to a first-person narration that often drops personal pronouns, presenting the entire tale as a series of lists that describe her character's emotional state as she seeks to understand her life. Each novella is marked by its direct and unique style and the raw intensity with which it relates the lives of its main characters.

In a review for *Slate* (6 July 2016), Nora Caplan-Bricker wrote of the two works, "It's reflective of Nors' style that the ecstatic and creative emerge, drolly and yet vividly, from the quotidian. . . . These modern forms and conveniences—social media, urban laundromats—are neither more nor less than structures for living around and among each other, for binding ourselves closer and drawing ourselves apart. Being human, we can't help but spin this mess into art, and that, Nors suggests, is enough to ennoble it."

MIRROR, SHOULDER, SIGNAL

Spejl, skulder, blink, Nors's 2016 novel, was published in English as *Mirror, Shoulder, Signal* in 2017. Like its predecessors, it focuses on the interior emotional life of a single middle-aged woman, in this case Sonja, the Danish translator for a popular Swedish crime novelist. Sonja's life has been upended of late: she is plagued by vertigo; her boyfriend, Paul, has deserted her for a woman in her twenties; and she has a difficult relationship with her sister, who lives in their childhood home in Jutland. Longing to reconnect with people, she begins to reexamine her life and concludes that every single bit of it needs a change. To that end, she decides that she needs to finally learn how to drive, but she soon discovers—both metaphorically and in actuality—that she has trouble changing gears. Sonja seeks to emulate her friend Molly, a married-with-children psychologist who also enjoys extramarital affairs and who changes everything about her life, including her name. But unlike Molly, Sonja's nonconformity and fatalism prevent her from having meaningful relationships.

Critics cheered *Mirror, Shoulder, Signal*. Reviewing the novel for the *Guardian* (4 Mar. 2017), Catherine Taylor wrote, "This 200-page lamentation on contemporary loneliness would quickly grate if it were not for the benevolent ingenuity of Nors's writing. When Sonja's narrative breaks free of the corner she has boxed herself into, the prose swoops and soars like her yearned-for whooper swans." In a review for the *Financial Times* (3 Mar. 2017), Isabel Berwick proclaimed, "Nors writes important modern women's fiction. It is an act of 21st century recovery and assertion: she gives back agency and centrality to older women, sidelined in all societies, even Scandinavian ones, where women are valued less than men, and childless, single women least of all." *Mirror, Signal, Shoulder* was short-listed for the 2017 Man Booker International Prize.

PERSONAL LIFE

Nors lived for several years in Copenhagen, the center of the Danish literary scene, but around 2013 she returned to Jutland, where she lives in a small house on the central western coast by the North Sea. Her experience in her native country—often touted in the media as being the happiest in the world, owing to its high standard of living—has informed her writing throughout her career. "We're fortunate if you look at the welfare system, and there isn't a great difference between poor and rich," Nors said to Mesure. "But nobody escapes living their lives, not even if you live in the happiest place in the universe, or the saddest. You still lose the ones you love. You still get ill. You can't escape your own existence. But you're not supposed to say that in Denmark. And I think that sometimes makes us a little bit unhappy."

SUGGESTED READING

Berwick, Isabel. "*Mirror, Shoulder, Signal* by Dorthe Nors: On the Road." Review of *Mirror, Shoulder, Signal*, by Dorthe Nors, translated by Misha Hoekstra. *Financial Times*, 3 Mar. 2017, www.ft.com/content/47c04802-fd9f-11e6-96f8-3700c5664d30. Accessed 29 Nov. 2017.

Caplan-Bricker, Nora. "'One Thing Is Inescapable: I Write.'" Review of *So Much for That Winter*, by Dorthe Nors, translated by Misha Hoekstra. *Slate*, 6 July 2016, www.slate.com/articles/arts/books/2016/07/dorthe_nors_so_much_for_that_winter_reviewed.html. Accessed 28 Nov. 2017.

"Dorthe Nors's Novel Is a Magnificent Exploration of Anxiety." Review of *Mirror, Shoulder, Signal*, by Dorthe Nors, translated by Misha Hoekstra. *The Economist*, 29 Apr. 2017, www.economist.com/news/books-and-arts/21721359-mirror-shoulder-signal-introduces-writer-who-both-funny-and-brave. Accessed 29 Nov. 2017.

Mesure, Susie. "Dorthe Nors: 'You Can't Escape Your Own Existence. But You're Not Supposed to Say That in Denmark.'" *The Independent*, 28 Feb. 2015, www.independent.co.uk/arts-entertainment/books/features/dorthe-nors-you-cant-escape-your-own-existence-but-youre-not-supposed-to-say-that-in-denmark-10076106.html. Accessed 5 Dec. 2017.

Nors, Dorthe. "Getting Slapped Around: An Interview with Dorthe Nors." Interview by Dwyer Murphy. *The Paris Review*, 18 Mar. 2014, www.theparisreview.org/blog/2014/03/18/getting-slapped-around-an-interview-with-dorthe-nors/. Accessed 28 Nov. 2017.

Nors, Dorthe. "A Wolf in Jutland: Dorthe Nors on the Writing Life in Denmark." *The Guardian*, 16 Dec. 2015, www.theguardian.com/books/the-writing-life-around-the-world-by-electric-literature/2015/dec/16/a-wolf-in-jutland-dorthe-nors-on-the-writing-life-in-denmark. Accessed 28 Nov. 2017.

Taylor, Catherine. "*Mirror, Shoulder, Signal* by Dorthe Nors Review: Coping Alone in Copenhagen." Review of *Mirror, Shoulder, Signal*, by Dorthe Nors, translated by Misha Hoekstra. *The Guardian*, 4 Mar. 2017, www.theguardian.com/books/2017/mar/04/mirror-shoulder-signal-by-dorthe-nors-review. Accessed 28 Nov. 2017.

SELECTED WORKS

Soul, 2001; *Stormesteren*, 2003; *Ann Lie*, 2005; *Kantslag* (*Karate Chop*), 2008; *Dage* (*Days*), 2010; *Minna mangler et øvelokale* (*Minna Needs Rehearsal Space*), 2013; *So Much for That Winter*, 2016; *Spejl, skulder, blink* (*Mirror, Shoulder, Signal*), 2016

—*Christopher Mari*

Lynn Novick

Date of birth: 1962
Occupation: Director, producer

Lynn Novick is happy to remain behind the scenes of the productions she codirects and coproduces with noted filmmaker Ken Burns. So it is no surprise that although, as writer and editor Daniel Okrent told Elizabeth Jensen for the *New York Times* (23 Sept. 2011), "she's a very gifted filmmaker . . . if you ask people who know documentary television but who are not in the business, they don't know her."

Burns has extended his contract with the Public Broadcasting System (PBS) into 2022, and as Novick continues to partner with him in the coming years, more people will know of her work. Speaking of their working relationship, Burns said to Jensen, "While some partners are more equal than others—i.e., and I think she would agree with this, I have the final creative say if there were a disagreement—I would be stupid not to listen very long and very hard to whatever she passionately believes in, and I think the films are better for that."

Novick has also begun pursuing her own documentary work, separate from Burns. One such project is a documentary about Bard Prison Initiatives, which helps prison inmates earn college degrees.

EDUCATION AND EARLY CAREER

Novick was born in London and raised in New York's Upper West Side. As a child, she did not aspire to filmmaking; her parents were both academics, and she thought she might follow that career path as well. She began her college career at Yale University as a premedical student, but she later changed her major to American studies, which gave her the chance to study the history of

By LBJ Library, via Wikimedia Commons

photography and how to make history attractive to nonhistorians.

Novick graduated from Yale magna cum laude in 1983 and, having no definite career plans, began working at the Smithsonian Institution's National Museum of American History as a research assistant. She catalogued materials, researched Eleanor Roosevelt, and created an exhibit on child photography of the nineteenth century, but she did not find the work fulfilling. "I needed something more hands-on, more engaging," she explained to Marilyn Armstrong for *Planet Vineyard* (Sept. 1998). "Academia was too theoretical, too out of touch. I'm not sure how I decided I wanted to make documentary films. I think it was a combination of things. I've always loved the movies. I study history. I need my work to have social value. Making documentary films brings all the strands together. I can bring history to life."

One major impetus for switching career paths was Burns's early documentary *Huey Long* (1985), about the larger-than-life 1930s-era Louisiana politician, which Novick saw while still working at the museum. "I don't remember having any idea of the filmmaker, just that this was an amazing story," she recalled to Jensen. Later, at a screening of another film by Burns, attended by both him and cinematographer Buddy Squires, she thought, "I would love to be them, I would love to do this."

A SPECTACULAR DEGREE OF COMPETENCY

Novick moved back to New York to live with her parents and found a job as a production assistant

at the public television station WNET. She was later hired to do picture research for Bill Moyers's series *Joseph Campbell and the Power of Myth* (1988) and subsequently became an associate producer on *A World of Ideas* (1988–90), also featuring Moyers. Working with Moyers gave her insight into conducting compelling interviews. When he did not hire her for the next project, Novick was deeply upset and planned to attend business school. Then Ken Burns called.

In June 1989, two months from completing his work on *The Civil War* (1990), Burns lost the associate producer in charge of clearing the rights for the historical photographs that would appear in the miniseries. In need of Novick's expertise, he hired her based on a recommendation. Although Novick had to wait to begin the job until mid-July due to scheduling conflicts, she completed the task in the allotted time, when her predecessor had estimated it would require eight months. "By late August all the work was done," Burns said to Jensen. "It represented a degree of competency that was so spectacular that you just went, 'Hmmm.'"

When Burns began making his next miniseries, the nine-episode *Baseball* (1994), he hired Novick again as an associate producer, the same job for which she had been credited in *The Civil War*. This time, her duties would extend beyond historical research, though she had no previous experience as a producer. "I literally had a stomachache for five years," she recalled to Alyssa Rosenberg for the *Washington Post* (21 Sept. 2017). Despite Novick's nerves, *Baseball*, which ran for over eighteen hours total, became the most-watched series in the history of public broadcasting and won the 1995 Primetime Emmy Award for outstanding informational series. The award cited Burns and Novick along with writer Geoffrey C. Ward and narrator John Chancellor.

Baseball was the beginning of a departure for Burns in terms of his directing and producing responsibilities. Having previously done most of the interviewing for his documentaries himself, he began delegating more and more of that task to Novick. "She's a total different interview style from me and I can remember sort of biting my lip a few times," he said to Rosenberg. "For me it's all about listening and moving in on a twitch or an eye thing and following it." However, he was soon impressed by the results produced by Novick's style of interviewing.

MORE DOCUMENTARIES

Novick subsequently served as both codirector and coproducer on the two-part documentary *Frank Lloyd Wright* (1998), about the titular architect. First presented at the Sundance Film Festival before being broadcast on PBS, the film was nominated for the Sundance Grand

Jury Prize and won several awards, including a 1998 Peabody Award. Novick also coproduced the ten-part PBS series *Jazz* (2001), which was nominated for five Emmy Awards.

The seven-part World War II series *The War*, which aired in 2007 and ran for a total of fifteen hours, was six years in the making. Novick was again coproducer and codirector. Instead of trying to present a global perspective on the war, Burns, Novick, and writer Ward decided to focus on how the war affected everyday Americans from four towns in different regions of the United States: Sacramento, California; Mobile, Alabama; Waterbury, Connecticut; and Luverne, Minnesota. Nearly forty people from these four locations were interviewed. This more localized focus represented a departure from the typical World War II documentary focus on the major players and decision makers. In another departure, the series did not shy away from highlighting errors made during the war, although it was ultimately an homage to those who fought in both the European and Pacific theaters, as well as to those who worked at home. The film won three 2008 Emmy Awards—for outstanding nonfiction writing, outstanding voice-over performance, and outstanding sound editing— and the 2007–8 Television Critics' Association (TCA) Award for outstanding achievement in news and information. Novick later joined Burns again as codirector and coproducer for *The Tenth Inning* (2010), a four-hour follow-up to *Baseball*. She was also credited as a writer alongside Burns and David McMahon.

Her next project as codirector and coproducer with Burns was the three-part, five-and-a-half-hour PBS series *Prohibition* (2011). The series, which was in part an outgrowth of conversations Novick had had with Daniel Okrent as he was researching material for his book *Last Call: The Rise and Fall of Prohibition* (2010), begins with the temperance movement of the 1820s and goes on to cover the passage of the Eighteenth Amendment, the thirteen years for which it was in effect, and its subsequent repeal. It also explores Prohibition's repercussions for life in the United States, particularly with respect to matters of taxation and of anti-German sentiment (at the time, many breweries were owned and operated by people of German descent).

The timing of the series' release was fortuitous, coinciding as it did with interest generated by *Boardwalk Empire* (2010–14), the HBO series about Prohibition-era bootleggers, and with the Occupy movement protests. As Tona Hangen wrote for the *Journal of American History* (June 2012), Burns and Novick "used *Prohibition* to argue that polarization over issues of morality and law pose a real danger to the American social contract." The producers joined with the National Constitution Museum in Philadelphia to create a website with educational materials that targeted the issues of civility and democracy in public discourse.

THE VIETNAM WAR

For their third collaboration on war, codirectors Burns and Novick looked at the Vietnam War in an eight-part series aptly titled *The Vietnam War* (2017), which lasted for eighteen hours total. As soon as they completed *The War*, they knew they had to cover Vietnam. They interviewed one hundred people connected to the war, including military personnel and antiwar protesters. Their research and filming took eleven years to complete.

Growing up, Novick had felt a strong personal connection to the Vietnam War. "I was born in 1962, so to me the Vietnam War is sort of the defining event of my whole coming-of-age," she said to James Fallows for the *National* (Oct.–Nov. 2017). "It was always happening. I don't remember a time when the Vietnam War wasn't happening when I was growing up. And I remember feeling that something very disturbing was happening, but I didn't understand as a child why." Part of this connection came through her father, who was involved in scientific opposition to the use of chemical agents in the war, particularly Agent Orange, a toxic herbicide that contained dioxin.

It was Novick who insisted that both sides of the conflict needed to be represented in the film. As Burns had recently had surgery and his doctor did not want him traveling, he never went to Vietnam; instead, Novick and producer Sarah Botstein traveled there to interview people from both the north and the south of the country, working with both American and Vietnamese directors. "One of the things we found so extraordinary was the scale of loss there," Novick recalled to Chuck Springston for *Vietnam Magazine* (Oct. 2017). "For Americans, the 58,000 names on the [Vietnam Veterans Memorial] Wall is an enormous, tragic loss for our country and it's unimaginable what those families went through. In Vietnam, there wasn't a single person I met who didn't know someone who died in the war. Imagine every American knowing someone who died in the Vietnam War." She made sure the film also had a version with Vietnamese subtitles and was shown in Vietnam.

"Some people have said, 'Why are you going to open old wounds? Can't we let sleeping dogs lie?'" Novick said to Springston. "We can't. This is too important. It's too painful. And it's still here. If we don't deal with it, it just eats away at our body politic in a really toxic situation."

PERSONAL LIFE

Novick married Robert I. Smith Jr. in 1989. They have a daughter, Eliza, and a son, James.

Novick, who took Eliza with her to Vietnam, told Rosenberg that she would like to return someday with James.

SUGGESTED READING

Armstrong, Marilyn. "Baseball: Interview with Lynn Novick—September 1998." *Planet Vineyard*, Sept. 1998. *Serendipity*, teepee12.com/2016/12/13/baseball-interview-with-lynn-novick-september-1998/. Accessed 4 Jan. 2018.

Burns, Ken, and Lynn Novick. "Ken Burns and Lynn Novick: Vietnam's Unhealed Wounds." *The New York Times*, 29 May 2017, www.nytimes.com/2017/05/29/opinion/ken-burns-lynn-novick-vietnam-war.html. Accessed 4 Jan. 2018.

Burns, Ken, and Lynn Novick. "The National Conversation: Ken Burns and Lynn Novick." Interview by James Fallows. *The National*, Oct.–Nov. 2017, www.amtrakthenational.com/the-national-conversation-ken-burns-and-lynn-novick. Accessed 4 Jan. 2018.

Burns, Ken, and Lynn Novick. Interview. By Chuck Springston. *Vietnam Magazine*, Oct. 2017, www.historynet.com/voices-ken-burns-lynn-novick.htm. Accessed 4 Jan. 2018.

Hangen, Tona. Review of *Prohibition*, directed by Ken Burns and Lynn Novick. *The Journal of American History*, vol. 99, no. 1, 2012, pp. 374–77. *Academic Search Complete*, search.ebscohost.com/login.aspx?direct=true&db=a9h&AN=75699955&site=ehost-live. Accessed 4 Jan. 2018.

Jensen, Elizabeth. "A Steady Presence out of the Limelight." *The New York Times*, 23 Sept. 2011, www.nytimes.com/2011/09/25/arts/television/lynn-novick-ken-burnss-partner-in-filmmaking.html. Accessed 4 Jan. 2018.

Rosenberg, Alyssa. "Meet Lynn Novick." *The Washington Post*, 21 Sept. 2017, www.washingtonpost.com/sf/opinions/2017/09/21/ken-burns-and-lynn-novick-directed-the-vietnam-war-together-why-is-only-one-of-them-famous/. Accessed 4 Jan. 2018.

SELECTED WORKS

The Civil War, 1990; *Baseball*, 1994; *Frank Lloyd Wright*, 1998; *Jazz*, 2001; *The War*, 2007; *The Tenth Inning*, 2010; *Prohibition*, 2011; *The Vietnam War*, 2017

—Judy Johnson

Nnedi Okorafor

Date of birth: April 8, 1974
Occupation: Author

Nnedi Okorafor straddles two worlds, in both her real life and in her fiction. During her childhood, she frequently returned with her parents to their native Nigeria from their home in the United States, which allowed her to sample life in both countries but not to feel entirely part of either. In her science fiction and fantasy, her main characters are often young women of African ancestry who find themselves in challenging and surreal circumstances. Her work has added a fresh variation to these speculative genres of fiction that often specialize in dislocation—placing characters in strange worlds and allowing them to reevaluate what it means to be human. Okorafor's writing has won numerous prestigious awards, including the World Fantasy, Nebula, and Hugo Awards. One of her most celebrated novels, *Who Fears Death* (2010), will be adapted into an HBO series executive-produced by famed fantasy writer George R. R. Martin, and she has completed work on the Binti series (2015–18), an award-winning trilogy of novellas about the adventures of a young girl at the most prestigious university in the galaxy.

In the *Los Angeles Review of Books* (13 Apr. 2016), Kinitra D. Brooks declared: "Okorafor's strengths lie in her vast abilities to weave worlds organically grounded in West African–based cosmologies. Nigerian-American Okorafor's considerable talent as a storyteller allows her to portray

By Bryan Alexander, via Wikimedia Commons

the richness of the African diaspora even as she exposes the limits Western modernity has placed upon the imaginations of her characters and her readers."

EARLY LIFE AND EDUCATION

Nnedi Okorafor was born in Cincinnati, Ohio, on April 8, 1974, the daughter of Igbo Nigerian parents who had immigrated to the United States to pursue their educations. Her father became a cardiovascular surgeon and chief of surgery at various Chicago-area hospitals; her mother was a nurse and midwife who later got a doctorate in health administration. Both parents were also excellent athletes: her father was a hurdler who had competed across Africa, while her mother had made the Nigerian Olympic javelin team. "As is the case with a lot of Nigerians, and immigrant families in general, there were only three career options: doctor, lawyer, and engineer," she said in an interview with Alexandria Alter for the *New York Times* (6 Oct. 2017). "And failure."

Okorafor's parents raised their four children to strive for excellence in their education and in their physical activity. Okorafor was an outstanding student and a superb athlete, competing at the national level in tennis and track through high school and into college. At age thirteen, however, she was diagnosed with scoliosis, a disease that can cause a severe curvature of the spine if not treated with a back brace or surgery. After completing her freshman year at the University of Illinois and being named Athlete of the Year, Okorafor opted to have her spine fused to correct the problem.

A CHANGE OF COURSE

The vast majority of people who undergo that surgical procedure have no complications afterward, but in a very small proportion of cases, paralysis can result—and that happened to nineteen-year-old Okorafor. In an interview with Elizabeth Hand for the University at Buffalo publication *UBNow* (29 Jan. 2016), Okorafor recalled: "I went from being the super athlete to being paralyzed within 24 hours. I could either have gone mad in that hospital bed or found some way to keep myself from going mad. The only way I could stop myself from going mad was by writing stories."

Throughout that summer Okorafor worked to restore the use of her legs once feeling began to return to them. When she returned to school in the fall, she was walking with a cane. But the biggest change, perhaps, was to her outlook on life: she began to imagine a life as a writer, a profession she once considered as not pragmatic. (Because of her love of insects, she had thought of becoming an entomologist.) She took a creative writing class at a friend's suggestion and

was hooked. After earning her undergraduate degree from the University of Illinois, she earned a master's degree in journalism from Michigan State University, then her doctorate in English from the University of Illinois at Chicago. In 2001, the Clarion Science Fiction and Fantasy Writers' Workshop beckoned; she attended it and was again transformed, now seeing how science fiction and fantasy as genres had as much literary merit as other forms of fiction.

BREAKTHROUGH

Okorafor's first novel was a young-adult fantasy, *Zahrah the Windseeker*. When it was first published in 2005, it sold fewer than a thousand hardback copies, in part because no one knew how to market a book with a Nigerian viewpoint. But it notably earned the 2008 Wole Soyinka Prize for Literature in Africa and the 2012 Black Excellence Award for Outstanding Achievement in Literature (Fiction). She subsequently published another young-adult fantasy, *The Shadow Speaker*, which earned the 2007 Carl Brandon Parallax Award. She also wrote a pair of children's books: *Long Juju Man* (2009), which won the Macmillan Writers' Prize for Africa, and *Iridessa and the Secret of the Never Mine* (2012).

If any of her standalone novels could be singled out for putting her on the literary map, it would likely be *Who Fears Death* (2010), which earned the 2010 Carl Brandon Kindred Award (given to works of speculative fiction dealing with issues of race and ethnicity) and the 2011 World Fantasy Award for Best Novel. Set in a postapocalyptic West Africa, the novel does not shy away from difficult topics, including genocide, rape, and racism, as the main character Onyesonwu (whose name means "who fears death") seeks to defeat her father using her magical powers. In her interview with Elizabeth Hand, the author, whose own father died in 2004, explained that "a lot of the rage in the novel [*Who Fears Death*] . . . came from me. It was also the result of stories I'd heard from family members throughout my life. It very much is an angry novel, but it's justifiable rage, a type of rage that brings change."

LATER STANDALONE NOVELS

Another notable standalone novel is Okorafor's *Lagoon*, first published in 2014. In it, an alien invasion begins in Lagos, Nigeria, the most populous city in Africa, when a giant fist-shaped wave pulls human beings below the surface, where the alien ship is at rest. The aliens begin by purifying the water and bioengineering the local marine life to its greatest potential. The three main human characters, Anthony, Agu, and Adaora, escort an alien ambassador named Ayodele in assumed human form to the surface world. The narrative is written in a wide variety of styles as Ayodele encounters the diversity of life on planet

Earth. Amal El-Mohtar, in a review for *NPR* (18 July 2015), declared: "Chaotic, enthralling, and moving fluidly from character voices to oral-style narration to gut-punchingly beautiful prose, *Lagoon* is almost less a novel than an experience: Of free-diving, of night-flying, of being cocooned in a spider's web."

Okorafor's 2015 novel *The Book of Phoenix* can serve either as a standalone novel or as a prequel to *Who Fears Death*. The main character of the novel is Phoenix, a genetically engineered black woman known as a "speciMen" who has been designed as a weapon by the Big Eye Corporation. Like her mythical namesake, Phoenix has wings and can burn herself out at will, only to be reborn sometime later to live—or fight and die again—as her corporate masters require. But Phoenix rebels against her programming and leads a resistance against the overarching power of Big Eye. In her *Los Angeles Review of Books* review, Brooks wrote that Phoenix "has been called to leadership, compassion, and even revolution amidst extraordinary circumstances," and that "the larger themes of rebellion, civil rights, and economic accountability do not get in the way of *The Book of Phoenix* taking the reader along on one hell of a fun ride."

THE BINTI TRILOGY

Okorafor is also the author of a pair of well-regarded series. The Binti trilogy—made up of the novellas *Binti* (2015), *Binti: Home* (2017) and *Binti: The Night Masquerade* (2018)—follows a young African girl of the Himba people who leaves her family on Earth to attend the greatest university in the galaxy, Oomza University. There she evolves, both emotionally and in powers and abilities, to become a synthesis of what she had been on her home world and what she has become in encounters with alien peoples. The author explained in an interview with *Wired* (1 Feb. 2017): "Oomza Uni is new territory for me. Space is new territory for me. Creatures outside of Earth—that's new territory for me. So when I'm thinking about aliens, my brain goes wild." She clarified that her inspiration came less from Earth's biodiversity than "the idea of what life would be like outside of our context. Once I sat down and started imagining the finest university in the galaxy, it was intense and immense."

The series met with considerable praise. In 2016 *Binti* won both the Nebula Award and the Hugo Award for best novella. Writing of the concluding novella for *NPR* (27 Jan. 2018), El-Mohtar declared that "what makes it [Oomza University] ideal is its diversity, its heterogeneous nature, its enormous capacity for accommodating difference." She added, "It's almost an invitation and a challenge to resist seeking unity or craft in this final piece of a three-part story

whose structure suggested it, and then shrugged it off."

THE AKATA SERIES

Okorafor's other series is the Akata series, which includes *Akata Witch* (2011) and *Akata Warrior* (2017). The main character is a Nigerian American girl named Sunny, who is an albino. Because of her condition, she is perceived as a witch by the more superstitious people around her—that is, until she learns that she has powers and belongs to a secret group with magical abilities, the Leopard Society. The series has been compared favorably to the Harry Potter series, because it uses traditional Nigerian myths in the same way that British author J. K. Rowling used traditional European myths and legends to spin her acclaimed fantasy series.

The series—as well as her other books—have helped Okorafor to develop a wide fan base, which includes such luminary speculative-fiction authors as Ursula K. Le Guin, Rick Riordan, George R. R. Martin, and Neil Gaiman. "The sheer joy of something like the 'Akata' series is the feeling that I simply have not read this before, and that is so rare," Gaiman said, as quoted by Alexandria Alter of the *New York Times*. "It's fantasy, yet it comes from a cultural place that isn't the stuff we've already seen 1,000 times before."

BLACK PANTHER

Okorafor has also branched into the realm of comic books, where, capitalizing on the runaway success of the rebooted Marvel superhero comic *Black Panther*, she has penned the digital series *Black Panther: Long Live the King*, released starting in late 2017. The comic furthers the adventures of Black Panther, king of the mythical and technologically advanced African nation of Wakanda. In March 2018 it was announced that Okorafor would also be writing a three-part series called *Wakanda Forever*, which centers on the Dora Milaje, the all-female bodyguards of the Wakandan king.

SUGGESTED READING

Alter, Alexandra. "Nnedi Okorafor and the Fantasy Genre She Is Helping Redefine." *The New York Times*, 6 Oct. 2017, www.nytimes.com/2017/10/06/books/ya-fantasy-diverse-akata-warrior.html. Accessed 14 Mar. 2018.

Anyangwe, Eliza. "'So Many Different Types of Strange': How Nnedi Okorafor Is Changing the Face of Sci-Fi." *The Guardian*, 18 Sept. 2017, www.theguardian.com/lifeandstyle/2017/sep/18/so-many-different-types-of-strange-how-nnedi-okorafor-is-changing-the-face-of-sci-fi. Accessed 14 Mar. 2018.

Brooks, Kinitra. "The Multiple Pasts, Presents, and Futures of Nnedi Okorafor's Literary

Nigeria." *Los Angeles Review of Books*, 13 Apr. 2016, lareviewofbooks.org/article/the-multiple-pasts-presents-and-futures-of-nnedi-okorafors-literary-nigeria/. Accessed 15 Mar. 2018.

El-Mohtar, Amal. "Binti's Story Is Finished—but Don't Expect Completion." *National Public Radio*, 27 Jan. 2015, www.npr.org/2018/01/27/577723899/bintis-story-is-finished-but-dont-expect-completion. Accessed 16 Mar. 2018.

El-Mohtar, Amal. "The Waters of 'Lagoon' Are Choppy but Enthralling." *National Public Radio*, 18 July 2015, www.npr.org/2015/07/18/418600412/the-waters-of-lagoon-are-choppy-but-enthralling. Accessed 15 Mar. 2018.

Hand, Elizabeth. "The Speculative Fiction of UB Faculty Member Nnedi Okorafor." *UB-Now*, 29 Jan. 2016, www.buffalo.edu/ubnow/stories/2016/01/profile_okorafor.html. Accessed 14 Mar. 2018.

"Wired Book Club: Nnedi Okorafor Finds Inspiration Everywhere—Including Jellyfish." *Wired*, 1 Feb. 2017, www.wired.com/2017/02/wired-book-club-nnedi-okorafor-interview. Accessed 14 Mar. 2018.

SELECTED WORKS

Zahrah the Windseeker, 2005; *The Shadow Speaker*, 2007; *Long Juju Man*, 2009; *Who Fears Death*, 2010; *Akata Witch*, 2011; *Lagoon*, 2014; *The Book of Phoenix*, 2015; *Binti*, 2015; *Akata Warrior*, 2017; *Binti: Home*, 2017; *Binti: The Night Masquerade*, 2018

—*Christopher Mari*

Yvonne Orji

Date of birth: December 2, 1983
Occupation: Actor; comedian

Actor and comedian Yvonne Orji made a name for herself as an actor in 2016, playing Molly Carter, a corporate lawyer with an active sex life, in HBO's hit comedy series *Insecure*. Before that, she had gained a following on the New York City and Los Angeles comedy circuits. Orji first fell in love with comedy after competing in the 2006 Miss Nigeria in America pageant, where she performed stand-up as her talent. After two years spent honing her performance skills in New York City, Orji landed an unpaid writing internship in Hollywood—a stint that led her to develop *First Gen*, a semiautobiographical half-hour sitcom pilot. "Standup was my gateway drug," she told Julie Schott for *Elle* (17 Jan. 2017). The pilot ultimately led to an audition for her role on *Insecure*, which earned Orji two National Association for the Advancement of Colored People (NAACP) Image Award nomination.

EARLY LIFE AND EDUCATION

Yvonne Orji was born on December 2, 1983, in Port Harcourt, the capital of Rivers State in southeastern Nigeria. She lived there for six years before relocating to the United States with her father and three older brothers in 1989. After reuniting with her mother, who had been working as a nurse in the United States, the family settled in Laurel, Maryland. Orji struggled to adjust to her new country and was frequently bullied during elementary and middle schools. "I got bullied because I had an accent and I was different. I got made fun of by white people and by black people," she told Jane Mulkerrins for the *Guardian* (16 Sept. 2017).

Orji attended high school at an all-girls international boarding school in Pennsylvania. Orji focused heavily on her studies at the urging of her parents, who wanted her to become a doctor. The self-described tomboy also participated in sports, playing tennis and softball and serving as power forward for the basketball team. Upon graduating high school in 2001, Orji was accepted at George Washington University (GWU) in Washington, DC. She earned her bachelor's degree in sociology with a double-minored in biology and public health in 2005, with the goal of pursuing medicine. However, she decided against going to medical school and instead returned to GWU to pursue a master's degree in public health.

FINDING COMEDY

In 2006, while attending graduate school, Orji entered the Miss Nigeria in America pageant, where she performed comedy for the first time during the competition's talent portion. "I created a five minute set based on my life, things my mom has said, things I feel like every Nigerian kid or immigrant kid could experience and lo and behold people laughed," she recounted to Schott. Although Orji's stand-up routine failed to win her the pageant, she soon began getting requests to perform at events. In 2007, Orji entered the campus comedy competition DC's Funniest College Student—and was named one of two contest winners for GWU. Her prize included the opportunity to tour the DC area college circuit and to compete at the competition finals, held at the DC Improv Comedy Club. Although she did not win, Orji recalled being complimented by two audience members who identified with her jokes about immigrants.

Upon completing graduate school in 2008, with a master's degree in public health, Orji accepted a position with the nonprofit global health organization Population Services International.

She then spent six months educating youths in postwar Liberia regarding teen pregnancy and HIV/AIDS prevention.

PURSUES COMEDY FULL TIME

Orji returned to Maryland in 2009. Despite her parents' disapproval, she decided to pursue comedy full time, with the goal of eventually becoming an actor. After working as a server at the Cheesecake Factory and earning enough money for acting lessons, Orji moved to New York City, where she joined an acting troupe and honed her comedic skills from 2009 to 2011. During that time, she launched and hosted *Momma, I Made It!*, a weekly clean comedy showcase in Midtown Manhattan, and reached the semifinals of NBC's 2010 Stand-Up for Diversity talent search.

In 2011, Orji landed a writers room internship in Los Angeles, California, for the TV One sitcom *Love That Girl!*, which involved punching up jokes for the script. Although the position was unpaid, she quickly realized its value. "I learned this is where the power is—you can create the story," she told Allison P. Davis for the *Ringer* (10 Oct. 2016). Show creator Bentley Kyle Evans and show writer Stacey Evans Morgan encouraged Orji to explore writing after hearing the story of how she chose comedy over medicine and her parents' disapproving reactions. Their positive feedback resulted in the initial draft of a TV pilot based on Orji's experience growing up as a first-generation African American.

After the conclusion of her internship in the fall of 2011, Orji returned to New York, where she briefly served as an artist-in-residence at the University of Richmond. She then collaborated with four fellow Nigerian American writers/actors on *First Generation Nigerian American Project*, a play depicting the African American immigrant experience. The performance was unveiled in March 2012 at the Women Center Stage Festival in downtown Manhattan.

FIRST GEN

In 2012, Orji relocated to Los Angeles. In addition to performing on the local comedy club circuit, she continued to develop the script for her prospective series. Acting also remained a priority for Orji, and—after making her television debut in a 2011 episode of *Love That Girl!*—she appeared in the comedic short *Sex (Therapy) with the Jones* in 2013. However, she was turned away from the majority of roles she auditioned for. The constant rejection and financial hardship eventually took their toll on Orji, who became discouraged. "I was five seconds from giving up," the actor wrote for *Teen Vogue* (20 Dec. 2017). "I had a meltdown on Sunset Boulevard. I kept thinking, I'm doing my best, but it's not working—I gotta renegotiate this plan." Orji subsequently focused her energy into

completing the final draft of her web series that she titled *First Gen*.

In 2015, Orji finished filming the pilot's trailer, which was financed by her neighbor and about thirty family friends. She uploaded it to her YouTube channel the same year, to largely positive reviews by public viewers. Around this time, Orji connected with the Senegalese American actor Issa Rae, who created and starred in the award-winning YouTube show *Awkward Black Girl*. Orji and Rae bonded over their shared African backgrounds and their mutual work projects. Rae soon recommended Orji for a role in her upcoming HBO project *Insecure*, a half-hour comedy chronicling the professional and private lives of a quirky twenty-something African American woman (Rae) and her best friend, a high-powered, sexually promiscuous corporate attorney. The pilot trailer of *First Gen* secured Orji an audition for the role of the best friend, Molly Carter, with network producers.

BREAKS THROUGH WITH *INSECURE*

For Orji, the audition process was a lengthy one. "I thought it would [take place] . . . tomorrow. [But] the next I heard about *Insecure* was July, seven months later," she shared with Nikita Richardson for *Fast Company* (26 Oct. 2016). "And then I went in for an audition and it took five auditions before I actually booked Molly. It was like a month-and-a-half long process." In late August 2015, Orji officially joined the cast of *Insecure*. The series debuted to critical acclaim on October 9, 2016. In a *Vanity Fair* review (6 Oct. 2016), Richard Lawson hailed Orji's portrayal as "an intriguing mix of glamorous poise and creeping despair" with "interesting dynamics to explore . . . from panicking about a love interest who admits that he fooled around with a guy in college to some pointed maneuvering through racial coding in an office that's largely white." By mid-November 2016, more than halfway through the eight-episode season, *Insecure* had earned a second-season renewal. For her performance as Molly in the first season, Orji earned a 2017 NAACP Image Award nomination for Outstanding Supporting Actress in a Comedy Series.

INSECURE RENEWED AND OTHER PROJECTS

Orji's success in *Insecure* helped her secure multiple guest and featured roles. She served as the host on *The Conversation: Talk Show Series* (2016), about love and relationships. In early 2017, she guest-starred in two episodes of the CW's hit sitcom *Jane the Virgin*. Orji then appeared in a minor role on the comedic web series *Flip the Script* (2017).

When *Insecure* returned in mid-2017, Orji's character's storyline tackled the gender pay gap, a major real-life issue facing women, particularly black women. When Molly realizes that her white male counterpart, who works less hours, is getting paid significantly more, she struggles to advocate for herself. "It's such a delicate space, especially for women of color, because you have to handle it where you're not perceived as the angry black girl and you're not emotional, but then you're one of a few brown faces in a sea of white men," Orji confided to Patrick Ryan for *USA Today* (9 Aug. 2017). During the second season, Orji also tackled other contemporary issues, including the stigma of mental health and infidelity. Her work on the show earned Orji her second NAACP Image Award nomination. In early August 2017, after only three episodes had aired, HBO renewed the show for a third season. *Insecure* was renewed for a fourth season in September 2018.

Also in 2017, Orji opened for comedian Chris Rock's Total Blackout 2017 comedy tour. The following year, she made her big-screen debut, opposite award-winning actors Kevin Hart and Tiffany Haddish, in *Night School* (2018), about a high-school dropout who returns to night school to get his GED. In July 2018, Orji started the podcast *Jesus and Jollof* with Nigerian author Luvvie Ajayi. The podcast features discussions on life, love, religion, and their experience as immigrants. Orji's web series, *First Gen*, was still in development in 2018.

PERSONAL LIFE

Orji lives in Los Angeles and is dating the Nigerian NFL player Emmanuel Ache. She serves as an ambassador for the Innocence Project. Orji has frequently stated that she is a devout Christian. She made headlines in March 2017, when she hosted a TEDx Talk titled "The Wait Is Sexy," during which she announced that she intends to remain a virgin until marriage.

SUGGESTED READING

Lawson, Richard. "HBO Leaps Ahead with *Insecure*—But Falls Behind with Divorce," *Vanity Fair*, 6 Oct. 2016, www.vanityfair.com/hollywood/2016/10/insecure-divorce-hbo-reviews. Accessed 15 Sept. 2018.

Mulkerrins, Jane. "*Insecure*'s Yvonne Orji: 'Our Show Is Relatable. We Are a Mess at Best.'" *The Guardian*, 16 Sept. 2017, www.theguardian.com/tv-and-radio/2017/sep/16/insecure-yvonne-orji-33-years-old-virgin. Accessed 15 Sept. 2018.

Orji, Yvonne. "*Insecure* Star Yvonne Orji on Creativity and Color on TV." Interview by Nikita Richardson. *Fast Company*, 26 Oct. 2016, www.fastcompany.com/3064972/insecure-star-yvonne-orji-on-creativity-and-color-on-tv. Accessed 15 Sept. 2018.

Orji, Yvonne. "*Insecure* Star Yvonne Orji on Following Her Dreams to Become a Comedian." *Teen Vogue*, 20 Dec. 2017, www.teenvogue.com/story/insecure-star-yvonne-orji-dreams-comedian. Accessed 15 Sept. 2018.

Orji, Yvonne. "*Insecure*'s Yvonne Orji on Inclusivity, Body Positivity, and Why She Shops in the Men's Section." Interview by Julie Schott. *Elle*, 17 Jan. 2017, www.elle.com/beauty/news/a42066/yvonne-orji-insecure-interview/. Accessed 15. Sept. 2018.

Orji, Yvonne. "Molly from *Insecure* Is Your New Favorite Single Lady." Interview by Allison P. Davis. *The Ringer*, 10 Oct. 2016, www.theringer.com/2016/10/10/16041734/yvonne-orji-interview-insecure-904c39efe72. Accessed 15 Sept. 2018.

Ryan, Patrick. "HBO's *Insecure* Breakout Yvonne Orji on Sex Scenes, Representation and the Gender Pay Gap." *USA Today*, 9 Aug. 2017, www.usatoday.com/story/life/tv/2017/08/09/yvonne-orji-insecure-hbo/551637001/. Accessed 15 Sept. 2018.

—*Bertha Muteba*

Ada Palmer

Date of birth: June 9, 1981
Occupation: Writer; historian

Ada Palmer is a professor, noted Renaissance historian, musician, and blogger, but she is perhaps currently best known as the winner of the 2017 John W. Campbell Award for Best New Writer, for her critically acclaimed debut science fiction novel, *Too Like the Lightning* (2016). The first in a series of four novels, it explores the promise and perils of a utopian society set in the twenty-fifth century. In this world, peace has been secured by eliminating differences between people: nationalities are abolished, along with gender identities, religious freedoms, and the freedom of expression. Throughout the books, Palmer explores what censorship has done to this overtly peaceful society and whether its leadership can maintain the peace at all costs. Each of the books has found admirers, who celebrate Palmer's ability to blend big-question concepts with immersive world building. Palmer herself states that this is exactly the type of science fiction she admires and was trying to emulate as she crafted her series. She remarked in an interview with Stephanie Palazzolo for the *Chicago Maroon* (17 Apr. 2017): "Great science fiction is full of ideas, not just one, or two, or five ideas, but new ideas on every page."

EARLY LIFE AND EDUCATION

Ada Palmer was born on June 9, 1981, and grew up in Annapolis, Maryland. She studied at the

By Aleksi Stenberg [CC BY-SA 4.0], via Wikimedia Commons

Key School in Annapolis and at the Bryn Mawr School in Baltimore. During her childhood, she gained a love of music from her mother, and studied Suzuki violin at age two as well as piano and the recorder. While still in elementary school she developed an appreciation for music theory with an instructor from the Peabody Institute. From this experience, she came to love Renaissance music. She also sang in school choirs.

Her passion for reading and writing came through her father, who read to her from J. R. R. Tolkien's *The Hobbit* when she was still enjoying the books of Dr. Seuss. From her father, she gleaned a love of science fiction, fantasy and comic books, as well as for Japanese anime and manga. She recalled on her website, *AdaPalmer. com*: "My interest in writing began in elementary school, and I was already working on my first novel project by fourth grade. I took summer classes on essay writing at Johns Hopkins through the Center for Talented Youth program, and a course on prose poetry at the Interlochen Center for the Arts."

Despite Palmer's love of reading and learning, she left high school in 1997, having become frustrated with it. She went to college early, studying at Simon's Rock College of Bard for two years, then finishing her final two years at Bryn Mawr College for her junior and senior years because she had set her mind on becoming a Renaissance historian and wanted to learn additional ancient Greek and Latin.

ACADEMIC CAREER

Upon graduating from Bryn Mawr College in 2001, Palmer began working toward her doctorate at Harvard University, because she wanted to study under James Hankins, a scholar respected for his work on the rediscovery of classical thought during the Renaissance. While earning her doctorate, she studied in Rome and Florence, including a period at the Villa I Tatti Harvard University Institute for Italian Renaissance Studies, and also as a Fulbright scholar. After completing her PhD in 2009, she taught at Texas A&M University as an assistant professor. In 2014, she left Texas A&M to take up a position at the University of Chicago's Department of History, where she is presently a member of the Stevanovich Institute on the Formation of Knowledge and an affiliate member of the Center for the Study of Gender and Sexuality.

Palmer continues to conduct research in Italy, including at the rare books libraries in the Vatican and at the Laurenziana Library in Florence. On her personal website, she wrote: "My research on intellectual history, or the history of ideas, is a way of exploring how our ideas affect what civilizations do, build and aim at, and how events change those ideas, history and thought shaping each other over time." She has published a number of academic works over her career including, most notably, the books *The Recovery of Classical Philosophy in the Renaissance* (2008), coauthored with James Hankins, and *Reading Lucretius in the Renaissance* (2014). This work also has allowed her to write *ExUrbe*, a travel and philosophy blog.

TERRA IGNOTA SERIES

In addition to her research and writing as an academic, Palmer also avidly composed fiction for much of her life. According to her website, she had written more than 900,000 words of fiction before she began work on the four-volume Terra Ignota series. The first book in the series, *Too Like the Lightning*, was published in 2016 to generally favorable acclaim. In 2017 the book was a finalist for the Hugo Award for Best Novel, and Palmer won the Hugo Awards' John W. Campbell Award for Best New Writer.

The novel takes place in the twenty-fifth century, in a utopian society in which people can travel from continent to continent with relative ease in flying cars, are without any nationalities, and are required to join organizations known as Hives. World peace has been achieved, but at a price: in addition to losing nationalities, gender identities have been extinguished, as have freedom of speech and public religious practices. Some people have been trained to be "set-sets"—beings who can use their bodies and minds as computer processors but who cannot feel the natural world. At the center of this narrative is Mycroft Canner, a convicted felon who is required to help anyone he meets, and Carlyle Foster, a spiritual counselor in a world in which public religious worship has been banned. Canner narrates the book, frequently breaking the fourth wall to address the reader directly in a style that NPR's Jason Heller (10 May 2016) compared to *Candide*, an eighteenth-century philosophical novel by Voltaire.

Reviewing Palmer's novel for NPR, Heller declared it to be an "awe-inspiring debut," adding: "*Lightning* is dizzying, and not always in a good way. Despite its frenetic intelligence, the first half of the book is bogged down by too much, too fast. It takes some work to get used to, but it's worth it. . . . The pace picks up considerably by book's end, and it becomes clear how much fun Palmer is having with her orchestrated onslaught of concepts, characters, language, and plot. It's a genius kind of energy, and it's infectious."

Seven Surrenders, the second volume in the series, was published in 2017. It continues the narrative of Canner's experiences, and what becomes clear is that the series is building toward a war, as political tensions grow while Canner claims that there is a theological basis to the miraculous powers of a child named Bridger—and that another character, J. E. D. D. Mason, is divine. Although many critics continued to praise Palmer's work, Liz Bourke remarked in a review published on *TOR.com* (10 Mar. 2017): "*Seven Surrenders* remains playfully baroque, vividly characterised, and possessed of a lively sense of humour, as well as a lively and argumentative interest in future societies and the problems of utopia. It's just not the *tour-de-force* second book I was hoping for."

Palmer's most recent book in the series is *The Will to Battle*, which was published in December 2017. In it, the peace and stability of the twenty-fifth century have proven to be built on lies: the leaders of the Hives have conspired for years to murder individuals systematically and selectively so that no single Hive could dominate. As news of the conspiracy continues to spread, long-held resentments begin to inflame every group in this civilization, who seem ready to gamble on warfare to set things right. A critic for *Publishers Weekly* (6 Nov. 2017) declared of this third volume: "Palmer's writing is decidedly difficult; upon a second and third reading, however, one appreciates the wry humor and the ingenious depth of her worldbuilding. The interplay between reader and narrator is especially enjoyable, calling into question reliability and truth. Growing accustomed to this future world and Mycroft's description of it takes time, but the payoff is rewarding."

PERSONAL LIFE

Palmer maintains her passion for music, primarily through her group Sassafrass, which she co-founded as an undergraduate at Bryn Mawr. She has also been composing her own Viking-themed music since her time at Harvard, in part because Viking culture conjures the sort of mythology and fantasy themes she has always enjoyed and studied. Her completed Viking song cycle was recorded by Sassafrass and released in 2015 as *Sundown: Whispers of Ragnarok*. Sassafrass also has two other albums: *Stories & Stone*, released in 2015, and *Friend in the Dark*, released in 2016. Palmer composed the music for these latter albums as well.

Palmer also maintains an avid interest in manga and anime. She has worked for several manga and anime publishers, blogs about the art form for *Tor.com*, and, from 2005 to 2007, wrote a biweekly column for Tokyopop about manga, cosplay, fashion and otaku culture. She is also the founder of Tezuka in English, a web resource about the life of Osamu Tezuka, who is widely known as the "the father of manga." She also creates, competes in, and often runs cosplay events and has staffed conventions related to these interests.

SUGGESTED READING

"About Ada Palmer." *Ada Palmer*, 2017, ada-palmer.com/about-ada-palmer/. Accessed 13 Nov. 2017.

Bourke, Liz. "An Overstuffed Narrative: Seven Surrenders by Ada Palmer." *Tor.com*, 10 Mar. 2017, www.tor.com/2017/03/10/book-reviews-seven-surrenders-by-ada-palmer/. Accessed 13 Nov. 2017.

Heller, Jason. "Science, Fiction and Philosophy Collide in Astonishing 'Lightning.'" *NPR*, 10 May 2016, www.npr.org/2016/05/10/476483675/science-fiction-and-philosophy-collide-in-astonishing-lightning. Accessed 13 Nov. 2017.

Palmer, Ada. "A Utopia with Caveats: Why Peace on Earth Might Require Big Sacrifices." Interview by Clara Moskowitz. *Scientific American*, 1 July 2016, www.scientificamerican.com/article/recommended-a-utopia-with-caveats-why-peace-on-earth-might-require-big-sacrifices/. Accessed 13 Nov. 2017.

Palmer, Ada. "Uncommon Interview: Hugo Award Nominee Ada Palmer." Interview by Stephanie Palazzolo. *The Chicago Maroon*, 17 Apr. 2017, www.chicagomaroon.com/article/2017/4/18/uncommon-interview-hugo-award-nominee-ada-palmer/. Accessed 13 Nov. 2017.

"The Will to Battle." *Publishers Weekly*, 6 Nov. 2017, www.publishersweekly.com/978-0-7653-7804-0. Accessed 14 Nov. 2017.

SELECTED WORKS

The Recovery of Classical Philosophy in the Renaissance, a Brief Guide (with James Hankins), 2008; *Reading Lucretius in the Renaissance,* 2014; *Too Like the Lightning,* 2016; *Seven Surrenders,* 2017; *The Will to Battle,* 2017

—*Christopher Mari*

Ashley Park

Date of birth: June 6, 1991
Occupation: Actor

Few Broadway performers in the early twenty-first century have made as strong an impression on theatergoers as Ashley Park has since debuting as a replacement in the long-running hit musical *Mamma Mia!* in 2014. Since that time, the award-winning actor, singer, and dancer has been seen in the featured role of Tuptim in the Lincoln Center Theater production of the revival of *The King and I* in 2015 and went on to star in another Broadway revival, *Sunday in the Park with George,* in 2017. However, her highest-profile role to date has been that of Gretchen Wieners, one of the villains in the original Broadway adaptation of the 2004 Tiny Fey–penned film *Mean Girls,* which debuted to rave reviews in 2018. The role earned Park—a childhood cancer survivor—a nomination for the 2018 Tony Award for Best Performance by an Actress in a Featured Role in a Musical.

When asked how she forged this successful path through the competitive theatrical world, Park told Casey Mink for *Backstage* (18 Apr. 2018), "Being a kind and genuine person and being as supportive to everybody as possible only nurtures the community, it only forges your own path forward. Someone else's success is not synonymous with your failure. The more we lift each other up—as cheesy as it sounds—it makes the work so much more fun."

EARLY LIFE AND EDUCATION

Ashley Jini Park was born in California on June 6, 1991, but was raised in Ann Arbor, Michigan. She has a younger sister, Audrey, who was an excellent athlete. Although her parents were not at all musical or in any way show-business oriented, they saw her budding potential as a performer early on. Even in her early childhood, all she ever wanted to do was to perform and to make people around her laugh. In speaking with Matt Mullen for *Interview* (1 May 2018), Park recalled, "[My parents] signed me up for dance classes very early on. I was always the runt of the class, but I was very, very dedicated. Then I started taking piano lessons. I've always been

super musical. But I never thought that musical theater was something I could pursue as a career until much later into high school."

During elementary school and while attending Pioneer High School, Park took on any roles she could, even playing such real-life figures as Scott Joplin, Chief Joseph, and Stevie Wonder at various points. However, it was during high school, partway through her sophomore year, that she ran into serious health problems. After she was diagnosed with acute myeloid leukemia, she spent much of that year in the hospital getting treatment. The Make-A-Wish Foundation granted her wish to see a Broadway show and took her and her family to see not one, but four: *The Lion King, Wicked, Spring Awakening,* and *A Chorus Line.* It was a life-changing experience for her.

When she was found to be cancer free following eight months in the hospital and six rounds of chemotherapy, she immediately returned to the stage to participate in high school productions. "I think I just missed being around people so much after being sick . . . and in the theater, you're constantly surrounded by people. . . . I never wanted cancer or any illness to define me. And in the theater, I could put on any hat (or in my case, wig) and explore different people and stories," she explained about her increased passion and dedication to performing in an interview for the website *Fit for Broadway* (30 Jan. 2016). As part of the theater program at her high school, she also got the chance to be mentored by musical theater students attending nearby University of Michigan who often directed productions.

Upon completing high school, Park majored in musical theater at the University of Michigan, graduating in 2013. She would not have to wait very long until she found her own place on the Great White Way.

EARLY ROLES ON BROADWAY

Park met with stage success early, being featured in such regional (during summer breaks) and university productions as *Jesus Christ Superstar, Miss Saigon, Bat Boy, Brigadoon, Jekyll & Hyde,* and *The Sound of Music* throughout her time in college. In 2014, within months after her graduation, Broadway beckoned when she landed a replacement role in the ensemble for the Broadway musical *Mamma Mia!* Written by British playwright Catherine Johnson and featuring the music of the 1970s Swedish pop group ABBA, the jukebox musical had debuted in 2001. She was eventually cast as the understudy for the role of Ali, one of the best friends of the main character, in the same production. Her time in the cast of *Mamma Mia!* helped her immensely as she continued to navigate New York's theater world. She noted to Mullen, "When I landed there I was just out of school and so green. To be in a show like that, which had been running for so long and where everyone had a routine, was incredibly valuable. I got to learn what life as a working actor is. Now I know what a call board is. Now I know how to do tax forms for a Broadway show." From there, beginning in late 2014, she gained recognition for playing the role of the wicked stepsister Gabrielle in the first national tour of Richard Rodgers and Oscar Hammerstein's *Cinderella*, which originally premiered on television in 1957.

In 2015, Park returned to the Broadway stage and moved on to even greater success playing the role of Tuptim, a slave brought from Burma (also known as Myanmar) to be one of the king's junior wives, in a critically acclaimed revival of Rodgers and Hammerstein's *The King and I* staged at the Lincoln Center Theater. During her time on *The King and I*, Park told Matthew Blank for *Playbill* (21 Apr. 2015), "[Director Bartlett Sher] challenged me, pushed me, and guided me to dig deep into every layer of this role and story. . . . Also getting to sing some of my favorite Rodgers and Hammerstein ballads with a 29-piece orchestra led by Ted Sperling still gives me giddy goosebumps. Working at Lincoln Center Theater is a dream come true, and doing it with over 50 brilliant, dedicated, disciplined, and lovely storytellers has made this experience incredibly fulfilling."

Following her run on *The King and I*, Park found herself playing and serving as the understudy for multiple roles in the Broadway revival of the musical *Sunday in the Park with George*, starring Jake Gyllenhaal and Annaleigh Ashford, with music and lyrics by Stephen Sondheim and book by James Lapine, in early 2017. This production marked the beginning of one of the busiest times in her career up to that point, as she began to take on roles that required overlapping auditions, performances, and rehearsals. She next appeared on stage as Maid Marian in *Hood*, a new musical about the classic character Robin Hood, which opened in July at the Dallas Theater Center, before immediately transitioning in September to be part of the cast of *KPOP*, a production about the world of Korean pop music, presented by Ars Nova in New York City.

BECOMING A MEAN GIRL

Park was in Dallas when she got a call that would considerably elevate her profile on Broadway. The celebrated and award-winning comedian and writer Tina Fey was adapting her acclaimed high school comedy film *Mean Girls* for Broadway as a musical and she wanted Park to audition for the role of Gretchen Wieners. Park, a longtime fan of the film, was eager to audition. There was only one problem: to make the audition, she would have to find a red-eye flight from Dallas to New York on the night of her opening for *Hood* and would not have the typical time to prepare. She managed to get a flight and came to the audition, sleep deprived but willing. The audition that morning took all of about seven or eight minutes, in which she performed some of the scenes and sang a song, as well as talked to Fey and the producers for a bit. Later that day, her agent called to tell her that she had gotten the part. For a time, she was beginning rehearsals for *Mean Girls* while she was still doing performances of *KPOP*.

Park believes she was able to land the role of Gretchen because she understood the character: an insecure girl who is fragile and flawed and wants, in the end, to be a good friend. In an interview with Victoria Myers for the *Interval* (15 May 2018), she said, "You can't play a villain honestly unless you really feel for them and have empathy, and I immediately felt empathy for Gretchen—and for all of the insecurities that we have growing up, and that we still carry as adults. That's why it's a part that everyone in the audience connects to."

MAKING AN IMPACT AND RECEIVING RECOGNITION

Being a part of *Mean Girls* has allowed Park to better appreciate a positive collaborative environment, particularly under the guidance of Fey, whom Park explained to Mink is not so "precious" with her writing as to want her actors simply to perform the parts without providing their own input. Park also believes the role is vitally important to her as an Asian American performer, because the role was not written for someone with Asian ancestry. Yet being in this role, she believes, helps to better demonstrate the modern diversity of American society. "I think it's really important to tell stories about race and racial divide and historical stories, but the fact that this truly does take place in a high school in 2018 and you see that represented on the stage, I think that's really important and I think that is subversive in its own way and political in its own way without calling any attention to it," she said to Myers.

In addition to earning a Tony Award nomination for her role as Gretchen, Park was nominated for the 2018 Drama League Distinguished Performance Award and the Drama Desk Award for Outstanding Actress in a Musical for her work in *KPOP*. She also won the 2018 Lucille Lortel Award for Outstanding Lead Actress in a Musical for *KPOP*. Furthermore, she won the 2018 Clarence Derwent Award for most promising female performer. She credits her mother with much of her success, telling Blank, "My mom is my champion. She has always been the most encouraging and resilient person. She teaches me by example to be smart, strong, humble, and above all else—to be kind."

PERSONAL LIFE

Park lives in New York City.

SUGGESTED READING

Park, Ashley. "Cue & A: *King and I* Star Ashley Park on Bartlett Sher, Onstage Tumbles and the Time She Played Stevie Wonder." Interview by Matthew Blank. *Playbill*, 21 Apr. 2015, www.playbill.com/article/cue-a-king-and-i-star-ashley-park-on-bartlett-sher-onstage-tumbles-and-the-time-she-played-stevie-wonder-com-347217. Accessed 9 Aug. 2018.

Park, Ashley. "Fit for *The King and I*." *Fit for Broadway*, 30 Jan. 2016, www.fitforbroadway.com/features/broadway/ffb-ashley-park/. Accessed 9 Aug. 2018.

Park, Ashley. "How Ashley Park Made 'Fetch' Happen—and Got Cast in *Mean Girls*." Interview by Casey Mink. *Backstage*, 18 Apr. 2018, www.backstage.com/interview/how-ashley-park-made-fetch-happenand-got-cast-mean-girls/. Accessed 9 Aug. 2018.

Park, Ashley. "An Interview with Ashley Park." Interview by Victoria Myers. *The Interval*, 15 May 2018, www.theintervalny.com/interviews/2018/05/an-interview-with-ashley-park/. Accessed 9 Aug. 2018.

Park, Ashley. "The Scene-Stealer: Ashley Park." Interview by Matt Mullen. *Interview*, 1 May 2018, www.interviewmagazine.com/culture/ashley-park-gretchen-weiners-mean-girls-interview. Accessed 9 Aug. 2018.

SELECTED WORKS

Mamma Mia! 2014; *The King and I*, 2015–16; *Sunday in the Park with George*, 2017; *Mean Girls*, 2018–

—*Christopher Mari*

Joc Pederson

Date of birth: April 21, 1992
Occupation: Baseball player

Baseball has long been described as a game of inches. Inches turn a fly ball into a home run, make a headlong slide safe or out, and make the difference between a fair or foul ball. Joc Pederson knows all about the power of inches, and then some. Those inches shaped his rise to Major League Baseball (MLB), where he became known for some of the longest home runs in the league. An All-Star by his mid-twenties, Pederson secured his place in Los Angeles Dodgers

By ATinySliver, via Wikimedia Commons

history as one of the highlights of the 2017 World Series against the Houston Astros.

However, he had to overcome numerous challenges along the way to success. Coming from a baseball family, Pederson excelled at the sport in high school and skipped college to sign with the Dodgers. He quickly became one of the best prospects in the minor leagues, known as a team player and hard worker who could both hit and play strong defense in center field. He enjoyed a spectacular start to his rookie season in 2015, but struggled significantly in the second half of the season, plagued by frequent strikeouts. This inconsistency, compounded by injuries, continued over the next two seasons. In mid-2017 he was demoted to the minors after a particularly brutal batting slump.

Almost forgotten while heading into the 2017 postseason, Pederson returned to etch his name in World Series history. Though the Dodgers ultimately lost to the Astros, he led the offense with three home runs and set a big-league record by having a hit and scoring a run in his first six World Series appearances. With this breakout performance and still four years left before free agency, Pederson was poised to cement his reputation as a star slugger. "I like to slug," he told Tyler Kepner for the *New York Times* (22 July 2015). "I take aggressive swings. I swing and miss because of it, and I think I still have a lot to improve."

EARLY LIFE AND EDUCATION

Joc Pederson was born on April 21, 1992, in Palo Alto, California, one of Stu and Shelly Pederson's four children. (Through his mother, Pederson is ethnically Jewish but does not identify as religiously Jewish.) His oldest brother, Champ, was born with the genetic disorder known as Down syndrome, which is characterized by intellectual disability and physical impairments. Pederson has noted that Champ's struggles, but overall happy disposition, inspired him to do his best throughout his life.

Another source of inspiration was his father, himself a baseball player. Stu Pederson played twelve seasons in the minor leagues, reaching the majors for just eight games with the Los Angeles Dodgers in 1985. Once his pro ball days were over, Stu continued to find work in the game, both as a high school and college coach and as a private hitting instructor. "He did everything he could to be the best player he could be. No regrets," Pederson said of his father to Jorge L. Ortiz for *USA Today* (18 May 2015). "That's what he's always told us, to go out there and make sure that when they take the uniform away from you, there's nothing you wish you could have done or should have done or worked harder."

Pederson played baseball and football throughout his childhood. Although he excelled at both, he made his reputation in baseball at Palo Alto High School, where he was named male athlete of the year in 2010, his senior season. By the time he graduated, scouts from MLB teams were on hand at every game the outfielder played. Despite the attention he was receiving, Pederson kept his head down and continued to hone his skills, spending roughly thirty-five hours a week working out. He also made sure to earn a scholarship to the University of Southern California (USC), in case the scouts decided to take a pass on him. "The sky is the limit for Joc and the future," his high school baseball head coach, Erick Raich, said at the time to Gracie Marshall for Palo Alto High's *Viking Magazine* (1 June 2010). "He has all of the ability to play professional baseball. . . . He is by far the best high school player I have ever coached."

MINOR LEAGUE PHENOM
During the 2010 MLB Draft, the Dodgers selected Pederson in the eleventh round. With a $600,000 signing bonus before him—much higher than normal for his relatively low draft position—he decided to skip college and instead sign with the Dodgers. In 2011, he began working his way through various teams in the Dodgers' minor league farm system. After early struggles, he worked with hitting coaches to change his swing and raise his batting average. The work soon paid off: he hit .353 in sixty-eight games of rookie ball, with eleven home runs.

From there Pederson steadily rose through the minors. He was promoted to the Dodgers' Class-A ball club, the Rancho Cucamonga Quakes, in April 2012. In September 2012 he made the AA Chattanooga Lookouts, and began the 2013 season as the youngest player on the team. After an impressive 2013 season, he was ranked as the Dodgers' top prospect by *Baseball America*.

In February 2014, the Dodgers' management invited him to spring training as a non-roster center fielder. Liking what they saw, they promoted him to their AAA team, the Albuquerque Isotopes in the Pacific Coast League (PCL). For the 2014 season he was voted the PCL Most Valuable Player (MVP), earned Rookie of the Year status, and was named to the postseason All-PCL team. In addition, *Baseball America* placed him on their 2014 Minor League All-Star team, while naming him AAA Player of the Year and an AAA All-Star.

Then, on September 1, 2014, Pederson got the call he had long been waiting for: the Dodgers had added him to their forty-man expanded roster and were bringing him up to the majors. At the time of the call up, Dodgers manager Don Mattingly described Pederson as the best center fielder in the team's organization.

ALL-STAR ROOKIE
Pederson played just eighteen games at the end of the 2014 season, with a mere four hits in twenty-eight at-bats. But what the Dodgers saw during that brief time impressed them enough to name Pederson as their starting center fielder for the 2015 season. The early returns were impressive. By May 2015, his offensive numbers ranked him in the top ten of the National League: 10 homers, 28 walks, .534 slugging percentage, and a .388 on-base percentage. From April 27 to May 6, all seven of Pederson's hits were home runs. By mid-July he had racked up 20 homers, many of them among the furthest-hit in the league, and had maintained a .356 on-base percentage. "This power is kind of new to me," Pederson told Kepner. "A lot of people have the same swing they've had since Little League and college, but I've kind of just created this. I didn't hit a home run until I was a junior in high school. It's all evolving."

Pederson's biggest offensive problem was strikeouts. As in the minors, the same aggressiveness that fueled his power stroke led to many swings-and-misses. At the major-league level, this kept his batting average well below his strong minor league level. Still, his numbers proved so good through the first half of the season that he was selected to the 2015 MLB All-Star Game, becoming the first Dodgers rookie chosen since 1995. While most of the attention came for his hitting, analysts gave Pederson high marks for his defensive play as well. "He's involved, and his angles are spot on," Dodgers broadcaster Rick

Monday, himself formerly a center fielder, told Kepner. "He's reading the ball off the bat. He gives himself a chance to get to the ball."

The latter half of the 2015 season, however, proved much more difficult. Pederson's bat cooled, and he entered an extended hitting slump that prompted management to pull him from the starting center fielder position. He ended the season with 26 homers but only 54 RBIs and a weak .210 batting average. Despite these challenges, he placed sixth in Rookie of the Year voting.

Pederson's 2016 season with the Dodgers proved he was a consistent player with the capacity to improve. He once again revamped his entire swing, which helped him make more contact and raise his batting average somewhat, ending the regular season at .246. His power also continued, with twenty-five home runs and twenty-six doubles. Despite a midseason shoulder injury, he appeared in 137 games, and posted above-average defensive ratings. He started all eleven games the Dodgers played in the 2016 postseason, hitting well in the National League Division Series (NLDS) but struggling as Los Angeles was eliminated in the National League Championship Series (NLCS).

2017 SEASON AND WORLD SERIES

Pederson's 2017 season opened with a blast—literally. On opening day in April against the San Diego Padres, he ripped a grand slam and collected five RBIs on the day. But what began so spectacularly was soon balanced by some disappointments. A groin strain in April put him on the disabled list for ten days, and then a collision with teammate Yasiel Puig in May again put him on the disabled list, this time with a concussion. But the worst was yet to come: after a 2-for-41 stretch at the plate in July and August, he was sent down to the minors. In 102 regular season games, he hit just .212 with 11 homers, 20 doubles, and 35 RBIs. His defensive performance also faltered.

Pederson continued to struggle at Triple-A. He returned to the Dodgers late in the season but was used sparingly and was left off the roster for the NLDS. Still, he remained determined to help the team in the postseason. "I think that his ability to stay the course and focus on things that he can control have helped him grow as a major league baseball player," Dodgers manager Dave Roberts said to Pedro Moura for the *Los Angeles Times* (31 Oct. 2017). "And to his credit, he didn't jump ship. I give all the credit to Joc and his growth. You're always trying to challenge guys to get better and not be complacent."

Pederson was added back to the Dodgers' roster for the NLCS. He recorded just one hit in five at-bats in that series, in which the Dodgers beat the Chicago Cubs to advance to the World

Series against the Houston Astros. It was there that Pederson returned to his star potential, essentially pacing the Los Angeles offense by getting at least one hit and one run scored in all six games he played. He also broke a Dodgers postseason record with five consecutive games with an extra-base hit, which tied the World Series record across the MLB. The most notable of his hits were his three home runs, including a three-run homer in Game 4. His overall postseason stats were equally impressive—a .304 batting average, an on-base percentage of .360, and five RBIs.

Although the Astros ended up winning the World Series in seven games, Pederson went into the off-season as a resurgent talent. Yet he remained humble, aware that it would take more work to sustain the success he had proven capable of. "I've still got a lot of work to do," he told Moura. "But it's encouraging to see some of the process and all of the hard work turn into some results in the game."

Pederson had earned $550,000 in 2017, and following the season was eligible for a raise under the MLB arbitration system for the first time. In that system, teams and eligible players negotiate a salary or have the matter decided by an independent panel of judges. Pederson and the Dodgers avoided an arbitration hearing by agreeing on a $2.6 million salary for the 2018 season. In the off-season Pederson married his girlfriend, Kelsey Williams.

SUGGESTED READING

Jaffe, Jay. "Houston Strong: Title-Starved Astros Deliver First Championship with World Series Game 7 Win Over Dodgers." *Sports Illustrated*, 2 Nov. 2017, www.si.com/mlb/2017/11/02/astros-world-series-champions-dodgers. Accessed 7 Mar. 2018.

"Joc Pederson." *MLB*, 2018, m.mlb.com/player/592626/joc-pederson. Accessed 7 Mar. 2018.

Kepner, Tyler. "Dodgers' Joc Pederson Hits Homers That Travel, but He Has a Long Way to Go." *The New York Times*, 22 July 2015, www.nytimes.com/2015/07/23/sports/baseball/dodgers-joc-pederson-already-a-power-has-far-to-go.html. Accessed 7 Mar. 2018.

Marshall, Gracie. "Palo Alto High School Male Athlete of the Year: Joc Pederson." *Viking Magazine*, 1 June 2010, vikingsportsmag.com/featured-athlete/2010/06/01/palo-alto-high-school-male-athlete-of-the-year-joc-pederson/. Accessed 7 Mar. 2018.

Moura, Pedro. "Joc Pederson's Season Included a Stint in Triple-A, and Now 3 World Series Home Runs." *Los Angeles Times*, 31 Oct. 2017, www.latimes.com/sports/mlb/la-sp-dodgers-joc-pederson-20171031-story.html. Accessed 7 Mar. 2018.

Ortiz, Jorge L. "Fueled by Family, Joc Pederson and His 'Ridiculous' Talent Power Dodgers." *USA Today*, 18 May 2015, www.usatoday.com/story/sports/mlb/2015/05/18/joc-pederson-dodgers-rookie-of-the-year/27531681/. Accessed 7 Mar. 2018.

Stephen, Eric. "Dodgers Sign Joc Pederson, Avoid Salary Arbitration with Everybody." *True Blue LA*, SBNation, 12 Jan. 2018, www.truebluela.com/2018/1/12/16880008/joc-pederson-contract-dodgers-salary-arbitration. Accessed 7 Mar. 2018.

—*Christopher Mari*

Bao Phi

Date of birth: February 1975
Occupation: Poet

Bao Phi is a Vietnamese American poet and spoken word artist. His second collection of poems, *Thousand Star Hotel* (2017), explores racism, police brutality, and the Asian American experience. The book was inspired by his young daughter Song. As a new father, Phi looked back on his own childhood in a family of Vietnamese refugees—he was three months old when his family fled Saigon in 1975—with new eyes. He has described the book as a survival "guidebook" for Song, he told Kat Chow for National Public Radio (20 July 2017), and as an act of political resistance. In it, he makes poor Asian Americans and Vietnamese Americans, who are often invisible, visible. Another work, a children's book called *A Different Pond* (2017), is based on Phi's experiences going fishing with his father. The book is illustrated by the Vietnamese American graphic artist Thi Bui. In 2018, *A Different Pond* was named a Caldecott Medal Honor Book by the American Library Association (ALA).

Phi, who was raised in Minneapolis, Minnesota, got his start as a slam poet, or performance poet, in the early 1990s. He is a two-time Minnesota Grand Slam champion and appeared on an episode of HBO's *Def Poetry Jam*, hosted by hip-hop mogul Russell Simmons. One of Phi's poems was included in the *Best American Poetry* anthology in 2006.

EARLY LIFE

Phi was born in Saigon in February 1975. The city fell to the North Vietnamese a few months later, in April, and Phi and his family were forced to flee. Phi's father was in the Southern Vietnamese military, and his mother worked in a gift shop at the university in Saigon, where his father and uncles had planned to attend school before the war broke out. Phi is the youngest of six children. The family moved through a series of refugee camps before settling in the United States in the Phillips neighborhood of South Minneapolis. "I'm in this strange position where I was present for that but I have no memory of it," Phi told Chow of his family's journey. In Minnesota, his father became a tailor and his mother owned a gift shop.

As Phi got older, his parents began to tell him more about their experiences during and after the war. Shared family trauma is an important thread in Phi's work. For young Phi, life in Phillips was not always easy. In the early years especially, neighbors took out frustrations with the failed war itself on Phi and his family. "People would routinely say things like 'go back to where you come from,'" he told Marianne Combs for Minnesota Public Radio's *MPR News* (17 May 2017). "People thought we were stealing their pets and eating them." Still, Phi's earliest childhood writings were mostly inspired by fantasy tales such as J. R. R. Tolkien's *The Lord of the Rings* and the role-playing game *Dungeons & Dragons*.

Phi began writing poetry as a student at South High School. He also became involved in social justice organizing. He learned about various movements through his fellow students and teachers, many of whom were Native American and African American. Inspired to speak on the common struggles of marginalized people, he joined the school speech team. "There were all these issues around me I couldn't ignore," he recalled to Crystal Duan for the Minneapolis *Star-Tribune* (14 Aug. 2017). "Around that time, there was this anti-racist group and protests against the [1990–91] Persian Gulf War. And I, as a young person, was trying to figure out being involved."

SLAM POETRY AND OTHER WORK

Phi's performances for the school speech team were early iterations of slam poetry. Slam poetry, Phi told Kathleen Janeschek for the magazine *Midwestern Gothic* (2017), taught him the importance of "urgency" in his writing. He recalled participating in speech events as a high schooler—he describes his young self as "intense" and "awkward"—in 1992 and 1993. Phi siphoned his budding activism into "angry poems about racism," he said. Performance poetry became an immediate way for him to express feelings and ideas. After high school, Phi won a full scholarship to Macalester College, a private university in St. Paul, Minnesota. He was not planning to pursue writing, but a professor, the poet Diane Glancy, encouraged him to take creative writing classes and keep writing poems. He decided to major in English. As a student at Macalester, Phi also made a formative connection to David Mura, a writer, poet, and performance artist. Phi joined Mura's group, Asian American Renaissance.

Phi stayed in St. Paul after graduation, becoming a fixture of the local slam poetry scene, where he encouraged the inclusion of diverse voices. "One of the best things about slam is that anybody can do it," he told Hannah Allam for the *Saint Paul Pioneer Press* (11 July 2000). "I want to hear other people's voices. I just go up there and do what I want to do. If it does well, it does well." Phi often did very well. He won the Minnesota Grand Slam twice and was a finalist for the National Poetry Slam in 2000. In 2004, he appeared on an episode of HBO's *Russell Simmons Presents Def Poetry*. He performed a poem called "You Bring Out the Vietnamese in Me," inspired by the Sandra Cisneros poem "You Bring Out the Mexican in Me." In 2006, former US poet laureate Billy Collins chose Phi's poem "Race" for inclusion in that year's edition of the *Best American Poetry* anthology.

Phi produced two EPs of his poetry in performance: *Refugeography* (2002) and *The Nguyens* (2008). In 2008, he appeared in a documentary called *The Listening Project*. In it, Phi and three other Americans travel to various countries interviewing citizens about what they think of the United States. In 2015, Phi published a short science fiction story called "Revolution Shuffle." It appeared in an anthology called *Octavia's Brood: Science Fiction from Social Justice Movements* (2015) and was nominated for a Hugo Award for best short story. One of his essays was published in an anthology called *A Good Time for the Truth: Race in Minnesota* in 2016.

SÔNG I SING AND A DIFFERENT POND

Reportedly, the late Allan Kornblum, the legendary founder of the indie Coffee House Press, approached Phi and offered to publish his work after seeing the young poet at a slam. Phi has said that he did not find the process of writing for print publication different than that of composing a poem to be performed aloud "I write poetry, and then I figure out what's the best way to perform that poetry in front of an audience," he explained to Janeschek. Phi published his first collection, *Sông I Sing*, with Coffee House Press in 2011. (Phi had previously published three poetry chapbooks: *Surviving the Translation: Collected Poems from 1993–2002* in 2002, *The Way We Pay* in 2004, and *Last Name First* in 2005.)

The book, its title a play on Phi's daughter's name, contains some of Phi's best-known poems, including "You Bring Out the Vietnamese in Me," "Race," and "The Nguyens," a collection of poems about different characters who all share the Vietnamese surname Nguyen. Dana Jennings, who reviewed the book for the *New York Times* (19 Dec. 2011), praised it highly, writing, "In this song of his very American self, in

every poem Mr. Phi writes rhymes with the truth." Phi sometimes uses the word "refugeography," a portmanteau of refugee and geography, to describe his work. The word comes from Phi's poem "You Bring Out the Vietnamese in Me." Critic Vinh Nguyen wrote about the term for the journal *MELUS: Multi-Ethnic Literature of the United States* (2016), describing it as the "spatial and psychic terrains of Vietnamese/American refugeehood." The poems in *Sông I Sing* evoke these two kinds of travel. Julie Thi Underhill, who reviewed the book for the arts magazine *diaCRITICS* (1 Dec. 2011), pointed out the double entendre of the title. The Vietnamese word "sông" means "river." Phi references actual rivers in Vietnam, "while reminding us that this collection stitches the refugee's 'over there' past with the 'over here' present via 'within here' simultaneity."

In 2014, Phi wrote a review for a children's book called *Here I Am* by Patti Kim and illustrated by Sonia Sánchez. Capstone, the book's publisher, was so impressed by the review that they reached out to Phi, asking him if he had ever considered writing a children's book. Since the birth of his daughter, Phi had. Adapting a poem he had written about fishing trips with his father, Phi wrote a children's book called *A Different Pond*. It was published in 2017 and was awarded a Caldecott Medal Honor in 2018. *A Different Pond* received starred reviews from both *Publishers Weekly* and *Kirkus*. The latter (24 May 2017) described it as a "powerful, multilayered story about family, memory, and the costs of becoming a refugee."

THOUSAND STAR HOTEL

Phi's second volume of poetry, *Thousand Star Hotel*, brought him further attention and critical acclaim. The book's title comes from a popular Vietnamese saying. One does not need to stay in a four-star hotel, the saying goes, because in Vietnam, one has a "thousand star hotel" every night. "It's sly," Phi told Chow of the saying and the theme of his book, "but it's also about survival and making the best of it."

The book was well received when it was published in 2017. Elizabeth Hoover, for the Minneapolis *Star-Tribune* (9 July 2017), called it both "heartbreaking" and "bitingly funny." She also identified Phi's poignant thesis, a line from the poem "Untitled / Father," in which, addressing his daughter, he says, "I just want a better world for you to be a small part of."

PERSONAL LIFE

Phi lives in the Powderhorn Park neighborhood of Minneapolis with his young daughter, Song. (He and Song's mother are separated.) He is also the program director of the Loft Literary Center, an arts organization in Minneapolis.

SUGGESTED READING

Chow, Kat. "The Poet Bao Phi, On Creating a 'Guidebook' For Young Asian-Americans." *National Public Radio*, 20 July 2017, www.npr.org/sections/codeswitch/2017/07/20/537580283/the-poet-bao-phi-on-creating-a-guidebook-for-young-asian-americans. Accessed 2 Mar. 2018.

Combs, Marianne. "For the Poet Bao Phi, a Violent Past Is Never Far Away." *MPR News*, 17 May 2017, www.mprnews.org/story/2017/05/17/for-the-poet-bao-phi-a-violent-past-is-never-far-away. Accessed 4 Mar. 2018.

Jennings, Dana. "Lyrical Renegades and Free-Range Sages." Review of *Sông I Sing*, by Bao Phi. *The New York Times*, 19 Dec. 2011, www.nytimes.com/2011/12/20/books/poems-by-bao-phi-roberto-bolano-and-simon-armitage-review.html. Accessed 6 Mar. 2018.

Nguyen, Vinh. "Refugeography in 'Post-Racial' America: Bao Phi's Activist Poetry." *MELUS: Multi-Ethnic Literature of the United States*, vol. 41, no. 3, 2016, pp. 171–93.

Review of *A Different Pond*, by Bao Phi. *Kirkus Reviews*, 24 May 2017, www.kirkusreviews.com/book-reviews/bao-phi/a-different-pond-capstone-young-readers/. Accessed 6 Mar. 2018.

Phi, Bao. "Interview Bao Phi." Interview by Kathleen Janeschek. *Midwestern Gothic*, 2017, midwestgothic.com/2017/09/interview-bao-phi/. Accessed 4 Mar. 2018.

Phi, Bao. "Star Poet Bao Phi on Racism, Writing and Why He Chooses to Stay in Minneapolis." Interview by Crystal Duan. *Star-Tribune* [Minneapolis], 14 Aug. 2017, www.startribune.com/star-poet-bao-phi-on-racism-writing-and-why-he-chooses-to-stay-in-minneapolis/440337213/. Accessed 2 Mar. 2018.

SELECTED WORKS

Sông I Sing, 2011; *Thousand Star Hotel*, 2017; *A Different Pond*, 2017

—*Molly Hagan*

Ben Platt

Date of birth: September 24, 1993
Occupation: Actor

Tony Award–winning actor Ben Platt is best known for his breakout turn as the star of the Broadway musical *Dear Evan Hansen*. A rising star in the entertainment industry, he launched his career with a supporting role in the popular 2012 film *Pitch Perfect*, a romantic comedy about college a cappella groups. He was named one of *Time* magazine's hundred most influential

By The Tony Awards on YouTube via Wikimedia Commons

people in 2017, and he became the youngest actor to date to be honored with the Drama League's Distinguished Performance Award, which an actor can only win once in their lifetime. As further proof that he is an accomplished singer as well as an actor, he landed a record deal with Atlantic Records in 2017.

Platt's first love has long been musical theater, particularly from the time he took the stage in his first musical production at the age of six. "I've spent every day since then just madly in love with musical theater," he said in his 2017 Tony acceptance speech, as quoted by Caty Szeto in the online edition of the student daily *Harvard-Westlake Chronicle* (31 Aug. 2017). "It's where I've found everything I've ever loved and where I belong." The show follows the story of Evan Hansen, a severely anxious teenager who begins the school year with a quest to make friends and ends up telling a huge lie about his relationship with a classmate who recently took his own life. It is unusually heavy fare for a Broadway musical, but critics and audiences deemed the show a resounding success. "I've never met an actor who has such emotional access," Steven Levenson, the writer of the show's book, said of Platt's performance on stage, as quoted by Joel Lovell in the *New York Times* (10 May 2017). "Yet every night, as intense as the role is internally, he hits each moment exactly the same. He's technically perfect, *every* time. I find it a mystery. He really is a unicorn."

EARLY LIFE AND EDUCATION

Platt was born the fourth of five children on September 24, 1993, in Los Angeles, California. His father, Marc Platt, is a veteran film, television, and theater producer best known for his work on the Academy Award–winning films *Bridge of Spies* (2015) and *La La Land* (2016) as well as the Tony Award–winning musical *Wicked*, which opened in 2003. Platt's mother, Julie, a former banker, chairs the Jewish Federation of Greater Los Angeles.

As a child, Platt often put on performances in the backyard, and his idea of ideal toys were things like fog machines and microphones. "I can't remember a time in Ben's life when I didn't think, 'This kid's a performer,'" his father told Gordon Cox for *Variety* (2017). In Platt's own recollection, he watched *The Wizard of Oz* (1939) every day and dressed up like Dorothy. "I had a blue jumper that was sort of close enough to what Dorothy was wearing, and I would carry around my giant Labrador retriever as Toto," he told Cox. When he was six years old, he was cast in a school production of *Cinderella* as the prince, and he went on to step into the roles of several other characters while at the school. About two years later, when he was eight, he appeared in his first professional production: *The Music Man*, starring Tony Award winner Kristin Chenoweth and television actor Eric McCormack, at the Hollywood Bowl (where he would continue to perform in subsequent years alongside veterans such as Jeremy Irons). In 2004, at the age of eleven, he played a leading role in a production of the musical *Caroline, or Change* at the Ahmanson Theatre. For a time, he went on a national tour with the show.

Platt attended high school at the prestigious Harvard-Westlake School in Los Angeles, where he befriended the actor Beanie Feldstein. (Feldstein, who has appeared on Broadway and in the Greta Gerwig film *Lady Bird*, is the younger sister of actor Jonah Hill.) As a student, he performed in musicals like *Pippin*—he played the title role—as well as with the school's improv troupe. His teachers remember him as inherently gifted and also a hard worker. "Ben was always early, always had done the work between rehearsals that needed to be done, was the first to learn his lines, to learn his music," Ted Walch, who directed Platt in *Pippin*, told Daryl H. Miller for the *Los Angeles Times* (11 June 2017). "Yes, he's wildly talented, but first and foremost he is on top of his game. He knows what it means to be prepared, to do the work you need to do so that your talent can shine through."

BREAKING INTO BROADWAY

Platt graduated from high school in 2011 but chose to defer his enrollment at Columbia University for a year to take a role in the film *Pitch Perfect* (2012), about dueling college a cappella groups. He played Benji Applebaum, the nerdy magician roommate of the film's male lead. Benji enjoys a breakout moment in a performance near the end of the film; the scene earned Platt a Teen Choice Award nomination for Choice Movie Scene Stealer. Actor Elizabeth Banks, who coproduced the film, told Michael Paulson for the *New York Times* (31 Mar. 2016): "He [Platt] really just felt like he was in that exact place between being a boy and being a man—*Pitch Perfect* was about that transitional time in people's lives, and he completely embodied that." *Pitch Perfect* performed modestly at the box office before really becoming a hit after landing on store shelves and HBO.

Platt attended Columbia for less than two months before getting cast (on the strength of his performance in *Pitch Perfect*) in late 2012 in the production of the Tony Award–winning musical satire *Book of Mormon*, about two young Mormon missionaries who travel to Uganda, staged at Chicago's Bank of America Theatre. He played Elder Cunningham, the nerdy sidekick to the unimpeachably perfect Elder Price. His interpretation deviated from that of the goofy Josh Gad, who originated the character, but won praise from critics. Chris Jones, writing for the *Chicago Tribune* (20 Dec. 2012), called Platt's performance the production's "true revelation." "Platt, whose comic instincts are exquisite, really leans into this part, throwing himself out there with the abandonment of youth," he wrote. After having owned the role on the Chicago stage for about a year before the production wrapped, in 2014, Platt made his Broadway debut as Elder Cunningham in the New York production; he left in 2015, the year in which he also reprised his role as Benji in the movie sequel *Pitch Perfect 2*.

DEAR EVAN HANSEN

Around the same time, Platt had begun working with songwriters Benj Pasek and Justin Paul. He had auditioned for their Off-Broadway musical *Dogfight* in 2012 but had been deemed too young for the role. The duo called Platt in 2014 and asked him to perform in a cold reading of a new musical. Though Platt was prohibited from reading the script until he set foot in the room for rehearsal, his performance still deeply impressed the creators. "I think Ben was officially attached to the project the minute he opened his mouth," producer Stacey Mindich told Cox of that initial meeting.

The musical, *Dear Evan Hansen*, premiered at Arena Stage in Washington, DC, in the summer of 2015. Peter Marks praised the musical in a review for the *Washington Post* (3 Aug. 2015) and singled out Platt's original take on the main character: "Platt's ability to elbow complicated

Evan so effortlessly into our affections attests to an achievement bordering on heroic," he wrote. The show soon moved Off-Broadway, to the Second Stage Theater, in March 2016. Later the same year, it transitioned to Broadway, playing at the Music Box Theatre. In a starred review for the *New York Times* (4 Dec. 2016), Charles Isherwood wrote that Platt's performance was one "not likely to be bettered on Broadway this season." The famously aloof critic seemed deeply moved by the musical and Platt, adding, "As Evan becomes more entangled in his deceptions, Mr. Platt's performance grows richer and more wrenching." Many critics picked up on the relatability of Evans's character, and Platt has explained in interviews his desire to portray such a complex character. "He's a brave kid, and he does what he thinks is best. Sometimes he's selfish, but we can all be selfish sometimes. I just like how imperfect he is," he told Paulson.

RECOGNITION AND OTHER WORK

Platt won the 2017 Tony Award for Best Performance by an Actor in a Leading Role in a Musical for the role before ultimately departing the production in November of that year. Also in 2017, he appeared on an episode of the revival of *Will & Grace* on NBC and had a role in the feature comedy *The Female Brain*. After signing with Atlantic Records that year as well, he planned for his eventual original album to have a "sort of Sam Smith/Adele narrative, very emotional pop music with a little bit of Donny Hathaway/Ray Charles, maybe throwing in some soul in there," he told Keith Caulfield for *Billboard* (7 Feb. 2018). He has written many of the songs himself.

In early 2018, Platt helped earn the original Broadway cast recording of *Dear Evan Hansen* a Grammy Award for Best Musical Theater Album; at that same event, he delivered a show-stopping performance of the song "Somewhere" from the classic musical *West Side Story*. Additionally, he and fellow Tony winner Lin-Manuel Miranda, the original star and creator of the popular musical *Hamilton*, teamed up to release a song titled "Found/Tonight," a mash-up of "You Will Be Found" from *Dear Evan Hansen* and "The Story of Tonight" from *Hamilton*. Proceeds from the single benefited the March for Our Lives against gun violence in Washington, DC, on March 24, 2018, at which the duo performed. At press time, Platt was in filming for *The Politician*, a new Netflix comedy series created by Emmy Award winner Ryan Murphy of *Glee* and *American Horror Story* fame.

PERSONAL LIFE

Platt resides in New York City. In his free time, he enjoys shopping, watching television, and spending time with friends.

SUGGESTED READING

Caulfield, Keith. "Ben Platt Talks Debut Album and Writing All Original Music for 'Very Emotional Pop' Set." *Billboard*, 7 Feb. 2018, www.billboard.com/articles/news/8098561/ben-platt-interview-debut-album-emotional-pop-grammys-video. Accessed 8 Sept. 2018.

Cox, Gordon. "Ben Platt on Meeting Beyoncé and Leaving *Dear Evan Hansen*." *Variety*, 2017, variety.com/2017/legit/features/ben-platt-beyonce-evan-hansen-1202579519/. Accessed 7 Sept. 2018.

Isherwood, Charles. "Review: In *Dear Evan Hansen*, a Lonely Teenager, a Viral Lie and a Breakout Star." Review of *Dear Evan Hansen*, directed by Michael Greif. *The New York Times*, 4 Dec. 2016, www.nytimes.com/2016/12/04/theater/dear-evan-hansen-review.html. Accessed 10 Sept. 2018.

Marks, Peter. "*Dear Evan Hansen* Radiates Charm and Wit, and That's No Lie." Review of *Dear Evan Hansen*, directed by Michael Greif. *The Washington Post*, 3 Aug. 2015, www.washingtonpost.com/entertainment/theater_dance/dear-evan-hansen-radiates-charm-and-wit-and-thats-no-lie/2015/08/03/9a263ee4-390b-11e5-8e98-115a3cf7d7ae_story.html. Accessed 7 Sept. 2018.

Miller, Daryl H. "Tony Winner Ben Platt's L.A. High School Days: He Shone in Different Ways Than Evan Hansen, Teachers Say." *Los Angeles Times*, 11 June 2017, www.latimes.com/entertainment/arts/la-et-cm-ben-platt-high-school-days-20170611-story.html. Accessed 7 Sept. 2018.

Paulson, Michael. "Ben Platt, from *Pitch Perfect* to an Anxious Teen on Stage." *The New York Times*, 31 Mar. 2016, www.nytimes.com/2016/04/03/theater/ben-platt-from-pitch-perfect-to-an-anxious-teen-on-stage.html. Accessed 10 Sept. 2018.

Szeto, Caty. "Ben Platt '11 Receives First Tony Award." *The Harvard-Westlake Chronicle*, 2017, hwchronicle.com/ben-platt-11-receives-first-tony-award. Accessed 13 Sept. 2018.

SELECTED WORKS

Pitch Perfect, 2012; *Book of Mormon*, 2012–15; *Dear Evan Hansen*, 2015–17; *Pitch Perfect 2*, 2015; *The Female Brain*, 2017

—Molly Hagan

Buster Posey

Date of birth: March 27, 1987
Occupation: Baseball player

When, as a teenage baseball player, Buster Posey was selected in the final round of the 2005 Major League Baseball (MLB) Draft, he made the pivotal decision to delay the start of his professional baseball career and instead develop his skills further as a student-athlete at Florida State University. There, he made an unexpected yet ultimately crucial transition from shortstop to catcher, a position in which he would thrive over the following years. Drafted by the San Francisco Giants in 2008, Posey was promptly moved from the team's minor-league affiliates to the major league, where he contributed to the Giants' World Series victories in 2010, 2012, and 2014. Along the way, Posey achieved impressive statistics as both a batter and a fielder, earning National League (NL) accolades such as Rookie of the Year, the Rawlings Gold Glove, the Hank Aaron Award, and multiple All-Star Game selections. Despite such recognition, however, Posey has never been content to let himself or his team spend too much time celebrating their past accomplishments. "We all start with a clean slate," he told Andrew Baggarly for the Bay Area *Mercury News* (14 Feb. 2011). "Each year, you come in with the same hunger and know you've got a long road ahead. That's what we're here to do."

EARLY LIFE AND EDUCATION

Gerald Dempsey "Buster" Posey III was born on March 27, 1987, in Leesburg, Georgia. He was the first child born to Traci Posey, a teacher, and Gerald Posey II, who worked in food distribution. Posey and his three younger siblings—Jack, Jess, and Samantha—grew up in Leesburg in the family's rural farmhouse. "We grew up on a piece of land kind of by ourselves," he recalled to Tom Verducci for *Sports Illustrated* (22 July 2013). "We grew up playing together. We had friends over occasionally. I think all of us were content to spend Friday night or Saturday night at home with each other. It was really a fun place to grow up."

As a youth, Posey enjoyed activities such as fishing and hunting but was particularly devoted to baseball, which was a common passion in his family: Jack and Samantha would go on to be successful college baseball and softball players, respectively. Posey proved to be a talented baseball player himself, drawing significant attention for his accomplishments with the Lee County High School baseball team. He played primarily as a pitcher and a shortstop. During Posey's junior season, he attracted the notice of professional baseball scouts due to achievements such

Ian D'Andrea, via Wikimedia Commons

as a 1.53 earned run average and a .544 batting average. He graduated from high school in 2005.

FLORIDA STATE

In June 2005, Posey was drafted by the Los Angeles Angels of Anaheim (later known as the Los Angeles Angels) in the fiftieth round of the MLB Draft. Although his selection raised the possibility that Posey could begin a career in baseball right out of high school, he ultimately chose to enroll at Florida State University (FSU) and play for the Florida State Seminoles baseball team. "I would have signed if it was the right situation—first round," he told Verducci of his decision. "But I wouldn't have been ready. I don't see how kids do it. I really don't. You're a kid still. You're under your parents' roof and then—bam!—you're an adult. At least with college there's a transition period." Posey began attending FSU in the fall of 2005 and made his debut with the Seminoles during the 2006 season.

Throughout his first season at FSU, Posey put forth a strong performance in the position of shortstop, and he was ultimately selected as a freshman All-American player in light of his work. During his second season, however, the team's leadership made the unexpected decision to switch Posey to catcher. "There's some good and bad about starting as late as I did," he told Heather Dinich for *ESPN* (15 Apr. 2008), speaking of the change in position. "The good being I didn't have any bad habits from little league. The bad is I did have to learn a lot to catch up." Despite Posey's late start, he excelled as a catcher and continued to play in that position during his junior year, which would be his final season with the team. At the end of that season, Posey won the 2008 Golden Spikes Award, which is given to the best amateur baseball player in the United States.

In addition to being an asset to his team, Posey was a strong student and made the university's dean's list on multiple occasions. He ultimately left the school after the 2008 season, prior to what would have been his senior year. In the summer of 2018, FSU announced that Posey would be inducted into the institution's hall of fame later that year.

SAN FRANCISCO GIANTS

In June 2008, Posey was drafted by a professional baseball organization for a second time, becoming the fifth overall draft pick in that year's MLB Draft. He was selected by the San Francisco Giants, with which he signed his first contract in August 2008. Posey began his professional baseball career with the Arizona League Giants, a rookie-level minor-league affiliate of the Giants, in mid-2008, but was quickly moved up to the Class A Short Season Salem-Keizer Volcanoes. During the 2009 season, he played with the advanced-A San Jose Giants and the triple-A Fresno Grizzlies, before being called up to the majors for seven games. He made his debut with the San Francisco Giants on September 11, 2009, in a game against the Los Angeles Dodgers.

Posey began the 2010 season with the Grizzlies but returned to the Giants in late May. Over the course of the regular season, Posey played in 108 games with the Giants, splitting his time between the positions of catcher and first base. He earned a batting average of .305 over the regular season and achieved fielding percentages of .991 as catcher and .995 as first baseman. In recognition of his performance, Posey was named the 2010 NL Rookie of the Year.

The Giants ended the 2010 regular season with ninety-seven wins and ranked first in the NL West. In the postseason—Posey's first with the team—the Giants defeated the Atlanta Braves in the National League Division Series (NLDS) before going on to beat the Philadelphia Phillies in the National League Championship Series (NLCS). Facing the Texas Rangers in the World Series, the Giants won four of the five games played, claiming the team's first championship since 1954. Although winning the World Series was a significant milestone for the Giants, as well as for Posey, he stressed the importance of continuing to work toward future successes. "Let's enjoy this today, tomorrow, maybe a week or a month," he said at the Giants' World Series victory parade, as quoted by Baggarly. "Then let's get back to work and make another run at it."

SETBACKS AND BREAKTHROUGH

Although Posey began the 2011 season with the Giants seemingly poised to play a key role on the team, his season ended after only forty-five games when he and another player collided at home plate during a game in May. The collision broke a bone in Posey's leg and tore multiple ligaments. His injuries, as well as other high-profile collisions, prompted intense debate among MLB leadership over the subsequent years, prompting the leagues to revise existing rules regarding player collisions.

Posey rebounded from his 2011 injury and achieved a string of major accomplishments, both on and off the field, during his first full season with the Giants in 2012. Over the course of 148 games, he earned the highest batting average in the NL with .336 and became the highest-ranked NL player in the Wins Above Replacement (WAR) metric for the season. He also earned an impressive fielding percentage of .991 for both positions played. At the end of the 2012 season, Posey was named the NL's Most Valuable Player (MVP). He also won his first NL Silver Slugger accolade, was selected for his first All-Star Game, and received the league's 2012 Hank Aaron Award.

Despite his extensive professional accolades, Posey maintained a low profile and sought to avoid recognition as a celebrity. "I like to keep things pretty simple," he told Verducci during the subsequent season. "I can go to cities and go to restaurants or the movies and occasionally I'll get recognized—but not for the most part." His attempts to stay under the radar were thwarted, however, when the Giants finished first in the NL West. During the 2012 postseason, the team beat the Cincinnati Reds and the St. Louis Cardinals in the NLDS and NLCS, respectively, and went on to play the Detroit Tigers in the World Series. The Giants swept the series, earning Posey his second championship win with the team.

FRANCHISE FIXTURE

Between the 2013 and 2017 seasons, Posey reinforced his status as a key member of the Giants' lineup. In 2013, he signed a nine-year, $167 million contract with the team, then the largest contract in the franchise's history. "It's hard to put into words what I feel right now, just an incredible feeling. . . .know that for the next nine years I'll be a part of this very storied franchise," he said following the agreement, as quoted by *Penn Live* (29 Mar. 2013). "I'm incredibly humbled to know I'll be a part of that." In 2014, Posey helped the Giants secure a spot in the postseason by beating the Pittsburgh Pirates in the NL Wild Card Game. The Giants went on to defeat the Washington Nationals, the Saint Louis Cardinals, and the Kansas City Royals to claim another World Series title.

Although the Giants failed to enter the postseason in 2015 and 2017 and lost to the Chicago Cubs—the ultimate World Series victors—in the NLDS in 2016, Posey remained a consistent performer in multiple roles. He had the second-highest fielding percentage among NL catchers and won the Wilson Defensive Player of the Year Award for catching in 2015; he received the NL Gold Glove Award in recognition of his performance as a catcher in 2016; and he achieved a batting average of .320, the second-highest of his major-league career, and won his fourth Silver Slugger Award in 2017. Posey was also selected to play in the All-Star Game every year from 2015 to 2017. Despite the Giants' struggles, Posey continued to take a positive approach. "We came in on a little rough patch, but baseball's funny," he told Matthew Jussim for *Men's Journal*. "Sometimes all it takes is one good game and it'll set you straight for a while, so the most important thing is try to come out and treat each game individually and do the best you can to try and win that one."

PERSONAL LIFE

Posey began dating his future wife, Kristen, when they were both in high school. They married in 2009, and their twins, Addison and Lee, were born in 2011. Posey and his family split their time between California and Georgia.

SUGGESTED READING

Baggarly, Andrew. "Much Has Changed Since Buster Posey's Last Training Camp with the San Francisco Giants." *The Mercury News*, 14 Feb. 2011, www.mercurynews. com/2011/02/14/much-has-changed-since-buster-poseys-last-training-camp-with-the-san-francisco-giants. Accessed 13 July 2018.

Dinich, Heather. "Posey, the Consummate Student-Athlete, Key to Florida State's Success." *ESPN*, 15 Apr. 2008, www.espn.com/college-sports/news/story?id=3337385. Accessed 13 July 2018.

Guardado, Maria. "Halos First Drafted Posey in '05 . . . as a Pitcher." *MLB*, 30 May 2018, www.mlb.com/news/buster-posey-was-first-drafted-by-angels/c-278458730. Accessed 13 July 2018.

Jussim, Matthew. "Iron Giant: Buster Posey Doesn't Feel Pressure, Because He's Too Busy Crushing Home Runs." *Men's Journal*, www. mensjournal.com/sports/iron-giant-buster-posey-doesnt-feel-pressure-because-hes-too-busy-crushing-home-runs/. Accessed 13 July 2018.

Kepner, Tyler. "Buster Posey, the Champions' Champion." *New York Times*, 29 Oct. 2012, www.nytimes.com/2012/10/30/sports/baseball/giants-posey-is-the-champions-champion.html. Accessed 13 July 2018.

"San Francisco Giants Sign Buster Posey to Nine-Year, $167M Contract." *Penn Live*, 29 Mar. 2013, www.pennlive.com/sports/index. ssf/2013/03/san_francisco_giants_sign_bust. html. Accessed 13 July 2018.

Verducci, Tom. "Country and Western." *Sports Illustrated*, 22 July 2013, www.si.com/vault/2013/07/22/106346383/country-and-western. Accessed 13 July 2018.

—Joy Crelin

Margo Price

Date of birth: April 15, 1983
Occupation: Singer-songwriter

Those wanting to learn about country singer-songwriter Margo Price can read any number of interviews and profiles—or they can just listen to the autobiographical tunes on her 2016 debut album, *Midwest Farmer's Daughter*, and her 2017 sophomore effort, *All American Made*. From the loss of her family farm to her struggles with alcohol and nights spent in jail, Price does not shy away from giving listeners an unvarnished picture of her life. "It's as close to memoir as you can get holding a guitar," Jonathan Miles wrote for the Southern culture magazine *Garden & Gun* (Oct./Nov. 2017).

Price was the first solo female artist in *Billboard* history to see her debut album appear in the top ten of the Top Country Albums chart before even landing a hit single, and she has since received much critical acclaim. Miles praised her "lemony voice that doesn't just slice through barroom chatter but can silence it midsentence" and described her sound as "vintage country—Telecaster twang, smears of pedal steel—but not replica country; there's no glaze of musical nostalgia, in fact no glaze whatsoever." He advised, "Queue up her songs while you're alone in your car, say, with no particular place to be, or wherever you've got space to focus not just on Price's singing but on what she's singing. Because the story Margo Price has to tell is an intense, turbulent one, a story rife with heartache and grit, and it's one she tells true." Similar sentiments come up again and again in discussions of her work. "In an era where authenticity is hard to come by and often murky at best," Matt Williams wrote for *Vice* (23 Mar. 2016), "it's tough to find a truer voice than Margo Price."

EARLY YEARS AND EDUCATION

Margo Rae Price was born on April 15, 1983, in Aledo, Illinois. Her mother was a teacher and her father ran a corn and soybean farm in the town of Buffalo Prairie. He lost the farm when a drought hit soon after he had invested in

By Levi Manchak, via Wikimedia Commons

expensive modern equipment. Price was about two years old at the time. "Big farming was coming in. And the banks weren't very generous in helping out the family after a hard year," she explained to Terry Gross for NPR's *All Things Considered* (22 Nov. 2017). Her father subsequently found work as a guard at a local prison. "Nobody wants to be working in a prison," Price recalled to Gross. "But he did what he had to do to put food on the table. And him and my mom worked very hard, very modest jobs to make sure that we were never without."

Price was raised in Aledo, a town with a population of under four thousand whose main claim to fame was its annual Rhubarb Festival. The family enjoyed listening to the local country radio station. Iconic singers such as Dolly Parton and Loretta Lynn, to whom Price would eventually sometimes be compared, provided the background music to much of her childhood.

Price sang in her church and school, and once her parents realized the extent of her talent, they did all they could to nurture it. Her mother regularly drove her an hour each way to take lessons with a voice coach named Sue Clark, acknowledged to be the best in the region. While still a preteen, Price learned to sing operatic pieces in the mezzo soprano range. She took up the guitar as a teenager.

Thanks to a cheerleading scholarship, Price, a generally rebellious and indifferent student in high school, attended Northern Illinois University. There she studied dance and theater, but never truly found her footing. In 2003, at the age of twenty, she decided to drop out and move to Nashville to explore a career in music. The move

was not as unrealistic as it may have seemed. Price had a close connection in the industry: her great-uncle Bobby Fischer, was a well-established Music Row songwriter, best known for his work with country stars Reba McEntire, George Jones, and Conway Twitty.

EARLY MUSICAL CAREER

Price described her move to Nashville in her popular song "Hands of Time," from her debut album. The lyrics include the lines: "When I rolled out of town on the unpaved road, I was $57 from being broke. . . . I want to buy back the farm. Bring my mama home some wine. And turn back the clock on the cruel hands of time." Initially, things did not go as planned. Price totaled her car her first week in the city, and she cycled through a series of odd jobs cleaning hotel rooms and working at the mall. One memorably bad gig found her wearing a Catholic schoolgirl uniform to wait tables at a chain tavern called the Flying Saucer. Early on, a potential manager lured her to his home and drugged her drink.

Nor did Fischer provide the easy introduction to the business she had envisioned. "I played a few songs for him, and he just sat there real quiet for a long time, and then he said, 'This is what you gotta do. You gotta get rid of your TV, get rid of your radio, get rid of your computer. Just write. Just keep writing,'" Price recalled to Miles. "It was his way of telling me my songs weren't good enough. It broke my heart, but it was so true."

One bright spot in an otherwise dismal period came when she met fellow aspiring musician Jeremy Ivey. Although he was then married, the pair became romantically involved, and together they founded a band, Buffalo Clover. The group traveled the country in an old Winnebago, toured the United Kingdom and Spain, and released three independent (and little-heard) albums before disbanding. For a time, Price also fronted a traditional country band she called Margo & the Pricetags, whose revolving lineup sometimes featured future star Sturgill Simpson.

Meanwhile, Ivey divorced, and when Price was twenty-five the couple wed. The newlyweds lived in a ramshackle house in a poor neighborhood, working at a catering company to make ends meet. Price has recalled to interviewers that they had so little money that they spent their first winter as a married couple huddled under a blanket next to a small space heater. When they tired of the city, they moved for a time to the Rocky Mountains, busking on the streets of Boulder, Colorado, to earn money for food.

TRAGEDY AND DETERMINATION

In 2010 Price gave birth to twin boys: Ezra and Judah. When Ezra died of a rare heart condition at just two weeks old, Price went into a downward spiral. "I denounced God," she admitted to Patrick Doyle for *Rolling Stone* (16 Mar. 2016). "I was so angry: 'Why would anybody do this to a person?'" She began drinking heavily, and one night, when a cab she had called to take her home after a night of bar-hopping did not arrive, she got behind the wheel of her car. She hit a telephone pole in full view of police officers, and the resulting arrest for drunk driving ended with her spending a weekend in Nashville's Davidson County Jail. She wrote about the experience in the song "Weekender," which includes the lines: "'Cause I'm just a weekender / In the Davidson County Jail / And my old man, he ain't got the cash / To even go my bail."

Price subsequently stopped drinking and entered therapy to deal with her grief. She continued to perform, even in the face of discouragement. She has recalled that she once played a gig in Macon, Georgia, for five people and, she quips, a cardboard cutout of country singer Kenny Chesney. "There was just something inside of me," she explained to Miles. "I'm just stubborn as hell."

Ivey shared her determination. With the goal of releasing a solo album of Price's music, in 2015 he sold the family car and pawned her wedding ring to finance a session at Nashville's famed Sun Studios, recording at night because the place was a major tourist attraction by day. "It kind of felt like there was the symbolism of it: We're willing to put up the car, the wedding ring," she told Jewly Hight for the *New York Times* (12 Oct. 2017). "We would rather have this album exist out here, even if nothing would have happened to it."

DEBUT ALBUM AND FOLLOW-UP

For a time, it looked like that prediction was coming true. Label after label passed on the chance to release the album. One day Price heard through the grapevine that musician and producer Jack White, formerly of the rock band the White Stripes, had heard her play a local showcase and was an admirer. Gathering up her courage, she approached his indie rock label Third Man Records, and in early 2016 *Midwest Farmer's Daughter* became the company's first-ever country release.

Having the well-respected White in her corner led to excited industry buzz. She was soon booked as a musical guest on *Saturday Night Live*, increasing her visibility considerably. She won Emerging Artist of the Year honors at the Americana Awards, watched Aledo put up a sign bragging about being her hometown, and lent the dress she wore on *SNL* to the Country Music Hall of Fame and Museum for an exhibit.

More important to Price than those accolades were the artistic freedom and backing she got to record her follow-up, *All American Made*, an album that, while still personal, more deeply explores broader themes of economic injustice and gender inequality. Discussing Price's oeuvre, Kitty Empire wrote for the *Guardian* (22 Oct. 2017): "Margo Price's 2016 debut . . . established Price as a penetrating new voice, drawing on her own heart-rending tribulations—poverty, jail, bereavement—and railing against fate and the sexual politics of Nashville, where Price had long toiled unrecognized. Price was only getting started, it turns out. *All American Made* finds her tour-honed band fleshing out 12 new songs in which errant lovers, 'cocaine cowboys,' and double standards get it in the neck."

Although many reviewers tend to focus heavily on Price's own story and the autobiographical nature of much of her work, Talia Schlanger, the host of NPR's *World Café* (3 Jan. 2018), cautions against that. "There's a danger, when an artist has as compelling a story as Margo Price has, that the personal will overshadow the musical," Schlanger asserted. "So let's just get one thing straight first: Margo Price writes really beautiful songs. And boy-oh-boy can she sing."

SUGGESTED READING

Doyle, Patrick. "Rising Country Star Margo Price on Why She Feels 'Like One of the Men.'" *Rolling Stone*, 16 Mar. 2016, www.rollingstone.com/music/features/rising-country-star-margo-price-on-why-she-feels-like-one-of-the-men-20160316. Accessed 10 Jan. 2018.

Empire, Kitty. "All American Made: Country Soaked in Serotonin." *The Guardian*, 22 Oct. 2017, www.theguardian.com/music/2017/oct/22/margo-price-all-american-made-review. Accessed 10 Jan. 2018.

Falcone, Dana Rose. "How Margo Price Overcame Struggles with Alcohol and Her Newborn's Death to Reach Country Stardom." *People*, 5 Jan. 2018. Accessed 10 Jan. 2018.

Gross, Terry. "Margo Price Sings about the Heartache and Beauty of Small-Town America." *Fresh Air*, NPR, 22 Nov. 2017, www.npr.org/templates/transcript/transcript.php?storyId=565670833. Accessed 10 Jan. 2018.

Hight, Jewly. "Margo Price, Nashville Outsider, Tells It Like It Really Is." *The New York Times*, 12 Oct. 2017, www.nytimes.com/2017/10/12/arts/music/margo-price-all-american-made.html. Accessed 10 Jan. 2018.

Miles, Jonathan. "Margo Price: Diamond in the Rough." *Garden & Gun*, Oct./Nov. 2017, gardenandgun.com/feature/margo-price/. Accessed 10 Jan. 2018.

Schlanger, Talia. "Margo Price on *World Café*." *World Café*, National Public Radio, 3 Jan. 2018, www.npr.org/sections/world-cafe/2018/01/03/575288454/margo-price-on-world-cafe. Accessed 10 Jan. 2018.

SELECTED WORKS
Midwest Farmer's Daughter, 2016; *Live at Rough Trade East*, 2016; *All American Made*, 2017

—*Mari Rich*

By Gina Prince-Bythewood, via Wikimedia Commons

Gina Prince-Bythewood
Date of birth: June 10, 1969
Occupation: Director, screenwriter

Since the beginning of her career as a filmmaker, Gina Prince-Bythewood has fought hard to make films on her own terms. A director and screenwriter who graduated from the University of California, Los Angeles film program and began her career writing for television shows such as *A Different World* (1992–93), she launched her feature-film career with the 2000 sports romance *Love & Basketball*, an ambitious work that was initially turned down by a multitude of studios due to factors such as its African American cast and romantic focus. Prince-Bythewood's persistence paid off, earning her multiple awards for directing and writing as well as a significant place in the history of independent filmmaking. Over the subsequent years, she would overcome rejection, studio demands, and limited budgets to complete a variety of projects that reflect her interests and concerns as a filmmaker, including 2008's *The Secret Life of Bees*, 2014's *Beyond the Lights*, and the 2017 television miniseries *Shots Fired*.

For Prince-Bythewood, making films in her own way is nonnegotiable. "People ask me all the time if I feel discriminated against as a black female director and I actually don't. I get offered a ton of stuff and if I wanted to get work all the time I could," she explained to David Greene for NPR (14 Nov. 2014). "But I like to direct what I've written. I feel what's discriminated against are my choices—which is to focus on people of color and more specifically women of color. Those are the films that are not getting made and those are the films that take a lot more fight." In addition to working on projects that reflect such choices, Prince-Bythewood has emphasized the importance of helping other would-be filmmakers and creative professionals achieve similar success. "I believe it's absolutely the responsibility of those who have made it through that door to reach back and pull others up," she told Bim Adewunmi for *BuzzFeed* (12 Nov. 2015). "We are very lucky to do what we do."

EARLY LIFE AND EDUCATION
Prince-Bythewood was born on June 10, 1969. She was adopted at three weeks old by Bob Prince, a computer programmer, and Maria Prince, a nurse. She and her older siblings grew up in Pacific Grove, California. She developed a love of sports at a young age and has credited her athletic activities with helping her develop a mindset that has enabled her to succeed in the competitive film industry. "My parents put me in sports when I was five years old, and they put my sisters in sports. So that's what I grew up with, that mentality: 'It's OK to want to be the best. Aggression is good,'" she told Inkoo Kang for *MTV News* (22 Mar. 2017). In addition to volleyball, softball, tennis, and cross country, she played basketball and ran track while attending Pacific Grove High School, where she set records that remained in place two decades after the end of her high school athletic career.

After graduating from Pacific Grove High School in 1987, Prince-Bythewood enrolled in the University of California, Los Angeles (UCLA), having refused to accept an initial rejection and subsequently writing a cogent letter to the head of the institution's film school that reversed the decision. A fan of soap operas, she initially aspired to become a soap opera screenwriter. However, her experience working on student films at UCLA sparked her desire to become a director, and she went on to direct a short thesis film titled *Stiches*, for which she received the Gene Reynolds Scholarship. She graduated from the UCLA School of Theater, Film and Television in 1991.

EARLY CAREER
Despite Prince-Bythewood's successful experiences as a director during her time at UCLA, she did not initially find work in that field, instead beginning her career in television writing.

"I knew I wanted to be a director, but I found out pretty damn quickly that nobody was just going to hand me a script to direct," she recalled to Kang. After completing an internship with Quincy Jones Entertainment, she was hired as a writer's assistant for the television show *A Different World*. Part of the show's apprenticeship program, she wrote for several episodes of the series prior to its conclusion in 1993.

Following her time writing for *A Different World*, Prince-Bythewood went on to write episodes for a variety of television series from 1994 to 1995, including *South Central* and *Courthouse*; she also directed and wrote a 1995 episode of *CBS Schoolbreak Special*, a series of after-school specials focused on teen issues. Her special, "What about Your Friends," was received well by critics, and she was nominated for Daytime Emmy Awards for outstanding writing and directing for her work. From 1997 to 1999, she directed several short films in addition to writing an episode of the television series *Felicity*.

LOVE & BASKETBALL

During the 1990s, Prince-Bythewood had also begun working on the script for what would become her first feature film, *Love & Basketball*. A love story that develops over more than a decade, the narrative heavily features the titular sport, which its two protagonists aspire to play professionally. For Prince-Bythewood, that premise had particular personal resonance. "Growing up, ball was everything to me," she told Lucy McCalmont for the *Huffington Post* (16 June 2015). "I'm an athlete first and always have been, and it's been so much a part of my life. And I just didn't feel that I ever saw that woman or girl reflected on screen."

Although Prince-Bythewood spent the better part of two years writing and refining the script, studios repeatedly turned down the screenplay, citing concerns about the film's African American cast and romance elements. However, after participating in the Sundance Institute's lab program and staging a table read in Los Angeles, she gained the support of veteran filmmaker Spike Lee, who joined the production as a producer, as well as distributor New Line Cinema. She went on to direct the film, which stars Sanaa Lathan and Omar Epps in the lead roles.

Love & Basketball premiered at the Sundance Film Festival in January 2000 and opened in US theaters in the spring of that year. Received well by many critics, the film was nominated for the Independent Spirit Award for Best First Feature. Prince-Bythewood herself won the Independent Spirit Award for Best First Screenplay as well as the Black Reel Award for Outstanding Director for her work on the film.

MAJOR MILESTONES

In addition to the premiere of *Love & Basketball*, the year 2000 also saw the debut of the HBO television film *Disappearing Acts*, which Prince-Bythewood directed and which also starred Lathan. Following the success of *Love & Basketball*, she set out to adapt the 1998 Wally Lamb novel *I Know This Much Is True*, but the project fell through due to studio demands that she cast a well-known actor in the lead role. Over the subsequent years, she continued to work in television, directing episodes of series such as *The Bernie Mac Show* (2003), *Girlfriends* (2005), and *Everybody Hates Chris* (2005).

Throughout that period, Prince-Bythewood worked to develop what would become her next two feature films, *The Secret Life of Bees* and *Beyond the Lights*. Released in 2008, *The Secret Life of Bees* was adapted from a 2002 novel by Sue Monk Kidd and features performances from actors Dakota Fanning, Jennifer Hudson, Queen Latifah, Alicia Keys, and Sophie Okonedo. For Prince-Bythewood, working with such well-regarded performers was initially a daunting process. "Going in, I was a little freaked out. I was thinking, 'How am I going to direct Oscar winners and nominees?'" she told Marc Cabrera for the *Monterey Herald* (17 Oct. 2008). "This film was my vision and fortunately they bought into that." She won numerous awards for the film, including the Image Awards for Outstanding Motion Picture and outstanding directing from the National Association for the Advancement of Colored People (NAACP). In 2009, her alma mater recognized her as UCLA filmmaker of the year.

For her next film, *Beyond the Lights*, Prince-Bythewood sought to tell a love story set against the backdrop of the music industry, through which she planned to critique the increased hypersexuality of young female performers as well as present a positive depiction of a romantic relationship between two black characters. "There's a perception in the world that black people don't love each other, that they don't get married. And it's because we don't see it, there are never any images of that in TV and film," she explained to Greene. "Without those images young black people have nothing to aspire to and the world continues to perpetuate this myth about the lack of black love. It's important for me to make us visible in universal stories."

When setting out to make the film, Prince-Bythewood faced difficulties securing studio support for the project, in part because of her plan to cast little-known actors Gugu Mbatha-Raw and Nate Parker in the lead roles. She ultimately made the film on a limited budget that required her and the actors to work for scale, the industry minimum for pay set by the actors' and directors' unions. "It's worth it because we got to make the movie we wanted to make," she told Adewunmi of the experience. Following the premiere of *Beyond the Lights* in 2014, Prince-Bythewood won the award for best screenplay from the African-American Film Critics Association (AAFCA) for her work on the film, which was also nominated for the Academy Award for best original song.

OTHER PROJECTS

In 2016, Prince-Bythewood announced that she would be directing and cowriting an adaptation of the 2014 novel *An Untamed State*, by Roxane Gay, which she hoped would ultimately star Mbatha-Raw. Prince-Bythewood became interested in adapting the novel after meeting Gay, who asked her to read the book. "I was in the middle of something and knew I didn't have time. Out of respect for her, I said I'll just read twenty pages to say, 'Hey, I read it,'" she recalled to Kang. "But I could just not put it down—it was so visceral. The story left me physically breathless. I thought, my god, if I could make a movie that makes an audience feel the way I feel, it would be incredible."

Prince-Bythewood returned to television in 2017 with the miniseries *Shots Fired*, cocreated with husband Reggie Rock Bythewood. The miniseries, which costars frequent collaborator Lathan, aired on the FOX television network between March and May of that year. Prince-Bythewood wrote and directed two episodes of the ten-part series. She likewise served as director for the pilot episode of the Marvel superhero television series *Cloak and Dagger*, which premiered at South by Southwest in March 2018. Continuing in this genre, she was also hired to direct and rewrite the script for a film focusing on the Marvel superheroes Silver Sable and Black Cat, which was scheduled for release in 2019.

PERSONAL LIFE

Prince-Bythewood first met her husband, Reggie Rock Bythewood, while they were both attending a taping of the sitcom *The Fresh Prince of Bel-Air*. The pair spent more time together while they were both writers on *A Different World*. "We were the younger writers on the show, they put us together a lot, to work on scenes and things like that and we just clicked," she recalled to Brittney Oliver for *Essence* (2 May 2017). The two later collaborated on projects such as *Beyond the Lights*, for which Bythewood served as a producer. They have two sons and live in California.

SUGGESTED READING

Cabrera, Marc. "Buzzing about *Bees*: Pacific Grove Native Turned Film Director Gina Prince-Bythewood Ushers New Project to Big Screen." *Monterey Herald*, 17 Oct. 2008, www.montereyherald.com/article/

zz/20081017/NEWS/810179948. Accessed 13 Mar. 2018.

Prince-Bythewood, Gina. "Director Gina Prince-Bythewood: 'Every Movie Starts with an Image.'" Interview by Bim Adewunmi. *BuzzFeed*, 12 Nov. 2015, www.buzzfeed.com/bimadewunmi/i-write-what-i-want-to-see-gina-prince-bythewood-interview. Accessed 13 Mar. 2018.

Prince-Bythewood, Gina. "Director Gina Prince-Bythewood: It's Time to 'Obliterate the Term Black Film.'" Interview by David Greene. *NPR*, 14 Nov. 2014, www.npr.org/sections/codeswitch/2014/11/14/363793023/director-gina-prince-bythewood-its-time-to-obliterate-the-term-black-film. Accessed 13 Mar. 2018.

Prince-Bythewood, Gina. "The Unstoppable Gina Prince-Bythewood." Interview by Inkoo Kang. *MTV News*, 22 Mar. 2017, www.mtv.com/news/2995885/the-unstoppable-gina-prince-bythewood/. Accessed 13 Mar. 2018.

Prince-Bythewood, Gina, and Reggie Rock Bythewood. "Married Hollywood Power Couple the Bythewoods Reminisce about Falling in Love on the Set of *A Different World*." Interview by Brittney Oliver. *Essence*, 2 May 2017, www.essence.com/gina-prince-bythewood-reggie-rock-bythewood-falling-love-story. Accessed 13 Mar. 2018.

Prince-Bythewood, Gina, et al. "Double or Nothing: An Oral History of *Love & Basketball*." Interview by Lucy McCalmont. *HuffPost*, 16 June 2015, www.huffingtonpost.com/2015/06/16/love-and-basketball-oral-history_n_7572140.html. Accessed 13 Mar. 2018.

SELECTED WORKS

Love & Basketball, 2000; *The Secret Life of Bees*, 2008; *Beyond the Lights*, 2014; *Shots Fired*, 2017

—Joy Crelin

Florence Pugh

Date of birth: January 3, 1996
Occupation: Actor

Although still in her early twenties, Florence Pugh has made a considerable impression on filmgoers and film critics for her remarkable performances in a pair of powerful films: *The Falling*, which premiered at the BFI (British Film Institute) London Film Festival in 2014 and was released in theaters in the United Kingdom in 2015, and *Lady Macbeth*, which premiered at the Toronto International Film Festival in 2016 before hitting theaters in both the United Kingdom and the United States in 2017; her work in the latter has cemented her place as

Photo by Matt Crossick/PA Images via Getty Images

an up-and-coming actor in the United States as well as in her native England. The strength of these performances has enabled her to gain roles in a wide variety of released and upcoming films, including ones featuring such well-known stars as Liam Neeson, Anthony Hopkins, Emma Thompson, and Chris Pine. In the press, she has been frequently compared to Kate Winslet, the veteran British actor who has won a number of awards throughout her career, including an Academy Award, and is perhaps best known for her role in James Cameron's 1997 film *Titanic*. As for Pugh herself, she hopes to find roles that are just as memorable during the course of her promising career. She said in an interview with Mark Olsen for the *Los Angeles Times* (7 July 2017), "I hope to create characters that people want to watch—and they either want to be or are or it's something that they recognize. Why shouldn't there be more epic, brilliant female characters onscreen?"

EARLY LIFE AND CAREER

Florence Pugh was born in Oxford, England, on January 3, 1996. During part of her childhood, she and her family lived in Spain. In an interview with Cath Clarke for the *Guardian* (28 Dec. 2017), she described her family, which includes three siblings, as "loud" and "creative." Her mother, Deborah, was a dancer; her father, Clinton, owned several restaurants and bars in Oxford—places where she earned pocket money or just enjoyed hanging out. She and her older brother and sister would all eventually end up in the entertainment industry. Reminiscing about growing up with a father in the restaurant

business, Pugh admitted to Clarke, "I can't remember a Friday when I was younger when I wasn't eating a pizza, flirting with the barman."

Pugh has always been interested in performance—singing and acting in nonprofessional capacities, often in school, from an early age. She had always hoped to become an actor but did not pursue it aggressively as a teenager, in part because she had seen how her brother had often endured rejection in his career. While she was studying at St. Edward's School in Oxford, casting agents began passing around leaflets for auditions to an independent film titled *The Falling*. As some of her classmates were auditioning and her mother had also encouraged her to do so, she decided to give it a shot as well. "I always knew I was going to get into the industry but when this opportunity came along I didn't think anything would come of it because, you know, it can take people years," she said to Gillian Orr for the *Independent* (18 Apr. 2015). "But I really was one of those annoying kids who was in every performance, doing every dance, singing in all the talent shows. I found academics really difficult."

OPENING DOORS WITH *THE FALLING*

The Falling, which world premiered at the BFI London Film Festival in 2014—serving as Pugh's first real exposure to the daunting red carpet experience—and was released in theaters in the United Kingdom the following year, was the brainchild of director Carol Morley, who had been inspired to develop the film after conducting research into the real-life phenomenon of mass psychogenic illness—a collective hysteria like the one she had heard of in a medieval village that had suffered from giggling fits. Morley's film takes place at a strict school for girls in England in 1969, where a strange, large-scale outbreak of fainting among the girls changes the dynamic between a pair of best friends, Lydia (played by Maisie Williams) and Abbie (played by Pugh). Pugh's character's sexual maturity—and the consequences of it—is at the center of the story.

Pugh wowed Morley and her staff during her audition for the crucial and complicated role of Abbie. "After you left the room I said, 'Oh wow,'" Morley stated to Orr in a joint interview with Pugh. "All the casting people were really quiet and I just said, 'Do you not think she's amazing?' And they all went, 'We've got goosebumps; that was like a young Kate Winslet walking into the room.'" In interviews, Pugh has explained how she learned to adapt to the grueling everyday life of working on a film set, including mastering the ability to stay in character for hours at a time and remain authentically emotive.

The film went on to receive critical acclaim, and for her performance, Pugh was nominated for Best British Newcomer at the 2014 BFI London Film Festival as well as for Young British/

Irish Performer at the London Critics' Circle Film Awards in early 2016. Before long, she was fielding offers and going on countless auditions, having secured an agent and deciding to forego pursuing a formal drama education. For several months after filming for *The Falling*, she worked with her agent to find the right scripts. She traveled to Los Angeles and shot a television pilot for the FOX network, *Studio City* (2015), in which she played an aspiring singer whose father (played by Eric McCormack) deals drugs to Hollywood celebrities; however, the series was ultimately not picked up. In 2016, she appeared on the British crime noir detective series *Marcella*.

LADY MACBETH

If *The Falling* had hinted at her acting potential, *Lady Macbeth* confirmed it. The debut feature-length film by veteran stage director William Oldroyd premiered at the Toronto International Film Festival in 2016. Eric d'Arbeloff, copresident of Roadside Attractions, was in large part inspired to fight for North American rights to the film after watching Pugh's performance on screen at the festival: "We were bowled over by luminous star-in-the-making Florence Pugh in the title role," he stated, as quoted by Etan Vlessing in the *Hollywood Reporter* (15 Sept. 2016).

In the film, which is based on Nikolai Leskov's 1865 work *Lady Macbeth of the Mtsensk District*, Pugh plays Katherine, a nineteenth-century woman married off to a much older man named Alexander (played by Paul Hilton), who lives in the English countryside. Alexander is a controlling menace who bars his wife from going outdoors and seeks to dominate her just as he himself is dominated by his overbearing father, Boris (played by Christopher Fairbank). Despite the prohibition, Pugh manages to get out, where she soon begins an affair with a stable hand named Sebastian (played by Cosmo Jarvis). Their relationship sets in motion a chain of events that has terrible repercussions for anyone who seeks to undo Katherine's well-laid plans. Though Pugh was initially intimidated by the part, she was also deeply intrigued by the character of Katherine: "She is bloody brilliant. Anybody would be stupid not to want the role. I am just delighted William thought I was up to it," she expressed to Donald Clarke for the *Irish Times* (28 Apr. 2017).

The film thrilled critics overall, as did Pugh's take on Katherine, specifically, including when it was screened at the Sundance Film Festival in Utah in January 2017 before its theatrical release later in the year in both the United Kingdom and the United States. Michael Phillips, writing for the *Chicago Tribune* (20 July 2017), stated, "Throughout *Lady Macbeth* we see Pugh's eyes, full of possibility and optimism at the outset, gradually darken. Even her breathing changes.

It's a wonderful performance in a very fine film." For her performance, Pugh earned the Malone Souliers Award for Breakthrough of the Year at the Evening Standard British Film Awards, the Dublin Film Critics Circle Award for Best Actress at the Dublin International Film Festival, and the British Independent Film Award for Best Actress.

UPCOMING PROJECTS

Since the release of *Lady Macbeth*, Pugh has been featured in two more films, a British horror film titled *Malevolent* (2017) and *The Commuter* (2018), a thriller that starred Liam Neeson. She also completed work on *Fighting with My Family* (2018), a biopic in which she portrays the real-life professional wrestler Paige and the journey she and her family took to superstardom in World Wrestling Entertainment (WWE). During the filming, Pugh had to perform in front of a large audience of wrestling fans to recreate some of Paige's most famous matches. "I was amazed at how calm and self-possessed she was," Stephen Merchant, the writer and director of *Fighting with My Family*, told Olsen. "I was more nervous than her. Paige's theme-tune played and she just strode out there like she was a superstar wrestler. . . . She didn't miss a beat."

In addition to these films and receiving a nomination for the EE Rising Star Award from the British Academy of Film and Television Arts (BAFTA) in 2018, Pugh has been attached to a number of upcoming projects. She will star as Cordelia in a BBC adaptation of *King Lear*, featuring Anthony Hopkins and Emma Thompson. She will also appear in *Outlaw King*, a film about the fourteenth-century Scottish king Robert the Bruce, which stars Chris Pine. The diversity of her upcoming films—from period pieces to Shakespeare to thrillers—is again drawing comparisons to Winslet, who has been well known throughout her career to take on a wide variety of roles. "The Kate Winslet thing has been a shocker," Pugh said with disbelief to Cath Clarke. "She's been my idol since I re-enacted *Titanic* and fell in love with Leo. And it's a privilege to be called the next anything. But I suppose to be the next you is all you can do. If I can make my mark just a little bit, then great."

SUGGESTED READING

Clarke, Cath. "Florence Pugh: 'Me, the Next Kate Winslet? That's Ridiculous.'" *The Guardian*, 28 Dec. 2017, www.theguardian.com/film/2017/dec/28/florence-pugh-me-the-next-kate-winslet-thats-ridiculous. Accessed 3 Apr. 2018.

Clarke, Donald. "Florence Pugh: The Best Actor You Haven't Heard Of." *The Irish Times*, 28 Apr. 2017, www.irishtimes.com/culture/film/florence-pugh-the-best-actor-you-haven-t-heard-of-1.3060858. Accessed 3 Apr. 2018.

Cusumano, Katherine. "Meet *Lady MacBeth's* Florence Pugh, a Truly Modern Feminist Hero in a Corset." *W*, 12 July 2017, www. wmagazine.com/story/florence-pugh-lady-macbeth-movie. Accessed 3 Apr. 2018.

Olsen, Mark. "In *Lady Macbeth*, Florence Pugh Is a Powerful, Placid Dynamo." *Los Angeles Times*, 7 July 2017, www.latimes.com/entertainment/movies/la-ca-mn-florence-pugh-lady-macbeth-20170629-story.html. Accessed 3 Apr. 2018.

Orr, Gillian. "'After You Left the Room I Said, Wow!': Director Carol Morley and Actress Florence Pugh on their Haunting New Film *The Falling*." *Independent*, 18 Apr. 2015, www.independent.co.uk/arts-entertainment/films/features/after-you-left-the-room-i-said-wow-director-carol-morley-and-actress-florence-pugh-on-their-haunting-10182952.html. Accessed 3 Apr. 2018.

Phillips, Michael. "*Lady Macbeth*: The 19th-century Postman Always Rings Twice." *Chicago Tribune*, 20 July 2017, www.chicagotribune.com/entertainment/movies/sc-lady-macbeth-mov-rev-0718-20170718-column.html. Accessed 3 Apr. 2018.

SELECTED WORKS

The Falling, 2014; *Lady Macbeth*, 2016; *Malevolent*, 2017; *The Commuter*, 2018

—Christopher Mari

Charles Randolph

Date of birth: ca. 1963
Occupation: Screenwriter

American screenwriter and producer Charles Randolph is known for "tackling difficult subjects with exuberance, zest, and a populist sensibility," as Todd Aaron Jensen wrote for the *Writers Guild of America West* website (8 Jan. 2016). A former college professor, Randolph did not embark on a screenwriting career until his mid-thirties but has since used his varied academic background to inform his work, which has been characterized by a preoccupation with important moral, social, and ethical issues. His screenplays have dealt with such weighty topics as the death penalty (*The Life of David Gale*, 2003), political violence and corruption (*The Interpreter*, 2005), the pharmaceutical industry (*Love & Other Drugs*, 2010), and the 2008 global financial crisis (*The Big Short*, 2015).

Randolph has earned the most attention and acclaim for *The Big Short*, which he cowrote with director Adam McKay. Adapted from Michael Lewis's best-selling 2010 nonfiction book of the same title, the farcical comedy uses an array of inventive narrative and stylistic devices to make complicated financial concepts accessible to audiences. For their script, Randolph and McKay earned a slew of honors, most notably the Academy Award for best adapted screenplay.

EARLY LIFE AND EDUCATION

The son of missionaries, Randolph was born around 1963 in Nashville, Tennessee. He spent the early years of his life abroad in Europe, where his parents did missionary work. Randolph's parents, however, were largely unsuccessful in their conversion efforts there; his father was expelled from both Jordan and Greece for trying to convert those countries' citizens. When Randolph was roughly six years old, his parents moved the family back to the United States.

Despite growing up in a strict religious household that shunned television, Randolph was exposed early on to the worlds of literature and film. His parents were fans of the mystery writer Agatha Christie and of the film director Alfred Hitchcock. Through their influence Randolph became particularly drawn to works that contained strong moral and social messages. He initially tried to follow in his parents' footsteps, aspiring to become, as he once put it to Dana Kennedy in a profile for the *New York Times* (23 Feb. 2003), a "James Bond for Jesus."

During the 1980s, after graduating from high school, Randolph traveled extensively in Europe as a missionary. There, his Bond-like endeavors included trying to smuggle Bibles into various Eastern European countries. He did so with limited success, however, and eventually grew dissatisfied with organized religion. Consequently, upon graduating from Yale Divinity School, he embarked on a career in academia.

From 1990 to 1999, Randolph taught at Webster Vienna Private University, in Austria, where he served as a cultural studies and philosophy professor. During that time, he immersed himself in a wide range of subjects, from advertising to political rhetoric to documentary filmmaking. He often practiced these subjects in a professional capacity; he created advertising campaigns for nonprofit organizations such as Amnesty International and made education documentaries for the consumer goods company Procter & Gamble.

ACADEMIA TO HOLLYWOOD

Randolph's academic studies eventually came to include feature films. He began studying various film genres and interviewing writers who worked within those genres. It was while conducting a series of lectures on this topic at the University of Southern California in Los Angeles that Randolph received his first big break. His lectures caught the attention of a producer for Peter and Bobby Farrelly, an American writer-director tandem collectively referred to as the Farrelly brothers, who by then had risen to Hollywood's mainstream following the runaway commercial success of their comedy film *Dumb and Dumber* (1994).

Randolph was promptly commissioned by the producer to write a comedy for the Farrelly brothers, which resulted in his first screenplay, titled "Fat," in 1998. Though the script, which has been likened to the zany works of cult filmmaker John Waters, did not get produced, it helped him land a deal with Creative Artists Agency (CAA), one of Hollywood's top talent firms. Attracted to film for its interdisciplinary nature, Randolph soon moved from Vienna to Los Angeles to pursue screenwriting as a career. He has attributed this decision, in part, to his growing unhappiness "with where academia in [his] field was headed," as he noted to Bill Graham for the *Film Stage* (19 Jan. 2016).

Nevertheless, Randolph drew on his academic background in writing the screenplay for *The Life of David Gale* (2003), which tackles the issue of the death penalty. Directed by two-time Academy Award nominee Alan Parker, the film stars Kevin Spacey as the titular David Gale, a philosophy professor and noted death penalty opponent who suddenly finds himself on death row after being convicted of murdering his friend, fellow death penalty opponent Constance Harraway (played by Laura Linney). Gale pleads his innocence, however, and in the days leading up to his execution, he summons an acclaimed New York–based investigative journalist, Bitsey Bloom (Kate Winslet), to Texas, where he is being held, in a last-ditch attempt for freedom.

Relying heavily on flashbacks, as Gale relates his story to Bloom across a glass partition in a visiting room and featuring a series of revelatory third-act plot twists, the film was widely panned by critics, most of whom found fault with its farfetched story and unsubtle anti–death penalty message. It also performed poorly at the box office, grossing only $38 million worldwide on a $38 million budget.

RISE TO SCREENWRITING PROMINENCE

For Randolph, the reaction to his first produced screenplay was humbling. The experience, though, helped reinforce to him the notion of film being a director's medium. In an interview with Scott Mendelson for *Forbes* (25 Jan. 2016), Randolph noted that his David Gale script was "genuinely beloved" throughout Hollywood before going into production. "Because the script had been so widely distributed, it made it easier when the film didn't perform," he told Mendelson. The poor reception of the film ultimately did little to harm Randolph's then rising reputation as a screenwriter.

Randolph's original screenplay for *The Interpreter* (2005), a political thriller directed by the late two-time Academy Award winner Sydney Pollack and starring Nicole Kidman and Sean Penn, was better received. He shared screenplay credit for the film with two of Hollywood's top script doctors, Scott Frank and Steven Zaillian. The film follows a United Nations (UN) interpreter, Silvia Broome (portrayed by Kidman), as she becomes unwittingly involved in a global conspiracy after overhearing a plot to assassinate the president of the fictional African country of Matobo. After reporting her discovery to the US Secret Service, Broome is targeted in an investigation led by hardened and recently widowed agent Tobin Keller (Penn), who suspects her to have deeper connections to the assassination subject than she lets on.

The first Hollywood film to be granted permission to shoot inside the high-security UN building in New York City, *The Interpreter* was generally praised by critics for its compelling plot, glossy production, tense action sequences, and high-minded message about peace. Many critics, however, had reservations about the film's handling of its fictional African country (for which a fictional language, Ku, was also created by African linguist Said el-Gheithy). It nonetheless amassed solid box office numbers for a film largely geared towards an older, more sophisticated audience, earning $162 million worldwide on an $80 million budget.

Following *The Interpreter*, which is noted for being Pollack's final film as a director, Randolph earned his first producing credit on the Russell Crowe vehicle *Tenderness* (2009). In the small-scale crime drama, helmed by Australian director John Polson, Crowe plays a detective who obsessively tracks the movements of a teenage murderer.

LOVE & OTHER DRUGS AND THE BIG SHORT

Randolph's next screenplay, for the film *Love & Other Drugs* (2010), is loosely based on Jamie Reidy's 2005 memoir *Hard Sell: The Evolution of a Viagra Salesman*. The book exposes the seedier aspects of the pharmaceutical drug industry, chronicling Reidy's lascivious adventures and sordid dealings while working as a Viagra salesman for drug giant Pfizer in the 1990s. Though his film adaptation delves heavily into that world, Randolph also created a multifaceted love story between Jamie Randall, the character based on Reidy (played by Jake Gyllenhaal), and Maggie Murdock (Anne Hathaway), a purely invented, free-spirited young woman who suffers from Parkinson's disease. "I didn't really use much of the book," he admitted to Aaron Ginsburg for *Script* (14 Apr. 2016), explaining that Reidy's book became "more of a background resource than story points."

Randolph initially sold his script to producer Scott Stuber, the former copresident of production at Universal Pictures, before having it passed on to the Academy Award–winning director-producer team of Edward Zwick and Marshall Herskovitz. He shared screenwriting credit with Zwick and Herskovitz, who, uncharacteristically, tried to retain much of his original draft. Straddling the line between romantic comedy and serious social commentary, the resultant film earned mixed reviews from critics, many of whom felt that it suffered from an unclear plot and indecisive tone, with its larger themes being overshadowed by the romance between Jamie and Maggie. Still, it fared well at the box office, raking in almost $103 million on a $30 million budget.

The same year *Love & Other Drugs* was released, Randolph began working on the screenplay for *The Big Short* (2015), a film about the 2008 financial crisis adapted from the 2010 best-selling nonfiction book of the same title by Michael Lewis. The book concentrates on the key players who defied conventional financial wisdom by betting against the US housing market, the collapse of which helped trigger the crisis. Speaking of what drew him to the project, Randolph told Jensen, "I really love very specific, very complicated worlds in storytelling," such as the largely abstract world of finance that Lewis's book sheds light on. As part of his research for the screen adaptation, which took approximately six months to write, Randolph read many financial books and articles and consulted with various mortgage and real-estate experts to familiarize himself with the industry.

AWARD-WINNING COLLABORATION

Randolph's script for *The Big Short* lagged in development for several years, largely due to studio concerns over whether audiences would flock to see a film with such abstruse content. It received new life, however, after writer-director Adam McKay, then best known for his comedy film collaborations with Will Ferrell, became involved in the project. McKay subsequently produced a draft that included voice-over narration by one of the script's central characters and interstitial sequences that cleverly elucidated complex financial concepts. This meta component to the script, as Randolph explained to Mendelson, "allowed the film to have a voice separate and apart from its characters, which was very likable."

Randolph and McKay were, as McKay told Jensen, a "chocolate and peanut butter" pairing—an odd-couple combination in which each nevertheless brings out the other's strengths. Randolph praised McKay for his significant script contributions, which helped shift the film's tone from satirical to farcical, giving it an energy that it had previously lacked. Randolph also noted that McKay, despite making changes, remained respectful to Randolph's original script, which itself stayed true to the richly drawn characters in Lewis's book. Speaking of his approach to writing screenplays, Randolph told Brianne Hogan for *Creative Screenwriting* (20 Jan. 2016), "I usually start with the characters. I try to see what defines and makes them specific and unique. I usually give them each a quirk and measure everything against that quirk. I try to arrive at that right tone."

The Big Short did in fact strike the right tone for both critics and audiences alike. Premiering in November 2015 at the American Film Institute (AFI) Fest, the film was almost universally hailed for its first-rate acting, free-associative editing, and unconventional yet highly entertaining handling of complicated financial material. It stars Christian Bale, Steve Carell, and Ryan Gosling (as the narrator), and features a plethora of celebrity cameos, from actor Margot Robbie to the late chef Anthony Bourdain, who address the audience directly to explain the intricacies behind esoteric terms such as "credit default swaps" and "collateralized debt obligations."

In a representative review for *Variety* (13 Nov. 2015), Andrew Barker commented that *The Big Short* turns "a dense economics lecture into a hyper-caffeinated postmodern farce, a spinach smoothie skillfully disguised as junk food." Randolph and McKay received numerous honors for their script, including an Academy Award, British Academy of Film and Television Arts (BAFTA) Award, and Writers Guild of America Award, all for best adapted screenplay. *The Big Short* received five Academy Award nominations in total, including one for McKay's direction, and was also a commercial success, grossing $133 million against a reported $28 million budget. In the Writers Guild of America West article, Randolph described Hollywood as "an uncertain town" and said that "you never know what's going to happen to your work," but "on *The Big Short*, it all went right."

In addition to film, Randolph has written and executive produced television pilots for HBO and ABC. Shortly after his *Big Short* Oscar win, he signed a deal with Amazon Studios to develop a drama series about a present-day civil war. He has since worked on unproduced film projects with such high-profile directors as Michael Mann and Doug Liman. In 2018, it was announced that he had penned the script for an upcoming drama, tentatively titled *Fair and Balanced*, about the sexual harassment allegations surrounding late, disgraced Fox News founder Roger Ailes.

PERSONAL LIFE

Since 2004 he has been married to the Israeli American actor Mili Avital, whom he thanked in Hebrew during his Academy Award acceptance speech. The couple have two children together, son Benjamin and daughter Fanny.

SUGGESTED READING

Barker, Andrew. Review of *The Big Short*, directed by Adam McKay. *Variety*, 13 Nov. 2015, variety.com/2015/film/reviews/the-big-short-review-1201639770/. Accessed 18 July 2018.

Ginsburg, Aaron. "Writers on Writing: Love and Other Drugs." *Script*, F+W, 14 Apr. 2016, www.scriptmag.com/features/writers-on-writing-love-and-other-drugs. Accessed 18 July 2018.

Kennedy, Dana. "In Film, Still a Missionary." *The New York Times*, 23 Feb. 2003, www.nytimes.com/2003/02/23/movies/film-in-film-still-a-missionary.html. Accessed 18 July 2018.

Randolph, Charles. "Banking on The Big Short." Interview by Brianne Hogan. *Creative Screenwriting*, 20 Jan. 2016, creativescreenwriting.com/banking-on-the-big-short/. Accessed 18 July 2018.

Randolph, Charles. "'The Big Short' Co-Writer Charles Randolph on Why He Left Academia, Adam McKay's Contributions, and More." Interview by Bill Graham. *The Film Stage*, 19 Jan. 2016, thefilmstage.com/features/the-big-short-co-writer-charles-randolph-on-why-he-left-academia-adam-mckays-contributions-and-more/. Accessed 18 July 2018.

Randolph, Charles. "Interview: Oscar-Nominated 'The Big Short' Screenwriter Charles Randolph." Interview by Scott Mendelson. *Forbes*, 25 Jan. 2016, www.forbes.com/sites/scottmendelson/2016/01/25/interview-oscar-nominated-the-big-short-screenwriter-charles-randolph/. Accessed 18 July 2018.

Randolph, Charles, and Adam McKay. "Coming Up Big." Interview by Todd Aaron Jensen. *Writers Guild of America West*, 8 Jan. 2016, www.wga.org/writers-room/features-columns/the-craft/2016/the-big-short-randolph-mckay. Accessed 18 July 2018.

SELECTED WORKS

The Life of David Gale, 2003; *The Interpreter*, 2005; *Love & Other Drugs*, 2010; *The Big Short*, 2015

—*Chris Cullen*

Rapsody

Date of birth: January 21, 1983
Occupation: Rapper

When recording artist Rapsody was nominated for the Grammy Award for Best Rap Album in late 2017, the nomination marked a crucial milestone in the career of a performer who was critically acclaimed but little known outside of specific hip-hop circles. A talented rapper since her years at North Carolina State University, during which she cofounded the student hip-hop club H2O and the rap collective Kooley High, Rapsody released numerous extended-play recordings and mixtapes after signing with the label Jamla Records. In 2012 she released her debut album, *The Idea of Beautiful*, which met with positive reviews but little mainstream attention. For Rapsody, however, fame and popularity were not the focus. "It's easy to get caught up in the rat race, you know? Trying to be this or that for popularity. You lose yourself in that," she told Jessi Roti for the *Chicago Tribune* (7 Dec. 2017). "I want to be able to wake up every day and be happy with the reflection that's looking back at me and know I gave something honest to this world and to whoever's on the receiving end listening."

A turning point in Rapsody's career came in 2017, following the release of her second full-length album, *Laila's Wisdom*. Earning the artist two Grammy nominations as well as widespread acclaim and recognition, the album highlighted Rapsody's vocal and lyrical skills while also calling attention to the social consciousness that

Photo by Richard Bord/WireImage/Getty Images

influences much of her work. "It's the times we're in," she told David Peisner for *Billboard* (19 Jan. 2018) of that facet of her music. "We can't afford to not say anything. We have so much to talk about."

EARLY LIFE AND EDUCATION

Rapsody was born Marlanna Evans on January 21, 1983, in North Carolina. The second-youngest of five children, she grew up in Snow Hill, a small town in the eastern part of the state. Her father worked as a mechanic, while her mother hand-painted fine china. Growing up, Rapsody was close to her extended family, including cousins who introduced her to a variety of new music. She would later name her second album, *Laila's Wisdom*, after her paternal grandmother.

Over the course of her childhood and teen years, Rapsody developed a fascination with the hip-hop genre. She was particularly inspired by the female rappers popular during the 1990s, including MC Lyte, Queen Latifah, and Lauryn Hill, the latter of whom was popular not only as a solo artist but also as a member of the group the Fugees. However, despite her love of hip-hop, she did not initially consider pursuing a career in music herself. "We weren't [raised] to think we could be musicians and artists," she recalled to Peisner of her upbringing. "You were taught the basic things: lawyer, doctor, teacher, accountant. Go to college, make some money, get married, have kids."

Rapsody attended Greene Central High School, where she played basketball and served as class president for a time. She graduated from the school in 2001 and went on to enroll in North Carolina State University in Raleigh, following the example set by her older sisters. She majored in accounting at the university.

KOOLEY HIGH

Among the factors that influenced Rapsody's decision to attend North Carolina State University were her older sisters' reports of the university and the Raleigh area's strong hip-hop scene, which not only promoted local music but also welcomed notable artists from out of state. Upon her arrival at the university, however, she found that hip-hop had waned in popularity since her sisters' time there and was disappointed by the music events available on campus. "The worst was when they had a country band playing homecoming," she told David Menconi for the *News & Observer* (13 Feb. 2016). "That was disappointing. But I got around the right group of people and we started organizing more hip-hop things around campus." Rapsody and her friends founded a hip-hop–focused student organization that they called H2O, which held a variety of events to promote the genre, including rap battles and other live performances.

In addition to her work with H2O during her time at North Carolina State, Rapsody joined Kooley High, a rap collective made up of some of the H2O's members. Rapsody began performing and recording music with the group, which included fellow rappers Charlie Smarts and Tab-One, a DJ known as DJ Ill Digitz, and producers Foolery and The Sinopsis. The collective would later be featured in the 2009 documentary *One Day: Introducing Kooley High*, which documented a day in the life of the group and explored their musical ambitions.

During Rapsody's time with Kooley High, the group captured the attention of producer Patrick Douthit, also known as 9th Wonder. He had previously worked with artists such as Jay-Z and was working closely with the North Carolina–based rap group Little Brother. Rhapsody was identified by 9th Wonder as the standout performer in the collective, and she began collaborating with the producer in 2008. Following her departure from Kooley High, the group continued to record and perform as a five-member collective.

SOLO DEBUTS

Following the establishment of 9th Wonder's record label Jamla Records, Rapsody signed with that label and began recording extensively. She also worked at a shoe store during her early career and at that time struggled to make ends meet while pursuing her musical dreams. "I was broke and hungry a lot," she told Peisner. "I'd only eat once a day. I spent three months living in the studio, hitting up friends: 'Hey, can I come take a shower?'" Rapsody released her first solo mixtape, *Return of the B-Girl*, in 2010 and followed that recording with two additional mixtapes, *Thank H.E.R. Now* and *For Everything*, in 2011. An extended-play (EP) recording, *The Black Mamba*, followed in 2012. In addition to showcasing her skills as a rapper and lyricist, Rapsody's early recordings notably featured guest appearances by several established and up-and-coming artists, including critically acclaimed rapper Kendrick Lamar.

In 2012, Rapsody released her first full-length studio album, *The Idea of Beautiful*. The album met with a largely positive reception, much of which compared the rapper to artists such as Lauryn Hill and emphasized her status as a female performer in a genre that is overwhelmingly male dominated. Indeed, over the course of her career, Rapsody has expressed a mixed view of her status as a female rapper, arguing at times against the use of such labels while also acknowledging the empowering aspects of women's trailblazing work in hip-hop. "As women, we can tap into our emotions in a way that men aren't always allowed to. But I can also show you the strength of a woman, talk about something like power, which is multi-dimensional," she explained to Rodney Carmichael for *NPR* (20 Dec. 2017). "It's dope to show people that women can go in these different places: We can be hard, we can be gritty, we can talk about pain, we can talk depression. I can talk about love. There's not a human on earth who doesn't feel those emotions." Rapsody likewise became known for socially conscious rap that deals with a variety of issues that affect people on a personal and political level.

INCREASING RECOGNITION

Following the release of *The Idea of Beautiful*, Rapsody returned to creating somewhat less structured recordings, releasing the mixtape *She Got Game* in 2013. The EP *Beauty and the Beast* followed in 2014, and in 2016, she released an additional EP titled *Crown*. In the summer of 2016, Rapsody announced that she had signed to the record label Roc Nation, founded by Jay-Z, in addition to maintaining her affiliation with Jamla Records.

In addition to releasing her own music, Rapsody made numerous guest appearances on songs during that period, collaborating with an array of artists. She gained recognition in 2015 following the release of the song "Complexion (A Zulu Love)," which appeared on Kendrick Lamar's album *To Pimp a Butterfly*. Having previously worked with Rapsody on a song from her mixtape *For Everything*, Lamar approached her about writing and performing a verse for the track, which deals with the issue of colorism. "He said, all races are important, but this is something special that we really need to address, especially within the black community, with colorism, and light-skinned versus dark-skinned. So, it wasn't a hard concept to get," Rapsody told Adam Fleischer for *MTV* (16 Mar. 2015). "I did the verse and sent it to him that night." *To Pimp a Butterfly* was ultimately nominated for the Grammy Award for album of the year, and Rapsody, as a cowriter of "Complexion (A Zulu Love)," was included in that nomination.

LAILA'S WISDOM

A major milestone in Rapsody's career came in 2017, when she released her second full-length album, *Laila's Wisdom*. Released on the Roc Nation label, the album featured guest appearances from artists such as Lamar, Black Thought, and Busta Rhymes. According to many of the critics who reviewed it, the album highlighted Rapsody's mastery of songwriting and performance. Widely acclaimed as one of the best rap albums of the year, *Laila's Wisdom* went on to be nominated for the Grammy Award for Best Rap Album, while the song "Sassy" was nominated for the award for best rap song. With her rap album nomination, Rapsody became one of only five solo female artists ever to be nominated for the award.

For the artist, the nominations were particularly meaningful because they were achieved without a major promotional push. "This was as organic as it could possibly be," she told Andreas Hale for the *Root* (2 Dec. 2017). "This is really hip-hop, and that's what makes it even more refreshing." Although the awards for best rap album and best rap song both ultimately went to Lamar, the nominations drew significant attention to Rapsody's work, establishing her further as an important figure in hip-hop.

Amid such recognition, Rapsody took note of the tendency of the media and some fans to pit female hip-hop artists against each other and frequently spoke out against that pattern in interviews. She noted that while male rappers have often been allowed by society to coexist without manufactured conflicts, female rappers often have not. "You see these tweets like, 'Yo, Rapsody's dope. When you gonna battle [fellow rapper] Nicki Minaj?'" she explained to Carmichael. "I'm thinking, why do I have to battle somebody just because they're a woman? You have all these guys coexisting, but because I'm a woman I've gotta be on my *Love & Hip Hop* confrontational thing and go after another woman just to entertain you? That's the silliest concept to me, ever." In light of her Grammy nomination for best rap song, Rapsody was especially compared to and contrasted with rapper Cardi B, the only other female artist nominated for that year's award, whose musical style and persona differed dramatically from Rapsody's. Despite media suggestions of a rivalry, however, Rapsody rejected such narratives, telling Hale, "I think there's room for everybody."

PERSONAL LIFE

When not performing elsewhere, Rapsody lives in North Carolina.

SUGGESTED READING

Carmichael, Rodney. "Define Your Line: Rapsody on Coexisting in Rap's Power Gap." *NPR*, 20 Dec. 2017, www.npr.org/sections/therecord/2017/12/20/569104375/define-your-line-rapsody-on-coexisting-in-raps-power-gap. Accessed 9 Mar. 2018.

Dyroff, Denny. "On Stage (Spotlight): Made in America." *The Unionville Times*, 2 Sept. 2017, www.unionvilletimes.com/?p=36430. Accessed 8 Mar. 2018.

Fleischer, Adam. "How Do You End Up Featured on Kendrick Lamar's Album? Rapsody Tells Her Story." *MTV*, 16 Mar. 2015, www.mtv.com/news/2106673/rapsody-kendrick-lamar-complexion-a-zulu-love-to-pimp-a-butterfly/. Accessed 9 Mar. 2018.

Hale, Andreas. "Rapsody on Her Grammy Nominations Being 'Good for the Culture,' Her Unconventional Journey and Thoughts on Cardi B." *The Root*, 2 Dec. 2017, www.theroot.com/rapsody-on-her-grammy-nominations-being-good-for-the-c-1820915173. Accessed 9 Mar. 2018.

Menconi, David. "Raleigh Rapper Rapsody Up for a Grammy Award." *The News & Observer*, 13 Feb. 2016, www.newsobserver.com/entertainment/arts-culture/article59457466.html. Accessed 8 Mar. 2018.

Peisner, David. "Rapsody's Grammy Breakout: How She Became the Only Woman Nominated for Best Rap Album." *Billboard*, 19 Jan. 2018, www.billboard.com/articles/news/grammys/8094901/rapsody-grammys-2018-best-rap-album-interview. Accessed 9 Mar. 2018.

Roti, Jessi. "Rapsody on Best Rap Album Grammy Nomination: 'Never Let Your Gender Define You or Limit You.'" *Chicago Tribune*, 7 Dec. 2017, www.chicagotribune.com/entertainment/ct-ott-rapsody-lailas-wisdom-1208-20171129-story.html. Accessed 9 Mar. 2018.

SELECTED WORKS

Return of the B-Girl, 2010; *Thank H.E.R. Now*, 2011; *For Everything*, 2011; *The Black Mamba*, 2012; *The Idea of Beautiful*, 2012; *She Got Game*, 2013; *Beauty and the Beast*, 2014; *Crown*, 2016; *Laila's Wisdom*, 2017

—Joy Crelin

Condola Rashād

Date of birth: December 11, 1986
Occupation: Actor

In the decade after graduating from college, Condola Rashād quickly established herself as one of the finest stage actors of her generation. She made her Off-Broadway debut in 2009, in Lynn Nottage's Pulitzer Prize–winning drama *Ruined*, before earning three featured Tony Award nominations: for *Stick Fly* in 2012; for the 2013 revival of *The Trip to Bountiful*; and for *A Doll's House, Part 2* in 2017. She had her first leading role on Broadway in 2018, starring as Joan of Arc in the historical play *Saint Joan*—a performance that earned Rashād her fourth Tony nomination. As a black actor, Rashād broke industry barriers by tackling traditionally white characters, including the roles of Juliet in the 2013 Broadway revival of William Shakespeare's *Romeo and Juliet*, Emmy in 2017's *A Doll's House*, and the

Joan Marcus, via Wikimedia Commons

fifteenth-century French heroine Joan of Arc in *Saint Joan*.

EARLY LIFE AND EDUCATION

Condola Phylea Rashād, the only daughter of award-winning actor Phylicia Rashād and former NFL player and sportscaster Ahmad Rashād, was born in New York City on December 11, 1986. Rashād was named after her paternal grandmother and has five half siblings from her parents' previous marriages. She grew up just north of New York City in Mount Vernon. As a young child, Rashād visited the set of NBC's hit comedy series *The Cosby Show*, where her mother portrayed high-powered attorney and matriarch Clair Huxtable. She was also a backstage presence at several of her mother's Off-Broadway and Broadway productions. "I fell in love with what goes on behind the scenes—the craft," she shared with Joseph V. Amodio for *Newsday* (4 Oct. 2013). "I watched my mother take a character from a page and create something. I think the best actors are the ones who . . . just want to tell you a story." Rashād attended the Ethical Culture Fieldston School, where she was a member of the track and soccer teams. She also took classical piano lessons after school.

Following her graduation from Fieldston's Upper School in 2005, Rashād turned down the music theater program at Carnegie Mellon University School of Drama in Pittsburgh, Pennsylvania, to study theater at the California Institute of Arts. "What was cool about Cal Arts was that it really gives you space to work on things that are quite avant-garde. That was exciting to me," she revealed to Emma Brown for *Interview* (11 Feb. 2016). In 2008, Rashād earned her BFA degree from Cal Arts and moved back to New York. "I think New York does a better job of taking chances on new faces," she confided to Benjamin Lindsay for *Backstage* (12 Apr. 2017).

HER BIG BREAK

Two months after graduating, Rashād joined the ensemble cast of playwright Lynn Nottage's *Ruined*. The play kicked off with a month-long world premiere at Chicago's Goodman Theatre on November 8, 2008, before moving Off-Broadway to the Manhattan Theatre Club in January 2009. After three weeks of previews, *Ruined* officially opened at the Manhattan Theatre Club in February 2009. Rashād earned critical acclaim for her role as Sophie, a mutilated rape survivor living in the war-ravaged Congo. For her performance, Rashād was rewarded with a Theatre World Award (2008–9) and a Drama Desk Award nomination.

Rashād had her television debut in an episode of the CBS legal drama *The Good Wife* in 2009, before appearing on a two-episode arc of NBC's *Law & Order: Criminal Intent* in 2010. The same year, she had a small part in the romantic comedy *Sex and the City 2* (2010). After costarring as an ambitious journalist in the unaired ABC drama pilot *Georgetown* (2011), Rashād auditioned for the female lead opposite Samuel L. Jackson in Katori Hall's play *The Mountaintop*. Although actor Angela Bassett eventually won the role, *The Mountaintop*'s director, Kenny Leon, was so impressed by Rashād's audition that he cast the newcomer in his next project, the play *Stick Fly*.

TAKES BROADWAY BY STORM

Stick Fly, a comedy about the tensions that surface between members of a well-to-do African American family during a presumably relaxing weekend at their Martha's Vineyard home, opened at the Cort Theater in December 2011. Running for ninety-three shows before closing on February 26, 2012, *Stick Fly* received mixed reviews. For her performance as Cheryl, the housekeeper's wisecracking teenage daughter who fills in for her ailing mother, Rashād received her first Tony Award nomination, for best featured actress in a play.

In mid-2012, Rashād had a recurring role on the first season of the NBC musical drama *Smash* and guested in two episodes of the web sitcom *Submissions Only*. She returned to the big screen the same year, starring in director Alexis Lloyd's feature-film debut, *30 Beats* (2012), which opened in limited release. Also in 2012, she appeared in Lifetime's all-black version of the 1989 drama *Steel Magnolias*, directed by *Stick Fly*'s Leon and costarring Rashād's mother.

In April 2013, Rashād returned to Broadway as part of an all-black production of playwright Horton Foote's *The Trip to Bountiful*, starring Tony Award–winning actress Cicely Tyson. Rashād stood out as Thelma, a young newly-wed who befriends Tyson's character during a bus trip. During the 2013 award season, Rashād earned her second consecutive Tony Award nomination, as well as a Drama Desk Award nomination for Outstanding Featured Actress in a Play.

In September 2013, Rashād starred in an interracial remake of *Romeo and Juliet* opposite film actor Orlando Bloom. Rashād was initially drawn to the production because of the decision to focus on the story itself, rather than the ethnically diverse cast. "At the end of the day I am a black woman and I'm a storyteller. The same way an Asian person is a storyteller, the same reason a white person's a storyteller," she told Karu F. Daniels for *NBC News* (9 June 2017). "To me what it means being an actor is I am a shape shifter, I am a time traveler. You give me any story, I can tell it to you. That's what I felt that I was really allowed to do."

Preview performances for David Leveaux's modern retelling of William Shakespeare's tragic love story began in August 2013. However, when *Romeo and Juliet* officially premiered at the Richard Rodgers Theatre a month later, it drew mixed reaction from critics and struggled to attract audiences. The play closed in December 2013—over a month earlier than planned.

CONQUERS A NEW STAGE

In 2014, Rashād accepted a starring role as an ancient Egyptian pharaoh's sister on Fox's straight-to-series drama *Hieroglyph*, but the show was ultimately scrapped in June 2014, before ever airing an episode. The same year, she successfully auditioned for a role in the Showtime drama *Billions*, about New York's hedge-fund industry. "Originally the character of Kate Sacher was for a guest star, possibly recurring, so I was just excited for that," she shared with Brown. "Then I got word that they were trying to make it into a regular, and about a month later we were shooting the pilot." When *Billions* premiered in January 2016, it drew nearly three million multi-platform viewers. Within a month, the show was renewed for its second season.

Rashād soon became more prominent in television. She guest-starred on two episodes of Aziz Ansari's sitcom *Master of None* in 2015 and 2017 and made big-screen appearances in the hostage drama *Money Monster* (2016), directed by Jodie Foster, and the thriller *Complete Unknown* (2016), alongside actor Rachel Weisz. In mid-2017, *Billions* was renewed for a third season.

CEMENTS BROADWAY STATUS

Following a four-year hiatus, Rashād returned to Broadway in March 2017. She appeared in playwright Lucas Hnath's *A Doll's House, Part 2*, the imagined sequel to Henry Ibsen's 1879 classic. She was cast as Emmy, an estranged adult daughter reunited with her mother, who abandoned her fifteen years earlier. "I was really moved by the fact that the character I was asked to play has such a very different standpoint on life than I did personally," she confided to Suzy Evans for *TodayTix* (7 June 2017). "I like to go far away from my own world view and really get into the mind of someone that feels the complete opposite."

A Doll's House, Part 2 began previews at the John Golden Theatre on March 30, 2017, before officially opening nearly a month later. Rashād held her own in a four-person cast that included industry veterans Laurie Metcalf, Chris Cooper, and Jayne Houdyshell, and she received critical acclaim for her performance. *A Doll's House, Part 2* garnered eight Tony Award nominations, including Rashād's third for best featured actress in a play.

After concluding her role in *A Doll's House, Part 2* in July 2017, Rashād starred in the independent feature *Bikini Moon* (2017), in which she played the title role—a shell-shocked Iraq war veteran. The next year, Rashād attended the 2018 Sundance Film Festival to promote her 2018 project. The biopic *Come Sunday*, in which Rashād plays the wife of a real-life Pentecostal preacher who becomes a pariah when he questions the existence of hell, premiered on the streaming service Netflix in April 2018. At the same time, Rashād also appeared on the third season of *Billions*.

In 2018, RRashād starred as the title role in the Broadway production of playwright George Bernard Shaw's *Saint Joan*. To prepare to play the French icon, Rashād thoroughly researched her part. "I think that often when people think of Joan of Arc they just think of this mercenary, this soldier. . . . when she was leading the army, there was a certain fire that came through her," she shared with Greg Evans for *Deadline* (1 June 2018). "When she was just in her life, she was described as quite graceful and quite simple. I think because of what she's come to represent it's easy to put her in one place, but she was a whole human being." *Saint Joan* debuted at the Samuel J. Friedman Theatre on April 25, 2018. The production had fifty-five performances before ending its run on June 10, 2018. For her performance, Rashād received a Tony Award nomination for Best Performance by an Actress in a Leading Role in a Play.

PERSONAL LIFE

The actor, who lives in Bushwick, Brooklyn, fronts the alternative rock group Condola and the Stoop Kids. The band has one album to their credit: 2014's *The Letter 9*. She became engaged to actor Sebastian Vallentin Stenhøj in 2016.

SUGGESTED READING

Chow, Andrew R. "Condola Rashad's Next Role to Tackle: Joan of Arc." *New York Times*, 12 Sept. 2017, www.nytimes.com/2017/09/12/theater/condola-rashad-saint-joan-broadway.html. Accessed 13 July 2018.

Daniels, Karu F. "'Shape Shifter': Condola Rashad on Third Tony Nomination." *NBC News*, 9 June 2017, www.nbcnews.com/news/nbcblk/shape-shifter-condola-rashad-third-tony-award-nomination-n769956. Accessed 13 July 2018.

Evans, Suzy. "Condola Rashad: Magic Lady." *TodayTix*, 7 June 2017, www.todaytix.com/insider/nyc/posts/condola-rashad-magic-lady. Accessed 13 July 2018.

Lindsay, Benjamin. "How Condola Rashad Quietly Became One of Her Generation's Finest Stage Actors." *Backstage*, 12 Apr. 2017, www.backstage.com/interview/how-condola-rashad-quietly-became-one-her-generations-finest-stage-actors/. Accessed 13 July 2018.

Rashād, Condola. "'Billions' Star Condola Rashad Talks Saints, Trolls and Being Joan of Arc—Tony Awards Watch." Interview by Greg Evans. *Deadline*, 1 June 2018, deadline.com/2018/06/condola-rashad-billions-broadway-tony-awards-saint-joan-1202401672/. Accessed 13 July 2018.

Rashād, Condola. "Condola Rashad on *Romeo and Juliet* Orlando Bloom: 'We Had a Connection from the Minute We Met.'" Interview by Joseph V. Amodio. *Newsday*, 4 Oct. 2013, www.newsday.com/entertainment/theater/condola-rashad-on-romeo-and-juliet-orlando-bloom-we-had-a-connection-from-the-minute-we-met-1.6176580. Accessed 13 July 2018.

Rashād, Condola. Interview. By Emma Brown. *Interview*, 11 Feb. 2016, www.interviewmagazine.com/film/condola-rashad. Accessed 13 July 2018.

SELECTED WORKS

Ruined, 2009; *Stick Fly*, 2011; *The Trip to Bountiful*, 2013; *Romeo and Juliet*, 2013; *A Doll's House, Part 2*, 2017; *Saint Joan*, 2018

—*Bertha Muteba*

Haley Lu Richardson

Date of birth: March 7, 1995
Occupation: Actor

Haley Lu Richardson began her acting career in guest roles on television shows such as *Ravenswood* and *Law and Order: Special Victims Unit*. Her role in the latter led to her role in the 2017 film *Columbus*; having seen Richardson's work, the wife of the film's director recommended her. Following the release of the *Columbus* film, Richardson explained one of the benefits of being an actor to Devan Coggan for *Entertainment Weekly* (10 Aug. 2017): "Every character I get into, I get to learn about a new place, a new person, a new life situation. I feel like it makes me more empathetic, just as a human." Richardson is one of the few performers to have had two full-length premieres the same year—*The Young Kieslowski* and *The Last Survivors*, in 2014—at the Los Angeles Film Festival.

By David Siegel, via Wikimedia Commons

EDUCATION AND EARLY CAREER

Born in Phoenix, Arizona, Richardson had parents who were supportive of her artistic interests. Her father, Forrest, is a golf course architect and her mother, Valerie, is a graphic designer. Richardson's first love was dance; she competed for ten years. She also played soccer and participated in musical theater. As an only child, Richardson created imaginary friends to fill the roles of siblings.

However, she wanted a movie career, which involved making arguments at dinner for and against moving to Los Angeles. As she told Emma Brown for *Interview* (19 Aug. 2015), "I ended up making a 3-D panel poster and writing up a list of pros and cons and how we were going to attack the cons. I gave them this whole presentation on how it was going to work. A week later, my mom moved to L.A. with me!" Realizing that the emotion she portrayed in dance was part of the acting world, she was convinced that acting would become her career. Richardson was sixteen. She dropped out of high school but completed the work online to get her diploma.

Some of Richardson's earliest acting credits included a guest appearance on the Disney Channel sitcom *Shake It Up* in 2013 and, also that year, a role in an ABC pilot alternately titled *Adopted* or *Keep Calm and Karey On*, which never got picked up. She was also a cast member in the 2013 Lifetime television movie *Escape from Polygamy*.

DOUBLE WORLD PREMIERES

In 2014, when she was seventeen, Richardson was cast as Kendal in the post-apocalyptic film *The Last Survivors*. At first titled *The Well*, it was one of fifty-nine nondocumentary entries that premiered at the twentieth Los Angeles Film Festival. Although Richardson had never held a weapon of any kind, after being cast she was taken to a shooting range for practice before filming the fight scenes. Her dance background was helpful in dealing with the film's fight choreography.

She spent the days of the shoot—done in the Mojave Desert to convey the landscape of a world without water—covered with mud and sand, along with makeup to appear as if she were covered in oil. As Richardson said in a press release for *PRLog* (21 May 2014), "My mom told me many times that it's hard work to be beautiful. Shooting *The Well* was really hard work and I am anything but beautiful and glamorous on screen!"

Director Tom Hammock featured his parents among the survivors. His father, Dr. Bruce Hammock of University of California's Division of Agriculture and Natural Resources, commented for his department's online publication *Bug Squad* (2 Feb. 2016): "We were on the set at 5:30 a.m. We worked until dark, in weather well below freezing, with high winds blowing sand. The professional actors and actresses put in amazing performances under quite adverse conditions."

Also in 2014, Richardson starred in the romantic comedy *The Young Kieslowski*, which also premiered at the Los Angeles Film Festival, where it won the Audience Award for Best Narrative Feature. She played Leslie Mallard, who becomes pregnant with twins while a Stanford student. Writer Kerem Sanga, not coincidentally, has a twin brother; they were conceived while his parents attended Stanford. (Sanga has made it clear, however, that his parents handled their situation better than the characters in his film.)

THE BRONZE

Richardson next won the role of gymnast Maggie Townsend in the 2015 film *The Bronze*, depicting the training of a young Olympic hopeful. She arrived twenty minutes late for her audition for the part, which would have normally disqualified her. However, as writer Winston Rauch explained to Liz Ohanesian for *KCET* (10 Mar. 2016), "The first thing you want to do when somebody shows up late like that is, you want to be like, 'Sorry, you lost it,' but . . . she was so good when she actually performed her monologue. She stopped herself, gave herself a moment, started over and gave us the most bubbly, effervescent [performance]. That's what we wanted."

The Bronze was Richardson's first venture into comedy; she learned about timing and improvising from more seasoned actors. In addition, although as a young child she had participated in gymnastics, she worked for two months with trainers to learn specific techniques of the sport. She performed some of the routines in the film herself, although she had a stunt double, National College Athletics Association (NCAA) gymnastics champion Katherine Grable, to perform the more challenging moves. As she told Lamarco McClendon for *Variety* (8 Mar. 2016), "Physically, this role was a lot of preparation because I had to train with a stunt coach for two months before we started filming. I had to get my body in shape so I looked like a believable gymnast, and I had to learn how to get into the moves so the stunt double could actually do the flips."

The film premiered on the first night of the Sundance Film Festival in January 2015. Despite having that prime slot, reviews were not favorable, and the movie was partially re-edited. It was not the first glitch in the process of releasing the film, which was shot in twenty-two days in Amherst, Ohio, a place that perfectly embodied the writers' concept of a small Midwestern town. After multiple delays, Sony Pictures Classics finally released the film in March 2016, to generally lackluster reviews.

TWO MORE FILMS

Meanwhile, Richardson picked up additional television credits, appearing in a 2015 episode of *Law and Order: Special Victims Unit* and in 2016 scoring a recurring role in the ABC addiction recovery drama *Recovery Road*. But she also kept her sights set on the big screen.

Richardson took a key role in the 2016 comedic drama *The Edge of Seventeen*, written and directed by Kelly Fremon Craig. Richardson plays Krista, the best friend of Nadine, played by Hailee Steinfeld. The film is set in high school, and centers around the conflicting tensions of dating and friendship. Richardson spoke to Jeff Mitchell for the *Phoenix Film Festival* website (18 Nov. 2016) about continually playing teenagers: "I have been acting professionally for five years, ever since I was 16. Since then, I've literally just played high school kids. I feel like that I'm constantly forced into all of those memories, and I'm just stuck there reliving it forever. So, yes, I could definitely relate to all of the (high school) characters."

One of the elements in the script that rang true for Richardson was the need for self-love. As she told Mitchell, "You really have to take care of yourself and love yourself (in order) to be giving to other people."

Richardson was next cast as Claire Benoit in M. Night Shyamalan's 2016 horror film *Split*, which opened in the United States in 2017. The protagonist, Kevin Wendell Crumb (played by James McAvoy), is a man with twenty-three different personalities, and Claire is one of three young women he kidnaps.

COLUMBUS

The 2017 independent drama *Columbus*, from Korean-born director Kogonada, gave Richardson her first major leading role, in which she impressed movie critics. As Richard Brody wrote for the *New Yorker* (19 June 2017), "Richardson in particular vaults to the forefront of her generation's actors with this performance, which virtually sings with emotional and intellectual acuity."

Richardson plays Casey, a young woman from Columbus, Indiana—a small town but a mecca of modern architecture. A year after high school graduation, she has not gone to college, in part because she is caretaker for her mother, a recovering drug addict. Casey is a tour guide to the city's architectural wonders and works part time in a library. She meets a young man from out of town and the two bond over a shared love of architecture.

Aware of the limitations of her education but remedying the situation with her acting, Richardson told Bob Strauss for *Los Angeles Daily News* (28 Aug. 2017), "I learned so much from doing this movie. I just tried to absorb everything because I never went to film school, I never studied cinema in any way, and Kogonada is such a cinephile. He appreciates it and dissects it as if it were truly an art and not just this business. So everything he did with the visuals of this place Columbus and of these buildings, why each scene was filmed in each place, everything was very purposeful and very symbolic."

FUTURE FOCUS

Richardson's work set for release in 2018 includes *The Chaperone*, a period drama and the first feature film produced by public television broadcaster PBS. Set in the 1920s and based on a novel by Laura Moriarty, the film features Richardson as Louise Brooks, the American actor and noted flapper who popularized the bob haircut. Richardson plays opposite Elizabeth McGovern, who plays the title role of a woman whose life is changed when she accompanies Brooks to New York City. The film reunites McGovern, director Michael Engler, and screenwriter Julian Fellowes, all noted for their work on the popular PBS series *Downton Abbey*.

Richardson stars in the role of Maci in the independent comedy *Support the Girls*, also expected for release in 2018. The film is directed by Andrew Bujalski and costars Regina Hall, with whom Richardson performed in *Split*. Filmed in Texas, *Support the Girls* focuses on the efforts of young women working at a restaurant—with Hall as manager and Richardson as wait staff—to host a fundraiser and the opposition they face from the eatery's owner.

PERSONAL LIFE

Richardson tries to keep a balance in her life, because, as she told Brown, "You take your craft seriously, but you don't have to take yourself seriously. It's so easy to judge yourself and be so hard on yourself and have all these expectations and demands." She has a line of unique hand-crocheted fashion items she designed, Hooked by Haley Lu. One of her handmade tops makes a brief appearance in the film *The Edge of Seventeen*. As she told Mitchell, "Crocheting is . . . a really good thing to have in a world where there is so much pressure. My mom taught me how to crochet when I was eight, and I've been doing it ever since and coming up with patterns and designs. It's something that I do just creatively and to have fun."

SUGGESTED READING

Brody, Richard. "The Precocious Genius of 'Columbus.'" *The New Yorker*, 19 June 2017, www.newyorker.com/magazine/2017/06/19/the-precocious-genius-of-columbus. Accessed 12 Mar. 2018.

Brown, Emma. "Discovery: Haley Lu Richardson." *Interview*, 19 Aug. 2015, www.interviewmagazine.com/film/discovery-haley-lu-richardson. Accessed 12 Mar. 2018.

Coggan, Devan. "Breaking Big: Haley Lu Richardson Heads from *The Edge of Seventeen* to *Columbus*." *Entertainment Weekly*, 10 Aug. 2017, ew.com/movies/2017/08/10/breaking-big-haley-lu-richardson-columbus/. Accessed 12 Mar. 2018.

McClendon, Lamarco. "Melissa Rauch Talks Fame, Petiteness and Free Pretzels at 'The Bronze' Premiere." *Variety*, 8 Mar. 2016, variety.com/2016/scene/vpage/melissa-rauch-the-bronze-premiere-1201724868/. Accessed 12 Mar. 2018.

Ohanesian, Liz. "The Bronze: Screenwriters Melissa and Winston Rauch Talk about the Olympics Comedy." *KCET*, 10 Mar. 2016, www.kcet.org/kcet-cinema-series/the-bronze-screenwriters-melissa-and-winston-rauch-talk-about-the-olympics-comedy. Accessed 12 Mar. 2018.

Richardson, Haley Lu. Interview. By Jeff Mitchell. *Phoenix Film Festival*, 18 Nov. 2016, www.phoenixfilmfestival.com/blog/2016/11/an-interview-with-haley-lu-richardson-from-the-edge-of-seventeen-by-jeff-mitchell. Accessed 12 Mar. 2018.

Strauss, Bob. "After 'Split' and 'Edge of Seventeen,' Haley Lu Richardson Takes on 'Columbus.'" *Los Angeles Daily News*, 28 Aug. 2017, www.dailynews.com/2017/08/02/after-split-and-edge-of-seventeen-haley-lu-richardson-takes-on-columbus/. Accessed 12 Mar. 2018.

SELECTED WORKS

The Young Kieslowski, 2014; *The Bronze*, 2015; *The Edge of Seventeen*, 2016; *Split*, 2016; *Columbus*, 2017

—*Judy Johnson*

Anthony Rizzo

Date of birth: August 8, 1989
Occupation: Baseball player

When first baseman Anthony Rizzo was traded to the Chicago Cubs in 2012, he could not have known that he would become a key contributor to one of the most significant events in franchise history—and Major League Baseball (MLB) history as a whole. By the time of the trade, the Cubs had not won a World Series since 1908, and the team had not even competed in baseball's top showcase since 1945. That record-length championship drought was finally ended in 2016, when Rizzo and his teammates claimed the National League pennant and went on to beat the Cleveland Indians in the World Series, becoming instant heroes to generations of long-suffering Cubs fans. For Rizzo, whose upbeat and optimistic approach to his sport became one of his defining characteristics during his tenure in Chicago, the victory was attributable both to the skills of his teammates and to their sheer determination to end a legendary losing streak once and for all.

By Keith Allison, via Wikimedia Commons

A professional baseball player since the age of eighteen, Rizzo was no stranger to challenges even more daunting than those on the field. While playing in the minor leagues in 2008, he was diagnosed with Hodgkin lymphoma and underwent several months of treatment before the cancer went into remission. Following that experience, Rizzo dedicated himself both to raising funds for pediatric cancer research and to putting forward the best possible performance in his sport. "Live every moment that you can because you never know," he told Tom Verducci for *Sports Illustrated* (10 Aug. 2016). "I feel like when I do things, I do them the best I possibly can."

EARLY LIFE AND EDUCATION

Anthony Vincent Rizzo was born on August 8, 1989, in Fort Lauderdale, Florida. The second son born to John and Laurie Rizzo, he was raised in Parkland, Florida. Rizzo grew up playing a variety of sports, including baseball and hockey, with the encouragement of his father. He soon demonstrated a talent for baseball in particular. "Once he got into T-ball, Little League, he was a freak," his father told Teddy Greenstein for the *Chicago Tribune* (30 Sept. 2016). "By end of the season, the kids were asking him to sign their ball. The parents were saying, 'He's gonna be in the pros.'"

As a teenager, Rizzo attended Marjory Stoneman Douglas High School, where he continued to excel as a baseball player. During that time, he attracted the attention of professional baseball scouts. This included Laz Gutierrez, a scout for the Boston Red Sox organization, who was impressed not only by the first baseman's talent but also by his personality and leadership. After graduating from high school in 2007, Rizzo opted not to attend college and instead entered the 2007 MLB Draft. On June 7 of that year, he was drafted by the Red Sox as the twentieth pick in the sixth round of the draft. He signed a contract two months later, with the team paying him more money than usual for his draft position.

MINOR-LEAGUE CAREER

Rizzo began his professional baseball career in the minor leagues, initially joining the Gulf Coast League Red Sox, the major-league team's rookie affiliate. He was promoted to the Class A–level Greenville Drive in 2008 and got off to a hot-hitting start but played only twenty-one games with the team that season. In the spring of 2008, Rizzo sought medical attention for symptoms he was experiencing and was diagnosed with Hodgkin lymphoma, a form of cancer. "I didn't know what anything was," he told Verducci. "I didn't know what chemotherapy was. I thought chemotherapy was cancer. I had no idea." Despite his unfamiliarity with the condition, Rizzo remained optimistic going into treatment. "They explained what they had to do, and I was like, OK, let's go," he recalled to Verducci.

After undergoing treatment for several months, Rizzo learned that the cancer had gone into remission. He returned to baseball in 2009, beginning the season with the Greenville Drive and later moving to the Salem Red Sox. In May of 2010, Rizzo moved on to the double-A Portland Sea Dogs, for which he posted 20 home runs, 80 runs batted in (RBIs), and a .263 batting average in 107 games. He was quickly becoming a notable power-hitting prospect. In December 2010, however, the Red Sox traded Rizzo to the San Diego Padres organization (whose front office included several former Red Sox executives) as part of a package for fellow first baseman Adrian Gonzalez, an established All Star. Nevertheless, Boston general manager Theo Epstein reportedly told Rizzo "Someday I'll get you back," as reported by Verducci.

SAN DIEGO PADRES

The Padres assigned Rizzo to their triple-A affiliate in Tucson, Arizona, for the start of the 2011 season. There he excelled, hitting .365 with 16 home runs, and before long he was called up to the major league club. He made his big-league debut with San Diego on June 9, 2011, in a winning home game against the Washington Nationals, during which he scored one of the team's seven runs.

Yet despite that strong start, Rizzo struggled to adjust to the team and performed uncharacteristically poorly during his first months with the Padres. "I know that it can only get better, that it can't get much worse," he told Chris Jenkins for the *San Diego Union Tribune* (18 July 2011) at the time. "I'm holding up, but I'm sure not happy about it. It's not fun to struggle, ever." However, he was determined to improve and fulfill his potential. "I know I'm a good player," he told Jenkins. "I'm going to be the player they say I am. Even with the pitchers up here, I'm going to hit well. It's just a matter of time."

With a low batting average and high strikeout rate, Rizzo was returned to Triple A. Back in the minors he hit well again, and he received a late-season call up to the majors. However, the 2011 season proved to be a challenging one for the Padres, and the team did not compete in the postseason. Over the course of his first two major-league stints in 2011, Rizzo played in forty-nine games with a meager .141 batting average. Although his fielding at first base was strong as it was in the minors, he was mainly heralded for his offensive potential, making these early results disappointing.

Despite these struggles, Rizzo was initially still considered the Padres' first baseman of the future. However, the team acquired other players in the offseason, making a spot for him on the roster less certain. Meanwhile, Epstein became general manager of the Chicago Cubs, and several Padres executives who had worked with him in the Red Sox organization joined him. Very familiar with Rizzo, this group of Cubs executives eagerly traded for him, sending pitcher Andrew Cashner to San Diego in return.

CHICAGO CUBS

Rizzo began the 2012 season with the AAA Iowa Cubs, where he again dominated at the plate. He was called up to the Cubs' major-league club on June 26, and this time his performance more closely matched his minor-league success. He was named the National League (NL) rookie of the month for July 2012 after hitting .330. Though he did not maintain quite that pace across the rest of the season, his final 2012 statistics of a .285 batting average, 15 home runs, and 48 RBIs in eighty-seven games established him as an everyday player. He was also seen as a key piece in Epstein's plans to rebuild the Cubs into World Series contenders. The historic franchise, already known for its legendary championship drought, was in the midst of several seasons of losing records, finishing 2012 with a dismal 101 losses.

The following year saw Rizzo's first complete season with the Cubs, during which he played in almost every game. His batting average regressed considerably, ending the season at .233, and the Cubs again finished last in the NL Central division, but he still managed 23 home runs, 40 doubles, and 80 RBIs. He also signed a $44 million contract extension early in the season, signing

him with the Cubs for seven years through 2019, with two extra years as team options. He rewarded the team for this confidence in him in 2014, when he was selected to the MLB All Star Game for the first time. Though the Cubs once again finished last in their division, Rizzo finished the regular season with a solid .286 batting average and 32 home runs. He even earned consideration for the NL Most Valuable Player (MVP) Award, coming in tenth in voting.

In 2015, Rizzo played in 160 games and made 701 plate appearances during the regular season, both the most of any player in the National League. He earned his second All Star appearance, and finished the regular season with 31 home runs, 101 RBIs, and 94 runs scored to go with a .278 average. Under new manager Joe Maddon, the Cubs played to a 97–65 record, third best across the MLB. However, the two teams with better records, the St. Louis Cardinals and the Pittsburgh Pirates, were also in the NL Central, forcing the Cubs into the wild card game to begin the postseason. Chicago beat the Pirates in that win-or-go-home contest, though Rizzo went hitless. The team proceeded to beat the Cardinals in the National League Division Series (NLDS), but ultimately were swept by the New York Mets in the National League Championship Series (NLCS).

In addition to making strong in-game contributions for the Cubs, Rizzo came to establish himself as a leader and a positive force on the team. He especially became known for his happy demeanor and optimistic attitude. "He's always upbeat, positive. He plays every day, plays with enthusiasm, is definitely not afraid and is very supportive of the rest of the group," Maddon told Greenstein. "He has a great outlook on the day."

2016 WORLD SERIES

Despite their defeat in the previous postseason, Rizzo and his teammates remained hopeful going into 2016. The Cubs had not won a World Series since 1908, the longest title drought in professional sports, but Rizzo was convinced that after years of losing Epstein and company had built a serious contender. "We saw the big picture. You never want to lose a game . . . but you do the best you can," he later told Al Yellon for the blog *Bleed Cubbie Blue* (20 Apr. 2017). "I knew they were putting together the talent and by 2014 and 2015 I knew we had the ability to win."

The 2016 season was a strong one for the Cubs, as the team achieved an MLB-best record of 103–58 to win the NL Central. An All Star for the third consecutive year, Rizzo compiled a .292 batting average, 32 home runs, 109 RBIs, and 94 runs scored along with his usual solid defense across the regular season. In recognition of his performance, he was awarded the NL Silver

Slugger and Gold Glove awards for top offensive and defensive play, respectively, at first base. He also came in fourth in NL MVP voting for the second year in a row.

During the postseason, the Cubs beat the San Francisco Giants in the NLDS and then proceeded to the NLCS against the Los Angeles Dodgers. Rizzo hit .320 in the NLCS with two home runs, helping to beat the Dodgers four games to two and earning the Cubs the National League pennant for the first time since 1945. In the World Series, the Cubs faced the Cleveland Indians. Again, Rizzo played a key role, scoring the most runs of any player on either team with seven and hitting .360. The tense series went the full seven games, with the Cubs ultimately winning the deciding contest 8–7 in the tenth inning. For his role in bringing the franchise its first championship in more than a century, Rizzo went from popular star to Cubs legend.

2017 AND BEYOND

Rizzo continued his strong play in 2017, finishing the regular season with a .273 average and matching his 32 home runs and 109 RBIs of the previous year. The Cubs won their division again at 92–70 and beat the Washington Nationals in the NLDS. However, the team lost its attempt to repeat as World Series champions by losing to the Dodgers in the NLCS.

Rizzo also began the 2018 season strong, hitting his first home run of the season in the opening-day game against the Miami Marlins. "I've hit a lot of home runs," he told Jorge L. Ortiz for *USA Today* (29 Mar. 2018). "That was probably the most out-of-body experience I've had hitting a home run in my life." He was placed on the disabled list for a back injury less than two weeks later but was scheduled to return shortly thereafter.

PERSONAL LIFE

Following his experience undergoing treatment for Hodgkin lymphoma, Rizzo became actively involved in promoting and raising funds for pediatric cancer research with the Anthony Rizzo Family Foundation. He received the Roberto Clemente Award from Major League Baseball in 2017 for his charitable efforts.

Rizzo also became an advocate for gun control in 2018, following the deaths of seventeen teenagers and adults in a shooting at his former high school in Parkland. "Every day, you think of them," he told Tony Andracki for *NBC Sports Chicago* (29 Mar. 2018). "Every day, you feel for what happened." He spoke out in support of the student protests that occurred after the event and left spring training to attend a vigil shortly after the shooting.

When not playing baseball elsewhere, Rizzo lives in Chicago. In addition to enjoying the city's restaurants, he enjoys boating on Lake Michigan. Rizzo announced his engagement to Emily Vakos in 2017.

SUGGESTED READING

Andracki, Tony. "8 Years After Cancer Remission, Anthony Rizzo Maintains Perspective." *NBC Sports Chicago*, 2 Sept. 2016, www.nbcsports.com/chicago/chicago-cubs/8-years-after-cancer-remission-anthony-rizzo-maintains-perspective. Accessed 13 Apr. 2018.

Andracki, Tony. "In Wake of Parkland Tragedy, Anthony Rizzo Has Transformed into an Icon That Transcends Baseball." *NBC Sports Chicago*, 29 Mar. 2018, www.nbcsports.com/chicago/cubs/wake-parkland-tragedy-anthony-rizzo-has-transformed-icon-transcends-baseball-stoneman-douglas-gun-control. Accessed 13 Apr. 2018.

Greenstein, Teddy. "Home Schooled: Anthony Rizzo Learned to Give It His All Early." *Chicago Tribune*, 30 Sept. 2016, www.chicagotribune.com/sports/baseball/cubs/ct-cubs-anthony-rizzo-spt-1002-20161001-story.html. Accessed 13 Apr. 2018.

Jenkins, Chris. "Rizzo's Hard Road Takes Him Home." *San Diego Union Tribune*, 18 July 2011, www.sandiegouniontribune.com/sports/padres/sdut-rizzos-hard-road-takes-him-home-2011jul18-htmlstory.html. Accessed 13 Apr. 2018.

Ortiz, Jorge L. "Anthony Rizzo's Home Run an 'Out-of-Body Experience' on Emotional Opening Day." *USA Today*, 29 Mar. 2018, www.usatoday.com/story/sports/mlb/2018/03/29/anthony-rizzos-home-run-out-body-experience-emotional-opening-day/471462002/. Accessed 13 Apr. 2018.

Rizzo, Anthony. "BCB Interview: Anthony Rizzo." Interview by Al Yellon. *Bleed Cubbie Blue*, 20 Apr. 2017, www.bleedcubbieblue.com/2017/4/20/15372322/bcb-interview-anthony-rizzo. Accessed 13 Apr. 2018.

Verducci, Tom. "Den Leader: Slugger and Cancer Survivor Anthony Rizzo Holds the Cubs Together." *Sports Illustrated*, 10 Aug. 2016, www.si.com/mlb/2016/08/09/anthony-rizzo-chicago-cubs-cancer-all-star. Accessed 13 Apr. 2018.

—Joy Crelin

Michael Rosbash

Date of birth: March 7, 1944
Occupation: Geneticist

"The circadian system has its tentacles around everything," researcher Michael Rosbash told

By Bengt Nyman [CC BY 2.0], via Wikimedia Commons

Sarah C. P. Williams for the *HHMI Bulletin* (Spring 2014). "It's ticking away in almost every tissue in the human body." Indeed, the circadian rhythm, which can be described as the body's natural sleep-wake cycle, plays a key role in a person's health, and scientists have increasingly linked disruptions in that rhythm to physical and mental health concerns, from metabolic disorder to cancers to depression. The mechanisms behind the circadian rhythm, however, were little understood and have long been a topic of interest for researchers. Among the scientists working in that field is Rosbash, who has been studying the circadian workings of fruit flies since the early 1980s.

A professor of biology at Brandeis University, Rosbash joined the institution in 1974 after completing his doctoral studies at the Massachusetts Institute of Technology (MIT) and a postdoctoral appointment at the University of Edinburgh. Over more than four decades, he established his Rosbash Lab as a major force in neuroscience and genetics while overcoming some scientists' skepticism about his and his colleagues' approach. "There are so many different ways to be successful in science, but probably persistence more than anything else is my guess," he told Marc Gozlan for *Medscape* (19 Oct. 2017). He added, "Just never give up." His decades of persistence proved fruitful: in addition to making groundbreaking observations in fruit fly genetics and neurobiology, Rosbash shared the 2017 Nobel Prize in Physiology or Medicine for his work in the field, becoming the

first Brandeis researcher to win that internationally renowned honor.

EARLY LIFE AND EDUCATION

Michael Morris Rosbash was born in 1944 in Kansas City, Missouri. He was the first of two sons born to Alfred and Hilde Rosbash, German Jews who had settled in the United States around 1938 after fleeing the Nazi regime. When Rosbash was two, his family moved to Massachusetts, where his father found work as a cantor at Temple Ohabei Shalom in Brookline. His mother later became a cytologist at Boston's Beth Israel Hospital. His father died when Rosbash was ten years old, and Rosbash spent the remainder of his childhood living in Newton, Massachusetts, with his mother and younger brother, James. As a youth, Rosbash exhibited some interest in biology but was not strongly drawn to science over any other academic pursuit. In fact, he recalled to Gozlan that he preferred baseball and his toy trains at the time.

Rosbash attended Newton High School, later renamed Newton North High School. After graduating in 1961, he enrolled in the California Institute of Technology (Caltech), an institution he chose less for its academic reputation and more for its geographical distance from his hometown. "I was a difficult kid and a somewhat indifferent student but realized somehow that a new start at a good place and far from home was important," he wrote for the *Shaw Prize* website (23 Sept. 2013). Although he first intended to study mathematics, Rosbash soon pursued studies in biology and chemistry and furthered his interest in those subjects through work at the research laboratory of pioneering molecular biologist Norman Davidson. Rosbash earned his bachelor's degree from Caltech in 1965. He would go on to be designated a Caltech Distinguished Alumnus in 2001.

Following his time at Caltech, Rosbash spent the 1965–66 academic year at the Institute of Physico-Chemical Biology (Institut de Biologie Physico-Chimique) in Paris, France. His year in France was funded through a Fulbright Fellowship, the first of many prestigious honors he would receive over the course of his career. During that period, Rosbash worked in a laboratory run by biochemist Marianne Grunberg-Manago, participating in research into protein synthesis and ribonucleic acid (RNA) processing. After returning from France, he enrolled in MIT to pursue doctoral studies in biophysics, researching RNA and protein synthesis under adviser Sheldon Penman. Rosbash earned his doctorate in 1971.

ACADEMIC CAREER

After earning his degree, Rosbash remained at MIT for six months, serving as a postdoctoral researcher. He next took a postdoctoral fellowship at the University of Edinburgh, with financial support from the Helen Hay Whitney Foundation Research Fellowship program. Rosbash remained in Edinburgh for three years, researching gene expression under scientist John Bishop. While Rosbash was still abroad, a hiring committee from Brandeis University recruited him for a position at the institution. Following the launch of its Rosenstiel Basic Medical Sciences Research Center in 1970, the university was actively seeking to attract talented researchers to its campus in Waltham, Massachusetts, and, after offering Rosbash a position there, agreed to defer his hiring until he had completed the final year of his postdoctoral appointment. Rosbash accepted the offer, which he later noted in interviews gave him a degree of security that many young scientists did not have. "I did not have to go on the job market, worried about where I was going to go, or spend 3 months touring different places," he told Gozlan. "It was a good place and I had good colleagues. It was a place I knew well because it is 5 miles from where I grew up." Rosbash joined Brandeis as an assistant professor in October 1974.

Over the subsequent decades, Rosbash remained at Brandeis, where he was promoted to associate professor in 1980 and full professor in 1986. During the early 1980s, he was denied tenure within the Rosenstiel Center but granted it by the biology department, which resulted in his laboratory moving into the biology building in August 1982. In March 2012, after nearly four decades at Brandeis, Rosbash became the first Peter Gruber Endowed Chair in Neuroscience. The position was established through a gift to Brandeis from the Peter and Patricia Gruber Foundation, which had previously awarded Rosbash a 2009 Gruber Neuroscience Prize.

Rosbash also received a 1976 Research Career Development Award from the National Institutes of Health (NIH), a 1988 Guggenheim Fellowship, and the 2013 Shaw Prize in Life Science and Medicine. In addition to conducting research at Brandeis, Rosbash taught courses in molecular biology at the university and served as an investigator with the Howard Hughes Medical Institute (HHMI) since 1989. He belongs to the American Association for the Advancement of Science, American Academy of Arts and Sciences (AAAS), and National Academy of Sciences (NAS).

RESEARCH

Since the 1970s, Rosbash has conducted research into such foundational topics as the genes regulating proteins in yeast, the cloning of genes, and the properties and functions of RNA. Much of his work has taken place at the intersection of fields such as biology, genetics, and neuroscience, with Rosbash exploring how different systems within the body and brain interact and influence the subject's behavior. "It's like being interested in who we are and the origin of our own appetites, failures, and personalities," he explained to Gozlan. "So when neurogenetics became possible to do, I started to pay attention."

A major turning point in his career came in October 1982, when Rosbash began a professional collaboration with fellow Brandeis professor Jeffrey C. Hall. The two professors, who had become friends not long after they both arrived at Brandeis, often played basketball together and discussed their respective research in the university's locker room. Although they had already carried out several years of research on their own, they determined that they could accomplish far more if they worked together.

Rosbash and Hall's collaboration focused primarily on *Drosophila melanogaster*, commonly known as the fruit fly. Building on earlier work by researchers such as Caltech's Seymour Benzer and Ronald Konopka, Rosbash and Hall sought to isolate a specific gene believed to control the circadian rhythm in *Drosophila*. In 1984, they identified and sequenced the gene in question, which was known in the field as *period*. Studying *period* further, the scientists found that the gene controls the production of the protein PER, a crucial component in the feedback system that regulates the circadian rhythm. Throughout the 1980s and 1990s, Rosbash and his colleagues continued their research and published papers on their findings in prominent publications such as *Cell* and *Nature*. Rosbash went on to study the ways in which neurons in a fruit fly's brain connect to its circadian clock, further illuminating the complex, interconnected nature of the brain and body's natural functions. Although focusing specifically on *Drosophila*, Rosbash's findings are thought to apply to a wider selection of animals and to have particularly significant implications for humans, as mismatches between humans' sleep patterns and circadian clocks may contribute to a variety of health concerns. Research on circadian rhythms in mammals has shown effects on humans' circulatory, metabolic, and endocrine functions as well as on body temperature and sleep cycles.

NOBEL PRIZE

On October 2, 2017, the Nobel Prize Committee announced that Rosbash, along with two other researchers, had been selected to receive that year's Nobel Prize in Physiology or Medicine. Arguably the most prestigious award in the sciences, the Nobel Prize not only draws international attention to its recipients but also grants a monetary award, 9 million Swedish krona, or about 1.1 million USD, in 2017. Rosbash split the award evenly with Hall, then professor emeritus, as well as with Michael W. Young of Rockefeller University, who had independently sequenced *period* and identified related genes known as *timeless* and *doubletime*. The Nobel Prize was not the first award the three researchers shared, their having previously received the 2009 Gruber Neuroscience Prize, the 2011 Louisa Gross Horwitz Prize for Biology or Biochemistry, and the 2013 Shaw Prize for their work.

Rosbash first learned that he had been selected by the prize committee through an early morning phone call, which he later joked to journalists had disrupted his own circadian rhythm. Despite the recognition his work had received over the years, he initially disbelieved what he was hearing. "It slowly dawned on me when I was dragged out of my stupor and out of my slumber that it was probably true," he told Deirdre Fernandes for the *Boston Globe* (2 Oct. 2017). Rosbash traveled to Stockholm, Sweden, in December 2017 to deliver his Nobel lecture, "The Circadian Clock, Transcriptional Feedback and the Regulation of Gene Expression," and to receive his prize in person. Although Rosbash received significant recognition following the prize announcement, he tends to shift attention to the research itself and to the tiny subjects that made the researchers' discoveries possible. "It's a great day for the fruit fly," he told Gina Kolata for the *New York Times* (2 Oct. 2017).

PERSONAL LIFE

Rosbash is married to Nadja Abovich, a retired researcher whom he met while she was a graduate student in the Rosbash Lab. He has two grown daughters. Rosbash lives in Newton, Massachusetts. An avid player of sports such as basketball, football, and tennis as a young man, he enjoys cycling and swimming.

SUGGESTED READING

Cha, Ariana Eunjung. "Nobel in Physiology, Medicine Awarded to Three Americans for Discovery of 'Clock Genes.'" *The Washington Post*, 2 Oct. 2017, www.washingtonpost.com/news/to-your-health/wp/2017/10/02/nobel-prize-in-medicine-or-physiology-awarded-to-tktk. Accessed 12 Jan. 2018.

Fernandes, Deirdre. "Brandeis Professors, Once 'Mocked' for Research, Win Nobel Prize for Medicine." *Boston Globe*, 2 Oct. 2017, www.bostonglobe.com/metro/2017/10/02/two-men-with-area-ties-receive-nobel-prize-medicine/HQWlBvoVk8b0ff0WGGlqxH/story.html. Accessed 12 Jan. 2018.

Kolata, Gina. "2017 Nobel Prize in Medicine Goes to 3 Americans for Body Clock Studies." *The New York Times*, 2 Oct. 2017, www.nytimes.com/2017/10/02/health/nobel-prize-medicine.html. Accessed 12 Jan. 2018.

Rosbash, Michael. "Autobiography of Michael Rosbash." *The Shaw Prize*, 23 Sept. 2013, www.shawprize.org/en/shaw.php?tmp=3&twoid=94&threeid=219&fourid=386&fiveid=183. Accessed 12 Jan. 2018.

Rosbash, Michael. "We'll Always Have RNA." *RNA*, vol. 21, no. 4, Apr. 2015, pp. 546–47. *PMC*, www.ncbi.nlm.nih.gov/pmc/articles/PMC4371273. Accessed 12 Jan. 2018.

Williams, Sarah C. P. "Around the Clock." *HHMI Bulletin*, vol. 27, no. 2, Spring 2014, pp. 13–17, www.hhmi.org/sites/default/files/around-the-clock-hhmi-bulletin-spring-2014.pdf. Accessed 12 Jan. 2018.

—*Joy Crelin*

Adam Rutherford

Date of birth: ca. 1975
Occupation: Scientist, author

"I love learning about science, and telling people about discoveries new and old," scientist Adam Rutherford told Plamena Malinova for *Brooklyn* magazine (2 Apr. 2018). "But I'm also very keen to shift the perception of science away from the idea that it is static, or a bank of facts. We don't know much more than we do, and finding new things opens more doors." Throughout his career as a geneticist, author, television and radio presenter, and science consultant, Rutherford has sought to open such scientific doors for the public, translating complex concepts into approachable language and demonstrating the roles that basic scientific principles play in the average person's everyday life. A former *Nature* editor who holds a doctorate in genetics from University College London (UCL), Rutherford found his calling in scientific outreach and has hosted the BBC Radio 4 program *Inside Science* as well as numerous science-related television documentaries. As the author of *Creation* (2013) and *A Brief History of Everyone Who Ever Lived* (2016), Rutherford shed light on the ongoing research into the origins of life and the evolution of humanity, while as a science consultant for film and television, he has contributed to the scientific plausibility of creative works such as Alex Garland's *Ex Machina* (2015) and *Annihilation* (2018). Above all, Rutherford emphasizes the importance of nurturing scientific curiosity and filling gaps in one's knowledge. "'We don't know' is a phrase that all scientists should say frequently, hopefully followed by 'but I know how to find out,'" he told Malinova.

By Your Funny uncle, via Wikimedia Commons

EARLY LIFE AND EDUCATION

Rutherford was born around 1975 in Ipswich, England, to a Guyanese Indian mother and a British father. His parents divorced when he was eight years old, and Rutherford spent the remainder of his childhood living with his psychologist father, stepmother, two stepbrothers, and a younger half-brother. As a youth, Rutherford enjoyed playing cricket and was also intrigued by science, both factual and fictional. In an interview with Daniel Bennett for *Science Focus* (27 Mar. 2018), he recalled finding a photograph of his childhood bedroom that showed a picture from a *Star Wars* film displayed alongside an image cut out of a David Attenborough nature book. "I was never pushed in a particular direction but it was clear from that photo, forty or so years after it was taken, that my interests are almost exactly as they were as a young boy," he told Bennett.

After completing his studies at the Ipswich School, Rutherford enrolled in University College London (UCL), initially to study medicine. He did not enjoy his studies aside from a module on genetics, and after a year, he decided to find a new major. Rutherford next considered pursuing a degree in psychology or classics but did not qualify to join those programs due to his grades. Inspired by his limited experience studying with Steve Jones, professor of human genetics in the UCL Department of Genetics, Evolution and Environment, Rutherford ultimately chose to pursue a degree in evolutionary biology. Rutherford not only identifies Jones as a key factor in his switch to evolutionary biology, but also as his

greatest intellectual influence. "He knows that because I've told him," Rutherford said in an interview for the *Scientific 23*, a website devoted to scientist interviews. "He also knows I'm waiting for him to die so I can fully inherit his career."

As an undergraduate, Rutherford had his first opportunity to work as a laboratory technician, assisting with research related to stalk-eyed flies. "It was my responsibility to feed the flies, which laid their eggs on rotten vegetable matter," he recalled for the *Scientific 23*. "I used to buy frozen sweetcorn from Budgens around the corner, liquidize it, leave it at 37 degrees C until it was rotten and let them lay their eggs in it, then remove them a week later—not deeply glamorous, but after that I was hooked on research." He also pursued work not related to science, serving for a time as a hand model and working as a photocopier salesperson for less than a day.

EARLY CAREER

After completing his undergraduate degree, Rutherford continued his education in genetics at UCL and pursued doctoral research at the UCL Great Ormond Street Institute of Child Health. His research focused on the relationships between genes and retinal development, and a portion of his work concerned a genetic cause of congenital blindness. Rutherford completed his doctoral thesis, "The Role of CHX10 in the Development of the Mammalian Retina," in 2002. He would later be named an honorary staff member at UCL.

Although Rutherford had succeeded in earning his doctorate, he found that he was "better at talking about science than doing it," as he told the *Scientific 23*. He opted to pursue a career outside of research and academia, instead taking a position at a scientific journal. He later moved on to *Nature*, a major scientific publication, where he worked for more than a decade. During that time, Rutherford held a number of different positions for the journal, including web editor and podcast manager.

In 2006, Rutherford began what would become an extensive career in science outreach with the television series *Men in White*. He took a four-month sabbatical from his full-time job to film the series, in which he, physicist Harry "Basil" Singer, and engineer Jem Stansfield sought to answer the public's scientific questions in a manner far more casual than that of existing science programs. "We spent ages thinking about how we could do something where people came to us with a problem and we could demonstrate how fun science is and dispel that ancient myth about scientists all being middle class, white geezers," he told the *East Anglian Daily Times* (4 Oct. 2006). The six episodes of *Men in White* aired for one season on the United Kingdom's Channel 4 in 2006.

SCIENCE IN THE MEDIA

In the years following the premiere of *Men in White*, Rutherford became known for his attempts to educate the public about scientific concepts through the media, particularly radio and television documentaries. For Rutherford, the key to successful scientific outreach is ensuring that the information provided is transmitted in a manner that fits the intended audience. "Science is highly technical and highly specific, and translating that appropriately to broader or different audiences is important," he told the *Scientific* 23. "You have to judge your audience and adjust to them—you don't always say the same things to adults and school children and teenagers, or to scientists and non-scientists." Rutherford expanded upon his earlier television appearances as the presenter of numerous television documentaries, including *The Cell* (2011), *The Gene Code* (2011), and *Will It Snow?* (2011). He likewise contributed to an episode of the long-running documentary series *Horizon*.

In addition to his television work, Rutherford has worked in radio. Since July 2013, he has hosted the BBC Radio 4 program *Inside Science*, which features interviews and other content related to a variety of scientific disciplines. Rutherford has likewise hosted other science-related radio programs, including *The Curious Cases of Rutherford & Fry* (2016–). In that program, he and fellow scientist Dr. Hannah Fry investigate science-related questions submitted by listeners, ranging from "Why do we dream and why do we repeat dreams?" to "What is the tiniest dinosaur?"

As a well-regarded science expert, Rutherford has consulted for media projects, including the television series *The Cat in the Hat Knows a Lot about That!* and the films *World War Z* (2013) and *Kingsman: The Secret Service* (2015). He became particularly known for his work with filmmaker Alex Garland, whom he advised during the making of the science-fiction films *Ex Machina* (2015) and *Annihilation* (2018). "Working with Alex has been the greatest joy of my professional life," Rutherford said in his interview for the website *52 Insights*. "He's a very intelligent guy, thorough and meticulous and he really cares about the idea, whether it's artistic or scientific because he's very scientifically literate." Rutherford went on to explain Garland sought to prevent his films from containing "anything that is so absurd that it's going to make people go, 'What the f—— was that?'"

PUBLICATIONS

Alongside his work in radio, television, and film, Rutherford is a prolific writer and has published numerous articles about science-related topics in the *Guardian* newspaper on topics ranging from whether scientific journal publications and books are trustworthy to the lack of genetic basis for race. His first book, *Creation*, was published in the United Kingdom in 2013. Subtitled *The Origin of Life* and *The Future of Life* in its original UK publication, the book consists of two separate but related sections, one dealing with the origins of life on Earth and one devoted to the concept of synthetic biology, a field of research focused on creating biological systems. *Creation* received largely positive reviews and went on to be published in the United States under the title *Creation: How Science Is Reinventing Life Itself.*

Rutherford followed *Creation* with the 2016 popular-science work *A Brief History of Everyone Who Ever Lived: The Stories in Our Genes*, published in the United States as *A Brief History of Everyone Who Ever Lived: The Human Story Retold through Our Genes* the following year. In that book, Rutherford explores the stories about humankind that are revealed through the study of genetics. "I wanted to tell the stories of our pasts that are enlightened by this new source text, which is DNA," he told Malinova, speaking of the book. "It's only been available to us for a few years now, but carries the history of our species. That's a rich seam to mine." Much like his previous work, *A Brief History* was received well by critics, and the book went on to be long-listed for the 2017 Wellcome Book Prize and become a 2017 National Book Critics Circle Award finalist.

In addition, Rutherford's book *Genetics* was published in 2018 as part of the newly created Ladybird Experts series of illustrated adult-oriented introductions to scientific subjects. His next book, *The Book of Humans: The Story of How We Became Us*, is scheduled for publication in September of 2018. *The Book of Humans* delves into what distinguishes humankind from the rest of the animal kingdom and the role of culture in human evolution.

PERSONAL LIFE

Rutherford lives in London with his wife, Georgia, who works in book publishing. They have three children. A lifelong fan of science fiction, Rutherford still loves that genre despite the scientific inaccuracies often found in science-fiction films. "People ask me a lot if I can just watch a film without thinking about the science and the answer is, I mostly don't care," he told Hannah McKee for *Stuff* (11 Mar. 2016). "I don't like things to be ridiculous, but films are not documentaries, they don't have to be scientifically accurate, it's great if they are, but if it's a great film, I don't care."

SUGGESTED READING

McKee, Hannah. "Geneticist Adam Rutherford's Talent for Breaking Down Big Ideas." *Stuff,*

11 Mar. 2016, www.stuff.co.nz/entertainment/77759722/geneticist-adam-rutherfords-talent-for-breaking-down-big-ideas. Accessed 12 May 2018.

"One of the Zany Men in White." *East Anglian Daily Times*, 4 Oct. 2006, www.eadt.co.uk/ealife/one-of-the-zany-men-in-white-1-77410. Accessed 12 May 2018.

Rutherford, Adam. "Adam Rutherford: How We Became the Data." Interview. *52 Insights*, 2 Nov. 2017, www.52-insights.com/adam-rutherford-how-we-became-the-data-genetics-interview-a-brief-history. Accessed 12 May 2018.

Rutherford, Adam. "Annihilation: Stranger than Fiction." Interview by Daniel Bennett. *Science Focus*, 27 Mar. 2018, www.sciencefocus.com/article/space/annihilation-netflix-adam-rutherford-interview. Accessed 12 May 2018.

Rutherford, Adam. *A Brief History of Everyone Who Ever Lived*. Experiment, 2017.

Rutherford, Adam. "Dr. Adam Rutherford." *The Scientific 23*, thescientific23.com/interview?id=29&name=Adam%20Rutherford. Accessed 12 May 2018.

Rutherford, Adam. "Interview with 2018 NBCC Non-Fiction Award Finalist Dr. Adam Rutherford." Interview by Plamena Malinova. *Brooklyn*, 2 Apr. 2018, www.bkmag.com/2018/04/02/nbcc-finalist-dr-adam-rutherford. Accessed 12 May 2018.

SELECTED WORKS

Creation: The Origin of Life / The Future of Life, 2013; *A Brief History of Everyone Who Ever Lived: The Stories in Our Genes*, 2016; *Genetics*, 2018

—Joy Crelin

Ahmed Saadawi

Date of birth: May 1973
Occupation: Author

Ahmed Saadawi is an award-winning Iraqi novelist best known for his third novel, *Frankenstein in Baghdad* (2013), a surrealist satire about Iraq after the 2003 US invasion. The book, which draws on elements of Mary Shelley's 1818 classic *Frankenstein*, won the International Prize for Arabic Fiction (IPAF) in 2014, a $50,000 award commonly described as an Arabic Booker Prize. Saadawi is the first Iraqi to receive this accolade. *Frankenstein in Baghdad*, which was published in English in 2017, was also short-listed for the Man Booker International Prize, awarded for fiction in translation, in April 2018.

Photo by AHMAD AL-RUBAYE/AFP, via Getty Images

Saadawi, a Baghdad-born novelist, screenwriter, and poet, wrote *Frankenstein in Baghdad* in response to the US occupation of his home city. The Iraq war, over in the minds of most Americans, is a constant presence in the lives of Iraqi citizens like Saadawi. In a profile of Saadawi for the *New York Times* (16 May 2014), Tim Arango wrote about Saadawi's former favorite haunt, a Baghdad café where the city's literary and artistic community would gather over tea. The place was "so special" to Saadawi, Arango wrote, that he wrote it into *Frankenstein*. One evening, after *Frankenstein* was published, a suicide bomber attacked the café. A few of Saadawi's friends were killed. Arango wrote about the incident to illustrate how fear and death have become central to life in Iraq. "The most important thing that has happened to me is that I am still alive," Saadawi told Arango. Saadawi further described modern life in Baghdad to Arango as a "dystopia"; his surrealist vision of the city in *Frankenstein* springs from this characterization. More literally, however, as he told Jean-Marc Mojon for *Gulf News* (29 Sept. 2016), a particular memory informed the concept of Saadawi's novel. At the height of the war, Saadawi visited a hospital that was overwhelmed by countless dead bodies. "One day, someone came asking about his brother.. . . They told him that all the bodies had already been collected by their families, except for these pieces," Saadawi said. "There were mismatched, unclaimed . . . body parts and they told him to assemble a man from them and take it away."

Saadawi is also the author of two previous novels—*al-Balad al-jamil* (The beautiful country, 2004) and *'Iinah yahlimu, 'aw yuleiba, 'aw yamut* (Indeed he dreams or plays or dies, 2008)—and four collections of poetry. In 2010, he was named one of the thirty-nine best Arab writers under forty in the Hay Festival's Beirut39 competition. His novel *Bab al-tabashir* (The chalk door) was published in Arabic in 2017. He has sold the film rights to *Frankenstein* to a British film company.

EARLY LIFE AND WORKS

Saadawi was born in Baghdad in May 1973. He grew up in Sadr City, a Shiite neighborhood in Baghdad. His father was a driving instructor who worked for the government. Saadawi learned to read and write by tagging along with his mother to literacy classes. "That got me writing earlier than other kids. . . . By the time I was seven, I was writing many stories about animals," he told Mojon. "I would read them to my friends and they would listen to me. It made me feel famous. So at that time I already had this idea that fiction was a part of real life." His parents encouraged him to write, giving him books and notebooks as a child. As a young man, Saadawi attended a local teacher's college. After graduation, he decided to pursue a creative life, writing and drawing cartoons. He incurred several debts in these pursuits—"I'm not good with money," he told Arango. He has also worked as a journalist—he was a correspondent for the BBC for a number of years—and as a documentary filmmaker to make ends meet. Journalism, he told the Ruya Foundation for Contemporary Culture in Iraq (13 Oct. 2014), taught him to be less precious about his writing. "As a journalist, I would go to a place and capture an impression of it, so I could write about it that same day," he said. "Before, I'd been waiting for the muse of inspiration to come down, but this is an illusion, a klawat as we say in Iraq. One's imagination matures as we become better writers."

Saadawi, who names Ernest Hemingway and Gabriel García Márquez as influences on his work, published his first book, a collection of poems called *al-Wathn al-ghazii*, in 1997. He followed this with three more volumes of poetry, *Najat zayida* in 1999, *Eid al-ughniat al-sayiya* in 2001, and *Surati wa'ana 'ahlim* in 2003. He published his first novel, *al-Balad al-jamil*, in 2004. The magazine *Al Sada*, based in the United Arab Emirates (UAE), awarded it a prize for best novel. Saadawi's second novel, *'Iinah yahlimu, 'aw yuleiba, 'aw yamut* (2008), caught the attention of the IPAF committee, who invited him to a writing workshop where he worked on what would become his third novel, *Frankenstein in Baghdad*. His second novel is also the one that earned him recognition from the British Hay

Festival's Beirut39. Bloomsbury published a collection of writing from the Beirut39 authors in 2011. Saadawi contributed two draft chapters of *Frankenstein in Baghdad*.

FRANKENSTEIN IN BAGHDAD (2013)

It took Saadawi four years to write *Frankenstein in Baghdad*. "I spent considerable time researching, conducting interviews, taking pictures and collecting information," he told Al-Mustafa Najjar for *Asharq al-Awsat*, a London-based Arabic newspaper (22 Mar. 2014). Before the Beirut39 publication, an even earlier excerpt appeared on *Kikah.com*, an online Arabic literary journal, in 2008. *Frankenstein in Baghdad* was published in Arabic in 2013 and was translated into English by Jonathan Wright in 2017. The book is set in Baghdad in 2005. Bombs and violence have decimated the city, and a junk peddler named Hadi al-Attag picks through the wreckage collecting stray body parts. Hadi intends to give each part a proper burial, and to this end, stitches the parts together, in the manner of Shelley's Dr. Frankenstein, to create an entire body. Like the monster in the original *Frankenstein*, Hadi's creation becomes sentient, after a security guard is killed by a bomb planted in a truck. Unable to find his former body, the guard's soul wanders to a nearby cemetery seeking advice, and the spirit of a teenage boy advises him to find a different body. The guard finds and inhabits Hadi's grotesque creation, slipping "inside the corpse" and "filling it from head to toe" while Hadi sleeps. When Hadi wakes up, the creature is already gone.

The creature, called "shesma" in the Arabic and its approximate equivalent "Whatsitsname" in the English translation, prowls Baghdad at night, seeking to kill those who killed the people to whom its parts once belonged. He uses his victims' body parts to replace his own putrid limbs. Inevitably, Whatsitsname "eventually kills innocents too," Arango wrote, "reflecting the madness and moral ambiguities of the war and its aftermath." Whatsitsname, with his hodgepodge of rotting limbs, also, according to Saadawi, represents the modern state of Iraq. "Because I'm made up of body parts of people from diverse backgrounds—ethnicities, tribes, races and social classes—I represent the impossible mix that never was achieved in the past," Whatsitsname bitterly muses in the book. "I'm the first true Iraqi citizen." In the book, Whatsitsname, referred to by the public as Criminal X, is pursued by a journalist named Mahmoud and a character named General Surur Majid of the Department of Investigation. Cults form around Whatsitsname, and participants assuage his murderous guilt. *Frankenstein in Baghdad* is an allegory that verges on the absurd. Saadawi incorporates elements of horror and fantasy to describe the real-life horror of Baghdad in 2005.

As Saadawi put it to Najjar: "The use of fantasy renders the book more entertaining to readers and also offers a chance to deal with reality in an untraditional way. The element of fantasy adds a touch of joy to the work, mitigating its cruelty."

Wright's English translation of *Franken-stein* was well received. Dwight Garner, writing for the *New York Times* (22 Jan. 2018), wrote that Saadawi "blends the unearthly, the horrific and the mundane to terrific effect." He added: "There's a freshness to both his voice and vision; he is working through a country's trauma from a series of unusual angles." Rayyan Al-Shawaf, for the *Chicago Tribune* (24 Jan. 2018), described *Frankenstein* as "an oblique and darkly humor-ous commentary on the self-perpetuating nature of violence," though he also offered a criticism, writing that the novel is "periodically drained of tension by the Whatsitsname's lengthy absences from the proceedings." Jason Heller, for the *At-lantic* (15 Oct. 2017), wrote that *Frankenstein* "startles and stuns." He further noted that, like Shelley, who only referred to her monster with words such as "wretch" and "demon," Saadawi chooses to leave his creature nameless. "Saadawi uses this namelessness to evoke the dehuman-ization that comes with totalitarianism and war, where whole populations are often seen as a single, faceless mass rather than as individuals," Heller wrote.

PERSONAL LIFE

Saadawi is married with four children. He lives in Baghdad, where he is a member of a thriving arts community.

SUGGESTED READING

Al-Shawaf, Rayyan. "'Frankenstein in Baghdad' by Ahmed Saadawi Offers Powerful Allegory." Review of *Frankenstein in Baghdad*, by Ahmed Saadawi. *Chicago Tribune*, 24 Jan. 2018, www.chicagotribune.com/lifestyles/books/sc-books-frankenstein-baghdad-ahmed-saadawi-0124-story.html. Accessed 10 May 2018.

Arango, Tim. "Baghdad Is a Setting, and a Char-acter, Too." *The New York Times*, 16 May 2014, www.nytimes.com/2014/05/17/world/middleeast/iraqi-novelist-dodging-bombs-writes-to-clear-the-fog-of-war.html. Accessed 5 May 2018.

Garner, Dwight. "In 'Frankenstein in Baghdad,' a Fantastical Manifestation of War's Cruelties." Review of *Frankenstein in Baghdad*, by Ahmed Saadawi. *The New York Times*, 22 Jan. 2018, www.nytimes.com/2018/01/22/books/review-frankenstein-in-baghdad-ahmed-saadawi.html. Accessed 10 May 2018.

Heller, Jason. "How Sci Fi Writers Imag-ine Iraq's Future." *The Atlantic*, 15 Oct. 2017, www.theatlantic.com/entertainment/archive/2017/10/how-sci-fi-writers-imagine-iraqs-future/541512/. Accessed 10 May 2018.

Mojon, Jean-Marc. "The Son of Baghdad Who Fathered Iraqi Frankenstein." *Gulf News*, 29 Sept. 2016, gulfnews.com/news/mena/iraq/the-son-of-baghdad-who-fathered-iraqi-fran-kenstein-1.1904053. Accessed 9 May 2018.

Saadawi, Ahmed. "Novelist Ahmed Saadawi Creates an Iraqi Frankenstein." Interview by Al-Mustafa Najjar. *Asharq al-Awsat*, 22 Mar. 2014, eng-archive.aawsat.com/m-najjar/lifestyle-culture/novelist-ahmad-saadawi-cre-ates-an-iraqi-frankenstein. Accessed 10 May 2018.

Saadawi, Ahmed. "Interview: Award-Winning Author Ahmed Saadawi on the Enemy of Writing and the Power of Words." Interview. *Ruya Foundation*, 13 Oct. 2014, ruyafoun-dation.org/en/2014/10/ahmed-saadawi/. Ac-cessed 10 May 2018.

SELECTED WORKS

'Iinah yahlimu, 'aw yuleiba, 'aw yamut, 2008; *Frankenstein in Baghdad*, 2014; *Bab al-tabashir*, 2017

—*Molly Hagan*

Cécile McLorin Salvant

Date of birth: August 28, 1989
Occupation: Singer

A singer whom jazz greats have described as one in a generation, Cécile McLorin Salvant initial-ly did not plan even to study jazz, let alone to pursue a career in that musical genre. Trained as a classical and baroque vocalist, the singer developed a passion for jazz while studying at a conservatory in France and soon began perform-ing with a band that included her jazz teacher as well as fellow students. The release of her de-but album, *Cécile*, and first-place finish at the Thelonious Monk Institute of Jazz International Vocals Competition in 2010 underscored her talent as a vocalist and brought her to the atten-tion of the international jazz community. Over the following years, she earned widespread criti-cal acclaim for her albums, which include the Grammy Award–winning recordings *For One to Love* (2015) and *Dreams and Daggers* (2017).

Born and raised in Miami, Florida, Salvant grew up in a household that valued music and was introduced to an array of genres and eras of music at an early age. Her diverse musical tastes are reflected in her albums and live performanc-es, which feature a mixture of original songs, jazz standards, songs from musicals, and songs that have fallen out of favor in the twenty-first

By David Becker, via Wikimedia Commons

century due to their subject matter. For Salvant, the latter songs provide a valuable opportunity to explore sides of jazz that may be less familiar to her audience. "I like songs that talk about identity and power dynamics in an unexpected way. I also like songs that are funny, or inappropriate in some way, to the extent that you might not expect to hear them in a jazz context," she explained to Grant Smithies for *Stuff.co.nz* (30 Jan. 2018). "People often think jazz means clean and family friendly, but really, this is music that began in the brothel. I like songs with a little edge."

EARLY LIFE

Cécile Sophie McLorin Salvant was born on August 28, 1989, in Miami, Florida. Her father, Alix Salvant, was a doctor, while her mother, Léna McLorin, was the founder and head of L'École Franco-Américaine de Miami (the French-American School of Miami), a private French-immersion elementary school. Salvant's parents were originally from Haiti and France, respectively, and she grew up speaking both French and English. She also has a sister named Aisha.

Music was a constant presence throughout Salvant's childhood, and her parents' wide-ranging musical tastes made her early musical education a substantial one. "Music was always playing in the house when I was growing up," she told Roseanna Vitro for *JazzTimes* (20 Jan. 2016), adding that her parents listened to music belonging to a vast range of genres, eras, and cultures. Salvant started playing the piano as a child and eventually began to sing with vocal groups such as the children's choir of the Miami Choral

Society. Although she continued to play piano into adulthood, she proved to be a particularly talented vocalist and began classical voice lessons during her early teens.

As a teenager, Salvant auditioned for a music-focused high school but ultimately chose to enroll in the International Baccalaureate program at Coral Reef High School, a magnet school in Miami. There, she served for a time as editor in chief of the school's literary and art magazine, *Elysium*, and received a prestigious National Achievement Scholarship. She graduated from Coral Reef High School in 2007.

MUSICAL EDUCATION

After graduating from high school, Salvant enrolled in the Conservatoire Darius Milhaud (Darius Milhaud Conservatory) in Aix-en-Provence, France, to study classical and baroque voice. She also enrolled in a law and political science program at another school, as she was unsure of her ability to make a living as a singer. She began studying jazz voice after her mother encouraged her to take a class at the conservatory led by Jean-François Bonnel. Although she was not particularly interested in the genre, Bonnel convinced her to join the class after hearing her sing.

Under Bonnel's tutelage, Salvant began to explore the long history of jazz music, related genres, and the singers who innovated within them. "He gave me recordings, twenty CDs at a time, which I played again and again," she recalled to Fred Kaplan for the *New Yorker* (22 May 2017). Salvant was inspired by the work of Bessie Smith, a noted blues and jazz singer who performed during the first several decades of the twentieth century. "She sang about sex and food and savages and the Devil and Hell and really exciting things you don't hear on 'Ella Fitzgerald Sings the Cole Porter Songbook,'" she told Kaplan. "I thought, This is great! All these great stories! I'd heard torch songs by Dinah Washington about 'I'll wait for you forever.' But here's Bessie Smith singing, 'You come around after you been gone a *year*? Good*bye*!' It was empowering."

In addition to studying jazz with Bonnel, Salvant formed a band with her instructor and several student musicians, performing with them in France and elsewhere. Although her career focus had shifted strongly toward music, she continued her studies in law and completed her bachelor's degree through a distance-learning program. After relocating to New York, she enrolled in music-related classes at the New School but ultimately left to focus on her singing career.

EARLY CAREER

Many of Salvant's earliest performances took place in France, where she and the newly formed Jean-François Bonnel Paris Quintet performed at local events and festivals. The group's early success proved instrumental in Salvant's decision to focus on jazz vocals rather than on the classical and baroque styles she had initially planned to study. "The reason I turned to jazz was the gigs were coming in," she explained to Kaplan. "If more gigs had come in with Baroque, I'd have tried to do both." She went on to perform concerts in Paris, which brought further attention to her vocal talents and fresh take on the genre. Her first album, *Cécile*, debuted in 2010. The album featured accompaniment by the Jean-François Bonnel Paris Quintet and songs by twentieth-century composers such as Cole Porter and Irving Berlin.

In addition to the release of her first album, 2010 brought a major turning point in Salvant's career in the form of her participation in the prestigious Thelonious Monk Institute of Jazz International Vocals Competition. Held yearly, the institute's competition highlights a different jazz instrument each year and in 2010 focused on talented jazz vocalists. Salvant traveled to Washington, DC, as one of twelve semifinalists and went on to be selected as one of the competition's three finalists. She claimed first place in the competition, winning substantial praise from the competition's judges, all critically acclaimed jazz singers.

AARON DIEHL TRIO AND *WOMANCHILD*
In 2012, Salvant moved to New York City to pursue her career as a performer and recording artist further. Soon afterward, she began working with Aaron Diehl, a pianist who would become a long-standing collaborator. Diehl, bassist Paul Sikivie, and drummer Lawrence Leathers formed the Aaron Diehl Trio, and the group began to accompany Salvant during her performances, which initially featured existing songs rather than original numbers for the most part. In addition to her distinctive voice, Salvant became known for performing with a degree of theatricality that enabled her to bring forth the hidden significance or even alternative interpretations of the songs she performed. She credited that approach in part to her long-standing interest in the forms of jazz in which "it doesn't really matter how pristine and agile the voice is, as long as there's a story being conveyed," she explained to Tom Vitale for *NPR* (18 Nov. 2017).

Salvant signed with the jazz record label Mack Avenue, releasing her second album, *WomanChild*, in 2013. Diehl and other artists accompanied her on the album, which featured covers of existing jazz numbers as well as original songs written by Salvant. *WomanChild* received significant critical praise following its release and was nominated for the 2013 Grammy Award for Best Jazz Vocal Album. Following *WomanChild*, Salvant was featured on several other albums,

including 2014's *It's Christmas on Mack Avenue* and 2015's *Big Band Holidays*. In addition to performing with the Aaron Diehl Trio, she joined the jazz trumpeter Wynton Marsalis in concert on multiple occasions, including performances with the Jazz at Lincoln Center Orchestra.

RECOGNITION, OTHER ALBUMS, AND AWARDS
As Salvant gained further public and industry recognition, jazz performers and genre experts widely praised her approach to the genre and unique vocal talent. "You get a singer like this once in a generation or two," Marsalis said, as quoted by Kaplan. For Salvant, her newfound recognition gave her the opportunity to promote the genre of jazz as one that is vibrant and accessible, contrary to its public perception. "I . . . like to challenge the misconception that jazz is some sort of musical museum piece, but I guess some artforms are doomed to be misunderstood and not attract the larger audiences they deserve," she told Smithies. "It's frustrating that people think of it as old and dusty and no fun and too challenging or whatever. And it's just not true."

Although Salvant has been pleased with the reception her work has received, she has called attention to the need to broaden the world of jazz further to make the genre more welcoming to fans from all demographics and backgrounds. "There are not enough people my age, people younger than me in the audience. There are not enough black people in the audience," she told Vitale. "I don't see people like me a lot in my audience. . . . To make things more inclusive and diverse, that would be a wonderful next step."

Continuing to perform and record with the Aaron Diehl Trio, Salvant followed *Woman-Child* with the album *For One to Love*, released in 2015. The album featured five original songs by Salvant, several interpretations of earlier jazz songs, and several songs from musicals. *For One to Love* received positive reviews from numerous publications and won the 2015 Grammy Award for Best Jazz Vocal Album. Salvant's next recording, 2017's *Dreams and Daggers*, earned the singer her second consecutive Grammy in that category. Unlike her earlier albums, *Dreams and Daggers* consisted of two discs and encompassed a total of twenty-three songs. Although several of the songs, primarily Salvant's originals, were recorded in a studio, the majority of the songs featured on *Dreams and Daggers* were recorded live during a performance at New York's Village Vanguard jazz club. In addition to the Grammy Award, Salvant received accolades following the release of *Dreams and Daggers*, including being named Female Vocalist of the Year by the Jazz Journalists Association in 2018.

PERSONAL LIFE

Salvant lives in New York City. In addition to her work as a singer and composer, she enjoys drawing. Her illustrations and visual art have been featured on her website as well as on the covers and inserts of albums such as *For One to Love* and *Dreams and Daggers*. She exhibited her work publicly at a one-night art party at New York's RAW Space in 2017.

SUGGESTED READING

Gonzalez, Fernando. "Cécile McLorin Salvant Displays Her Jazz Vocals Friday, Dec. 20 at Arsht Center." *Miami.com*, 13 Dec. 2013, www.miami.com/things-to-do-in-miami/ce-cile-mclorin-salvant-displays-her-jazz-vocals-friday-dec-20-at-arsht-center-15066/. Accessed 9 June 2018.

Kaplan, Fred. "Cécile McLorin Salvant's Timeless Jazz." *The New Yorker*, 22 May 2017, www.newyorker.com/magazine/2017/05/22/cecile-mclorin-salvants-timeless-jazz. Accessed 9 June 2018.

Salvant, Cécile McLorin. "Grammy Award-Winning Jazz Singer Ahead of Hong Kong Concerts: Interview with Cécile McLorin Salvant." Interview by Robin Lynam. *South China Morning Post*, 20 Mar. 2018, www.scmp.com/culture/music/article/2138058/grammy-award-winning-jazz-singer-ahead-hong-kong-concerts-interview. Accessed 9 June 2018.

Salvant, Cécile McLorin. "An Interview with Cécile McLorin Salvant." Interview by Roseanna Vitro. *JazzTimes*, 20 Jan. 2016, jazztimes.com/columns/voices/an-interview-with-ceci-le-mclorin-salvant/. Accessed 9 June 2018.

Smithies, Grant. "Cecile McLorin Salvant: Race, Sex and All That Jazz." *Stuff.co.nz*, 30 Jan. 2018, www.stuff.co.nz/entertainment/100809799/cecile-mclorin-salvant-race-sex-and-all-that-jazz. Accessed 9 June 2018.

Tanasychuk, John. "Cecile McLorin Salvant: Daydream Believer." *SouthFlorida.com*, 10 Apr. 2014, www.southflorida.com/music/sf-go-cecile-mclorin-salvant-miami-beach-041214-20140410-story.html. Accessed 9 July 2018.

Vitale, Tom. "The Vast, Versatile Range of Cécile McLorin Salvant." *NPR*, 18 Nov. 2017, www.npr.org/2017/11/18/561380228/the-vast-versatile-range-of-c-cile-mclorin-salvant. Accessed 9 June 2018.

SELECTED WORKS

Cécile, 2010; *WomanChild*, 2013; *For One to Love*, 2015; *Dreams and Daggers*, 2017

—*Joy Crelin*

Sampha

Date of birth: November 16, 1988
Occupation: Singer

British singer-songwriter and producer Sampha has worked with some of music's biggest stars, including Beyoncé, Kanye West, and Frank Ocean, but the success of his 2017 debut album *Process* proves Sampha to be a formidable artist in his own right. *Process*, among other feats, showcases Sampha's beautiful and plaintive singing voice. Writing for the *Fader* (28 June 2016), Ruth Saxelby called it "a voice that scratches the soul." It occasionally breaks or frays, she added, "almost like his emotions are so close to the surface that they're bruising his vocal cords." The critically acclaimed album won the prestigious Mercury Prize, awarded each year for best album in the United Kingdom and Ireland, and the music website *Pitchfork* ranked it number four on their list of the twenty best pop and R & B albums of 2017. Sampha's talents as a musician, and his surplus of emotion, have made him one of the most sought-after artists working in hip-hop and R & B.

Sampha got his start on the Internet, meeting an early mentor, South London producer Kwes, through the social networking site *MySpace* in 2007. Kwes introduced Sampha to the British indie label Young Turks, and a few years later, Sampha found himself meeting the rapper Drake, who was interested in using one of Sampha's beats. After the release of two critically acclaimed EPs, and collaborations with the

Photo by David Wolff - Patrick/Redferns/Getty Images

musical elite, Sampha seemed poised to seize his moment. But after his mother was diagnosed with cancer for a second time, Sampha decided to put his career, and his first album, on hold. His mother's eventual passing made the making of *Process* all the more difficult, and grief informs the album in profound ways.

EARLY LIFE

Sampha Sisay was born in London on November 16, 1988. His parents, Binty and Joe Sisay, were originally from Kenema, Sierra Leone. Sampha is the youngest of five boys by nearly a decade. His older brothers, Junior, John, Sanie, and Ernest, spent their formative years in Kenema, where their father worked as a diamond evaluator. His new job brought the family to England in 1982. They settled in Morden in southwest London. Sampha's father loved music. He brought home a new CD or single nearly every week. His tastes were eclectic. One week he would proffer a new song from the British pop group the Spice Girls; another week he would have something by the Italian opera singer Luciano Pavarotti. One record, *Worotan* (1996) by the Malian singer Oumou Sangaré left a lasting impression on Sampha. "I listen to it now and it's a big influence on the way I view melodies and scales," he told Saxelby for *Pitchfork* (8 July 2013). "That immediacy of melody, those rhythms, and the production awakened something in me."

Sampha's father died of lung cancer in 1998, when Sampha was nine years old. After his father's death, Sampha sought to express his emotions through music, particularly through playing the piano. His father had bought the family's old piano from a neighbor when Sampha was three, in hopes of tempting his sons away from the television. Sampha cut his musical teeth on and emptied his youthful sorrows into that piano. He later wrote a song with it as the central image. In "(No One Knows Me) Like the Piano," he sings: "No one knows me like the piano in my mother's home / You would show me I had something some people call a soul." The lyrics describe both the piano itself and the losses it contains.

SUNDANZA AND *DUAL* EPS

Sampha discovered music production when he was about thirteen years old. At his brother's house, he taught himself to use digital music programs like Cubase and Reason. He was inspired by his cousin Flirta D, a well-known MC in London's underground grime scene (grime being a genre developed in London in the early 2000s, combining electronic music with hip-hop and reggae-derived genres). Sampha developed a grime persona called Kid Nova (after a Marvel Comics character) and began posting beats on the social media website *MySpace*. "I used to try

and give beats to people," Sampha recalled of his early musical endeavors to Kieran Yates for *Beat Magazine* (23 Dec. 2016), "but I just didn't leave enough room for anyone to rap over my beats, they were just so full of piano, and synths, so it wasn't really a vehicle for lyricists." When he was nineteen, Sampha briefly embarked on a university career studying music production at the University of Chester at Warrington but dropped out because he felt like his own musical goals were at odds with what he was studying. But he found other ways to forward his career. Through *MySpace*, Sampha came across a South London producer named Kwes. Kwes made R & B music—not rap like Sampha—but Sampha was drawn to his music. After hearing a song called "Tissues," in which a tissue is personified as an empathetic figure, Sampha decided to reach out to Kwes. "At the time I was writing songs as well, and wouldn't really share them, but I would send him songs," Sampha said to Ashley Monáe for *Paper* magazine (2 Feb. 2017). Kwes's unique sound and lyrics made Sampha feel more comfortable with his own work. Kwes sent Sampha's music to the indie label Young Turks, and introduced him to artists like hip-hop musician Ghostpoet, rapper DELS, and composer Micachu. Sampha released his first EP, *Sundanza*, with Young Turks in 2010. The six tracks are mostly instrumental beats. (The EP was released in a limited run of handmade CD-Rs. Years later, Sampha's brother accidentally deleted the digital master file of the project. Today, all that remains of *Sundanza* are unmastered mp3s.)

That same year, Sampha worked with London producer SBTRKT (Aaron Jerome) on SBTRKT's 2011 self-titled debut album. Sampha has singing, writing, and/or production credits on more than half the tracks on the album. His contributions garnered attention, particularly his aching vocals on the song "Hold On." In 2011, he sang with singer-songwriter Jessie Ware on a dreamy pop song called "Valentine." He spent most of 2012 on tour with SBTRKT, and in early 2013, he released an EP with electronic producer Koreless for a side project called Short Stories.

At about this time, Sampha's collaborators included Drake and Beyoncé. He traveled to Toronto to work with Drake on his 2013 album *Nothing Was the Same*, where he was featured on the single "Too Much" as guest singer, writer, and producer. Sampha also appeared, as both a singer and producer, on the song "The Motion," later released as a bonus track on the album. During their collaboration, Sampha contributed backing vocals to the Drake and Beyoncé song "Mine" that appears on Beyoncé's self-titled 2013 album.

Sampha also traveled to Ghana to work with Solange Knowles on what would become "Don't

Touch My Hair," a hit track from her 2016 album *A Seat at the Table*. He also went to Los Angeles and Italy to work with Kanye West. West added one of the tracks they made together, a piano-driven song called "Saint Pablo," to his 2016 album *The Life of Pablo* a few months after it was released. In July of that year, Sampha released his second and breakthrough EP *Dual*. A far cry from *Sundanza*, the piano is the central musical element of *Dual*. "These ruminative, revealing songs paint a more intimate portrait of Sampha," Zach Kelly wrote for *Pitchfork* (14 Aug. 2013). One popular song, a ballad called "Indecision," was written after the tragic death of singer Amy Winehouse in 2011.

THE PROCESS OF *PROCESS*
As Sampha steadily rose to fame, his family life was rocked by hardship and tragedy. When he was in his late teens, one of his older brothers had a stroke that left him seriously disabled, and Sampha often served as his caretaker. In 2010, Sampha's mother was diagnosed with cancer. Sampha did his best to divide his time between his career and his family. His mother's cancer went into remission in 2012. Sampha resumed work on his debut and moved into his own apartment, but in 2014, his mother's cancer returned, and he moved back home again. She died in 2015. Grief made his return to work difficult. In 2016, Sampha worked with R & B virtuoso Frank Ocean on Ocean's album *Endless*. He appears on the song "Alabama." The collaboration gave Sampha the confidence to pursue his ideas. He decided to return to a song he had set aside called "Blood on Me." The song later became one of the standout tracks on his debut. Sampha was similarly inspired by his work with Solange. Her album, in part a political manifesto, inspired Sampha to be a "little more brave in terms of creating a dialogue and not necessarily feeling like what you are saying is perfect," he told Harriet Gibsone for the London *Guardian* (6 Feb. 2017).

Sampha released his debut album *Process* in February 2013. Anchored by the song "(No One Knows Me) Like the Piano," a tribute to his mother, *Process* is a "remarkable, meditative work" about processing grief, Marcus J. Moore wrote for *Pitchfork* (3 Feb. 2017). "In a way," Moore wrote, "*Process* feels like a concept album on which Sampha rediscovers himself." Jonny Ensall, who reviewed the album for the British music magazine *NME* (1 Feb. 2017), praised Sampha's delicate creations and the way they mirror the sensibility of the artist himself. "*Process* might not be as bold or as inventive or as life-changing as some of the other records Sampha's had a hand in during his career, but it does have a quiet, dignified impact that suits its maker," Ensall wrote. "He hasn't stepped out

of his shadowy, background world; instead, he's invited us to join him there."

PERSONAL LIFE
Sampha lives in northwest London with his girlfriend, Jojo, a personal trainer.

SUGGESTED READING
Ensall, Jonny. Review of *Process*, by Sampha. *NME*, 1 Feb. 2017, www.nme.com/reviews/album/sampha-process-album-review. Accessed 7 Mar. 2018.

Gibsone, Harriet. "Sampha: I Was Like, 'Mum! Drake Wants My Beat!' And She Was Like, 'Who?'" *The Guardian*, 6 Feb. 2017, www.theguardian.com/music/2017/feb/06/sampha-drake-kanye-west-frank-ocean. Accessed 7 Mar. 2018.

Kelly, Zach. Review of *Dual EP*, by Sampha. *Pitchfork*, 14 Aug. 2013, pitchfork.com/reviews/albums/18419-sampha-dual-ep/. Accessed 7 Mar. 2018.

Monaé, Ashley. "UK Singer, Songwriter and Producer Sampha Steps into the Spotlight." *Paper*, 2 Feb. 2017, www.papermag.com/uk-singer-songwriter-and-producer-sampha-steps-into-the-spotlight-2233945936.html. Accessed 7 Mar. 2018.

Moore, Marcus J. Review of *Process*, by Sampha. *Pitchfork*, 3 Feb. 2017. Accessed 7 Mar. 2018.

Saxelby, Ruth. "Sampha." *Pitchfork*, 8 July 2013, pitchfork.com/features/rising/9164-sampha/. Accessed 7 Mar. 2018.

Saxelby, Ruth. "Sampha's Search for Magic." *The Fader*, 28 June 2016, www.thefader.com/2016/06/28/sampha-cover-story-interview. Accessed 7 Mar. 2018.

SELECTED WORKS
Sundanza, 2010; *Dual*, 2013; *Process*, 2017

—*Molly Hagan*

Samanta Schweblin
Date of birth: 1978
Occupation: Writer

Samanta Schweblin is an Argentinian novelist and short story writer. Her first novel, *Fever Dream*, translated into English by Megan McDowell, won the Tigre Juan Prize for Fiction in 2015, and was short-listed for the Man Booker International Prize in 2017. (The book was originally published in Spanish as *Distancia de rescate* in 2014.) In 2010, Schweblin was named one of the twenty-two best Spanish-language writers under thirty-five by the British literary magazine *Granta*. Schweblin has written three

Photo by Simone Padovani/Awakening/Getty Images

collections of shorts stories including *El núcleo del disturbio* (The core of disturbance) in 2002, *Pájaros en la boca* (Birds in the mouth) in 2009, and *Siete casas vacías* (Seven empty houses) in 2015. Only a handful of Schweblin's stories have received English translations. She is best known to English-speaking readers for *Fever Dream*, a cryptic dialogue between a woman in a hospital bed named Amanda and a young boy named David. Schweblin is known for her fantastical and unsettling, yet bare-bones style. Mysterious forces called the worms figure heavily into *Fever Dream*, which *New Yorker* critic Jia Tolentino wrote (4 Jan. 2017) "filled [her] with unease."

EARLY LIFE

Schweblin was born in 1978 in Buenos Aires, Argentina. She traces her love of writing to her childhood, when, at five years old, she told her mother stories. She discovered pacing, tension and how to build suspense. "I remember discovering the sensation that I could really touch someone else with storytelling," she told Bethanne Patrick for the writing website *lithub.com* (12 Jan. 2017). "There aren't many moments in life when another person wants to hear you, when you can capture that person's attention completely. It's an amazing feeling, and when I'm writing, I'm trying to go for that moment." She was enthralled by the power of literature; she recalls watching her grandfather crying while reciting Latin American poetry. At seventeen, with her mother's encouragement, she began attending literary workshops taught by famous authors. Buenos Aires has a long tradition of

such workshops, held in writers' homes. Schweblin began to write seriously, though she studied film at the University of Buenos Aires. She chose the degree because she felt that screenwriting and editing best taught her how to craft a story. Meanwhile, she continued to attend novelist Liliana Heker's writing workshops, also attended by such professional authors as screenwriter Pablo Ramos, novelist Guillermo Martínez, and novelist Inés Garland. The workshops introduced her to the publishing world; she landed Barcelona-based agent Glòria Gutiérrez and published her first collection of short stories, *El núcleo del disturbio* (*The Core of the Disturbance*), in 2002.

SHORT STORY COLLECTIONS

El núcleo del disturbio earned Schweblin awards through the National Fund for the Arts and the Haroldo Conti National Competition. The collection includes one of Schweblin's best-known stories, translated as "To Kill a Dog." Schweblin wrote it when she was just eighteen. She later said that the idea came to her fully formed. She sat down and wrote the whole thing in a few hours. It was her first published story. An English translation appears in a 2014 issue of the London literary magazine *The White Review*. The story was adapted into an award-winning short film in 2013. In "To Kill a Dog," an unnamed narrator must undergo a terrible test administered by an agent known only as the Mole. To pass the test, the narrator must beat a dog to death to prove that he is capable of murdering a person. The gruesome initiation takes place in an unknown city for an unknown organization. The narrator is prepared to complete the task, but early on struggles to select the proper victim from a pack of stray dogs. When he does, a man approaches him. "Between the trees a shadow moves, a drunkard approaches me and says, you can't do that sort of thing, the dogs know who the guilty one is and will get even. They know, he says, don't you get it?" Schweblin's disturbing story—with an ominous ending that recalls the warning of the drunkard—suggests the cyclical nature of violence, but invites more than one interpretation. One English editor was sure that the story was an allegory about the Argentinean military coup. "He explained why it was about that with such concrete examples that I was completely fascinated because that was never my intention," Schweblin told Cara Benson for *Full Stop* magazine (29 Mar. 2017).

Schweblin received a National Council for Culture and Arts (CONACULTA) scholarship in Oaxaca, Mexico, in 2008. She published her second story collection, *Pájaros en la boca* (*Birds in the Mouth*), in 2009; the collection won the prestigious Casa de las Américas Prize. It contains a story called "Preserves," which employs elements of magical realism. In it, a pregnant woman struggles to take control over her life. Her husband, Manuel, seems distant, while her mother and mother-in-law overwhelm her with their anxieties about the new baby, Teresita. The narrator and Manuel visit a doctor and devise a birth plan—but the plan is not what it seems. The story explores the anxiety of motherhood and questions what it means to be "ready" to have children. Like "To Kill a Dog," Schweblin's "Preserves" is sparse and swiftly paced. Both stories have a fable-like quality, shaped by a few well-chosen details—such as Mole's unusual sunglasses in "Dog" and the "little colored sheets" in "Preserves." This is all by design. "When you are writing a story you really need to make most of the time you have," Schweblin told theshort-form.com literary website in 2010. "You can't waste it describing what a character is wearing, things must happen quickly and precisely."

In 2010 Schweblin was named one of the twenty-two best Spanish-language writers under thirty-five by the literary magazine *Granta*, and in 2012 she won the Juan Rolfo Story Prize for a story called "Un hombre sin suerte" (A man with no luck). The same year, she was invited to teach a workshop in Berlin, where she subsequently decided to live. Schweblin published her third book, *Siete casas vacías* (Seven empty houses), in 2015. Paul Doyle, for his literary blog *By the Firelight* (16 Jan. 2017), noted that the book marked Schweblin's shift from the overtly fantastical to the uncanny and strange. "The fantastic is no longer an external element or force that one can interact with," like the tiny seed pod that the narrator spits out at the end of "Preserves." "Instead," he wrote, "it's an open question, perhaps of motivation, perhaps of perspective." Doyle cites a story in the collection called "La respiración cavernaria" (Deep breathing), in which an aging woman loses touch with the world around her. The lack of concrete reality destabilizes the reader as well.

FEVER DREAM (2017)

Schweblin published her first novel, *Distancia de rescate* (literally translated as "rescue distance"), in 2014. Her trusted collaborator McDowell translated the book into English, under the title *Fever Dream*, in 2017. "Some translators can be so obsessed and so perfectionist they ask you for a map of the house where your characters live," Schweblin told Mark Reynolds for the website *bookanista.com* in 2017, while others ask no questions at all. McDowell, meanwhile, "is just in the middle—in a good way," Schweblin said. "You can see that she's thinking carefully not only about each word but also the complete form of the book." *Fever Dream* is written as a dialogue between Amanda, a woman dying in a hospital bed, unable to move, and a young boy named David. Amanda does not have long to live, so David peppers her with questions about how she got there. Amanda talks about David's mother, Carla, and her daughter, Nina. There are two thematic elements to the impressionistic and hallucinatory tale, a reviewer for the *Economist* (22 Apr. 2017) wrote. It is both a "study in maternal anxiety" and "an ecological horror story." Amanda frets over something she calls "rescue distance"—the book's original title—by which she means the amount of time it would take for her to reach her child in the event of disaster. Meanwhile, the book also refers to Argentina's soy fields, whose toxic pesticides ravage rural communities.

Critics were nearly unanimous in their praise, describing *Fever Dream* as both dream-like and tightly plotted. The novel, the reviewer for the *Economist* wrote, "is almost as if [great American novelist] Henry James had scripted a disaster movie about toxic agribusiness." Tolentino consumed the book in a single sitting, writing, "The genius of *Fever Dream* is less in what it says than in how Schweblin says it, with a design at once so enigmatic and so disciplined that the book feels as if it belongs to a new literary genre altogether." The book was shortlisted for the prestigious Man Booker International Prize in 2017, though the award ultimately went to David Grossman's *A Horse Walks into a Bar*. That same year, a translated version of Schweblin's story "The Size of Things" appeared in the *New Yorker*. (She wrote it when she was twenty-two or twenty-three.) The story, about a man regressing to childhood, bears a resemblance to F. Scott Fitzgerald's story "The Curious Case of Benjamin Button" and Roald Dahl's "The Man from the South." The story is ambiguous about whether the transformation involved is metaphorical or literal. "Writing it, I was at a stage when I felt as though ideas, to be strong, needed the power of more classic forms," Schweblin told Deborah Treisman for the *New Yorker* (22 May 2017), referring to the classical idea of metamorphosis. "It was a learning stage—though I'm still learning, really."

PERSONAL LIFE

Schweblin lives in Berlin with her boyfriend, who runs a local bar. In keeping with the tradition in which she learned to write, Schweblin holds writing workshops three times a week at her house in Berlin.

SUGGESTED READING

Doyle, Paul. Review of *Siete casas vacías*, by Samanta Schweblin. *By the Firelight*, 16 Jan. 2017, bythefirelight.com/2017/01/16/siete-casas-vacias-seven-empty-houses-by-samanta-schweblin-a-review/. Accessed 1 Nov. 2017.

"Samanta Schweblin's Blistering Debut Novel." Review of *Fever Dream*, by Samanta Schweblin. *Economist*, 22 Apr. 2017, www.economist.com/news/books-and-arts/21721118-fever-dream-suspenseful-eco-horror-samanta-schweblins-blistering-debut-novel. Accessed 2 Nov. 2017.

Schweblin, Samanta. Interview. By Cara Benson. *Full Stop*, 29 Mar. 2017, www.full-stop.net/2017/03/29/interviews/cara-benson/samanta-schweblin/. Accessed 30 Oct. 2017.

Schweblin, Samanta. Interview. *The Short Form*, 2010, www.theshortform.com/interview/samanta-schweblin. Accessed 30 Oct. 2017.

Schweblin, Samanta. "Samanta Schweblin on Revealing Darkness through Fiction." Interview by Bethanne Patrick. *Literary Hub*, 12 Jan. 2017, lithub.com/samanta-schweblin-on-revealing-darkness-through-fiction/. Accessed 30 Oct. 2017.

Schweblin, Samanta. "This Week in Fiction: Samanta Schweblin on an Adult Man's Infantilization." Interview by Deborah Treisman. *The New Yorker*, 22 May 2017, www.newyorker.com/books/page-turner/this-week-in-fiction-samanta-schweblin-2017-05-29. Accessed 2 Nov. 2017.

Tolentino, Jia. "The Sick Thrill of 'Fever Dream.'" Review of *Fever Dream*, by Samanta Schweblin. *The New Yorker*, 4 Jan. 2017, www.newyorker.com/books/page-turner/the-sick-thrill-of-fever-dream. Accessed 2 Nov. 2017.

SELECTED WORKS

El núcleo del disturbio, 2002; *Pájaros en la boca*, 2009; *Distancia de rescate*, 2014 (*Fever Dream*, 2017)

—*Molly Hagan*

The Secret Sisters

Occupation: Band

LAURA ROGERS
Date of birth: April 5, 1986
Occupation: Vocalist

LYDIA ROGERS
Date of birth: ca. 1988
Occupation: Vocalist

Most often referred to as performers of Americana or roots music, Laura and Lydia Rogers, the two siblings who make up The Secret Sisters, have released three albums: an eponymous debut in 2010, *Put Your Needle Down* in 2014, and *You Don't Own Me Anymore* in 2017. That

By Bryan Ledgard via Wikimedia Commons

last effort, which was nominated for a Grammy Award for best folk album of the year, came after a grueling period during which they were sued by their manager, dropped by their record label, and forced to declare bankruptcy, leading many music journalists to paint them as beneficiaries of a distinctly American ethos of second chances and come-from-behind success.

EARLY YEARS AND EDUCATION

Laura Rogers was born on April 5, 1986. Her sister, Lydia Rogers, who is sometimes referred to by her married name, Lydia Slagle, is about two years younger, making the year of her birth approximately 1988. The sisters were raised outside of Florence, Alabama, near Muscle Shoals, a small city located along the Tennessee River that is home to two iconic recording studios, FAME Studios and Muscle Shoals Sound Studio, that have helped shape American pop music. (Among the artists who contributed to what is now known as the Muscle Shoals sound are Aretha Franklin, Wilson Pickett, Otis Redding, and the Staple Singers.) "Even as kids, our dad told us stories about Muscle Shoals," Laura recalled to Monica Collier for the local Florence *TimesDaily* (1 Dec. 2016). "But you don't realize the worldwide impact it has when you're so close to it geographically."

The siblings hail from a musical family. Their grandfather and his brothers formed a gospel group called the Happy Valley Boys that gained widespread popularity during the 1940s and 1950s, and their father, Ricky Rogers, is the bassist in the band Iron Horse, which blends bluegrass with the music of artists such as Modest Mouse, Guns & Roses, Ozzy Osbourne, and Metallica.

"Our dad was always dragging us to these bluegrass festivals," Laura recalled to Collier. "As kids, you kind of hate it and are only there for the craft booths and food. We didn't realize when we were kids it was burying itself into us and the music we would eventually make." Reunions of the large, deeply devout family typically involved pulling out instruments and hymn books, and those gatherings also exerted a marked influence on the two. In the car, the sisters would harmonize with their parents—Ricky singing bass, their mother as alto, Lydia as tenor, and Laura as soprano—and they still consider the memories of those trips among the fondest of their youth.

Despite that background, the sisters never intended to forge careers as professional musicians. It was in 2009, just after Laura had completed her business studies at Middle Tennessee State University and started working as a nanny, that she heard about an open audition being held at the Indigo Hotel in downtown Nashville. Although she had never performed in front of any large crowd not composed of family members, she decided to attend. The judges were impressed, and, by then somewhat comfortable and emboldened, she asked if her sister could also audition. When the organizers agreed, she quickly summoned Lydia to make the two-hour drive from Alabama.

After Lydia finished with her own tryout, Dave Cobb, a Nashville-based producer known for his work with such artists as Shooter Jennings and the Zac Brown Band, asked if the two had ever considered forming a musical duo. They did, and named themselves The Secret Sisters after finding out that the name "the Rogers Sisters" was already taken; the name, they have told interviewers, references their sudden and seemingly mysterious appearance on the music scene.

MUSIC CAREER

With Cobb's help, within two months The Secret Sisters had signed a recording deal with Universal Republic. "We thought it was a fluke, or even a scam, like they were trying to get us on a TV show or something, and it would be a horrible deal for us," Laura said in an interview by Chuck Armstrong for the *Boot* (9 June 2017). "People told us, 'You better be careful, they want something from you.' But what would they have gotten? I was 22 years old and didn't have anything!"

The Secret Sisters, their first album, was released in 2010 and contained mainly cover material, as the label had moved so rapidly that there had been little time to pen new tunes. "We

realized, in the moment, that we were very fortunate," they admitted to Armstrong. "We knew bands and artists who were trying for years and years and years to get somewhere, and here we were with this dream experience." Produced by industry legend T-Bone Burnett and recorded with a team of seasoned Nashville session players on analog 1950s equipment, the album garnered positive reviews. "Their harmonies are a work of art, their grip on their material unerring: If the Andrews Sisters had recorded an album of Carter Family songs during World War II, it would sound just like this," Allison Stewart wrote for the *Washington Post* (27 Dec. 2010). "The Sisters never break character, never let on that they know it's really 2010. *The Secret Sisters* is a cheerful anachronism: Impossible to replicate, tough to forget, it's the year's loveliest museum piece."

Their sophomore effort, *Put Your Needle Down*, was recorded during a whirlwind period that found the two touring and collaborating with such artists as Jack White, Paul Simon, and Bob Dylan. Like their debut, it won praise from critics. "*Put Your Needle Down* is as old-fashioned as a handwritten letter," Kevin Harley wrote for the *Independent* (25 May 2014). "But there is more to it than that. Because with T Bone Burnett at the helm, this is no lazy exercise in nostalgia. These songs bounce, buzz and bubble along with timeless life. And jeez louise, those harmonies!"

At about this time, the sisters decided to seek a change in management—not an uncommon occurrence in the music business. Their manager, however, chose to initiate a lawsuit that proved devastating to them on both a practical and an emotional level. "More than anything else, I think it hurt our creativity," Lydia recalled to Armstrong. "There would be times where we'd need to be writing a song and gearing up for the next record, but we just didn't feel like writing because all of this stuff was happening." Fortuitously, not long after they had been forced to declare personal bankruptcy due to legal fees, fellow artist Brandi Carlile, whom they had long admired, agreed to produce their next album. Because money was tight, the duo hit upon the solution of using the crowdfunding site *PledgeMusic*, which had been gaining in acceptability and popularity in recent years. They promised fans who donated to their cause various perks, from an autographed CD for $25 and a signed lyric sheet for $75 all the way up to a private concert for $5,000.

With funding secured and a producer they deeply respected on board, the sisters recorded the aptly named *You Don't Own Me Anymore*. "I think Lydia and I had to discover our strength as artists and writers and women," Laura told Armstrong. "I feel like we've gone through this renaissance on our own, and this new record really expresses that."

The album—released by Americana-focused label New West as the act was dropped by Universal Republic during the lawsuit—contained several evocative tracks, including the haunting "Tennessee River Runs Slow." The video for that song took place at Alabama folk artist Butch Anthony's Museum of Wonder, the regular site of the Doo-Nanny, a version of Burning Man. Folk artists like Anthony, as Ann Powers wrote for National Public Radio's (NPR) *Songs We Love* (30 Mar. 2017), "are as crucial to the soul of Alabama as is anyone who fulfills more unsavory (and currently prevalent) stereotypes. So is the sound of The Secret Sisters, running true like a river current, soaring like the eagles who fly above their nestled homes."

You Don't Own Me Anymore received a Grammy nod in the category of best folk album of 2017 but ultimately lost to *Mental Illness* by Aimee Mann. The nomination brought The Secret Sisters increased attention outside Americana music circles, though some wider audiences already knew them from the inclusion of their song "Tomorrow Will Be Kinder" on the soundtrack to the blockbuster film *The Hunger Games* (2012) and the use of "Let There Be Lonely," a tune they cowrote, on the ABC show *Nashville* in 2013.

PERSONAL LIFE

Lydia's husband, Mark Slagle, is a filmmaker who has contributed his talents to their music videos. They live in Birmingham, Alabama. Laura's husband, Kyle, is a member of the National Guard; they live in the town of Killen, Alabama, in a home built by Laura's grandfather in the 1950s. Laura has said in interviews that she hopes to someday have a "hobby farm" on which to raise goats, chickens, cows, and donkeys.

SUGGESTED READING

Armstrong, Chuck. "A Brief History of The Secret Sisters, as Told by the Secret Sisters." *The Boot*, 9 June 2017, theboot.com/the-secret-sisters-you-dont-own-me-anymore-interview-2017/. Accessed 15 July 2018.

Collier, Monica. "Secret Sisters: Hometown Magic." *TimesDaily*, 1 Dec. 2016, www.timesdaily.com/life/entertainment/the-secret-sisters-making-a-big-statement/article_dcb8086c-ec6c-5563-a07c-ee2d73420532.html. Accessed 15 July 2018.

Harley, Kevin. Review of *Put Your Needle Down*, by The Secret Sisters. *Independent*, 25 May 2014, www.independent.co.uk/arts-entertainment/music/reviews/album-reviews-neil-young-royksopp-robyn-sharon-van-etten-the-secret-sisters-9424829.html. Accessed 15 July 2018.

Niesel, Jeff. "Folk Duo the Secret Sisters Get a Well-Deserved Second Chance." *Cleveland Scene*, 18 May 2017, www.clevescene.com/scene-and-heard/archives/2017/05/18/folk-duo-the-secret-sisters-get-a-well-deserved-second-chance. Accessed 15 July 2018.

Powers, Ann. "The Secret Sisters, 'Tennessee River Runs Low.'" *Songs We Love*, NPR, 30 Mar. 2017, www.npr.org/2017/03/30/521937695/songs-we-love-the-secret-sisters-tennessee-river-runs-low. Accessed 15 July 2018.

Stewart, Allison. "Quick Spin: The Secret Sisters' Pretty and Pristine Self-Titled Album." Review of *The Secret Sisters*, by the Secret Sisters. *The Washington Post*, 27 Dec. 2010, www.washingtonpost.com/wp-dyn/content/article/2010/12/27/AR2010122703732.html. Accessed 15 July 2018.

Wake, Matt. "Secret Sisters Overcome Lawsuit, Bankruptcy, Being Dropped by Label to Make New LP." *AL.com*, 17 Mar. 2016, www.al.com/entertainment/index.ssf/2016/03/secret_sisters_overcome_lawsui.html. Accessed 15 July 2018.

SELECTED WORKS

The Secret Sisters, 2010; *Put Your Needle Down*, 2014; *You Don't Own Me Anymore*, 2017

—Mari Rich

Luis Severino

Date of birth: February 20, 1994
Occupation: Baseball player

"The best feeling in the world is waking up in the morning and remembering that you're a New York Yankee," pitcher Luis Severino wrote for *Players' Tribune* (5 Sept. 2017). Indeed, for Severino that feeling was the culmination of a lifelong dream. As a baseball-loving child growing up in the Dominican Republic, he idolized the Yankees and dreamed of one day playing for the iconic team. After training hard to get himself noticed among the many young Dominicans hoping for a chance to play professional baseball, he received offers to play for other major-league teams, but ultimately signed with the Yankees in December 2011.

Over the next several years, Severino moved up in the Yankees organization, playing for minor-league affiliate teams and progressing quickly from the rookie level to the highly ranked triple A. His debut with the Yankees in 2015 signaled his potential as a starting pitcher, but a disappointing 2016 season and temporary demotion to the minor leagues presented a tough challenge

By Arturo Pardavila III, via Wikimedia Commons

for the young player to overcome. Upon his return to the Yankees in 2017, however, Severino again demonstrated his substantial talents with an All-Star season. Elevated to the position of staff ace, he embraced the high expectations of the notoriously passionate New York fanbase. "When you're doing stuff bad, everybody knows it," he told Steve Serby for the *New York Post* (27 May 2017). "But when you're doing good, everybody knows it too, so I love that."

EARLY LIFE AND EDUCATION

Severino was born on February 20, 1994, in Sabana de la Mar, Dominican Republic. Baseball was a common passion in his neighborhood, and Severino grew up playing the sport with his father, brother, and neighbors. An avid viewer of televised Major League Baseball (MLB) games, Severino found himself drawn to the New York Yankees. "There was just something about that uniform, and the pinstripes, and that logo, and . . . New York," he wrote for the *Players' Tribune*. "When I went to the field, I'd sometimes try to be like the guys I saw on TV, or pretend I was playing in Yankee Stadium." Although he initially played positions such as third base and outfield, he soon learned to pitch and quickly took to the role of pitcher. He trained to throw baseballs as fast as he could, and by the time he was in his late teens he could reach up to ninety-seven miles per hour.

Determined to play baseball professionally, Severino attended MLB tryouts whenever possible and also enrolled in a baseball academy. Coming from a modest background, he viewed the numerous scouts and recruiters in the Dominican Republic as opportunities and worked hard to impress them. He soon attracted attention from various teams, including the Miami Marlins and the Colorado Rockies. Despite feeling pressure to take the first offer that came his way, he followed the advice of his agent to wait for better terms. He very nearly signed with the Rockies, but the Yankees matched the offer at the last minute and Severino jumped at the chance to join his favorite franchise. "When I met up with friends and family, I was more excited than I've ever been in my life," he recalled in his piece for the *Players' Tribune*. "I was practically shouting to everyone: 'I am a New York Yankee! I'm going to play in New York. I'm a Yankee!' And they just sort of looked at me. They didn't know what to do." Severino officially signed with the Yankees as an amateur free agent on December 26, 2011.

MINOR LEAGUES

After signing with the Yankees, Severino began his professional baseball career in the Dominican Summer League, joining that league's Yankees 1 team in 2012. The following season, he moved to the United States to play with the Yankees' rookie league Gulf Coast League team but transitioned to a higher level of play after appearing in six games, moving up to the class-A Charleston RiverDogs. Although the move to the United States and subsequent shifts from team to team presented a challenge for Severino, he adjusted to such major life changes with the help of fellow players with roots in the Dominican Republic. "I struggled to find the time to improve my English, and had a hard time eating McDonald's hamburgers every single day," he wrote for the *Players' Tribune*. "But there were always other Dominican players around to help me out. . . . After a while, with some help, you just sort of get the hang of things."

Severino began the 2014 season with the RiverDogs, starting fourteen games and recording a solid 2.79 earned run average (ERA). He quickly moved on to the Class A Advanced Tampa Yankees and then the Double A Trenton Thunder, continuing to excel at both levels. He remained with the Thunder into 2015 but soon moved up yet again, joining the Triple A Scranton/Wilkes-Barre RailRiders. There he had a perfect 7–0 record with an excellent 1.91 ERA.

Although aware that his fast progression through the Yankees organization boded well for his chances of playing in the majors, Severino acknowledged the valuable experience he was gaining in the minor leagues and expressed that he was not in a rush to move on. "Every time you go out there, you learn," he told Jamal Collier for the Yankees' official website (24 July 2015). "It's the same baseball." Nevertheless, Severino had come to be considered one of the most impressive pitchers in the minor leagues and the Yankees' top prospect, and his promotion seemed virtually assured.

NEW YORK YANKEES

Several months into the 2015 season, the Yankees called Severino up to the major leagues. He made his debut with the Yankees on August 5, 2015, in a home game against the rival Boston Red Sox. Although the Yankees ultimately lost that game 2–1, Severino pitched well, allowing only two hits, no walks, and one earned run and one unearned run over five innings. "He did a pretty good job," Yankees manager Joe Girardi told Bill Madden for the *New York Daily News* (6 Aug. 2015) following Severino's debut. "I didn't think the surroundings would affect him, and it didn't. It was a positive for him and showed what he could mean for us going forward." Severino spent the remainder of the 2015 season with the Yankees, going 5–3 in eleven starts with a very promising 2.89 ERA. He did not pitch in the Yankees' sole postseason game, an unsuccessful wild card match against the Houston Astros.

Severino opened the 2016 season as part of the Yankees' starting rotation, but soon struggled; across his first seven starts he posted a rough 7.46 ERA and no wins. Following a dismal performance in a game against the Chicago White Sox, he was diagnosed with an arm injury and placed on the disabled list. He was then demoted back to the minor leagues, rejoining the Scranton/Wilkes-Barre RailRiders. Severino was deeply disappointed by the sudden drop in his performance. "The Yankees gave me opportunity to be in the rotation and I lost it," he recalled to Serby. "I know I have the skill and the stuff to be here in the big leagues, and I lost it." He did manage to regain something of his former dominance at Triple A, going 7–1 with a 3.25 ERA, and was eventually called back up to the majors. He was primarily used as a reliever for the rest of the season and did well, though he remained intent on winning back his starting role.

After the 2016 season concluded, Severino focused on regaining the command of several types of pitches to be an effective starter. To that end, he sought the advice of retired player Pedro Martinez, a fellow Dominican-born pitcher whose Hall-of-Fame-worthy career included a notable stint as the ace of the Red Sox and a Yankees nemesis. "We focused on mechanics," Severino told Brendan Kuty for *NJ.com* (29 Jan. 2017) of his work with Martinez. "My mechanics, my release point—trying to fix it all." Severino's off-season work paid off, as he not only made the Yankees' big-league club for the 2017 season, but also regained his job as a starter.

BECOMING AN ACE

Over the course of the 2017 season, Severino reestablished himself as a top-flight starter and helped lead a young Yankees club to a surprisingly strong campaign. He started thirty-one games and almost reached the 200-inning milestone, serving as a key pillar in the Yankees rotation with a 14–6 record. He achieved an ERA of 2.98, the third best in the American League (AL), and his 230 strikeouts were fourth-most in the league. His significantly improved performance drew widespread praise and saw him named as a reserve to the 2017 MLB All-Star Game. It even led some baseball analysts to proclaim him the new ace of the Yankees, but Severino tended to downplay his accomplishments and praise his fellow pitchers. "Like I always say, there are a lot of guys here that I know are way better," he told Wallace Matthews for the *New York Times* (26 July 2017), citing pitchers C. C. Sabathia and Masahiro Tanaka as key members of the team. "I got to keep doing this for five or six years and we'll see what happens."

The 2017 regular season ended with the Yankees in second place in the American League East, but their 91–71 record secured a wild card spot going into the postseason. Severino was chosen to start the single-elimination wild card game against the Minnesota Twins based on his strong regular season. However, he was pulled after allowing three runs and recording just one out. The Yankees managed to still win the game and went to play the Cleveland Indians in the American League Division Series (ALDS). They won that series 3–2, with Severino earning the win in game four with seven innings and three runs allowed. The Yankees then entered the American League Championship Series (ALCS), which they lost in seven games to the eventual World Series champion Houston Astros. Severino started two games in the ALCS, pitching four innings with one earned run for a no decision in game two and taking the loss in game six with three runs allowed over 4.2 innings. After the season was over it was announced that Severino came in third in voting for the AL Cy Young Award, given to the league's top pitcher.

Severino began the 2018 season widely considered the Yankees' ace, earning the start in the season opener as typically given to a team's best pitcher. He began the season strong, allowing no runs and just one hit over five and two-thirds innings, helping the Yankees win 6–1. Over the opening months of the season he continued to pitch well, ranking at or near the top of the AL and MLB in wins and ERA much of the time and playing a major role in the Yankees' close divisional race with the Red Sox. "This is a young man who wants to be great," Yankees manager Aaron Boone told Wallace Matthews for *Forbes*

(31 May 2018) of Severino during the season. "He relishes matchups against the best teams and the best pitchers."

PERSONAL LIFE

Severino and his wife, Rosmaly (Porro Frechel) Severino, have a daughter named Abigail. He has homes in Santo Domingo, Dominican Republic, and in New York City, the latter of which he came to enjoy greatly after joining the Yankees. "The food's very good. I like Times Square. A lot of people, a lot of lights and stuff like that. I love that," he told Serby.

SUGGESTED READING

Collier, Jamal. "Yanks Prospect Severino Handling Triple-A." *New York Yankees*, MLB Advanced Media, 24 July 2015, www.mlb.com/news/yankees-prospect-luis-severino-pitching-well/c-138565290. Accessed 9 June 2018.

Kuty, Brendan. "How Red Sox Hero Helped Yankees' Luis Severino Fix Problems." *NJ.com*, 29 Jan. 2017, www.nj.com/yankees/index.ssf/2017/01/how_red_sox_hero_helped_yankees_luis_severino_fix.html. Accessed 9 June 2018.

Madden, Bill. "Luis Severino Lives Up to the Hype in Yankee Debut, Looks Ready for Impact." *Daily News*, 6 Aug. 2015, www.nydailynews.com/sports/baseball/yankees/madden-luis-severino-lives-hype-yankee-debut-article-1.2316246. Accessed 9 June 2018.

Matthews, Wallace. "Elevated to Ace, Luis Severino Shows His Electric Stuff." *The New York Times*, 26 July 2017, www.nytimes.com/2017/07/26/sports/baseball/elevated-to-ace-luis-severino-shows-his-electric-stuff.html. Accessed 9 June 2018.

Matthews, Wallace. "Luis Severino Gives the Yankees a Weapon to Match Up with the Astros." *Forbes*, 31 May 2018, www.forbes.com/sites/wallacematthews/2018/05/31/luis-severino-gives-the-yankees-a-weapon-to-match-up-against-the-astros/#482037404b2c. Accessed 9 June 2018.

Severino, Luis. "Luis Severino on Hating Bullpen, Pedro's Tip and Making Mom Proud." Interview with Steve Serby. *New York Post*, 27 May 2017, nypost.com/2017/05/27/luis-severino-on-hating-bullpen-pedros-tip-and-making-mom-proud/. Accessed 9 June 2018.

Severino, Luis. "My Journey to the Bronx." *Players' Tribune*, 5 Sept. 2017, www.theplayerstribune.com/en-us/articles/luis-severino-yankees-my-journey-to-the-bronx. Accessed 9 June 2018.

—*Joy Crelin*

Yara Shahidi

Date of birth: February 10, 2000
Occupation: Actor

Yara Shahidi is an actor, model, and activist best known for her role on the popular ABC sitcom *Black-ish*. She plays Zoey Johnson, the eldest daughter of an upper-middle-class African American family living in a mainly white neighborhood in Los Angeles. The show's protagonist, Andre (played by actor and comedian Anthony Anderson), struggles to instill in his suburban, technology-obsessed children a sense of cultural identity—though no one in his family can seem to completely agree on what it means to be African American. Shahidi's character, Zoey, is smart, but also, at her worst, materialistic and entitled; the plot of her emotional maturation will continue in a spin-off titled *Grown-ish*, in which Zoey leaves home to go to college. As of the fall of 2017, the show was slated to premiere on Freeform in January 2018.

Though Shahidi and her character are the same age, the two young women could not be more different. Shahidi, who committed to attend Harvard University, is a prominent social activist and political voice for the up-and-coming Generation Z. In 2015, she partnered with *DoSomething.org* to promote a game to encourage young people, particularly young women, to pursue degrees in science, technology, engineering, and mathematics (STEM) fields and participated in a panel discussing the need for diversity in Hollywood and STEM fields. Shahidi,

Photo by Jason LaVeris/FilmMagic

who maintains a blog devoted to James Baldwin, called *Mainstream Anarchist*, also founded her own online mentoring program, Yara's Club, through the Young Women's Leadership Network in 2016. "I know my normal is different than other peoples' normal, but acting, it's just something I am passionate about," she told Kristin Tice Studeman for *W* magazine (22 Nov. 2016). "Acting doesn't define who I am, it's not my whole life. I have been able to have all these amazing experiences driven by ten million other interests and being able to have access to that because of acting balances it out."

EARLY LIFE AND CAREER

Shahidi was born in Minneapolis, Minnesota, on February 10, 2000. Her mother, Keri, who is of African American and Choctaw descent, is an actor and model. She has a master's degree in business and also serves as a consultant for parents of child actors. Shahidi's father, Afshin, who is Iranian, is a cinematographer and photographer who worked for a long time as a personal photographer for the late legendary musician Prince. In 2017, he published a book of photographs from their collaboration titled *Prince: A Private View*. Prince is not the only musical connection in Shahidi's life, however; her cousin is the rapper Nas. She is the eldest of three children and her two younger brothers, Sayeed and Ehsan, are also actors. After she was born, her mother gave a photograph to her agents as a greeting. The agents then called with a print booking for Shahidi, who was only six weeks old. As a young child, Shahidi, like her mother, worked in commercials and print. The family moved to Los Angeles, primarily to accommodate Afshin's job with Prince, when she was four years old.

Many of Shahidi's early jobs involved modeling in commercials as well as advertisements for toy companies such as Disney and Mattel. "I'd go into the Disney store and literally see me," she recalled in a dual interview with her close friend, actor Rowan Blanchard, for *Teen Vogue* (11 Nov. 2016). She appeared as characters like Cinderella and Tinkerbell, but "being the black version of so many characters brought up problems. I was happy to be black, but at the same time there were moments of, 'Why is this a separate collection?' There was this realization that being black meant I was the 'off-brand' version because Cinderella wasn't made to look like me," she said. Such early experiences have informed her activism about representation.

EXPANDING HER ACTING HORIZONS

When Shahidi was seven, her agent sent her a script for the Eddie Murphy film *Imagine That*, about a financial executive (Murphy) who is offered a glimpse into his daughter's imaginary world. Content with the versatile world of commercials and print advertising, she insists that she was not specifically looking to appear in a film—she remembers wondering how one could maintain the portrayal of a single character for months of shooting—but as a child herself, the script intrigued her. "As a seven-year-old with a crazy imagination it was cool for my first character to be literally a girl with an imaginary world," she told Studeman. The film, released in 2009, flopped at the box office and with critics, but Shahidi earned some serious praise. Roger Ebert wrote for the *Chicago Sun-Times* (10 June 2009) that her "charming" performance was the key to the father-daughter relationship at the heart of the movie. Ebert marveled that she was really only seven years old, writing, "She's a natural. I never caught her trying to be 'cute.' She played every scene straight and with confidence, and she's filled with personality."

Shahidi also appeared on several episodes of the short-lived ABC sitcom *In the Motherhood* (2009) and played bit parts in a handful of television shows and films including *Unthinkable* (2010) with Samuel L. Jackson and *Salt* (2010) with Angelina Jolie. Her next major role came in *Butter* (2011), a political satire set at a highly competitive butter-sculpting contest in Iowa, featuring a star-studded cast including Jennifer Garner and Emmy Award winner Ty Burrell. Shahidi's character, an inspirational butter-sculpting prodigy named Destiny, is a nod to then president Barack Obama; the film was moderately well received. Shahidi credited her upbringing when it came to winning the part, citing trips back to her home state to visit her paternal grandfather, who owns a Persian rug store in Minneapolis, and attend the state fair. Her Minnesota roots gave her an edge; she was the only girl auditioning for *Butter* who had actually witnessed a butter-sculpting contest. In 2012, she had a role in the first season of the syndicated sitcom *The First Family*, which imagines the life of the second African American president and his family. In 2013, she appeared on two episodes of the hit ABC drama *Scandal*; she played a younger version of the show's protagonist, Olivia Pope (Kerry Washington).

BLACK-ISH

Shahidi landed her biggest break yet when she earned the role of Zoey Johnson on the ABC sitcom *Black-ish*, which premiered in 2014. "Before I auditioned for *Black-ish*, I received scripts that portrayed black people in a negative and stereotypical way," she told Hannah Seligson for the *New York Times* (27 Nov. 2015). "But *Black-ish* is a more positive portrayal of what it's like to be black in America." Like *The Cosby Show* (1984–92) before it, *Black-ish* focuses on a prosperous

African American family—the father, Andre, is an advertising executive and the mother, Rainbow (played by Tracee Ellis Ross), is a doctor—but the show seeks to present the African American experience more generally by covering a variety of topics, including those that are more volatile. The show was created by Kenya Barris (who also cowrote the box-office smash hit comedy *Girls Trip* in 2017) with input from Anderson and was inspired by Barris's own experience growing up in poverty and raising his children in bourgeois privilege. The show explores generational differences—Andre's father is played by Laurence Fishburne—as well as issues of class and race. With *Black-ish* and its cast receiving critical acclaim almost immediately, Shahidi was honored with an Image Award for Outstanding Supporting Actress in a comedy series from the National Association for the Advancement of Colored People (NAACP) in 2015.

In subsequent seasons, the comedy also began to tackle real-world political topics more directly. In early 2016, the show aired an episode, called "Hope," about police brutality. In it, the family gathers around the living room television, waiting for a grand jury decision to indict or not indict a police officer for excessively tasing an unarmed African American man. Barris explained to Emily Nussbaum in an interview for the *New Yorker* (25 Apr. 2016) that the episode grew in part out of his anguish after the murder of twelve-year-old Tamir Rice in Cleveland in 2014. A year later, in January 2017, the show aired an episode, called "Lemons," about the aftermath of the 2016 presidential election. Both episodes were largely well received and widely discussed on social media, and the show continued to draw a strong audience in its fourth season.

COLLEGE AND *GROWN-ISH*

In early 2017, Barris announced that Shahidi would star in a spin-off series called *Grown-ish*—initially titled *College-ish*—for the Disney-owned channel Freeform. The show will follow Zoey as she leaves home to attend Southern California University. As Barris put it in the official pitch for the series, as quoted by Kate Stanhope in the *Hollywood Reporter* (2 Aug. 2017), "Where *Black-ish* examines what it means to be black, *Grown-ish* is an examination of what it is and what it means to be grown." Shahidi was excited at the prospect of playing the lead role and expanding her character further. "I feel like college campuses are highly politicized right now. And to be in that kind of environment, especially when Zoey has grown up in her perfect socioeconomic, liberal bubble . . . those are kind of going to be shattered and she has to figure out who she is in the larger context of the world around her," she explained to Michael Rothman for *ABC News* (16 Aug. 2017).

Shahidi herself had been taking high school courses through New York City's Dwight School's online program—including several advanced placement and honors courses in a variety of subjects—and had attended the school's prom with Blanchard. She celebrated her graduation in June 2017; academics and reading have always been deeply important to her. After being accepted to every college she applied to, she ultimately committed to attending Harvard University, though she elected to defer her enrollment for at least one year to allow her to get settled into the production of the first episodes of *Grown-ish*. When she arrives in Cambridge, Massachusetts, one of her classmates will be Obama's daughter Malia; former first lady Michelle Obama, a Harvard Law School graduate whom Shahidi had worked with on the Let Girls Learn education initiative, wrote one of Shahidi's college recommendation letters. Her plan is to double major in social studies (a combination of sociology, anthropology, philosophy, and economics) and African American studies. She will also continue to pursue activist causes, a devotion that is in large part derived from her own identity as a biracial young woman. "By being on a show called *Black-ish*, race became an unavoidable conversation," she said in the interview for *Teen Vogue*. "It gave me this platform to address these topics, and that opened the doors to develop my voice in an intentional way."

PERSONAL LIFE

Shahidi lives in Los Angeles and enjoys cooking and going to the beach when she is not working.

SUGGESTED READING

Ebert, Roger. Review of *Imagine That*, directed by Karey Kirkpatrick. *RogerEbert.com*, 10 June 2009, www.rogerebert.com/reviews/imagine-that-2009. Accessed 15 Nov. 2017.

Nussbaum, Emily. "In Living Color." *The New Yorker*, 25 Apr. 2016, www.newyorker.com/magazine/2016/04/25/blackish-transforms-the-family-sitcom. Accessed 15 Nov. 2017.

Seligson, Hannah. "*Black-ish* Star Yara Shahidi Is a Role Model Off-Screen." *The New York Times*, 27 Nov. 2015, www.nytimes.com/2015/11/29/fashion/black-ish-star-yara-shahidi-is-a-role-model-off-screen.html. Accessed 15 Nov. 2017.

Shahidi, Yara. "For Yara Shahidi, Style Is a Family Affair." Interview by Andi Teran. *Glamour*, 5 Apr. 2017, www.glamour.com/story/yara-shahidi-style-family. Accessed 15 Nov. 2017.

Shahidi, Yara, and Rowan Blanchard. "Introducing Our December Cover Stars: Yara Shahidi and Rowan Blanchard, Feminist Teen Icons and BFFs." *Teen Vogue*, 11 Nov. 2016, www.

teenvogue.com/story/rowan-blanchard-yara-shahidi-cover-interview-december-issue-representation-activism. Accessed 15 Nov. 2017.

Studeman, Kristin Tice. "Sixteen-Year-Old Actress and Activist Yara Shahidi Is Normal-*ish*." *W*, 22 Nov. 2016, www.wmagazine.com/story/yara-shahidi-16-year-old-actress-and-activist. Accessed 15 Nov. 2017.

SELECTED WORKS

Imagine That, 2009; *Butter*, 2011; *The First Family*, 2012–13; *Black-ish*, 2014–

—Molly Hagan

Amy Sherald

Date of birth: August 30, 1973
Occupation: Painter

In October 2017, the Smithsonian Institution's National Portrait Gallery in Washington, DC, announced that it had commissioned Baltimore-based artist Amy Sherald to paint the official portrait of former First Lady Michelle Obama. The resulting portrait, along with artist Kehinde Wiley's portrait of President Barack Obama, was unveiled on February 12, 2018, to great critical acclaim. "The artists, chosen by the Obamas, have combined traditional representation with elements that underscore the complexity of their subjects, and the historic fact of their political rise," Philip Kennicott wrote of both portraits for the *Washington Post* (12 Feb. 2018). "And both painters have managed to create compelling likenesses without sacrificing key aspects of their signature styles. The Obamas took a significant chance on both artists and were rewarded with powerful images that will shake up the expectations and assumptions of visitors to the traditionally button-down presidential galleries."

Sherald has traveled a long and difficult road to success. After earning her master of fine arts degree and studying with two famous painters, she was diagnosed with congestive heart failure in 2004, just before she had to quit painting entirely for three years to care for ailing family members in Georgia. She returned to Baltimore, and to painting, in 2007, developing her style as an artist while supporting herself by waiting tables. Five years later, she passed out in a pharmacy, signaling a lack of heart function that qualified her for a transplant. She received her new heart in late 2012 but did not regain enough energy to paint for another year. Her personal tragedies and triumphs changed her both as a person, prompting her to volunteer for a youth center and a prison arts program, and as an artist.

In 2016, Sherald won the Outwin Boochever Portrait Competition at the National Portrait Gallery and enjoyed her first solo exhibit at the Monique Meloche Gallery in Chicago. In 2017, she joined the faculty of her alma mater, the Maryland Institute College of Art (MICA). Her paintings are in collections across the country, including the National Museum of Women in the Arts and the National Museum of African American History and Culture.

EARLY LIFE

Sherald was born in Columbus, Georgia, on August 30, 1973. Her parents, a dentist and a stay-at-home mother, hoped their daughter would grow up to be a doctor, but Sherald's true calling presented itself early; as a child, she would draw pictures at the end of her sentences at school. She recalls one particularly transformative moment: on a sixth-grade field trip to an art museum, Sherald saw a painting called *Object Permanence* (1986) by artist Bo Bartlett, in which Bartlett, who is white, painted himself as a black man. "I've forgotten a lot of things," Sherald said to Mary Carole McCauley for the *Baltimore Sun* (19 Dec. 2016). "I've forgotten how to play the piano and how to speak Arabic, though I studied it for two years. But I'll never forget how much it meant to me to see myself in that museum."

Despite her love of art—the naturally shy Sherald told Marlisa Sanders for the *International Review of African American Art* (1 May 2013) that "art class was [her] safe haven" in high school—Sherald enrolled at Clark Atlanta University, a historically black university, as a premedical student. One day, she stopped to talk to a man who was selling his artwork outside the campus library. She told him she liked art herself and, at his request, brought him one of her paintings from high school the next day. The man gave her a warning, she told Sanders: "If you don't use your talent, you'll lose your talent." Though Sherald was already in her third year of college at the time, she chose to heed his advice and switched her major to painting.

ART EDUCATION

As an art student, Sherald began working with artist and art historian Arturo Lindsay at nearby Spelman College. She graduated from Clark Atlanta in 1997 but continued to work as Lindsay's apprentice for several years after. "I begged to work for him for free," she recalled to Joan Cox for *BmoreArt* magazine (29 Nov. 2012). In exchange, in addition to helping Sherald continue to develop her skills as a painter, Lindsay introduced her to the inner workings of the art world. She traveled with him to shows and even oversaw the installation of one show at the Museum of Contemporary Art Panama on her own. "He showed me what it really meant to be an artist, what the world was like for an artist inside of a working system," she said to Cox.

In 2000, not long after her apprenticeship ended, Sherald's father died of Parkinson's disease. She moved to Baltimore on a whim and enrolled as a graduate student at MICA, where she studied with the late Grace Hartigan, an abstract expressionist painter. Looking back, Sherald told Cox, she was not quite ready for graduate school; her most formative art training happened just after she graduated, in 2004. In her final year at MICA, Sherald met Norwegian painter Odd Nerdrum and, exhibiting the drive with which she had pursued her apprenticeship with Lindsay, introduced herself to the artist before he delivered a planned lecture at the school. "He asked me what I was going to do after grad school," she recalled to Cox. "And I was like, 'I'm coming to Norway to study with you!' and then I ended up giving him a ride to the train station that night."

Nerdrum agreed to take Sherald on as an apprentice, and she won a $3,000 grant to travel to Norway. Nerdrum's paintings are strange and sometimes horrifying or grotesque; his style is strongly reminiscent of seventeenth-century painters such as Rembrandt and Caravaggio, and his figures are rendered in deep reds and browns. But Sherald was drawn to something else in his work. "It's his sense of the timelessness," she said to Cox. "I was attracted to that sense of timelessness and spirit in his work. His work looks like he could've painted it five hundred years ago or painted it yesterday. You can't really place it in time."

Years later, Sherald's paintings are also described as timeless. She works from contemporary models but clothes her subjects in outfits that give them a sense of temporal ambiguity. Speaking to Robin Pogrebin for the *New York Times* (23 Oct. 2017), she attributed this timelessness to her subjects more than to her own style, noting that she is extremely selective about whom she chooses to paint and that "there has got to be something about them that only [she] can see." Elaborating on those subjects who catch her eye, Sherald added, "They exist in a place of the past, the present and the future. It's like something I sense with my spirit more than my mind."

A DIFFICULT ROAD

Sherald spent only a few months in Norway, and when she returned to Baltimore, she decided to begin training for a triathlon. Having long had a recurring dream about running a marathon and dying at the end, she went to the doctor for a check-up first, and was shocked to learn that she had congestive heart failure. "I would have been one of those athletes whose heart just stops and no one knows why," she said to Gabriella Souza

for *Baltimore* magazine (17 Oct. 2016). "I didn't have any symptoms, but my heart functioning was down to 18 percent."

Around the same time, Sherald was called home to Georgia to help her mother care for ailing relatives. For the next three years, she did not paint at all, though she did gain something from the experience. "I got to know my brother as a person," she said to McCauley. "We had great conversations about life and religion and philosophy." Their time together took on a new significance to Sherald when her brother was diagnosed with lung cancer and died several years later.

Sherald returned to Baltimore in 2007 but struggled to find artistic inspiration. "That year was the world year of my life because my self-esteem was shot," she said to Cox. She would spend eight-hour days in the studio but could not figure out what she wanted to paint. Then a moment of inspiration came from an unexpected source. Sherald had been grappling, again, with issues of racial history and identity that had been stirred up by her time in Georgia, and she considered doing a series of paintings about lynching—she even completed one such work, *Hangman* (2007), which she described to Cox as a "reverse lynching" painting—but she felt she should try to establish a theme that she would still want to engage with years later, and it was not in her nature to dwell on the negative. "I'm an escapist," she said to Cox. "I love the Teletubbies—the idea of grass with no bugs make[s] me happy, you know, I like feeling like I have the ability to dream and fantasize." She decided to take a break one night and watch a movie she had already seen, Tim Burton's magical realist tale *Big Fish* (2003). Suddenly, everything fell into place. "I just had this light bulb moment watching it!" she recalled. "And I thought, this is what I want. . . . I want the freedom to have this kind of experience inside of myself."

COMING INTO HER OWN

After her "light bulb moment," Sherald took off confidently in her chosen artistic direction, incorporating a sense of magic realism and elements of whimsy into her work. Her early paintings from this period include *The Rabbit in the Hat* (2009), which shows a man pulling a rabbit from a hat, and *Maybe If I Wore a Mask* (2009), featuring a woman wearing an unlaced corset, puffy skirt, and white tiger mask. Later works are less overtly circus-like. One of Sherald's most popular pieces, *High Yella Masterpiece: We Ain't No Cotton Pickin' Negroes* (2011), features two men in white suits holding cones of pink cotton candy.

Sherald's portraits feature ordinary people, typically people whom she sees on the street, all of them African American. "Having studied

European art history," Pogrebin wrote of her choice of subjects, "she is keenly aware of the scarcity of black faces. 'There's not enough images of us,' she said." She often portrays her subjects in colorful clothes that contrast with the neutral grays in which she renders their skin tones—a stylistic choice intended "to exclude the idea of color as race from [her] paintings by removing 'color,'" according to her artist statement. "The gray skin tone works for a number of reasons," Sherald explained to Cox. "It works because of all the other colors I am using and then it works because it helped me play with that idea of taking away color and what it meant."

While coming into her own as an artist, Sherald was experiencing worsening health problems; she lost weight, and she began to have difficulty breathing. Doctors told her that her heart was functioning at 5 percent capacity and scheduled an appointment for a transplant consultation. In October 2012, the day before the consultation (and shortly after Cox conducted her interview for *BmoreArt*), she passed out in a pharmacy while picking up a prescription and was taken to the hospital. She later told Souza that the reality of her situation began to hit her while she was in the ambulance. "I felt like I could die then," she said. "I actually felt that for the first time, and it did scare me. I thought, 'I can't be afraid to die,' so I just made peace with it at that moment. I said, 'I'm not going to be afraid, it's all going to be okay.'"

Sherald spent two months in the hospital waiting for a heart transplant; she received one just eleven days after her brother's death from lung cancer. Recovery set her back another year. She struggled with depression and anxiety and adopted a Pekingese–Jack Russell terrier mix, whom she named August Wilson. When she eventually returned to the canvas, one of the first paintings she completed was a portrait of a young woman in a navy dress, wearing a bright red fascinator and holding a large teacup. That painting, *Miss Everything (Unsuppressed Deliverance)*, would later win the 2016 Outwin Boochever Portrait Competition at the National Portrait Gallery, earning her a $25,000 award and effectively launching her national career.

PAINTING THE FIRST LADY

Sherald's Outwin Boochever win, which attracted the attention of museums and art critics nationwide, also landed her on the radar of First Lady Michelle Obama, who, in the last year of her husband's second presidential term, was in the process of selecting the artist who would paint her official portrait for the National Portrait Gallery. The selection process begins with the gallery providing the president and First Lady with portfolios of potential artists. When gallery curators first began compiling the list for the Obamas, they were unaware of Sherald's work; following the portrait competition, which took place in October 2016, her name was added to the list "at the very last minute," museum director Kim Sajet said to Roberta Smith for the *New York Times* (16 Oct. 2017).

The selection of Sherald and Wiley was announced in October 2017; their completed portraits were unveiled in February 2018. "It's easy to forget the historical importance of Monday's unveiling," Kennicott wrote of the event. "Intellectually, we all know that the White House was a white man's exclusive preserve until 2008. But a stroll through the National Portrait Gallery emphasizes that fact in a visual and emotional way that recalls not just the racism built into this country's founding document, but the racism that has shaped the history of art and portraiture since the Renaissance."

Sherald's painting shows Michelle Obama seated against a light blue background—one that conveys a sense of "calm, clarity and Wedgwood-hued enlightenment," according to Kennicott—wearing a capacious full-length dress created by designer Michelle Smith. The dress, which features bold red, pink, yellow, gray, and black geometric shapes against a white background, was originally part of Smith's spring 2017 Milly collection, which, she told Robin Givhan for the *Washington Post* (12 Feb. 2018), was intended to represent the "desire for equality, equality in human rights, racial equality, LGBTQ equality," as well as the "feeling of being held back . . . that we're not quite there yet."

SUGGESTED READING

Kennicott, Philip. "The Obamas' Portraits Are Not What You'd Expect, and That's Why They're Great." *The Washington Post*, 12 Feb. 2018, www.washingtonpost.com/entertainment/museums/obamas-portraits-unveiled-for-americans-presidents-exhibition/2018/02/12/d9f3691a-1000-11e8-8ea1-c1d91fcec3fe_story.html. Accessed 15 Feb. 2018.

McCauley, Mary Carole. "Equipped with New Heart, Baltimore's Amy Sherald Gains Fame with Surreal Portraiture." *The Baltimore Sun*, 19 Dec. 2016, www.baltimoresun.com/entertainment/arts/bs-ae-amy-sherald-20161216-story.html. Accessed 6 Feb. 2018.

Pogrebin, Robin. "After a Late Start, an Artist's Big Break: Michelle Obama's Official Portrait." *The New York Times*, 23 Oct. 2017, www.nytimes.com/2017/10/23/arts/design/amy-sherald-michelle-obama-official-portrait.html. Accessed 6 Feb. 2018.

Sanders, Marlisa. "Amy Sherald, a Second Life." *IRAAA+: The International Review of African American Art Plus*, 1 May 2013, iraaa.museum.hamptonu.edu/page/

Amy-Sherald%2C-A-Second-Life--. Accessed 6 Feb. 2018.

Sherald, Amy. "Amy Sherald, in Depth." Interview by Joan Cox. *BmoreArt*, 29 Nov. 2012, www.bmoreart.com/2012/11/amy-sherald-in-depth-by-joan-cox.html. Accessed 6 Feb. 2018.

Smith, Roberta. "Why the Obamas' Portrait Choices Matter." *The New York Times*, 16 Oct. 2017, www.nytimes.com/2017/10/16/arts/design/obamas-presidential-portraits.html. Accessed 15 Feb. 2018.

Souza, Gabriella. "A Wonderful Dream." *Baltimore*, 17 Oct. 2016, www.baltimoremagazine.com/2016/10/17/a-wonderful-dream-baltimore-artist-amy-sherald-finds-success. Accessed 15 Feb. 2018.

SELECTED WORKS

Hangman, 2007; *The Rabbit in the Hat*, 2009; *Maybe If I Wore a Mask*, 2009; *High Yella Masterpiece: We Ain't No Cotton Pickin' Negroes*, 2011; *Wellfare Queen*, 2012; *Miss Everything (Unsuppressed Deliverance)*, 2014; *Freeing Herself Was One Thing, Taking Ownership of That Freed Self Was Another*, 2015; *The Make Believer (Monet's Garden)*, 2016; *Listen, You a Wonder. You a City of a Woman. You Got a Geography of Your Own*, 2017; *Michelle LaVaughn Robinson Obama*, 2018

—Molly Hagan

Tye Sheridan

Date of birth: November 11, 1996
Occupation: Actor

Tye Sheridan is an actor best known for his starring role in the Steven Spielberg action film *Ready Player One* (2018). Sheridan was born and raised in a small town in East Texas. He dreamed of becoming a baseball player before he was discovered by noted auteur Terrence Malick when he was just ten years old. Sheridan made his acting debut in Malick's celebrated 2011 film *Tree of Life*. Several years and countless auditions later, Sheridan landed a role in the Jeff Nichols film *Mud* (2012) opposite Matthew McConaughey and has been steadily employed ever since.

In 2016, Sheridan joined the blockbuster X-Men franchise as a young Cyclops in *X-Men: Apocalypse*, but his star turn in *Ready Player One* is considered his true breakout role. Based on the 2011 Ernest Cline novel of the same name, the film is set in the year 2045 and involves a virtual reality video game. "I was completely obsessed with VR before I even heard about *Ready*

By Gage Skidmore via Wikimedia Commons

Player One, or even knew that Steven was doing a film," Sheridan told Dana Goodyear for *W Magazine* (19 Apr. 2018). "So when the script came around and I had the opportunity to audition for it, I was like, 'Hoooly sh—t. This is going to be huge!'" Working on the film, Sheridan met a young Serbian visual-effects designer named Nikola Todorovic. The two have since launched a VR production company called Aether. In the film, Sheridan plays Wade Watts, who escapes his impoverished and abusive household through a virtual reality simulator called the OASIS. The OASIS was created by a reclusive billionaire named James Halliday, played by Mark Rylance. Before he died, Halliday created a three-part quest through the OASIS, each part informed by his love of 1980s culture. The player that unlocks the final "Easter egg" wins control of the OASIS and Halliday's fortune. Sheridan's character Watts is determined to complete the quest at any cost.

EARLY LIFE AND FIRST AUDITION

Sheridan was born in Elkhart, a tiny town in East Texas, on November 11, 1996. His family has lived in East Texas since the early 1800s. Sheridan grew up in a trailer on an eighty-acre piece of land that his parents shared with his grandparents. "I had such a pure upbringing—my childhood was a really happy time," he told Rebecca Haithcoat for *GQ* magazine (28 Mar. 2018). His mother owns a beauty shop, and his father worked as a UPS driver. Sheridan, who has a younger sister named Maddie, recalls that his father would always toss a baseball with him when he got home from work. He dreamed of becoming a baseball player, but when he was in the fourth grade, he received a letter from the independent filmmaker, Terrence Malick, inviting him to audition for a film. Talent scouts had traveled through Texas visiting public schools, and Sheridan, just ten years old at the time, caught their eye. At his first audition, with A. J. Edwards, Malick's second-unit director, Edwards gave Sheridan a tennis ball to bounce against the wall as a distraction. Edwards saw something special in Sheridan. "He was a little ten-year-old James Dean," Edwards recalled to Goodyear. Sheridan went on to be invited to a number of callbacks.

TREE OF LIFE

Sheridan won a role in Malick's surreal and meditative *Tree of Life* (2011) over 10,000 other young actors. He played Steve O'Brien, the brother of protagonist Jack O'Brien. His parents are played by actors Jessica Chastain and Brad Pitt. The film, set in 1950s Waco, Texas, and based on Malick's own life, explores the nature of existence, intercutting the story of one man's coming-of-age and the story of the birth and death of the universe. The film received enthusiastic praise from critics and won the prestigious Palme d'Or when it premiered at the Cannes Film Festival. It was nominated for three Academy Awards, including best picture. In his review for the *New York Times* (26 May 2011), A. O. Scott compared Malick's achievement to the work of *Moby Dick* novelist Herman Melville or poet Walt Whitman, writing that the "movie stands stubbornly alone, and yet in part by virtue of its defiant peculiarity it shows a clear kinship with other eccentric, permanent works of the American imagination." Sheridan recalls the experience of working on the film as fluid. "What I retained from that experience is, it's good to rehearse and work things through, but when you overwork something and you dig yourself so deep and invest yourself in one style, it's hard to dig yourself out," he told Zack Sharf for *IndieWire* (29 Mar. 2018).

MUD

After shooting *Tree of Life*, Sheridan returned to Elkhart. He continued to play ball, but also worked to secure another acting job. For the next three years, he sent out scores of audition tapes but faced variations of the same criticism: his Southern accent was too strong. Then Sheridan auditioned for and won a role in the Jeff Nichols film *Mud* (2012). Sheridan starred alongside Academy Award winners Matthew McConaughey and Reese Witherspoon in that film, playing an Arkansas teenager who befriends a fugitive named Mud (McConaughey). Nichols was more than pleased with Sheridan's

performance. He told Aaron Hillis for *Variety* (13 Sept. 2012), "He's the best of both worlds. He came out of the invaluable Terrence Malick boot camp, where he was put in situations and told to play and be himself in front of a camera. That came naturally to him, but my style of filmmaking is heavily scripted. There was some question about how he's going to take on this dialogue, and I was shocked to see he could do both marvelously."

The critical success of *Mud* helped accelerate Sheridan's career. He moved in with his aunt, uncle, and cousins in Austin, Texas. He landed a role in a film called *Joe*, alongside Nicolas Cage, in 2013. In that film, Sheridan plays a young teenager working on a lumber crew with an abusive father. Next came a role in the thriller *The Forger* (2014), about an art forger, starring John Travolta and Christopher Plummer. The same year, Sheridan appeared in a handful of episodes of the CBS comedy series *Last Man Standing* with comedian Tim Allen. In 2015, Sheridan appeared in a film called *Entertainment*, a drama about a stand-up comedian; *Last Days of the Desert*, starring Ewan McGregor as Jesus; and the award-winning *Stanford Prison Experiment*, based on a real 1971 psychological experiment about the ways that having power affects people. He also appeared in the drama *Dark Places*, starring Charlize Theron, and starred in the comedy horror *Scouts Guide to the Zombie Apocalypse*. In 2016, he starred in a noir thriller called *Detour*, about a law student who blames his stepfather for an accident that left his mother comatose.

X-MEN: APOCALYPSE

That same year, Sheridan appeared in *X-Men: Apocalypse*. Alongside such actors as Oscar Isaac, Jennifer Lawrence, and Michael Fassbender, Sheridan played a young Cyclops. According to director Bryan Singer, Sheridan took the role very seriously, even when he felt silly doing so. In the film, Cyclops shoots laser beams out of his eyes. The beams, of course, are edited in later in computer-generated imagery (CGI), so Sheridan had relatively little to do in action scenes. "Everyone else's moves are kinda cool, and I just take off my glasses and stare at someone really intensely and growl," he told Tim Stack for *Entertainment Weekly* (27 Apr. 2016). The film itself, the ninth in the franchise, received middling reviews. "For every lively moment, there's a reminder that the franchise is tiring," Glenn Kenny wrote for the *New York Times* (26 May 2016). The movie fared much better with audiences, however, becoming one of the top-grossing X-Men movies, raking in $543.9 million worldwide.

READY PLAYER ONE

In 2018, Sheridan starred in the Spielberg-helmed *Ready Player One*, based on the book of the same name. Of working on the movie, Sheridan told Christina Radish for *Collider* (2 Apr. 2018), "I grew a lot, as an actor and as a person, and I grew a lot with my knowledge of filmmaking, in general." He was particularly in awe of Spielberg, whom he described to Good-year as "the greatest film nerd of all time." The film is an adventure story that explores identity and the perils of the Internet. (Each character creates their own avatar in the OASIS. Watts's avatar Parzival is named for Percival, the Arthurian knight who sought the Holy Grail.) The film's main theme—which Sheridan described to Radish as "How do you balance your digital self, or your virtual profile or image, and your real world self?"—resonated with Sheridan. "I have a seventeen-year-old sister, so I'm very sensitive to this stuff because she has social media," Sheridan told Radish. "People can get very sucked into a digital world and how people perceive them, on their social media, versus how they perceive them, in real life." *Ready Player One* received positive, if not enthusiastic, reviews. Most noted that it was an improvement over the dense and overly nostalgic book.

After *Ready Player One*, Sheridan starred in a crime drama called *Friday's Child*, written and directed by A. J. Edwards, the same second-unit director who years ago described him as a young James Dean when he auditioned for *Tree of Life*. In June 2017, it was announced that Sheridan would be reprising the role of Cyclops in the film *X-Men: Dark Phoenix* (2019).

SUGGESTED READING

Goodyear, Dana. "*Ready Player One*'s Tye Sheridan Is Hollywood's Most Talented Chameleon." *W Magazine*, 19 Apr. 2018, www.wmagazine.com/story/tye-sheridan-ready-player-one-w-magazine-cover-story. Accessed 8 Sept. 2018.

Haithcoat, Rebecca. "*Ready Player One*'s Tye Sheridan Is from Another World." *GQ*, 28 Mar. 2018, www.gq.com/story/ready-player-one-tye-sheridan-profile. Accessed 8 Sept. 2018.

Hillis, Aaron. "Tye Sheridan: 'Tree' Star Impresses in 'Mud.'" *Variety*, 13 Sept. 2012, variety.com/2012/film/news/tye-sheridan-tree-star-impresses-in-mud-1118058879/. Accessed 8 Sept. 2018.

Kenny, Glenn. "Review: 'X-Men: Apocalypse,' a Sequel 5,000 Years in the Making." Review of *X-Men: Apocalypse*, directed by Bryan Singer. *The New York Times*, 26 May 2016, www.nytimes.com/2016/05/27/movies/x-men-apocalypse-review.html. Accessed 9 Sept. 2018.

Scott, A. O. "Heaven, Texas and the Cosmic Whodunit." Review of *The Tree of Life*, directed by Terrence Malick. *The New York Times*, 26 May 2011, www.nytimes.com/2011/05/27/movies/the-tree-of-life-from-terrence-malick-review.html. Accessed 8 Sept. 2018.

Sharf, Zack. "Tye Sheridan Looks Back on 'The Tree of Life' and What He Learned from Terrence Malick at 11 Years Old." *IndieWire*, 29 Mar. 2018, www.indiewire.com/2018/03/tye-sheridan-lessons-terrence-malick-tree-of-life-1201944989/. Accessed 8 Sept. 2018.

Sheridan, Tye. "Tye Sheridan on 'Ready Player One' and Looking Ahead to 'X-Men: Dark Phoenix.'" Interview by Christina Radish. *Collider*, 2 Apr. 2018, collider.com/ready-player-one-tye-sheridan-interview-x-men-dark-phoenix/. Accessed 9 Sept. 2018.

SELECTED WORKS

Tree of Life, 2011; *Mud*, 2012; *X-Men: Apocalypse*, 2016; *Ready Player One*, 2018

—*Molly Hagan*

Suzanne Simard

Date of birth: ca. 1961
Occupation: Ecologist

Few PhD students discover something during the course of their research that will radically alter humanity's scientific understanding of living systems. Fewer still have their doctoral dissertations published in an esteemed scholarly journal because of that discovery. Yet that is exactly what happened to Suzanne Simard, now a professor of forest ecology and silvics at the University of British Columbia (UBC), in 1997, when *Nature* published part of her dissertation on how certain tree species communicate with one another and share nutrients and water via a belowground fungal network.

Simard's radical discovery has helped researchers better understand the interconnectivity of ecosystems and the symbiotic nature of plants. "A forest is a cooperative system, and if it were all about competition, then it would be a much simpler place," she explained to Diane Toomey for *Yale Environment 360* (1 Sept. 2016). "Why would a forest be so diverse? Why would it be so dynamic? To me, using the language of communication made more sense because we were looking at not just resource transfers, but things like defense signaling and kin recognition signaling. We as human beings can relate to this better. If we can relate to it, then we're going to care about it more. If we care about it more, then we're going to do a better job of stewarding our landscapes."

Her work also has applications regarding how forests and other natural habitats, such as grasslands, need to be protected and maintained. In 2016, Simard was awarded a C$929,000 Strategic Partnership Grant by the Natural Sciences and Engineering Research Council of Canada (NSERC) to investigate and reassess forest renewal practices in the context of climate change.

EARLY LIFE

Simard's family originally hailed from Quebec before moving to the inland rainforest of British Columbia, where Simard and her siblings, sister Robyn and brother Kelly, grew up. Her father's family had long relied on the forests to make their living, a preoccupation that deeply influenced her upbringing. "My grandfather and my uncles all horse logged," she recalled to Anne Strainchamps for the radio show *To the Best of Our Knowledge* (28 Apr. 2018), referring to a type of forestry management that employs horses to pull felled trees to a collection area for use by humans. "Every summer we would spend in the cedar hemlock forests that were so rich and diverse and huge playgrounds for kids that just became part of me. I think I was always wired for forests and wired for Earth, so it's just a natural calling." Forestry was in the family on her mother's side as well; her great-uncle Joseph Gardner was the dean of UBC's Faculty of Forestry from 1965 to 1983—a period that would overlap with Simard's undergraduate studies there, though the two kept their relationship confidential at the time.

In an essay for Marc Guttman's anthology *We Discover* (2016), excerpted in the UBC Faculty of Forestry's newsletter *Branchlines* (Spring 2016), Simard recounted a formative incident in her childhood, in which the family dog fell into the outhouse and had to be dug out. "I become entranced as the men dig down through the layers, starting with the dark forest floor, then the white then red then yellow mineral soil horizons underneath. The men curse. The fine roots have formed an impenetrable mat and the coarse ones are jutting at awkward angles deep in the soil," she wrote. "The interwoven pallet of roots and soil also serve to anchor and connect the colorful mix of birch, hemlock and cedar trees. . . . Thus began my serendipitous journey of discovery about the unseen world of the forest."

EDUCATION AND EARLY CAREER

After earning her bachelor of science in forestry (BSF) degree from UBC in 1983, Simard began working as a silviculturist for a logging company in the Lillooet Ranges on British Columbia's west coast. "When I started studying forestry and working in the forest industry, I noticed that we were managing forests as though they were just a bunch of trees," she recalled in an interview for the quarterly newsletter *Leaf Litter* (Winter 2016). "I always say that the whole is greater than the sum of its parts, yet we manage the forest as though it is just a bunch of parts. I was doing basic silviculture back then, trying to figure out how to get trees to grow better, and trying to understand why a managed forest looked so different from an old growth forest." She credited an early supervisor of hers, forester Alan Vyse at the BC Ministry of Forests, with encouraging her to conduct forest research. "That," she said, "ultimately led me to ask the question, 'What is going on below ground?'"

To answer that question, Simard pursued graduate studies at Oregon State University, earning first her master of science degree in 1989 and then her doctorate in 1995. During her doctoral studies, she belonged to the Cosmo Eco Society, a group that would meet over drinks to debate the larger meaning of ecosystems and of science in general. These freewheeling conversations allowed her to step out of the confines of the scientific method and try to understand things that were occurring in ecosystems on a more instinctive level.

Upon completing her PhD, Simard continued her work as a research scientist for the BC Ministry of Forests until 2002, when she joined UBC's Department of Forest Sciences (now the Department of Forest and Conservation Sciences) as an associate professor. Now a full professor, in addition to teaching, she conducts research projects on a wide variety of topics, including forest ecology, complex adaptive systems, and ecological resilience to global climate change.

DISCOVERING UNDERGROUND COMMUNICATION NETWORKS

Simard's success in the field of forest ecology came early. In 1997 the esteemed journal *Nature* agreed to publish part of her PhD dissertation, which looked at underground carbon exchanges in mixed-species forests. "For my doctoral research, I wanted to understand why the planted monocultures were less resilient and productive than the mixed primary forests," she wrote in her essay for *We Discover*. To that end, she and her colleagues used radioisotope markers to determine if Douglas fir and paper birch trees were, as she suspected, exchanging carbon via belowground fungi lattices.

The experiment demonstrated that the tree systems had a symbiotic relationship with the fungi in the soil. "Trees are connected below ground by these mutualistic fungi called mycorrhizal fungi," she explained to Strainchamps. "You can think of them as extensions of the root system. The plant or the tree depends on that fungus to go out and explore the soil and the fungus goes and explores and grows into all these little teeny tiny niches or accesses nutrients that are unavailable to the tree." In exchange, the fungus benefits by absorbing photosynthesis products from the tree, as it is unable to produce its own.

Perhaps what is most remarkable about Simard's discovery is that this network not only connects fungi to a tree system, but also different types of trees to one another—in this case, Douglas firs and paper birches—for the trees' mutual benefit. "It really turns upside down how we've traditionally thought [about] and managed forests," she said to Strainchamps. "And we still manage them to this very day on this competition model, that there are individuals competing for resources. But what I've found is that they're all connected together and that they're sharing these resources. It doesn't mean competition is not going on as well, but there's a multiplicity of interactions."

The scientific results have been popularized to a three-word sentence: Trees can talk. And while they do not talk as people do, Simard likens the underground network to a neural network in the human brain, with similar patterning. This is particularly noticeable between what she and her fellow researchers call the "hub tree" or the "mother tree"—the largest, oldest, and most connected tree in the area—and the younger trees surrounding it.

Further research conducted by Simard and the graduate students under her supervision has found that mother trees demonstrate a preference for trees that are genetically related to them—a phenomenon already observed among animals known as "kin recognition." "We've done some experiments to show that these mother trees will actually send more carbon to genetically related individuals than strangers," she said to Strainchamps. "So that means that the mother tree is nurturing her young to pass on her genes to future generations." In addition, a mother tree that is about to die will pass its remaining resources directly to those genetically related trees. These discoveries have wider implications: just as research has found that human beings with good social networks tend to have longer and healthier lives, so, too, do trees with strong connections in diverse local communities.

FOREST RESILIENCE FOR THE FUTURE

Simard believes that a better understanding of the interconnectivity of forest systems will play an important part in mitigating the effects of climate change on these systems. "There's a lot that can be done to facilitate [the resilience of forests] because of these mycorrhizal networks, which we know are important in allowing trees to regenerate. It's what we leave behind that's so

important," she explained to Toomey. "If we leave trees that support not just mycorrhizal networks, but other networks of creatures, then the forest will regenerate. I think that's the crucial step is maintaining that ability to regenerate trees."

She also believes that forest maintenance needs to now take into account the importance of mother trees in supporting the health of the tree systems around them, as well as the larger animal networks. One of her ongoing research projects is the Mother Tree Project, an investigation of the role of mother trees in at least two dozen forests throughout British Columbia. "How do you conserve mother trees in logging, and use them to create resilient forests in an era of rapid climate change?" Simard said to Richard Grant for *Smithsonian* magazine (Mar. 2018), speaking of the project's goals. "Should we assist the migration of the forest by spreading seeds? Should we combine genotypes to make the seedlings less vulnerable to frost and predation in new regions? . . . This is a way of giving back what forests have given to me, which is a spirit, a wholeness, a reason to be."

PERSONAL LIFE

Simard married Donald L. Sachs, a forest research consultant and her occasional coauthor, in 1990. They have two daughters, Hannah and Nava.

A breast cancer survivor, Simard told Strainchamps of her experience with the disease, "The thing that really got me through was my connections, the friends I made. It was this incredible magical network where you could just feel the love going from person to person and we're all doing great. For me it was like I was living the very thing I was seeing in the forests. . . . I know I'm going to be okay, just like that tree is going to be okay as long as it stays within its community."

SUGGESTED READING

Grant, Richard. "Do Trees Talk to Each Other?" *Smithsonian*, Mar. 2018, www.smithsonianmag.com/science-nature/the-whispering-trees-180968084. Accessed 19 July 2018.

McNeely, Marie, host. "Dr. Suzanne Simard: Getting to the Root of Underground Signaling in Forest Ecosystems." *People Behind the Science*, episode 210, 23 Jan. 2015, www.people-behindthescience.com/dr-suzanne-simard. Accessed 19 July 2018.

Petersen, Allura. "Web of the Woods." *The Planet*, 16 Mar. 2017, theplanetmagazine.net/web-of-the-woods-350f64b7f637. Accessed 19 July 2018.

Simard, Suzanne. "Expert Q&A: Suzanne Simard." *Leaf Litter*, vol. 14, no. 4, Winter 2016, www.biohabitats.com/newsletter/fungi/expert-qa-suzanne-simard. Accessed 12 July 2018.

Simard, Suzanne. "Exploring How and Why Trees 'Talk' to Each Other." Interview by Diane Toomey. *Yale Environment 360*, Yale School of Forestry & Environmental Studies, 1 Sept. 2016, e360.yale.edu/features/exploring_how_and_why_trees_talk_to_each_other. Accessed 12 July 2018.

Simard, Suzanne. "Listening to the Mother Trees." Interview by Anne Strainchamps, article by Shannon Henry Kleiber. *To the Best of Our Knowledge*, Wisconsin Public Radio / PRX, 28 Apr. 2018, www.ttbook.org/interview/listening-mother-trees. Accessed 12 July 2018.

Simard, Suzanne. "Unseen Connections." *Branchlines*, vol. 27, no. 1, Spring 2016, pp. 18–19, forestry.sites.olt.ubc.ca/files/2011/11/bl-72.11.pdf#page=18. Accessed 19 July 2018.

—*Christopher Mari*

Christian Slater

Date of birth: August 18, 1969
Occupation: Actor

Christian Slater is a Golden Globe Award–winning American actor known for his roles in *Heathers* and *Mr. Robot.*

EARLY LIFE AND EDUCATION

Christian Slater was born on August 18, 1969, in New York City. He was born into a performing arts family, the only son of actor Thomas Knight Slater (also known as Michael Hawkins) and casting director Mary Jo Slater. Slater was raised in New York's Upper West Side neighborhood. Interested in acting from an early age, Slater asked his father to bring him along on acting jobs so he could watch his father perform in New York theaters.

Slater's first acting appearance was in a Pampers commercial as a young child. When Slater was eight years old he landed his first television role, a brief appearance on the long-running daytime soap opera *One Life to Live.* At age nine, he joined the company of a traveling production of *The Music Man*, starring Dick Van Dyke. Slater spent nine months traveling and performing with the production. It was around this time that Slater started drinking alcohol.

He later attended the Fiorello H. LaGuardia High School of Music and Art and Performing Arts in New York. At age sixteen, his family moved to Los Angeles.

HOLLYWOOD ACTOR

It was not long before Slater made his first appearances in films. He debuted in 1985's *The Legend of Billy Jean* and was cast opposite Sean Connery in *The Name of the Rose* in 1986. He starred as JD, the misanthropic high schooler who starts a suicide fad in the dark comedy *Heathers* (1988). *Heathers* became a cult hit and provided Slater with his breakout role. It also defined Slater's early career roles, many of which presented him as a cynical or rebellious youth. He reprised this persona in *Gleaming the Cube* (1989) and *Pump Up the Volume* (1990).

By the early 1990s, Slater was in high demand as an actor. In his initial major blockbuster films, he had supporting roles in *Robin Hood: Prince of Thieves* (1991) and *Interview with the Vampire* (1994). He starred as the lead in the cult hit *True Romance* (1993) and the drama *Untamed Heart* (1993). Slater appeared with John Travolta in the action film *Broken Arrow* in 1996 and directed his first feature, *Museum of Love*, the same year.

For much of his early career, Slater's alcohol and drug abuse, and the resulting behavior and legal trouble they caused, threatened his work as an actor. He already had a number of arrests when, in 1994, he was detained for trying to board an airplane with a handgun. His trouble came to a head in 1997 when he was arrested on suspicion of assault with a deadly weapon and battery after he fought with police officers at a Los Angeles party. He was sentenced to ninety days in jail and was later put on parole and required to go to rehab. Slater did not find steady work for several years after his stint in jail and only appeared in a handful of poorly received films.

In the early 2000s, Slater appeared in mostly minor films or in supporting roles while working on several television programs. His significant work in this period included a recurring role in *The West Wing* (2002) and the Academy Award–nominated film *The Good Shepherd* (2004).

In 2005, Slater was arrested again after an altercation in a New York deli in which he was charged with sexually abusing a stranger. The charges were later dropped. In 2006, Slater appeared in Emilio Estevez's acclaimed *Bobby*, a film about the assassination of Robert F. Kennedy. Slater briefly starred as the lead in *My Own Worst Enemy* (2008), a short-lived primetime television drama, and in *Breaking In* (2011), a television comedy series.

He was cast in *Mr. Robot* in 2015, a television drama series that became his first major success since his 1990s teen film era. Slater plays the titular character, who leads a group of anarchist computer hackers. For his performance, Slater won a 2015 Golden Globe Award for best supporting actor.

Slater made headlines in 2016 over his tumultuous relationship with his father. After an estrangement of nearly a decade, Slater's father sued Slater in a twenty-million-dollar defamation claim over Slater's public assessment of his father's mental health.

IMPACT

Slater was an iconic teen idol of the 1980s and 1990s, starring in many popular youth culture films. His off-screen life has been a source of tabloid fascination since his rise to fame. His 2015 Golden Globe win was his first major critical award of his career.

PERSONAL LIFE

Slater's half-brother, Ryan Slater, is also a Hollywood actor. Slater has been in highly publicized romantic relationships with fellow actors Winona Ryder and Samantha Mathis. He married journalist Ryan Haddon in 2000. Together they had two children: Jaden and Eliana. The couple divorced in 2006. Slater married Brittany Lopez in 2013. They live in New York City's Hell's Kitchen neighborhood with his son, Jaden.

SUGGESTED READING

"Christian Slater." *Bio.com*. A&E Television Networks, n.d. Web. 24 Apr. 2016.

Heawood, Sophie. "Christian Slater: 'When You're Drinking and Doing Drugs, You're Going to Be Lying.'" *Guardian*. Guardian News and Media, 9 Oct. 2015. Web. 24 Apr. 2016.

Jacobs, Andrew. "Christian Slater, Starring in an Unscheduled Courtroom Drama." *New York Times*. New York Times, 1 June 2005. Web. 24 Apr. 2016.

Murray, Noel. "Christian Slater on *Mr. Robot* and Why He's Returning to TV." *Rolling Stone*. Rolling Stone, 22 June 2015. Web. 5 May 2016.

Slater, Christian. "Christian Slater." Interview by Lars von Trier. *Interview*. Interview, 11 June 2015. Web. 24 Apr. 2016.

SELECTED WORKS

The Name of the Rose, 1986; *Heathers*, 1988; *Gleaming the Cube*, 1989; *Pump Up the Volume*, 1990; *Robin Hood: Prince of Thieves*, 1991; *Untamed Heart*, 1993; *True Romance*, 1993; *Interview with the Vampire*, 1994; *Broken Arrow*, 1996; *The West Wing*, 2002; *The Good Shepherd*, 2004; *Bobby*, 2006; *My Own Worst Enemy*, 2008; *Breaking In*, 2011–2012; *Mr. Robot*, 2015–

—*Richard Means*

Clint Smith

Date of birth: August 25, 1988
Occupation: Writer

Award-winning writer and educator Clint Smith strives to promote change by increasing people's understanding of those who are discriminated against. In his poems and essays, he has drawn extensively from his experience as an African American man to share intimate and revealing firsthand stories that confront such themes as racial identity, prejudice, family, love, and education. "The question I always ask myself," Smith noted to Tosin Oyekoya in an undated interview for *Blavity*, "is how can I create work that will constantly push both me and my audience to think of the world beyond ourselves? Because ultimately that's what empathy is."

A graduate of Davidson College, Smith taught high school English in Maryland through the prestigious Teach for America program from 2011 to 2014. During that time, he also became an acclaimed spoken-word artist, serving as a member of the winning team at the 2014 National Poetry Slam. He has since delivered two popular TED Talks and published a poetry collection, *Counting Descent* (2016), which received several honors. As of 2018, he was a doctoral candidate in education at Harvard University.

EARLY LIFE

Clinton "Clint" Ward Smith III was born on August 25, 1988, in New Orleans, Louisiana. Along with his younger brother and sister, he was raised in a Catholic family and enjoyed an economically privileged upbringing. His father is a lawyer, and his mother is a doctor. In an interview with Robin Young for the National Public Radio (NPR) radio program *Here & Now* (28 Nov. 2016), Smith said that he and his siblings "grew up in a home full of joy, affirmation, [and] laughter."

Nevertheless, from a very young age, Smith was also made fully aware of his racial identity. His father told him early on of the frightening social implications of being black in America. As a result, Smith learned how to navigate the challenges of balancing an idyllic home life and the cold realities of the outside world. He has recalled many instances of being reminded of those realities while innocently playing with his childhood friends, "an interracial assemblage of young boys that would have made the Disney Channel proud," as he described them in an essay for the *TED* website (1 May 2015).

Like many of his friends, Smith played soccer, but his involvement in the sport inadvertently helped reinforce his outsider status. He was often the only black kid on his youth-league and school teams growing up. Still, this did little to diminish his love for the sport. A seminal moment in Smith's life occurred when he was twelve, while on an overnight soccer trip. He and his teammates were chasing each other around in their hotel parking lot with water guns when Smith's father intervened. Taken back to his room, Smith was chided by his father for his naivete and warned of the potentially fatal consequences of playing with fake guns. (This incident is recalled in Smith's poem "Counterfactual" from *Counting Descent* and also mentioned in his TED Talk "How to Raise a Black Son in America.")

That chilling message resonated with Smith throughout his adolescence, which was also marked by a love of reading and writing. Smith became an avid reader largely thanks to the influence of his mother, who collected encyclopedias; she would tell her son to consult one whenever he had a question about something. Meanwhile, he started writing regularly as a means of channeling his curiosity about the world.

SHAPED BY HURRICANE KATRINA
Smith attended Benjamin Franklin High School in New Orleans, the top public high school in Louisiana. He played on the school's varsity soccer team and helped lead them to a state championship as a sophomore. Smith's senior year, however, was interrupted by Hurricane Katrina, which struck New Orleans on August 29, 2005. The storm forced Smith to flee with his family to Houston, Texas, where they stayed with Smith's aunt and uncle.

While waiting for the storm to subside, Smith was contacted by Davidson College, a small liberal arts college near Charlotte, North Carolina. He was recruited to play soccer at the school, which he visited with his father one week later. Impressed with its prestigious academic reputation, Smith committed to Davidson during his trip. The school's admissions office then helped secure him placement at the Awty International School, a large private school in Houston, so he could complete high school.

Though Smith joined the soccer team at Awty, which waived his tuition fees, to help assimilate into his new community, Hurricane Katrina had a profound and lasting effect on his sense of identity and his outlook for the future. Two months after the storm, he returned to New Orleans to visit his childhood home, which suffered extensive flood damage. In an essay for *Seven Scribes* (31 Aug. 2015), Smith reflected on this experience, writing that he had no words to describe "how it felt to be rendered refugee by the rest of the world, to be made more charity case than human."

Smith graduated from Awty in 2006. He was one of seventy students from his senior class at Benjamin Franklin High to not graduate from the school, which did not reopen until January of that year because of storm-related damage. He received an honorary diploma from the school in 2018.

UNEXPECTED CALLING
By the time Smith arrived at Davidson, soccer had already begun to take a backseat to other endeavors. Thanks to a collection of inspiring English professors, Smith developed a newfound passion for the arts. That passion took on a new dimension during the summer of 2008, while he was interning at a publishing company in New York. A colleague invited him to attend a spoken-word event at the city's famed Nuyorican Poetry Café, which resulted in "one of the most transformative evenings of my life," as he recalled to Oyekoya.

Deeply moved by what he heard, Smith immediately resolved to become a poet and began writing in earnest. Upon returning to Davidson, he immersed himself in the history of spoken-word and slam poetry and started doing open mic nights at local venues. He also helped found a campus spoken-word collective called FreeWord, which began competing in national college competitions. The beauty of art forms like spoken word, Smith explained to Oyekoya, lies in their power to "push us beyond what we know, or even beyond the possibilities of what we thought we knew."

Smith also spent time studying in Senegal before graduating from Davidson with a bachelor's degree in English in 2010. Afterward, he deferred a commitment to the Teach for America program so he could accept an internship with Grassroots Soccer, an organization that aims to educate South African youths about HIV/AIDS. He spent the next year working with that organization in Soweto, South Africa, where he used his soccer and spoken-word skills to raise awareness about the virus.

After returning to the United States in 2011, Smith began teaching tenth-grade English at Parkdale High School in Riverdale Park, Maryland, through Teach for America. He taught there for three years, winning the 2013 Christine D. Sarbanes Teacher of the Year Award from the Maryland Humanities Council. During that time, he regularly performed spoken-word and poetry readings around the Washington, DC, area. In 2012, he won the Graffiti DC poetry slam title. That same year he became the US cultural ambassador to Swaziland, where he conducted youth poetry workshops.

HARVARD AND TED TALKS
In the summer of 2014, Smith entered Harvard University in Cambridge, Massachusetts, to pursue a doctoral degree in education. His research

focuses there have included mass incarceration and the sociology of racism, among other topics. As part of his research, Smith began working with incarcerated people at various Massachusetts state prisons, where he taught creative writing to prisoners serving life sentences. "I don't want to be the person who moves into the proverbial ivory tower [of academia]," he explained to Andrew Bauld for the *Harvard Graduate School of Education* website (6 Feb. 2018).

Meanwhile, Smith became a member of the DC Beltway Poetry Team, which won the 2014 National Poetry Slam. That year he showcased his spoken-word chops during a TED Talk in New York, titled "The Power of Silence," in which he discussed instances of when he failed to speak up for people who were being discriminated against or disparaged, from a gay friend to his own students. In his second TED Talk, "How to Raise a Black Son in America," which he gave in 2015, Smith shared important life advice that his parents had given him growing up to ensure his safety. His two TED Talks have generated more than six million combined views.

COUNTING DESCENT AND OTHER PUBLICATIONS

Smith's debut poetry collection, *Counting Descent*, was published by Write Bloody Publishing in 2016. The collection comprises fifty-six poems—many of which previously appeared in other literary publications—that create a mosaic of personal and shared black experiences. They collectively explore what Smith has called the "cognitive dissonance" of "grow[ing] up in a home in which you feel loved, affirmed, and celebrated, and then going out into a world that has been taught to fear you," as he put it to Robin Young. Poems like "Ode to the Only Black Kid in the Class," "My Jump Shot," "For the Taxi Cabs That Pass Me in Harvard Square," and "For the Boys Who Never Learned How to Swim" give insight into the kind of systemic racism, prejudice, and stereotyping black people encounter daily.

Counting Descent received the 2017 Literary Award for Poetry from the Black Caucus of the American Library Association. It was also a finalist for a National Association for the Advancement of Colored People (NAACP) Image Award. Smith was additionally awarded the 2017 Jerome J. Shestack Prize for a group of poems that included *Counting Descent*'s opening piece, "Something You Should Know."

In addition to his poetry and spoken-word performances, Smith has written essays and scholarly articles for prominent publications, including the *New Yorker*, the *Atlantic*, the *New Republic*, and the *Harvard Educational Review*. He also contributes regularly to the political podcast *Pod Save the People*. He earned a place on *Forbes* magazine's 2018 list of thirty influential people under the age of thirty in media for his art and activism.

PERSONAL LIFE

Smith described himself to Oyekoya as a "pretty awkward guy" who has never really felt comfortable with public speaking. He has nonetheless worked tirelessly at his craft to deliver flawless recitations of his poems. Smith's personal favorite of his own poems is "My Father Is an Oyster," which traces his father's lifelong influence on him. He first recited it for his family in a hospital room right before his father underwent a second kidney transplant.

Smith resides in Washington, DC, with his wife, Ariel, with whom he has a son.

SUGGESTED READING
Bauld, Andrew. "Looking Beyond a Life Sentence." *Harvard Graduate School of Education*, 6 Feb. 2018, www.gse.harvard.edu/news/18/02/looking-beyond-life-sentence. Accessed 21 July 2018.

"Bigger Than the Work: Clint Smith '10 Brings Message to Davidson." *Davidson Journal*, Davidson College, 11 Feb. 2015, www.davidson.edu/news/news-stories/150211-clint-smith-in-advance-of-lecture. Accessed 21 July 2018.

"Clint Smith '10: Game Changers." *Davidson Journal*, Davidson College, gamechangers.davidson.edu/people/clint-smith-10. Accessed 21 July 2018.

Smith, Clint. "Clint Smith: Behind the Mic." Interview by Tosin Oyekoya. *Blavity*, blavity.com/clint-behind-mic. Accessed 21 July 2018.

Smith, Clint. "My Hopes, Dreams, Fears for My Future Black Son." *TED*, 1 May 2015, ideas.ted.com/my-hopes-dreams-fears-for-my-future-black-son. Accessed 21 July 2018.

Smith, Clint. "Strangers in Our Home." *Seven Scribes*, 31 Aug. 2015, sevenscribes.com/strangers-in-our-home-why-writing-about-hurricane-katrina-is-both-impossible-and-necessary. Accessed 21 July 2018.

Smith, Clint. "Through Poetry and TED Talks, Clint Smith Probes Racism in America." Interview by Robin Young. *Here & Now*, WBUR, 28 Nov. 2016, www.wbur.org/hereandnow/2016/11/28/clint-smith-poetry. Accessed 21 July 2018.

—Chris Cullen

Jussie Smollett

Date of birth: June 21, 1982
Occupation: Actor, singer, songwriter

"I used to hear people say nobody can prepare you for fame, and it's actually very true," actor Jussie Smollett told Luis Gomez for the *Chicago Tribune* (30 Mar. 2015). "But there is such beauty that comes with it when you're able to use your platform in a positive way." After earning considerable attention with his role as singer Jamal Lyon in the television drama *Empire*, Smollett sought to do just that, speaking out against racial injustice and homophobia as well as contributing to a variety of nonprofit organizations focused on issues such as justice and public health.

The child of two activists, Smollett grew up as one of six performer siblings and first found success as a child actor, appearing in projects such as the film *The Mighty Ducks* (1992) and the short-lived sitcom *On Our Own* (1994–95). After spending the better part of two decades out of the acting business, he returned to the spotlight with the 2015 premiere of *Empire*, which enabled him not only to explore a powerful new role but also to share his musical talents with the world. His increased recognition led to a variety of opportunities, including roles in major films such as *Alien: Covenant* (2017) and a highly anticipated debut album. Smollett, however, emphasized the importance staying true to himself in the face of his newfound fame. "I'm just enjoying my moment on *Empire* and just taking it all in," he told Paul Chi for *Vanity Fair* (17 Mar. 2015). "I wake up every day the same man just wanting to work hard and do the best work that I can do."

EARLY LIFE AND EDUCATION
Smollett was born on June 21, 1982, in Santa Rosa, California. His father, Joel, worked as a cable splicer, while his mother, Janet, oversaw the Smollett children's performing careers. Smollett was one of six siblings, all of whom acted, performed music, or modeled as children. All six of the children starred in the 1990s sitcom *On Our Own*, and several of them continued to act as adults: Smollett's sister Jurnee went on to the highest-profile career with numerous television and film roles, while his younger brother Jake appeared in the series *The Middleman* and later hosted his own cooking show on Food Network. In addition to performing professionally, Smollett and his siblings grew up watching classic films and often put on shows for their own amusement. "We had a whole damn production, because we had all these kids," he recalled to Melena Ryzik for the *New York Times* (9 Mar. 2016).

By Dominick D [CC BY-SA 2.0], via Wikimedia Commons

Due to Smollett's and his siblings' careers, the family split their time between New York and California throughout much of his childhood. His parents separated when he was fifteen, and Smollett lived primarily with his mother for the next several years. As a teenager, he attended multiple high schools in the Los Angeles area, including Calabasas High School and Malibu High School. Smollett would later note that he struggled to fit in at these predominantly white schools because of his race, and he told Shana Naomi Krochmal for *Out* magazine (28 Jan. 2016) that he once won and then abruptly lost the lead in a school musical due to racist attitudes among the school's population. "People were uncomfortable that I would be kissing this white girl," he told Krochmal. "It was 2000. After that, I left the school, because why subject myself to that bulls——?" Although Smollett had already been involved in activism from an early age due to the influence of his parents, who had first met while campaigning for civil rights, his experiences impressed on him the importance of speaking out against injustice.

EARLY CAREER
An actor from a young age, Smollett initially found roles in television commercials and went on to appear in the 1991 television film *A Little Piece of Heaven*. The following year, he had a small role in the comedy *The Mighty Ducks*, playing a member of the titular youth hockey team. A variety of additional film and television projects followed, including the animated

television series *Cro*, the miniseries *Queen*, and the 1994 film *North*.

During the early 1990s, Smollett and his siblings caught the attention of executives at the network ABC, who considered developing a television series around the children. "We had a meeting with ABC, and my mom had us perform 'Shut 'Em Down' by Public Enemy," he recalled to Aimee Cliff for *Fader* (28 Apr. 2015). "Don't ask me why, these five little children went in this ABC office with all of these old white executives, and we did it." Following the meeting, the five performing children as well as their baby brother were cast in the series *On Our Own*, which premiered on ABC in 1994. A family sitcom, the show focused on a young man, played by actor Ralph Louis Harris, who attempts to care for his six younger siblings after the death of their parents. *On Our Own* struggled to gain viewership, even after being moved to ABC's popular TGIF programming block, and it was ultimately canceled in 1995 after one season.

EVOLVING FOCUS

Following the cancelation of *On Our Own*, Smollett stopped acting professionally for nearly fifteen years. "I wasn't a child star. I was just a working actor," he explained to Krochmal. "And then I wasn't a cutesy kid anymore, but I also wasn't a leading man." As an adult, he worked as a fundraiser for the nonprofit Artists for a New South Africa, for which he would later serve as a board member. He also held a variety of different jobs, including stints as a bartender and a clown. A singer and songwriter, Smollett also began recording music in a home studio, releasing the EP *Poisoned Hearts Club* in 2011.

Smollett returned to acting in 2009 with a role in the short comedy film *Pitch This*, written by and costarring his brother Jake. He resumed pursuing acting work over the next several years, taking on roles in episodes of television series such as *The Mindy Project* and *Revenge*. He likewise returned to film, appearing in the 2012 movie *The Skinny* and the 2014 direct-to-video project *Born to Race: Fast Track*.

EMPIRE

A turning point in Smollett's career came in 2015, when he began to costar in the drama *Empire*. The show, which premiered on Fox in January of that year, follows music executive Lucious Lyon (Terrence Howard), who, after learning that he is terminally ill, must decide who will take over his entertainment company after he dies. Smollett plays Lucious's middle son, openly gay singer and songwriter Jamal, who has a strained relationship with his father due to Lucious's homophobic behavior. Smollett first learned of the role from his sister Jazz and, after reaching out to Empire cocreator Lee Daniels,

claimed the role of Jamal, whose relationship with Lucious was inspired, in part, by Daniels's relationship with his own father.

Empire proved popular among viewers and was renewed for a second season less than two weeks after its premiere. A third season followed, and the fourth season of *Empire* premiered in September of 2017. Critics and viewers particularly praised Smollett's performance as Jamal, noting that the character eschewed stereotypes of gay men and gay African Americans common in the media. For Smollett, the opportunity to play Jamal was meaningful on both a professional level and a personal one. "I received a letter from a kid that said Jamal gave him the courage to come out to his parents," he told Chi. "It touched me deeply and it's an honor to help people."

Smollett was nominated for a variety of awards in recognition of his performance on *Empire*, including the Image Award for outstanding supporting actor in a drama series, the BET Award for best actor, and the Teen Choice Award for television actor in a drama. He was also widely recognized for the songs he wrote and performed for the show, winning the Guild of Music Supervisors Award for best song recorded for television for the song "You're So Beautiful" in 2016.

OTHER PROJECTS

Having become well known for his musical talents through his work on *Empire*, Smollett soon began fielding questions about his own musical projects. "I have been recording my album but I'm taking my time," he told Joan Wallace for the *Latin Times* (18 May 2017). "I want to do things in the right way and not any other way." In January of 2018 Smollett released the song "Freedom," the first single from the album. His debut full-length album, *Sum of My Music*, is scheduled for release in March of 2018.

In addition to his ongoing work on *Empire*, Smollett appeared in a variety of other film and television projects, including collaborations with his siblings. In 2016 he appeared in two episodes of the historical series *Underground*, which starred his sister Jurnee Smollett-Bell, and also contributed to the Food Network series *Smollett Eats*, starring his brother Jake and featuring all six Smollett siblings. Smollett returned to film in the 2017 science-fiction project *Alien: Covenant*, an installment in the long-running *Alien* franchise. A fan of the original film *Alien* (1979) as a child, he was excited to work with acclaimed director Ridley Scott. "He is so phenomenal because he is aware of the most outstanding technology . . . and all the effects that we have in cinema but he also wanted to give the movie a certain level of realness," Smollett explained to Wallace. "He had this seven feet guy inside an alien costume and literally that was our alien. It was not fake, that was real." Smollett also made a brief appearance as poet Langston Hughes in the 2017 biopic *Marshall* and expressed his desire to reprise that role in a Hughes biopic.

PERSONAL LIFE
Smollett lives in Los Angeles and spends much of his time in Chicago, where *Empire* is filmed. Like many of his siblings, he enjoys cooking, which he has attributed to his mother's Southern heritage. "You can always come to my house and I will cook for you," he told Chi. "I make the best macaroni and cheese that you will ever have in your life and I make a mean gumbo."

Long involved with a variety of charitable causes, Smollett remains affiliated with Artists for a New South Africa and has also worked with the Black AIDS Institute, which seeks to prevent HIV in African American communities. After gaining widespread fame for his role in Empire, he sought to use his platform to support LGBTQ rights as well as racial justice and the Black Lives Matter movement. "People were telling me, 'Don't do it,'" he told Krochmal of his decision to speak out on violence against African Americans. "But I felt like, *If I lose my career based on this, then I don't need that career.*"

SUGGESTED READING
Chi, Paul. "*Empire*'s Jussie Smollett Opens Up about Being a Gay Icon and His Cooking Skills." *Vanity Fair*, 17 Mar. 2015, www.vanityfair.com/hollywood/2015/03/empire-jussie-smollett-gay-icon. Accessed 12 Jan. 2018.

Cliff, Aimee. "*Empire*'s Jussie Smollett: I Want to Help Fix America." *Fader*, 28 Apr. 2015, www.thefader.com/2015/04/28/jussie-smollett-interview. Accessed 12 Jan. 2017.

Gomez, Luis. "Interview: 'Empire' Has Made Kings of Stars Yazz and Jussie Smollett." *Chicago Tribune*, 30 Mar. 2015, www.chicagotribune.com/entertainment/celebrity/chi-empire-yazz-jussie-smollett-20150330-column.html. Accessed 12 Jan. 2018.

Hawkins, Kayla. "'Empire's Jamal, Jussie Smollett, Comes from a Famous Family in Real Life Too & Here's What They're Up To." *Bustle*, 14 Jan. 2015, www.bustle.com/articles/58266-empires-jamal-jussie-smollett-comes-from-a-famous-family-in-real-life-too-heres-what. Accessed 12 Jan. 2018.

Krochmal, Shana Naomi. "Jussie Smollett on How a Black Gay Man Can Save the World." *Out*, 28 Jan. 2016, www.out.com/entertainment/2016/1/28/exclusive-jussie-smollett-being-black-and-gay-hollywood. Accessed 12 Jan. 2017.

Ryzik, Melena. "The Smollett Family Business: Acting and Activism." *The New York Times*, 9 Mar. 2016, www.nytimes.com/2016/03/13/arts/television/the-smollett-family-business-acting-and-activism.html. Accessed 12 Jan. 2018.

Smollett, Jussie. "Jussie Smollett Talks 'Alien Covenant' Experience: 'Empire' Actor Reveals Scariest Shooting Moment, New Projects." Interview with Joan Wallace. *Latin Times*, 18 May 2017, www.latintimes.com/jussie-smollett-talks-alien-covenant-experience-empire-actor-reveals-scariest-417988. Accessed 12 Jan. 2018.

SELECTED WORKS
The Mighty Ducks, 1992; *Cro*, 1993–94; *On Our Own*, 1994–95; *Empire*, 2015– ; *Smollett Eats*, 2016– ; *Alien: Covenant*, 2017; *Marshall*, 2017

—Joy Crelin

Somi

Date of birth: June 6, 1981
Occupation: Singer-songwriter

Somi is an American-born jazz singer of East African descent. She has described her music, which blends jazz, gospel, and traditional African music, as new African soul. It is a sound Farai Chideya for National Public Radio's (NPR) *News & Notes* (5 June 2007) called as "diverse as the five languages" the singer speaks. Somi was raised in Champaign, Illinois, and Ndola, Zambia, by Rwandan and Ugandan parents, and her particular blend of African and American music was inspired by her roots. To Chideya, she described the titular song on her 2007 debut *Red Soil in My Eyes*, as a "kind of a conversation I'm having with my ancestors." Somi has released a handful of albums, including the critically-acclaimed *The Lagos Music Salon* (2014) and the award-winning *Petite Afrique* (2017). Somi has served as the artist-in-residence at the University of California, Los Angeles' (UCLA) Center for the Art of Performance and the Robert Rauschenberg Foundation. She has also twice received the Doris Duke Foundation's French-American Jazz Exchange Composer's Grant.

EARLY LIFE AND EDUCATION
Somi, the sixth of seven children, was born Laura Kabasomi Kakoma on June 6, 1981, in Champaign, Illinois. (Her name, Kabasomi, means "child of scholarship.") Her father, Dr. Ibulaimu Kakoma, was Rwandan, but raised in Uganda. During his life, he worked as a professor of veterinary medicine and immunology at the University of Illinois at Urbana-Champaign. Somi's mother, Elizabeth Nyarubona Kakoma, was born and raised in Uganda. She was an

oncology nurse and a talented singer. "She has a beautiful voice and is a great keeper of Ugandan folk songs. She sang me a lot of songs from her home. She constantly breaks into song. But she also loves '50s and '60s pop. She played Elvis Presley and Perry Como around our house all the time," Somi recalled to Will Layman for *Pop Matters* (25 Sept. 2014). Her father introduced her to reggae and roots music. Somi was drawn to classical music and began learning to play the cello when she was eight years old. As a child, she watched Julie Andrews sing in the musical film *The Sound of Music* and dreamed of becoming a singer herself. "I loved singing so much, but I didn't think it was a viable career choice," she told Layman. "Everyone in my family had a more traditional job, and immigrant families don't usually encourage you to be an artist."

Somi's family traveled all around the world when she was a child. When she was three years old, they moved to Ndola, Zambia, where her father worked for the World Health Organization (WHO). They returned to Champaign several years later. Somi attended the University Laboratory School and Champaign Central High School. She earned a bachelor's degree in cultural anthropology and African studies at the University of Illinois. After graduating, she spent a year and a half doing research in Kenya, Tanzania, and Uganda, working for a time with children with human immunodeficiency virus (HIV). She had originally planned to become a medical anthropologist, but the trip reacquainted her with her heritage in a way that made her reexamine her future. "Now that you know where you are from you can see where you want to go," she recalled telling herself to Siddhartha Mitter for the *Boston Globe* (15 Nov. 2009). "And I chose to come to New York, and music became the first thing for me."

RED SOIL IN MY EYES

Somi released an album called *Eternal Motive* in 2003, but she dismissed the project as a wrong-footed start. "I was actually shying away from the African and world side of things," she told Mitter. "I was getting advice that people just wouldn't get it. I didn't take many risks vocally. I was also very young in the journey." Somi eventually earned a master's degree in performance studies from the New York University Tisch School of the Arts, where she began performing for live audiences. "My first performance was terrifying but totally thrilling," she recalled to Doreen Umutesi for the Rwandan *New Times* (11 Sept. 2013). "The best word I can use to describe how I feel when performing for an audience is FREE. You are at once vulnerable yet disarming. There is something about performance that both humbles and strengthens you simultaneously. It is where I am happiest and most liberated."

While studying at Tisch, Somi began working on her second album, *Red Soil in My Eyes* (2007). She told Mitter, "I started singing in other languages. I began to tell a full story." Songs from the album include "My Mother's Daughter," about life lessons passed between generations; "Mbabzi," about her mother's life; and "African Lady," a song musically influenced by the late Nigerian musician Fela Kuti about domestic violence. The most popular song on the album, "Ingele," is a slow jazz, Swahili song about heartbreak. The song provided Somi with her first breakthrough hit and peaked in the top ten on US world music charts. Somi describes "Ingele" as a love song. "I was kind of—you find yourself in one of those relationships where, you know, you started off so much love and the best of intentions, and then it's kind of deteriorated into something else," she told Chideya. "And that song is really kind of speaking to my lover asking him to kind of come back, return to that place we once were."

IF THE RAINS COME FIRST

Somi signed with the New York City record label ObliqSound in 2009. That year, she released the album *If the Rains Come First*, which peaked at number two on the Billboard World Album chart. Christopher Loudon reviewed the album for *Jazz Times* (1 Mar. 2010), writing, "Whether exploring hope or heartache, personal lesson or universal truth, each of the original compositions that fill her third album is solid as earth and vital as air." The album's title came from one of Somi's mother's maxims about the unpredictable nature of life: when the rain comes it can bring either plentitude or devastation. The songs reflect this theme. "Jewel of His Soul" is about a once-respected Senegalese intellectual who became homeless after moving to Paris, France, and "Be Careful, Be Kind" recalls the death of Somi's cousin in a car accident. The album also features a performance from the South African trumpeter Hugh Masekela, Somi's longtime mentor, on the song "Enganjyani." A song called "Kuzunguka" captures the happiness she felt when her father became free from cancer; unfortunately, he died later that year.

THE LAGOS MUSIC SALON

In 2011, Somi released a live album called *Somi: Live at Jazz Standard*, to mostly positive reviews. Somi traveled to Lagos, Nigeria, that year for a seven-week teaching artist residency. Partly due to her grief after losing her father, she ended up staying for eighteen months. Somi later said, in multiple interviews, that the energy of Lagos reminded her of New York City.

Somi's experiences in the city served as the basis for her third studio album. After returning to New York in 2013, Somi signed with Sony

Music's jazz imprint OKeh Records and released *The Lagos Music Salon* with the label the following year. The album included guest appearances by Grammy Award–winning rapper Common on the song "When Rivers Cry" and the Grammy Award–winning Beninese singer Angélique Kidjo on "Lady Revisited." The album's title was inspired by the intimate shows that Somi hosted in Lagos, in nontraditional spaces like art galleries. "Somi delivers vocal performances of striking tonal clarity and expressiveness, shedding light on the lives of the people of Lagos by delving into their struggles, pain, pride, and joys," Ken Capobianco wrote in his review of the album for the *Boston Globe* (6 Aug. 2014). The song "Two Dollar Day" is about domestic workers, while "Brown Round Things" is about sex workers. "Four African Women" is about surviving genocide, and "When Rivers Cry" is about environmental destruction.

DREAMING ZENZILE AND PETITE AFRIQUE

In 2016, Somi wrote and appeared in the jazz opera *Dreaming Zenzile / A Work-in-Progress*, about the life of Miriam Makeba, the famous South African singer and activist. The show featured reinterpretations of Makeba's music, as well as original songs based on Makeba's life and career. *Dreaming Zenzile* premiered at the Apollo Theater in New York City.

Somi's next album, *Petite Afrique* (2017), is a tribute to her neighborhood, Harlem's Little Africa. It also serves as a commentary on how the neighborhood has changed and gentrified over time. Like *The Lagos Music Salon*, many of the songs on *Petite Afrique* are character studies. "The Gentry," featuring singer Aloe Blacc, is about the tension between new residents and a long-running drum circle in Marcus Garvey Park. Somi's neighbors are from different countries in Africa and they speak different languages, but the singer was drawn to their stories because they reminded her of her own. She told Mitter for the *Village Voice* (28 Mar. 2017) that her father, a Pan-Africanist, would have encouraged her line of inquiry. "He would have said yes, tell their story—this is our story too!" *Petite Afrique* received critical acclaim and won the National Association for the Advancement of Colored People (NAACP) Image Award for Outstanding Jazz Album in 2018.

PERSONAL LIFE

Somi splits her time between New York City and Lagos. In 2008, she founded a nonprofit that supports contemporary African artists called New Africa Live. She was invited to perform for the United Nations General Assembly in 2013, to commemorate the International Day of Remembrance of the Victims of Slavery and the Transatlantic Slave Trade. Somi is a TED senior fellow and speaker, and was selected as one of the first Association of Performing Arts Presenters fellows, among other honors.

SUGGESTED READING

Capobianco, Ken. Review of *The Lagos Music Salon*, by Somi. *The Boston Globe*, 5 Aug. 2014, www.bostonglobe.com/arts/music/2014/08/04/somi-the-lagos-music-salon/N5atuuj9K9zW1btzPEzDLI/story.html. Accessed 16 Sept. 2018.

Layman, Will. "Singing Across Continents: An Interview with Somi." *Pop Matters*, 25 Sept. 2014, www.popmatters.com/185767-singins-across-continents-an-interview-with-somi-2495616221.html. Accessed 10 Sept. 2018.

Loudon, Christopher. Review of *If the Rains Come First*, by Somi. *Jazz Times*, 1 Mar. 2010, jazztimes.com/reviews/vox/somi-if-the-rains-come-first/. Accessed 13 Sept. 2018.

Mitter, Siddhartha. "Somi's *Petite Afrique* Celebrates Her Favorite Slice of the City." *The Village Voice*, 28 Mar. 2017, www.villagevoice.com/2017/03/28/somis-petite-afrique-celebrates-her-favorite-slice-of-the-city/. Accessed 16 Sept. 2018.

Mitter, Siddhartha. "To Another Place: Somi." *The Boston Globe*, 15 Nov. 2009, archive.boston.com/ae/music/articles/2009/11/15/somi_takes_her_sound_to_a_new_level_that_captures_where_shes_been____and_is_now/. Accessed 10 Sept. 2018.

Somi. "A Musical Meeting of Africa and America." Interview by Farai Chideya. *News and Notes*, NPR, 5 June 2007, www.npr.org/templates/story/story.php?storyId=10741482. Accessed 13 Sept. 2018.

Somi. "Know Yourself, Listen to Your Heart, and Take Risks—Singer Laura Kabasomi Kakoma." Interview by Doreen Umutesi. *The New Times*, 11 Sept. 2013, www.newtimes.co.rw/section/read/69101. Accessed 10 Sept. 2018.

SELECTED WORKS

Red Soil in My Eyes, 2007; *If the Rains Come First*, 2009; *The Lagos Music Salon*, 2014; *Petite Afrique*, 2017

—*Molly Hagan*

Tyshawn Sorey

Date of birth: July 8, 1980
Occupation: Musician, composer

Tyshawn Sorey, a multitalented musician and composer from Newark, New Jersey, won the prestigious MacArthur Fellowship in 2017. The

By Nomo michael hoefner [CC BY-SA 3.0], via Wikimedia Commons

fellowship, which is also known as the "genius grant," and comes with an award of $625,000, is awarded annually to around twenty or thirty "talented individuals who have shown extraordinary originality and dedication in their creative pursuits and a marked capacity for self-direction," according to the MacArthur Foundation (*macfound.org*) website. An accomplished percussionist, pianist, and trombonist, Sorey has collaborated with such diverse figures as the late free-jazz pianist Muhal Richard Abrams; the mercurial, genre-defying saxophonist Steve Coleman, who won a MacArthur Fellowship in 2014; jazz trumpeter Dave Douglas; MacArthur-winning jazz pianist Vijay Iyer; and experimental composer John Zorn. These artists, like Sorey, seek to explore the outer fringes of jazz and sound.

Sorey has an uncanny musical ability—he is able to read a score once and know it by heart—but, as he told Anastasia Tsioulcas for National Public Radio (NPR) (11 Oct. 2017), "I wasn't necessarily only interested in rhythm, melody, and harmony. Music is really a manifestation of our life experiences, expressed in sound—melody, rhythm, harmony, all of these things exist together." In 2017, Sorey earned his doctorate from Columbia University, took over a professorship in the music department at Wesleyan University that was once held by his former mentor, and released *Verisimilitude*, an album that showcases the qualities for which Sorey is best known—among them his ability to integrate complex compositions with on-the-spot improvisations. The album, which Giovanni Russonello described for the *New York Times* (2 Aug. 2017) as Sorey's "most captivating album yet," captures some of the minimalism of his earlier work but also suggests, as Seth Colter Walls wrote in his review for the online magazine *Pitchfork* (15 Aug. 2017), a "delicate chaos."

EARLY LIFE

Sorey was born on July 8, 1980, and grew up in Newark, New Jersey. He was obsessed with music from a young age—"always turning the radio dial," as he said to Joseph Atmonavage for *NJ.com* (23 Oct. 2017). His late-night listening expeditions introduced him to bluegrass, country, and classical music. "I was the odd person," he recalled to Atmonavage. "I didn't do much socially. All I did was focus my energy on music—practicing, listening, and studying." Sorey's family did not have much money when he was growing up, so his musical education was largely dependent on his own motivation and efforts. His father played him records and helped him build a makeshift drum kit; his grandfather bought him his first real kit at fourteen. Sorey taught himself to play piano in the basement of his church, and he learned to play the trombone as well, if only because it was one of the few instruments available at Camden Street Middle School.

Sorey's innate talent won him a place at Newark Arts High School, a magnet school, where he begged teachers to open the school doors at 5:00 a.m. so that he could practice for three hours before classes began. When Sorey was eighteen, he was preparing to audition for a Star-Ledger Scholarship for the Performing Arts, made available to college-bound Newark high school seniors through the New Jersey Performing Arts Center (NJPAC), where Sorey was attending the Jazz for Teens program. Though Sorey was best known as a trombonist at the time, he planned to play a piece he had composed for the piano. NJPAC faculty member Mark Gross had agreed to coach him for his audition, but at their first session, Sorey had forgotten his score at home. He assured Gross that he could perform the fifteen-minute piece from memory. Gross was shocked when Sorey played the complicated piece, which he described to Atmonavage as "unbelievably orchestrated," without error. Gross told Atmonavage that there was nothing more he could do to prepare Sorey for the audition, other than to "make sure he had a good suit and good shoes." Sorey won the scholarship and went on to attend William Paterson University, in Wayne, New Jersey, as a classical trombone major.

MUSICAL EDUCATION

Even at William Paterson, Sorey was recognized by his professors as unusually gifted, often placing out of required classes in favor of self-directed study. During his tenure, he switched his major from trombone to jazz drumming and became increasingly interested in nontraditional composition. After earning his bachelor of music degree in jazz studies in 2004, Sorey went on to pursue a master's degree in composition at Wesleyan University, where he would study under composer and 1994 MacArthur Fellowship recipient Anthony Braxton.

Braxton had been an early member of the Chicago-based Association for the Advancement of Creative Musicians (AACM), an avant-garde nonprofit musical organization formed in the mid-1960s that, as Russonello wrote, "aims to nurture visionary black composers without accommodating the classical or jazz establishments." Sorey and Braxton had previously met while Sorey was an undergraduate; in fact, it was Braxton who had inspired the young musician to actively pursue and study composition. Of this early encounter, Sorey recalled to Daniel Lehner for the website *Allaboutjazz.com* (26 June 2012), "I had a conversation with . . . Braxton about how to begin a body of work that I actually believe in, because I had thought, 'Well, who cares? I'm just a drummer and I'll be playing in so-called jazz bands and that's all I'm going to be doing and nobody's going to be playing my music.'" He continued, "I had given up on the idea of being a composer, and Braxton said, 'Well, you should keep writing your music, because there's somebody out there who will believe in your work, whether or not it's somebody you want to believe in it. There's going to always be people out there who will want to do your music.'"

Braxton, and the ideas he helped shape, deeply influenced Sorey and his development as a composer. "All of the founding members of the AACM, and also people from the second wave of that collective, all of them had a very high impact on my work as a composer and also as a student of music," he said to Howard Reich for the *Chicago Tribune* (11 Oct. 2017). "Anthony Braxton, specifically, what he has done in terms of paving the way for African American composers like myself to basically show me that, yes, you can do this too. You have a voice also." He added, "I never thought of being a black composer until I got in touch with their music."

EARLY CAREER

Sorey played with a number of groups and ensembles while at Wesleyan, most notably Fieldwork, a trio consisting of him, Iyer, and saxophonist Steve Lehman. (Sorey replaced previous drummer Elliot Humberto Kavee.) Fieldwork released *Door*, the group's third album and the first one to feature Sorey, in 2008. Sorey was coming into his own as a composer after making a name as a sideman for artists such as Coleman and Douglas, and his influence can be felt throughout the expansive and sophisticated *Door*, for which he wrote six of the album's eleven pieces. Troy Collins, in his review of the album for *All About Jazz* (4 June 2008), praised Sorey for his "egoless compositions" that "[downplay] his own role in favor of atmospheric restraint" and "[eschew] ego for the sake of the group dynamic." It is a challenging record, Collins wrote, but "true innovation never comes without a price, as the group moves well beyond its comfort zone, exploring previously untapped sound worlds."

Sorey's contributions to Fieldwork built on his growing reputation after his own debut album, *That/Not*, which he had released in 2007. *That/Not* established Sorey as a composer and musician who loved both the freedom of improvisation and the mathematics of complex composition. Mark F. Turner, also writing for *All About Jazz* (13 Nov. 2007), praised Sorey's assertion of his own voice and wrote that the album "exposes the inner workings of a young musician with the ability to play in any context, but the boldness to do his own thing."

Sorey's second album, *Koan* (2009), is among his best known. He recorded the album with another trio, this one with Todd Neufeld on guitar and Thomas Morgan on bass. Like *That/Not*, *Koan* features interplay between precise composition and improvisation, but it is also an exploration of space, silence, and quietness. Ben Ratliff, writing for the *New York Times* (7 Aug. 2009), described a live performance of songs from the album as having "one foot in ultra-minimalism and one in the free-jazz performance tradition." *Koan* was also heavily influenced by Zen Buddhism. Sorey had visited a Japanese monastery in 2006, and the experience inspired him to practice meditation and use elements of that practice in his work.

Sorey continues to be interested in the experience of listening. "I never listen to music passively," he told Russonello, and implied that he expects the same engagement from his own listeners. After *Koan*, Sorey formed an improvisational jazz trio with pianist Kris Davis and tenor saxophonist Ingrid Laubrock called Paradoxical Frog. They released an eclectic self-titled debut album in 2010.

MASTER MUSICIAN

Sorey earned his master's degree from Wesleyan in 2011. That same year, he released his third album, *Oblique–I*, which was a notable departure from his first two albums. In his review for NPR's *Fresh Air* (11 Oct. 2011), Kevin Whitehead described it as "the kind of rollicking band album you'd expect from a powerhouse drummer." Sorey recorded the album with Neufeld, saxophonist Loren Stillman, pianist John Escreet, and bassist Chris Tordini. This album was followed by *Alloy* (2014), recorded with Sordini and pianist Corey Smythe, which marked a return to the reflective quietness of *Koan*, with the exception of a melodic groove called "Template."

Sorey, Tordini, and Smythe recorded their next album, *The Inner Spectrum of Variables* (2016), with a string trio consisting of violinist Fung Chern Hwei, violist Kyle Armbrust, and cellist Rubin Kodheli. Sorey estimated that nearly 90 percent of the album was improvised using a system of "conduction" devised by another of Sorey's mentors, Lawrence D. "Butch" Morris, in which gestural cues are used to conduct a piece spontaneously as it occurs. Released as a two-disc album, *Inner Spectrum* is sweeping in its scope; it is made up of six movements, ranging in style from classical to avant-garde. In a review for *All About Jazz* (25 May 2016), Karl Ackermann wrote, "Sorey doesn't so much blur the line between the conventional roles of the ensemble and jazz trio, as he does allow their individual voices tell two sides of the same story," and went on to deem the album "the vision of a modern master."

The breadth of *Inner Spectrum* laid the groundwork for Sorey's 2017 album, *Verisimilitude*, which, though sold as a single disc, "has an epic scale that follows from the wide-ranging air of" its predecessor, according to Walls. Also in 2017, Sorey earned his doctorate in music from Columbia University, with a concentration in composition, and in the fall he joined Wesleyan University's faculty as an assistant professor of music.

Then, in October, the news came that he had been selected to receive a coveted MacArthur Fellowship for his achievements in "assimilating and transforming ideas from a broad spectrum of musical idioms and defying distinctions between genres, composition, and improvisation in a singular expression of contemporary music," according to the citation. Though dubious about being labeled a "genius," Sorey viewed the award as a validation of his choice to pursue his passion and stay true to himself. "You get it for just being who you are," he said to Tsioulcas. "I've been recognized for doing something that I truly have believed in, and worked on for the past twenty-odd years. It's a blessing."

PERSONAL LIFE

Sorey met Amanda Scherbenske, an ethnomusicologist and scholar of Jewish music, when they were both students at Wesleyan. The couple married in 2011. Their first child was born in 2017.

SUGGESTED READING

Atmonavage, Joseph. "Everyone Knew This Newark Native Was Special. Now He's Officially a Genius." *NJ.com*, Advance Digital, 23 Oct. 2017, www.nj.com/entertainment/index.ssf/2017/10/tyshawn_sorey_newark_jazz_musician_macarthur_grant.html. Accessed 13 Nov. 2017.

Lehner, Daniel. "Tyshawn Sorey: Composite Reality." *All About Jazz*, 26 June 2012, www.allaboutjazz.com/tyshawn-sorey-composite-reality-tyshawn-sorey-by-daniel-lehner.php. Accessed 13 Nov. 2017.

Ratliff, Ben. "Improvised Silence amid the Sounds." Review of performance by Tyshawn Sorey, 5 Aug. 2009, The Stone, New York. *The New York Times*, 7 Aug. 2009, www.nytimes.com/2009/08/08/arts/music/08guitar.html. Accessed 13 Nov. 2017.

Reich, Howard. "MacArthur Fellow Tyshawn Sorey Stretches Musical Definitions." *Chicago Tribune*, 11 Oct. 2017, www.chicago-tribune.com/entertainment/music/reich/ct-ent-tyshawn-sorey-jazz-macarthur-genius-1011-20171009-story.html. Accessed 13 Nov. 2017.

Russonello, Giovanni. "Is It Jazz? Improvisation? Tyshawn Sorey Is Obliterating the Lines." *The New York Times*, 2 Aug. 2017, www.nytimes.com/2017/08/02/arts/music/tyshawn-sorey-verisimilitude-interview.html. Accessed 13 Nov. 2017.

Tsioulcas, Anastasia. "Tyshawn Sorey, a Musical Shapeshifter, Wins MacArthur 'Genius' Prize." *The Record*, NPR, 11 Oct. 2017, www.npr.org/sections/therecord/2017/10/11/556828177/tyshawn-sorey-a-musical-shapeshifter-wins-macarthur-genius-prize. Accessed 13 Nov. 2017.

SELECTED WORKS

That/Not, 2007; *Door*, 2008; *Koan*, 2009; *Oblique-I*, 2011; *Alloy*, 2014; *The Inner Spectrum of Variables*, 2016; *Verisimilitude*, 2017

—Molly Hagan

Vince Staples

Date of birth: July 2, 1993
Occupation: Rapper

In an interview with Vince Staples for the *New York Times* (29 June 2017), Joe Coscarelli described the twenty-four-year-old musician as "one of the most prolific, consistent and prodigious rappers to emerge in recent years." Hailing from Long Beach, California (also the home of rappers Snoop Dogg and his cousin Nate Dogg), Staples began rapping after a chance meeting with former Odd Future member Syd tha Kyd in 2010. After releasing his first mixtape, *Shyne Coldchain Vol. 1*, in December 2011, Staples

By digboston, via Wikimedia Commons

released three more mixtapes and an extended-play (EP) album before dropping his critically acclaimed double debut album, *Summertime '06*, in 2015.

Staples has been heralded as "a last-gasp protector of many things thought to be endangered," including "hip-hop lyricism, West Coast gangster rap, in-the-trenches protest songs, [and] social-media authenticity," according to Coscarelli, who also noted that the rapper "wants no part" of any of these titles. Staples's writing voice is sometimes wry, sometimes cynical, and sometimes sad, while his social media presence reveals a playful and sharp wit. His politics, worldview, and music have been shaped by an upbringing steeped in gang culture, and his driving motivation is his desire to convey his lived experience accurately. "I been through hell and back, I seen my momma cry / Seen my father hit the crack then hit the set to flip a sack / I done seen my homies die then went on rides to kill 'em back / So how you say you feel me when you never had to get through that?" he raps on "Like It Is," the penultimate track on *Summertime '06*. "No matter what we grow into, we never gonna escape our past."

EARLY LIFE

Staples was born in Compton, California, on July 2, 1993, and grew up in Long Beach. The youngest of five siblings, he was a quiet, studious child. "Late one night when he was in elementary school, I saw the bathroom light on and yelled, 'What are you doing in there?'" his mother, Eloise, recalled to Jeff Weiss for the *Fader* (20

June 2016). "He said, 'Nothing.' When he finally came out, there was a book in his hand that he tried to hide. It was past bedtime, but he had a test the next day and was just trying to study. He was always wise beyond his years."

When Staples was in first grade, his father was arrested on Christmas Day. Staples rarely talks about his father, though he tells part of the story in his song "Nate," from his fourth mixtape, *Shyne Coldchain II* (2014). After the arrest, Staples and his mother and siblings moved in with an aunt in Compton, where he became close with his maternal grandfather, Andrew Hutchins, a retired construction worker and truck driver from Haiti who is now deceased. Hutchins, Staples told Weiss, had "accidentally helped start a gang" when he settled in Compton's East Side years before, and gang life was a natural part of Staples's upbringing. "There's no better way to put it than: my family came from the streets," he said to Weiss. "My whole family was gang members. I never knew what I wanted to do besides that."

In Compton, Staples ran with the 2N Gangsta Crips. At the same time, he flourished at a black-owned private school called Optimal Christian Academy, winning an essay contest in the sixth grade. Staples—who, according to his mother, did an uncannily accurate Ray Charles impression—was not yet interested in music; instead, he was drawn to writing, particularly about politics and current events.

"THE POWER OF FEAR"

When he was thirteen, Staples began attending Mayfair High School, a majority-white school in the Los Angeles suburb of Lakewood. He enjoyed skateboarding, played basketball and football, and dreamed of going to college and then graduate school. When he was a freshman, however, he was caught with a stolen cell phone. Multiple witnesses, including the owner of the phone, told the school that Staples did not steal it, but his gang affiliation was more compelling evidence to school authorities. "When my mom went to pick me up [from the school], they showed her a file with my picture on it that said 'Active gang leader,'" Staples recalled to Weiss. "I was thirteen. You ain't leading nothing at thirteen."

Staples was charged with four felonies, including aggravated assault and armed robbery, but the school and the police agreed to drop the charges if he agreed to drop out of the school. The event marked the beginning of a difficult period in his life, the profound effect of which is attested by the title of his acclaimed debut album: *Summertime '06*, referring to the time in which it happened. "That was the point in time where I understood the power of fear," Staples said to Ali Shaheed Muhammad and Frannie

Kelley for NPR's *Microphone Check* podcast (1 July 2015)—not just feeling fear, but also instilling it in others. "It's either they're scared of you or they're better than you," he explained of his worldview at the time. "And no one wants to feel like anyone else is better than them. So we established fear."

Staples found himself in the thick of the gang violence that was endemic in his community. "Everybody was gang banging. . . . I did it, my daddy did it, my momma did that s——, and all my brothers did it," he said to Dharmic X for *Complex* (7 Oct. 2013). He added, "It's really the culture. I don't try to push that with my music because it's nothing I feel like anybody needs to be pushing. I'm from here so that's corny to me. . . . You won't last six months in this before you see a n—— die or go to jail. After that, it gets old real fast."

SCHOOL WOES

In 2008, Staples's mother sent him to live with one of his sisters in Atlanta. "I was only out there for eight months at the most, but it made me not want to go to school anymore," he told Dharmic X. "I was over that s——. I used to do dumb s——, but seeing black ignorance on a large scale, seeing that in school all day really had me analyzing myself. . . . I just felt like I wanted to be a better person after moving there because I saw the most extreme ends of the spectrum. It really got to the point where I understood racism."

After those eight months, he returned to California and moved in with his aunt in La Palma. By his own estimation, he attended six or seven different schools over the next two years, during which time, he frequently got into trouble for fighting and missing classes. "Eventually, I stopped going to school because I didn't feel like dealing with that," he said to Dharmic X. "It became a headache. It went from getting used to knowing everybody at your school and having no problems—like a real family environment—to being around a bunch of people I had never met before. It was a hard transition to make."

EARLY CAREER

Staples's life took an unexpected turn in 2010 when he met rapper Dijon Samo, who then performed under the name Lavi$h. At the time, Staples only rapped for fun, but Samo introduced him to producer Sydney Bennett—better known as Syd tha Kyd, a member of the explosive shock-rap hip-hop collective Odd Future Wolf Gang Kill Them All ("Odd Future" for short), which would soon rocket to fame. "[Samo and his friends would] go to Syd's house to record, and me and Syd clicked automatically," Staples told Dharmic X. He began hanging out at her house every day, and through her he met and similarly bonded with fellow Odd Future

member Earl Sweatshirt. Staples's vocals were featured on Earl's track "epaR," from his self-titled debut mixtape, released in March 2010; both men have since disavowed the song for its violent depiction of rape. Regardless, the collaboration put Staples on the map, especially after Odd Future's mainstream breakthrough in 2011.

With the encouragement of Syd and others, Staples began to make music of his own. He released his first mixtape, *Shyne Coldchain Vol. 1*, in December 2011; the following year, he signed with veteran manager Corey Smyth and collaborated with producer Michael Uzowuru on his second mixtape, *Winter in Prague* (2012). In August 2012, Smyth negotiated a deal for Staples to sign with Def Jam's ARTium imprint.

Staples released his breakout mixtape *Stolen Youth*, recorded with rapper and producer Mac Miller (using the pseudonym Larry Fisherman), in June 2013. "Staples' voice is slack but unflappable and his outlook is coolly cynical," Naomi Zeichner wrote of the release for the *Fader* (20 June 2013). In a brief interview accompanying the announcement, Staples rejected the label of "conscious rapper," telling Zeichner, "I don't see myself as a conscious rapper, I doubt anyone really does. My subjects ain't the most positive. That conscious s—— is corny to me anyway, and nine times out of ten it's a front."

In March 2014, Staples released *Shyne Coldchain II*, his fourth mixtape and his first solo project since his debut. Later that year, he released the EP *Hell Can Wait* (2014), featuring the tracks "Hands Up" and "Blue Suede." The former, as Abby Aguirre wrote for *Vogue* (9 Sept. 2016), "proved prescient," as the EP's release came less than a month after the death of unarmed black teenager Michael Brown at the hands of police in Ferguson, Missouri, and the subsequent adoption of "Hands up, don't shoot" as a rallying cry of the protests that followed. Aguirre also made particular mention of the critically lauded "Blue Suede," which includes the lines "All I wanted was them Jordans with the blue suede in 'em" and "Young graves get the bouquets / Bouquets, the bouquets, the bouquets / Hope I outlive them red roses."

SUMMERTIME '06 (2015) AND BIG FISH THEORY (2017)

Staples's debut studio album, the double-disc *Summertime '06*, was released in June 2015. In his rapturous review of the album for the music website *Pitchfork* (29 June 2015), Jayson Greene opened with an assessment that also fairly encapsulates Staples's artistic persona: "The Long Beach rapper expresses complex ideas in plain, hard sentences, ones that can be handed to you like a pamphlet. His rapping is conversational, but these are the conversations you have when all optimism has been burned away." The album explores Staples's past as well as the political present. On the track "C. N. B."—the title of which stands for "coldest n—— breathing"—he raps, "The sheets and crosses turned to suits and ties / In Black America, can you survive? / They made a nuisance once the noose is tied / We gentrified, we victimized, we fighting for survival."

Staples released his second studio album, *Big Fish Theory*, in June 2017. Taking a cue from the mercurial David Bowie, an artist whom he has often cited in interviews, Staples deliberately created for the album an entirely different sound from that of *Summertime '06*. "I wouldn't want to repeat my steps—I want something different every time," he explained to Coscarelli. "A lot of artists are like that: Kanye [West] is like that; Donald Glover is like that; Tyler, the Creator. That's definitely what I want to do."

Jack Hamilton, reviewing *Big Fish Theory* for *Slate* (26 June 2017), called it "an audacious and genre-defying work, a startling turn from Staples as we thought we knew him." Sheldon Pearce, writing for *Pitchfork* (23 June 2017), appreciatively described it as a "collection of sleek club-rap bangers" and concluded, "*Big Fish Theory* is a compact rap gem for dancing to or simply sitting with, an album that is as innovative as it is accessible; if not a glimpse into the future, then it's at least an incisive look at the present." Stand-out tracks include "BagBak," featuring the lines "Until the president get ashy, Vincent won't be votin' / We need Tamikas and Shaniquas in that Oval Office / Obama ain't enough for me, we only getting started."

PERSONAL LIFE

Staples follows a straight-edge lifestyle, meaning he abstains from alcohol, tobacco, and recreational drugs. "I just never started," he explained to Kyle Eustice for *Thrasher* magazine (7 June 2017). "It's easier to not do it. . . . I don't have the blessing or luxury of just being able to have that strength to stop. I just never got around to it." He has also requested that his fans refrain from smoking at his shows while he is onstage, as it aggravates his asthma.

SUGGESTED READING

Aguirre, Abby. "Vince Staples Is the Anti-Rapper for Our Time." *Vogue*, 9 Sept. 2016, www.vogue.com/article/vince-staples-prima-donna-summertime-alexander-wang. Accessed 14 Apr. 2018.

Staples, Vince. "Download Vince Staples' Album *Stolen Youth*." Interview by Naomi Zeichner. *The Fader*, 20 June 2013, www.thefader.com/2013/06/20/download-vince-staples-album-stolen-youth. Accessed 14 Apr. 2018.

Staples, Vince. Interview. By Kyle Eustice. *Thrasher*, 7 June 2017, www.thrashermagazine.com/articles/music-interviews/vince-staples-interview. Accessed 19 Apr. 2018.

Staples, Vince. "Vince Staples: 'My Job Is to Keep My Sanity." Interview by Ali Shaheed Muhammad and Frannie Kelley. *Microphone Check*, NPR, 1 July 2015, www.npr.org/sections/microphonecheck/2015/07/01/419169611/vince-staples-my-job-is-to-keep-my-sanity. Accessed 17 Apr. 2018.

Staples, Vince. "Vince Staples Prefers to Speak Only for Himself." Interview by Joe Coscarelli. *The New York Times*, 29 June 2017, www.nytimes.com/2017/06/29/arts/music/vince-staples-interview-big-fish-theory.html. Accessed 14 Apr. 2018.

Staples, Vince. "Who Is Vince Staples?" Interview by Dharmic X. *Complex*, 7 Oct. 2013, www.complex.com/music/2013/10/who-is-vince-staples. Accessed 14 Apr. 2018.

Weiss, Jeff. "Vince Staples, Regular Genius." *The Fader*, 20 June 2016, www.thefader.com/2016/06/20/vince-staples-cover-story-interview. Accessed 14 Apr. 2018.

SELECTED WORKS

Shyne Coldchain Vol. 1, 2011; *Stolen Youth* (with Mac Miller/Larry Fisherman), 2013; *Shyne Coldchain II*, 2014; *Summertime '06*, 2015; *Big Fish Theory*, 2017

—Molly Hagan

Sloane Stephens

Date of birth: March 20, 1993
Occupation: Tennis player

In the late summer of 2017, tennis player Sloane Stephens made what could be considered one of the more dramatic comebacks in her sport. Having spent nearly a year off the court while recovering from a foot injury, Stephens entered her second Grand Slam tournament since returning to play and proceeded to dominate the competition, moving through the rounds of the US Open until she defeated fellow American player Madison Keys to claim the title. Having previously experienced some success in Grand Slam events, including an unexpected defeat of superstar Serena Williams in the quarterfinals of the 2013 Australian Open, Stephens's US Open victory decisively demonstrated that she was a real contender despite a record that some tennis commentators argued did not reflect her full potential. "We play a very long season. There's no one that is going to win every single week," she told Alyssa Roenigk for *ESPN* (2 July 2018) in response to such arguments. "I believe that if you just work on yourself and focus on yourself, you'll allow yourself to have success, no

By si.robi via Wikimedia Commons

matter what else is going on around you. Life does go on."

Indeed, Stephens's tennis career grew as she overcame a host of setbacks. These included not only her 2016 injury but also the personally devastating deaths of her stepfather and her father during her junior career. "There are going to be struggle moments," she told Ben Rothenberg for the *New York Times* (6 Sept. 2017). "But if you keep a good attitude, it will all eventually come together."

EARLY LIFE AND EDUCATION

Stephens was born on March 20, 1993, in Plantation, Florida. Her mother, Sybil Smith, was a former All-American college swimmer who went on to become a psychologist, while her father, John Stephens, was a football player who had spent several years as a running back with the New England Patriots. Stephens's parents separated not long after she was born, and she and her mother moved to Smith's home state of California when Stephens was two years old. Her mother later married Sheldon Farrell. Stephens spent much of her childhood in Fresno, with her mother, stepfather, and younger brother, Shawn.

When Stephens was a child, her mother and stepfather both enjoyed playing recreational tennis at a local country club. By the time Stephens was nine years old, she began to play the sport herself and quickly demonstrated a talent for the game. She began training with coach and former tennis player Francisco Gonzalez at Sierra Sport and Racquet Club in Fresno but soon left California to pursue further training, moving back

to Florida with her family. Stephens went on to enroll in the Saviano High Performance Tennis Academy, where she trained with Nick Saviano, a former player and longtime coach.

Stephens returned to California with her family in her teen years, and she resumed training there. Homeschooled from the age of twelve on, Stephens initially decided to focus on her tennis career rather than attend college. However, she later enrolled in a bachelor's degree program with Indiana University East, which had partnered with the Women's Tennis Association (WTA) to enable professional tennis players to pursue undergraduate studies. Stephens earned her degree in communication studies in the winter of 2017.

EARLY CAREER

Stephens was active as a junior competitor, playing in major tennis events such as the United States Tennis Association's Girls' National Championships, the Junior Fed Cup, and various World TeamTennis events. Throughout her early career, she played in both singles and doubles competitions but was particularly successful as a doubles player. In 2008, Stephens and her partner, Christina McHale, claimed a doubles championship at an International Tennis Federation (ITF) Women's Circuit event. She continued to compete in doubles matches during the subsequent years and in 2010 managed her greatest success to that point, partnering with Tímea Babos to win three junior Grand Slam titles.

Despite Stephens's success on the court, her early career was marked by personal challenges, beginning with the death of her stepfather in 2007. Another painful loss came in 2009, when Stephens's father, with whom she had reconnected as a teenager, died unexpectedly. The news of his death came while Stephens was competing in the 2009 US Open juniors competition, and she left the competition between matches to attend his funeral. She later returned to the competition and won her next match, although she was ultimately eliminated in the third round. Both her father and stepfather shaped her life and outlook both in life and in death. "I still wonder who's going to walk me down the aisle," she said to Shaun Assael for *ESPNW* (4 Jan. 2013) several years later. "And I can't make a call and say, 'Pick up this month's copy of *Vogue*, Daddy, I'm in it.' But both of them helped me learn how to be happy and live my life."

GOING PRO

During her late teens, Stephens began to compete in senior-level events overseen by professional tennis organizations such as the ITF and the WTA. She officially began her professional career in 2009, having gained the motivation and confidence to do so through her successful performance on the junior circuit. As a professional player, Stephens competed in national and international tournaments that varied in prestige, including the four major tournaments known as Grand Slams. Encompassing the Australian Open, the French Open (also known as Roland Garros), Wimbledon, and the US Open, the Grand Slam events offer the highest monetary prizes in professional tennis, and players who perform well in such events receive significant international attention as well as a major boost in their global player rankings.

Stephens tried unsuccessfully to qualify for the US Open's women's singles tournament for several years. Then, in 2011, Stephens made her first Grand Slam singles appearance on the senior level in the French Open, during which she was eliminated in the first round. In May of that year, she won her first ITF title at Italy's Camparini Gioielli Cup. Stephens also played in the US Open, progressing past the first two rounds of the competition before being eliminated in the third. The following year saw Stephens compete in all four Grand Slam events. She put forth her strongest performance at the French Open, where she progressed to the fourth round before being defeated by Australian Samantha Stosur.

2013 AUSTRALIAN OPEN

A key point in Stephens's career came in January 2013, when she made it to the quarterfinals of the Australian Open. During that round, she faced off against Serena Williams, an acclaimed American tennis star who had won fifteen Grand Slam titles prior to that point. Stephens stunned onlookers when she beat Williams, ending the established player's twenty-match win streak and securing herself a spot in the semifinals. Although she lost in the semifinal to Belarusian Victoria Azarenka, who would go on to win the tournament, Stephens gained widespread attention for her defeat of Williams, especially as she was nineteen years old at the time. Stephens went on to impress tennis fans further by making it to the quarterfinals at Wimbledon in July of that year.

For Stephens, the high scrutiny and expectations she faced following her defeat of Williams made playing tennis more stressful than fun. "When someone says, 'Just have fun, enjoy it,' at that time in 2013, I'd say: 'You're crazy! This is not fun, this is stressful, this is prize money, this is ranking, this is you're-the-only-young-American, this is Oh-my-God-you-beat-Serena,'" she recalled to Rothenberg. "There were just so many things happening that I couldn't really stop." Nevertheless, she continued to play well throughout 2013 and by the end of the year ranked twelfth in the world in the WTA's singles rankings.

VICTORIES AND SETBACKS

The years following the 2013 Australian Open were less productive for Stephens, who ended 2014 with a WTA ranking of thirty-seven. She competed in the Grand Slam events during the 2014 season, moving on to the fourth round in both the Australian Open and the French Open, but failed to duplicate the success of the previous season. Stephens ended her 2014 season early after injuring her wrist. Her fortunes improved in 2015, when she began working with Chicago-based coach Kamau Murray. During the season, Stephens made it to the fourth round in the French Open and the third at Wimbledon. She also succeeded outside of the Grand Slam events, claiming top place at the Citi Open in Washington, DC.

The 2016 season was initially successful for Stephens. Despite not progressing past the third round at the first three majors, she performed well in other competitions, winning women's singles titles at tournaments in New Zealand, Mexico, and the United States. She also traveled to Rio de Janeiro, Brazil, to compete in her first Olympic Games as a member of the US national tennis team. Stephens competed in the women's singles event but lost to Canadian Eugenie Bouchard in the first round.

As the year progressed, however, Stephens began experiencing pain in her foot, which was later revealed to be caused by a stress fracture. The injury required surgery and extensive rest, forcing her to stop playing tennis for nearly a year. The experience was difficult for Stephens, who at times feared being unable to return to professional play. "It was hard to see the light at the end of the tunnel," she told Rothenberg. "But I think once I kind of bought into that light, it's been good since then." Stephens ultimately returned to the professional circuit in mid-2017.

US OPEN TITLE

In August 2017, having recovered fully from her injury and played in several tournaments since returning to the court, Stephens entered the women's singles tournament at the US Open. Despite being unseeded, she performed well in the early stages of the competition, defeating Roberta Vinci, Dominika Cibulková, Ashleigh Barty, and Julia Görges in the first four rounds. She then beat Latvian Anastasija Sevastova in the quarterfinals and fellow American Venus Williams in the semifinals, before moving on to her first Grand Slam finals. There, she faced off against friend and fellow American Madison Keys. Stephens decisively defeated Keys, claiming her first Grand Slam title along with $3.7 million in prize money.

Not only did this reestablish Stephens as a force to be reckoned with, but her Grand Slam victory was especially meaningful as it came at the same venue where she had received the news of her father's death eight years before. "If someone told me when my dad died that I would end up winning the US Open years later, I would've been, like, You're crazy," she told S. L. Price for *Sports Illustrated* (12 Sept. 2017). "It is crazy. But I've had so many great moments here, and so many sad moments here, that winning, here, makes it even more special." In addition to winning the US Open in 2017, Stephens was a member of the US team that won that year's Fed Cup.

During the 2018 season, Stephens entered the Australian Open but was eliminated in the first round. She went on to claim the women's singles title at the Miami Open that spring and later made it to the final round of the French Open, where she lost to Simona Halep of Romania. In July 2018, Stephens lost to Donna Vekić of Croatia in the first round of Wimbledon. The upset prompted some tennis commentators to claim that Stephens was insufficiently committed to excelling at her sport. Stephens herself, on the other hand, demonstrated a more relaxed, pragmatic attitude toward the loss. "I said to my coach, 'Man, that was unfortunate. She played well,'" she told Roenigk. "Not too much you can do. I'm not going to, like, go cry and bang my racket. Can't dwell on it. Can't take it back."

In August 2018, Stephens reached the final of Canada's Rogers Cup but again lost to Halep. At the end of the month, Stephens was seeded third as she defended her title at the 2018 US Open, held at Arthur Ashe Stadium in New York. Stephens made it to the quarterfinals, but was eliminated from the competition after losing to nineteenth seed Sevastova on September 4. Despite the loss, Stephens was proud of making it to the quarterfinals and looking forward to upcoming matches.

PERSONAL LIFE

Stephens, a dog lover, enjoys cooking and watching basketball. In 2016, she began dating professional soccer player Jozy Altidore, whom she first met as a child in Florida. In addition to playing tennis professionally, she established the Sloane Stephens Foundation, which seeks to promote tennis among young people in California and Florida.

SUGGESTED READING

Assael, Shaun. "Stephens Trying to Take Control of Path Ahead." *ESPNW*, 4 Jan. 2013, www.espn.com/espnw/news-commentary/article/8765814/espnw-headliners-why-sloane-stephens-women-tennis. Accessed 10 Aug. 2018.

Goodman, Lizzy. "Is Sloane Stephens the Future of American Tennis?" *Elle*, 16 July 2014, www.elle.com/culture/career-politics/a12790/sloane-stephens-profile. Accessed 10 Aug. 2018.

Pfahler, Laurel. "Stephens on the Rise in Girls' Tennis." *RivalsHigh*, Yahoo! Sports, 14 Apr. 2009. *Internet Archive*, web.archive.org/web/20130707022017/http://highschool.rivals.com/content.asp?CID=935426. Accessed 14 Aug. 2018.

Price, S. L. "The Complex Rise of Sloane Stephens." *Sports Illustrated*, 12 Sept. 2017, www.si.com/tennis/2017/09/12/sloane-stephens-us-open-title-family-kamau-murray-injury-recovery. Accessed 10 Aug. 2018.

Pucci, Mike. "New Haven Open: Sloane Stephens on Her Way Up." *New Haven Register*, 19 Aug. 2011, www.nhregister.com/news/article/NEW-HAVEN-OPEN-Sloane-Stephens-on-her-way-up-11574607.php. Accessed 10 Aug. 2018.

Roenigk, Alyssa. "Nonchalant Reaction to Wimbledon Loss a Blessing and Curse for Sloane Stephens." *ESPN*, 2 July 2018, www.espn.com/tennis/story/_/id/23976703/nonchalant-reaction-wimbledon-loss-blessing-curse-sloane-stephens. Accessed 10 Aug. 2018.

Rothenberg, Ben. "Sloane Stephens Beat Stress, Physical and Mental. Can She Beat Venus Williams?" *The New York Times*, 6 Sept. 2017, www.nytimes.com/2017/09/06/sports/tennis/sloane-stephens-venus-williams-us-open.html. Accessed 10 Aug. 2018.

—*Joy Crelin*

Tim Sweeney

Date of birth: 1970
Occupation: CEO, Epic Games

Epic Games founder and chief executive officer Tim Sweeney devoted relatively little of his life to playing video games. Sweeney stated that he found figuring out how to create games was far more compelling than playing them. "I would play games long enough to discover what games were doing and how they were doing it," he explained to Stephen Totilo for *Kotaku* (7 Dec. 2011). "And then I'd spend the rest of my time building." After launching the company that would become Epic Games out of his parents' Maryland home at the age of twenty-one, Sweeney soon established himself as a talented and creative developer with games such as *ZZT* (1991) and *Jill of the Jungle* (1992). He went on to recruit a skilled team of video game creators whose efforts throughout the 1990s shaped the evolution of the video game industry for the next two decades. With the release of Unreal Engine, a powerful game-development tool, Epic Games

By Official GDC via Wikimedia Commons

gave both major game studios and independent developers the ability to create sophisticated games that could be played on a variety of platforms. For Sweeney, the success of the Unreal Engine and Epic's later video game titles, such as the popular 2017 game *Fortnite*, spoke to the company's commitment to making video game creation and play as widely accessible as possible. "We release the whole Unreal Engine source code because we feel anybody who wants to make a game should have all the benefits an engine developer has when they make their game," he explained to Dean Takahashi for *VentureBeat* (3 Aug. 2018). "*Fortnite's* the same thing. We want to democratize the participation in these events, make it all based on merit."

EARLY LIFE AND EDUCATION
Timothy Sweeney was born in 1970, and grew up in Potomac, Maryland. His father worked for the US Department of Defense. As a child, Sweeney demonstrated a strong interest in hands-on involvement with technology. "I was always interested in technical things, building go-karts out of engines, boards and whatever pieces I could find," he recalled to Totilo. "The people with my skill-set . . . there was a transition point. If you were born five years earlier than me, you were an auto mechanic. You did souped-up cars and drag-racing and all of these other crazy things. If you were born five years later, you were into computers. It was the same audience." Introduced to computers early in life, Sweeney began programming and made his first game on his Apple II computer at the age of eleven.

Sweeney's fascination with programming continued into his teen years. "For my first 10,000 hours of programming it was entirely on my own and entirely self-directed," he told Totilo. "In those early days I didn't really have anybody to share my programming experiences with. I was the weird computer guy and nobody really cared." After graduating from Potomac's Winston Churchill High School in 1988, Sweeney enrolled in the University of Maryland, where he studied mechanical engineering. Although he lived in the university's dorms in College Park, he often returned to his parents' home on weekends to use his computer. The family home later became the headquarters of Potomac Computer Systems, a company Sweeney founded with the intent of becoming a computer consultant. Sweeney ultimately left the University of Maryland before completing his bachelor's degree.

EPIC GAMES
Sweeney's longstanding passion for programming and interest in the concept of shareware—software distributed for free and encouraged to be shared—soon turned Potomac Computer Systems into a video game development company. His first professional foray into video games was ZZT, a puzzle game that incorporated elements of programming into the game itself. Designed to be played on MS-DOS systems and created over the course of nine months, ZZT was officially released by Potomac Computer Systems in late 1991. Following the game's release, Sweeney changed the name of his company to Epic MegaGames, which he described to Benj Edwards for *Gamasutra* (25 May 2009) as "kind of a scam to make it look like we were a big company." ZZT proved popular among players, who purchased copies of the game by mail, directly from Sweeney's base of operations at his parents' house. "I was selling about three or four copies a day, which is a hundred dollars a day. It was income you could live on, actually," he told Edwards. "I decided I was going to try to do that full-time and make a living from it, so I started working on *Jill of the Jungle*, this 2D side-scrolling game." Released in 1992, *Jill of the Jungle* became Epic MegaGames' second successful title.

As Epic MegaGames' offerings met with a positive reception among fans of video games, Sweeney began to recruit other video game professionals, including programmers and artists, to join the company and work on new projects, both alongside Sweeney and independently. "I've always looked for people who do something really important better than me, and then get them to do that and don't mess with them," he told James Brightman for *GamesIndustry.biz* (13 Mar. 2012) of his recruitment and leadership approach. Throughout the 1990s, Epic MegaGames produced a variety of titles, including *Xargon* (1993), *Jazz Jackrabbit* (1994), and *7th Legion* (1997). After moving out of the Sweeney family home, the company spent brief periods in Rockville, Maryland, and in Canada before establishing its headquarters in North Carolina in 1999. The company also simplified its name to Epic Games. Sweeney served as chief executive officer of the company and remained actively involved in its operations throughout its expansion. He retained a controlling interest in the company following the Chinese company Tencent's acquisition of 40 percent of Epic Games in 2012.

UNREAL ENGINE

In the mid-1990s, Sweeney began developing the game engine technology Unreal Engine, which became the underpinning of Epic's later video games as well as one of the company's most profitable products. Inspired in part by the rise of video games with three-dimensional graphics, the Unreal Engine was a tool used by developers to create and render video games. For Sweeney and his colleagues, the Unreal Engine represented an "editor-centric approach to game development, where you had this integrated editor that used the game engine for real-time display of everything," as he explained to Edwards. Sweeney personally completed much of the programming for the first incarnation of the tool, Unreal Engine 1, which Epic Games went on to use to create the 1998 game *Unreal*, the first installment of a series.

Although Sweeney and his colleagues initially planned to use the Unreal Engine solely in house, demand for the tool soon arose among other game developers, and Epic began to license the engine for use by other video game companies. Over the subsequent decades, the various incarnations of the Unreal Engine were used not only to produce Epic Games' properties but also numerous popular games from other major companies, including *Deus Ex* (2000), *BioShock* (2007), *Batman: Arkham Asylum* (2009), and *Rocket League* (2015). Following the release of Unreal Engine 4 in 2014, Epic Games made the engine available to an even wider audience, releasing the tool for free while implementing royalty fees that applied only to financially successful commercial projects, thus granting independent developers, novices, and students the ability to use one of the industry's powerful tools with little financial risk. In addition to Unreal Engine, Epic created the Unreal Engine Marketplace, in which game developers could purchase game-making components such as visual assets from creators for use in their own games.

Following the introduction of the Unreal Engine, Epic Games continued to develop its own video game properties, to significant success. The company released the third-person shooter game *Gears of War* to critical acclaim in 2006 and went on to develop several sequel games before selling the rights to the property to Microsoft in 2014. Particularly focused on making games created using the Unreal Engine playable on a wide range of devices, Epic Games released the first Unreal Engine based iOS game, *Infinity Blade*, in 2010. The company launched the multiplayer online game *Paragon* in 2016, but ultimately shut it down in 2018, after the game proved to be less successful than expected.

FORTNITE

In 2017, the company released two games under the title *Fortnite*. The first, *Fortnite: Save the World*, was a cooperative game in which players work together to survive and build shelters in a hostile environment. Released in the summer of 2017, the game required players to pay for access like many other video games. The second, *Fortnite Battle Royale*, allowed players to play for free but included the option to pay for cosmetic upgrades through microtransactions. Released for a variety of platforms, including PC and PlayStation 4, in late 2017, the free-to-play version of *Fortnite* pitted up to one hundred players against each other in a fight to the death. After proving global popularity, *Fortnite Battle Royale* was made available for the Nintendo Switch in mid-2018. In August of that year, a beta version of the game became available for Android devices.

The success of *Fortnite*, and particularly *Fortnite Battle Royale*, provided a significant financial boost for Epic Games, earning the company more than $160 million per month as of May 2018, and reportedly made Sweeney himself a billionaire. For Sweeney, however, the success of *Fortnite* was particularly significant because it demonstrated the desire of gamers to be able to play games on multiple platforms, an issue about which he felt strongly. "I think we will see, over the next two years—a huge theme in the whole game industry will be connecting all of the platforms together and reaching the entire base of gamers," he told Takahashi. "It's going to lead to huge growth. When gamers can play a game together with all of their friends, regardless of the devices they own, you have a much more compelling social experience. That applies to all multiplayer games." The financial success of *Fortnite* also enabled Epic Games to reinvest much of the company's profits in key areas of interest, including Unreal Engine, esports, and future projects.

PERSONAL LIFE

Sweeney lives in Cary, North Carolina. In addition to creating video games and related technology, he is a committed conservationist and has dedicated his time and money to protecting some of North Carolina's most diverse ecosystems from potential development. He began buying undeveloped land in the state around 2008. By 2016, he owned more than forty thousand acres in the state, including a tract of land known as Box Creek Wilderness, a Registered National Heritage Area home to a diverse array of plants and wildlife. The same year, the land's undeveloped status was threatened when a power company sought to build a power line across the property. To ensure that the Box Creek Wilderness would be protected, Sweeney, in late 2016, arranged for the land to be covered by a conservation easement, effectively donating the land to the United States Fish and Wildlife Service. "It's still in private ownership but the easement ensures it can never be developed," Sweeney told Karen Chávez for the *Citizen Times* (8 Nov. 2016). "It's not open to anyone in the public at any time, but people can email and get a permission card and go and enjoy it." In addition to the Box Creek Wilderness, Sweeney has donated more than one thousand additional acres of land for conservation purposes.

SUGGESTED READING

Chávez, Karen. "Box Creek Wilderness Permanently Protected." *Citizen Times*, 8 Nov. 2016, www.citizen-times.com/story/news/local/2016/11/08/box-creek-wilderness-permanently-protected/93443704/. Accessed 10 Aug. 2018.

Pendleton, Devon, and Christopher Palmeri. "*Fortnite* Mania Fuels Epic Growth to $8.5 Billion." *Bloomberg*, 24 July 2018, www.bloomberg.com/news/features/2018-07-24/fortnite-phenomenon-turns-epic-game-developer-into-billionaire. Accessed 10 Aug. 2018.

Sweeney, Tim. "An Epic Interview with Tim Sweeney." Interview by James Brightman. *GamesIndustry.biz*, 13 Mar. 2012, www.gamesindustry.biz/amp/2012-03-13-an-epic-interview-with-tim-sweeney. Accessed 10 Aug. 2018.

Sweeney, Tim. "From the Past to the Future: Tim Sweeney Talks." Interview by Benj Edwards. *Gamasutra*, 25 May 2009, www.gamasutra.com/view/feature/132426/from_the_past_to_the_future_tim_.php. Accessed 10 Aug. 2018.

Sweeney, Tim. "Tim Sweeney: Epic's CEO on *Fortnite* on Android, Skipping Google Play, and the Open Metaverse." Interview by Dean Takahashi. *VentureBeat*, 3 Aug. 2018, venturebeat.com/2018/08/03/tim-sweeney-epics-ceo-on-fortnite-on-android-skipping-google-play-and-the-open-metaverse/. Accessed 10 Aug. 2018.

Totilo, Stephen. "The Quiet Tinkerer Who Makes Games Beautiful Finally Gets His Due." *Kotaku*, 7 Dec. 2012, kotaku.com/5865951/the-quiet-tinkerer-who-makes-games-beautiful-finally-gets-his-due. Accessed 10 Aug. 2018.

—*Joy Crelin*

SZA

Date of birth: November 8, 1990
Occupation: Singer

Solána Imani Rowe, who performs under the name SZA, is a Saint Louis–born, New Jersey–raised R & B singer and songwriter. Her years-in-the-making debut album, *Ctrl*, was released to both popular and critical acclaim in June 2017. Prior to *Ctrl*, Rowe was well known in indie circles for her extended-play albums (EPs) *See. SZA.Run* (2012), *S* (2013), and *Z* (2014). She collaborated with Nicki Minaj and Beyoncé to write the hit song "Feeling Myself," which appeared on Minaj's 2014 album *The Pinkprint*, and she worked with Rihanna and producer Tyran Donaldson to develop her song "Consideration," which she gave to Rihanna (if somewhat reluctantly) for her album *Anti* (2016).

Rowe, a science lover who came to singing and songwriting almost by accident, was signed to the rap label Top Dawg Entertainment in 2013. Her stage name (pronounced "sizzah") is an acronym derived from the Supreme Alphabet created by former Nation of Islam member and Five Percent Nation founder Clarence 13X: the S stands for "savior" (although Rowe sometimes prefers "sovereign" instead); the Z stands for "zig-zag-zig," representing the sometimes convoluted path from knowledge to wisdom and understanding; and the A stands for "Allah," the Arabic word for God.

Rowe's ever-evolving sound, a blend of smooth R & B vocals and ethereal pop and electronic beats, defies easy description. Soulful and strange, it combines ultra-sincere lyrics about insecurity and loneliness with a smattering of images that verge on the absurd. "I am not human / I am bacon," she sings in 2013's "Aftermath."

EARLY LIFE

Rowe was born in Saint Louis, Missouri, on November 8, 1990. She was raised in the predominantly white neighborhood of Maplewood, New Jersey—the same affluent suburb in which Grammy Award–winning singer and rapper Lauryn Hill grew up. Her father was an executive producer at CNN, and her mother was a global account executive at AT&T.

By The Come Up Show [CC BY 2.5], via Wikimedia Commons

Rowe was interested in music from an early age, but her protective father forbade her from watching television or listening to the radio. She loved his old jazz records and developed an affinity for Miles Davis, Billie Holiday, and Louis Armstrong. Still, she seized on sources of new music when she could—a mix CD from a friend's Bat Mitzvah, a broken iPod she found at gymnastics camp, or the rap music her older half-sister sometimes played. She once bought a Lil Jon CD because she had heard one of his songs on her sister's answering machine; when her father discovered it, he grounded her.

Other early interests of Rowe's included dancing and gymnastics. She danced pointe ballet with the American Ballet Theatre and modern contemporary dance with the Alvin Ailey American Dance Theater. She trained as a gymnast for thirteen years and even considered training for the Olympics at one point. In 2005, while a student at Columbia High School in Maplewood, she was ranked the fifth-best gymnast in the nation.

Rowe's father is Muslim, and she has described her upbringing as "orthodox Muslim." (Her mother is Christian.) She attended a Muslim preparatory school, wore leggings and long sleeves while practicing cheerleading and gymnastics, and, as an adolescent, briefly wore a hijab. The latter ended "somewhere around the seventh grade," she told Insanul Ahmed for *Complex* (8 Sept. 2013), after the September 11, 2001, terrorist attacks. "I was attacked at school and taunted," she recalled. "It got really uncomfortable and I started to get embarrassed.

. . . At school, I wanted to fit in so I would take my hijab off."

Rowe began covering again as a sophomore in high school. "I don't know why I did that again," she said to Ahmed. "I think I was starting to feel like ungrounded or losing my mind. I was upset and had to go back to something that was familiar to me so I started covering again." The harassment this time was worse, and eventually Rowe separated from the faith—and, for a time, from her father—altogether. She has since reconciled with both her father and, to some extent, her faith. "I go to Jumu'ah [Friday prayer] when I can with my dad," she told Ahmed. "Some things never change. I'll feel most comfortable with Islam forever."

COLLEGE INTERRUPTED

After graduating from high school in 2008, Rowe attended Delaware State University as a marine biology major, but she failed out in her first year. Though a good student, Rowe was bored by school, preferring to skip class and smoke marijuana with her roommate. "I was just high every day," she said to Ahmed. "I never had that much weed in my face before and it was free. . . . Both of us failed out of class and we just sat on the curb in front of our dorms and made occasional trips to the café." She moved to New York City, where she worked a number of odd jobs, including as a bartender at a strip club, and spent time with her older brother, Daniel, a rapper who performs under the name Mnhattn. "He was having me sing Biggie lyrics over MF Doom, or like introducing me to the Dum Dum Girls," Rowe recalled to Alex Morris for *Rolling Stone* (30 Aug. 2017). "I was depressed and he was depressed, and I didn't have s—— else to do."

She had never considered herself a singer, Rowe told Ahmed, because her voice did not have the "soft" quality of singers such as Aaliyah or Ashanti. In numerous interviews, Rowe has emphasized the serendipity of her life's path. Her music career began by chance; Daniel was recording an album and asked her to sing a hook on one of his songs. "When I sang for the first time on my brother's track, I was like, 'It doesn't sound that bad,'" she said to Ahmed. "Listening to it now, it's horrendous and the worst song I've ever made." But, she said, "That was the beginning of hearing my voice and being like, 'I can do something.'"

Rowe would return to college at least twice more, though by that time she was more interested in pursuing music than her studies. "I was doing music on the side, I had to fail out of school for my parents to really understand," she said to Raj Anand for the website *uproxx.com* (18 Apr. 2014). "They were pissed. . . . So disappointed. Then I went back to school out of guilt for one semester. I took a loan out on my name, which is why I owe like $30,000 in student loans, because I left again."

MIXTAPES AND EPS

In 2011, Rowe's boyfriend was the creative director for the clothing brand 10.Deep, which was sponsoring one of rapper Kendrick Lamar's shows at Gramercy Theatre in Manhattan. After the show, Rowe offered to deliver free clothes to Lamar and members of his label, Top Dawg Entertainment (TDE). She brought along her friend Ashley—"I was afraid to go by myself," she told Ahmed—who happened to be listening to one of Rowe and her brother's songs when they made the delivery. TDE executive Terrence "Punch" Henderson, was impressed by her voice and said he might call her into the studio later. Nearly an hour later, however, the label's founder, Anthony "Top Dawg" Tiffith, called her to complain that she had not brought them the right sizes, and Rowe felt her chance at a connection had slipped away.

Still, Punch and Rowe kept in touch; she occasionally sent him tracks she was working on, and he became a mentor to the anxiety-prone perfectionist. "One thing Punch has taught me is that when talent fails you, all you have is skill," she said to Ahmed. She worked to build her skills as a songwriter and musician, and in October 2012 she released her first EP, *See.SZA.Run*, as a mixtape online. ("Mixtape" in this context refers to a self-produced, independently released album that is made available free of charge.)

See.SZA.Run features indie producers such as Brandun DeShay, formerly of the hip-hop collective Odd Future. Rowe admitted to Chris Kelly for *Fact* magazine (24 Apr. 2013) that her collaboration with DeShay only came about after she stole some of his beats for the mixtape. The recording process was "experimental," she said; she freestyled the songs, writing them in the studio in real time. "I don't believe in doing more than one take or drafting," she explained. "If the song isn't the way I want it before I leave, it's probably not going to get there."

A few months later, in spring 2013, Rowe released her second mixtape, S. Peppered with audio clips from the horror film *Rosemary's Baby* (1968), the album is more confident and mystical than her first release and shows Rowe honing her artistic voice. In a review of S for the online magazine *Consequence of Sound* (22 Apr. 2013), Adam Kivel wrote that Rowe's "dreamy, warped R & B manages to exude confidence and fragility, brushing against your skin just as it evaporates icy cold into the mist."

In July 2013, Rowe was picked up by TDE, becoming the first woman and the first non-rapper signed by the label. She released Z, her third EP and her first retail release, in spring 2014. Featuring guest appearances by Lamar,

Rashad, and Chance the Rapper, the finished product was far glitzier than her previous work. "After *See.SZA.Run* and S, I originally thought I would do another EP and that it would be this little thing," Rowe said to Reggie Ugwu for *Billboard* (7 Apr. 2014). But, she said, "then everything blew up. It's different now. I feel like I owe people more."

CREATIVE DIFFICULTIES

Throughout 2015, Rowe toured the festival circuit, playing Bonnaroo, Coachella, Lollapalooza, and Afropunk, and worked on her full-length debut album. She has said that at least three totally different versions of the album existed at one time. As the project was repeatedly delayed, first by Rowe and then by TDE, she reworked it over and over again.

One unexpected setback came when Rowe was called into a writing camp for superstar musical artist Rihanna. "I'd made no material for her for, like, the last three hours," she recalled to Ryan White for *i-D* (26 Oct. 2017). "Then [producer] Pharrell [Williams] walks in and is like, 'So what've you been doing?' and I'm like, 'S——'. I get to play *Pharrell* my music.'" Wanting to impress him, she played a song she had been working on for her own album. Rihanna decided she wanted the song; Rowe offered to write her a new one, but Rihanna was adamant. The song became Rihanna's "Consideration," the highly acclaimed opening track of her 2016 album *Anti*. Though Rowe was featured on the track and was praised for her performance, the incident forced her to completely rethink her album. "I think I needed that song on my album," she said to White. "But then I do also think it was supposed to work out the way it worked out." Still, she said, her album "probably would have been completed a year earlier had I kept 'Consideration.' That was the centerpiece. I shot a video for it and everything."

In October 2016, frustrated and overwhelmed by delays on the part of TDE, Rowe posted on Twitter, "I actually quit. [Punch] can release my album if he ever feels like it. Y'all be blessed." She deleted the post later the same day, but it was reported on by several media outlets. A week later, speaking about the incident to Karizza Sanchez for *Complex* magazine (28 Nov. 2016), Rowe revealed that the album was not the only thing causing her stress. "My life has just been falling the f—— apart," she said. "I buried, like, three ex-boyfriends, my granny died, I buried someone two days ago. . . . I'm devastated by the state of the world and the hatred."

CTRL AT LAST

Despite her frustrations, Rowe was determined to complete her album, if uncertain about her plans after its release. Finally, *Ctrl* was released in June 2017. (At one point, the album had been rumored to be titled *A*, to complete the trilogy begun by *S* and *Z*; Rowe told White that *A* is actually an unreleased EP, insisting, "Yes it does exist!") The release came only after TDE "cut [her] off," Rowe said to Rebecca Nicholson for the *Guardian* (29 July 2017), by simply removing her hard drive from the studio when they decided she was taking too long. "I just kept f—— everything up," she said. "I just kept moving s—— around. I was choosing from 150, 200 songs, so I'm just like, who knows what's good anymore?"

Ctrl enjoyed early and emphatic endorsements from stars such as P. Diddy, Lamar, Drake, and Solange. The album's title comes from Rowe's desire for control over her life. "Four years ago, I was hoping for a lot but not *being* a lot," she said to White. "I didn't feel in control of my life, I felt like, 'I hope this works out,' but I wasn't invested in the result. Now I'm acknowledging that I'm scared, and I'm invested."

PERSONAL LIFE
Rowe lives in Los Angeles with her French bulldog, Piglet.

SUGGESTED READING

Kelly, Chris. "New Talent: Alt-R&B Vocalist SZA on 'Snatching' Tracks and Putting Her Music in the Universe." *Fact*, 24 Apr. 2013, www.factmag.com/2013/04/24/new-talent-alt-rb-vocalist-sza-on-snatching-tracks-and-putting-her-music-in-the-universe/. Accessed 14 Nov. 2017.

Morris, Alex. "How SZA Beat Depression and Cracked the Top 10 with *Ctrl*." *Rolling Stone*, 30 Aug. 2017, www.rollingstone.com/music/features/sza-talks-ctrl-depression-discrimination-top-dawg-w500004. Accessed 14 Nov. 2017.

Nicholson, Rebecca. "SZA: 'The Record Company Took My Hard Drive from Me.'" *The Guardian*, 29 July 2017, www.theguardian.com/music/2017/jul/29/sza-record-company-took-my-hard-drive-beyonce-kendrick-lamar. Accessed 14 Nov. 2017.

Sanchez, Karizza. "Why SZA's Next Album May Be Her Last." *Complex*, 28 Nov. 2016, www.complex.com/music/2016/11/sza-interview-quitting-music-dec-jan-2017-issue. Accessed 14 Nov. 2017.

SZA. "Who Is SZA?" Interview by Insanul Ahmed. *Complex*, 8 Sept. 2013, www.complex.com/music/2013/09/who-is-sza/. Accessed 14 Nov. 2017.

Ugwu, Reggie. "SZA Talks Z Album & Being the Only Girl in Top Dawg Entertainment." *Billboard*, 7 Apr. 2014, www.billboard.com/articles/columns/the-juice/6041313/sza-talks-z-album-being-the-only-girl-in-top-dawg-entertainment. Accessed 15 Nov. 2017.

White, Ryan. "How SZA Became the Definitive Sound of 2017." *i-D*, 26 Oct. 2017, i-d.vice.com/en_us/article/j5jed3/how-sza-became-the-definitive-sound-of-2017. Accessed 15 Nov. 2017.

SELECTED WORKS
See. *SZA.Run*, 2012; *S*, 2013; *Z*, 2014; *Ctrl*, 2017

—*Molly Hagan*

Mya Taylor

Date of birth: March 28, 1991
Occupation: Actor

Mya Taylor is a transgender actor who won the 2016 Film Independent Spirit Award for best supporting female for her role in *Tangerine* (2015).

EARLY LIFE
Named Jeremiah James Bonner on March 28, 1991, in Houston, Texas, Mya Taylor grew up in Richmond, Texas. When she was thirteen, her mother, Cecelia Bonner, was jailed and Taylor and her brother and sister moved in with their maternal grandmother and her husband. The grandmother's husband was abusive and beat Taylor.

When she was young, Taylor considered herself gay, but she was unaware she was transgender. She knew she wanted long hair, and she frequently dressed in women's clothes, but until she learned an aunt was transgender, she lacked knowledge about transgender people. When she was eighteen, Taylor told her family that she was a transgender woman. They rejected her, so she left home to live with her aunt in Los Angeles, California.

Rather than supporting Taylor's desire to transition, her aunt cautioned her not to, saying that she lacked the looks to be attractive as a woman. Taylor frequently slept elsewhere—on the street or at friends' places—until she was able to obtain housing through the assistance of a youth center.

Obtaining a job proved more difficult. Taylor applied for nearly two hundred jobs, running the gamut from house cleaner to personal assistant, and had dozens of interviews, but was unable to land a job. Unable to find any other type of work, Taylor worked as a sex worker in Hollywood until 2014. She dressed as a woman and worked on the corner of Santa Monica Boulevard and Highland Avenue. The work was high risk, and Taylor was arrested and jailed four times.

LIFE'S WORK

By 2014, Taylor had begun hormone therapy for her transition. She lived in an apartment in Compton with a trans roommate, Kitana Kiki Rodriguez, who also worked as a sex worker. They both hung around at the Los Angeles LGBT Center, and it was there that independent filmmaker Sean Baker first met Taylor. Baker was intrigued with the activity at Santa Monica Boulevard and Highland Avenue and wanted to interview sex workers to learn their stories. Although most sex workers were reluctant to talk with him, Taylor was willing. Baker was drawn to her enthusiasm and spirit, and they began a collaboration that eventually resulted in the movie *Tangerine*.

Tangerine is a comedy about a woman released from prison on Christmas Eve (Sin-Dee, played by Rodriguez) and her best friend (Alexandra, played by Taylor), who go on a quest to find the pimp/boyfriend who cheated on Sin-Dee. It is set in the subculture of transgender sex workers working the intersection of Santa Monica Boulevard and Highland Avenue in Hollywood, and was written specifically for its two costars.

Taylor encouraged Baker to incorporate humor in the film. Initially reluctant, he eventually agreed—and decided also to make the film so it would appeal to mainstream audiences instead of the smaller, select audiences he had originally intended. The low-budget film was shot entirely on an iPhone 5S. The film premiered at the Sundance Film Festival in January 2015 and was a hit with the audience. While *Tangerine* failed to win any awards at Sundance, it went on to play at film festivals around the world and was nominated for numerous awards, winning many. For her performance in *Tangerine*, Taylor won the Film Independent Spirit Award for best supporting female in 2016, the 2015 Seattle Film Critics Award for best supporting female and the 2015 Gotham Independent Film Award for breakthrough actor. The film's executive producers, Mark and Jay Duplass at Magnolia Pictures, also led an unsuccessful campaign to nominate Taylor and her costar for Academy Awards.

Following her role in Tangerine, Taylor appeared in two short films: *Diane from the Moon* (2016) and *Happy Birthday, Marsha!* (2016). In each of them she played the role of a trans woman. She was also at work on another short film, *Viva Diva*.

IMPACT

Mya Taylor welcomed the attention *Tangerine* brought to transgender issues and has used her newfound celebrity to be an activist and spokesperson to educate people about these issues. She also has embraced acting and hopes to have the opportunity to play roles that are not about a transgender person, knowing that once she fulfills that goal, she will have broken another barrier.

PERSONAL LIFE

Taylor lives in North Dakota with her fiancé, James Behnke.

SUGGESTED READING

Bahr, Lindsey. "Meet the Transgender Women Who Inspired, Star in *Tangerine*." *AP: The Big Story*. Assoc. Press, 9 July 2015. Web. 21 Apr. 2016.

Hess, Taylor. "'I Can't Try to Be an Activist if People Don't Know My Real Story': *Tangerine*'s Mya Taylor." *Filmmaker*. Filmmaker Magazine, 29 Oct. 2015. Web. 21 Apr. 2016.

Ruiz, Michelle. "Mya Taylor and the Trans Actress's Dream of Going to the Oscars." *Cosmopolitan*. Hearst Communications, 26 Feb. 2016. Web. 21 Apr. 2016.

Taylor, Mya, and Sean Baker. "A Downtrodden LA Corner Inspires Comedy and Friendship in *Tangerine*." Interview by Terry Gross. *NPR*. National Public Radio, 21 July 2015. Web. 21 Apr. 2016.

Taylor, Mya, and Sean Baker. "*Tangerine* Director Sean Baker and Star Mya Taylor on Making the Most Exciting Film of the Year." Interview by Peter Macia. *Vogue*. Condé Nast, 9 July 2015. Web. 22 Apr. 2016.

Travers, Andrew. "Academy Screenings: 'Tangerine' Star Mya Taylor on Her Breakthrough." *Aspen Times*. Swift Communications, 1 Jan. 2016. Web. 21 Apr. 2016.

SELECTED WORKS

Tangerine, 2015; *Diane from the Moon*, 2016; *Happy Birthday, Marsha!*, 2016

—Barb Lightner

Chrissy Teigen

Date of birth: November 30, 1985
Occupation: Model

Since coming into prominence following her first appearance in the magazine *Sports Illustrated*'s annual swimsuit issue in 2010, model Chrissy Teigen has established herself as one of modeling's crossover success stories. Known for her humorous take on everyday life and relatable public persona—both evident in her frequent posts to social networks such as Twitter and Instagram—Teigen has built upon her success as a model and established herself as a television personality, cookbook author, and media brand. At the same time, she has remained close to her

By David Shankbone, via Wikimedia Commons

modeling roots, while maintaining her signature irreverent take on the industry that made her famous. "Some people, I think, think that because I don't take it as seriously as a lot of the girls do, that I frown upon modeling or think it's stupid," she told Erin Cunningham for the *Daily Beast* (21 July 2014). "I don't at all. This is my life. I would be nothing without this. But I really don't take it seriously."

Born in Utah and raised in Washington and California, Teigen was discovered by a photographer while in her late teens. She found work as a catalog model before a series of *Sports Illustrated* appearances made her increasingly in demand. She went on to appear in a variety of reality and talk-focused television programs, and, since 2015, has served as a cohost and commentator for the Emmy-nominated series *Lip Sync Battle*. Teigen's true passion, however, is food, which became the focus of her long-running blog, *So Delushious*. She published her first cookbook, *New York Times* Best Seller *Cravings*, in 2016. For Teigen, food is a passion that she tends to approach with the same degree of humor and flexibility as the other areas of her life. "I always get to eat what I want, because if I don't, I go insane," she told Laurie Sandell for *Cosmopolitan* (28 Apr. 2014). "If you're going to choose to do something like the Paleo Diet, then you choose not to enjoy your nights out."

EARLY LIFE AND EDUCATION
Christine Teigen was born in Delta, Utah, on November 30, 1985. Her mother, Vilailuck, is Thai, while her father, Ron, is Norwegian American. She has four half-siblings. As a child, Teigen and her parents lived in a number of different states. The family eventually settled in Snohomish, a city north of Seattle, Washington. Teigen grew up playing a variety of sports and was a member of the cheerleading squad at Snohomish High School. She spent her first three years of high school in Snohomish but transferred to Huntington Beach High School for her senior year, following her family's move to Huntington Beach, California. Teigen graduated from high school in 2003.

As a child and teenager, Teigen did not consider pursuing a career in modeling or the entertainment industry, and instead focused on other interests. "I always wanted to be a teacher or wanted to do something with food," she recalled to Cunningham. However, her trajectory shifted dramatically during her late teens, when a photographer spotted her while she was working at a surf shop in Huntington Beach and asked her to model for him. Although Teigen was initially skeptical of the opportunity and insisted that her father accompany her to that first photoshoot, the photographer was legitimate. The experience would open numerous doors for Teigen over the subsequent years.

MODELING CAREER
In the years following her first photoshoot, Teigen began to explore the possibility of modeling as a career despite initial doubts that she was suited for the job. "I just never thought I could do it myself really ever," she explained to Cunningham. "I just never thought I was tall enough or skinny enough. [When I was starting] it was the time of the very thin, waify runway models. So, I knew I couldn't do that." In spite of such trends in the modeling industry, Teigen eventually signed with the agency IMG Models. She initially found work as a catalog model, working primarily out of Miami, Florida, where she spent part of the year sharing a home with other models while booking jobs. In addition to shooting photographs for use in advertisements, Teigen appeared in music videos. In 2007 and 2008, she served as a briefcase-holding model on the television game show *Deal or No Deal*.

A turning point in Teigen's career came after friend and fellow model Brooklyn Decker, who had previously modeled for *Sports Illustrated*'s annual swimsuit issue, connected Teigen with the individuals in charge of the issue. Modeling for *Sports Illustrated 2010 Swimsuit*, Teigen was given the title of Rookie of the Year for her work, which brought her widespread attention as a model. Over the following years, she became a fixture in the swimsuit issue, appearing in each installment through 2017. In 2014, Teigen was featured on the magazine's cover, along with models Nina Agdal and Lily Aldridge. After her

Sports Illustrated debut, Teigen appeared in a variety of other magazines, including *Vogue*, and modeled in advertising campaigns for companies such as Gillette, Gap, and Nike. As she became increasingly known for her personality and sense of humor, she likewise appeared in advertisements that drew on her relatable humor and point of view, including television commercials for companies such as McDonald's, Google, and Smirnoff.

A PASSION FOR FOOD

Long interested in food and cooking, Teigen began a food blog called *So Delushious* in 2011. The blog became an outlet for her interest in food and an opportunity to discuss subjects other than modeling and her relationship with singer John Legend, both of which were topics of interest in the media. Over the course of several years, Teigen posted to *So Delushious* on a regular basis, sharing pictures of meals she cooked and ate, links to her favorite recipes, and musings about her everyday life. Teigen has noted in interviews that she was largely disinterested in her mother's Thai cooking during her early life; as an adult, however, she expressed an interest in a vast range of cuisines, and her blog reflects her diverse culinary tastes.

Although Teigen has no formal culinary training, she found that readers appreciated her relatable approach and willingness to admit her unfamiliarity with cooking tricks and techniques. "I don't think you understand how many simple things I learn all the time that I'm almost embarrassed to share that I didn't know. Then I realize that if I didn't know that, then there's probably 1.7 million people on the Internet who probably didn't know that either," she explained to Catherine Kast for *People* (23 Feb. 2016). "It's the tiniest little things that I feel so dumb not knowing. Then I share it, and I'm in this whole world of people who are like, 'That's awesome!'" Having established herself as both a passionate foodie and a talented cook in her own right, Teigen wrote the *New York Times* best-selling cookbook *Cravings: Recipes for All the Food You Want to Eat*, with author Adeena Sussman, in 2016. Soon afterward, she began work on a second cookbook, which Teigen announced she had completed in the spring of 2018.

TELEVISION AND TWITTER

In addition to her modeling work and forays into the culinary industry, Teigen has become known for her appearances on numerous television shows. She has made guest appearances on entertainment news programs such as *Access Hollywood*, *Extra*, and *Entertainment Tonight*; she also hosted the 2013 television series *Model Employee* and served as a judge for the 2014 cooking competition show *Snack-Off*. In 2015, she began to serve as a cohost and commentator for the competition series *Lip Sync Battle*, in which celebrities perform elaborate lip sync routines. Teigen has likewise served as a guest cohost on the food-focused talk show *The Chew* and, in 2015 and 2016, cohosted the talk show *FABLife*.

Although she initially found television appearances to be nerve-wracking, Teigen quickly adjusted to being a fixture on reality and talk-focused programs. "Three years ago I would have been terrified to go on a show like 'The Chew' or 'The View.' I would have been shaking and sweating," she revealed in an interview for *A Drink With* (14 Apr. 2015). "There was actually a pill that I used to take to stop me from sweating because I would get so nervous that I would be covered in sweat, under my nose and all over my arms. I would be so scared! Now that kind of stuff is nothing to me." Although projects such as *Model Employee* and *FABLife* proved to be short lived, *Lip Sync Battle* remained popular among television viewers and was nominated for two consecutive Emmy Awards for Outstanding Structured Reality Program, in 2016 and 2017.

Teigen is also known for her extensive social media presence that she uses to comment on food, work, family, and her day-to-day life through her distinctive comedic lens. Although social media is regarded by some primarily as a promotional tool, Teigen has noted that she genuinely enjoys connecting with others through services such as Twitter and Instagram. "I've always been crazy about—even like, remember AOL chat rooms?" she told Cunningham. "I always loved message boards and I was always interacting on the computer." Teigen's Twitter presence became the focus of further attention after President Donald Trump's official government Twitter account blocked her for criticizing him.

PERSONAL LIFE

Teigen met her husband, singer John Legend, when she starred in the music video for his song "Stereo." "I walked into John's dressing room to meet him, and he was ironing in his underwear," she told Sandell of their first meeting. "I said, 'You do your own ironing!?' He said, 'Of course I do.' I gave him a hug." After keeping in touch while Legend was on tour, the pair began dating in 2007. They married in Italy in September 2013. Teigen and Legend have two children, Luna and Miles, and split their time between New York and Los Angeles.

In the years following the birth of her first child, Teigen spoke candidly about the difficult aspects of pregnancy and motherhood, including her struggle with infertility and the decision to pursue in vitro fertilization, as well as her later experiences with postpartum depression and anxiety. She has likewise spoken out against the practice of "mom shaming," in which critics go out of their way to comment negatively on a mother's parenting decisions. "You can call me anything—you can talk about my face, my make-up, my clothes, whatever," Teigen told Gibson Johns for *AOL* (1 Apr. 2018). "But once you say my food looks bad or I'm not doing something correctly with my child, that's when I launch."

SUGGESTED READING

Cunningham, Erin. "Chrissy Teigen and the Rise of the Social Supermodel." *Daily Beast*, 21 July 2014, www.thedailybeast.com/chrissy-teigen-and-the-rise-of-the-social-supermodel. Accessed 9 June 2018.

Jacobs, A. J. "Everyone, Chrissy. Chrissy, Everyone. Have Fun." *Esquire*, 7 Aug. 2014, www.esquire.com/entertainment/interviews/a29618/chrissy-teigen-interview-0914/. Accessed 9 June 2018.

Kast, Catherine. "Chrissy Teigen on Her New Cookbook, Cravings: I Spent 'Years Trying to Prove to People That I Love Food.'" *People*, 23 Feb. 2016, greatideas.people.com/2016/02/23/chrissy-teigen-cookbook-cravings-love-cooking/. Accessed 9 June 2018.

Sandell, Laurie. "Chrissy Teigen Is a Member of the Mile-High Club." *Cosmopolitan*, 28 Apr. 2014, www.cosmopolitan.com/entertainment/news/a24251/chrissy-teigen-on-june-2014-cosmo/. Accessed 9 June 2018.

Teigen, Chrissy. "Chatting Up Chrissy Teigen." Interview by Abby Gardner. *Marie Claire*, 2 Mar. 2012, www.marieclaire.com/beauty/news/a6968/chrissy-teigen-gillette-interview/. Accessed 9 June 2018.

Teigen, Chrissy. "Chrissy Teigen Reveals Two Topics She Won't Take Any Criticism for on Social Media." Interview by Gibson Johns. *AOL*, 1 Apr. 2018, www.aol.com/article/entertainment/2018/04/01/chrissy-teigen-reveals-two-topics-she-wont-take-any-criticism-for-on-social-media/23400499/. Accessed 9 June 2018.

Teigen, Chrissy, and John Legend. "Chrissy Teigen and John Legend." *A Drink With*, 14 Apr. 2015, adrinkwith.com/chrissyteigen-johnlegend/. Accessed 9 June 2018.

—*Joy Crelin*

Jeanine Tesori

Date of birth: November 10, 1961
Occupation: Composer

Jeanine Tesori is an American Tony Award–winning composer known for her Broadway musical-theater productions *Thoroughly Modern Millie*, *Shrek*, and *Fun Home*.

EARLY LIFE AND EDUCATION

Jeanine Tesori was born on November 10, 1961, in Manhasset on Long Island, New York, and grew up in the nearby town of Port Washington. Her father was a doctor and her mother was a nurse. She studied piano from the age of three, but a piano teacher who, she felt, stifled her creativity led her to quit the lessons at thirteen.

Tesori abandoned music briefly as a teenager, focusing on playing sports while attending high school. She later coached at a children's theater camp, which helped to renew her interest in the performing arts. However, she did not intend to pursue it professionally, instead enrolling as a premed student at Barnard College.

In 1981, Tesori attended a production of *Lena Horne: The Lady and Her Music* conducted by Linda Twine, which she later cited as an influential event in her life, saying that before seeing the production, she was unaware that writing music could be a career for women. She later changed her major to music. She graduated in 1983 and began working as a musical theater arranger, pianist, and conductor in New York. Tesori worked as a pit conductor for several major productions, including *Gypsy!* in 1989, *The Secret Garden* in 1991, and *The Who's Tommy* in 1993.

BROADWAY COMPOSER

In 1993, Tesori took a break from conducting and began writing her first musical score. The musical, *Violet*, was produced Off-Broadway in 1997. The play, which centers on a disfigured young woman, was a success, winning the Drama Critics' Circle Award for best musical and the Lucille Lortel Award for outstanding musical. Tesori received her first of five Tony Award nominations in 1998 for her contribution to the Lincoln Center production of *Twelfth Night*, which starred actors Paul Rudd and Helen Hunt.

Tesori's next major success came in 2002, with her adaptation of the film *Thoroughly Modern Millie*. The play, which featured actor Sutton Foster in the lead role, was a Broadway hit and earned Tesori her second Tony nomination. Though Tesori's best score nomination did not lead to a win, the show was awarded the Tony for best musical. Her next feature, *Caroline, or Change*, debuted in 2004 and was another success, earning her a Drama Desk Award for outstanding music. The play was one of several in which Tesori collaborated with acclaimed American playwright Tony Kushner.

Tesori composed scores for several other major Broadway musicals, including the stage adaptation of the children's animated film *Shrek*, which debuted in 2008. The play was the largest-scale and highest-budget production Tesori had worked on and featured all original music. During the run of *Shrek*, Tesori also wrote instrumental music for John Guare's *A Free Man of Color*, which opened on Broadway in 2010. Her musical *Violet* had a brief Broadway run in 2014.

With Lisa Kron, Tesori wrote the original score for 2015's *Fun Home*. The play, adapted from Alison Bechdel's 2006 graphic novel, was a major critical success. For their work, the duo won the 2015 Tony Award for original score.

In addition to her musical theater productions, Tesori has authored musical scores for films such as *Shrek the Third* (2007), *Nights in Rodanthe* (2008), *Every Day* (2010), and several animated Disney films.

Tesori lectures at Yale University in the undergraduate music department. She serves as the creative director of A Broader Way, an arts program cofounded by singer Idina Menzel that offers arts education to girls from underserved communities in New York. She also serves as the founding director of the Encores! Off-Center program at New York City Center, which presents a series of Off-Broadway musicals in concert each summer.

IMPACT

Tesori's musical theater compositions have been critically and commercially successful and have won two Drama Desk Awards and a Tony Award.

PERSONAL LIFE

Tesori met conductor and music arranger Michael Rafter in 1989, when they were both working on a Broadway revival of *Gypsy!*. They later married, eloping to Siena, Italy. They live in New York with their daughter, Siena.

SUGGESTED READING

Finn, Robin. "The Words Rule, but Her Music Sets Them Free." *New York Times*. New York Times, 15 Dec. 2003. Web. 20 Apr. 2016.

Hamedy, Saba. "Tonys 2015: Jeanine Tesori, Lisa Kron Lead a Big Night for Women in Theater." *Los Angeles Times*. Los Angeles Times, 8 June 2015. Web. 20 Apr. 2016.

Herstein, Beth. "Talking to Jeanine Tesori and Veanne Cox about *Caroline, Or Change*." *Talkin' Broadway*. Talkin' Broadway, 25 Nov. 2003. Web. 20 Apr. 2016.

Heyman, Marshall. "Shrek's Theater Queen." *W*. Condé Nast, Dec. 2008. Web. 20 Apr. 2016.

Stephens, Stephanie. "'Fun Home' Composer Jeanine Tesori Hits High Notes of a Healthy Life." *Parade*. AMG/Parade, 2 Apr. 2015. Web. 20 Apr. 2016.

Tesori, Jeanine. Interview by Marc Snetiker. "From *Fun Home* to *Millie*: Composer Jeanine Tesori Looks Back on 10 of Her Songs." *Entertainment Weekly*. Entertainment Weekly, 18 May 2015. Web. 20 Apr. 2016.

Tesori, Jeanine. Interview by Ted Sod. *Roundabout Blog*. Roundabout Theatre Company, 25 Mar. 2014. Web. 20 Apr. 2016.

SELECTED WORKS

Violet, 1997; *Twelfth Night*, 1998; *Thoroughly Modern Millie*, 2002; *Caroline, or Change*, 2004; *Shrek the Musical*, 2008; *A Free Man of Color*, 2010; *Fun Home*, 2015

—*Richard Means*

Eric Thames

Date of birth: November 10, 1986
Occupation: Baseball player

Eric Thames, a first baseman and outfielder for the Milwaukee Brewers, took a circuitous journey to Major League Baseball (MLB) stardom. He was drafted by the Toronto Blue Jays in the seventh round of the 2008 MLB Draft and made his major-league debut with that team in 2011. Over the next two years, however, he bounced around three other MLB teams, thanks to a combination of inconsistent playing time, lackluster performance, and injuries. In an effort to revive his flagging career, Thames signed with the NC Dinos of the Korea Baseball Organization (KBO) League, the top professional baseball league in South Korea, in 2014. In three seasons with the Dinos, he transformed himself into a power-hitting superstar, achieving several noteworthy distinctions and earning—thanks to his muscular physique, thick beard, and plethora of tattoos, as well as his performance—the nickname "God."

Thames, a left-handed batter and right-handed thrower, made a dramatic return to the majors in 2017 after signing a contract with the Brewers. He opened the first month of that season in blistering fashion, helping to launch one of the more interesting second acts in modern MLB history. Speaking of Thames's revamped game and approach, the Brewers' manager Craig Counsell told Dave Sheinin for the *Washington Post* (18 May 2017), "His at-bats are just deeply personal to him . . . He never takes one off, and he almost never gets himself out [by swinging at bad pitches]. It's this intense focus he has. That's what stands out."

EARLY LIFE AND EDUCATION

Eric Allyn Thames was born on November 10, 1986, in Santa Clara, California. His family had a strong military background; his grandfather was a drill sergeant who served in the Vietnam War

Keith Allison, via Wikimedia Commons

and his father was a US Marine. Consequently, Thames was instilled with a strong and unwavering work ethic at an early age. This would prove fruitful for him in his baseball career.

As a twelve-year-old, Thames caught the attention of a local hitting instructor, Joe Bettencourt, who recognized his potential after, ironically, watching him strike out three times in a youth-league game. After receiving Bettencourt's phone number, Thames, determined to hone to his raw, unpolished skills, arrived at the instructor's home the very next day for his first lesson. Soon afterward, the two began working together daily. Thames "thirsted for instruction," as Bettencourt recalled to Adam McCalvy for *MLB.com* (27 Apr. 2017). "He wanted to hit every day. . . . Baseball was everything to him."

Still, Thames was deemed not good enough to play shortstop on the freshman team at Bellarmine Preparatory School in San Jose, California, and initially was used mainly as a pinch runner. Undaunted, he spent the subsequent summer working tirelessly at his craft, taking hundreds of swings every day in the backyard of Bettencourt's home, where Bettencourt ran a baseball training facility. Thames's hard work paid off, and as a sophomore, he earned the starting shortstop spot on Bellarmine's junior-varsity squad. He made the school's varsity roster as a junior and won team Most Valuable Player (MVP) honors during his 2004 senior season, which saw him move from shortstop to the outfield.

Despite being a two-time all-conference selection, Thames went undrafted out of high school and was overlooked by top college baseball programs. As a result, he attended two small schools in California, Cabrillo College and West Valley College, respectively, before making his way to Pepperdine University in 2007.

RISE TO THE MAJOR LEAGUES

Thames's winning mentality immediately won over his coaches at Pepperdine, where he first began to show flashes of his star potential. As a redshirt sophomore outfielder and designated hitter, he batted .320 and led the Waves with forty-four runs batted in (RBIs) and five triples. These numbers resulted in him being selected by the New York Yankees in the thirty-ninth round of the 2007 MLB Draft. Hoping to further improve his draft stock, however, Thames opted to return to Pepperdine for the 2008 season.

He did just that, earning conference MVP honors after hitting a remarkable .407 with thirteen home runs and fifty-nine RBIs. One week before the 2008 draft, however, Thames's stock dropped significantly after he tore his right quadriceps muscle while beating out an infield hit. Following the injury, which required surgery, MLB teams that had initially shown early-round interest in Thames balked at drafting him. The Toronto Blue Jays were ultimately enticed enough by his skills to take him in the draft's seventh round.

Despite being sidelined for nearly a year, Thames rose rather quickly through the Jays' farm system. In 2010, he performed outstandingly for the Jays' AA affiliate, the New Hampshire River Cats of the Eastern League, batting .288 with twenty-seven home runs and 104 RBIs. He was then promoted to AAA Las Vegas in the Pacific Coast League before the start of the 2011 season. After hitting .342 in thirty-two games for Las Vegas, Thames was called up to the Jays in May. Starting at designated hitter, he recorded an RBI single in his major-league debut.

Appearing in ninety-five games for the Jays as a rookie, Thames put up respectable numbers, hitting .262 with twelve home runs and posting a .769 on-base plus slugging percentage (OPS). He opened the 2012 season as the Jays' Opening Day left fielder but was soon cast into a platoon role. "People don't realize when you're playing every day it's easier," Thames explained to Tom Verducci for *Sports Illustrated* (25 Apr. 2017), "But platooning . . .? You don't play for a week. It's tough."

The lack of consistent playing time hampered Thames's play, and following an early-season slump, he was demoted back to AAA Las Vegas. Despite returning to form there, he was dealt to the Seattle Mariners at the 2012 trade deadline.

ROAD TO KOREA

Thames's tenure in Seattle was similarly brief. He batted a paltry .220 in forty games with the Mariners in 2012 and then failed to make the team's twenty-five-man roster out of spring training in 2013. That summer the Mariners traded Thames to the Baltimore Orioles, who immediately assigned him to their triple-A team, the Norfolk Tides. Thames was released by the Orioles, however, just two months later, after which he was picked up on waivers by the Houston Astros; he did not appear in a major-league game for either team. Along the way, he suffered a broken hand after it was accidentally stepped on.

During the 2014 off-season, Thames played in the Venezuelan Winter League, partly to recover from his hand injury. It was then when the KBO League's NC Dinos reached out to his agent, Adam Karon, with a one-year contract offer of near $800,000, which at the time was more than double his annual major-league salary. Thames initially rejected the offer, with the belief that Korea—and Asian baseball in general—was a last-ditch stop for aging MLB veterans and underperforming castoffs. Karon, though, eventually persuaded him to go there for a year, at which point the Dinos purchased his rights from the Astros. As Thames recalled to Verducci, "I put so much pressure on myself, and I was at rock bottom when I went to Korea and I said, 'You know what? I'm just going to have fun.'"

Thames's "fun" meant overhauling his entire game. By then, he had established himself as "a hitter of formidable power but little else of use," as Sheinin wrote. Known for having poor plate discipline with a tendency to chase balls out of the strike zone, Thames began studying visualization techniques and the hitting approaches of perennial All-Star players like Barry Bonds and Miguel Cabrera. Meanwhile, he adjusted to the culture shock of living in a foreign country by learning rudimentary Korean and reading self-help books, including ones on mindfulness and meditation. "I was able to let go of being a perfectionist and embrace becoming result-independent," he said to Sheinin. "Not worrying about what happens. Just doing what you have to do to be prepared. The rest is up to fate."

BASEBALL GOD IN KOREA

Armed with a flatter, or more level, swing and a sounder mind, Thames put up numbers in Korea that were often described as "Ruthian," after the iconic slugger Babe Ruth. In three seasons with the Dinos, he hit .348, averaged forty-one home runs and 126 RBIs, and, demonstrating baserunning ability that had hitherto been unseen, stole sixty-four bases. In 2015, he won the KBO's MVP Award after amassing forty-seven home runs and 140 RBIs, to go along with a .381 batting average, 103 walks, forty-two doubles, and

forty stolen bases. He became the first player in KBO history to hit forty homers and steal forty bases in a season and became just the third foreign-born player to earn league MVP honors.

A below-average outfielder in the majors, Thames was moved to first base in Korea. Making a seamless transition to the position, he also won the league's equivalent of the Golden Glove Award for his stellar defensive play in 2015. Following another forty-homer, 120-RBI campaign for the Dinos in 2016, he began fielding offers to play baseball in Japan's more lucrative and competitive professional baseball league, in addition to interest from a handful of MLB teams. By that time, Thames had become a major celebrity in Korea, earning the nickname "God" for his prodigious production. Standing out with his physically imposing, bearded, and tattooed appearance, he was often hounded everywhere he went. "Going anywhere with him is insane in that country," Karon told Jerry Crasnick for *ESPN.com* (29 Nov. 2016). "It's like going out with the Beatles."

Compared to a comic-book superhero, Thames's likeness appeared on everything from beer bottles to a line of watches in South Korea. He was ready to return to the majors, however; and in November 2016, Thames agreed to terms with the Milwaukee Brewers on a three-year contract worth $16 million. Sold on Thames's reinvented game, the Brewers, who had scouted him overseas solely through video, released first baseman Chris Carter, then the reigning National League (NL) home run champion, to make room for him on their roster. For Thames, the decision was an "easy" one, as he told Adam McCalvy in another article for *MLB.com* (10 Apr. 2017). "I'm a ballplayer. I know I'm pretty much a mercenary. It's not often a player gets to choose where he wants to go, so to be in that situation, I was truly blessed."

UNLIKELY SECOND ACT WITH BREWERS

Receiving the unequivocal organizational support that had eluded him during his first go-round in the majors, Thames rewarded the Brewers' faith in him by authoring a memorable 2017 campaign. He hit safely in his first twelve games and smashed eleven home runs in his first twenty games, both of which were Brewers franchise records. One of the biggest stories and most productive players in the league during the first quarter of the season, Thames finished the month of April with a .345 batting average and a remarkable 1.276 OPS. His sudden power surge led some to suspect he was taking performance-enhancing drugs, allegations of which he vehemently denied. (He passed numerous random drug tests during the season.)

Thames's production, not surprisingly, tapered off during the second half of the season.

He nonetheless finished with solid numbers, tying for the Brewers lead with thirty-one home runs and leading the team in slugging percentage (.518), OPS (.877), and walks (75). Appearing in 138 games, Thames served as the Brewers' primary starting first baseman but also spent time playing in both left and right field. He credited his unlikely MLB resurgence to playing on a regular basis and to his vastly improved plate discipline honed while in Korea. As Thames explained to Sheinin, "I'm not looking for revenge on old GMs and coaches. This is all about pride for me. Coming back here was a challenge to myself. I wanted to come back here, embrace the challenge and apply everything I learned over there."

Thames returned as the Brewers' starting first baseman during the 2018 season. He hit seven home runs in twenty-two games before tearing a ligament in his left thumb while making a diving defensive play at first. The injury required surgery and sidelined him for six weeks. Upon his return in early June, Thames was moved back to the outfield to accommodate the Brewers' All-Star first baseman Jesús Aguilar. The following month, he was placed on the disabled list a second time after straining his hamstring. He entered the 2018 season midpoint batting .250 with thirteen home runs and twenty-eight RBIs.

PERSONAL LIFE
Known for his gregarious, outgoing personality, Thames has a wide range of interests, which include everything from Eastern philosophy to video games to professional wrestling. A voracious reader, he makes an effort to read approximately thirty minutes to an hour every day to help clear his mind.

SUGGESTED READING

Crasnick, Jerry. "A Sensation in Korea, Can Eric Thames Make It in the Majors?" *ESPN*, 29 Nov. 2016, www.espn.com/mlb/story/_/id/18066579/a-sensation-korea-eric-thames-make-most-chance-milwaukee-brewers. Accessed 16 July 2018.

Kepner, Tyler. "For Brewers' Eric Thames, Stint in South Korea Goes a Long Way." *New York Times*, 29 Apr. 2017, www.nytimes.com/2017/04/29/sports/baseball/eric-thames-brewers-home-runs-milwaukee.html. Accessed 25 June 2018.

McCalvy, Adam. "Mix of Old, New Schools Brought Thames Home." *MLB.com*, MLB Advanced Media, 10 Apr. 2017, www.mlb.com/news/brewers-got-eric-thames-using-old-new-schools/c-223467354. Accessed 16 July 2018.

McCalvy, Adam. "Thames' Tear Unsurprising to Childhood Coach." *MLB.com*, MLB Advanced Media, 27 Apr. 2017, www.mlb.com/news/eric-thames-childhood-coach-unsurprised/c-226897050. Accessed 16 July 2018.

Sheinin, Dave. "At His Breaking Point in South Korea, Eric Thames Made a Pact with Himself and Revived His Career." *Washington Post*, 18 May 2017, www.washingtonpost.com/news/sports/wp/2017/05/18/eric-thames-learned-patience-in-south-korea-and-returned-as-one-of-baseballs-hottest-hitters/?utm_term=.e06517d4f361. Accessed 16 July 2018.

Verducci, Tom. "'Adapt or Die': Home Run Sensation Eric Thames Goes Deep on the Keys to His Success." *Sports Illustrated*, 25 Apr. 2017, www.si.com/mlb/2017/04/25/eric-thames-milwaukee-brewers-breakout-star. Accessed 16 July 2018.

—*Chris Cullen*

Tessa Thompson

Date of birth: October 3, 1983
Occupation: Actor

Tessa Thompson is an actor best known for her roles in the films *For Colored Girls*, *Dear White People*, and *Creed*.

EARLY LIFE AND EDUCATION
Tessa Lynne Thompson was born on October 3, 1983, in Los Angeles, California. Her father, Marc Anthony Thompson, is a musician from Panama. She attended Santa Monica High School, where she participated in school plays, including a performance of William Shakespeare's *A Midsummer Night's Dream*, in which she played the role of Hermia.

Following high school, Thompson continued her education at Santa Monica College in Santa Monica, California. There she studied cultural anthropology and took acting classes. She did not have enough credits to graduate and elected to take a lecture course given by members of the Los Angeles Women's Shakespeare Company. The group's founder, Lisa Volpe, asked Thompson to do a reading and subsequently cast her as Ariel in their production of Shakespeare's *The Tempest*.

Through her role in *The Tempest*, Thompson was cast in a production of Shakespeare's *Romeo and Juliet* produced by the Boston Court Performing Arts Center in Pasadena, California, in 2003. This version, called *Romeo and Juliet: Antebellum New Orleans, 1836*, took the play out of Verona and set it in the French Quarter. The production was successful with critics, and Thompson received an Image Award nomination from the National Association for the Advancement of

Colored People (NAACP) for her performance as Juliet.

LIFE'S WORK

Thompson starred in two succeeding shows at the Boston Court, *Summertime* (2004) and *Pera Palas* (2005), before making her transition to film and television. After two weeks of auditions in Los Angeles, she received her first television role. She guest starred on the crime drama series *Cold Case* (2005), on which she played the victim of an unsolved 1930s murder in one episode. That same year, she secured a recurring role on the comedy drama series *Veronica Mars* (2004–7). That series ran for three seasons, and Thompson appeared in the second season as Jackie Cook, the daughter of a famous baseball player. While shooting *Veronica Mars*, Thompson continued to work in theater with a role in the play *Indoor/Outdoor* (2006).

Thompson also made her big screen debut in 2006, in the horror film *When a Stranger Calls* (2006). She received her first film accolade for her role in the drama *Mississippi Damned* (2009); based on the director Tina Mabry's experiences growing up in Tupelo, Mississippi, the film was praised by critics, and Thompson won the grand jury prize for best actor at the American Black Film Festival that year for her role as a struggling pianist. Following *Mississippi Damned*, Thompson appeared on several television series, including the law drama *Private Practice* in 2009, the superhero drama *Heroes* in the same year, and in a few episodes of the police drama *Detroit 1-8-7* in 2010 and 2011.

Her next major film role was in the drama *For Colored Girls* (2010). Based on the play by Ntozake Shange, the film looks at the lives of nine African American women and the challenges they face. Thompson plays Nyla Adrose, a dance student who lies to her family and friends about getting an abortion. Although the film received generally negative reviews, the cast was applauded for their performances, including Thompson, who won a Black Reel Award for best breakthrough performance. Thompson stated that the role was very special for her because she had been a fan of the original play since she was a teenager.

Thompson landed her next two recurring roles in television series in 2012 with the period drama *Copper* and *666 Park Avenue*. On the big screen, Thompson starred in the satirical comedy *Dear White People* (2014), about racial hypocrisy at a college. For her role as a biracial student, she received numerous accolades, including an Image Award nomination for outstanding actress in a motion picture and a 2014 Gotham Independent Film Award for best breakthrough actor.

After appearing in the period drama *Selma* (2014) as civil rights activist Diane Nash, Thompson costarred in the boxing drama *Creed* (2015). An installment in the popular Rocky series (1976–2015), *Creed* was critically acclaimed, and Thompson won an Image Award and an African American Film Critics Association Award for best supporting actress.

IMPACT

Since becoming involved in acting in the early 2000s, Thompson has worked consistently in theater, film, and television. For her critically acclaimed performances, she has won an Image Award, a Black Reel Award, and a grand jury prize at the American Black Film Festival.

PERSONAL LIFE

Thompson lives in Los Angeles and enjoys traveling solo in her spare time to India and Europe.

SUGGESTED READING

Behrens, Deborah. "Tessa Thompson Returns to Shakespeare as Rosalind." *This Stage Magazine*. LA Stage Alliance, 11 July 2012, this-stage.la/2012/07/tessa-thompson-returns-to-shakespeare-as-rosalind/. Accessed 28 July 2018.

Dockterman, Eliana. "Creed's Tessa Thompson on Why She's More Than Just a Cliché Movie Girlfriend." *Time*, 30 Nov. 2015. time.com/4129487/creed-tessa-thompson-cliche-movie-girlfriend/. Accessed 29 July 2018.

Houston, Shannon M. "Tessa Thompson Breaks the Mold." *Paste Magazine*, 28 May 2014, www.pastemagazine.com/articles/2014/05/the-hollywood-race-tessa-thompson-and-the-myth-of.html. Accessed 29 July 2018.

Lange, Maggie. "Creed Star Tessa Thompson: Hollywood's Miss Independent." *GQ*, 25 Nov. 2015, www.gq.com/story/tessa-thompson-wcw. Accessed 29 July 2018.

Peoples, Lindsay. "Tessa Thompson on Race, Hollywood, and Her Impending Stardom." *New York Magazine*, 12 Feb. 2016, www.the-cut.com/2016/02/meet-tessa-thompson.html. Accessed 29 July 2018.

SELECTED WORKS

Veronica Mars, 2005–6; *Damned*, 2009; *For Colored Girls*, 2010; *Detroit 1-8-7*, 2010–11; *Copper*, 2012–13; *Mississippi Dear White People*, 2014; *Creed*, 2015

—*Patrick G. Cooper*

Olga Tokarczuk

Date of birth: January 29, 1962
Occupation: Author

The humanist author Olga Tokarczuk is one of Poland's most acclaimed writers. She tackles the complexities of her country's history and modern life with a dexterity and humor that has earned her numerous awards and critical acclaim across Europe. In recent years, her popularity has spread to the English-speaking world, in which three of her novels have been translated thus far, with more promised to come. Included among her awards are the Nike Award, one of Poland's highest literary honors, which she won twice, in 2008 and 2015; the 2013 Vilenica Prize, presented to Central European authors for outstanding works of literature; the 2015 Brückepreis, an international prize given to authors who contribute to better understanding between peoples in Europe; and the 2018 Man Booker International Prize, which she won for *Flights*, the 2017 English translation of her 2007 novel *Bieguni*.

Although she is thrilled to have been embraced by English-language literary circles, she also acknowledges that there is a considerable difference between the ways in which British or American authors write and the way Polish authors do. Tokarczuk told Claire Armitstead for the *Guardian* (20 Apr. 2018), "The first thing is that we don't trust reality as much as you do. Reading English novels I always adore the ability to write without fear about inner psychological things that are so delicate. In such a form you can develop a story in a very linear way, but we don't have this patience. We feel that in every moment something must be wrong because our own story wasn't linear. Another difference is that you are rooted in psychoanalysis while we're still thinking in a mythical, religious way."

EARLY LIFE AND CAREER

Olga Tokarczuk was born on January 29, 1962, in Sulechów, which is near Zielona Góra, in Poland. Amid the student revolts of 1968 and ensuing Communist government repression, Tokarczuk quickly came to understand the political turmoil in the country, even though she was then just six years old. Her parents were bookish leftists—"but not communists," she clarified to Armitstead—and she grew up in a literate, intellectual environment. She also became fascinated with psychology at a very young age. She recalled reading Sigmund Freud and Carl Jung and realizing how, as she told Helen Brown for the *Financial Times* (6 Apr. 2018), "every tiny thing you did had a deeper meaning . . . those ideas turned the world into a book I could read."

When it came time to go to college, she entered Warsaw University with the idea of

By Borys8, via Wikimedia Commons

becoming a psychologist herself. Upon her graduation, she became an addiction specialist at a hospital, married, and had a son. After five years, however, she quit. Tokarczuk recalled to Armitstead, "I was working with one of my patients and realised I was much more disturbed than he was."

Writing became her therapy, and Tokarczuk wrote in earnest. In 1989, she published a collection of poetry, *Miasta w lustrach* (Cities in mirrors). Two novels quickly followed: *Podróż ludzi księgi* (The journey of the book-people), in 1993, and *E. E.* in 1996. None of these early works have yet been translated into English.

HOUSE OF DAY, HOUSE OF NIGHT AND PRIMEVAL AND OTHER TIMES

Tokarczuk's sixth book, *Dom dzienny, dom nocny* (1998), was the first of her works to receive an English translation. It was published as *House of Day, House of Night*, translated by Antonia Lloyd-Jones, in 2002. Although often described as a novel, the book may also be seen as a collection of short pieces, all nominally linked by a narrator who settles in a small village in western Poland on the Czech border. She lives there with her husband, known only as R. Through the narrator, the reader learns some of the town's history: the fact that it has at various times been part of Poland, Germany, and the former Czechoslovakia; that it is populated by Poles from the eastern part of the country who had fled the Soviets at the end of World War II; and that it is watched closely by border guards in the nearby Czech Republic. Readers also learn of a host of local characters, described by the narrator in short narrative bursts.

House of Day, House of Night wowed reviewers upon its translation into English by Lloyd-Jones. Writing for the *Guardian* (20 Oct. 2002), Philip Marsden declared, "Tokarczuk's prose is simple and unadorned. She tells her stories with a natural fluency that easily accommodates the hopes, drudgery, and absurdities of the world she is describing. Real lives mingle with the imagined, dreams with day, past with present in an entirely plausible way. A lot of nasty things happen and many people die but the tone is by no means gloomy in tone. As Marta, the voice of folk wisdom in the book, points out: 'If death were nothing but bad, people would stop dying immediately.' *House of Day, House of Night* opens its doors on a very fresh and vibrant Polish talent."

Primeval and Other Times, Tokarczuk's next novel to debut in the English-speaking world, was in fact an older one. Originally titled *Prawiek i inne czasy*, it was first published in Polish in 1996 but did not come out in English until 2010. Lloyd-Jones again served as translator. In the novel, the author creates a mythical Polish village, known as Prawiek (Primeval). Through the eyes of four archangels who protect Primeval, the reader observes changes in the village over eight decades, beginning in 1914, the first year of World War I.

English-language critics again found much to savor in Tokarczuk's work. "The book struck deep chords in readers, who responded to it as if a luminous new way of presenting twentieth-century Poland had been found," a writer noted for the *Economist* (10 Mar. 2016). "'Primeval is the place at the centre of the universe' it begins—and that universality, packed as the narrative is with offbeat characters and one strange episode after another, was the secret of its success."

The author has published numerous other works in Polish that have yet to be translated into English. They include, among others, *Lalka i perła* (The doll and the pearl) in 2000; *Gra na wielu bębenkach* (Playing on many drums) in 2001; *Ostatnie historie* (The last stories) in 2004; and *Anna w grobowcach świata* (Anna in the tombs of the world) in 2006. Each of these works has helped to cement her reputation as one of the leading lights of modern Polish literature.

WINNING THE MAN BOOKER FOR *FLIGHTS*

Bieguni, Tokarczuk's 2007 novel, already had a sterling reputation when Jennifer Croft translated it into English as *Flights* in 2017. *Flights* had won the 2008 Nike Award, one of Poland's most prestigious literary prizes. The novel takes its thematic cues from wandering and movement, by people and items moving through space and history. Among these seemingly random stories are tales such as the one in which Polish composer Frédéric Chopin's heart is returned to Warsaw by his loving sister. In another, a seventeenth-century doctor learns of the existence of the Achilles tendon by dissecting his own severed leg. Also included are stories of a woman returning to Poland to help an old friend take his own life and a man losing his grip on reality when his wife and child disappear, then suddenly reappear.

Reviewing the novel for the *Guardian* (3 June 2017), Kapka Kassabova declared, "It is a novel of intuitions as much as ideas, a cacophony of voices and stories seemingly unconnected across time and space, which meander between the profound and the facetious, the mysterious and the ordinary, and whose true register remains one of glorious ambiguity. Olga Tokarczuk is a household name in Poland and one of Europe's major humanist writers, working here in the continental tradition of the 'thinking' or essayistic novel. *Flights* has echoes of W. G. Sebald, Milan Kundera, Danilo Kiš, and Dubravka Ugrešić, but Tokarczuk inhabits a rebellious, playful register very much her own."

Flights would go on to win the Man Booker International Prize in 2018. The prize is given to outstanding works of fiction in English translation, with its stipend divided equally between author and translator. "Tokarczuk is a writer of wonderful wit, imagination and literary panache," Lisa Appignanesi, who led the judging panel, said in a statement quoted by Anna Codrea-Rado in the *New York Times* (22 May 2018). "[Tokarczuk] flies us through a galaxy of departures and arrivals, stories and digressions, all the while exploring matters close to the contemporary and human predicament—where only plastic escapes mortality."

FORTHCOMING WORKS IN ENGLISH TRANSLATION

English translation of more of Tokarczuk's works are forthcoming. *Prowadź swój pług przez kości umarłych*, her 2009 novel, will be published as *Drive Your Plow over the Bones of the Dead* in the fall of 2018, with Lloyd-Jones as translator. *Księgi Jakubowe*—to be known as *The Books of Jacob*—will be published in 2019 in the United Kingdom. This latter novel, which was first published in 2014, also won Poland's Nike Prize, but it was also a matter of some controversy in the author's homeland shortly after its publication.

The Books of Jacob describes the life of a contentious eighteenth-century religious leader named Jacob Frank who helped forcibly convert Jewish Poles to Catholicism. Although the book met with critical acclaim in Poland and was even a best seller, many Poles took offence at the way the author presented Poles as anti-Semitic and as oppressors at a time when, during the Polish-Lithuanian Commonwealth of 1569–1795, Jews and other minority groups enjoyed a considerable amount of religious freedom. She particularly outraged members of Poland's increasingly powerful right wing. Extremists even issued death threats. Her publishers were so concerned for her safety that they hired bodyguards to protect her and her partner, the translator Grzegorz Zegadlo. Despite the controversy, Tokarczuk remained defiant and outspoken, and quite willing to take on what she perceived as patriarchal elements in Poland who were unwilling to look at the country's history, both good and bad. She told Brown, "I opened a history that was taboo from a number of perspectives: it was swept under the carpet by Catholics, Jews and communists. It took me eight years to research such fragile and contentious facts. But after I won the Nike Award [Poland's most prestigious literary prize], I was attacked by people who didn't want to know about Poland's dark past."

SUGGESTED READING

Armitstead, Claire. "Olga Tokarczuk: 'I Was Very Naive. I Thought Poland Would Be Able to Discuss the Dark Areas of Our History.'" *The Guardian*, 20 Apr. 2018, www.theguardian.com/books/2018/apr/20/olga-tokarczuk-interview-flights-man-booker-international. Accessed 24 May 2018.

Brown, Helen. "Olga Tokarczuk: 'It's Time for Us to Look at Poland's Relationship with the Jews.'" *Financial Times*, 6 Apr. 2018, www.ft.com/content/076bb888-372b-11e8-8b98-2f31af407cc8. Accessed 24 May 2018.

Codrea-Rado, Anna. "Olga Tokarczuk of Poland Wins Man Booker International Prize." *The New York Times*, 22 May 2018, www.nytimes.com/2018/05/22/books/booker-international-winner-olga-tokarczuk.html. Accessed 24 May 2018.

Kassabova, Kapka. "The Ways of Wanderers." Review of *Flights*, by Olga Tokarczuk. *The Guardian*, 3 June 2017, www.theguardian.com/books/2017/jun/03/flights-by-olga-tokarczuk-review. Accessed 24 May 2018.

Marsden, Philip. "Poles Apart." Review of *House of Day, House of Night*, by Olga Tokarczuk. *The Guardian*, 20 Oct. 2002, www.theguardian.com/books/2002/oct/20/fiction.features2. Accessed 24 May 2018.

"Olga Tokarczuk's Polish Narrative." *The Economist*, 10 Mar. 2016, www.economist.com/prospero/2016/03/10/olga-tokarczuks-polish-narrative. Accessed 24 May 2018.

Tokarczuk, Olga. "Where History's March Is a Funeral Procession." *The New York Times*, 15 Apr. 2010, www.nytimes.com/2010/04/16/opinion/16tokarczuk.html. Accessed 24 May 2018.

SELECTED WORKS

Prawiek i inne czasy (*Primeval and Other Times*), 1996; *Dom dzienny, dom nocny* (*House of Day, House of Night*), 1998; *Bieguni* (*Flights*), 2007

—Christopher Mari

Joshua Topolsky

Date of birth: October 19, 1977
Occupation: Journalist

"Joshua Topolsky is the very model of a modern news editor," Thornton McEnery wrote for *Crain's New York Business* (30 Mar. 2015). During his time as editor-in-chief of the popular tech blog *Engadget*, known for its insightful reviews of new phones, gaming systems, and other essentials of digital life, he held a post that "[put] him at the center of the schism between old and new media," as McEnery wrote. Topolsky later cofounded and edited *The Verge*, a splashy multimedia effort devoted to the intersection of culture, the arts, science, and technology. Although he was an instrumental part of *The Verge*'s success and had helped create Vox Media, its parent company, he walked away in 2014 to join Michael Bloomberg's financial news business, charged with revamping the tradition-bound company's digital strategy.

His squabbles with the iconoclastic mogul were widely reported, however, and his tenure with Bloomberg turned out to be short-lived.

By nrkbeta via Wikimedia Commons

Undaunted, Topolsky went on to create *The Outline*, a digital media company that he started with $5 million in venture capital. With its launch in 2016, Topolsky wanted "to establish a next-generation version of the *New Yorker* while also fixing many of the ills facing digital publishing and advertising," according to Mike Shields for the *Wall Street Journal* (5 Dec. 2016). "The new venture-backed site is aiming for a smart, high-brow readership—an audience that falls somewhere between traditional brands like the *New York Times* and digital natives like BuzzFeed." Discussing the mixture of long-form reportage and snappily aggregated links to other compelling stories, Topolsky explained to Shields, "We want to help people discover things, and keep moving. We don't want to rewrite lots of stories or just do hot takes."

Topolsky was hopeful that readers would appreciate the colorful site, which is heavily optimized for viewing on mobile devices and features a Snapchat-inspired method of swiping to navigate between stories rather than scrolling. "I want to build a product for people," he asserted to Benjamin Mullen during an interview for the Poynter Institute (8 Aug. 2016). "I want them to be part of this thing. I want people to love to love it. Frankly, I want them to be angry about it if they don't like it. I want them to feel something."

EARLY YEARS AND EDUCATION

Joshua Topolsky was born on October 19, 1977, in Pittsburgh, Pennsylvania. He was always deeply interested in technology, and as a child, he enjoyed taking apart household gadgets, including the family's rotary telephone, to see how they worked. He received his first computer—a Texas Instruments TI-99/4A—when he was six years old, and, as a self-described "nerd" with few friends, he often convinced his mother and father to take him to the local electronics store so that he could peruse the shelves. "I would buy random combos of little lights, toggles, and minuscule motors and build meaningless machines, which I found endlessly fascinating," he wrote in an autobiographical piece for *The Outline* (7 Feb. 2018). "I was extremely curious."

Topolsky also spent much of his time playing with his brother, Eric, on their ColecoVision game system, which, excitingly, had a computer add-on, the Coleco Adam, whose software came on slow-to-load cassette tapes. (He remembers the sci-fi game *Buck Rogers* as a particular favorite.) He eventually graduated to a PC with a 10 MB hard drive and a four-color monitor. It was, he wrote, "the most incredible piece of technology that I had ever used. It was the first line of 'personal computers' produced by IBM, when IBM still cared about consumers, and it was magic. It had expansion slots in the back. It had a 5 1/4-inch floppy disk drive. It beeped loudly if you pressed on too many keys at once. And it would do pretty much anything a computer was capable of doing in the mid-80s to early-90s—which put unbelievable control into my greedy, nerdy hands."

Topolsky spent some time as a DJ, spinning trance music using the stage name Joshua Ryan. Sources reporting on his music career are notoriously unreliable, however, with the *AllMusic* website reporting that he was born in Sicily, and others listing conflicting information about his discography. Most list his most popular recording as a 1999 track called "Pistolwhip," which reached the UK pop charts. Along with his brother, who goes by the name Eric Emm, he formed a production team called the Brothers. (Eric is now best known for his work with the band Tanlines).

JOURNALISM

In 2008 Topolsky became the editor-in-chief of *Engadget*, an online publication founded by Peter Rojas, who had made his name at the early tech publication *Gizmodo*. He also became known to television viewers as the technology correspondent for *Late Night with Jimmy Fallon* and, later, *The Tonight Show Starring Jimmy Fallon*, both of which aired on NBC. In that capacity, he demonstrated new devices, made recommendations, and bantered with the host.

Topolsky remained at *Engadget* until 2011, when he left to cofound *The Verge*, an ambitious multimedia effort. In the interim, he started a temporary news and review site called *This Is My Next*, whose title was drawn from a phrase he regularly used when discussing a product: "This is my next phone," or "This is my next laptop," for example. Many of his *Engadget* colleagues joined him at *This Is My Next* and subsequently followed him to *The Verge*, which officially launched on November 1, 2011. Topolsky served as editor-in-chief, wrote articles, and appeared in regular podcasts. The company's mission, as stated on its website at the time, was "to offer breaking news coverage and in-depth reporting, product information, and community content via a unified, modern platform." The site now states, "Our original editorial insight was that technology had migrated from the far fringes of the culture to the absolute center as mobile technology created a new generation of digital consumers."

Thanks in some part to Topolsky's reputation and television recognition, *The Verge* gained 4 million unique monthly viewers during its earliest days. Within a few years that number had jumped to 10 million, and by 2014, Vox Media, its parent company, was valued at an estimated $200 million. That success caused something of a buzz in digital media circles, and in 2014 Topolsky was lured away from the media outlet he had founded by Bloomberg Media, whose

CEO, Justin Smith, hoped to invigorate the venerable company's digital strategy.

Bloomberg was a behemoth, as Ravi Somaiya wrote for the *New York Times* (10 July 2015): "The media company consists of different fiefs, encompassing television, radio, a consumer website, *Businessweek* magazine and a financial newswire, all built around a newsroom of about 2,400 journalists and funded by the lucrative terminal business, which serves subscribers who pay about $21,000 a year. Revenue from subscriptions equaled $9 billion in 2014, or 85 percent of the company's total revenue."

Topolsky's title was Editor, Bloomberg Digital, and Chief Digital Content Officer, Bloomberg Media, but he did not hold it for long. One day, Michael Bloomberg, a no-nonsense billionaire who had served as the mayor of New York City from 2002 to 2013, suggested in a meeting that the company might not need a website, given that most of its revenue came from its financial data and trading desk terminals. Topolsky reportedly responded in a sarcastic manner, angering the older man. Soon after, the company announced that it was parting ways with its upstart editor.

Topolsky cast the news in a positive light, writing on his personal website (11 July 2015), "We accomplished ridiculous things in a tiny period of time. Let this sink in a bit: we launched two completely new (award-winning, beautiful, inventive) websites and founded our first regional site (hi Europe!); hit new traffic records (like surpassing the *WSJ* for the first time); became the leader in business digital video (we grew audiences nearly 350% YoY); nearly doubled our social traffic (all-time highs in every metric, a 358% increase in Facebook traffic YoY); PLUS we saw double digit revenue growth in digital. But more important than revenue or numbers, the editorial work I had a chance to be a part of was some of the strongest and most interesting stuff anyone anywhere has been doing." (YoY is an acronym used in the financial industry meaning "year over year.")

In early 2015, Topolsky had begun recording a weekly podcast about technology trends, but still unsatisfied, he sought venture capital for a new media company of his own. He called it Independent Media and announced that its first publication would be *The Outline*. He explained on his site, "You may not know this about me so I will tell you: I love building new things. I love looking at tough problems and figuring out a way to make them work. I love making something beautiful and useful and smart and engaging. I love the potential I see in news and media and modern storytelling and how that works on the web / mobile / apps / whatever—but I don't often love what I see being done with it. And I get particularly bored and anxious when I feel like I'm not working towards making something more interesting than the last thing I made."

Cadillac, Method, and Under Armour Sportswear signed on as charter sponsors for the visually interesting, graphics-heavy publication, and Topolsky has announced that he'd like to keep the audience small and selective—in the tens of millions per month rather than the billions per month a site like Buzzfeed attracts. "Talk to a twenty-five-year-old and ask them if what they see in their feed every day is good," he told Mullen. "I literally can't remember the last time I asked someone that question and they said yes."

PERSONAL LIFE

Born into a Jewish family, Topolsky identifies as an atheist. He is married to the writer Laura June Topolsky, who was once also an editor at *The Verge*. In 2018, she published a memoir, *Now My Heart Is Full*, which examines her relationship with her late mother, an alcoholic, set against the backdrop of the birth of her own daughter, Zelda June Topolsky.

The family lives outside of New York City.

SUGGESTED READING

Abbruzzese, Jason. "Josh Topolsky on Leaving *The Verge* and His Future at Bloomberg." *Mashable*, 24 July 2014, mashable.com/2014/07/24/josh-topolsky-on-the-verge/. Accessed 6 Sept. 2018.

McEnery, Thornton. "40 under 40: Class of 2015." *Crain's New York Business*, 30 Mar. 2015, www.crainsnewyork.com/40under40/2015. Accessed 6 Sept. 2018.

Mullen, Benjamin. "Josh Topolsky Wants You to Love *The Outline* . . . Or Hate It." *Poynter*, 8 Aug. 2016, www.poynter.org/news/josh-topolsky-wants-you-love-outlineor-hate-it. Accessed 6 Sept. 2018.

Shields, Mike. "Former Bloomberg Editor Joshua Topolsky Launches *The Outline*." *Wall Street Journal*, 5 Dec. 2016, www.wsj.com/articles/former-bloomberg-editor-joshua-topolsky-launches-the-outline-1480935601. Accessed 6 Sept. 2018.

Somaiya, Ravi. "Web Chief Joshua Topolsky to Leave Bloomberg as Staff Tensions Surface." *New York Times*, 10 July 2015, www.nytimes.com/2015/07/11/business/media/joshua-topolsky-web-chief-bloomberg-leaving.html. Accessed 6 Sept. 2018.

Topolsky, Joshua. "This Tweet Could Be My Life." *The Outline*, 7 Feb. 2018, theoutline.com/post/3288/this-tweet-could-be-my-life-ibm-pc-xt-at-3d-render-1980s-1990s-daniel-karner. Accessed 6 Sept. 2018.

—*Mari Rich*

Rebecca Traister

Date of birth: 1975
Occupation: Author; journalist

Author and journalist Rebecca Traister has devoted much of her career to documenting inequality in society, as well as the ways in which both historical and contemporary individuals—particularly women—have sought to change that inequality. Traister told Peter Kafka on the *Recode Media* podcast, as reported by Eric Johnson for *Recode* (29 June 2017), "Everything about our every day—the jobs, education, early childhood education, paid leave, minimum wage, our health insurance, our infrastructure—everything that we live in this country every day is shaped by policy that is influenced by racial and gender inequality." A longtime contributor to publications such as *Salon*, the *New Republic*, and *New York* magazine, Traister has written extensively on topics such as women in politics, navigating twenty-first-century society as a single woman, and motherhood. With her journalistic work and multiple books, including *Good and Mad: The Revolutionary Power of Women's Anger* (2018), Traister has made a name for herself as a key contributor to the vital ongoing discussion of equality in the United States.

EARLY LIFE AND EDUCATION

Rebecca E. Traister was born in Pennsylvania in 1975. She grew up outside of Philadelphia, Pennsylvania. Her mother, Barbara, held a doctorate from Yale University and spent many years as an English professor at Lehigh University. Traister's father, Daniel, likewise held a PhD, as well as multiple master's degrees, and spent more than three decades as curator of research services at the University of Pennsylvania's rare book and manuscript library. Both of Traister's parents published widely in their respective fields, and her brother, Aaron, also became a writer.

As a child, Traister was greatly influenced by her mother's high level of education and successful career, which suggested the possibilities available for women in academia and the workplace. However, she also observed that her mother carried out all of the domestic work in her family's household, which, as she told Terry Gross for *National Public Radio* (NPR) (1 Mar. 2016), sent "mixed messages about the possibility for equality within marriage." Such childhood observations shaped Traister's later interest in the social, political, and economic factors related to life as an unmarried woman.

Traister attended Germantown Friends School, a day school in the Germantown neighborhood of Philadelphia. After graduating in 1993, she enrolled in Northwestern University's

By Photo by Dana Meilijson. Jewish Women's Archive via Wikimedia Commons

Weinberg College of Arts and Sciences, where she majored in American studies. Traister earned her bachelor's degree from the college in 1997. After graduating, she moved to New York City, where she began her career in journalism as an assistant for *Talk* magazine.

JOURNALISM AND *BIG GIRLS DON'T CRY*

Over the course of her career as a journalist, Traister held a variety of positions at print and online publications. After leaving *Talk*, she spent several years at the *New York Observer*, beginning her tenure there as a fact checker. She eventually began writing for the publication and went on to serve as a film critic and film industry writer. In 2003, Traister joined the publication *Salon* as a staff writer. Over the course of nearly a decade with the publication, she established herself as a journalist particularly concerned with issues surrounding women, including feminism, gender equality, and the role of women in politics and the media. She also began to write about issues surrounding single women and the institution of marriage through, as she described to Caitlin Schiller for the *Blinkist* podcast *Simplify* (21 Dec. 2017), "a certain amount of first-person writing."

Having established herself as a key voice in the conversation surrounding women in politics and the media through her news and magazine publications, Traister continued to explore such topics in her first book, *Big Girls Don't Cry: The Election that Changed Everything for American Women*, published in 2010. Incorporating portions of articles originally published in *Salon*,

Elle, and the *Nation*, *Big Girls Don't Cry* chronicles the role of women in the 2008 US presidential election. In addition to focusing on politicians such as Hillary Clinton and Sarah Palin, Traister explores the events and issues surrounding spouses of politicians, like Michelle Obama, as well as a variety of women working in the media. Upon its publication, *Big Girls Don't Cry* earned extensive acclaim from critics and was named a New York Times Notable Book of 2010. The book also won the 2012 Ernesta Drinker Ballard Book Prize, which recognizes achievement in books concerning women's rights.

WRITING FOR THE *NEW REPUBLIC*

In 2014, Traister joined the *New Republic* as a writer and senior editor, and was also named a contributing editor for *Elle* magazine, for which she had written on a freelance basis since 2003. Traister left the *New Republic* in 2015 to join *New York* magazine as a writer at large for both the main magazine and its affiliate *The Cut*.

Throughout that time, Traister explored the multitude of ways in which society hampers the efforts of women to navigate issues of pregnancy and motherhood. "If you're a person who has worked ambitiously, energetically, and efficiently for decades, it can be wildly discombobulating to find yourself suddenly tripped up by your own body, especially when it's not illness or disability that's stopping you, but among the most common and human of conditions," she wrote in the article "Why Women Can't Break Free from the Parent Trap," published in the *New Republic* in 2015. "Yet this is a regular, lived reality for more women than ever before." In "Why Women Can't Break Free from the Parent Trap," as well as other articles, Traister called attention to the widespread lack of parental leave and flexible schedules in the United States. She also wrote about the discrimination pregnant women and women with children face in the workplace, particularly in regard to hiring and promotions.

Also in 2015, Traister wrote the articles "The Violence Didn't Start with the Baltimore Riots" and "Our Racist History Isn't Back to Haunt Us. It Never Left Us" for the *New Republic*. Both articles focused on racial violence in the 2010s. For those articles, as well as "Why Women Can't Break Free from the Parent Trap" and others, Traister was awarded the 2016 Hillman Prize for Opinion and Analysis in journalism.

ALL THE SINGLE LADIES

Traister published her second book, *All the Single Ladies: Unmarried Women and the Rise of an Independent Nation*, in 2016. She had begun considering the topic for the book around 2010, when—while she was preparing for her own wedding—Traister was struck by the way in which getting married was widely viewed as synonymous with beginning adult life. It was a concept that was at odds with the fact that Traister had been living an independent adult life for more than a decade.

Drawing from her own experiences as well as those of other women, *All the Single Ladies* traces the history of single womanhood in the United States and documents the experiences of unmarried women from a variety of backgrounds navigating life in the twenty-first century. Traister notes that the number of unmarried women in the United States increased in the 2000s and 2010s, and that among those who do marry, the median age of first marriage increased dramatically from the median age in the mid-twentieth century. "The choice not to marry isn't necessarily a conscious rejection of marriage," she explained to Gross. "It is the ability to live singly if an appealing marriage option doesn't come along."

Despite these changing trends, however, Traister makes it clear that much of twenty-first century society in the United States is still structured in a way that makes marriage the default state. "Our school days operate so that you assume that somebody is there to pick up children at three o'clock in the afternoon," she told Schiller as an example. "Who do we assume is there? We can't even begin to count the number of sort of basic daily realities in our lives that are built around the idea that we're organized into hetero married pairs." *All the Single Ladies* debuted on the New York Times Best Seller list to critical acclaim and was named a Best Book of 2016 by the *Boston Globe*.

CLINTON PROFILES, *THE CUT*, AND *GOOD AND MAD*

During and after the 2016 presidential election, Traister produced notable work about the role of women in government. Although she had previously been unable to make contact with Clinton during the 2008 race, Traister succeeded in gaining access in 2016, with the goal of profiling the Democratic candidate. "I made very clear that the piece I wanted to write was putting [Clinton] in the context of American history," Traister told Kafka. "There was no promise about, 'It's going to be good, it's going to be bad,' of course. But I did say, 'This is a crucial historic moment, and I thought there would be more coverage that made careful note of that.'" The resulting profile, "Hillary Clinton vs. Herself," was published by *New York* magazine in May 2016. Traister followed that article with the profile "Hillary Clinton Is Furious. And Resigned. And Funny. And Worried," published a year later, six months after Clinton's 2016 defeat.

In 2017, Traister wrote a series of articles for *New York* magazine's *The Cut* about the rising number of allegations of sexual assaults by politicians, Hollywood executives, and other prominent men. Titled "Why the Harvey Weinstein Sexual-Harassment Allegations Didn't Come Out Until Now," "Your Reckoning. And Mine," and "This Moment Isn't (Just) About Sex. It's Really About Work," the trio of articles won Traister the 2018 National Magazine Award for Columns and Commentary. The same year, Traister was elected a member of the American Academy of Arts and Sciences for the field of journalism and communications.

In 2018, Traister published her third book, *Good and Mad: The Revolutionary Power of Women's Anger*. Expanding upon some of the topics touched on in *All the Single Ladies*, the book documents the role of women's anger in social and political movements, including movements like the 2017 Women's March. The book also explores how women's anger is perceived, particularly in comparison to anger expressed by men.

PERSONAL LIFE

Traister is married to defense attorney Darius Wadia. They have two daughters, Rosie and Bella, and live in New York. Traister's personal life notably intersected with her writings on life as a working parent in 2015, when she gained significant attention for making a television appearance while wearing her sleeping infant daughter in a chest carrier. Following her appearance, both Traister and the news program on which she appeared received praise for demonstrating the possibility of creating a supportive work environment for new parents.

SUGGESTED READING

Bronzite, Sarah. "Women No Longer Need to Be Married." *The Jewish Chronicle*, 14 Apr. 2016, www.thejc.com/culture/books/women-no-longer-need-to-be-married-1.64145. Accessed 14 Sept. 2018.

Hoder, Randye. "This Little-Seen MSNBC Interview Has Big Implications for Working Moms." *Fortune*, 11 Mar. 2015, www.fortune.com/2015/03/11/this-little-seen-msnbc-interview-has-big-implications-for-working-moms/. Accessed 14 Sept. 2018.

Johnson, Eric. "How *New York* Magazine's Rebecca Traister Convinced Hillary Clinton to Start Talking." *Recode*, 29 June 2017, www.recode.net/2017/6/29/15887768/rebecca-traister-hillary-clinton-new-york-magazine-profile-recode-media-peter-kafka-podcast. Accessed 14 Sept. 2018.

Traister, Rebecca. "Rebecca Traister: The Power of Being Single—Transcript." Interview by Caitlin Schiller. *Blinkist*, 21 Dec. 2017, www.blinkist.com/magazine/posts/rebecca-traister-the-power-of-being-single-transcript. Accessed 14 Sept. 2018.

Traister, Rebecca. "Single by Choice: Why Fewer American Women Are Married Than Ever Before." Interview by Terry Gross. *NPR*, 1 Mar. 2016, www.npr.org/templates/transcript/transcript.php?storyId=468688887. Accessed 14 Sept. 2018.

Traister, Rebecca. "30 Was the Year I Vowed to Start Living Like an Adult." *Elle*, 25 Aug. 2015, www.elle.com/life-love/sex-relationships/amp30004/rebecca-traister-essay-on-turning-30/. Accessed 14 Sept. 2018.

Traister, Rebecca. "Why Women Can't Break Free from the Parent Trap." *New Republic*, 2 Feb. 2015, newrepublic.com/article/120939/maternity-leave-policies-america-hurt-working-moms. Accessed 14 Sept. 2018.

SELECTED WORKS

Big Girls Don't Cry: The Election That Changed Everything for American Women, 2010; *All the Single Ladies: Unmarried Women and the Rise of an Independent Nation*, 2016; *Good and Mad: The Revolutionary Power of Women's Anger*, 2018

—Joy Crelin

Basil Twist

Date of birth: ca. 1969
Occupation: Puppeteer

Basil Twist is an American puppeteer and stage director best known for his abstract performance *Symphonie Fantastique*.

EARLY LIFE AND EDUCATION

Basil Twist was born and raised in San Francisco, California. Puppets were a family tradition for Twist. His mother, Lynne, was the founder of a troupe of amateur puppeteers who performed at schools and hospitals in the area, and his maternal grandfather, band leader Griff Williams, often used puppets in his music performances. Twist's grandmother, Dorothy B. Williams, for whom a New York City theater is named, gave Twist his grandfather's puppets when he was a child and had begun to take an interest in puppetry. Twist also began making his own puppets at an early age, creating a full cast of *Star Wars* puppets following the first film's release in 1977.

Despite it being his hobby and creative interest as a child, Twist stopped puppeteering in high school out of social shame. When he graduated from high school, he briefly attended Oberlin College, but could not maintain an interest in academics, knowing he would rather be making puppets.

Twist moved to New York City, where he took a few courses at New York University, but soon returned to his true passion of puppetry and began searching for opportunities with local theaters. He soon met theater and film director Julie Taymor, who later invited him to work on one of her productions.

Certain that he would pursue a career in puppetry, Twist moved to France and attended the École Nationale Supérieure des Arts de la Marionnette in Charleville-Mezieres. He earned a Doctor of Musical Arts degree in 1993 and was the first American to graduate from the institute. Twist returned to New York City and began working on his first onstage puppetry production.

PUPPETEER

Twist began making puppets using discarded materials found on the streets of New York City. His puppets are often constructed using reclaimed fabrics. He prefers silk above all other puppet fabrics due to its texture and "life." His puppets are not always representational; some of the things he manipulates onstage are merely objects such as a piece of cloth or a feather.

As a puppeteer, Twist's performances are abstract and expressionist, incorporating broad, choreographed movements and musical scores. Twist's performances have been noted for their dream-like sequences and use of vibrant color. He often requires up to three puppeteers to perform a single puppet's motions.

In 1998 he debuted with *Symphonie Fantastique*, an underwater puppetry performance that has become his best-known work. The piece, which features bubbles, feathers, and glitter in a five-hundred-gallon water tank, began when Twist found an unused aquarium on the street and started experimenting with underwater puppetry.

Symphonie Fantastique was a critical success. He quickly earned larger opportunities to collaborate and stage his performances. He was hired to create the Dementors sequence in the film *Harry Potter and the Prisoner of Azkaban*. The final edit of the film used computer animation based on the puppet modeling Twist created for the sequence.

Twist's subsequent performances continued the thematic approach he established with *Symphonie Fantastique*, while also drawing on such diverse influences as ballet in *Petrushka* (2001) and *The Rite of Spring* (2013), opera in *Hansel and Gretel* (2006), and Japanese Awaji puppetry in *Dogugaeshi* (2004). ("Dogugaeshi" means "set-flipping," a major element of that performance, which demonstrates Twist's fascination with manipulating everything onstage, not only the puppets.) Some of his inspiration also came from closer to home: in his 2008 show, *Arias with a Twist*, he incorporated his grandfather's puppets into the performance.

Twist acknowledges that puppeteering is not a modern interest, particularly in the United States, so he is reserved about his profession. He often carries puppets in saxophone cases to dissuade conversation about puppetry with strangers.

Twist has created puppets for other stage performances, including Broadway's *The Pee-Wee Herman Show* (2010) and *The Addams Family* (2010). In addition to creating and staging performances, Twist teaches the art of puppetry at the Dream Music Puppetry Program at the HERE Arts Center in New York.

IMPACT

Twist has won many awards for his puppetry, including an Obie, five UNIMA Awards, a Guggenheim Fellowship, and two Bessie Awards. He was awarded a MacArthur Foundation fellowship in 2015.

PERSONAL LIFE

Twist lives New York, and works in a Greenwich Village studio where he creates his puppets. As of 2011 he was in a relationship with poet and photographer Bobby Miller, who has been involved in some of Twist's productions.

SUGGESTED READING

Acocella, Joan. "Puppet Love." *New Yorker*. Condé Nast, 15 Apr. 2013, www.newyorker.com/magazine/2013/04/15/puppet-love. Accessed 27 Sept. 2018.

Blair, Elizabeth. "Basil Twist: A Genius, With Many a String Attached." *NPR*, 23 May 2012, www.npr.org/2012/03/24/148922534/basil-twist-a-genius-with-many-a-string-attached. Accessed Sept. 27, 2018.

Green, Jesse. "Theater Review: Puppets à la Russe, in Basil Twist's *The Rite of Spring*." *Vulture*. New York Media, 17 Oct. 2014, http://www.vulture.com/2014/10/theater-review-basil-twists-the-rite-of-spring.html. Accessed 27 Sept. 2018.

Mckinley, Jesse. "A Puppeteer Thrives in a Watery Wonderland." *New York Times*, 7 Jan. 1999, https://www.nytimes.com/1999/01/08/movies/a-puppeteer-thrives-in-a-watery-wonderland.html. Accessed 27 Sept. 2018.

"Meet a Puppeteer with a Gift for Pulling Strings." *CBSNews*, 11 Oct. 2015, www.cbsnews.com/video/meet-a-puppeteer-with-a-gift-for-pulling-strings/. Accessed 27 Sept. 2018

SELECTED WORKS

Symphonie Fantastique, 1998; *Petrushka*, 2001; *Master Peter's Puppet Show*, 2002; *La Bella Dormente nel Bosco*, 2005; *Hansel and Gretel*, 2006; *Dogugaeshi*, 2004; *Arias with a Twist*, 2008; *The*

Rite of Spring, 2013; *Sisters' Follies between Two Worlds*, 2015

—*Richard Means*

Michael W. Twitty

Date of birth: 1977
Occupation: Culinary historian, food writer

For cook, food writer, and culinary historian Michael W. Twitty, the culinary perspective for which he has become well known—kosher/soul—is far more than simply fusion cuisine. "It's culinary intermarriage," he told Hillary Eaton for the *Los Angeles Times* (10 Apr. 2017). "It's a dialogue, really. The way these African American, African diasporic, and Jewish food cultures interact with others." As a researcher long intrigued by the interconnections between food and culture, Twitty is particularly interested in the ways in which such cuisines have developed, reflecting not only the necessities of life as a member of a diaspora but also the influences of family traditions and historical context.

Throughout the first decades of the twenty-first century, Twitty has established himself as an independent scholar with an expertise in African American and Southern culinary history—areas that for Twitty are inextricably linked, as most of the cooking in what he terms the Old South was carried out by enslaved African Americans. Through projects such as the Cooking Gene project and the Southern Discomfort Tour, he has sought to investigate the African roots of Southern cuisine as well as his own ancestors' history in the South, both of which feature heavily in his 2017 work *The Cooking Gene: A Journey through African American Culinary History in the Old South*. For Twitty, food and cooking are closely tied to identity, and his work in that area enables him both to assert his own identity and combat the forces that have erased the contributions of African American cooks from the antebellum period through Twitty's own lifetime. "My whole path as a culinary historian and as a writer has been a resistance and a rebellion against every voice that I've ever come across," he wrote in a piece for the *Washington Post* (10 July 2013). "My form of rebellion is cooking my own identity. Identity cooking is when you cook what you are. That's how you can best understand me."

EARLY LIFE AND CAREER

Michael William Twitty was born in 1977 to William Lee Twitty and Patricia Anita Townsend. Born in Washington, DC, he grew up in Wheaton, Maryland. Twitty developed

Photo by *The Washington Post* via Getty Images

an interest in food and cooking at an early age and was particularly immersed in Southern cuisine. "I always had the sense that being a black Washingtonian meant having one foot in the South," Twitty wrote for the *Washington Post*. "There was iced tea on the table every night; there was pot liquor and corn bread." He was particularly influenced by his maternal grandmother, who passed down the culinary traditions she had learned during her early life in Alabama. "No one had to tell me about 'organic' or 'sustainable,' because that was the tradition that was passed down to me," he recalled for the *Washington Post*.

After graduating from high school, Twitty enrolled in Howard University, where he majored in Afro-American studies and anthropology. He was unable to complete his studies at Howard for financial reasons but continued his education independently, focusing particularly on culinary history. Beginning in 1995, Twitty worked intermittently as an intern for the Smithsonian, where he contributed to events such as the Smithsonian Folklife Festival and at times participated in the institution's living-history programs. In addition to his historical work, Twitty found work as a Hebrew school teacher and enjoyed teaching young students and challenging preconceived notions of who a Hebrew school teacher could be. "I was young, male, African American and of Jewish descent by conversion," he told Vivian Henoch for the website *myJewishDetroit* (Sept. 2009). "They learned quickly not to put their seventh grade stuff over on me, and I loved the challenge of teaching students across all streams of Orthodox, Conservative, Reconstructionist, Renewal, and Reform Judaism." Twitty continued teaching into 2013 but moved away from that work when he began to focus on his culinary and historical initiatives full time.

INDEPENDENT SCHOLAR

In the early twenty-first century, Twitty established himself as an independent scholar focused on African American Southern cooking as well as Sephardic and Ashkenazi Jewish cuisines. He was particularly interested in documenting the African roots of well-known Southern dishes, as these roots had been largely ignored by later white chefs and culinary scholars. In addition to offering consulting services, lectures, and workshops to museums and other institutions, Twitty operated the website *AfroFoodways* and the blog *Afroculinaria*, making his writings on such topics available to read online. *Afroculinaria* gained attention in 2013, when Twitty wrote an open letter to celebrity chef and television personality Paula Deen about the legacy of culinary injustice in Southern cuisine and invited her to cook a meal with him at a North Carolina plantation after Deen became embroiled in scandal for having used a racial slur. Although Deen did not respond to the letter, Twitty's blog post garnered him numerous new readers as well as the attention of the culinary community in the United States.

Alongside his blog, Twitty was active on the social media website *Twitter* both as himself, under the handle @koshersoul, and as his alter ego, @antebellumchef. "My role as the persona of @antebellumchef is to interrogate the current brand of Southern food because it often relegates our ancestors to a tertiary position in the genealogy of Southern cuisine," he wrote of the latter social media account for the *Washington Post*. Twitty was particularly concerned with the erasure of black cooks from Southern cuisine, despite ample historical evidence that most cooking in the South during the antebellum period was performed by cooks of African descent. In light of that erasure, Twitty sought to call attention to such historical individuals through speaking appearances and culinary events, some of which featured Twitty and other historical re-enactors cooking in period clothing. "I do what I do to honor those people who were not formally educated but had formal experience—who *created* Southern cuisine," he explained in his piece for the *Washington Post*. "I do this to honor them, because so many of them are nameless, faceless and uncredited for the genius that they had in making the American table work."

For his contributions to the fields of food writing and culinary history, Twitty was selected as a 2016 fellow by the TED (Technology, Entertainment, Design) organization. He delivered a TED Talk titled "Gastronomy and the Social Justice Reality of Food" in late 2016. In addition to his online work and public appearances, Twitty has published articles in a variety of magazines and books and in 2006 self-published the short book *Fighting Old Nep: The Foodways of Enslaved Afro-Marylanders 1634–1864*.

THE COOKING GENE

Perhaps Twitty's most significant research and educational project was an initiative known as the Cooking Gene project, which focused on his own family's history in the South, the development of Southern cuisine, and the connections between those topics. As part of that effort, Twitty sought to take a trip throughout the South, visiting and cooking at a variety of locations such as the plantation houses where his ancestors had been enslaved. He began crowdfunding that project, the Southern Discomfort Tour, in 2011 and the following year began his journey, during which he visited Virginia, South Carolina, Georgia, Alabama, and Louisiana. The extended Cooking Gene project also encompassed genealogical and genetic research as Twitty sought to determine the origins of his ancestors. He likewise worked to document culinary traditions that endured among African American cooks and families that he encountered during his travels.

In addition to documenting portions of the Cooking Gene project and Southern Discomfort Tour online, Twitty went on to publish a full-length book dealing with his findings and the links between family, history, culture, and food. *The Cooking Gene: A Journey through African American Culinary History in the Old South* was published by the Amistad imprint of HarperCollins in 2017. Following the publication of the book, Twitty made numerous speaking engagements, at times wearing the period clothing that he had worn on various occasions during the Southern Discomfort Tour. For Twitty, it was especially important to bring history to life and emphasize the humanity of his ancestors and other enslaved people. "I want people to see the soot smudges and smell the lingering wood smoke," he explained to Andrea King Collier for *NBC News* (21 July 2017). "I want them to understand the irony of doing something so incredibly skilled, but still not being seen as a person, a human being. And yet, these men and women cooked day-in and day-out for both fellow enslaved and their enslavers. I want people to see part of that in living color." Following its publication, *The Cooking Gene* received largely positive reviews from critics and was named one of the best nonfiction works of 2017 by publications such as *Kirkus Reviews*.

KOSHER/SOUL

In addition to his work as a culinary historian, Twitty has become known for a culinary perspective that he has termed "kosher/soul," blending elements of African, African American, Sephardic Jewish, and Ashkenazi Jewish cuisines in his own cooking. "I take blander Ashkenazi foods and jazz them up with African and Sephardic ingredients and spices or take African foods and soften them into plain-Jane Ashkenazi foods or Sephardic foods," he told Eaton. "I'm constantly trying to remake dishes and flavors and trying unusual things out: a lot of lemon, ginger, mint, rosewater, rhubarb, juniper berries."

In addition to influencing Twitty's cooking, the kosher/soul concept reflects his understanding of the similarities between African American and Jewish food cultures and the relationships between food and cultural identity. "They're both oppressed cultures—where the luxury of terroir isn't a reality," he explained to Eaton. Although the word *terroir* is typically used in discussions of the relationship between food and the region in which it is produced, Twitty has a broader understanding of the term. "It's what's in your blood and your memory," he told Eaton. "It's what's in your heritage and your family history."

PERSONAL LIFE

Twitty lives in Rockville, Maryland.

SUGGESTED READING

Bolton-Fasman, Judy. "One Book, One Read, Many Stories." *JewishBoston*, 4 Apr. 2018, www.jewishboston.com/one-book-one-read-many-stories. Accessed 13 Apr. 2018.

Henoch, Vivian. "Michael Twitty: A Kosher Soul." *MyJewishDetroit*, Sept. 2016, myjewishdetroit.org/2016/09/michael-twitty-a-kosher-soul Accessed 13 Apr. 2018.

Roig-Franzia, Manuel. "Tracing His Urge to Cook through Slavery and the South." *The Washington Post*, 18 Aug. 2017, www.washingtonpost.com/outlook/tracing-his-urge-to-cook-through-slavery-and-the-south/2017/08/18/1aeaa6de-6e19-11e7-96ab-5f38140b38cc_story.html. Accessed 13 Apr. 2018.

Twitty, Michael W. "First Person: Michael W. Twitty, 36, Culinary Historian and Food Blogger from Rockville." *The Washington Post*, 10 July 2013, www.washingtonpost.com/lifestyle/magazine/first-person-michael-w-twitty-36-culinary-historian-and-food-blogger-from-rockville/2013/07/10/a9ac8d08-d91f-11e2-9df4-895344c13c30_story.html. Accessed 13 Apr. 2018.

Twitty, Michael W. "Michael Twitty, the African American Jewish Writer, Is Poised to Give Us a New Way to Think about Passover." Interview by Hillary Eaton. *Los Angeles Times*, 10 Apr. 2017, www.latimes.com/food/dailydish/la-dd-michael-twitty-20170410-story.html. Accessed 13 Apr. 2018.

Twitty, Michael W. "Michael Twitty's 'The Cooking Gene' Explores Intersection of Culture and Cuisine." Interview by Andrea King Collier. *NBC*, 21 July 2017, www.nbcnews.com/news/nbcblk/blk-book-club-michael-twitty-cooking-gene-intersect-culture-cuisine-n784251. Accessed 13 Apr. 2018.

Weissman, Michaele. "His Paula Deen Takedown Went Viral. But This Food Scholar Isn't Done Yet." *The Washington Post*, 16 Feb. 2016, www.washingtonpost.com/lifestyle/food/his-paula-deen-takedown-went-viral-but-this-food-scholar-has-more-on-his-mind/2016/02/12/f83900f8-d031-11e5-88cd-753e80cd29ad_story.html. Accessed 13 Apr. 2018.

—Joy Crelin

Nora Twomey

Date of birth: October 31, 1971
Occupation: Animator, director

When Nora Twomey cofounded the animation studio Cartoon Saloon with former classmates Tomm Moore and Paul Young in 1999, she could not have known that within a decade, the studio would produce a feature-length animated film that would not only draw widespread attention to the company but also earn international acclaim and numerous award nominations. Codirected by Twomey and Moore, that first feature, 2009's *The Secret of Kells*, further demonstrated the quality of the work produced by the studio—which had previously created short films such as *From Darkness* (2002) and television series such as *Skunk Fu!* (2007–8)—as well as Cartoon Saloon's viability as a force in the international animation industry. "The idea that we can do it is exciting in itself," Twomey told Tara Brady for the *Irish Times* (19 May 2018) of the studio's work. "That an independent studio can team up with other independent studios around the world and pool resources, and that you're not dependent on merchandise or sales."

As a creative director of Cartoon Saloon and a core member of the studio, Twomey has filled a variety of roles for the studio's projects, including serving as voice director and head of story for the company's second feature, 2014's *Song of the Sea*. She made her debut as sole director of a feature film in 2017 with *The Breadwinner*, an adaptation of a young-adult novel about a girl who disguises herself as a boy in Taliban-era Afghanistan. In addition to its intriguing

Boungawa, via Wikimedia Commons

imagination was her only form of entertainment during her work hours.

Twomey eventually enrolled in Coláiste Stiofáin Naofa, a further education institution in Cork, to study art. She later moved to Dublin to attend Ballyfermot College of Further Education, an institution that was known for its animation program and admitted students based on talent and portfolios rather than their previous educational history. At the college, she learned about a variety of artistic techniques from the school's faculty, which included "really great life-drawing teachers," as she told Claire Scott for the website *Dublin Live* (27 Jan. 2018). "We looked very carefully at the details of human gesture and anatomy; the little things that show you what's human," she told Scott. "And it was some work—you'd be drawing the entire day and you'd be knackered going home but I think that focus was what did it for me and also meeting people who were equally as enthusiastic, people who loved drawing—it's contagious."

CARTOON SALOON

After completing her studies in animation and graduating from Ballyfermot College in 1995, Twomey initially remained in Dublin and took a position with Brown Bag Films, an animation studio founded in 1994 that would go on to specialize in animated television programs and short films. However, she disliked living in the city and ultimately left Dublin for Kilkenny, a smaller town in southeastern Ireland. In Kilkenny, she and Ballyfermot College classmates Tomm Moore and Paul Young founded their own independent animation studio, Cartoon Saloon, in 1999. "They were my peers in the classroom, so it's wonderful to still be in Ireland working together," she told Scott of her work with Moore and Young. "Certainly at the time we graduated the temptation was to go off and work in the big studios or the games' industry." Although the animation industry was largely dominated by large companies, Ireland was experiencing a small boom in animation during the late twentieth century and beginning of the twenty-first, and Cartoon Saloon was among the small companies offering new opportunities for the country's talented animators. "There are so many people that set up their own businesses that are working away here and it's really encouraging and lovely to see," Twomey told Scott.

As one of Cartoon Saloon's founders, Twomey served in a variety of roles for the company's projects over its first decades of existence in addition to holding the position of creative director. She, at times, directed projects for the studio, helming the short films *From Darkness* (2002) and *Backwards Boy* (2004), and also filled the roles of animator, producer, writer, and art director for various productions. In addition to

subject matter, the film was particularly significant thanks to the work of its animators, who blended traditional hand-drawn styles of animation with cutting-edge techniques that nevertheless resemble long-established styles. "We wanted to do something that would feel classical, timeless," Twomey told John Meagher for the *Independent* (11 June 2017) of her team's strategy. "There are sophisticated techniques that can be used now, but they might date it and we didn't want that." Twomey and Cartoon Saloon's approach undoubtedly paid off. In addition to receiving overwhelmingly positive reviews from film critics, *The Breadwinner* was nominated for numerous major awards, including the Academy Award for best animated feature, following the film's premiere in September 2017.

EARLY LIFE AND EDUCATION

Nora Twomey was born on October 31, 1971, in Cork, Ireland. She was interested in art from an early age and was often drawing but did not initially consider pursuing a formal education in any art form, instead choosing to leave school at the age of fifteen and join the workforce. Her first job involved manufacturing porcelain dolls, and the experience emphasized her passion for hands-on artistic work. "I loved making things," she recalled to Brady. "I loved that something existed at the end of the day that didn't exist when you started in the morning." She went on to take a position at a vegetable-processing factory, where she worked twelve-hour night shifts. She would later credit the job with helping to develop her imaginative capabilities, as her own creating short films and other content, Cartoon Saloon would later move into animated television programming with the children's show *Skunk Fu!*, which aired between 2007 and 2008.

FEATURE FILMS

A decade after the founding of Cartoon Saloon, the company released its first feature-length animated film, 2009's *The Secret of Kells*. Inspired by Irish history and legend and deeply influenced by the ninth-century illuminated manuscript known as the Book of Kells, the film tells the story of a boy named Brendan who works to complete the Book of Kells while also dealing with threats in the form of a Celtic god and Viking raiders. Twomey and Moore served as co-directors of the film, which was based on a story by Moore and a screenplay written by Fabrice Ziolkowski, and Twomey was also a member of the film's voice cast.

As Cartoon Saloon's first feature film, *The Secret of Kells* drew significant attention for its status as an independently produced animated work, its connection to Irish culture, and the quality and distinctive style of its animation. After premiering at France's Gérardmer Film Festival in January 2009, *The Secret of Kells* played at festivals and in theaters in Ireland and beyond. The film earned widespread acclaim from critics, with A. O. Scott writing in a review for the *New York Times* (4 Mar. 2010) that "it is only fitting that a movie concerned with the power and beauty of drawing . . . should be so gorgeously and intricately drawn." It was also nominated for numerous awards, including the Academy Award for Best Animated Feature Film, the Irish Film and Television Academy (IFTA) Awards for Best Film and Best Animation (the latter of which it won), and the animation-focused Annie Award for Best Animated Feature.

Following the success of *The Secret of Kells*, Cartoon Saloon went on to release its second feature film, *Song of the Sea*, in 2014. Twomey served as voice director and head of story for the film, which drew from Celtic legends about the mythological creatures known as selkies that were said to shift between human and seal forms. Much like *The Secret of Kells*, *Song of the Sea* was nominated for the Academy Award for Best Animated Feature Film, and it further claimed the IFTA Award for Best Film. The following year, Twomey also began a role as creative producer of Cartoon Saloon's animated children's television series *Puffin Rock*, which was ultimately acquired by the popular streaming platform Netflix.

THE BREADWINNER

Cartoon Saloon's next feature film, *The Breadwinner*, differed significantly from the studio's previous features in terms of its subject matter and origins. Based on the 2000 book by Canadian writer Deborah Ellis, the film tells the story of Parvana, a girl living in Taliban-era Afghanistan who disguises herself as a boy to help her family survive after her father is imprisoned. The film rights to the original novel had previously been optioned with the goal of making a live-action film, but after reconsidering on the basis that animation would help to keep audiences engaged despite the heavier nature of the subject matter and having admired work such as *The Secret of Kells*, those holding the rights saw Cartoon Saloon as an appropriate studio to adapt the work.

The Breadwinner was likewise particularly significant for Twomey, as the film was the first feature-length work for which she served as the sole director, and she also found herself particularly drawn to the source material. "As soon as I read it, I knew that I wanted to make this film," she told Meagher. "It's such a captivating story, but I wanted to make sure that whatever we did would truly do justice to it." To create *The Breadwinner*, she worked with a team of more than three hundred professionals based in Ireland, Luxembourg, and Canada and benefited from the assistance of actor and director Angelina Jolie, who served as one of the film's executive producers and played an important role in promoting the film. For Twomey, the involvement of film-industry figures such as Jolie was essential to a small studio such as Cartoon Saloon, which faced the substantial challenge of creating animated features in an industry largely—although not entirely—dominated by a handful of large companies. "I'm an animator," she explained to Meagher. "It's what I'm trained to do and it's my passion, but you have to learn to be a diplomat and a salesperson too because you're trying to sell the idea of this story and why it's worth investing in it."

First shown at the Toronto International Film Festival in September 2017, *The Breadwinner* opened in US theaters in November of that year and in several other countries, including Ireland and the United Kingdom, during the first half of 2018. Although somewhat of a departure from Cartoon Saloon's previous efforts, the film's compelling story and innovative mingling of hand-drawn animation and digitally animated sequences inspired by stop-motion appealed to film critics as well as fans of animation, and Twomey and her team were widely recognized for their efforts. In addition to being nominated for the Academy Award for Best Animated Feature Film, *The Breadwinner* won the Annie Award for best independent animated feature, and Twomey herself was nominated for the Annie for outstanding achievement in directing for an animated feature. After *The Breadwinner*, Twomey planned to work on a feature-length animated adaptation of American writer Ruth

Stiles Gannett's 1948 children's book *My Fa-ther's Dragon*, which she was set to codirect with Moore.

PERSONAL LIFE

Twomey lives in Kilkenny with her husband, Michael McGrath, and their sons, Oliver and Patrick. She has noted that her experiences as a parent were essential in shaping her approach to *The Breadwinner*, which focuses heavily on family. "I don't think I could have told this story ten years ago. I don't think I would have been open enough to try it," she explained to Brady. "Something happened to me when I became a parent. I couldn't listen to the news for six months. I couldn't cope with the fact that—in two sentences—someone would relate the loss of a life to the loss of hundreds of lives while you are there doing your best to nurture one single baby. The effect of that, that idea of the preciousness of children, has never left me."

Twomey was diagnosed with breast cancer in 2016. She continued working through chemotherapy and treatment as *The Breadwinner* was being completed.

SUGGESTED READING

Brady, Tara. "Angelina Jolie, *The Breadwinner* and Me. By Nora Twomey." *The Irish Times*, 19 May 2018, irishtimes.com/culture/film/angelina-jolie-the-breadwinner-and-me-by-nora-twomey-1.3494812. Accessed 16 July 2018.

Meagher, John. "From School Drop-Out to Oscar-Nominated Animator with Cartoon Saloon—Nora Twomey." *Independent*, 11 June 2017, www.independent.ie/entertainment/movies/from-school-dropout-to-oscarnominated-animator-with-cartoon-saloon-nora-twomey-35798523.html. Accessed 16 July 2018.

Scott, Claire. "Oscar Nominee Reveals How Her Time in Ballyfermot Paved the Road to Success." *Dublin Live*, 27 Jan. 2018, www.dublinlive.ie/news/dublin-news/oscar-nominee-reveals-how-time-14201401. Accessed 16 July 2018.

Twomey, Nora. "Animator Nora Twomey: 'Factory Work Was Incredible Training for My Imagination.'" Interview by Tim Lewis. *The Guardian*, 20 May 2018, www.theguardian.com/film/2018/may/20/film-director-nora-twomey-interview-new-review-q-and-a-breadwinner. Accessed 16 July 2018.

SELECTED WORKS

The *Secret of Kells* (with Tomm Moore), 2009; *Song of the Sea*, 2014; *The Breadwinner*, 2017

—Joy Crelin

James Tynion IV

Date of birth: December 14, 1987
Occupation: Comic book writer

James Tynion IV is an award-winning comic book writer best known for his work on Batman comics within the DC Universe, including the series *Batman Eternal*. In 2016, his crossover series for DC Comics and IDW Publishing featuring Batman and the Teenage Mutant Ninja Turtles became a *New York Times* Best Seller. He writes for DC's continuation of the long-running biweekly *Detective Comics*. In addition to his work on well-known comic franchises, Tynion has a growing body of original work garnering acclaim. His epic supernatural mystery adventure series *The Woods* won the GLAAD Media Award for Outstanding Comic Book in 2017, and a Syfy television drama based on the series is in development.

Tynion, who identifies as bisexual, makes a conscious effort to portray queer and trans characters in his work. One of his most recent comics, *The Backstagers*, a young-adult fantasy about a group of teenage boys working on a theater stage crew, features characters with a variety of different sexual identities. Tynion told Jon Erik Christianson for *Comics Alliance* (31 Aug. 2016) that the comic industry is experiencing a massive and positive shift in terms of who gets to tell their story: "There are still tremendous issues in terms of queer representation, but we're also getting to the point where—not to toot my own horn—but I'm an openly queer creator as

Photo by Michael Stewart/WireImage, via Getty Images

the head writer on Detective Comics, which is co-starring a queer lead." He continued, "The queer voices are coming forward, and I think in terms of the young generation of comics writers and artists, they're, frankly—and this just might be the bubble I live in—but it seems like queer is the new majority. And there is something very exciting about that. And I'm excited to see where it all leads."

EARLY LIFE AND EDUCATION

Tynion was born in New York City on December 14, 1987, and grew up in Milwaukee, Wisconsin. As a kid, he begged his father to make up new stories about his favorite character, Peter Pan. He discovered comic books, and the joy of ongoing story lines, when he was in middle school. Around the same time, Tynion realized that he was bisexual. He came out to a friend, but as he later said, the admission did not go well. Tynion attended Marquette University High School, a private, Catholic all-boys school in Milwaukee. He joined the theater department's stage crew "where I found myself and my voice," he told Brigid Alverson for the *School Library Journal* (10 July 2017). Of the friends he made on the crew, Tynion added, "They didn't care that I liked guys. They were interested in things I was interested in. They didn't want to be anything or fit any role; they just wanted to hang around and build sets." At Marquette, Tynion helped found the school's first gay student alliance support group. He graduated in 2006.

Tynion attended Sarah Lawrence College in Bronxville, New York. He studied writing with author Scott Snyder, who had then recently published an acclaimed collection of literary short stories featuring superheroes called *Voodoo Heart* (2006). Tynion and Snyder became friends, and Snyder told him that comic book publishers DC and Marvel had approached him about writing comics. Snyder told Tynion about a concept that would eventually become the Eisner Award–winning DC series *American Vampire*. "We bonded pretty quickly and I started lending him some of my favorite comics, and he started lending me his," Tynion recalled to Jeffrey Renaud for the website *CBR.com* (29 Feb. 2012). "Being friends with Scott has been the greatest writing master class that I ever could have hoped for."

BATMAN, NIGHT OF OWLS, AND TALON

After graduating from Sarah Lawrence in 2010, Tynion interned with Vertigo, an imprint of DC Comics, where he worked under editor Shelly Bond. About a year later, in 2011, Snyder approached him about cowriting back-ups, or one-off stories that have no bearing on a comic's ongoing plot, for the *Batman* series. "After he spent a half-hour reassuring me that it wasn't a joke, I said, 'Yes,' and that very night we started talking

about all the different ways we could approach the back-ups to make them the best they could possibly be," Tynion told Renaud. The back-ups were a part of Snyder's series *Night of Owls*. Together, Snyder and Tynion delved into Bruce Wayne's past, through the character of Jarvis Pennyworth, the Wayne family's longtime servant and father of their loyal butler, Alfred Pennyworth. Snyder and Tynion's back-up "The Fall of the House of Wayne" is set when Wayne (later known as Batman) is just an infant.

Soon after that, Tynion worked with Snyder to write *Batman Annual #1*, which is notable for the reintroduction of a classic Batman villain, Mr. Freeze. In 2012, they launched *Talon*, a spin-off of *Night of Owls*. That series, which ran for eighteen issues, featured the Talons, a group of assassins introduced in the *Night of Owls*. *Talon* tells the story of an escaped assassin named Calvin Rose, on the run from his former allies. Tynion lobbied hard for the series. When he first suggested it to Snyder, Snyder was skeptical. Tynion wrote a draft of the story in a weekend. "Then Scott and I went back and forth for a few weeks, until we got something we were both really happy with, and then we took it to DC, and they decided to [give] it the green light," Tynion recalled to Eric Diaz for *Nerdist* (4 Sept. 2013). Tynion also worked on the DC series *Red Hood and the Outlaws*, which also features characters from the Batman universe.

ORIGINAL WORKS AND BATMAN ETERNAL

In 2013, Tynion created his first original series, *The Eighth Seal*, a political horror story for the digital comics website *Thrillbent*. In an interview for the blog *Bloody Disgusting*, he described the series as the classic horror film *Rosemary's Baby* (1968) meets the early-2000s presidential television drama *The West Wing*. In it, a woman named Amelia Greene is plagued by debilitating, horrific visions. To further complicate her psychological struggles, she is also the First Lady of the United States. The series delves into political conspiracy.

The following June, Tynion published another comic for *Thrillbent* called *The House in the Wall*. The series, cowritten with Noah J. Yuenkel, follows the story of Ariel Carpenter, a twenty-something living in Brooklyn. Ariel, aimless and unemployed, dreams of a magical house, but when she discovers the door to that house in the wall of her crumbling apartment, untold horrors are unleashed.

Between these two series, Tynion was named one of the head writers for the new DC weekly comic *Batman Eternal*, which launched in 2014. When the series was announced, Snyder, the comic's creator, told Brian Truitt for *USA Today* (20 Oct. 2013) that he and Tynion would plan the series' first arc. He described his former student as a "great world builder" with an "incredible expansive mind."

Tynion's endeavors for DC continued in 2015 and 2016. These included cowriting DC's *Constantine: The Hellblazer* and serving as head writer for the crossover series *Batman & Robin Eternal*. At this time, Tynion also wrote a six-issue crossover miniseries featuring Batman and the Teenage Mutant Ninja Turtles. Tynion was more than happy to take on the project, describing the concept to Vaneta Rogers for the comic book website *Newsarama* (13 Oct. 2015) as "too good to be true."

THE WOODS AND WORK WITH BOOM! STUDIOS

When Tynion was still working on *Talon*, he was approached by BOOM! Studios. The publisher was looking for a four-issue series pitch, but Tynion pitched them a three-year epic instead. BOOM! liked the idea, and ordered twelve issues of Tynion's supernatural mystery, *The Woods*. In the series, an entire high school—including teachers, students and staff—in Milwaukee are suddenly and mysteriously transported to an alien planet. *The Woods* proved to be one of BOOM!'s most successful original series launches, and in 2014 the first printing of the first issue sold out in a few weeks. In his review of the first issue, *The Arrow*, for the *School Library Journal* (8 Oct. 2014), J. Caleb Mozzocco wrote, "Tynion seems to find a good balance between seeding the mystery with clues and focusing on the inherent drama of the situation." In late 2016, Syfy announced that it was developing an hour-long drama based on *The Woods*, with producer and director Brad Peyton and writer Michael Armbruster.

In 2015, BOOM! released the first two miniseries in Tynion's Apocalyptic Trilogy. The first miniseries, *Memetic* follows a college-aged man named Aaron and his boyfriend, Ryan, as they try to make their way through Manhattan and the hordes of undead that seek to eat them. The source of the zombie infection is an internet meme. The second miniseries, *Cognetic*, is about a creature that can control human minds like a singular hive mind. The third and final miniseries in the trilogy, *Eugenic*, launched in 2017.

In 2016, Tynion and artist Rian Sygh published a BOOM! comic about a group of teenage boys working on their school's theater stage crew called *The Backstagers*. The concept was inspired by his own experiences as a high schooler. "It's very important to me to explore things that are more personal," he told George Gene Gustines for the *New York Times* (15 May 2016). "I was a stage crew kid growing up myself. It's a very strange place that always held a special part of my heart."

PERSONAL LIFE

Tynion lives in Brooklyn, New York, with his partner and dog.

SUGGESTED READING

Christianson, Jon Erik. "Bi the Books: James Tynion Pulls Back the Curtain on Erasure and Queer Haircuts [Flame Con]." *Comics Alliance*, 31 Aug. 2016, comicsalliance.com/james-tynion-flame-con-interview. Accessed 12 May 2018.

Diaz, Eric. "Comic Book Day: James Tynion IV Talks *Talon* and *Red Hood & The Outlaws*." *Nerdist*, 4 Sept. 2013, nerdist.com/comic-book-day-james-tynion-iv-talks-talon-and-red-hood-the-outlaws. Accessed 11 May 2018.

Gustines, George Gene. "Boom Box Comics Tell Stories of Teenagers, with a Light Heart." *The New York Times*, 15 May 2016, www.nytimes.com/2016/05/16/business/media/boom-box-comics-tell-stories-of-teenagers-with-a-light-heart.html. Accessed 12 May 2018.

Mozzocco, J. Caleb. Review of *The Woods, Volume 1: The Arrow*, written by James Tynion IV and drawn by Michael Dialynas. *School Library Journal*, 8 Oct. 2014, blogs.slj.com/goodcomicsforkids/2014/10/08/review-the-woods-vol-1-the-arrow. Accessed 11 May 2018.

Rogers, Vaneta. "DC Gives BATMAN Even More New TEENAGE Allies, but This Time They're MUTANT NINJA TURTLES." *Newsarama*, 13 Oct. 2015, www.newsarama.com/26327-dc-gives-batman-even-more-new-teenage-allies-but-this-time-they-re-mutant-ninja-turtles.html. Accessed 11 May 2018.

Tynion, James, IV. "Interview James Tynion IV on 'Backstagers.'" Interview by Brigid Alverson. *Good Comics for Kids*, School Library Journal, 10 July 2017, blogs.slj.com/goodcomicsforkids/2017/07/10/interview-james-tynion-iv-on-backstagers. Accessed 11 May 2018.

Tynion, James, IV. "[Interview] James Tynion IV Talks Political Horror in 'The Eighth Seal.'" Interview by Lonnie Nadler. *Bloody Disgusting*, 23 Apr. 2013, bloody-disgusting.com/news/3229919/interview-james-tynion-iv-talks-political-horror-in-the-eighth-seal. Accessed 11 May 2018.

SELECTED WORKS

The Eighth Seal, 2013; *The House in the Wall*, 2014; *The Woods*, 2014–17; Apocalyptic Trilogy, 2015–17; *The Backstagers*, 2016

—Molly Hagan

Kali Uchis

Date of birth: July 17, 1994
Occupation: Singer

Kali Uchis is a Colombian American singer, rapper, and producer. In 2017 Uchis was nominated for a Latin Grammy Award for Record of the Year for "El Ratico," a collaboration with Colombian singer Juanes. Uchis was also nominated for a Grammy Award for Best R & B Performance for her song "Get You" with Daniel Caesar. She released her debut album, *Isolation*, in 2018. The album includes the hit single "After the Storm," featuring rapper Tyler the Creator and funk legend Bootsy Collins. The video for the song features an aggressively apathetic Uchis placidly moving through a retro-styled house. Collins, wearing his trademark top hat and sunglasses, appears on a cereal box. The ever-eccentric Tyler the Creator raps with his face poking out from Uchis's AstroTurf lawn. The off-kilter aesthetic of the video is a good introduction to the difficult-to-classify Uchis, whose voice recalls that of a midcentury cabaret singer or the late neo-soul singer Amy Winehouse and whose sound ranges from chillwave to reggaeton to 1950s doo-wop.

Uchis, who was born near Washington, DC, but spent much of her early childhood living in Colombia, released her first mixtape, *Drunken Babble*, in 2012, when she was just eighteen. A swaggering and playful music video for the song "What They Say" caught the attention of Snoop Dogg, who helped launch her career by inviting her to collaborate on his 2014 mixtape *That's My Work, Vol. 3*. With a slew of collaborations (including Snoop and Gorillaz), an EP, and a critically acclaimed album under her belt, Uchis has made it clear that she is an artist with a unique vision. Her influences range from French actor Brigitte Bardot to Brazilian singer Astrud Gilberto to filmmaker Wes Anderson. "I grew up listening to so many different types of music," she told Alex Weiss for *Paper* magazine (6 Apr. 2018). "I'm just drawn to artists who are total individuals and independent thinkers, artists who have their own style and are just very authentic about who they are and what they stand for."

EARLY LIFE AND EDUCATION

Uchis was born Karly-Marina Loaiza outside of Washington, DC, on July 17, 1994. (Her stage name, Kali Uchis, is a nickname her father gave her.) Her parents moved to the United States from Pereira, Colombia, in the early 1990s. "There was too much going on in the country at the time, there was a lot of guerrilla warfare," Uchis explained to Jaquira Díaz for the *Fader* (13 July 2017). The family—Uchis, her parents, and her three brothers—moved between Colombia and the United States. Uchis started elementary

By Alice.Umusic, via Wikimedia Commons

school in Pereira, but the family moved back to the United States again, this time permanently, when Uchis was in the third grade. They settled in a suburb of northern Virginia. Uchis did poorly in high school, skipping classes to spend time in the photo lab making short films. She wrote poetry and songs but was mostly interested in visual art and directing. Her general rebelliousness irked her father, who threw her out of the house for breaking curfew when she was seventeen. A note left on her bed said, as Uchis recalled to Díaz, "Even though I love you, you continue to be disrespectful. You have to learn what it's like to really be on your own. When I get home, I don't want to see you. Go figure it out." Uchis began living out of her car and sleeping in parking lots. After two weeks, her father begged her to come back, but Uchis realized that she needed to learn to take care of herself. She took a succession of odd jobs to make ends meet, working as a cashier at a grocery store and selling clothes, while attending T. C. Williams High School in Alexandria. She also began, during this time, to write songs. As Díaz told it, Uchis wrote and recorded an early version of her 2018 song "Killer" in the middle of the night in a twenty-four-hour grocery store parking lot: "If you loved me, you wouldn't put me through this," the song's lyrics say. Uchis and her father made amends several months later; she has a tattoo of his name on her bicep as a symbol of their bond.

DRUNKEN BABBLE

Uchis was just eighteen when she released her debut mixtape, *Drunken Babble*, on the free download site *DatPiff* in 2012. It was the summer after she graduated high school. "I literally put it together in a month," Uchis recalled to Briana Younger for the music website *Bandwidth* (22 Apr. 2014). "I initially didn't make it to put it out. I was just using it as a creative outlet . . . I'm saying everything that's hurting me and bothering me," she said. Eventually she decided to release the tape, she told Younger, because "I felt like people would actually appreciate something real." Díaz described the tape as "a psychedelic multi-genre collection that recalls an earlier decade, the likes of Billie Holiday mixed with talk-rap, old school hip-hop, and dancehall reggae." In 2013, while holding down a job at Whole Foods, Uchis released a video for her song "What They Say." The song's dreamy production recalls 1950s doo-wop groups. In the video, Uchis and her friends steal a man's car and drive around, smoking weed and having a good time. "You don't gotta listen to what they say," Uchis sings. "It ain't real."

The video garnered Uchis attention from rapper Snoop Dogg, who reached out to her on Twitter. He asked her to collaborate on a song called "On Edge" for his 2014 mixtape, *That's My Work, Vol. 3*. She also heard from Odd Future rapper Tyler the Creator and appeared on his song "Aunt Wang Syrup Theme Song," also in 2014. Tyler collaborated with Uchis on her 2015 EP *Por Vida* (*For Life*). That record also featured producers Diplo, BADBADNOTGOOD, and Kaytranada. In his review for the Latin music website *Remezcla* (2015), Marcos Hassan wrote that *Por Vida* "is a slow jam extravaganza, one that's not quite pop, not quite girl group/Northern soul, and not quite Nineties R & B but everything in between. [Uchis] creates a sound you'll swear you've heard before but can't quite put your finger on—at once familiar and fresh." *Rolling Stone* named *Por Vida* one of their top twenty best R & B albums of 2015. That year, Uchis also toured with soul singer Leon Bridges.

ISOLATION

In 2017, Uchis appeared on the song "El Ratico (The Root)" with Colombian superstar Juanes. Her family in Colombia had been skeptical of her success before then, doubting she could make a living from music alone; the collaboration convinced them that Uchis really had made it. A testament to Uchis's versatility, she also appeared on the song "Caramelo Duro (Hard Candy)" from Miguel's album *War & Leisure* and the Gorillaz songs "Ticker Tape" and "She's My Collar" the same year. She released "Tyrant," featuring British singer Jorja Smith, in 2017, as the first single from her debut album. Beca Grimm (22 June 2017) described the song for NPR as a "love letter . . . to summer 2017" that also nods at the political turmoil of that summer,

less than a year after the election of President Donald Trump. The song is an ode to a new lover, "a romantic banger flecked with self-awareness," Grimm wrote. In it, Uchis sings, "When everything's on fire / You're my peace and quiet." Uchis released her second single, "Nuestra Planeta (Our Planet)," featuring reggaeton singer Reykon, a few months later. The song, recorded in Medellín, Colombia, is sung entirely in Spanish.

Uchis performed her third single, "After the Storm," on the *Tonight Show Starring Jimmy Fallon* on March 14, 2018, and released her debut album, *Isolation*, in April of that year. The album, featuring production from Thundercat, Damon Albarn, and Kevin Parker of Tame Impala, opens with a gentle bossa nova intro. "I like being able to open a project with a mysterious, flowy, dainty moment—a feather brushing on the top of your skin," Uchis explained to Claire Lobenfeld for *Pitchfork* (11 Apr. 2018). The sounds on the rest of the album are diverse but united by a common feeling that Julianne Escobedo Shepherd described in her review for *Pitchfork* (11 Apr. 2018) as "a slinky desert vibe, a document of the way young Angelenos have opened up the way for sounds and genre to gloop in on each other like a lava lamp." (Uchis has always cultivated a California sound, but now also lives in Los Angeles.) Shepherd praised Uchis's precision and restraint in crafting the album. She concluded: "*Isolation* is a star turn from an artist who has proven she's ready for it." Joe Levy for *Rolling Stone* (5 Apr. 2018) was similarly impressed, awarding the album four out of five stars. He compared it to early offerings from Beck and iconic hip-hop duo Outkast, describing Uchis as "a pop weirdo who works grooves that seem vintage and futuristic at the same moment." Much like Shepherd, he offered an emphatic conclusion: "Uchis is a woman on the verge."

SUGGESTED READING

Díaz, Jaquira. "Who Is the Real Kali Uchis?" *The Fader*, 13 July 2017, www.thefader.com/2017/07/13/kali-uchis-cover-story-album-tyrant-interview. Accessed 12 May 2018.

Grimm, Beca. "Songs We Love: Kali Uchis, 'Tyrant (Feat. Jorja Smith).'" *NPR*, 22 June 2017, www.npr.org/2017/06/22/533847772/songs-we-love-kali-uchis-tyrant-feat-jorja-smith. Accessed 12 May 2018.

Hassan, Marcos. Review of *Por Vida*, by Kali Uchis. *Remezcla*, 2015, remezcla.com/features/music/review-kali-uchis-por-vida/. Accessed 12 May 2018.

Levy, Joe. "Review: Kali Uchis' 'Isolation' Proves She's an Exciting Young Talent." Review of *Isolation*, by Kali Uchis. *Rolling Stone*, 5 Apr. 2018, www.rollingstone.com/music/

albumreviews/review-kali-uchis-isolation-w518725. Accessed 12 May 2018.

Shepherd, Julianne Escobedo. Review of *Isolation*, by Kali Uchis. *Pitchfork*, 11 Apr. 2018, pitchfork.com/reviews/albums/kali-uchis-isolation/. Web. 12 May 2018.

Uchis, Kali. "Kali Uchis: 'I'm an Artist in Every Sense of the Word.'" Interview by Briana Younger. *Bandwidth*, 22 Apr. 2014, bandwidth.wamu.org/kali-uchis-im-an-artist-in-every-sense-of-the-word/. Accessed 12 May 2018.

Weiss, Alex. "Kali Uchis is a Self-Made Pop Star." *Paper*, 6 Apr. 2018, www.papermag.com/kali-uchis-beautiful-people-2-2556830986.html. Accessed 12 May 2018.

—*Molly Hagan*

Gabrielle Union

Date of birth: October 29, 1972
Occupation: Actor

Gabrielle Union is a television and film actor whose work includes the movies *Bad Boys II* (2003) and *Deliver Us from Eva* (2003) and the television series *Being Mary Jane* (2013–). She is known for playing strong and seductive women as well as for her ability to convey humor in her performances.

EARLY LIFE AND EDUCATION

Gabrielle Union was born on October 29, 1972, in Omaha, Nebraska, to Sylvester Union, then a high school basketball coach, and Theresa Glass Union, a social worker and phone company manager. The second of three daughters, she spent her early years in an Omaha community where her family had long-standing roots. When she was eight, her family moved to California to the town of Pleasanton, about twenty-five miles east of Oakland. She attended Foothill High School, where she was on the soccer, basketball, and track teams. After graduating in 1991, she attended the University of Nebraska–Lincoln, where she was on the soccer team. After one semester, she returned to California and briefly studied at Cuesta College. She later enrolled at the University of California, Los Angeles (UCLA) and graduated in 1996 with a degree in sociology.

Union worked as an intern at a modeling agency during her senior year of college. Although she had planned to go to law school, when she finished the internship, she was invited to model for the agency and agreed, seeing it as a quick way to pay off her school loans and earn money for her future education.

LIFE'S WORK

While working as a model, Union was asked to audition for an acting role and landed a guest role on the television comedy series *Saved by the Bell* in 1995, appearing for two seasons. She soon was offered guest roles on many other shows, including *Moesha*, *Malibu Shores*, and *Goode Behavior* in 1996; *Dave's World* and *Sister, Sister* in 1997; and as Dr. Courtney Ellis in eleven episodes of *City of Angels* in 2000. She also had a recurring role in *7th Heaven* from 1996 to 1999.

Union landed her first film role in the 1998 television movie *1973*, which then led the following year to her first feature film role as Katie in *She's All That*. Also in 1999, Union appeared in the film *10 Things I Hate About You*.

Union's big break came when she played the role of a cheerleading captain in the teen flick *Bring It On* in 2000, starring Kirsten Dunst. She then appeared in a string of movies, including the romantic comedies *Two Can Play That Game* and *The Brothers* in 2001 and the 2002 comedy *Welcome to Collinwood*. All the while, Union continued to guest star in television shows, and in 2001 she had a guest role on the popular sitcom *Friends*.

In 2003 Union was given her first starring role in the romantic comedy *Deliver Us from Eva*, and that same year she appeared in the action film *Cradle 2 the Grave* and the comedy drama *Bad Boys II*. Nominated for BET (Black Entertainment Television) Awards for all three movies, she won the 2004 BET Comedy Award for outstanding lead actress in a box office movie for *Deliver Us from Eva*.

In recognition of her acting talent, Union received the AOL Time Warner Rising Star Award at the 2003 American Black Film Festival. She had earned a reputation for playing roles of strong, opinionated women and was appearing mainly in comedies and romantic dramas, including *Breakin' All the Rules* (2004), costarring Jamie Foxx, and the starring role of Alice Kramden in the 2005 remake of the 1950s sitcom *The Honeymooners*.

After guest spots on shows such as *The Proud Family* (2003), *The West Wing* (2004), and voice work on *Family Guy* (2005), Union landed a starring role as a crime reporter on the television series *Night Stalker* in 2005. The series was cancelled after one season, but Union kept a busy schedule, appearing in the memoir *Running with Scissors* (2006), the drama *Daddy's Little Girls* (2007), and the biographical *Cadillac Records* (2008). Returning to television, she appeared in several episodes of *Ugly Betty* in 2008, *Life* in 2009, and *Flashforward* in 2009 and 2010.

While many critics predicted that Union seemed poised to become "the next big star," she continued to appear in B films in the early

2010s. This trend changed in 2013 when she landed the starring role in the television series *Being Mary Jane*. The series became a hit, with reviewers crediting Union for her performance as a multidimensional character who was both competent and vulnerable, successful and flawed. The series was renewed for its fourth season in 2016.

IMPACT

Gabrielle Union has used her celebrity to advocate for issues important to her. In 2006, for instance, she met with congressional leaders to promote funding for rape crisis centers, and in 2009, she testified before Congress in support of the Violence Against Women Act. She also has served as an ambassador for the Susan B. Komen Foundation.

PERSONAL LIFE

Union was married to former professional football running back Chris Howard from 2001 to 2006. She married professional basketball player Dwayne Wade in 2014. Union legally changed her name to Union-Wade in 2016.

SUGGESTED READING

Abrahamson, Rachel Paula. "Gabrielle Union: My Advice on Being a Stepmom." *US Weekly*. US Weekly, 29 Feb. 2016. Accessed 26 May 2016.

"American Black Film Festival Announces 2003 Honorees Russell Simmons and Gabrielle Union." *ABFF*. ABFF Ventures, 30 May 2003. Accessed 24 May 2016.

Barney, Chuck. "'Being Mary Jane': Gabrielle Union Relishes a Career High Point." *Mercury News*. Digital First Media, 3 Mar. 2015. Accessed 18 May 2016.

Biga, Leo Adam. "Being Gabby." *Reader*. Reader, 23 Sept. 2012. Accessed 26 May 2016.

Stedman, Alex. "Gabrielle Union Channels Soledad O'Brien in BET's 'Being Mary Jane.'" *Variety*. Variety Media, 17 Dec. 2013. Accessed 18 May 2016.

SELECTED WORKS

Bring It On, 2000; *City of Angels*, 2000; *Deliver Us from Eva*, 2003; *Bad Boys II*, 2003; *Cradle 2 the Grave II*, 2003; *Running with Scissors*, 2006; *Night Stalker*, 2005; *Being Mary Jane*, 2013–;

—*Barb Lightner*

Lil Uzi Vert

Date of birth: July 31, 1994
Occupation: Rapper

Philadelphia-born rapper Lil Uzi Vert is a self-proclaimed rock star with an Atlanta sound. A controversial figure in the hip-hop world from his earliest recordings, he skyrocketed to fame in 2016 with the popular crossover mixtape *Lil Uzi Vert vs. the World*. Later that year came an appearance on the smash hit single "Bad and Boujee" by the rap group Migos, which reached number one on the Billboard Hot 100 chart in January 2017. Uzi continued his rapid ascent to stardom with his own hit single, "XO TOUR Llif3," which also appeared on his debut full-length album *Luv Is Rage 2* (2017). In 2018 he was nominated for Grammy Awards for best new artist and for best rap performance on "Bad and Boujee."

Born Symere Woods, Uzi's stage name is derived from a comparison of his rapid-fire lyrical flow to that of an Uzi submachine gun. The "vert" part of his name is short for "vertical," referring to his planned trajectory to the top of the charts. Uzi got his start posting music online and soon gained attention not only for his modern sound but also for his mercurial and often challenging persona, with a penchant for onstage stunts and fashion outside of traditional hip-hop style. Citing goth rocker Marilyn Manson as his greatest influence, he came to represent a new breed of rapper, one that mixes genres in ways that have drawn both praise and scorn. For example, Uzi's

Photo by Scott Dudelson/Getty Images

music has been derisively categorized as a mumble rap or emo rap, while he has been dismissed as a "SoundCloud rapper" after the music-sharing website that launched his career.

Yet Uzi's fans and collaborators are unbothered by such labels. As record producer Don Cannon, who helped break Uzi into the mainstream, told Gavin Godfrey for the music website *Pigeons & Planes* (23 May 2017), "Every time artists turn the page in rap it's always going to have some kind of criticism." Indeed, Uzi himself took a more philosophical approach to his career. "I ain't competing with nobody," he told Felipe Delerme for *Fader* (14 Feb. 2017). "Only person I'm competing with is myself. I'm competing with time."

EARLY LIFE

Uzi was born on July 31, 1994, in Philadelphia, Pennsylvania. His parents were separated, so Uzi split his time between his mother, a nurse, and his father, who lived in the North Philadelphia neighborhood of Francisville. He was introduced to rap by his grandmother, with whom he was very close. She gave him his first CD, an album by the Atlanta-based crunk rappers the Ying Yang Twins.

Despite his relatively average upbringing, in his own estimation Uzi was an oddball among his peers. He liked rap, but he was also into acts like the emo pop-punk band Paramore and his idol, Marilyn Manson, notorious for shock-value industrial metal. It took some time for him to merge these influences and pursue making his own music. When he was in tenth-grade, one of Uzi's friends, a teenager named William Aston, recorded a freestyle over a song by hip-hop artist Chris Brown. Aston was so lauded among their classmates that Uzi got jealous. "I'm like, if he made a song, I can make a song," Uzi recalled to Kyle Kramer for *Noisey* (2 Mar. 2016).

Uzi started recording over beats he found on the video-sharing website *YouTube*. He and Aston joined forces, calling themselves Steaktown or the Steak Town Zombies. In 2012, they posted a video for their "Steaktown Anthem" on *YouTube*. In it, one can see Uzi (nearly unrecognizable without his trademark short dreadlocks and face tattoos) perform a proto-version of his nasally, stuttering flow. At the time, he went by the name Sealab Vertical.

EARNING ATTENTION

Steaktown caught the attention of local Philadelphia DJ Buzz Worthy, who offered to manage the crew. Aston declined, but Uzi accepted the offer. The DJ introduced Uzi to a producer named Charlie Heat—later a collaborator with superstar Kanye West—who produced Uzi's first breakthrough song, "U.Z.I.," released in 2014.

By the time the song was released, Uzi had adopted the moniker Lil Uzi Vert.

As he began to get serious about music, however, Uzi faced difficult prospects. He hated school and quit the only job he had ever held—stocking goods at the retailer Bottom Dollar—after four days. His mother was so upset over his lack of ambition in pursuing a stable career that she kicked him out of her house. He moved in with his grandmother. He also got his first face tattoo, the word "Faith" on his forehead, as a personal challenge to himself: keep the faith. "It was like, If I get this face tattoo, I got to focus," he told Delerme. "I can't go in nobody's office with a suit on with this . . . on my face. I got to focus on what I want to do."

Fortunately for Uzi, he did not have long to wait before his music made an impression. Don Cannon and DJ Drama, the producers behind the Generation Now record label, first heard "U.Z.I." on the well-known Philadelphia radio show of DJ Diamond Kuts. They quickly moved to sign the young rapper. "I knew he was a star," Cannon told Delerme. "And I wanted to make his life better for him and his family." The producers encouraged Uzi to work with beat makers in Atlanta, Georgia, advice based at least in part on Uzi's sound. While hip-hop has long been categorized geographically, Uzi was among a wave of younger artists who had grown up consuming music online regardless of where it originated, and reflected various influences in their own work. According to the ears of Cannon and Drama, Uzi had more in common with the pop-crossover dance rappers of Atlanta than the more traditional street rappers of Philadelphia. In particular, his style incorporated elements of the increasingly popular trap subgenre, originally developed in the South.

RISE TO FAME

Backed by Cannon and Drama, Uzi began a run of prodigious musical output that kicked his career into overdrive. In 2014 he released the mixtape *The Real Uzi*, helping him earn a distribution deal with the major label Atlantic Records, and his songs started to see thousands, rather than hundreds, of plays online. Early in 2015, he appeared on the successful single "WDYW" by fellow rapper Carnage, further raising his profile. He then toured with rapper Wiz Khalifa (an early influence who became something of a mentor) and the rock band Fall Out Boy. Later that year he released another mixtape, *Luv Is Rage*, with guests including Khalifa and Young Thug.

In early 2016, Uzi released yet another mixtape, *Lil Uzi Vert vs. the World*, which gained significant buzz and became a crossover hit. Two of its singles broke the Billboard Hot 100 chart, with the breakout "Money Longer" peaking at number eight. The tape itself made it onto the

Billboard 200 Top 50. Critics were quick to note how the work represented a major shift in hip-hop: as Sean Romano wrote in his review for the pop culture site *The Young Folks* (9 Dec. 2016), "Uzi might be the first rapper whose influences are exclusively post Y2K." The hip-hop magazine *Complex* ranked "Money Longer" number nineteen on their fifty best songs of 2016.

Later in 2016, Uzi was featured on the single "Bad and Boujee" by the rap group Migos. In early 2017, the track hit number one on the Billboard Hot 100, giving him his highest chart success to that point. Critics and tastemakers hailed him as one of hip-hop's most exciting acts, poised for true superstardom. Meanwhile, however, Uzi's outlook on making music evolved. He freely admitted his original goal had been simply to make money, but as his success snowballed he became more aware of industry pressures and the need to please his growing fan base. "Being a rapper is a facade," he told Delerme. "I hate it."

LUV IS RAGE 2 (2017)

Regardless of his doubts about the music industry, Uzi continued to build his brand in 2017. Among his collaborations early that year was an appearance on Playboi Carti's "Woke Up Like This," in which he memorably rapped about being a rock star. Perhaps even more anticipated, however, were his releases under his own name. In February 2017, Uzi put out four songs, including the single "XO TOUR Llif3," on an EP called *Luv Is Rage 1.5*, intended as a preview of his delayed full-length album debut.

"XO TOUR Llif3" went on to become a massive hit, peaking at number seven on the Billboard Hot 100. The slow-burning track solidified Uzi's position in the public imagination as an emo rapper, with references to the breakup of a romantic relationship, depression, and substance abuse. "I was speaking authentic on 'XO TOUR Llif3,'" Uzi told Chris Martins in an interview with *Billboard* magazine (21 Dec. 2017). "Anyone can relate: I was in a dark space, so I went with it." The official video for the song, released in September, features artists from the XO record label, for which Uzi had been on tour—also the source of the song's title. The spooky, sadistic imagery of the video was reminiscent of Uzi's old inspiration, Marilyn Manson. Around the time the video premiered, Manson himself expressed admiration for the rapper, and discussed potentially contributing to Uzi's next album.

Uzi's debut album, *Luv Is Rage 2*, was finally released in August 2017. It debuted at number one on the Billboard 200 and Top Rap Albums charts. Paul A. Thomas, reviewing the record for *Pitchfork* (30 Aug. 2017), called it Uzi's "most musically developed work to date." The album features appearances by top names such as

Pharrell and the Weeknd, and a later remix of the song "The Way Life Goes" features Nicki Minaj. But most critics agreed Uzi was at his best doing his own thing and taking risks. "Whether he's full of joy or howling into the void, he pushes his songs to their edge, which helps deliver on the promise shown in his earlier work," Thomas wrote. "We knew Lil Uzi Vert would become one of rap's biggest stars, but *Rage 2* suggests he may spend his time on top experimenting rather than retreating to a comfort zone."

PERSONAL LIFE

At the beginning of his career, Uzi dated fashion designer Brittany Byrd. Byrd served as Uzi's stylist and muse; their turbulent relationship and subsequent breakup are discussed in several of his songs. Uzi is also known for his unorthodox fashion taste, which combines emo and skater elements with traditional hip-hop looks and has been analyzed by fans and detractors alike almost as much as his music.

SUGGESTED READING

Bruner, Raisa. "How Rap Became the Sound of the Mainstream." *Time*, 25 Jan. 2018, time.com/5118041/rap-music-mainstream/. Accessed 8 Feb. 2018.

Cannon, Don, and DJ Drama. "DJ Drama and Don Cannon Break Down the Rise of Lil Uzi Vert." Interview by Gavin Godfrey. *Pigeons & Planes*, 23 May 2017, pigeonsandplanes.com/in-depth/2017/05/lil-uzi-vert-dj-drama-don-cannon. Accessed 8 Feb. 2018.

Delerme, Felipe. "Lil Uzi Vert Can't Be Bothered." *Fader*, 14 Feb. 2017, www.thefader.com/2017/02/14/lil-uzi-vert-cover-story-interview-hawaii. Accessed 8 Feb. 2018.

Kramer, Kyle. "Lil Uzi Vert Is Living in the Future of Rap." *Noisey*, 2 Mar. 2016, noisey.vice.com/en_ca/article/695vmy/lil-uzi-vert-noisey-next. Accessed 8 Feb. 2018.

Martins, Chris. "2017 No. 1s: Lil Uzi Vert on How Being 'Authentic' Took 'XO Tour Llif3' to Pop Radio." *Billboard*, 21 Dec. 2017, www.billboard.com/articles/events/year-in-music-2017/8071114/lil-uzi-vert-xo-tour-llif3-interview-no-1s-2017. Accessed 9 Feb. 2018.

Romano, Sean. Review of *Lil Uzi vs. The World*, by Lil Uzi Vert. *The Young Folks*, 9 Dec. 2016, www.theyoungfolks.com/music/92977/album-review-lil-uzi-vert-lil-uzi-vs-the-world/. Accessed 8 Feb. 2018.

Thompson, Paul A. Review of *Luv is Rage 2*, by Lil Uzi Vert. *Pitchfork*, 30 Aug. 2017, pitchfork.com/reviews/albums/lil-uzi-vert-luv-is-rage-2/. Accessed 9 Feb. 2018.

SELECTED WORKS

The Real Uzi, 2014; *Luv Is Rage*, 2015; *Lil Uzi Vert vs. the World*, 2016; *The Perfect Luv Tape*, 2016; *Luv Is Rage 2*, 2017

—*Molly Hagan*

Grace VanderWaal

Date of birth: January 15, 2004
Occupation: Musician

Grace VanderWaal first came to widespread public attention as a twelve-year-old, when she appeared on the eleventh season of the hit television show *America's Got Talent* in September 2016. Accompanying herself on the ukulele, she sang "I Don't Know My Name"—a song she had written—in a high, distinctive voice that immediately captured the judges' attention. The famously acerbic Simon Cowell compared her to pop star Taylor Swift, and VanderWaal ultimately won the top prize of $1 million, beating out a mind-reading duo called the Clairvoyants.

"VanderWaal, a hiccupy, preternaturally poised, unusually good folk-pop singer who could be the offspring of [singer-songwriters] Jewel or Feist, may be the closest thing to a ready-made star the show—or any reality talent show—has ever produced," Allison Stewart wrote for the *Chicago Tribune* (9 Nov. 2017). "Now comes the hard part: protecting her greatest asset, her stripped-down, unforced naturalness, from a record industry that wants to turn her into somebody else, preferably Taylor Swift."

Asked by Ella Ceron for *Teen Vogue* (20 Sept. 2017) if she ever wearied of the near-constant comparisons to Swift, VanderWaal replied: "You obviously want to accept it and be happy about it and embrace it. When you look at Arianna Grande, she always had the Mariah Carey comparisons and that's kind of followed her throughout her career. She still made her name though, and I admire that. I would want to mirror the same thing."

The release of her first full-length album, *Just the Beginning*, in 2017, did little to quell the comparisons. "Flashes of vintage Swift shine through the album's twelve tracks, which has much grander musical ambitions than VanderWaal's uke-strumming may have initially shown," Maeve McDermott wrote for *USA Today* (2 Nov. 2017), echoing the sentiments of many others. "There's a certain chirp in VanderWaal's voice that's reminiscent of Swift." Nor was McDermott alone among observers in lauding VanderWaal for not falling into the trap of many aspiring artists. In the midst of the Swift comparisons, she wrote, "While so many pop stars

Photo by Gonzalo Marroquin/Patrick McMullan via Getty Images

seem to bypass their tweenage phases, skipping from child-star status to full-grown adulthood, VanderWaal sounds like a thirteen-year-old in her songs, in the best possible way."

Critics have also praised the refreshingly relevant lyrics the young songwriter has penned. Of "I Don't Know My Name," a tune that touches upon adolescent confusion and identity, VanderWaal explained to Brittany Spanos for *Rolling Stone* (9 June 2016) that inspiration had hit one night while she was doing her homework. "It's about how I've gone through so many different phases and styles and friendships," she said, "and it's about how now, I think that this is who I want to be and this is what I want my life path to be."

CHILDHOOD

The future singer was born to Tina and David VanderWaal on January 15, 2004, in Kansas, where her father's job as a marketing executive for LG Electronics was then based. Grace was the youngest of the couple's three children; she has one older brother, Jakob, and an older sister, Olivia. (The family name is Dutch in origin.) They lived in the small metropolitan area of Lenexa, Kansas, until moving to Suffern, a bucolic town in upstate New York.

VanderWaal began singing at about the age of three, and when she was ten, Tina arranged for her to begin piano lessons. That pursuit was quickly abandoned after VanderWaal realized the amount of time and patience it would take to achieve any level of proficiency. When a family friend introduced her to the ukulele, however, she became hooked. Although Tina refused to buy VanderWaal the instrument she asked for, thinking it was merely a passing whim, she used her own birthday money to purchase an inexpensive model and began teaching herself to play by watching YouTube videos. VanderWaal has told reporters that even though she was using her own money, her mother still insisted on giving input, recommending that a larger, brown ukulele be purchased because VanderWaal would have too quickly grown out of the baby-blue one she initially coveted.

AMERICA'S GOT TALENT

In short order, VanderWaal became good enough to try her hand at local open-mic nights, often performing covers of songs by the band Twenty One Pilots, and she dreamed of appearing on the reality television juggernaut *American Idol*. That show required performers to be at least fifteen, however. By contrast, *America's Got Talent* had fewer restrictions—during the show's first season, in 2006, an eleven-year-old singer named Bianca Ryan had even taken home the top prize. Unbeknownst to VanderWaal, Tina, tired of hearing her daughter talk about entering a televised competition, filled out the application for *America's Got Talent*.

VanderWaal auditioned in March 2016, bringing the studio audience to its feet in an enthusiastic ovation and eliciting the Taylor Swift comparison from Cowell. Another judge, Howie Mandel, pushed the show's "golden buzzer," an honor signifying his belief that the young performer should advance directly to the next stage of *America's Got Talent*, where she would compete for viewer votes. "I honestly can't remember that moment—it's all a blur," VanderWaal admitted to Lindsay Peoples for the *Cut* (5 Dec. 2016). "It feels like I was just watching the episode and not in it. But when I was onstage or in the back room I got really nervous. And I kept telling myself that I didn't care what the judges said, it's just an audition—but I was still so nervous!"

Back at school while awaiting the next stage of the competition, VanderWaal—who played the saxophone in the marching band and who had never enjoyed any great level of popularity—was puzzled by the reaction of many of her classmates. "[It] is very great but it gets kind of confusing," VanderWaal told Spanos after her episode aired. "I used to sit alone at lunch with only [my best friend] Caroline, and now all these people are coming. I don't know if they genuinely want to be my friend or they want to be the girl from *America's Got Talent*'s friend." Even dinner at a local restaurant with her family found her surrounded by people who had seen the show and wanted to interact in some way with her.

Once VanderWaal garnered first place, in September of that year, the attention increased exponentially. The YouTube channel on which she had been posting videos quickly passed 50 million views, her Instagram account got well over two million followers, and her home town mounted a parade in her honor.

PROFESSIONAL MUSIC CAREER

Of all the perks of fame, VanderWaal was most eager to experience leaving school behind; it was, however, not all she had hoped for. "School used to be the enemy for me," she told Hardeep Phull for the *New York Post* (21 Dec. 2017). "I was always dying to get out, but then I did get out, and I started to be home-schooled. I thought I would sleep in, wake up with the birds chirping, do two hours of school, stay in my jammies and eat waffles. But I would have so many arguments with my parents because I had the ability to put off [my work]." She then began to fall behind, nearly failing to complete the seventh grade. It was eventually decided that she would return to conventional schooling for eighth grade, despite the demands of a burgeoning professional career.

Soon after her win, VanderWaal had signed a recording contract with major label Columbia, and in early December of that year, she released a five-track EP, *Perfectly Imperfect*, which included one new song, "Gossip Girl," as well as the four songs she had performed on *America's Got Talent*: "I Don't Know My Name," "Clay," "Light the Sky," and "Beautiful Thing." The EP debuted in the top ten of the Billboard 200 chart and earned VanderWaal a reputation as a recording-industry natural. "I wasn't sure what I was walking into by working with Grace in the studio," her producer, Greg Wells, admitted to Spanos for a follow-up article in *Rolling Stone* (6 Jan. 2017). "Within the first ten minutes of working on music together, I was happily surprised to find that I was working with a real artist who could speak the language of record making." He said that her level of musical intuition "takes most of us years to hone and develop, yet somehow this was pouring out of her at age twelve during her first time in the studio."

VanderWaal—who promoted the EP with several high-profile appearances, including one at a Knicks game at Madison Square Garden and another during the nationally televised Macy's Thanksgiving Day Parade—followed that effort with a full-length album, *Just the Beginning*, which was released in early November 2017. The album debuted on the Billboard 200 chart at number twenty-two and earned generally favorable reviews.

Among the laurels VanderWaal has received are a Radio Disney Music Award in the category of Best New Artist, a Teen Choice Award in the

"Next Big Thing" category, and inclusion on the Billboard 21 under 21 list. Always interested in fashion, she was signed to a contract by IMG Models, has been named the face of Fender Guitars, and has collaborated on a collection of accessories with the youth-oriented retail chain Charming Charlie.

PERSONAL LIFE

VanderWaal insists that despite her newfound fame, she remains an ordinary teen. She is a fan of such television shows as *New Girl* and *Bob's Burgers* and still enjoys riding her bike and playing with her family's two dogs.

She has given a portion of her *America's Got Talent* prize money to charity and is particularly interested in donating to causes related to music and art education. She announced her intention to use another portion to build lavish tree houses for herself and her sister, who helped design all the packaging for her albums.

While she is adjusting to her new life, she has told interviewers that she continues to be somewhat shy. "I'm an indoors person," she explained to Ceron. "I always have been. I've always liked to be alone, I like silence."

Discussing her ultimate goals with Phull, VanderWaal said: "I'm thinking about being an art therapist when I grow up. Mental health is such an interesting thing, and it's something I've wanted to [explore] for a while. The singing? I'm just going to see where it goes!"

SUGGESTED READING

Corinthios, Aurelie. "*America's Got Talent* Winner Grace VanderWaal Says She's Just a Normal Kid." *People*, 21 Sept. 2016, people.com/tv/grace-vanderwaal-americas-got-talent-winner-on-her-life-offstage/. Accessed 18 Jan. 2018.

McDermott, Maeve. "Grace VanderWaal's *Just the Beginning* Shows a Taylor Swift in Training." Review of *Just the Beginning*, by Grace VanderWaal. *USA Today*, 2 Nov. 2017, www.usatoday.com/story/life/music/2017/11/02/grace-vanderwaals-just-beginning-album-review-shows-taylor-swift-training/822378001/. Accessed 18 Jan. 2018.

Peoples, Lindsay. "*America's Got Talent* Star Grace VanderWaal Is Just Getting Started." *The Cut*, 5 Dec. 2016, www.thecut.com/2016/12/singer-grace-vanderwaal-debuts-her-first-album.html. Accessed 18 Jan. 2018.

Spanos, Brittany. "*America's Got Talent* Star Grace VanderWaal Talks Songwriting, Katy Perry." *Rolling Stone*, 9 June 2016, https://www.rollingstone.com/music/news/americas-got-talent-star-grace-vanderwaal-talks-songwriting-katy-perry-20160609. Accessed 18 Jan. 2018.

Spanos, Brittany. "Meet Grace VanderWaal: Pop Prodigy on the Edge of 13." *Rolling Stone*, 6 Jan. 2017, www.rollingstone.com/music/features/meet-grace-vanderwaal-pop-prodigy-on-the-edge-of-13-w459126. Accessed 18 Jan. 2018.

Stewart, Allison. "Grace VanderWaal Is a Ready-Made Star, from TV to Stage." *Chicago Tribune*, 9 Nov. 2017, www.chicagotribune.com/entertainment/music/ct-ott-grace-vanderwaal-1110-story.html. Accessed 18 Jan. 2018.

VanderWaal, Grace. "Grace VanderWaal on Body Image and Why Her New Album Really Is 'Just the Beginning.'" Interview by Ella Ceron. *Teen Vogue*, 20 Sept. 2017, www.teenvogue.com/story/grace-vanderwaal-interview-body-image-school-just-the-beginning-new-album. Accessed 18 Jan. 2018.

—*Mari Rich*

Katharine Viner

Date of birth: January 1971
Occupation: Journalist

Katharine Viner was named the twelfth editor of the British-based newspaper the *Guardian* in 2015, succeeding longtime editor Alan Rusbridger. Viner previously established the *Guardian*'s Australian edition with great success and then served as editor in chief of the paper's online American edition. She helped make the *Guardian* a leading online news source in Australia, the United States, and elsewhere around the world. Her savvy digital leadership was considered a major factor in her ascent to the paper's top position.

Viner has often acknowledged the transformative power of online journalism. Writing for the *Huffington Post* (27 May 2015), Paul Blanchard quoted a speech in which she reflected on the changes facing her profession: "We are no longer the all-seeing all-knowing journalists, delivering words from on high for readers to take in, passively, save perhaps an occasional letter to the editor. Digital has wrecked those hierarchies almost overnight, creating a more levelled world, where responses can be instant, where some readers will almost certainly know more about a particular subject than the journalist, where the reader might be better placed to uncover a story."

EARLY LIFE AND EDUCATION

Viner was born in 1971 and grew up in Yorkshire, England. Her grandfather, Vic Viner, was a World War II veteran who was part of the Operation Dynamo rescue effort at Dunkirk. He married Viner's grandmother, Winnie Simpson,

Photo by Angel Manzano / Getty Images

only two weeks before his work at Dunkirk began. His son, Michael, became Viner's father. Her parents were both teachers employed in the public sector.

Viner enjoyed a middle-class lifestyle as a teenager in the 1980s, as she would later document in an article revisiting her 1988 diary. "Like many teenagers, I couldn't see far beyond my own boundaries and the outside world had limited influence," she wrote for the *Guardian* (26 Nov. 2004). Among her interests were alternative rock music, literature, liberal politics, and feminism. She attended the prestigious Ripon Grammar School, where she became head girl, a student leader and representative of the school. At Ripon, Viner was a debater who, with fellow student Simon Stockill, won the national final of the Observer Mace Schools' Debating Competition.

Viner also developed an interest in journalism during her student days, though it took some time for her to consider it as a career. While at Ripon in 1987, she published her first article in the *Guardian*, a piece on the legacy of the O-level exams. She also worked for a week at the local paper, the *Ripon Gazette*. She then attended Pembroke College, Oxford University, studying English. While at Oxford, she won a *Guardian* contest that awarded her editorship of the paper's women's page for a week. "I came in and did it and I was clueless, I hadn't done any student journalism and I really didn't know about it," she told Julie Tomlin for the *Press Gazette* (5 May 2005). "But I did this thing and it was like a

revelation, I just loved it so much." Viner graduated from Oxford in 1989.

BEGINNING A CAREER IN JOURNALISM

Following the advice of Louise Chunn, then the editor of the *Guardian*'s women's page, Viner decided to seek a career in journalism. Her first professional job was a brief stint at *Cosmopolitan* magazine's UK edition, serving first as an intern before being hired as an assistant on feature stories and then as an editor. In 1994 she became a newspaper features writer and commissioning editor at the *Sunday Times*. Then, in 1997, she began working at the *Guardian*. Her initial assignment was on the lifestyle pages.

Proving herself competent and versatile, Viner quickly began moving through the ranks at the *Guardian*. For an eighteen-month stint she served as deputy editor of the paper's G2 magazine under Roger Alton. She then became editor of another publication, the *Guardian Weekend* magazine, in 1998. Her work brought her the distinction of being named the British Society of Magazine Editors' newspaper magazine editor of the year in 2002. In her role, she enjoyed the freedom to publish "absolutely anything that's interesting," as she told Tomlin. However, she strove to include a variety of voices on a variety of subjects, to avoid making the magazine simply a platform for her own interests.

Among those interests was a longstanding fascination with the Middle East, which Viner fed through travel and research. The connections she made through this activity led her to what would become a signature accomplishment outside of journalism: developing a play.

MY NAME IS RACHEL CORRIE

Viner became a board member of London's Royal Court Theatre, where a friend who shared her interest in the Middle East worked. In 2003, G2 published excerpts from the diaries and correspondence of Rachel Corrie, a young activist who had been killed that year by an Israeli bulldozer in the contested Gaza Strip. Actor Alan Rickman contacted the Royal Court, interested in seeing Corrie's writings turned into a theatrical work. Eventually, Viner was chosen to work with Rickman on a script, as the theater wanted a journalist's touch on the project and knew Viner was knowledgeable about the Middle East conflict.

Viner and Rickman compiled and edited Corrie's writings, including otherwise unpublished pieces from throughout Corrie's life that were provided by her family. As Viner wrote for *Broadway.com* (17 Oct. 2006), "We were both staggered by the quality of Rachel's writing . . . This was a delight for us, and helped provide the structure for the piece." The resulting play, *My Name is Rachel Corrie*, debuted in 2005.

The one-woman show, originally directed by Rickman, was a considerable success in Britain, earning strong reviews and running at two other theaters in addition to the Royal Court. It also attracted significant controversy due to the politically charged material, especially in the United States, where an initial planned debut was canceled before the show appeared Off-Broadway in 2006.

Viner's experience working on *My Name is Rachel Corrie* also led to a lasting friendship with Rickman. Although the two butted heads during the collaboration itself, once they viewed their final project they came to understand how their backgrounds complemented each other. As Viner recalled in the *Guardian* (14 Jan. 2016) in a tribute to Rickman, who died in 2016, "On the opening night we each admitted that we couldn't have done justice to Rachel's words without the other. We'd been a partnership, we agreed, however crotchety."

DIGITAL SUCCESS AT THE *GUARDIAN*

In 2008 Viner was promoted to deputy editor of the *Guardian*. She served in that role through 2012, and in 2013 was placed in charge of launching the *Guardian Australia*, a digital edition of the paper for the Australian market. Working essentially from scratch, she and her team built an online presence that became a leading news provider in the country, critically acclaimed for work in areas such as immigration and climate change. In less than a year, the *Guardian Australia* website had more than five million individual visitors per month.

Meanwhile, however, the Guardian News & Media company as a whole was experiencing financial trouble. The paper had invested heavily in its international operations and found considerable journalistic success, including in the United States. For example, it earned attention for coverage of documents released by WikiLeaks, and it won a Pulitzer Prize for its reporting on Edward Snowden's National Security Agency (NSA) leaks. Yet this success did not translate into increased revenues, and the paper, funded by the nonprofit Scott Trust, was losing money.

With her track record of success, in 2014 Viner was appointed the editor in chief of the *Guardian US*, the paper's American digital platform based in New York City, while remaining an overall deputy editor as well. In the US role, she succeeded Janine Gibson, who returned to the *Guardian*'s British operations. Viner entered her new position with the chief goal of increasing US readership, and soon she began to show signs of success. Even as print circulation in Britain continued to fall, the *Guardian*'s web traffic in the United States rose by 30 percent from early 2014 to early 2015.

Viner's experience and success in digital media proved important in the 2015 election to become editor in chief of the *Guardian* and a director of Guardian Media Group. The paper's top position was known for low turnover, with retiring incumbent Alan Rusbridger serving since 1995. While Gibson had been seen as Rusbridger's protégé and a natural choice to succeed him, internal politics at the *Guardian* had grown increasingly divisive in light of the paper's financial struggles. In a nonbinding preliminary vote, 53 percent of the *Guardian* staff voted in favor of Viner, who had campaigned for a focus on the paper's strengths in areas of culture and special features. Emily Bell, a candidate with previous decades of work at the *Guardian* and a platform focused on ethics, came in second place, while Gibson was third. The vote was a clear repudiation of Gibson and Rusbridger's journalistic status quo, embodied by the Snowden coverage.

EDITOR IN CHIEF

Although the staff vote established Viner as a preferred editor in chief candidate, it did not guarantee her the job. The ultimate decision was to be made by the Scott Trust, which developed its own shortlist of candidates. This was eventually narrowed to Viner and Ian Katz, who had served as a *Guardian* deputy editor before leaving to become editor of *Newsnight* on *BBC News*. Finally, the trust followed the staff in choosing Viner as the paper's new editor in chief. She became the twelfth editor in the history of the *Guardian*, and the first woman to hold the position.

Viner's new position also saw her appointed the director of the Guardian Media Group, including the *Guardian* and the *Observer* weekly paper. She faced the challenge of a company operating in the red, despite having online operations making it one of the most-read English newspapers throughout the world. In 2015 the media group had a deficit of over $64 million. However, it resisted establishing a paywall that would limit free online access to content, remaining committed to open journalism and growing overall readership.

Viner took several steps to improve the *Guardian*'s financial fortunes in the first years of her tenure. With a grant from the John S. and James L. Knight Foundation, the news group established an innovation lab to share expertise in digital publishing. The lab also focused on more effective use of mobile devices to deliver news.

In early 2016 Viner unveiled a plan designed with Guardian Media Group chief executive David Pemsel with the aim of reducing costs by 20 percent and breaking even within three years. As quoted by Ravi Somaiya for *New York Times* (25 Jan. 2016), Viner stated that "Over the next three years a growing and far deeper set of relationships with our audience will result in a reimagining of our journalism, a sustainable business model and a newly focused digital organization that reflects our independence and our mission." The restructuring did result in job cuts, with 100 editorial jobs among 250 total planned cuts announced in March 2016.

PERSONAL LIFE

Viner has maintained a largely private life outside of her career. Her appointment as the first female editor in chief of the *Guardian* won her status as a feminist role model among some observers. She has commented on social issues, such as in delivering the keynote speech at Oxford University's second annual Women of Achievement lecture in 2016, discussing the ways to make the Internet a better place. In that speech, Viner decried the fact that social media and clickbait articles serve as major sources of news for many people, rather than old-fashioned investigative journalism.

SUGGESTED READING

Blanchard, Paul. "What Does Katharine Viner's Appointment Mean for the 'Guardian'?" *Huff-Post*, 27 May 2015, www.huffingtonpost.co.uk/paul-blanchard/what-does-katharine-viners-appointment-mean_b_6956954.html. Accessed 17 Oct. 2017.

"Katharine Viner." *The Guardian*, 2017, www.theguardian.com/profile/katharineviner. Accessed 7 Nov. 2017.

Somaiya, Ravi. "*Guardian* to Slash Costs and Renew Online Focus." *The New York Times*, 25 Jan. 2016, www.nytimes.com/2016/01/26/business/media/guardian-announces-cost-cutting-effort-to-reduce-losses.html. Accessed 25 Oct. 2017.

Somaiya, Ravi, and Stephen Castle. "*Guardian* Names Katharine Viner as Editor." *The New York Times*, 20 Mar. 2015, www.nytimes.com/2015/03/21/business/media/guardian-names-katharine-viner-as-new-editor.html. Accessed 17 Oct. 2017.

Viner, Katharine. "Alan Rickman: The Most Loyal, Playful and Generous of Friends." *The Guardian*, 14 Jan. 2016, www.theguardian.com/film/filmblog/2016/jan/14/alan-rickman-the-most-loyal-playful-and-generous-of-friends. Accessed 16 Oct. 2017.

Viner, Katharine. "Dear Diary. . ." *The Guardian*, 26 Nov. 2004, www.theguardian.com/lifeandstyle/2004/nov/27/weekend.katharineviner. Accessed 7 Nov. 2017.

Viner, Katharine. "Katharine Viner: Channeling Rachel Corrie." *Broadway.com*, 17 Oct. 2006, www.broadway.com/buzz/6203/katharine-viner-channeling-rachel-corrie/. Accessed 23 Oct. 2017.

—*Judy Johnson*

Lena Waithe

Date of birth: May 17, 1984
Occupation: Screenwriter, actor, and producer

Although the relatively sudden professional success of screenwriter and actor Lena Waithe may suggest she is having what the entertainment media might term "a moment," Waithe herself is reluctant to use that terminology. "It's scary when they say you're having a moment because moments are momentary," she told Christina Radish for the *Collider* (3 Feb. 2018). "I get it, though. It's a culmination of things that have come together." Indeed, the years 2017 and 2018 in many ways pulled together the separate threads of Waithe's career, which encompasses writing for television, creating her own projects, and acting. An entertainment professional since her move to Los Angeles in 2006, Waithe began her career working behind the scenes as an assistant and crew member for various projects before branching out into writing for television shows such as *Bones* and creating her own projects, including the short film *Save Me*. After joining the cast of the award-winning Netflix comedy series *Master of None* when it launched in 2015, Waithe gained attention as an actor for her portrayal of the character of Denise; she also demonstrated her talents as a writer with the 2017 episode "Thanksgiving," for which she shared with Ansari the 2017 Emmy Award for outstanding writing for a comedy series. The creator of the television series *The Chi*, Waithe achieved another major goal with the premiere

By Gage Skidmore, via Wikimedia Commons

of that show on Showtime in early 2018, and in the spring of that year, she made her film debut as an actor with a role in the blockbuster *Ready Player One*. Her slate of creative projects and other initiatives in development further suggest that describing Waithe's success with the word "moment" is an egregious understatement. "I feel like I wanna have a series of moments," she told Radish.

EARLY LIFE AND EDUCATION

Lena Diane Waithe was born on May 17, 1984, in Chicago, Illinois. Her parents divorced when she was three years old, and Waithe and her older sister remained with their mother. The family moved in with Waithe's maternal grandmother, who lived in Chicago's South Side. "It was really cool because I got to grow up in the same house that my mom grew up in," Waithe recalled to Carrie Schedler for *Chicago* magazine (4 Jan. 2018). "And I was in a neighborhood of kids who were the children of kids my mom grew up with."

As a child, Waithe enjoyed going to the movies but was particularly drawn to television. While still in elementary school, she determined that she wanted to become a television writer, and Waithe later came to be particularly interested in ensuring that television reflected the realities and potential of children who rarely see their lives represented on television. "If you come from a poor background and you have a single parent, TV becomes what you dream about," she told Rebecca Haithcoat for the *Guardian* (5 Jan. 2018). "It's really important for young brown kids to see other brown kids on television because it's like you're seeing a version of yourself that you hoped to be."

When Waithe was twelve, her family moved to Evanston, a city north of Chicago. She attended Evanston Township High School, from which she graduated in 2002. Following her graduation, Waithe enrolled in Columbia College Chicago to study television. In addition to her studies, she had a variety of entertainment-adjacent jobs as a young adult, including stints at a movie theater and a Blockbuster video-rental store. During her senior year at Columbia College, Waithe traveled to Los Angeles, California, and completed a five-week program that gave her hands-on experience in various aspects of the entertainment industry. She earned her bachelor's degree in 2006.

EARLY CAREER

After college, Waithe moved to Los Angeles, where she worked a variety of jobs in television and film. Beginning in 2007, she served as an assistant to one of the executive producers of the television series *Girlfriends*. Waithe later worked as assistant to director and screenwriter Gina Prince-Bythewood, assisting the filmmaker

during the production of the 2008 film *The Secret Life of Bees*. She went on to work behind the scenes on films such as *Notorious* (2009), a biopic of the rapper Notorious B. I. G., and *I Will Follow* (2010), the feature film debut of acclaimed director Ava DuVernay.

In addition to her work as an assistant and crew member, Waithe remained focused on her goal of becoming a television writer and one day running her own projects. In addition to writing episodes for the Nickelodeon television series *How to Rock*, she wrote and directed the 2011 short film *Save Me* and cocreated the web series *Hello Cupid*. Her strong work on an early draft of the pilot for what would become her series *The Chi* demonstrated her talent as a writer for television, and in 2014, she was hired on as a writer for the long-running crime procedural *Bones*. She remained part of that series' writing team into 2015. Waithe likewise made her television debut as an actor during that period, appearing in an episode of the HBO series *The Comeback* in 2014.

MASTER OF NONE

Waithe gained widespread attention beginning in 2015, when she joined the cast of the new Netflix original series *Master of None*, which premiered in November of that year. The series follows the life of a New York–based actor named Dev (show cocreator Aziz Ansari) and his interactions with his group of friends, which includes Waithe's character, Denise. Although the character was initially conceived of as a future love interest for Dev, Waithe's casting led the writers to reshape the character to reflect more of Waithe's own background, personality, and sexual orientation. Although the idea of playing one of the few African American lesbian characters on television might have been daunting for some, Waithe viewed her character as an opportunity. "I've never been a person that has had fear of, like, 'Oh, I don't want to be the poster child for all black lesbian women,'" she told Lisa Weidenfeld for the *Hollywood Reporter* (18 Nov. 2015). "I want to be someone in the public eye that they can be proud of. I don't feel like, 'Oh her character can't do anything bad.' I just wanted her to feel like a real human being."

Master of None received critical acclaim following the release of its first season, earning a nomination for the Emmy Award for outstanding comedy series. The second season of the show premiered on Netflix in May 2017. Unlike the first season, the second season of *Master of None* featured an episode, titled "Thanksgiving," that was cowritten by Waithe. Documenting Denise's coming-out story, the episode drew heavily from Waithe's own life. "[Series cocreator] Alan [Yang] asked me, 'Hey, how did you come out?' We had this long conversation about it, and how religion didn't play a huge role in my family, and I grew up in a house of women," she told E. Alex Jung for *Vulture* (17 May 2017) of the events that led up to the episode's creation. "I didn't even make it back to my hotel when Aziz called and said, 'We have to tell that story, and I need you to write it.' I'm like, 'I already have a full plate, I trust you guys,' and they're like, 'No, you have to write it.'" The episode's personal touch and strong writing led it to be identified by many critics as one of the show's best, and Waithe and Ansari went on to win the Emmy Award for outstanding writing for a comedy series for their work. In addition to being a major professional milestone for Waithe, the victory had broader significance as well, as Waithe was the first black woman to claim that award.

ACTING WORK

Although acting "wasn't on the list" of things Waithe wanted to accomplish, "it was a wonderful surprise," she told Weidenfeld. Following the debut of *Master of None*, Waithe appeared on screen in a number of additional projects, including episodes of television series such as *Transparent* and *This Is Us*. She also appeared in several 2018 episodes of the Netflix show *Dear White People*, created by Justin Simien. Waithe had previously served as a producer for Simien's 2014 film of the same name, and the two have frequently described themselves as best friends.

Waithe made her debut as a film actor in 2018, with a role in the science fiction film *Ready Player One*. Based on a novel by writer Ernest Cline, the film was directed by legendary filmmaker Steven Spielberg. Waithe was initially surprised at being cast, as she typically brings much of her own personality to roles rather than blending into a character, as some filmmakers would prefer. However, as her success in *Ready Player One* and other projects has demonstrated, Waithe herself is a compelling draw for many. "I think people really like the sauce that I bring to things, my cadence, and my sensibility," she explained to Radish. "To be yourself is truly a revolutionary act, and I think more and more people should try it because it's gotten me a pretty cool life."

THE CHI

As early as 2014, Waithe began working on a proposed series that would take place in her hometown of Chicago and accurately represent life in that city, which has widely been portrayed in the media as a violent and dangerous place to live. "They act like it's a jungle or that the young black males are the problem. In actuality, I think it's the system. A lot of these problems are way above our pay grade," Waithe told Haithcoat. "It's a complex city. There's a lot of beauty there.

There's a lot of humanity there. A lot of light, a lot of joy." Waithe particularly wanted to show the city from the perspective of a Chicago native rather than that of an outsider. The resulting series, *The Chi*, premiered on the premium cable channel Showtime in January 2018. The show was received well by critics and viewers, and Showtime quickly ordered a second season to air in 2019.

In addition to her work on *The Chi*, Waithe is developing a half-hour series, *Twenties*, based on her early years in Los Angeles. A proponent of the Time's Up initiative, which seeks to combat sexual harassment in the entertainment industry, as well as efforts to support talented writers from marginalized communities, Waithe has been outspoken about issues such as representation and seeks to use her newfound influence to help aspiring screenwriters through her production company. "We're going to put our money where our mouths are to help make sure new writers' projects have the funding and the development they need before they get taken out to the market," she explained to Caroline Framke for *Vox* (7 Jan. 2018) of her efforts. Although Waithe has already experienced significant professional success, she remains committed to pursuing her goals further. "This is definitely a time when I'm very aware of the space I'm in," she told Schedler. "But I don't want people to say, 'Oh, Lena had a great year.' Because I'm trying to make 2018 bigger."

PERSONAL LIFE

Waithe met her fiancée, entertainment executive Alana Mayo, at a meeting of entertainment professionals. They became engaged in 2017, during their first Thanksgiving celebrated together. Waithe and Mayo live in the Echo Park neighborhood of Los Angeles.

SUGGESTED READING

Haithcoat, Rebecca. "'Master of None's' Lena Waithe: 'If You Come from a Poor Background, TV Becomes What You Dream About.'" *The Guardian*, 5 Jan. 2018, theguardian.com/tv-and-radio/2018/jan/05/master-of-nones-lena-waithe-if-you-come-from-a-poor-background-tv-becomes-what-you-dream-about. Accessed 12 May 2018.

Waithe, Lena. "Lena Waithe Comes Home." Interview by Carrie Schedler. *Chicago*, 4 Jan. 2018, www.chicagomag.com/Chicago-Magazine/February-2018/Lena-Waithe/. Accessed 12 May 2018.

Waithe, Lena. "Lena Waithe on Creating 'The Chi' & Working on 'Ready Player One.'" Interview with Christina Radish. *Collider*, 3 Feb. 2018, collider.com/lena-waithe-the-chi-interview/. Accessed 12 May 2018.

Waithe, Lena. "Lena Waithe Wrote Her Most Personal Story for 'Master of None.'" Interview by E. Alex Jung. *Vulture*, 17 May 2017, www.vulture.com/2017/05/lena-waithe-master-of-none-thanksgiving-episode-conversation.html. Accessed 12 May 2018.

Waithe, Lena. "'Master of None's' Lena Waithe Talks Accidental Stardom, 'Failure to Launch.'" Interview by Lisa Weidenfeld. *Hollywood Reporter*, 18 Nov. 2015, www.hollywoodreporter.com/live-feed/master-nones-lena-waithe-talks-841476. Accessed 12 May 2018.

Waithe, Lena. "'That's My Mission—to Level the Playing Field': Lena Waithe on Lifting Marginalized Voices." Interview by Caroline Framke. *Vox*, 7 Jan. 2018, www.vox.com/platform/amp/culture/2018/1/7/16858590/lena-waithe-interview-the-chi. Accessed 12 May 2018.

Woodson, Jacqueline. "Lena Waithe Is Changing the Game." *Vanity Fair*, 22 Mar. 2018, www.vanityfair.com/hollywood/2018/03/lena-waithe-cover-story/. Accessed 12 May 2018.

—*Joy Crelin*

Photo by Paul Zimmerman/Getty Images

Dana Walden

Date of birth: ca. 1965
Occupation: CEO of Fox Television Group

Dana Walden is the cochair and CEO of the Fox Television Group. She and her longtime business partner, Gary Newman, gained oversight of Fox Broadcasting in 2014 after fifteen years at the helm of 20th Century Fox Television. The California-born Walden began her career in public relations, but made the leap into programming after an impassioned speech at a Fox company retreat in 1995. In the late 1990s, Walden oversaw the development of such hit shows as *Ally McBeal* and *Buffy the Vampire Slayer*. She was named copresident, with Gary Newman, of 20th Century Fox Television in 1999. Their partnership has yielded several popular shows, including *Glee, Modern Family, Homeland, New Girl*, and most recently, the dramas *Empire* and *This Is Us*. Walden has a knack for finding good shows. Her method starts with identifying good talent. "When I get behind a project or a creator or an actor, I think I'm a powerful advocate," she told David Garber for *CSQ Magazine* (25 June 2014). "I believe deeply in the work of the people we're in business with." This position is evident in her support for such Emmy Award–winning artists as Ryan Murphy, the creator of *Glee, American Horror Story*, and *American Crime Story*, and Howard Gordon, the creator of *Homeland*. Gordon described Walden

to Garber as "the person who both held my hand the tightest and slapped me on the back of the head the hardest." Walden considers the description a compliment. "We're making stories that impact people around the world," she told Garber. "There should be a level of passion about it."

EARLY LIFE AND EDUCATION

Dana Walden (née Freedman) was born the eldest of three girls in Studio City, California. Her mother, Sheril, was a professional dancer. Her father, Robert, worked in the travel industry, though he was also a member of the celebrity-filled Friar's Club of Beverly Hills. He often took Walden to the club's headquarters after school. Sometimes she sat at the front desk helping connect calls to famous members such as comedian Milton Berle and late-night television show host Johnny Carson. Entertainment was an important part of her childhood. "Television was definitely my babysitter," she joked to Lacey Rose for the *Hollywood Reporter* (5 Dec. 2012). Growing up, Walden loved watching the cartoon *Speed Racer* and the sitcom *Happy Days*. She did some performing herself with an after-school theater program, though her dreams of becoming a leading lady were stymied by her mother, who ran the program and did not want to seem as though she was giving preference to her daughter. Walden also loved riding horses. As a teenager she rode in competition, but quit after college. It was a quintessential California upbringing; Walden reportedly hung out with Moon Zappa, Frank Zappa's daughter, who was featured on her father's

1982 hit single "Valley Girl." Walden graduated with a communications degree from the University of Southern California (USC) in 1986.

EARLY CAREER

A sour early meeting that Walden had when she was a senior in college set the tone for her unlikely rise in the male-dominated entertainment industry. Her father helped secure her a meeting with a top Hollywood agent. The agent asked Walden how well she could type. Surprised, she told him that she was not very good at it. "What's a pretty girl like you doing not knowing how to type?" he chided her, Walden recalled to Joe Flint for the *Los Angeles Times* (2 Oct. 2011). She decided that one day, the agent was going to regret talking to her that way. After college, Walden took a job with the publicity firm Bender, Goldman & Helper, where she worked as Larry Goldman's assistant. She helped him oversee campaigns for such shows as *Star Trek: The Next Generation* and the extraordinarily popular *The Arsenio Hall Show*. Hall's show, which ran from 1989 to 1994, cultivated a young and diverse audience, offering an antidote to the more old-fashioned *Tonight Show* with Carson. Hall hired Walden to handle marketing and publicity for his show in 1990. Working for the show, Walden met Lucie Salhany, who was then running the Paramount Pictures television division and was considered one of the most powerful female executives in the industry. Walden was in awe of Salhany, who famously championed *The Oprah Winfrey Show* in the 1980s. "To see a woman being the boss was inspirational," Walden told Flint. In 1993 Salhany was hired as the chair of Fox Broadcasting, and recruited Walden to join her.

"JERRY MAGUIRE MOMENT"

Walden worked in public relations for 20th Century Fox Television, getting "an education that most executives who come up the creative path don't get," she told Flint. After a few years, she was named the company's head of corporate communications and publicity. At a company retreat in 1995, Walden made a risky decision that she now refers to as her "*Jerry Maguire* moment," she told Garber. In the 1996 movie *Jerry Maguire*, sports agent Maguire (Tom Cruise) gives an unexpected and impassioned plea to his bottom-line-focused colleagues. For Maguire, it is a come-to-Jesus moment about the nature of his work. He wants to be more honest and serve his young athlete clients better. His unwelcome opinions get him fired, but his new mission statement sets him on a course for success and self-fulfillment. At the corporate retreat, Walden, along with every other Fox executive, was required to give a "state of the studio" address to the rest of the company. Waiting backstage

at the event, Peter Chernin, then CEO of Fox Television, approached her. Walden had met Chernin a handful of times, but as he walked toward her, he held out his hand and introduced himself again. It seemed like a fated moment. If she had not made enough of an impression on the boss in the past, Walden decided, she was going to make up for it right then.

When Walden took the stage, she said a number of things that she knew her colleagues would not want to hear. She told the crowd that company was not doing very well, and that they only had themselves to blame. Fox talked about taking programming risks, she said, but never seemed to follow through. "I felt we were not real competitors in network television," she recalled of her speech to Laurie Sandell for *Marie Claire* (12 Mar. 2013). "The studio wasn't prolific; we didn't have much of a brand." Walden was certain that her screed was going to get her fired. Instead, Chernin immediately hired her as the vice president of current programming. It was an outcome worth celebration, but Walden's life is not a movie, and her early programming career proved to be a challenge. Some coworkers, including those positioned directly above her, resented her and the speech that had won her the job. Eventually, Walden found a friend in Ken Horton, the head of 20th Century Fox Television development. Horton taught her about the creative side of the industry—scripts, writers, and feedback—but also encouraged her to trust her instincts with regard to a project. Her "gut," she told Sandell, remains her guide.

PARTNERSHIP WITH GARY NEWMAN

During the late 1990s, Walden's gut picked several hit shows, including two David E. Kelley shows: the comedy *Ally McBeal*, starring Calista Flockhart, and the law firm drama *The Practice*. Walden also oversaw the development of Joss Whedon's *Buffy the Vampire Slayer*. In 1999, the president of 20th Century Fox Television, Sandy Grushow, was promoted, and Walden was one of three candidates in the running to replace him. In the end, the studio made an unusual decision. They hired Walden and another candidate, Gary Newman, to run the studio together. Newman began his career as a lawyer, but had made a name for himself as a superior deal-maker. Fox reasoned that Walden, who knew every writer and producer in television, and Newman would make a perfect team. This was the case, Walden recalled to Garber, and then some. She described their early partnership as "One plus one equaled one and a half." They both had the skills to run the company alone, so there was significant overlap in their workload. They devised a management plan that allowed them to divide the work more efficiently. The two developed a habit of constant communication that fostered a sense of deep trust, freeing each other to make decisions without the other's explicit approval. When they do disagree, Walden told Garber, "Who believes more strongly in their position is whose choice or decision we ultimately go with."

During their fourteen years together as co-presidents, Walden and Newman oversaw the development of the drama *24*, the breakout high school musical hit *Glee*, the multiple Emmy Award–winning comedy *Modern Family*, the comedy *How I Met Your Mother*, the animated comedy *Family Guy*, the Emmy Award–winning drama *Homeland*, the drama *Sons of Anarchy*, and the comedy *New Girl*. In 2014, the Fox network's cash cow, the reality singing competition show *American Idol*, fell in the ratings. Kevin Reilly, the head of entertainment programming at the network resigned, and Walden and Newman floated a proposal. They advocated for merging the studio 20th Century Fox TV, of which they were presidents, and Fox's broadcasting company to create a new company: the Fox Television Group. The higher-ups at Fox liked the idea; in fact, competitors NBC and ABC had already combined their network and studio companies. Fox hired Walden and Newman as joint chairs and CEOs of the Fox Television Group in 2014. Since then, Walden and Newman have overseen the development of the hit show *Empire*, and, in 2016, sold the now hit show *This Is Us* to NBC. In December 2017, Walt Disney bought most of 21st Century Fox, prompting many to speculate about whether or not Walden would stay with Fox TV. She recently joined the board of directors at the streaming service Hulu.

PERSONAL LIFE

Walden married Matthew Walden, a former Arista Records executive, on December 17, 1995. They have two daughters, Aliza and Casey, and live in Los Angeles. Walden enjoys traveling with her family, and is fond of ski trips. She sits on the board of the Los Angeles Zoo and supports the nonprofit Chance for Bliss, which rescues elderly animals.

SUGGESTED READING

Flint, Joe. "Dana Walden Is Obsessed with TV." *Los Angeles Times*, 2 Oct. 2011, articles.latimes.com/2011/oct/02/business/la-fi-ct-himi-walden-20111002. Accessed 14 Dec. 2017.

Garber, David. "Dana Walden: Hollywood's Leading Lady." *CSQ Magazine*, 25 June 2014, csq.com/2014/06/dana-walden-hollywoods-leading-lady/. Accessed 14 Dec. 2017.

Rose, Lacey. "20th TV's Dana Walden on Her Career-Changing 'Jerry Maguire' Moment." *Hollywood Reporter*, 5 Dec. 2012, www.hollywoodreporter.com/news/women-entertainment-dana-walden-fox-397427. Accessed 14 Dec. 2017.

Walden, Dana. "MC@Work: Confessions of a Hit Woman." Interview by Laurie Sandell. *Marie Claire*, 12 Mar. 2013, www.marieclaire.com/career-advice/tips/a7537/dana-walden-interview/. Accessed 15 Dec. 2017.

—*Molly Hagan*

Emily Warren

Date of birth: August 25, 1992
Occupation: Singer-songwriter

Emily Warren first became well known in the music industry as a hit-making songwriter and went on to shine as a solo music star in her own right. After signing as a songwriter with Dr. Luke's Prescription Songs in 2013, she became a one-woman hit machine, cowriting songs for such artists as Frenship, the Chainsmokers, Dua Lipa, Charli XCX, Astrid S, and Shawn Mendes, among others. With the release of so many multiplatinum songs copenned by Warren, including Frenship's "Capsize" and Dua Lipa's "New Rules," *Forbes* named her to its 30 Under 30 Music Class of 2018. Since 2017, she has released four singles under her own name—"Something to Hold On To," "Hurt by You," "Poking Holes," and "Paranoid"—and is planning to release her debut solo album in 2018. Of her forthcoming album, she told Kelly Wynne for *Atwood Magazine* (11 Jan. 2018): "I want a collection of music for people to sink into, should they want to. . . . I

hope that each track can serve a different function and that they can come together and mean something as a whole."

EARLY LIFE AND MUSICAL AMBITIONS

Emily Warren Schwartz was born on August 25, 1992, and raised on the Upper West Side of Manhattan in New York City. She developed her love of music thanks to the influence of her father, a lawyer who has played in a 1960s cover band since his college days. As a child, she would frequently watch him and his bandmates rehearse for shows around New York City. Later, she developed an understanding of songwriting from her piano teacher, Jen Bloom, who inspired her to write her own compositions.

Warren attended the prestigious prep school Trinity from kindergarten through high school. She found the school challenging because it was not, as she has described in interviews, a school with a rigorous art program, but rather a place that prepared students to go to Ivy League colleges such as Harvard University or Yale University. She often clashed with her teachers and needed extensions for her assignments because her attention was focused on her development as a musician. Finding time to make music while dealing with her academically rigorous high school was not easy—but this may have helped, rather than hindered, her musical ambitions. "Sometimes I think that the fact that it wasn't easy is what taught me my drive and motivation," she told Wynne. "I felt like I had something to prove and that made me work ten times harder."

While attending high school, she started the band Emily Warren & the Betters, with bassist Gab Bowler, drummer Etienne Bowler, and Matt Porter. The group played shows around New York City and released a self-titled EP in October 2010. Their biggest success was having their song "Not at All" featured on *Skins*, a drama that ran briefly on MTV in 2011. Although not a commercial hit, the band did allow Warren to demonstrate her budding songwriting talents. Reviewing the band's show at Webster Hall in New York City for the *Huffington Post* (18 Feb. 2011), Dan Alford declared: "Much of her material presents an appealing combination of intimacy and recognizable pathos—it leaves you wanting to know more, even though the feeling is familiar—but it doesn't whine or simper. If anything her songwriting is characterized by a rejection of rejection."

COLLEGE AND DR. LUKE'S PRESCRIPTION SONGS

Upon graduating from Trinity in 2011, Warren enrolled in New York University's (NYU) Tisch School of the Arts, where she studied songwriting and recorded music. Her time at NYU was very fruitful. She recalled in an interview with

Rob LeDonne for *Billboard* (27 Jan. 2017): "During my freshman year, I remember [mega producer and Dr. Luke protégé] Benny Blanco came in and spoke about what he did and how he got his start. . . . It was then I started to realize there was this whole world of pop songwriting."

Although upset that her band had not had the success she liked, she continued her undaunted efforts to break into the music industry. She discovered that she knew a former intern at Atlantic records named Rhea Pasricha, who had just landed a job in artists and repertoire (A&R) at Dr. Luke's Prescription Songs. Remembering Warren's work with her band, Pasricha asked Warren to fly out to Los Angeles to see if she might be a good fit in Dr. Luke's songwriting stable. After meeting with staffers and sitting in on sessions, they agreed that they should wait until Warren finished at NYU, but then about two weeks later Dr. Luke called Warren and asked her to sign with him right away. She did so, and in the summer of 2013 joined the songwriting staff of Prescription Songs but completed her undergraduate degree at NYU on schedule in 2015.

AN IN-DEMAND SONGWRITER

The song that brought Warren considerable success was "Capsize," which she wrote with Scott Hoffman and the pop duo Frenship, who performed the song. The song was written on the day of her graduation from NYU. She recalled how she heard the song for the first time on the radio to LeDonne: "I remember I was driving to pick my friends up from the airport in L.A. I turned the radio on and it was the chorus of 'Capsize' with me singing and I started hysterically crying." "Capsize" became a streaming megahit, with more than 300 million plays by 2017.

Even prior to "Capsize," Warren had proved to be more than a one-hit wonder. She penned "Masterpiece," a single off Jessie J's 2014 album, *Sweet Talker*. With her friend Scott Harris, she cowrote four songs on Shawn Mendes's album *Handwritten* (2015): "Strings," "Aftertaste," "Air," and "Lost." She worked with the Chainsmokers on a series of songs, some of which also featured her vocals. They include "Don't Say," "My Type," "Side Effects," "Until You've Been Gone," and "Paris." "Don't Let Me Down," another collaboration with the Chainsmokers, peaked at number three on the Billboard Hot 100 chart and earned a Grammy Award for Best Dance Recording. Other artists she has written for—frequently alongside Scott Harris—include Dua Lipa, Charli XCX, Astrid S, Little Mix, and Melanie Martinez. In November 2017, owing largely to her tremendous and continuing success as a pop songwriter, Warren made *Forbes* magazine's 30 Under 30 list for people in the music industry.

Warren described her songwriting process to Nicole White for *Omnisound Magazine* (26 Jan. 2018): "It starts with a long conversation with whoever I am writing with and [I] figure out . . . what is happening in their lives. We then make a song about that." She noted that this method is successful because if she and the artist can speak in an "honest or real" way about the artist's experiences, the audience is likely to be able to relate to it.

BREAKING OUT ON HER OWN

In 2017 Warren began exploring the idea of performing some of her own material. She explained her transition from songwriter to solo artist in her interview with White: "When people started leaving my voice on songs . . . it sort of felt like an organic, natural moment. Like, alright, if I still want to put songs out, this is kind of the time."

Her solo efforts, similar to her songs for other artists, feature infectious pop beats and lyrics that draw a listener in. Wynne wrote of Warren's solo work: "The raw, emotional content displayed in Warren's releases are compelling. . . . The sound is clean and uninterrupted, which allows for all vocals to be the center stage."

As of August 2018, Warren was at work on completing her debut solo album, which was scheduled to be released later that year. She has also continued to write for other artists alongside her work for her own album. In 2018 she co-wrote all four tracks of the Chainsmokers' *Sick Boy* EP as well as penning and producing songs for a wide range of other artists, including electronic-music duo Galantis, pop artist Bebe Rexha, K-pop star Taeyeon, Grammy Award–winner Jason Mraz, and dancehall singer Sean Paul.

PERSONAL LIFE

Warren lives in Los Angeles. When not writing songs, she enjoys traveling, visiting museums, and reading.

SUGGESTED READING

Alford, Dan. "Review: Emily Warren & the Betters at Webster Hall." *Huffington Post*, 18 Feb. 2011, www.huffingtonpost.com/dan-alford/emily-warren-the-betters-_b_825183.html. Accessed 23 July 2018.

LeDonne, Rob. "How I Got Started: Chainsmokers Co-Writer & 'Paris' Singer Emily Warren Shares Her Story." *Billboard*, 27 Jan. 2017, www.billboard.com/articles/columns/pop/7669763/emily-warren-capsize-chainsmokers-paris-singer-interview. Accessed 23 July 2018.

Spreyer, Simon. "Emily Warren." *AllMusic*, www.allmusic.com/artist/emily-warren-mn0002251220. Accessed 20 July 2018.

Warren, Emily. "Emily Warren Talks Working with the Chainsmokers, Singing on 'Paris.'" Interview by Taylor Weatherby. *Billboard*, 13 Jan. 2017, www.billboard.com/articles/news/dance/7655252/emily-warren-chainsmokers-paris-credit-interview. Accessed 23 July 2018.

Warren, Emily. "From Hits to Heart: A Conversation with Emily Warren." Interview by Kelly Wynne. *Atwood Magazine*, 11 Jan. 2018, atwoodmagazine.com/emily-warren-2018-interview/. Accessed 20 July 2018.

Warren, Emily. Interview by Nicole White. *Omnisound Magazine*, 26 Jan. 2018, www.omnisoundmagazine.com/interview-emily-warren.html. Accessed 20 July 2018.

SELECTED WORKS

"Until You Were Gone," 2015; "Capsize," 2016; "Phone Down," 2016; "Don't Say," 2017; "My Type," 2017; "New Rules," 2017; "Something to Hold On To," 2017; "Hurt by You," 2017; "Poking Holes," 2018

—*Christopher Mari*

David Weigel

Date of birth: September 26, 1981
Occupation: Journalist

Journalist, blogger, and author David Weigel made his career by reporting on conservative political viewpoints, particularly the shifting trends within the US Republican Party in the first decades of the twenty-first century. Unlike many political commentators, however, he avoided espousing either of the two major political parties in an increasingly partisan landscape. Instead, he acknowledged casting votes for both Republicans and Democrats, and aligned with many libertarian or otherwise third-party policies. This independent streak has made him a popular voice in an age of party upheaval—a development that also reflects the evolving nature of news coverage. Commenting on the changes in the media, Weigel told Keach Hagey for *Politico.com* (23 July 2010), "Any interview anywhere, any bit of hustle on any kind of story, if people can verify it, it can explode. You don't need anymore to make sure that your story gets to ABC News or a nightly broadcast somewhere."

EDUCATION AND EARLY CAREER

Weigel was born in Wilmington, Delaware, in 1981 and grew up there. He joined the junior Reserve Officers' Training Corp (ROTC) in high school, but did not enjoy the experience. He

Photo by Robert Daemmrich Photography Inc/Corbis via Getty Images

also served as music review editor for his school paper. He knew from his teenage years that he wanted to write, though he considered it might take a different form, such as teaching or research. In 1998 he moved to England, where he finished his secondary schooling.

Weigel returned to the United States in 2000 to attend Northwestern University's Medill School of Journalism. While there he became editor-in-chief of *Northwest Chronicle*, the conservative paper on campus, and continued to write about music for that publication. He also had pieces appear in *The Daily Northwestern*, another student-run paper. He graduated with a bachelor's degree in political science and journalism in 2004. Weigel received an internship as an editorial assistant at *USA Today* paid for by the Collegiate Network, another conservative group. Launching his journalism career, he became a reporter for the trade magazine *Campaigns & Elections*.

From 2006 to 2008, Weigel worked for *Reason*, a magazine with a libertarian slant. During that time he and fellow blogger Julian Sanchez roomed together in Washington, DC, in a house they named Casa de Libertarios. As part of a fertile scene of young political reporters living in the capital, the arrangement provided inspiration for his writing. As Ashley Parker reported for the *New York Times* (9 Mar. 2008), "Mr. Weigel said he remembers bumping into his roommate doing laundry and ending up in a fifteen-minute discussion about immigration policy, the sort of conversation that might later make it into one of his posts."

Weigel then moved to the *Washington Independent*, where he developed a blog on conservative politics. He remained there until 2014.

CONTROVERSY AND CAREER BREAKTHROUGH

The *Washington Post* hired Weigel in 2010 to blog about the Republican Party, and particularly the Tea Party movement within it, for a column titled "Right Now." His tenure lasted only three months, however, before he was caught up in a scandal regarding private messages he had posted on Journolist, a liberal email list. The messages, some of which predated his tenure at the *Washington Post*, were leaked, revealing his often unflattering comments about many of the conservative figures he was covering. Conservatives had already been upset by a post from Weigel on the social media platform Twitter that called those who opposed gay marriage "bigots," prompting him to apologize. In the wake of the controversy, Journolist was shut down.

Weigel immediately offered to resign from the *Washington Post*, an offer that management at first refused. By the next day, however, in the light of further leaks, the paper accepted his resignation. Some managers reportedly feared Weigel did not have enough objectivity to perform the job. Rather than attempt to justify himself, Weigel expressed regret over what he had written. As quoted by Ross Douthat for the *New York Times* (28 June 2010), he said: "I was cocky, and I got worse. I treated the list like a dive bar, swaggering in and popping off about what was 'really' happening out there, and snarking at conservatives . . . . I was stupid and arrogant, and needlessly mean."

Despite leaving the *Washington Post* under a cloud, Weigel's credibility and employability did not suffer. In fact, the scandal raised his profile and in many ways boosted his career to a new level. As he told Hagey, the general reaction to his resignation was "more sympathy than anything else from politicians, from spokesmen, from journalists, from people in think tanks." He netted a job as a contributor with MSNBC immediately after leaving the *Washington Post*. Within months, the online publication *Slate* (owned, ironically, by the *Washington Post*) hired Weigel as senior political reporter. He spent four years there, developing a self-titled column and a podcast of political interviews. *Time* named his blog one of the best blogs of 2011.

MOVING TO BLOOMBERG

In the fall of 2014, Weigel was hired by Bloomberg Media, which was set to expand its political coverage with the newly developed Bloomberg Politics platform. The company sought reporters who would bring value not only to print publications, but also across television, radio, web, and mobile content. Weigel, who had developed a reputation as a leading political journalist in the online sphere, with a sizable Twitter following, fit the bill. He explained his departure from *Slate* to readers in a post in which he suggested he only took the new position for the opportunity to be part of an ambitious new venture.

Bloomberg Politics indeed proved to be an ambitious project, and the organization leveraged Weigel as a key asset. As Michael Calderone reported for the *Huffington Post* website (2 Sept. 2014), Bloomberg Media's editorial director Josh Tyrangiel lauded the new hire: "Driven by his own curiosity, he eschews the pack to write and report some of the smartest pieces about how real people perceive their politicians. He loves the far right and the far left—in part for their commitment to their beliefs and in part because there are such great stories there. Dave also radiates a passion for writing that manifests itself in more than just a freakishly intimidating number of bylines. The man knows how to twirl a word and turn a phrase."

At Bloomberg, Weigel created a blog, "Whoa, If True," that was well regarded. The launch of Bloomberg Politics was not as successful as envisioned, however, in part because it was beset by internal conflicts between the Washington and New York offices. Weigel would spend only nine months there before his next move brought his journalism career full circle.

RETURN TO THE *WASHINGTON POST*

In 2015 Weigel returned to the *Washington Post* to cover national politics, with a focus on grassroots groups. Much coverage of his new position revolved around his previous history with the paper, but the he preferred to look to the future. "I think they were right to accept my resignation in 2010," he told Erik Wemple for the *Post* itself (8 July 2015). "I've changed and worked a lot harder since then. I'm a different and more responsible person."

Weigel's initial area of focus upon his hiring was conservative grassroots movements, including the presidential campaign of libertarian politician Rand Paul, whom he had previously covered for Bloomberg. He expressed much enthusiasm for the new opportunity, and the potential for collaborating with others on the staff. "What the Post is now is just the most exciting newsroom in the country, if that's not too hyperbolic," he told Hadas Gold for *Politico* (7 July 2015). "The people who write about politics are writing these definitive stories, and I want to be part of that. I'm hoping to add a focus on that to what they have already."

With his career as a journalist reinvigorated at the *Washington Post*, Weigel also pursued other interests. In the fall of 2016, amid the US presidential election, he served as public affairs writer in residence at the University of Wisconsin's Robert M. La Follette School of Public Affairs. In that role he spoke to classes and appeared with other political commentators to discuss the election and other issues. Following the upset result of the election, he was part of on-campus panel discussions with academics and other prominent figures attempting to analyze aspects of the vote.

THE SHOW THAT NEVER ENDS

One of Weigel's longstanding personal interests—music—formed the basis for a departure from his political writing that opened a new side of his career. After working on it for several years, he released his first book, *The Show That Never Ends: The Rise and Fall of Prog Rock*, in 2017. The work had its genesis in a five-part series at *Slate*, where writers were encouraged annually to write something not in their usual area. As a fan of the often-maligned genre of progressive (or prog) rock, Weigel set about documenting its history. As he told David Greene for *NPR Music* (18 July 2017), "I've always liked this progressive rock that is not critically respected or has been written out of rock history—not completely, but written as sort of a hilarious little hurdle for real musicians to get over."

In discussing prog, Weigel highlights its fusion of classical music with improvisation, rock instrumentation, and challenging lyrics or instrumentals. He touches on everything from the technological advances, such as synthesizers, that drove the music to the genre's demise at the hands of punk rock. Throughout, he argues for critical acceptance of prog as an important bridge between music of the mid-1960s, including garage bands and psychedelic music, and many later genres. The book focuses primarily on British progressive rock groups, which Weigel considers more creative than the groups from the United States.

Although he had been working on the book for years, Weigel finished it while covering the 2016 presidential election. That timing was fortuitous, as he told Alex Shephard for *New Republic* (15 June 2017): "I think it saved my sanity, quite honestly. I had been interested in progressive rock forever. I was into it before I was into politics. But once I got all the way, neck-deep into politics, I realized I needed this refuge."

PERSONAL LIFE

In addition to music, Weigel enjoys baseball and dancing at concerts and weddings. He wears the military dog tags of his grandfather, a World War II veteran, on a chain around his neck. Weigel is active on Twitter, with hundreds of thousands of followers, but tries to avoid allowing his job and personal views to create conflicts on social media. "I don't start fights and I don't punch in a particular direction," he told Wemple. "I will mute people if they're trying to bait me . . . I'm very conscious that you can turn off the screen and you don't have an argument anymore." He lives in Washington, DC.

SUGGESTED READING

Calderone, Michael. "Bloomberg Politics Hires Slate's Dave Weigel as New Venture Prepares for Launch." *HuffPost*, 2 Sept. 2014, www.huffingtonpost.com/2014/09/02/dave-weigel-bloomberg-launch_n_5752388.html. Accessed 6 Dec. 2017.

Douthat, Ross. "Weigel on Weigel." *The New York Times*, 28 June 2010, douthat.blogs.nytimes.com/2010/06/28/weigel-on-weigel/. Accessed 6 Dec. 2017.

Gold, Hadas. "Dave Weigel Returns to The Washington Post." *Politico*, 7 July 2015, www.politico.com/blogs/media/2015/07/dave-weigel-returns-to-the-washington-post-210107. Accessed 6 Dec. 2017.

Greene, David. "Can't Prog Rock Get Any Respect Around Here?" *NPR Music*, 18 July 2017, www.npr.org/2017/07/18/534577902/can-t-prog-rock-get-any-respect-around-here. Accessed 6 Dec. 2017.

Hagey, Keach. "Media Stars." *Politico*, 23 July 2010, www.politico.com/story/2010/07/media-stars-040044. Accessed 6 Nov. 2017.

Weigel, David. "Beyond Dragons and Nonsense: A Q&A with David Weigel about Prog Rock." Interview by Alex Shephard. *New Republic*, 15 June 2017, newrepublic.com/article/143317/beyond-dragons-nonsense-qa-david-weigel-prog-rock. Accessed 6 Dec. 2017.

Wemple, Erik. "Washington Post Nabs Dave Weigel from Bloomberg Politics." *The Washington Post*, 8 July 2015, www.washingtonpost.com/blogs/erik-wemple/wp/2015/07/08/washington-post-nabs-dave-weigel-from-bloomberg-politics. Accessed 6 Dec. 2017.

—*Judy Johnson*

Hassan Whiteside

Date of birth: June 13, 1989
Occupation: Basketball player

In 2017, Hassan Whiteside, the Miami Heat's seven-foot tall center with a seven-feet, seven-inch wingspan, led the National Basketball Association (NBA) in rebounds. In 2016, his first full professional season, he led the league in blocks. "What he does is really unique," Heat coach Erik Spoelstra told Zach Buckley for *Bleacher Report* (25 Oct. 2017). "He's a dominant defensive player that makes your entire team defense better, and he's as impactful as any center in the

By Keith Allison [CC BY-SA 2.0], via Wikimedia Commons

league offensively." Despite a nagging injury in the middle of his 2018 season, Whiteside, a big, agile man in league that prizes the quick and the small, is poised to become the leader the Heat have been seeking since the departure of superstars LeBron James, Dwayne Wade, and Chris Bosh. Whiteside's rise has been far from smooth, however. "I wish everything went perfect, you know," Whiteside told Ethan Skolnick for *Bleacher Report* (31 Jan. 2015). "Everybody wants to be the No. 1 pick, go to the NBA and just kill that rookie year on. But I didn't have that path. I had a lot tougher path." Born in North Carolina, Whiteside played ball for a handful of different schools before spending a year at Marshall University. He was drafted, thirty-third overall, by the Sacramento Kings in 2010, but immaturity and a reportedly poor attitude saw him demoted to the D-League. In 2013, Whiteside took his talents abroad, dodging AK-47–wielding security guards in Lebanon and struggling to find a good interpreter in China. The two-year odyssey changed Whiteside. He gained the confidence to harness his considerable skill, and he returned to the United States with an eye toward an NBA comeback in 2014.

EARLY LIFE AND EDUCATION

Hassan Niam Whiteside was born in Gastonia, North Carolina, on June 13, 1989. His father, Hasson Arbubakrr, was a defensive end for the Tampa Bay Buccaneers in the early 1980s. He separated from Whiteside's mother, Debbie Whiteside, and moved to New Jersey when Whiteside was a toddler. Debbie Whiteside worked multiple jobs—including building transmissions for tractor trailers, delivering newspapers, and catering—to support Whiteside and his six siblings.

Whiteside was an athletic child. He wrestled and played football, but he loved basketball most of all. He found it hard to find a team because his family was constantly moving as his mother tried to make ends meet. Whiteside, who ultimately attended three middle schools and six high schools, did not play for a regular team, but he was certain that a middle school teacher's prediction—that one day he would play for the NBA—would come true, if only because he had no other plan. "What's the Plan B?" Whiteside recalled to Jonathan Abrams for *Bleacher Report* (28 June 2016). "I didn't have a Plan B. I didn't." When Whiteside was a teenager, he invited his father to see one of his games. Arbubakrr was horrified. There were no referees, no stands with fans. It was just a pick-up game in an old gym.

Arbubakrr brought Whiteside to live with him in New Jersey, where he played for East Side High School in Newark. Coaches Bryant Garvin and Anthony Tavares made Whiteside, then about six-foot-six, a center. The teen, who had always considered himself a stealthy guard, was displeased. "I didn't like fighting for the rebounds, not getting the ball," he told Abrams. Whiteside learned to play the position and then he learned to love it. During his eighteen months at East Side he averaged 18 points, 10 rebounds, and 5.5 blocks per game. In 2008 Whiteside, a senior, returned to North Carolina, enrolling first at Hope Christian Academy in Charlotte and then the elite Patterson School in Lenoir. Over the course of the season Whiteside grew another three inches, gained thirty pounds, and led the team to a number one national ranking among prep school teams and a 34–2 record. By the time he graduated in 2009, Whiteside was ranked nineteenth among centers in his class, but he had committed to attend Marshall University in Huntington, West Virginia, before major teams like Kentucky showed an interest. Whiteside, who was not used to playing for a losing team, did not initially do well at Marshall. "His talent could outdo somebody who worked harder," his coach, Donnie Jones, told Abrams. "It was hard for him to even understand that if you played hard and had talent, how good you could become, and he started figuring that out."

EARLY NBA CAREER

At the end of his first and only year at Marshall, Whiteside averaged 13.1 points, 8.9 rebounds, and 5.4 blocks. He was named Defensive Player of the Year and Freshman of the Year in his conference. Whiteside initially planned to remain at Marshall, but after Jones and his staff left for another school, Whiteside declared for the NBA draft in 2010. He fared unexpectedly poorly, called in the second round, the thirty-third pick overall, by the Sacramento Kings. The transition to professional ball was a difficult one for Whiteside, who did not know, for instance, that it is customary for players to warm up before a game even if they do not expect to play. To make matters more difficult, the Kings that year also drafted another center, star DeMarcus Cousins. Whiteside chafed against the structure of the NBA and his second-fiddle status. A month into his rookie season, the Kings demoted Whiteside to the Reno Bighorns, a D-League team. It was a demoralizing turn of events made worse by a knee injury. By the season's end he had only played two full minutes during his rookie season with the NBA.

"WORLDWIDE WHITESIDE"

The next season, Whiteside, plagued by an ankle sprain, played only seven games with the Kings and eleven with the Bighorns. In the summer of 2012, the Kings let him go. Whiteside continued, at first, to play on D-League teams, such as the Sioux Falls Skyforce and the Rio Grande Valley Vipers. But rumors of Whiteside's poor attitude had traveled. No one it seemed, wanted to invest in the young player, and wherever he went, he got little time on the court. By 2012, money had grown tight. Desperate, he signed a contract with Lebanon's Amchit Club. It was the beginning of Whiteside's global odyssey back to the NBA. "I call him Worldwide Whiteside," his father told Abrams. "Him going around the world grew him up." Whiteside's initial experience in Lebanon was a frightening and disappointing one. During his second game, several players started fighting, and the fans rushed the floor. Security, armed with riot gear and assault rifles, shielded the players as they ran off the court and back to the locker room. After that, the entire season was canceled, and Whiteside signed a contract with a team in China's second-tier league, the Sichuan Blue Whales. Whiteside's first successful professional season in 2012–13 was fueled by his determination to prove himself to executives who did not think he was good enough for the top-tier Chinese Basketball Association (CBA). He averaged 25.7 points, 16.6 rebounds, and 5.1 blocks, leading the Blue Whales, undefeated in the playoffs, to a championship. He was named Chinese NBL Finals MVP and won *Asia-Basket.com* All-Chinese NBL Center of the Year, Defensive Player of the Year, and other honors. For the 2013–14 season, Whiteside returned to Lebanon, where he spent six months playing for United Club Tripoli. The same season he also returned to China, where he played seventeen games with the Jiangsu Tongxi in the CBA.

NBA COMEBACK

Whiteside made his NBA comeback in September 2014, signing a contract with the Memphis Grizzlies, but the team dropped him back to the Vipers, who still held his D-League contract. His manager then brokered a trade deal, sending Whiteside to the Iowa Energy. Chastened by his past NBA experience and his years abroad, Whiteside vowed to work his way back toward the NBA one step at a time. In his first game with the team, he almost made a triple double with 30 points, 22 rebounds, and eight blocks. Whiteside's performance caught the attention of the Miami Heat, and he was invited to a closed-door workout. Although the Heat decided not to sign him at the time, the Grizzlies re-signed him. A traveling delay prevented Whiteside from playing in his first game with the Grizzlies, and the team dropped him, again, the next day. After some more negotiation, Whiteside signed with Miami. Two weeks into his tenure with the Heat, Whiteside scored 14 points and 13 rebounds and blocked a franchise-record 12 shots in a game against the Chicago Bulls. Nick Schwartz, writing for *USA Today* (25 Jan. 2015) called Whiteside's showing "arguably the best minute-by-minute performance of any player in the NBA this season." When asked by a reporter about his stunning turn after the game, Whiteside, in seriousness, replied that he was just hoping to boost his rating on the video game *NBA 2K*.

By the end of his breakout 2015–16 season, Whiteside led the league in blocks with an average 3.68 per game, and finished third on the Defensive Player of the Year ballot. Poised to become the team's star, he signed a four-year $98 million contract with the Heat in July 2015. During the 2016–17 season, Whiteside became the first Heat player to record 1,000 points and 1,000 rebounds in a season. At season's end, he led the league in rebounds, the first Heat player ever to do so. He began his 2017–18 season with high hopes; in the season opener against the Orlando Magic on October 18, 2017, he scored 26 points and made 22 rebounds—the eighth such "20/20" of his career. But in late November 2017, Whiteside suffered a bone bruise on his left knee. As of mid-December, Whiteside's knee was improving, but it was unclear when he would return to the court.

PERSONAL LIFE

When he was young and his mother was struggling to earn a living for herself and her children, Whiteside promised her that he would buy her a house one day. In May 2017 Whiteside made good on his promise by purchasing a new six-bedroom house for her.

SUGGESTED READING

Abrams, Jonathan. "From Forgotten to Coveted: Hassan Whiteside's NBA Journey." *Bleacher Report*, 28 June 2016, thelab.bleacherreport.com/from-forgotten-to-coveted/. Accessed 15 Dec. 2017.

Buckley, Zach. "Can Hassan Whiteside Become the All-Star Leader Miami Heat Need?" *Bleacher Report*, 25 Oct. 2017, bleacherreport.com/articles/2740247-can-hassan-whiteside-become-the-all-star-leader-miami-heat-need. Accessed 16 Dec. 2017.

"Hassan Whiteside Bio." *NBA*, NBA Media Ventures, 2017, www.nba.com/heat/player-bios/hassan-whiteside. Accessed 18 Dec. 2017.

Navarro, Manny. "Heat's Hassan Whiteside Surprises Mother with Six Bedroom Home." *Miami Herald*, 1 June 2017, www.miamiherald.com/sports/nba/miami-heat/article153754164.html. Accessed 18 Dec. 2017.

Schwartz, Nick. "Miami's Hassan Whiteside after Blocking 12 Shots: 'I'm Just Trying to Get My 'NBA 2K' Rating Up.'" *USA Today*, 25 Jan. 2015, ftw.usatoday.com/2015/01/miami-heat-hassan-whiteside-12-blocks-triple-double. Accessed 15 Dec. 2017.

Skolnick, Ethan. "Hassan Whiteside Has Gone from Novelty to Necessity for Miami Heat." *Bleacher Report*, 31 Jan. 2015, bleacherreport.com/articles/2342029-hassan-whiteside-has-gone-from-novelty-to-necessity-for-miami-heat. Accessed 16 Dec. 2017.

—*Molly Hagan*

Jodie Whittaker

Date of Birth: June 3, 1982
Occupation: Actor

"I am part of an amazing profession," British actor Jodie Whittaker told Phil Penfold for the *Yorkshire Post* (21 Mar. 2013). "I love my job—even if it is pretty scary at times, walking out on a stage or on a set and knowing that you could make yourself look a total imbecile." Since making her film debut in 2006's *Venus*, Whittaker has walked out onto numerous stages and sets and put forth engaging, multidimensional performances that have earned her widespread acclaim both within and outside of the United Kingdom. Having established herself with a wide range of film and television roles, she gained significant notice for her work in such projects as the 2011 science-fiction film *Attack the Block* and the television drama *Broadchurch*, which began airing in 2013. A new milestone for Whittaker came in the summer of 2017, when it was announced that she would be the

By Ibsan73 [CC BY 2.0], via Wikimedia Commons

next actor—and first woman—to play the character of the Doctor in the long-running science-fiction series *Doctor Who*. Whittaker was thrilled to have the opportunity to fill the iconic role. "To be asked to play the ultimate character, to get to play pretend in the truest form: this is why I wanted to be an actor in the first place," she told the BBC (17 July 2017) upon the announcement.

EARLY LIFE AND EDUCATION
Whittaker was born on June 3, 1982, to Adrian and Yvonne Whittaker. Her father is the co-owner of a company that sells and installs window film, and her mother worked as a nurse and later as a magistrate. Whittaker and her older brother, Kris, grew up in and near Skelmanthorpe, a village in the county of West Yorkshire in northern England. As a child, Whittaker enjoyed drama classes in school and had little interest in academic subjects, instead demonstrating an early interest in performing. "I was the attention-seeking child in class who needed everyone to look at meeee!" she recalled to Esther Addley for the *Guardian* (21 July 2017).

By the time Whittaker was in her mid-teens, she hoped to pursue a career in acting, an aspiration her parents encouraged despite a career adviser's warning that Whittaker make backup plans. After attending secondary school at Shelley College, Whittaker enrolled in Kirklees College to complete a diploma in the performing arts and subsequently spent a year traveling abroad. "All my mates were going to university, and that wasn't for me, so I decided that seeing other places, other cultures would broaden my mind a bit," she explained to Penfold. "And boy, it certainly did that! I certainly had no plan at all—I just pointed myself towards the US, and went."

Following her return to the United Kingdom, Whittaker decided to pursue studies in acting and relocated to London, where she enrolled in the prestigious Guildhall School of Music and Drama. She graduated from the institution in 2005 and won a medal during her final year. "I got it for most improved, which basically means I was s—— when I started and left not embarrassing the school," she told Gerard Gilbert for the *Independent* (17 June 2011). Despite her somewhat self-deprecating attitude toward her dramatic abilities, Whittaker was among the first students in her year to secure representation by an agent.

EARLY CAREER
Whittaker began her professional acting career in the theater, playing the part of Ampelisca in the Shakespeare's Globe production of the Peter Oswald play *The Storm* while still studying at Guildhall. The play, which starred actor and then artistic director of the theater Mark Rylance, opened at Shakespeare's Globe in the summer of 2005. Whittaker remained active in theater throughout the following years, appearing in productions of *Bash* at London's Trafalgar Studios and *Awake and Sing!* at the Almeida Theatre. She also found work on television, securing small roles in shows such as the anthology series *The Afternoon Play*, the medical soap opera *Doctors*, and the crime drama *Dalziel and Pascoe*.

Whittaker made her feature film debut in 2006's *Venus*, playing a troublemaking teenager who befriends an elderly man played by veteran actor Peter O'Toole. The presence of well-known actors such as O'Toole and Vanessa Redgrave garnered *Venus* significant attention within the film community, and Whittaker's status as a talented newcomer prompted further interest. "Everyone kept asking: 'Where did the director find you?' Like he had picked me up on a train platform or something," she recalled to Tara Brady for the *Irish Times* (24 June 2016).

For Whittaker, filming *Venus* was not only a major step in her career but also a valuable opportunity to learn from the film's more established stars. "The thing I noticed about [O'Toole and Redgrave] was, even though they had absolutely nothing to prove, they worked so hard on the script, they worked so hard on their choices," she told Brady. "And I remember thinking: 'If you're still learning and discovering and studying this long into your career, then this job will never be boring.'" Over the following years, Whittaker's own career was far from boring as she found numerous roles in films such as 2007's *St. Trinian's* and the 2009 sequel, *St. Trinian's 2: The Legend of Fritton's Gold*, as well as television projects such as the miniseries *Tess of the D'Urbervilles* (2008) and *Marchlands* (2011).

MAJOR PROJECTS

Whittaker gained notice among moviegoers in 2011, when she costarred in the science-fiction film *Attack the Block*. Set in a London public housing estate, the film chronicles a group of residents' attempt to fight off an alien invasion. Whittaker plays Sam, a young nurse and a new resident of the estate, and was drawn to the role thanks to filmmaker Joe Cornish's realistic approach to the character. "I loved Sam because I usually go up for quite neurotic, on the brink women and she was incredibly practical and really straight and un-flappy," she told Rob Carnevale for *IndieLondon*. "She didn't have a wet-look T-shirt, she didn't suddenly have these outlandish skills that I'd never had before and I wasn't crying and reaching out for someone to save me. [Cornish] wrote Sam like he wrote everyone else—as a real person in a very heightened situation."

The year 2011 proved to be a productive one for Whittaker, including not only the premiere of *Attack the Block* but also the release of the romantic drama *One Day*, based on the 2009 novel by David Nicholls. For Whittaker, who played a supporting role in the film, *One Day* presented a daunting challenge. "There's a lot of pressure because everyone I meet says, 'Oh my God, it's one of my favorite books.' Terrifying," she told Gilbert. Whittaker also starred in a 2011 episode of the science-fiction anthology series *Black Mirror* and the following year costarred in the biopic *Good Vibrations*, about Irish record label owner Terri Hooley. She likewise remained active in theater during that period, playing the title role in a 2012 production of the Greek tragedy *Antigone* at the National Theatre.

Among her many projects, Whittaker enjoyed working on the comedy *Adult Life Skills*, which premiered at New York's Tribeca Film Festival in 2016. An expanded version of the 2014 short film *Emotional Fusebox*, which had been nominated for the British Academy of Film and Television Arts (BAFTA) Award for best British short film, *Adult Life Skills* was written and directed by Whittaker's friend Rachel Tunnard, and featured actor Rachael Deering, Whittaker's friend since early childhood. For Whittaker, making *Adult Life Skills* was significant not only because of those friendships but also because of the film's unique perspective. "It's not one of those films where [the protagonist] needs to get money and a boyfriend," she told Brady. "It's not about living as a high-flier. It's about learning to live. It's a brave pitch for a comedy." *Adult Life*

Skills ultimately won two British Independent Film Awards and was nominated for four others, including the award for best actress for Whittaker. Tunnard received the Nora Ephron Prize at the Tribeca Film Festival, among other honors, in recognition of her work.

TELEVISION DRAMAS

Beginning in 2013, Whittaker received widespread acclaim for her performance in the first season of the television crime drama *Broadchurch*, in which the murder of a local boy prompts an investigation that reveals many of the town's darkest secrets. Whittaker plays Beth Latimer, the mother of the murdered boy and a major figure in the events of the season. As the former resident of a small town, she was drawn to *Broadchurch*'s approach to the murder investigation and mystery. "Everyone knows everyone else," she told Penfold. "But, think about it, when something like this child's death occurs, everyone becomes a suspect. Who do you trust, who do you believe?" Whittaker reprised the role of Beth in the show's second and third seasons, which focuses on the murder trial and an unrelated case, respectively.

In 2017, Whittaker starred in another high-profile television project, the medical drama *Trust Me*. A four-episode miniseries, *Trust Me* follows a nurse, Cath, who assumes a new identity and impersonates a doctor after losing her job. "I love the fact that [Cath's] choices are quite morally dubious—they certainly aren't black and white," Whittaker told the BBC (26 July 2017). "She makes decisions that are quite challenging to justify, even though we know her reasons." To prepare for the role, Whittaker underwent some basic medical training and even had the opportunity to insert a tube into one of show creator Dan Sefton's veins. "I did it right, thank God!" she told the BBC.

DOCTOR WHO

In July 2017, the team behind the long-running British science-fiction show *Doctor Who* announced that Whittaker had been chosen as the next actor to play the time-traveling eccentric known as the Doctor, who regenerates into a new body—played by a new actor—when seriously injured. First aired between 1963 and 1989 and revived in 2005, the show had previously featured twelve different actors in the lead role. Whittaker was selected to take over from actor Peter Capaldi, who had himself taken over from Matt Smith in 2014. Her casting was significant because she was the first woman to play the Doctor, widely considered one of the most iconic characters in British popular culture. Whittaker made her debut in the role in the 2017 *Doctor Who* Christmas special and was set to begin her first season as the Doctor in 2018.

PERSONAL LIFE

Whittaker met her husband, the American-born actor Christian Contreras, while attending Guildhall. They married in 2008. Contreras has appeared in such films as *Zero Dark Thirty* and *Adult Life Skills*. Whittaker and Contreras live in London with their daughter, who was born in 2015.

In addition to her acting work, Whittaker enjoys sports and is an avid runner who has participated in the London and New York marathons. Although seemingly separate from her professional career, running nevertheless taps into Whittaker's creative side. "I can't listen to music because headphones don't fit my ears properly. So I have to pretend," she told Brady. "Usually something ridiculous, like: 'I'm in medieval England and I have to run for four hours to get medicine to the dying.' I'm doolally like that."

SUGGESTED READING

Addley, Esther. "Jodie Whittaker: The Force of Nature Taking On *Doctor Who*." *The Guardian*, 21 July 2017, www.theguardian.com/tv-and-radio/2017/jul/21/jodie-whittaker-the-force-of-nature-taking-on-doctor-who. Accessed 12 Nov. 2017.

Brady, Tara. "Jodie Whittaker: 'It's about Learning to Live.'" *The Irish Times*, 24 June 2016, www.irishtimes.com/culture/film/jodie-whittaker-it-s-about-learning-to-live-1.2695130. Accessed 12 Nov. 2017.

Gilbert, Gerard. "Jodie Whittaker: 'I Work a Lot and No One Knows Who I Am.'" *Independent*, 17 June 2011, www.independent.co.uk/news/people/profiles/jodie-whittaker-i-work-a-lot-and-no-one-knows-who-i-am-2297790.html. Accessed 12 Nov. 2017.

Penfold, Phil. "Jodie Whittaker: The Rise of a Venus with Her Feet on the Ground." *The Yorkshire Post*, 21 Mar. 2013, www.yorkshirepost.co.uk/news/jodie-whittaker-rise-of-a-venus-with-her-feet-on-the-ground-1-5518411. Accessed 12 Nov. 2017.

Treadaway, Luke, and Jodie Whittaker. "*Attack the Block*—Luke Treadaway and Jodie Whittaker Interview." By Rob Carnevale. *IndieLondon*, www.indielondon.co.uk/Film-Review/attack-the-block-luke-treadaway-and-jodie-whittaker-interview. Accessed 12 Nov. 2017.

Whittaker, Jodie. Interview. *BBC*, 26 July 2017, www.bbc.co.uk/mediacentre/mediapacks/trustme/jodie. Accessed 12 Nov. 2017.

Whittaker, Jodie. "Introducing Jodie Whittaker—The Thirteenth Doctor." *BBC*, 17 July 2017, www.bbc.co.uk/mediacentre/latestnews/2017/jodie-whittaker-13-doctor. Accessed 12 Nov. 2017.

SELECTED WORKS

Venus, 2006; *Tess of the D'Urbervilles*, 2008; *Marchlands*, 2011; *Attack the Block*, 2011; *Black Mirror*, 2011; *Good Vibrations*, 2012; *Broadchurch*, 2013–17; *Adult Life Skills*, 2016; *Trust Me*, 2017; *Doctor Who*, 2017–

—Joy Crelin

Samira Wiley

Date of birth: April 15, 1987
Occupation: Actor

Samira Wiley is an actor who is best known for her supporting role in the Netflix series *Orange Is the New Black*, in which she played inmate Poussey Washington from 2013 to 2016. Beginning in 2017, she appeared as Moira in the Hulu series *The Handmaid's Tale*, which is based on the acclaimed 1985 dystopian novel by Canadian author Margaret Atwood. She has earned three Screen Actors Guild Awards (SAG), in 2015, 2016, and 2017, for her role as part of the *Orange Is the New Black* cast, and she was nominated in 2017 for a Primetime Emmy Award for Outstanding Supporting Actress in a Drama Series for her role as Moira.

Grateful for the success she has achieved and the opportunities she has been given, Juilliard-trained Wiley hails from a theatrical background. She has one desire above all others for her career, as she noted in an interview with Durga Chew-Bose for the *Guardian* (23 June 2014): "I never want to pigeonhole myself or get typecast. I'm looking forward to my career and showing all of my range as an actress, and I'm looking at other mediums too. I'm a theater actress first. And I cannot wait to return to the stage."

In addition to her acting career, Wiley has modeled for various magazines and has won awards for her advocacy concerning lesbian, gay, bisexual, and transgender (LGBT) issues.

EARLY LIFE AND EDUCATION

Samira Wiley was born on April 15, 1987, and raised in Washington, DC, alongside her brother and sister. Her parents, Christine and Dennis W. Wiley, served as the copastors of the Covenant Baptist United Church of Christ in Washington, DC, for some years and are well known for their outreach to the LGBT community. Their church, in which Wiley spent much of her time growing up, has been performing same-sex unions for more than a decade. In interviews, Wiley has said that she has always admired her parents' convictions and has felt nothing but

Photo by Dia Dipasupil/Getty Images for New York Fashion Week: The Shows

support from them and her religious community since she came out as a lesbian.

From about age ten, Wiley knew that she wanted to become an actor. After hearing an advertisement on a local radio station about the summer arts program at Howard University, she got her parents to take her. At the same time, she searched for concrete inspiration to reaffirm her desired career path: "All I wanted to do was to be able to look to TV, look to film to see someone who looked like me so that I knew that it was possible," she explained to Benjamin Lindsay for *Backstage* (25 May 2017). That moment came, she told Lindsay, when she watched a film featuring Angela Bassett, in which she felt the actor portrayed real-life figure Tina Turner with "dedication" and "authenticity."

Wiley attended high school at the Duke Ellington School of the Arts in Washington, DC. Though she did not receive any special recognition while in school, she determinedly applied to several theater programs. Optimistic but practical, upon receiving rejection letters from all of them, she enrolled at Temple University in Philadelphia, Pennsylvania, with the idea that she could still work in the industry but perhaps in a background role. However, at the insistence of one of her professors, she warily but hopefully auditioned for the famed Juilliard School and was ultimately accepted. After transferring out of Temple and moving to New York City, she began her training as a stage actor. "Juilliard gave me confidence in a way that I had never had before," she wrote in an article for *Glamour* (10 Aug. 2017).

ORANGE IS THE NEW BLACK

Upon graduating from Juilliard in 2010, Wiley found mostly walk-on roles in various television series, with her most notable role in the film comedy *The Sitter* in 2011. While she worked, she also bartended most nights, never sure if a plum role was waiting for her.

As luck would have it, she landed an audition for a dream role in a show involving a friend from Juilliard, Danielle Brooks, who had already secured a part on the Netflix adaptation of Piper Kerman's 2010 prison memoir *Orange Is the New Black*. The comedy-drama series looks at the lives of female inmates at a minimum-security federal prison, where most are incarcerated for low-level offenses. After encouragement from and line reading with Brooks, Wiley auditioned for the role of Poussey Washington, the best friend of Brooks's character. Though she won the role, her early experiences in the industry, particularly in one show in which it seemed that she had earned a recurring role until she was never called back after two episodes, prompted her to keep tending bar throughout the first season. Her performance as an intelligent, brave, and loyal friend with a wicked sense of humor won her immediate praise from viewers and critics, however, and as her fears quickly proved unfounded, she accepted that she could make it in acting full time. "I felt like from the moment I got that role, I was doing what I was supposed to be doing," she told Glenn Whipp for the *Los Angeles Times* (22 June 2017).

PLAYING A FAN FAVORITE

During Wiley's four seasons on *Orange Is the New Black*, viewers continued to learn more about her character, both from her experiences in prison and through flashbacks to her previous life. As her character's popularity grew, so, too, did Wiley's fame: "The biggest change I guess for me is that I've lost my anonymity when I walk down the street," she noted to Chew-Bose. At the same time, she has expressed in interviews that she appreciated that as the cast was largely composed of lesser-known actors, they experienced the increasing fame together.

In the fourth season, the show's writers decided that they wanted to kill off her character to use her senseless death as a commentary on the real-life deaths that inspired the Black Lives Matter movement. At first, Wiley was upset that her character was being killed off; she felt as if she had done something wrong as a performer. However, she quickly understood the motivations behind this unexpected plot twist and that it had to be her character. She said, as quoted by Victoria Ahearn for the Toronto *Star* (5 July 2016), that her character's death "very much echoed the deaths of Eric Garner, Mike Brown and other senseless deaths caused by police and brutality," and she added that she was "really honoured to be able to be a part of a television show that's not afraid to tackle those issues."

THE HANDMAID'S TALE

After leaving *Orange Is the New Black*, Wiley had a role in the television series *You're the Worst* (2016) and the period drama *Detroit* (2017). Though she initially worried about being typecast, she auditioned and, after winning the role, went on to again catch the public's imagination with her riveting performance as one of the handmaids in the Hulu series *The Handmaid's Tale* beginning in April 2017. Based on Margaret Atwood's award-winning and best-selling novel, the series looks at a dystopian world following a second American Civil War, in which the Republic of Gilead is formed in what had been the United States. In Gilead, a military dictatorship, employing a perverted form of Christianity, takes away women's rights and freedoms and forces all fertile women into sexual servitude to the ruling class of men, whose wives are unable to bear children. In the show, Wiley plays Moira, the best friend of the main character, June (Elisabeth Moss), who plots to escape her life as a handmaid and flee to Canada.

The first season of the series won eight Emmy Awards, and Wiley herself was nominated for best supporting actress. Many critics and viewers of the show have found timely comparisons in it to real-life events, including the Me Too movement, in which women and men have described their experiences with sexual harassment and assault. In an interview with Leigh Blickley for the *Huffington Post* (9 Mar. 2018), Wiley remarked, "I'm so surprised and in awe of the writers on our show. It just seems that they are so in tune with exactly what is happening right now in our country, in our world. Every time I read a script, it feels like I'm watching a new episode for the audience: I feel it in my gut. It feels so close and so relevant to what we're living every day, what we're seeing on the news, the stories we're hearing from our colleagues and people we meet."

In the show's second season, which premiered in April 2018, the action moves both outside the Republic of Gilead and beyond the plot of Atwood's original novel. Wiley's Moira has managed to escape to Canada. Despite having come to a better place, however, all is not well with Moira. "On the surface, it looks so wonderful. She's gotten access to health care, she's gotten money—things that women aren't even allowed to possess. But there's also the other side of it, which is that she is a refugee in a new country where she's never been before. She's lonely and going through a lot of depression, PTSD, from being in that horrible, horrible

place," Wiley explained to Jessica Kegu for *CBS News* (3 May 2018).

In addition to her work on television, Wiley appeared in the comedy *Social Animals* and had finished production on the heist drama *Vault* by the summer of 2018.

PERSONAL LIFE AND ADVOCACY

During her time on *Orange Is the New Black*, Wiley met and fell in love with one of the show's screenwriters, Lauren Morelli, who was then married to a man. Morelli separated from her husband to pursue a relationship with Wiley, whom she married on March 25, 2017. The couple live in Los Angeles.

A staunch supporter of LGBT rights throughout her career, Wiley has received the 2015 Human Rights Campaign's Visibility Award and the 2018 Vito Russo Award at the GLAAD Media Awards, among other accolades, for her civil rights advocacy. She told Blickley that she has embraced this role as well: "It's really a dream. I feel super lucky especially when it comes to me getting much more comfortable in terms of who I am in the LGBT community. I think visibility is of the utmost importance and to know I've somehow been 'picked' to be a voice, I feel like it's a real responsibility that I have and I want to be able to portray these characters in a way that is inspiring to young women."

SUGGESTED READING

Ahearn, Victoria. "*Orange Is the New Black* Star Samira Wiley on How Black Lives Matter Inspired Poussey Washington." *The Star*, 5 July 2016, www.thestar.com/entertainment/television/2016/07/05/orange-is-the-new-black-star-samira-wiley-on-how-black-lives-matter-inspired-the-show.html. Accessed 4 June 2018.

Kegu, Jessica. "Why Samira Wiley Almost Passed on *The Handmaid's Tale*." *CBS News*, 3 May 2018, www.cbsnews.com/news/samira-wiley-on-the-handmaids-tale-season-two/. Accessed 4 June 2018.

Wiley, Samira. "How Angela Bassett Inspired a Young Samira Wiley to Become an Actor." Interview by Benjamin Lindsay. *Backstage*, 25 May 2017, www.backstage.com/interview/how-angela-bassett-inspired-young-samira-wiley-become-actor/. Accessed 4 June 2018.

Wiley, Samira. "*Orange Is the New Black*'s Samira Wiley: 'Prison Is Not a Funny Place.'" Interview by Durga Chew-Bose. *The Guardian*, 23 June 2014, www.theguardian.com/tv-and-radio/tvandradioblog/2014/jun/23/orange-is-the-new-black-samira-wiley-interview. Accessed 4 June 2018.

Wiley, Samira. "Samira Wiley Says *Handmaid's Tale* Season 2 Will Show Parts of Gilead We've Never Seen." Interview by Leigh Blickley.

HuffPost, 9 Mar. 2018, www.huffingtonpost. com/entry/samira-wiley-handmaids-tale-season-2_us_5aa168fbe4b0e9381c168625. Accessed 4 June 2018.

Wiley, Samira. "Samira Wiley Talks *Orange, Handmaid's Tale* and Doing the Electric Slide at Disneyland." Interview by Glenn Whipp. *Los Angeles Times*, 22 June 2017, www.latimes.com/entertainment/envelope/la-en-st-samira-wiley-handmaids-tale-orange-is-the-new-black-20170622-htmlstory.html. Accessed 4 June 2018.

SELECTED WORKS

The Sitter, 2011; *Orange Is the New Black*, 2013–16; *The Handmaid's Tale*, 2017–

—Christopher Mari

WondaGurl

Date of birth: December 28, 1996
Occupation: Record producer

In 2005, the Oshunrinde family of Ontario, Canada, got their first home computer. The arrival of a new computer would be exciting for many children, but for nine-year-old Ebony Oshunrinde—later known as WondaGurl—the moment represented the start of what would become a life-changing career in beat-making and record production. Over the next several years, Oshunrinde, a fan of established producers such as Timbaland and an avid user of the music software FL Studio, honed her skills as a beat maker and impressed members of the Toronto hip-hop community when she won the 2012 Battle of the Beat Makers at the age of fifteen. The following year, the name WondaGurl reached new audiences when rapper Jay-Z selected one of the young producer's beats for his album *Magna Carta Holy Grail*. Although still in high school at the time, WondaGurl found that her musical goals were nevertheless within her reach. "I used to not feel very confident, but it developed over time," she told Emily Laurence for *Seventeen* (19 July 2013). "Now I believe you can accomplish your dreams no matter how old you are. I'm doing it!"

Over the years following the release of "Crown," the Jay-Z track featuring her beat, WondaGurl has worked with an array of rappers and singers, including Travis Scott, Drake, and Rihanna. Her popular work has established her as a major new force within the industry and likewise earned her recognition from publications such as *Forbes* magazine. Despite her success, however, WondaGurl continues to aspire to greater things. "I dream about completely taking

over the game, in a Timbaland kind of way," she told Anupa Mistry for the *Fader* (25 May 2016).

EARLY LIFE AND EDUCATION

Ebony Naomi "WondaGurl" Oshunrinde was born on December 28, 1996, in Ontario, Canada. Her mother, Jozie Oshunrinde, is a travel agent. One of four children, WondaGurl spent her early years in Scarborough and Mississauga before moving to the city of Brampton as a teenager. Beginning in eleventh grade, she attended Chinguacousy Secondary School, a high school known for its science and technology program, which grabbed her attention.

WondaGurl began experimenting with music early in life, making her first beats when she was as young as nine. Initially creating beats using a small Casio keyboard, she moved on to using beat-making computer software after her household got its first computer. Although she had no formal education in making beats and found structured music lessons unappealing, she found that the Internet—particularly the website YouTube—provided all the tutorials a determined aspiring beat maker could need. "If you really want to learn, you will sit there and learn it," WondaGurl told Slava Pastuk for *Noisey* (10 July 2014). "I was a bored kid. I had no friends, so I said, OK I'm going to make beats."

By the time she was ten years old, WondaGurl had set up a studio in her bedroom, demonstrating how seriously she took her work as a beat maker. Initially influenced by the work of producer Timbaland, she came to incorporate numerous influences into her music, including elements of the dancehall genre that she noted was popular in her Nigerian family. She posted her early work online under the name EO Muzik but later took on the name WondaGurl prior to making her first appearance at Toronto's Battle of the Beat Makers.

EARLY CAREER

As a teenager, WondaGurl sought to demonstrate her beat-making process in person in addition to on the Internet. However, when she attempted to join the Battle of the Beat Makers challenge in Toronto at the age of thirteen, she was barred from competing because of her age. WondaGurl persisted and succeeded in convincing the event's organizers to eliminate the previous age restriction so that she could compete the following year. She made her first appearance at the 2011 Battle of the Beat Makers and placed third in the competition at the age of fourteen. The appearance brought her to the attention of Toronto producer Boi-1da, whose pseudonym had inspired her own. Boi-1da came to serve as a mentor to WondaGurl, introducing her to other members of the thriving Toronto producing and rap scene. In 2012, WondaGurl returned to the

Battle of the Beat Makers, where she faced off against more than thirty other producers. She impressed the judges with her work during the competition and ultimately claimed first place. The victory earned her significant attention within the beat-making community, and she went on to pursue a career in music seriously following the win.

In addition to competing at the Battle of the Beat Makers, to which she would return as a guest judge several years later, Wonda-Gurl became involved with a local organization called the Remix Project during her early career. Dedicated to helping creative youth from disadvantaged communities meet their goals, the organization provides mentoring, educational programs, creative facilities, and equipment. For WondaGurl, the Remix Project helped her build connections that would prove crucial to her later success. "Remix is what helped me get into Toronto and its music scene," she recalled to Brandon Brown for *NOW* (3 Nov. 2017). As she gained recognition for her beats, she began to work with Canadian hip-hop artists as a producer, creating the beats that formed the basis of their songs. Early tracks included the 2012 song "Money Money" by rappers Rich Kidd and Son-Real. For WondaGurl, working with local artists gave her the opportunity to stand out and create the kinds of music she would want to listen to. "No one in Toronto was making feel-good music," she told Mistry. "I like to hear things I've never heard before."

PROCESS

As a producer and beat maker, WondaGurl frequently makes use of samples and draws influence from an array of musical genres and sounds. "I like weird sounds," she explained to Pastuk. "I sample dancehall songs sometimes just by going on YouTube and searching for new artists. I'm never really into what they're talking about, but I like their flow, the way they sound on the beat, and the bass. I don't care for new school reggae. Old school reggae is the most important thing, since it's all about the bass and drums." In addition to such sources of inspiration, WondaGurl has also been inspired by electronic music and Bollywood music as well as by elements of contemporary hip-hop.

Although she used several different beat-making programs in the early stages of her career, WondaGurl is perhaps best known for using the program FL Studio, which became her software of choice by the time she entered her teens. Formerly known as FruityLoops, FL Studio enables producers to create complex tracks by editing and manipulating music and other sounds. WondaGurl has noted that while such programs enable her to do her work quickly, completing a track typically takes "a couple days," as she told

Brown. "I like sitting on them and going back," she explained. WondaGurl also owns a Roland GAIA synthesizer that she received as a prize at the 2012 Battle of the Beat Makers, although she has noted that she uses it infrequently.

BREAKTHROUGH

A key moment in WondaGurl's career came in 2013, after she emailed a beat she had made to American rapper Travis Scott. The two had worked together on Scott's song "Uptown," from his 2013 mixtape *Owl Pharaoh*, and would later collaborate on the 2015 song "Antidote," among other projects. While WondaGurl had initially expected that Scott would use the beat himself, the events that instead unfolded would shape the young producer's career from that point on. "[Scott] said he was going to add some stuff to it," she told Jessica Herndon for the *Hollywood Reporter* (13 Aug. 2013). "But when he was in the studio with Jay-Z, he showed it to him and Jay liked it." Among the most popular and critically lauded rappers of all time, Jay-Z was in the process of completing his twelfth studio album, *Magna Carta Holy Grail*, at the time of his interaction with Scott. He ultimately used the beat for the song "Crown," for which WondaGurl was credited as a cowriter and coproducer. *Magna Carta Holy Grail* went on to be nominated for the Grammy Award for best rap album in addition to being certified double platinum by the Recording Industry Association of America.

Following the debut of *Magna Carta Holy Grail*, WondaGurl became the center of widespread media coverage, much of which emphasized the fact that she was still a high school student at the time. For the producer, the success of her beat was both indescribable and motivating. "When I listen to the song now, knowing I produced it, it feels unreal," she told Laurence. "My next goal is to win a Grammy." WondaGurl's increased profile within the hip-hop community proved beneficial, enabling her to work with numerous additional artists, although she noted in interviews that she had to balance her beat-making work and her responsibilities at home and at school carefully. Among other projects during that period, WondaGurl worked on two songs featured on Canadian rapper Drake's 2015 mixtape *If You're Reading This It's Too Late*. She also noted in interviews that she took her sudden rise in fame and increase in income from producing as an opportunity to upgrade her recording equipment.

RISING STAR

In the years following her breakthrough with "Crown," WondaGurl became increasingly in demand as a producer and worked with a variety of well-known artists, including rappers Big Sean and Lil Uzi Vert and singers Usher and

Rihanna. She remained closely affiliated with Travis Scott and served as a producer for two tracks from his 2018 album *ASTROWORLD*. In keeping with her longtime involvement with the Toronto music scene, she likewise continued to work with up-and-coming Canadian rappers such as KILLY, for whom she produced the 2018 extended-play (EP) recording *KILLSTREAK*.

In addition to producing music with popular artists, WondaGurl has personally appeared in advertisements for brands such as Sprite and was featured as a model in the fall Window Book for the retailer Barneys New York. In 2018, she was included in *Forbes* magazine's 30 Under 30 list for the field of music. While pleased with her success in her industry, WondaGurl remains focused on the process rather than its rewards. "Just work hard and stay humble," she told Laurence of her mindset.

SUGGESTED READING

Barmak, Sarah. "A Drumroll, Please, for WondaGurl." *Toronto Star*, 29 Dec. 2013, www.pressreader.com/canada/toronto-star/20131229/281865821303967. Accessed 14 Sept. 2018.

Brown, Brandon. "Making a Beat with Wondagurl." *NOW*, 3 Nov. 2017, nowtoronto.com/music/features/making-a-beat-with-wondagurl/. Accessed 14 Sept. 2018.

Herndon, Jessica. "16-Year-Old 'Magna Carta Holy Grail' Producer 'Wondagurl' Now Working on Beats for Drake." *Hollywood Reporter*, 13 Aug. 2013, www.hollywoodreporter.com/earshot/16-year-old-magna-carta-604250. Accessed 14 Sept. 2018.

Mistry, Anupa. "Meet WondaGurl, the Quiet Hustler Behind Rap's Loudest Beats." *Fader*, 25 May 2016, www.thefader.com/2016/05/25/wondagurl-producer-ebony-oshunrinde-interview/amp. Accessed 14 Sept. 2018.

Pastuk, Slava. "Wondagurl: Already Graduated." *Noisey*, 10 July 2014, noisey.vice.com/en_us/article/6vaqmr/wondagurl-interview. Accessed 14 Sept. 2018.

WondaGurl. "Meet Jay-Z's 16-Year-Old Producer." Interview with Emily Laurence. *Seventeen*, 19 July 2013, www.seventeen.com/celebrity/gmp500/jay-z-wondagurl/. Accessed 14 Sept. 2018.

WondaGurl. "Meet WondaGurl, the 16-Year-Old Producer Behind Travi\$ Scott's 'Uptown.'" Interview by Lauren Nostro. *Complex*, 5 June 2013, www.complex.com/music/2013/06/wondagurl-producer-travis-scott-uptown. Accessed 14 Sept. 2018.

—*Joy Crelin*

Alina Zagitova

Date of birth: May 18, 2002
Occupation: Figure skater

In the lead-up to the 2018 Winter Olympic Games, Russian figure skater Alina Zagitova may have seemed an unlikely contender for a gold medal. Only fifteen years old at the time of the competition, she was still in her first season on the senior-level figure-skating circuit, following several years of successful competition on the junior level. In addition to facing off against skaters from a range of countries, Zagitova faced competition from fellow Russian and training partner Evgenia Medvedeva, who was several years her senior and more experienced in high-level competition. While Medvedeva was widely favored to place first in the women's singles competition, Zagitova put forth a record-breaking effort that ultimately won her the gold to Medvedeva's silver. She likewise competed in the team skating competition, helping her team achieve a silver-medal finish.

The daughter of an ice hockey coach, Zagitova began skating as a young child and began training for a career in figure skating shortly after. A talented junior-level competitor, she moved to Moscow, Russia, in 2015, to train with noted coach Eteri Tutberidze. Tutberidze also trained Medvedeva, as well as several other successful skaters. Following wins at competitions such as the Russian Junior Figure Skating Championships and the World Junior Figure Skating Championships, Zagitova began her

By David W. Carmichael, via Wikimedia Commons

first professional season in September 2017, less than six months before her victories at the Olympics. Despite her success on the ice, Zagitova remained aware of the need for constant self-improvement, particularly as new challengers entered international competition. "There are no limits in figure skating, and it is good that it is developing, that a new generation of skaters is coming up that is better and more technical than the one before," she told Tatjana Flade for *Golden Skate* (9 June 2017). "I am trying not to stay behind the younger ones in our group. I am watching them. If they are doing something better than me, I am trying to do it even better."

EARLY LIFE AND EDUCATION

Zagitova was born on May 18, 2002, in Izhevsk, Russia. She was the first of two daughters born to Ilnaz Zagitov and Leysan Zagitova. Zagitova was not initially given a first name when she was born, due to her parents remaining undecided on what name to choose, but at the age of one was named Alina after the Russian gymnast Alina Kabaeva. She later came to admire Kabaeva, the winner of two Olympic medals and numerous world and European championships, and expressed a desire to meet her namesake.

Zagitova's father played ice hockey and later coached the sport during her childhood, and the family moved to towns such as Leninogorsk and Almetyevsk due to his career. They later returned to Izhevsk, where Zagitova lived until she was thirteen. Thanks to her father's work in hockey and her mother's own interest in figure skating, Zagitova was introduced to skating at a young age and began participating in figure skating by the time she was five. Having demonstrated her talent in the sport, she soon began extensive training in the hope of pursuing a career in competitive figure skating.

EARLY CAREER

In 2015, Zagitova moved to Moscow, Russia, to live with her grandmother while training with retired figure skater and accomplished coach Eteri Tutberidze at the Sambo 70 sports training school. Tutberidze was known for coaching accomplished skaters such as Olympic medalists Yulia Lipnitskaya and Evgenia Medvedeva. Early on in Zagitova's time with Tutberidze, Tutberidze expelled the young skater, as Zagitova was struggling to adjust to the coach's training style. However, Tutberidze ultimately decided to give Zagitova a second chance, a decision that would prove to be significant for the skater and coach.

While training with Tutberidze, Zagitova began to compete in major figure-skating competitions at the junior level. In 2016, she competed in the Russian Junior Figure Skating Championships, placing ninth in the women's division. The same season, she skated in two Junior

Grand Prix events, competitions overseen by the International Skating Union (ISU). Zagitova claimed first place at the Junior Grand Prix event in Saint-Gervais-les-Bains, France, and placed third in the Junior Grand Prix in Ljubljana, Slovenia. In December 2016, she won the ladies' singles division at the 2016–17 Junior Grand Prix Final in Marseille, France.

For Zagitova, her national and international junior-level competitions were a valuable learning experience that not only enabled her to adjust to the experience of competing in major events, but also allowed her to gain a greater understanding of the work needed to succeed on that level. "I learned about myself that I have character," she told Flade. "And while I was not able to cope with nerves the season before, I now with experience realize what I need to do." Zagitova competed in both the senior and junior divisions of the 2017 Russian Figure Skating Championships. She earned a silver medal in the senior division and a gold medal in the junior division. She then won her division at the 2017 World Junior Championships in Taiwan.

SENIOR CAREER

Zagitova began her first official senior season in late 2017. Based on Zagitova's talents and intensive training, Tutberidze had high hopes for the young skater. "I think her chances are very high," she told Flade. "If Alina is not slacking off in her work, I think she probably can fight for number two [in Russia]." Zagitova's first major competition of the season was the 2017 Lombardia Trophy in Italy, a competition within the ISU's Challenger Series. Zagitova placed first in the ladies' singles division at that event.

In addition to Challenger Series events and non-ISU competitions such as the Japan Open, Zagitova was selected to compete in two senior-level 2017 Grand Prix events, the Cup of China, held in Beijing, China, and the Internationaux de France, held in Grenoble, France. Zagitova claimed first place in both competitions. She then competed in the 2017–18 Grand Prix Final in Nagoya, Japan, where she earned a gold medal in the ladies' singles competition. Following the conclusion of the Grand Prix, Zagitova won a gold medal at the 2018 European Figure Skating Championships in Moscow. She later placed fifth in her division at the 2018 World Figure Skating Championships in Milan, Italy.

During events such as the Grand Prix Final, Zagitova became known for performing routines in which all of the jumps were confined to the second half of her program, or routine, a strategy known as "backloading." Zagitova herself called attention to that characteristic of her programs, telling Flade, "I do all my jumps in the second half and for it not to look like I'm doing only jumps, I had to do them exactly on the music with the other elements to make the components visible." The design of her programs proved controversial among some figure-skating commentators, as they appeared specifically designed to take advantage of a scoring rule stipulating that jumps performed during the second half of a skater's program receive a 10 percent scoring bonus. Nevertheless, Zagitova's performances received widespread acclaim, earning her both numerous medals and significant international attention.

2018 OLYMPICS

In 2018, Zagitova competed in the Winter Olympic Games in Pyeongchang, South Korea. Prior to the 2018 Games, the International Olympic Committee (IOC) suspended the Russian Olympic Committee for its handling of the use of performance-enhancing drugs among Russian athletes. The Russian Olympic Committee's suspension banned high-ranking Russian Olympic officials from appearing at the Olympics, as well as most Russian athletes from competing. The IOC later determined that Russian athletes without a history of using performance-enhancing drugs would be allowed to compete in the 2018 Olympics. The athletes competed as the Olympic Athletes from Russia (OAR), a neutral team competing under the Olympic flag, rather than as members of the Russian national team. Zagitova joined Medvedeva—widely considered a favorite to win her events before incurring a foot injury in 2017—as well as a number of other Russian figure skaters as members of the OAR.

Zagitova competed in two events during the 2018 Olympics, beginning with the team figure skating event. She placed first in the ladies' free skate competition during the team event, helping the OAR claim a silver medal. Following the team event, Zagitova competed in the ladies' single figure skating event, which consisted of the short program and free skating competitions. Zagitova achieved a world record score of 82.92 points in the short program, breaking the previous world record set by Medvedeva earlier in competition. She then tied with Medvedeva in the free skating phase of the competition, with a score of 156.65. Zagitova's combined total score of 239.57 points earned her the first-place finish. In addition to winning her first Olympic gold medal, the win made Zagitova the second-youngest woman to win an Olympic gold medal in ladies' single figure skating, after American skater Tara Lipinski in 1998.

As in earlier competitions, Zagitova backloaded her jumps in the programs she performed during the Olympics. Her decision to do so proved controversial in light of her victory over Medvedeva. Some figure-skating commentators who favored Medvedeva argued that the older skater's routines showed artistry, while Zagitova

won on technicality. "I think it's very obvious that I have the most difficult program in the world," Zagitova said in defense of her routines, as quoted by Chuck Culpepper for the *Washington Post* (21 Feb. 2018). Despite facing some criticism, she won praise from accomplished figure skaters such as Lipinski, who provided commentary during the 2018 Olympics. "What sets her apart is she has this fearlessness and the technical brilliance," Lipinski said of Zagitova, as quoted by Jeré Longman and Victor Mather for the *New York Times* (22 Feb. 2018). "I think she knows in a confident way that she's the best."

PERSONAL LIFE

Zagitova lives in Moscow. In addition to figure skating, she enjoys drawing. A lover of animals, Zagitova has several pets, including an Akita puppy named Masaru, who was given to her following her success at the Olympics by a Japanese organization dedicated to the breed, and a chinchilla.

SUGGESTED READING

Culpepper, Chuck. "When Researching Olympic Skater Alina Zagitova, It's Best Not to Read the Fine Print." *The Washington Post*, 21 Feb. 2018, www.washingtonpost.com/sports/olympics/when-researching-olympic-skater-alina-zagitova-its-best-not-to-read-the-fine-print/2018/02/21/cb6dc500-16dd-11e8-92c9-376b4fe57ff7_story.html. Accessed 9 June 2018.

Flade, Tatjana. "Russia's Alina Zagitova Prepares for Senior Debut." *Golden Skate*, 9 June 2017, goldenskate.com/2017/06/alina-zagitova/. Accessed 9 June 2018.

Janes, Chelsea, and Des Bieler. "Alina Zagitova Edges Past Evgenia Medvedeva to Win Gold, Canadian Kaetlyn Osmond Takes Bronze." *The Washington Post*, 23 Feb. 2018, www.washingtonpost.com/news/early-lead/wp/2018/02/22/pyeongchang-olympics-womens-figure-skating-live-updates-results-schedule-scores-analysis/. Accessed 9 June 2018.

Longman, Jeré, and Victor Mather. "Figure Skating: Alina Zagitova Wins Russia's First Gold Medal." *The New York Times*, 22 Feb. 2018, www.nytimes.com/2018/02/22/sports/olympics/womens-figure-skating.html. Accessed 9 June 2018.

Lutz, Rachel. "Who Is Alina Zagitova?" *NBC Olympics*, 11 Dec 2017, www.nbcolympics.com/news/who-alina-zagitova. Accessed 9 June 2018.

Turner, Amanda. "Figure Skating Star Alina Zagitova Most Admires Namesake Kabayeva." *International Gymnast*, 20 Feb. 2018, www.intl-gymnast.com/index.php?option=com_content&view=article&id=5014:figure-skating-star-alina-zagitova-most-admires-namesake-kaba

yeva&catid=2:news&Itemid=53. Accessed 9 June 2018.

Zaccardi, Nick. "Coach: Yevgenia Medvedeva Asked If Alina Zagitova Could Be Held Out of Olympics." *NBC Sports*, 7 May 2018, olympics.nbcsports.com/2018/05/07/yevgenia-medvedeva-alina-zagitova-eteri-tutberidze/. Accessed 9 June 2018.

—*Joy Crelin*

Henrik Zetterberg

Date of birth: October 9, 1980
Occupation: Hockey player

A fixture on the Detroit Red Wings since 2002, team captain Henrik "Hank" Zetterberg credits much of his success to his teammates and mentors within the franchise. "I played with many good leaders since I got here," he told *NHL.com* (15 Jan. 2013). "You try to take bits and pieces from all the guys that you play with, and they really formed the player who I am now." Indeed, over the course of two decades with the team, Zetterberg has become a force to be reckoned with. A consistent contributor who has often led his team both in points scored and number of games played in a season, he played a key role in the Red Wings' 2008 Stanley Cup victory as well as the team's many other appearances in the National Hockey League (NHL) playoffs.

A hockey player since childhood, Zetterberg first gained international notice as a member of Timrå IK and the national hockey team of his native Sweden before being drafted by the Red Wings in 1999. In addition to becoming a crucial member of that team over the years, he has likewise competed internationally for Sweden at events such as the Winter Olympics, helping claim a gold medal at the Torino games in 2006. Following the retirement of captain Nicklas Lidström, Zetterberg was named captain of the Red Wings in 2013. Although he has faced numerous challenges in his time as captain, including the Red Wings' disappointing 2016–17 and 2017–18 seasons, Zetterberg remains determined to help his teammates improve and tap into the team's true potential. "When you're done, you want to leave this place for the young kids who are going to take over, in a good spot," he told Alex Prewitt for *Sports Illustrated* (14 Feb. 2017).

EARLY LIFE

Zetterberg was born on October 9, 1980, in Njurunda, Sweden, to Ulla and Goran Zetterberg. His mother worked as an office supervisor, while his father, a former professional hockey player, coached the local hockey team. Zetterberg

By Michael Miller, via Wikimedia Commons

played both soccer and hockey as a child but began to focus exclusively on hockey in his early teens, having demonstrated significant talent on the ice while playing for local youth teams. In addition to playing hockey, the young Zetterberg worked for a time as a cleaner at a bowling alley in Njurunda. He also spent his early years watching horse racing with his father and grandfather, and as an adult he would buy stakes in several racing horses.

When Zetterberg was seventeen, he spent more than seven months serving in the Swedish military in accordance with the policy of compulsory military service for young men that was in place in Sweden at that time. Zetterberg soon determined that he was not well suited for military work. "We were supposed to sneak up on a group that was out in the woods," he recalled to Andrea Nelson for the website of the *Detroit Red Wings* (11 Nov. 2013). "All of a sudden we were surrounded by everyone else and they just started shooting, not real ones, but the fake machine gun. We were pretty scared then we realized we were probably not the best guys of sneaking up on the enemy." Despite such incidents, Zetterberg found his brief military service to be a valuable part of his late teen years. "It was kind of the first time we really had to take orders and do stuff like that and I think that's a good experience for us," he told Nelson.

EARLY CAREER

Zetterberg began playing high-level hockey in his late teens, joining the Timrå IK junior team at seventeen. He later played for the Timrå IK team in the Swedish Elite League, which named him rookie of the year in 2001 and player of the year in 2002. In addition to playing for Timrå IK, Zetterberg competed on an international level as a member of the Swedish national team, appearing in world championships and other major international tournaments.

Perhaps the most significant competition in Zetterberg's early career came in 2002, when he and his teammates on the Swedish national team took part in the Winter Olympics in Salt Lake City, Utah. The Swedish team defeated its opponents in the group stage but ultimately lost to Belarus in the quarterfinals. Despite that defeat, the Olympics was a formative experience for Zetterberg, in part because it was his first time playing against formidable players from the United States' National Hockey League. "I remember going on the ice for the first time to take a faceoff at the Olympics in Salt Lake City and when I looked up, there was [Canadian-born New York Rangers player] Eric Lindros standing across from me," he recalled to Larry Wigge for *NHL.com* (22 May 2008). "I must have been giving him five inches and about forty pounds in that matchup." The experience impressed on Zetterberg the importance of competing on an equal level with NHL veterans. "I knew I had to get bigger and stronger," he told Wigge.

DETROIT RED WINGS

Although Zetterberg played primarily in Sweden during his early career, he was eligible for the NHL Entry Draft and put himself forward for selection in 1999 despite his doubts about his chances. To the surprise of Zetterberg, who was on vacation with his parents at the time, he was chosen by the Detroit Red Wings in the seventh round of the draft. Following his selection, he resumed playing hockey in Sweden and did not initially join the Red Wings. He made his eventual debut with the team on October 10, 2002, in a game against the San Jose Sharks. Zetterberg spent nearly fifteen minutes on the ice and scored an assist during that first game. Over the course of his first season with the Red Wings, Zetterberg played in seventy-nine games and scored twenty-two goals and twenty-two assists. He was named rookie of the month in February 2003 and went on to be named to the NHL All-Rookie Team for the 2002–3 season. In April 2003, Zetterberg competed in his first Stanley Cup playoffs, scoring one goal over the course of the Red Wings' four unsuccessful games against the Mighty Ducks of Anaheim.

Throughout the subsequent years, Zetterberg established himself as a key member of the Red Wings, contributing to the team's successes during both the regular seasons and the playoffs. Although the life of a professional hockey player was challenging, Zetterberg continued to learn

and adjust. "It's a tough schedule. It's tough mentally. It's tough to be on it all the time," he told Prewitt. "But the more you play and the more time you spend in the league, that's what you learn, and that's what you have to get better at." Although primarily an NHL player by 2004, he returned to Sweden to play for Timrå IK again during the 2004–5 NHL lockout, in which a labor dispute led to the cancellation of the entire season. Regular NHL play resumed in the fall of 2005. During the 2006–7 season, Zetterberg (along with Teemu Selanne and Dany Heatley) led the league in game-winning goals achieved with ten.

STANLEY CUP

The Red Wings made regular appearances in the playoffs during Zetterberg's early years with the team, and in 2007, the team made it to the conference finals before falling once again to Anaheim. The following year, however, proved particularly significant for the franchise, which had last won the Stanley Cup in June 2002. After a successful regular season in which Zetterberg led the team in goals, the Red Wings entered the playoffs as the number-one team in the NHL's Central Division. After defeating the Nashville Predators, Colorado Avalanche, and Dallas Stars in the first stages of the competition, the team moved on to face the Pittsburgh Penguins in the Stanley Cup Finals. The Red Wings won four of the six games played in the finals, defeating the Penguins to claim the Stanley Cup. Named the most valuable player (MVP) of the tournament, Zetterberg was awarded the Conn Smythe Trophy for his contributions. "It's been unbelievable," he said following the deciding game of the finals, as quoted by *CBC Sports*. "It was tough losing that last game but we battled through that and came back today and played an unbelievable game."

Following the Red Wings' Stanley Cup win, the team managed another highly successful season, again claiming the top spot in the Central Division. In January 2009, midway through the season, Zetterberg signed a twelve-year contact extension worth about $72 million with the team. During the playoffs, the Red Wings again proceeded to the Stanley Cup Finals and once again faced the Pittsburgh Penguins. Although the team was unable to claim the Stanley Cup for a second year in a row, Zetterberg again made significant contributions to the team's postseason performance, leading the Red Wings in points scored during the playoffs.

In addition to experiencing success with the Red Wings, Zetterberg continued to compete for Sweden in international competitions, including the 2006 and 2010 Winter Olympic Games. In 2006, he was part of the Swedish team that claimed the gold medal in men's hockey at the games in Torino, Italy. Sweden was less successful at the 2010 games in Vancouver, Canada, losing to Slovakia in the quarterfinals. The Swedish men's hockey team fared far better at the 2014 games in Sochi, Russia, winning the silver medal in the tournament. Zetterberg, however, was unable truly to take part in that victory, as a painful back injury forced him to leave the competition after one game. He did not return to the Olympics in 2018, as the NHL opted not to pause its season to allow players to participate.

TEAM CAPTAIN

In January 2013, Zetterberg was named captain of the Red Wings following the retirement of former captain and fellow Swedish player Nicklas Lidström. For Red Wings leadership, Zetterberg was the natural choice for the position. "We have a good guy who's a real good human being, who loves hockey, who has a mind for the game, he's really good to his teammates and he's demanding of himself and he doesn't mind speaking his mind," the team's coach at the time, Mike Babcock, told *NHL.com* (15 Jan. 2013). "To me, that's pretty good leadership."

Zetterberg's tenure as captain was marked by significant changes for the team, including a shift from the Central Division to the Atlantic Division in 2013 and the team's move from the Joe Louis Arena to the Little Caesars Arena in 2017. Zetterberg also faced several difficult seasons for the Red Wings, during which the team struggled to win games. The team's performance during the 2016–17 season prevented the Red Wings from making it into the playoffs for the first time since 1990, and the team was again unable to secure a spot in that tournament the following year. Despite such setbacks, Zetterberg sought to remain positive. "You've just got to enjoy it as much as you can," he told Prewitt. "And not be as down as you've probably been before when you haven't played as good enough. Or, when the team's not doing well, you've got to find the good things and the happy things and try to keep your head up."

In the summer of 2017, hockey journalists reported that Zetterberg was considering retiring after the 2018–19 season. However, he later announced that he had no set plans for retirement and intended to keep playing for as long as he was physically able. "I'll go in the offseason and try to have a good summer, work on my health and hopefully I can come back and be better," he told Ted Kulfan for the *Detroit News* (3 Apr. 2018). "Health is the key," he added. "If I'm not healthy, it's over."

PERSONAL LIFE

Zetterberg married Swedish model and television personality Emma Andersson in 2010. Their son, Love, was born in 2015. Zetterberg and his wife are the founders of the Zetterberg Foundation, an organization dedicated to charitable work in the Detroit area as well as elsewhere in the world. He has received multiple awards in honor of his philanthropic efforts, including the 2012–13 NHL Foundation Player Award and the 2014–15 King Clancy Memorial Trophy.

SUGGESTED READING

Custance, Craig. "Henrik Zetterberg: Leaving a Lasting Impact on the Franchise." *The Athletic*, 18 Dec. 2017, theathletic.com/184069/2017/12/18/henrik-zetterberg-leaving-a-lasting-impact/. Accessed 13 Apr. 2018.

"Detroit Red Wings Win Stanley Cup." *CBC Sports*, 5 June 2008, www.cbc.ca/sports/hockey/detroit-red-wings-win-stanley-cup-1.700492. Accessed 13 Apr. 2018.

Kulfan, Ted. "Wings' Henrik Zetterberg Not Eyeing Retirement." *Detroit News*, 3 Apr. 2018, www.detroitnews.com/story/sports/nhl/redwings/2018/04/03/wings-henrik-zetterberg-eyeing-retirement/33517585/. Accessed 13 Apr. 2018.

Nelson, Andrea. "Zetterberg Remembers His Military Service." *Detroit Red Wings*, 11 Nov. 2013, www.nhl.com/redwings/news/zetterberg-remembers-his-military-service/c-691018. Accessed 13 Apr. 2018.

Prewitt, Alex. "Henrik Zetterberg Staying Upbeat as He Leads the Red Wings through a Frustrating Year." *Sports Illustrated*, 14 Feb. 2017, www.si.com/nhl/2017/02/14/henrik-zetterberg-red-wings-career-retirement. Accessed 13 Apr. 2018.

"Red Wings Name Henrik Zetterberg as Captain." *NHL.com*, 15 Jan. 2013, www.nhl.com/news/red-wings-name-henrik-zetterberg-as-captain/c-650507. Accessed 13 Apr. 2018.

Wigge, Larry. "Zetterberg Has Grown into an NHL Superstar." *NHL.com*, 22 May 2008, www.nhl.com/news/zetterberg-has-grown-into-an-nhl-superstar/c-371725. Accessed 13 Apr. 2018.

—*Joy Crelin*

Jenny Zhang

Date of birth: 1983
Occupation: Writer

Author Jenny Zhang won the 2018 PEN/Robert W. Bingham Prize for Debut Fiction, which carried a $25,000 prize, for her 2017 collection of short stories, *Sour Heart*. She became the first writer to be published by Lenny, an imprint of

Random House founded by actor Lena Dunham. Dunham said of Zhang, as quoted by Olivia Aylmer for *Vanity Fair* (31 July 2017), "Jenny is fatally honest, profoundly funny, and totally unafraid. What if Judy Blume and Salvador Dali took on immigrant life in America? You'd have Jenny Zhang." Zhang's writing crosses genres, including essay, poetry, and fiction. Her influences include the French and Greek poets she grew up reading, who wrote embodied literature. She told Nate Brown for the *Los Angeles Review of Books* (12 Aug. 2016), "Not every reader only has an appetite for the 'great' subjects. And now people with different appetites are finally being seen as a viable reading audience and also as viable creators of new writing that speaks to these other appetites."

EARLY LIFE AND EDUCATION

Zhang's family emigrated from Shanghai to the United States when she was five. The family lived among other Chinese families, and Zhang thought of herself as Chinese. She had to begin again with language to learn English, an experience that she says shaped her. Her Chinese remains at what she considers a third-grade level.

Zhang told Brown that she knew at an early age that she wanted to be a writer: "I have such a large fantasy world, and that world was what, very early on, made me want to be a writer. Writing was the space in which I could completely control and create that fantasy world. . . . I can't help but play with what is acceptable and what is unacceptable. In my writing-fantasy world, I get to decide that."

As a child, Zhang found validation in writing stories, where her ethnicity did not matter, and her intelligence could shine. Shy, she was able to express herself on the page and gain the notice of teachers who complimented her work. She also enjoyed reading narratives about growing up in the United States; Laura Ingalls Wilder's books were among her favorites.

Zhang attended Stanford University, from which she graduated in 2005. She went on to earn a master of fine arts from the prestigious Iowa Writers' Workshop. She told Stephanie Newman of *Los Angeles Review Books* (27 Sept. 2017) about the perils of graduate school: "I'm not sure how useful it's been for me to think of myself as just a poet or just a fiction writer. It was when I went to Iowa for grad school that the genres became so divided and defined. You were either a fiction writer or a poet, and you couldn't take a poetry workshop if you went for fiction and vice versa." It was only in her third year, when she took a class in translation and a group of thirty international writers visited campus, that she observed each had published in multiple genres.

Another effect of her graduate school experience was to move her away from minimalist literature. The voices in her later prose are speaking in run-on sentences, truer to life than the spare dialogue of many fiction writers. She spoke of her extravagance in language with T. Kira Madden for *Asian American Writers' Workshop* (7 Sept. 2017): "Why save and scrimp on language? It never made any sense to me. I want to be wasteful with language. I don't want to save up."

Zhang taught at the middle school and high school levels, as well as at the college level. In talking with Brown about teaching challenges, Zhang said, "It gets really intense to teach an intro to creative writing class—because you're not just asking them to change their habits as a reader, you're asking them to change the way that they relate to humanity and the way that they think about themselves."

POETRY AND NONFICTION

With Esmé Wang, whom Zhang met while they were in graduate school in the Midwest, she cofounded the blog *Fashion for Writers* in 2007. The two documented their outfits, worn far from the fashion world. Zhang also wrote nonfiction essays as a staff writer for *Rookie* magazine, an online publication whose target audience is adolescent girls. As she told Daniel Poppick for *Bomb Magazine* (24 Aug. 2017), writing for teenagers "sobered me up to the responsibility of having an audience. None of my poems were instantly viewed 100,000 times like my 2,000-word essays for *Rookie*. Whether I liked it or not, it changed the way I wrote. I still fiercely guard my illusion of freedom, but over time I've felt less free."

Zhang does feel free to write of her political beliefs and ideas in her essays, claiming to be more interested in questions than answers and not averse to mysteries. She focuses her attention on issues such as misogyny, white supremacy, and racism.

She resists attempts to turn her into a spokesperson for the experience of Asian Americans. As she told Madden, "It's very odd to be made so symbolic by these publications that are looking for me to speak more symbolically, looking for me to be representative of an entire group of people."

Although Zhang's emphasis at Iowa was in fiction, she wrote poetry on the side as well. Her first collection, *Dear Jenny, We Are All Find*, was published in 2012. *Hags*, a nonfiction chapbook, followed in 2014.

SOUR HEART

Zhang describes actor Lena Dunham as her fairy godmother. Dunham is perhaps best known for the HBO series *Girls*, but she also is a writer.

She and producer and writer Jenni Konner began the online feminist platform Lenny Letter in 2015, which published fiction and nonfiction. Random House published Dunham's memoir *Not That Kind of Girl*. Later, when the publishing house offered Dunham a Lenny imprint, she selected Zhang's short story collection as her first title.

Dunham was interested in young voices. Aylmer quoted Dunham as saying of her decision to publish Zhang, "We have always said we want to push the ball forward for women, for diversity, for L.G.B.T.Q. voices, and we aren't wavering from that mission. We want the Lenny Books logo to signify that you're about to dive into a world you have never entered before, or never entered with such humanity."

Dunham sent Zhang a tweet admiring her work. She later emailed, asking Zhang to be her opening act at Dunham's reading from *Not That Kind of Girl* in Iowa City. Despite misgivings that the email was fake, Zhang accepted. Dunham then asked if she had ever thought of working with an editor. At that point, Zhang had neither editor nor agent, but Dunham connected her with Andy Ward, the editor of Dunham's memoir. Zhang then reworked the stories she had written in graduate school. As she told Adalena Kavanagh for the website *Electric Literature* (7 Aug. 2017), "I had to mutilate most of these stories, cut entire pages out, add entire pages in, change almost every word on the page, but more than just aesthetic improvements, I had to re-envision what these stories were about. I had to change the story in some of the stories."

The 2017 collection contains seven loosely linked short stories set in the outer boroughs of New York City during the 1990s. The narrators are young Chinese American women who either immigrated to the United States as children or are the US–born children of immigrants. These are not typical stories of "model minority" immigrants, however. The parents in these stories were well-educated mainland Chinese people whose lives were disrupted by the Cultural Revolution of the 1960s and 1970s. They came to the United States and worked menial jobs, living with ten people in a small apartment, to survive. Zhang based some of the narratives on stories she had grown up hearing of life during the Cultural Revolution, though she was not attempting to write historical fiction.

The details of the characters are often based on Zhang's own experience: there are girls in the stories who were born in Shanghai, were raised in New York, or attended Stanford. In fact, Zhang used her early diaries as she wrote the stories during college and graduate school. Describing the compilation, Zhang told Newman, "I was interested in exploring four or five big questions in different ways over and over again."

Rather than create some kind of epic road for the reader to follow, I tried to create a house with many rooms. You can wander in and look here and there, and instead of feeling like you took a journey, you feel like you explored a house."

ON HER WRITING CRAFT

Frank Guan, in an interview for *Vulture* (1 Aug. 2017), asked Zhang if, in writing *Sour Heart*, she felt she was perhaps writing a novel rather than simply linked stories. Zhang responded, "I always felt I wasn't writing a pure short story—or maybe it felt like I was writing failed short stories? . . . But I also felt, at the same time, that I wasn't writing a novel. In the American conception of short fiction, the short story packs a wallop, and the novel is supposed to be this meandering epic."

In that book, Zhang deliberately chose to write her characters speaking as her own family does, in a mix of Chinese and English. The text contains Chinese characters, not set apart by italic or any special type, and sometimes not translated.

Zhang discovered that although she regarded writing about the female body as a craft-based choice rather than a political one, readers and critics did not always see it that way. As she told Newman, "It was not something that could actually be treated as an aesthetic choice. . . . Bodies gendered as women become political because they're so contested, and they're used as a proxy in all these cultural and political fights."

PERSONAL LIFE

Zhang lives in the Williamsburg neighborhood of Brooklyn, New York, although she still has family in Shanghai and visits there. She returned for the first time when she was nine, and then in four-year intervals. As an adult, concerned with the health of aging family members, she tries to visit annually.

Zhang told Guan, "My parents are very protective of me, and because we don't speak the same language fluently, I can seem very small and sheltered by my mother. . . . She doesn't get to see me excel as a person because she doesn't speak or read English very well. Even if I'm dazzling, she'll never really get to see that because I can only dazzle in the English language."

SUGGESTED READING

Aylmer, Olivia. "How Jenny Zhang Discovered Her Literary Fairy Godmother in Lena Dunham." *Vanity Fair*, 31 July 2017, www.vanityfair.com/culture/2017/07/jenny-zhang-book-sour-heart-lena-dunham-lenny. Accessed 23 Feb. 2018.

Zhang, Jenny. "Every Day a Funeral: Jenny Zhang and Nate Brown in Conversation." Interview by Nate Brown. *Los Angeles Review of Books*, 12 Aug. 2016, lareviewofbooks.org/article/every-day-funeral-jenny-zhang-nate-brown-conversation/. Accessed 22 Feb. 2018.

Zhang, Jenny. "Author Jenny Zhang on China, Family, Class, and Her Short-Story Collection *Sour Heart*." Interview by Frank Guan. *Vulture*, 1 Aug. 2017, www.vulture.com/2017/08/author-jenny-zhang-talks-her-new-book-sour-heart.html. Accessed 1 Mar. 2018.

Zhang, Jenny. "Daniel Poppick and Jenny Zhang." Interview by Daniel Poppick. *Bomb Magazine*, 24 Aug. 2017, bombmagazine.org/articles/daniel-poppick-and-jenny-zhang/. Accessed 28 Feb. 2018.

Zhang, Jenny. "Wasteful with Language: An Interview with Jenny Zhang." Interview by T. Kira Madden. *Asian American Writers Workshop*, 7 Sept. 2017, aaww.org/wasteful-with-language-jenny-zhang/. Accessed 1 Mar. 2018.

Zhang, Jenny. "Writing 'Goopily' about the Body: An Interview with Jenny Zhang on 'Sour Heart.'" Interview by Stephanie Newman. *Los Angeles Review of Books*, 27 Sept. 2017, lareviewofbooks.org/article/writing-goopily-about-the-body-an-interview-with-jenny-zhang-on-sour-heart/. Accessed 22 Feb. 2018.

SELECTED WORKS

Dear Jenny, We Are All Find, 2012; *Hags*, 2014; *Sour Heart*, 2017

—*Judy Johnson*

Chloé Zhao

Date of birth: March 31, 1982
Occupation: Director

Chloé Zhao believes in the universality of human storytelling and the power of the human spirit in overcoming obstacles, no matter how difficult. The Chinese-born, US-educated film director is particularly enamored with telling the stories of people in the American West, where, in her view, the open country provides individuals the opportunity to discover their own identities. Zhao did that herself, when she moved from New York to the Pine Ridge Reservation in South Dakota.

Her first two feature-length films, *Songs My Brothers Taught Me* (2015) and *The Rider* (2017), are both set on the Pine Ridge Reservation and explore the dynamic of characters struggling with identity and belonging. In particular, *The Rider*—a fictionalized account of Brady Blackburn (Brady Jandreau), a Lakota rodeo star in his teens who is trying to return to riding after a life-threatening injury—garnered critical acclaim and a host of accolades. The film has

Photo by Amanda Edwards/Getty Images

been lauded for its presentation of the triumph of the human spirit, without the sentimentality depicted in many more traditional Westerns. "At a time like this, there's a need to see that there's good in America," she said in an interview with John Powers for *Vogue* (22 Mar. 2018). "We're always being told that we have to win all the time. But that's not real life. Our film's message isn't the typical Hollywood ending. Brady has lost something, but he doesn't give up. He never would. . . . I would never want to make a film without hope."

EARLY LIFE, EDUCATION AND CAREER

Chloé Zhao was born Zhao Ting in Beijing, China, on March 31, 1983. Her father was a manager of a steel company; her mother was a hospital worker who had previously been in a performance troupe for the People's Liberation Army (PLA). During her formative years, she wrote fan fiction and drew manga, but was an indifferent student. Her one passion was going to the movies. She fell in love with *Happy Together*, a 1997 Hong Kong romance film directed by Wong Kar-wai that has since served as a touchstone for her career. When she was fifteen, her parents sent her to a boarding school in England, which she has described in interviews as being something like Hogwarts, the imaginary school of wizardry from the Harry Potter book series by J. K. Rowling.

Zhao then attended college in the United States. She enrolled at Mount Holyoke in Massachusetts, where she studied political science, but was not inspired to pursue a career in public service as she had hoped. "When you're 18 years old, you feel very passionate and also try to understand how we treat each other and why things happen," she said to Sandy Cohen for *American Way* (Mar. 2018). "But I just felt discouraged about the idea of working in politics."

When she graduated, Zhao settled in New York and took on odd jobs as a bartender, party promoter, and real estate agent, before deciding to apply to the film program at New York University's Tisch School of the Arts. It was here that she found her calling. As a novice filmmaker, Zhao produced a number of short films, including *Post* (2008), *The Atlas Mountains* (2009), and *Benachin* (2011). But it was her short film *Daughters* (2010) that garnered her early attention. After debuting at the Clermont-Ferrand International Short Film Festival, it won best student live-action short at the 2010 Palm Springs International ShortFest and the special jury prize at the 2010 Cinequest Film Festival.

SONGS MY BROTHERS TAUGHT ME

Zhao was living in a trendy part of Brooklyn, New York, and feeling somewhat at odds with the frenetic pace of life in the city, when her life again made a sudden shift. She was reading a newspaper account of an outbreak of suicides among American Indian teens and was inspired to get her driver's license, move west, and look for stories to tell via film. "I came across some images of a reservation, and even within one frame, there's so much contradiction," Zhao said to Matt Mullen for *Interview*. "You see this young Lakota boy on a horse, but in an urban hip-hop outfit, and it's next to this really rundown government housing. But then behind that is the most beautiful landscape."

Zhao eventually found her way to the Pine Ridge Reservation in South Dakota, where she stayed for months at a time, in motels or teacher housing, even in the basement of a church. In time, the people there came to accept her as someone who was not looking to use or exploit them for their stories, but who really wanted to get to know them. During her time on the reservation, the kernels of a story began to gel and inspired her first feature-length film, *Songs My Brothers Taught Me* (2015), about a teenager named Johnny Winters (John Reddy), who is debating whether to stay on the reservation, which is plagued by poverty and alcoholism, or follow his girlfriend Aurelia (Taysha Fuller). Aurelia is heading to college in California, where she hopes to become a lawyer one day. Johnny is one of twenty-five children from nine wives of a deceased bull rider. Part of what is keeping him on the reservation is his eleven-year-old sister, Jashaun (Jashaun St. John), who loves him dearly.

Shot in a documentary style and lightly fictionalized to fit a film narrative, *Songs My Brothers Taught Me* was praised when it was first released. In a review for the *New York Times* (1 Mar. 2016), Stephen Holden wrote: "Because [Zhao's] laissez-faire approach makes little effort to fit the fragmentary scenes into a tidy portrait of reservation life, 'Songs My Brothers Taught Me' feels more authentic than if she had chosen to impose a tighter structure. You come at the story, such as it is, as a visitor from the outside world, picking up information as the movie goes along." Holden also touted Joshua James Richards's cinematography: "Whether the camera observes horseback riders atop a bluff or a distant thunderstorm on the horizon, you are mesmerized by the desolate beauty of the Great Plains and the changing sky overhead."

THE RIDER

The promise Zhao showed as a filmmaker with *Songs My Brothers Taught Me* was fulfilled in her next feature-length production, *The Rider*, which premiered at the 2017 Director's Fortnight at the Cannes Film Festival, where it won the top prize, the Art Cinema Award, presented by the International Confederation of Art Cinemas. The film also earned Zhao nominations for best feature and best director at the Independent Spirit Awards, where, in January 2018, Zhao was presented with the inaugural American Airlines Bonnie Award, named for Bonnie Tiburzi Caputo, the first female pilot to fly for a major US airline. The award is given to promising female directors, and comes with a $50,000 grant.

Like her previous film, *The Rider* was set on the Pine Ridge Reservation. It follows the life of a rodeo horseman named Brady Blackburn. Blackburn's story is based on events in the life of the actor who portrays him, Brady Jandreau. In the film, Blackburn is nearly killed after having his head trampled by a bucking bronco. The story follows his attempts to find his way in life again after being told by doctors that his bronco riding days are over. The wound in his head—more than three inches wide and an inch deep—leaves him with a steel plate and occasional seizures, including an inability to use his left hand properly. Blackburn attempts to work ordinary jobs and comes close to selling his prize saddle before meeting a horse named Apollo, with whom he has an immediate and instinctive bond. The remainder of the film occupies itself with what Blackburn will do now that he has met the horse of his dreams.

In addition to earning awards, *The Rider* was also met with nearly universal acclaim. In a review for the *Washington Post* (18 Apr. 2018), Ann Hornaday wrote: "'The Rider' reinvigorates tropes from the western genre of men, horses, honor codes and vast expanses of nature with a refreshing lack of sentimentality, without sacrificing their inherent lyricism and poetry. . . . Zhao is a filmmaker of extraordinary tact and insight: She has taken a story that could have been unremarkable or too romanticized and made it into something honest, magnificent and lasting." Similarly, Justin Chang of the *Los Angeles Times* (10 Apr. 2018), remarked: "With its gorgeous frontier lyricism and its wrenchingly intimate story of a young man striving to fulfill what he considers his God-given purpose, 'The Rider' comes as close to a spiritual experience as anything I've encountered in a movie theater this year."

FORTHCOMING PROJECTS

Zhao was tapped by Amazon Studios in 2018 to direct a biopic of Bass Reeves, the first black man to become a United States deputy marshal. After being born into slavery, Reeves became one of the most esteemed lawmen of the Old West.

Zhao is also at work on a science fiction feature film that takes place in northwestern China. Although the project is a departure for Zhao from the Western stories she has focused on thus far, she welcomes the change. "I'm not someone who takes on one identity and lets it form my whole being," Zhao told Matt Mullen for *Interview*. "I think I'm more a jack of all trades. It would be very freeing to be like, 'This is the one thing I do, and this is who I am.'" At the same time, the project continues her exploration of setting and identity, including her own. As she said to Cohen, "One of the identities I feel like I'm questioning is my identity as a human, not even as a woman or a woman of color—but as a human being."

PERSONAL LIFE

Zhao lives in Ojai, California, with her partner, cinematographer Joshua James Richards. The two met while they were film students at New York University. Richards shares Zhao's interest in the American West, and was the director of photography on both *Songs* and *The Rider*.

SUGGESTED READING

Chang, Justin. "Chloé Zhao's Cowboy Drama 'The Rider' Is a Moving, Lyrical Tale of Loss and Recovery." Review of *The Rider*, directed by Chloé Zhao. *Los Angeles Times*, 10 Apr. 2018, www.latimes.com/entertainment/movies/la-et-mn-the-rider-review-20180410-story.html. Accessed 13 Aug. 2018.

Cohen, Sandy. "Filmmaker Chloé Zhao Is the Accidental Realist." *American Way*, Mar. 2018. magazines.aa.com/en/features/2018/02/filmmaker-chloy-zhao-is-the-accidental-realist. Accessed 13 Aug. 2018.

Holden, Stephen. "Review: In 'Songs My Brothers Taught Me,' Reservation Dreams and Their Limits." *The New York Times*, 1 Mar. 2016, www.nytimes.com/2016/03/02/movies/songs-my-brothers-taught-me-review.html. Accessed 13 Aug. 2018.

Hornaday, Ann. "'The Rider,' Starring a Real Rodeo Horseman, Is a Breath of Fresh Prairie Air for Westerns." Review of *The Rider*, by Chloé Zhao. *The Washington Post*, 18 Apr. 2018, www.washingtonpost.com/goingoutguide/movies/the-rider-starring-a-real-rodeo-horseman-is-a-breath-of-fresh-prairie-air-for-westerns/2018/04/18/85e1e6de-3dce-11e8-a7d1-e4efec6389f0_story.html. Accessed 18 Apr. 2018.

Mullen, Matt. "The Rider Is an Early Contender for Best Film of 2018." *Interview Magazine*, 13 Apr. 2018, www.interviewmagazine.com/film/the-rider-chloe-zhao-is-an-early-contender-for-best-film-of-2018. Accessed 13 Aug. 2018.

N'Duka, Amanda. "Amazon Studios Lands Biopic on Bass Reeves, First Black U.S. Deputy Marshal, from 'The Rider' Helmer Chloé Zhao." *Deadline*, 20 Apr. 2018, deadline.com/2018/04/amazon-bass-reeves-biopic-the-rider-chloe-zhao-1202373293/. Accessed 13 Aug. 2018.

Powers, John. "How Chloé Zhao Reinvented the Western." *Vogue*, 22 Mar. 2018, www.vogue.com/article/chloe-zhao-the-rider-vogue-april-2018. Accessed 13 Aug. 2018.

SELECTED WORKS

Daughters, 2010; Songs *My Brothers Taught Me*, 2016; *The Rider*, 2017

—*Christopher Mari*

OBITUARIES

Amsale Aberra

Born: Addis Ababa, Ethiopia; March 1, 1954
Died: New York, New York; April 1, 2018
Occupation: Fashion designer

Amsale Aberra is most well known for her simple, minimalist wedding dress designs. Celebrities like Julia Roberts, Halle Berry, and Katharine Gershman have worn her dresses, and her work has also appeared in films such as *Runaway Bride*, *27 Dresses*, and *The Hangover*.

Amsale Aberra was born in 1954 in Addis Ababa, Ethiopia, to Aberra Moltot and Tsadale Assamnew. Her father, Moltot, was the vice minister of national community development in Emperor Haile Selassie's government. In 1974, Aberra moved to Poultney, Vermont, to study commercial art at Green Mountain College. However, during her first year of studies, Haile Selassie's government was overthrown, and her father was imprisoned. Unable to pay for her college tuition, Aberra moved to Boston to live with her half-sister, Aster Yilma. By working small jobs, Aberra was able to support herself in attending Boston State College where she received a degree in political science in 1981. While waitressing at a coffee shop, Aberra met her husband, Clarence O'Neil Brown III. After graduating, Aberra moved with Brown to New York City where she attended the Fashion Institute of Technology (FIT), graduating in 1982 with a degree in fashion design. After graduation Aberra began working as a showroom manager for designer Harvé Benard and eventually became his design assistant. While planning her wedding in 1985, Aberra discovered that no designers were making the simple, elegant wedding dresses she desired, so she designed her own dress. After her success, Aberra placed an advertisement in a national bridal magazine. Receiving many calls for gowns, Aberra and her husband launched the Amsale Bridal Collection, operating out of her loft apartment. In 1990, Aberra sold her first designs to Kleinfeld's, the country's largest wedding-dress retailer. In 1997 she opened her own boutique, Nouvelle Amsale, on Madison Avenue, selling evening gowns, cocktail dresses, and evening separates. Aberra became a leader in New York's black business community and has received many awards, including the Legacy Award at the 2012 Black Enterprise Women of Power Summit. She has twice been listed among *Ebony* magazine's Power 150 list of influential African Americans. She also served on the board of the Ethiopian Children's Fund.

Aberra is survived by her husband and their daughter, Rachel. Her father, Moltot, and her half-sister, Aster, also survive.

See *Current Biography* 2005

Daniel K. Akaka

Born: Honolulu, Hawaii; September 11, 1924
Died: Honolulu, Hawaii; April 6, 2018
Occupation: US Senator

Daniel Akaka was the first native Hawaiian to serve in either house of the US Congress. A liberal Democrat, Akaka spent much of his career dedicated to advocating for the rights of native Hawaiians, welfare, and environmental protection.

Daniel Akaka was born in Honolulu, Hawaii, to Annie and Kahikina Akaka. He attended Kamehameha School and graduated in 1942 before joining the US Army Corps of Engineers at the end of World War II. After serving, Akaka attended the University of Hawaii and received a bachelor's degree in education in 1952. From 1953 to 1960, Akaka taught elementary school and eventually became a vice principal. He was appointed as principal of the school in 1963. Akaka received a master's degree in education from the University of Hawaii in 1966 and then went to work as the chief programming planner for the Hawaii Department of Education. From 1971 to 1974, Akaka served as the director of the Office of Economic Opportunity and then from 1975 to 1976, served as the director for the Progressive Neighborhoods program. During this same year, Akaka served as the human-resources special assistant to the governor of Hawaii. In 1976, Akaka won the Democratic nomination for Hawaiian Second District Congressman and thus became the first native Hawaiian to serve in either house of the US Congress. Akaka served for fourteen years in the US House of Representatives and held a seat on the Appropriations Committee. In 1990, Akaka was elected to the US Senate and was re-elected in 1994, 2000, and 2006. Akaka decided to retire in 2011. During his time in Congress, Akaka pushed for legislation for the US government to apologize for overthrowing the Hawaiian government in 1893 and for compensation to restore homelands wrongfully taken by the US government.

Akaka is survived by his wife, Mary Mildred Chong, their five children, Millannie, Daniel Jr., Gerard, Alan, and Nicholas, and several grandchildren and great-grandchildren.

See *Current Biography* 2001

Azzedine Alaïa

Born: Tunis, Tunisia; February 26, 1935
Died: Paris, France; November 18, 2017
Occupation: Fashion designer

The world-renowned fashion designer, Azzedine Alaïa, was sometimes referred to as an artist or sculptor. Many famous women, from Michelle Obama to Lady Gaga, wore his designs.

The date of Azzedine Alaïa's birth is not known for certain. Some reports have his birth year as 1935, whereas others consider 1939 or 1940 as his true birth year. He was born to a Tunisian wheat farmer and had a twin sister and a younger brother. From a very early age, Alaïa enjoyed art, and his mother's French midwife introduced him to *Vogue* magazine and encouraged him to study sculpture at the École nationale supérieure des Beaux-Arts. His career in fashion began when he began sewing hems for a dressmaker's shop. Along the way, he began designing fashion for individuals, two of whom introduced Alaïa to a dressmaker specializing in making copies of haute couture designs. In 1957 Alaïa landed a job with Christian Dior, and several years later he moved to Guy Laroche. He also spent five years as a housekeeper for the Marquise de Mazan, cooking Tunisian dishes and looking after the children. Through the influential family Alaïa gained access to a wealthy clientele, and he began a made-to-order business. With the social upheavals of 1968, young women were abandoning haute couture, and Alaïa picked up a market for his body-hugging, curvaceous designs. *Elle* magazine featured his work in the 1980s. In 1982 he held his first show in the United States at Bergdorf Goodman, and sales skyrocketed. In 1984 and 1985 the Museum of Modern Art (MoMA) in Bordeaux gave him a retrospective. From 1988 to 1992, Alaïa's boutique flourished at 131 Mercer Street in New York City. Stars and dignitaries around the world were wearing his designs. Following the year 2000, Alaïa began picking up investors, including Compagnie Financière Richemont, a Swiss group known for investing in Van Cleef & Arpels and Cartier. Alaïa also created work for the opera and ballet, and he began holding art exhibitions.

Azzedine Alaïa never married, but his life partner, Christoph von Weyhe, a painter, survives.

See *Current Biography* 1992

Samir Amin

Born: Cairo, Egypt; September 3, 1931
Died: Paris, France; August 12, 2018
Occupation: Economist, educator

Samir Amin was the former director of the Third World Forum, a group of intellectuals dedicated to promoting social and economic growth in third world regions of the world. A modern Marxist, Amin was sometimes referred to as a radical economist. He published over thirty books and numerous scholarly articles.

Samir Amin was born in Cairo, Egypt, to two medical doctors. His mother, Odette, was of French descent. She charged higher rates to her wealthy patients, so she could also treat the poor for free. Amin's Egyptian father, Farid, was a public health official in Port Said. As a boy, Samir Amin was deeply affected after seeing a child dig through the trash for food and vowed he would change society. He moved to Paris in 1949 where he studied economics and political science at the secondary school, Lycée Henri IV. In 1952 he received a diploma from the Institute of Political Science and a law degree the following year. He joined France's Communist Party and the French students' union, while also editing the student paper, *Etudiants anticolonialistes*. He received a graduate degree in political economics and a mathematical statistician's diploma from the French Institute of Statistics. He was invited to Mali where he became an economic adviser to the government. In 1963 Amin left Mali for a position at the African Institute for Economic Development and Planning (IDEP), an institute formed by the United Nations in 1962, which trained African policy makers and development officials. He was director of the organization from 1970 to 1980. While there, he also helped found the Council for the Development Research in Africa. In 1980 he became the director of the Third World Forum, a think tank that studied the impact of capitalism on people of the Third World. In 1997 the organization expanded to worldwide concerns, becoming the World Economic Forum, which congregates world leaders. Amin coined the term "Eurocentrism," to describe how non-European histories are perceived through a European lens. Amin's most important publications include *The Accumulation on a World Scale: A Critique of the Theory of Underdevelopment*. In 1990 he published his autobiography, *Itinéraire intellectuel*.

See *Current Biography* 2012

Kofi Annan

Born: Kumasi, Ghana; April 8, 1938
Died: Bern, Switzerland; August 18, 2018
Occupation: Former secretary-general of the UN, Ghanaian diplomat, Nobel laureate

Kofi Annan was a Ghanaian diplomat who served two five-year terms as the secretary-general of the United Nations (UN) from 1997 to 2007. He was the first black African to serve as secretary-general. He was awarded the Nobel Peace Prize in 2001.

Kofi Annan was born to an aristocratic family in Ghana, then known as the Gold Coast, the first British colony in Africa to gain independence. He attended the prestigious Methodist Mfantsipim boarding school and then studied economics at the University of Science and Technology in Kumasi, Ghana, and at Macalester College in St. Paul, Minnesota, before continuing his graduate studies at the Institut des Hautes Études Internationales, in Geneva, Switzerland, and at the Massachusetts Institute of Technology (MIT). Annan spent nearly his entire working career at the UN, first with the World Health Organization (WHO), and with the UN Economic Commission for Africa. In the early 1990s, Boutros Boutros Ghali, then UN secretary-general, appointed him first deputy in charge of peacekeeping, placing Annan in the middle of the Rwandan genocide in 1994 and the Bosnian genocide in 1995, events that would haunt him for the rest of his life. On January 1, 1997, Annan took office as the UN secretary-general, where he established his reputation as a peacekeeper, always seeking diplomacy over force, and consensus building over discord. He instituted organizational reform, streamlining UN bureaucracy. At the time, the UN employed more than 50,000 workers in thirty agencies worldwide. Writing for The New York Times (18 Aug. 2018), Alan Cowell quoted author Michael Ignatieff as writing of Annan, "Few people have spent so much time around negotiating tables with thugs, warlords and dictators. He has made himself the world's emissary to the dark side." Annan came out vehemently against the US invasion of Iraq in 2003, claiming it was an illegal action, winning him no friends in the US Bush administration. Upon retiring from the UN, he joined Nelson Mandela's group of humanitarians and world leaders known as "the Elders," who are dedicated to peace and humanitarian rights. He chaired the organization from 2013 until his death. He also created the Kofi Annan Foundation, dedicated to overcoming obstacles to peace, development, and human rights.

Kofi Annan's death was a shock to world leaders. His survivors include his wife, Nane Lagergren, his three children, and his brother Kobina Annan.

See *Current Biography* 2002

Shoko Asahara

Born: Yatsushiro, Kumamoto, Japan; March 2, 1955
Died: Tokyo, Japan; July 6, 2018
Occupation: Cult leader

Shoko Asahara was the founder and leader of the Japanese cult, Aum Shinrikyo. Asahara was sentenced to death in 2004 after orchestrating the 1995 sarin gas attack on the Tokyo subways, killing thirteen people and injuring over 6,000.

Born Chizuo Matsumoto, Asahara was born on the southern Japanese island of Kyushu, with four brothers and two sisters. Born blind in one eye and visually impaired in his second, Asahara went to a government-run school for the blind until he was twenty years old. In 1982 Asahara and his wife founded the Heavenly Blessing, and two years later Asahara founded Aum Shinsen no Kai, the precursor to Aum Shinrikyo. Aum Shinsen no Kai ran several businesses, including a yoga school, a health drink company, and a book publishing firm, all managed by Asahara. Specifics of the cult's actions at this time are still not fully known. Asahara traveled to the Himalayas on 1987 and claimed to have received from the Dalai Lama secret teachings enabling him to levitate, see through objects, meditate underwater for up to six hours, and to have achieved full enlightenment. Upon his return he adopted his present name, Shoko Asahara. In his 1989 book, *The Destruction of the World*, Asahara described a disastrous war, which he predicted would take place around 1997, between the United States and Japan. In August 1989, after extensive lobbying, Aum Shinrikyo was officially recognized as a religious organization under the religious corporation law. After Asahara's failure to win election to the Japanese legislature, the cult began administering drugs to many of the members to increase compliance. A series of violent terrorist activities led up to the 1995 sarin gas subway attack, in which five Aum Shinrikyo members placed eleven packets of sarin gas on three separate Tokyo subway lines on March 20, 1995. A total of thirteen people died and an estimated 6,000 were injured. After two months, Asahara was arrested, along with over one hundred of his members. He was charged with seventeen criminal acts, including masterminding the March 1995 subway attack, ordering the June 1994 Matsumoto attack, killing two cult members, and murdering the lawyer Tsutsumi Sakamoto and his family. He was convicted and sentenced to death in 2004.

Shoko Asahara is survived by his wife, Tomoko Ishii, their two sons and four daughters, all of whom were involved with the cult. Tomoko Ishii was arrested along with Asahara but was released in 2002.

See *Current Biography* 2003

Charles Aznavour

Born: Paris, France; May 22, 1924
Died: Mouriès, France; October 1, 2018
Occupation: Songwriter, singer, actor

Charles Aznavour was a world-renowned French songwriter, composer, and singer, who wrote more than a thousand songs (by his own estimation) and sold records in the hundreds of millions. He appeared in more than sixty films. He was often referred to as the French Frank Sinatra.

Though born in Paris, Charles Aznavour was an Armenian at heart. His parents, who were thought to be singers themselves certainly instilled a love of music in their son, went to France to avoid Turkish persecution in Armenia. They enrolled their son in acting school when he was just nine, and he became part of a troupe of child actors. In his younger years, Aznavour wrote for Édith Piaf, arguably France's greatest pop singer, spending eight years in her entourage, even following her to New York, working as her secretary. Though considering himself more of a songwriter than performer, Aznavour still performed his songs throughout Belgium and France, in working-class cafés. (Some of his songs were deemed too risqué for radio.) In 1956 he was touring in North Africa when the director of the Paris Moulin Rouge heard him sing at a casino in Marrakesh and signed him. From then on, he was never out of work. In 1963 he rented out Carnegie Hall and performed before a sold-out audience. Other New York venues included Radio City Music Hall and Madison Square Garden. Some of his most recognized songs in the United States are "She" and "Yesterday When I Was Young," which was also the title of his 2003 autobiography. Aznavour also never forgot his Armenian roots, becoming an ambassador and spokesman for Armenian refugees, and raising funds for the victims of a 1988 earthquake that killed 45,000.

At the time of his death at age 94, Aznavour still had singing engagements on his calendar. His survivors include his wife Ulla (nee Thorsel) and five children.

See *Current Biography* 1968

Dennis Banks

Born: Leech Lake Reservation, Minnesota; April 12, 1937
Died: Rochester, Minnesota; October 29, 2017
Occupation: Native American activist, co-founder of the American Indian Movement

In 1968 Dennis Banks helped co-found the American Indian Movement (AIM) with the mission of promoting Native American self-sufficiency and drawing attention to the deplorable plight of US Native Americans. Along with other AIM leaders, Banks staged the occupation of the former California state penitentiary at Alcatraz Island, the Bureau of Indian Affairs in Washington DC, and the hamlet of Wounded Knee, to earn recognition of century-old treaty rights the United States had been ignoring.

Dennis Banks was born on the Leech Lake Indian Reservation in Minnesota and was abandoned to his grandparents who raised him. He spent most of his childhood in boarding schools run by the Bureau of Indian Affairs (BIA) in accordance with the Indian Reorganization Act of 1934. In 1953 Banks joined the United States Air Force and was stationed in Japan where he married a Japanese woman and had a child. He went absent without leave (AWOL), was arrested and returned to the United States, never to see his wife and child again. At home in Minnesota Banks engaged in petty crime serving two and a half years in jail. Upon his release he and a fellow inmate, Clyde Bellecourt, formed the AIM to help fight poverty, exercise their civil rights, and fight for equal treatment under the law. The organization came to fame by staging an occupation of Alcatraz to call attention to the plight of life on Indian reservations. In 1973, after a white man killed an Indian in Custer, South Dakota, Banks led a group of two hundred Indians in a protest that turned into a riot. Several weeks later, the AIM launched a standoff at Wounded Knee where shots were fired. Banks was charged and became a fugitive from the law. He eventually turned himself in and served fourteen months of a three-year sentence.

Following his incarceration, Banks became an addiction counselor. He also appeared in several movies and documentaries. In addition to his wife and child in Japan, Dennis Banks is survived by nineteen children and one hundred grandchildren.

See *Current Biography* 1992

Roger Bannister

Born: London, England; March 23, 1929
Died: Oxford, England; March 3, 2018
Occupation: Athlete, physician

On 6 May 1954 Roger Bannister broke the four-minute mile, with a time of 3:59.4. He was the first man to do so. In June of 1955, Queen Elizabeth made him a Commander of the British Empire. Shortly thereafter, Bannister retired from competition to focus on his medical studies.

Roger Bannister was born to Ralph and Alice (Duckworth) Bannister. His father was a treasury official. Bannister claimed that he was driven to athletics out of his fear of "not belonging." At thirteen he won his first race at a cross-country match near Bath, England. He attended University College School in London where he continued his running practice. In 1946 he entered Exeter College at Oxford University to study medicine. There he discovered his athletic ability was greater than most runners. He became the captain of a joint Oxford-Cambridge track team. In 1952, after earning his degree at Oxford, he attended the Olympic games in Helsinki, Finland, where he finished in a disappointing fourth place. His perceived failure motivated Bannister to train hard, though he remained out of competition for a year while attending St. Mary's Hospital Medical School in London. In the spring of 1954, Bannister broke the four-minute mile at the Iffley Road track in Oxford with the time of 3:59.4 minutes. His career in international athletic competition was short-lived, however, as he chose to focus on his medical career rather than continuing with the extensive training regimen his sport required. In addition to becoming a medical doctor, Bannister became the director of the National Hospital for Nervous Diseases in London. He continued his association with sports by serving as the chairman of the British Sports Council. Later he served as president of the International Council of Sport Science and Physical Recreation.

In 1955, Roger Bannister married Moyra Jacobsson, the daughter of the economist and soon-to-be managing director of the International Monetary Fund (IMF), Per Jacobsson. Bannister and his wife, Moyra had four children. His wife and children survive.

See *Current Biography* 1956

Art Bell

Born: Jacksonville, North Carolina; June 17, 1945
Died: Pahrump, Nevada; April 13, 2018
Occupation: Radio broadcaster and author

Arthur Bell is most known for his nightly broadcasts of "Coast to Coast AM," a five-hour radio show on the paranormal. He notoriously spoke with listeners and aired unscreened recounts of paranormal encounters. Broadcasting throughout the 1990s, Bell created a large, enthusiastic following. He penned several books in the late 1990s.

Arthur Bell III was born in Jacksonville, North Carolina, to Arthur William Bell, Jr. and Jane Lee Gumaer Bell. At the age of twelve, Bell received his first ham radio license and at thirteen, he received his radio technician's license from the Federal Communications Commission (FCC). Bell had his first radio job reading news for a religious channel in New Jersey at the age of fifteen. He briefly attended the University of Maryland but quit to join the US Air Force, based in Texas. There, Bell and a friend set up a pirate (illegal) radio station for the base camp. After leaving the Air Force, Bell worked for several different radio stations. In 1970, while working at KENI radio station in Anchorage, Alaska, he broke the world record for longest consecutive hours broadcast by a single individual, totaling 116 hours. The same year, Bell chartered a DC-8 to rescue orphaned children left behind during the Vietnam War. Following a brief television stint, Bell joined the radio station KDWN, outside of Las Vegas, Nevada. There he began broadcasting about paranormal activities, including UFO sightings. Due to the increasing popularity of his show, Bell was offered a syndication for his program in 1984, which led to the creation of his well-known radio program, "Coast to Coast AM." The show ended in 1998, after Bell announced his departure to fans, spurring fear and suspicion from his fans. It was later determined that Bell left the show due to a family emergency pertaining to his son's involvement in a lawsuit. Bell announced his retirement from radio in 2000 following rumors that he molested children. The rumors were misguided, conflating the facts of his son, Art Bell IV's, lawsuit against a former teacher.

Art Bell married four times. He is survived by his fourth wife, Airyn Ruiz, their two children, Asia and Alexander, and three children from his previous marriages, Vincent, Lisa, and Arthur.

See *Current Biography* 2000

Lerone Bennett

Born: Clarksdale, Mississippi; October 17, 1928
Died: Chicago, Illinois; February 14, 2018
Occupation: Writer, editor, historian, poet

Though some of his positions on African American history were controversial, Lerone Bennett was a leading scholar and author on the subject. He wrote eight books on African American history and was the senior editor at *Ebony* magazine for nearly forty years. He earned numerous awards and accolades including the Patron Saints Award, a Lifetime Achievement Award from the Nation Association of Black Journalists, the Candace Award from the National Coalition of 100 Black Women, a Salute of Greatness Award from the Martin Luther King Jr. Center for Nonviolent Social Change, a trumpet Award from Turner Broadcasting, and a Candle in the Dark Award from Morehouse College.

Lerone Bennett was born and raised in the Deep South in Mississippi. At an early age he was taught the value of education and reading, and he was most proud of the fact his grandmother, with thirteen children, made sure any of her children who wanted to could go to college, in spite of her husband's indifference. Bennett originally wanted to study law but following his graduation from Morehouse College with an AB degree, he got a job as a reporter for the African-American owned *Atlanta Daily World.* He became the city editor in 1952 and a year later, he worked as an associate editor at *Jet* magazine. Finally, in 1954 he joined *Ebony* magazine as an associate editor, working his way up to senior editor by 1958. While at *Ebony* he authored eight books, most notably *Before the Mayflower,* which grew out of a series of essays he wrote for the magazine. In 1968 he was a visiting professor of history at Northwestern University, where he also authored *Pioneers in Protest,* a book of biographical sketches of African American abolitionists. His work offered new perspectives, sometimes stirring great controversy, as in his assertion in *Forced to Glory: Abraham Lincoln's White Dream,* that Abraham Lincoln was a racist who actively campaigned against freedom and opportunity for African Americans. In the early 2000s, Bennett became involved in the hearings about monetary reparations for descendants of American slaves. Bennett's work has been translated into more than six languages.

Lerone Bennett's survivors include his three daughters and three grandchildren. His wife, Gloria Sylvester, predeceased him in 2009, as did his son, Lerone III, in 2013.

See *Current Biography* 2001

Günter Blobel

Born: Waltersdorf, Silesia, Germany; May 21, 1936
Died: New York, New York; February 18, 2018
Occupation: Biologist, professor, Nobel laureate

The Nobel Assembly awarded Günter Blobel its prize in medicine in 1999 for his contributions to understanding the inner workings of antibody cells, which has led to breakthroughs in the treatment of AIDS, cancer, and Alzheimer's disease. In addition to his research, Blobel was a full professor at Rockefeller University until his death.

Born in 1936, Günter Blobel's childhood was overwhelmed by the mayhem of World War II. His father had been a veterinarian in Dresden. Blobel was born one of seven children, though a sister was killed in the final days of the war. Witnessing the bombing in Dresden, Blobel developed a passion for architecture, which eventually contributed to his interest in cell structure. After the war, the family found itself in Soviet-occupied East Germany. Refusing to join the Communist Party, Günter Blobel escaped to West Germany in the early 1950s after graduating from high school. In 1960 he earned an MD from the University of Tübingen. While interning at a small hospital, he realized his true passion was in research. Blobel's brother, Hans had won a Fulbright-sponsored faculty post at the University of Wisconsin and urged his brother to join him and study for a PhD. Blobel took his brother's advice and earned a PhD in oncology in 1967. Shortly thereafter, he joined the staff at Rockefeller University as a post-doctoral fellow in the cell biology lab, working with George Palade who would win a Nobel Prize in 1974. With the advent of the electron microscope, the two were able to study the internal structure of a cell. Dr. Blobel and his colleague, Dr. David Sabatini, surmised that some sort of "signal" was transmitted between cells and any error or misdirection of those signals led to diseases like cancer and AIDS. Blobel further discovered that these signals comprised a chain of amino acids. His discovery was a monumental breakthrough in treating diseases. Upon receiving the $960,000 Nobel Prize, Blobel donated the money to "Friends of Dresden," an organization committed to the restoration of artistic and architectural works that were damaged or destroyed in World War II. He became a US citizen in 1980.

Günter Blobel married restaurateur Laura Maioglio in 1976. His survivors include his wife and five siblings.

See *Current Biography* 1999

Steven Bochco

Born: New York, New York; December 16, 1943
Died: Los Angeles, California; April 1, 2018
Occupation: Television producer and writer

Steven Bochco won numerous Emmys over the course of his career as a writer and producer. Some of his most famous television shows include *Hill Street Blues*, *LA Law*, *Doogie Howser, M.D.*, and *NYPD Blue*.

Steven Bochco was the oldest of two children born to Rudolph and Mimi Bochco. He attended the High School for Music and Art in Manhattan and received a scholarship to study at New York University (NYU). He transferred after his first year to the Carnegie Institute of Technology (now Carnegie-Mellon University), where he met several acting students who would eventually star in his most popular television series. He also met his first wife, Barbara Bosson, who introduced Bochco to her father, Louis Blau, a prominent show-business lawyer, who introduced Bochco to Universal Studios, where he interned during his time at Carnegie. After receiving his Bachelor of Fine Arts degree from Carnegie in 1966, Bochco returned to Universal Studios as an assistant to the head of the story department. His first credit was for an augmentation of the original Chrysler Theater script for *A Fade to Black*. In 1968, Bochco wrote a screenplay for *The Counterfeit Killer*, and from 1968 to 1972, Bochco wrote full-length scripts for the NBC original series *The Name of the Game*. In 1971, he became the story editor for the popular show *Columbo*, earning him his first Emmy for outstanding writing achievement in drama. In 1978 he was hired by MTM Enterprises, where he and a colleague, Michael Kozoll, created the police drama *Hill Street Blues*, one of the most celebrated series in television history. In 1985 Bochco joined Twentieth Century Fox. With Terry Louise Fisher, Bochco created *LA Law*, a very popular series that won numerous Emmys. In 1987, with the help of Fox, Bochco became an independent producer. In 1989, he created the show *Doogie Howser, M.D.*, based on his father's experience as a child prodigy violinist. From 1993 to 2005 Bochco and colleague David Milch wrote another popular police drama, *NYPD Blue*. In 2007, Bochco announced his decision to step away from television dramas.

Steven Bochco is survived by his wife, Dayna, his three children, Jesse, Sean, and Melissa, and his two grandchildren.

See *Current Biography* 1991

Paul Bocuse

Born: Collonges-au-Mont-d'Or, France; February 11, 1926
Died: Collonges-au-Mont-d'Or, France; January 20, 2018
Occupation: French chef, restaurateur

Though he would deny it, chef Paul Bocuse has been credited with the title "father of Nouvelle cuisine." His cuisine comprised lighter, fresher ingredients, with fewer traditional heavy sauces. Nicknamed the "Lion of Lyon," Bocuse has also been credited with creating the "chef's liberation movement," introducing the image of the chef as celebrity and restaurateur. He was awarded France's Legion of Honor in 1975.

Paul Bocuse was born into a long line of chefs going back seven generations. His family had been in the restaurant business since 1765. It has been reported that he created his first serious dish, veal kidneys, at the age of eight. During World War II, Bocuse was drafted into the Vichy youth camp where he worked in the canteen and slaughterhouse. In 1944 he joined the Free French Division. He was wounded in combat and received the Croix de Guerre (military cross). He apprenticed in a number of prestigious restaurants including at La Mère Brazier in Le col de la Luère, outside Lyon, Lucas-Cartin in Paris, and under Fernand Point, who had trained Bocuse's father, at Point's three-star La Pyramide (The Pyramid) in Vienne. He returned to the family restaurant and was able to repurchase the ancestral inn his grandfather had lost, transforming it into the grand banquet facility, L'Abbaye de Collonges. He converted the family's smaller restaurant that his father built into the L'Auberge Paul Bocuse. Within a year he had received a star in the Michelin Guide, an accolade most chefs spend a lifetime trying to earn. During the next decade he would win several more stars. Bocuse credited his great success to his insistence on the freshest ingredients and reducing cooking time to maintain flavor. His signature creations include a pastry-crusted truffle and foie gras chicken soup, and sea bass stuffed with lobster mousse, also encased in pastry. Bocuse was also among the first chefs to leave the kitchen to mingle with his guests, creating something of a "chef's liberation movement." He appeared on the covers of *Newsweek* and *The New York Times Magazine*. In the 1980s, he worked with Epcot Center (in Walt Disney World) in Florida to create restaurants at the French Pavilion. Bocuse published four cookbooks and a memoir.

Paul Bocuse's survivors include his wife, Raymonde, and his two children.

See *Current Biography* 1988

Anthony Bourdain

Born: New York, New York; June 25, 1956
Died: Kaysersberg, France; June 8, 2018
Occupation: Chef, writer, television host

Anthony Bourdain was a world-renowned chef, television series host, and author. Throughout his life Bourdain strived to find the best food available, sometimes in little-known, remote places, prompting the creation of his various television series and many of his books. He wrote over fifteen books, both fiction and non-fiction, that were inspired by his life working in kitchens and traveling the world.

Anthony Bourdain was the oldest son born to Pierre and Gladys Bourdain. Bourdain attended Dwight-Englewood High school and then Vassar College, where he started working in kitchens as a dishwasher. After his sophomore year, he transferred to the Culinary Institute of America. Bourdain's first job after graduating was at the prestigious Rainbow Room in Manhattan. From there he had several jobs at some of the top restaurants in New York City, until his drug habit left him without a job or home. In 1988 Bourdain was able to overcome his drug addiction and began working at restaurants once again. At this time he also began writing, and in 1995 his first book of fiction, *Bone in the Throat*, was published. By this time, Bourdain held some of the top chef positions at exclusive restaurants in New York. He gained extreme popularity after writing a piece for the *New Yorker*, called "Don't Eat Before Reading This," which exposed many truths about kitchens and restaurant practices. He was immediately offered a book deal for *Kitchen Confidential: Adventures in the Culinary Underbelly* (2000). He then wrote two more books, including *A Cook's Tour: In Search of the Perfect Meal* (2001), which was published alongside a TV series, *A Cook's Tour*, which aired on the Food Network. His show, *Anthony Bourdain: No Reservations*, aired in 2005, a show where he would introduce viewers to cuisine around the world. During this time, he also wrote several fiction books, which often encompassed his life experiences. Bourdain had a series of shows and cookbooks including *The Layover* (2011), *The Mind of a Chef* (2012) and *Anthony Bourdain: Parts Unknown* (2013), *The Taste* (2013). Many of his shows received awards, including several Emmys and a Peabody Award for *Parts Unknown*.

Anthony Bourdain is survived by his daughter, Ariane. His suicide prompted international campaigns for mental health and suicide awareness.

See *Current Biography* 2006

T. Berry Brazelton

Born: Waco, Texas; May 10, 1918
Died: Barnstable, Massachusetts; March 13, 2018
Occupation: Pediatrician, professor, author

Thomas Berry Brazelton, a prominent pediatrician and child psychiatrist of the twentieth century, is most well-known for his development of the Neonatal Development Assessment Scale. He became a comforting presence for new parents; rivaling the popularity of Dr. Benjamin Spock in earlier generations. Brazelton published numerous, seminal books on child development.

Born in Waco, Texas, Brazelton was the second child of Thomas Berry Brazelton, Sr. and Pauline Battle Brazelton. His fondness and appreciation for children is said to stem from his time babysitting his younger cousins when he was a child. After completing his secondary education at Episcopal High School, Brazelton attended a pre-medical program at Princeton. He then attended Columbia University's College of Physicians and Surgeons and received his MD in 1943. From 1944–1945 Brazelton served in the United States Naval Reserve. After World War II, he attended the medical residency program at Massachusetts General Hospital (MGH) from 1945–1947. His interest in human behavior prompted him to join a child psychiatry residency at Boston's James Jackson Putnam Children's Center. In 1950, Brazelton established his first private pediatric practice in Cambridge, Massachusetts. At this same time, he became an instructor at Harvard Medical School (HMS) and began his research on newborns, infants, toddlers, and their parents. After studying major milestones in infant development, Brazelton published the "Brazelton Scale," or the Neonatal Development Assessment Scale, now used worldwide as a diagnostic test to determine a newborn's responses to the environment to better understand these developmental problems. During his research, Brazelton established that infants are complex and responsive individuals, who react according to the way their parents or caregivers interact with them. Using this knowledge, Brazelton published his first book, *Infants and Mothers: Individual Differences in Development* in 1969. Since this initial publication, Brazelton has published dozens of other books on child psychiatry and development, being careful to make these publications accessible to the general public. Brazelton established the Children's Development Unit at the Children's Hospital in Boston, in 1972. He has received many awards and honorary degrees for his work in child development.

Brazelton's wife, Christina Lowell, died in 2015. They are survived by their four children, daughters Katherine, Pauline, and Christina, and son Tom, and their seven grandchildren.

See *Current Biography* 1993

Maria Bueno

Born: São Paulo, Brazil; October 11, 1939
Died: São Paulo, Brazil; June 8, 2018
Occupation: Tennis player

Maria Bueno is celebrated as one of Brazil's most decorated tennis players. Often referred to as one of the most graceful tennis players, Bueno won three Wimbledon singles titles and nineteen Grand Slam titles during her tennis career.

Maria Esther Audion Bueno was born to Pedro and Esther Bueno. Bueno began playing tennis at the age of five and gained her skills by copying champion players at her local sports club, players who were primarily men. She won a girls' tournament in São Paulo, and by the age of fourteen Bueno was the women's tennis champion of Brazil. In 1955, at the age of fifteen, Bueno defeated Maria Weiss in the Pan-American Games. At this same time, her father insisted she study to become a teacher, and Bueno earned a teacher's certificate at the Colegio Santa Inés and began teaching primary school. However, Bueno continued to play tennis and participated in several international championships. During the years of 1958 and 1959, Bueno's main commentator and, at times, double's partner was Althea Gibson of the United States. However, at the end of 1959, Gibson retired, helping to move Bueno to the top of the international women's tennis rankings. That same year, Bueno won at Wimbledon against Darlene Hard, the first of three Wimbledon victories. After winning her second Wimbledon title, Bueno contracted hepatitis in 1961, leaving her unable to compete for one year. When she appeared at the Masters Invitational tournament at St. Petersburg, Florida, she lost to several of her rivals. She was said to have lost some of her "spark" after her bout with hepatitis, though by 1964 Bueno won her third Wimbledon title. However, in 1965, a knee injury forced Bueno into retirement. She did return to tour for the Japan Open in 1974, and in 1978 Bueno was inducted into the International Tennis Hall of Fame. She continued working in the tennis world by becoming a commentator for the Sports TV channel and BBC World Service. The 2015 Olympic Tennis Centre in Rio was named after her.

Maria Bueno is survived by her nephew, Pedro.

See *Current Biography* 1965

Barbara Bush

Born: New York, New York; June 8, 1925
Died: Houston, Texas; April 17, 2018
Occupation: Former first lady of the United States

Barbara Bush was the forty-first first lady of the United States and only the second woman in US history to have both a husband and son become a US president. She and her husband, George HW Bush, were the longest-married Presidential couple, having been married over seventy-three years.

Barbara Bush was born to Pauline and Marvin Pierce and lived in Rye, New York, during her childhood. Bush's great-great-great-uncle, Franklin Pierce, was the fourteenth President of the United States. Bush attended Milton School, Rye Country Day School, and then Ashley Hall Boarding School for her final two years of high school. She met George Herbert Walker Bush at a dance during her winter break in 1941. In 1943, Bush enrolled in Smith College but dropped out in 1944. During the summer of 1944, Bush worked in a nuts-and-bolts factory. She and George Bush married in January of 1945. In 1946, Bush gave birth to George Walker Bush. She worked at a Yale co-op for one year, before moving to Texas and then California due to George HW Bush's work with the oil industry. Once in California, Bush had five more children: Pauline (known as Robin, who died after her fourth birthday), Jeb (John Ellis), Neil, Marvin, and Dorothy. In 1950, the Bushes moved back to Texas, where George HW Bush established the first oil-and-gas dealership. In 1966, the Bushes moved to Washington DC as George HW Bush was elected to the US House of Representatives for the Seventh Congressional District. During this time, Bush had become very involved in various charities, especially following her daughter, Pauline's, battle with leukemia. In the mid-1970s, George HW Bush began to consider running for president, and Bush decided to focus her volunteerism on literacy. During her time campaigning for widespread literacy, Bush authored two books, *C. Fred's Story: A Dog's Life*, published in 1984, and *Millie's Book: As Dictated to Barbara Bush*, published in 1990. George HW Bush was Vice President from 1981 to 1989, and then became the forty-first President until 1993. In 2000, Bush's son, George W Bush, became the forty-third President.

Barbara Bush is survived by her husband, five children, seventeen grandchildren, and seven great-grandchildren.

See *Current Biography* 1989

Brendan T. Byrne

Born: West Orange, New Jersey; April 1, 1924
Died: Livingston, New Jersey; January 4, 2018
Occupation: Former governor of New Jersey

Brendan Byrne was voted into office as governor of New Jersey by a landslide with a margin of nearly two to one, against incumbent Governor Cahill whose office was plagued by corruption. He is credited with bringing the Giants football team to New Jersey and for supporting the building of the Meadowlands Sports Complex. After a Supreme Court decision forced New Jersey to find new ways to finance public education, Byrne supported the state's first income tax and was still re-elected for a second term. He was the first New Jersey governor to serve two terms while his party also held the legislature the entire time.

Brendan Byrne's father had been the public safety commissioner of the family's hometown of West Orange, and he served on the Essex County tax board. Byrne served in the US Air Force during World War II. Upon his return he graduated from Princeton University in 1949 and earned his LL.B. degree from Harvard Law School in 1951. He served as assistant counsel to then Governor Robert Meyner, who later appointed him executive secretary. The governor later named him the prosecutor of Essex County where he gained a reputation fighting against corrupt construction contractors. He served as president of the public utilities commission until 1970 when he was appointed judge to the New Jersey Superior Court. Most famously, as Byrne was investigating organized crime, a recorded phone conversation between gangsters revealed that Byrne "couldn't be bought." The incident served him well in his 1973 bid for New Jersey governor. He won the election. He worked to create a public advocate's office and to simplify voter registration. His administration was remarkably free from scandal though he drew criticism for flying to Washington, DC, ordering his car to follow him there to provide local transportation, and then return, empty, to New Jersey, all during the gasoline shortages of the early 1970s. After retiring from politics in 1982, Byrne became a partner in a law firm.

Byrne's first marriage to Jean Featherly ended in divorce. Byrne's second wife, the former Ruthi Zinn, his six children, and nine grandchildren survive him. One daughter predeceased him in 2006.

See *Current Biography* 1974

Montserrat Caballé

Born: Barcelona, Spain; April 12, 1933
Died: Barcelona, Spain; October 6, 2018
Occupation: Spanish opera singer

Montserrat Caballé was one of the greatest opera singers of the second half of the twentieth century. She was known especially for the breadth of her repertoire with more than one hundred roles at her command, and for her longevity, singing on stage well into her sixties.

Montserrat Caballé was born into poverty as the Great Depression and the Spanish Civil War had decimated the fortunes of her family, who had formerly been comfortably middle class. Her father had been a chemist. The entire family loved music, and her father had an extensive record collection, some of which he had to sell to feed his family. Caballé first learned to sing by listening to and accompanying those albums. Recognizing that she had tremendous talent, even as a nine-year-old child, the family sent her to the Conservatori Superior de Música del Liceu in Barcelona where she completed a six-year-course. She then studied voice technique for six years with Eugenia Kemeny. At age twenty-one Caballé won the Liceu Conservatory Gold Medal, Spain's highest singing award. In 1957 she made her operatic debut as Mimi in *La Bohème* at the Basel Opera in Basel, Switzerland, where she had a three-year contract. She then had a two-year contract at the Bremen Opera in Germany. Her first appearance in the Americas was in Mexico City in 1964. She made her way to a US audience on April 20, 1965, when the American Opera Society needed to replace mezzo-soprano Marilyn Horne who had fallen ill just before she was to perform Lucrezia Borgia at Carnegie Hall. That same night, RCA Victor Red Seal Records signed Caballé on for a US-exclusive contract. Later that year she debuted at the Metropolitan Opera singing Marguerite in Gounod's Faust. Throughout her career Caballé's performances would be interrupted, even mid-song, by adoring audiences. In 1988 she famously recorded an album with Freddie Mercury, British front man for the rock band Queen.

Montserrat Caballé's survivors include her husband, Bernabé Martí, a Spanish tenor, and their two children.

See *Current Biography* 1967

Peter Alexander Rupert Carington

Born: Buckinghamshire, England; June 6, 1919
Died: July 9, 2018
Occupation: Statesman, British Duke of Carrington

Lord Carrington served as Secretary of State for Defense of Great Britain under six British Prime Ministers. Lord Carrington was known as one of the Conservative Party's most influential policy makers through the 1970s and 1980s. (His family name, Carington, differed from his title, Lord Carringon, in the House of Lords.)

Peter Alexander Rupert Carington was born to Rupert Victor John Carington, the fifth Baron Carrington, and Sibyl Colville, the daughter of the second Viscount Colville. He was educated at Eton preparatory school for boys. After the death of his father in 1938, Carington became the sixth Baron Carrington, and once nineteen trained at the Royal Military College and served as a Major in the army during World War II. In 1946 Lord Carrington became a member of the Buckinghamshire County Council and deputy chairman of the agricultural executive committee, and he took his hereditary seat in the House of Lords. In 1951 Winston Churchill appointed Lord Carrington as joint parliamentary secretary to the Ministry of Agriculture and Fisheries, becoming the youngest member of Churchill's government. He was then appointed parliamentary secretary to the Ministry of Defence in 1954. From 1956 to 1959, Lord Carrington served as British High Commissioner in Australia, before becoming Privy Councillor and First Lord of the Admiralty. In 1963 Lord Carington became the Conservative party leader in the House of Lords; and when the labour party won the 1964 elections, Lord Carrington was opposition leader in the House of Lords and an adviser in the consultative committee or "Shadow Cabinet" formed by Edward Heath. After the 1970 elections, Prime Minister Heath appointed Lord Carrington Secretary of State for Defence. In 1982 he served as foreign secretary under Prime Minister Margaret Thatcher from 1979 to 1982 and was appointed secretary general of the North Atlantic Treaty Organization (NATO) in 1984, where he served for four years. Lord Carrington was given a life peerage in 1999 after most hereditary peers were removed from the House of Lords.

Peter Alexander Rupert Carington Carrington is survived by his three children The Honorable Alexandra Carington, The Honorable Virginia Carington, and Rupert Francis John Carington, 7th Baron Carrington, and six grandchildren.

See *Current Biography* 1971

Frank Charles Carlucci

Born: Scranton, Pennsylvania; October 18, 1930
Died: Washington, DC; June 3, 2018
Occupation: Cabinet member, US diplomat

Frank Charles Carlucci was the Secretary of Defense during the Reagan administration and served as a top government official and US diplomat during his career.

Frank Charles Carlucci III was born to Frank Charles Carlucci Jr. and Roxanna Bacon Carlucci. He graduated from Wyoming Seminary College Preparatory School before attending Princeton University, where he received a BA in 1952. The following two years he served in the US Navy. In 1955 he enrolled at the Harvard Graduate School for Business Administration, but he left after just one year. Carlucci joined the United States Foreign Service in 1956 and in 1957 received his first overseas assignment as vice-consul and economic officer at the American Embassy in Johannesburg, South Africa. He also held posts in Belgian Congo (now Zaire), Zanzibar, Tanzania, and Brazil. A former classmate offered Carlucci a post in the Office of Economic Opportunity (OEO) in Washington, DC, where he became Deputy Director for Operations. In 1970, under the Nixon administration, Carlucci became Director of the OEO. In 1972, he was the number two man under Caspar W. Weinberger, at the Office of Management and Budget (OMB), and then in 1973, he was the Under Secretary of Health, Education, and Welfare (HEW). The next year, Carlucci was again appointed United States Ambassador to Portugal, where the US State Department observers gave Carlucci much of the credit for having kept Portugal allied with the West by resisting Kissinger's inclination to write off that nation. In 1978, Carlucci obtained the post of CIA Deputy Director, under the Carter administration, where he criticized the 1974 Freedom of Information Act, which provides access to government information on demand except for certain sensitive materials, and he pushed for punishment of unlawful disclosure of government sources. After the election of Ronald Reagan, Carlucci was appointed as Deputy Secretary of Defense. After the resignation of Weinberger in 1987, Carlucci became Secretary of Defense and served until 1989. Frank Carlucci worked under five presidents, total, and received several awards for his work with the US Army. He has received two honorary college degrees.

Frank Charles Carlucci is survived by his wife, Marcia, their three children, Frank IV, Karen, and Kristin, and six grandchildren.

See *Current Biography* 1981

Luigi Luca Cavalli-Sforza

Born: Genoa, Italy; January 25, 1922
Died: Belluno, Italy; August 31, 2018
Occupation: Geneticist, scientist

Luigi Luca Cavalli-Sforza was a pioneer in the field of what he called "genetic geography" and "cultural evolution." He was the first scientist to posit that by using the genetics of blood types and statistics, he could trace where different populations originated. By taking data from disparate fields such as anthropology, genetics, statistics and even geology, he concluded that genetically there is no such thing as separate races, and he helped trace the origins of humanity to a single region in Africa.

Italian-born scientist, Luigi Luca Cavalli-Sforza was introduced to the study and analysis of evolution while attending the University of Pavia in the early 1940s, and learned the science of heredity, immunology, and blood groups while in graduate school during the war. As a medical student he was exempted from fighting. Following the war, Cavalli-Sforza was a research assistant at the Istituto Sieroterapico, a blood serum institute in Milan where he studied immunology and blood groups. From 1948 to 1950, Cavalli-Sforza was a researcher at Cambridge University where he worked with famed statistician and creator of the mathematical theory of evolution, Sir Ronald Fisher. Cavalli-Sforza initially studied genetic traits in towns in northern Italy, while working as a lecturer at the University of Parma and the University of Pavia. He also gathered information about blood types and heredity from three centuries of church records in Italy. This initial study would launch his groundbreaking studies and publications several decades later. In 1978 Cavalli-Sforza and two colleagues, Paolo Menozzi and Alberto Piazza, embarked on an enormous project studying more than 100,000 individuals from 2,000 communities. Their study resulted in their enormously influential book *The History and Geography of Human Genes*, which essentially presented a new human family tree based on 110 genetic markers and establishing Africa as the cradle of humanity. An underlying question or tangent running throughout Cavalli-Sforza's work was the question of racial superiority. He famously debated the Nobel Laureate and physicist, William Shockley, publicly, after Shockley declared blacks were not as intelligent as whites. Cavalli-Sforza has published numerous books and professional papers on subjects such as the history of the spread of agriculture and the cultural transmission of behavior and cultural norms. Cavalli-Sforza taught at Stanford University from 1972 to 1992.

Dr. Cavalli-Sforza's survivors include his four children and three grandchildren.

See *Current Biography* 1997

Jill Conway

Born: Hillston, New South Wales, Australia; October 9, 1934
Died: Boston, Massachusetts; June 1, 2018
Occupation: Historian, college president

Jill Conway was an historian and the first female president of Smith College. Her research and publications are used as core curriculum in women's studies courses across the country.

Jill Kathryn Ker Conway was born to William Innis Ker and Evelyn Mary Ker. She attended Abbotsleigh private school for girls and in 1952 entered the University of Sydney on a scholarship. Conway graduated with a BA and a University Medal in 1958, and then returned to the same university to receive her MA in Australian history. In 1960 Conway left Australia for Harvard University, where she received her PhD in history in 1969, while also teaching at the University of Toronto with her husband. For much of her academic career, Conway focused on the gender roles of women and the development of these roles in history. She also studied the ways in which the environment influenced people's mythic images. She gave a series of radio talks on the subject, entitled *Myths and National Culture*. At this time she was also an associate professor of history at the University of Toronto, and from 1973 to 1975, she served as the university's first vice-president for internal affairs. During her time at the university she contributed to several publications, including *Academic Transformations: Seventeen Institutions under Pressure* (1973), *Notable American Women* (1971), and *The Modern Period* (1980). In 1975, Conway became the seventh President of Smith College, making her the first female president of the country's largest privately endowed women's liberal-arts college. Conway helped establish the Smith Society of Scholars Studying Women's Higher-Education History and the research program, Women and Social Change. She published *The Female Experience in Eighteenth and Nineteenth-Century America: A Guide to the History of American Women* in 1982, and then her memoir, *The Road from Coorain*, in 1989. She remained president of Smith College for ten years, until 1985, when she became a visiting scholar and professor in the Program in Science, Technology, and Society of the Massachusetts Institute of Technology. She was awarded the National Humanities Award Medal by President Barack Obama in 2013.

Jill Conway has no immediate survivors.

See *Current Biography 1991*

Frank Corsaro

Born: New York, New York; December 22, 1924
Died: Suwanee, Georgia; November 11, 2017
Occupation: American director

Frank Corsaro was a maverick director who was the first to posit that opera singers should also act. In later productions Corsaro included video and other multimedia in his operatic stage productions.

According to Corsaro, he was born on a ship outside New York harbor as his Italian immigrant parents moved to the United States from Argentina. He attended the Yale School of Drama where he directed his first production of Sartre's *No Exit* in 1947. In 1950 he joined the famous Actors Studio while he pursued a short career in acting, even starring opposite Joanne Woodward in the 1968 film *Rachel, Rachel* (directed by Paul Newman). He would later serve as the artistic director at the famous method acting school. In 1953 he directed *The Scarecrow,* off Broadway, starring James Dean, Patricia Neal, and Eli Wallach. His first Broadway production, *The Honeys,* starred Hume Cronyn and Jessica Tandy. His career breakthrough was the 1966 production of *La Traviata* for the City Opera, starring Patricia Brooks and Plácido Domingo. He also worked closely with the set designer, author, and illustrator Maurice Sendak famous for his children's book *Where the Wild Things Are.* Corsaro taught and directed at the American Opera Center at Juilliard. In 1988 he became the artistic director at the Actors Studio.

In 1971 Corsaro married City Opera mezzo-soprano Mary Cross Lueders (referred to as "Bonnie"). His survivors include one son, two brothers, and two grandsons.

See *Current Biography 1975*

Ronald Dellums

Born: Oakland, California; November 24, 1935
Died: Washington, DC; July 30, 2018
Occupation: Former congressman, mayor of Oakland

Ronald Dellums was a self-avowed radical, a fire-brand representative when he entered Congress in 1970. He was staunchly anti-war and anti-war machine through most of his tenure and fought for civil rights, including those of black South Africans during apartheid. He was the first African American and the first African American chairman to serve on the Armed Services Committee. He ended his political career serving as mayor of Oakland, California.

Ronald Dellums's father was a Pullman car porter turned longshoreman, and his mother was a clerk-typist. His uncle was a labor organizer with the Brotherhood of Sleeping Car Porters. In high school, Ronald Dellums had dreams of playing professional baseball and trained with future players Curt Flood and Frank Robinson. But blatant racism in the coaching staff kept him from his dream. Unable to find work after graduating from Oakland Technical High School, he joined the US Marine Corps in 1954. Two years later he attended Oakland City College on the GI Bill. He earned a BA degree from San Francisco State College in 1960, and a master's degree from the University of California at Berkeley in 1962. He was a social worker until 1967 when he launched his political career, running for the Berkeley City Council. Several years later, anti-war activists persuaded him to run for Congress. He would win re-election a dozen times. Within his first year, Dellums called for an investigation into war crimes committed by the US armed services, and when the Armed Services Committee refused, he launched his own investigation. He remained a staunch critic of the ever-increasing military budget at the expense of domestic programs. He was a staunch critic of the Reagan administration. In the mid-1980s Dellums called on Congress to sanction South Africa for its apartheid policies. He was arrested in 1984 for demonstrating at the South African embassy. In 1991 Dellums won a seat on the Intelligence Committee and became chairman of the black caucus. In 1993 he was seated on the Armed Services Committee. In 1997 he announced his retirement from Congress only to reluctantly run for mayor of Oakland at the insistence of the Democratic electorate. He served one term.

Ronald Dellums survivors include his wife, Cynthia, his five children, six grandchildren, and two great-grandchildren.

See *Current Biography 1993*

George Deukmejian

Born: Mendes, New York; June 6, 1928
Died: Long Beach, California; May 8, 2018
Occupation: Governor

George Deukmejian was a two-term governor of California, known for his support on stricter crime legislation and anti-government spending policies. Though a Republican, he was admired by both Republicans and Democrats for his willingness to negotiate and work across party lines.

Born Courken George Deukmejian Jr., Deukmejian was the son of Courken George Deukmejian Sr. and Alice Gairdan. Deukmejian attended high school in Watervliet, New York, and then attended Siena College, where he graduated with a BA in Sociology in 1949. He later attended St. John's University and received his JD degree in 1952. After serving in the army from 1953 to 1955, Deukmejian moved to California to practice law. In 1962, Deukmejian was elected state assemblyman. Four years later, he was elected to the state senate and then became leader of the upper chamber's Republicans. In 1978, Deukmejian became attorney general for the state of California. He was known for being very "hands-on" while in office and established a Special Prosecutions Unit to fight organized crime in the state. Deukmejian also spent much of his time pushing for anti-crime legislation. Then, in 1982, Deukmejian won the general election for Governor of California. Immediately upon being sworn in, Deukmejian had to deal with an extreme fiscal crisis, a crisis which lead to the California unemployment rate reaching 11.2 percent. Throughout the crisis, Deukmejian did not raise taxes, but instead pared spending and balanced the budget. In 1986, Deukmejian took a public stand against the University of California's investments in South Africa during Apartheid. Deukmejian's urging led to the University being one of the first major institutions to take a stand against Apartheid.

George Deukmejian is survived by his wife, Gloria, their children, Leslie, George, and Andrea, and their six grandchildren.

See *Current Biography* 1983

Bradford Dillman

Born: San Francisco, California; April 14, 1930
Died: Santa Barbara, California; January 16, 2018
Occupation: Actor, author

Bradford Dillman is most remembered for his role in the movie *Compulsion*, which also starred Orson Welles and Dean Stockwell. The three actors shared best actor awards at the 1959 Cannes Film Festival. Dillman also won the award for most promising newcomer for his role in the 1958 film, *A Certain Smile.*

Bradford Dillman was born to a wealthy stockbroker, Dean Dillman. He attended private schools in California and Connecticut before earning a degree in literature from Yale University in 1951. Soon thereafter he served in the US Marines in the Korean War. He began his acting career early, appearing in student productions throughout his schooling. At Yale he performed in eight productions of the Yale Dramatic Association. He received a scholarship to attend the London Royal Academy of Dramatic Arts but turned down the offer so he could appear in an off-Broadway production of *The Scarecrow.* In late 1955 Dillman was accepted into the Actors Studio. Among his classmates was Marilyn Monroe. In 1959 Dillman was selected, out of more than five hundred applicants, for the role of Edmund Tyrone in José Quintero's production of *Long Day's Journey into Night.* Over the course of his career, Dillman appeared in over one hundred and forty roles in movies and television. Some of the most prominent movies he appeared in include *Dirty Harry, Sudden Impact,* and *The Enforcer.* He won a daytime Emmy Award for his appearance in the 1975 ABC *Afternoon Playbreak.* He was a regular guest in the wildly popular series *Murder, She Wrote,* starring his friend Angela Lansbury. Dillman also authored several non-fiction books about sports, as well as several novels. In 1997 he published his memoir, *Are You Anybody? An Actor's Life.*

Bradford Dillman's first marriage, to Frieda Harding McIntosh, ended in divorce. His second wife, actress Suzy Parker, predeceased him in 2003. His survivors include his five children, a stepdaughter, eight grandchildren, and two step-grandchildren.

See *Current Biography* 1960

Alene Duerk

Born: Defiance, Ohio; March 29, 1920
Died: Lake Mary, Florida; July 21, 2018
Occupation: US Navy officer

Alene Duerk was the first female to achieve flag rank in the US Navy. She was named Rear Admiral in 1972.

Alene Duerk's father died of tuberculosis when she was just four, which factored heavily in her mother raising her two daughters to be self-sufficient women. Though she was quite young, Duerk remembered the nurses who came into her home to treat her father, inspiring her to go into nursing when she was an adult. After graduating from high school, she studied nursing at the Toledo Hospital School of Nursing and was commissioned to serve as a nurse on the naval ship Benevolence during World War II. She remained in the US Naval Reserve after the war and worked on her BS in nursing at the Frances Payne Bolton School of Nursing at Western Reserve University. She graduated in 1948 and was called to active duty in 1951 during the

Korean War. Following the war, Duerk became a nursing instructor at the Portsmouth Naval Hospital, and eventually, Interservice Education Coordinator at the Philadelphia Naval Hospital. In 1958 she was quickly promoted from lieutenant to lieutenant commander, and finally commander while working as a Nurse Programs Officer in Chicago. Throughout the early 1960s, she worked her way up the ranks in various nursing administration capacities and was promoted to captain on July 1, 1967. By 1970 she was made director of the Navy Nursing Corps, and on April 27, 1972 she was nominated for flag rank, or rear admiral. Duerk retired from the Navy in 1975, having achieved the rank of admiral.

Alene Duerk was awarded an honorary doctorate from Bowling Green State University in 1973. Information about survivors was not immediately available.

See *Current Biography* 1973

David Douglas Duncan

Born: Kansas City, Missouri; January 23, 1916
Died: Grasse, France; June 7, 2018
Occupation: Photojournalist

David Duncan was a celebrated photojournalist who captured significant moments in history on camera, including soldiers on the battlefield during World War II, the wars in Korea and Vietnam, life at the Kremlin, to even his close friend, Pablo Picasso. Throughout his career, Duncan published photos and articles with *National Geographic* and *Life* magazines and published over two dozen books of his work.

David Douglas Duncan was born to Kenneth Stockwell and Florence Watson Duncan, the fourth son and second youngest of the family. Duncan attended the University of Arizona, where in 1934, he unwittingly captured a photo of a notorious criminal, John Dillinger, at a burning hotel. The next year however, Duncan transferred to the University of Miami in Coral Gables to study zoology. After graduating, Duncan traveled, working as a freelance photographer, most often filming marine-centric subjects. He was hired to work on the Chile-Peru Expedition of the American Museum of Natural History, and his photographs were published in editions in 1941 and 1943. Duncan joined the US Marine Corps in 1943 and, having been assigned to photograph operations, covered the guerrilla fighting of the Fijians against the Japanese on the Solomon Islands in early 1944 and later Marine combat aviation on Okinawa and other islands. In 1945, aboard the USS Missouri, he photographed the official surrender of Japan. Many of these wartime photos were

also published in *National Geographic*. In 1946, Duncan joined *Life* magazine as a photographer and traveled to several countries in the Middle East. He then went to Japan and Korea, where he photographed men on the battlefield, calling his work *This Is War!* Afterwards he captured photos of the departure of King Farouk from Egypt after his overthrow by Egyptian army officers, and the Solar Boat of Cheops, in Egypt, which had not been seen since 3000 B.C. In 1955, Duncan persuaded Egypt's President, Gamal Abdel Nasser, to let him photograph Arab refugees in the Gaza Strip. In 1956, Duncan met Pablo Picasso, of whom Duncan took over 10,000 photos, and wrote two books: *The Private World of Pablo Picasso* and *Picasso's Picassos*.

David Duncan is survived by his wife, Sheila Macauley.

See *Current Biography* 1968

Samuel Epstein

Born: Middlesbrough, England; April 13, 1926
Died: Chicago, Illinois; March 18, 2018
Occupation: Physician

Samuel Epstein spent his life as a crusader against common cancer-causing behaviors and products. He spent his time researching and alerting the public to household products that contained carcinogens, and released the "dirty dozen" list of products consumers should avoid. He wrote numerous articles and books about the nature of cancer prevention and the influences of the media and politics on adequate education and prevention.

Samuel Epstein was the son of Isidore Epstein, a rabbi and world-renowned Hebraic and Talmudic scholar. Epstein attended Guys Medical School for his pre-med education. He graduated from the University of London in 1947 with a BS in physiology. Epstein then returned to Guys Medical School and received additional bachelor's degrees in Medicine and Surgery in 1950. After working briefly, he went back to the University of London to receive his degree in bacteriology, parasitology, pathology, and then his MD. During this same time, Epstein served as a pathologist for the Royal Army Medical Corps. He moved to the United States in 1960 and established the first toxicology and cancer lab in the country. In 1966 Epstein discovered that griseofulvin, an antibiotic used to treat athlete's foot, caused cancer. He continued to appear before congressional committees to end sales of harmful products, including the use of DDT, aldrin, and other harmful pesticides like Agent Orange during the Vietnam war. When not researching or teaching, Epstein spent much of his time criticizing the world of medicine, politics, and the media for not being forthcoming with the nature of cancer in society (acknowledging common cancer-causing chemicals and reporting increases in cancers world-wide). In 1994, Epstein launched the Cancer Prevention Coalition, to make cancer prevention a top priority in the country. Epstein researched the health risks posed by Monsanto's genetically engineered bovine growth hormone (rBGH), which increases milk production, and on the dangers of sex hormones used to fatten cattle. He worked to have these chemicals banned from use in Europe. Epstein received dozens of awards for his work.

Samuel Epstein is survived by his second wife, Catherine, their sons, Julien and Mark, and a daughter, Emily, from his previous marriage. He is also survived by two grandchildren.

See *Current Biography* 2001

Nanette Fabray

Born: San Diego, California; October 27, 1920
Died: Palos Verdes, California; February 22, 2018
Occupation: American actor

A star on Broadway and television, Nanette Fabray was a Tony and Emmy Award-winning actor, who is most remembered for her comedic roles.

By the time she was four years old, Nanette Fabray was appearing on the vaudeville stage. She was born the youngest of five children. She attended Los Angeles Junior College to study acting with the noted director, Max Reinhardt, but due to an undiagnosed hearing problem she did not do well and left school. Her impairment was later surgically corrected, and she became an advocate to the hearing-impaired. When she was twenty-one, Fabray appeared in her first Broadway show, *Let's Face It*, starring Eve Arden and Danny Kaye. At twenty-eight she won a Tony Award for best actress for her role in her seventh Broadway show, *Love Life*. Her roles and accolades kept coming. In 1956 she won two Emmy Awards for best comedian and best actress for her work on *Caesar's Hour*, starring Sid Caesar. Ironically, she won another Emmy after she had been released from the show. In 1955 Fabray was injured by falling debris backstage and spent several weeks in the hospital. Fabray's first movie role was alongside Betty Davis in *The Private Lives of Elizabeth and Essex*. As she received more and more recognition, Fabray was bothered by so many mispronunciations of her name (which was spelled Fabares) that she changed it to Fabray, a phonetic spelling. She made numerous appearances on such shows as *The Carol Burnette Show*, *The Mary Tyler Moore Show*, and *The Dean Martin Show*. She made regular appearances on game shows like *What's My Line* and *Hollywood Squares*. In 1986 the Screen Actors Guild (SAG) awarded Fabray a life achievement award. As a spokesperson and representative of the hearing impaired, Fabray was awarded the President's Distinguished Service Award and the Eleanor Roosevelt Humanitarian Award.

Fabray's first marriage to David Tebet, an advertising executive who later became the president of NBC ended in divorce. In 1957 she married the screenwriter Ranald MacDougall who later became president of the Writers Guild of America. He predeceased her in 1973. Her survivors include her stepson and two grandchildren.

See *Current Biography* 1956

Miloš Forman

Born: Caslav, Czechoslovakia; February 18, 1932
Died: Warren, Connecticut; April 13, 2018
Occupation: Film director

Miloš Forman was an Oscar winning Czech-American director whose most notable works include *Black Peter, One Flew Over the Cuckoo's Nest, Ragtime,* and *Amadeus.*

Miloš Forman was born, the youngest of three boys, to Rudolf and Anna Forman. In 1940, both of his parents were seized by Nazis and transferred to concentration camps, where they both died. He later learned that he was the illegitimate son of a Jewish architect with whom his mother had an affair. Years later he would contact his biological father who survived the Holocaust. After their parents' arrests, Forman and his brothers were taken in by relatives and family friends. The boys attended numerous schools throughout Czechoslovakia due to their lack of a stable home. Forman graduated secondary school in 1950 and attended film school in Prague. He first worked as a director of film presentations at Czechoslovak Television, where he wrote and worked as assistant director on several films. In 1963, Forman made his first film, a documentary-like short, called, *The Audition*, with a companion piece called *Competition*. In 1963, Forman also completed his first feature-length film, *Black Peter*, which won several European film awards. In 1964, Forman completed the award-winning *The Loves of a Blonde*, which gained him increased international recognition, especially in the United States. Forman's next film, *The Fireman's Ball*, drew heavy criticism from Czechoslovakian politicians but was financially supported by European and American supporters and thus gained popularity outside of Czechoslovakia. In 1971 Forman released *Taking In*, which was filmed in New York where Forman had moved after the Soviet invasion of Czechoslovakia in 1968. A few years later, in 1975, Forman directed *One Flew Over the Cuckoo's Nest*, which won five Oscars. Forman directed *Hair*, a screen adaptation of the Broadway musical, in 1979. *Amadeus* was released in 1984, winning eight oscars, including best director and best picture. Additional films include, *Valmont* (1989), *The People vs. Larry Flynt* (1996), *Man on the Moon* (1999), and *Goya's Ghost* (2006).

Miloš Forman married three times. He is survived by his four children: Petr and Matěj (from his first marriage to Věra Křesadlová) and James and Andrew (from his second marriage to Martina Formanová).

See *Current Biography* 1971

Clarence Fountain

Born: Tyler, Alabama; November 28, 1929
Died: Baton Rouge, Louisiana; June 3, 2018
Occupation: Gospel singer

Clarence Fountain was the founding member of the Grammy-Award winning gospel group, The Blind Boys of Alabama. Started in the 1940s, Fountain and his band toured for over fifty years.

Clarence Fountain was born into a singing family in Selma, Alabama. At the age of eight, he enrolled in the Alabama Institute for the Negro Deaf and Blind, where he and four other boys started a band called the Happy Land Jubilee Singers, with Fountain as their lead singer. The band was quite successful, and the group left school in 1944 to pursue their music full-time. They released their first song in 1948, called "I Can See Everybody's Mother But Mine," and officially changed the band's name to The Five Blind Boys of Alabama. The band and another band, The Five Blind Boys of Mississippi, had a friendly rivalry and would often perform with one-another at concerts. The band toured extensively throughout the 1960s, 1970s, and 1980s. They received their first Grammy nomination for "Deep River" in 1992. They won Grammys in 2001, 2002, 2003, and 2004, and were given the Grammy Lifetime Achievement Award in 2009. However, Fountain stopped touring with the band in 2007, due to declining health.

Clarence Fountain is survived by his wife, Barbara.

See *Current Biography* 2001

Aretha Franklin

Born: Memphis, Tennessee; March 25, 1942
Died: Detroit, Michigan; August 16, 2018
Occupation: American singer

Aretha Franklin was arguably one of the greatest soul singers in history. She was dubbed the "Queen of Soul," a cultural icon of contemporary pop music. More than one hundred singles made it to the Billboard charts, and she received eighteen Grammy Awards, as well as a lifetime achievement award. She sang at Barack Obama's 2009 inauguration and performed at pre-inauguration concerts for Presidents Jimmy Carter and Bill Clinton. She also sang at the memorial service for Dr. Martin Luther King, Jr. in 1968. *Rolling Stone* magazine included her in its list of the "100 Greatest Singers of All Time." She was the first female artist to be inducted into the Rock & Roll Hall of Fame.

Aretha Franklin was born, one of five children, to Reverend C. L. Franklin and Barbara Siggers Franklin. Franklin's father was a popular Baptist pastor whose sermons were broadcast nationwide, and his daughter, Aretha, learned to sing in the church's gospel choir. Her parents separated when Franklin was six, and her mother died several years later. The Franklin home often welcomed well-known musicians like Art Tatum and Mahalia Jackson who became her mentors. Aretha was a self-taught pianist who never learned to read music. She dropped out of school at twelve, after giving birth to a son, and she had a second child two years later. In the late 1950s, Franklin moved to New York to pursue her singing career, signing on with Columbia Records when she was just eighteen. After the release of her first album, *Aretha*, *Downbeat* magazine named her the best new female star of the year. She recorded her iconic hit, "Respect," in 1967, which won Franklin her first two Grammy Awards. Though her husband, Ted White, was her manager, he was physically abusive, and the two divorced in 1969. The disco era of the late 1970s saw a slump in Franklin's popularity, and in 1979, her father was shot and left in a coma after his home was broken into. Franklin had a bout of heavy drinking before sobering up, but her career stayed flat until the mid-1980s. In 1986, Michigan lawmakers declared her voice to be one of the state's natural resources.

Franklin's survivors include her four sons, and four grandchildren.

See *Current Biography* 1992

John Gagliardi

Born: Trinidad, Colorado; November 1, 1926
Died: Collegeville, Minnesota; October 7, 2018
Occupation: College football coach

John Gagliardi was the winningest coach in the history of college football, with 489 wins, 189 losses, and 11 ties. In 2006 he was inducted into the College Football Hall of Fame. Gagliardi received the National College Football Awards Association (NCFAA) Contributions to College Football Award in 2013. In 2003 President George Bush had Gagliardi visit the White House.

John Gagliardi was born in the small Colorado town of Trinidad, the fifth of nine children. His father, who immigrated from southern Italy in 1910, was a coal miner, before opening his own blacksmith shop; and when demand for blacksmiths slackened, he opened an auto repair shop. His son, John, was one of only seven boys in his class. He was a gifted athlete who was the captain and quarterback for the school football team. So, when the football coach was called to active duty in 1943 and the football team was about to be cut, he offered to fill in as coach. He led the team to its first-ever league championship. He was just sixteen years old. Gagliardi remained the high school coach while attending Trinidad Junior College, leading his team to four conference titles in six years. He enrolled at Colorado College where he earned his degree in education in 1949. Gagliardi was hired to coach football, basketball, and baseball at Carroll College in Helena, Montana, where he led all three teams to league championships. What made Gagliardi so unique was his coaching style. He called it "winning with no's." Among the "No's" (which numbered in the hundreds) were no calisthenics, no tackling during practice, no playbooks, no compulsory weightlifting program, no captains (all seniors were considered captains), and, significantly, no calling him "coach." His record at Carroll caught the eye of a scout from St. John's University in Collegeville, Minnesota, home of Johnny McNally who would become a charter member of the Professional Football Hall of Fame. At the time, St. John's had not won a conference title in fifteen years. Gagliardi would remain at St. John's for another sixty-four seasons, retiring in 2012.

John Gagliardi is survived by his wife, Peg, four children, and numerous grandchildren.

See *Current Biography* 2008

William H. Gass

Born: Fargo, North Dakota; July 30, 1924
Died: St. Louis, Missouri; December 6, 2017
Occupation: Writer, philosopher, university professor

William H. Gass wrote three novels, several collections of short stories and novellas, and three volumes of essays. He was a writer who experimented with a new kind of fiction, foregoing the conventions of plot and character, using metaphor to develop storylines. He opposed the idea that art is an imitation of life.

William Gass was born in North Dakota, though he spent his childhood in Warren, Ohio, where his father taught drafting at the local high school. By all accounts he had a difficult childhood. He claimed his father was a bigot, crippled by arthritis, and his mother was an alcoholic. Upon graduating from high school, Gass attended Kenyon College, but World War II had him serving in the Pacific theater as an ensign in the navy for several years. Following the war, Gass attended Columbia University, studying under the noted philosopher Ludwig Wittgenstein, learning the interrelationships between reality, language, and the mind. He completed his PhD in 1954 and began teaching at the College of Wooster in Ohio, followed by a stint at Purdue University, and finally settling at Washington University in St. Louis where he taught for more than thirty years. In 1958 Gass reached nationwide acclaim when the literary magazine *Accent* devoted an entire issue to his short stories. Eight years later, he published *Omensetter's Luck,* a highly acclaimed, historical novel. Gass was best known for his approach to literature, coining the term "metafiction" to describe a story in which an author becomes a character in his own fiction. Gass wrote only three novels: *Omensetter's Luck, The Tunnel,* and *Middle C.* However, he published numerous collections of novellas, short stories, and essays. He was a great influence on such noted modern writers as Jonathan Safran Foer and David Foster Wallace.

William Gass won numerous accolades over his career including three National Book Critics Circle Awards, the Truman Capote Award for Literary Criticism, the William Dean Howells Medal, four Pushcart Prizes, the Pen-Faulkner Prize, and a lifetime achievement award from the Lannan Foundation.

Gass was married twice. His first marriage ended in divorce. His survivors include his second wife, Mary Henderson, his five children, five grandchildren, and two great-grandchildren.

See *Current Biography* 1986

John Gavin

Born: Los Angeles, California; April 8, 1931
Died: Beverly Hills, California; February 9, 2018
Occupation: Actor, US ambassador to Mexico

While John Gavin had once been marketed as the next Rock Hudson, he had more success as the US ambassador to Mexico, and as a corporate executive with the Atlantic Richfield Company, and as president of Univisa Satellite Communications. He served as president of the Screen Actors Guild (SAG) from 1971 to 1973.

John Gavin's birth name was Juan Vincent Apablasa. His father was of Chilean descent and his mother's family was from Mexico, so Gavin was fluent in Spanish from an early age, a characteristic that would serve him well as an adult. His parents divorced when he was quite young, and his mother married Harold Golenor who adopted him. Gavin attended St. John's Military Academy in Los Angeles, Beverly Hills High school, and Villanova Preparatory School in Ojai, California before entering Stanford University where he earned a degree in Latin American economic history. Gavin was tall and quite handsome, which had talent agents calling him the next Rock Hudson. However, he had limited success playing opposite such great female leads as Lana Turner, Sophia Loren, and Katharine Hepburn. He also played Janet Leigh's lover in the Alfred Hitchcock thriller *Psycho*. He had been considered for the role of James Bond in *Diamonds Are Forever,* and *Live and Let Die* but lost out to Roger Moore and Sean Connery. While still growing his career in entertainment, he became involved in the political campaigns of his friend Ronald Reagan. He became the secretary general of the Organization of American States under President John F. Kennedy and was later named US ambassador to Mexico under Ronald Reagan. His relationship with the Mexican government soured after he expressed relief that more Americans weren't killed in the devastating 1985 earthquake that killed thousands. He was spotted having lunch with members of the opposition National Action Party, which did not endear him to Mexican President José López Portillo. He resigned in 1986 and launched a successful business career.

John Gavin had divorced his first wife, actress Cicely Evans in 1965. They had two children. In 1974 he married the singer and actress Constance Towers. His survivors include his second wife, his children and stepchildren and numerous grandchildren.

See *Current Biography* 1962

Hubert de Givenchy

Born: Beauvais, Picardy, France; February 21, 1927
Died: Paris, France; March 10, 2018
Occupation: Fashion designer

A renowned fashion designer, Hubert De Givenchy's most iconic designs have been worn by stars including Jacqueline Kennedy Onassis, Grace Kelly, and by Audrey Hepburn in her iconic role as Holly Golightly in the movie *Breakfast at Tiffany's*. After partnering with Hepburn for many of her films, Givenchy gained fame and notoriety for his signature elegant designs.

Hubert James Marcel Taffin de Givenchy was born to Beatricé Badin and Lucien Taffin de Givenchy in Beauvais, France in 1927. At the age of three his father passed away and Givenchy, his mother and brother moved into his maternal grandparents' home. Givenchy was heavily influenced by the Parisian fairs near his home, where he was introduced to fashion by Coco Chanel and Elsa Schiaparelli. He attended the École nationale supérieure des Beaux-Arts in Paris, where he studied law. However, at the age of seventeen, Givenchy showed his fashion designs to Jacque Fath and was immediately asked to be Fath's apprentice-designer. In 1949 Givenchy joined Elsa Schiaparelli's staff, and gained a reputation for his notable cardigans, dresses, blouses, and interchangeable "separates," which attracted the attention of many American clients. In 1952 he opened his own House of Couture; and during a Spring fashion show in the same year, his designs exploded in popularity. His shop remained successful due to Givenchy's use of cheaper materials, while ensuring high-quality stitching and ready-to-wear designs. In 1954, Audrey Hepburn first contacted Givenchy to design costumes to inspire the character Sabrina in *Roman Holiday*. His designs appeared in several of her films and in Hepburn's daily life. Givenchy retired from fashion in 1995 but remained active in the arts, as an antiques expert for prominent museums. In 2005, Givenchy's label was handed to Riccardo Tisci, who took the label in directions Givenchy did not approve of. The title of artistic director was handed to Clare Waight Keller in 2017.

Givenchy is survived by his lifelong partner and couture fashion designer, Philippe Venet. Information about additional survivors is not available.

See *Current Biography* 1955

Richard Goodwin

Born: Boston, Massachusetts; December 7, 1931
Died: Concord, Massachusetts; May 20, 2018
Occupation: Presidential advisor and speech-writer

Richard Goodwin was an influential speech writer and assistant to several presidents and senators. Referred to as the "Voice of the 1960s," Goodwin wrote and advised on many historic occasions. He was also an author of several books on public policy.

Richard Goodwin was born to Joseph and Belle Goodwin in Brookline, Massachusetts. He attended Tufts University where he graduated summa cum laude. He then attended Harvard Law School and became President of the *Harvard Law Review*. Goodwin graduated in 1958, again at the top of his class, and worked for one year as a law clerk to Supreme Court Justice Felix Frankfurter. In 1959 Goodwin joined the US House of Representatives subcommittee and was then introduced to Robert Kennedy, who arranged for Goodwin to join John F. Kennedy's staff as a speechwriter. He wrote a large percentage of Kennedy's speeches during his presidential campaign in 1960. Once Kennedy won the presidency, Goodwin was appointed assistant special counsel in the White House (his area of responsibility being Latin America). At the end of 1961, Goodwin was appointed Deputy Assistant Secretary of State for Inter-American Affairs. Goodwin took temporary leave from the State House to work as international secretariat for the Peace Corps. During this time away, he continued to write speeches for Kennedy. After Kennedy's assassination, Goodwin returned to the White House and became Johnson's special assistant in 1964. His last speech for Johnson was the 1966 State of the Union address. Soon after the Johnson address, Goodwin wrote *Triumph or Tragedy: Reflections on Vietnam*, which was published by Random House. The book detailed his doubts of the Johnson administration and its involvement in Vietnam. From 1966 to 1967, Goodwin served as Jacqueline Kennedy's attorney against William Manchester's publications on the President's death. Goodwin assisted both in Robert Kennedy and Senator Eugene McCarthy's campaigns for President. After Robert Kennedy's assassination, Goodwin joined McCarthy's team until Humphrey was nominated. Much later, Goodwin helped write Al Gore's 2000 concession speech and was a consultant to both Senator John Kerry and President Barack Obama.

Richard Goodwin is survived by his wife, Doris Kearns, his children, Richard (from his first marriage to Sandra Leverant), Michael, and Joseph, and two grandchildren.

See *Current Biography* 1968

Sue Grafton

Born: Louisville, Kentucky; April 24, 1940
Died: Santa Barbara, California; December 28, 2017
Occupation: Author, screenwriter

Sue Grafton is most remembered for her hugely successful series of detective novels, twenty-five in all, that feature her private investigator protagonist, Kinsey Millhone.

Sue Grafton credits her "benign neglect" as a child for her success as a creative writer. Both of her parents were functional alcoholics. Her father was a lawyer who also wrote mystery novels. Her mother was a high school chemistry teacher. Grafton was an avid reader from an early age. Though she read the requisite Nancy Drew and Agatha Christie novels, she was particularly inspired by Mickey Spillane's work. She graduated from the University of Louisville in 1961 with a degree in English, a failing marriage, and a daughter. She moved to California with her second husband and worked in a series of clerical jobs including her job as a secretary at Danny Thomas Productions. She also began to write her own fiction. In 1967 her first novel, *Keziah Dane*, was published. Her second novel, *The Lolly-Madonna War*, was published in 1969, and was picked up by Metro-Goldwyn-Mayer, which hired Grafton to write the movie script. Though the movie starred top talent, including Rod Steiger and Jeff Bridges, it did not do well. During the 1970s Grafton wrote numerous scripts for television and the film industry and was nominated for an Edgar Award in 1987 for the script she wrote for the movie, *Love on the Run*. However, she came to abhor the Hollywood environment to the extent that, after her success with the Millhone novels, she vowed never to have them adapted for the screen. Her unhappiness with the industry provided the impetus she needed to start writing detective fiction. The first Millhone novel, *A is for Alibi*, was published in 1982, winning the 1983 Mystery Stranger Award from the Cloak and Clue Society. The book was the first in the abecedarian series. Grafton claimed she got the titles for her series from an old Victorian nursery rhyme that began "A is for Amy who fell down the stairs; B is for Basil assaulted by bears…"

Sue Grafton's many writing awards include numerous Shamus and Anthony Awards and starred reviews from *Publishers Weekly*, *Kirkus*

Review, and *Booklist*. Sue Grafton was married three times. Her survivors include her husband, Steven Humphrey, three children, four granddaughters, and a great-grandson.

See *Current Biography* 1995

Billy Graham

Born: Charlotte, North Carolina; November 7, 1918
Died: Montreat, North Carolina; February 21, 2018
Occupation: Evangelist, author

Sometimes referred to as America's pastor, Christian evangelist Billy Graham was the confidant to many modern US presidents and offered prayers at five presidential inaugurations. Graham penned nearly a dozen books about his faith. In addition to countless awards, Graham received the Presidential Medal of Freedom in 1983. In a rare acknowledgement of his service, Graham was one of only four private citizens to lie in state at the US Capital Rotunda in Washington, DC.

William Franklin Graham, Jr, was born into a long line of Scottish pioneers, and his two grandfathers fought for the Confederacy during the Civil War. He was born and raised on the family dairy farm. Though the family was Christian, Graham was more interested in history and baseball than he was in religion. In fact, his greatest aspiration was to play professional baseball. However, in his sixteenth year he was inspired by an itinerant preacher, Mordecai Ham, to give his life to Christ. He attended Bob Jones College and the Florida Bible College. In 1939 he became an ordained minister. Later, he earned a bachelor's degree in anthropology from Wheaton College. While ministering to his first congregation at the Village Church in Western Springs, Illinois, Graham also took over a Christian radio hour called *Songs in the Night* and began a traveling ministry called Youth for Christ. His first book, *Calling Youth to Christ* was published in 1947. He gained nation-wide attention as evangelism's rising star following his successful "Canvas Cathedral" revival meetings. In the mid-1950s he founded the magazine *Christianity Today*, and held rallies, which he called "crusades," around the world, including a sixteen-week stint at Madison Square Garden in New York, which was attended by millions. He refused to preach in South Africa because of the country's segregation. At one notable event in Tennessee, he tore down ropes that organizers had erected to separate his black and white audience. Graham worked to remain non-partisan, becoming an advisor to presidents on both sides of the political aisle, including John F. Kennedy and Richard Nixon. He became a regular fixture in Lyndon Johnson's White House. His reign was not without controversy though. He was caught on tape in conversation with Richard Nixon, discussing how the "Jewish media" was hurting the country.

Billy Graham married a Wheaton classmate, Ruth Bell. The marriage lasted sixty-four years until her death in 2007. They had five children who survive him in addition to numerous grandchildren and great-grandchildren.

See *Current Biography* 1973

Robert Guillaume

Born: St. Louis, Missouri; November 30, 1927
Died: Los Angeles, California; October 24, 2017
Occupation: American actor

Robert Guillaume is most remembered for his portrayal of Benson Dubois on the television show *Soap*, from 1977 to 1979. The role won him the 1979 Emmy Award for best supporting actor. He earned another Emmy in 1985 for his title role in the *Soap* spinoff, *Benson*. He also provided the voice for Rafiki in the Disney animated hit movie *The Lion King*. He earned a Grammy Award for his part in the movie's audiobook version.

Robert Guillaume was born Robert Williams in 1927. He was abandoned by his parents and raised, along with three siblings, by his maternal grandmother, Jeannette Williams, who worked as a laundress at a Christian school. He was expelled from school and entered the US army in 1945, but barely earned an honorable discharge. He finished high school and worked in a series of jobs. He enrolled at St. Louis University, but soon transferred to the music school at Washington University, also in St. Louis, where he studied under opera singer Leslie Chabay. He moved to New York where he took voice lessons and began auditioning for roles on Broadway and Off-Broadway. As an African American man, Broadway roles did not come easy. His attitude was to offer alternative interpretations for the roles he auditioned. In 1976 he earned a role in an all-black revival of Frank Loesser/Abe Burrows' musical *Guys and Dolls*. The hit won Guillaume a 1977 Tony Award. During the 1970s Guillaume performed in a number of television shows including *All in the Family*, *Sanford and Son*, *Good Times*, and *The Jeffersons*. In 1977 he was offered the role of Benson, a butler in the hit series *Soap*. He also starred in the title role in *Benson*, a *Soap* spin off. In 1990 he appeared in the title role of *Phantom of the Opera*. In 1999

Guillaume suffered a stroke on the set of Aaron Sorkin's series *Sports Night*. Sorkin rewrote Guillaume's role to that of a stroke victim. He would become a spokesman for the American Stroke Association.

Robert Guillaume's first marriage ended in divorce. His second wife, Donna Brown, survives along with Guillaume's four children.

See *Current Biography* 2000

Donald Hall

Born: New Haven , Connecticut; September 20, 1928
Died: Wilmot, New Hampshire; June 23, 2018
Occupation: Poet, essayist, critic, children's writer

Donald Hall was a celebrated US poet laureate, writer, and essayist known for his plain-spoken writing and themes of nature's beauty and love and loss.

Donald Hall, Jr. was born the only child to Donald Andrew and Lucy Hall who were dairy farmers. He wrote extensively throughout his childhood and submitted poems to major magazines and his local literary magazines. He attended Hamden High School and then Phillips Exeter Academy, where he graduated in 1947. He then attended Harvard University, where he befriended Robert Frost. After graduating in 1951 with a BA, Hall went to Oxford University, where he received the Newdigate Prize for narrative poetry for his poem "Exiles" (1952). He then attended Stanford University as a Creative Writing Fellow from 1953 to 1954. In 1955 Hall published his first book of poetry, Exiles and Marriage, which was a finalist for the National Book Award in poetry. In 1957 Hall became an assistant professor of English at the University of Michigan, where he continued publishing his poetry. In 1975 he left his teaching job to pursue writing full-time, and moved to Eagle Pond Farm in New Hampshire, an environment which inspired many of his writings. Hall published over fifty books throughout his life, with some of his most celebrated works being, *Writing Well* (1973), *Ox-cart Man* (1979), *The One Day* (1988), and *Without* (1998). Hall received two Guggenheim fellowships, the 1991 Robert Frost Medal, and the 1994 Ruth Lilly Poetry Prize. He served as US poet laureate from 2006 to 2007 and in 2010 was awarded the National Medal of the Arts from President Barack Obama.

Donald Hall is survived by his daughter, Philippa, and son, Andrew. He is also survived by five grandchildren and one great-grandchild.

See *Current Biography* 1984

Roy Halladay

Born: Denver, Colorado; May 14, 1977
Died: Gulf of Mexico, Florida; November 7, 2017
Occupation: Major league baseball player

Roy Halladay was one of the greatest baseball pitchers of his time, pitching a near no-hitter in his second major league appearance for the Toronto Blue Jays. He was included in eight All-Star selections in his sixteen-year career and won two Cy Young Awards. In 2010 he was only the second player to pitch a no-hitter in post-season play. (The first was Don Larsen who pitched a no-hitter in the 1956 World Series.)

Roy Halladay was raised in Arvada, a Denver suburb and was only three years old when he began tossing a baseball with his father, and joined a T-ball team when he was five. In high school Halladay was selected an All-Conference, All-State player for three years, leading his team to a state championship in 1994 and second place in 1995. He was voted the state Most Valuable Player (MVP) during his junior and senior seasons. Upon graduating from high school at Arvada West High School, he entered the Major League Baseball (MLB) draft and was picked up by the Toronto Blue Jays in the 1995 amateur draft. He had a rough season in 2000 and the Blue Jays sent him to the Syracuse class AAA team where he began a rigorous rework of his pitching style and physical conditioning, putting special focus on his mental game, seeking the counsel of the noted sports psychologist Harvey A. Dorfman. Back in the majors, Halladay had a breakout season, compiling a 19-7 record. He played in an All-Star Game for the first time. Unfortunately, Halladay was injury prone and had to sit out most of the 2004 season. Just a week before his anticipated appearance in another All-Star Game, he was hit by a line drive. His injuries kept him out for the rest of the 2005 season. Nevertheless, he led the American League (AL) that year. He played for the Phillies for one year, in 2012, and retired in 2013.

Halladay married his wife Bonnie in 1998, and they had two children. Roy Halladay earned his pilot's license several years before the plane crash that claimed his life. His survivors include his wife and two sons.

See *Current Biography* 2010

Johnny Hallyday

Born: Malasherbes, Paris, France; June 15, 1943
Died: Marnes-la-Coquette, France; December 5, 2017
Occupation: French rock and roll performer

Johnny Hallyday was a French musical super star for more that fifty years. He was sometimes referred to as a French Elvis Presley and sold more than one hundred and ten million records. He was so popular in France that Jimi Hendrix performed as a supporting act for Hallyday.

Shortly after his birth, Johnny Hallyday's parents split up and abandoned him to a paternal aunt who raised him. As his extended family were stage performers, Hallyday grew up backstage at theaters, traveling across Europe, and sleeping in hotels. Because this lifestyle was so mobile, Hallyday acquired his education in correspondence schools. By the age of nine, Hallyday performed on stage while his cousins changed costumes for their act. He was a great fan of Elvis Presley and began cultivating an image like that of Presley, covering Presley songs in French. He also followed Presley's forays into movies. Over the course of his career, Hallyday produced an eclectic variety of albums with everything from French ballads to American country and western songs. Though he had a rock and roll "bad boy" image, he was also somehow vulnerable. He was good friends with a number of other rock and roll royalty, including Rod Stewart, Mick Jagger, and John Lennon. His personal life was tumultuous. He was married five times, twice to one woman, and survived two suicide attempts.

Information about survivors is unavailable. At the time of his death he lived with his wife, Laeticia Hallyday, and two young daughters.

See *Current Biography* 2003

Barbara Harris

Born: Evanston, Illinois; July 25, 1935
Died: Scottsdale, Arizona; August 21, 2018
Occupation: Actress

Barbara Harris was an actress and a founding member of Second City improvisational theater. She won a Tony Award for her role as the lead in *The Apple Tree.*

Barbara Harris's father, Oscar Harris, was a tree surgeon and her mother, Natalie, taught piano. Harris had originally planned to be a dancer, but she became more interested in theater after graduating from high school. After a brief stint at Wright Junior College in Chicago, Harris signed on as an apprentice with the Playwright's Theatre Club, a repertory formed by students from the University of Chicago. When their building was condemned, the group decided to try improvisation at a local coffeehouse. Soon thereafter, Harris married fellow actor, Paul Sills who was awarded a Fulbright grant to study European theater. The couple studied in England and in Germany—a time that Harris acknowledged as formative in exposing her to different styles of acting. In 1959, after a brief time in Hollywood, where Harris turned down a seven-year contract with Twentieth Century Fox because she didn't want such a long commitment, she joined with her improvisational cohorts to form The Second City theater group. They soon received offers from Broadway and opened in 1961. In 1965 Harris played the role of Daisy in the Broadway musical, *On a Clear Day You Can See Forever.* Her performance won her a Tony nomination. Two years later she won a Tony Award for her performance as Eve in *The Apple Tree.* (Alan Alda played Adam.) By the late 1960s, she left Broadway and began acting in film. She won an Oscar nomination for her role in *Who Is Harry Kellerman and Why Is He Saying Those Terrible Things About Me?* (which also starred a young Dustin Hoffman). Harris shunned fame, claiming she always enjoyed the people and the process of creating a character, rather than the finished product.

Barbara Harris's marriage to Paul Sills was short-lived. She had no immediate survivors.

See *Current Biography* 1968

Stephen William Hawking

Born: Oxfordshire, England; January 8, 1942
Died: Cambridge, England; March 14, 2018
Occupation: Physicist, professor

Dr. Stephen Hawking is widely known as one of the most prominent scientists of the twentieth century. He was the author of *A Brief History of Time: From the Big Bang to Black Holes,* written for the general public, inciting popular interest into the field of physics and the history of the universe.

Born to Frank Hawking and Isobel Walker, Hawking was the eldest of four siblings. He was an average student at St. Albans School in London. However, as an undergraduate at University College, Oxford, Hawking began exploring concepts within cosmology, including the major question: where did the universe come from? He earned his PhD from Cambridge University in 1977 and remained there as a professor for the rest of his life. After his twenty-first birthday, in

1963, Hawking was first diagnosed with amyotrophic lateral sclerosis (ALS), also known as Lou Gehrig's disease, an incurable disease characterized by the slow deterioration of motor neurons, affecting muscles and movement. At the time he was given a life expectancy of three years; however, after two years Hawking's condition stabilized, and he was able to continue his studies and research. In the year 1965, Hawking married Jane Wilde, an event that he claims gave him something to live for. Building on Albert Einstein's Theory of Relativity and the concept of black holes, Hawking and his colleague, Roger Penrose, proved that space-time can reach a singularity at the center of a black hole. Within this singularity the presence of matter becomes so great that the force of gravity becomes infinite, creating a point of infinite density, which creates a hole through the fabric of the universe. By inverting this theory, Hawking proposed that, during an event called the "Big Bang," time and space began around sixteen or seventeen million years ago. In the 1970s, Hawking presented findings that proved black holes could become smaller (as opposed to only larger, as previously thought) via the interaction of particles and antiparticles at the edge of a black hole. The particles which escape the black hole are known as "Hawking radiation." Eventually, enough pairs of particles and antiparticles have been separated into the black hole, causing the hole to explode from existence. In 1985, after being hospitalized with pneumonia, Hawking lost use of his voice and was forced to use a computerized program to speak for him. Though he lost use of his voice, Hawking continued his research and wrote *A Brief History of Time: From the Big Bang to Black Holes* in 1988. Throughout his career, Hawking has received numerous awards for his contributions to science.

Hawking separated from his wife and mother of his three children, Jane Wilde, in 1990 and later married Elaine Mason, who had been his nurse for many years. Hawking and Mason divorced in 2006. Stephen Hawking's survivors include his three children and three grandchildren.

See *Current Biography* 1984

Margaret Heckler

Born: New York, New York; June 21, 1931
Died: Arlington County, Virginia; August 6, 2018
Occupation: US politician

Margaret Heckler served eight terms as a delegate to the US House of Representatives for Massachusetts. In 1983 President Ronald Reagan named her Secretary of the Department of Health and Human Services, though her tenure was short-lived. She also served as the US Ambassador to Ireland from 1986 to 1989, the first woman to hold the post.

Margaret O'Shaughnessy was born, the only child, to Irish immigrants, John and Mary O'Shaughnessy. Her father was a doorman at a New York City hotel and her mother was a homemaker. Margaret won a scholarship to Albertus Magnus College where she majored in political science while also serving as a delegate to the Connecticut Intercollegiate Student Legislature and later, as the speaker of the group. She received her BA degree in 1953, then attended Boston College Law School, earning her LL.B in 1956. She married her political strategist and fellow student, John Heckler, in 1953. While setting up her own legal practice, she also served on the Wellesley, Massachusetts Governor's Council, a position she held from 1958 to 1966. In 1962 she declared candidacy for the Governor's Council. In 1966, defying the stalwarts of the Massachusetts Republican Party, Heckler ran against the twenty-one-term incumbent congressman for the Tenth Congressional District, and former Speaker of the House, Joseph W. Martin, Jr. She won and then set out to win the election over her Democrat rival, Patrick Harrington, Jr. She was a strong advocate for veteran's affairs, child welfare, and women's rights, though her staunch anti-abortion stance alienated her among feminists. In 1983, President Ronald Reagan named her to head the Office of Health and Human Services; however, Reagan ousted her in 1985 and named her the new US Ambassador to Ireland, where she was widely praised for her promotion of industry in Ireland.

After a thirty-one-year marriage, the Heckler's divorced in 1984. He remarried three weeks later. Margaret Heckler's survivors include her three children and four grandchildren.

See *Current Biography* 1983

Philip Hoff

Born: Turners Falls, Massachusetts; June 29, 1924
Died: Shelburne, Vermont; April 26, 2018
Occupation: Politician

Philip Hoff was the first Democrat elected as Governor in the state of Vermont in over one hundred years. He is credited with making changes and setting agendas that influenced the states' politics for decades to follow.

Philip Hoff was born to Olaf and Agnes Hoff, one of four children. Hoff attended Williams College in Massachusetts, but entered the

U.S. Navy submarine branch during World War II, from 1943 to 1946. He returned to Williams College and received his BA in english literature in 1948. Hoff received his law degree from Cornell Law, after which he worked in a law office in New York City. He was then asked by a friend to join a law practice in Burlington, Vermont, where he worked until he became governor in 1962. Once in Vermont, Hoff served as chairman of the Burlington zoning board and as the Burlington representative to the Vermont State General Assembly. Hoff was elected Governor of Vermont in 1962, making him the first Democratic governor elected in Vermont in over one hundred years. He served three two-year terms in office and in 1970 ran for US Senate. Though he lost in 1970, Hoff was elected to the state senate in 1982 and served for two more terms. During his time in office, Hoff focused on racial equality and environmental protection.

Philip Hoff is survived by his wife, Joan, their four children, Susan, Dagny, Andrea, and Gretchen, six grandchildren, and two great-grandchildren.

See *Current Biography* 1963

Raymond Hunthausen

Born: Anaconda, Montana; August 21, 1921
Died: Helena, Montana; July 22, 2018
Occupation: US Catholic prelate

Bishop Raymond Hunthausen was the last remaining American bishop to participate in the Second Vatican Council from 1962 to 1965. He gained worldwide attention when he withheld part of his income taxes in protest to US nuclear proliferation.

Raymond Hunthausen was born the eldest of seven children in the small mining town of Anaconda, Montana, where his family ran a grocery store. As a child Hunthausen wanted to be a pilot. In high school he loved science and entered Carroll College in Helena, Montana, as a chemistry major. However, his mathematics teacher persuaded him to try the priesthood. Following graduation, Hunthausen enrolled at St. Edwards Seminary in Seattle. He was ordained as a priest in 1948. After receiving his master's degree in chemistry from Notre Dame University, he taught chemistry and coached football and basketball teams at his alma mater Carroll College. He became president of the college from 1957 to 1962. While teaching at Carroll, he earned an LLD degree from DePaul University. In 1962 Pope John appointed him bishop of Helena. In 1975 he was named archbishop of Seattle. During the late 1970s the Vatican started receiving complaints about Hunthausen from conservative Catholics who considered his implicit acceptance of contraception and his leniency with matters of divorce to be unacceptable. In 1981 it was reported he had advocated withholding part of one's taxes as an act of civil disobedience to protest US policies of nuclear weapons proliferation. The Vatican responded with an "apostolic investigation." Ultimately Cardinal Ratzinger lauded Hunthausen's efforts to "be a good bishop." Hunthausen's was one of the first dioceses in the country to address sexual abuse by priests.

Raymond Hunthausen leaves behind five siblings, thirty-four nieces and nephews, over one hundred great-nieces and nephews, and sixty-four great-great nieces and nephews.

See *Current Biography* 1987

Dmitri Hvorostovsky

Born: Krasnoyarsk, Siberia, Russia; October 16, 1962
Died: London, England; November 22, 2017
Occupation: Russian opera singer

Dmitri Hvorostovsky was a world-renowned opera singer whose natural talent as a baritone had him performing on the world's greatest stages.

Dmitri Hvorostovsky was born in an isolated city in Siberia, which was closed to foreigners due to its role in Russia's defense industry. He was an only child who was raised primarily by his grandparents. His mother was a gynecologist and his father, a chemical engineer who worked very long hours, and he saw them only on weekends. He began cultivating his natural musical talent as a musician, taking piano lessons as a child. However, as he grew to adolescence, he abandoned his lessons and began rebelling, getting into street fights, and drinking. Alcoholism would later cost him his first marriage. He became obsessed with rock music and joined a rock band, but his voice was too rich. At age sixteen Hvorostovsky's father sent him to a school that trained music teachers and choral conductors, where he found his new passion for classical singing. At age nineteen Hvorostovsky entered the Krasnoyarsk State Arts Institute where he studied under the instructor Yekaterina Yofel who taught him the extraordinary breath control he became known for. He graduated from the conservatory in 1986, and in 1987 he won the Glinka National Competition in Russia. In 1988 he made his first trip outside of the Soviet Union to attend the Concours International de Chant competition, which he won. He had also become the principal singer at the

Krasnoyarsk Opera. Following his 1989 win at the BBC Singer of the World competition in Cardiff, he began receiving invitations to perform at prestigious opera houses throughout the world. He debuted at the New York Metropolitan Opera in 1995. In 2005 he gave a concert in the Red Square in Moscow to commemorate the sixtieth anniversary of the end of World War II, with Russian President Vladimir Putin in attendance. In the summer of 2015 Hvorostovsky announced he had been diagnosed with a brain tumor.

Dmitri Hvorostovsky was married twice. His first marriage ended in divorce. His survivors include his parents, his second wife, Florence Illi, a Swiss-born soprano, and his four children.

See *Current Biography* 2006

Robert Indiana

Born: New Castle, Indiana; September 13, 1928
Died: Vinalhaven, Maine; May 19, 2018
Occupation: Pop artist

Robert Indiana created one of the most iconic sculptures of the twentieth century, a sculpture that reads "LOVE," that has been reprinted in many forms and plagiarized worldwide.

Born Robert Clarke, Indiana was born to Earl and Carmen Clarke, though his father left while Indiana was still a child. He attended Arsenal Technical High School but painted extensively during his free time after school and when not working. Indiana attained a university scholarship by joining the Army Air Corps. He was discharged in 1949 and attended the Art Institute of Chicago for his BFA degree. Indiana moved to New York City in 1954 and quickly befriended, and was heavily influenced by, the artists Ellsworth Kelly, Jack Youngerman, and James Rosenquist. He began creating artwork using found objects, such as paper, wood planks and wheels. He also began creating paintings using bright colors and large stencil letters, spelling words such as HUB, SOUL, PAIR, and MOON (which was exhibited in the Museum of Modern Art). He would often use quotes from his favorite writers: Walt Whitman and Herman Melville. He also created works influenced by the charged political nature of the 1960s. Many of these pieces were included in a collection he called "American Dream." In 1965, Indiana created several painted canvases spelling LOVE, with the O tilted to the side. The following year, he was given a major retrospective exhibition consisting of twenty-two paintings, twelve sculptures, and drawings, prints, and posters, which were displayed at several universities and

galleries across the country. In 1970, Indiana created a twelve-foot steel sculpture of the word LOVE, again with the O tilted, for Indianapolis Museum of Art. The sculpture grew in popularity and traveled to cities across the world. In 1978, Indiana returned to Maine to escape the public eye and often resented the popularity of the LOVE sculpture, believing it ruined his reputation. He continued to work on art, and in 2008, creating a similarly designed poster for Barack Obama's presidential campaign, using the word HOPE.

Robert Indiana has no remaining survivors.

See *Current Biography* 1973

Asma Jahangir

Born: Lahore, Pakistan: January 27, 1952
Died: Lahore, Pakistan; February 11, 2018
Occupation: Pakistani human rights advocate, lawyer

Asma Jahangir was a leading human rights lawyer who co-founded AGHS, the first all-female law firm in Pakistan, the Women's Action Forum, and the Human Rights Commission of Pakistan.

The name Asma means "innocence" in Urdu, Pakistan's official language. She was born into a distinguished, active political family. Her father, Malik Ghulam Jilani, was a rehabilitation commissioner who processed Muslim refugees who crossed into Pakistan following the 1947 partition of India. He was a prominent voice for progressive reform in Pakistan's National Assembly. Two of his daughters, Asma and Hina Julani, became lawyers and human rights activists. Asma Jahangir, the second of four children, attended the Convent of Jesus and Mary Catholic school. Her father, Malik, was arrested several times for his political views. In 1970 he could not find legal representation so his daughter filed a constitutional petition in the Supreme Court challenging the legality of his arrest. The court ruled in her favor, going so far as to delegitimize the government that had him arrested, and a lawyer was born. She received her law degree from Punjab University in 1978, and established the law firm, AGHS, along with her sister and two other female lawyers, with the mission of representing women in an increasingly hostile atmosphere towards women. The group also co-founded the Women's Action Forum, which advocated for women's rights. Because of her controversial work on behalf of women, Jahangir's life was always in jeopardy, and a fatwa (religious edict) called for her death. In one case, a gunman entered her office and murdered a young mother who was seeking a divorce from an abusive husband. The incident was deemed an "honor killing." In 1986 Jahangir set up the first legal aid center in Pakistan and, with her sister, co-founded the Human Rights Commission of Pakistan. After Benazir Bhutto was elected President, she asked Jahangir to become Pakistan's first female judge, but Jahangir refused saying she could not defend laws she didn't believe in. In 1998 she was appointed a United Nations Rapporteur, serving on the human rights commission.

Asma Jahangir received numerous awards including the Millennium Peace Prize and the Ramon Magsaysay Award for public service. She married Mian Tahir Jahangir in 1974, and they had three children. Her husband, three children, and three siblings survive.

See *Current Biography* 2003

Ingvar Kamprad

Born: Agunnaryd, Sweden; March 30, 1926
Died: Småland, Sweden; January 27, 2018
Occupation: Swedish entrepreneur, founder of IKEA

Ingvar Kamprad founded the furniture outlet IKEA in 1943 when he was just seventeen. He was frequently listed as one of the world's top-ten richest people. His honors include His Majesty the King's Badge for Merit.

Ingvar Kamprad was born to a Swedish farmer in the small village of Agunnaryd, in southeastern Sweden. He attended a type of trade high school and, at a very young age, became interested in how factories manufacture their products and get them to consumers. While still a teenager, Kamprad began selling small sundries such as ballpoint pens and matches, and named his enterprise IKEA, a name created using the first initials of his name and the initials of his family's farm and the town—Elmtaryd and Agunnaryd—where he was raised. He traveled to Paris at the invitation of his ballpoint pen manufacturer. The trip inspired him to expand his business through advertisements and a simple mail-order catalogue business.

In 1950 he began selling locally manufactured home furnishings through his catalogue. The first IKEA furniture catalogue was published in 1951, and the first IKEA showroom was opened in 1953. At the suggestion of some of his furniture designers, he adopted the concept of customer-assembled furniture that could be more readily shipped in flat packages rather than unwieldy furniture crates. By reducing his storage and shipping costs, he was able to keep prices lower than competitors. He also reduced costs by minimizing sales staff. His showrooms were built to accommodate customer's needs to wander through the displays, deciding for themselves what they needed. Over the next decades he began installing showrooms throughout the world. The first IKEA store in the United States was opened in 1985 in Philadelphia. By 1994, IKEA had one hundred and twenty-five stores in twenty-six countries. Kamprad's image was damaged in 1994 by reports that he had a past acquaintance with the ultra-right, pro-Nazi activist Per Engdahl. Kamprad responded with regret and honesty, blaming the naiveté of his youth and the influence of his German grandmother who had been drawn into Engdahl's pre-World War II vision of a "non-Communist, Socialist Europe."

Kamprad married his wife, Margaretha in 1960. They had three sons. Kamprad had an adopted daughter from a previous marriage. All his children survive him.

See *Current Biography* 1998

Charles K. Kao

Born: Shanghai, Republic of China; November 4, 1933
Died: Sha Tin, Hong Kong; September 23, 2018
Occupation: Optics engineer

Dr. Charles Kuen Kao was often referred to as the "Father of Fiber Optics," a technological advancement that made way for modern telecommunications, including the Internet. He and fellow scientists, Willard Boyle and George Smith, shared the 2009 Nobel Prize in Physics.

Charles Kao was born to a wealthy family in Shanghai, China. His father was a judge in the court of international law, and his grandfather had been a Confucian scholar, a poet, and calligrapher. The family moved to Shanghai when Kao was fourteen, just prior to China's Communist Revolution in 1949. Kao received his BS and PhD in electrical engineering from Woolwich Polytechnic School of London before joining International Telephone and Telegraph (ITT), where he would remain for over thirty years, working in Britain, across Europe, and the United States. In 1966 Kao and his colleague, George Hockham published a groundbreaking paper that determined the reason light dissipated when pulsed through glass fiber was due to imperfections in the fiber itself. They unveiled a prototype fiber-optic strand that could carry a gigacycle of information, roughly equivalent to 200 television channels or 200,000 phone calls. In 1970 Kao took a short leave to help establish an electronics department at the Chinese University of Hong Kong. Later, in 1987, he would become president of the university through 1996. In 1982 ITT designated Kao an executive scientist, and in 1985 he taught as an adjunct professor at Yale University.

In 1985, the United Nations awarded Kao with the Marconi International Fellowship and, in 1999, he was awarded the Draper Prize by the National Academy of Engineering. He was knighted in 2010.

His survivors include his wife, Gwen Wong, and their two children.

See *Current Biography* 2001

Isabella Karle

Born: Detroit, Michigan; December 2, 1921
Died: Alexandria, Virginia; October 3, 2017
Occupation: American physical chemist and crystallographer

Isabella Karle invented methods to study the structures of molecules using electron and x-ray diffraction. Her work helped her husband, Jerome Karle and his partner, Herbert Hauptman win the 1985 Nobel Prize in Chemistry. Her work had a significant impact in the fields of molecular biology, chemistry, physics, metallurgy, geology, genetics, and pharmacology. She was the first woman to win the $250,000 Bower Award and Prize for Achievement in Science, and in 1995 President Bill Clinton awarded her the National Medal of Science.

Isabella Karle was born to Polish, working class immigrants. She was a precocious child who skipped several grades in elementary school. By the age of twenty-three, she had earned her bachelor's, master's, and doctoral degrees from the University of Michigan, which she attended on scholarship. She was the first American woman to receive a doctorate in chemistry from the university. Karle met her husband, Jerome Karle at the university when the two shared a course in physical chemistry. They married in 1942 and then worked together in Chicago on the Manhattan Project. While there, Isabella Karle developed a process to convert lumps of plutonium oxide into plutonium chloride. Her discoveries provided greater ease and accuracy in deducing the structures of molecules and helped prove the work of her husband and Herbert Hauptman, who were awarded the 1985 Nobel Prize in chemistry. (Jerome Karle was deeply disappointed his wife had not been included in the award as her work was indispensable to his work.) Her work also helped scientists understand the chemical processes taking place inside the body, contributing to the development of disease fighting pharmaceuticals.

Isabella Karle had three daughters who survive her along with four grandchildren and a great granddaughter.

See *Current Biography* 2003

Carl Kasell

Born: Goldsboro, North Carolina; April 2, 1934
Died: Potomac, Maryland; April 17, 2018
Occupation: Radio newscaster

Known for his reassuring baritone voice on National Public Radio's (NPR) *Morning Edition* show, Carl Kasell was also a judge and scorekeeper on NPR's game show, *Wait, Wait...Don't Tell Me*, where he would leave humorous outgoing phone messages for winning contestants.

Carl Kasell was born in Goldsboro, North Carolina, one of four children. From a young age Kasell was interested in radio, and at the age of sixteen, Kasell and his radio class were invited to give weekly reports at the local radio station, WGBR-AM. The station allowed Kasell to DJ his own late-night music show. He graduated from Goldsboro High School in 1952 and attended the University of North Carolina (UNC). While in school, Kasell was one of the first hosts of UNC's new radio station, WUNC. After graduating with a bachelor's degree in english in 1956, Kasell was drafted into the army and stationed in Italy. While there, he met and married his wife, Clara de Zorzi. After completing his time with the army, Kasell moved back to Goldsboro and took up his job with WGBR-AM. In 1965 he moved to Virginia for a job at WAVA-FM where he began working for NPR as a morning anchor on *All Things Considered*. In 1977, Kasell joined NPR full-time, and two years later, he became the newscaster for *Morning Edition*. He held that job for over thirty years. In the 1990s, Kasell became the judge and scorekeeper for NPR's comedic game show, *Wait, Wait...Don't Tell Me!* His wife died in 1997 after thirty-seven years of marriage, but Kasell later remarried in 2003. Kasell was inducted into the National Radio Hall of Fame in 2010, and in 2014 published a book by the same name as his game show, *Wait, Wait... Don't Tell Me!* That same year he announced he would step down as judge and was succeeded by Bill Kurtis.

Carl Kasell is survived by his second wife, Mary Ann Foster. He is also survived by his son from his first marriage, Joe, a stepson, Brian, and four grandchildren.

See *Current Biography* 2002

Oliver Knussen

Born: Glasgow, Scotland; June 12, 1952
Died: Snape, England; July 8, 2018
Occupation: Composer, conductor

Oliver Knussen was a renowned composer and conductor, known especially for his operatic composition *Where the Wild Things Are*, based on the popular children's story. During his career, Knussen wrote three symphonies, many chamber works, and recorded over fifty albums.

Stuart Oliver Knussen was born to Stewart and Ethelyn Knussen, the inheritor of a long line of family musicians. He began composing music at the age of six, and until 1968 took private music lessons at the Royal Academy of Music. He also attended the central tutorial School of Young Musicians for his primary education. In 1968 Knussen was allowed to compose a piece for the London Symphony Orchestra, entitled Knussen's Symphony No. 1, and after the conductor fell ill, Knussen was asked to conduct the piece himself. He was fifteen years old at the time. In 1970 Knussen joined Tanglewood Music Center, in Lenox, Massachusetts, where he eventually became Head of Contemporary Music. From 1977 until 1982, Knussen worked as an instructor in composition at the Royal College of Music in London. During this same time, Knussen began working with children's author, Maurice Sendak, author of *Where the Wild Things Are*. Knussen began writing the score for the Opera version of the book in 1979. It was officially performed in 1984 at the Royal National Theatre in London by the Glyndebourne Festival Opera. The show was performed at the New York City Opera during the 1987–88 season and the Chicago Opera Theatre in 1989. Knussen and Sendak also worked in the creation of the Opera version of *Higglety Pigglety Pop!*, which was first staged by the Glyndebourne Festival Opera in 1985, on a double bill with *Where the Wild Things Are*. Knussen returned to Tanglewood from 1986 until 1993. He had been the co-artistic director of the Aldeburgh Festival of Music and the Arts, in England, since 1983. He was a guest conductor for the Residentie Orchestra, the BBC Symphony Orchestra, the Philharmonia Orchestra, and the London Sinfonietta. Between 1991 and 1993 he was composer in residence with the Chamber Music Society of Lincoln Center, for whom he composed the octet *Songs Without Voices* (1992). He won the Queen's Medal for Music in 2016.

Oliver Knussen is survived by his daughter, contralto Sonya Alexandra Knussen.

See *Current Biography* 1994

Charles Krauthammer

Born: New York, New York; March 13, 1950
Died: Atlanta, Georgia; June 21, 2018
Occupation: Columnist, television commentator

Charles Krauthammer was a Pulitzer-prize winning columnist for *The Washington Post* and a conservative commentator for *Fox News*. Though he began his career as a Democrat, Krauthammer developed more conservative views, and coined the title "Neoconservative."

Charles Krauthammer was born to Shulim and Thea Krauthammer, and was raised in Montreal, Canada. He attended McGill University and received his degree in political science and economics in 1970. He then attended Oxford University for one year before deciding to pursue medicine at Harvard Medical school. After one year at Harvard, Krauthammer had a swimming accident, leaving him paralyzed and wheelchair bound. He did his residency at Massachusetts General Hospital (MGH) after graduating with his MD and served as the Chief resident of psychiatry from 1977 to 1978. In 1978, Krauthammer moved to Washington, DC to become the director of sciences for the Alcohol, Drug Abuse, and Mental Health Administration with the US Department of Health and Human Services. Once there, Krauthammer started writing speeches and joined the *New Republic*, serving from 1981 to 1982 as associate editor, and from 1982 to 1988 as senior editor. He wrote several pieces for *Time* and *The Washington Post,* many of which received awards. In 1987 Krauthammer won a Pulitzer Prize for his writing with *The Post*. During this time, his political leanings shifted from Democrat to Republican, and finally, to what he called neoconservatism. In 2004, the American Enterprise Institute for Public Policy Research gave Krauthammer its Irving Kristol Award. He was known for being very vocal of his support for the War in Iraq. In 2008 Krauthammer wrote extensively on his support for the Republican candidate, John McCain, and during the Obama administration, Krauthammer criticized many policies in his writings and during his appearances on *Fox News*. During the 2016 election, he made several statements that he thought neither Hillary Clinton, nor Donald Trump would be fit for office.

Charles Krauthammer is survived by his wife, Robyn, and their son, Daniel.

See *Current Biography* 2008

Mathilde Krim

Born: Como, Lombardy, Italy; July 9, 1926
Died: Kings Point, New York; January 15, 2018
Occupation: Geneticist, philanthropist

Dr. Mathilde Krim is most remembered for her research into, and social activism about, the AIDS virus. She was likely the first scientist to view the structure of chromosomes in an Electron Microscope. Before her AIDS research, Dr. Krim was a specialist in cancer research at the Sloan-Kettering Institute for Cancer Research and at Cornell Medical College. She helped found the American Foundation for AIDS Research (amfAR), now known as the Foundation for Aids Research, in 1983, and served as its founding chairwoman. She was awarded the Presidential Medal of Freedom in 2000.

Mathilde Krim was born, one of four children, to a Swiss agronomist and a Czechoslovakian mother. She claimed that by the age of six, she had decided to be a biologist. She attended the University of Geneva, graduating with a degree in genetics in 1948, and a PhD in 1953. It was at Geneva that she was introduced to the Electron Microscope. Upon seeing the images of Nazi concentration camps, Krim joined Irgun, the Zionist underground movement, and spent a summer smuggling weapons across the French border. She married a fellow Zionist, converted to Judaism, and moved to Israel. Her family disowned her. She became a research associate at the Weizmann Institute of Science in Rehovot, where she worked with the team that discovered amniocentesis could determine fetal diseases, as well as the sex of an unborn child. After she divorced her first husband, she met and married Arthur Krim, a trustee of the institute and chairman of United Artists in the United States. She followed her husband to New York, where she worked as a research associate in the virus research division at Cornell Medical College, studying the role of the natural protein interferon in inhibiting the growth of tumors. Eventually, she helped found the interferon laboratory at the Sloan-Kettering Institute and lobbied for support by the National Institutes of Health (NIH) and the National Cancer Institute, which agreed to sponsor her research. With the introduction of AIDS in the early 1980s, Krim helped found the AIDS Medical Foundation and became a key player in advocating for research into the disease. She promoted safe sex practices and needle exchanges and fought the discrimination against people with the disease.

Dr. Krim had one daughter, Daphna, from her first marriage. Her daughter and two grandchildren survive. Arthur Krim predeceased his wife in 1994.

See *Current Biography* 1987

Henri Landwirth

Born: Antwerp, Belgium; March 7, 1927
Died: Jacksonville, Florida; April 16, 2018
Occupation: Hotel executive and philanthropist

Henri Landwirth is most well known for his hotel and philanthropic organization, Give Kids the World, which provides children with life-threatening diseases the chance to experience theme parks, such as Walt Disney World.

Henri Landwirth was born to a Jewish couple, Max and Fanny, in Antwerp, Belgium. Landwirth had a twin sister, Margot. At the age of three, Landwirth and his family moved to Poland. When he was twelve, the Second World War began and Landwirth was separated from his family and sent to concentration camps. Over five years, Landwirth was moved among concentration camps, but was eventually saved from execution and set free by a soldier at the end of the war. He discovered that his sister, Margot had survived the war and returned to Belgium, though both of his parents had died. In 1949, both Landwirth and his sister immigrated to the United States and became citizens. Shortly after arriving, Landwirth was drafted into the army to serve in the Korean war and was honorably discharged in 1952. After returning, he attended the New York Hotel Technology School. After graduating he worked at several New York hotels as a clerk and bellhop. In 1954, Landwirth married and moved to Florida to work in a hotel where he eventually became the general manager. In 1956, Landwirth became manager of the Starlite Hotel and hosted the seven original Project Mercury astronauts from the nearby American space program. In 1970, Landwirth bought into the Holiday Inn franchise near the Walt Disney theme park. As the park grew in popularity, Landwirth bought more hotels in the area. In 1986, Landwirth founded Give Kids the World, which allows children with life-threatening diseases, and their families, to visit the Kissimmee resort village next to Walt Disney World. In 1999, Landwirth tried to retire but returned after five weeks to found Dignity-U-Wear, an organization which partners with large retail stores to provide clothing to the homeless. Landwirth wrote and published an autobiography in 1996, titled *Gift of Life*. He has received numerous awards for his philanthropic work.

Henri Landwirth is survived by his three children, Gary, Greg, and Lisa, and four grandchildren.

See *Current Biography* 2005

Felicia Langer

Born: Tarnów, Poland; December 9, 1930
Died: Tübingen, Germany; June 21, 2018
Occupation: Lawyer, human rights activist

Felicia Langer was a human rights lawyer who had defended Palestinians in Israel since the 1960s. A survivor of the Holocaust, Langer believed in protecting the rights of all.

Felicia Langer was born to wealthy Polish lawyers, and in 1939 they fled to Russia during the Nazi invasion of Poland. After returning to Poland at the end of World War II, Langer, her new husband, and her mother moved to Israel. Langer attended the Hebrew University in Tel Aviv for her law degree and began practicing in 1965. After the 1967 Six Day War, Langer opened her own practice in Jerusalem, intending to represent Arabs displaced during the Israeli occupation and those she believed were mistreated by the Israeli military. In 1968 she began representing Palestinian families whose homes are targeted for demolition by the Israeli army. Langer was one of the first attorneys to petition the Israeli High Court of Justice to rule against the use of torture during interrogations by the Shin Bet, Israel's internal security agency. She also fought against deportation and police brutality. Langer's only son left Israel because of the extreme hostility of Israelis towards her and her family. Langer became overwhelmed after the Palestinian uprising in 1987, known as the Intifada. By 1990, tired of constant defeat, Langer left Israel for Tübingen, Germany, and joined the University of Bremen and Kassel as a teacher. In 1990 she received the Right Livelihood Award, and a year later she received the Bruno Kreisky Prize for the defence of human rights. Langer was awarded membership of the German Federal Order of Merit in 2009 and the Palestinian Order of Merit and Excellence in 2012. She has written several books including, *With My Own Eyes: Israel and the Occupied Territories 1967–1973* (1975), *These Are My Brothers: Israel and the Occupied Territories, Part II* (1979), *An Age of Stone* (1988), *Fury and Hope: The Memoirs of Felicia Langer* (1993), *Appearance and Truth in Palestine* (1999), and *Quo Vadis Israel* (2001).

Felicia Langer is survived by her son, Michael, and three grandchildren.

See *Current Biography* 2004

Paul Laxalt

Born: Reno, Nevada; August 2, 1922
Died: McLean, Virginia; August 6, 2018
Occupation: US politician

Paul Laxalt was the former governor of Nevada and a US senator. He was a close confidante of Ronald Reagan; he served as Reagan's campaign chairman and as the general chairman of the Republican National Committee (RNC) while Reagan was president.

Paul Laxalt was born the eldest of six children, to French Basque immigrants. His father was a sheep herder who spent months away from the family, grazing sheep in the high meadows of the Sierra Nevada mountains. His mother attended the French Cordon Bleu culinary institute and was widely recognized for her cooking skills used in the family-owned hotel restaurant. Paul Laxalt attended Santa Clara University, though his education was interrupted while he worked as a medic in the Philippines during World War II. After returning home he earned a law degree from the University of Denver. The following year, Laxalt won election as the district attorney for Ormsby County. Though he never lost a case, he chose to only serve one term. He was elected lieutenant governor in 1962. Two years later he ran for the senate, losing to his opponent by a mere forty-eight votes. However, he won his bid for governor two years later. As governor, Laxalt took special interest in reducing the power of organized crime in the state. He pushed through legislation that allowed corporations to invest in Las Vegas and advocated for legislation for tighter accounting rules for gambling control. This move brought in Howard Hughes who bought six of the largest hotels. The move then brought in more investors. By mid-1969, sixteen out of the eighteen largest hotels were owned by public corporations. Laxalt also signed a bill raising gambling taxes by an average of twenty percent. Just as Laxalt was gaining national attention, especially from then president Nixon, he decided to retire, citing family concerns. He returned to private law practice for several years, only to return to politics in the 1974 race for the senate. This time Laxalt won—by the slim margin of 626 votes. Soon thereafter he became the campaign manager for Ronald Reagan. Laxalt himself made a brief try for the presidency in 1987.

Paul Laxalt's first marriage ended in divorce. His survivors include his wife, Carol, seven children, twelve grandchildren, and seven great-grandchildren.

See *Current Biography* 1979

Ursula K. Le Guin

Born: Berkeley, California; October 21, 1929
Died: Portland, Oregon; January 22, 2018
Occupation: Fantasy and science fiction writer

Ursula Le Guin was one of the foremost fantasy and science fiction writers of the twentieth century. She wrote more than twenty novels, twelve books of poetry, and several volumes of short stories, as well as more than a dozen children's books and several books of translation. Her book *The Left Hand of Darkness* won the Hugo and Nebula Awards, two of the most prestigious prizes for science fiction. In 2014 Le Guin earned the Medal for Distinguished Contribution to American Letters from the National Book Awards.

The youngest of four children, Ursula Le Guin was born into a family of intellectuals. Her anthropologist father, Alfred L. Kroeber specialized in the Native Americans of California. Her mother, Theodora Kracaw Kroeber, wrote the book about his work called *Ishi in Two Worlds*, about the life of the "last wild Indian." Le Guin attended Radcliffe College, graduating in 1951. A year later she earned her master's degree in literature of the Middle Ages and Renaissance from Columbia University. She won a Fulbright fellowship to study in Paris, where she met and married another Fulbright scholar, Charles Le Guin, the following year. Le Guin's first novel, *Rocannon's World*, was published in 1966, and she then set to work on her *Earthsea* trilogy. As Gerald Jonas writes for *The New York Times*, on 23 January 2018, "the magic of Earthsea is language-driven…instead of a holy war between Good and Evil, Ms. Le Guin's stories are organized around a search for 'balance' among competing forces." Her book *Lathe of Heaven* was made into two made-for-television movies, one in 1980, and the other in 2002. Her *Earthsea* trilogy was also adapted in 2006 for a Japanese animated movie and was made into a mini-series on the Sci Fi channel in 2004.

Le Guin's survivors include her husband, three children, and four grandchildren.

See *Current Biography* 1983

Robin Leach

Born: Perivale, London, England; August 29, 1941
Died: Las Vegas, Nevada; August 24, 2018
Occupation: Television personality

Robin Leach is most recognized as the voice and host of the television series *Lifestyles of the Rich and Famous*.

Robin Leach was born into a middle-class family in the London suburb of Harrow. His first job out of high school was as a general assignment reporter for the small, local newspaper, the *Harrow Observer*. He had a natural ability to bring drama to even the most mundane stories. His first celebrity story happened when the paper editor had thrown a dart at a town map and sent Leach to the targeted location to knock door-to-door until he found a story. One door he knocked on belonged to the English composer and playwright, Leslie Bricusse, who was writing the score for *Stop the World, I Want to Get Off*. After publishing the story Leach was invited backstage after the opening. He was shocked to find a despondent Bricusse, lamenting the quality of his work. Leach was struck by the contrast between what an average Joe perceives a celebrity's life to be and how the celebrity perceives his life. Leach became an entertainment reporter, first at London's *Daily Mail*, and eventually in the United States, at the *New York Daily News*. In 1969, while also working freelance, Leach was named show business editor at *The Star*, where he remained until 1979. By dint of what Leach would call "cheekiness," he got many scoops, most notably becoming an "aid" to Margaret Trudeau, wife of the Canadian prime minister, who was said to be having an affair with Mick Jagger. After a heated confrontation with her husband, witnessed by Leach, Mrs. Trudeau went into seclusion in Leach's Connecticut home. Leach sold the story all around the world. Leach's television career took off when he was hired as a reporter for a daily half-hour magazine-style pilot called *Entertainment Tonight*. In 1983 he approached the show's creator, Al Masini with his idea for a show that delves into the private lives of celebrities, that shows celebrities' homes, yachts, even bedrooms. Within three months the show premiered as a syndicated series. It remained hugely popular, with several spinoffs, and remained in syndication from 1984 to 1995.

Robin Leach's three sons survive him.

See *Current Biography* 1990

Leon M. Lederman

Born: New York, New York; July 15, 1922
Died: Rexburg, Idaho; October 3, 2018
Occupation: Physicist, educator

In collaboration with fellow physicists Melvin Schwartz and Jack Steinberger, Leon Lederman helped usher in a new era in particle physics. They shared the Nobel Prize for physics in 1988.

Leon Max Lederman was born into a working-class family. His parents were Russian-Jewish immigrants who owned their own laundry business. Though his brother, Paul, never completed high school, Lederman credited him for his interest in science, as the two brothers tinkered with mechanical equipment his brother brought home. Lederman earned his BS degree in chemistry from City College in New York (CCNY) in 1943, then served two years as a lieutenant in the US Army Signal Corps. Using the GI Bill, Lederman continued his education in physics at Columbia University, graduating with his PhD in 1951. He stayed at the university, working as a research associate at the school's Nevis Laboratory, using the particle accelerator there to discover a new particle known as the neutral K-meson. Shortly thereafter, he worked with two associates, Melvin Schwartz and Jack Steinberger, to determine that "left-right symmetry" or "parity" had been violated. In other words, the interaction of the almost identical particles "tau" and "theta" did not behave as expected, leading them to wonder about a paradox that seemed to show a difference between neutrinos that arose with muons and those arising from electron neutrinos. Using the powerful new accelerator at the Brookhaven Institute, they determined there was a new or different category of matter. Their experiments provided evidence that antimatter obeys the same forces that matter does, and they discovered the Upsilon (or Upsilon meson), the heaviest particle ever detected. Several years after his team's groundbreaking research, Lederman was named the director of the Fermi National Accelerator Lab. There he oversaw the construction of the powerful Tevatron accelerator. Through the 1980s Lederman continued to lobby the government for funding for the Superconducting Super Collider. His hopes were dashed in 1993 when funding was canceled. After retiring from the Fermi lab, Dr. Lederman taught physics at the University of Chicago.

Dr. Lederman's survivors include his wife, Ellen Carr, his three children and five grandchildren.

See *Current Biography* 1989

Judith Leiber

Born: Budapest, Hungary; January 11, 1921
Died: Springs, New York; April 28, 2018
Occupation: Handbag designer

Judith Leiber was known for her whimsical and artfully crafted handbags, which have been displayed at galleries including the Metropolitan Museum of Art, the Smithsonian Institution, and the Chicago Historical Society. Depicting a variety of subjects like fruits, animals, and natural objects, many celebrities and several first ladies have been known to favor Leiber's designs.

Judith Leiber was born to Emil and Helen Peto. She was sent to study chemistry at King's College in London, but at the start of World War II, she was forced to return home. Through forging documents, her family was able to remain in Hungary for the duration of the war, even during the Nazi occupation. After the war, Leiber began making handbags at her home in Hungary, but soon met her husband, Gerson Leiber, and the two moved to New York. For over fourteen years Leiber worked for a firm making handbags until it closed, and Leiber decided to start her own company, Judith Leiber, Inc. in 1963. Her first customers were the stores Bullock's and Bergdorf Goodman, and by 1973, Leiber won the Coty American Fashion Critics Award, the first ever given to a handbag maker. In the 1980s, Leiber started making her now iconic animal purses and other objects using materials such as leather, beads, crystals, animal skins, and even carved wood. Her handbags ranged in price from $700 to $7,500, and many people compare them to pieces of artwork. In March 1993, Time Products Inc., purchased Judith Leiber, Inc. for a reported $18 million, though Leiber remained as president and chief designer of the firm.

Judith Leiber has no immediate survivors.

See *Current Biography* 1996

Ruud (Rudolphus) Lubbers

Born: Rotterdam, Netherlands; May 7, 1939
Died: Rotterdam, Netherlands; February 14, 2018
Occupation: Dutch prime minister, diplomat

Ruud Lubbers was the youngest and longest-serving Dutch prime minister. He was elected in 1982 at the age of forty-three and served until 1994. In 2001 he was named the United Nations (UN) high commissioner for refugees.

Rudolphus Lubbers was born to a wealthy Roman Catholic family in Rotterdam, Netherlands. He graduated from Erasmus University with a degree in economics. Though he had hoped for a career in academia, his father's untimely death left Ruud and his brother to manage the family business, Lubber's Hollandia Engineering Works. He decided to run for Parliament, and in 1972 he was elected as the candidate to represent the Catholic People's Party, which joined a coalition of other parties to become the Christian Democratic Appeal (CDA). Lubbers served as the economics minister under Prime Minister Johannes (better known as Joop) den Uyl of the Labor party. In addition, he was the party whip for the CDA. He served again under Prime Minister Andreas van Agt, who unexpectedly resigned in 1982 leaving Lubbers to replace him. Lubbers inherited a budget deficit and high unemployment. He turned out to be a keen negotiator, working with industry to produce more jobs, working with trade unions on a compromise on wage increases, and instituted cuts to welfare and unemployment benefits. In the mid-1980s he resisted attempts by the North Atlantic Treaty Organization (NATO) to place medium-range nuclear missiles on Dutch soil. In 2001 Lubbers was named United Nations (UN) high commissioner for refugees and refused the salary he was entitled to. He was an important leader in the negotiations to form the European Union (EU) and its single currency, the Euro. An agreement was signed in 1992 in the Dutch city of Maastricht. In 2003 Lubbers was accused of sexual harassment; and though he denied the charge, he resigned in 2005 after an investigation corroborated his accuser's claims.

Ruud Lubbers married the economist, Ria Hoogeweegen, in 1962. She and their three children survive.

See *Current Biography* 2003

received the 1977 Olivier Award for best musical. In 1981, Lynne choreographed *Cats*, which opened on Broadway and became the longest running show in Broadway history. Lynne was awarded a 1984 Austrian Silver Order of Merit for her direction of *Cats* in Vienna and the 1989 Moliere Award for best musical of the year for *Cats* in Paris. Following this, she choreographed the dance work for the film *Yentl* (1983); and in 1986 Lynne again teamed with Andrew Lloyd Webber to choreograph *The Phantom of the Opera*, another award-winning production. In 1997 Lynne was awarded the Commander of the Order of the British Empire by Queen Elizabeth II. She received a Lifetime Achievement Award from the Dance Teachers' Benevolent Fund in 1999, and in 2001 she was honored by the Royal Academy of Dance with the Queen Elizabeth II Coronation Award. Lynne was given the title of Dame Commander of the Most Excellent Order of the British Empire in 2014. She also won an Olivier Award for achievement in a musical on *Cats* and earned a special lifetime achievement Olivier in 2013.

Gillian Lynne is survived by her husband, Peter Land.

See *Current Biography* 2002

Gillian Lynne

Born: Bromley, England; February 20, 1926
Died: London, England; July 1, 2018
Occupation: Dancer, choreographer

Gillian Lynne was a tony-nominated dancer and choreographer, known for her work choreographing the hit Broadway musicals *Cats*, and *The Phantom of the Opera*.

Gillian Lynne was the only child born to Leslie and Barbara Pyrke. She began taking dance lessons at the age of five; and, after being evacuated to Somerset due to the Blitz during World War II, Lynne was enrolled at the Cone Ripman School. At sixteen, Lynne was given the opportunity to dance as the Swan Queen in *Swan Lake* at the People's Palace, after which she was invited to join the British Royal Ballet company. She danced with the company for seven years as principal dancer, until she left to be lead dancer for the London Palladium. During the 1950s, Lynne performed in a variety of showcases, including in film. She choreographed her first ballet, *The Owl and the Pussycat*, for the Western Theatre Ballet in 1962. Throughout the 1960s and 1970s, Lynne choreographed many pieces until, in the mid-1970s, she joined the Royal Shakespeare Company, where she choreographed the musical *A Comedy of Errors*, which

Winnie Madikizela-Mandela

Born: Bizana, South Africa; September 26, 1936
Died: Johannesburg, South Africa; April 2, 2018
Occupation: Anti-apartheid activist

Many South Africans considered Winnie Mandela to be "the mother of the nation." Through her political activism and marriage to Nelson Mandela, Winnie Mandela committed her life to anti-apartheid efforts.

Named Nomzamo Winifred Zanyiwe Madikizela, Winnie Mandela was born to a noble family called Pondo. She was one of nine children, who grew up in a very poor village in the eastern Cape Province. After graduation from high school, she moved to Johannesburg to attend the Jan Hofmeyr School of Social Work, where she received a degree in pediatric social work in 1955, making her the first black medical social worker in the country. She met Nelson Mandela at a Christmas party in 1956. In 1957, Mandela joined and became chairwoman of the Women's League of the African National Congress (ANC). Winnie and Nelson Mandela married in 1958, and the couple moved to a small house in the black township of Soweto. Later that same year, Mandela, then pregnant, was arrested and imprisoned after joining a protest with the Federation of African Women. She was fired from her job at Baragwanath Hospital because of her imprisonment. Once released, she worked for the Child Welfare office in Soweto. In 1962, Mandela was given a ban order for membership on the national executive board of the Women's Federation and was restricted from leaving Johannesburg for two years. In 1964, Mandela's husband, Nelson Mandela, was sentenced to life in prison for treason, sabotage, and violent conspiracy. Mandela continued to be quietly involved in political works and was arrested again in 1969 and imprisoned for nine months. Upon release, she was immediately re-detained for eight more months due to alternate sections under the Terrorism Act. During her imprisonment, Mandela was beaten and tortured. In 1977 she was banished to the town of Brandfort, where she was not allowed to meet with more than one person at a time. When Mandela's house and clinic in Brandfort were firebombed, she was blamed for the arson and forced to move back to her home in Soweto. At this time, Mandela's anti-apartheid involvement became more radical, and she formed the United Football Club, a group of bodyguards who would enforce justice on Mandela's opponents. Nelson Mandela was released from prison in 1990, and apartheid ended in 1994. The Mandelas divorced in 1996. At the same time, Winnie Mandela and her "Football Club" were put under investigation and found to have engaged in human rights violations. Mandela made a public apology and was later convicted of kidnapping, due to the actions of her bodyguards. She served in the South African Parliament from 1994 to 2003 but was convicted of obtaining fraudulent loans and spent five years in prison. She was released early and returned to parliament from 2009 until her death in 2018.

Winnie Mandela's two daughters, Zindziswa and Zenani, and nine grandchildren survive.

See *Current Biography* 1986

John Mahoney

Born: Blackpool (Lancashire), England; June 20,1940
Died: Chicago, Illinois; February 4, 2018
Occupation: Actor

Though he had a rich career as a character actor in such movies as *Moonstruck Reality Bites,* and *Say Anything,* John Mahoney is most remembered for his role as Frasier's cranky, retire police officer father in the popular television show, *Frasier* from 1993 until 2004.

John Mahoney was born to a large family, the seventh of eight children. He had an early interest in theater, performing Gilbert and Sullivan roles in drama festivals around England when he was just eleven years old. He nearly quit school altogether, but his parents persuaded him to get his high school diploma. He followed a sister, who had married an American soldier, to the United States and joined the army to serve in Europe. After leaving the military, he attended Quincy College to earn a bachelor's degree and then continued for a master's degree at Western Illinois University in Macomb. Working there as a teaching assistant convinced Mahoney that academia was not for him. He worked as an orderly at St. Mary's Hospital, which was helpful when he was hired as an editor at a small-circulation medical journal. On a trip back to England, Mahoney saw a Tom Stoppard production of *Jumpers,* which renewed his interest in theater. At the age of thirty-five, Mahoney quit his editing job and began training as an actor with the St. Nicholas Theater in Chicago. He was eventually invited to join Chicago's famed Steppenwolf Ensemble, which became his new home as he appeared in more than thirty productions. He supplemented his income with bit parts in film. He earned a Tony Award for best feature actor in a play in 1986 for his role in John Guare's American Playhouse production of *The House of Blue Leaves.* He was cast for the role that made him a household name in 1993 in the *Cheers* spin off, *Frasier,* the most successful spinoff in television history. He appeared on Broadway in 2007 in a revival of *Prelude to a Kiss.*

John Mahoney never married. Information about survivors is unavailable.

See *Current Biography* 1999

Judy Martz

Born: Big Timber, Montana; July 28, 1943
Died: Butte, Montana; October 30, 2017
Occupation: Former governor of Montana

Judy Martz was the first female governor of the state of Montana from 2001 to 2005.

Judy Martz was born Judy Helen Morstein. Her parents were originally cattle ranchers, but the family moved to Butte, Montana, when Judy was still a child, and her father was a miner and livestock inspector. In 1963 Judy Martz qualified for the US World Speed Skating Team and participated in the 1964 Winter Olympic Games in Innsbruck, Austria. Though she failed to win, she set her sights on the 1968 games. After her longtime boyfriend, Wayne Estes, an All-American basketball player at Utah State University, was killed, Judy was devastated and decided she wanted to make a difference in people's lives. She reconnected with her old friend, Harry Martz who was in the military. The two married in 1965, and he spent several years in Germany while his wife attended Eastern Montana College. In 1971 the couple bought a Butte garbage collection firm, renaming it Martz Disposal. In 1995, Martz told her friend, Marc Racicot she was interested in being his running mate for his second term. Upon their win in 1997, she became Montana's first female lieutenant governor. Once Racicot's second term ended, Martz ran for governor and won. Though she managed to reverse the state's deficit into a surplus, cut taxes, and increase funding for education, her term was rife with scandal and an ethics complaint. By the end of her term, Martz's approval was an abysmal twenty percent. She did not run for re-election.

They had two children. Information about survivors is unavailable.

See *Current Biography* 2005

Hugh Masekela

Born: Witbank, Mpumalanga, South Africa; April 4, 1939
Died: Johannesburg, South Africa; January 23, 2018
Occupation: South African trumpeter, flugelhornist, singer

Hugh Masekela was a world-renowned musician who is most widely recognized for his fusion of American jazz and polyrhythmic, indigenous African dance and folk music. He was a contemporary and student of the world's greatest jazz musicians such as Dizzy Gillespie, who gave Masekela his first trumpet, and Miles Davis.

One of four children, Hugh Masekela was born in a mining town near Johannesburg. His father was a health inspector and his mother was a social worker. His sister, Barbara would eventually lead the African National Congress's arts and culture departments. He and his siblings were raised primarily by their grandmother, Johanna, where they were surrounded by music, and Masekela was an early jazz enthusiast. He was a troublemaker who was sent to an Anglican school for black children where a benevolent priest, Father Trevor Huddleston, took special interest in him. Masekela made a bargain with Huddleston; he would stop making trouble if Huddleston would help him learn to play the trumpet. He and several other students formed the Huddleston Jazz Band. After the government closed the school, Masekela and some fellow students toured for several years and became the first black band to record an album in South

Africa. To his chagrin, audiences wanted to hear mbaqanga, a rough-and-ready music of South Africa's black villages. Masekela left South Africa following the Sharpeville massacre in 1960 and came to the attention of noted American musician Harry Belafonte, who helped him enroll in the Manhattan School of Music where he watched performances by John Coltrane, Thelonious Monk, and Miles Davis. In 1963 he released his first solo album, *Trumpet Africaine*. He appeared at the Monterey Festival with Janis Joplin and The Who, and afterwards his single "Grazing in the Grass" became a mega-hit, topping the US charts. He returned to Africa after twelve years in the United States, traveling across the continent. He settled in Botswana in 1980. In 1987 he teamed with Paul Simon on a tour to promote his album *Graceland*. Masekela fought for civil rights in both America and South Africa. He put out his last album, *No Borders*, in 2016. He received South Africa's highest civilian award, the Order of Ikhamanga.

Masekela was married four times and had two children who survive him.

See *Current Biography* 1993

Peter Mayle

Born: Brighton, England; June 14, 1939
Died: Ménerbes, France; January 18, 2018
Occupation: British writer

Though he wrote numerous children's books and collections of essays, Peter Mayle is most remembered for his humorous, autobiographical account of his life in Provence, France, fixing up an eighteenth-century farmhouse. The book, titled *A Year in Provence*, spent a year at the top of the bestseller lists in England and the United States, as did the sequel, *Toujour Provence*. In 1989 *A Year in Provence* won the British Book Awards' "Best Travel Book of the Year."

Peter Mayle was born in Brighton, England, one of three children. When Mayle was still a child, the family moved to Barbados where his father was an employee of the British Foreign Office. Mayle attended school there and, according to one report, college. He returned to England and began a career in advertising at Ogilvy, Bensen & Mather, soon moving to the firm's New York office, where he worked for thirteen years. (He later recalled that period of his life in his 1990 book, *Up the Agency*.) In 1975 he became a freelance writer after he had published several children's books, including *Where Did I Come From?* (about the facts of life), and *What's Happening to Me?* (about puberty). Mayle and his wife enjoyed annual vacations in

Provence, France, and in 1986, came upon their "dream house," an eighteenth-century "fixer upper" stone farmhouse. After moving there, Mayle had intended to write a novel, but was too distracted by his tasks in renovating the house. His agent suggested heput aside the novel and begin chronicling his experiences. The resulting *A Year in Provence* was a humorous account of life in the South of France. The book became a major bestseller, to such an extent that fans of his work regularly showed up at his doorstep for autographs. The book did much to bolster the tourism in Provence.

Peter Mayle's survivors include his wife of more than forty years, Jennie Mayle, his five children, and several grandchildren.

See *Current Biography* 1992

John McCain

Born: Panama Canal Zone, Panama; August 29, 1936
Died: Cornville, Arizona; August 25, 2018
Occupation: American congressman and senator

John McCain served two terms in the US House of Representatives and six terms in the senate. He sought the presidency twice. In 2008 he was the Republican nominee for president.

By all accounts, John McCain was considered a hero, a naval pilot shot down and captured by the North Vietnamese in 1965. Tortured and held in solitary confinement for years, McCain famously refused to take the release the North Vietnamese offered him (as a publicity stunt), as the son of a high-ranking navy admiral, instead choosing to stay with his fellow soldiers until they were all released years later. He emerged from the experience, permanently disabled, weighing just over one hundred pounds. McCain was born into a military family. Both his father and grandfather were four-star admirals, the first father-son duo with such a distinction. (They each had navy ships named after them.) His paternal grandfather was the commander of all naval aircraft carriers in World War II, and his father was the commander in chief of US forces in the Pacific during the Vietnam War. McCain was the middle child of three siblings; and as with most military families, he moved a great deal as a child. He attended Episcopal High School, an all-white, all-male boarding school, before entering the US Naval Academy in Annapolis, where he studied electrical engineering. Shortly thereafter he entered flight school at the Naval Air Station in Pensacola, Florida. On October 26, 1967, on his twenty-third flying

mission, after a twenty-plane attack on a power facility in Hanoi, McCain's plane was shot down. He ejected but was severely injured with broken arms and a shattered knee. He was dragged from the lake where he landed and severely beaten by a mob. He then landed at the *Hỏa Lò* prison camp, which was labeled the "Hanoi Hilton" by American prisoners of war. He remained there until March 14, 1973. Upon his return, McCain was awarded the Silver and Bronze Stars, a Distinguished Flying Cross, and other honors, and was named the Navy's senate liaison. He retired from the military in 1981 and set about making a life as a civilian in Phoenix, Arizona, working for his father-in-law's beer distributorship. However, when it was clear thirty-year Congressman John Rhodes was retiring, McCain easily won the seat and served two terms. He ran for the senate several years later. Senator McCain was considered a Republican "maverick," following his own convictions, sometimes to the chagrin of his fellow conservative Republicans. One of his last votes on the senate floor was his dramatic thumbs down ("no" vote), which scuttled Republican plans to fully repeal the Affordable Care Act. McCain sat on several powerful congressional committees during his tenure. For McCain, outside his desire to serve as commander in chief as president, his greatest honor was to serve as Chairman of the Armed Services Committee. He was a member of the Select Committee on POW/MIA Affairs, the Commerce Committee, and the Indian Affairs Committee.

McCain's survivors include his wife, Cindy, his 106-year-old mother, his two siblings, seven children, and five grandchildren.

See *Current Biography* 2006

Donald McKayle

Born: New York, New York; July 6, 1930
Died: Irvine, California; April 6, 2018
Occupation: Dancer and choreographer

Donald McKayle is best known for his work as a prominent modern dance choreographer and performer. From an early age, McKayle incorporated aspects of black culture into his performances. He worked with numerous dance companies, worldwide, and choreographed and directed musicals on Broadway, including *Raisin* (1973), based on the novel, *A Raisin in the Sun*, by Lorraine Hansberry.

Donald McKayle was born to Philip and Eva McKayle in the Bronx borough of New York City. After graduating from DeWitt Clinton High School in 1946, McKayle attended City College of New York (CCNY), but dropped out after two years to pursue dance full-time. McKayle's first performance was in 1948, in a work by Sophie Maslow and Jean Erdman at the Mansfield Theatre. In addition to working with several choreographers, McKayle danced on Broadway throughout the 1950s, and with his wife, Esta Beck, he choreographed works at the Henry Street Playhouse, and premiered his work, *Games*, at the Hunter College Playhouse. Though he choreographed concert pieces throughout his career, McKayle also choreographed several films and televisions shows. He was nominated for an Antoinette Perry award for his fight choreography in *Golden Boy* (1964), and choreographed scenes in *A Time for Singing* (1966), *I'm Solomon* (1968), and in London, *The Four Musketeers* (1967). In 1967 McKayle produced a concert using many of his previous pieces, retitling the composition, *Black New World*. McKayle became the first black man to direct and choreograph a Broadway musical with *Raisin*, in 1974, which won him a Tony award. In 1989, McKayle join the faculty at the University of California, Irvine, as a professor of dance, where he remained until shortly before his death. He also served as faculty at Juilliard, Sarah Lawrence, Bennington, and Bard College.

Donald McKayle is survived by his wife, Leah Levine, their son, Guy, his two children from his first marriage to Esta Beck, Liane and Gabrielle, and two grandchildren.

See *Current Biography* 1971

Michael I, King of Romania

Born: Sinaia, Prahova, Romania; October 25, 1921
Died: Aubonne, Switzerland; December 5, 2017
Occupation: King of Romania

King Michael I of Romania is credited with saving thousands of lives during World War II when he had the Romanian dictator and Hitler puppet, Ion Antonescu, arrested. He also had the rare distinction of both preceding and succeeding his father as king of the country.

Not yet six years old, Prince Michael (Mihai) of Romania succeeded his grandfather, the late King Ferdinand I. Michael's father, the former playboy and Crown Prince Carol, abdicated his right to the throne to continue his love affair with Magda Lupescu. Michael's mother, Princess Helen, was from the Greek royal family. Michael's great-great-grandmother was England's Queen Victoria. In 1930, Michael's father, claiming his exile had been forced, returned to the throne. At the beginning of World War II, King Carol declared a royal dictatorship but was bested by German and Soviet forces that seized Romanian territory. In an effort to appease Romanian fascists, King Carol assigned

the brutal General Antonescu to head his government. Antonescu then had King Carol exiled. Finding himself king once again, the eighteen-year-old Michael I secretly amassed antigovernment forces. He asked Antonescu to surrender to the Soviets. When he refused, King Michael had the general and his followers arrested and imprisoned. Romania was thus the first Axis nation to abandon Hitler. Following the war, the Soviet Union occupied Romania, and Stalin ordered the end of the monarchy. Under pressure to save the lives of thousands of his supporters, King Michael abdicated in 1947 and lived the rest of his life in Switzerland. Attending the wedding of Britain's Princess Elizabeth and Prince Philip of Greece, Michael met Princess Anne of Bourbon-Parma whom he later married in 1948. They had five daughters. King Michael was one of the few recipients of the Order of Victory from Moscow for his assistance to the Red Army. He also received the Legion of Merit from the United States. He remained highly popular in his country and was allowed to visit several times.

King Michael's wife predeceased him in 2016. Their five daughters survive.

See *Current Biography* 1944

Stan Mikita

Born: Sokolče, Vlachy, Czechoslovakia (now Slovakia); May 20, 1940
Died: Chicago, Illinois; August 7, 2018
Occupation: Major league hockey player

Stan Mikita was one of the most widely-respected players in the National Hockey League (NHL). He was the first player to achieve hockey's "triple crown" by winning the Lady Byng Memorial Trophy, the Hart Memorial Trophy for most valuable player (MVP), and the Art Ross Trophy for being the league's leading scorer. He is widely credited with inventing the curved hockey stick. He made the All-Star team nine times and was inducted into the Hockey Hall of Fame in 1983. He finished his career with 541 goals, second only to fellow teammate and friend, Bobby Hull.

Stan Mikita was born Stanislav Gvoth in Sokolče, a small in what was then Czechoslovakia (now Slovakia). His father worked in a textile mill, and his mother worked in the fields of their small farm. In 1948 the Communists were encroaching into Czechoslovakia, and Mikita's parents sent their son away with visiting relatives from St. Catharine's, an industrial town in Ontario, Canada. His uncle Joe and aunt Ann Mikita adopted their nephew, giving him their surname. In 1956 Mikita joined a "junior A" hockey team in the Ontario Association. He quickly became a star player and was offered several athletic scholarships; however, at eighteen, Mikita dropped out of school and followed his teammate, Bobby Hull, to the big league, signing a two-year contract with the Black Hawks. He would remain with the team for the duration of his twenty-two-season career. In the 1967 and 1968 seasons, Mikita became the first player to win hockey's "triple crown," after being the league's highest scorer, named the most valuable player in the NHL, and then receiving the Lady Byng Memorial award for outstanding performance and "gentlemanly conduct."

See *Current Biography* 1970

Arjay Miller

Born: Shelby, Nebraska; March 4, 1916
Died: Woodside, California; November 3, 2017
Occupation: Corporate executive, Stanford University graduate school dean

When Henry Ford, Jr. advertised his search for executive talent in *Life* magazine, Arjay Miller and nine of his Army Air Force and Harvard colleagues answered the call, earning a reputation as "quiz kids" as they learned the ropes. Later they were referred to as "whiz kids" as their economic talent was credited with rescuing the company from its steady decline. He was also credited with designing the wildly successful Ford Mustang. He later served as the dean of Stanford's Graduate School of Business.

Arjay Miller was born the youngest in a family of eight children to a Nebraska farmer in a small town outside of Omaha. Shortly after he graduated as the high school class valedictorian, he and his family moved to California where he attended the University of California in Los Angeles (UCLA), specializing in business and finance. Though originally rejected from military service due to poor eyesight, he taught prospective pilots in the Army Air Force throughout World War II. He entered the Air Force Statistical Control School at Harvard University and worked at the statistical control office in the Pentagon. Upon his discharge, he and several colleagues from Harvard applied to the Ford Motor Company where they spearheaded a reorganization at the company. One of his colleagues was Robert S. McNamara who would become Ford's president, and later, the US Secretary of Defense for presidents Kennedy and Johnson. Miller became Ford's president in 1963. After riots broke out in the slums of Detroit, Miller founded the Economic Development Corporation of Greater Detroit to help support black business development and went so far as to support a negative income tax to help alleviate poverty.

In 1940 Miller married the economist Frances Fearing who predeceased him in 2010. Survivors include their two children, three grandchildren, and seven great-grandchildren.

See *Current Biography* 1967

Warren Miller

Born: Los Angeles, California; October 15, 1924
Died: Orcas Island, Washington; January 2018
Occupation: Sports filmmaker

Warren Miller considered himself a "ski bum" who made his fortune filming amateur and professional skiers all over the world. He was an entrepreneur who built his own media enterprise, Warren Miller Entertainment, Inc., which has featured film, television, and video productions. He was partly responsible for the popularization of snow skiing and snow boarding.

Warren Miller was born in Hollywood, California, and became interested in skiing at a very young age. After serving in the navy during World War II, he attended the University of Southern California but dropped out to become a "ski bum." During the winter of 1948 to 1949 he worked as a ski instructor in Sun Valley, Idaho. Two young executives from Bell & Howell, Harold Geneen and Charles Percy, took lessons from Miller and hearing about his dream to make ski films, loaned him one of the company's sixteen-mm cameras. He worked in his spare time filming skiers. He traveled with a projector and amplifier to any ski club that would have him, showing his work to fellow skiers anxious for the next season. Eventually his work became an institution among the ski crowd, helping to turn skiing from an obscure "niche" sport to the multi-billion dollar, wildly popular winter sport it has become. His witty baritone voice-over narration was entertaining as he reported on trends like snowboarding and extreme skiing and fads like ski ballet and snow kayaking. Miller made a new ski film every year from 1949 to 2004. In 2002 his company was traded to Time Warner. As of 2013, Active Interest Media owns his brand.

Warren Miller was the honorary director of skiing at the exclusive Yellowstone Club in Big Sky, Montana. His survivors include his wife of thirty years, Laurie, three children, a stepson, and five grandchildren.

See *Current Biography* 1997

Zell Miller

Born: Young Harris, Georgia; February 24, 1932
Died: Young Harris, Georgia; March 23, 2018
Occupation: Politician

Zell Miller was known for being a Democratic senator and governor of Georgia. Though he remained a member of the Democratic party for his entire career, Miller was known for supporting Republican party members and even gave a speech at the Republican National Convention (RNC) in 2004 on behalf of President George W. Bush.

Only seventeen days after the birth of his son, Zell Bryan, Stephen Miller, died, leaving his wife, Birdie Miller, to raise their two children alone. Zell Miller attended Young Harris College for two years before transferring to Emory University in Atlanta, Georgia. He spent several years in the Marine Corps, from 1953 to 1956, before completing his college education at the University of Georgia, with an AB degree in political science, and an MA in history. Between the years of 1958 and 1964 he taught history and political science at the University of Georgia. He also taught at Young Harris College, Emory, and DeKalb Community College. In 1958, at the age of twenty-six, Miller successfully ran for mayor of Young Harris, thus beginning a life-long career as a politician. Throughout the 1970s and 1980s, Miller served the state of Georgia as a senator and as lieutenant governor, and in 1991 he became Georgia's 79th governor. He was re-elected in 1994.

During his time as governor, Miller focused on issues such as crime reduction and public education. In 1992, Miller started a program with lottery revenues to finance a scholarship called Helping Outstanding Pupils Educationally (HOPE), which would provide grants and loans for student tuitions. He also fought to have the Confederate battle emblem removed from the Georgia state flag. In 2000, after the death of Senator Paul Coverdell, Miller was elected to the senate. Though he remained a life-long Democrat, Miller supported Republican initiatives and candidates. During his time in the senate, Miller supported several of President George W Bush's decisions and in 2004 spoke at the Republican National Convention. Following the speech, Miller received significant backlash from the press. In his later years, Miller continued to endorse Republican party leaders.

Zell Miller is survived by his wife, Shirley Carver, their two children, Murphy and Matthew, four grandchildren, and eight great-grandchildren.

See Current Biography 1996

Arthur Mitchell

Born: New York, New York; March 27, 1934
Died: New York, New York; September 19, 2018
Occupation: Dancer, choreographer

Arthur Mitchell was the first African American dancer to perform as a principal with a major ballet company. He co-founded the Dance Theatre of Harlem.

Arthur Mitchell was born in Harlem, New York. His father was a janitor and his mother stayed home to raise their five children. While still a child, Mitchell delivered newspapers and shined shoes to help support the family. He began learning tap dancing through the local police Athletic League. A counselor there suggested he audition for a spot in the New York School for the Performing Arts. He did so and was accepted to the school. Upon graduation in 1952, Mitchell received a scholarship to the School of American Ballet, which eventually led to his acceptance as a dancer with the New York City Ballet. He rose to soloist in 1958 and principal in 1962, putting him in the unusual position of being an African American man dancing with white ballerinas during the civil rights era. He became known for choreographing movement using the contrast between skin tones as part of his performance. He also began using tights and shoes that matched a dancer's skin tone rather than the traditional pink tights. In 1968, using a storage garage lent to him by the Harlem School of the Arts, Mitchell founded the Dance Theatre of Harlem. By keeping the doors open, Mitchell attracted youth from the street. Within a matter of a few months, the school had attracted eight hundred students and would become one of the most popular dance schools in the world. The Guggenheim Museum hosted the school's debut performance in 1971. Nelson Mandela invited the Dance Theatre group in 1992 to perform in front of an integrated audience. Through his experience working with the children of the townships, Mitchell started the Dancing Through Barriers outreach program in South Africa.

In 1975, Mitchell received the Dance Magazine Award. He also received a Kennedy Center Honor and Handel Medallion from the city of New York in 1993. He received the MacArthur Genius Award in 1994 and a National Medal of the Arts in 1995.

Mitchell's nephew survives him.

See Current Biography 1966

Malcolm Morley

Born: London, England; June 7, 1931
Died: New York, New York; June 1, 2018
Occupation: Painter

Malcolm Morley was an award-winning artist of the twentieth-century, known for his pioneering the photorealist and neo-expressionism movements. During the height of his career, Morley was using "superreal" techniques, even utilizing grid-lines to create paintings from smaller photos or postcards.

Malcolm Morley was born to Dorothy Morley, and he never knew his father's name. He left London for the United States in 1958 and became fascinated with the ocean. Morley was expelled from school; and at the age of fourteen, joined the crew of a tugboat in Newfoundland, Canada. He then returned to London, where he got arrested several times for misdemeanors and criminal activity. While in prison, Morley took several art classes and once released, decided he would be an artist. He went to St. Ives in Cornwall to join an artist's colony and was offered a position at the Royal College of Art, where he graduated in 1957. Morley then moved to New York City in 1958 and met several influential artists of the 1950s, including Andy Warhol and Mark Rothko. His first solo exhibition was in 1964, at the Kornblee gallery, where he showed a series of abstract works. From there, Morley began experimenting with his painting style and developed what is called *photorealism*, paintings of realistic monochromes of battleships and sailors, sometimes tracing them from photographs and then applying a grey ink wash to produce a hazy image like a newspaper photograph. He first exhibited this style of painting at a show in 1967 and in 1970 painted an intricate and detailed painting of the South African Greyville Race course and painted a large red X through the entire piece. It was thought the painting referred to Malcolm X and the anti-apartheid message, but it was also speculated it represented Morley's rejection of his photorealist style. At this point, Morley began using drugs and painting in a much more erratic way, as depicted in his piece, Los Angeles Yellow Pages (1971), taking on more expressionist styles. His work has been shown worldwide, and Morley has received many awards, including the prestigious Turner Prize, for his work shown at his 1984 show at Whitechapel gallery in London.

Malcolm Morley is survived by his fifth wife, Lida.

See *Current Biography* 1984

Makio Murayama

Born: San Francisco, California; August 10, 1912
Died: Michigan; January 8, 2012
Occupation: American biochemist

Dr. Makio Murayama is most remembered as the primary expert in the structure and treatment of sickle cell anemia, a blood disorder that afflicts black people almost exclusively.

Makio Murayama's father died when he was just four years old. He was sent to Japan to live with a great aunt where he remained for ten years before returning to the United States. While he was in high school he was employed as an assistant medical photographer at the San Francisco County Hospital. He attended the University of California at Berkeley as a biochemistry and bacteriology student, graduating with a bachelor's degree in 1938. He continued graduate work, majoring in biochemistry. He minored in nuclear physics under professors Ernest O. Lawrence and Robert Oppenheimer at Berkeley's Radiation Laboratory. He received his master's degree in biochemistry and nuclear physics in 1940. After the United States declared war with Japan, Murayama's family was sent to an internment camp in Idaho, and Murayama was ordered to report for the Manhattan Project in Chicago as a physicist, though he was turned away when they learned he was Japanese. He found work at the Children's Hospital of Michigan, where he began as a research biochemist and was first exposed to the disease sickle cell anemia. Murayama followed the director, Dr. James L. Wilson, to Bellevue Hospital in New York City in 1943 where he became the director of the hospital's pediatric laboratory. Two years later, he followed his mentor once more to the University of Michigan where Murayama developed several methods for micro chemical blood analysis in sickle cell patients. He received a National Institutes of Health (NIH) fellowship that allowed him to finish his PhD degree in 1953. For two years he attended the California Institute of Technology (Caltech) where he studied under the leading authority in sickle cell anemia, Dr. Linus Pauling. In 1958 the NIH hired Murayama as a biochemist where he became the only scientist in the huge organization to study sickle hemoglobin. In 1966 Murayama published what would later be recognized as his landmark paper on sickle cell anemia, making him one of the world's foremost authorities on the disease. In 1969 he received the Association of Sickle Cell Anemia Award, and in 1972 he received the Martin Luther King Jr. medical achievement award. He co-authored the book *Sickle Cell Hemoglobin: Molecule to Man*, published by Little Brown in 1973.

Murayama was married twice. His first wife died in 1972. Later that year, he married Diane Louise Diehl Robertson. They had three children. Information about survivors is unavailable.

See *Current Biography* 1974

Jim Nabors

Born: Sylacauga, Alabama; June 12, 1930
Died: Honolulu, Hawaii; November 30, 2017
Occupation: American actor, singer

Actor Jim Nabors is most remembered for his portrayal of the amiable hayseed, country bumpkin, Gomer Pyle, originally a minor character on the popular television comedy *The Andy Griffith Show*. Nabors starred in the popular spinoff military comedy, *Gomer Pyle, USMC*. He also starred in his own variety show, *The Jim Nabors Hour*. Nabors recorded a dozen albums with his deep, baritone singing voice, a surprising contrast to his nasal, southern twang. He also acted in several movies with his long-time friend Burt Reynolds.

Jim Nabors was the only son of policeman, Fred Canada Nabors, and Mavis (Newman) Nabors. He had two older sisters. Childhood asthma sometimes kept Nabors home from school and from participating in school sports. He was a gifted singer, however, and was drawn to the theater. He sang in the glee club at his high school and as a student at the University of Alabama where he earned his bachelor's degree in business administration. Following college, he worked as a typist at the United Nations (UN) in New York where he hoped to break into the theater world. He briefly worked as an assistant film editor at a television studio in Tennessee before moving to Los Angeles where he worked in film editing for NBC studios. He was "discovered" by comedian Bill Dana while performing at the Horn, a Santa Monica cabaret. Dana was head writer for Steve Allan and had Nabors perform several times on the show. In 1963 and 1964, Nabors began portraying the warmhearted, bumbling bumpkin, Gomer Pyle on *The Andy Griffith Show*. He soon had his own shows, *Gomer Pyle USMC* and *The Jim Nabors Hour*. He was also in increasing demand to appear on various comedy variety shows like *The Smothers Brothers*, *Danny Thomas*, and occasionally on *The Carol Burnett Show*. He made his first record album in 1966 selling over a million copies.

Jim Nabors married his long-time partner, Stan Cadwallader once gay marriage was legalized in Washington State. Cadwallader and a niece and nephew survive.

See *Current Biography* 1969

Vidiadhar Surajprasad (V.S.) Naipaul

Born: Chaguanas, Trinidad and Tobago; August 17, 1932
Died: London, England; August 11, 2018
Occupation: Writer

Vidiadhar Surajprasad, known by his initials, V. S., Naipaul was an award-winning author and Nobel laureate. Naipaul was knighted in 1990.

V. S. Naipaul was born in Chaguanas, Trinidad, the grandson of an Indian Brahmin from Uttar Pradesh, India, who traveled to Trinidad as an indentured worker on the sugar plantations. His father was an aspiring fiction writer and newspaper reporter for the *Trinidad and Tobago Guardian*. Naipaul attended an English school. In 1952 he moved to England where he attended University College at Oxford on a scholarship, studying English literature. After college he began writing fiction and made a living as a freelance broadcast announcer and eventually edited a literary program for the BBC Colonial Service. By 1957 Naipaul was writing freelance essays and articles, primarily for the *New Statesman*. His first few novels relied a great deal on his experiences in the West Indies, and he began earning recognition with prizes such as the John Rhys Memorial prize for *The Mystic Masseur*, and the Somerset Maugham Award for *Miguel Street*. His breakthrough novel was *A House for Mr. Biswas*, published in 1961. Naipaul was widely traveled, especially during the early 1960s. He developed as a writer of non-fiction, focusing on travel writing, and earning himself the description as a "writer without roots," also, in part, because his characters were often immigrants struggling with a new identity in a new environment. He was overwhelmed by his ancestral land of India, about which he wrote three travelogues. He also traveled across East Africa in the 1970s. His 1971 collection, *In a Free State*, about his African sojourns won him the 1971 Booker Prize. Naipaul was a great critic of Islam, which he felt inherently lead to tyranny. He was awarded the Nobel Prize for literature in 2001.

V. S. Naipaul was married twice. He had no children of his own but adopted his second wife's adult daughter. His wife, Nadir Khannum Alvi, survives.

See *Current Biography* 1977

Henri Namphy

Born: Cap-Haïtien, Nord, Haiti; November 2, 1932
Died: Dominican Republic; June 26, 2018
Occupation: Former president of Haiti

Henri Namphy became the President of Haiti, after the exile of the thirty-year dictator Duvalier. Though he attempted to install a democratic government, he was ousted from office after being met by demonstrations and protests.

Henri Namphy grew up as one of three children in Cap-Haïtien, where he attended a Roman Catholic elementary and primary school. He graduated from the Military Academy in 1954 and quickly rose through the ranks under dictators François Duvalier and Jean-Claude Duvalier. In 1984 he was made Lieutenant General of the country's army. In 1986, before going into exile Duvalier named Namphy his successor. Namphy instituted some reforms and permitted the adoption of a new liberal constitution by referendum in March 1987. But Haiti degenerated once more into violence and repression, exacerbated by the reemergence of the Duvalier's notorious private army known as Tonton Macoute (and culminating in a massacre of civilians that resulted in the cancellation of presidential elections in November 1987). A civilian president, Dr. Leslie F. Manigat, took office in February 1988 after rescheduled elections, but he soon came into conflict with Namphy, who had retained the post of commander in chief of the armed forces. On June 20, 1988 Namphy seized control of the government, proclaimed himself president, and dissolved the legislature. Nineteen days later he abrogated the constitution. His actions prompted the United States Department of State to issue a pronouncement condemning what it called a "serious blow to hopes for democracy" in a troubled land. Namphy was forced to relinquish the presidency once more and go into exile following a coup on September 17, 1988 that brought a new military junta, headed by Lieutenant General Prosper Avril, the commander of the presidential guard, into power. Namphy continued to live in exile in the Dominican Republic until the time of his death. Henri Namphy is survived by his two daughters.

See *Current Biography* 1988

Charles Neville

Born: New Orleans, Louisiana; December 28, 1928
Died: Huntington, Massachusetts; April 26, 2018
Occupation: Saxophonist

Charles Neville was the saxophonist and fourth member of the band the Neville Brothers. Along with three of his brothers, Neville cultivated a devoted audience by playing Grammy-award winning soul and funk music.

Charles Neville was the second oldest of four brothers, born to Art, Sr. and Amelia Neville. He also had two sisters though the four boys made up the band, Neville Brothers. Neville began his career as a saxophonist by playing backup in the 1950s. He served in the US Navy from 1956 to 1958. Neville played alongside BB King and the Bobby Blues Band in the 1960s, and then began teaching at Goddard College in the 1970s. He was arrested and spent more than three years in the Louisiana penitentiary (Angola) for possession of marijuana. The Neville Brothers began playing together in 1976, when they joined an uncle, Big Chief Jolly Landry, calling themselves the Wild Tchoupitoulas, but by 1977 they started going by the Neville Brothers. Some of their albums include *Fiyou on the Bayou* (1981), *Nevillization* (1984), *Treacherous* (1986), and *Uptown* (1987). Much of their music included sounds of Indian chants, Afro-Caribbean rhythms, and parade-drum virtuosity. Their album *Yellow Moon* (1989) attracted much more mainstream attention, and this was followed by *Brother's Keeper* (1990), *Treacherous Too* (1991), *Family Groove* (1992), *Live on Planet Earth* (1994), *Mitakuye Oyasin Oyasin (All My Relations)* (1996), and a retrospective, *The Very Best of the Neville Brothers* (1997). Though they were all in the band, each brother, including Charles Neville, would work on side projects outside of the Neville Brothers.

Charles Neville is survived by his wife Kristin, daughter Charmaine, sons Talyn and Khalif, and brothers Art, Cyril and Aaron.

See *Current Biography* 1999

Miguel Obando y Bravo

Born: La Libertad, Chontales, Nicaragua; February 2, 1926
Died: Managua, Nicaragua; June 3, 2018
Occupation: Cardinal

Miguel Obando y Bravo was the Roman Catholic Archbishop of Managua and the first Cardinal in Central American history. He was also a prominent political activist and mediator in tumultuous political events in Nicaragua.

Miguel Obando y Bravo was born in La Libertad, Nicaragua. He attended a Catholic high school in El Salvador; and after entering the Salesian order and completing the seminary course, Obando y Bravo was ordained in 1958. His first assignment was to a Catholic high school in Guatemala, where he taught mathematics and physics and served as principal and baseball coach. In 1968 Obando y Bravo returned to Nicaragua as auxiliary bishop of Managua. In 1970 he became archbishop of Managua, and as a result, prelate of Nicaragua. At this time, Obando y Bravo spoke out against the Somoza regime and inspired several conferences to engage the Catholic populations of Central America in social justice activism. Obando y Bravo was asked to mediate debates between Somoza and the leftist Frente Sandinista de Liberación Nacional (FSLN). Although Obando y Bravo denounced the Somoza regime and tried to remain outside of the Sandinista actions, he allowed Catholic priests and nuns to join Sandinista political affiliates. However, in 1980, the Sandinista leaders tried cutting Obando y Bravo's television and radio air time to redistribute leadership within the Protestant and Catholic churches, and Obando y Bravo interpreted this to mean they were trying to silence him. Through his protests, they canceled his broadcasts. A series of incidents in 1983 and 1984 inflamed the enmity between Archbishop Obando y Bravo and the Sandinistas and were worsened by Obando y Bravo's support of the US government and the counterrevolutionaries (commonly referred to as "Contra") cause. Pope John Paul II named him to the Sacred College of Cardinals in 1985, and he continued his condemnation of the Sandinista regime and their steps toward totalitarianism. A regional peace agreement in 1987 helped to ease tensions between the Sandinistas and the Catholic Church, and Obando y Bravo again acted as a mediator between the Sandinistas and the Contras. Afterwards, he supported the campaigns of Violeta Chamorro (1990) and Arnoldo Aleman (1996), and in 2006, supported the return of Ortega and the Sandinistas to the Liberal Party.

Miguel Obando y Bravo has no immediate survivors.

See *Current Biography* 1988

Idrissa Ouédraogo

Born: Banfora, Burkina Faso; January 21, 1954
Died: Ouagadougou, Burkina Faso; February 18, 2018
Occupation: Burkinabe filmmaker

Idrissa Ouédraogo was an African filmmaker who achieved worldwide recognition with his film Yaaba, about village life in his native Burkina Faso, one of the poorest countries in the world. His work won the International Federation of Film Critics (FIPRESCI) Prize at Cannes in 1989. His masterpiece, Tilai, about family honor in his native village, won the Cannes Jury Prize in 1990.

Idrissa Ouédraogo grew up in Banfora, a small village outside Ouagadougou, Burkina Faso's capital. He was bright and was one of the few children admitted to the government high school. He became interested in filmmaking only because he had no desire to teach, and because the African Institute for Film Education (INAFEC) was nearby. At the time, Burkina Faso was becoming known as an important cultural center for the African continent due to its hosting the biennial Pan-African film Festival (FESPACO). Following graduation Ouédraogo worked in the government's film production office. He eventually moved to Paris where he studied at the Institut des hautes études cinématographiques and received a degree in cinematography in 1985. As he released his short films, he began to win numerous prizes and international attention. His first major feature-length film success was *Yam Daabo*, which centered on a family leaving its native village. Ouédraogo's work attracted the attention of a Swiss producer, Pierre-Alain Meier, and the two began closely following each other's work. Meier was so taken by Ouédraogo's next project that he offered to help produce it. The film *Yaaba*, became one of the more talked about films of 1989, and was honored at the Cannes Film Festival, winning the International Critics' Award. As it was shown at film festivals around the world, the film began amassing prizes. Ouédraogo's next film, *Tilai*, released in 1990, came to be known as Ouédraogo's masterpiece, winning the Grand Prix at Cannes. Ouédraogo also directed *The Tragedy of King Christopher*, a stage production at the Paris Comédie-Française.

A list of immediate survivors was not available. Ouédraogo had a large extended family, many of whom worked on his films with him.

See *Current Biography* 1993

Peter George Peterson

Born: Kearney, Nebraska; June 5, 1926
Died: New York, New York; March 20, 2018
Occupation: Financier, philanthropist

A tycoon of the financial industry, Peter G. Peterson cultivated his career during some of the most financially turbulent times in US history. After working with many presidential candidates, Peterson was able to understand and articulate to the public the instability of the financial crisis of 2008. Publishing several books, Peterson explained topics such as tax reform, government entitlement, social security inflation, and aging societies.

Peter Peterson was born to George and Venet Peterson on June 5, 1926. The son of two Greek immigrants, Peterson grew up working at the family's small restaurant. For his undergraduate degree, Peterson attended Nebraska State Teachers College for one year, then attended the Massachusetts Institute of Technology (MIT) until he was expelled. He finished his BS degree at Northwestern University in 1947. While simultaneously pursuing a master's in business administration from the University of Chicago, Peterson became a market analyst for Market Facts, Inc. and within four years became executive vice president. He then moved to McCann-Erickson Inc. and within two years became vice president there. In 1958, Peterson became director of Bell and Howell, and by 1961 became the company's president. At the age of 36 he was named chairman and chief executive, a title he held until 1971. At this point, Peterson was offered a position as President Nixon's assistant on international economic affairs and then became commerce secretary in 1972. Peterson only held the position for one year due to his conflicting views as a liberal Republican. Peterson chose to then join Lehman Brothers as the company's chairman. He restructured the business, earning them five years of record-breaking profits. In 1985, Peterson and a Lehman colleague created Blackstone, which grew to become a world-class private equity investment firm, worth over eighty-eight billion dollars by the time it went public in 2007. In 2008, Peterson retired from Blackstone. Throughout his career, Peterson was also very involved in the fiscal integrity of the United States. In 1994, Peterson founded the Concord Coalition and was appointed by President Clinton to the Bipartisan Commission on Entitlement and Tax Reform. Peterson wrote many books on a variety of topics surrounding the financial security of the country. He was heavily involved in philanthropy and fiscal advocacy in his later years.

Peterson married three times. His first two marriages ended in divorce. He is survived by his five children, from his second marriage to Sally Hornbogen, and nine grandchildren. He is also survived by his brother, John, and his wife, Joan Ganz Cooney.

See Current Biography 1972

Robert D. Ray

Born: Des Moines, Iowa; September 26, 1928
Died: Des Moines, Iowa; July 8, 2018
Occupation: Politician

Robert Ray was the first governor of Iowa to serve five consecutive terms in office. Though a Republican, Ray introduced several liberal-leaning pieces of legislation during his time in office.

Robert Ray was born to Clark and Mildred Ray, and has one sister, Novelene. He attended Roosevelt High School and after graduation joined the army for two years, until 1948. Upon his return from the military, Ray attended Drake University, where he received his BA in 1952, and his Law degree in 1954. He joined the firm Lawyer, Lawyer, Ray, & Crouch in 1954. Ray became a member of the Iowa Republican central committee in 1960 and in 1963 was chosen chairman of the state party, a post that he held until 1967. In 1968, Ray was elected as Governor of Iowa and served for five consecutive terms, a total of fourteen years. During his time as Governor, Ray expanded funding for K-12 education, created a merged Department of Transportation (DOT), and eliminated the sales tax on food and drugs. In the late 1970s, Ray led the way for bottle and can deposit legislation, dramatically cleaning up Iowa's roadsides. He established the Iowa Commission on the Status of Women and issued Executive Orders advancing civil rights. In 1976, Ray became chairman for the Republican National Convention (RNC). He later became a leader in the humanitarian resettlement of refugees from Laos, Cambodia, Thailand, and Vietnam by helping them relocate, find jobs, and start new lives in Iowa. In 1979, Ray was a member of the U.S. delegation to the Special United Nations Conference of Refugees in Geneva, Switzerland. He served as a U.S. Representative to the United Nations in 1983. Ray then returned to Des Moines to become president and CEO of Blue Cross and Blue Shield of Iowa, where he also served as Acting Mayor of Des Moines in 1997, and as Interim president of Drake University in 1998. In 2005, Ray became the only governor to ever receive the Iowa Award.

Robert Ray is survived by his wife, Billie, their three children, Randi, Lu Ann, and Victoria, and eight grandchildren.

See Current Biography 1977

Della Reese

Born: Detroit, Michigan; July 6, 1931
Died: Encino, California; November 19, 2017
Occupation: Singer, actor

Though Della Reese was an award-winning singer in her early career, she is most remembered for the role she played in the popular television series *Touched by an Angel,* where she was an older "supervisor" to the younger angel, Monica, played by Roma Downey. The show placed in the Nielsen ratings' Top 10 from 1996 to 2000. Late in her life, Ms. Reese became an ordained minister.

Della Reese was born Delloreese Patricia Early to a steelworker father and a mother who was a domestic helper. She was the youngest child in a family of six girls and one boy. She got an early start on her career as the featured singer in her church's gospel choir. When Reese was thirteen, the gospel singer Mahalia Jackson heard her and had the young girl fill in for an ailing soprano in her gospel choir. Reese later entered Wayne State University where she studied psychology and planned to become a psychiatrist. However, her mother died, and Reese had a falling out with her father. She had to drop out of school to support herself. Her big break happened when she won a singing contest at Detroit's Flame Show Bar. She moved to New York where she became a singer with the Erskine Hawkins Orchestra. During the 1960s and 1970s, Reese acted in several popular television series, including *The Mod Squad* and *Chico and the Man.* She sometimes filled in as a guest host on Johnny Carson's *The Tonight Show.*

Della Reese was married three times. (Another marriage to Duke Ellington's son, Mercer Ellington was annulled.) She had three children and one adopted daughter who predeceased her in 2002. Reese's survivors include her husband, Franklin Lett, and three children.

See *Current Biography* 1971

Uwe Reinhardt

Born: Osnabrück, Germany; September 24, 1937
Died: Princeton, New Jersey; November 13, 2017
Occupation: Economist, educator

Uwe Reinhardt was a world-renowned economist who specialized in healthcare policies. He was the James Madison Professor of Political Economy, teaching economics and public affairs at the Woodrow Wilson School of Public and International Affairs at Princeton University from 1968 until his retirement in 2015. He was instrumental in devising some of the healthcare reforms in the Affordable Care Act, also known as Obamacare.

Uwe Reinhardt was born in Germany in 1937, just as Adolph Hitler was rising to power. Reinhardt's home was near the Hürtgen forest and the Belgian border where some of the most brutal, hand-to-hand combat took place, over several months, between American and German forces. At age eighteen, rather than be drafted into the German army, Reinhardt immigrated to Montreal, Canada. He earned his undergraduate degree from the University of Saskatchewan in Saskatoon. He then earned his PhD in economics from Yale University in the United States. Thereafter, he taught at Princeton University. He felt the United States should try to emulate the healthcare systems in Canada and Germany to make healthcare universal and foolproof rather than having such benefits tied to employment. Reinhardt served on many governmental commissions and committees such as the National Council on Healthcare Technology associated with the US Department of Health, Education, and Welfare (HEW). He also served as a Commissioner on the Physicians Payment Review Commission. He has served on a number of editorial boards and published numerous articles.

Reinhardt married Tsung-Mei Cheng, a health policy research analyst at Princeton University. Cheng, their three children, and two grandchildren survive.

See *Current Biography* 2004

Burt Reynolds

Born: Lansing, Michigan; February 11, 1936
Died: Jupiter, Florida; September 6, 2018
Occupation: American actor

Burt Reynolds is most remembered for his roles on television and at the box office, as a rugged, mustachioed and wry, tough guy in films like *Deliverance, Smokey and the Bandit,* and *The Cannonball Run.* He was nominated for an Oscar for his performance in *Boogie Nights* in 1997.

Burt Reynolds spent most of his childhood in West Palm Beach and Waycross, Florida, where his father, a former cowboy, was police chief. By all accounts, Reynolds's father was a tough disciplinarian who often clashed with his son. Reynolds was reported to have run away from home at least once. He played football in high school and in college where he was an All-Southern Conference halfback at Florida State College. However, an injury kept him off the field for good. After moderate success in acting at school, Reynolds dropped out of college and briefly moved to New York with dreams of an acting career. However, he soon returned to take acting classes at Palm Beach Junior College, and in 1958 he won the Florida Drama Award, which included an opportunity to work at the Hyde Park Playhouse where actress Joanne Woodward recognized his talent and recommended him to an agent. He signed with Universal Pictures Television and began appearing in minor television roles on popular shows like *Gunsmoke* and *Flipper*. When he could not find acting roles, he performed as a stunt man. He claimed his best acting lessons happened when he appeared on late night talk shows like Johnny Carson's *Tonight Show* and *The Merv Griffin Show*, where he learned to relax, and his appearances brought national exposure. His big breakthrough into film happened when he was cast in the role of Lewis Medlock in John Boorman's 1972 film *Deliverance*. That same year, he appeared nude in the centerfold of *Cosmopolitan* magazine, which he claimed was an act of satire. Reynolds started getting roles in more high-profile films. His iconic role was as Bandit in the movie *Smokey and the Bandit*, and as J. J. McClure in *The Cannonball Run*. However, through a series of bad business decisions and bad professional choices—he could have played Jack Nicholson's role in *One Flew Over the Cuckoo House*, and Harrison Ford's Hans Solo role in *Star Wars*—his career declined precipitously during the 1970s and 1980s. His personal life fared no better. He and wife, Loni Anderson, launched a bitter and very public divorce. Reynolds found moderate success again, in the 1990s. In 1992 he appeared in the movie *Boogie Nights*, which won him an Academy Award nomination for best supporting actor.

Burt Reynolds's son, Quinton, is his only survivor.

See *Current Biography* 1973

with his undergraduate professor, Francis Bitter, in the magnet laboratory, studying isotopic shifts. As a graduate student he held a Dupont Fellowship, in 1952–53, and a National Science Foundation (NSF)Fellowship, from 1953 to 1955. In 1956 he completed his PhD thesis on the photoproduction from hydrogen of pi-mesons, unstable elementary particles that have rest masses between those of the electron and the proton. Richter joined the Department of Physics at Stanford University as a research associate in 1956 and was promoted to assistant professor in 1960, and associate professor three years later. With his team, Richter spent six years building a colliding-beam device for trapping and storing counter-rotating beams of electrons in a magnetic guide field and allowing electron-electron scattering to be studied at a center-of-mass energy twenty times larger than the one envisioned in his original plan. In 1965 the Stanford Linear Accelerator Center (SLAC) team completed work on the complicated colliding-beam accelerator, and with their first successful experiment with the new accelerator, Richter and his associates extended the validity of quantum electrodynamics down to less than 10–14 centimeters. In 1973 the Stanford Positron Electron Asymmetric Ring (SPEAR) was completed, along with a large magnetic detector, and the experiments leading to Richter's Nobel prize-winning discovery began. Richter and Dr. Samuel Ting received a Nobel prize for his discovery in 1976. Dr. Richter directed the Department of Energy's SLAC National Accelerator Laboratory at Stanford from 1984 to 1999. He received the nation's highest scientific honor, the National Medal of Science, in 2014.

Burton Richter is survived by his wife, Laurose, their two children, Elizabeth and Matthew, and two grandchildren.

See *Current Biography* 1977

Burton Richter

Born: New York, New York; March 22, 1931
Died: Palo Alto, California; July 18, 2018
Occupation: Physicist

Burton Richter was a Nobel-prize winning physicist for his work discovering a subatomic particle, named "charm quark," that became a foundation for understanding matter.

Burton Richter was born to Abraham and Fanny Richter, the older of two siblings. He attended Far Rockaway High School and then Mercersburg Academy, before attending the Massachusetts Institute of Technology (MIT). Richter graduated with a BS in 1952 and continued onto the MIT graduate program, working

---

Joël Robuchon

Born: Poitiers, Vienne, France; April 7, 1945
Died: Geneva, Switzerland; August 6, 2018
Occupation: French chef, restaurateur

Joël Robuchon was a French haute cuisine super star, whose restaurants won more Michelin stars than any chef in history. The 1990 *Gault-Millau* guide named him one of the best chefs of the century.

Joël Robuchon, the son of a stonemason and housekeeper, had originally planned to become a priest. In fact, at age twelve, he entered a seminary but was unable to continue his studies when his parents divorced three years later.

To help his mother, Robuchon took a job as an apprentice cook at a local restaurant, the Relais de Poitiers. In 1963 Robuchon became a Compagnon of the Tour de France, a program for aspiring chefs who learn their trade by traveling around the country, working in restaurants. He spent ten years in the program, while also competing in cooking contests. In 1974 Robuchon was named head chef at Hotel Concorde-Lafayette where he managed ninety chefs, producing three thousand meals a night. He won the Meilleur Ouvrier, France's highest culinary award in the country. In 1978 he became head chef at the Paris Hotel Nikko. Robuchon opened his own restaurant, Jamin, in 1981, a restaurant that accommodated forty guests with a forty-person staff. Jamin earned a 19.5 rating, out of 20, in the German *Gault-Millau* guide, and winning Robuchon the prestigious Taittinger Prize. In 1993 Robuchon opened a larger, more formal restaurant, which soon surpassed Jamin's popularity. Several years later, Robuchon decided to retire due to the physical stress of the job, only to reemerge in 2003 after publishing several popular cookbooks and an autobiography. In 2003, Robuchon opened a new series of restaurants called L'Atellier de Joël Robuchon, an informal, convivial dining area, with a central, open kitchen surrounded by a U-shaped dining counter with stools.

Joël Robuchon is survived by his wife of more than fifty years, Janine Pallix, as well as their two children.

See *Current Biography* 2003

Philip Roth

Born: Newark, New Jersey; March 19, 1933
Died: New York, New York; May 22, 2018
Occupation: Writer

Philip Roth was a Pulitzer-Prize winning writer, known for infusing his fictional characters with aspects from his own life as a Jewish boy raised in Newark, New Jersey. Throughout his life, Roth published many short stories, novellas, novels, and works of non-fiction. He earned three National Book Awards (along with several additional books making the finalists' cut), several PEN/Faulkner Awards, and the National Book Foundation's Award for Distinguished Contribution to American Letters. In 2011 he was awarded the National Humanities Medal by President Barack Obama.

Philip Roth was born to Herman and Bess Roth and has an older brother, Sandy. Roth attended Jewish Weequahic High School and then Rutgers University, before transferring to Bucknell University, where he received his BA in English in 1954. Roth obtained his MA in English from the University of Chicago the following year, before serving briefly in the US Army. He returned to the University of Chicago to teach for two years, during which time he began writing fictional short stories. His first publication was "The Day It Snowed," in the *Chicago Review* in 1955. His first novella, *Goodbye, Columbus*, was published four years later. His writing was met with both admiration and criticism, mostly coming from the Jewish community. Though Jewish himself, Roth wrote very candidly and often portrayed his Jewish characters in an unflattering manner. Many Jews thought these portrayals were borderline anti-Semitic. In the late 1960s Roth began teaching at the University of Pennsylvania, and in 1969, *Goodbye, Columbus* was made into a film. At this same time, almost contemporaneously, he published *Portnoy's Complaint, Our Gang, In the Breast, The Great American Novel*, and *My Life as a Man*, which was his most popular publication up to that date. By the 2000s Roth had published over seventeen books, including a biography of his then wife, Claire Bloom.

Information about Philip Roth's survivors was not immediately available.

See *Current Biography* 1991

Otis Rush

Born: Philadelphia, Mississippi; April 29, 1935
Died: Chicago, Illinois; September 29, 2018
Occupation: Guitarist, vocalist

Otis Rush was a Grammy Award-winning blues guitarist who was a major influence on younger blues guitarists such as Jimmy Page of Led Zeppelin and Eric Clapton. Though he would not claim the label, Rush was the progenitor of what became known as the "West Side Sound."

Otis Rush was born into abject poverty, one of seven children, to a share cropper in the deep South. His father was rarely around, and he and his siblings often had to leave school to work in the fields. According to Rush, he picked up the guitar at a young age out of sheer boredom—something to do when not working. He played the guitar left-handed and upside down because he liked the sound. Visiting a sister in Chicago, Rush saw Muddy Waters perform. He moved to Chicago in 1949 working odd jobs and spending his nights roaming the blues clubs on Chicago's West side. He began playing at the popular 708 Club for five dollars a night and was eventually able to quit his day jobs. One night in 1956, Willie Dixon saw him perform and signed him with Cobra Records. His first hit single was "I Can't Quit You Baby," which reached number six on the Billboard R&B charts and would eventually be picked up by Led Zeppelin for their debut album, *Led Zeppelin*. Rush's recording career, however, was sporadic. Cobra went bankrupt, and his recordings for big names like Chess and Delmark remained delayed or never released. His album *Right Place, Wrong Time*, now considered a classic, wasn't released until 1976. Rush developed a reputation for being unpredictable, even erratic in his live performances—sometimes brilliant and sometimes lackluster. He retired from recording in 1970, though he re-emerged in the 1980s. In 1999 he won a Grammy Award for best traditional blues album for *Any Place I'm Going*. The same year he was inducted into the Blues Hall of Fame.

Otis Rush was married twice and had six children. Rush's wife, six children, and numerous grandchildren survive.

See *Current Biography* 2002

Red Schoendienst

Born: Germantown, Illinois; February 2, 1923
Died: Town and Country, Missouri; June 6, 2018
Occupation: Baseball player and manager

Red Schoendienst was a major league baseball player, manager, and then coach for over seventy-four years. Playing for the Cardinals, the Giants, and the Braves, Schoendienst won two National League (NL) pennants and five World Series games with his teams.

Albert Fred Schoendienst was born to Mary and Joseph Schoendienst. His father was a coal miner who played semiprofessional baseball. Schoendienst attended New Baden High School, but left school at the age of fourteen. He held several odd jobs during the depression, until he joined the Civil Conservation Corps at the age of sixteen. In 1942 Schoendienst decided to try for the St. Louis Cardinals, and was asked to sign a class-D contract. He played six games as second baseman with Union City, then went to Albany in the Georgia-Florida League and played the rest of the 1942 season there, with the exception of the nine final games that he played as a shortstop with Lynchburg in the Piedmont League. Schoendienst then joined the Rochester International League, where he was voted Most Valuable Player (MVP). He joined the major League in 1945, playing left-field for the Cardinals. In 1956 he was traded to the New York Giants, with whom he played one hundred games. In 1957 Schoendienst was then traded to the Milwaukee Braves, but in 1958 he was admitted to the hospital with tuberculosis and did not return to the Braves until 1960. However, due to many injuries and his worsening vision, Schoendienst returned to the Cardinals as a player-coach in 1963. In 1964, Schoendienst was appointed manager of the Cardinals. He then served as a coach from 1979 until 1995 before moving to the front office. Schoendienst finished his career with a .289 batting average, 2,449 hits, 427 doubles, 1,223 runs and a .983 fielding percentage. He set a major league record with eight doubles in a three-game span. Schoendienst was inducted into the Baseball Hall of Fame in 1989.

Red Schoendienst is survived by his four children; Colleen, Cathleen, Eileen, and Kevin, eight grandchildren, and seven great grandchildren.

See *Current Biography* 1964

Ed Schultz

Born: Norfolk, Virginia; January 27, 1954
Died: Washington, DC; July 5, 2018
Occupation: Radio/television talk show host

Ed Schultz was a popular radio/television talk show host and news broadcaster.

Ed Schultz was born to George and Mary Schultz in Norfolk, Virginia. His father was an engineer, and his mother was a high school English teacher. He was a high school football player who graduated in 1972 before attending Moorhead State University (currently Minnesota State University at Moorhead). Schultz played football for the university, and in 1977 he was the passing champion in the National Collegiate Athletic Association (NCAA), Division II. He briefly played professionally for the Oakland Raiders. His broadcasting career started in the late 1970s in Fargo, North Dakota. He was a raucous, outspoken, and sometimes irascible sportscaster. In 1992 he launched a daily, two-and-a-half-hour regional talk show, the conservative *News and Views*, on station KFGO. He often berated his Democrat representatives and derided the poor and homeless. That all changed when he met Wendy Noack, a psychiatric nurse who worked at a homeless shelter. When he asked her to lunch, she insisted they meet at the Salvation Army cafeteria near her work. He was humbled when some of the homeless recognized him and praised his radio show. Schultz realized that he had it all wrong. After he and Noack married, they traveled around the country broadcasting from small towns along the way, exposing Schultz to the poverty and suffering of middle-America and the working poor. He decided to change his message and change his political affiliations. In 2004 his nationally syndicated talk show, *The Ed Schultz Show*, debuted, supported by the non-profit group, Democracy Radio. That same year he published his book *Straight Talk from the Heartland*. In 2009 the Schultz's moved to New York where he hosted *The Ed Show* on MSNBC.

Ed Schultz is survived by his wife of twenty years, Wendy Noack, his son from his first marriage, and five stepchildren.

See *Current Biography* 2005

Francisco (Pancho) Segura

Born: Guayaquil, Ecuador; June 20, 1921
Died: Carlsbad, California; November 18, 2017
Occupation: Ecuadorian tennis player

Pancho Segura was one of the first South American tennis players to win prestige as one of the world's greatest tennis players. For three years straight, he won the National Collegiate Athletic Association (NCAA) singles tennis championships, and he won the prestigious US Pro Tennis Championships from 1950 to 1952. He later became a mentor to a young Jimmy Connors. He was inducted into the International Tennis Hall of Fame in 1984.

Francisco (Pancho) Segura was born on a steamboat on the Guayas River en route to Guayaquil, Ecuador. He was one of ten children. His father, Domingo Segura, was the caretaker of the exclusive Guayaquil Tennis Club, where Pancho worked as a ball boy on the courts. The family lived on the club grounds, and Pancho earned extra money for the family by running errands and doing small chores for club members. Segura has several major illnesses as a child. He suffered from rickets, which left his legs bowed, and contracted malaria. A double hernia affected him so profoundly that the only way for him to practice his powerful tennis swings was to do so double-handed. The University of Miami recruited Segura in 1940 where he played on the tennis team. He won the US NCAA singles title from 1943 to 1945, as well as the singles semifinals of the US Nationals in Forest Hills, Queens, from 1942 to 1945. He turned pro in 1947 and traveled the world with such tennis greats as Bobby Riggs, Pancho Gonzalez, and Tony Trabert. From 1950 to 1952, Segura won the prestigious US Pro Tennis singles championships. He left the pro tour in 1962 and began teaching at the Beverly Hills Tennis Club and, later, at the Omni LaCosta Resort and Spa, where he lived until his death. In the late 1960s he began mentoring the soon-to-be champion, Jimmy Connors.

Segura became a US citizen in 1991. Pancho Segura was married twice and had two children. His second wife, Beverly Moylan, two children, and four grandchildren survive.

See *Current Biography* 1951

Anita Shreve

Born: Boston, Massachusetts; October 7, 1946
Died: Newfields, New Hampshire; March 29, 2018
Occupation: Writer

Anita Shreve was an award-winning novelist and writer, publishing seventeen books and numerous articles and short stories. Some of her most noted works included *The Pilot's Wife* (1998), which was made into a CBS television movie, and *The Weight of Water* (1996).

Anita Shreve was born to Richard and Bibiana Shreve and raised outside of Boston, Massachusetts. She attended Tufts University and graduated with a BA in english in 1968. After graduating, Shreve worked as a high school teacher in the Boston area, and wrote short stories for small publications. In 1975, one of her stories won the O. Henry Award. Shortly thereafter, she and her husband moved to Kenya, where Shreve's husband was a graduate student, and Shreve continued writing as a journalist for American publications. Upon returning to the United States, she became deputy editor of *Viva* magazine in 1986. Many of Shreve's articles and stories focused on issues of feminism, motherhood, and children's health. She co-wrote three books with Lawrence Balter, including *Dr. Balter's Child Sense: Understanding and Handling the Common Problems of Infancy and Early Childhood* (1985), *Dr. Balter's Baby Sense* (1985), and *Who's in Control? Dr. Balter's Guide to Discipline Without Combat* (1988). Shreve co-wrote another book with Patricia Lone, titled *Working Woman: A Guide to Fitness and Health* (1987). Shreve's first solo book was *Remaking Motherhood: How Working Mothers Are Shaping Our Children's Future* (1987). In the late 1980s, Shreve began writing works of fiction, though the novels continued to contain themes of her earlier works. Her first work of fiction, *Eden Close*, was published in 1989. Her best-known books were *The Weight of Water* (1996), *The Pilot's Wife* (1998), and *Fortune's Rocks* (1999). *The Pilot's Wife* was the Oprah Winfrey Book Club's choice in 1999. While writing her numerous novels, Shreve also worked as a visiting lecturer at Amherst College.

Anita Shreve is survived by her second husband, John Osborn, her children, Chris and

Katherine Clemens, stepchildren, Whitney, Allison, and Molly, and three grandchildren. She is also survived by two sisters, Janet Martland and Betsy Shreve-Gibb.

See *Current Biography* 2000

Neil Simon

Born: New York, New York; July 4, 1927
Died: New York, New York; August 26, 2018
Occupation: American playwright

A playwright with over thirty plays, and nearly as many screenplays to his name, Neil Simon was one of the most prolific writers in Broadway history. He was nominated for seventeen Tony Awards, winning three, and was nominated for four Academy Awards. In 1961 he had four plays running on Broadway simultaneously. In 1983 he became the only living playwright to have a theater named after him.

Neil Simon was born in the Bronx borough of New York City. When he was five, the family moved to Washington Heights in Manhattan. His parents fought often and Simon's father, Irving Simon, who worked in the garment district, abandoned his family several times during Simon's childhood. When his parents finally divorced, Neil Simon went to live with cousins, while his brother, Danny, went to live with an aunt. Simon graduated from DeWitt Clinton High School and then enlisted in the Army Air Forces Air Reserve training program, while attending New York University (NYU). (His military experience would factor heavily in his hit play, *Biloxi Blues*.) He was assigned to an air base near Denver, and he continued his studies at the University of Denver. Simon credits his brother with getting him into writing. Danny, eight years his senior, worked for Warner Brothers in New York, and in their spare time, the two began writing comedy sketches for early television greats like Sid Caesar, Jackie Gleason, and Phil Silvers. He befriended other comedic writers like Mel Brooks, Carl Reiner, and Woody Allen, making what Charles Isherwood, writing for *The New York Times* (26 August 2018), called the "comedy of urban neurosis." His first play was *Come Blow Your Horn*, produced in 1961, and though it was relatively short-lived on Broadway, Simon gained important connections. His second play, *Barefoot in the Park*, was a hit and made Robert Redford a star. The movie adaptation starred Redford and Jane Fonda in the lead roles. Simon's play *The Odd Couple*, was a great stage success, winning Simon one of his Tony Awards. It was also made into a successful movie starring Walter Matthau and Jack Lemmon. It was even made into a popular television series.

Neil Simon was married five times, twice to the same woman, Diane Lander. His survivors include his wife, Elaine Joyce, three daughters, three grandchildren, and one great-grandson. His son, Danny Simon, predeceased him in 2005.

See *Current Biography* 1989

Louise M. Slaughter

Born: Lynch, Kentucky; August 14, 1929
Died: Washington, DC; March 16, 2018
Occupation: Congresswoman

Louise Slaughter held her position in Congress for sixteen consecutive terms, spanning more than thirty years. During her time in Congress, Slaughter advocated for women's rights, campaign-finance reform, breast cancer research, educational opportunities for homeless children, and the National Endowment for the Arts and Humanities.

Dorothy Louise McIntosh Slaughter was born in Harlan County, Kentucky, to Oscar Lewis McIntosh and Daisy Grace Byers McIntosh. Slaughter attended Somerset High School and then received a BS in microbiology and a master's degree in public health (MPH) from the University of Kentucky. Following her receiving her MPH, Slaughter worked as a bacteriologist at the Kentucky Department of Health and at the University of Kentucky. From 1953 to 1956, Slaughter worked at Procter and Gamble as a market researcher, until she married her husband, Robert Slaughter, and moved to Rochester, New York. Slaughter began her political career in 1976 when she was elected to the Monroe county legislature. In 1982 she won a seat in the New York State Assembly. Then in 1986, Slaughter was elected to the House of Representatives, the first Democrat from her district to do so in forty-two years. Slaughter was re-elected, and held almost sixteen consecutive terms, until the time of her death. Slaughter was appointed the first chairwoman of the House Committee on Rules in 1989, a position she held until 1994. She again became chairwoman for the rules committee from 2007 until 2010. In 1991 Slaughter and six other congresswomen marched on the floor of the Senate to delay the appointment of Clarence Thomas, who had been accused of sexual harassment by Anita Hill. Though Thomas was appointed, this march helped raised awareness about attitudes toward women in Congress. Throughout her career, Slaughter campaigned for numerous pieces of legislation that related to her background in biology. Such topics included genetic information nondiscrimination, reduction in the use of antibiotics in livestock, and the advancement of the Affordable Care Act.

Slaughter's husband predeceased her in 2014. Her survivors include their three daughters, Megan, Amy, and Emily, their seven grandchildren, and one great-grandchild.

See *Current Biography* 1999

Liz Smith

Born: Fort Worth, Texas; February 2, 1923
Died: New York, New York; November 12, 2017
Occupation: Journalist, author

Liz Smith was a popular, highly regarding gossip columnist who wrote for numerous papers, including the *New York Daily News, Newsday,* and the *New York Post.* Her work was syndicated in over sixty other newspapers. Her acclaim and celebrity rivaled that of the stars she wrote about.

Liz Smith was born Mary Elizabeth Smith in Fort Worth, Texas. She attended Hardin-Simmons University, a Baptist college in Abilene, Texas, eventually transferring to the University of Texas where she worked on a literary magazine and the university's newspaper. She graduated with a journalism degree in 1948 and moved to New York and worked as a typist and proofreader for *Newsweek.* During the 1950s she worked as an associate producer with the journalist, Mike Wallace. During the 1960s she worked as an entertainment editor for *Cosmopolitan* magazine, and was a staff writer for *Sports Illustrated,* as well as a freelance contributor to a number of popular magazines, including *Vogue, Esquire, American Home,* and *Ladies Home Journal.* In 1975 the editors at the *New York Daily News* decided to reintroduce a "gossip column." Smith was selected due to her easy-going manner and sense of humor. She redefined the form and, in the words of Gloria Steinem, "transcended a whole art form." Because her writing was free of malice, was fair and honest, celebrities trusted her with their secrets, and she became close friends with many of her subjects. She was also credited with several "hard news" scoops, including her story about high-echelon embezzlement at Columbia Pictures in 1977. Smith also began writing twice-weekly commentary for WNBC-TV in New York City. In 1978 she published her book, *The Mother Book,* a collection of "facts, fancies, overblown sentimentalities...profundities, and curiosities." She contributed to many charities and non-profit organizations including Literacy Volunteers and the Woman's Action Alliance.

Liz Smith married a football player while in college at the University of Texas, but the marriage didn't last. Her second marriage to New York travel agent Fred Lister likewise ended in divorce. She had no children. Information about survivors is not available.

See *Current Biography* 1987

Orin C. Smith

Born: Ryderwood, Washington; June 26, 1942
Died: Jackson, Wyoming; March 1, 2018
Occupation: Coffee executive

Orin C. Smith is best known for his role as the CEO of Starbucks, a world renowned coffee roaster chain. He was instrumental in its success as a public company and dedicated his time at Starbucks to ensuring environmental protection and fair compensation of groups involved with coffee farming.

Orin C. Smith was born to Curtis and Vernetta Smith on June 26, 1942 in Ryderwood, Washington. Shortly after his birth, the family moved to Chehalis, Washington. He attended W. F. West High School and then attended Centralia Community College, before receiving a BA in Business Administration from the University of Washington. In 1967, Smith received an MBA from Harvard University and joined the financial consulting firm, Touche-Ross (later, Deloitte and Touche). He worked for the firm on and off for over twelve years until 1985, while simultaneously working for Washington state's Office of Management and Budget from 1977 to 1980, and 1985 to 1987. In 1987 Smith went to work for Northern Air Freight and was then hired by Starbucks in 1990 as the executive vice president and chief financial officer. In 1992 Smith oversaw the company's initial public offering of stock; and in 1994, he became president and chief operating officer. In 2000, Smith was made CEO of Starbucks. During his time at Starbucks, Smith ensured that coffee bean farmers were paid more than the average commercial rate for quality beans, and that environmental protection regulations were upheld. In 2000 Smith also became director of Conservation International to uphold environmental protection and humanity within the coffee industry. From 2006 to 2018, Smith served on the board of the Walt Disney Company, and from 2004 to 2015 he also served on the board of directors of Nike, Inc. In 2009 he was appointed to the University of Washington Board of Regents. Throughout his career, Smith contributed to several philanthropic organizations and set up several scholarships for students at the University of Washington.

Smith is survived by his wife, Janet, their two sons, and their grandchildren. He is also survived by his three siblings, Kevin, Michael, and Vicki.

See *Current Biography* 2003

Kate Spade

Born: Kansas City, Missouri; December 24, 1962
Died: New York, New York; June 5, 2018
Occupation: Fashion designer

Kate Spade was an internationally recognized handbag and fashion designer, known for her bold color choices and tasteful, simple designs. She was known by many in the fashion world as a style icon.

Katherine Noel Brosnahan was the fifth of six children born to Earl Brosnahan Jr. and June Therese Mullen Brosnahan. She attended the University of Kansas before transferring to Arizona State University, where she majored in broadcast journalism. While at school, Spade worked at Johns and Co., a clothing store where she met her husband, Andy Spade. In 1985, after graduating, Spade moved to New York City and began working for *Mademoiselle* Magazine, as a temporary employee. By the time she was twenty-eight, Spade became the senior fashion editor for the magazine. Her then boyfriend, Andy, suggested Spade start a handbag company, with his financial and business know-how and Spade's eye for design and knowledge of the fashion market. In 1992 Spade quit her job to launch the company, Kate Spade LLC, and entered her first show in 1993. After her second show, many luxury department stores began buying her designs, and the brand received mentions in fashion magazines such as *Elle* and *Vogue*. That year, Andy quit his job to join full-time as CEO, and the couple opened their first store in Soho, New York City. The company began to face many challenges, after the couple sold over half the company to Neiman Marcus, a company which then went through a workers' union controversy following the purchase. Additionally, the brand faced setbacks with the high percentage of counterfeits being sold. At the same time, the Kate Spade LLC brand continued to expand to include additional accessories and clothing and received a number of fashion guide book deals. In 2006 Liz Claiborne Inc. bought out the rest of Spade and her husband's shares in Kate Spade LLC, with Spade and her husband deciding to remain with the company as members only. She and her original investors started a new company, Frances Valentine, in 2014, an accessories and shoes company.

Kate Spade committed suicide on June 25, 2018. Her survivors include her husband, Andy, and their daughter, Frances Beatrix Spade. News of Spade's suicide sparked international campaigns for suicide and depression awareness.

See *Current Biography* 2007

Tony Sparano

Born: West Haven, Connecticut; October 7, 1961
Died: Eden Prairie, Minnesota; July 22, 2018
Occupation: Football coach

Tony Sparano was a well-traveled professional football coach. In 2008 he led the Dolphins to the greatest single-season turnaround in National Football League (NFL) history, when the team became the only team to reach the playoffs after losing sixteen games in the previous season. That year he received the NFL Alumni Coach of the Year Award.

Anthony Joseph Sparano III was the first of three children born to a close-knit family in West Haven, Connecticut. He was raised in a three-story row house with both sets of grandparents. His father worked at several blue-collar jobs, from driving a liquor truck to furniture upholstery. His mother worked as a waitress and school crossing guard. He graduated from Richard C. Lee High School, where he lettered all four years as an offensive lineman on the football team. He attended the University of Central Florida for one semester before transferring to the University of New Haven. He earned his BA in criminal law in 1982. In 1984 the university hired him to work as an offensive line coach and recruiting coordinator. In 1988 he moved to Boston University (BU) where he likewise served as offensive team coach and coordinator. He remained at BU for six years. He then returned to New Haven as the team's head coach where he overhauled their football program and brought their four-year record to 41-14-1. He was named the New England Football Writers Division II/III Coach of the Year. In 1999 he joined the big league as offensive quality control coach of the Cleveland Browns. He remained there in several capacities through the 2002 season. His first head coach job in professional ball came in 2008 when he signed a four-year contract with the Miami Dolphins, winning the American Football Conference (AFC) East title in 2008. Sparano was named NFL Alumni Coach of the Year. Sparano would move on to serve as offensive line coach for a number of pro teams, including the Oakland Raiders, New York Jets, and Minnesota Vikings.

Tony Sparano's survivors include his wife, three children, and four grandchildren.

See *Current Biography* 2010

John Sulston

Born: Cambridge, England; March 27, 1942
Died: Buckinghamshire, England; March 6, 2018
Occupation: Geneticist

A Nobel Prize-winning geneticist, John Sulston is most well-known for his work sequencing the first full genome of a multicellular organism, the *C. elegans*. After his work with *C. elegans*, Sulston was instrumental in the completion of the sequencing of the human genome in 2000.

John Edward Sulston was born to Arthur Edward Aubrey Sulston and Josephine Muriel Frearson (Blocksidge) Sulston. Though he was not known as a particularly good student, Sulston attended the University of Cambridge for his bachelor's degree and then continued at Cambridge for his doctorate. After receiving his PhD in 1966, Sulston moved to San Diego, California, for a fellowship at the Salk Institute for Biological Studies. At the institute, Sulston was able to meet Francis Crick, one of the men responsible for constructing the first molecular model of the double-helix of DNA. In 1969 Sulston moved back to England to work at the British Medical Research Council's (MRC) Cambridge laboratory. There, Sulston began to study *C. elegans* and eventually mapped the species genome, in what was called the "Worm Project." Sulston was responsible for documenting the lineage of every cell in adult *C. elegans* from the time of conception, as well as the development of *C. elegans* embryos. From this research, Sulston discovered some of the main reasons for apoptosis, or cell death. In 1990, Sulston and his team were able to write out the full sequence of the organism's genome. The entire project was completed in 1998, with support from James Watson and the Human Genome Project, and was the first-ever sequencing of a multicellular organism. In 1992 the MRC started the Wellcome Trust to fund genome research, and Sulston was named director of the facility (called the Sanger Centre). The Sanger team and a team at the Genome Sequencing Center at Washington University worked together to fully sequence the human genome by 2000. For his work on the human genome, Sulston was Knighted by Queen Elizabeth II in 2001. On October 7, 2007, Sulston and his two colleagues, Sydney Brenner and H. Robert Horvitz, received the Nobel Prize in Physiology or Medicine. Sulston received numerous other awards for his research in genetics. After completion of the human genome sequencing, Sulston wrote and published, with Georgiana Ferry, *The Common Thread: A Story of Science, Politics, Ethics, and the Human Genome.*

Sulston is survived by his wife, Daphne, his two children, Ingrid and Adrian, and two grandchildren. He is also survived by his sister, Madeleine.

See *Current Biography* 2007

Cecil Taylor

Born: New York, New York; March 25, 1929
Died: New York, New York; April 5, 2018
Occupation: Jazz pianist, composer, poet

Cecil Taylor is most famously known for his unique jazz music and compositions. Influenced from a young age by many different styles of music, Taylor created his own sound of free jazz. He was known for incorporating his own poetry into his concerts and performances.

Cecil Taylor was born in Queens, New York, an only child to a chef and housewife. His mother was highly educated and played a major role in influencing his musical aspirations. However, she died when he was just fourteen. In high school, Taylor won a performance contest with radio station WHN, and through this show, was offered a job with a local booking agent. However, Taylor was quickly dropped due to clients not wanting a black musician to play at their events. Taylor decided to attend New York College of Music, and in 1952 entered the New England Conservatory of Music, where he was classically trained. His exposure to many diverse musicians gave Taylor a unique sound, including his addition of percussive elements to his piano playing. During his early career in the mid-1950s, Taylor made a living delivering goods for coffee shops and by washing dishes. He recorded his first album, *Jazz Advance*, in 1956. He played with his band (Steve Lacy, Buell Neidlinger, and the drummer, Dennis Charles) at a few local music festivals and restaurant gigs. In the late 1950s, his unique sound began to attract the attention of wider audiences, beyond the local New York music scene. His album, *Into the Hot*, was recorded and released in 1961, and his album, *Unit Structures*, was released in 1966. In the early 1970s, Taylor was an instructor at the University of Wisconsin, then at Madison, and Antioch College. In 1973, he received the Guggenheim Fellowship, which was the first of many notable awards Taylor would receive later in the 1980s and 1990s. His albums *Silent Tongues, Unit*, and *3 Phasis* were released in the mid-1970s, during which time Taylor began to really grow in popularity. He performed at the White House Jazz Festival in 1978 and at Carnegie Hall in 1977. Taylor has received numerous awards and honors for his works, most recently, in 2014, he was awarded the coveted Kyoto Prize.

Cecil Taylor has no surviving family members.

See *Current Biography* 1986

Paul Taylor

Born: Wilkinsburg, Pennsylvania; July 29, 1930
Died: New York, New York; August 29, 2018
Occupation: Dancer, choreographer

Award-winning choreographer, Paul Taylor, was one of the most influential dance storytellers in the world. He disclaimed allegiance to any single style of dance; his compositions embraced modern experimentation and avant-garde with classical ballet. He was popular with ballet audiences as well as with modern dance aficionados. His dance company, the Paul Taylor Dance Company, was one of the world's foremost, and long-lasting dance institutions.

Paul Taylor was born to physicist, Paul Belville Taylor and Elizabeth (Pendleton Rust) Taylor. Although he had step-siblings through his mother's previous marriage, Taylor was essentially raised as an only child. During the Depression, the family moved to Washington, DC where his mother managed the Brighton Hotel, and her son entertained himself observing the stream of humanity that came through the hotel. While in school, Taylor participated in sports and attended Syracuse University on a partial swimming scholarship and a partial painting scholarship. He majored in painting, but a summer job as a chauffeur for a dance school in Bar Harbor, Maine, introduced him to the world of dance. The following summer he enrolled in Connecticut College where he trained with Martha Graham, Doris Humphrey, and José Limón. Instead of returning to Syracuse, he went to Julliard on a partial scholarship. He originally became a male understudy for Martha Graham, then worked his way up to regular dancer, and finally to soloist. He also began working with George Balanchine, the artistic director of the New York City Ballet. Taylor began choreography in 1955. In 1962, he created his own dance company, the Paul Taylor Dance Company, which became one of the first to perform worldwide, partially sponsored by the US State Department. In 1974 Taylor contracted hepatitis and became addicted to Dexamyl, a drug that reduced anxiety, particularly with stage fright. He decided to retire as a performer and focus on his choreography. He was commissioned by dance organizations, worldwide, including the American Ballet, the Royal Danish Ballet, and the Paris Opera Ballet. He received many accolades including a "genius award" fellowship from the MacArthur Foundation, National Medal of the Arts, Kennedy Center honors, and an Emmy Award in 1992.

Paul Taylor had no immediate survivors.

See *Current Biography* 1964

Morgan Tsvangirai

Born: Gutu, Masvingo, Rhodesia (now Zimbabwe); March 10, 1952
Died: Johannesburg, South Africa; February 14, 2018
Occupation: Former prime minister of Zimbabwe

Morgan Tsvangirai was a political leader in Zimbabwe who once nearly toppled the dictatorial regime of President Robert Mugabe.

Morgan Tsvangirai was one of nine children born to a poor bricklayer in the country now known as Zimbabwe. His education was limited as he left school at age sixteen. He was never able to attend the university, though later in life, he attended the Harvard Kennedy School Executive Leadership program. In 1988 he was elected secretary general of the Zimbabwe Congress of Trade Unions (ZCTU), a position that would eventually make him a life-long political opponent of Zimbabwe's dictator president, Robert Mugabe. In 1999 Tsvangirai founded and led the Movement for Democratic Change (MDC), and he launched serious opposition to Mugabe's Zanu-PF government. He was arrested several times in the early 2000s and was unsuccessfully tried for treason in 2003. In 2007 he was severely beaten while in police custody as Mugabe tried to paint Tsvangirai as a puppet of the West, who risked a return to colonialism for Zimbabwe. The 2008 election was pivotal when Tsvangirai arguably won the presidential election, but Mugabe called for extensive recounting, eventually forcing a runoff election, resulting in violence. The compromise left Tsvangirai as Zimbabwe's prime minister and Mugabe retaining his position as president.

Morgan Tsvangirai's first wife, Susan, was killed in a car accident under suspicious circumstances in 2009. His survivors include his wife, Elizabeth Macheka, and his six children.

See *Current Biography* 2005

John V. Tunney

Born: New York, New York; June 26, 1934
Died: Los Angeles, California; January 12, 2018
Occupation: US senator from California

The son of heavyweight boxing champion, Gene Tunney, John Tunney was a California congressman and US senator.

John Tunney was born the second of four children to the heavyweight boxing champion, Gene Tunney. His mother was Polly Lauder, heiress to the Carnegie family fortune. He grew up primarily in Stamford, Connecticut, attending Yale University for his degree in anthropology. He attended the University of Virginia Law School where he was a roommate to Edward M. Kennedy. In 1957 Tunney attended the Academy of International Law at the Hague. He earned his LL.B. in 1959. In 1960 he joined the US Air Force and worked in the Advocate General's Office in Riverside, California, where he also taught law part-time at the University of California, Riverside. He eventually opened a law practice in California. In 1964 Tunney was elected to the US Congress, representing the 38th congressional district of California. While in Congress he served on the House Committee on Interior and Insular Affairs, and the powerful house Committee on Foreign Affairs. He served until January of 1971 when he was sworn in as a California senator. At that time, Tunney was the youngest senator serving in Washington. He was thirty-six.

John Tunney's survivors include his wife, his four children, two stepchildren, and three grandchildren.

See *Current Biography* 1971

Stansfield Turner

Born: Chicago, Illinois; December 1, 1923
Died: Redmond, Washington; January 18, 2018
Occupation: Director of the CIA, Admiral

Stansfield Turner was the director of the Central Intelligence Agency (CIA) in the Carter administration, from February 1977 to 1981. He overhauled the CIA, which had been drawn into the corruption of the Nixon era, by dismissing over eight hundred officers at the height of the Cold War with Russia. His decorations include the Legion of Merit.

Stansfield Turner was born and raised, one of two children, in Chicago, Illinois. He attended Amherst College for two years before transferring to the US Navy Academy where he was a brigade commander. He and Jimmy Carter were in the same class at Annapolis though they did not know each other at the time. After a year serving on a navy cruiser, Turner attended Oxford University as a Rhodes scholar, graduating in 1950 with a master's degree in philosophy, politics, and economics. He served aboard destroyers in both the Atlantic and Pacific during the Korean War, earning a Bronze Star. He advanced through the naval grades becoming a commander in 1967 when he guided a missile frigate off the coast of Vietnam. In the early 1970s Turner was appointed president of the Naval War College in Newport, Rhode Island. A few years later he served as commander of the US Second Fleet and the National Atlantic Treaty Organization (NATO) Striking Fleet Atlantic. In 1977 the new President Jimmy Carter named Turner his primary advisor on foreign intelligence and head of the Central Intelligence Agency (CIA). His express goal was to restore the reputation of the United States intelligence community. Two major world events caught Turner's CIA by surprise: the 1979 Soviet invasion of Afghanistan and the fall of the Shah of Iran. During the Iranian revolution fifty-two Americans were held hostage, including four CIA members, for 444 days until Ronald Reagan became president in January of 1981. Following his dismissal from the CIA, Turner continued lecturing on national security and the CIA at the Graduate School of Public Policy at the University of Maryland. He was highly critical of the Bush administration's use of the CIA for overly harsh interrogations following the attacks of September 11, 2001.

Turner was married three times. His second wife, Karin Gilbert was killed in a plane crash in 2000 that left Turner critically injured. Turner's survivors include his wife, Marion Weiss Turner, his two children, four stepchildren, twelve grandchildren, and four great-grandchildren.

See *Current Biography* 1978

Atal Bihari Vajpayee

Born: Gwalior, Madhya Pradesh, India; December 25, 1924
Died: Delhi, India; August 16, 2018
Occupation: Former prime minister of India, poet, writer

Atal Bihari Vajpayee was a powerful Indian politician for more than fifty years, having served several decades in parliament. He was the foreign minister from 1977 to 1980. He served three terms as prime minister, though two were not full terms.

Atal Bihari Vajpayee's father was a Hindu scholar and school teacher. His family was of the Brahmin caste. As a young man, Vajpayee was drawn to Communism and was jailed for several weeks for leading anti-British activities with the Rashtriya Swayamsevak Sangh (RSS), a nationalist Hindu organization that fought colonial rule. He graduated from Victory College in Gwalior and earned his master's degree in·political science from Dayanand Anglo-Vedic College in Kanpur. He studied law but did not graduate. In the early 1950s Vajpayee joined the Jana Sangh and worked as a private secretary for the group's president, Shyama Prasad Mukherjee. Within a few years he was made president and would remain president of the party until 1977, when a coalition of political groups called the Janata (People's) party, which included Jana Singh, came into power. Vajpayee served as external affairs minister (under the prime minister, Morarji Desai) and established relationships with China and the Soviet Union. In 1980 Vajpayee helped found the Bharatiya Janata (Indian People's Party) (BJP) and served as party president until 1986. In 1996 BJP won 161 seats in the 545-seat Parliament, and Vajpayee was made prime minister. However, due to a very tight majority, he resigned after thirteen days rather than undergo a vote of no confidence launched by an opposing party's coalition. In 1998 the BJP had established enough alliances to take the clear majority, and Vajpayee was sworn in once more. Within his first year, India conducted underground nuclear tests, establishing itself as a nuclear power and setting international relations on edge, particularly for the United States and Pakistan, which immediately detonated their own nuclear weapons tests. With the end of the Cold War, India welcomed then president Bill Clinton in 2000, and strengthening their bonds after the September 2001 terror attacks in the United States.

Atal Bihari Vajpayee never married. He had one adopted daughter, Namita Bhattacharya. She and her daughter, Neharika, survive.

See *Current Biography* 2000

Robert Venturi

Born: Philadelphia, Pennsylvania; June 25, 1925
Died: Philadelphia, Pennsylvania; September 18, 2018
Occupation: American architect

Architect Robert Venturi was often considered the father of postmodern architecture and urban design, rejecting the modern boxy facades of glass and steel. He wrote several books, including his 1966 seminal work, Complexity and Contradiction in Architecture, which fostered a post-modern movement in architecture, though Venturi would reject the characterization as the "father" of the movement. In 1991, Venturi won the Pritzker Prize, often considered the "Nobel Prize" of architecture. In 1992 President Bill Clinton awarded Venturi and his wife, Denise Scott Brown, the National Medal of Arts.

Robert Venturi was the only child of Robert Charles Venturi, a wholesale fruit merchant in Philadelphia. He entered Princeton University in 1944, graduating Phi Beta Kappa in 1947 with a degree in architecture. He continued his graduate studies at Princeton, winning the Palmer scholarship in 1948 and the American Institute of Architects student medal in 1949. He graduated with a Master of Fine Arts degree in 1950. From there he studied architecture at the American Academy in Rome, having won the Rome Prize Fellowship in 1954 and 1956. His studies there culminated in his ground-breaking book *Complexity and Contradiction in Architecture*. Venturi's was a "people first" theory of architecture—people and all their messy contradictions. Early on, Venturi inspired rage from more established colleagues who considered his ideas, and Venturi's relationships with pop artists, too radical. His 1972 book, *Learning from Las Vegas* examined the city's layout, considering the effects of the automobile on city structure. Venturi's first important building, the Vanna Venturi House was a home for his mother in Philadelphia. In 2005 the house was featured on a US postage stamp.

Robert Venturi's survivors include his wife, Denise, and a son.

See *Current Biography* 2000

Paul Virilio

Born: Paris, France; January 4,1932
Died: Paris, France; September 10, 2018
Occupation: French philosopher, architect

Paul Virilio was a French philosopher whose work explored the effects of warfare and technology on human history, and how high-speed computer technology and media might affect humanity's future.

Paul Virilio was an art student at the École des Métiers d'Art, where he became a skilled stained-glass artisan, creating windows for several churches. Henri Matisse and Georges Braque were fellow students. Though his father was an Italian Communist, Virilio converted to Christianity in 1950. In 1954 Virilio was drafted to fight in the Algerian war for independence.

His experiences there would inform his later writings. After the war, he enrolled at the Sorbonne studying phenomenology under Maurice Merleau-Ponty. As his philosophy started to take shape, he became captivated by, and began examining the Atlantic Wall, constructed by the Nazis to hinder American and British Troops during World War II. In 1975 his first major publication, Bunker Archeology, would be about these structures. Once he had completed his studies at the Sorbonne, he set up his own architecture practice in Paris and founded the architecture and artist association, Architecture Principe. In 1963 through 1966 he and fellow artisan Claude Parent designed the cathedral of-Sainte-Bernadette du Banlay, in Nevers, France, a "bunker church" styled after military architecture. In 1968 he was nominated for a full professorship at the École Spéciale d'Architecture (ESA) in Paris. He became the director of studies in 1973, the general director in 1975, and chairman of the board in 1989. One of Virilio's most important works was published in 1977, titled *Vitesse et Politique: Essai de Dromologie* (*Speed and Politics: Dromology Essay*), which attempted to argue that speed, physically and mentally, was a defining force in civilization. He explored the impact of literal technologies of motion on politics, economies, and cultures, and suggested a "war model" was integral to the growth of modern cities. Most his publications examined the interrelationship between war and the need for speed, rather than commerce and wealth, as the foundation of human society. He would later examine how people have become dissociated from one another and their immediate surroundings through ever-increasing speed of travel and information. In 1989 Virilio became the director of the program of studies at the Collège International de Philosophie de Paris, which was headed by Jacques Derrida. In 1992 he would become a member of the High Committee on the Housing of the Disadvantaged, an organization dedicated to helping the homeless.

See *Current Biography* 2005

George Walker

Born: Washington, DC; June 27, 1922
Died: Montclair, New Jersey; August 23, 2018
Occupation: Composer, pianist, educator

George Walker was the first African American composer to win a Pulitzer Prize in music for his composition, *Lilacs*, which is based on the Walt Whitman poem, "While Lilacs Last in the Dooryard Bloom'd," about the death of Abraham Lincoln. Walker's life comprised a series of firsts: the first African American to graduate from the Curtis Institute of Music, the first African American to debut at the prestigious Town Hall in New York City, the first black instrumentalist to play with the Philadelphia Orchestra, and the first black student to earn a doctorate from the Eastman School of Music.

George Walker's parents were highly accomplished and nearly as inspiring as their son. His father immigrated from Jamaica with little money and no contacts or family in the United States. He put himself through medical school; and because the American Medical Association (AMA) did not accept black people, he started his own black medical association. He was also a self-taught pianist. But it was Walker's mother who most cultivated her son's musical talent. An important family ritual was her singing along with her son's piano accompaniment. She had him taking piano lessons from age five. He performed his first recital at Howard University when he was just fourteen—the same year he was admitted to Oberlin College on a full scholarship. He graduated in 1941 with highest honors and was then accepted into the famous Curtis School of Music where he studied under Rudolf Serkin and Rosario Scalero. He graduated in 1945. In spite of his extraordinary talent, Walker had great difficulty finding an agent or work as a concert pianist—there just weren't any African American classical pianists in the music world, and it was assumed white audiences wouldn't attend. In 1953 Walker abandoned his dream of playing and turned to composition and teaching. He enrolled in the doctoral program at the Eastman School of Music. Shortly after graduating, Walker won a Fulbright fellowship and a Jay Hay Whitney grant, which allowed him to study under Nadia Boulanger at the American Academy at Fontainebleau, France. Shortly thereafter, Walker began teaching at a series of colleges, including the New School for Social Research, the Dalcroze School of Music, Smith College, and the University of Colorado (as a visiting professor). He became a distinguished professor and chair of the music department at Rutgers University and also taught at the Peabody Institute at Johns Hopkins University. While teaching, Walker continued composing. In 1968 he was invited to participate in a symposium of black composers, sponsored by the Rockefeller Foundation. In 1996, Walker learned he had won a Pulitzer Prize.

Walker's marriage to Helen Siemens ended in divorce. His survivors include his two sons, and three grandsons.

See *Current Biography* 2000

Mort Walker

Born: El Dorado, Kansas; September 3, 1923
Died: Stamford, Connecticut; January 27, 2018
Occupation: American cartoonist

As the creator of such popular comic strips as Beetle Bailey and Hi and Lois, Mort Walker was one of the country's most successful cartoonists. He won the Ruben Award from the National Cartoonists Society, the US Army Decoration for Distinguished Civilian Service, Sweden's Adamson Award, and was made a Chevalier in the French Order of the Legion of Honor. He also founded the International Museum of Cartoon Art in 1974.

Mort Walker's parents were both artists, but to feed the family, Walker's father worked in construction, building schools as they followed the oil boom from town to town, from Texas to Ohio. They finally settled in Kansas City, Missouri. Walker claimed to have known he would be a cartoonist from the age of three and published his first cartoon in a magazine when he was just eleven, He continued to produce work for such magazines as *Child Life, Inside Detective,* and *Flying Aces.* He briefly attended Kansas City Junior College and worked for Hall Brothers Greeting Cards (now known as Hallmark cards). He attended one semester at the University of Missouri but was drafted into the Army Corp. in 1943. Leaving the military as a commissioned officer, he continued his education at the university, graduating in 1948 with a degree in arts and sciences. He moved to New York with big dreams of becoming a full-time cartoonist, while supporting himself with a magazine-editing job. Within a few years, he was becoming well known for his single-panel cartoons that appeared in magazines like *The Saturday Evening Post.* His Beetle Bailey character, originally a college student named Spider, debuted in twelve newspapers on September 4, 1950. Within a year Spider had morphed into the now well-loved, gangly, and lazy army private named Beetle Bailey. Since its inception, the comic strip upended the army's strict hierarchy, which got it dropped several times from the military newspaper *Stars & Stripes.* But as the military culture evolved with the times, so did Walker's comic strip, introducing the African American character, Lieutenant Jack Flap, and characters of Greek, Italian, French, and Asian descent. He even introduced a technology geek named Gizmo. The comic strip Hi and Lois was a spin-off of Beetle Bailey since Lois was Beetle's sister.

Mort Walker was married twice. Between the two of them, Walker and his second wife, Cathy, had ten children, with six of them working to produce Walker's cartoons. Walker's survivors include his wife, Catherine Carty, two stepchildren, his six children from his first marriage.

See *Current Biography* 2002

Randy Weston

Born: New York, New York; April 6, 1926
Died: New York, New York; September 1, 2018
Occupation: Jazz pianist, composer

Randy Weston was a musician most recognized for combining traditional West African rhythms with American jazz. He received the Jazz Masters award from the National Endowment for the Arts in 2001 and was inducted into *DownBeat* magazine's hall of fame in 2016. Weston received two Grammy nominations: one in 1973 for his album titled *Tanjah* and another in 1995 for *The Splendid Master Gnawa Musicians of Morocco,* which was performed largely by Moroccan musicians.

Randy Weston's parents separated when he was just three years old, though they remained a relatively tight-knit family. His father, Frank Edward Weston, a native of Panama, owned a diner that catered to many local jazz musicians, thus exposing his son to the rhythms of the African American music scene. He constantly played jazz in their home, including the classics of Count Basie, Andy Kirk, and Duke Ellington. Weston's mother exposed her son to gospel music. At his father's insistence, Weston began taking piano lessons, though he had little interest in the beginning. However, hearing and eventually befriending Thelonious Monk had a great impact on him. Explaining to Fred Bouchard of *DownBeat* (November 1990) Monk played "like they must have played in Egypt 5,000 years ago." While most people might consider jazz to be distinctly African-American, generated from the grief of slavery, Weston considered the roots of jazz to be distinctly African. In 1959 he became a member of the United Nations (UN) Jazz Society, which sought to spread jazz worldwide, especially in Africa. He released an album in 1960 entitled *Uhuru Afrika* (a Swahili phrase meaning "Free Africa.") The album was banned in South Africa, a heavily segregated nation, ruled by white colonialists. During the early 1960s, Weston partnered with Marshall Stearns touring universities, teaching, and presenting a history of jazz in a series of roundtable discussions, while immersing himself in research of West African music. Weston moved to Morocco in 1968 where he ran the African Rhythms Cultural Center. In 1972 he moved to Paris, France, and for the next decade, divided his time between three continents, teaching about the connections between jazz and African music. He received fellowships from the Guggenheim Foundation, the Doris Duke Charitable Trust, and United Artists. He released his fiftieth and last album in 2016.

See *Current Biography* 2000

Richard Wilbur

Born: New York, New York; March 1, 1921
Died: Belmont, Massachusetts; October 14, 2017
Occupation: Poet, critic, translator, university professor

Richard Wilbur was an award-winning poet and US poet laureate from 1987 to 1988. He won two Pulitzer Prizes as well as the Bollingen Prize and the Ruth Lilly poetry prize for lifetime achievement.

Richard Wilbur grew up on a farm in New Jersey, which factored into the general tenor of his appreciation for the natural world and humanity's place in it. He attended Amherst College in Massachusetts. During World War II, he had hoped to serve as a cryptographer in the army, but his history as a left-wing student activist meant he was transferred to the infantry where he served in France and Germany. After the war Wilbur earned a master's degree from Harvard University, where he met Robert Frost who became something of a mentor for him. He taught briefly at Wellesley College than transferred to Wesleyan University for the bulk of his teaching career. He was a writer-in-residence at Smith College for ten years, from 1977 to 1987. Wilbur's first Pulitzer was for his third book of poetry, *Things of This World*, in 1957. He won a second Pulitzer in 1988 for his *New and Collected Poems*. From 1957 through 1987, Wilbur published five collections of poetry. He also established a reputation as a translator of Molière's plays, and wrote the lyrics for Leonard Bernstein's 1956 production of the opera *Candide*. Wilbur also published five children's books.

In 1942 Wilbur married the granddaughter of Robert Frost's first publisher, Mary Charlotte Hayes Ward. They had four children, all of whom survive. His wife Charlotte died in 2007.

See *Current Biography* 1966

Tom Wolfe

Born: Richmond, Virginia; March 2, 1930
Died: New York, New York; May 14, 2018
Occupation: Author, journalist

Tom Wolfe was a celebrated journalist and author known for his unique writing style, using many exclamation marks, elongated words, and unusual capitalization. He helped originate a "New Journalism," a hybrid of novelistic techniques and non-fiction.

Thomas Kennerly Wolfe, Jr. was born to Thomas K. Wolfe Sr., a professor of agronomy at Virginia Technical Institute, and Helen Perkins Hughes Wolfe, a garden designer. As a young child, Wolfe would write his own stories about his childhood or about themes from his favorite books at the time. He attended St. Christopher's School for his secondary education and then attended Washington and Lee University, where he received a BA in English in 1951. Wolfe then earned his PhD from Yale University in 1956, in American Studies. Within a few years, he had joined *The Washington Post* as a local and Latin American reporter. In 1960, just one year after joining *The Post*, Wolfe won the Washington Newspaper Guild award for foreign news in reporting and humor. Wolfe became an artist-reporter for the *New York Herald Tribune* in 1962, where he was able to be much more experimental with his writing style and quickly became quite popular. Twenty-three of his articles and eighteen satiric drawings were collected and published as a book in 1966, called *The Kandy-Kolored Tangerine-Flake Streamline Baby*, which was quickly a best seller. He wrote the cult classic *The Electric Kool-Aid Acid Test*, a chronical of his travels with counterculture icon, Ken Kesey and his "Merry Pranksters." Wolfe continued writing for *New York* and at the same time, several different collections of his articles were published as books. His first full-length novel, *The Bonfire of Vanities*, published in 1987, was a best-seller and was adapted for film. His nonfiction book, the National Book Award-winning *The Right Stuff*, about the Mercury space program, was also adapted for film and received four Academy Awards. Wolfe didn't publish another book until eleven years later, with *A Man in Full*.

Tom Wolfe is survived by his wife, Sheila Berger, and their two children, Alexandra and Tommy.

See *Current Biography* 1971

John Young

Born: San Francisco, California; September 24, 1930
Died: Houston, Texas; January 5, 2018
Occupation: Astronaut

Commander John Young was a career Naval officer and test pilot who flew with Virgil (Gus) Grissom in America's first two-man, maneuverable Gemini 3 space flight in 1965. He ran the National Aeronautics and Space Administration's (NASA) office of astronauts for thirteen years and was an executive at the Johnson Space Center. He was honored by the Smithsonian's Air and Space Museum upon his retirement in 2004.

Though born in California John Young's family moved east during the Depression and Young spent his childhood in Orlando, Florida, where his father was a Naval commander in the "Seabees," naval construction force. Young graduated from Orlando High School and entered the Georgia Institute of Technology where he earned his BS degree in aeronautical engineering in 1952. He then enlisted with the US Navy, serving in Korea in 1959. In 1962 he was sent to the naval air station at Point Mugu, California, where he trained in Project Jump High, flying an F4B jet. In 1962 he was selected, one of seven, out of two hundred and fifty-three qualified volunteers, to take part in future space missions. In 1972 he explored the moon's surface in a lunar rover vehicle. He flew twice in Gemini space missions, once in an Apollo mission, and later, in several space shuttle missions. He was the only astronaut to fly in all three space endeavors. Upon retiring from space flight, he headed the NASA astronauts' office for thirteen years, and became an executive with the Johnson Space Center in Houston, Texas. He retired in 2004.

John Young was married twice. His survivors include his wife, Susy Feldman Young, two children, and numerous grandchildren and great-grandchildren.

See *Current Biography* 1965

Malcolm Young

Born: Glasgow, Scotland; January 6, 1953
Died: Elizabeth Bay, Australia; November 18, 2017
Occupation: Rhythm guitarist

Malcolm Young and his brother, Angus Young, founded the raucous hard rock band, AC/DC, which would be inducted into the Rock and Roll Hall of Fame in 2003. AC/DC won their first Grammy Award in 2010 for their song "War Machine." Their album *Back in Black* was inducted into the Grammy Hall of Fame in 2013.

Malcolm Young was born, the sixth of nine children, in Glasgow, Scotland. The family moved to Australia in 1963. He left school at the age of fifteen to work as a machine maintenance engineer for a company that manufactured brassieres. In the meantime, Malcolm and his brother, Angus, learned to play guitar and decided to form a band. It was their sister, Margaret, a huge rock and roll fan who suggested the name AC/DC (the acronym for electricity's alternating current and direct current). They held their first concert in a pub in Sydney in 1973. Their first single, "Can I Sit Next to You," became a local hit in Australia. In 1975 they released their first album, *High Voltage*. Within a year, they would produce their second album, *TNT*, which hit the number two position on Australia's charts. In 1976 the band signed with Atlantic Records and moved to England. Writing for the *All Music Guide*, Steven Huey characterized them and their music as a "stripped down collection of loud, raw, rude rockers, mostly odes to rock and roll," a description appropriate for most metal bands. Their first big international hit was their album *Highway to Hell*, which would become a hard rock classic. The band was struck by tragedy in 1980 when band member, Bon Scott, was found dead after a night of hard drinking. The band would continue to lose and gain new members through the decades, but the two Young brothers remained the core of the band.

Malcolm Young gave his last performance in 2010 after being diagnosed with dementia. It was reported that during the tour he had to relearn songs that he had written himself. Young's survivors include his brother, Angus, a sister, his wife, O'Linda, two children, and three grandchildren.

See *Current Biography* 2005

CLASSIFICATION BY PROFESSION

ACTIVISM
Pushpa Basnet
Tarana Burke
Yvonne Chaka Chaka
Aaron Maybin

ANIMATION
Nora Twomey

ART
Guy Delisle
Julie Dillon
Awol Erizku
Emil Ferris
Dominique Goblet
Olivia Locher
Aaron Maybin
Amy Sherald

BUSINESS
Beth Comstock
Patricia Harris
Mina Lux
Tim Sweeney
Dana Walden

COMEDY
Yvonne Orji

ECONOMICS
Angus Deaton
Robert J. Gordon

EDUCATION
Emily Graslie
Erin Entrada Kelly
Jeanne Marie Laskas
Clint Smith

ENTERTAINMENT
Basil Twist

ESSAYS
Rachel Kaadzi Ghansah

FASHION
Virgil Abloh
Matthew Henson

FICTION
Elliot Ackerman
Jesse Ball
Robin Benway
Mathias Énard
Emily Fridlund

Rivka Galchen
Roxanne Gay
Dominique Goblet
Lisa Halliday
Sheila Heti
Roy Jacobsen
Kapka Kassabova
Erin Entrada Kelly
Lisa Ko
Valeria Luiselli
Fiona Mozley
Antonio Muñoz Molina
Dorthe Nors
Nnedi Okorafor
Ada Palmer
Ahmed Saadawi
Olga Tokarczuk
James Tynion IV
Jenny Zhang

FILM
Caitriona Balfe
Lake Bell
Aline Brosh McKenna
Rachel Brosnahan
Millie Bobby Brown
Sterling K. Brown
Timothée Chalamet
Hong Chau
Auli'i Cravalho
Jacqueline Durran
Joel Edgerton
Bryshere Y. Gray
Liz Hannah
Laura Harrier
Sandra Hüller
Patty Jenkins
Leslie Jones
So Yong Kim
Danielle Macdonald
Samuel Maoz
Kleber Mendonça Filho
Reed Morano
Lynn Novick
Gina Prince-Bythewood
Florence Pugh
Charles Randolph
Haley Lu Richardson
Tye Sheridan
Christian Slater
Jussie Smollett
Mya Taylor
Tessa Thompson
Nora Twomey
Gabrielle Union

Lena Waithe
Jodie Whittaker
Samira Wiley
Chloé Zhao

GRAPHIC NOVELS
Guy Delisle
Emil Ferris

HISTORIAN
Erica Armstrong-Dunbar
Ada Palmer
Michael W. Twitty

JOURNALISM
John Carreyrou
Nima Elbagir
Ronan Farrow
Maggie Haberman
Jazmine Hughes
Jodi Kantor
Antonio Muñoz Molina
James Nachtwey
Joshua Topolsky
Rebecca Traister
Katharine Viner
David Weigel

LITERATURE
Samanta Schweblin

MODELING
Chrissy Teigen

MUSIC
Joshua Abrams
Brothers Osborne
Kane Brown
BTS
Daniel Caesar
Yvonne Chaka Chaka
Luke Combs
Jack Conte
Damien Escobar
Phil Elverum
Jackie Evancho
Florida Georgia Line
GoldLink
Haim
Sam Hunt
Lindsey Jordan
Kelela
Khalid
King Krule
Greg Kurstin
Dua Lipa
Logic
London Grammar
Robert Lopez
Zayn Malik

Julia Michaels
Maren Morris
Carla Morrison
Kacey Musgraves
Margo Price
Rapsody
Cécile McLorin Salvant
Sampha
The Secret Sisters
Jussie Smollett
Somi
Tyshawn Sorey
Vince Staples
SZA
Jeanine Tesori
Kali Uchis
Grace VanderWaal
Lil Uzi Vert
Emily Warren
WondaGurl

NONFICTION
Erica Armstrong-Dunbar
Roxanne Gay
Sheila Heti
Kapka Kassabova
Jeanne Marie Laskas
Adam Rutherford
Rebecca Traister
Michael W. Twitty

POETRY
Jesse Ball
Bao Phi
Eve Ewing
Ross Gay
Kapka Kassabova
Layli Long Soldier
Clint Smith

POLITICS, FOREIGN
Boyko Borisov
Horacio Cartes
Andrzej Duda
Juan Orlando Hernández
Katrín Jakobsdóttir
Ewa Kopacz
Danilo Medina
Tomislav Nikolić

POLITICS, U.S.
Alejandro García Padilla
John Kitzhaber

PUBLISHING
Radhika Jones

SCIENCE
Joseph Acaba
Barry Barish

Natalie Batalha
Jennifer Doudna
Marcus du Sautoy
Jacques Dubochet
David G. Haskell
Clifford V. Johnson
Yves Meyer
Michael Rosbash
Adam Rutherford
Suzanne Simard

SOCIOLOGY
Eve Ewing

SPORTS
José Altuve
Craig Anderson
Mookie Betts
Sergei Bobrovsky
Devin Booker
Alex Bregman
Zach Britton
Malcolm Brogdon
Kris Bryant
Jimmy Butler
Kam Chancellor
Anthony Davis
Rafael Devers
Jessica Diggins
Skylar Diggins-Smith
Grigor Dimitrov
Joel Embiid
Sabina-Francesca Foişor
Nick Foles
Sylvia Fowles
Shelly-Ann Fraser-Pryce
Fu Yuanhui
Red Gerard
Rudy Gobert
Marcin Gortat
Shayne Gostisbehere
Kareem Hunt
Kyrie Irving
Aaron Judge
Case Keenum
Evgeny Kuznetsov
Francisco Lindor
Hideki Matsuyama
Auston Matthews
Kei Nishikori
Aaron Nola
Joc Pederson

Buster Posey
Anthony Rizzo
Luis Severino
Sloane Stephens
Eric Thames
Hassan Whiteside
Alina Zagitova
Henrik Zetterberg

TECHNOLOGY
Jack Conte
Susan Fowler

TELEVISION
Caitriona Balfe
Janine Sherman Barrois
Lake Bell
Rachel Brosnahan
Millie Bobby Brown
Sterling K. Brown
Timothée Chalamet
Hong Chau
Felicia Day
Joel Edgerton
Bryshere Y. Gray
Laura Harrier
Freddie Highmore
Patty Jenkins
Leslie Jones
Cush Jumbo
Danielle Macdonald
Simone Missick
Lynn Novick
Yvonne Orji
Condola Rashād
Haley Lu Richardson
Yara Shahidi
Christian Slater
Jussie Smollett
Tessa Thompson
Gabrielle Union
Lena Waithe
Jodie Whittaker
Samira Wiley

THEATER
Sandra Hüller
Cush Jumbo
Ashley Park
Ben Platt
Condola Rashād
Samira Wiley

LIST OF PROFILES

List of Profiles